Cisco Network Security Troubleshooting Handbook

Mynul Hoda, CCIE No. 9159

Cisco Press

800 East 96th Street
Indianapolis, Indiana 46240 USA

Cisco Network Security Troubleshooting Handbook

Mynul Hoda

Published by:
Cisco Press
800 East 96th Street
Indianapolis, IN 46240 USA

Printed in the United States of America 1 2 3 4 5 6 7 8 9 0

First Printing November 2005

Library of Congress Cataloging-in-Publication Number: 2003116568

ISBN: 1-58705-189-3

Trademark Acknowledgments

Warning and Disclaimer

This book is designed to provide information about troubleshooting Cisco network security through the eyes of a Technical Assistance Center (TAC) Support Engineer. Every effort has been made to make this book as complete and as accurate as possible, but no warranty or fitness is implied.

The information is provided on an "as is" basis. The authors, Cisco Press, and Cisco Systems, Inc. shall have neither liability nor responsibility to any person or entity with respect to any loss or damages arising from the information contained in this book or from the use of the discs or programs that may accompany it.

The opinions expressed in this book belong to the author and are not necessarily those of Cisco Systems, Inc.

Corporate and Government Sales

Cisco Press offers excellent discounts on this book when ordered in quantity for bulk purchases or special sales.

For more information please contact: **U.S. Corporate and Government Sales** 1-800-382-3419 corpsales@pearsontechgroup.com

For sales outside the U.S. please contact: **International Sales** international@pearsoned.com

Feedback Information

At Cisco Press, our goal is to create in-depth technical books of the highest quality and value. Each book is crafted with care and precision, undergoing rigorous development that involves the unique expertise of members from the professional technical community.

Readers' feedback is a natural continuation of this process. If you have any comments regarding how we could improve the quality of this book, or otherwise alter it to better suit your needs, you can contact us through e-mail at feedback@ciscopress.com. Please make sure to include the book title and ISBN in your message.

We greatly appreciate your assistance.

Publisher	John Wait
Editor-in-Chief	John Kane
Cisco Representative	Anthony Wolfenden
Cisco Press Program Manager	Jeff Brady
Executive Editor	Mary Beth Ray
Acquisitions Editor	Michelle Grandin
Production Manager	Patrick Kanouse
Development Editor	Betsey Henkels
Project Editor	Marc Fowler
Copy Editor	Interactive Composition Corporation
Technical Editors	Qiang Huang, Nadeem Khawaja, and Jonathan Limbo
Editorial Assisant	Raina Han
Book/Cover Designer	Louisa Adair
Composition	Interactive Composition Corporation
Indexer	Tim Wright

Corporate Headquarters
Cisco Systems, Inc.
170 West Tasman Drive
San Jose, CA 95134-1706
USA
www.cisco.com
Tel: 408 526-4000
800 553-NETS (6387)
Fax: 408 526-4100

European Headquarters
Cisco Systems International BV
Haarlerbergpark
Haarlerbergweg 13-19
1101 CH Amsterdam
The Netherlands
www-europe.cisco.com
Tel: 31 0 20 357 1000
Fax: 31 0 20 357 1100

Americas Headquarters
Cisco Systems, Inc.
170 West Tasman Drive
San Jose, CA 95134-1706
USA
www.cisco.com
Tel: 408 526-7660
Fax: 408 527-0883

Asia Pacific Headquarters
Cisco Systems, Inc.
Capital Tower
168 Robinson Road
#22-01 to #29-01
Singapore 068912
www.cisco.com
Tel: +65 6317 7777
Fax: +65 6317 7799

Cisco Systems has more than 200 offices in the following countries and regions. Addresses, phone numbers, and fax numbers are listed on the **Cisco.com Web site at www.cisco.com/go/offices.**

Argentina • Australia • Austria • Belgium • Brazil • Bulgaria • Canada • Chile • China PRC • Colombia • Costa Rica • Croatia • Czech Republic
Denmark • Dubai, UAE • Finland • France • Germany • Greece • Hong Kong SAR • Hungary • India • Indonesia • Ireland • Israel • Italy
Japan • Korea • Luxembourg • Malaysia • Mexico • The Netherlands • New Zealand • Norway • Peru • Philippines • Poland • Portugal
Puerto Rico • Romania • Russia • Saudi Arabia • Scotland • Singapore • Slovakia • Slovenia • South Africa • Spain • Sweden
Switzerland • Taiwan • Thailand • Turkey • Ukraine • United Kingdom • United States • Venezuela • Vietnam • Zimbabwe

Printed in the USA

About the Author

Mynul Hoda, CCIE No. 9159 for both Routing and Switching and Security, CISSP, is one of the lead engineers in High Touch Technical Support (HTTS) based in San Jose, California, where he has been working as a senior Security/VPN support engineer for the last two years. In his current role, he is involved in troubleshooting Security/VPN issues in some of the biggest and most critical networks in the industry around the world. Before joining HTTS, Mynul was a senior support engineer in Cisco Technical Assistance Center (TAC) bases in San Jose, CA, for three years. Mynul routinely provides escalation support to his immediate team and other security support teams within Cisco, provides training and boot camps, and answers customer questions on the Networking Professionals Connection e-community. Along with this, he writes and reviews Cisco.com docs, constantly maintains, updates, and presents training materials for Security/VPN Boot Camp for internal CA organization and the Premium Partner. His areas of expertise are configuring and troubleshooting all forms of Security/VPN technologies such as AAA, IPS, Firewall, and VPN. Mynul holds a bachelor's degree in chemical engineering from the University of South Alabama, and a master's in Computer Science from the University of Alabama. Before joining Cisco Systems, Mynul worked as an Internet consultant at American Computer Consultants, where he was responsible for designing and implementing the E-Commerce site architecture, and network security architecture. Among other exciting things, he is also currently reviewing and understanding the source code for Firewall and AAA technologies, which is giving him an edge in understanding the security technologies in depth and providing the very best customer support. Mynul has eight years of experience altogether in the IT industry, including five years exclusively in Cisco Network Security Troubleshooting.

Mynul is living happily in San Jose, CA, with his wife, Rashida, and 20-month-old baby boy, Rayaadh.

About the Technical Reviewers

Qiang Huang, CCIE No. 4937 (ISP Dial, Routing and Switching, and Security), CISSP, is a technical marketing engineer in the Cisco Systems Security Technology Group. He currently focuses on competitive analysis of various vendors in the network security market. Before that, Qiang worked in the security consulting group, conducting security posture assessment, security design review, and technical support operation as the technical lead in the VPN and network security group. Qiang has extensive experience with many security products and technologies, including firewalls, VPNs, intrusion detection and prevention, and identity management. Qiang received his master's degree in electrical engineering from Colorado State University.

Nadeem Khawaja, CCIE No. 9069, has worked as a Customer Support Engineer in the Security Solutions team within the Cisco System TAC since early 2001. At Cisco, Nadeem supports the PIX Firewall, Intrusion Detection Systems, Router-based IOS Firewalls, and Cisco Secure Access Control Servers. Nadeem has more than nine years of experience in the computer networking field and is currently pursuing a master's degree in computer science at San Jose University. In addition to his Routing and Switching CCIE, Nadeem also has the CCIE Security certification and holds the CCNP and CCDP certifications.

Jonathan Limbo, CCIE No. 10508 (Security) is currently an IPS Signature developer for the Asia Pacific region. He currently focuses on vulnerabilities, evolving attack vectors, and exploits. Previous roles include working on the APAC Security team for Technical Support Services specializing in DDoS Attack mitigation, and various technical network and system administrator roles. Jonathan has been in the security space for six years and has extensive experience within security, including security policies, security tools, and Cisco Secure technologies, including authentication and authorization access control, perimeter defense, encryption, and self-defending network strategies. Jonathan is a CISSP and is certified in ethical hacking (CEH).

Dedications

This book is dedicated to my loving parents, whose care, unconditional love, and sacrifice resulted in where I stand today. They are the best parents in the world—true blessings from God, indeed!!!

And,

My wife, Rashida, whose sincerity, love, care, and thoughtfulness gave me the energy to complete this project. She is a true friend, a very best life partner, and a very fine human being.

And,

My 20-month-old son, Rayaadh, whose cute and innocent face brings me a new level of energy every day—I can walk any difficult path for that innocent smile on the face of my baby boy.

Acknowledgments

All praises and thanks go to God almighty for giving me the opportunity to complete this project. Without His mercy and His compassion, the writing of this book simply would not be possible. I can never be humble enough to show my gratitude to Him for everything He blessed me with.

A big thanks goes to my manager, Tony Moreland, who helped me so much during this project. He is one of the best technical managers (if not the best) at Cisco. Throughout the writing of this book, he has been as supportive and flexible as he could be. I could not have asked more. Thanks to Dale Miller, Director of HTTS, and Curtis Hill, Senior Director, for giving me the opportunity to learn and grow in the HTTS organization. Their unmatched and superior leadership makes HTTS a fun place to learn, work, and grow professionally.

Special thanks go to Technical Reviewers Qiang Huang, Nadeem Khawaja, and Jonathan Limbo. They are all my friends, colleagues, and some of the finest troubleshooters for Security/VPN products in the industry. Thanks for taking time and editing the book character by character for technical accuracy. You guys are simply superb!!

This acknowledgment would not be complete without mentioning two names from Cisco Press—Acquisitions Editor Michelle Grandin, who trusted me with this project, and helped me tremendously during the initial phase of writing, and Developmental Editor Betsey Henkels, who edited and corrected the writing of the book character by character. I am impressed with her level of energy and patience in this endeavor. I don't want to miss the opportunity to thank other Cisco Press folks involved—Executive Editor Mary Beth Ray, for keeping me on track throughout the writing process; Executive Editor Brett Bartow, for trusting me with the project; Christopher Cleveland, Sr. Development Editor, for his careful editing; and Marc Fowler, Project Editor, for all of his flexibility.

Technical contents of the book are based on developers' discussions, internal training materials, chalk talks, networkers presentations, and my on-the-job training. Several engineers' names come to mind who helped me in developing my technical skills, which directly and indirectly influenced the contents of the book. Among many, some of them are Christopher Paggen (two case studies in Chapter 4 are taken directly from his notes); David White, Jr. (Dave is a true expert in PIX/ASA; Chapter 3 would have not been completed without borrowing some great content from Dave's work); Mike Sullenberger; and Frederic Detienne for DMVPN and VPN in general. I would like to thank those individuals, among others, whose names are unknown.

On the family front, I would like to thank my younger brother, Tipu, for encouraging me to move into the field of networking; my elder sister, Parvin, and her husband, Ripon, for their love and affection; and my uncle, Abdul Mannan, whose guidance helped in building the foundation of my educational background.

This book is the result of the direct and indirect contributions of all these individuals. I am ever grateful to them.

This Book Is Safari Enabled

The Safari® Enabled icon on the cover of your favorite technology book means the book is available through Safari Bookshelf. When you buy this book, you get free access to the online edition for 45 days.

Safari Bookshelf is an electronic reference library that lets you easily search thousands of technical books, find code samples, download chapters, and access technical information whenever and wherever you need it.

To gain 45-day Safari Enabled access to this book:

- Go to http://www.ciscopress.com/safarienabled
- Enter the ISBN of this book (shown on the back cover, above the bar code)
- Log in or Sign up (site membership is required to register your book)
- Enter the coupon code WKCK-VYAE-7RJI-55EG-LVG6

If you have difficulty registering on Safari Bookshelf or accessing the online edition, please e-mail customer-service@safaribooksonline.com.

Contents at a Glance

Introduction xxxv

Part I **Troubleshooting Tools and Methodology 3**

Chapter 1 Troubleshooting Methods 5

Chapter 2 Understanding Troubleshooting Tools 15

Part II **Troubleshooting Cisco Secure Firewalls 27**

Chapter 3 Troubleshooting Cisco Secure PIX Firewalls 29

Chapter 4 Troubleshooting Firewall Services Module 113

Chapter 5 Troubleshooting an IOS Firewall 177

Part III **Troubleshooting Virtual Private Networks 221**

Chapter 6 Troubleshooting IPsec VPNs on IOS Routers 223

Chapter 7 Troubleshooting IPsec VPN on PIX Firewalls 297

Chapter 8 Troubleshooting IPsec VPNs on VPN 3000 Series Concentrators 347

Part IV **Troubleshooting Network Access Control 417**

Chapter 9 Troubleshooting AAA on IOS Routers 419

Chapter 10 Troubleshooting AAA on PIX Firewalls and FWSM 477

Chapter 11 Troubleshooting AAA on the Switches 541

Chapter 12 Troubleshooting AAA on VPN 3000 Series Concentrator 587

Chapter 13 Troubleshooting Cisco Secure ACS on Windows 615

Part V **Troubleshooting Intrusion Prevention Systems 673**

Chapter 14 Troubleshooting Cisco Intrusion Prevention System 675

Chapter 15 Troubleshooting IDSM-2 Blade on Switch 787

Chapter 16 Troubleshooting Cisco IDS network Module (NM-CIDS) 831

Chapter 17 Troubleshooting CiscoWorks Common Services 861

Chapter 18 Troubleshooting IDM and IDS/IPS Management Console (IDS/IPS MC) 883

Chapter 19 Troubleshooting Firewall MC 931

Chapter 20 Troubleshooting Router MC 959

Chapter 21 Troubleshooting Cisco Security Agent Management Console (CSA MC) and CSA Agent 983

Chapter 22 Troubleshooting IEV and Security Monitors 1039

Index 1079

Table of Contents

Introduction xxxv

Part I Troubleshooting Tools and Methodology 3

Chapter 1 Troubleshooting Methods 5

Proactive Actions for Handling Network Failure 5

Types of Failure 7

Problem-Solving Model 8
- Step 1: Define the Problem 9
- Step 2: Gather the Facts 10
- Step 3: Consider Possible Problems 12
- Step 4: Create an Action Plan 12
- Step 5: Implement the Action Plan 12
- Step 6: Observe Results 12
- Step 7: Repeat if Necessary 13
- Step 8: Document the Changes 13

Summary 13

Chapter 2 Understanding Troubleshooting Tools 15

Using Device Diagnostic Commands 15
- show Commands 15
- debug Commands 16

Test Commands 17
- ping Command 17
- traceroute Command 18
- telnet Command 18
- nslookup Command 19

Network Analyzers 20

Trivial File Transfer Protocol (TFTP) Server 20

FTP Server 21

Syslog Server 21

Audit and Attack Tools 21

Core Dump 22
- Using TFTP 22
- Using FTP 22
- Using rcp 23

Using a Flash Disk 23
Additional Configuration 23
"Exception Memory" Command 23
debug sanity Command 24
Testing the Core Dump Setup 24

Part II Troubleshooting Cisco Secure Firewalls 27

Chapter 3 Troubleshooting Cisco Secure PIX Firewalls 29

Overview of PIX Firewall 29
PIX Packet Processing 30
File System Overview 32
Access-List 34
time-range Keyword 34
Enable/Disable 35
Outbound ACL 35
nat-control 36
Modular Policy Framework (MPF) Objective 37
Transparent Firewall 38

Diagnostic Commands and Tools 39
show Commands 39
show xlate [detail] 39
show connection [detail] 40
show local-host 40
show service-policy 41
show asp drop 41
show cpu usage 42
show traffic 42
show blocks 43
show output filters 44
show tech-support 45
Debug Commands 45
debug icmp trace 46
debug application_protocol 47
debug pix process 47
debug fixup tcp | udp 47
capture Command 47
Sniffer Capture 49
Syslog 50
Traceback/Crashinfo 53
Other Tools 53

Problem Areas Breakdown 54
Licensing Issues 54
Password Recovery Issue 56
Software Upgrade and Downgrade Issues 60
Standard Upgrade Procedure 61
Upgrade using ROM Monitor Mode 63
Downgrade Procedure 66
Upgrading PIX Firewall in a Failover Setup 68
Connection Issues Across PIX Firewall 68
Configuration Steps 69
Troubleshooting Steps 72
Transparent Firewall Issues 78
Configuration Steps 79
Troubleshooting Steps 82
Virtual Firewall 84
Security Context 84
How the Virtual Firewall Works 84
Limitations of Virtual Firewall 86
Configuration Steps 87
Troubleshooting Steps 90
Quality of Service (QoS) Issues 90
Policing 90
Low Latency Queuing (LLQ) 93
Troubleshooting Steps 94
Performance Issues 94
High CPU Utilization 95
High Memory Utilization 98
Large ACL 101
Reverse DNS & IDENT Protocol 101

Case Studies 102
Active/Standby Model 102
Active/Active Model 102
Hardware and License Requirements 104
System and User Failover Group 104
Initialization, Configuration Synchronization/Command Replication 104
Configuration Examples 105
Asymmetrical Routing Support 106
Troubleshooting Steps 108

Common Problems and Resolutions 109

Best Practices 110
Protecting the PIX Firewall Itself 110
Protecting Network Resources 111

Chapter 4 Troubleshooting Firewall Services Module 113

Overview of FWSM Firewall 113
FWSM Architecture 113
Control Plane (CP) 113
Network Processors (NP) 114
Packet Flows 116

Diagnostic Commands and Tools 119
Show Commands 120
show Commands on the Switch 120
show Commands on the FWSM 120
Debug Commands 122
Sniffer on the FWSM 123
Syslog on the FWSM 124
Sniffer Capture 125

Analysis of Problem Areas 125
Licensing Issues 126
Hardware Issues 127
Firewall Module Administration Issues 128
Flash 128
Setting the Boot Device (Route Processor) 129
Maintenance Partition 130
Password Recovery Procedure 132
Upgrading a New Image 133
Upgrading Software Images 133
Connection Problems 134
Configuration Steps 135
Troubleshooting Steps 139
AAA Issues 142
Virtual and Transparent Firewall 142
High CPU Issues 143
Intermittent Packet Drops Issues 144
Failover Issues 144
Failover Operations 146
Configuration Steps 149
Troubleshooting Steps 155

Case Studies 157
Case Study 1: Multiple SVI for FWSM 157
Why Change the Existing Model? 159
Scenario One: DHCP Helper with FWSM 1.1(x) 160
Scenario Two: Alternate Configuration 162
Case Study 2: Understanding Access-List Memory Utilization 164
The Compilation Process: Active and Backup Trees 164

How Memory Is Allocated: Release 1.1(x) or 2.2(1) in Single Mode 165
How memory is Allocated: Release 2.2(1) in Multiple Mode 166
Trees and contexts: A Matter of Mapping 168
FWSM Release 2.3: The ACL Partition Manager 168
Examples of ACL Compilation 170
Access-lists: Best Practices 172

Common Problems and Resolutions 173

Best Practices 174

Chapter 5 Troubleshooting an IOS Firewall 177

Overview of IOS Firewall (CBAC) 177
Single Channel Protocol Inspection 182
UDP and CBAC 182
ICMP and CBAC 182
Application Layer Protocol (TCP-based) and CBAC 183
Multi-Channel Protocol Inspection 187
NAT/PAT and CBAC 188
Port Application Mapping (PAM) and CBAC 188
Denial of Service (DoS) Detection And Prevention 189
TCP Syn Flood and DoS Attack Launched by UDP 189
Fragmentation 191
Real-Time Alerts and Audit Trails 192
Interaction of CBAC with IPsec 193
Transparent Cisco IOS Firewall 193

Diagnostic Commands and Tools 194
show Commands 194
debug commands 195
Syslog 199
Packet Capture (Sniffer Traces) 199

Categories of Problem Areas 199
Selection of Software for IOS Firewall Issues 199
Unable to Connect (Inbound and Outbound) across CBAC 201
Packet Failure to Reach the Router's Incoming Interface 201
Misconfigured ACL 202
Misconfigured NAT and Routing 202
IP Inspection Applied In the Wrong Direction 202
UDP Inspection Is Not Configured 203
Return Traffic Might Not Be Coming Back to the Router 203
ICMP Traffic Is Not Inspected 203
There Is a Problem with Inspecting Single Channel Protocol 204
Required Multi-Channel Protocol is Not Inspected 205
IP URL Filtering Blocking The Connection 205

Redundancy or Asymmetric Routing Problems 205
Performance Issues 205
Timeouts for TCP, UDP, and DNS 207
Short Threshold Values for Half-open and New Connections 208
HTTP Inspection Dilemma 208
Switching Path 208
Large ACL 209
Reverse DNS and IDENT Protocols 209
Running Older Code 209
Intermittent Packet Drops 210
IP URL Filtering Is Not Working 211

Case Studies 211
How auth-proxy Works 212
Method of Authentication 212
Supported Platform 213
Configuration Steps 213
Troubleshooting auth-proxy 216

Common Problems and Resolutions 217

Best Practices 218
Basic Router Security 218
Anti-spoofing Configuration 219

Part III Troubleshooting Virtual Private Networks 221

Chapter 6 Troubleshooting IPsec VPNs on IOS Routers 223

Overview of IPsec Protocol 223
Encryption and Decryption 223
Symmetric Algorithms 224
Asymmetric Algorithms 224
Digital Signatures 225
Security Protocols 225
Authentication Header (AH) 226
Encapsulating Security Header (ESP) 226
Transport Mode 226
Tunnel Mode 227
Security Associations (SAs) 228
SA and Key Management with IKE Protocol 229
IKE Phase 1 229

Diagnostic Commands and Tools 233
show Commands 233
show Command for Phase I 234
show Commands for Phase II 235

show Commands for Interface Counters 237
show Command for Verifying IPsec Configuration 237
Commands for Tearing Down Tunnel 238
debug Commands 238

Analysis of Problem Areas 239
Basic LAN-to-LAN Troubleshooting 239
Successful LAN-to-LAN Tunnel Establishment Process 240
Tunnel Establishment Fails at Phase I 247
Tunnel Establishment Fails at Phase II 252
Tunnel Is Established but Unable To Pass Traffic 254
GRE over IPSec 255
Configuration Steps 256
Troubleshooting Steps 257
Public Key Infrastructure (PKI) Troubleshooting 258
Configuration Steps 258
Troubleshooting Steps 261
Remote Access Client VPN Connection 265
Configuration Steps 265
Troubleshooting Steps 267

Case Studies 270
DMVPN Architecture 271
Multipoint GRE Tunnel Interface (mGRE Interface) 271
Next Hop Resolution Protocol (NHRP) 271
Configuration Steps 272
Troubleshooting DMVPN 278
NHRP Mapping Problem 278
Crypto Socket Creation Problem 279
Crypto VPN problem 279
Passing Data Across an Established Tunnel Problem 281

Common Problems and Resolutions 281
NAT With IPsec Issues 281
NAT in the Tunnel End Points 282
NAT in the Middle 284
Firewall and IPsec Issues 284
Maximum Transmission Unit (MTU) Issues 285
Split Tunneling Issues 286

Best Practices 287
Stateful Failover 287
Stateless Failover 288
Loss of Connection Detection Mechanism 288
Stateless Failover Mechanism Options 291

Chapter 7 Troubleshooting IPsec VPN on PIX Firewalls 297

Overview of IPsec Protocol 297

Diagnostic Commands and Tools 297
show Commands 297
debug Commands 300

Categorization of Problem Areas 302
LAN-to-LAN Troubleshooting 302
Configuration Steps 302
Troubleshooting Steps 308
Remote Access VPN Troubleshooting 323
Configuration Steps 323
Troubleshooting Steps 328

Case Studies 334

Common Problems and Resolutions 337
NAT with IPsec Issues 338
NAT in the tunnel End Point 338
NAT Device In the Middle of Tunnel End Points 338
Firewall and IPsec 340
Maximum Transmission Unit (MTU) Issues 340
Split Tunneling Issues 342

Best Practices 344
Dead Peer Discovery (DPD) 344
Reverse Route Injection (RRI) 345
Stateful Failover For VPN Connections 345

Chapter 8 Troubleshooting IPsec VPNs on VPN 3000 Series Concentrators 347

Diagnostic Commands and Tools 347
Debug Tool 347
Monitoring Tool 350
Administer Sessions 352
Configuration Files 354
LED Indicators 354
Crash Dump File 354
VPN Client Log 354

Analysis of Problem Areas 356
LAN-to-LAN Tunnel Issues 356
Configuration Steps 356
Troubleshooting Steps 357
Remote Access VPN Connection 363
Configuration Steps 364
Troubleshooting Steps 365

Digital Certificate Issues 382
Digital Certificate on the VPN Client 383
Digital Certificate on the VPN Concentrator 383

Case Studies 389
Clientless SSL VPN 390
Configuration Steps for Basic SSL VPN Connection 390
Troubleshooting Steps for Basic SSL VPN Connection 391
Configuration Steps for Web Server Access 392
Troubleshooting Steps For Web Server Access 393
Configuration Steps for CIFS Access 394
Troubleshooting Steps for CIFS Access 395
Thin Client 395
Configuration Steps for Port Forwarding 396
Java Applet Debugging 397
Troubleshooting Steps for Port Forwarding 397
Configuration Steps for MAPI Proxy 399
Troubleshooting Steps for MAPI Proxy 400
Configuration Steps for E-mail Proxy 401
Troubleshooting Steps for E-mail Proxy 401
Thick Client (SSL VPN Client) 402
Configuration Steps for SSL VPN Client 403
Troubleshooting Steps for SSL VPN Client (SVC) 403

Common Problems and Resolutions 406

Best Practices 410
Redundancy Using VRRP 410
Redundancy and Load Sharing Using Clustering 412
Redundancy Using IPsec Backup Servers 415

Part IV Troubleshooting Network Access Control 417

Chapter 9 Troubleshooting AAA on IOS Routers 419

Overview of Authentication, Authorization, and Accounting (AAA) 419
AAA Architecture 420
AAA Communication Protocols 421
TACACS+ 421
RADIUS 425
Difference between RADIUS and TACACS+ 428

Diagnostic Commands and Tools 429
show Commands 429
debug Commands 430

Analysis of Problem Areas 432
Router Management Troubleshooting 432
Login Authentication 432
Configuration Steps 432
Troubleshooting Steps 435
Enable Password Authentication 438
Exec Authorization 440
Command Authorization 443
Accounting 445
Dialup Networking Troubleshooting 446
Authentication and Authorization for Dialup Networking 446
Accounting for Dialup Networking 457
X-Auth Troubleshooting for IPsec 457
Auth-proxy Troubleshooting 457

Case Studies 458
Router Configuration 458
LAC Configuration 458
RADIUS Server Configuration 462
LAC RADIUS Configuration 462
LNS RADIUS Configuration 463
Troubleshooting Steps 464
LAC Router Troubleshooting 464
LNS Router Troubleshooting 468

Common Problems and Resolutions 472

Best Practices 474

Chapter 10 Troubleshooting AAA on PIX Firewalls and FWSM 477

Overview of Authentication, Authorization, and Accounting (AAA) 477
Authentication 478
Authorization 480
Authorization for an Administrative Session 480
Authorization for VPN Connection (X-Auth) 481
Accounting 482

Diagnostic Commands and Tools 483
show commands 483
debug Commands 484
Syslog 485
Other Useful Tools 486

Problem Areas Analysis 486
Firewall Management with AAA Troubleshooting 487
Login Authentication Issues 487
Enable Authentication 496

Command Authorization 499
Troubleshooting Steps 503
Accounting 504
Cut-Through Proxy Authentication 505
Authentication for Cut-Through Proxy 506
Troubleshooting Cut-Through Proxy Authentication 511
Authorization for Cut-Through Proxy 514
Accounting for Cut-Through Proxy 526
Extended Authentication (X-Auth) Issues for Remote Access VPN Connection 526
Configuration Steps 527
Troubleshooting Techniques 529
Case Studies 530
Case Study 1: AAA Exemption 530
Case Study 2: Virtual Telnet 532
Configuring Virtual Telnet 533
Troubleshooting Virtual Telnet 534
Case Study 3: Virtual HTTP 535
Common Problems and Resolutions 536
Best Practices 538
Chapter 11 Troubleshooting AAA on the Switches 541
Overview of AAA 541
Switch Management 541
Identity-Based Network Services (IBNSs) 541
IEEE 802.1x Framework 542
Extensible Authentication Protocol (EAP) 545
RADIUS IN 802.1x 546
What Is Authenticated 547
Machine Authentication 548
Authorization 548
Accounting 548
Extension of IEEE 802.1x Standard by Cisco IBNS Initiative 550
Diagnostic Commands and Tools 552
Switch Management 552
Identity-Based Network Services (IBNSs) 555
Categorization of Problem Areas 558
Switch Management Troubleshooting 558
Login Authentication 559
Enable Password Authentication 562
Authorization 564
Accounting 565

Identity-Based Network Services (IBNSs) 566
Configuration Steps 567
Authorization 570
Troubleshooting Steps 570

Case Studies 574
Configuring Automatic Client Enrollment on AD and Installing a Machine Certificate on a Windows Client 574
Generating and Installing the CA Root Certificate on the ACS Server 576
Generating and Installing an ACS Server Certificate on the ACS Server 579

Common Problems and Resolutions 582

Best Practices 585
For Switch Management 585
For Identity-Based Network Services (IBNSs) 585

Chapter 12 Troubleshooting AAA on VPN 3000 Series Concentrator 587

AAA Implementation on the Concentrator 587
VPN Concentrator Management 587
Tunnel Group and User Authentication 587

Diagnostic Commands and Tools 589

Analysis of Problem Areas 590
VPN Concentrator Management Troubleshooting 590
Configuration Steps 590
Group/User Authentication (X-Auth) Troubleshooting 594
Both Group and User Authentication Are Performed Locally on the VPN 3000 Concentrator 595
Group Authentication Is Done Locally and No User Authentication Is Done 596
Group Authentication Is Done Locally on VPN 3000 Concentrator and User Authentication Is Done with RADIUS Server 596
Group Authentication Is Done with a RADIUS Server and User Authentication Is Done Locally 597
Both Group and User Authentications Are Performed with the RADIUS Server 599
User Is Locked to a Specific Group 601
Dynamic Filters on the VPN 3000 Concentrator 602
Configuration of Dynamic Filters on CiscoSecure ACS 604
Troubleshooting Steps 607

Case Studies 608
VPN 3000 Concentrator Configuration 608

Group Configuration on the VPN 3000 Concentrator 608
Defining the CS ACS RADIUS Server on VPN 3000 Concentrator 609
CS ACS Windows Configuration 609
AAA Client Definition for VPN 3000 Concentrator 609
Configuring the Unknown User Policy for Windows NT/2000 Domain Authentication 609
Testing the NT/RADIUS Password Expiration Feature 610

Common Problems and Resolutions 611

Best Practices 612

Chapter 13 Troubleshooting Cisco Secure ACS on Windows 615

Overview of CS ACS 615
CS ACS Architecture 615
The Life of an AAA Packet in CS ACS 619

Diagnostic Commands and Tools 621
Reports and Activity (Real-time Troubleshooting) 621
Radtest and Tactest 622
Package.cab File 622

Categorization of Problem Areas 625
Installation and Upgrade Issues 625
CS ACS on Windows Platform 625
CS ACS with Active Directory Integration 627
Configuration Steps 628
Troubleshooting Steps 629
CS ACS with Novell NDS Integration 630
Configuration Steps 630
Troubleshooting Steps 631
CS ACS with ACE Server (Secure ID [SDI]) Integration 636
Installation and Configuration Steps 637
Troubleshooting Steps 638
Replication Issues 639
Configuration 640
Troubleshooting Steps 644
Network Access Restrictions (NARs) Issues 648
Configuration Steps 648
Troubleshooting Steps 651
Downloadable ACL Issues 652
Downloading ACL per User Basis Using Filter-id 652
Using Cisco AV-Pair 653
Using Shared Profile Components 653
Troubleshooting Steps 654

Case Studies 655
Back Up and Restore the CS ACS Database 656
Creating a Dump Text File 657
User/NAS Import Options 658
Import User Information 658
Import NAS Information 659
Compact User Database 660
Export User and Group Information 660
Common Problems and Resolutions 661
Best Practices 670
Part V Troubleshooting Intrusion Prevention Systems 673
Chapter 14 Troubleshooting Cisco Intrusion Prevention System 675
Overview of IPS Sensor Software 675
IPS Deployment Architecture 676
IPS Software Building Blocks 677
MainApp 677
AnalysisEngine 678
CLI 678
Communication Protocols 678
Modes of Sensor Operation 681
Inline Mode 681
Inline Bypass Mode 682
Promiscuous Mode 682
Combined Modes 683
Hardware and Interfaces Supported 683
Diagnostic Commands and Tools 685
show Commands 686
show version 686
show configuration 687
show events 687
show statistics service 687
show interfaces 689
show tech-support 689
cidDump Script 690
tcpdump command 690
iplog 691
packet Command 692
Classification of Problem Areas 692
Initial Setup Issues 693

User Management Issues 696
Creation and Modification of User Profiles 696
Creating the Service Account 697
Software Installation and Upgrade Issues 699
Obtaining Sensor Software 699
IPS Software Image Naming Conventions 700
Installing or Re-imaging the IPS Appliances System Image 703
Disaster Recovery Plan 707
Upgrading Major/Minor Software or Service Pack/Signature Update 710
Upgrading to IPS 5.0 715
Licensing Issues 717
How Do I Know if I have A Valid License? 717
How to Procure The License Key From Cisco.com 718
Licensing the Sensor 719
Communication Issues 720
Basic Connectivity Issues 720
Connectivity Issues Between IPS Sensor and IPS MC or IDM 725
Connectivity Issues Between IPS Sensor and Security Monitor 725
Issues with Receiving Events on Monitoring Device 726
SensorApp Is Not Running 726
Physical Connectivity, SPAN, or VACL Port Issues 728
Unable to See Alerts 731
Blocking Issues 733
Types of Blocking 733
ACL or VACL Consideration on the Managed Devices 734
Supported Managed Devices and Versions 735
Proper Planning for Blocking 736
Master Blocking Sensor (MBS) 737
Configuration Steps for Blocking 737
Configuring Steps for the Master Blocking Sensor (MBS) 741
Troubleshooting Steps for Blocking 743
TCP Reset Issues 754
Inline IPS Issues 757
Configuration Steps 757
Troubleshooting Steps 762

Case Studies 763
Capturing IPS Traffic with a Hub 763
Capturing IPS Traffic with SPAN 763
SPAN Terminology 764
SPAN Traffic Types 764
SPAN on Catalyst 2900/3500XL 765
SPAN on Catalyst 2950, 3550 and 3750 767
SPAN on Catalyst 4000/6000 with Cat OS 770
SPAN on Catalyst 4000/6000 with Native IOS 771

Capturing IPS Traffic with Remote SPAN (RSPAN) 773
Hardware Requirements 773
Configuration Steps 774
Capturing IPS Traffic with VACL 775
Capturing IPS Traffic with RSPAN and VACL 776
Capturing IPS Traffic with MLS IP IDS 776

Common Problems and Their Resolution 777

Best Practices 781
Preventive Maintenance 782
Creation of Service Account 782
Back up a Good Configuration 782
Recommendation on Connecting Sensor to the Network 784
Recommendation on Connecting the Sniffing Interface of the Sensor to the Network 784
Rating IPS Sensor 784
Recommendation on Connecting Command and Control Interface 784
Recommendation on Settings of Signature on Sensor 784
Recommendation on Inline-Mode Deployment 785

Chapter 15 Troubleshooting IDSM-2 Blade on Switch 787

Overview of IDSM-2 Blade on the Switch 787
Software and Hardware Requirements 788
Slot Assignment on the Switch 788
Front Panel Indicator Lights and How to Use Them 789
Installing the IDSM-2 Blade on the Switch 789
Removing the IDSM-2 Blade from the Switch 790
Ports Supported on IDSM-2 Blade 790

Diagnostic Commands and Tools 791
show Commands in Both Modes 791
show Commands in CatOS 792
show Commands in Native IOS 792

Common Problems and Resolutions 793
Hardware Issues 793
IDSM-2 Hardware Issues on Native IOS 793
IDSM-2 HW Issue on CatOS 797
Communication Issues with IDSM-2 Command and Control Port 800
Configuration Steps 801
Troubleshooting Steps 803
Failing to Get Traffic from the Switch with Promiscuous Mode 805
Configuration Steps 805
Troubleshooting Steps 814
Issues with Inline Mode 816

Not Generating Events Issues 817
TCP Reset Issues 818

Case Study 818
How to Re-image the IDSM-2 with System Image 818
How to Upgrade the Maintenance Partition 823
How to Upgrade the Signature/Service Packs/Minor/Major Software Upgrade 824
How to Upgrade the IDSM-2 Blade from IDSM 4.x to 5.x 826

Common Problems and Resolutions 826

Best Practices 829

Chapter 16 Troubleshooting Cisco IDS Network Module (NM-CIDS) 831

Overview of NM-CIDS on the Router 831
Software and Hardware Requirements 832
Front Panel Indicator Lights and How to Use Them 833
Slot Assignment on the Router 833
Installing NM-CIDS Blade on the Router 833
Removing NM-CIDS Blade from the Router 833
Ports Supported on NM-CIDS 834

Diagnostic Commands and Tools 835

Common Problems and Resolutions 835
Hardware Issues 836
NM-CIDS Console Access Issues 839
Assigning IP Address to the IDS-Sensor Interface on the Router 839
Connecting to NM-CIDS 840
Disconnecting from NM-CIDS 842
Troubleshooting Console Access Issues 843
Communication Issues with NM-CIDS Command and Control Port 844
Issues with Not Receiving Traffic from the Router Using the Sniffing Port 846
Configuration Steps 846
Troubleshooting Steps 847
Managing NM-CIDS from an IOS Router 848
Software Installation and Upgrade Issues 849

Case Studies 850
CEF Forwarding Path 850
IPS Insertion Points 851
Network Address Translation (NAT) 851
Encryption 852
Access List Check 852
IP Multicast, UDP Flooding, IP Broadcast 852

Generic Routing Encapsulation (GRE) Tunnels 852
Address Resolution Protocol (ARP) Packets 853
Packets Dropped by the IOS 853
Forwarding the Packets to the IDS at a Rate Higher Than the Internal Interface Can Handle 853

Common Problems and Resolutions 853
Re-imaging the NM-CIDS Application Partition 854
Performing the Re-image of Application Partition 854
Troubleshooting Steps 857
Configuring Time on the NM-CIDS 857
Default Behavior for Time Setting on NM-CIDS 857
Using Network Time Protocol (NTP) Server 858

Best Practices 858

Chapter 17 Troubleshooting CiscoWorks Common Services 861

Overview of CiscoWorks Common Services 861
Communication Architecture 861
User Management on CiscoWorks Common Services 862

Diagnostic Commands and Tools 863
How to Collect mdcsupport on a Windows Platform 863
Categorization and Explanation of MDCSupport-Created Log Files 863

Categorization of Problem Areas 865
Licensing Issues 865
Registration for CiscoWorks Common Services 867
Installing/Upgrading the License Key for CiscoWorks Common Services 868
Registration for the Management Center for Cisco Security Agents (CSA MC) 868
Installing the License Key for the Management Center for Cisco Security Agents (CSA MC) 869
Common Licensing Issues and Work-Arounds 869
Installation Issues 870
Installation Steps 870
Troubleshooting Installation Problems 871
User Management Issues 873
Database Management Issues 873
CiscoWorks Common Services Backup 874
CiscoWorks Common Services Restore 875

Case Studies 876

Common Problems and Resolutions 877

Best Practices 881

Chapter 18 Troubleshooting IDM and IDS/IPS Management Console (IDS/IPS MC) 883

Overview of IDM and IDS/IPS Management Console (IDS/IPS MC) 883
IDS/IPS MC and Security Monitor Processes 884
Communication Architecture 884

Diagnostic Commands and Tools 885
Audit Reports 885
MDCSupport File 886
How to Collect MDCSupport on a Windows Platform 886
What to Look for and What Is Important in the MDCSupport File 886
Enable Additional Debugging on IDS/IPS MC 887

Analysis of Problem Areas 888
Important Procedures and Techniques 889
Verifying Allowed Hosts on the Sensor 889
Adding Allowed Hosts on the Sensor 890
Verifying the SSH and SSL Connection Between IDS/IPS MC and a Sensor 893
Resolving SSH and SSL Connection Problems Between IDS/IPS MC and a Sensor 893
Verifying If the Sensor Processes Are Running 893
Verifying That the Service Pack or Signature Level Sensor Is Running 895
Verifying the Service Pack or Signature Level on IDS/IPS MC 895
Verifying That the IDS/IPS MC (Apache) Certificate Is Valid 896
Regenerating IDS/IPS MC (Apache) Certificate 897
Resolving Issues with the IDS/IPS Sensor Being Unable to Get the Certificate 897
Changing the VMS Server IP Address 898
Manually Updating the Signature Level on the Sensor 899
Unable to Access the Sensor Using IDM 901
IDS/IPS MC Installation and Upgrade Issues 902
IDS/IPS MC Licensing Issues 904
Corrupted License 904
Determining If a License Is Expired 905
Importing Sensor Issues with IDS/IPS MC 905
Configuration Steps 906
Troubleshooting Steps 907
Signature or Service Pack Upgrade Issues with IDS/IPS MC 908
Upgrade Procedure 909
Troubleshooting Steps 910
Configuration Deployment Issues with IDS/IPS MC 917
Configuration Steps 917
Troubleshooting Steps 918
Database Maintenance (Pruning) Issues 920

Case Study 920
Launch the Attack and Blocking 923
Troubleshooting Steps 924
Common Problems and Resolutions 925
Best Practices 929
Chapter 19 Troubleshooting Firewall MC 931
Overview of Firewall MC 931
Firewall MC Processes 931
Communication Architecture 932
Diagnostic Commands and Tools 932
Collecting the Debug Information (Diagnostics) 932
Using GUI 932
Using CLI 933
What Does the CiscoWorks MDCSupport Utility Generate? 933
Other Useful Log Files Not Collected by mdcsupport 933
Analysis of Problem Areas 934
Installation Issues 934
Installation Verifications 934
Installation Troubleshooting 934
Initialization Issues 936
Browser Issues 937
Authentication Issues 938
Firewall MC Authenticated by the Firewall During Configuration Import and Deployment 939
Firewall MC Authenticated by the Auto Update Server During Configuration Deployment 940
Firewalls Authenticated by the Auto Update Server During Configuration or Image Pulling 940
Activity and Job Management Issues 941
Unlocking of an Activity 941
Stopping a Job from Being Deployed 942
Device Import Issues 943
Configuration Generation and Deployment Issues 947
Firewall MC is Unable To Push the Configuration to the AUS 947
Getting "Incomplete Auto Update Server contact info." Message when Pushing The Configuration to AUS 947
Memory Issues with Firewall Services Module (FWSM) during Deployment 947
Database Management Issues 948
Backing up and Restoring Databases 948
Scheduling Checkpoint Events for the Database 950

Compacting a Database for Performance Improvement 952
Disaster Recovery Plan 953

Common Problems and Resolutions 954

Best Practices 956

Chapter 20 Troubleshooting Router MC 959

Overview of Router MC 959
Router MC Processes 959
Communication Architecture 960
Features Introduced on Different Versions of Router MC 960

Diagnostic Commands and Tools 960
Setting the Logging Level 961
Collecting the Debug Information (Diagnostics) 961
Using a Graphic User Interface 961
Using a Command Line Interface 961
Collecting the Router MC Database 962
Using the Log Files 962
Reports 963

Analysis of Problem Areas 963
Installation and Upgrade Issues 963
Initialization Issues 964
Browser Issues 965
Authentication Issues 967
Authentication Issues with the Router MC 967
Authentication Issues with the Managed Device Using SSH 968
Activity and Job Management Issues 968
Device Import Issues 969
Configuration Generation and Deployment Issues 970
Database Management Issues 972
Backing up and Restoring Database 972
Troubleshooting Router MC Backup/Restore Operations 973

Case Study 974
Understanding User Permissions 974
CiscoWorks Server Roles and Router MC Permissions 974
ACS Roles and Router MC Permissions 975
Setting up Router MC to Work with ACS 979
Step 1: Define the Router MC Server in ACS 979
Step 2: Define the Login Module in CiscoWorks as TACACS+ 979
Step 3: Synchronize CiscoWorks Common Services with the ACS Server Configuration 980
Step 4: Define Usernames, Device Groups, And User Groups in ACS 980

Best Practices 980

Chapter 21 Troubleshooting Cisco Security Agent Management Console (CSA MC) and CSA Agent 983

Overview of CSA MC and Agent 983
Management Model for CSAgent 983
CSA MC Directory Structure 985
Communication Architecture 986
How Cisco Security Agents Protect Against Attacks 987

Diagnostic Commands and Tools 987
CSA MC Log 987
Windows System Information 988
Server Selftest Information 988
CSA MC Log Directory 988
CSA Agent Log 988
CSA Agent Log Directory 988
Turning on Debug Mode 989
Details Log—csainfo.log file 989
Logs for Blue Screen 990
Rtrformat Utility 990
Additional Logs Controlled by the Sysvars.cf file 991

Categorization of Problem Areas 992
Installation and Upgrade Issues 993
New Installation Issues with CSA MC 993
New Installation Issues with CSAgent 997
Upgrade Issues with CSA MC 1002
CSAgent Update Issues 1004
Licensing Issues 1005
How to Procure the License 1007
How to Import the License 1007
Determining the Number of Desktop/Server Licenses That Are in Use 1008
Troubleshooting Licensing Issues 1009
CSA MC Launching Issues 1010
CSA MC Not Launching 1010
CSA MC Is Launching, but Slowly 1013
CSAgent Communication, Registration, and Polling Issues with CSA MC 1014
Application Issues with CSAgent 1016
How to Create Exceptions 1016
How to Disable Individual CSAgent Shims 1016
Disabling csauser.dll 1018
Creating Buffer Overflow Exclusions 1018
Troubleshooting Steps 1020
Report Generation Issues 1021

Profiler Issues 1022
Database Maintenance Issues 1023
Disaster Recovery Plan (DRP) for CSA MC 1023
Purging Events from the Database 1028
Compacting the Database 1029
Checking and Repairing the CSA MC MSDE Database 1031

Common Problems and Resolutions 1032

Best Practices 1036
Recommendation on Installation 1036
Test Mode 1036
Disaster Recovery for CSA 1036

Chapter 22 Troubleshooting IEV and Security Monitors 1039

Overview of IEV and Security Monitor 1039
Communication Architecture 1040
How Does It Work? 1041
RDEP/SDEE Collector Management 1042
XML Parsing 1044
Alert Inserter 1044
IDS/IPS MC and Security Monitor Processes 1044
User Management for Security Monitor 1045

Diagnostic Commands and Tools 1046

Categorization of Problem Areas 1046
Installation Issues 1047
Issues with Launching 1047
DNS Issues 1048
Issues with Enabling SSL 1049
Getting Internal Server Error While Opening Security Monitor 1050
Security Monitor Takes a Long Time to Launch 1050
Page Cannot Be Found Error While Trying to Launch Security Monitor 1050
IDS/IPS MC Launches But Security Monitor Does Not 1050
Security Monitor Behaves Strangely 1051
Licensing Issues 1051
Device Management Issues 1051
Importing IDS Sensors from IDS/IPS MC 1051
Adding Other Devices 1052
IEV and Security Monitor Connect with Sensor 1053
Notification Issues 1055
Event Viewer Issues 1055
Launching the Event Viewer 1055
Using the Event Viewer 1056

Generating Events for Test 1057
Troubleshooting Steps 1057
Report Generation Issues 1060
Report Generation Fails 1060
Report Fails to Complete 1061
Database Maintenance Issues 1062
Proactive Measures Immediately After Installing the Security Monitor 1062
Reactive Measures During Run Time 1064
Case Study 1068
Configuration Steps 1068
Troubleshoot E-mail Notification 1071
Common Problems and Resolutions 1072
Best Practices 1077
Index 1079

Icons Used in This Book

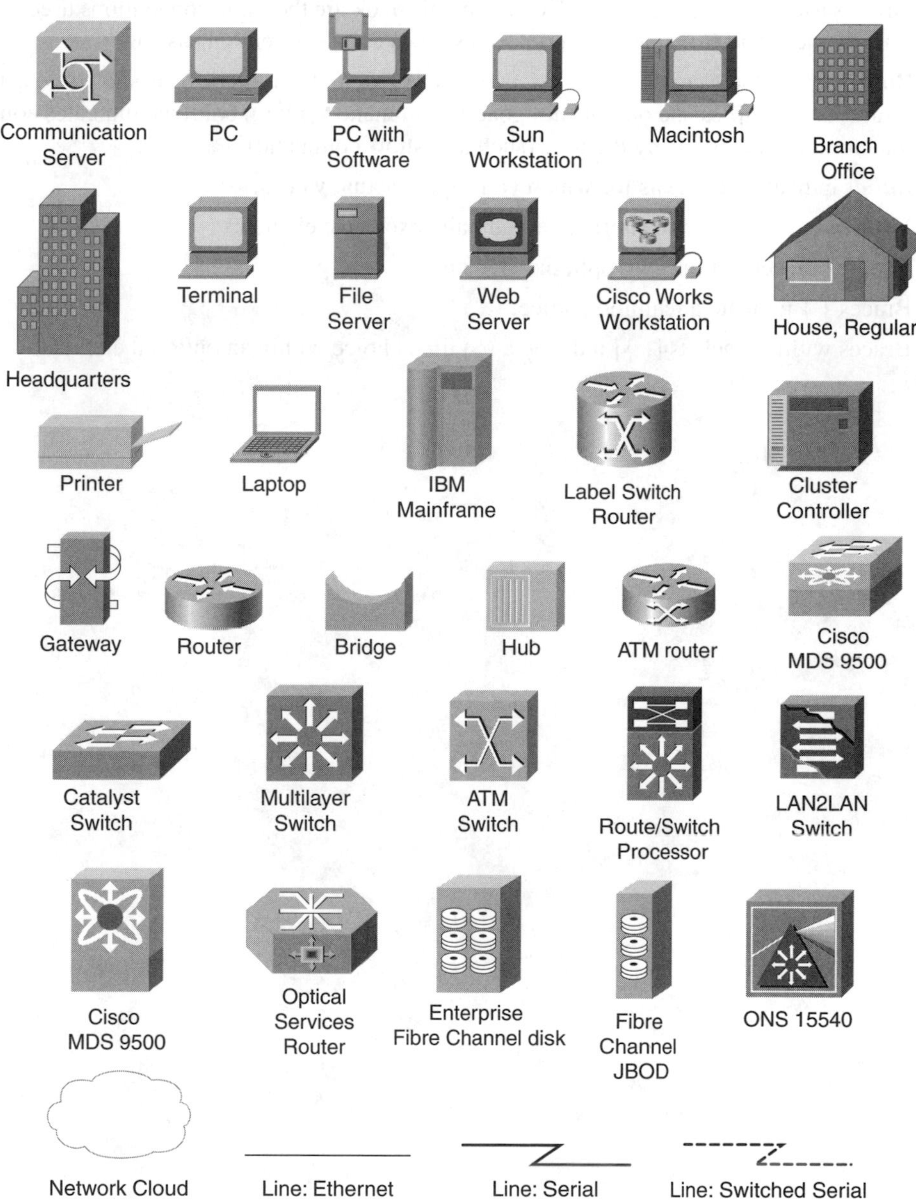

Command Syntax Conventions

The conventions used to present command syntax in this book are the same conventions used in the IOS Command Reference. The Command Reference describes these conventions as follows:

- **Boldface** indicates commands and keywords that are entered literally as shown. In actual configuration examples and output (not general command syntax), boldface indicates commands that are input manually by the user (such as a **show** command).
- *Italics* indicate arguments for which you supply actual values.
- Vertical bars (|) separate alternative, mutually exclusive elements.
- Square brackets [ ] indicate optional elements.
- Braces { } indicate a required choice.
- Braces within brackets [{ }] indicate a required choice within an optional element.

Introduction

Learning and implementing effective troubleshooting techniques is essential to protect your network. Cisco Network Security Troubleshooting Handbook prepares you to systematically troubleshoot your network's security devices and presents step-by-step procedures for tackling issues that arise so that you can protect your network and avoid costly down time for your enterprise.

Goals and Methods

Cisco.com documentation, along with other texts on Cisco network security devices, is invaluable in providing information that is required in understanding different products. Unfortunately, this information is scattered in different places, and different text. My motivation in writing this book is to give you the technique and approach that I and other TAC engineers use to troubleshoot an issue on different Cisco network security devices. The book brings all the tools and techniques scattered around different places in Cisco.com into a centralized location, which not only will help readers to quickly identify the tools and commands required to diagnose a problem, but will help in escalating the issue to the Cisco Support team in a timely manner, with all the required information to resolve the issue faster.

Every chapter of this text will help you understand the configuration and troubleshooting of Cisco network security products on the following topics:

- Overview of every product
- Diagnostic tools and commands available
- Categorization of the problem areas of every product
- Case studies
- Common problems and resolutions
- Best practices

Who Should Read This Book?

This book is not designed to be a general security design or configuration topics book, although it can be used for that purpose. This book is intended to tremendously increase your ability to troubleshoot Cisco network security products efficiently. You can also use this book for preparing for the CCIE Security exam, but that's not the ultimate intention. The main purpose of this book is to provide a one-stop, comprehensive troubleshooting solution for Cisco network security products deployed in the enterprise network.

Strategies for Becoming an Efficient Troubleshooter

There are several ways that you can develop the skills required to be an efficient Cisco network security troubleshooter. While some people take a systematic approach and try to understand the products in greater depth, and then troubleshoot the issue efficiently; others learn it on the job without in-depth understanding of the product. This book can be used in both ways.

How This Book Is Organized

Although this book could be read cover-to-cover, it is designed to be flexible and allow you to move easily between chapters, and sections of chapters, to cover just the material that you need more work with.

The chapters cover the following topics:

- **Chapter 1, "Troubleshooting Methods"**—This chapter discusses the Troubleshooting techniques for Cisco network security and some of challenges that need to be overcome for troubleshooting problems efficiently.
- **Chapter 2, "Understanding Troubleshooting Tools"**—This chapter discusses some of the basic tools available to determine the facts of the problem. More product-specific tools and commands are discussed in the product-specific chapter.
- **Chapter 3, "Troubleshooting Cisco Secure PIX Firewalls"**—This chapter discusses the new features available on PIX Firewall Version 7.0 and ASA platform. In-depth troubleshooting tips and techniques are discussed thoroughly in this chapter. This chapter provides the foundation knowledge required to understand Chapters 4 and 5.
- **Chapter 4, "Troubleshooting Firewall Services Module"**—Firewall Services Module provides the same functionality as PIX Firewall with complex architecture. This chapter doesn't repeat the information discussed in Chapter 3, but discusses the configuration and troubleshooting of the issues that are specific to FWSM.
- **Chapter 5, "Troubleshooting an IOS Firewall"**—This chapter examines the configuration and troubleshooting of CBAC, one of the IOS firewalls, in detail. Auth-proxy is discussed in the case study section of this chapter.
- **Chapter 6, "Troubleshooting IPSec VPNs on IOS Routers"**—This chapter provides a brief overview of the IPSec protocol, which is the foundation information required for Chapters 7 and 8. Configuration and troubleshooting aspects are examined in greater depth for both LAN-to-LAN and Remote Access VPN connection using IPSec protocol only. DMVPN, an extension of LAN-to-LAN IPSec VPN tunnel, is discussed in this chapter in greater detail.
- **Chapter 7, "Troubleshooting IPSec VPN on PIX Firewalls"**—This chapter covers configuration and troubleshooting of IPSec VPN on the PIX Firewalls/ASA platform.
- **Chapter 8, "Troubleshooting IPSec VPNs on VPN 3000 Series Concentrators"**—This chapter covers configuration and troubleshooting of both LAN-to-LAN and Remote Access VPN connections using the IPSec protocol on VPN 3000 Series Concentrators. Web VPN and SSL VPN are discussed in greater detail in this chapter.
- **Chapter 9, "Troubleshooting AAA on IOS Routers"**—AAA and the protocols that implement AAA framework are discussed in this chapter, which is the foundation knowledge required for Chapters 10, 11, and 12. Specific AAA implementation and troubleshooting of the RADIUS and TACACS+ protocols are discussed in greater detail.
- **Chapter 10, "Troubleshooting AAA on PIX Firewalls and FWSM"**—Based on the knowledge gained from Chapter 9, this chapter explores configuration and troubleshooting issues in AAA implementation for PIX management and cut-through proxy authentication (for the traffic through the PIX firewall). This discussion is based on PIX Firewall Version 7.0.

- **Chapter 11, "Troubleshooting AAA on the Switches"**—Configuration and troubleshooting of AAA implementation for both Switch management and Identity-based Network Services (IBNS) are discussed in greater detail.
- **Chapter 12, "Troubleshooting AAA on VPN 3000 Series Concentrator"**—AAA can be used for both VPN 3000 Series Concentrator management and VPN connections. Both of these options are discussed in detail in this chapter.
- **Chapter 13, "Troubleshooting Cisco Secure ACS on Windows"**—This chapter discusses the configuration and troubleshooting of Cisco Security ACS on Windows. This same information also can be used for ACS Appliance.
- **Chapter 14, "Troubleshooting Cisco Intrusion Prevention System"**—This chapter discusses the configuration and troubleshooting of IPS 5.0 version on the IPS Appliance. This chapter also builds up the foundation for Chapters 15 and 16.
- **Chapter 15, "Troubleshooting IDSM-2 Blade on Switch"**—IDSM-2 runs the same software on the appliance that is discussed in Chapter 14, so the same information is not discussed in this chapter. IPS specific to IDSM-2 blade is discussed in this chapter.
- **Chapter 16, "Troubleshooting Cisco IDS network module (NM-CIDS)"**—NM-CIDS is an IPS blade that runs on the router, which is discussed thoroughly in this chapter. The IPS feature is discussed in Chapter 14.
- **Chapter 17, "Troubleshooting Common Services"**—Common Services is a component of the VMS bundle that installs other reporting and management components, such as Firewall MC, Router MC, Security Monitor, and so on. Troubleshooting of Common Services is discussed thoroughly in this chapter.
- **Chapter 18, "Troubleshooting IDM and IDS/IPS Management Console (IDS/IPS MC)"**—This chapter discusses the configuration and troubleshooting of IDM and IPS Console (IPS MC), which is part of VMS to manage sensors.
- **Chapter 19, "Troubleshooting Firewall MC"**—This chapter discusses the configuration and troubleshooting of Firewall MC, which is a component of VMS to manage the PIX firewall, FWSM, and ASA 5500 series appliances.
- **Chapter 20, "Troubleshooting Router MC"**—This chapter discusses the configuration and troubleshooting of Router MC, which is used to manage VPN configuration on the router.
- **Chapter 21, "Troubleshooting Cisco Security Agent Management Console (CSA MC) and CSA Agent"**—This chapter discusses configuration and troubleshooting of the host-based IPS solution, which is used to protect the hosts from malicious activities.
- **Chapter 22, "Troubleshooting IEV and Security Monitors"**—The primary focus of this chapter is to discuss the configuration and troubleshooting of Security Monitor, which is a component of VMS that can be used to receive events from Firewall, CSA, IPS sensors, and so on. Based on the events received, user-friendly reports can be generated based on different criteria. This chapter focuses on some of issues that may arise during run time.

PART

Troubleshooting Tools and Methodology

Chapter 1 Troubleshooting Methods

Chapter 2 Understanding Troubleshooting Tools

CHAPTER 1

Troubleshooting Methods

Providing users with networks that demonstrate high availability has never been as important as it is today. A single moment of network downtime may cost an organization a considerable amount of money and represent, as well, intangible losses that are not acceptable to today's executives. So, it is important to have the methods and tools at your disposal to troubleshoot any critical issues that you might experience in your network. While this is true for all network components, it is even more important for the security devices, because security devices embed into different parts of the network in the traffic path to provide security. Therefore the problems that arise from security devices often are critical and their impact on the overall network is huge. For example, a simple misconfiguration of Access Control lists (ACLs) on Firewall in the direction of Internet-bound connections could block all Internet-bound traffic for the whole network. For these reasons, knowing the products and the available commands and tools for identifying the problem quickly is a must. To be successful as a Cisco network security troubleshooter, you need the following:

- Clear understanding of security devices
- An accurate and complete network topology which shows a detailed view of the network, packet paths, and the position of the security devices in the packet path
- Method to diagnose the problem and select the tools for diagnosis

This chapter focuses on a generic troubleshooting method for security products in the network (a method that also is useful for other networking devices). Chapter 2, "Understanding Troubleshooting Tools," focuses on the most important components of the "Troubleshooting Methodology" which is the primary topic of this chapter.

Proactive Actions for Handling Network Failure

Network failure is extremely undesirable; nevertheless, it is unavoidable. Network failure is caused by the constant additions and changes to the network that are necessary because of the increasing demand for rapid throughput, the addition of advanced service features (for example, Voice over IP [VoIP]), and the evolution of new technologies such as wireless LANs. Additional security services and protocols are constantly being developed to meet the security needs and requirements of these new technologies and products. The best approach is to be prepared and equipped with all the tools and techniques you need to cope with network failure. It is always easier and faster to recover from a network failure if you are fully prepared ahead of time.

As a self-test, review the following list to check if you are fully prepared for a network failure:

- **Proper documentation**—Clear documentation that is easy to follow is a must for any network and in particular for troubleshooting network devices. It is also important during troubleshooting to document any changes being made to the network so that it is easier to back out of an operation if troubleshooting has failed to identify the problem within the maintenance window. Having good backup copies of all the devices before the start of a troubleshooting session can help to restore the network to working condition more quickly.

  Solutions to every problem that is solved should be documented, so that you can create a knowledge base that others in your organization can follow if similar problems occur later. Invariably this will reduce the time to troubleshoot your networks and, consequently, minimize the business impact.

- **Having a network baseline**—You must baseline your network, and document normal network behavior and performance as follows: at different times of the day, different days in the week, and different months in the year. This is very important, especially for the security aspects of the network. You might also consider deploying external auditing or logging tools such as Syslog, MCP, and so on, for defining the baseline. Another good practice is to constantly collect logs for comparison with the baseline to uncover any abnormal behavior that requires investigation and troubleshooting. For example, you baseline a network that has connection counts across a PIX firewall of 10K in rush hours. Suddenly, on Saturday night, your PIX experiences connections substantially above 10K. You know something is wrong, and this knowledge should trigger further investigation before a worm could possibly spread and cause more harm to the network.

- **Backup of working configuration and version information of devices on controlled areas in the network**—You must back up working copies of every device's configuration and version information, and keep them in a secured location that is readily accessible to selected personnel, so that you can revert back if needed.

- **Clear, concise and updated network topology**—Undoubtedly, one of the most important requirements in any network environment is to have current and accurate information about that network (both physical and logical topology) available to the network support personnel at all times. Only with complete information can we make intelligent decisions about network change. In addition, only with complete information can we troubleshoot as quickly and as easily as possible. The network topology should include at a minimum, the names, types, and IP address of the devices. Additionally, it is advisable to know the types of protocols, links, and services configured on the devices.

- **Tools Readily Available**—It is not acceptable to have to wait to download or install tools that might be required during troubleshooting. At a minimum, be sure to have available external Syslog servers and sniffer software, in addition to an FTP

Server and a Trivial File Transfer Protocol (TFTP) server. For example, most PIX firewall issues can be diagnosed with the syslog server. Under some rare circumstances, you might need the sniffer capture if the syslog is not giving you any conclusive result.

- **Cohesive teamwork between Security Operation (SecOp) and Network Operation (NetOp) personnel**—In a mid- to large-sized network, network operations and security operations are divided. As the security is a component that goes hand-in-hand with every technology and product, it is extremely important that you have a cooperative professional relationship with those involved in troubleshooting issues that involve technologies beyond security. For example, if you have a GRE over IPSec tunnel between two sites, Security Operations might be responsible for the IPSec VPN, whereas Network Operations handles routing and switching. If you have problems with unstable VPN tunnel and packet drops, the problem might be either with the VPN or the underlying IP network. If the IP network is not stable, the tunnel will not be stable. Or the problem might simply be with the hardware encryption. In nutshell, to come up with the fastest diagnosis and resolution, both teams should form a cohesive work team.
- **Change control review**—You must produce a change control for all the following: every component you add to the network; every new service you turn on; and every new command you add to the devices. Change control includes documentation and thorough review with senior engineers and management. If possible, simulate the setup in the lab network before introducing the changes to production. Schedule a maintenance window within which to perform the task. Formally establish a change control review board with the senior members of the team if required.
- **Clear and concise escalation procedure**—This is often one of the most important and overlooked proactive measures. You should document and make available to every member of the troubleshooting team a clear and concise escalation procedure. You should also list the points of contact to external networks, including the connections to the Internet. This not only helps you as a senior engineer in the company, but helps others who are new to your network. Escalation procedures could include information on how to engage the next tier of engineering in your organization, and guidelines on when and how to engage the Cisco Support team.

Types of Failure

So far you have learned what actions you may take to make yourself completely ready to recover fully from any type of security-related network failure. Although it is important to recover quickly from every failure, some types are more important than others, and therefore failures are handled differently. Network failures can also occur at different times:

- **During the configuration/deployment phase**—As previously discussed, any addition, deletion, or change to the network (for example, a software upgrade, or adding a new device such as a PIX) should be accomplished during a scheduled maintenance window. If the change control is not implemented in due time, you must have a rollback capability to the working condition. If you encounter problems during configuration/deployment, most of the time this is considered to be a non-service affecting failure, and you have more time to analyze and troubleshoot the problem. For example, if you wanted to protect a segment of your network which is currently unprotected with a PIX firewall, and during PIX deployment you encounter problems with traffic, you could roll back to the previous setup (that is, leaving the network without PIX) until the root cause was known. With this type of failure, it is extremely important to collect the required information to get to the root cause of the problem.

- **In the production network**—You could experience a failure in the production network. For example, traffic has been flowing without problems, when suddenly a user from the internal network cannot access the Internet across the PIX firewall. This type of failure is unexpected and requires in-depth knowledge of the product and a systematic approach to troubleshooting this type of failure. The next section covers these topics.

Problem-Solving Model

While troubleshooting a production network problem, it is best to use a systematic troubleshooting approach. It is not uncommon to see a network security troubleshooter take an unsystematic approach, which might work sometimes, but could introduce other problems to the network. Besides, troubleshooting takes enormous amounts of time unless you know about the product and technology, and take a systematic approach.

This section explains the systematic troubleshooting approach that you can use to help isolate your problems.

Step 1 Define the problem.

Step 2 Gather facts about the problem.

Step 3 Consider possibilities.

Step 4 Create an action plan.

Step 5 Implement the action plan.

Step 6 Observe the results.

Step 7 Repeat Steps 1 through 6 if necessary.

Step 8 Document the changes after the issue is resolved.

The sections that follow provide additional information about each of these steps.

Step 1: Define the Problem

This is the first step in the process. Based on the information available, you must define your problem precisely. You should define the problem in terms of a set of symptoms and potential causes. Every problem should have an element (for example, PIX firewall, translation, connection, and so on) and one or two lines outlining the problem statement. Sometimes you have to deal with multiple problems. In that case, it is important to define each problem individually and address each one in the order of priority. This is especially important because without solving the problem of highest priority, you might not be able to address the next issue.

For instance, users might complain that the PIX firewall was not allowing their traffic from inside to the Internet. There could be multiple reasons for this. It could be that the translation is not formed that is required for the connection to be formed. This, in turn, results in an unsuccessful connection across the PIX firewall. Or, it could be that translation is formed but the connection is not formed. So, under that circumstance, you might define two problem statements. The first statement could be this: "The PIX is not building up translation." The second statement could be this: "The PIX is not building up a connection." Now you need to prioritize which is more important. Obviously, without translation, there are no connections. So, you need to work on translation first, because resolving translation may resolve the connection. From this example you can see that setting priorities is important. So, to properly analyze the problem, identify the general symptoms, and then ascertain what kinds of problems (causes) could result in these symptoms. The problem statement should follow this format: *What is wrong with what?*

Here are some of the questions that will help you define a good problem statement:

1 Identify the concerns end users have by asking these questions:

   a What is wrong in the network?

   b What actions do I want to take in the network?

   c How do I know there is a problem? Is it based on hard data like debugs, traces, screen shots, and show commands, or is it based on users' experiences?

   d What do I see in the network that indicates that there is a problem?

2 Once you have answers to these preliminary questions, you might need to prioritize the problem by answering the following questions:

   a What has the biggest impact on my network operations?

   b What is the impact on my network or operations?

   c What is the impact on my business?

   d What are my deadlines, and what is the timeframe or maintenance window I am working in?

   e When are my users coming into work?

   f What is the impact on our business or operations if we do not get this fixed?

   g What signs do I see that this impact will be changing?

3 After going through steps 1 and 2, you should be able to define the problems and prioritize them if needed. The problem statement can now be as narrowed to the following: "Translation is not getting built up on the PIX firewall for inside host x."

Step 2: Gather the Facts

Gathering facts is a step that will help to isolate the possible causes. The following actions should be taken to uncover the facts:

1 What are the reported problems?

   To find out the problems reported, take the following steps:

   a Ask questions of affected users, network administrators, managers, and other key people.

   b Collect information from sources such as network management systems, protocol analyzer traces, output from router diagnostic commands, or software release notes. Chapter 2, "Understanding Troubleshooting Tools," covers the tools required for collecting and verifying facts.

2 Where is the problem reported?

   Once you identify symptoms of the problems, you need to find out exactly where the problem is reported. This deals with the location of the device and the problems in the device. The following questions, along with a topology diagram of the network, will help you find information about where the problem is reported:

   a Which device (VPN concentrator, PIX, and so on) is having a problem?

   b What country, city, wiring closet is it in? A topology map also will give you this information.

   c What interface (for example on PIX, is it DMZ, outside, or the inside interfaces) is experiencing problems?

   d Which functions in the software are problematic (for example is it connection, translation, etc. on the PIX Firewall)?

   e Which perimeter of the network is the source of the problem?

3 When is the problem reported?

   It is very important to know when the problem is reported. This might help in identifying what changes have occurred at the time of the problem occurrence. The following question will help in getting this information:

   a When did you first notice the problem? (Refer to timestamps in the syslog.) You can ask the end users for the time when the problem occurred and see if the time stamp on the log correlates with the time end users report.

   b When was the problem was first reported and logged?

   c Is the problem intermittent (appearing and disappearing at different parts of the day for example), or continuous?

   d At which stage of the protocol negotiation does the failure occur? (For example, in the case of IPSec, is it failing on phase 1 or phase 2?)

   e What changes were made to the network before, after, or at the time the problem was reported by syslog or an end user.

   f Which devices are affected? Are there any other similar or different types of devices that possibly may be affected but are not affected, and what are the key differences?

4 What is the scope of the problem?

   Understanding the magnitude of the problem is important. The following questions will assist you in identifying the magnitude of the problem:

   a How many network/security devices experience the problem?

   b How big is the issue? How many users are affected?

   c How many issues are there on any specific device? For example, are you experiencing both high CPU and failover issues on the PIX? One might be responsible for the other, but you need to include all possibilities.

   d Is there any specific pattern or trend? Is the problem becoming aggravated, reducing, or staying the same? For example, if you have a connection problem across the PIX firewall for a specific host, are there multiple hosts having problems with connection? Is the problem reduced at a specific time of the day?

5 Use baseline information.

After collecting as many facts as possible, use the baseline information (configuration, statistics, and so on) to find out what has changed in terms of configurations and statistics. For example, you might have baselined the Port Address Translation (PAT) to be 30K during a busy hour. And if you find the translation number has crossed more than 30K at any given time, this could be a potential problem.

Step 3: Consider Possible Problems

If you do a good job in fact-finding, know your network well, and have topology and baseline information on hand, this step is easier. In other words, the success or failure of this step depends heavily upon the previous steps.

Using the facts, you can eliminate some of the potential problems from the list you defined in Step 1. Depending on the data, for example, you might be able to identify whether a problem involves software or configuration. At every opportunity, try to decrease the number of potential problems, so that you can create an efficient plan of action, which is discussed next.

Step 4: Create an Action Plan

Based on the remaining potential problems deduced from the previous step, prioritize the issues. Then start making the changes one by one, based on the list you have created, with highest priority first. Working with only one variable at a time enables you to reproduce a given solution to a specific problem. If you alter more than one variable simultaneously, you might be able to solve the problem, but identifying the specific change that eliminated the symptom becomes far more difficult, and will not help you solve the same problem if it occurs in the future.

Step 5: Implement the Action Plan

Perform each step carefully while testing to see whether the symptom disappears.

Step 6: Observe Results

Whenever you change a variable, be sure to gather results. Generally, you should use the same method of gathering facts that you used in Step 2 (that is, working with the key people affected, in conjunction with using your diagnostic tools).

Step 7: Repeat if Necessary

Analyze the results to determine whether the problem has been resolved. If it has, then the troubleshooting is complete.

Step 8: Document the Changes

If the problem has not been resolved, you must create an action plan based on the next most likely problem in your list. Return to Step 4, change one variable at a time, and repeat the process until the problem is solved. However, if the problem is resolved, be sure to document the changes you make. This step is very important and often is ignored. Every change you make to the network poses the potential of creating another problem (although this does not often happen). So, if you have the documentation on the changes you make, you can always refer back to them. Besides, this process produces a good knowledge base for others in the department who are not involved with the specific troubleshooting that you have performed.

Summary

As you have seen in this chapter, a systematic troubleshooting approach coupled with sound knowledge of the Cisco Network Security products can make a troubleshooter's life painless. One very important piece in this systematic approach is the tools and techniques without which fact-findings might be inaccurate or incomplete. Chapter 2, "Understanding Troubleshooting Tools," discusses a summary version of the commands and tools available for the security devices to be successful in a fact-finding process. Subsequent chapters discuss troubleshooting tools and techniques in greater detail based on specific products to make Cisco network security troubleshooting efficient. So, buckle up and start this exciting and challenging journey through Cisco network security troubleshooting.

CHAPTER 2

Understanding Troubleshooting Tools

As discussed in Chapter 1, fact finding is the most important aspect of the troubleshooting life cycle. In today's complex networks, without proper tools and commands, it is extremely difficult to verify essential details. Other chapters in this text present the tools and commands specific to a product, but this chapter presents a general overview of all those tools.

Using Device Diagnostic Commands

Cisco Security Network devices have numerous integrated commands to assist you in monitoring and troubleshooting your network. The following sections describe the basic use of these commands:

- **show** commands
- **debug** commands

show Commands

The **show** commands are powerful monitoring and troubleshooting tools. You can use the **show** commands to perform several functions:

- Monitor device behavior during initial installation
- Monitor normal network operation
- Isolate problems with interfaces, nodes, media, or applications
- Determine when a network is congested
- Determine the status of servers, clients, or other neighbors

The **show** commands have different effects for different devices as explained in this text, chapter by chapter. However, some common commands are used in every device. For instance, the **show version** command displays the configuration of the system hardware, the software version, the names and sources of configuration files, and the boot images. The **show running-config** command displays the router configuration currently running.

Some of the Cisco Network Security devices have a convenient Graphical User Interface (GUI) for obtaining status and various statistics which is equivalent to the output of **show** command using CLI. One such tool is the PIX Device Manager (PDM). You can use either the **show** command or the PDM to obtain statistics and configuration information on the PIX firewall.

debug Commands

The **debug** commands can provide a wealth of information about the traffic being seen (or *not* seen) on an interface, error messages generated by nodes on the network, protocol-specific diagnostic packets, and other useful troubleshooting data. Exercise care when using **debug** commands. Many **debug** commands are processor-intensive and can cause serious network problems (such as degraded performance or loss of connectivity) if they are enabled on an already heavily loaded router. When you finish using a **debug** command, remember to disable it with its specific **no debug** command (or use the **no debug all** or **undebug all** command to turn off all debugging).

It is best to use **debug** commands to isolate problems, not to monitor normal network operation. Because of high processor overhead, **debug** commands can disrupt device operation, and therefore you should use them only when you are looking for specific types of traffic or problems, and have narrowed your problems to a likely subset of causes.

Output formats vary with each **debug** command. Some generate a single line of output per packet, and others generate multiple lines of output per packet. Some frequently generate large amounts of output, and others generate only occasional output. Some generate lines of text, and others generate information in field format.

To minimize the negative impact of using **debug** commands, follow this procedure:

Step 1 Use the **no logging console** global configuration command on your router. This command disables all logging to the console terminal.

Step 2 Use Telnet to access the network devices (for example, router, PIX, and so on) and go into **enable** mode. For a router, you then execute the **terminal monitor** command to copy **debug** command output and system error messages to your current terminal display. By redirecting output to your current terminal display, you can remotely view the output of the **debug** command, without being connected through the console port. If you use **debug** commands at the console port, character-by-character processor interrupts are generated, maximizing the processor load already caused by using **debug**. If you intend to keep the output of the **debug** command, spool the output to a file.

Step 3 You can also send the debug output to the buffer or a syslog server for reliability checks and capturing debug output, especially when you cannot remain in front of the Telnet window of the device. For collecting debug output or other syslog messages in real time, the Telnet window (the monitor mode on the router for syslog) is preferred. However, if you need to collect the debug output or other syslog messages on the router over a period of time, the only choices are sending the debug and other syslog messages to a buffer or the syslog servers. Sometimes, because of buffer limitations on the device, syslog server is the only choice.

Test Commands

There are few test commands available that can be used for various purposes. Following is a list of such commands:

- **ping**—Helps to determine the connectivity between devices on your network.
- **traceroute**—Provides a method of determining the route by which packets reach their destination from one device to another.
- **telnet**—Helps to find out if a TCP-based application is running and listening on a specific port.
- **nslookup**—Helps to determine if name resolution for a domain name or IP address is working correctly.

ping Command

To check host reachability and network connectivity, use the **ping** command, which can be invoked from any network device that has a TCP/IP stack. For IP, the **ping** command sends Internet Control Message Protocol (ICMP) Echo messages. ICMP is the Internet protocol that reports errors and provides information relevant to IP packet addressing. If a station receives an ICMP Echo message, it sends an ICMP Echo Reply message back to the source.

The extended command mode of the **ping** command permits you to specify the supported IP header options. Different Cisco security devices implement the **ping** command in different ways. For example, in a router, **extended ping** allows the router to perform a more extensive range of test options. To enter **ping** extended command mode, enter **yes** at the extended commands prompt of the **ping** command on the router.

There are various other usages for the **ping** command than just connectivity testing. For example, extended ping on the router can be used to initiate a LAN-to-LAN IPsec tunnel by generating interesting traffic. This helps in verifying if the tunnel configuration is correct, and if the tunnel is working as expected on the routers. If the tunnel is working with extended ping, then this indicates that the problem may be somewhere else in the network. You can use count, MTU, and DF bit option to find out the packet loss and fragmentation issues. More specific usage of the **ping** command is discussed in the chapter that is specific to each product.

traceroute Command

The **traceroute** (in a Windows platform, it is **tracert**) command discovers the routes that a packet follows when traveling to its destination. The **traceroute** command permits the supported IP header options to be specified, allowing the router to perform a more extensive range of test options.

The **traceroute** command works by using the error message generated by routers when a datagram exceeds its time-to-live (TTL) value. First, a probe datagram is sent with a TTL value of 1. This causes the first router to discard the probe datagram and send back "time exceeded" error messages. The **traceroute** command then sends several probes and displays the round-trip time for each. After every third probe, the TTL is increased by 1.

Each outgoing packet can result in one of two error messages. A "time exceeded" error message indicates that an intermediate router has seen and discarded the probe. A "port unreachable" error message indicates that the destination node has received the probe and discarded it because it could not deliver the packet to an application. If the timer goes off before a response comes in, **traceroute** prints an asterisk (*).

The **traceroute** command terminates when the destination responds, when the maximum TTL is exceeded, or when the user interrupts the trace with the escape sequence. Note that for **traceroute** to function correctly, you must ensure that you are allowing all the ICMP types **traceroute** command uses ("Time Exceeded" for example); otherwise, **traceroute** will not work. If that happens, you are limited to using only the **ping** command if only **Echo** and **Echo Reply** are allowed. For details on different ICMP types, go to the following link:

http://www.cisco.com/warp/public/110/31.html#messtype

Just as with **ping**, you can use the **traceroute** command for connectivity testing. But the real use of the **traceroute** command is to find out which device in the network is dropping the packets if there is a connectivity issue. Also, if you have a routing loop in the network or an asymmetric routing setup in the network, you can discover this by performing the trace a few times and comparing the hops the packet is taking each time.

telnet Command

As you know, Telnet is primarily used to log in to a specific device for configuration purposes. However, the **telnet** command also can check the status of a specific TCP port of an application to see if the application is working on that specific port. For instance, to find out if the mail server is alive and listening on port 25 for SMTP, use the **telnet** command with mail server IP address or the domain name along with the port number 25 as an argument, as follows:

```
D:\>telnet xxx.xyz.com 25
220 xxx.xyz.com ESMTP Sendmail ......
```

You can also check to see if the web server is alive by using Telnet to access the web server with port **80**, and after that executing the **get** command. Example 2-1 shows output from a live web server with the **telnet** command on port **80**:

Example 2-1 *Shows the Output of Telnet Test for a Live Web Server*

```
D:\>telnet www.xyz.com 80
HTTP/1.0 200 OK
Cache-Control: no-store
Pragma: no-cache
Cache-Control: no-cache
X-Bypass-Cache: Application and Content Networking System Software 4.2.9
Connection: Close

<HTML><HEAD><META HTTP-EQUIV="REFRESH" CONTENT="0" URL=""></HEAD><BODY>
</BODY></HTML>
Connection to host lost.
D:\>
```

Just as with a mail server and web server, you can find out if a TCP-based application is running and listening on a specific TCP port with the **telnet** command in a similar fashion as shown earlier.

nslookup Command

This command is used to obtain the IP address of a domain name or a domain name of an IP address of a specific server application (for instance, Web application running on a server). This is an extremely useful command, because while troubleshooting issues with e-mail or Web packets connectivity, you may not know if you have a problem with the domain name resolution or the actual packet flow. Example 2-2 shows how to use this command to perform the resolution from domain name to IP address and vice versa.

Example 2-2 *Use* **nslookup** *Command for Domain Name to IP Address Resolution and Vice Versa*

```
! The following line is trying to find out the ip address of the www.xyz.com web
! server's IP address
D:\>nslookup www.xyz.com
Server:  dns-xxx.dummy.com
Address:  x.x.x.x

Non-authoritative answer:
Name:    www.xyz.com
Address:  10.1.1.100
! The following line is trying to find out the name from the IP address which results in
! www.xyz.com name
D:\>nslookup 10.1.1.100
Server:  dns-xxx.dummy.com
Address:  x.x.x.x

Name:    www.xyz.com
Address:  10.1.1.100
D:\>
```

Network Analyzers

A network analyzer, also known as a protocol analyzer, decodes the various protocol layers in a recorded frame and presents them as readable abbreviations or summaries. These results detail which layer is involved (physical, data link, and so forth) and what function each byte or byte content serves. Most network analyzers can perform many of the following functions:

- Filter traffic that meets certain criteria so that, for example, all traffic to and from a particular device can be captured.
- Time stamp-captured data.
- Present protocol layers in an easily readable form.
- Generate frames and transmit them onto the network.
- Incorporate an expert system in which the analyzer uses a set of rules, combined with information about the network configuration and operation, to diagnose and solve, or offer potential solutions to, network problems.

As all the Cisco Network Security devices have extensive **show** and **debug** commands and syslog capability, most of the problems that arise in those devices can be diagnosed and troubleshot without the help of any external tool such as a network analyzer. However, there are some instances where using the network analyzer is required. For example, if users from a private network cannot access the Internet through the PIX firewall, and with the **show** command and syslog you have discovered that the packets are not hitting the PIX inside interface, you can isolate this problem with the network analyzer. The problem might be in Layer 2 with an ARP corruption, Content-Addressable Memory (CAM) table problem on the switch, and so on.

Many commercial and freely downloadable network analyzers are available in the market. A very popular and free downloadable network analyzer (Ethereal) can be downloaded from the following location: http://www.ethereal.com/

Certain Cisco Network Security devices have built-in packets capturing capability very much like sniffer software. One such example is the **capture** command on the PIX firewall. More details on specific **capture** commands are explained in the respective product-specific chapters.

Trivial File Transfer Protocol (TFTP) Server

TFTP is used to load different images on the security devices. You may be able to install or upgrade IOS, PIX, and Firewall Services Module (FWSM) images from these servers. A very popular and free TFTP server can be downloaded from the following location: http://www.solarwinds.net/Tools/Free_tools/TFTP_Server/

It is important to have the TFTP server loaded and ready, because it may be needed at any time.

FTP Server

Software for most of the Cisco Security or other network devices can be installed or upgraded with a TFTP server as discussed in the preceding section. However, some security devices require FTP to install or upgrade the software. One such example is the Intrusion Prevention System (IPS). Hence, you need to have one of the supported FTP servers ready and running in your network for an immediate installation or upgrade of the IPS software.

Syslog Server

Syslog servers can be used for logging syslog messages from various devices. This can be used either for troubleshooting issues or for archival purposes. Most of the Cisco Security devices support syslog to capture debug command output for troubleshooting. Although capturing the debug output using a Telnet or SSH session is a preferred method for many troubleshooters, this may not work for a specific problem type. For instance, if you run into an intermittent connectivity issue through FWSM, you may not be able to capture the debug output at the time the problem occurs with a real-time Telnet or SSH session. However, you may turn on the debug, and configure syslog server with debugging on the FWSM, so that you do not miss the window of opportunity for capturing the debug output at the time of the problem. There are quite a few syslog servers available as both commercial and free downloads. A very popular free downloadable syslog server can be found from the following location: http://www.kiwisyslog.com/

Audit and Attack Tools

The bootable Knoppix security CD, which provides access to a bootable CD image, includes most of the common security/attack tools that are available. You can download this image to create your own CD that you can use on any system (since it is bootable). You do not need any specific operating system to install this software. Just reboot your PC with this CD. This removes the normal requirement to have a Linux box on which to build the security tools.

This tool can be extremely useful for auditing your network to see if the Network Security devices are working as expected. One such example would be to simulate attack, using this tool, to the segment of the network where Network IPS sensor is deployed. You can determine if the IPS signature tuning is working properly. For example, if one of your signatures is tuned on IPS to fire an alarm with a specific attack launched by the tool, you should get an alarm if the signature tuning is working properly.

For more details on the Knoppix tool, refer to the following link: http://www.knoppix-std.org/

Core Dump

Core dump is basically a complete memory dump of a device. In the event of a core dump, there is nothing much you can do. You need to share this information with Cisco for further analysis. However, it's important to know how many different ways the core dump can be collected. In PIX firewall, the **crashinfo** (core) goes into flash. The only way to retrieve this file is with the command **show crashinfo**. In IPS, you can get the core file in text format with the **show tech-support** command. This section explains the router core dump. For other device-specific core dumps, refer to the respective chapters.

You can use four methods to set up the router to generate a core dump:

- Trivial File Transfer Protocol (TFTP)
- File Transfer Protocol (FTP)
- Remote Copy Protocol (RCP)
- Flash disk

Using TFTP

If TFTP is used to dump the core file to the TFTP server, the router will dump only the first 16 MB of the core file. This is a limitation of most TFTP applications. Therefore, if your router's main memory is more than 16 MB, do not use TFTP.

The following is the router configuration needed for getting a core dump using TFTP:

```
exception dump a.b.c.d
```

Here, *a.b.c.d* is the IP address of the TFTP server.

The core dump is written to a file named *hostname*-core on the TFTP server, where *hostname* is the name of the router. You can change the name of the core file by adding the **exception core-file** *filename* configuration command.

Depending on the TFTP server application used, it may be necessary to create on the TFTP server an empty target file to which the router can write the core. Also, be sure that you have enough memory on your TFTP server to hold the complete core dump.

Using FTP

To configure the router for core dump using FTP, use the following configuration commands:

```
ip ftp username username
ip ftp password password
exception protocol ftp
exception dump a.b.c.d
```

Here, *a.b.c.d* is the IP address of the FTP server. If the username and password are not configured, the router will attempt anonymous FTP.

Using rcp

Remote Copy Protocol (RCP) can also be used to capture a core dump. Enabling RCP on a router will not be covered in this text. Refer to the Cisco IOS Software Configuration document for configuring RCP.

After RCP is enabled on the router, the following commands must be added to capture the core dump using RCP:

```
exception protocol rcp
exception dump a.b.c.d
```

Here, *a.b.c.d* is the IP address of the host enabled for RCP.

Using a Flash Disk

Some router platforms support the Flash disk as an alternative to the linear Flash memory or a Personal Computer Memory Card International Association (PCMCIA) Flash card. The large storage capacity of these Flash disks makes them good candidates for another means of capturing core dump. For information on the router platforms and IOS versions that support the Flash disk, refer to the Cisco IOS Release Notes.

The following is the router configuration command needed to set up a core dump using a Flash disk:

```
exception flash [procmem | iomem | all ] [device-name[:partition-number]] [erase |
  no_erase]
```

The **show flash all** command will give you a list of devices that you can use for the **exception flash** command.

Additional Configuration

The configuration commands in this section may be used in addition to those described in the preceding section.

"Exception Memory" Command

During the debugging process, you can cause the router to create a core dump and reboot when certain memory size parameters are violated. The following **exception memory** commands are used to trigger a core dump:

```
exception memory minimum size
```

This command defines the minimum free memory pool size.

```
exception memory fragment size
```

This command defines the minimum size of contiguous blocks of memory in the free pool.

The value of *size* is in bytes and is checked every 60 seconds. If you enter a size that is greater than the free memory, and if the **exception dump** command has been configured, a core dump and router reload is generated after 60 seconds. If the **exception dump** command is not configured, the router reloads without generating a core dump.

debug sanity Command

In some cases, the technical support representative will request that **debug sanity** be enabled when setting up the core dump. This is a hidden command in most IOS releases, but it is sometimes necessary to debug memory corruption. With **debug sanity**, every buffer that is used in the system is sanity-checked when it is allocated and when it is freed.

The **debug sanity** command must be issued in privileged exec mode (enable mode) and involves some CPU utilization. However, it will not significantly affect the router's functionality.

Not all types of crashes require **debug sanity** to be enabled. Use this command only when your technical support representative requires it. To disable **debug sanity**, use the privileged exec command **undebug sanity**.

Testing the Core Dump Setup

When the router is configured for core dump, it may be useful to test whether the setup works.

The IOS provides a special command to test or trigger a core dump:

```
write core
```

Use this command in privileged EXEC mode (enable mode). This command causes a crash, and the content of the memory is dumped accordingly. If no core dump is generated, the whole setup and config must be reviewed. The **write core** command will affect a production network. It will cause the router to crash and will prevent it from coming up before dumping the content of its memory. This might take some time, depending on the amount of Dynamic Random Access Memory (DRAM) present on the router. Use the command with utmost caution.

As you have seen, this chapter discusses some of the generic tools that are used in day-to-day troubleshooting of Cisco Network Security. The purpose of this high-level overview is to make you familiar with some of the practical reasons to use different troubleshooting tools efficiently and provide you with the links that are hard to find in, around, or during the troubleshooting session. Tools such as the **syslog**, **show**, and **debug** commands are everyday friends for an efficient troubleshooter. As mentioned earlier, there are many more product-specific tools available within the products to debug and troubleshoot a problem, and these are discussed in the product-specific chapters. This chapter familiarizes you with the generic tools that will be used in rest of the text.

PART II

Troubleshooting Cisco Secure Firewalls

Chapter 3 Troubleshooting Cisco Secure PIX Firewalls

Chapter 4 Troubleshooting Firewall Services Modules

Chapter 5 Troubleshooting an IOS Firewall

CHAPTER 3

Troubleshooting Cisco Secure PIX Firewalls

A PIX firewall falls into the category of stateful firewall. It provides security to the perimeter network by creating and maintaining the state information of connections. PIX boosts performance because its OS is embedded and runs directly from RAM for packet processing. Cisco Adaptive Security Appliance (ASA 5500 Series), is the next-generation security appliance, which runs the same OS as the PIX, but provides more security services (for example, an SSM blade for IPS, SSL VPN, and so on) than PIX Firewall. Beginning with Version 7.0, the ASA 5500 (minimum version requirement on the ASA is 7.0), and PIX platforms (running Version 7.0), provide the same firewall features. As the primary focus of this chapter is to discuss firewall features, additional services provided by the ASA 5500 (IPS, SSL, VPN, and so on) will not be discussed. The troubleshooting discussion in this chapter is based on the PIX platform, which also can be used for ASA 5500.

PIX Firewall has a very flexible and robust command-line interface (CLI) parser that is very similar to a router (in particular on PIX Version 7.0). In addition, a GUI such as Adaptive Security Device Manager or ASDM (formally known as PIX Device Manager or PDM) and a firewall management console (MC) can be used to manage the PIX firewall. Most troubleshooting, however, is performed using the CLI; hence the primary focus on the chapter is using the CLI on the new version of PIX, which is 7.0.

Overview of PIX Firewall

The architecture of PIX Firewall is based on the Adaptive Security Algorithm (ASA), which maintains the state information and provides security to your connection. ASA is a set of rules and policies that the packet has to conform to while traversing the firewall. As mentioned before, PIX is a stateful firewall, which means it works based on connections, not on a per-packet basis. It remembers every connection through the firewall.

ASA

ASA has the following characteristics:

- ASA provides a *stateful* connection.
- ASA allows return packets for established connections.

- ASA tracks source and destination ports and addresses, Transmission Control Protocol (TCP) sequences, and additional TCP flags.
- TCP sequence numbers are randomized.
- The inside interface has a security level of 100.
- The outside interface has a security level of 0.
- Demilitarized zone (DMZ) interfaces have user-settable security levels from 1 through 99.
- Starting with PIX OS 5.2, users are allowed to change the default security levels of both the outside and inside interfaces, but it is not recommended.
- By default, the PIX allows traffic to pass from higher security interfaces to lower security interfaces, and in the case of TCP and User Datagram Protocol (UDP) connections, it allows the return traffic back through. The same does not hold for Internet Control Message Protocol (ICMP).

PIX Packet Processing

Packet flow across the PIX firewall is depicted in Figure 3-1. Work through the following steps to understand the packet flow:

1 Packets are received on the ingress interface

Packets arrive on the ingress interface, which is indicated by input counters of the interface.

Figure 3-1 *PIX Firewall Packet Flow*

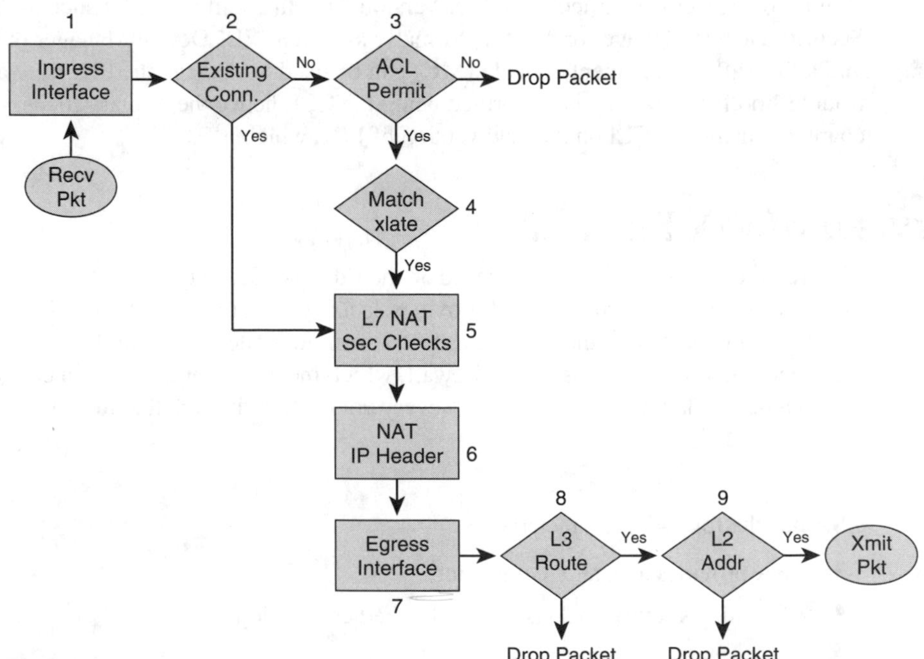

2 Existing connection checks

Packets go through the existing connection check. If the connection exists, the ACL check is bypassed. If there is no existing connection, TCP non-SYN packets will be dropped and logged. If PIX receives a TCP SYN or UDP request packet, packets are passed to ACL checks.

3 Interface ACL check

The initial packet in the flow of packet is processed through interface ACLs. Packets that are denied by interface ACLs are dropped and logged.

4 NAT check

The initial packet in the flow must match a translation rule. To perform NAT, it is important to know the egress interface. Hence a quick route lookup is performed. If the translation is turned off, the translation is skipped. If the NAT is configured and the translation rule is matched, the connection is created on the PIX firewall. If an overlapping NAT is configured, the following order of NAT operations is performed:

a **nat 0 access-list** (nat-exempt).

b Match existing xlates.

c Match static commands (first match). Static NAT with and without access-list is checked before Static PAT with and without an access-list.

d Match nat commands. **nat <id> access-list** is matched first. Then **nat <id> <address> <mask>** is checked. If the ID is 0, create an identity xlate. Use a global pool for dynamic NAT. Use a global pool for dynamic PAT.

5 Inspection check

Inspections are applied to NAT embedded IPs in the payload. Commands in control channels are inspected for compliance and secondary data channels. Additional security checks are also applied to the packet with inspection.

6 Perform NAT

Perform IP address or the port translation.

7 Packets forwarded to egress interface

Packets are forwarded to the egress interface. The egress interface is determined by the translation rules first. If translation rules do not specify the egress interface, the global route lookup is performed to determine the egress interface.

8 Interface route lookup

Once the packet is on the egress interface, an interface route lookup is performed. Only routes pointing out the egress interface are used to forward the packet. Remember that the translation rule can forward the packet to the egress interface, even though the routing table may point to a different interface.

9 Layer 2 address lookup for the next-hop address

After the interface route lookup is performed, the next-hop address is identified. At this stage, ARP resolution is performed. Then the packets are put in the wire, and the interface counters are incremented.

File System Overview

When upgraded to PIX 7.0, PIX Flash memory is reformatted. The contents of the files are different than in the older versions. Table 3-1 shows the different files that go into Flash on PIX Firewall Version 6.3 and earlier, and on PIX Firewall Version 7.0 and later.

Table 3-1 *Different Files Go Into Flash On Different Versions*

Release 6.3 and Earlier	Release 7.0 and Later
SW Image	SW Image
Config File	Config File
Private Data File	Private Data
PDM Image	ASDM Image
Crash Information	Backup Image (If disk and flash space are available) Backup config file (if disk and flash space are available) Virtual Firewall Config File Crash Info (Internal Only) 1M/ASA, 128K/PIX

The Flash file system can be viewed with either the **dir** or **show flash** command as shown in Example 3-1.

Example 3-1 *Flash File System on PIX 7.0*

```
PIX# dir
Directory of flash:/
3      -rw-  4902912     13:37:33 Nov 24 2004  cdisk.7.0.0.89
4      -rw-  6748932     13:21:13 Nov 24 2004  ASDM
16128000 bytes total (4472832 bytes free)
PIX(config)#
! Boot [system | config} <url> is the command that needs to be used to define the file
! using which the system should boot. It is possible to store more than one system
! image and config file. Designate which system image and start-up config file to boot.
```

Example 3-1 *Flash File System on PIX 7.0 (Continued)*

```
PIX(config)# boot system flash:/cdisk.7.0.0.89
! Verify the start-up System Image. Display the system boot image.
PIX# show bootvar
BOOT variable = flash:/cdisk.7.0.0.89
Current BOOT variable = flash:/cdisk.7.0.0.89
CONFIG_FILE variable =
Current CONFIG_FILE variable =
PIX#
```

Table 3-2 shows the commands available to work with the Flash File System CLI.

Table 3-2 *Commands Available for PIX Flash File System*

Command	Meaning
cd	Change the current working directory to the one specified.
delete	Deletes a file. If a path is not specified, the file would be deleted from the current working directory. When deleting files the user would be prompted with the filename and asked to confirm the delete. The /recursive option would delete files recursively.
dir	Displays the content of the current directory.
format	Formats the disk using File Allocation Table (FAT).
mkdir	Creates a new directory.
more	Displays the contents of a specified file. more [/ascii] [/binary] [disk:][<path>]
rename	Renames a specified file.
rmdir	Removes a specified directory. Use will be prompted.
pwd	Shows the present working directory.
copy	Copies a file from flash: ftp, http, https, running and startup config tftp, system.

Example 3-2 shows the debug command available for troubleshooting the Flash file system.

Example 3-2 **debug** *Command For Troubleshooting File System*

```
PIX# debug disk ?
  file
  file-verbose
  filesystem
PIX# debug disk
```

You might receive the following warnings and errors related to file system misbehavior: Out of space, run fsck, filename too long, no such file. The solution for these is self evident.

Access-List

The implementation of access-list is same as before on the PIX firewall, with some additional features that are discussed in the sections that follow.

time-range Keyword

The **time-range** keyword provides a way for the Network Security Manager to specify a time interval when connectivity to the specified destinations is permitted or denied. Multiple time ranges can be defined. The command allows easy and routine control of traffic connectivity through the firewall device.

The **time-range** keyword is used to control the execution of various features in the PIX/ASA. The **time-range** feature is available in access control and VPN access hours (an attribute of group policy).

First, define a period of time—start/stop, certain days, and so on, that can be evaluated to a true/false condition when compared to the current appliance time.

Then, place the keyword qualifier Time-Range with the *name* as one of the last parameters on an access-list statement that describes the connectivity path.

The Time-Range keyword, when applied on an access-list statement, identifies a statement that is applied only when the current time of the **security appliance clock** is in the time period specified by the command (a true condition). Example 3-3 shows how to configure the time-range option.

Example 3-3 *Using the* **time-range** *Command*

```
! Choose a time-range name:
PIX(config)# time-range ?
  WORD < 64 char  Time range name
PIX(config)# time-range sevt
PIX(config-time-range)# ?
! More than one periodic entry can be defined. Decide how to specify the time period:
PIX(config-time-range)# ?
Time range configuration commands:
  absolute  absolute time and date (one per time-range)
  exit      Exit from time-range configuration mode
  help      Help for time-range configuration commands
  no        Negate a command or set its defaults
  periodic  periodic time and date (multiple are permitted)
! More than one TIME-RANGE entry can be made Absolute Time Start and End, or just start
! with no end, . . . or end with no start (immediate start)
PIX(config-time-range)# absolute ?
  end    ending time and date
  start  starting time and date
PIX(config-time-range)# periodic ?
  Friday     Friday
  Monday     Monday
  Saturday   Saturday
```

Example 3-3 *Using the* **time-range** *Command (Continued)*

```
  Sunday     Sunday
  Thursday   Thursday
  Tuesday    Tuesday
  Wednesday  Wednesday
  daily      Every day of the week
  weekdays   Monday thru Friday
  weekend    Saturday and Sunday
! And finally a configuration
. . .
time-range BusinessHours
 absolute start 10
 periodic weekdays 7
. . .
access-list outside_mpc_in remark Only WWW traffic goes to DMZ
access-list outside_mpc_in extended permit tcp any 1.1.1.0 255.255.255.0 eq www
time-range BusinessHours
. . .
! "show time-range", "show clock" and "show access-list" are useful debugging commands
! when trying to determine if a time-range or ACE is active at the current time. e.g
! (note the inactive label in the ace below):
PIX# show access-list
access-list cached ACL log flows: total 0, denied 0 (deny-flow-max 4096)
            alert-interval 300
access-list ACL1; 2 elements
access-list ACL1 line 1 extended permit ip any any time-range TR1 (hitcnt=0)
  (inactive)
access-list ACL1 line 2 extended deny ip any any (hitcnt=0)
PIX#
```

Enable/Disable

Access Control Lists (ACLs) are common traffic control commands. PIX OS 7.0 provides more control, especially in troubleshooting, by providing an easy way to "turn on" or "turn off" the processing of a specific access policy (access-list entry). This aids greatly in troubleshooting.

The keyword INACTIVE is applied at the end of an access-list entry to remove it from processing.

The command syntax for applying the access-list is as follows:

```
access-list outside_access_in extended permit tcp any object-group mail-servers eq
  smtp inactive
```

There are no **debug** commands, output, logging outputs, caveats, or limitations specifically related to this keyword. Debug information comes from the **access-list** command features.

Outbound ACL

PIX OS 7.0 provides more granular access control by allowing both "incoming at interface" and "outgoing at interface" access policies to be configured.

The OUT keyword is applied on the access-group command. It identifies an access policy (access-list) that applies to outgoing traffic at the specified interface. The OUT keyword can reduce the number of commands in a configuration and make its logical interpretation easier.

To bind an access-list to an interface, use the access-group command in global configuration mode. To unbind an access-list from the interface, use the "no" form of this command.

```
access-group access-list {in | out} interface interface_name [per-user-override]
  no access-group access-list {in | out} interface interface_name
```

Example 3-4 shows how to use the access-list and apply that as outbound.

Example 3-4 *Using an Outbound ACL*

```
PIX# configure terminal
PIX(config)#
PIX(config)# names
PIX(config)# name user_net 10.1.1.0
PIX(config)# name dev_net 20.1.1.0
PIX(config)# name 24mask 255.255.255.0
. . .
PIX(config)# access-list acl_outbound permit tcp user_net 24mask any eq 80
PIX(config)# access-list acl_outbound deny tcp dev_net 24mask any
. . .
PIX(config)# access-group acl_outbound out interface outside
. . .
```

NOTE The per-user-override option allows downloaded access-lists to override the access-list applied to the interface. If the per-user-override optional argument is not present, PIX preserves the existing filtering behavior.

The per-user access list is governed by the timeout value specified by the uauth option of the timeout command, but it can be overridden by the AAA per-user session timeout value.

nat-control

The PIX always has been a device supporting, even requiring, Network Address Translation (NAT) for maximum flexibility and security. **NAT** is introduced as an option in PIX OS 7.0.

Configuring **nat-control** on the PIX forces the PIX firewall to require NAT for a source address (for outbound traffic) and for a destination address for inbound traffic.

If you upgrade PIX firewall from 6.x to Version 7.x, **nat-control** is enabled on the PIX. For new configurations, **nat-control** is disabled by default. If **no nat-control** is specified, only hosts that require NAT need to have a NAT rule configured.

The **nat-control** statement is valid in routed firewall mode and in single and multiple security context modes. No new NAT functionality is provided with this feature. All existing NAT functionality remains the same.

If you have **no nat-control** configured, and if there is a nat matching, it will go through the NAT engine. Otherwise, the packet will go through without NATing. In PIX 6.3 and earlier, the packet is dropped if there is no NAT match.

Table 3-3 shows the comparison between nat-control and no nat-control.

Table 3-3 *Comparison Between* **nat-control** *and* **no nat-control**

	nat-control	no nat-control
No inside nat rule No outside nat rule	Deny	Continue
No inside nat rule outside nat rule	Continue	Continue
No inside nat rule No outside nat rule	Deny	Continue

The difference between the **no nat-control** command and the **nat 0** (identity NAT) command is that identity NAT requires that traffic be initiated from the more secure interface. The **no nat-control** command does not have this requirement, nor does it require a static command to allow communication to inside hosts. It relies on access-policies.

Modular Policy Framework (MPF) Objective

There is a growing need to provide greater granularity and flexibility in configuring network policies. For example, it is extremely important to have the ability to include a destination IP address as one of the criteria to identify traffic for Network Address Translation, or the ability to create a timeout configuration that is specific to a particular TCP application, as opposed to the current timeout scheme, which applies a timeout value to all TCP applications, and so on. **MPF** provides the tools to meet these and other needs.

MPF features are derived from quality of service (QoS) as implemented in IOS. Not all features have been carried across. **MPF** is built on three related CLI commands:

- **class-map**—This command identifies the traffic that needs a specific type of control. Class-maps have specific names, which tie them into the policy-map. This just selects the traffic.
- **policy-map**—This command describes the actions to be taken on the traffic described in the class-map. Class-maps are listed by name under the appropriate policy-map. Policy-maps have specific names too, which tie them into the service-policy. They specify what action needs to be taken.
- **service-policy**—This command describes where the traffic should be intercepted for control. Only one service-policy can exist per interface. An additional service-policy, **global-service-policy**, is defined for traffic and general policy application. This policy applies to traffic on all interfaces. The command applies the policy. You can have only one service policy per interface.

PIX 7.0 has the following restrictions for match/policy and class statements.

- Number of Policy-map: 64.
- Number of Class-map: 255.
- Number of Classes in a policy-map: 63.
- Number of match statements in a class-map: 1. For match tunnel-group and default-inspect, allow two statements.

Transparent Firewall

Transparent Firewall works based on Layer 2 information. This provides the ability to deploy a PIX firewall in a secure bridging mode. It provides rich Layer 2 through 7 security services as a Layer 2 device.

Remember these points while implementing a Transparent Firewall on the PIX Firewall:

- One inside and outside interface is supported for the transparent firewall.
- Each directly connected network must be on the same subnet.
- A management IP address must be configured and should be on the same subnet as the connected network.
- This management IP address cannot be a default gateway for connected devices, so you should point to the other router's IP address as your default gateway.
- The PIX uses this IP address as the source address for packets that originate on the outside interface.
- You can pass non-IP traffic such as Internetwork Pack Exchange (IPX) traffic using an **EtherType** ACL to allow non-IP traffic through.
- Dynamic routing protocols will run on the device and will pass through the PIX.
- NAT is not supported. NAT is performed on the upstream router. You must use an extended ACL to allow Layer 3 traffic, such as IP traffic, through the PIX.

If you configure multiple contexts with Transparent Firewall, you must note the following points:

- A management IP address is required for each context, even if you do not intend to use Telnet to the context.
- For multiple context modes, each context must use different VLANs; you cannot share a virtual LAN (VLAN) across contexts.
- For multiple context mode, each context can use the same (overlapping) subnet or different subnets under different VLANs.
- Be sure that the upstream router performs NAT if you use overlapping subnets.

You might encounter several limitations with Transparent Firewall and VPN implementations:

- VPN tunnels are allowed only when configured for single (Routed) context mode.
- **To-the-box** IPsec traffic is supported.

- **Through-the-box** IPsec data, or data carried through a tunnel destined for the secure side of the transparent firewall, is not supported.
- Only **static crypto maps** are supported.
- The IP address configured for the management access is the VPN peer address.
- WebVPN is not supported while the device is operating in transparent mode.
- Only L2L tunnels are supported, and only one tunnel at a time.
- X-Auth and mode config attributes should not be used during tunnel negotiation, but are configurable.
- VPN tunnel cannot be initiated from the firewall (answer only).
- VPN Load Balancing and VPN Stateful Failover are not supported.
- QoS of VPN data is not supported.
- NAT over the tunnel is not supported.

Diagnostic Commands and Tools

Several tools and commands are available on the PIX Firewall to troubleshoot all kinds of issues with PIX Firewall. In this section, we will attempt to go through all such tools and commands, which will be used in the rest of the chapter for troubleshooting specific issues.

show Commands

show commands on PIX Firewall are used to display statistics and information about the PIX firewall both current and past. **show** commands are used mainly for troubleshooting and the monitoring the health of the PIX firewall. Some of most useful **show** commands are shown in the sections that follow.

show xlate [detail]

This command shows the translation details through the PIX firewall. Example 3-5 shows both the summary and details of translation that are built up on the PIX firewall. It is recommended to look at the details of the translation which gives the interfaces involved the flow of a packet. This is useful to identify and correct any NAT related mis-configuration.

Example 3-5 *Translation Through the PIX Firewall*

```
PIX (config) # show xlate
3 in use, 3 most used
PAT Global 20.1.1.50(0) Local 10.1.1.50 ICMP id 340
PAT Global 20.1.1.50 (1024) Local 10.1.1.50(1028)
PAT Global 20.1.1.50 (1024) Local 10.1.1.50(516)
PIX (config) # show xlate detail
3 in use, 3 most used
Flags: D -DNS, d - dump, I - identity, I - inside, n - no random,
          o - outside, r - portmap, s - static
TCP PAT from inside:10.1.1.50/1026 to outside:20.1.1.50/1024 flags ri
UDP PAT from inside:10.1.1.50/1028 to outside:20.1.1.50/1024 flags ri
ICMP PAT from inside:10.1.1.50/21505 to outside:20.1.1.50/0 flags ri
PIX(config)#
```

Table 3-4 describes the Xlate flags.

Table 3-4 *Xlate Flags Table*

Flag	Description
s	Static Translation Slot
d	Dump Translation Slot on Next Clearing Cycle
r	Port Map Translation
n	No Randomization of TCP Sequence Number
o	Outside Address Translation
I	Inside Address Translation
D	DNS A RR Rewrite
I	Identity Translation from NAT 0

show connection [detail]

This command shows the connection details output on the PIX firewall. Connection will not be built up without translation. So, if you do not see any connection, you need to find out if the translation is built up. Example 3-6 shows the translation that is built up on the PIX firewall.

Example 3-6 *Shows the* **show connection [detail]** *Output from the PIX Firewall*

```
PIX (config) # show connection
2 in use, 2 most used
! Idle time, bytes transferred and the flags are shown in the following connection
TCP out 192.150.49.10:23 in 10.1.1.15:1026 idle 0:00:22 bytes 1774 flags UIO
UDP out 192.150.49.10:31649 in 10.1.1.15:1028 idle 0:00:14 bytes 540 flags d
! Following command shows the interface details of the connection
PIX (config) # show connection detail
2 in use, 2 most used
Flags: A - awaiting inside ACK to SYN, a - awaiting outside ACK to SYN,
           B - initial SYN from outside, D - DNS, d - dump,
           E - outside back connection, F - outside FIN, f - inside FIN,
           G - group, H - H.323, I - inbound data, M - SMTP data,
           m - SIP media, O- outbound data, P - inside back connection,
           q - SQL*Net data, R - outside acknowledged FIN,
           R - UDP RPC, r - inside acknowledged FIN, S - awaiting inside SYN,
           s - awaiting outside SYN, T - SIP, t - SIP transient, U - up
TCP outside: 192.150.49.10/23 dmz:10.1.1.15/1026 flags UIO
UDP outside: 192.150.49.10/31649 dmz:10.1.1.15/1028 flags d
PIX#
```

show local-host

A **local-host** is an entry that is created for any source IP on a higher security level interface. The **show local-host** command displays the translation, connection, and AAA information together. Example 3-7 shows a **local-host** information for local host IP address of **10.1.1.50**.

Example 3-7 **show local-host** *Command Output*

```
PIX# show local-host 10.1.1.50
Interface inside: 822 active, 823 maximum active, 0 denied
local host: <10.1.1.50>,
    TCP connection count/limit = 0/unlimited
    TCP embryonic count = 0
    TCP intercept watermark = unlimited
    UDP connection count/limit = 63/unlimited
  AAA:
  Xlate(s):
    PAT Global 20.1.1.50(41166) Local 10.1.1.50(39075)
  Conn(s):
    UDP out 198.133.219.25:8943 in 10.1.1.50:63556 idle 0:01:31 flags -
PIX#
```

show service-policy

This command is used to see what inspection policies are applied and the packets matching them, as shown in Example 3-8.

Example 3-8 *Output of the* **show service-policy** *Command*

```
PIX# show service-policy
Global policy:
  Service-policy: global_policy
    Class-map: inspection_default
      Inspect: dns maximum-length 512, packet 0, drop 0, reset-drop 0
      Inspect: ftp, packet 0, drop 0, reset-drop 0
      Inspect: h323 h225, packet 0, drop 0, reset-drop 0
      Inspect: h323 ras, packet 0, drop 0, reset-drop 0
      Inspect: http, packet 0, drop 0, reset-drop 0
      Inspect: netbios, packet 0, drop 0, reset-drop 0
      Inspect: rsh, packet 0, drop 0, reset-drop 0
      Inspect: rtsp, packet 0, drop 0, reset-drop 0
      Inspect: skinny, packet 0, drop 0, reset-drop 0
      Inspect: esmtp, packet 0, drop 0, reset-drop 0
      ...
Interface outside:
  Service-policy: VoIP
    Class-map: voice_marked
      Priority:
        Interface outside: aggregate drop 0, aggregate transmit 0
PIX#
```

show asp drop

This command is used to identify the number of packets dropped by the PIX while processing the packet as shown in Example 3-9.

Example 3-9 **show asp drop** *Command Output*

```
PIX# show asp drop
Frame drop:
   Invalid tcp length                                          9382
   Invalid udp length                                            10
   No route to host                                            1009
   Reverse-path verify failed                                    15
   Flow is denied by access rule                           25247101
   First TCP packet not SYN                                   36888
   Bad option length in TCP                                     731
   TCP MSS was too large                                      10942
   TCP Window scale on non-SYN                                 2591
   TCP Dual open denied                                          11
   TCP data send after FIN                                       62
   TCP failed 3 way handshake                                328859
   TCP SEQ in SYN/SYNACK invalid                                142
   TCP ACK in SYNACK invalid                                    278
   TCP packet SEQ past window                                 46331
   DNS Inspect packet too long                                    5
   DNS Inspect id not matched                                  8270
   ...
PIX#
```

show cpu usage

This command is first introduced in PIX OS Version 6.0(1). Under normal conditions, the PIX CPU should stay below 30 percent, and can go as high as 60 percent. Anything above 60 percent is high. If the CPU reaches 100 percent, the PIX will start dropping packets. The **show cpu usage** command displays the CPU over time as a running average as shown below:

```
PIX# show cpu usage
CPU utilization for 5 seconds = 1%; 1 minute: 2%; 5 minutes: 1%
PIX#
```

NOTE The percentage usage prints as NA (Not Applicable) if the usage is unavailable for the specified time interval; this can happen if you try to find out CPU Usage before the 5-second, 1-minute, or 5-minute intervals.

show traffic

The **show traffic** command displays the traffic transmitted and received on each interfaces of the PIX as shown in Example 3-10.

Example 3-10 **show traffic** *Command Output*

```
PIX# show traffic
outside:
        received (in 124.650 secs):
                295468 packets  167218253 bytes
                2370 pkts/sec   1341502 bytes/sec
        transmitted (in 124.650 secs):
                260901 packets  120467981 bytes
                2093 pkts/sec   966449 bytes/sec
inside:
        received (in 124.650 secs):
                261478 packets  120145678 bytes
                2097 pkts/sec   963864 bytes/sec
        transmitted (in 124.650 secs):
                294649 packets  167380042 bytes
                2363 pkts/sec   1342800 bytes/sec
PIX#
```

show blocks

The **show blocks** command and the **show cpu usage** command are useful in determining whether the PIX is being overloaded. The blocks are internal storage locations, similar to queues on a router; a packet is stored in a block until the PIX can process it and place it on the outbound interface xmit queue. Example 3-11 shows the **show blocks** output.

Example 3-11 **show blocks** *Command Output*

```
PIX# show block
  SIZE    MAX    LOW    CNT
     4    100     99    100
    80    100     98    100
   256    600    592    600
  1550   1704   1362   1448
  2048    100    100    100
  2560     40     40     40
  4096     30     30     30
  8192     60     60     60
 16384    104    104    104
 65536     10     10     10
PIX#
```

In the **show blocks** command output, **SIZE** is the block size, **MAX** is the total number of block available, **LOW** is the lowest number of blocks available on PIX since the last reboot, and the CNT is the current number of blocks available for specific task. Both **LOW** and **CNT** for any block size hit to zero indicate a low memory condition, which requires further investigation. To determine which features are responsible for memory block utilization, refer to Table 3-5, which summarizes the different memory blocks and the purpose of different sizes of blocks.

Table 3-5 *Showing Different Sizes of Memory Blocks and Their Usage*

Block Size	Used For	Created at boot up time	MAX
4	Duplicating existing blocks in DNS, isakmp, url-filtering, uauth, h323, tftp, and TCP modules	1600	1600
80	Used in TCP Intercept to generate an ACK packet, failover hello messages.	400	400
256	Stateful Failover, Syslog, TCP module	8192	500
1550	Ethernet Packets, buffering url filtered packets.	8192	400
1552	QoS Metrics	4096	0
2560	IKE Messages	8192	0
4096	QoS Metrics	200	0
8192	QoS Metrics	150	0
16384	Only used for the Livengood (i82543) Gig Ethernet cards	9216	0
65536	QoS Metrics	16	0

show output filters

Sometimes, it is very important to view the **show** command output to specific lines for specific information. You can do this with the Output filter option. The syntax is as follows:

```
show command | begin | include | exclude | grep [-v] <regular_exp>
```

Following is a list of definitions for the arguments of this command:

- **begin**—Start displaying the output beginning at the First Match of the RegEx, and continue to display the remaining output.
- **include**—Display any line that matches the RegEx.
- **exclude**—Display any line that does not match the RegEx.
- **grep**—This is the same as **include**.
- **grep –v**—This is the same as **exclude**.

For example, to display the interface stats starting with ethernet1, execute the following command:

```
PIX# show interface | begin ethernet1
```

To display only the route statements from the running-config, execute the following command:

```
PIX# show running-config | include route
```

To display the whole configuration except for the access-lists, you can execute the following command:

```
PIX# show running-config | exclude access-list
```

Displaying the access-list entries that contain address 10.1.1.50 can be achieved with the following command:

```
PIX# show access-list | grep 10.1.1.50
```

To display only access-list entries that have non-zero hit counts, execute the following command:

```
PIX# show access-list | grep -v hitcnt=0
```

show tech-support

show tech-support collects output of a list of **show** commands. The command for **show tech-support** is as follows:

```
show tech-support [no-config | detail | tftp:]
```

Example 3-12 summarizes how to use the **show tech-support** command.

Example 3-12 *How to Use the* **show tech-support** *Command*

```
! Following command will collect all the information including the running-config for
! Troubleshooting
PIX# show tech-support
! The following command collect the same output without the running-config
PIX# show tech-support no-config
! The following allows you to redirect the output into different location
PIX# show tech-support file ?
  flash:  Write output to flash: file system
  ftp:    Write output to ftp: file system
  tftp:   Write output to tftp: file system
PIX#
! The following command allows you to collect the detail show tech-support information
PIX# show tech-support detail
. . . . . .
PIX#
```

Debug Commands

Although **show** commands are very useful to identify the problem quickly, **debug** commands are required to see more detailed information about the problem under some circumstances for the connectivity issues. As **debug** commands affect the CPU of the PIX negatively, use the **debug** command as a last resort. Before turning on the respective **debug** command, it is very important to know how much traffic is flowing through the firewall of a specific type.

In this section, we discuss several **debug** commands available on PIX that will help you troubleshoot connectivity problems across the PIX firewall.

debug icmp trace

This **debug** command is used to see the debug output of the ping going across the PIX firewall. Ping is usually used to check the IP connectivity across the firewall.

While using ping for connectivity tests, remember these points:

- You can ping only the local interface of the PIX. For example, if your PC is on the inside network, you can ping only to the inside interface of the PIX.
- You cannot ping the remote interface of the PIX. For example, if you are on an inside network, you cannot ping to the DMZ or the outside interface of the PIX firewall. If you are on outside, you can ping only on the outside interface.
- ICMP echo-replies must be permitted explicitly thru the PIX unless you have ICMP inspection enabled.

Figure 3-2 demonstrates that Bob is able to ping to the inside interface, not the DMZ or outside interface.

Figure 3-2 *Inside Users Ping Ability to PIX Firewall*

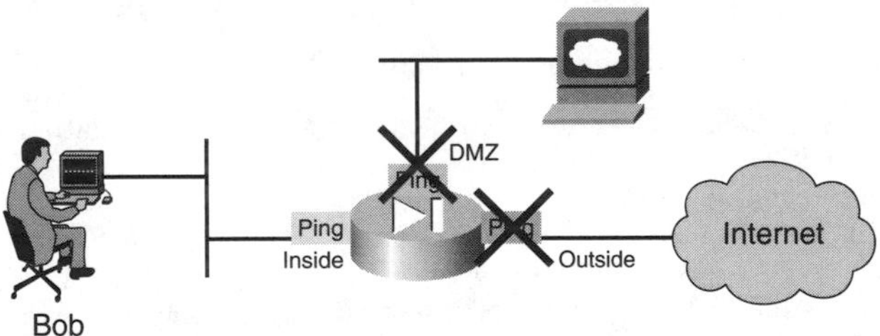

For a successful ping across the PIX firewall, you should see the **request** and **reply** packets on the **debug icmp trace** command output as shown in Example 3-13.

Example 3-13 debug icmp trace *Output of a Successful IP Connection*

```
PIX# debug icmp trace
PIX#
! In the following line, the ingress interface is inside, inside untranslated IP
! address, and destination address of the packet is 192.168.1.50
ICMP echo-request from inside:10.1.1.50 to 192.168.1.50 ID=3239 seq=4369 length=80
! Following line shows that 10.1.1.50 is translated to IP address 172.16.10.1
ICMP echo-request: translating inside:10.1.1.50 to outside:172.16.10.1
! The following lines are reply packets
ICMP echo-reply from outside:192.168.1.50 to 172.16.10.1 ID=3239 seq=4369 length=80
ICMP echo-reply: untranslating outside:172.16.10.1 to inside:10.1.1.50
PIX#
```

The **debug icmp trace** command output shows enough details of the ingress, egress, source, destination IP/port, and the protocol information which can be used to define the packet flow.

NOTE You can turn off all debugs globally on the PIX firewall by issuing the **no debug all** or **undebug all** (**u all** is the short form) command.

---

debug application_protocol

To troubleshoot any application-specific issues, for example, Session Initiation Protocol (SIP) across the PIX firewall, you may run the debug for the corresponding protocol. For instance, to troubleshoot the issue pertaining to Media Gateway Control Protocol (MGCP) for voice over IP (VoIP) traffic between a phone and Call Manager, run the **debug mgcp** command.

debug pix process

To debug NAT within the payload of the packet, run **debug pix process** to see if the NAT is working correctly. For instance, if there is NAT in for MGCP, **debug mgcp** will not show the NAT details from the payload. For the NAT details, you must run **debug pix process**.

debug fixup tcp | udp

Use this command to find any inspection-related issue of a protocol. For example, to debug a problem with an FTP connection, you might need to run **debug fixup tcp**, which shows the FTP connection-related issue.

capture Command

The **capture** command (introduced in Version 6.2) allows for sniffing the packet hits at the interface of the PIX firewall. The command **debug packet** is deprecated by this **capture** command. The **capture** command must be executed from the enable mode (not the configuration mode), and optionally, you can configure an access-list to define the interesting traffic. Traffic can be captured both before and after it passes through the PIX; one capture on the inside interface, one capture on the outside interface. You can copy captures via TFTP or HTTPS.

Following is the syntax to enable **capture** on the PIX Firewall for traffic analysis:

```
capture capture-name [access-list acl-name] [buffer buf-size] [circular-buffer]
  [ethernet-type type] [interface if-name] [packet-length bytes]
```

Table 3-6 summarizes the meaning of the arguments of the **capture** command.

Table 3-6 **capture** *Command Arguments*

Arguments	Meaning
Capture name	This is the name of the capture that is used to view the information after the capture is completed.
Access-list	Used to define the traffic that needs to be captured.
Buffer	Capture buffer saved in RAM (default size 512kb).
Circular-Buffer	The default is to stop capturing when the buffer is full. Overwrites the buffer from beginning when full. The default is non-circular.
Ethernet-type	Used to ca Ethernet packets of a particular type. The default is IP.
Interface	Used to c packets on a specific interface. The default is all interfaces.
Packet-length	Used to configure the maximum length to save from each packet. The default is 68 bytes.

To illustrate how to use the **capture** command on the PIX firewall, examine an example. Assume that an inside host (10.1.1.100) is unable to go through Telnet to the server with IP address 200.1.1.100 on the outside. Additionally, assume that the host address 10.1.1.100 is translated to 50.1.1.00. Work through the following steps to enable **capture** on the PIX firewall:

Step 1 Create an ACL for both the inside and outside interfaces.

You must create two separate ACLs to apply with the capture for the inside and outside interfaces.

The inside interface ACL should use the untranslated source IP address and the destination IP address:

```
PIX(config)# access-list 100 permit tcp host 10.1.1.100 host 200.1.1.100
  eq 23
PIX(config)# access-list 100 permit tcp host 200.1.1.100 eq 23 host
  10.1.1.100
```

The outside interface ACL should use the translated source address and the destination IP address.

```
PIX(config)# access-list 101 permit tcp host 50.1.1.100 host 200.1.1.100
  eq 23
PIX(config)# access-list 101 permit tcp host 200.1.1.100 eq 23 host
  50.1.1.100
```

Step 2 Create captures on both inside and outside interfaces.

```
PIX(config)# capture out-telnet access-list 101 interface outside
  packet-length 1500
PIX(config)# capture in-telnet access-list 100 interface inside packet-
  length 1500
```

Step 3 Perform the test.

Initiate a Telnet session from the inside host (10.1.1.100) to access 200.1.1.100 on the outside.

Step 4 Copy the captures off to a TFTP Server or use HTTP server on the PIX.

You can display the capture output on the PIX firewall with the following commands:

```
PIX# show capture in-telnet
PIX# show capture out-telnet
```

To download the capture output to a TFTP server, use the following commands:

```
PIX# copy /pcap capture:out-telnet tftp://10.1.1.5/out.pcap
PIX# copy /pcap capture:in-telnet tftp://10.1.1.5/in.pcap
```

If the HTTP server is enabled on the PIX firewall for the ASDM access, you can use the following command to download the pcap files from the PIX firewall using the web browser:

```
https://<PIX_IP>/capture/out/pcap
```

Step 5 Analyze captures with sniffer software.

After downloading the captures from the PIX firewall, you can analyze the captures with sniffer capture software such as Ethereal.

The capture command has been enhanced to capture packets dropped by security policies.

```
PIX# capture mycapture type asp-drop ?

  acl-drop                 Flow is denied by access rule
  all                      All packet drop reasons
  bad-crypto               Bad crypto return in packet
  bad-ipsec-natt           Bad IPSEC NATT packet
  bad-ipsec-prot           IPSEC not AH or ESP
  bad-ipsec-udp            Bad IPSEC UDP packet
  bad-tcp-cksum            Bad TCP checksum
  bad-tcp-flags            Bad TCP flags
  conn-limit               Connection limit reached
  . . .
PIX#
```

Sniffer Capture

The **capture** command on the PIX firewall is useful only if the packets are reaching to the PIX interface. So you need to rely on external sniffer capture software. Besides, the **capture** command output can be converted and saved in pcap format, which later can be opened and analyzed by sniffer capture software. Ethereal is very popular free downloadable sniffer software (www.ethereal.com).

Syslog

Syslog is the best troubleshooting tool for the PIX firewall. It logs traffic both to and through the firewall. The level of detail provided by syslog is controlled by the level of detail at which PIX is configured for syslog. Seven syslog logging levels can be set on the PIX firewall as shown in Table 3-7.

Table 3-7 *Syslog Messages*

Log Level	Description	# of Messages (Sum)
0	Emergencies	0
1	Alerts	41 (41)
2	Critical	21 (62)
3	Errors	74 (136)
4	Warnings	56 (192)
5	Notifications	21 (213)
6	Informational	95 (308)
7	Debugging	15 (323)

Work through the steps that follow to configure logging on the PIX firewall.

1 Define what you want to capture.

The first step is to enable syslog on the PIX firewall to define the amount of logging you want to capture. There are two ways to define what you want to capture: first with the **syslog level**, and second with the **event_list**. The general syntax for enabling logging is as follows:

```
PIX(config)# [no] logging console|buffered |monitor |trap|mail|asdm
  event_list | level
```

While defining a different level of syslog, you can direct the logging to a monitor, console, buffer, ASDM, syslog server, or e-mail. For example, to enable the logging level to debug and capture the information in the buffer, configure the following:

```
PIX(config)# logging buffer debug
```

The No form of the command which follows will turn off debug level buffer logging.

```
PIX(config)# no logging buffer debug
```

You can change the default buffer size with the following command:

```
PIX(config)# [no] logging buffer-size <bytes>
```

For example, to set up the buffer size to be 8192 bytes, use the following command:

```
PIX(config)# logging buffer-size 8192
```

If you connect to the PIX with Telnet or SSH and want to display the level 6 logging on the monitor, use the following command:

```
PIX(config)# logging monitor 6
```

This can be written as follows:

```
PIX(config)# logging monitor informational
```

To send debug level logging to a syslog server, use the following command:

```
PIX(config)# logging trap debug
```

The following commands send the critical level information to e-mail recipient

```
PIX(config)# logging mail critical
```

You can configure the "Modifiable syslog" feature on the PIX to reduce the amount of syslog. For example, to determine what commands are being executed on the PIX, message 111009 records this information, but by default it is at level 7 (Debug).

```
%PIX-7-111009: User 'xyz' executed cmd: show run
```

So, to capture this syslog ID, the PIX must have the debug level enabled. With debug level logging, PIX generates a huge amount of logging. To cut this down, use the following command to bring the syslog ID down to some lower level, for example, level 1, which will reduce the number of messages substantially with the following command:

```
PIX(config)# logging message 111009 level 1
```

You also can use the following command:

```
PIX(config)# logging message 111009 level alerts
```

Now your syslog message should look like this:

```
%PIX-1-111009: User 'xyz' executed cmd: show run
```

To disable the modifiable syslog, you can use the following command:

```
PIX(config)# no logging message 111009 level alerts
```

Or, you can use the following command:

```
PIX(config)# logging message 111009 level 7
```

With a modifiable syslog, you will still get some logs in different lower levels (for example level 0, 1, 2, and so on). If you just want to see a specific syslog message, use the event class configuration.

An event list can be configured to allow only the specific syslog ID to be logged. An event_list provides you the flexibility to track events by class, severity, or syslog message ID. If you just want to capture syslog for ID 101001 only, you can use the following commands:

```
PIX(config)# logging list mylist message 101001
PIX(config)# logging buffered mylist
```

2 Define the syslog server.

You must define the external syslog server IP address to forward the syslog message to the external syslog server. If your syslog server resides on the inside network with an IP address of 10.1.1.5, use the following command:

```
PIX (config) # logging host inside 10.1.1.5
```

3 Define the mail server.

If you decide to send out syslog information to e-mail addresses, you need to configure the mail server and the e-mail addresses to forward the syslog information.

```
PIX(config)# logging from-address pixbldg3@xyz.com
PIX(config)# logging recipient-address admin@xyz.com level critical
PIX(config)# smtp server pri-smtp-host sec-smtp-host
PIX(config)#
```

4 Turn on the time stamp for syslog.

You can configure the time stamp for logging with the following command:

```
PIX(config)# logging timestamp
```

Use the following command to turn off the timestamp:

```
PIX(config)# no logging timestamp
```

5 Redirect debug to syslog if needed.

To redirect the debug output to syslog, execute the following command:

```
PIX(config)# logging debug-trace
```

To turn off the redirection, use the following command:

```
PIX(config)# no logging debug-trace
```

The syslog message number used is 711011.

6 Turn logging on.

Finally, turn logging *ON* with the following command:

```
PIX(config)# logging enable
```

The following command turns off logging:

```
PIX(config)# no logging enable
```

Once logging is configured, you can verify the syslog configuration with the following command:

```
PIX# show running logging
```

To remove the logging configuration, use the following command:

```
PIX(config)# clear config logging
```

To display buffer logging syslog messages, use the following command:

```
PIX# show logging
```

To display only the syslog configuration settings, use the following command:

```
PIX# show logging setting
```

System syslog messages on PIX/ASA 5500 are found at the following link:

http://www.cisco.com/univercd/cc/td/doc/product/multisec/asa_sw/v_70/syslog/saslmsgs.htm

Syslog messages based on different severity levels on PIX/ASA 5500 can be found at the following link:

http://www.cisco.com/univercd/cc/td/doc/product/multisec/asa_sw/v_70/syslog/saslapa.htm

Get the syslog message ID from the syslog server, find the meaning, and perform the recommended action suggested by the syslog message ID in the previously listed links.

Traceback/Crashinfo

Traceback is a record of abnormal function calls that is usually shown on the console of the PIX firewall, when an abnormal situation occurs. Problems with PIX normal functionality may produce a console traceback message. Not every traceback is serious; some are cosmetic. But, every traceback should be decoded and analyzed. Because the traceback is in hexadecimal values, you will not be able to decode it. Therefore, you need to engage the Cisco Support team for decoding and analyzing it. The problematic function (routines) that causes the traceback might have severe effects, such as crashing the whole PIX and thereby requiring a reboot.

The method of traceback information collection depends on the version PIX is running. If your PIX is running a version earlier than 6.2, you need to connect the console to collect the traceback information for analysis. This is extremely inconvenient and poses security risks to the PIX, as you have to leave the console port connected for hours or even days to collect the traceback, as you do not know when the PIX will crash. Beginning with Version 6.2, the crash information is saved to Flash memoryby default. If saving the crash information to Flash is disabled manually, you can enable it with the following command:

```
PIX(config)# crashinfo save
```

Other Tools

Several often overlooked tools can help minimize the implementation and downtime of network availability. In this section, we will go through these tools:

- **Conduit to Access-list Converter**—Cisco's recommendation is to convert all conduits into access-lists. Access lists are more flexible and more efficient in terms of processing packets. Because conduits work globally on the PIX, if you have multiple interfaces, the packet coming through one of those interfaces has to go through the sequential search to find a match, whereas with an access-list this is more specific to the interface. In PIX Version 7.0, this command is deprecated completely, so you must convert your existing conduit into access-list before proceeding with the upgrade. You can download occ-121.gz for UNIX and occ-121.zip for Windows for a conduit to access-list conversation from the following location: http://www.cisco.com/cgi-bin/tablebuild.pl/pix. The output interpreter can be used as well for conversion.

- **Output Interpreter**—This is a great tool for finding common configuration errors very quickly. Here is the link for the Output interpreter:

  https://www.cisco.com/cgi-bin/Support/OutputInterpreter/home.pl

  Paste the **write terminal** or **show running-config** under the text box of **Enter show command(s) output** from your device for analysis.

- **Bugs Tracker**—Bugs Tracker allows you to look for a possible bug on a specific release. Search by using the string **Bug Toolkit** in the following link: http://www.cisco.com/kobayashi/support/tac/tools.shtml
- **Field Notices**—Field Notices contain information on whether you have severe hardware or software issues on any specific platform or version of the PIX firewall. The following link contains the field notices for the PIX firewall: http://www.cisco.com/en/US/customer/products/hw/vpndevc/ps2030/prod_field_notices_list.html
- **PSIRT Pages**—This security advisory contains Security Vulnerabilities and remedies for all Cisco products. The link for the PSIRT is: http://www.cisco.com/en/US/customer/products/products_security_advisories_listing.html

Problem Areas Breakdown

Troubleshooting PIX Firewall is rewarding because of its extensive syslog capabilities, with many useful **show** and **debug** commands. This section addresses in detail the troubleshooting steps you can take that use the flexible tools and commands that are available. The following functional areas are covered:

- Licensing issues
- Software upgrade/downgrade issues
- Password recovery issues
- Connection issues
- Performance issues
- Transparent firewall issues
- Quality of service (QoS)

More detail discussion follow in the next sections.

Licensing Issues

PIX licensing is accomplished through the activation key, which dictates what features are available for use on the PIX firewall. All available features that are turned on by the activation key can be viewed with the **show version** command. One important distinction between router and PIX firewall licensing is that for turning on additional features, you must download a new image for the router, whereas on the PIX firewall, you need to a get a new activation key. PIX Firewall has a single image for all the platforms, and all the features are included in the same image, with certain features enabled or disabled based on the activation key. The activation key is tied to the serial number displayed by using the

show version command. Hence, when you request the activation key, it's advisable to provide the **show version** output to the Cisco Licensing department (licensing@cisco.com).

The activation key is saved to Flash, so if you replace the Flash, a new activation key comes with it with default features turned on. So if you need additional features, you will need to get a new activation key.

Requests for the DES/3DES can be made (free) from the following location:

http://www.cisco.com/kobayashi/sw-center/internet/pix-56bit-license-request.shtml

The activation key can be a four-octet number as shown in Example 3-14 or a five-octet number, which can be viewed with the **show version** output. Example 3-14 also shows how to enter an activation key from the **Enable** mode.

Example 3-14 *Version Output from PIX 515E*

```
! Following command will enter the activation key to the system. Note that this command
! is entered from enable mode not from configuration mode.
PIX# activation-key 0x0106cb46 0x440feea5 0xac91a4a0 0xad38381c 0x0d08e782
! Show version output which shows the running activation key and the features available
PIX# show version
Cisco PIX Firewall Version 7.0(0)67
Device Manager Version 5.0(0)42
PIX (7.0.0.67) #0: Tue Nov  9 19:14:14 PST 2004
    morlee@caldina:/vws/wza/build/f1/7.0.0.65_branch/7.0.0.67/Xpix/target/f1
PIX up 12 days 17 hours
Hardware:   PIX-515E, 64 MB RAM, CPU Pentium II 433 MHz
Flash E28F128J3 @ 0xfff00000, 16MB
BIOS Flash AM29F400B @ 0xfffd8000, 32KB
 0: Ext: Ethernet0            : media index  0: irq 10
 1: Ext: Ethernet1            : media index  1: irq 11
! Following are the features available
License Features for this Platform:
Maximum Physical Interfaces : 6
Maximum VLANs               : 25
Inside Hosts                : Unlimited
Failover                    : Enabled
VPN-DES                     : Enabled
VPN-3DES-AES                : Enabled
Failover active/standby only: Disabled
Failover active/active only : Disabled
Cut-through Proxy           : Enabled
Guards                      : Enabled
URL-filtering               : Enabled
Security Contexts           : 5
GTP/GPRS                    : Disabled
VPN Peers                   : Unlimited
This machine has an Unrestricted (UR) license.
Serial Number: 807204118
! Four octet activation key is shown below
Running Activation Key: 0x0106cb46 0x440feea5 0xac91a4a0 0xad38381c 0x0d08e783
Configuration last modified by enable_15 at 01:10:18.238 UTC Mon Jan 17 2005
PIX#
```

The following list describes different types of activation keys for the PIX firewall:

- **Before Version 5.0**—Licensing was done based on the number of connections, not based on features that must be turned on in versions earlier than PIX Firewall Version 5.0. The connection was counted towards the maximum number of inbound connections through the PIX firewall.
- **Version 5.0 and later**—From Version 5.0 and more recently, the licensing is based on features.
- **Restricted versus Unrestricted**—On certain PIX platforms (PIX 515, 525, and 535), licensing can be based on Restricted (R) or Unrestricted (UR). Restricted has less interface support and failover is disabled.
- **For Failover Pair**—One PIX must have an unlimited license, and the other one can be either Unlimited or Failover only.
- **Version 7.0 and later**—PIX firewall Version 7.0 supports two kinds of license keys:
  - Existing 4-tuple license key available for PIX Version 6.3
  - New 5-tuple license key for PIX Version 7.0 only

  Unlike PIX Version 6.3, which always requires a valid license key to run, PIX Version 7.0 can run without a license key, but it runs in default settings. When upgrading from PIX Version 6.3 to PIX Version 7.0, the existing license key for PIX Version 6.3 is preserved and is saved in a central location on the Flash file system. When downgrading from PIX Version 7.0 to PIX Version 6.2 or 6.3, the existing license key for the original PIX Version 6.2 or 6.3 that was saved during the upgrade procedure is retrieved and saved to the PIX Version 6.2 or 6.3 image.
- **PIX Security Context Licenses**—Context licensing can be 5, 10, 20, 50, 100, 5–10, 10–20, 20–50, or 50–100 contexts.

NOTE If you want to upgrade from one version to another, you do not need to get a new activation key. However, be sure to write down the key from the **show version** output to proceed with the upgrade. The activation is needed only to enable additional features of the PIX firewall.

Password Recovery Issue

Password recovery needs to be performed on the PIX firewall under following circumstances:

- If you have defined AAA for login purposes, and you lost the username and password. If the AAA server is down, you still can log in with **pix** as the username and **enable password** as the password. If the AAA server is down and you forgot **enable password**, you must perform password recovery.
- If AAA is not configured, but you have lost the login **password**.

PIX performs password recovery in the **ROM** monitor mode by loading a utility called **npdisk** which removes the AAA configuration, and enables password configuration lines from the startup-config file. This, therefore, allows the users to be able to log in to the PIX and get access to the running configuration.

Beginning with PIX Version 7.0, you can disable the password recovery ability, to provide extra security to the PIX firewall. For example, if intruders were to get physical access to the PIX and connect to the console port to perform the password recovery, they could gain access to the PIX configuration and bring the PIX into production. If the password recovery ability was disabled, even though intruders who had physical access to the PIX could get into the ROM monitor mode, and load **npdisk** image, PIX would wipe out the whole configuration before giving access. So, your PIX configuration would not be compromised, and intruders would not be able to bring the PIX online. It is extremely important to provide stringent physical security for your PIX firewall.

The "allow password recovery" option can be set during the preconfiguration template work-through as follows, or with the **no service password-recovery** command.

```
Allow password recovery? [yes]

WARNING: entering 'no' will disable password recovery and disable access to password
  recovery via the npdisk utility. The only means of recovering from lost or
  forgotten passwords will be for npdisk to erase all file systems including
  configuration files and images.

If entering 'no' you should make a backup of your configuration and have a mechanism
  to restore images from the Monitor Mode command line...

Allow password recovery? [yes]
```

To enable password recovery on the CLI, execute the following command:

```
PIX(config)# service password-recovery
```

The following command will turn off the password recovery option:

```
PIX(config)# no service password-recovery
```

Be sure to write this configuration to the startup configuration for changes to be effective.

```
PIX# write memory
```

Work through the following steps to perform the password recovery:

1 Boot PIX firewall into a ROM monitor by pressing the Escape key while the PIX is rebooting.

  Download the **npdisk** image from the following location:

  http://www.cisco.com/warp/public/110/34.shtml

Note The npdisk is backward-compatible, so if you have np63.bin image, that can be used for PIX running Version 6.3 and earlier.

2 Download and install any flavor of the Trivial File Transfer Protocol (TFTP) server if you haven't done so already. You can download TFTP server for free from the Internet.

3 Connect the TFTP server to one of the interfaces (for example, ethernet1) of the PIX using a crossover cable. This will ensure the reliability of the image downloaded to the PIX, as the TFTP is an unreliable protocol. However, you can use the TFTP server in different network segments as depicted in Figure 3-3.

Figure 3-3 *A TFTP Server Setup for PIX Firewall Upgrade*

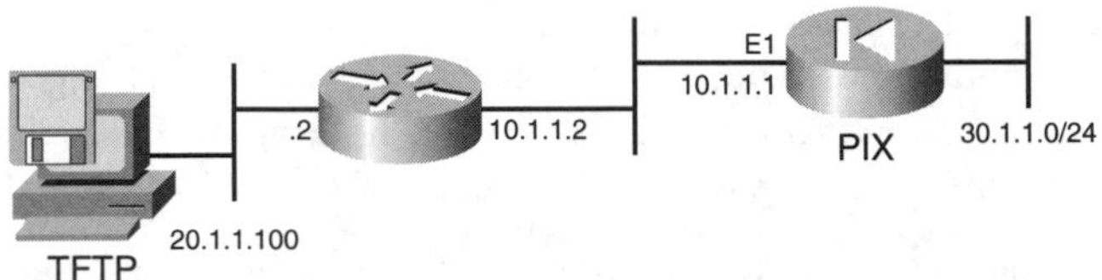

4 Load the **npdisk** image in the root directory of the TFTP server.

5 From the **ROM** monitor mode of PIX firewall, configure the network parameters for the interface where the TFTP server is connected. For example, if the **ethernet1** interface is connected to the TFTP server, the configuration should like the following (based on Figure 3-3):

```
Use BREAK or ESC to interrupt boot.
Use SPACE to begin boot immediately.
Boot interrupted.
Use ? for help.
monitor> interface 1
monitor> address 10.1.1.1
monitor> file np63.bin
monitor> gateway 10.1.1.2
monitor> server 20.1.1.100
```

6 Initiate the TFTP download of the **npdisk** image.

At this stage, you can initiate the download process for **npdisk** image. If the password recovery is allowed as per configuration, you will see the following output:

```
monitor> tftp
tftp np63.bin@20.1.1.100 via 10.1.1.2........... Received 92180 bytes
Do you wish to erase the passwords? [yn] y
The following lines will be removed from the configuration:
        enable password 8Ry2YjIyt7RRXU24 encrypted
        passwd 2KFQnbNIdI.2KYOU encrypted
        aaa authentication serial console LOCAL
        aaa authentication telnet console LOCAL
        aaa authentication ssh console LOCAL
        aaa authentication enable console LOCAL
```

```
Do you want to remove the commands listed above from the configuration?
  [yn] y
Passwords and aaa commands have been erased.
Rebooting..
```

When **npdisk** is loaded via the monitor mode, npdisk will read the startup-config file. If **service password-recovery** is present in the configuration, it will operate as it does in previous versions—it will remove only the startup-config lines that are used to configure the enable password, as in the above output.

If **no service password-recovery** is configured on the PIX firewall, the following sequence will occur:

```
monitor> tftp
! Following is what's shown when you no password recovery option is
  configured.
Cisco Secure PIX Firewall password tool (3.0) #3: Wed May 5 16:20:53 EDT
2004
. . . . .
Using the default startup configuration
WARNING: Password recovery has been disabled by your security policy.
Choosing YES below will cause ALL configurations, passwords, images,
and files systems to be erased and a new image must be downloaded via
monitor mode.
Erase all file systems? y/n [n]:
! Answering 'yes' to this question will result in a prompt to verify
! deletion and overwriting of all local file systems (flash: for PIX
! platforms). After all file systems are erased the system will reboot
! and a new image must be downloaded via monitor mode.
WARNING: Password recovery has been disabled by your security policy.
Choosing YES below will cause ALL configurations, passwords, images,
and files systems to be erased and a new image must be downloaded via
monitor mode.
Erase all file systems? y/n [n]: yes
Permanently erase flash:? y/n [n]: yes
Erasing Flash:
..............................
Rebooting...
! Answering 'no' to the question above will result in the system rebooting and
! loading the image on flash:
WARNING: Password recovery has been disabled by your security policy.
Choosing YES below will cause ALL configurations, passwords, images,
and files systems to be erased and a new image must be downloaded via
monitor mode.
Erase all file systems? y/n [n]: no
Rebooting...
```

When you have password recovery option disabled, when **npdisk** is loaded, it will detect **no service password-recovery** in the startup-config file. Hence, the user will be prompted to erase the Flash file system. If the user chooses not to erase the Flash, the system will reload. This is because password recovery depends on maintaining the existing configuration; this erasure prevents you from recovering a password. However, if you choose Yes, the configuration will be removed and you will need to load a new image.

Software Upgrade and Downgrade Issues

Before proceeding with the upgrade to PIX Firewall Version 7.x, it's important to understand the minimum requirements in terms of hardware, software and the memory. Also it's important to understand different types of releases, which are as follows:

- **Major Feature Releases**—Major feature releases contain, of course, all the new major features. Typically these releases are not frequent. PIX Firewall Versions 6.0(1), 6.1(1), 6.2(1), 6.3(1), and 7.0(1) are examples of major releases.
- **Maintenance Releases**—Maintenance releases introduce minor features of PIX Firewall. PIX Versions 6.0(2), 6.0(3), and 6.0(4) are examples of maintenance releases. Also, bugs are fixed in maintenance releases, which are published on the Cisco web site more frequently than the major releases. In addition, the maintenance release features are combined to form the next major release.
- **Interim Releases**—Interim releases are for bug fixes. All the interim releases, along with additional new minor features, are combined to form the next maintenance release. Examples of interim releases are 6.0(2.100), 6.0(2.101), and 6.0(2.122).

Once you become comfortable with the release process, quickly go through the following list to understand the minimum hardware, software, memory, and flash requirement:

- **Minimum hardware Requirements**—PIX Version 7.0 software can be upgraded on PIX 515/515E, PIX 525, and PIX 535 platforms. This version is not currently supported on PIX 501 or PIX 506/506E platforms.
- **Minimum software Requirements**—You must be running Version 6.2 or later to upgrade to PIX Version 7.0. So, if you are running a PIX version earlier than 6.2, you must first upgrade to PIX Version 6.2 or PIX Version 6.3 before you can proceed with the upgrade.
- **Minimum Memory Requirements**—To upgrade the PIX 515 or PIX 515E, you need to upgrade the memory before performing an upgrade. The PIX 515 and PIX 515E memory upgrades do not require a BIOS update. The minimum flash memory requirement is 16 MB. The memory requirement is based on the types of licenses you have on the PIX as shown in Table 3-8.

Table 3-8 *Memory Requirements Based On License on PIX 515 and PIX 515E*

Restricted License	Unrestricted License
64 MB—Add an additional 32 MB module to your current 32 MB	128 MB—Remove your two 32 MB modules and install a single 128 MB module

Note For PIX 515 and PIX 535 platforms that use 8 MB of Flash memory on versions earlier than PIX Version 7.0, the Flash size automatically expands to 16 MB when upgrading to PIX Version 7.0, which is sufficient for PIX Version 7.0 operation. However, you need to perform the upgrade from ROM Monitor mode.

- **Minimum connectivity requirements**—The minimum connectivity requirements to perform an upgrade to PIX Version 7.0 are:
  — A PC that is connected to any network port of the PIX and is running TFTP software. (Your PC can be connected to the PIX using a switch or a crossover cable).
  — A console connectivity program to talk to the PIX (HyperTerminal or another Terminal Emulation program, DB-9 connector, and rollover cable).

Depending on the platform, you can upgrade the PIX firewall in one of the two following ways:

- Standard upgrade procedure
- ROM Monitor upgrade procedure

Standard Upgrade Procedure

You can a use standard upgrade procedure for any model of PIX other than PIX 515 (not PIX 515E), and PIX 535 to upgrade the PIX from 6.x to 7.x.

1 Ensure the IP connectivity between the PIX and the TFTP server with the **ping** command:

```
PIX# ping 20.1.1.100
```

Replace 192.168.2.200 with your TFTP server IP address.

2 Save the current configuration with the **write net <ip address> <file name>** command to the TFTP server.

```
PIX# write net 20.1.1.100:pix63config.txt
```

3 Copy the PIX Firewall binary image (for example, pix702.bin) to the root directory of the TFTP server.

4 Execute the following command to initiate the upgrade process:

```
PIX# copy tftp flash:image
```

5 Enter the IP Address of the TFTP server at the following prompt:

```
Address or name of remote host [0.0.0.0]? <tftp_server_ip_address>
```

6 Enter the name of the file on the TFTP server that you wish to load. This will be the PIX binary image file name.

```
Source file name [cdisk]? <filename>
```

7 Type **yes** when prompted to start the TFTP copy.

```
copying tftp://172.18.173.123/pix701.bin to flash:image
[yes | no | again]? yes
```

The image will now be copied over from the TFTP server to Flash. You should see the following messages indicating that the transfer was successful, the old binary image in Flash is being erased, and the new image is written and installed.

```
!!!!!!!!!!!!!!!!!!!!!!!!!!!!!!!!!!!!!!!!!!!!!!!!!!!!!!!!!!!!!!
Received 5124096 bytes
Erasing current image
Writing 5066808 bytes of image
!!!!!!!!!!!!!!!!!!!!!!!!!!!!!!!!!!!!!!!!!!!!!!!!!!!!!!!!!!!!!!
Image installed
PIX#
```

8 Check and set the correct boot variable.

After copying the file to Flash, confirm the configuration boot command with the following command:

```
PIX# show running-config | grep boot
boot system flash:/pix701.bin
PIX#
```

If the boot system is pointing to the correct file, execute the **write memory** command to retain this configuration.

```
PIX# write memory
```

The correct *<filename>* is the name of the file on Flash that was copied from the TFTP server earlier. It should show something like boot system flash:/<filename>.

9 If boot system file is set up incorrectly, remove and set this up in the configuration mode:

```
PIX# configure terminal
PIX(config)# no boot system flash:pix701.bin
PIX(config)# boot system flash:pix.702.bin
PIX(config)# exit
PIX# write memory
```

10 Reload PIX Firewall to boot the new image.

```
PIX# reload
Proceed with reload? [confirm]  <enter>


Rebooting....
```

The PIX will now boot the 7.0 image.

Upgrade using ROM Monitor Mode

If you try to upgrade PIX 515 (not PIX 515E) and PIX 535 from Version 6.3 to 7.0, you might run into a problem with the Flash as shown in Example 3-15. The problem is that PIX Version 6.3 can access only 8 MB of onboard Flash out of 16 MB Flash under normal mode of operation. This means that if you have PIX 515 and 535 that have a PDM images installed, you will not be able to upgrade via "copy tftp flash", because there is not enough available space in Flash. You must copy the image over from Monitor mode, and then boot up into 7.0, which will convert the file system, and then you will have to copy the same 7.0 image over again to save it in Flash. If you attempt to upgrade via "copy tftp flash", you will receive the following error:

Example 3-15 *Insufficient flash*

```
PIX# copy tftp://20.1.1.100/cdisk flash:
copying tftp://20.1.1.100/cdisk to flash:image
!!!!!!!!!!!!!!!!!!!!!!!!!!!!!!!!!!!!!!!!!!!!!!!!!!!!!!!!!!!!!!!!!!!!!!!!!!!!!!!!!!!!!!!
!!!!
! Output is suppressed
!!!!!!!!!!!!
Received 4902912 bytes
Erasing current image
! Insufficient flash space available for this request:
Size info:request:4849720 current:1941560 delta:2908160 free:1310720
Image not installed
PIX#
```

Work through the following steps to upgrade the PIX firewall to Version 7.0 from ROM Monitor mode on PIX 515 and PIX 535:

1 Download the PIX 7.x image from the following location and copy it to the root directory of the TFTP server: http://www.cisco.com/cgi-bin/tablebuild.pl/pix

2 Enter into Monitor Mode.

Work through the following steps to enter into the Monitor mode:

a Connect a console cable to the console port on the PIX using the following communication settings:

```
9600 bits per second
8 data bits
no parity
1 stop bit
no flow control
```

b Power cycle or reload the PIX. During bootup you will be prompted to use BREAK or ESC to interrupt Flash boot. You have 10 seconds to interrupt the normal boot process.

c Press the **ESC** key or send a *BREAK* character to enter monitor mode. If you are using Windows Hyper Terminal, you can press the **ESC** key or send a *BREAK* character by pressing **Ctrl+Break**. If you are telnetting through a terminal server to access the console port of the PIX, you will need to press **Ctrl+]** (Control + Right bracket) to get to the Telnet command prompt. Then enter the **send break** command.

d This will bring the monitor mode with the **monitor>** prompt.

e Define interface settings in the ROM Monitor mode.

Enter the interface number that the TFTP server is connected to. The default is interface 1 (Inside).

```
monitor> interface <num>
```

The command to use the inside interface should look like the following:

```
monitor> interface 1
```

Remember that in Monitor Mode, the interface will always auto-negotiate the speed and duplex. The interface settings cannot be hard-coded. Therefore, if the PIX interface is plugged into a switch that is hard-coded for speed and duplex, you must reconfigure it to auto-negotiate while you are in Monitor Mode. Also be aware that the PIX firewall cannot initialize a Gigabit Ethernet interface from Monitor Mode. You must use a Fast Ethernet interface instead.

Enter the IP address of the interface just defined with the following command:

```
monitor> address <PIX_ip_address>
```

To assign IP address 10.1.1.1, use the following command:

```
monitor> address 10.1.1.1
```

3 (Optional) Enter the IP address of your gateway. A gateway address is required if the PIX's interface is not on the same network as the TFTP server.

```
monitor> gateway <gateway_ip_address>
```

If your TFTP server is on a different network (for example, the 172.16.171.0/24 network) define the default gateway so that you know how to get there.

```
monitor> gateway 10.1.1.100
```

4 Enter the IP Address of the TFTP server with the following command:

```
monitor> server <tftp_server_ip_address>
```

If the TFTP server IP address is 172.16.171.1, configure the following:

```
monitor> server 172.16.171.50
```

5 Enter the name of the file on the TFTP server that you wish to load. This will be the PIX binary image file name.

```
monitor> file <filename>
```

For example, if you are trying to install Version pix702.bin, your configuration will look like this:

```
Monitor> file pix702.bin
```

6 Verify IP connectivity by pinging from the PIX to the TFTP server. If the pings fail, double-check the cables, IP address of the PIX interface, and the TFTP server, and the IP address of the gateway (if needed). The pings must succeed before continuing.

```
monitor> ping <tftp_server_ip_address>
```

For example, if you have the TFTP server with IP address 20.0.0.101, you can ping as follows:

```
monitor> ping 172.16.171.50
Sending 5, 100-byte 0xc56 ICMP Echoes to 20.0.0.101, timeout is 4 sec
!!!!!
Success rate is 100 percent (5/5)
monitor>
```

7 Start the TFTP download by typing "**tftp**" as follows:

```
monitor> tftp
```

The PIX will download the image into RAM and will automatically boot it. During the boot process, the file system will be converted along with your existing configuration. However, you are not finished yet. Note the following warning message after booting.

```
*************************************************************************
**                                                                     **
**   *** WARNING *** WARNING *** WARNING *** WARNING *** WARNING ***   **
**                                                                     **
**            ----> Current image running from RAM only! <----         **
**                                                                     **
**  When the PIX was upgraded in Monitor mode the boot image was not   **
**  written to Flash.  Please issue "copy tftp: flash:" to load and    **
**  save a bootable image to Flash.  Failure to do so will result in   **
**  a boot loop the next time the PIX is reloaded.                     **
**                                                                     **
*************************************************************************
```

After the image has been copied, wait for the PIX to return to the normal prompt. (This may take from 3 minutes on a PIX 525 to 10 minutes on a PIX 515.)

8 Once booted, you enter enable mode and copy the same image over to the PIX again, but this time using the **copy tftp flash** command. This will save the image into the

Flash file system. Failure to perform this step will result in a boot loop the next time the PIX is reloaded.

```
PIX> enable
PIX# configure terminal
PIX(config)# interface ethernet 1
PIX(config-if)# ip address 10.1.1.1 255.255.255.0
PIX(config-if)# exit
PIX(config)# exit
```

Use the following command to upgrade the PIX with the following command:

```
copy tftp[:[[//location] [/tftp_pathname]]] flash[:[image | pdm]]
```

The following command will show the upgrade procedure:

```
PIX# copy tftp://20.0.0.101/cdisk.7.0.80.245 flash:
Address or name of remote host [20.0.0.101]?
Source filename [cdisk.7.0.80.245]?
Destination filename [cdisk.7.0.80.245]?
```

9 Once the image is copied over using the **copy tftp: flash:** command, the upgrade process is complete.

10 Execute the following command to verify that the image file is loaded in Flash:

```
PIX# show flash
Directory of flash:/
-rw- 2024 05:31:23 Apr 23 2004 downgrade.cfg
-rw- 4644864 06:13:53 Apr 22 2004 cdisk.7.0.80.245
```

11 Set the boot system flash:/ command with the following command:

```
PIX# configure terminal
! In this case "boot system flash:cdisk.7.0.80.245" to boot from the new
  image.
PIX(config)# boot system flash:/cdisk.7.0.80.245
! Enter the write memory command to update the flash configuration file.
PIX(config)# write memory
```

12 Enter the reload command:

```
PIX(config)# reload
```

13 Execute the **show version** command and make sure the new version is shown in Flash.

Downgrade Procedure

To downgrade PIX from Version 7.x to Version 6.x, use the **downgrade** command instead of the **copy tftp flash** command. Failure to use the **downgrade** command will cause the PIX to go into a boot loop.

When the PIX is upgraded from 6.x to 7.x, the 6.x startup configuration is saved in Flash with the file name **downgrade.cfg**. This configuration can be reviewed before downgrade by issuing the command **more flash:downgrade.cfg** from an enable prompt in 7.0. When you follow the downgrade procedure, which is outlined in the steps that follow, this configuration will be restored to the device when it is downgraded.

Additionally, if the PIX is upgraded via Monitor Mode, the previous 6.x binary image will be saved in Flash as **image_old.bin**. You can verify that this image exists by issuing the **show flash:** command on 7.0. If the image exists on Flash, you can use this image, instead of loading the image from a TFTP server.

Work through the following steps to downgrade the version from 7.x to 6.x on the PIX firewall:

1 Enter the **downgrade** command and specify the location of the image that you want to downgrade to.

```
PIX# downgrade tftp://<tftp_server_ip_address>/<filename>
```

For example, to downgrade to Version 6.3.4 from TFTP server, execute the following command:

```
PIX# downgrade tftp://10.1.1.50/pix634.bin
```

If you upgraded your PIX from Monitor Mode, the old binary image is still saved in Flash. Use the following command to downgrade back to that image:

```
PIX# downgrade flash:/image_old.bin
```

2 A Warning message appears alerting you that the Flash is about to be formatted. Press **enter** to continue.

```
This command will reformat the flash and automatically reboot the system.
Do you wish to continue? [confirm]  <enter>
```

The image will now be copied over into RAM, and the startup configuration is also copied into RAM.

```
Buffering image
!!!!!!!!!!!!!!!!!!!!!!!!!!!!!!!!!!!!!!!!!!!!!!!!!!!!!!!!!!!!!!!!!!!!
!!!!!!!!!!!!!!!!!!!!!!!!!!!!!!!!!!!!!!!!!!!!!!!!!!!!!!!!!!!!!!!!!!!!

Buffering startup config

All items have been buffered successfully.
```

3 A second warning message appears indicating that the Flash will now be formatted. Do NOT interrupt this process or the Flash may become corrupt. Press **enter** to continue with the format.

```
If the flash reformat is interrupted or fails, data in flash will be lost
and the system might drop to monitor mode.
Do you wish to continue? [confirm] <enter>
```

The Flash is now formatted and the old image installed, and the PIX is rebooted.

```
Acquiring exclusive access to flash
Installing the correct file system for the image and saving the buffered
  data
```

```
!!!!!!!!!!!!!!!!!!!!!!!!!!!!!!!!!!!!!!!!!!!!!!!!!!!!!!!!!!!!!!!!!!!!!!
!!!!!!!!!!!!!!!!!!!!!!!!!!!!!!!!!!!!!!!!!!!!!!!!!!!!!!!!!!!!!!!!!!!!!!
Flash downgrade succeeded


Rebooting....
```

4 The PIX will now boot up to the normal prompt.

Upgrading PIX Firewall in a Failover Setup

Upgrading the PIX Appliance from 6.x to 7.x is a major upgrade. It cannot be accomplished without downtime, even for PIXen in a failover set. Note that many of the failover commands change with the upgrade. The recommend upgrade path is to power down one of the PIXen in the failover set. Then follow the preceding instructions to upgrade the powered-on PIX. Once the upgrade is complete, verify that traffic is passing, and also reboot the PIX once to verify it comes back up without issue. Once you are satisfied that everything is working properly, power off the newly upgraded PIX and power on the other PIX. Then follow the instructions above to upgrade the PIX. Once the upgrade is complete, verify that traffic is passing, and also reboot the PIX once to verify that it comes back up without issue. Once you are satisfied that everything is working properly, power on the other PIX. Both PIXen should now be upgraded to 7.0 and powered on. Verify that they establish failover communications properly by issuing the **show failover** command.

NOTE The PIX now enforces the restriction that any interface passing data traffic cannot also be used as the LAN failover interface, or the stateful failover interface. If your current PIX configuration has a shared interface that is being used to pass normal data traffic and the LAN failover information or the stateful information, then if you upgrade, the data traffic will no longer pass through this interface. All commands associated with that interface also will fail.

From PIX 6.x to 7.x upgrade, you require a minimum downtime of the network because of the incompatibility between different image versions. From 7.0 to 7.0x, you can upgrade without downtime if the stateful failover is configured.

Connection Issues Across PIX Firewall

Figure 3-4 shows a typical deployment of the PIX firewall in the network.

Figure 3-4 *A Typical PIX Firewall Deployment in the Network*

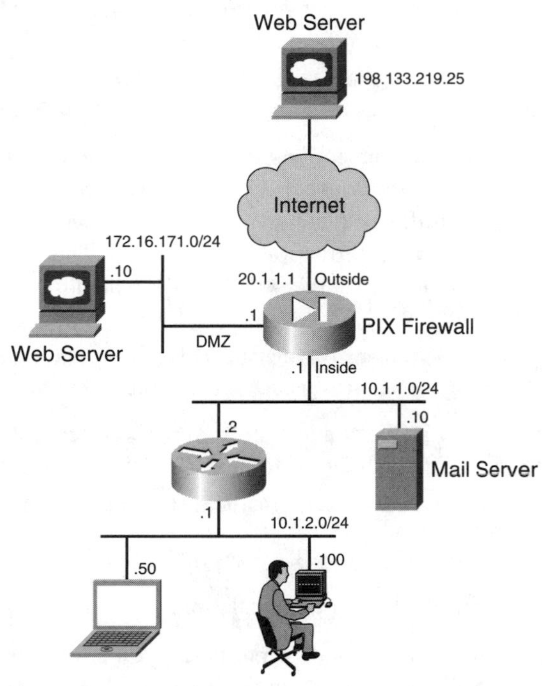

This section discusses the configuration and the troubleshooting steps of the firewall configuration based on Figure 3-4.

Configuration Steps

Connections initiated from higher security going to lower security (for example, inside to Internet or inside to DMZ interface) are considered to be outbound connections. And the traffic from the lower- to higher-security interface network is considered to be inbound traffic. Work through the following steps to configure PIX Firewall for inbound and outbound traffic:

1 Configure access-list on ingress (incoming) interface (optional).

By default, outbound connections are allowed through the PIX firewall if you have the proper translation (if **nat-control** is turned on) and the routing configured. If nat-control is turned off, you do not need any translation. However, if you prefer to create an ACL and apply it on the ingress (incoming) interface, be sure to allow the initial traffic so that translation (if nat-control is turned on and NAT is configured for the traffic) and connections can be created on the PIX firewall. This translation and connection information is maintained on the PIX firewall. To allow the outbound web traffic only from the inside network to a single web server IP address 198.133.219.25 (see Figure 3-4), use the following command:

```
PIX (config) # access-list 101 permit tcp any host 198.133.219.25 eq www
PIX (config) # access-group 101 in interface inside
```

By default, inbound connections are denied on the interface. You must configure an access-list to allow the connection on the interface. However, you must be sure to allow the initial traffic so that translation and connections can be created on the PIX firewall and the state information is maintained. The following ACL will allow SMTP traffic to the mail server (10.1.1.10), which has translated IP address 20.1.1.10:

```
PIX (config) # access-list 102 permit tcp any  host 20.1.1.10 eq smtp
PIX (config) # access-group 102 in interface outside
```

If you want to allow the connection from the web server (172.16.171.10) to the mail server on the inside with the IP address of 10.1.1.10, use the following ACL:

```
PIX (config)# access-list 103 permit tcp host 172.16.171.10 host 10.1.1.10
  eq smtp
PIX (config)# access-group 103 in interface dmz
```

2 Configure for translation or no translation.

Beginning with PIX Firewall Version 7.0, you have the option to turn NAT on or off with the **NAT-control** command. If the **NAT-control** command is turned on (off is default unless the PIX is upgraded from 6.3), PIX Firewall requires you to configure the NAT for source address translation by default for outbound traffic, and destination address translation for the inbound traffic. If **NAT-control** is turned off, NAT will be performed only if the packet matches the source or destination NAT rules.

3 Configure NAT for the outbound connection.

There are many options available to configure source address translation depending on your need for the outbound connection.

To configure Dynamic NAT, use the following command:

```
PIX(config)# global (outside) 1 20.1.1.20-20.1.1.50 netmask 255.255.255.0
PIX(config)# global (outside) 1 20.1.1.51
PIX(config)# nat (inside) 1 10.10.1.0 255.255.255.0
PIX(config)# nat (inside) 1 10.10.2.0 255.255.255.0
```

For outbound connection, you can also configure Dynamic PAT with the interface IP address as follows:

```
PIX(config)# global (outside) 1 interface
PIX(config)# nat (inside) 1 10.10.1.0 255.255.255.0
PIX(config)# nat (inside) 1 10.10.2.0 255.255.255.0
```

To configure policy NAT for outbound connection, use the following command:

```
PIX(config)# access-list 101 permit 10.1.1.0 255.255.255.0 any
PIX(config)# access-list 101 permit 10.1.2.0 255.255.255.0 any
PIX(config)# nat (inside) 1 access-list 101
PIX(config)# global (outside) 1 20.1.1.20-20.1.1.50 netmask 255.255.255.0
```

To configure Policy PAT, use the following commands:

```
PIX(config)# access-list 101 permit 10.1.1.0 255.255.255.0 any
PIX(config)# access-list 101 permit 10.1.2.0 255.255.255.0 any
PIX(config)# nat (inside) 1 access-list 101
PIX(config)# global (outside) 1 interface
```

To use static for the source address translation, use the following command:

```
PIX(config)# static (inside,outside) 20.1.1.100 10.1.1.100 netmask
  255.255.255.255
```

Note that the same static translation can be used for the inbound connection to the 10.1.1.100 address which has external IP address 20.1.1.100.

If you do not want to perform the NAT for the source address, you can configure identity NAT, which is also known as **nat 0** with the following command:

```
PIX(config)# nat(inside) 0 10.1.1.0 255.255.255.0
PIX(config)# nat(inside) 0 10.1.2.0 255.255.255.0
```

The same can be configured with the following command:

```
PIX(config)# access-list 101 permit 10.1.1.0 255.255.255.0 any
PIX(config)# access-list 101 permit 10.1.2.0 255.255.255.0 any
PIX(config)# nat (inside) 0 access-list 101
```

The difference between the **nat 0 ACL** vs. **nat 0 network** is that with **nat 0 ACL**, the translation will be bypassed for both inbound and outbound connections. For inbound connections, the destination address will be bypassed and for outbound connections, the source address will be bypassed. But when you have **nat 0 network** statement, only the source address translation will be bypassed.

4 Configure NAT for inbound connection if required.

For an inbound connection you must configure PIX to perform destination address translation. This usually is accomplished with the static command on the PIX firewall as follows:

```
PIX(config) # static(inside,outside) 20.1.1.100 10.1.1.100 netmask
  255.255.255.255
```

You must allow the traffic to 20.1.1.100 on the outside interface of the PIX for the inbound connection.

To use the interface IP address for the inside host address 20.1.1.100, configure static PAT with the following command:

```
PIX(config)# static (inside,outside) tcp interface 80 10.1.1.100 80
  netmask 255.255.255.255
```

On the ACL applied to the ingress interface, you must create an ACL to allow the traffic to the 20.1.1.1 address for the web access.

To configure policy static NAT to define additional criteria for the NAT to be triggered for the destination address translation, use the following command:

```
PIX(config)# access-list 101 permit tcp host 10.1.1.100 eq 80 host any
PIX(config)# static (inside, outside) 20.1.1.100 access-list 101
```

You also can configure bi-directional NAT on the PIX firewall. The details of bi-directional NAT are beyond the scope of this book.

5 Configure routes for outside and inside networks.

You can configure static or dynamic routing protocol on the PIX to populate the routing table. Usually, if PIX performs the NAT/PAT for the Internet-bound traffic, a default gateway is configured to point to the next-hop router. You can have a single default gateway on the PIX firewall. The following command will configure the default gateway for the Internet-bound traffic:

```
PIX(config)# route outside 0.0.0.0 0.0.0.0 20.1.1.10
```

As the network 10.1.2.0/24 network is not directly connected to the PIX firewall, but off the inside router, you must configure the following route pointing to 10.1.1.2.

```
PIX(config)# route inside 10.1.2.0 255.255.255.0 10.1.1.2
```

You also must have a default gateway on the inside router to point to PIX inside interface IP address (10.1.1.1).

6 Turn on protocol inspection.

By default, several protocol inspections are enabled, which are sufficient to process traffic across the PIX firewall. If there is a protocol that is not inspected, you might need to turn it on.

Troubleshooting Steps

Before delving into the details of how to troubleshoot connectivity problems, it is important to understand the meaning of different connection flags to quickly identify the problem with connections. You can use combinations of **show**, **debug**, and the syslog message that are discussed in this section, to troubleshoot connectivity problems.

Figure 3-5 shows the connection flags for both inbound and outbound connections across the PIX firewall for TCP connections.

Figure 3-5 *PIX Firewall Connection Flags Information for Both Inbound and Outbound Connections*

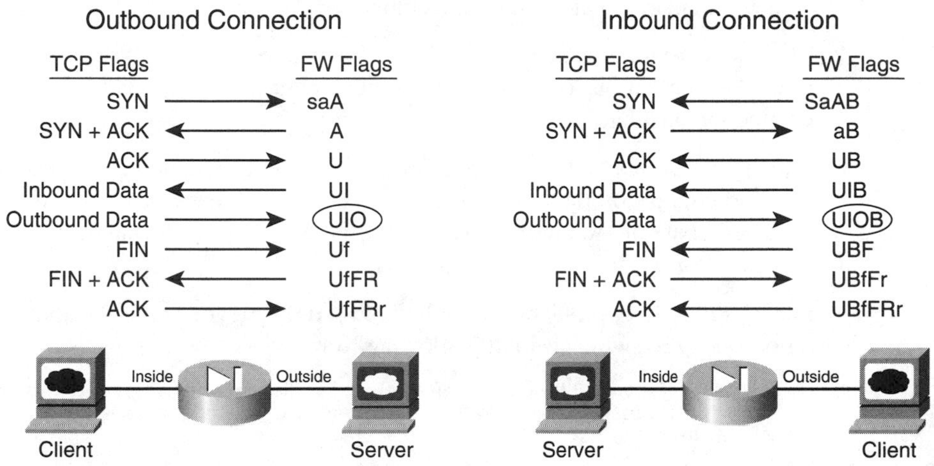

Outbound Connection

TCP Flags		FW Flags
SYN	→	saA
SYN + ACK	←	A
ACK	→	U
Inbound Data	←	UI
Outbound Data	→	UIO
FIN	→	Uf
FIN + ACK	←	UfFR
ACK	→	UfFRr

Client — Inside — Outside — Server

Inbound Connection

TCP Flags		FW Flags
SYN	←	SaAB
SYN + ACK	→	aB
ACK	←	UB
Inbound Data	←	UIB
Outbound Data	→	UIOB
FIN	←	UBF
FIN + ACK	→	UBfFr
ACK	←	UBfFRr

Server — Inside — Outside — Client

The following numbered steps show the sequence of the packets and the connections flags for the outbound connection (see Figure 3-5) through the PIX firewall:

1 When PIX receives an initial **SYN** packet from the inside network, the **SYN** packet is permitted by the access-list on the ingress interface, a translation (xlate) is built up (if NAT is configured), and the connection is created with the flag **saA**, which can be verified with the **show connection** command.

2 The outside device responds to the **SYN** packet with a **SYN+ACK**. The connection flags are updated to reflect this, and now show **A**. Again, this information can be verified with **show connection** command output.

3 The inside device responds to the **SYN+ACK** with an **ACK**, and this completes the TCP 3-way handshake. The connection is now considered **up** (the **U** flag will be shown with the **show connection** command).

4 When the outside device sends the first data packet, the connection is updated, and an **I** is added to the connection flags to indicate that the PIX received inbound data on that connection.

5 Finally, after the inside device sends a data packet, the connection is updated to include the **O** flag.

Understanding the connection flags for the teardown of the connection is very important. Following is the sequence of packets and the corresponding connection flags for the outbound connection:

1 When PIX receives a **FIN** packet from the inside, PIX updates the connection flags by adding an **f**.

2 The outside device immediately responds to the **FIN** packet with a **FIN+ACK**. The connection flags are updated to reflect this with **UfFR** flags.

3 The inside device responds to the **FIN+ACK** with a final **ACK**, and the PIX tears down the connection. Thus, there are no more connection flags, because the connection no longer exists.

The sequence of events that takes place for the inbound connection is similar to that of the outbound connection on the PIX firewall but it has different flags. Details are not discussed here, but refer to Figure 3-5 for a summary of connection flags for the inbound connection.

If you have connectivity problems through the PIX firewall, you need to analyze the connection syslog ID, which is in the following form:

```
PIX-6-302014: Teardown TCP connection number for interface_name:real_address/
  real_port to interface_name:real_address/real_port duration time bytes number
  [reason] [(user)]
```

The reason field is important to understand. Table 3-9 outlines the reasons for connection terminations.

Table 3-9 *Reasons for Connection Termination*

Connection Flags	Meaning
Reset-I	Reset was from Inside
Reset-O	Reset was from Outside
TCP FINs	Normal Close Down Sequence
FIN Timeout	Force Termination After 15 Seconds
SYN Timeout	Force Termination After 2 Minutes
Xlate* Clear	Command Line Removal
Deny	Terminate by Application Inspection
SYN Control	Back Channel Initiation from Wrong Side
Uauth Deny	Deny by URL Filter
Unknown	Catch All Error

*An **xlate** is created dynamically when a packet from a high-security-level interface initiates an outbound connection to a lower-security-level interface.

If you cannot make connection across the PIX firewall, the problem might be with the access-list, NAT, routing, and so on. Work through the following steps to correct the connectivity problem:

1 Is the initial packet reaching the PIX firewall?

This is the first and most important step to troubleshoot the connectivity problem across the firewall. You must be sure the PIX is receiving the initial packet on its interface. If ACL is configured on the interface, you can find out if the packet is reaching to the PIX interface by executing the **show access-list** command. You should see the hit counts incrementing on the **show access-list** command output. Another way you can verify if the packets are reaching is by executing the **show interface** command as shown in Example 3-16. You should see that the **Input counters** are incrementing. The software input queue is an indicator of traffic load, and "No buffers" indicates packet drops, typically due to bursty traffic.

Example 3-16 *Interface Statistics of Inside Interface*

```
PIX-A# show interface inside
Interface Ethernet1 "inside", is up, line protocol is up
  Hardware is i82559, BW 100 Mbps
        Auto-Duplex(Full-duplex), Auto-Speed(100 Mbps)
        MAC address 000d.2807.097a, MTU 1500
        IP address 192.168.1.1, subnet mask 255.255.255.0
        32 packets input, 2100 bytes, 0 no buffer
        Received 0 broadcasts, 0 runts, 0 giants
        0 input errors, 0 CRC, 0 frame, 0 overrun, 0 ignored, 0 abort
        36 packets output, 2304 bytes, 0 underruns
        0 output errors, 0 collisions, 0 interface resets
        0 babbles, 0 late collisions, 0 deferred
        0 lost carrier, 0 no carrier
        input queue (curr/max blocks): hardware (128/128) software (0/1)
        output queue (curr/max blocks): hardware (0/1) software (0/1)
        Received 35 VLAN untagged packets, 1610 bytes
        Transmitted 36 VLAN untagged packets, 1008 bytes
        Dropped 0 VLAN untagged packets
PIX-A#
```

To see the details of the packet going across or reaching the PIX firewall, run the **capture** command as shown in the "Diagnostic Commands and Tools" section.

2 Is the initial packet allowed by the ACL?

For outbound connection across the PIX firewall, you do not have to configure an ACL to allow the traffic. By default, all traffic is allowed. However, for the inbound connection, you must configure an ACL to allow the traffic. Execute the **show access-list** command and be sure that you see that the hit count on ingress interface ACL increases over time. Remember that creating an ACL is not sufficient; you also must apply the ACL on the interface in the proper direction. Execute **show running-config access-group** command to verify if indeed the access-list is applied to the correct interface.

3 Is translation being built up?

If Steps 1–2 are verified, the next step is to verify if the translation is being built up for the connection (this is mandatory when the **nat-control** is turned on or when **nat-control** is turned off but NAT is configured to perform the translation). If the translation is not being built up, first be sure the nat/global is configured correctly. For example, to verify that the nat/global is configured for the outbound connection, execute the following commands:

```
PIX# show run nat-control
PIX# show running-config nat
```

```
PIX# show running-config global
PIX# show running-config static
PIX# show run alias
```

You need to ensure that the NAT identification corresponds to the global identification.

If some hosts are able to connect through the PIX, but some are not, the problem might be that you are running short of addresses from the global pool. To be on the safe side, it is recommended to configure a PAT address along with the NAT pool (when the **nat-control** is turned on).

To verify that a host is building up translation, use the following command:

```
show xlate [global | local <ip1[-ip2]> [netmask <mask>]] [gport | lport
  <port1[-port2]>] [debug]
```

For example, to find out if inside host 10.1.1.70 is building up the translation, execute the following command:

```
PIX# show xlate local 10.1.1.70 debug
NAT from inside:10.1.1.70 to outside:20.1.1.70 flags - idle 0:00:10
timeout 3:00:00
PIX#
```

For translation issues, the following syslog message will be generated:

```
PIX-3-305005: No translation group found for tcp src inside:10.1.1.70/
  11039 dst outside:198.133.219.25/80
PIX-3-305006: regular translation creation failed for tcp src
  inside:10.1.1.70/11040 dst outside:198.133.219.25/80
```

To find out the translation and connection entry created for a specific host (10.1.1.70), execute the following command:

```
PIX# show local 10.1.1.70
```

If the NAT is not working as expected, run the following debug command to get the details of the NAT translation process:

```
PIX# debug pix process
```

4 Is the connection being built up?

If the translation is built up, next make sure that the connection is built up. This can be verified with the **show conn** or **show conn detail** commands to find the connection flag. The meaning of different connection flags is in Figure 3-5. You also need to analyze the syslog to see why the connection is being reset. Refer to Table 3-9 to find out the meaning of different connection resets. For example, if you see connection reset reason as Reset-I, the inside host is resetting the connection.

5 Is routing set up correctly on PIX?

If you see the translation being built up on the PIX but it does not know where to forward the traffic, you must ensure that you have the route set up correctly. For outbound traffic towards the Internet, you must ensure that the default gateway is set up on the outside interface. If the default route is missing to reach to 198.133.219.25 from the inside host 10.1.1.1, you will get the following syslog message:

```
PIX-6-110001: No route to 198.133.219.25 from 10.1.1.70
```

Use the following commands to find out if the route indeed exists:

```
PIX(config)# show route | include 198.133.219.25
```

In Figure 3-4, if you want the users from network 10.1.2.0/24 to be able to access 198.133.219.25, in addition to a default gateway configured on the outside interface, you must configure a static route pointing to the inside router as follows:

```
PIX(config)# route inside 10.1.2.0 255.255.255.0 10.1.1.2
```

6 Is the return traffic coming back to the PIX?

If the global pool or the translated IP address of the initial packet is not part of the same network as the outside interface network of the PIX, the next-hop router will not get the proxy Address Resolution Protocol (ARP) from the PIX. Hence, it is mandatory to create a static route on the next-hop router for the translated network so that the next hop router directs the packets back to the outside interface of the PIX Firewall. For example, in Figure 3-4, if you are using any address on the global pool which is part of network 20.1.1.0/24, you do not need any route defined on the router where the PIX outside interface is connected. This is because, with nat/global, PIX will proxy ARP the MAC address from the global pool to the router that is connected to the outside router. If the global pool is defined with the IP address not part of the outside interface network (20.1.1.0/24), for example, the 30.1.1.0/24 network, you must define a static route on the outside router for network 30.1.1.0/24 pointing to the outside interface (20.1.1.1) of the PIX firewall.

7 Is the router or the PIX ARPing correctly?

If everything else is set up correctly, and you are still unable to make connection across the PIX firewall, execute the **show arp** command on the PIX to see if the next-hop address has an ARP entry. For example, if you have a default gateway setup pointing to 20.1.1.10, on the PIX you should see an ARP entry for the 20.1.1.10 address. If the ARP entry is built as shown by the **show arp** command, execute the **debug arp** command and then execute the **clear arp** command to see if the ARP is having issues. ARP can be a problem for the next-hop router (especially on the outside router). When you make changes to the global pool, static and so on, it is recommended to clear the ARP on the outside router.

8 Packets are dropped by Accelerated Security Path (ASP).

PIX Firewall contains a system for packet inspection, called the Accelerated Security Path (ASP). All packets have to go through the ASP logic, and if any packet violates the logic, that packet will be dropped by the PIX firewall. Sometimes what the ASP considers to be illegitimate packets may be legitimate for you. So it's important to find out what packets the ASP is dropping. This section presents some techniques that you can use to help troubleshoot the problem.

Execute the **show asp drop** command to find out counter values for the reasons for packet drops by the ASP. Issue the command **clear asp drop** then **show asp drop** to get a baseline of the drops so far, then send the traffic that is not making it through the firewall, and then issue **show asp drop** again, and check which counters are incrementing. Following is a sample output of the **show asp drop** command.

```
PIX# show asp drop
Frame drop:
Flow is denied by access rule 3001
First TCP packet not SYN 3000
Bad TCP flags 30
TCP failed 3 way handshake 51
TCP RST/FIN out of order 71
TCP SEQ in SYN/SYNACK invalid 10
TCP ACK in SYNACK invalid 10
TCP packet SEQ past window 40
TCP RST/SYN in window 60
TCP DUP and has been ACKed 16
DNS Guard id not matched 80
PIX#
```

To find the details on what packets are dropped by the ASP, turn on capture with the following command:

```
PIX# capture capture_name type asp-drop drop-code all packet-length 1518
```

Drop-code can be **all** or a specific one in the preceding command. However, because you typically don't know why the PIX is dropping the packet, you cannot specify a specific drop-code; therefore you will usually use **all** as drop-code. You might need to run **interface capture** in addition to **ASP drop capture** to troubleshoot ASP drop issues.

Additionally, instead of sending the debug output to the console, redirect it to the logging buffer with the following commands:

```
PIX(config)# logging list mylist message 711001
PIX(config)# logging buffered mylist
PIX(config)# logging debug-trace
PIX(config)# debug fixup tcp
PIX(config)# debug pix process
```

After going through the preceding steps, you should be able to resolve most of the connectivity problems. However, if you run into a problem with the PIX Firewall version, you might need to engage the Technical Assistance Center (TAC) for further analysis.

Transparent Firewall Issues

Beginning with PIX Firewall Version 7.0, the transparent firewall feature is supported. This section explains the configuration and troubleshooting steps of transparent firewall on the PIX firewall. Configuration is based on Figure 3-6.

Figure 3-6 *Transparent Firewall Deployment*

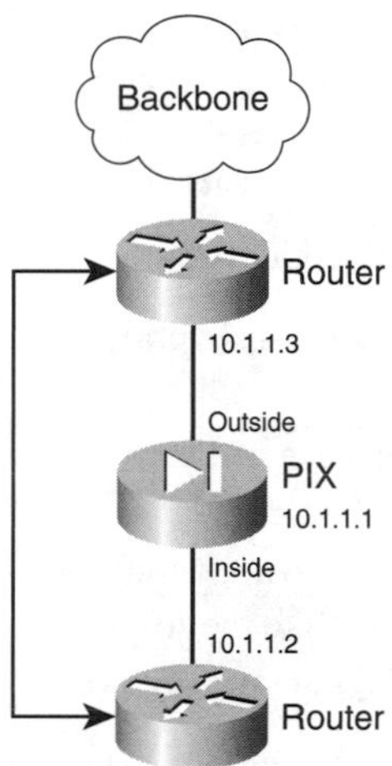

Configuration Steps

Work through the following steps to configure transparent firewall based on Figure 3-6:

1 Turn on transparent firewall.

Convert the PIX firewall with the following command:

```
PIX(config)# show firewall
Firewall mode: Router
PIX(config)# firewall transparent
Switched to transparent mode
PIX(config)#
```

2 Assign an IP address for management.

Configure the IP address for the PIX firewall for management purposes. This address cannot be used as a default gateway for the host. The IP address should be of the same subnet of the other hosts.

```
PIX(config)# ip address 10.1.1.1 255.255.255.0
```

3 Configure interfaces (inside and outside).

Bring up both inside and outside interfaces and be sure not to use the IP addresses on the interface. The following command will turn on the outside interface:

```
PIX(config)# interface Ethernet 0
PIX(config-if)# nameif outside
PIX(config-if)# security-level 0
PIX(config-if)# no shutdown
```

Configure the inside interface with the following commands:

```
PIX(config)# interface Ethernet 1
PIX(config-if)# nameif inside
PIX(config-if)# security-level 100
PIX(config-if)# no shutdown
```

4 Configure an access-list (optional).

You can configure an access-list optionally, and filter the traffic. The command syntax is as follows:

```
PIX(config)# [no] access-list <acl-name> ethertype <permit | deny> <ether-value> [unicast | multicast | broadcast]
```

For example, if you want to allow only the IPX traffic, and deny the rest, your ACL configuration will be the like the following:

```
PIX(config)# access-list 100 ethertype permit ipx
```

Then, you need to apply the access-list on the interface. If the access-list 100 needs to be applied on the inside interface, the configuration will look like this:

```
PIX(config)# access-group 100 in interface inside
```

5 Configure ARP inspection.

ARP inspection is turned off by default, which means that all ARP packets are allowed through the PIX firewall. You can control the flow of ARP packets by enabling ARP inspection. When you enable ARP inspection, PIX Firewall compares the MAC address, IP address, and source interface in all ARP packets to static entries in the ARP table, and takes the actions as follows:

a If the IP address, MAC address, and source interface match an ARP entry, the packet is allowed through.

b If there is a mismatch between the MAC address, the IP address, or the interface, the PIX firewall drops the packet.

c If the ARP packet does not match any entries in the static ARP table, you can set the PIX firewall to either forward the packet out all interfaces (flood), or to drop the packet.

ARP inspection prevents network devices from ARP spoofing. ARP spoofing can lead an attacker to a **man-in-the-middle** attack. For example, a host sends an ARP request to the gateway router; the gateway router responds with the gateway router MAC address. The attacker, however, sends another ARP response to the host with the attacker's MAC address instead of the router's MAC address. The host, thinking that the hacker's MAC address is the valid destination, starts forwarding the packet. The attacker can now intercept all the host traffic before forwarding it on to the router.

ARP inspection ensures that an attacker cannot send an ARP response with the attacker MAC address, if the correct MAC address and the associated IP address are in the static ARP table.

Note In multiple context mode, the commands in this chapter can be entered in a security context, but not in the system context. The dedicated management interface, if present, never floods packets even if this parameter is set to flood.

You can add a static ARP Entry with the following command:

```
arp interface_name ip_address mac_address
```

ARP inspection compares ARP packets with static ARP entries in the ARP table. The following command allows ARP responses from the router at 10.1.1.1 with the MAC address 0009.7cbe.2100 on the outside interface. Enter the following command.

```
PIX(config)# arp outside 10.1.1.3 0009.7cbe.2100
```

Note that the transparent firewall uses dynamic ARP entries in the ARP table for traffic to and from PIX Firewall, such as management traffic. To enable ARP inspection, use the following command:

```
PIX(config)# arp-inspection interface name enable flood | no-flood]
```

Here **flood** forwards non-matching ARP packets out all interfaces, and **no-flood** drops non-matching packets. Note that the default setting is to flood non-matching packets. To restrict ARP through the PIX firewall to only static entries, set this command to **no-flood**. The following command enables ARP inspection on the outside interface, and to drop all non-matching ARP Packets.

```
PIX(config)# arp-inspection outside enable no-flood
```

To view the current settings for ARP inspection on all interfaces, enter the following command:

```
PIX(config)# show arp-inspection
```

6 Configure the MAC address table.

Just as with a normal bridge or switch, PIX Firewall learns and builds a MAC address table by inserting the MAC address with the source interface. Unlike a normal bridge or switch, if the destination is not present on the MAC table, PIX does not flood on all interfaces. Instead it does the following:

a If the packets are for devices directly connected, PIX firewall generates an ARP request for the destination IP address so that it can learn which interface receives the ARP response.

b If the packets for devices are not directly connected, PIX Firewall generates a ping to the destination IP address so that PIX Firewall can learn which interface receives the ping reply. The original packet is dropped.

You can build up the MAC table dynamically or statically. By default, each interface automatically learns the MAC addresses of entering traffic, and PIX Firewall adds corresponding entries to the MAC address table. You can disable MAC address learning if desired; however, unless you add MAC addresses to the table statically, no traffic can pass through the PIX Firewall.

To disable MAC address learning, enter the following command.

```
PIX(config)# mac-learn interface_name disable
```

The **no** form of this command re-enables MAC address learning. The **clear configure mac-learn** command re-enables MAC address learning on all interfaces.

You can add static MAC addresses to the MAC address table if desired. One benefit to adding static entries is to guard against MAC spoofing. If a client with the same MAC address as a static entry attempts to send traffic to an interface that does not match the static entry, the security appliance drops the traffic and generates a system message.

To add a static MAC address to the MAC address table, enter the following command:

```
PIX(config)# mac-address-table static interface_name mac_address
```

The interface name is the source interface. The default timeout value for dynamic MAC address table entries is five minutes, but you can change the timeout. To change the timeout, enter the following command.

```
PIX(config)# mac-address-table aging-time timeout_value
```

The *timeout_value* (in minutes) is between 5 and 720 (12 hours). The default is 5 minutes.

Troubleshooting Steps

There are a combination of show and debug commands available to troubleshoot problems with transparent firewall. You can determine the mode of firewall with the following command:

```
PIX# show firewall
```

You can find out the mac-address-table on the PIX in transparent mode with the following command:

```
PIX# show mac-address-table [interface_name]
```

The following is sample output from the **show mac-address-table** command that shows the entire table:

```
PIX# show mac-address-table
interface mac address type Time Left
-----------------------------------------------------------------------
outside 0009.7cbe.2100 static -
inside 0010.7cbe.6101 static -
inside 0009.7cbe.5101 dynamic 10
PIX#
```

The following command displays the mac-address-table only for inside interface:

```
PIX# show mac-address-table inside
interface mac address type Time Left
-----------------------------------------------------------------------
inside 0010.7cbe.6101 static -
inside 0009.7cbe.5101 dynamic 10
PIX#
```

Use the following debug command in addition to the **show** commands to troubleshoot the transparent firewall issues:

- **debug arp-inspection**—To track the code path of arp forwarding and arp inspection module in transparent firewall.
- **debug mac-address-table**—To track insert/delete/update to the bridge table maintained for transparent firewall.
- **debug l2-indication**—To track code path for processing of layer 2 (l2) indications.

You need to turn on syslog level 4 to see all messages pertaining to transparent problem. This can help in identifying problems pertaining to transparent firewall.

- **MAC Spoofing**—If you receive a MAC address entry that conflicts with the existing static entry (MAC address to a specific interface), you will get the following syslog message:

  ```
  %PIX-3-321001: Deny MAC address <mac-address>, possible spoof attempt on
    interface <interface>
  ```

  For example, if you have a static MAC address defined pointing to the DMZ interface, and if you receive the same MAC address dynamically from the inside interface, then it will be considered as MAC spoofing.

- **ARP Inspection**—If the ARP inspection module drops a packet, the following syslog message will be generated:

  ```
  %PIX-3-321002: ARP inspection check failed for arp <request | response>
    received from host <mac-address> on interface <interface>. This host is
    advertising MAC Address <mac-address-1> for IP Address <ip-address>,
    which is currently statically assigned to MAC Address <mac-address-2>.
  ```

- **Host Movement**—If a MAC address of a host is moved from one interface to the other, the following syslog message will be generated:

  ```
  %PIX-4-411001: MAC <mac-address> moved from <interface-1> to <interface-2>
  ```

  Here interface-1 is the name of the interface from where the host has moved. Interface-2 is the name of the interface to where the host has moved.

- **L2 Table Flooding**—When the bridge table is full and an attempt is made to add one more entry by the Mac-address of the host, the following syslog message will be generated:

  ```
  %PIX-4-411002: Detected bridge table full while inserting MAC
    <mac-address> on interface <interface>. Number of entries = <num>
  ```

Virtual Firewall

Beginning with PIX Firewall Version 7.0, you can logically partition a single PIX firewall into multiple logical PIX firewalls. Each logical PIX firewall can have its own security policy and administration control. This logical PIX firewall is called a Security Context, which is discussed next.

Security Context

Depending on your type of platform and the license, you can have up to 50 security contexts on the PIX, which means you can create up to 50 logical PIXen out of a single PIX firewall. As mentioned before, each security context is an independent firewall with its own security policy, interfaces, and administrators. Almost all the required features to provide the firewalling are possible with multiple contexts: firewall features, IPS, and management, to name a few. Note, however, that with multiple mode some of the features are not supported, including VPN (you can still establish VPN for management purposes only), Web VPN, Dynamic Routing protocols, and Multicast.

As soon as you convert the PIX firewall from single to multiple mode, it creates the system resource space and the **admin** context:

- **System Resource**—After converting into multiple mode, when you log in to the PIX, you are taken to the **System Resource** space. From **System Resource**, the system administrator adds and manages contexts. The System Resource configuration identifies basic settings for the PIX firewall. The system Resource space does not include any network interfaces or network settings for itself; rather, when the system needs to access network resources (such as downloading the contexts from the server), it uses the admin context, which can have interface and network connectivity.
- **Admin Context**—The **admin** context is created as soon as you convert the PIX firewall into multiple mode. It is just like any other context, except that users for **admin** context can access system administrator rights and can access the system and all other contexts. Typically, the **admin** context provides network access to network-wide resources, such as a syslog server or a context configuration server.
- **User Security Context**—Apart from the admin context, you can create an individual security context. The limit is up to 50 based on your PIX model. Each security context is just like a single PIX firewall.

How the Virtual Firewall Works

When PIX operates in multiple context mode, each packet that enters the PIX firewall must be classified, so that the PIX can determine to which context it should send a packet. This is the job of a component of the PIX software called **classifier**. To classify the packets, the classifier goes through the following order to check with the destination IP address of the packet:

1. Context Interface IP Address

If the destination address of the packet is the interface IP address of the context (for instance, outside the interface IP address of a context) that means the packet is for a specific context, hence the classifier marks the packet for that context. An example of these types of packets is an SSH connection to a specific context to mange the context.

2 Source Interface (VLAN)

If the destination address of the packet is not one of the interface IP addresses of the context, the next check is performed based on the source VLAN of the packet. For example, if Ethernet 1 and Ethernet 2 interfaces are connected to VLAN100 and VLAN200, respectively, and if these interfaces are mapped to the context 1 and context 2, when the packet enters into PIX through Ethernet 1, the classifier will forward the packet to context 1, which is obvious. To make it little more complex, assume that Ethernet 1 is configured as trunks for VLAN100 and VLAN200, and VLAN100 is mapped to context1 and VLAN200 is mapped to context 2. With this setup, if the packet reaches to the PIX using VLAN 200, the classifier will forward the packet to context 2. Figure 3-7 shows an example to illustrate this point.

Figure 3-7 *Source VLAN Varies with Multiple Contexts*

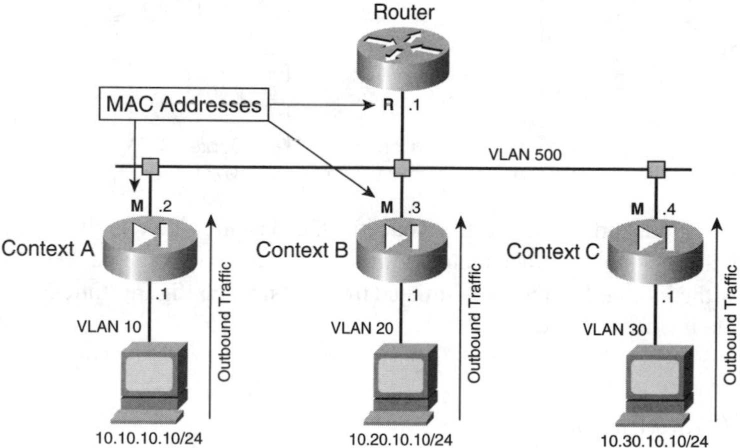

This example shows VLAN 10, 20, and 30 mapped to separate contexts, so for outbound traffic; the classification will be made based on these sources' VLAN. Note that the PIX inside interface can be configured as a trunk for these VLANs, and then mapped to the individual VLAN to the respective contexts. For example, VLAN 10 should be mapped to Context A. For return traffic, the classifier would already know which context the return traffic belongs to. Even though the outside VLAN 500 is shared for the outside interface across all three contexts, the classifier builds up the knowledge base on which context the return packet should belong to based on the source address translation of the initial outbound traffic.

3 Destination Address

If the packet is not destined for the interface IP address of any context, and if the source VLAN of the packet is shared as shown in Figure 3-8 for the inbound connection, the classifier makes the decision on which context the packet needs to be forwarded based on the destination IP address.

Therefore, PIX classifier needs to have the knowledge of the destination network for each context. The classifier learns this destination network based on the translation configured on the contexts. Figure 3-8 illustrates this point.

Figure 3-8 *VLAN Sharing with Multiple Contexts*

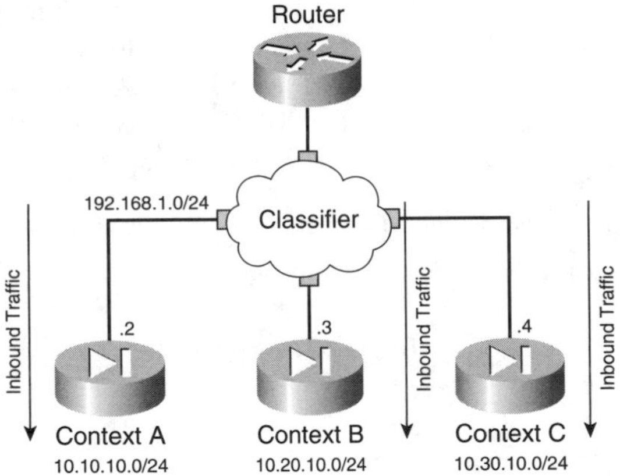

For inbound traffic initiated from outside, the classifier looks only at static statements where the global interface matches the source interface of the packet. So in Figure 3-6, to allow the inbound connection initiated from outside, configure static NAT on each classifier for the inside network.

Limitations of Virtual Firewall

Before delving into the details of configuration and troubleshooting of Virtual Firewall, it is important to understand some of the limitations of the Firewall implementation:

- **Transparent Firewall in Multiple Contexts**—In routed mode, the classifier classifies the packet based on source VLAN, or destination IP address. So it is possible to share the same VLAN across multiple contexts with the help of NAT. But, in transparent mode, NAT cannot be configured. Therefore, classification is based only on source VLAN. This means it is not possible to share the same VLAN across multiple contexts.
- **NAT Zero Access List and Shared Interfaces in routed mode**—On the PIX Firewall, you can configure "NAT zero access-list" to bypass the NAT for the traffic defined on the ACL. If you do that and if the VLAN is shared, the classifier will not know the destination address per context, so communication will fail.

- **Hosts on Shared Interfaces Cannot Initiate Outbound Connections**—If you share the inside VLAN among multiple contexts, this will cause problems, unless you have the destination address translation configured. Usually outbound traffic is Internet-bound, and configuration address translation may not be possible. Therefore, it is strongly recommended not to share the inside VLAN for outbound traffic among multiple contexts.

Configuration Steps

Figure 3-9 shows two context deployments of the PIX firewall.

Figure 3-9 *Two Context Deployment of the PIX Firewall*

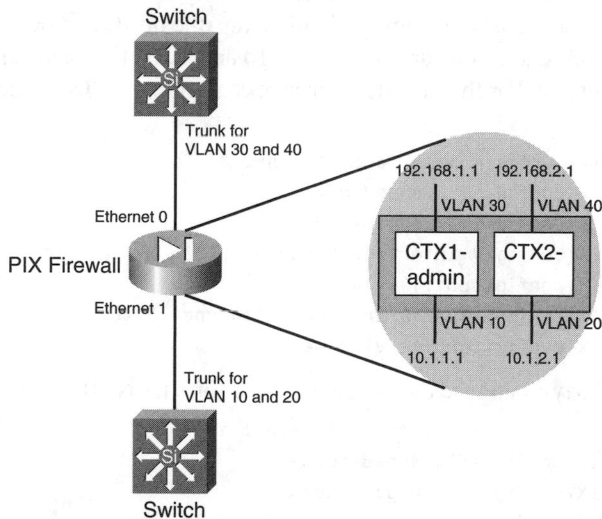

Work through the following steps to configure multiple contexts on the PIX firewall based on Figure 3-9:

1 Change the mode of operation from the **single** to **multiple** with the following command:

```
PIX(config)# mode multiple
WARNING: This command will change the behavior of the device
WARNING: This command will initiate a Reboot
Proceed with change mode? [confirm]
Convert the system configuration? [confirm]
. . . . . .
```

Once the PIX is booted up, execute the following **show** command and be sure that the security context mode is shown as multiple:

```
PIX# show mode
Security context mode: multiple
PIX#
```

After the PIX is converted to the multiple context, once you log in to the PIX, you will be taken to the System Resource Space (context). From here, you can configure the rest of the other contexts. The context **admin** will be created by default, which can be verified with the following command:

```
PIX# show running-config context admin
context admin
  config-url flash:/admin.cfg
!
PIX#
```

2 Configure interfaces.

You need to configure all interfaces on the system context before they can be mapped to the user security context. For this setup, the inside and outside (both interfaces) are configured as trunk carrying VLAN 10 and 20 on the inside and VLAN 30 and 40 on the outside. For the outside interface, configure the PIX in the system context as follows:

```
PIX(config)# interface Ethernet 0
PIX(config-if)# speed auto
PIX(config-if)# duplex auto
PIX(config)# interface Ethernet 0.30
PIX(config-subif)# vlan 30
PIX(config-subif)# interface Ethernet 0.40
PIX(config-subif)# vlan 40
```

Similarly, configure the inside interface for VLAN 10 and 20 as follows:

```
PIX(config)# interface Ethernet 1
PIX(config-if)# speed auto
PIX(config-if)# duplex auto
PIX(config)# interface Ethernet 1.10
PIX(config-subif)# vlan 10
PIX(config-subif)# interface Ethernet 0.20
PIX(config-subif)# vlan 20
PIX(config-subif)#
```

3 Create contexts.

From system context, you can create a new context or change the role of admin context. To do this, you need to create a new context that you want to designate as admin context. For instance, if you want to configure contexts ctx1 and ctx2, and want to make ctx1 your admin context, you need to create the two new contexts as follows:

```
PIX(config)# context ctx1
PIX(config-ctx)# config-url flash:/ctx1.cfg
PIX(config)# context ctx2
PIX(config-ctx)# config-url flash:/ctx2.cfg
PIX(config-ctx)#
```

Now assign the admin context role to ctx1 context as follows:

```
PIX(config)# admin-context ctx1
```

Finally remove the admin context that was created by default as follows:

```
PIX(config)# no context admin
```

Verify the contexts you have just created:

```
PIX# show context
Context Name      Interfaces                          URL
*ctx1                                                 flash:/ctx1.cfg
 ctx2                                                 flash:/ctx2.cfg

Total active Security Contexts: 2
PIX#
```

4 Associate interfaces to the contexts.

You need to associate the interfaces from the system context with the **allocate-interface** commands. For example, to allocate interfaces Ethernet0.30, and Ethernet1.10, you can use the following commands:

```
PIX(config)# context ctx1
PIX(config-ctx)# allocate-interface Ethernet0.30
PIX(config-ctx)# allocate-interface Ethernet1.10
```

Similarly, the following interface mappings are for context ctx2:

```
PIX(config)# context ctx2
PIX(config-ctx)# allocate-interface Ethernet0.40
PIX(config-ctx)# allocate-interface Ethernet1.20
```

After creation of context, verify it with the following command:

```
PIX# show context
Context Name      Interfaces                          URL
*ctx1             Ethernet0.30, Ethernet1.10                   flash:/ctx1.cfg
 ctx2             Ethernet0.40, Ethernet0.20                   flash:/ctx2.cfg

Total active Security Contexts: 2
PIX#
```

5 Configure the interfaces on the context.

From system context, go to the respective contexts to configure the interfaces with **changeto** command. The following commands show how to configure the interfaces on the context ctx1:

```
PIX(config)# changeto context ctx1
PIX/ctx1(config)# interface Ethernet0.30
PIX/ctx1(config-if)# ip address 192.168.1.1 255.255.255.0
PIX/ctx1(config-if)# nameif outside
PIX/ctx1(config-if)# exit
```

The following commands are used to configure the inside interface on context ctx1:

```
PIX/ctx1(config)# interface Ethernet1.10
PIX/ctx1(config-if)# ip address 10.1.1.1 255.255.255.0
PIX/ctx1(config-if)# nameif inside
PIX/ctx1(config-if)# exit
```

Configure interfaces for context ctx2 in the same way as for context ctx1:

```
PIX(config)# changeto context ctx2
PIX/ctx2(config)# interface Ethernet0.40
PIX/ctx2(config-if)# ip address 192.168.2.1 255.255.255.0
PIX/ctx2(config-if)# nameif outside
PIX/ctx2(config-if)# exit
PIX/ctx2(config)# interface Ethernet1.20
PIX/ctx2(config-if)# ip address 10.1.2.1 255.255.255.0
PIX/ctx2(config-if)# nameif inside
PIX/ctx2(config-if)# exit
```

6. At this stage, you can treat both ctx1 and ctx2 contexts as individual firewalls and define the policies, NAT, and so on just as you would do for a regular PIX firewall.

   To go back to the system context, execute the following command:

```
PIX(config-ctx)# changeto context system
PIX(config)#
```

Troubleshooting Steps

Troubleshooting techniques for multiple contexts are the same as for a single context, so the same information will not be repeated here. Most of the problems that arise with multiple context are caused by a lack of understanding of how multiple context works. It is strongly recommended that you work through the preceding section to understand how multiple context works and how to configure the PIX firewall correctly.

Quality of Service (QoS) Issues

Beginning with PIX Version 7.0, there are two QoS features available on PIX Firewall:

- Policing
- Low Latency Queuing (LLQ)

Policing

Policing is used to control the amount of traffic that can flow through an interface. On the PIX, policing is supported for outbound traffic only. The example that follows illustrates this concept.

Assume that you have a LAN-to-LAN connection between the main office (hub), and a remote office (spoke). The communication between the LAN of the hub, 10.1.1.0/24 and LAN of the spoke, 10.1.2.0/24 is protected by the LAN-to-LAN IPsec tunnel. Assume that you want to limit traffic from the main office to remote office traffic so that the VPN data link does not become oversubscribed. To achieve this, work through the steps that follow to configure outbound policing on the PIX firewall on the main office (hub):

Step 1 Create a class-map to classify the traffic subject for policing.

Use the **class-map** command to enter class-map configuration mode. From class-map configuration mode, you can define what traffic should be included in the class using the **match** command.

The following is an example that shows how to classify the VPN traffic (tunnel group name is spoke1) for policing for destination IP address flow:

```
PIX(config)# class-map remote-VPN-traffic
PIX(config-cmap)# match flow ip destination-address
PIX(config-cmap)# match tunnel-group spoke1
PIX(config-cmap)#
```

The following commands are available in class-map configuration mode:

- **description**—It describes the class-map.
- **match any**—It specifies all traffic to be matched.
- **match access-list**—Traffic classification is made based on the access-list.
- **match port**—It specifies that traffic should be matched using a TCP/UDP destination port.
- **match precedence**—This specifies that the precedence value represented by the Type of Service (TOS) byte in the IP header should be matched.
- **match dscp**—It specifies that the Internet Engineering Task Force (IETF)-defined DSCP value in the IP header should be matched.
- **match rtp**—This specifies that an RTP port should be matched.
- **match tunnel-group**—It specifies that the security-related tunnel groups should be matched.
- **match flow**—It specifies that the IP destination address should be matched.
- **Match default-inspection-traffic**—This specifies that the default traffic for the **inspect** commands should be matched.

Step 2 Create a policy-map describing the action you want to perform on the data flow.

To define the policy map, use the following command syntax:

```
PIX(config)# policy-map mypolicy
PIX(config-pmap)# ?

MPF policy-map configuration commands:
  class         Policy criteria
  description   Specify policy-map description
  exit          Exit from MPF policy-map configuration mode
  help          Help for MPF policy-map configuration commands
  no            Negate or set default values of a command
  rename        Rename this policy-map
  <cr>
PIX(config-pmap)#
```

The descriptions of keywords are as follows:

— **class**—Specifies a class-map for traffic classification.

— **clear configure policy-map**—Specifies that all policy-map configurations should be removed with one exception: if a policy-map is in use in a service-policy command, that policy-map is not removed.

— **description**—Specifies a description for the policy-map.

— **help policy**—The map shows syntax help for the **policy-map** command.

For your example, if you want to configure police rate 10,000 bps, and burst 15,000 bytes, and if VPN traffic exceeds the burst and then drops, your policy-map can be configured as follows:

```
PIX(config)# policy-map vpn-Policy
PIX(config-pmap)# class remote-VPN-traffic
PIX(config-pmap-c)# police 10000 15000 conform-action transmit exceed-
action drop
```

Once the policy-map is configured, you can verify it with the following command:

```
PIX# show running-config policy-map
```

Step 3 Attach the policy map to a service-policy.

The service-policy identifies the interface at which the action is performed.

Use this command to apply the service policy:

```
PIX(config)# service-policy policy-map-name interface interface-name
```

For example, to apply a service policy globally, use the following command:

```
PIX(config)# service-policy global-policy global
```

To apply the policy on the outside interface, use the following configuration:

```
PIX(config)# service-policy vpn-Policy interface outside
```

Low Latency Queuing (LLQ)

Low Latency Queuing is important for latency-sensitive traffic such as VoIP traffic. If you want to make sure VoIP phones at the main office have the lowest latency possible through the firewall and VPN to the remote office, you need to configure LLQ. To be effective, you must configure LLQ in both directions both on the Main and the Remote sites.

Just as with Policing, assume that you have a LAN-to-LAN between the main office (hub), and the remote office (spoke). The communication between the LAN of hub, 10.1.1.0/24 and LAN of spoke, 10.1.2.0/24 is protected by the LAN-to-LAN IPsec tunnel. Assume that you want to apply LLQ for the voice traffic across the tunnel. Work through the following steps to accomplish this task:

Step 1 Create a class-map describing the data flow. More than one class-map is required; one for voice traffic, and other one for the rest of the other traffic.

All voice traffic can be classified with the following class-map, which requires LLQ:

```
PIX(config)# class-map remote-Voice
PIX(config-cmap)# match tunnel-group spoke1
PIX(config-cmap)# match dscp ef
PIX(config-cmap)#
```

The following class-map classifies the rest of the other traffic that doesn't require LLQ:

```
PIX(config)# class-map remote-Other-traffic
PIX(config-cmap)# match tunnel-group spoke1
PIX(config-cmap)# match flow ip destination-address
PIX(config-cmap)#
```

Step 2 Create a policy-map describing the action on the previously created class-map.

Create a policy-map and apply priority queue for the VOICE traffic and the policing for the other traffic as follows:

```
PIX(config)# policy-map vpn-Policy
PIX(config-pmap)# class remote-Voice
PIX(config-pmap-c)# Priority
```

```
PIX(config-pmap)# class remote-Other-Traffic
PIX(config-pmap-c)# police outside 200000 37500 conform-action transmit
  exceed-action drop
```

Note You cannot combine priority and police in the same class map.

Step 3 Attach the policy-map to a new or existing service-policy that identifies where the action is performed.

Bind the policy-map outside-policy to the interface with the following command:

```
PIX(config)# service-policy vpn-Policy interface outside
```

Step 4 Configure priority queues for LLQ and Best Effort traffic.

Use the following command to configure priority queue on the interface:

```
priority-queue interface name
tx-ring-limit value
queue-limit value
```

Example 3-17 shows a sample of priority queue on the outside interface of the PIX firewall.

Example 3-17 *Priority Queue Applied to the Outside Interface*

```
PIX(config)# priority-queue outside
! <max allowed no of packets queued at the tx-ring for the priority-queue>
PIX(priority-queue)# tx-ring-limit 20
! <max # of packets queued at the priority queue>
PIX(priority-queue)# queue-limit 20
PIX(priority-queue)#
```

Troubleshooting Steps

Use the **show service-policy** command to get statistics, and observe their behavior to determine operational status. There is no low latency queue or priority queue in multiple context modes.

Performance Issues

When you run into high CPU or low memory on the PIX, you might observe one or more of the following symptoms:

- A packet drops across the firewall.

- You are unable to log in to PIX either via Telnet, SSH or even the console.
- You are unable to execute any command on the CLI even if you can connect to it.

This high CPU and low memory condition on the PIX firewall can be caused by normal or abnormal traffic. Examples of abnormal traffic are attacks, worms, viruses, and so on, in the network. However, if you have just deployed a new PIX in the network, and you are having performance issues, you might be reaching the CPU or memory limit on the PIX. This can happen if you have an additional feed or bandwidth increment for your existing PIX. It can also happen because of misconfiguration on the switch that causes the redirecting of all traffic into the port of the PIX firewall. However, if performance deteriorates suddenly, chances are that either you are running into a configuration issue on the PIX or your network is under attack. This section describes troubleshooting steps for isolating issues with CPU and memory problems.

High CPU Utilization

It is important to keep the CPU utilization under 60 percent. If utilization exceeds 60 percent, you must examine the traffic and see if you need to consider a firewall with higher performance, or if you are under attack.

Work through the following steps to identify and correct high CPU utilization problem:

Step 1 Find out the summary of CPU utilization.

In both single and multiple mode, execute the following command to obtain the summary of the CPU usage at any time:

```
PIX# show cpu [usage] [context {all | context_name}]
```

A sample output of the **show cpu usage** command is as follows:

```
PIX# show cpu usage
CPU utilization for 5 seconds = 1%; 1 minute: 0%; 5 minutes: 0%
PIX#
```

A sample output of CPU usage for a specific context in multiple context mode follows:

```
PIX/context_name(config)# show cpu usage context admin
CPU utilization for 5 seconds = 1%; 1 minute: 0%; 5 minutes: 0%
PIX/context name(config)#
```

You can find out the same information by executing the command from the context itself as follows:

```
PIX/context_name(config)# show cpu usage context admin
CPU utilization for 5 seconds = 1%; 1 minute: 0%; 5 minutes: 0%
PIX/context name(config)#
```

The following command shows how to display the CPU utilization for all contexts:

```
PIX(config)# show cpu usage context all
CPU utilization for 5 seconds = 1%; 1 minute: 0%; 5 minutes: 0%
```

```
5 sec 1 min 5 min Context Name
0% 0% 0% admin
59% 59% 59% system
41% 41% 41% <kernel>
PIX#
```

If the CPU utilization is showing high, move to the next step to find out which process is causing the high CPU utilization.

Step 2 Identify the process that is utilizing maximum CPU cycles.

Execute the **show process** command on the PIX firewall and find out the run time of the process. You should compare the other processes with different poll processes, for example, the **557poll** process. Example 3-18 shows that the **Logger** process is utilizing the maximum CPU cycles other than **557poll.**

Example 3-18 *Output of* **show processes** *on PIX Firewall*

```
PIX(config)# show processes
    PC       SP       STATE          Runtime    SBASE     Stack Process
Hsi 001eab19 008a5a74 00557910             0 008a4aec 3628/4096 arp_timer
Lsi 001f00bd 00a28dbc 00557910             0 00a27e44 3832/4096 FragDBGC
Lwe 00119abf 02d280dc 0055b070             0 02d27274 3688/4096 dbgtrace
Lwe 003e4425 02d2a26c 00557dd8         74440 02d28324 6936/8192 Logger
Crd 001e26fb 0533940c 00557d88       6070290 05338484 3684/4096 557poll
Lsi 00300a29 04c0f504 00557910             0 04c0e57c 3944/4096 xlate clean
....
PIX(config)#
```

As it is not clear how severely CPU cycles are utilized by the **Logger** process, take a **show process** command output in one-minute intervals. Now take the difference, and list the difference of CPU utilization as shown in Example 3-19.

Example 3-19 *The Differences in CPU Utilization by Different Process*

```
Process_Name            Runtime (msec)
Logger                  35340
pix/intf3               28410
557poll                  8250
i82543_timer             5180
i82542_timer             2330
```

As you can see, the **Logger** process is utilizing the maximum CPU cycles. Starting with PIX firewall version 7.0, you can find out the same information just discussed on which process is utilizing the highest CPU cycles by executing show processes cpu-hog. This is preferred to the method that was just explained.

Step 3 Examine the process and take corrective action.

As the **Logger** process is using the maximum CPU, review the configuration for syslog as shown in Example 3-20.

Example 3-20 *The Output of the* **show log** *Command*

```
PIX(config)# show log
Syslog logging: enabled
    Standby logging: disabled
    Console logging: disabled
    Monitor logging: disabled
    Buffer logging: level alerts, 0 messages logged
! Following line shows huge amount of trap level logging, which mean this much
! of syslog information is written to the syslog server. But this in total since
! the PIX is rebooted last.
    Trap logging: level warnings, 6929312 messages logged
        Logging to inside 172.16.171.10
    History logging: disabled
 . . .
PIX(config)#
```

In Example 3-20, it is not conclusive how quickly the PIX is generating so many messages to the syslog. Therefore, execute the **show log** command again as shown in Example 3-21 and compare the new output with the previously taken output that was shown in Example 3-20.

Example 3-21 *The* **show log** *Output Taken After a Few Minutes*

```
PIX(config)# show log
Syslog logging: enabled
    Buffer logging: level alerts, 0 messages logged
!Notice the amount of messages logged after few minutes
    Trap logging: level warnings, 9152372 messages logged
        Logging to inside 172.16.171.10
PIX(config)#
```

Step 4 Investigate the Syslog messages.

At this stage, you should be fairly certain that the syslog is causing the high CPU utilization problem. So you need to determine if it is because of attack or misconfiguration. If the syslog server is available, perform the analysis from the syslog server, or turn on the buffer logging.

For this specific example, assume that the syslog server is down, which will cause the PIX to generate the syslog messages as shown in Example 3-22.

Example 3-22 **show log** *Output When the Syslog Server Is Unreachable*

```
PIX(config)# show log
     Buffer logging: level warnings, 41527 messages logged
     Trap logging: level warnings, 9553127 messages logged
        Logging to inside 172.16.171.10
. . .
400011: IDS:2001 ICMP unreachable from 172.16.171.10 to 172.16.171.1 on interface
  inside
400011: IDS:2001 ICMP unreachable from 172.16.171.10 to 172.16.171.1 on interface
  inside
```

continues

Example 3-22 **show log** *Output When the Syslog Server Is Unreachable (Continued)*

```
400011: IDS:2001 ICMP unreachable from 172.16.171.10 to 172.16.171.1 on interface
  inside
400011: IDS:2001 ICMP unreachable from 172.16.171.10 to 172.16.171.1 on interface
  inside
400011: IDS:2001 ICMP unreachable from 172.16.171.10 to 172.16.171.1 on interface
  inside
400011: IDS:2001 ICMP unreachable from 172.16.171.10 to 172.16.171.1 on interface
  inside
PIX(config)#
```

In the previous example, ICMP Unreachable is generated by the syslog server for each syslog message PIX is sending to the syslog server. The problem is aggravated when the Intrusion Prevention System (IPS) is configured, because for every ICMP unreachable message, PIX is generating an IPS message and sending it to the syslog server, which in turn generates another similar message. And this cycle continues until the syslog server is rechargeable.

To correct the problem, you need to bring up the syslog server or turn off logging. You might consider turning of IPS until the syslog server is up again.

Step 5 Follow the same procedure to correct other problems. For example, if you are under attack, examining the syslog along with sniffer capture will assist in finding the hosts that are infected, so that you can correct the problem by patching the host, or, as a temporary work-around, configuring the PIX with ACL to drop the bad packets on the interface. Actions that need to be taken differ depending on the problem.

Step 6 Re-examine the CPU output, and repeat as necessary.

For additional details on troubleshooting performance issues on the PIX firewall, refer to the following link:

http://www.cisco.com/en/US/products/hw/vpndevc/ps2030/products_tech_note09186a008009491c.shtml

To find out the function of different processes on the PIX, refer to the following link:

http://www.cisco.com/en/US/partner/products/hw/vpndevc/ps2030/products_tech_note09186a008009456c.shtml

High Memory Utilization

If you cannot make a new connection across the PIX firewall, but your existing connections are working well, most likely you are running into low memory issues. Work through the steps that follow to identify and correct the problem:

Step 1 Check the amount of free memory available with the following command:

```
PIX# show memory
Free memory:        40955872 bytes (61%)
```

```
Used memory:        26152992 bytes (39%)
-------------      ----------------
Total memory:       67108864 bytes (100%)
PIX#
```

This output will show the memory available. If free memory is low, investigate the reason for the low memory.

Step 2 Analyze the syslog message to find out if you received the following message for running short of memory:

```
%PIX-3-211001: Memory allocation Error
%PIX-3-211001: Memory allocation Error
```

Step 3 Identify what is utilizing the memory (RAM) most heavily on the PIX. Before you can make that identification, you must know how memory is utilized on the PIX. Several things use up memory, such as the PIX image (run from RAM), configuration, the IPsec database, Xlates (translations), and connections. Most of the time, if the problem appears suddenly, the problem is with either translations or connections.

So, you need to check the translations count with the **show xlate** command as shown below:

```
PIX# show xlate count
350 in use, 400 most used
PIX#
```

The translation count in this example looks normal.

Now, quickly find the connection count with the following command:

```
PIX# show conn count
161723 in use, 161723 most used
PIX#
```

So, it appears that with only 350 translations, 16,1723 connections are made, which is an indication that your network may be infected by a virus or worm.

Step 4 Now analyze the traffic load and find out from which interface the vast majority of traffic is coming. You can find this information with the command shown in Example 3-23.

Example 3-23 *Examining Traffic Load with the* **show traffic** *Command*

```
PIX# show traffic
! Following statistics is for outside interface
outside:
        received (in 50.000 secs):
                2170 packets    501050 bytes
                65 pkts/sec     21752 bytes/sec
        transmitted (in 50.000 secs):
                187629 packets  9455480 bytes
                7601 pkts/sec   394156 bytes/sec
```

continues

Example 3-23 *Examining Traffic Load with the* **show traffic** *Command (Continued)*

```
! Following statistics is for outside interface
inside:
        received (in 25.000 secs):
                180224 packets  10410480 bytes
                7208 pkts/sec   416419 bytes/sec
        transmitted (in 50.000 secs):
                7500 packets     124631 bytes
                65 pkts/sec      6725 bytes/sec
PIX#
```

As you can see in the previous example, the inside interface is receiving the vast majority of traffic very fast (7208 pkts/sec). So, at this point, you can be fairly certain that a virus or a worm has infected the inside hosts.

Step 5 Identify the hosts that are generating all the connections. Example 3-24 shows how to find out the hosts that are generating all these connections:

Example 3-24 *Identifying Hosts that Are Generating All These Connections*

```
PIX# show local-host | include host|count/limit
local host: <10.1.1.10>,
    TCP connection count/limit = 2/unlimited
    UDP connection count/limit = 0/unlimited
local host: <10.1.1.20>,
    TCP connection count/limit = 5/unlimited
    UDP connection count/limit = 0/unlimited
local host: <10.1.1.50>,
    TCP connection count/limit = 12/unlimited
    UDP connection count/limit = 0/unlimited
. . .
local host: <10.1.1.100>,
    TCP connection count/limit = 151501/unlimited
    UDP connection count/limit = 0/unlimited
PIX#
```

The previous example shows that the majority of the traffic is indeed coming from 10.1.1.100.

Step 6 Now that you have found the host that is generating all this traffic, look at the connections, and find the details of the type of connection as shown in Example 3-25.

Example 3-25 *Connections Generated by the Host*

```
PIX# show local-host 10.1.1.100
Interface inside: 300 active, 300 maximum active, 0 denied
local host: <10.1.1.100>,
    TCP connection count/limit = 166108/unlimited
    TCP embryonic count = 166108
    UDP connection count/limit = 0/unlimited
  Xlate(s):
    Global 209.165.201.21 Local 10.1.1.100
```

Example 3-25 *Connections Generated by the Host*

```
  Conn(s):
    TCP out 65.101.32.157:135 in 10.1.1.100:34580 idle 0:01:43 Bytes 0 flags saA
    TCP out 65.103.108.191:135 in 10.1.1.100:8688 idle 0:01:43 Bytes 0 flags saA
    TCP out 65.100.205.160:135 in 10.1.1.100:7774 idle 0:01:43 Bytes 0 flags saA
    TCP out 65.101.182.19:135 in 10.1.1.100:39193 idle 0:01:43 Bytes 0 flags saA
. . . . ...
PIX#
```

The preceding example shows that all connections are embryonic connections, which reaffirms that the host is infected.

Step 7 To cure the problem, patch the machine, and take any other actions recommended by the anti-virus software vendor. If the patch is not possible immediately, shut down the machine and unplug it from the network.

Step 8 As a temporary work-around, you can limit the maximum number of connections for the specific host as follows:

```
PIX(config)# nat (inside) 1 10.1.1.100 255.255.255.255 50 0
```

For the remainder of the network, configure for unlimited connections as follows:

```
PIX(config)# nat (inside) 1 0.0.0.0 0.0.0.0 0 0
```

Finally, be sure to clear the local host with the following command:

```
PIX(config)# clear local-host 10.1.1.100
```

Step 9 If the memory is leaked by a specific process, you may run into problem with memory on the PIX firewall even under normal load of traffic. Under this circumstance, use the output of **show process memory** over time to see which process is continually getting more memory allocated, but not freeing it back. Then look for specific bug on the code.

Large ACL

ACL comprises multiple Access Controls Elements (ACEs), which are processed sequentially in top-down fashion. So, it is very important that you configure the entries that are most likely to be matched towards the top of the access-list. The performance impact of an access-list increases linearly with the increase in the number of ACEs. So, try to summarize the address ranges of the ACEs as much as possible. The smaller the list is, the less the CPU is used and the shorter the time required to search sequentially for an entry. If you have a huge number of ACEs even after summarization, configure turbo ACL. Note that the turbo ACL feature is available only on PIX Firewall Version 6.2 and above.

Reverse DNS & IDENT Protocol

If you can connect to the servers but need to wait a long time before the data comes back, you might run into a problem with reverse DNS or IDENTD. To work around the problem with DNS issues, be sure to allow UDP/53 to the DNS server from the destination server, provided that the DNS server is behind the PIX firewall. To get around the problem for IDENT protocol, be sure to allow TCP/113 through the PIX firewall so that the server can communicate with the client on TCP/113.

Case Studies

This section explores the failover features available on PIX Firewall in greater detail (the discussion is based on information from the New Product Introduction training by PIX marketing team with modification to be able to easily comprehend).

The resiliency of the connections through the PIX firewall can be achieved with failover, which means that if one PIX failed, the other PIX still would be available to process the packets. Starting from PIX Version 7.0, PIX can be configured in one of the following two failover modes:

- Active/standby model
- Active/active model

Active/Standby Model

In this model, one PIX acts as the active PIX that processes the traffic at the time, and the other unit acts as standby. In the event of failure of the active unit, the standby unit becomes active and starts processing packets. If stateful failover is configured, the transition of connections from active to standby is very smooth. The new features added to Version 7.0 are as follows:

- **Stateful failover for VPN traffic**—This release introduces stateful failover for VPN connections. All security association (SA) state information and key material is synchronized automatically between the failover pair members, and this provides a highly resilient VPN solution.
- **Non-Stop Online Software Upgrades**—This version allows you to perform software upgrades of failover pairs without affecting network uptime or connections flowing through the units. This is because of the ability being introduced in this version to perform inter-version state sharing between PIX failover pairs. This allows you to perform software upgrades to maintenance releases (for example, 7.0(1) upgrading to 7.0(2)) without affecting traffic flowing through the pair. There is no impact in both active/standby failover environments and active/active environments.

Active/Active Model

The active/standby model is not the best way to use the resources. Ideally, both of the units in the failover should be used, and act as backups for each other in the event of failure. This is exactly what active/active failover can provide, as introduced in Version 7.0. In this model, both units can actively process firewall traffic while at the same time serving as backups for each other. In PIX Version 7.0, only a two-node setup is possible, in which each device handles 50 percent of the traffic. When one unit fails, the remaining unit takes over and processes 100 percent of the traffic.

Remember that in this model, PIX itself does not perform the load balancing of the traffic. So, it is your responsibility to engineer the network to route 50 percent of the traffic to each unit. This can be accomplished either by static routes or dynamic routing protocols on both upstream and downstream routers.

A new command, **failover groups**, is being introduced to support active/active failover. Conceptually it is very similar to the Cisco's Multi-Group Hot Standby Router Protocol (HSRP) or Virtual Router Redundancy Protocol (VRRP). As mentioned before, PIX 7.0 supports a two-node active/active failover configuration with two failover groups.

The active/active failover feature leverages the Security Context feature. Figure 3-10 shows a typical two-node cluster. On unit A, ctx1 is active and ctx2 is standby. Unit B has ctx2 as active and ctx1 is standby. If unit A fails, unit B will have both contexts active and will process 100 percent of the firewall traffic.

Figure 3-10 *Active/Active FO setup*

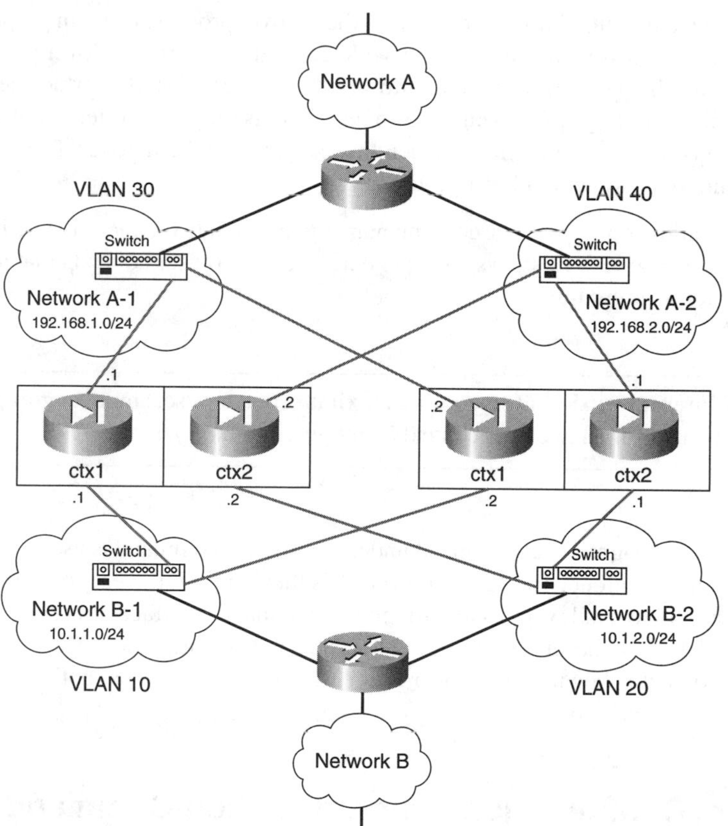

Each failover group contains separate state machines to keep track of the failover state. The command **failover active group** <group#> can be used to change the active state of a failover group.

Hardware and License Requirements

You must have the following minimum requirement for hardware and licensing to configure active/active failover:

- Both units need to have the same hardware configuration.
- Both units must have an unrestricted (UR) License, or the primary unit must have a UR license and the secondary unit must have an active/active failover-only license.

System and User Failover Group

To support active/active failover, PIX 7.0 failover added support for failover groups. Each failover group has its own state machine and can switch over independently. There are two types of failover group: system failover group and user failover group. The concept is similar to the system and user context.

The system group is used internally by the failover process. Its main purpose is to allow the failover process to manage the unit-wide activities under the failover group scheme. These activities include: unit health monitoring, failover command interface health monitoring, running config synchronizing, and so on. There is only one system failover group per unit, and it is created automatically when the user enables the failover. The system context is bound to the system failover group.

User failover groups are used to manage the user contexts under the active/active failover scheme. Figure 3-10 shows a simple example of two user contexts that are bound to two user failover groups.

NOTE PIX Firewall Version 7.0 supports a maximum of two (user) failover groups. However, there can be more than two user contexts configured in the system.

The **failover-group** subcommand under the **context** command is used to bind a user context to a failover group. The failover group 1 is the default failover group. If a user context is not bound to a failover group through the command interface, it is bound to failover group 1 by default. Failover group 1 must be created first and must be the last group to be removed. If a context is bound to a failover group, the failover group cannot be deleted unless the binding is removed.

Initialization, Configuration Synchronization/Command Replication

When a unit boots up, the system failover group will contact the active peer to obtain the running configuration. If both units boot up at the same time, the System failover group of the Primary unit will become active and synchronize its configuration to the Secondary unit. After configuration syncing has finished, the state machine of the user failover group will start running to elect the active unit for each group and start the Active/Active failover.

Even though both units could be actively processing user traffic, the command replication is uni-directional. The command will be replicated to the peer only if **failover group 1** is in active state. Users will be warned if they try to enter a configuration command from the standby unit. This means that a user context can be in the active state, but the user will need to enter commands from the user context of the standby unit if it is bound to failover group 2.

Configuration Examples

Work through the steps that follow to configure Active/Active Failover:

Step 1 Verify that both units have exactly the same hardware configuration and proper license.

Step 2 If a unit is in single context mode, use the command: **mode multiple** to bring it to multiple security contexts mode.

Step 3 Configure the basic failover parameters in the system context of the primary unit. Example 3-26 shows the configuration needed for active/active failover.

Example 3-26 *Active/Active Failover Setup*

```
PIX(config)# failover lan unit primary
PIX(config)# failover lan interface folink ethernet2
PIX(config)# failover link stfo Ethernet3
PIX(config)# failover interface ip folink 1.1.1.1 255.255.255.0 standby 1.1.1.2
PIX(config)# failover interface ip stfo 2.2.2.1 255.255.255.0 standby 2.2.2.2
! This command is optional but recommended
PIX(config)# failover key cisco123
PIX(config)# failover lan enable
PIX(config)#
```

Step 4 Use the failover group command to configure a failover group. Example 3-27 shows how to configure two failover groups with the preemption option.

Example 3-27 *Failover Group Configuration*

```
! Execute failover group command that will take you to the subcommand mode
PIX(config)# failover group 1
! Primary unit has higher priority
PIX(config-failover)# primary
! Preempt peer if bootup as Standby
PIX(config-failover)# preempt
PIX(config-failover)# exit
PIX(config)# failover group 2
! Secondary unit has higher priority
PIX(config-failover)# secondary
PIX(config-failover)# preempt
PIX(config-failover)# exit
PIX(config)#
```

Step 5 Bind the user contexts to the failover group. Assume there are two contexts, **ctx1** and **ctx2,** in addition to admin.

```
PIX(config)# context ctx1
PIX(config-context)# join-failover-group 1
PIX(config-context)# exit
PIX(config)# context ctx2
PIX(config-context)# join-failover-group 2
PIX(config-context)# exit
PIX(config)#
```

Step 6 Type the **failover** command to enable active/active failover.

Step 7 Configure the bootstrap failover configuration on the secondary unit as shown in example 3-28.

Example 3-28 *The Initial Configuration on the Standby PIX*

```
PIX(config)# failover lan unit secondary
PIX(config)# failover lan interface folink ethernet2
PIX(config)# failover link stfo Ethernet3
PIX(config)# failover interface ip folink 1.1.1.1 255.255.255.0 standby 1.1.1.2
PIX(config)# failover interface ip stfo 2.2.2.1 255.255.255.0 standby 2.2.2.2
! This command is optional but recommended
PIX(config)# failover key cisco123
PIX(config)# failover lan enable
PIX(config)# failover
```

Step 8 After failover is up, on the Primary unit (i.e., Active for failover group 1), issue the **write memory** command to save the configuration to flash.

Asymmetrical Routing Support

For better performance and reliability, you may have the network set up with redundant connections to the same Internet Service Provider (ISP) or two different ISPs as shown in Figure 3-11. This poses a problem for PIX, as the ISP may receive traffic from one PIX but might return traffic back to the other PIX. This is because these two PIX firewall units (or pairs) do not share session information. Therefore, while the return packet is allowed by the PIX that allowed the initial connection, it is denied by the other PIX. This is also how it works in Failover mode when it is deployed with Active/Standby Mode.

The same problem can occur when running active/active failover. A unit may receive a packet that belongs to its peer. If this happens, the receiving unit will forward the packet back to its peer for processing. Stateful failover must be enabled to support asymmetric routing.

Figure 3-11 shows two units running Active/Active failover, where Unit 1 has context ctx1 active and Unit 2 has context ctx2 active. An inside host initiates a connection through context ctx1 of Unit 1 (solid line). Context ctx1 creates the connection, replicates the connection to Unit 2, and then forwards the packet. If the return packet is routed through context ctx2 of Unit 2, connection information already exists in Unit 2's connection table. But, because context ctx1 is not active in Unit 2, it forwards the packet back to Unit 1 (arrows).

Figure 3-11 *Asymmetric Routing Support with Active/Active FO Setup*

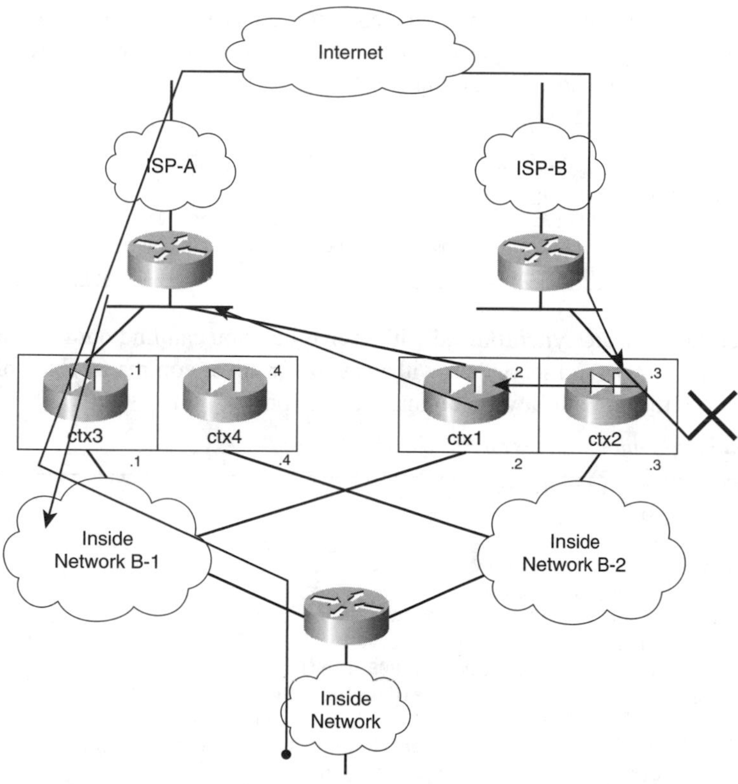

Following are some of the restrictions and cautions you should remember when configuring asymmetric routing in Active/Active Failover mode.

- Remember that multiple context PIX does not support VPN, IPS, and other features.
- Shared interface setup requires NAT.
- Under the asymmetric routing A/A FO, packets are forwarded by Layer 2.
- The supported scenario is for outbound traffic being routed through one unit and inbound traffic being routed to a different unit for a given connection. The scenario where traffic traveling in the same direction for a connection gets routed to different units should not happen if routing is configured properly. The upstream or downstream router should set up the load-balancing policy such that routers are not performing *per packet load balancing* to the High Availability (HA) cluster.

To configure asymmetric routing support, you need to use **asr-group** command under the interfaces of contexts. Asymmetric routing support is needed for the outside interface only; you need to have the following commands configured on both ctx1 and ctx2:

```
PIX/ctx1(config)# interface Ethernet 0.30
PIX/ctx1(config-if)# asr-group 1
PIX/ctx2(config)# interface Ethernet 0.40
PIX/ctx2(config-if)# asr-group 1
```

Troubleshooting Steps

Before working through some of the common scenarios, it would be helpful for you to examine the syslog messages that are shown on the secondary PIX firewall after you turn on logging *on* as shown in Example 3-29.

Example 3-29 *Syslog on the Secondary PIX*

```
PIX(config)# logging on
PIX(config)# logging monitor 7
PIX(config)# 111008: User 'enable_15' executed the 'logging con 7' command.
        Detected an Active mate.  Switching to Standby
        Switching to Standby.
```

After the units are synchronized with each other, you can find out the status of a unit on both the primary and secondary with the **show failover** command. Example 3-30 shows the output of the **show failover** command on the primary unit.

Example 3-30 *Monitoring Failover Status on Primary PIX Firewall*

```
PIX(config)# show failover
Failover On
Cable status: Normal
Reconnect timeout 0:00:00
Poll frequency 5 seconds
Last Failover at: 14:52:29 EST Wed Feb 9 2005
        This host: Primary - Active
                Active time: 14805 (sec)
                Interface outside (192.168.1.1): Normal
                Interface inside  (10.1.1.1): Normal
                Interface stateful (1.1.1.1): Normal
        Other host: Secondary - Standby
                Active time: 250 (sec)
                Interface outside (192.168.1.2): Normal
                Interface inside  (10.1.1.2): Normal
                Interface stateful (1.1.1.2): Normal

Stateful Failover Logical Update Statistics
        Link : stateful
        Stateful Obj    xmit        xerr        rcv         rerr
        General         34036       0           1054        0
PIX#
```

Work through the following steps to troubleshoot the failover problem:

Step 1 Level 1 syslog will give the reasons for a failover. So always check the syslog to determine the root cause. For example, if the switch port failed on the inside interface of Active Firewall, you would see the following message on the Primary (Active) firewall.

```
411002: Line protocol on Interface inside, changed state to down
105007: (Primary) Link status 'Down' on interface 1
104002: (Primary) Switching to STNDBY—interface check, mate is
  healthier
```

Syslog from Secondary (Standby) Firewall will report the following message:

```
104001: (Secondary) Switching to ACTIVE—mate want me Active
```

Step 2 Execute **show interface** on both PIX firewalls to make sure they are up.

Step 3 Test the connectivity by pinging to the Failover interface IP. Be sure to allow the ICMP for the interfaces.

Step 4 If the primary and secondary are connected in two different switches, be sure that all VLANS are trunked between the switches.

Step 5 Be sure to turn on dot1Q across the board on the switch.

Common Problems and Resolutions

This section looks into some confusions and commonly asked questions regarding PIX firewall in a question-and-answer format.

1 Can a PIX firewall function in both transparent and routed modes?

   Answer: No, it can function either in routed or transparent Mode.

2 Is load balancing possible with a PIX firewall?

   Answer: Yes, with Version 7.0, you can configure asymmetric routing with active/active failover setup. However, the load balancing must be configured on upstream or downstream routers.

3 Is **NAT-control** turned on by default on PIX firewall?

   Answer: In PIX Firewall Version 7.0, the **NAT-control** command is turned off by default, which means that unless there is a matching source/destination NAT statement for the packet, NAT will not occur. However, unlike the older version of the code, if there is no match on the source or destination NAT, the packet will be allowed.

4 Can non-IP protocols be routed through the PIX firewall?

   Answer: Yes, other protocols such as Internetwork Packet Exchange [IPX] and AppleTalk can function, but only if you configure transparent firewall, which is new in Version 7.0.

5 Is it possible to configure a transparent firewall in multiple contexts? If so, are there any restrictions?

   Answer: Yes, a transparent firewall can be configured in multiple contexts. In both single and multiple contexts, there can be only one inside and one outside interface, unlike the routed mode, in which more than two interfaces are possible. However, in multiple contexts mode with a transparent firewall, you cannot share the same interface into multiple contexts.

6 Can policing traffic be configured inbound on the PIX firewall?

Answer: No. Unlike with routers, only outbound policing is possible on PIX Version 7.0.

7 Is ESMTP supported through the PIX firewall?

Answer: Yes, with Version 7.0, it is possible to send ESMTP traffic across PIX firewall inspected.

8 Is it possible to pass traffic between equal security level interfaces?

Answer: You can permit communication between interfaces with equal security levels by using the following command:

```
PIX(config)# same-security-traffic permit inter-interface
```

9 Is it possible route the packets back to the same interface as PIX learns the packet from?

Answer: Yes, permitting traffic in and out of the same interface is possible with the following command:

```
PIX(config)# same-security-traffic permit intra-interface
```

10 Can I configure time-based access-list on the PIX firewall?

Answer: Yes, beginning with PIX Firewall Version 7.0, time-based access-lists are available.

Best Practices

This section looks into some of the best practices for PIX Firewall when deployed to the production network, including:

- **Protecting the PIX firewall itself**—Physical and logical security
- **Protecting the network resources**—Anti-spoofing configuration, and denial of service (DOS) attacks

Protecting the PIX Firewall Itself

The PIX firewall protecting your network should be secured by itself. Following are some of the recommendations for securing the firewall that is protecting your network from the hostile environment:

- **Physical security**—As the firewall is one of the most critical network devices in your network, proper action should be taken to protect it from a hacker's physical access. Having console access can help the hackers to change the policy, which can cause severe harm to the network. It is recommended that you turn off the password recovery ability on the PIX with Version 7.0.
- **Link bandwidth policing**—Under no circumstances should you allow more traffic to

flow to a PIX firewall interface than it can handle. This can happen when your network or ISP is affected with a virus such as code red, and so on. So, proper QoS needs to be configured to police the bandwidth on both upstream and downstream routers. Though PIX Firewall has a good mechanism for protecting against DoS attacks, the mechanism is for protecting internal network resources, not for the PIX from DoS. Therefore, an effective method to implement QoS on upstream and downstream routers is to police bandwidth.

- **Secure access for management purposes**—There are multiple ways to allow access for managing the PIX Firewall. Among them, Telnet is the only one that is not secured. Arguably, the console is not secured either if it is connected via reverse Telnet. So, for remote management, it is best to configure SSH instead of Telnet on the PIX firewall.
- **Access control and password**—Be sure to configure access control for the Console port before providing access for managing the PIX. In a non-AAA environment, use **passwd**, and **enable password** commands. If AAA is configured on the PIX, be sure to apply AAA for connections. SSH with AAA is highly recommended for device management.
- **Regular monitoring by an IPS device**—Though PIX has IPS capacity, it is very limited. IPS devices such as the sensor or IDSM blade could be useful for analyzing the exploitation. In the absence of an IPS monitoring device, you might rely on PIX syslog to analyze the traffic, which is not a very effective solution in a large network due to the amount of syslog.
- **Syslog monitoring if IPS is absent**—In the absence of IPS devices, syslog may be used to monitor the traffic coming in or going out of your network. However, while configuring the syslog, you might need to pay extra attention to the level of detail you want to configure to collect syslog. If you leave the debug-level logging on, that might cause slow performance, because of the amount of CPU cycles it uses. Move messages you want to see to lower levels, instead of raising logging levels and capturing messages you do not want to see.

Protecting Network Resources

To protect the network resources behind the PIX firewall, you must undertake the following actions:

- **Anti-spoofing configuration**—You can accomplish anti-spoofing configuration with the command **ip verify reverse-path** on all interfaces of the PIX firewall. This means that the firewall rejects any packet that has a source address that is not expected to be on that interface. If the PIX is an Internet firewall, it should reject all packets coming from the Internet that claim to be from a private network. Similarly, it should reject all packets coming from the private network with source addresses that are not part of the private network, as anti-spoofing is not optional in either direction.
- **Prevention from DOS attack**—Set embryonic and maximum connection counts on static and nat statements to prevent network resources from DoS attack.

Chapter 4

Troubleshooting Firewall Services Module

Firewall Services Module (FWSM) is designed and implemented based on the PIX Firewall code; hence most of the troubleshooting techniques shown in Chapter 3, "Troubleshooting Cisco Secure PIX Firewalls" also apply to FWSM, with a few exceptions. However, as the FWSM module interoperates with the switch, the packet flows from point A to point B through the FWSM are more complex than that of the PIX/ASA platform because of its complex architecture. To troubleshoot issues with FWSM, you must understand FWSM architecture. This will help you to understand FWSM packet flows. So this chapter starts with a discussion of FWSM Architecture, which leads to a discussion of packet flows through the FWSM. Then we will discuss the tools available to troubleshoot complex issues, and how to use these tools to analyze logs efficiently. Issues are then broken down into different categories such as connection issues, performance issues, and so on, for simplicity. The chapter concludes with a Best Practices Section.

Overview of FWSM Firewall

As previously mentioned, the FWSM is like the PIX Firewall/ASA in that they are both stateful, as discussed in detail in Chapter 3. The difference between the FWSM and PIX/ASA lies in the unique and complex architecture of the FWSM, which is discussed next.

FWSM Architecture

A block diagram (Figure 4-1) best explains the architecture of FWSM.

The different components of the FWSM that are pictured in Figure 4-1 are discussed in the sections that follow.

Control Plane (CP)

The FWSM module comprises primarily two elements: a CP, and a daughter card that hosts three Network Processors (NPs). Most of the memory-intensive tasks and complex operations are performed in the CP. The high performance is achieved by moving the frequently used simple tasks within the packet processing to the Network Processors. The CP is responsible for the following tasks:

- Layer 7 fixups
- Overall management of the blade
- Supervisory functions for each NP
- Running of routing protocols
- Preliminary compilation of the access rules before downloading them into the slow NP

Figure 4-1 *FWSM Hardware Block Diagram*

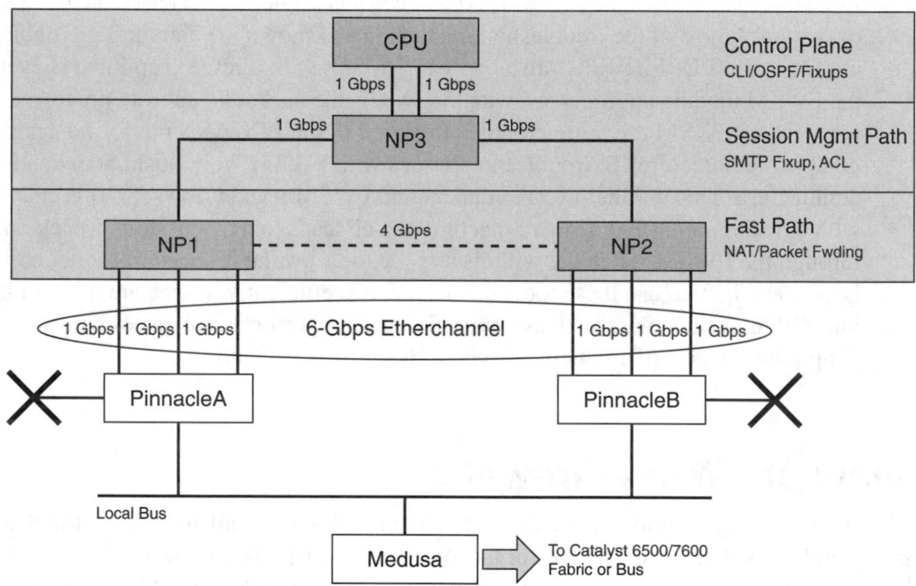

CP has two Gigabit Ethernet ports connected to the Session Management Path NP (NP3), which is discussed next. You can verify the Gigabit Ethernet ports on the CP by executing the **show nic** command.

Network Processors (NP)

The Network Processor performs a subset of functions for the FWSM. Each NP has four Gigabit Ethernet interfaces. FWSM consists of the following three NPs:

- **Session Management Path Network Processor (NP3)**—Session Management Path, which is shown in Figure 4-1, is referred to as NP3. NP3 connects to the CP using two Gigabit Ethernet ports—ports 3 and 4. Ports 1 and 2 are connected to the Fast Path Network Processors (NP1 and NP2).

- **Fast Path Network processors (NP1 and NP2)**—The Fast Path NPs are referred to as NP1 and NP2. The fourth Gigabit Ethernet port of each NP connects to Port 1 and 2 of NP3. This leaves three available Gigabit Ethernet ports for each Fast Path NP—NP1 and NP2—to connect with the Catalyst 6500/7600 switching crossbar-SFM (offers 256 GBps) or backplane (offers 32 GBps). Hence, there are a total of six Gigabit Ethernet ports from Fast NPs—NP1 and NP2 form an EtherChannel to connect with the Switch (cat6500/7600) bus/crossbar. The EtherChannel that is formed uses six Gigabit ports with Fast Path NPs.

EtherChannel

For maximizing the efficiency of the six Gigabit Ethernet interfaces between the FastPath NPs and the Pinnacle, the switch software automatically bundles them together and creates an 802.1Q trunking Etherchannel connection. With a FWSM installed in slot 3, Example 4-1 shows the Etherchannel characteristics for that slot 3.

Example 4-1 *The Etherchannel Characteristics*

```
CAT6503# show etherchannel summary
Flags:  D - down        P - in port-channel
        I - stand-alone s - suspended
        H - Hot-standby (LACP only)
        R - Layer3      S - Layer2
        U - in use      f - failed to allocate aggregator
Number of channel-groups in use: 1
Number of aggregators:           1
Group  Port-channel  Protocol    Ports
------+-------------+-----------+-----------------------------------------------
272    Po272(SU)        -        Gi3/1(P)   Gi3/2(P)   Gi3/3(P)   Gi3/4(P)
                                 Gi3/5(P)   Gi3/6(P)
CAT6503# show firewall module 3 state | include trunk
Administrative Mode: trunk

Operational Mode: trunk
Vlans allowed on trunk: 1
CAT6503#
```

Figure 4-2 is a logical depiction of the connection between a Catalyst 6500/7600 and an FWSM located in slot 3.

Figure 4-2 *6500/FWSM 6Gbps 802.1Q Etherchannel*

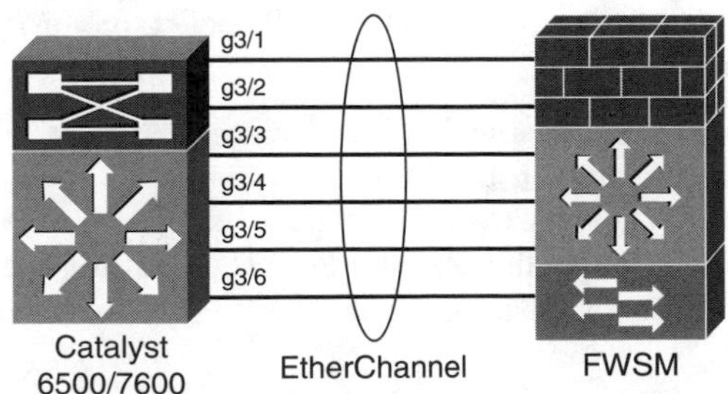

Traffic destined to the FWSM is subjected to the standard user-configurable Etherchannel traffic distribution algorithm. That algorithm determines which interface should be used to transmit traffic belonging to a given session. An interface in this case corresponds to one of the Gigabit Ethernet ports of either NP1 or NP2. Traffic is never load-balanced on a per-packet basis; rather, a session-based hash algorithm is used. Example 4-2 shows the user's choices for load-balancing traffic.

Example 4-2 *Choices for Etherchannel Load-Balancing Algorithm on the Switch*

```
CAT6503(config)# port-channel load-balance ?
  dst-ip          Dst IP Addr
  dst-mac         Dst Mac Addr
  dst-port        Dst TCP/UDP Port
! This is the default setting for algorithm
  src-dst-ip      Src XOR Dst IP Addr
  src-dst-mac     Src XOR Dst Mac Addr
  src-dst-port    Src-Dst TCP/UDP Port
  src-ip          Src IP Addr
  src-mac         Src Mac Addr
  src-port        Src TCP/UDP Port
CAT6503#
```

The FWSM is responsible for ensuring that the return traffic (from the FWSM back to the switch) follows the same path as the original traffic.

If you see that an undesirable event occurs specifically to one port on the NP and not to the other, you can change the load-balancing algorithm on the cat6k, and see whether the pattern then looks different.

Packet Flows

In the preceding section, you learned the architectural details. This section presents the packet flows through the FWSM as illustrated in Figure 4-3.

The following sequence illustrates the packet flow through the FWSM:

1. The packets from the switch are forwarded from the Pinnacle buffer through one of the Etherchannel ports to the Fast Path.
2. Fast Path Packet Flow

   When the fast path receives a Dot1Q IP packet, the fast path performs the following actions on the packet:

   a. It verifies if the destination MAC address is one of Firewall MAC Addresses / Broadcast / Multicast.

   b. It checks whether the destination IP is one of the firewall interface IP Addresses, and if so, sends the packets to Control Plane, for example, a Telnet session to the FWSM.

Figure 4-3 *Packet Data Flows Through FWSM*

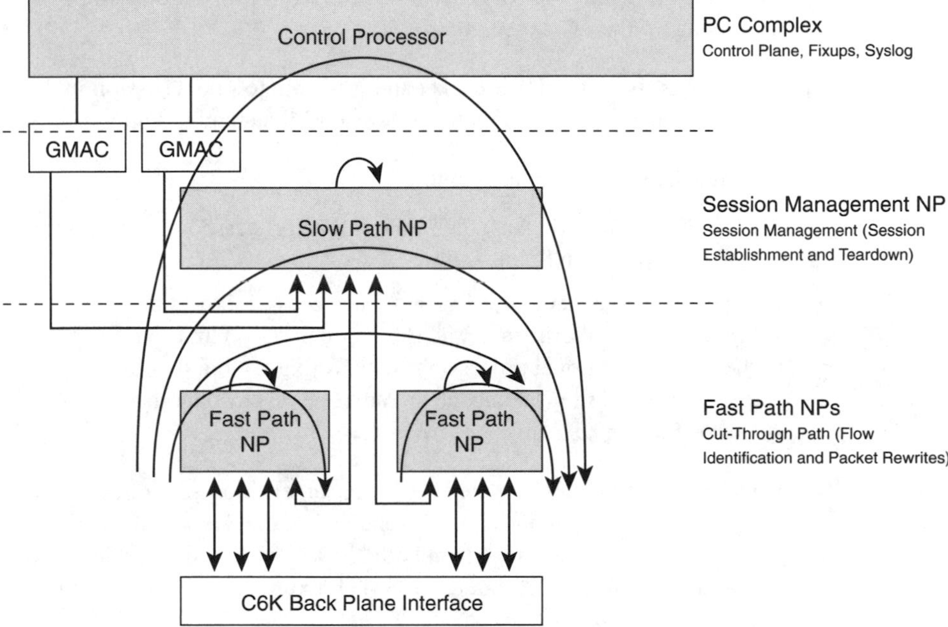

c If packets are routing packets (for example, RIP/OSPF packets), they are forwarded to the Control Plane.

d If the packets are fragmented, they are sent to the Virtual Reassembly Module.

e Non-TCP/UDP protocol packets are sent to the Session Management Path NP or the Control Plane (for example, ICMP packets).

f If packets are TCP/UDP packets, session lookup is performed.

g If the session lookup is successful (a matching entry found), the state retrieved from the session lookup will indicate what action should be taken with the packet. If the fragmentation flag was set, send the packet back to the "IP virtual reassembly" module. If the packet needs to be processed in the Fast Path, then rewrite the packet appropriately (NAT), and update the state if necessary (sequence Number / Window update / FIN Processing / Statistics / Time Stamps . . .). If the state is marked as an Intercepted Session / AAA Session (for updating the inactivity timer) and so on, send the packet to the Session Management Path NP (NP3). If SMTP fixup is required, send the packet to the Session Management Path (NP3); otherwise, for all other fixups, send the packet to the CP.

h If the Session lookup fails (a miss), then depending on the type of packet, actions will be taken accordingly. If the packet is not a SYN TCP packet, the packet is dropped. If it is an Internet Control Message Protocol (ICMP) and not an ECHO request from inside, the packet will be dropped (or an action will be taken depending on the ACL configured).

i If the packet is a TCP/UDP packet and is unable to find a session in the session table, the packet is forwarded to the Session Management Path NP.

2 Session Management Path Packet Flow

A packet received from the Fast Path NPs will be processed in the Session Management Path NP (NP3) as follows:

a If required, the packet will go through the access control list (ACL) checking, authentication, authorization, and accounting (AAA) and so on before it is sent to the CP for additional processing, such as fixup. Note that SMTP fixup is performed in the Session Management Path. The rest of the other traffic fixup is performed in the CP.

b If the packet received from the Fast Path is an existing session, the Fast Path NP will include the Session ID when sending it to the Session Management Path NP. The state in Session Management Path NP will be found, and the appropriate action will be taken (TCP intercept, SMTP fixup, AAA Timestamp Updates) based on the state information.

c A packet with no session (TCP SYN, UDP, Internet Control Message Protocol (ICMP) ECHO Request) will be processed on the Session Management Path (for example, the ACL will be checked for the packet). For additional processing, the packet will be sent to the CP. For example, the control connection of the FTP packet will be sent to the CP for the FTP fixup. If additional processing is not required by the CP (for example smtp fixup) the packet will be completely processed by the Session Management Path NP. Session information will be inserted, so that subsequent packets can be short-circuited.

3 Control Plane (CP)

Control Plane performs all the intelligent and sophisticated activities. For example, the CP takes care of the fixup for Multi Channel Protocol, which helps in dynamically inspecting and opening up the necessary ports for the data connection. Control Plane also processes the traffic destined for it. The CP takes care of the overall NP management—syslogging, routing and so on.

To understand the previous steps clearly, take an example of packet flow across the FWSM for FTP connection, as depicted in Figure 4-4. FTP connection requires packet processing on the CP and all network processors (both fast and Session Management NPs). This section walks through the packet flow of an FTP session when fixup is turned on for FTP as shown in Figure 4-4.

Figure 4-4 *Packet Flow for FTP Session*

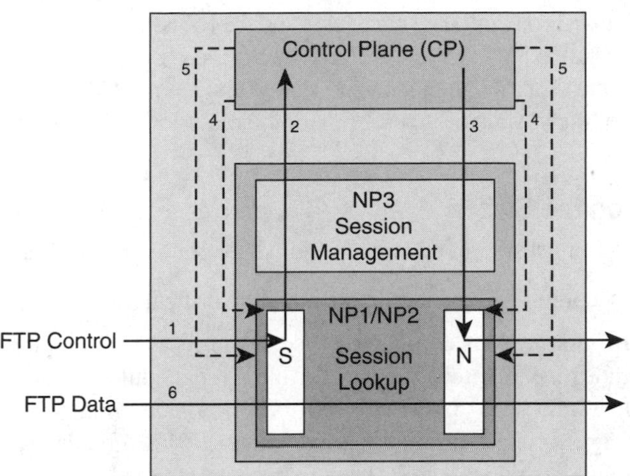

Step 1 When the first FTP control packet arrives, the session lookup fails in Fast Path NP (NP1 or NP2), and the packet is directed to the Session Management Path (NP3).

Step 2 After passing the ACL tests in NP3, the packet is then forwarded to the CP for fixup, as this is an FTP packet.

Step 3 The CP processes the packet and sends it out through the NAT module.

Step 4 The CP inserts the control channel session entry in the fast path's session, and NAT modules indicating all the control channel packets should be directed to CP.

Step 5 On seeing the payload of the subsequent packets (PORT / PASV command), the CP inserts the necessary rule for allowing the data channel in the session module.

Step 6 All packets corresponding to the data channel are short-circuited in the fast path (NP1 & NP2).

Diagnostic Commands and Tools

The importance of the **show** commands cannot be overemphasized for troubleshooting FWSM. Under some rare circumstances, you may require to run the **debug** commands. Details about the **show** and **debug** commands are discussed in the following sections.

Show Commands

show commands on both the switch side and the FWSM side are important for diagnosing problems with FWSM. As the FWSM is a multi-processor system, much information cannot be viewed on the Control Plane; it can be viewed and interpreted only with the **show** command. This section shows you how to use some of the **show** commands on switches and on the FWSM.

show Commands on the Switch

The following list summarizes the use of **show** commands on a switch:

- **show** command for module installation verification

  show module This command is used to verify the installation of the FWSM module on the switch. You can find out if the module is coming online or not, and view the status information. This is a very important first-hand command to diagnose any HW-related issue with the FWSM blade. You can find the slot number, which can be used to session into the blade.

- **show** command for firewall VLAN mappings verification on the switch

  show firewall Use this command, with additional arguments, to find VLAN mappings that are configured on the switch to the firewall modules so that the VLANs can be downloaded and used by the FWSM. Example 4-3 shows the VLAN mappings in Native IOS.

Example 4-3 *Using the* **show firewall** *Command Efficiently*

```
! To Verify the VLAN groups configured in the RP
Router# show firewall vlan-group
Group vlans
-----   ------
  2      10,100
! To verify the VLAN groups associated with a particular module.
Router# show firewall module 7 vlan-group
Module Vlan-groups
  7           2,
Router#
```

show Commands on the FWSM

There are several important **show** commands available on the FWSM to verify the configuration and statistics of different components and the features of the FWSM. The following list contains some of those commands:

- **show** command for VLAN download verification on the FWSM

  The **show vlan** command is used on the FWSM side to find out if or what VLANs are downloaded to the module from the switch. If the VLAN mappings from the switch to the FWSM are functioning correctly, the output shown in Example 4-4 should be same as the information reported on the switch in Example 4-3.

Example 4-4 *VLANS Downloaded to the FWSM From the Switch*

```
FWSM# show vlan
10, 100,
FWSM#
```

- **show** command for statistics on different NPs

  The **show np**[*#*] **stats** command is by far the most important debug command to troubleshoot issues on the NPs. The NP1 and NP2 are fast paths, and NP3 is the Session Management Path.

- **show** commands to find out ACL limitations in NP3

  Different ACLs have different maximum size limitations in the NP. To view the ACL limits, use the following commands:

  ```
  show np 3 acl stats
  show np 3 acl count
  show np 3 acl tree
  ```

- **show** commands for connections

  Connections are distributed into different Network Processors on FWSM. To find the details of the connections, execute the following command:

  ```
  show conn long x
  ```

  The "x" parameter specifies the amount of the connection information you want to display. Actually the only meaningful values are "0" (default), "1", "2", and "3". More than "3" will give you the same amount of information as "3". Therefore, this is the command you will commonly use:

  ```
  Show conn long 3
  ```

  To find the connection information that is made up to the CP complex, execute the following command:

  ```
  show pc conn
  ```

- **show** commands for checking the Gigabit Ethernet Port Statistics on the CP

  Two Gigabit Ethernet ports (ports 3 and 4 of NP3 processors) are connected to the CP. This information, and additional statistics, can be verified with the following command:

  ```
  Show nic
  ```

- **show** command for retrieving console message from buffer

  There is no external console port visible on the FWSM. For debugging, there is a console port (inside the blade), which works with a baud rate of 19600. When no Telnet session is available, the output is saved to a buffer. The buffer output can be examined subsequently when a Telnet connection is made using the following command:

  ```
  show console-output  [m-n]
  ```

Here m-n refers to message numbers. Example 4-5 displays the **show console-output** command.

Example 4-5 *The* **show console-output** *Command*

```
FWSM(config)# show console-output 6-8
Message #6 : Found PCI card in slot:4 bus:1 dev:5 (vendor:0x1014 deviceid:0x1e8)
Message #7 : Ignoring PCI card in slot:4 (vendor:0x1014 deviceid:0x1e8)
Message #8 : Found PCI card in slot:5 bus:1 dev:4 (vendor:0x1014 deviceid:0x1e8)
FWSM(config)#
```

NOTE Buffer size is limited to 4K bytes.

Debug Commands

debug commands display only the information of the packets that hit the Control Plane (CP). Information of the packets that are short-circuited in the NPs are not displayed on the CP.

One of the most important debug commands is the following:

```
FWSM# debug icmp trace
```

With this ICMP debug command, FWSM shows only the messages for pings to the FWSM interfaces, and not for pings through the FWSM to other hosts. If you are connected to the FWSM with Telnet/SSH, and want to display the debug messages on the monitor for the connectivity problem from a host to the FWSM interface, use the following commands:

```
FWSM(config)# debug icmp trace
FWSM(config)# logging monitor debug
FWSM(config)# terminal monitor
FWSM(config)# logging on
FWSM(config)#
```

Example 4-6 shows a sample output of the **debug icmp trace** command.

Example 4-6 *A Sample ICMP Trace*

```
FWSM(config)# debug icmp trace
FWSM(config)# 1: ICMP echo request (len 56 id 26120 seq 0) 10.6.69.30 > 10.6.69.124
2: ICMP echo reply (len 56 id 26120 seq 0) 10.6.69.124 > 10.6.69.30
3: ICMP echo request (len 56 id 26120 seq 256) 10.6.69.30 > 10.6.69.124
4: ICMP echo reply (len 56 id 26120 seq 256) 10.6.69.124 > 10.6.69.30
5: ICMP echo request (len 56 id 26120 seq 512) 10.6.69.30 > 10.6.69.124
FWSM(config)#
```

As shown in this example, you must see the request and reply packets. Pinging to the interface of the FWSM ensures that the FWSM interfaces are active and that the VLAN configuration is correct.

Use the following **debug** command to see the debug output on the interface of any types of IP packets:

```
[no] debug packet interface_name [src s_ip [netmask m]] [dst d_ip [netmask m]]
  [[proto icmp] | [proto tcp [sport s_p ] [dport d_p]] [proto udp [sport s_p]
  [dport d_p]] [rx | tx | both]
```

NOTE As most of the packets flowing through FWSM are shot-circuited and never reached to the CP, this **debug packet** command may be ineffective as it will not show you any output. The **debug packet** command will be effective if you debug output when the packets are handled by the CP (for example, FTP fixup).

Other than specifying the interface name, the other arguments are optional. The following command will throw debug output to the inside interface of the IP packets:

```
FWSM# debug packet inside
```

To know the details of fixup interactions on the FWSM, execute the following command:

```
FWSM# debug fixup <tcp|udp>
```

For the details of a specific protocol, run the following **debug** command:

```
FWSM# debug rtsp | sip | skinny | ils | sqlnet | h323 h225|h245|ras  asn|event
```

Sniffer on the FWSM

The FWSM has built-in sniffer capture capability, which you can use to get the details of the packets flowing through the FWSM in both directions.

To enable packet capturing, attach the capture to an interface with the *interface* option. Multiple interface statements attach the capture to multiple interfaces.

A packet must pass both the Ethernet and access-list filters before the packet is stored in the capture buffer.

NOTE The capture command is not saved to the configuration and the capture command is not replicated to the standby unit during failover.

To capture packets between host A and B traversing both the inside and outside interfaces, work through the following steps to turn on capture:

Step 1 To enable packet capture traversing the inside interface, use the following commands on the FWSM:

```
FWSM(config)# access-list capture_in permit <protocol> host A host B
FWSM(config)# access-list capture_in permit <protocol> host B host A
FWSM(config)# capture inside access-list capture_in buffer 2000000
  interface inside packet-length 1500
```

With the this configuration, FWSM will capture packets of 1500 bytes or less in size with a maximum file size of 2 MB.

Step 2 To enable packet capture traversing the outside interface, use the following configuration on the FWSM:

```
FWSM(config)# access-list capture_out permit <protocol> host A host B
FWSM(config)# access-list capture_out permit <protocol> host B host A
FWSM(config)# capture outside access-list capture_out buffer 2000000
  interface outside packet-length 1500
```

Step 3 Retrieve the **pcap** format file from the PIX firewall by browsing to the PIX.

On the FWSM, you must have the web server turned on. If it's not turned on, run the **setup** command and run through the prompts. Next, open a browser and enter **https://<pix_ip>/capture/<capture_name/pcap** to connect to the web server on the FWSM. After connecting to the PIX, you will be prompted to save the file.

Step 4 Transfer the **pcap** file to the TFTP server.

To send a **pcap** format file from the FWSM to a tftp server, execute the following command:

```
FWSM# copy capture:<capture_name> tftp://<pix_ip>/temp pcap
```

Step 5 View the capture buffer on the FWSM.

If the *capture_name* is specified, it displays the capture buffer contents for that capture. Issue **show capture** *<capture_name>* to see the capture buffer.

Step 6 Reset and Remove the capture command.

To clear the capture buffer, enter the following **clear capture** command:

```
FWSM# clear capture inside
FWSM# clear capture outside
```

To remove the **capture** command

```
FWSM# no capture inside
FWSM# no capture outside
```

When you are finished capturing, be sure to remove the capture access-lists.

```
FWSM# no access-list capture_in
FWSM# no access-list capture_out
```

Syslog on the FWSM

Syslog implementation on FWSM is very similar to PIX Firewall with a few exceptions. Syslog is processed by the Control Plane (CP), whereas other processors might generate so many syslog messages that it could overwhelm the Control Plane (CP). So FWSM has an option for rate limiting for the Syslog on the FWSM. You can configure up to 16 Syslog servers to forward the syslog messages. There are eight levels of syslog you can configure:

- **Emergencies**—level 0
- **Alerts**—level 1
- **Critical**—level 2
- **Errors**—level 3
- **Warnings**—level 4
- **Notifications**—level 5
- **Informational**—level 6
- **Debugging**—level 7

The recommended syslog level is 4. Syslog messages generated in the NPs are processed by the CP before being forwarded to the Syslog servers (if any have been configured). Because the NPs can generate many Syslog messages, these Syslog messages can be rate-limited.

```
[no] logging rate-limit {unlimited | {num [interval]}} message syslog_id
[no] logging rate-limit {unlimited | num [interval]} level syslog_level
```

The rate-limiting applies for all syslog destinations (console, buffer, monitor). By default, rate limit is disabled. Interval is optional, and default is 1 second. You can disable rate-limiting with the following command:

```
clear logging rate-limit
```

You can configure the rate-limiting configuration with the following command:

```
show logging rate-limit
```

Sniffer Capture

Sometimes you might find that the syslog, after running the debug commands, might not give very conclusive results because other network-related issues could be affecting the packet flow. In this rare circumstance, capturing the sniffer traces simultaneously from incoming and outgoing interface segments might help to isolate the problem (as discussed earlier, the capture command can be used if the packets are reaching to the FWSM, but if the packets are getting dropped in another part of the network, then capture on the FWSM is ineffective). A very popular and freely downloadable sniffer software is Ethereal (www.ethereal.com)

Analysis of Problem Areas

FWSM problem areas can be broken down into the following areas:

- Licensing issues
- Hardware issues

- Firewall module administration issues
- Connection issues
- AAA issues
- Virtual and transparent firewall
- High CPU issues
- Intermittent packet drops issues
- Failover issues

A more detailed discussion of the previously listed items follows in the coming sections.

Licensing Issues

You do not need a license to run FWSM in single firewall mode. If you use the following command to convert FWSM to multiple mode, you can use two contexts in addition to an admin context:

```
FWSM# configure terminal
FWSM(config)# mode multiple
FWSM(config)# show mode
Firewall mode: multiple
The flash mode is the SAME as the running mode.
FWSM(config)#
```

Every context is mapped to a virtual firewall. If you require more than two virtual firewalls (contexts), you will need an activation key. Activation keys can be obtained from licensing@cisco.com, once you purchase the license. For security contexts, you can purchase up to 100 licenses in increments of 20.

The activation key comes in number form with four octets that can be entered into the FWSM with the **activation-key key** command as follows:

```
FWSM(config)# activation-key 0xaaaaaaaa 0xbbbbbbbb 0xcccccccc 0xdddddddd
FWSM(config)#
```

Then you can verify the number of contexts available with the **show version** command or the **show activation-key** command as follows:

```
FWSM(config)# show activation-key
Running Activation Key: 0xaaaaaaaa 0xbbbbbbbb 0xcccccccc 0xdddddddd

Licensed Features:
Failover:            Enabled
VPN-DES:             Enabled
VPN-3DES:            Enabled
Maximum Interfaces:  256 (per security context)
Cut-through Proxy:   Enabled
Guards:              Enabled
URL-filtering:       Enabled
Throughput:          Unlimited
ISAKMP peers:        Unlimited
! Following line indicates how many Virtual FW can be configured
Security Contexts:   20
```

```
This machine has an Unrestricted (UR) license.

The flash activation key is the SAME as the running key.
FWSM(config)#
```

You can simply override an activation key with the **activation-key** command, or you can clear the old activation key with the **clear activation-key** command and enter the new one.

Hardware Issues

Troubleshooting an FWSM blade hardware problem on the switch is very similar to troubleshooting an IDSM-2 blade. Hence, the troubleshooting techniques discussed in the "Hardware Issues" section of Chapter 15, "Troubleshooting IDSM-2 Blade on Switch," are not repeated here. Only information specific to the FWSM blade is discussed. If you cannot session into the FWSM blade, first execute the **show module** command to determine the status of the module. The module can be in any of the following conditions:

- Module is not recognized
- Module status shows faulty/other
- Module shows OK but you cannot session into it

To troubleshoot issues with any of these three conditions or more, follow these troubleshooting steps:

Step 1 Ensure that you are running a supported version of code on your switch for FWSM. You can find this information in the Release note of the corresponding version. For example, for FWSM Version 2.3(2), you can find the "Chassis System Requirements" from the following link: http://www.cisco.com/univercd/cc/td/doc/product/lan/cat6000/mod_icn/fwsm/fwsm_2_3/fwsm_rn/fwsmrns.htm#wp73044

Step 2 Ensure that the FWSM can coexist with other blades in the same chassis. Refer to the Catalyst 6500 Release note in the following location:

http://www.cisco.com/univercd/cc/td/doc/product/lan/cat6000/relnotes/index.htm

In addition, you can look at the Software Advisor for additional information (only available to registered customers):

http://www.cisco.com/pcgi-bin/Support/CompNav/Index.pl

Beginning with Native IOS Version 12.2(14)SY, FWSM, VPN, IDSM-2, and NAM modules can coexist in the same chassis. There is no CatOS available to support all these modules in the same chassis.

Step 3 If you are running CatOS (Hybrid) code on your switch, reset the configuration for the slot that is occupied by the FWSM module. To do this, use the following commands:

(a) Type **set module power down mod** to power down the FWSM.

(b) Clear the switch's configuration associated with that slot and to power up the module.

Step 4 For additional troubleshooting refer to Chapter 15, "Troubleshooting IDSM-2 Blade on Switch," and consult the following links:

For Hybrid Mode, refer to the following link: http://www.cisco.com/en/US/products/hw/switches/ps700/products_tech_note09186a0080134734.shtml

For Native IOS, refer to the following link: http://www.cisco.com/en/US/products/hw/switches/ps700/products_tech_note09186a00801751d7.shtml

Firewall Module Administration Issues

To administer the Firewall module effectively and efficiently, it is important to be familiar with the following items below:

- Flash
- Setting the boot device
- Maintenance partition
- Password recovery procedure
- Upgrading a new image

The following section explores each these items in more detail.

Flash

FWSM contains a 128 MB Compact Flash, which is partitioned into six sizes for different tasks as shown in Table 4-1.

Table 4-1 *The Partitions of Compact Flash Memory*

Partition Number	Size (MB)	Description
First (cf:1)	16	Maintenance Partition
Second (cf:2)	7	Network Configuration
Third (cf:3)	1	Crash Dump Partition

Table 4-1 *The Partitions of Compact Flash Memory (Continued)*

Partition Number	Size (MB)	Description
Fourth (cf:4)	20	Application Partition1—FWSM file system—image, configuration, and PDM file
Fifth (cf:5)	20	Application Partition2—FWSM file system—image, configuration, and PDM file
Sixth (cf:6)	64	Reserved

Typically, you will be working with cf:1, cf:4 or cf:5 partitions. If you set the boot device for cf:4 or cf:5, the FWSM will boot up in normal mode (application partition). However, if you set the boot device for cf:1, the module will boot up as Maintenance, which can be used to re-image or perform the password recovery for the Application partition (cf:4 or cf:5). More details on setting up the Boot Device follow in the next section.

Setting the Boot Device (Route Processor)

In native IOS mode, to boot the Firewall to Application Partition (Firewall module), set the Compact Flash Partition to 4 or 5 with the following command:

```
Cat6509(config)# boot device  module mod-num cf:4
```

To boot from the Maintenance Partition, set the Compact Flash partition to 1 with the following command:

```
Cat6509(config)# boot device  module mod-num cf:1
```

To display the Boot Partition that is configured, execute the following command:

```
Cat6509# show boot device  module mod-num
```

Example 4-7 shows the module 6 boot to Application Partition.

Example 4-7 *FWSM Boot to Application Partition Setting*

```
Router# show boot device module 6
[mod:6 ]: cf:4
Router#
```

By default, the FWSM module is set to boot to Application partition. To change this to maintenance partition, change the boot variable, then reset the module.

To work on a specific partition temporarily, regardless of the boot variable setup, use the following command for Native IOS (to reset the module for Maintenance partition):

```
Router# hw-module module mod_num reset cf:1
```

For Catalyst operating system software, execute the following command to go to the Maintenance partition:

```
Console> (enable) reset mod_num cf:1
```

For Application partition, use either cf:4 or cf:5 instead of cf:1.

Then to session into the FWSM, enter the following command in Native IOS:

```
Router# session slot mod_num processor 1
```

For Catalyst operating system software, enter the following command:

```
Console> (enable) session mod_num
```

A more detailed discussion follows in the next section for the Maintenance partition.

Maintenance Partition

You can use the Maintenance Partition for the following purposes:

- If the modules application partition is corrupted, use the maintenance partition to recover and reprogram the application partition.
- Use the **show crashdump** command from the Maintenance Partition to obtain the crash dump, for debugging purposes.
- The application module can be upgraded from the Maintenance Partition.
- The enable password for the module can be cleared from the Maintenance Partition command line interface (CLI).

To get into the Maintenance partition, use either the **session** command or **telnet*** command from the switch. It can be accessed by Telnetting to 127.0.0.x1 (x = slot # of the FWSM module). Example 4-8 shows a sample output of how to connect to the FWSM if it is on slot 3 on the switch.

Example 4-8 *Connecting to the Maintenance Partition*

```
System> telnet 127.0.0.31
Maintenance image
localhost.localdomain login: root
Password: cisco
Maintenance image version: 1.1(0.4)
root@localhost.localdomain#
```

When asking for login information, you can use either a **root** or **guest** user account. Table 4-2 summarizes the purpose of these two users' accounts, and what rights each user account has.

Table 4-2 *User Accounts for Maintenance Partition Access*

Users/Password	Description
root/Cisco	Used for normal access. It provides a restricted shell and allows users to upgrade Application Partition images. It also allows users to display version/image information.
guest/cisco	Guest account is meant for Cisco Support team operations, such as retrieving the diagnostic results and upgrading the BIOS image. Guest account access can be enabled/disabled from the root account. However, guests cannot change the root password. So, a guest is a superset of root level commands.

The default password for root and guest accounts is **Cisco,** and this can be reset by the **passwd** command from the maintenance partition. This can also be reset on the Application partition.

Once you are in the maintenance partition, you need to set up the networking parameters, so that the FWSM blade on the Maintenance partition can communicate with the rest of the network or the TFTP/FTP server. Remember that the IP address that you set on the MP partition is *always part of VLAN 1 on the switch*. So, you need to ensure that the TFTP/FTP server for the image download has a proper route from the VLAN1 on the switch. Table 4-3 summarizes the configuration commands available on the Maintenance partition.

Table 4-3 *Maintenance Partition Commands*

Commands	Description
ip	To set IP parameters (root and guest)
show	To show system parameters (root and guest)
passwd	To set the password for the current user (root and guest)
upgrade	To download and install new application image (root and guest)
clear ip	To clear network configuration for the interface (root and guest)
clear log upgrade	To clear the log file for upgrade operation (root and guest)
logout	To log out of the shell (root and guest)
passwd-guest	To set password for guest account (root)
enable-guest	To enable the guest account (root)
Disable-guest	To disable the guest account (root)
clear passwd	To clear the enable password for application (root and guest)
upgrade-bios	To install new BIOS image (guest)
debug	To use Network Processor (NP) debug utility (guest)

Table 4-4 lists and describes the different **show** commands available on the Maintenance Partition.

Table 4-4 **show** *Commands Available in MP*

Commands	Description
show ip	Shows network configuration for the interface (root and guest)
show images	Shows images on the application partition (root and guest)
show version	Shows system parameters (root and guest)
show log upgrade	Shows upgrade log file (root and guest)
show diaglog	Shows diagnostics log file (guest)
show ethif	Shows Ethernet interface info (guest)
show crashdump	Shows the contents of crashdump file (guest)

Based on the command syntax listed in Tables 4-3 and 4-4, configure your FWSM Maintenance partition to set initial networking parameters as shown in Example 4-9.

Example 4-9 *Initial Networking Configuration for Maintenance Partition*

```
Cisco Maintenance image
login: root
Password:
Maintenance image version: 1.1(0.3)
root@localhost# ip address 10.1.1.1 255.255.255.0
root@localhost# ip broadcast 10.1.1.254
root@localhost# ip host FWSM
root@localhost# ip gateway 10.1.1.100
root@localhost# ip domain cisco.com
root@localhost# ip nameserver 10.1.1.150
root@localhost# show ip
IP address: 10.1.1.1
Subnet mask: 255.255.255.0
IP Broadcast: 10.1.1.254
DNS Name: FWSM.cisco.com
Default Gateway: 10.1.1.100
Nameserver(s): 10.1.1.150
root@localhost#
```

Password Recovery Procedure

If you forget or lose the passwords for the FWSM application partition, you can reset the password to default values from the Maintenance Partition. Clearing the password with the following command from the Maintenance partition will reset the Telnet password to **cisco** and will clear the enable password:

```
guest@localhost# clear passwd cf:partition_number>
```

Here *partition_number* refers to the number of the application partition whose password has to be reset. The following example shows the resetting of the password for the application partition in slot 4.

```
guest@localhost# clear passwd cf:4
Do you wish to erase the passwords? [yn] y
The following lines will be removed from the configuration:
       enable password 8Ry2YjIyt7RRXU24 encrypted
       passwd 2KFQnbNIdI.2KYOU encrypted
Do you want to remove the commands listed above from the configuration? [yn] y
Passwords and aaa commands have been erased.
guest@localhost#
```

Upgrading a New Image

The Application partition and Maintenance partition use two separate images. This section discusses the new image upgrade on both the Maintenance and Application partitions:

- Upgrading the Maintenance partition
- Upgrading the Application partition

Upgrading the Maintenance Partition

To upgrade MP, you must use the Application partition using the following command:

```
upgrade-mp  tftp-url
```

Here *tftp-url* is the Trivial File Transfer Protocol (TFTP) server location and name of the FWSM Maintenance software image file. You can download the Maintenance image from the following link:

http://www.cisco.com/cgi-bin/tablebuild.pl/cat6000-fwsm

Example 4-10 shows the upgrade procedure for Maintenance partition.

Example 4-10 *MP Upgrade from the Application Partition*

```
FWSM# upgrade-mp
Address or name of remote host [10.1.1.150]? 10.1.1.150
Source file name []? mp-1.0.1-bin.gz
copying tftp://192.168.253.79/mp-1.0.1-bin.gz to flash [yes|no|again]?y
!!!!!!!!!!!!!!!!!!!!!!!!!!!!!!!!!!!!!!!!!!!!!!!!!!!!!!!!!!!!!!!!!!!!!!!!!!!!!!!!!
!!!!!!!!!!!!!!!!
Received 7700916 bytes. Maintenance partition upgraded.
FWSM#
```

Upgrading Software Images

You can download the Application partition image from the same location as the Maintenance partition:

http://www.cisco.com/cgi-bin/tablebuild.pl/cat6000-fwsm

You can upgrade the Application partition in either of the following ways:

- **From the Application partition**—The usual upgrade procedure performed on the Application partition is by the Application partition itself. File transfer for the upgrade on the Application partition is possible with the TFTP protocol only. Use this command for upgrade:

```
FWSM# copy tftp[:[[//location][/pathname]]] flash[:[image | pdm]]
```

The following example shows how to upgrade the Application partition from the Application partition itself:

```
FWSM# copy tftp://10.1.1.150/cdisk flash:image
```

- **From the Maintenance Partition**—If the Application Partition is corrupted, use the Maintenance partition to re-image the Application partition. You can also upgrade the Application partition from the MP. The following command is used in both the re-imaging and upgrading of application partition from the Maintenance partition.

  ```
  Guest@localhost# upgrade ftp://username@server/path/image device
  ```

  The following example shows how to upgrade the Application partition from the Maintenance partition:

  ```
  FWSM# upgrade ftp://username@10.1.1.150/tftpboot/c6svc-fwm-k9.1.1.0.127.bin cf:4
  ```

Connection Problems

A typical FWSM is depicted in Figure 4-5, in which MSFC is situated on the outside interface of the FWSM.

Figure 4-5 *A Typical FWSM Deployment*

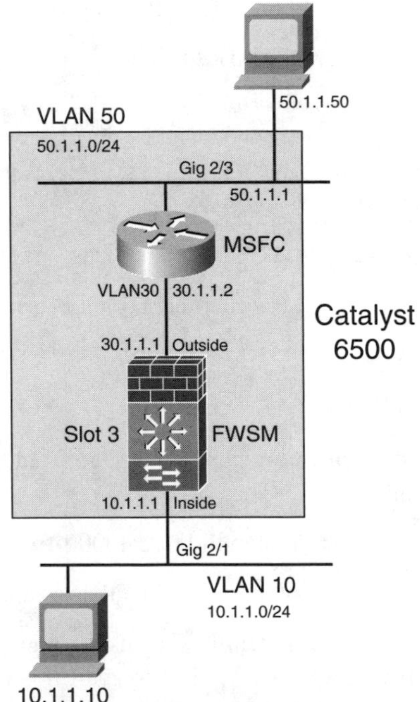

As shown in Figure 4-5, VLAN 10 is sitting on the inside, and VLAN 50 is the SVI interface on MSFC. The outside interface of the FWSM is configured to be part of VLAN 30 on the switch. Hence, this interface VLAN 30 on the MSFC is used by the FWSM to communicate with MSFC and any other VLANs configured on the MSFC.

This section examines the following two topics in detail based on Figure 4-5.

- Configuration steps
- Troubleshooting steps

Configuration Steps

Work through the following steps to configure the switch and the FWSM with two interfaces (inside and outside) based on Figure 4-5:

Step 1 Configure the VLAN, and the ports on the switch.

First, configure the interface and the VLAN on the switch. If you are running Native IOS, configure the interfaces and VLANs as shown Example 4-11.

Example 4-11 *VLAN and Interfaces on the Native IOS Switch*

```
CAT6509# configure terminal
Enter configuration commands, one per line.  End with CNTL/Z.
! Create the VLANs 10, 30, and 50 on the switch with the following command
CAT6509(config)# vlan 10,30,50
CAT6509(config-vlan)# exit
! Following interface is connected to the inside network - VLAN 10
CAT6509(config)# int g2/1
CAT6509(config-if)# switchport
CAT6509(config-if)# switchport mode access
CAT6509(config-if)# switchport access vlan 10
CAT6509(config-if)# spanning-tree portfast
CAT6509(config-if)# no shut
CAT6509(config-if)# exit
! The following interface is connected to the outside - VLAN 50. Note that this is
! not SVI interface
CAT6509(config)# int g2/3
CAT6509(config-if)# switchport
CAT6509(config-if)# switchport mode access
CAT6509(config-if)# switchport access vlan 50
CAT6509(config-if)# spanning-tree portfast
CAT6509(config-if)# no shut
CAT6509(config-if)# exit
CAT6509(config)#
! The following layer III VLAN interface is the SVI interface which is connected
! with the outside interface of the FWSM. You must have already created the layer
! II VLAN for the VLAN interface 30.
CAT6509(config)# interface vlan 30
CAT6509(config-if)# description To FWSM's outside interface
CAT6509(config-if)# ip address 30.1.1.2 255.255.255.0
CAT6509(config-if)# no shut
CAT6509(config-if)#^Z
```

Example 4-12 shows the same configuration in the Hybrid mode as shown in Example 4-11 in the Native IOS mode.

Example 4-12 *Showing VLAN and Interface Configuration on the CatOS*

```
! Create the VLANs on the Supervisor first (make sure your VTP mode allows it)
cat6509> (enable) set vlan 10,30,50
! Put physical ports 2/1 and 5/6 in their vlans; set ports as host ports
cat6509> (enable) set vlan 10 2/1
cat6509> (enable) set vlan 50 2/3
cat6509> (enable)
! Session into the MSFC and create VLAN 30 interface for the SVI interface for
! FWSM
cat6509> (enable) session 15
Trying Router-15...
Connected to Router-15.
Escape character is '^]'.
MSFC> enable
Password:
MSFC# configure terminal
! create a "point-to-point" vlan (30) between the MSFC and the FWSM
MSFC(config)# interface vlan 30
MSFC(config-if)# ip address 30.1.1.2 255.255.255.0
MSFC(config-if)# no shut
! create VLAN 50 interface so that this VLAN can communicate with VLAN 10 through
! the FWSM
MSFC(config-if)# int vlan 50
MSFC(config-if)# ip address 50.1.1.1 255.255.255.0
MSFC(config-if)# no shut
```

Note Always create the firewall VLANs on the Supervisor first. Then session to the MSFC and bring up the VLAN interface between the MSFC and the FWSM. If you perform the operation in the reverse order, you might run into a situation in which the VLAN will fail to come up. If so, clear all firewall VLANs on the Supervisor, remove the VLAN interface on the MSFC, and create the firewall VLANs on the Supervisor again.

Step 2 Map the VLANs on the switch to the FWSM.

Once the VLANs and interfaces are configured on the switch, configure the switch to map the VLANs to the FWSM blade. The syntax to map the VLANs is different in Native IOS and Hybrid modes on the switch.

If you are running Native IOS, use the following command to group VLANs with the first line and map the VLAN group to the FWSM that is seated on slot 3 of the FWSM:

```
CAT6509(config)# firewall vlan-group 1 10,30
CAT6509(config)# firewall module 3 vlan-group 1
```

If you are running the switch in Hybrid mode, use the following command:

```
cat6509> (enable) set vlan 10,30 firewall-vlan 3
Vlans  30,40 declared secure for firewall module 3
CAT6509> (enable)
```

Step 3 Configure the interfaces on the FWSM.

By now, VLANs 10 and 30 should be downloaded to the FWSM. The download can be verified by using the following command:

```
FWSM# show vlan
10, 30
FWSM#
```

Map the downloaded VLANs on the FWSM to the corresponding interfaces of the FWSM with the following command:

```
FWSM(config)# nameif vlan_number if_name security_level
```

VLAN10 is mapped to **inside** interface, and the VLAN30 is mapped to the **outside** interface as follows:

```
FWSM(config)# nameif vlan10 inside security100
FWSM(config)# nameif vlan30 outside security0
```

After defining the interface, assign the IP address to the interfaces with the following command:

```
FWSM(config)# ip address if_name ip_address [netmask]
```

The following commands show the IP address configuration of the inside and outside interfaces:

```
FWSM(config)# ip address inside 10.1.1.1 255.255.255.0
FWSM(config)# ip address outside 30.1.1.1 255.255.255.0
```

Step 4 Define routes on the FWSM.

By default you can create a single Switched Virtual Interface (SVI) on the MSFC and point to that as the default gateway on the FWSM. The syntax for configuring the static route is as follows:

```
FWSM(config)# route if_name ip_address netmask gateway_ip metric
```

The following command shows a default route pointing to the SVI interface (VLAN interface 30):

```
FWSM(config)# route outside 0 0 30.1.1.2
```

Step 5 Configure NAT/PAT/Static.

For outbound traffic (traffic from inside to outside, for instance), the source address translation is required by default. You may configure nat/global or static NAT to translate the source address. Alternatively, you may bypass NAT checking with a **nat zero ACL** command. Nat/global is used for dynamic translation, but static NAT is used to create permanent mapping.

Static is used mainly for inbound connections to perform the destination address translation. Dual nat/alias is used to support bi-directional NAT.

The following commands are used to configure nat/global and static:

```
FWSM(config)# nat [(if_name)] nat_id local_ip [netmask [max_conns
  [em_limit]]] [norandomseq]
FWSM(config)# global [(if_name)] nat_id {global_ip [-global_ip]
  [netmask global_mask]} | interface
FWSM(config)# static [(internal_if_name, external_if_name)] global_ip
  local_ip [netmask network_mask] [max_conns [em_limit]] [norandomseq]
```

The following commands show the PAT configured for the outbound connection:

```
FWSM(config)# nat (inside) 1 10.1.1.0 255.255.255.0
FWSM(config)# global (outside) 1 interface
```

To allow an inbound connection, either exempt the NAT with the **nat zero acl** command or with the **static** command. The following command shows the static translation for the inbound connection to the VLAN10.

```
FWSM(config)# static (inside,outside) 30.1.1.110 10.1.1.110 netmask
  255.255.255.255 0 2
```

Step 6 Configure an access-list.

Unlike the PIX firewall, you must allow the outbound traffic with an access-list applied on the higher security interface (for example, inside interface). Otherwise, packets are denied in both directions (inbound and outbound). The syntax for an access-list configuration is as follows:

```
FWSM(config)# access-list acl_ID [deny | permit] protocol {source_addr |
  local_addr} {source_mask | local_mask} operator port {destination_addr |
  remote_addr} {destination_mask | remote_mask} operator port
```

Then, apply the ACL to the interface with the following command.

```
FWSM(config)# access-group acl_ID in interface interface_name
```

Example 4-13 shows the access-list configuration and how to apply it on the interface.

Example 4-13 *ACL Configuration and How to Apply it on the Interface*

```
! Following ACL will allow all traffic from inside to outside network
FWSM(config)# access-list 101 permit ip any any
! Following ACL is to allow only web traffic to 30.1.1.110 which is translated to
! inside IP address of 10.1.1.110 (actual web server IP on the inside network.
FWSM(config)# access-list 102 permit any host 30.1.1.110 eq 80
```

Example 4-13 *ACL Configuration and How to Apply it on the Interface (Continued)*

```
! ACL 101 is applied on the inside interface
FWSM(config)# access-group 101 to the inside interface
! ACL 102 is applied to the outside interface
FWSM(config)# access-list 102 in interface outside
FWSM(config)#
```

Step 7 Turn on fixups.

To turn on fixup for a specific protocol, you can use the **fixup protocol** command. For example, to turn on fixup for the ICMP, which is off by default, use the following command:

```
FWSM(config)# fixup protocol icmp
```

Troubleshooting Steps

If you follow the configuration steps carefully, you usually will not run into any problem with connections across the FWSM. If you run into connection problems, work through the following steps to correct the problems:

Step 1 Be sure you can ping to the directly connected interface of the FWSM.

If you cannot pass traffic across the FWSM, you must ensure that you can ping to the interface of the FWSM from a host in the same VLAN. For example, if you mapped the inside interface to VLAN 10, a host (10.1.1.10) on VLAN 10 must be able to ping to the FWSM inside interface (10.1.1.1). If you cannot ping, work through the following steps to correct the problem; otherwise proceed to the next step:

(a) Make sure the ICMP is allowed on the interface of FWSM by using the **icmp** command. You can execute the **show icmp** command to verify whether the icmp is allowed on the interface. To enable ICMP on the inside interface, use the following command:

```
FWSM(config)# icmp permit 0 0 inside
```

(b) If the ping is still unsuccessful, run the **debug icmp trace** command and see if FWSM displays any debug output. If there are no debug messages on ICMP on the FWSM, go to the next step.

(c) Ping to other devices in the same VLAN and subnet. If you are not successful, check the port that is connected to the device. If the ping is successful, move to the next step.

(d) Execute the **show interface** command and ensure that the interfaces are shown up/up. If they are shown in any other state, verify that the **nameif** command used the proper VLAN number with the commands that follow:

```
FWSM# show nameif
nameif vlan10 inside security100
nameif vlan30 outside security0
FWSM#
```

(e) If you still have problems with the interface, execute the **show vlan** command and be sure the correct VLANs are downloaded properly on the FWSM.

```
FWSM# show vlan
10, 30
FWSM#
```

(f) If you have FWSM set up with Hybrid mode, be sure to configure the VLANS on the switch before defining the SVI on the MSFC. If you have configured an SVI interface on the MSFC before configuring the VLAN on the switch, you must remove the SVI from the MSFC and VLANs from the switch. Reconfigure VLANs on the switch first and then configure the SVI interface on the MSFC.

(g) If the packets still do not flow, change the Ether channel algorithm on the switch.

Step 2 If you can successfully ping the inside and outside interface from the corresponding VLANs, the next step is to make sure that you can ping across the FWSM. If you cannot do so, follow the next step.

Step 3 By default, FWSM denies all packets from higher to lower security, and lower to higher security networks. So you must configure the ACL to allow this traffic on both directions. You can execute **show access-list** in conjunction with **show access-group** commands to verify whether the ACL is configured, and applied to the correct interface. You must also allow the return packet from the opposite direction. For example, to ping the outside from the inside, you must allow the ICMP on the inside interface and on the outside interface. If you do not want to allow ICMP packets on the outside interface, you can configure **fixup protocol icmp**. If the packets are dropped by the ACL, this information will be logged in the syslog, if you turn on syslogging to level 4. If with the **show access-list** command packet, counters are incrementing, you know that the ACL is allowing the packets that the NAT may not be configuring or may be configuring incorrectly. So, go to the next step.

Step 4 Check to see if the translation is not being built.

If the hit counters are incrementing on the ACL, make sure you are not running with a translation issue. As the NAT is taken care of by the NP3 processor, you can execute the **show np3 nat|global|static|alias** command to verify the configuration. You can execute **show xlate detail** command to see if the translation is being built up as follows:

```
FWSM(config)# show xlate detail
Flags: D - DNS, d - dump, I - identity, i - inside, n - no random,
       o - outside, r - portmap, s - static
1 in use, 2 most used
ICMP PAT from inside:10.1.1.10/45 to outside:30.1.1.1/1036 flags r
FWSM(config)#
```

Step 5 Verify that the route exists in the routing table for the destination network.

If the ACL and translation are fine, execute the **show route** command to verify that the routing table is in the firewall module. Example 4-14 is an example of a routing table.

Example 4-14 *Showing a Routing Table on the FWSM*

```
FWSM(config)# show route

S    0.0.0.0 0.0.0.0 [1/0] via 30.1.1.2, outside
C    10.1.1.0 255.255.255.0 is directly connected, inside
C    30.1.1.0 255.255.255.0 is directly connected, outside
C    127.0.0.0 255.255.255.0 is directly connected, eobc
FWSM(config)#
```

Step 6 Verify whether the route exists on the outside router or MSFC for the return traffic.

The MSFC or the outside router must have the route pointing back to the outside interface of the FWSM. You can run the **debug ip packet detail ACL** on the MSFC or the router to make sure that a route is defined on the MSFC or router pointing back to the outside interface of the FWSM. Note that if you want the communication to take place between these VLANs and outside network, you must have a route for every VLAN defined on the FWSM. The following commands show how to run the **debug ip packet detail ACL** command. Assume that you want to verify the connection from the source address of 30.1.1.1, and destination address of 50.1.1.50 on the MSFC. You can configure the ACL as follows and turn on debug using this ACL.

```
MSFC(config)# access-list 101 permit ip host 30.1.1.1 host 50.1.1.50
MSFC(config)# access-list 101 permit ip host 50.1.1.50 host 30.1.1.1
```

```
MSFC(config)# exit
MSFC# debug ip packet detail 101
```

Step 7 Finally, verify the connection establishment with the following command:

```
FWSM(config)# show local 10.1.1.10
local host: <10.1.1.10>, tcp conn(s)/limit = 1/0, embryonic(s)/limit =
0/0 udp c
onn(s)/limit = 0/0
    Xlate(s):
        PAT Global 30.1.1.1(1042) Local 10.1.1.10(11003)
FWSM(config)#
```

To determine the details of the connection, use the following commands:

```
FWSM(config)# show conn
1 in use, 2 most used
 Network Processor 1 connections
TCP out 50.1.1.50:23 in 10.1.1.10:11003 idle 0:00:42 Bytes 4672 FLAGS - U
 Network Processor 2 connections
```

If you want more details, you can use the **show conn long 3** command.

AAA Issues

AAA implementation on the FWSM is the same as on PIX Firewall. For Version 1.x, AAA implementation is based on PIX OS 6.0 and 6.2. However, for Version 2.x, AAA implementation is based on PIX 6.3.x. The implementation difference between the FWSM and PIX Firewall varies for where the authentication information caches. If there are new connection requests, and the cut-through proxy is turned on, the initial connection will be processed by the Control Plane. Once the user authentication is successful, it will be cached in the NP processors. So, subsequent requests will not go to the PC complex. For troubleshooting AAA on the FWSM, you can refer to Chapter 10, "Troubleshooting AAA on PIX Firewalls and FWSM."

Virtual and Transparent Firewall

Virtual Firewall and Transparent Firewall work the same way on the FWSM as does PIX Firewall. So, for details on configuration, and on troubleshooting on Virtual and Transparent firewalls, refer to Chapter 3.

High CPU Issues

FWSM may experience high CPU utilization for many reasons: misconfiguration, fixup of certain protocols, and too much traffic going across the FWSM. Work through the following steps to correct the high CPU utilization problems on the FWSM:

Step 1 Take two **"show processes"** command outputs, about one minute apart. This will give you the difference in CPU utilization at intervals of one minute.

Step 2 Calculate the difference in the number of processes taking the maximum amount of CPU in a one-minute interval. The values displayed are in milliseconds **(ms)**. Be sure to exclude any polling thread.

Step 3 Because the CPU shown is what is running on the CP (not the NPs), this limits the scope to:

- Traffic sourced from the FWSM (mgmt, routing protocols, AAA, websense, syslog, and so on)
- Traffic requiring L7 fixups (VoIP, PortMapper, ils, and so on)

Step 4 Find out what and how many connections are on the CP by issuing the **show pc conn** command.

Step 5 Typically high CPU utilization is caused by syslog, or the type of traffic hitting the CPU. Disable syslog or disable individual fixups until you uncover the utilization problem.

Remember that if the CP is experiencing high CPU utilization, this should not affect the flow of traffic across the FWSM that is processed by the NPs. However, if the NPs become busy (high CPU), then you could experience packet drops. There is no command available to show the CPU utilization on the NPs. However, if the NPs start sending **PAUSE** frames towards the two Pinnacle ASICs, that indicates how busy they are. You can get this information by using the following command:

```
FWSM(config)# show np 1 stats | include pause
! The following number should stay 0
PF_MNG: pause frames sent (x3)                              : 0
FWSM(config)# sh np 2 stats | include pause
PF_MNG: pause frames sent (x3)                              : 0
FWSM#
```

Ideally, you should see zero in the output of the previous command. If you see a number higher than zero, you should check the command output a few times to see if the number is incrementing. If it is incrementing, you might consider sniffing the traffic to analyze what is causing this extra overload.

Additionally, you can check the ingress queue on NP1 and NP2, as shown in Example 4-15, to see if they are filling up (another indication of high CPU utilization).

Example 4-15 *Check the Ingress Queue for the NP1*

```
FWSM(config)# show np 1 ingress | include count
! The column for the following three lines should be zero
   bcb_fq_th_0_count       0x10080040   0x00000000   --> here
   bcb_fq_th_1_count       0x10080020   0x00000000   --> here
   bcb_fq_th_2_count       0x10080010   0x00000000   --> here
   bcb_fq_arr_count        0x10100400   0x000c0000
   dmu_rx_counters         0x00000000   0x00000000
FWSM(config)#
```

If you see non-zero values in the last column, it means that the NPs are dropping incoming frames.

Intermittent Packet Drops Issues

Intermittent packet drops can occur for various reasons. You need to go through the "High CPU Issues" troubleshooting steps to make sure that you are not encountering any performance issues. Additionally, you might need to check the following to troubleshoot the intermittent packet drops issue:

1 Fragmentation issues

   By default, fragmented packets cannot traverse the FWSM if you are running a version earlier than FWSM 2.2. You can use the fragment command to configure this feature as described in this link:

   http://cco/en/US/products/sw/secursw/ps2120/products_command_reference_chapter09186a00801727a8.html#wp1029667

   http://www.cisco.com/en/US/products/sw/secursw/ps2120/products_command_reference_chapter09186a00801727a8.html#wp1029667

   This behavior differs from that of the PIX firewall. Common protocols that use fragmented packets are Open Shortest Path First (OSPF) and Network File System (NFS).

2 If you are running IP URL filtering, be sure that the policy defined in the URL server is not denying the packet.

Failover Issues

Failover helps to avoid the single point of failure in your network and provides the constant security to your network. The stateful failover feature provides a seamless connectivity experience through the firewall for the end users. As of the writing of this book, FWSM operates in Active/Standby mode, which means that at any point in time, one unit will be active and the other unit will be standby. Only one unit can be a standby unit for an active unit. Unlike the PIX firewall, FWSM can function only in LAN-based Failover mode, in which a LAN interface carries the failover messages from one unit to the other. As there is no dedicated serial cable available for the LAN-based Failover, the active unit is selected based on configuration of the FWSM. You can configure one unit as primary and other unit as secondary. When both units boot up at the same time, the primary will become active and the secondary will becomes standby. However, if the secondary boots up before the primary, the secondary becomes active, and stays as active until it fails or you manually make the active unit primary. There is no automatic preemption.

Failover for FWSM can be deployed in one of the following two ways, as shown in Figure 4-6:

- Intra Chassis Redundancy
- Inter Chassis Redundancy

Figure 4-6 *Intra/Inter Chassis Redundancy*

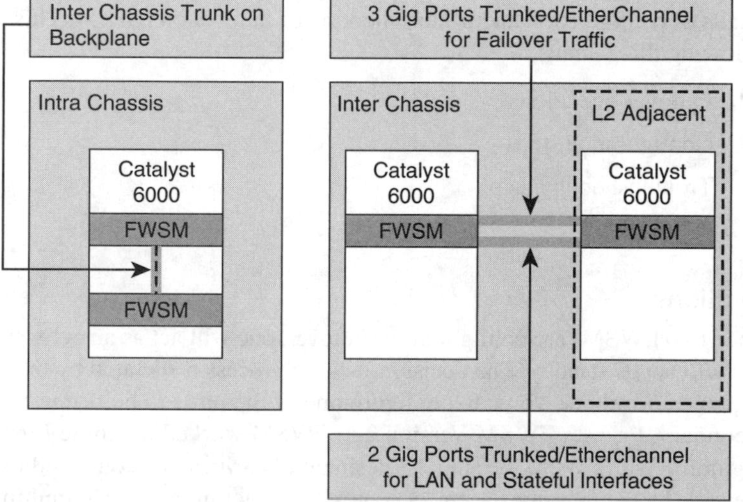

- **Intra Chassis Redundancy (Single Chassis)**—For Intra Chassis Failover setup, two FWSMs are inserted into the same chassis. One of the FWSMs acts as the primary and the other FWSM acts as the secondary unit. From a network point of view, there is no issue in supporting Active and Standby Firewall blades in the same chassis, but the risk is the single point of failure. Note that there is a dedicated failover interface between active and standby units.
- **Inter Chassis Redundancy (Multi Chassis)**—As shown in Figure 4-6, for Inter Chassis setup (the figure on the right), the Catalyst Switch on the left has the Active Firewall, whereas the one on the right has the Standby Firewall unit. All Firewall interfaces between active and standby Firewall are Layer 2 apart, which requires a 6 Gb dot1q Etherchannel link between the two switches. The 6 Gb channel is not mandatory, because all Firewall interfaces are virtual. It also can be of smaller bandwidth, with the obvious side effect of degradation in bandwidth after switchover. In this case, this link can be a bottleneck after switchover. Also it is not mandatory to

have an Etherchannel link between Active and Standby Firewall modules. The only requirement is to have all corresponding interfaces of Active and Standby Firewall Layer 2 of OSI model apart.

Both FWSMs (with Active and Standby Firewall modules) should have identical definitions of the firewall and normal router interfaces on MSFC. After switchover, that is, when the Active Firewall fails and the Standby unit becomes the new Active Firewall, all (and *only*) the Firewall traffic is bridged to the active Firewall over the Etherchannel between the two switches. Traffic coming out of Firewall will have to cross Etherchannel (or any other layer 2 connectivity to the other switch for Firewall interfaces) to go to the actual hosts.

It is extremely important to understand how failover operates, before delving into the details of configuration and troubleshooting of failover on FWSM. This section covers the following three items:

- Failover operations
- Configuration steps
- Troubleshooting steps

Failover Operations

Once two FWSMs are configured for failover, one will act as an active unit and the other one will act as standby. The decision-making process is dictated by the configuration and sequence of reboot. You can configure one of the units to be primary and other to be secondary. Prior to FWSM Version 2.x, FWSM worked in single firewall mode, but beginning with FWSM Version 2.x, a single FWSM can be converted to multiple virtual firewall (by configuring a security context). If you run failover in multiple mode, failover is *not* virtualized in release 2.x, which means that failover is not determined on a per-context basis, but rather as a whole for the module. A single context cannot be active when another context is standby on the same FWSM; rather all contexts are either active or standby. During the initialization phase, active and standby roles are decided. It is, however, possible to change the role of failover manually after the initialization process.

Initialization Phase

After both FWSM modules have booted and failover is enabled, the modules will attempt to communicate with each other. Once the communication is established, the primary will become active and the secondary will become standby. The active will then synchronize its configuration to the standby. The system is now in a steady state with both active and standby modules.

Failover Conditions

The standby unit can become active under one of the following conditions:

- If the active FWSM is removed or shut down
- If the active FWSM reboots due to manual or forced reset
- If communication over failover and firewall interfaces is lost
- If the number of healthy firewall interfaces on active falls to a number that is below half the number on standby
- If you force failover through CLI

Forced Reboot Conditions

An FWSM will self-reboot under one of the following three conditions:

- If the standby is unable to sync interfaces from Active properly
- If the standby is unable to complete the configuration sync from Active
- Either on active or standby, if a pool of 1550 size blocks is exhausted

Monitoring

As you have seen, failover can trigger either because one FWSM unit fails or one standby unit becomes healthier than the active unit. An FWSM unit's health depends on the interface's health. So to detect unit failure, or to decide which unit is healthier, both unit monitoring and interface monitoring needs to be performed as follows:

- **Unit Monitoring**—Each FWSM will monitor the unit health of its failover peer by sending a Hello message to the other unit. If a unit has not received a Hello message from the other unit for 30 seconds, it will perform the following test:
  - Send ARP request for failover interface and each Firewall interface

    If a reply is heard on a Firewall interface, but *not* the failover interface, *no* failover will take place, and the Active/Standby state will remain as it is. If no replies are heard on either of the Firewall interfaces and on the failover interface, the other unit is marked as "Failed" and this unit will become Active, if it is not already. Conditions which can cause this type of failure include:
  - Removal of peer FWSM module
  - Reboot of peer FWSM module
  - Removal or failure of the physical medium carrying failover interface and Firewall interface traffic for FWSMs in separate chassis
  - Shutdown of failover interface and Firewall interface VLANs
  - Traffic overload on the failover interface and Firewall interfaces causing packet loss

- **Interface Monitoring**—Each unit monitors the health of its own Firewall interfaces and those of its failover peer by sending Hello messages on the Firewall interfaces. If a unit does not receive any messages on a particular interface for *three consecutive poll intervals*, the unit will run the following tests on that interface for 30 seconds:

  1. Check for link status of that interface
  2. Check for any incoming traffic on that interface
  3. Send the ARP for the most recent hosts (up to 2) learned from that interface
  4. Broadcast ping to the interface's subnet

  If all of these tests fail, and the interface on the other FWSM is receiving traffic, or is able to ARP/PING a host on that interface, this unit's interface is marked as **Failed**.

  Remember that in FWSM version 1.x, if a unit finds that it has *fewer than half* the number of healthy interfaces as the other unit, it will mark itself as *Failed*. The Standby will take over if it is determined that the Active has failed. This is referred to as *the 50 percent rule*.

  The biggest drawback with the 50 percent rule is that that the failure of an *important* link does not necessarily trigger a unit failover. To understand this point, look at an example. Assume that you have three interfaces—inside, outside, and DMZ for FWSM, which is set up as a failover. If the outside link is down, you will lose all connectivity to the outside world. Although this is an important link, due to the 50 percent rule, the Primary unit that is currently active will not failover, even though the secondary unit is healthier (as all three interfaces are up on the secondary unit). So you need to rely on Layer 1 or 2 redundancy schemes, such as Etherchannel and the Spanning-Tree protocol, to avoid this type of failure.

  To address this 50 percent rule shortcoming, FWSM release 2.x introduces the capability to modify the fixed 50 percent rule that applies to the 1.1(x) release. This is achieved using interface tracking. You can designate monitored interfaces across contexts. Each time a monitored interface fails, a counter (N) is incremented. It is compared against a global counter (M) that is specified by the user. Whenever N exceeds M, a module failover is triggered. Using this property, a module failover could be initiated when, for instance, all the interfaces of a context fail, or when the interface leading to the ISP router fails. This feature is available both in single and multiple modes.

  Interface failure might occur for one of the following reasons:

  — The VLAN interface is shut down or the VLAN is cleared from the switch.

  — The port/ports or the cable carrying the interface's VLAN between a pair of FWSMs in separate chassis is removed or becomes faulty.

— The interface is overloaded with traffic and experiencing packet drops.

— No failover IP address is configured.

Interface failover can be determined either by using the **show failover** or **show interface** command.

Configuration Steps

Two protocols that help in attaining redundancy between two FWSMs are a failover protocol, and a logical update (LU) protocol. The failover protocol monitors the health of both FWSMs and their interfaces at fixed intervals, whereas the LU protocol ensures the replication of the connection table to the Secondary unit, to maintain the data flow of existing connections upon failover. Work through the following steps to configure Failover:

Step 1 Be sure to fulfill the minimum requirements.

Before attempting to configure for Failover, you must fulfill the following minimum requirements for it to operate correctly:

(a) Both FWSMs must be running the same version of FWSM software.

(b) Both must have the same number of VLANS mapped from the switch. Also be sure to configure the same number of interfaces on both units.

(c) Both units must be Layer 2 adjacent on all their interfaces. In other words, all interfaces must be capable of exchanging Layer 2 broadcast packets (Address Resolution Protocol [ARP] and so on) between each other, as the failover protocol packets cannot be routed.

(d) When running multiple modes, both modules must have the same licensing characteristics—for example, the number of contexts, and so on. (This is not applicable for FWSM 1.x.)

(e) Both modules must run in the same mode; a single mode unit cannot be paired with a multiple mode unit. (This is not applicable for FWSM 1.x.)

(f) Both firewalls must agree on operating either as routed or transparent. (This is not applicable for FWSM 1.x.)

Step 2 Configure two additional VLANs on the switch and map them to FWSM for the failover interface and the stateful failover link.

You must create a VLAN on the switch and map this VLAN to the failover interface of both primary and secondary FWSMs. If your FWSMs are in different chassis, you must configure a trunk link to carry the VLAN to the other switch. If the FWSM modules are in the same chassis, be sure to map the VLANs that you have created to both of the FWSMs. The same thing applies for the stateful failover link. It is strongly recommended to create two separate VLANs for the failover interface and the stateful failover link. In the native IOS, you can create a layer 2 VLAN with the **vlan** command in configuration mode. In hybrid mode, you can do the same with the **set vlan** command.

The LU protocol can generate large (up to 700Mbps) amounts of traffic. If the LAN and link interfaces are not dissociated, providing guaranteed output queue servicing to the failover protocol can be difficult when there is congestion. For instance, VLAN 100 could be dedicated to carrying the LU traffic, while VLAN 101 takes care of the failover protocol. Both VLANs can be trunked using 801.Q between the two switches.

Step 3 Configure the failover LAN interface and the failover link.

For failover to operate on the FWSM, a failover communication interface must be configured. This is the LAN interface over which failover protocol packets will travel. To configure stateful failover, use the same interface or a different one to carry LU traffic. With the previous steps, be sure to configure the VLANs for the failover interface and stateful failover link. Execute **show vlan** on both FWSMs to ensure that both VLANs (among other VLANs) are downloaded to the FWSM. Once the VLANs are downloaded, you can configure the failover interfaces with the following commands if you are running a FWSM version earlier than 2.x:

```
nameif VLAN_NUMBER interface_name security_level
ip address interface_name IP_address netmask
failover lan interface <if_name>
failover link <if_name>
```

Example 4-16 shows the primary FWSM's configuration in single mode with the inside VLAN10, the outside VLAN30, and the failover VLAN 400 with FWSM version 1.x.

Example 4-16 *Failover Configuration for the Primary FWSM*

```
FWSM(config)# nameif 400 fover 50
FWSM(config)# nameif 450 flink 60
FWSM(config)# ip address fover 1.1.1.1 255.255.255.0
FWSM(config)# ip address flink 2.1.1.1 255.255.255.0
FWSM(config)# failover ip address fover 1.1.1.2 255.255.255.0
FWSM(config)# failover ip address flink 2.1.1.2 255.255.255.0
FWSM(config)# failover lan interface fover
FWSM(config)# failover link interface flink
FWSM(config)#
```

On the secondary unit, if you are running FWSM Version 1, all you need is the failover interface configured as shown in Example 4-17. (You can simply copy and paste the failover interface configuration from the primary to the secondary unit.)

Example 4-17 *Failover Configuration for the Secondary FWSM*

```
FWSM(config)# nameif 400 fover 50
FWSM(config)# nameif 450 fover 60
FWSM(config)# ip address fover 1.1.1.1 255.255.255.0
FWSM(config)# failover ip addr fover 1.1.1.2 255.255.255.0
FWSM(config)# failover lan interface fover
FWSM(config)# failover link interface flink
FWSM(config)#
```

Beginning with Version 2.x, this is configured with the following command:

```
failover lan interface <if_name> vlan <vlan>
failover link <if_name> [vlan <vlan>]
```

Unlike in Version 1.x, you do not need to first **nameif** the VLAN interfaces and then associate them with failover functions. This is now performed using a single command that was described previously.

If the firewall is operating in multiple mode, the failover interface and the stateful link interface are configured at the system execution space as shown in Example 4-18 (in single mode, the configuration is the same).

Example 4-18 *Two VLANS for the LAN Interface and the LU Interface*

```
FWSM(config)# failover lan interface fover vlan 400
FWSM(config)# failover link flink vlan 450
FWSM(config)#
```

Assign IP addresses to these interfaces. The configuration is performed on both units (copy and paste from the primary unit to the secondary unit) as shown in Example 4-19.

Example 4-19 *Failover Interface IP Address Configuration*

```
FWSM(config)# failover interface ip fover 1.1.1.1 255.255.255.0 standby 1.1.1.2
FWSM(config)# failover interface ip flink 2.1.1.1 255.255.255.0 standby 2.1.1.2
FWSM(config)#
```

Step 4 Assign IP addresses for the failover interfaces.

You must assign standby IP addresses for each failover and Firewall interface. This is configured with the following command in FWSM Version 1.x:

```
FWSM(config)# failover ip address <if_name> <IP_Address>
```

The Standby FWSM will use these IP addresses as the addresses for its interfaces. The Active will use the IP addresses specified by the **ip address** command. The only exception to this is the failover communication interface, for which the primary will **always** use the IP address specified by the **ip address** command, and the secondary will always use the IP specified by the **failover ip address** command as shown in Example 4-20.

Example 4-20 *IP Address Configuration in Single Mode Running FWSM 1.x*

```
FWSM(config)# nameif 30 outside 0
FWSM(config)# nameif 10 inside 100
FWSM(config)# ip address inside  10.1.1.1 255.255.255.0
FWSM(config)# ip address outside 10.30.1.1 255.255.255.0
FWSM(config)# failover ip addr inside 10.1.1.2 255.255.255.0
FWSM(config)# failover ip addr outside 10.30.1.2 255.255.255.0
```

You do not need to configure the interfaces shown in Example 4-20 on the secondary. This information will be replicated to the secondary unit.

If you are running FWSM 2.2, the same interface is configured with the following command:

```
failover interface ip <if_name> <ip_address> <mask> standby
  <ip_address>
```

The **failover interface ip** command now assigns an IP address to both the active and standby units, deprecating the 1.1(x) **failover ip address** syntax. Example 4-21 shows the interface configuration on the Primary unit.

Example 4-21 *Primary Unit's Interface IP Address Configuration*

```
FWSM(config)# failover interface ip inside 10.1.1.1 255.255.255.0 standby 10.1.1.2
FWSM(config)# failover interface ip outside 10.30.1.1 255.255.255.0 standby
 10.30.1.2
FWSM(config)#
```

If you are running multiple firewall mode, within a context, the same rule applies. The **failover ip address** command is deprecated in favor of an extension to the regular **ip address** command:

```
ip address <if_name> <ip_address> <mask> [standby <ip_address>]
```

In multiple firewall mode, create contexts, assign interfaces to them, and associate VLANs to interfaces within those contexts. Use the new **ip address** CLI when assigning IP addresses to interfaces. These steps are only performed on the primary unit. Example 4-22 shows a single context configuration in multiple mode.

Example 4-22 *Context Configuration on Multiple Mode*

```
FWSM(config)# context engineering
Creating context 'client'... Done. (4)
FWSM(config-context)# logical-interface vlan10
FWSM(config-context)# logical-interface vlan30
FWSM(config-context)# config-url tftp://10.10.1.101/engineering.cfg
FWSM(config-context)# changeto context engineering
FWSM/client(config)# nameif vlan10 inside 100
FWSM/client(config)# ip address inside 10.1.1.1 255.255.255.0 standby 10.1.1.2
FWSM/client(config)# nameif vlan30 outside 0
FWSM/client(config)# ip address outside 10.30.1.1 255.255.255.0 standby 10.30.1.2
! Monitor all contexts' interfaces
FWSM(config)# changeto context engineering
FWSM/client(config)# monitor-interface inside
FWSM/client(config)# monitor-interface outside
! Switch back to system execution space and enable failover on the primary unit:
FWSM-Prod(config)# changeto system
```

Step 5 Designate primary and secondary units.

Unlike serial cable-based Failover on PIX Firewall, in LAN-based failover there is no physical cable to distinguish the Primary and Secondary units. This is determined through configuration. You can use the following command to elect which FWSM should become Primary and which one should be the Secondary unit:

```
FWSM(config)# failover lan unit {primary|secondary}
```

On the primary FWSM, execute the following command:

```
FWSM(config)# failover lan unit primary
```

On the secondary unit, execute the following command to turn it to a standby unit:

```
FWSM(config)# failover lan unit secondary
```

The FWSM configured as primary will become Active, and the secondary will become Standby if both units are booted up at the same time. In a running system, there will be *no* preemption. In other words, if a secondary is currently the Active module and a primary has finished booting, the primary will become Standby, rather than forcing a failover and becoming Active.

Step 6 Configure interface policy (optional).

Beginning with FWSM Version 2.x, the global interface policy can be specified either as a percentage or as an absolute number. When the number of monitored interfaces that have failed reaches or exceeds the interface policy, a module failover is triggered. The failover interface policy is configured within the system execution space using the following command:

```
failover interface-policy <n> [percent]
```

Assuming a failover interface policy of 1 interface, here is the sequence of events that occurs as soon as one monitored interface fails:

```
Switching to Standby
104002: (Primary) Switching to STNDBY - Interface check
```

Remember that a set of criteria needs to be met to fail an interface.

Step 7 Configure poll interval (optional).

A poll interval is the amount of time that elapses between each failure detection attempt. That interval is specified using the **failover poll <interval>** command. The poll interval is used for both unit and interface health monitoring:

```
failover polltime [unit|interface] [msec] <x> [holdtime [msec] <y>]
```

For example, failover poll time 15 can be configured with the following command:

```
FWSM(config)# failover poll 15
```

In release 1.1(x) the **failover polltime** command is used to configure the frequency of failover Hello messages exchanged between two units. The value in 1.1(x) can range from 3 to 15 seconds. The hold timer is always fixed to three times the poll time value. In release 2.1(x), the poll interval can be adjusted independently for the interface and the unit. The unit poll interval is fixed to 1 second by default, but can be modified to any value. The interface poll time can be set between 3 to 15 seconds and does not have a configurable hold time.

Step 8 Turn on stateful failover for http traffic (optional).

HTTP replication is not *on* by default. The **Failover replication http** command turns on HTTP replication. Enabling HTTP replication reduces performance dramatically. It is not recommended in FWSM. The failover LAN interface should be dedicated.

Step 9 Turn on the failover.

You should turn on the failover on the primary unit first with the following command:

```
FWSM(config)# failover
! No Response from Mate
FWSM(config)#
```

Once the **no response from mate** message appears, enable failover on the secondary unit by using the **failover** command with no parameters. From here on, no configuration is performed on the secondary unit. The following messages appear on the primary unit:

```
709003: (Primary) Beginning configuration replication: Send to mate.
709004: (Primary) End Configuration Replication (ACT)
```

A series of SYSLOG messages 105003 and 105004 should quickly follow on the primary unit:

```
105003: (Primary) Monitoring on interface 1 waiting
105004: (Primary) Monitoring on interface 1 normal
```

Meanwhile, the secondary unit should display the following sequence as shown in Example 4-23.

Example 4-23 *Messages that Will Appear on the Secondary Unit After Turning FO on*

```
FWSM(config)# failover
        Detected an Active mate.  Switching to Standby
        Switching to Standby.
Beginning configuration replication from mate.
This unit is in syncing state.  'failover' command will not be effective at this time
End configuration replication from mate.
709006: (Secondary) End Configuration Replication (STB)
FWSM(config)#
```

NOTE If the **write memory** command is performed from the system execution space, the standby module deletes all its existing contexts and syncs the entire system execution space configuration from the active firewall. If the **write memory** command is performed from within a context, the standby module adds the context to its system execution space and synchronizes the context's configuration in addition.

Troubleshooting Steps

Before working through some of the common scenarios, it will be helpful for you to examine the syslog messages that are shown on the secondary FWSM after you enable logging on as shown in Example 4-24.

Example 4-24 *Syslog on the Secondary FWSM*

```
FWSM(config)# logging on
FWSM(config)# logging monitor 7
FWSM(config)# logging console 7
FWSM(config)# 111008: User 'enable_15' executed the 'logging con 7' command.
        Detected an Active mate.  Switching to Standby
        Switching to Standby.
FWSM(config)#
Beginning configuration replication from mate.
This unit is in syncing state.  'failover' command will not be effective at this time
End configuration replication from mate.
709006: (Secondary) End Configuration Replication (STB)
Access Rules Download Complete: Memory Utilization < 1%
105003: (Secondary) Monitoring on interface 2 waiting
105003: (Secondary) Monitoring on interface 1 waiting
105004: (Secondary) Monitoring on interface 2 normal
105004: (Secondary) Monitoring on interface 1 normal
FWSM#
```

After the units are synchronized with each other, you can find the status of a unit on both the primary and secondary with the **show failover** command. Example 4-25 shows the output of the **show failover** command on the primary unit.

Example 4-25 *Monitoring Failover Status on Primary FWSM*

```
FWSM(config)# show failover
Failover On
Failover unit Primary
Failover LAN Interface fover
Reconnect timeout 0:00:00
Poll frequency 15 seconds
        This host: Primary - Active
                Active time: 29925 (sec)
                Interface outside (10.30.1.1): Normal
                Interface inside (10.1.1.1): Normal
        Other host: Secondary - Standby
                Active time: 285 (sec)
                Interface outside (10.30.1.2): Normal
                Interface inside (10.1.1.2): Normal
Stateful Failover Logical Update Statistics
        Link : Unconfigured.
FWMS#
```

Example 4-26 shows the same on the secondary unit.

Example 4-26 *The Status of FO With the* **show failover** *Command*

```
FWSM(config)# show failover
Failover On
Failover unit Secondary
Failover LAN Interface fover
Reconnect timeout 0:00:00
Poll frequency 15 seconds
        This host: Secondary - Standby
                Active time: 285 (sec)
                Interface inside (10.1.1.2): Normal
                Interface outside (10.30.1.2): Normal
        Other host: Primary - Active
                Active time: 30750 (sec)
                Interface inside (10.1.1.1): Normal
                Interface outside (10.30.1.1): Normal
Stateful Failover Logical Update Statistics
        Link : Unconfigured.
FWSM(config)#
```

Work through the following steps to troubleshoot the failover problem:

Step 1 Level 1 syslog specifies a reason for failover. So always check the syslog to determine the root cause. For example, if the switch port failed on the inside interface of Active Firewall, you would see the following message on the Primary (Active) Firewall.

```
411002: Line protocol on Interface inside, changed state to down
105007: (Primary) Link status 'Down' on interface 1
104002: (Primary) Switching to STNDBY—interface check, mate is healthier
```

Syslog from Secondary (Standby) Firewall will report the following message:

```
104001: (Secondary) Switching to ACTIVE—mate want me Active
```

Step 2 Issue the **show failover history** command to see the reasons for the past state changes, which will help narrow the possibilities for the failover.

```
FWSM# show fail history
==========================================================================
>From State    To State                        Reason
==========================================================================
  Init         Disabled  Set by the CI config cmd
  Disabled     Listen    Set by the CI config cmd
  Listen       Active    No Active unit found
  Active       Active    Other unit got stuck in learn state after sync
==========================================================================
```

Step 3 Execute **show vlan** on both FWSM units and make sure you have the same VLANs downloaded on both units.

Step 4 Execute **show interface** on both FWSM units to make sure they are up. Map the VLANs to the right interfaces.

Step 5 Test the connectivity by pinging to the Failover interface IP. Be sure to allow the ICMP for the interfaces.

Step 6 Verify that the Failover interface VLAN is configured on the switch, and is not removed from the switch accidentally.

Step 7 Make sure all VLANS are trunked between the switches.

Step 8 Be sure to turn on dot1Q across the board on the switch.

Case Studies

In this section, we discuss two important features of FWSM in detail:

- Multiple SVI for FWSM
- Understanding access-list memory utilization

Case Study 1: Multiple SVI for FWSM

In this case study, you will learn the concept of SVI interfaces on the MSFC and the need for configuring multiple SVI interfaces.

As previously stated, SVI stands for Switched Virtual Interface. It represents a logical Layer 3 interface on a switch. For Catalyst Operating System (CatOS) versions earlier than 7.6(1) and Cisco IOS Software releases earlier than 12.2(14)SY, only one SVI is allowed as part of the Firewall VLANs. In other words, only one Layer 3 interface can be configured between the FWSM and Multilayer Switch Feature Card (MSFC). Attempting to configure multiple SVIs produces a command-line interface (CLI) error message.

For CatOS Versions 7.6(1) and later and Cisco IOS Software releases 12.2(14)SY and later, the FWSM supports multiple SVIs. By default, only one SVI is supported. To enable support for multiple SVIs on your switch on Native IOS, use the following command:

```
Cat6509(config)# firewall multiple-vlan-interfaces
Warning: enabling multiple VLAN interfaces may result in traffic bypassing the F
WSM - use with caution!
Cat6509(config)#
```

On the hybrid mode, you can use the following command to turn on the multiple SVI interface:

```
Cat6509# set firewall multiple-vlan-interfaces {enable | disable}
```

Traffic is sent to the Firewall Services Module (FWSM) by way of Virtual LANs (VLAN) exclusively. The FWSM has no concept of physical ports of its own. Instead, you need to map VLANs to the FWSM interface. For instance, VLAN 30 in Figure 4-7 is mapped to the *inside* interface, whereas VLAN 20 represents the *outside* interface. Physical switchports are then placed into either VLAN, and hosts connect to those ports. When communication occurs between VLANs 20 and 30, the FWSM is the only available path, forcing traffic to be inspected statefully.

Figure 4-7 *One SVI Interface Typical Setup*

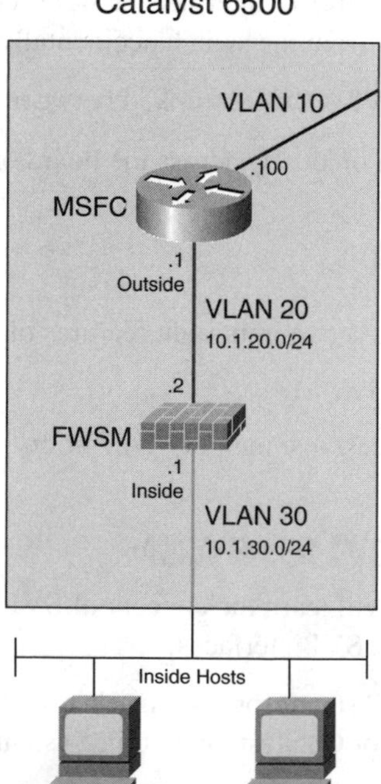

In Figure 4-7, the default gateway for the two hosts on VLAN 30 exists only on the FWSM. In other words, no **interface VLAN 30** is ever created on the MSFC. VLAN 30 is mapped directly to the **inside** interface on the FWSM. Software that supports the FWSM (CatOS 7.5(1) or higher; Supervisor IOS 12.1(13)E or higher) automatically includes a built-in security check that prevents a user from creating a second connection to the MSFC, **interface VLAN 30**. If a user can create such an interface, traffic from the hosts can bypass the FWSM as shown in Figure 4-8.

Figure 4-8 *Host Bypassing in Multiple SVI Interfaces*

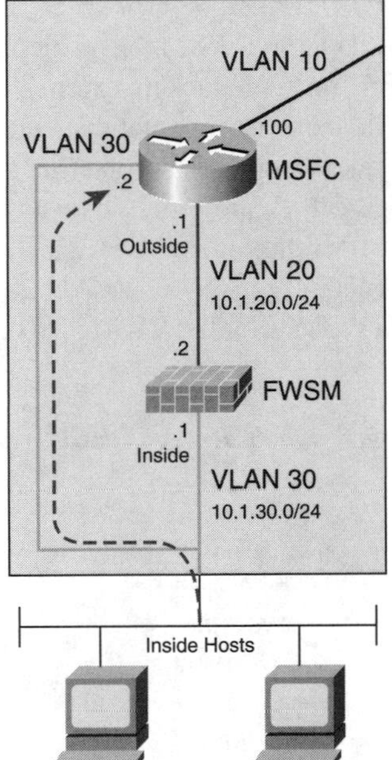

In Figure 4-8, **interface VLAN 30** is created on the MSFC and is assigned an IP address 10.1.30.2/24. Hosts at the bottom of the figure also reside in VLAN 30. Either accidentally or intentionally, the inside users may bypass the FWSM altogether. Besides, discovering these multiple paths may be achieved without much grief, if insiders have bad intentions. The more serious problem is whether outside traffic from non-secure VLAN 10 can reach the **inside** subnet directly through the MSFC, which creates a major security breach.

Why Change the Existing Model?

As discussed earlier, the automatic check preventing more than one VLAN interface between the MSFC and the FWSM is extremely valuable to prevent accidental security holes. However, there are a few scenarios in which being able to bypass that check is required.

CatOS release 7.6(1) or higher and Supervisor IOS 12.2(14)SY has the option of turning on the ability of multiple SVI interfaces to bypass the check. The commands used for both CatOS and Sup IOS are listed in Table 4-5.

Table 4-5 *Commands For Multiple SVI Interfaces*

CatOS 7.6(1)	Supervisor IOS 12.2(14)SY
set firewall multiple-vlan-interfaces <enable|disable>	[no] firewall multiple-vlan-interfaces

Scenario One: DHCP Helper with FWSM 1.1(x)

When running release 1.1(x), the FWSM drops incoming UDP broadcasts. Protocols such as DHCP (RFC 2131) rely on such packets extensively, and the lack of DHCP helper functionality in the FWSM can be problematic in certain designs. This section explains how the multiple VLAN interfaces can work around that shortcoming. Take a look at the sample topology depicted in Figure 4-9. Suppose two hosts on VLAN 30 (*inside* screened subnet) would like to acquire an IP address using DHCP. The enterprise's DHCP server is located off another screened subnet on VLAN 10. VLAN 20 represents the *outside* network and binds the MSFC to the FWSM. Finally, VLAN 500 connects the Catalyst 6500 switch to the "outside world."

Figure 4-9 *Hosts Bypassing In Multiple SVI Interfaces for DHCP*

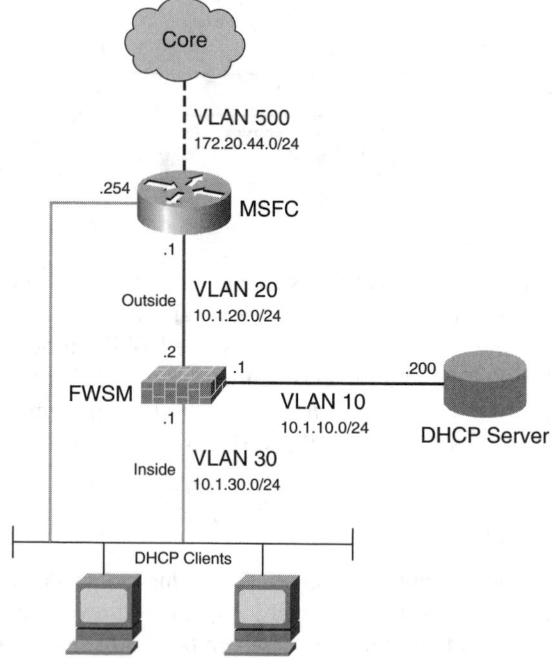

First, enable the multi-VLAN knob. Then create an interface VLAN 20 on the MSFC and assign the IP address 10.1.20.1/24 to it. You can also create an interface VLAN 30 and assign 10.1.30.254/24 to it. By doing this, you have actually connected the inside subnet directly to the MSFC. This means that your two hosts can bypass the firewall. To prevent this, apply an inbound access-list to interface VLAN 30 to allow only DHCP requests. Here is a quick background on the operation of the DHCP protocol:

1 Clients broadcast a DHCPDISCOVER.
2 Servers unicast a DHCPOFFER back.
3 Clients broadcast a DHCPREQUEST.
4 Servers unicast a DHCPACK back.

DHCP messages from a client to a server are sent *to* the UDP port 67, and DHCP messages from a server to a client are sent *to* UDP port 68. Therefore, in the scenario, a simple input access-list needs to be applied to VLAN 30 **on the MSFC** to allow only UDP broadcasts where source port=68 and destination port=67. This takes care of allowing client-sourced messages to reach the DHCP server. You then add an IP helper-address statement to point to the DHCP server, as shown in Example 4-27.

Example 4-27 *Configuring* **ip helper-address** *on MSFC*

```
MSFC(config)# access-list 150 permit udp host 0.0.0.0 eq 68 host 255.255.255.255 eq 67
MSFC(config)# interface Vlan 30
MSFC(config-if)# ip address 10.1.30.254 255.255.255.0
! Following assign the dhcp's IP address
MSFC(config-if)# ip helper-address 10.1.10.200
MSFC(config-if)# ip access-group 150 in
MSFC(config-if)#
```

You also need to tell the MSFC how to reach the DHCP server (via the Firewall). Example 4-28 shows the route configuration that is needed to accomplish this.

Example 4-28 *Route Needed on the MSFC*

```
MSFC(config)# ip route 10.1.10.200 255.255.255.255 10.1.20.2
MSFC(config)#
```

This configuration allows the MSFC to receive UDP broadcasts on VLAN 30 and transform them into IP unicast requests destined to 10.1.10.200 (source IP address 10.1.30.254). You need to verify that this traffic is allowed to cross the firewall.

This takes care of the traffic between the client and the server. What about the opposite direction? The server unicasts its replies back to the relay agent's IP address, always. In this case, these packets look like that shown in Table 4-6.

Table 4-6 *Packet Format for DHCP*

Source IP address	10.1.10.200
Destination IP address	10.1.30.254
Protocol	UDP
Source Port	67
Destination Port	68

Firewalls in general do not support asymmetric routing. That is, in this case, you have to force the DHCP offer from the DHCP server to go back out VLAN 20, even though VLAN 30 is connected directly. You need to add the route shown in Example 4-29.

Example 4-29 *Route Needed for Proper Routing*

```
FWSM(config)# route vlan20 10.1.30.254 255.255.255.255 10.1.20.1
FWSM(config)#
```

Return traffic from the DHCP server enters VLAN 10 and is routed onto VLAN 20 directly by the firewall. The relay agent receives the offer packet and in turns hands out an IP address to the DHCP client.

There is still one problem that needs to be solved, however. We have to ensure that traffic originated from the core (off VLAN 500) that is destined to the inside screened subnet (VLAN 30) does not bypass the firewall. By default, it will bypass the firewall because the MSFC has an interface connected to VLAN 30 (admin distance 0). Policy routing comes to the rescue. Apply an incoming policy routing rule on interface VLAN 500 that reads **any traffic destined to 10.1.30.0/24, your next-hop is 10.1.20.2.** Example 4-30 shows the configuration for policy routing.

Example 4-30 *Configuration Needed For Policy Routing*

```
MSFC(config)# ip access-list extended internet-to-inside
MSFC(config-ext-nacl)# permit ip any 10.1.30.0 0.0.0.255
MSFC(config-ext-nacl)#exit
MSFC(config)# route-map internet-to-inside-policy-routing permit 10
MSFC(config-route-map)# match ip address internet-to-inside
MSFC(config-route-map)# set ip next-hop 10.1.20.2
MSFC(config)# interface Vlan 500
MSFC(config-if)# ip address 172.20.44.70 255.255.255.192
MSFC(config-if)# ip policy route-map internet-to-inside-policy-routing
MSFC(config-if)#
```

Scenario Two: Alternate Configuration

An alternate configuration is depicted in Figure 4-10.

Figure 4-10 *Host Bypassing in Multiple SVI Interfaces for DHCP*

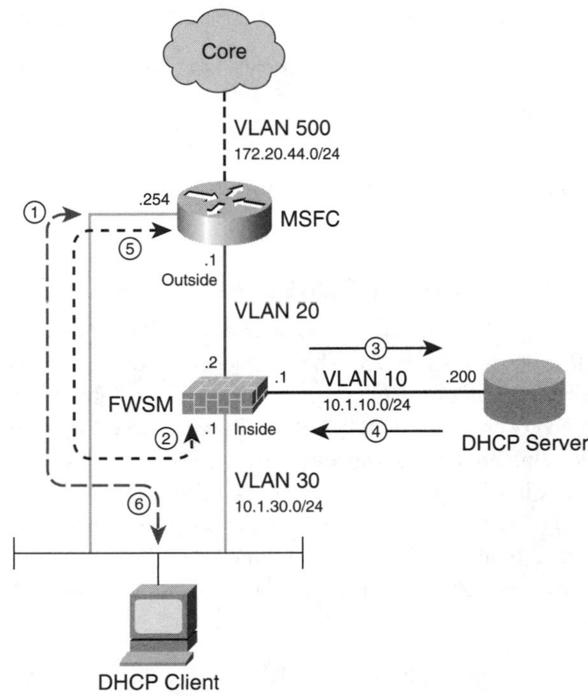

It is also possible to instruct the relay agent (10.30.1.254) to send packets destined to the DHCP back out interface VLAN 30. This is done by configuring this static route on the MSFC as shown in Example 4-31.

Example 4-31 *Route Configuration Needed on the MSFC*

```
MSFC(config)# no ip route 10.1.10.200 255.255.255.255 10.1.20.2
MSFC(config)# ip route 10.1.10.200 255.255.255.255 10.1.30.1
MSFC(config)#
```

This way, the **inside** interface of the FWSM receives all traffic sourced from 10.99.99.254 this time, in contrast to the previous example in which that traffic comes in via interface VLAN 20. This means the static route previously installed on the FWSM can be removed, as shown in Example 4-32.

Example 4-32 *Route Removal on MSFC*

```
FWSM(config)# no route vlan20 10.1.30.254 255.255.255.255 10.1.20.1
FWSM(config)#
```

That is because traffic returning from the DHCP server will naturally prefer the directly connected interface to reach 10.99.99.254. The router access-list needs to be slightly modified to resemble Example 4-33, to allow DHCP offer and ack messages sent by the DHCP server.

Example 4-33 *Access-list Needed on the MSFC*

```
MSFC(config)# access-list 150 permit udp host 0.0.0.0 eq 68 host 255.255.255.255
 eq 67
MSFC(config)# access-list 150 permit udp host 10.1.10.200 eq 67 host 10.1.30.254
 eq 67
MSFC(config)#
```

The policy routing configuration still applies.

Case Study 2: Understanding Access-List Memory Utilization

As stated previously, the Network Processors for the FWSM are used as hardware assistants to the generic CPU, relieving it from heavy packet processing such as access-list verification, network address translation, TCP sequence number randomization, and so on. One of these three network processors—namely NP3—is responsible for permitting or rejecting initial packets depending on the rules specified by the security policy. In other words, NP3 enforces access-list decisions in hardware. To do so, access-lists encoded via the command line interface (CLI) or graphical user interfaces (GUI) are compiled into a form that the hardware can recognize. NP3 comes equipped with 20MB of on-board memory (non-expandable) reserved for rules storage. Those 20MB are reserved for security policy rules exclusively:

- URL filtering statements
- Configured fixups
- Established rules
- AAA authentication policies
- Remote access to the FWSM (SSH, Telnet, HTTP)
- ICMP to the FWSM (as configured using the ICMP CLI)
- Policy NAT configuration
- Access-list entries

It is worth noting that translation entries or connection entries do not borrow from that memory space. The goal of this application note is to provide further details regarding the way access-lists are stored and processed on the FWSM.

The Compilation Process: Active and Backup Trees

NP3 carves that 20MB memory space differently depending on the operating mode (single or multiple mode). With the FWSM running in single mode (release 1.1(x) or 2.2(x)), NP3 uses a dual-tree structure and halves the 20MB into two equal-sized chunks. One tree is called the active tree, and the other is called the backup tree. A tree contains a certain number of nodes. A node is a 64-byte data structure used to store IP addresses and masks, and a corresponding action (permit/deny).

Shortly after a new access-list entry has been entered, modified or deleted, a compilation process is run on the generic CPU to transform the human-readable ACL into a form that the hardware can digest. The compilation process is automatically started by default—that is, once an access-list entry has been entered, it is shortly thereafter compiled into NP3. The following sequence captured from the CLI illustrates this:

```
FWSM(config)# access-list test permit udp host 10.1.1.1 any eq 69
Access Rules Download Complete: Memory Utilization: < 1%

FWSM(config)#
```

At the end of a successful compilation, rules are pushed down to NP3. During the compilation process, it is important that through-traffic still undergoes security checks using the access-list entries already in place. This is the reason for the backup tree. The backup tree is a mirror of the active tree. It is switched to active mode once the compilation process is running, so the compilation can run in the background without interrupting traffic currently switched by the FWSM. Once the compilation is finished, trees are switched back again.

How Memory Is Allocated: Release 1.1(x) or 2.2(1) in Single Mode

With release 1.1(x) or when running 2.2(1) in Single mode, the 20MB memory space is carved up evenly into two 10MB chunks. When the FWSM is running in single mode, a maximum theoretical limit of 63078 ACEs can be configured out of a total of 82819 rules (see Example 4-34 for the breakdowns of this number).

Example 4-34 *Breakdowns in the Number of Nodes in NP3 Processors for Memory*

```
FWSM(config)# show np 3 acl stats | include Total nodes
! 157696*64B = ~10MB
Total nodes         :        1 (max 157696)
FWSM(config)# show np 3 acl count
-------------- CLS Rule Current Counts --------------
! used for URL filtering
CLS Filter Rule Count        :             0
! one per fixup
CLS Fixup Rule Count         :             15
! for the "established"
CLS Est Ctl Rule Count       :             0
! statements
CLS Est Data Rule Count      :             0
! used for AAA auth
CLS AAA Rule Count           :             0
! for http/tnet/ssh/icmp
CLS Console Rule Count       :             0
! for policy nat
CLS Policy NAT Rule Count    :             0
! for actual ACEs
CLS ACL Rule Count           :             1
```

continues

Example 4-34 *Breakdowns in the Number of Nodes in NP3 Processors for Memory (Continued)*

```
---------------- CLS Rule MAX Counts ---------------
CLS Filter MAX               :            3942
CLS Fixup MAX                :              32
CLS Est Ctl Rule MAX         :             788
CLS Est Data Rule MAX        :             788
CLS AAA Rule MAX             :            7884
CLS Console Rule MAX         :            2365
CLS Policy NAT Rule MAX      :            3942
CLS ACL Rule MAX             :           63078
```

NOTE In 2.2 Single mode, there are 2 extra partitions reserved for downloadable ACLs (one active and one backup).

Note that connection entries or NAT translations do *not* borrow from this memory space. When a modification is made to an ACE (new entry, deletion, modification), the entire tree is recompiled. This is the reason for the sustained high CPU utilization when a substantial amount of ACE is present. The compilation task runs on the generic CPU, but the final result is pushed down to the hardware. Note that the mapping between ACE and node utilization is not necessarily one-to-one. This means that some ACEs such as **permit udp 10.0.0.0 255.0.0.0 172.16.0.0 255.255.0.0** can expand into multiple nodes in a tree, resulting in fewer than 63078 total ACEs—your mileage may vary. Optimizations for certain types of ACEs were brought into release 2.2(1.11), significantly reducing the expansion of ACEs using wildcards such as **permit udp any any**.

How memory is Allocated: Release 2.2(1) in Multiple Mode

When running in Virtual Firewall mode, both the carving scheme and the compilation process are slightly different and optimized for larger configurations. Instead of a dual tree structure, the memory is organized into 15 trees. Out of these 15 trees, two are used for user-downloadable ACE (one active + one backup). This leaves 13 trees: 12 active and one backup.

The 20MB are divided unevenly between the 15 trees: trees 13 and 14 are smaller (3071 entries) because they are reserved for user-downloadable ACEs. Within each one of the 13 other trees, space is allocated as shown in Example 4-35.

Example 4-35 *Allocation of Memory Space on One of the Thirteen Trees*

```
FWSM(config)# sh np 3 acl count 0

---------------- CLS Rule MAX Counts ---------------
CLS Filter MAX               :             606
CLS Fixup MAX                :              32
CLS Est Ctl Rule MAX         :             121
CLS Est Data Rule MAX        :             121
```

Example 4-35 *Allocation of Memory Space on One of the Thirteen Trees (Continued)*

```
CLS AAA Rule MAX              :         1213
CLS Console Rule MAX          :          363
CLS Policy NAT Rule MAX       :          606
CLS ACL Rule MAX              :         9704
FWSM(config)#
```

Where 1.1(x) and 2.2(1) single mode offered a total of 82819 rule entries, multiple mode nearly doubles that figure: (12 x 12766) + (2 x 3071) = 159334. That is normal because the allocation scheme no longer reserves an entire 10MB of space for the backup tree. Each tree being now much smaller, a backup size of 1/13 of the total space is sufficient. This also implies that in multiple mode each tree is compiled independently.

The following formula generally works to compute the maximum number of rules available per FWSM:

- Total number of nodes = 2 x 160K (64 bytes each = 20MB memory allocated for nodes)
- Total Number of Trees = X
- Nodes available per tree = 320K/X

  Best case number of rules = (320K / X)/2 = 160K/X (one rule takes at least two nodes)

With 12 active trees X = 13 (because of the backup tree), so the maximum number of *rules* per tree with 12 active trees is 160K/13 = roughly 12300. Keep in mind that this includes the number of filter, AAA, ICMP, Telnet rules, and so on. Table 4-7 records the exact maximum numbers per partition.

Table 4-7 *Exact Number of Rules Per Part/ Blade, and Maximum Number of ACEs Per Part Based on Partition*

partitions	rules/part	Rules/blade	max ACEs/part
1	79633	79633	62289
2	53087	106174	41526
3	39815	119445	31144
4	31850	127400	24915
5	26541	132705	20762
6	22750	136500	17797
7	19906	139342	15572
8	17694	141552	13841
9	15923	143307	12457
10	14476	144760	11325
11	13270	145970	10381
12	12248	146976	9582

Trees and contexts: A Matter of Mapping

As contexts (virtual firewalls) are created, they are assigned to an ACL memory pool in a round-robin fashion. Although this satisfies a large majority of applications, in some cases this fixed 12-tree allocation of memory space is no longer optimum. Examine the following examples:

- Three contexts: the first context is assigned to pool 1, the second context to pool 2, and the third context to pool 3. Each context can use a maximum of 9704 ACEs. Nine-twelfths of the total memory cannot be used by these contexts.
- One context with a very large ACL configuration, five contexts with only 20 ACEs each: each context is assigned to a pool in a round-robin fashion. With six contexts, 50 percent of the rule memory space cannot be used—even though contexts 2 to 6 use only a total of 100 rules, context 1 cannot borrow from their pools. Context 1t has to deal with the 9704 entries its pool offers.
- Twenty contexts: after the 12th context is created, the next context shares rule memory space with the first context. Also, if a change is made to an ACE in either context, the first tree is recompiled.

FWSM release 2.3 brings a better ACL partition management scheme to better address the three scenarios just discussed.

FWSM Release 2.3: The ACL Partition Manager

Starting with release 2.3, the system administrator is given the possibility to modify the ACL memory space-carving scheme. Instead of the default 12-pool model plus two trees for downloadable ACLs, the administrator can choose to divide the space into only three large chunks, or eight, or only one, depending on the needs of a particular configuration. Suppose, for instance, that it has been determined that there are never going to be more than six contexts on this FWSM: the super-user can opt for a six-pool allocation scheme.

A new command line interface is introduced for this purpose. It is available only from the system context, for obvious reasons. Note that the module must be reloaded before a new allocation scheme takes effect. Up to 12 partitions can be created, and if you try to create more than 12, following message will be displayed:

```
FWSM(config)# resource acl-partition 144
ERROR: Incorrect number of partitions. Allowed range is 1 - 12
Usage: resource acl-partition <number-of-partitions>
```

The following example shows allocating three partitions:

```
FWSM(config)# resource acl-partition 3
WARNING: This command leads to re-partitioning of ACL Memory.
It will not take affect until you save the configuration and reboot.
FWSM(config)# write memory
FWSM(config)# reload
```

When the system comes back online, the command in Example 4-36 displays the context-to-partition mapping. Note that even though three partitions were specified via the CLI, six partitions are actually created: three as required by the administrator, one backup, and two for downloadable ACLs. By default, a round-robin scheme is applied to map contexts to ACL partitions:

Example 4-36 *Resource Allocation for ACL after Changing the ACL-partition to 3*

```
FWSM(config)# show resource acl-partition
Total number of configured partitions = 3
Partition #0
        Mode                      : non-exclusive
        List of Contexts          : admin
        Number of contexts        : 1(RefCount:1)
        Number of rules           : 3(Max:41393)
Partition #1
        Mode                      : non-exclusive
        List of Contexts          : none
        Number of contexts        : 0(RefCount:0)
        Number of rules           : 0(Max:41393)
Partition #2
        Mode                      : non-exclusive
        List of Contexts          : none
        Number of contexts        : 0(RefCount:0)
        Number of rules           : 0(Max:41393)
FWSM(config)#
```

However, contexts can be manually mapped to a given partition. This is achieved in the context definition, as shown in Example 4-37.

Example 4-37 *Allocating Different Partitions from the Context*

```
FWSM(config-context)# ?

At the end of show <command>, use the pipe character '|' followed by:
begin|include|exclude|grep [-v] <regular_exp>, to filter show output.

allocate-acl-partition  Indicates which acl-partition the context belongs to
allocate-interface      Indicate interfaces assigned to the context
member                  Indicate class membership for a context
config-url              Indicate URL for a context configuration
description             Provide a description of the context
FWSM(config-context)#
FWSM(config-context)# allocate-acl 2
FWSM(config-context)# show resource acl
Total number of configured partitions = 3
Partition #0
        Mode                      : non-exclusive
        List of Contexts          : admin
        Number of contexts        : 1(RefCount:1)
        Number of rules           : 3(Max:41393)
Partition #1
        Mode                      : non-exclusive
        List of Contexts          : none
        Number of contexts        : 0(RefCount:0)
        Number of rules           : 0(Max:41393)
```

continues

Example 4-37 *Allocating Different Partitions from the Context (Continued)*

```
Partition #2
        Mode                        : exclusive
        List of Contexts            : acl-test
        Number of contexts          : 1(RefCount:1)
        Number of rules             : 0(Max:41393)
FWSM(config-context)#
```

Examples of ACL Compilation

Starting from a clean, empty configuration (Version 1.11–2.2 single mode), the ACL statistics report 0 is as follows:

```
FWSM(config)# show np 3 acl stats
----------------------------
    ACL Tree Statistics
----------------------------
Rule count          :      0
Bit nodes (PSCB's):        0
Leaf nodes          :      0
Total nodes         :      0 (max 157696)
Leaf chains         :      0
Total stored rules:        0
Max rules in leaf :        0
Node depth          :      0
----------------------------
FWSM(config)#
```

A simple ACL usually translates to one entry in the hardware, as illustrated in Example 4-38.

Example 4-38 *ACL Stats After Creating Just A Single ACL*

```
FWSM(config)# access-l simple permit tcp host 10.1.1.1 host 10.1.1.2
FWSM(config)# Access Rules Download Complete: Memory Utilization: < 1%
Access Rules Download Complete: Memory Utilization: < 1%

FWSM(config)# show np 3 acl stats
----------------------------
    ACL Tree Statistics
----------------------------
Rule count          :      1
Bit nodes (PSCB's):        0
Leaf nodes          :      1
Total nodes         :      1 (max 157696)
Leaf chains         :      0
Total stored rules:        1
Max rules in leaf :        1
Node depth          :      1
----------------------------
FWSM(config)#
```

ACEs that use object-groups expand in multiple lines. Example 4-39 results in 12 actual ACEs (3 hosts x 4 ports):

Example 4-39 *ACL Statistics Using Object Groups in the ACL*

```
FWSM(config)# show object
object-group network my_servers
  network-object host 10.80.2.24
  network-object host 10.80.2.25
  network-object host 10.80.2.26
object-group service common_ports tcp
  port-object eq www
  port-object eq https
  port-object eq telnet
  port-object eq ftp
FWSM(config)#
FWSM(config)# access-l simple permit tcp obj my_servers 10.0.0.0 255.0.0.0 obj
 common_ports
!
FWSM(config)# show np 3 acl stats
----------------------------
    ACL Tree Statistics
----------------------------
Rule count          :     12
Bit nodes (PSCB's):      11
Leaf nodes          :     12
Total nodes         :     23 (max 157696)
Leaf chains         :      0
Total stored rules:       12
Max rules in leaf :       1
Node depth          :      5
----------------------------

FWSM(config)#
! Another example using object-groups
FWSM(config)# show object
object-group network my_servers
  network-object host 10.80.2.24
  network-object host 10.80.2.25
  network-object host 10.80.2.26
object-group service common_ports tcp
  port-object eq www
  port-object eq https
  port-object eq telnet
  port-object eq ftp
object-group network my_nets
  network-object 10.48.0.0 255.255.0.0
  network-object 171.68.0.0 255.255.0.0
  network-object 10.144.0.0 255.255.0.0
object-group service port_range tcp
  port-object eq telnet
  port-object eq ftp
  port-object eq 1501
  port-object eq ssh
```

continues

Example 4-39 *ACL Statistics Using Object Groups in the ACL (Continued)*

```
  port-object range 8101 8115
  port-object range 8210 8214
  port-object range 8250 8252
  port-object eq 6502
  port-object eq 2100
  port-object eq 7091
  port-object eq 6000
  port-object eq 4900
FWSM(config)#
FWSM(config)# access-l simple permit tcp obj my_servers obj port_range obj my_nets
 obj common_ports
!
FWSM(config)# sh np 3 acl stats
----------------------
    ACL Tree Statistics
----------------------------
Rule count          :    432
Bit nodes (PSCB's):      431
Leaf nodes          :    432
Total nodes         :    863 (max 157696)
Leaf chains         :      0
Total stored rules:      432
Max rules in leaf :        1
Node depth          :     11
----------------------------

FWSM(config)#
```

One ACE expands into 432 entries, using relatively simple object-groups. This is normal because the ACL would require 432 individual ACEs anyway, if object-grouping was not used:

```
FWSM(config)# show access-list | include elem
access-list simple; 432 elements
FWSM(config)#
```

Access-lists: Best Practices

The following is a list of rules of thumb that will help you reduce the hardware resources occupied by ACEs:

- Use contiguous hosts addresses whenever possible. Aggregate host statements in ACEs/object-groups into networks.
- Use "any" instead of networks, and networks instead of hosts when possible.
- Try to simplify object-groups. Potentially this can save hundreds of ACEs when the ACLs are expanded. Grouping together individual port statements into a range is an example.

The time it takes to compile a tree is largely irrelevant because while the compilation is taking place, the "old" tree is still in place. Given that compilation time is not a critical factor, the use of a single partition is recommended. For backward compatibility, 2.3(1) ships with 12+2 partitions by default.

Common Problems and Resolutions

This section examines some of common confusions and questions asked regarding FWSM.

1. Can I run the FWSM, Intrusion Detection System Module-2 (IDSM-2), and VPN Service Module (VPNSM) in the same chassis?

   Answer: Yes, you can run all of these modules in the same chassis if the switch is running in Native IOS mode with versions 12.2(14)SY (Sup2) or 12.2(17a)SX10 (Sup720). There is no version available in hybrid mode to support all the modules in the same chassis.

2. Why am I unable to ping my FWSM on a directly connected interface?

   Answer: By default, each interface denies Internet Control Message Protocol (ICMP) on FWSM. Use the **icmp** command to allow ping to the interface. This behavior differs from that of the PIX firewall, where ping is allowed by default.

3. I can ping the FWSM interface that is directly connected to my network, but I am unable to ping other interfaces. Is this normal?

   Answer: Yes, this is designed as a built-in security mechanism that also exists on the PIX firewall.

4. Can I configure failover between two FWSMs running different versions of code?

   Answer: No. Failover requires that both FWSMs run the same version of code. A mechanism within the failover feature verifies the peer version and prevents failover if the versions of code are different. For this reason, you must upgrade both FWSMs at the same time.

5. Where can I find information on the error messages I am seeing on my FWSM?

   Answer: The Error Message Decoder can be found at the following location (only available for the registered customers):

   http://www.cisco.com/pcgi-bin/Support/Errordecoder/index.cgi

   Product documentation on system messages also contains useful information, which can be found in the following location: http://www.cisco.com/univercd/cc/td/doc/product/lan/cat6000/cfgnotes/fwsm/fwmsgs.htm

6. Where can I find information on existing bugs for my FWSM?

   Answer: Details on existing bugs can be found in the Bug Toolkit, which is in the following location (only available for the registered user):

   http://www.cisco.com/pcgi-bin/Support/Bugtool/launch_bugtool.pl

7. Does the FWSM support the IOS Open Shortest Path First (OSPF) auto-cost reference-bandwidth command?

   Answer: No. The FWSM is not aware of the physical ports connected to it. OSPF cost must be configured manually per interface using the **ospf cost** command.

8 What routing protocols are supported by the FWSM?

Answer: Open Shortest Path First (OSPF) and Routing Information Protocol (RIP) are the supported routing protocols.

9 Can I terminate VPN connections on my FWSM?

Answer: VPN functionality is not supported on the FWSM. Termination of VPN connections is the responsibility of the switch and/or VPN Services Module. The 3DES license is provided for management purposes only, such as connecting to a low-security interface via Telnet, Secure Shell (SSH), and Secure HTTP (HTTPS).

10 Are fragmented packets dropped by the FWSM?

Answer: This depends on the FWSM version. If you are running FWSM 1.1, fragmented packets can not traverse the FWSM by default. You can use the **fragment** command as shown in the following link to configure this feature:

http://www.cisco.com/en/US/products/sw/secursw/ps2120/products_command_reference_chapter09186a00801727a8.html#wp1029667

However, if you are running FWSM 2.2 and above, fragmented packets are allowed by default on the FWSM as in PIX Firewall (200).

11 How are the Access Control Lists compiled on the FWSM?

Answer: ACL is created and compiled on the PC complex. The maximum node that can be compiled and downloaded is 128K. It is important to note that this is the number of nodes, not the number of ACL or the number of Access Control Entries (ACEs) for a single ACL. ACL is compiled in the PC complex, and once compilation is completed successfully, it is downloaded to the NP slow processors as binary and in tree format, so that matching against the tree can be performed efficiently. If the compilation fails, it will not be downloaded to the slow NP processor; however, this will not affect the traffic flowing through the FWSM, as there are two tables maintained for old and new compiled trees in the slow NP processor. The slow NP has 20 MB for storing the tree of nodes created by the ACL compilation in the Control Plane (CP).

Best Practices

Following are some important considerations to consider while deploying FWSM:

- Do not configure multiple SVI interfaces unless absolutely necessary.
- Configure Active/Standby on two different chassis to avoid the single point of failure. If both Active and Standby units are in the same chassis, and if the switch fails, then both FWSMs fail.

- As the ACL is compiled on Control Plane and downloaded to Slow Network Processor, if you have large ACL, be sure to compile it manually to avoid CPU spikes during busy hours. The default option is Automatic compilation, and if you make a single line change in the ACL, the compilation will occur for every change. Hence, make the changes at once, and load the ACL on the FWSM. After that compile the access-list.
- Configure Port Fast for the convergence of the Spanning Tree Protocol change if the STP is configured (this is on by default on all Cisco Switches).
- Do not configure syslog to debug level unless you are troubleshooting an issue, as this may cause performance issues on the FWSM. This is because Control Plane has to process all the syslog activities and retrieve the syslog information from different Network Processors (NP).

CHAPTER 5

Troubleshooting an IOS Firewall

In addition to its primary role of routing, a router can provide security to the perimeter of the network. And depending on how you deploy it, a router can provide security to an intranet between different departments, or to an extranet between partners.

Routers provide several security services, which are commonly known as the IOS firewall feature set. The most important component of the IOS Firewall feature set is the Advanced Firewall Engine called Context-Based Access Control (CBAC), which turns a router into an effective enterprise-class firewall (FW). So, the primary focus of this chapter is CBAC, and how it interoperates with other security features such as auth-proxy, Network Address Translation (NAT), Port to Application Mapping (PAM), and so on. Cisco IOS Intrusion Prevention System (IPS), another important security feature of Cisco IOS firewall feature set that works in conjunction with CBAC, is discussed in greater detail in Chapter 16, "Troubleshooting Cisco IDS Network Module (NM-CIDS)," and is therefore not discussed here. The Case Study section looks into a rarely used IOS firewall feature called auth-proxy, which can work in conjunction with CBAC to provide user authentication of the traffic going through the firewall (the user-based firewall feature). This chapter covers all aspects of troubleshooting tools and techniques that are required to troubleshoot any issues pertaining to CBAC, followed by the Common Problems and Resolutions. The chapter concludes with best practices for implementing CBAC.

Overview of IOS Firewall (CBAC)

Because you can filter traffic using an access control list (ACL) on the router, you may wonder why CBAC is necessary. What shortcoming is CBAC addressing for the traditional ACL? That deserves an answer before we proceed any further with the CBAC discussion.

ACL has many limitations that keep it from being an effective firewall mechanism. The most important limitation is that ACL is a packet filtering mechanism based on Open System Interconnection (OSI) network and transport layer information. On the other hand, CBAC is a stateful firewall just like Private Internet Exchange (PIX), which filters traffic based on state information rather than just on network or transport layer information.

For example, assume there is an inside and outside network with a dotted line as the perimeter, and there is a firewall router with an Ethernet 0 interface going to the protected network (inside) and an interface Serial 0 going to the unprotected network (Internet) as shown in Figure 5-1.

Figure 5-1 *Limitation of Static ACL*

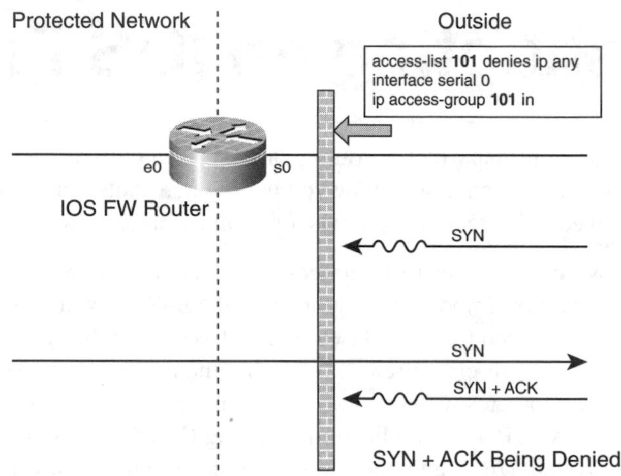

For the router to protect the inside network, two conditions must be met:

- Allow connections to initiate from the protected (inside) network.
- Deny connections initiated from the Internet (unsafe) network from entering the inside network.

To fulfill the second requirement, configure an ACL 101 on the serial 0 interface that denies all traffic from outside. This effectively sets up a wall to block outside traffic. Then, take a look at the first requirement, that is, to allow traffic from the protected network to the Internet. As shown in Figure 5-2, when Telnet is initiated from the inside to the outside, being a Transmission Control Protocol (TCP), the synchronize (SYN) packet from the inside makes it to the outside. This is because there is no access list applied in this example on the inside interface towards the direction of the initial packet. It is a good security practice, however, to configure ACL on the inside interface facing towards the protected network to stop anti-spoofing. You should, however, watch carefully that the reply SYN-ACK packet from outside is blocked by the ACL that you have applied on the serial 0 interface and the connection fails to set up. The result will be the same for the User Datagram Protocol (UDP) reply packet. So, as you can see with the static ACL, if this connection needs to be successful, you need to create an Access Control Entry (ACE) entry on ACL 101 that is applied earlier on the serial 0 interface with a source port 23 and destination port greater than 1023. Doing so opens up several holes to your network, because anyone from outside can also initiate connections using those ports). This is where CBAC plays an important role.

How can CBAC solve this problem? To turn on CBAC, create and apply a simple CBAC rule: inspect only TCP traffic for this example. This rule is turned on for the Ethernet 0 interface towards the direction of SYN packet (inspection must always be applied in the direction of the traffic initiation) as shown in Figure 5-2.

Figure 5-2 *An Example of CBAC Implementation for Telnet*

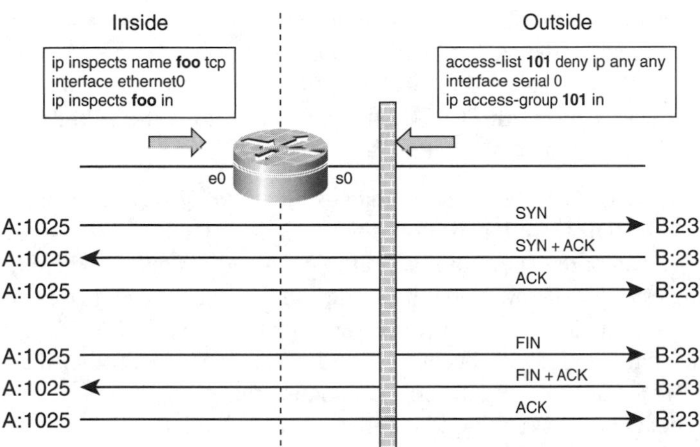

As before, if the Telnet connection is initiated from inside the host to outside, once the SYN packet goes through the router after ACL checking (in this example there is no ACL configured in the traffic initiation direction), the CBAC inspects it. The CBAC inspects it because the initiation packet is moving in the same direction in which the inspection rule is applied (on the Ethernet 0 interface as inbound). CBAC performs the following functions:

- It extracts transport layer information such as source and destination address and port from the packet.
- It determines the input and output interfaces.
- It adds a dynamic entry in the ACLs (after swapping the addresses) for return traffic to *allow* traffic back for this connection.

This, in effect, creates a tiny hole in the ACL, which is specific to this connection only. As a result, the reply SYN-ACK packet makes it through this hole and reaches the inside end host. The inside end host then replies with the final ACK, and the connection is established. As a result, the first requirement is also met (remember, the first requirement is to allow connections to initiate from the protected network). Once the connection is established, CBAC examines traffic in both directions for this particular connection. CBAC recognizes when the end hosts close connection using FIN (Finish) Exchange or RST (Reset), and the CBAC removes the dynamic ACL entries accordingly. So CBAC not only resolves the issue of creating ACL statically, it also opens up a very specific hole in the ACL that is required, and closes it when finished.

So far we have seen how CBAC helps with single-channel protocol by creating a dynamic ACL. With static ACL, to accomplish this result, leave the outside interface ACL wide open and thereby permit everything. Permitting everything, of course, defeats the purpose of configuring the ACL on the router in the first place. To address this security issue, you may be able to configure the *established* keyword on the ACL applied on the serial 0 interface. The *established* keyword filters TCP packets based on whether the ACK or RST bits are set. The setting of ACK or RST bits indicates that the packet is not the first in the session, and therefore, that the packet belongs to an established session. Although this effectively blocks the SYN packet (that is, packet initiation from outside to inside is blocked) for TCP traffic, it works only with TCP and filters based on only the TCP flag, and is therefore vulnerable to a spoof attack.

Reflexive ACL is a better solution than using an *established* keyword in static ACL, as it works with UDP as well, and creates the dynamic ACL based on source and destination IP addresses and ports. Therefore the traffic is filtered not only by the flag, as in static ACL with the *established* option, but by source and destination addresses and ports in addition to flags. The biggest drawback, however, with Reflexive ACL is that it does not work with a multi-channel protocol, because the additional channels (other than the first control channel) are built up using the port negotiation that occurs when using the control channel, and Reflexive ACL is unable to learn about this negotiation. Therefore, Reflexive ACL is unable to create dynamic ACE in the ACL for the data channel in the case of a multi-channel protocol. This failure is one of the serious shortcomings of Reflexive ACL. The following section examines how CBAC is better able to handle this multi-channel issue.

To understand how CBAC addresses the shortcoming of Reflexive ACL with multi-channel protocol, examine how CBAC works with multi-channel protocols such as File Transfer Protocol (FTP), H323, Session Initiation Protocol (SIP), and so on. As the name implies, multi-channel typically creates more than one connection for transferring data. Typically, the first connection acts as a control connection. The address and port information for the secondary connections (also known as data connection) are dynamically negotiated by end hosts over this control connection. To illustrate this, study an example of a two-channel protocol, Active FTP with CBAC as shown in Figure 5-3.

Just as before, the ACL 101 is on the outside interface (serial 0), and CBAC is configured on the inside interface (Ethernet 0). An inside host initiates the connection for the control channel by sending a SYN, and CBAC creates a dynamic hole for the return traffic, which allows the reply SYN-ACK packet through the hole. After the client sends the ACK, the connection completes as before.

Now, the inside host negotiates the address and port information for the second channel (data channel) by sending the PORT A: 5560 command. This means that the inside host listens on the source address A and on source port 5560. Hence, the FTP server should try to connect to the client to create the data channel. Note that the FTP client can use the **port** command to offer an address other than A to create a data connection from the FTP server, which is on the outside.

Figure 5-3 *An Example of CBAC Implementation for FTP*

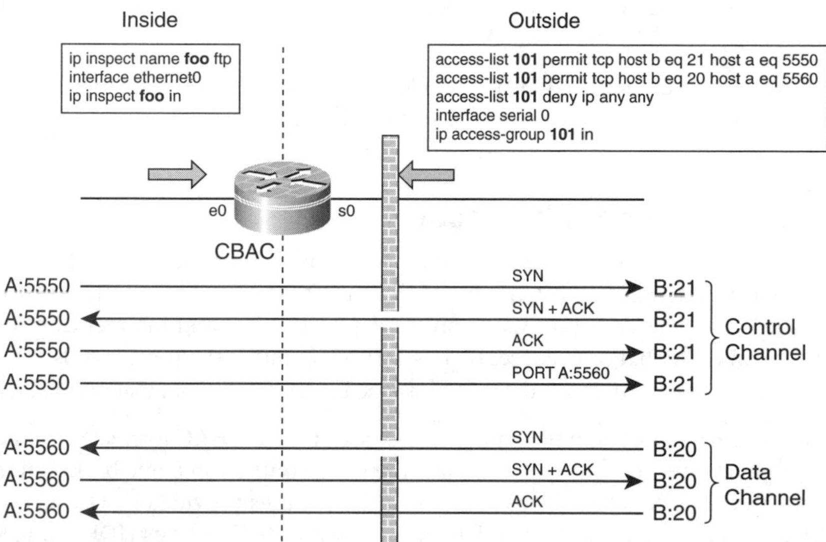

Even though the data channel is initiated from the FTP server sitting on the outside, the CBAC should allow this connection. Otherwise FTP application functionality will fail. CBAC does this by extracting the PORT A:5560 data from the packet (note that this information lies in the packet's Layer 7 payload and not in the Layer 4 header). After extracting this information, CBAC creates another dynamic ACL entry. The destination address/port in the ACL entry are set to A:5560, whereas the source address/port are set to "any" because CBAC does not know what address/port the outside host will use to initiate the data connection.

This creates another hole in the ACL, which is sometimes known as a wide hole because the src address/port are set to "any". When the outside host actually sends the SYN packet to initiate the connection, CBAC extracts the src information from this packet as B:20. It then uses this information to update the second dynamic ACL and changes the src address/port info from "any" to B:20, thus narrowing the hole to match only this connection. Now the rest of the three-way handshake completes successfully, and the second connection also succeeds. The first connection from A:5550 to B:21 is known as the control connection, and the second connection from B:20 to A:5560 is known as the data connection. Without CBAC, if you configure reflexive or static ACL, you must permit everything from outside to inside for the data connection. In summary, CBAC understands more than Layer 3 and Layer 4 of the OSI model; CBAC understands up to Layer 7. And because of its intelligence of application, CBAC can dynamically open and close the ports needed by the applications using dynamic ACLs.

The discussion in the preceding paragraph focuses primarily on how CBAC handles Active FTP connection, where data connection is initiated by the FTP server sitting on the outside. In passive FTP mode, both the control and data connections are initiated from inside to outside if the FTP clients are located on the inside. More details on Active and Passive FTP can be found in the following location: http://www.cisco.com/en/US/about/ac123/ac147/ac174/ac199/about_cisco_ipj_archive_article09186a00800c85a7.html

Details on how CBAC handles Passive FTP can be found in the following location: http://www.cisco.com/en/US/products/sw/secursw/ps1018/products_qanda_item09186a008009464d.shtml#qa5

Being a stateful firewall, CBAC provides several security services to your network. The most important are discussed in the sections that follow.

Single Channel Protocol Inspection

As discussed in the preceding section, for single channel protocols (Telnet, Hypertext Transfer Protocol [HTTP], Simple Mail Transfer Protocol [SMTP], etc.) you need to inspect only the Transport Layer protocol—TCP, UDP, and Internet Control Message Protocol (ICMP). For instance, to pass TELNET traffic, the router needs to perform just TCP inspection. There is no need to inspect Telnet, and in fact that option is not available.

As we learned earlier based on Figure 5-2, we can use CBAC to create a session and based on that, create a dynamic ACL, so that the return traffic can come back. Before you go though the discussion of some of the security features provided by CBAC for the single channel TCP protocol, it is worth reviewing how CBAC handles UDP and ICMP protocol. In the preceding section, we have seen how CBAC handles TCP-based protocol both for single- and multi-channel protocol. The following discussion focuses on how CBAC handles UDP and ICMP protocols.

UDP and CBAC

Unlike TCP, UDP is a connectionless protocol. Hence, CBAC's generic UDP inspection cannot detect when a client connection request is satisfied. Therefore, generic UDP inspection simply creates a channel when it recognizes the first request packet from the client, and keeps that channel open until no traffic has been detected between the client and the server for a set time. This approximates session maintenance. To turn on UDP inspection, use the **ip inspect myfw UDP** command in the global configuration mode (myfw is the name of the inspection rule). Although approximation of UDP connections works most of the time, it may fail in one of the two following ways:

- It can keep the channel open for too long, which may use the router's memory unnecessarily.
- It may close the channel too soon. If the client and server do not communicate for a long time, and UDP timeout value elapses, CBAC closes the channel, even though the application may not be finished with the conversation.

ICMP and CBAC

Stateful inspection of ICMP protocol was introduced in version 12.2(11)YU, and integrated in IOS version 12.2(15)T. Before this version, to allow the ping, you had to allow the

ECHO for the ping request traffic and ECHO-REPLY for ping reply traffic. With the introduction of stateful inspection in the ICMP protocol, static ACL does not have to be created for the ICMP Packet Types shown in Table 5-1.

Table 5-1 *ICMP Packet Types Supported by CBAC*

ICMP Packet Types	Name	Description
0	Echo Reply	Reply to Echo Request (Type 8)
3	Destination Unreachable	Possible reply to any request
8	Echo Request	Ping or traceroute request
11	Time Exceeded	Reply to any request if the time to live (TTL) packet is 0
13	Timestamp Request	Request
14	Timestamp Reply	Reply to Timestamp Request (type 13)

A more detailed description of stateful inspection of ICMP protocol can be found at: http://www.cisco.com/en/US/products/sw/iosswrel/ps5012/products_feature_guide09186a0080146558.html

Application Layer Protocol (TCP-based) and CBAC

Because CBAC can parse commands for some TCP-based application layer protocols, and has intelligence built in concerning these protocols, it can provide the security features outlined in the sections that follow.

Preventing from Invalid Command Execution

As mentioned previously, CBAC can parse commands of some TCP-based application layer protocols. SMTP and Extended Simple Mail Transfer Protocol (ESMTP) fall into this category. Although it is sufficient to inspect TCP for SMTP/ESMTP connections, you must inspect SMTP/ESMTP to ensure protocol conformation as per Request For Comment (RFC) through the CBAC router. To block the illegal commands execution by users using SMTP/ESMTP, you need to inspect SMTP/EMTP using the following commands:

```
ip inspect myfw smtp
ip inspect myfw esmtp
```

For SMTP inspection, CBAC effectively checks for command violation based on RFC 821 and issues alerts when it detects an SMTP attack (there is more on alerts in a later section). The RFC 821 commands allowed are **HELO MAIL**, **RCPT**, **DATA**, **RSET**, **NOOP**, and **QUIT** by CBAC when SMTP is inspected.

For ESMTP inspection, CBAC inspects the commands defined in RFC 1869, which are AUTH, DATA, EHLO, ETRN, HELO, HELP, MAIL, NOOP, QUIT, RCPT, RSET, SAML,

SEND, SOML and VRFY. All others are considered illegal, and when CBAC encounters others it generates alerts.

The CBAC router detects a limited number of SMTP attack signatures. A signature in a SYSLOG message indicates a possible attack against the protected network, such as the detection of illegal SMTP commands in a packet. Whenever a signature is detected, the connection is reset.

There are 11 "IDS Sensor" attack signatures. Five have always been integrated into the Cisco IOS Firewall SMTP implementation, which is shown in Table 5-2.

Table 5-2 *Signatures Available in CBAC*

Signature	Description
Mail: bad rcpt	Triggers on any mail message with a "pipe" (|) symbol in the recipient field.
Mail: bad from	Triggers on any mail message with a "pipe" (|) symbol in the "From:" field.
Mail: old attack	Triggers when "wiz" or "debug" commands are sent to the SMTP port.
Mail: decode	Triggers on any mail message with a ": decode@" in the header.
Majordomo	A bug in the Majordomo program allows remote users to execute arbitrary commands at the privilege level of the server.

Protection from Malicious Java Applets

With the rapid increase of Java applets on the Internet, protecting networks from malicious Java applets has become a major concern for every network administrator. Java blocking can be configured to intelligently filter or completely deny access to Java applets that are not embedded in archives or compressed files. If Java applets are embedded in archives or compressed files, they are not inspected by CBAC. When Java blocking is enabled on an interface, the firewall monitors contents of HTTP packets from HTTP servers, and when a Java applet is identified in the connection, the firewall immediately resets the connection to block that Java applet, preventing it from crossing the firewall.

While configuring CBAC, as soon as you turn on HTTP inspection (as shown in the commands that follow), it blocks the Java applet by default.

```
ip inspect name <rule> http [java-list <num>] [audit <on|off>] [alert <on|off>]
  [timeout <sec>]
access-list <num> <deny | permit> <src-addr> <src-wildcard>
```

Some of the important points to note here are:

- Inspecting TCP traffic is sufficient for HTTP unless Java applet blocking is needed. If Java applet is required, then you must inspect HTTP.
- If you trust some sites with Java applets and want to allow applets to be downloaded to the users' stations from these trusted sites, you need to configure a standard ACL (not an extended ACL) to permit these sites. Then apply the ACL to HTTP inspection with the Java-list option to trigger this. For instance, if you trust Java applets from server 20.1.1.1, then you need to configure CBAC as shown in Example 5-1.

Example 5-1 *Sample of Allowing Java Applet from only Site 20.1.1.1*

```
Router(config)#access-list 10 permit host 20.1.1.1
Router(config)#ip inspect myfw java-list 10
```

- If Java-list is not configured, java blocking is ON by default.

URL Filtering

In addition to Java applet filtering, IOS Firewall can also be configured to filter the web traffic based on other criteria such as address, userid, group, and so on to websites on the internet. This feature is called URL Filtering or Destination URL Policy Management and is introduced in versions 12.2(11) YU and 12.2(15) T and above.

Now look at the details of how URL filtering works with CBAC. The following sequence of events occurs when a CBAC router is configured with URL filtering as shown in Figure 5-4:

Step 1 The CBAC router configured with URL filtering receives an HTTP request from a user wanting to go to a specific website.

Step 2 The router simultaneously forwards the request to the destination websites and a query to the URL filter server. The query contains the requested URL destination Domain Name System (DNS) or Internet Protocol (IP) address.

Step 3 The server replies with a permit or denial of access to the router that is based on the policy setup on the server.

Step 4 The router either allows or denies (when it denies, the URL server redirects the users to information that indicates which category the user is denied) based on the response from the URL server.

Figure 5-4 *Limiting a Static ACL*

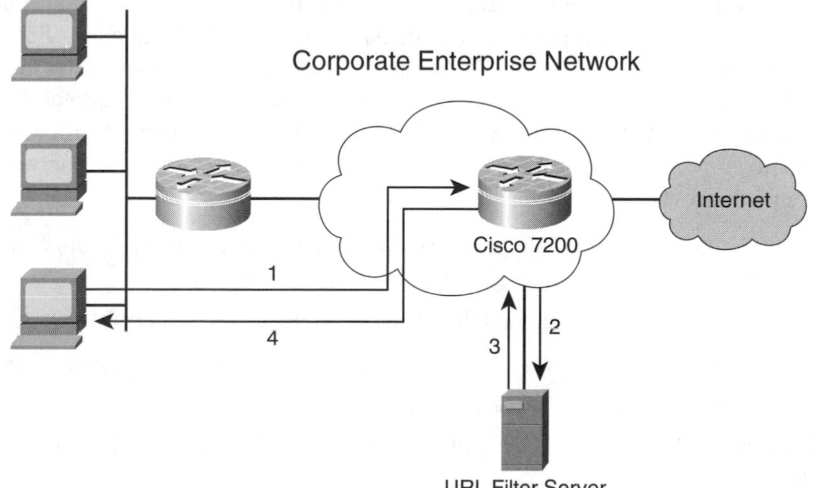

Step 2 needs little more elaboration. Before the router queries the server (if configured) it goes through two local tables on the router that contain the URLs of the destination web servers. Based on the tables, either all users are always permitted or always denied. If no entries or matches are found, the router checks its local cache to determine if the request has been made at an earlier time. If so, it studies the results. To improve the performance, this caching is enabled by default, and does not need to be explicitly configured. By default, the cache table can hold 5000 IP addresses. This can be modified with the following command:

```
ip urlfilter cache size
```

Caching enriches the URL filtering by minimizing the number of URL query requests that are sent to the filter server. It is interesting to note that the filter server makes decisions about caching an IP address. When the filter server receives a query request from Cisco IOS Software, it checks whether the request needs to be cached. If it does, the filter server sets a bit map in the response, which indicates that the IP address needs to be cached.

The URL server is a large detailed knowledge base of the Internet and has categorized many URLs into one of the more 80 categories including gaming, pornography, MP3s, freeware, shareware, and so on. You can define the policy based on one of the following categories:

- Allowable URL categories
- Users and groups that can access the content
- Timeframes in which access to content is allowed
- Additional content restrictions (that is, content is permitted by a time-based quota, with a warning message)
- Indication of whether the filtering is enforced or content is just monitored and stored in a database

Any degradation of network traffic performance due to URL filtering is not noticed by the user. For performance reasons, the GET request is forwarded to the desired URL destination if nothing triggers the local mechanisms, and to the URL server simultaneously. If the router has not received permission or denial by the time the destination URL replies with a web page, the router does not forward it, but instead holds it in its buffer until the reply comes from the URL server. If the URL server permits, the router allows the connection and maintains that URL in the cache. If the URL server denies, the router drops the connection, redirects the users, and gives them the reason the connection was denied. This cache improves the performance dramatically.

- Cisco IOS Firewall supports two URL filtering application vendors: Websense www.websense.com, and N2H2 www.n2h2.com.

The commands for turning on URL filtering on the CBAC router follow:

```
[no] ip urlfilter server vendor websense/n2h2 <IP address> [port <num>] [timeout
<secs>] [retrans <num>]
[no] ip urlfilter exclv-domain <domain>
```

Example 5-2 shows an example of how to turn on URL filtering. The url-cache is by default 5000.

Example 5-2 *Turning on URL Filtering*

```
router(config)# ip inspect name firewall http urlfilter
router(config)# interface e1
router(config-int)# ip inspect firewall in
```

NOTE A more detailed discussion on URL filtering is beyond the scope of this chapter. For more details, refer to the following URLs:

http://www.cisco.com/univercd/cc/td/doc/product/software/ios122/122newft/122limit/122y/122yu11/ftwebsen.htm

http://www.cisco.com/univercd/cc/td/doc/product/software/ios122/122newft/122limit/122y/122yu11/ft_n2h2.htm

One final and important point on IP URL filtering: User-based restriction is not possible with N2H2. However, it is possible with Websense because Websense has a mechanism for getting the username to correspond to an IP address. In addition to recognizing the users based on IP, Websense also can redirect the users for authentication before permitting the access to the website.

This concludes the discussion on security services that are provided by the CBAC for the single channel protocols. In the following sections, you will learn some of the security features that are applicable for both single- and multi-channel protocols. But before that, it is important to re-visit the discussion of multi-channel protocols.

Multi-Channel Protocol Inspection

Unlike the single-channel protocols discussed earlier, multi-channel protocols require you to configure for inspection on the application layer protocol. For example, if you inspect only TCP for FTP connection, the control channel becomes built up, because FTP is a TCP protocol. However, the data channel may not become built up because it depends on the port negotiation using the control channel, and if only TCP is inspected, CBAC does not watch the payload of the packet to gain knowledge of this port negotiation.

Hence, the TCP engine will not have any knowledge about the port and IP address information negotiated and agreed upon by the FTP client and server to build up the data channel. Consequently, CBAC does not open any hole on the ACL. So, if the data connection is initiated from outside, it will be dropped. Therefore, to inspect the payload and get all the necessary information for the data channel, you need to inspect the application layer protocol, which is in this case **ip inspect name myfw FTP**. Note that application inspection takes precedence over Layer 4 protocol inspection. In the example, because you inspect FTP protocol, you do not need inspection for TCP protocol. However if you inspect both TCP and FTP, only the FTP inspection engine is used, not TCP.

The section that follows discusses some of the important security services available for both single- and multi-channel protocols.

NAT/PAT and CBAC

CBAC interoperates with both static and dynamic NAT (source and destination). Static and Dynamic NAT with CBAC turns Cisco IOS Router into a very powerful enterprise class firewall. Here are a couple of the benefits NAT adds to CBAC:

- Hides your internal addresses from the outside world.
- Helps stop spontaneous attacks from the Internet because no traffic is allowed (static translation is an exception). Dynamic NAT allocates addresses only for nodes that have actually sent traffic through the router.

Port Application Mapping (PAM) and CBAC

Port Application Mapping (PAM) allows you to change the standard application port on the router. This is important for hiding well-known port numbers for different applications such as TCP/80 for the HTTP protocol. By default, PAM generates a table of information that identifies specific applications with specific TCP or UDP port information. The PAM table initially is populated with system-defined mapping information, when the firewall router first starts. Example 5-3 shows the output of the default port to application. CBAC works well with this standard port and creates session information based on this.

Example 5-3 *Output of System Defined Port CBAC Works With*

```
Router#show ip port-map
Default mapping: dns                port 53                   system defined
Default mapping: vdolive            port 7000                 system defined
Default mapping: sunrpc             port 111                  system defined
Default mapping: netshow            port 1755                 system defined
Default mapping: cuseeme            port 7648                 system defined
Default mapping: tftp               port 69                   system defined
Default mapping: rtsp               port 8554                 system defined
Default mapping: realmedia          port 7070                 system defined
Default mapping: streamworks        port 1558                 system defined
Default mapping: ftp                port 21                   system defined
Default mapping: telnet             port 23                   system defined
Default mapping: rtsp               port 554                  system defined
Default mapping: h323               port 1720                 system defined
Default mapping: sip                port 5060                 system defined
Default mapping: smtp               port 25                   system defined
Default mapping: http               port 80                   system defined
Default mapping: msrpc              port 135                  system defined
Default mapping: exec               port 512                  system defined
Default mapping: login              port 513                  system defined
Default mapping: sql-net            port 1521                 system defined
Default mapping: shell              port 514                  system defined
Default mapping: mgcp               port 2427                 system defined
```

However, you may change the default port for an application to something different. For example if you want to change the Telnet port from 23 to 1025, you need to use the following command:

```
ip port-map telnet port 1025
```

Without PAM, the firewall is limited to inspecting traffic using only the well-known or registered ports associated with an application. PAM enables you to customize network access control for specific applications and services.

PAM supports host- or subnet-specific port mapping, which allows PAM to be applied to a single host or subnet using ACL. Host- or subnet-specific port mapping is done using standard ACLs. Example 5-4 shows how to change the default port for FTP.

Example 5-4 *Sample Configuration Required to Change the Port*

```
! Following command shows the default port used for telnet
Router#show ip port-map ftp
Default mapping: ftp            port 21                  system defined

Router#configure terminal
Enter configuration commands, one per line.  End with CNTL/Z.
! Following access-list will be used to use a different FTP port for host IP address
  20.1.1.1
Router(config)#access-list 10 permit host 20.1.1.1
! Following command configure port 1022 for FTP connection based on ACL just created.
Router(config)#ip port-map ftp port 1022 list 10
Router(config)#end
! Following command verifies the FTP port just defined for the access-list 10
Router#show ip port-map ftp
Host specific:   ftp                port 1022   in list 10   user defined
Default mapping: ftp                port 21                  system defined

Router#
```

Note that with PAM, if you need to define multiple ports for an application, you need to define them with multiple commands.

Denial of Service (DoS) Detection And Prevention

DoS attack may be launched against a network in many different ways. Some of the most common DoS attacks that can be mitigated by CBAC are discussed in the sections that follow.

TCP Syn Flood and DoS Attack Launched by UDP

For a normal TCP connection to be considered established, TCP three-way handshakes must be completed (SYN, SYN-ACK, and ACK). For UDP, you need both REQUEST and REPLY packets to establish the connection. While waiting for the ACK to the SYN ACK, a connection queue of finite size on the destination host keeps track of connections waiting to be completed. The TCP SYN attack exploits this design by having an attacking source host generate TCP SYN packets with random source addresses toward a victim host. The victim destination host sends a SYN ACK back to the random source address and adds an entry to the connection queue. Because the SYN ACK is destined for an incorrect or non-existent host, the last part of the "three-way handshake" is never completed, and the entry remains in the connection queue until a timer expires. By generating invalid TCP SYN packets from random IP addresses at a rapid rate, it is possible to fill up the connection queue and deny TCP services (such as e-mail, file transfer, or WWW) to legitimate users. This affects the router's performance, which can result in the slowness of legitimate traffic and sometimes packet drops due to shortage of memory and high CPU utilization. It is not very easy to mitigate these types of attack. However, CBAC has a couple mechanisms to deal with these types of attacks:

- **Timeout values**—CBAC has different timeout values to clear up the unnecessary sessions that use up a lot of memory and buffer. To choose timeout values carefully, you must baseline your network under normal conditions. Selecting appropriate timeouts can help to mitigate the stress on the router and on the victim hosts from DoS attacks. Here are the timeout values available on the CBAC router:

```
ip inspect tcp idle-time seconds
ip inspect udp idle-time seconds
ip inspect dns-timeout seconds
ip inspect tcp synwait-time seconds
ip inspect tcp finwait-time seconds
```

- **Threshold Values**—Along with selecting appropriate timeouts, CBAC has the following options to define threshold values to mitigate the DOS attack.

```
ip inspect max-incomplete high number
ip inspect max-incomplete low number
ip inspect one-minute high number
ip inspect one-minute low number
ip inspect tcp max-incomplete host number block-time minutes
```

  The first and second lines define the max incomplete high and max incomplete low thresholds. If the high threshold is crossed, the oldest half of the open session is deleted to make way for each new coming session, until half of the open count falls under the low threshold. The third and fourth lines define the high and low threshold per minute. This means that when the half-open connection reaches the high mark, the router goes into aggressive mode, sends alerts to syslog, and starts deleting the oldest half-open connection until it reaches to the low mark. Max-incomplete and one-minute apply to both TCP and UDP half-open sessions. A one-minute value is calculated by taking a reading every 15 seconds (4 times a minute) of the connection attempts to the router. The fifth line, TCP max-incomplete, works on a per host basis and is restricted only to TCP traffic. This means that the fifth line does not count UDP traffic. TCP max-incomplete replaces sessions if block-time is not specified or zero. If a value is specified, CBAC deletes all sessions and blocks the connection for the specified amount of time.

Example 5-5 shows that the CBAC router has detected a DoS attack, going to aggressive mode, and then calming down:

Example 5-5 *Sample Alert Output of a DoS Attack*

```
%FW-4-ALERT_ON: getting aggressive, count (550/500) current 1-min rate: 250
%FW-4-ALERT_OFF: calming down, count (0/400) current 1-min rate: 0
```

A combination of %FW-4-ALERT_ON and %FW-4-ALERT_OFF error messages indicates a single attack. Example 5-5 shows a single DoS attack.

Example 5-6 shows that a sample output of a denial-of-service attack has occurred on a specific TCP host:

Example 5-6 *Sample Output of a DoS Attack Against a Single TCP Host*

```
%FW-4-HOST_TCP_ALERT_ON: Max tcp half-open connections (50) exceeded for host
172.21.127.242.
%FW-4-BLOCK_HOST: Blocking new TCP connections to host 172.21.127.242 for 2 minutes
(half-open count 50 exceeded)
%FW-4-UNBLOCK_HOST: New TCP connections to host 172.21.127.242 no longer blocked
```

Fragmentation

Fragmentation of IP packets is handled differently depending on the version of the IOS you are running on the router. The following discusses two options available on an IOS Firewall for handling fragmented packets:

- **Without Virtual Reassembly Option**—Before version 12.3(8) T, this Virtual Reassembly of fragmented packets was not available. The router maintains a table of fragmented IP packets. It protects aggressively by dropping secondary fragments unless the first fragment is seen. It also drops fragments that make total IP length greater than 65535. If there are fewer than 32 entries free in the table, configured timeout value is internally halved, and if there are fewer than 16 entries free in the table, timeout is set to 1 second. Fragmented packets are *not* inspected for L4 and L7 inspection.
- **With Virtual Reassembly Option**—As discussed earlier, before version 12.3(8) T, CBAC could not identify the contents of the IP fragments nor could it gather port information from the fragment. These inabilities allowed the fragments to pass through the network without being examined, or without dynamic access control list (ACL) creation. From version 12.3(8) T and above, virtual fragmentation reassembly (VFR) enables the Cisco IOS Firewall to create the appropriate dynamic ACLs, thereby protecting the network from various fragmentation attacks. VFR is on by default when NAT is configured on an interface. Otherwise, you can turn it on/off with the following commands under the interface.

  ```
  ip virtual-reassembly [max-reassemblies number] [max-fragments number]
    [timeout seconds] [drop-fragments]
  ```

  A more detailed discussion of this feature can be found at:

  http://www.cisco.com/en/US/products/sw/iosswrel/ps5207/products_feature_guide09186a00802299fb.html

NOTE Keep in mind that after you apply the CBAC rule in an interface to a specific direction, DoS prevention is on by default only for that interface and for that direction.

Real-Time Alerts and Audit Trails

Alerts identify suspicious activities such as protocol violation, DoS attack, and so on. Alerts is on by default, and the alerts are by default sent to the console. If syslog is configured, alerts can also be sent to a syslog server.

The following commands can be used to turn off the global alert and can be turned on/off per protocol basis.

```
ip inspect alert-off
ip inspect name <rule> protocol [alert <on | off>]
```

Note that alert configuration per protocol configuration gets higher priority than the global alert. Global alert configuration is on by default, so if you want to turn off alert configuration for a specific protocol, you need to execute the second line shown in the previous code sample. Example 5-7 shows the alerts of various protocols:

Example 5-7 *Sample Output of Alerts by Different Protocols*

```
! Sample HTTP (Java Block) alert
%FW-3-HTTP_JAVA_BLOCK: JAVA applet is blocked from (172.21.127.218:80) to
(171.69.57.30:44673)
! Sample FTP alerts
%FW-3-FTP_SESSION_NOT_AUTHENTICATED: Command issued before the session is
authenticated -- FTP client 30.0.0.1
%FW-3-FTP_PRIV_PORT: Privileged port 1000 used in PORT command -- FTP client
30.0.0.1 FTP server 40.0.0.1
%FW-3-FTP_NON_MATCHING_IP_ADDR: Non-matching address 92.92.92.92 used in PASV
response -- FTP client 171.69.63.26 FTP server172.21.127.195
! Connection is reset for all of the above alerts except FW-! 3-
FTP_SESSION_NOT_AUTHENTICATED
! Sample SMTP alerts
%FW-4-TCP_SENDMAIL_BAD_FROM_SIG: Sig:3102:Sendmail Invalid Sender -192.168.1.13 to
192.168.101.14
%FW-4-TCP_SENDMAIL_BAD_TO_SIG: Sig:3101:Sendmail Invalid Recipient -192.168.1.13 to
192.168.101.14
%FW-4-TCP_SENDMAIL_OLD_SIG: Sig:3104:Archaic Sendmail Attacks -192.168.18.215 to
192.168.118.216
%FW-4-TCP_SENDMAIL_DECODE: Sig:3105:Sendmail Decode Alias - 192.168.18.215 to
192.168.118.216
%FW-4-TCP_MAJORDOMO_EXEC_BUG: Sig:3107:Majordomo Execute Attack -192.168.18.215 to
192.168.118.216
%FW-3-SMTP_INVALID_COMMAND: Invalid SMTP command (ABCD\r\n)(total 6 chars) from
initiator (192.168.22.5:32952)
! Connection is reset for all of the above alerts
```

An audit trail is generated every time a session closes (gracefully or by timeout) with the following information:

- Source and destination IP addresses and ports
- Number of bytes exchanged in each direction

Unlike alerts, the audit trail is not on by default. You need to turn it on either in the global configuration or per protocol basis with the following commands.

```
ip inspect audit-trail
ip inspect name <rule> protocol [audit <on | off>]
```

Example 5-8 shows how to turn on syslog on a Cisco router:

Example 5-8 *Sample of How To Turn on Audit-Trail with Syslog on Router*

```
Router(config)#logging on
Router(config)#logging 192.168.1.11
! To enable audit-trail of Firewall messages.
FWRouter(config)#ip inspect audit-trail
```

Just as with alerts, audit configuration per protocol receives higher priority than the global configuration.

Example 5-9 shows a sample output of audit trail:

Example 5-9 *Sample Output of an Audit Trail*

```
%FW-6-SESS_AUDIT_TRAIL: tcp session initiator (192.168.1.13:33192) sent 22 bytes
-- responder (192.168.129.11:25) sent 208 bytes
%FW-6-SESS_AUDIT_TRAIL: http session initiator (172.16.57.30:44673) sent 1599 bytes
-- responder (172.21.127.218:80) sent 93124 bytes
```

Interaction of CBAC with IPsec

Cisco IOS Firewall does not inspect IPsec (Internet Protocol Security) traffic that traverses it. You need to allow AHP, ESP and UDP/500 to allow from unprotected to protected network for the IPsec tunnel to be built up and process data across CBAC. Example 5-10 shows an ACL that allows all the ports/protocols needed to build up IPsec tunnel between 10.1.1.1 and 20.1.1.1 peers:

Example 5-10 *Sample Output Of Configuration To Allow IPSEC*

```
Router(config)#access-list 100 permit ahp host 10.1.1.1 host 20.1.1.1
Router(config)#access-list 100 permit esp host 10.1.1.1 host 20.1.1.1
Router(config)#access-list 100 permit udp host 10.1.1.1 host 20.1.1.1 eq isakmp
```

Although CBAC does not inspect IPsec going through it, it works well with IPsec end devices. So, if you configure CBAC on the peer routers, CBAC inspects the tunneled traffic before encryption and after decryption.

Transparent Cisco IOS Firewall

The transparent firewall works on Layer 2 information, not Layer 3 of the OSI model. From version 12.3(8) T, IOS Firewall is designed to simultaneously interoperate in both Layer 2 and Layer 3 modes.

You can configure a transparent firewall just like the current L3 firewall using the **ip inspect** command. The **inspect in/out** command can be configured on any of the bridged interfaces for Layer 2 protection while also being configured on any LAN or serial interfaces to provide traditional Layer 3 protection. The transparent firewall operates on the bridged packets, and the Layer 3 firewall continues to operate on the routed packets.

To understand the CBAC fully, you must be knowledgeable about all the commands and tools available to troubleshoot the CBAC issues. The section that follows leads you through a discussion of the tools and commands available to troubleshoot CBAC effectively and efficiently.

Diagnostic Commands and Tools

The importance of the **show** and **debug** commands cannot be overemphasized for IOS firewall troubleshooting. Although **show** commands are useful to find the actual status of a connection, **debug** commands provide the details of the connections. Details about the **show** and **debug** commands are discussed in the following sections:

show Commands

The **show** command for CBAC that is available on the Cisco IOS router has the following options:

```
show ip inspect {name inspection-name|config|interfaces|session [detail] | all}
```

The most commonly used command is **show ip inspect session detail,** which shows the status of the session and other meaningful information as shown in Example 5-11:

Example 5-11 *Sample Output Of Show IP Inspect Session Detail*

```
Router# show ip inspect session detail
Established Sessions
! The status SIS_OPEN means the session is established
 Session 817298C4 (10.1.1.2:11005)=>(200.1.1.1:23) tcp SIS_OPEN
   Created 00:00:06, Last heard 00:00:03
   Bytes sent (initiator:responder) [37:83] acl created 1
   Inbound access-list 101 applied to interface FastEthernet0/1
Half-open Sessions
! The status SIS_OPENING means the session is not established. In the case of TCP, three
! -way handshake is not completed. In the case of UDP, the reply packets have not seen by
! the inspection engine.
 Session 81729A34 (10.1.1.2:11006)=>(200.1.1.10:23) tcp SIS_OPENING
   Created 00:00:03, Last heard 00:00:01
   Bytes sent (initiator:responder) [0:0] acl created 1
   Inbound access-list 101 applied to interface FastEthernet0/1
```

The most important information is the connection status. The connection status across CBAC can be in one of the following four states:

- **SIS_OPENING**—This is the state of the session when a SYN has been received but the complete three-way handshake is not over.
- **SIS_OPEN**—This is the state of the session when the intial three-way handshake is over and the session has moved to an established state.

- **SIS_CLOSING**—This is the state of the session when a FIN is received but the entire closing sequence has not been achieved.
- **SIS_CLOSE**—This is is that state of the session when the FIN and FINACKs have been received by both sides and the session is closed.

If you want to view the configuration, you can execute **show ip inspect all** as shown in Example 5-12:

Example 5-12 *Sample Output of* **show ip inspect all**

```
Router# show ip inspect all
Session audit trail is disabled
Session alert is enabled
one-minute (sampling period) thresholds are [400:500] connections
max-incomplete sessions thresholds are [400:500]
max-incomplete tcp connections per host is 50. Block-time 0 minute.
tcp synwait-time is 30 sec -- tcp finwait-time is 5 sec
tcp idle-time is 3600 sec -- udp idle-time is 30 sec
dns-timeout is 5 sec
Inspection Rule Configuration
 Inspection name myfw
    tcp alert is on audit-trail is off timeout 3600

Interface Configuration
 Interface FastEthernet0/0
  Inbound inspection rule is myfw
    tcp alert is on audit-trail is off timeout 3600
  Outgoing inspection rule is not set
  Inbound access list is not set
Outgoing access list is not set
Router#
```

show access-list shows if the access controls element (ACE) is created for the return traffic on the opposite direction of the inspection rule as shown in Example 5-13:

Example 5-13 *Displaying a Dynamic Access-List Created by CBAC*

```
Router# show access-list 101
!ACL 101 before CBAC created dynamic ACE
Extended IP access list 101
    10 deny ip any any (1563 matches)
Router# show access-list 101
Extended IP access list 101
! The following ACE is dynamically created by the CBAC
     permit tcp host 200.1.1.1 eq telnet host 10.1.1.2 eq 11015 (12 matches)
    10 deny ip any any (1571 matches)
Router#
```

debug commands

Before getting into the discussion of any **debug** command, you should understand how the packet flows through the router when CBAC is configured. Figure 5-5 shows the flow chart of the packet flow with CBAC configuration.

Figure 5-5 *Packet Flow Across a Router with CBAC Configuration*

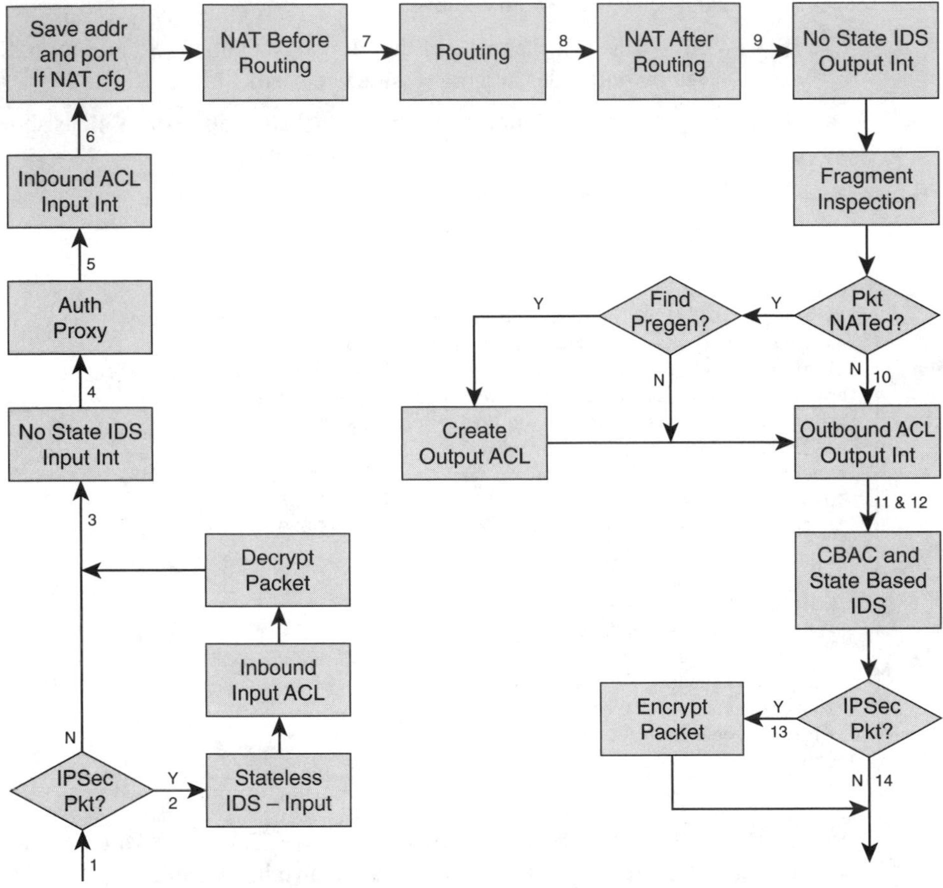

Following is a brief description of the packet flow based on Figure 5-5 when CBAC is configured.

1. The packet comes into the input interface.
2. If it is an IPsec packet, the IPsec packet goes through the IDs checking for atomic signatures in the input interface. The auth-proxy is not called for an IPsec packet, but the inbound ACL of the input interface is applied. IPsec decrypts the packet, and the decrypted packet is put back in the input queue.
3. The decrypted packet goes through the IDS checking for atomic signatures for the input interface.
4. Authentication-proxy starts here.
5. The inbound ACL of the input interface is applied. If it is a decrypted IPsec packet ACL, and you are running version 12.3.8(T) and above, then ACL check will be skipped at this stage. Otherwise, this ACL will be performed.

6 NAT inbound is applied.

7 Routing occurs.

8 NAT outbound is applied.

9 IDS checking for atomic signatures for output interface occurs.

10 Outbound ACL of the output interface is applied.

11 Firewall processing occurs.

12 IDS checking for composite signatures occurs.

13 If IPsec is required, then IPsec encrypts the packet.

14 The packet goes out the output interface.

An important point to note here is that the preceding flow is applied for both inbound and outbound direction on both outside and inside interfaces.

debug commands are used to see the details of the sequence of events that is discussed in the preceding section. The mostly frequently used **debug** commands are:

- **debug ip inspect object-creation**
- **debug ip inspect object deletion**
- **debug ip inspect events**
- **debug ip inspect tcp**
- **debug ip inspect application_protocol**

The first three commands are used in conjunction with either of the last two commands depending on requirements. If Application layer protocol is inspected, then the last command is used; otherwise **debug ip inspect tcp** is used.

Example 5-14 shows a sample output of **debug ip inspect object-creation, debug ip inspect object deletion,** and **debug ip inspect events.** This information is extremely important to see when you have any issues with CBAC.

Example 5-14 *Sample Output of Object Creation And Deletion*

```
Router#debug ip inspect object-creation
Router#debug ip inspect object-creation
Router#debug ip inspect events
! The asterisk means it's getting process switched
*Apr  3 01:53:30.707: CBAC Pak 8161F0B0 sis 81729A34 initiator_addr (10.1.1.2:11
007) responder_addr (200.1.1.1:23)
initiator_alt_addr (10.1.1.2:11007) responder_alt_addr (200.1.1.1:23)
! Session is getting created based on the above layer IV information
*Apr  3 01:53:30.711: CBAC OBJ_CREATE: create sis 81729A34
! Access list of getting created for return traffic
*Apr  3 01:53:30.711: CBAC OBJ_CREATE: create acl wrapper 8172EB80 -- acl item 8
16C8CFC
```

continues

Example 5-14 *Sample Output of Object Creation And Deletion (Continued)*

```
*Apr  3 01:53:30.711: CBAC Src 200.1.1.1 Port [23:23]
*Apr  3 01:53:30.711: CBAC Dst 10.1.1.2 Port [11007:11007]
*Apr  3 01:53:30.711: CBAC OBJ_CREATE: create host entry 817AC174 addr 200.1.1.1
 bucket 201
*Apr  3 01:53:30.847: CBAC OBJ_DELETE: delete host entry 817AC174 addr 200.1.1.1
! Once the connection is done, the following 2 lines will be shown
*Apr  3 01:59:01.907: CBAC OBJ_DELETE: delete sis 81729A34
*Apr  3 01:59:01.907: CBAC OBJ_DELETE: delete create acl wrapper 8172EB80 -- acl
 item 816C8CFC
```

Example 5-15 shows a sample output of **debug ip inspect tcp** for a successful TCP connection.

Example 5-15 *Sample Output of* **debug ip inspect tcp**

```
Router#debug ip inspect tcp
! TCP 3-way handshake is getting done
*Apr  3 02:01:35.742: CBAC sis 81729A34 pak 81455E10 TCP SYN SEQ 1004792293 LEN
0 (10.1.1.2:11008) => (200.1.1.1:23)
*Apr  3 02:01:35.746: CBAC* sis 81729A34 pak 81534BC0 TCP SYN ACK 1004792294 SEQ
 354756859 LEN 0 (200.1.1.1:23) <= (10.1.1.2:11008)
*Apr  3 02:01:35.750: CBAC* sis 81729A34 pak 814E8284 TCP ACK 354756860 SEQ 1004
792294 LEN 0 (10.1.1.2:11008) => (200.1.1.1:23)
*Apr  3 02:01:35.750: CBAC* sis 81729A34 pak 814E8284 TCP PSH ACK 354756860 SEQ
1004792294 LEN 12 (10.1.1.2:11008) => (200.1.1.1:23)
*Apr  3 02:01:35.750: CBAC* sis 81729A34 pak 814E8284 TCP ACK 354756860 SEQ 1004
792306 LEN 0 (10.1.1.2:11008) => (200.1.1.1:23)
*Apr  3 02:01:35.750: CBAC* sis 81729A34 pak 81534BC0 TCP PSH ACK 1004792294 SEQ
 354756860 LEN 12 (200.1.1.1:23) <= (10.1.1.2:11008)
*Apr  3 02:01:35.754: CBAC* sis 81729A34 pak 814E8284 TCP PSH ACK 354756872 SEQ
1004792306 LEN 3 (10.1.1.2:11008) => (200.1.1.1:23)
….
….
!Upon seeing the FIN, connections are getting torn down.
*Apr  3 02:02:00.378: CBAC* sis 81729A34 pak 81534BC0 TCP FIN PSH ACK 1004792337
 SEQ 354756955 LEN 0 (200.1.1.1:23) <= (10.1.1.2:11008)
*Apr  3 02:02:00.382: CBAC* sis 81729A34 pak 814E8284 TCP ACK 354756956 SEQ 1004
792337 LEN 0 (10.1.1.2:11008) => (200.1.1.1:23)
*Apr  3 02:02:00.386: CBAC* sis 81729A34 pak 814E8284 TCP FIN PSH ACK 354756956
SEQ 1004792337 LEN 0 (10.1.1.2:11008) => (200.1.1.1:23)
*Apr  3 02:02:00.390: CBAC* sis 81729A34 pak 81534BC0 TCP ACK 1004792338 SEQ 354
756956 LEN 0 (200.1.1.1:23) <= (10.1.1.2:11008)
Router#
```

If you have NAT configured with CBAC, you can run **debug ip nat** in conjunction with **debug ip packet detail ACL.** The *ACL* can be the name or number that defines the source and destination of the traffic that you want to troubleshoot.

Syslog

The **debug** commands discussed in the preceding section might overwhelm the router if they are sent to the console or monitor. So, it is better to send the commands to the buffer and capture the debug output if syslog server is not available:

- Disable the console and monitor logging for debug messages

```
router(config)# no logging console debugging
```

- Enable buffered logging and increase the buffer size to 1000000

```
router(config)# logging buffered 1000000
router(config)# logging buffered debugging
```

- Enable the required CBAC-related debug as discussed earlier.
- When the problem occurs, collect the debug output in the buffer and examine the output with the following command:

```
router# show logging
```

Packet Capture (Sniffer Traces)

Sometimes you may run into a problem, in which syslog, after running the debug commands, may not give very conclusive results because there may be other network-related issues that may affect the packet flow. Under this rare circumstance, capturing the sniffer traces simultaneously from incoming and outgoing interfaces segments may help in isolating the problem. A very popular and free downloadable sniffer software is Ethereal, www.ethereal.com

Categories of Problem Areas

CBAC problems arise mainly from lack of understanding and misconfiguration. This section discusses the problems you may run into while running CBAC in your network. It shows a step-by-step troubleshooting process for isolating and fixing any problem. The following list outlines the most typical problems in running CBAC:

- Selection of software for IOS firewall issues
- Inability to connect (inbound and outbound) across CBAC
- Performance problems
- Intermittent packet drops
- Non-functioning of IP URL filtering

Selection of Software for IOS Firewall Issues

To turn the router's IOS firewall on, you need a special IOS image that has the firewall feature set, which is a paid feature. Example 5-16 shows the output of the router with the IOS Firewall features.

Example 5-16 shows a Cisco 2600 router with 64 MB of RAM (60416 K + 5120 K), 16 MB of flash memory (16384 K), and a code image called flash: c2600-ik9o3s3-mz.122-15.T5.bin.

Example 5-16 show version *Output from an IOS Firewall Router*

```
Router# show version
Cisco Internetwork Operating System Software
IOS (tm) C2600 Software (C2600-IK9O3S3-M), Version 12.2(15)T5,  RELEASE SOFTWARE
 (fc1)
TAC Support: http://www.cisco.com/tac
Copyright (c) 1986-2003 by Cisco Systems, Inc.
Compiled Thu 12-Jun-03 14:32 by eaarmas
Image text-base: 0x80008098, data-base: 0x81934B78

ROM: System Bootstrap, Version 11.3(2)XA4, RELEASE SOFTWARE (fc1)

2-2-3-2621e uptime is 4 weeks, 18 hours, 39 minutes
System returned to ROM by power-on
System image file is "flash:c2600-ik9o3s3-mz.122-15.T5.bin"

cisco 2621 (MPC860) processor (revision 0x102) with 60416K/5120K bytes of memory
.
Processor board ID JAD04490M1N (972686017)
M860 processor: part number 0, mask 49
Bridging software.
X.25 software, Version 3.0.0.
2 FastEthernet/IEEE 802.3 interface(s)
32K bytes of non-volatile configuration memory.
16384K bytes of processor board System flash (Read/Write)
Configuration register is 0x2102
Router#
```

If for any reason you have changed the name of the IOS code, and **show version** is not giving you the right information, a quick way to find out if you have the IOS Firewall features or not is to execute **ip inspect ?** in the global configuration mode. If you have the IOS Firewall feature set, the output shows the options available; otherwise, you receive a message such as "command not recognized."

It is important to note that if the image name contains the letter "o," you have only the CBAC feature on the IOS image. If the image name contains "o3," you have CBAC, IDS and auth-proxy.

Before upgrading or changing an IOS image on the router to add the firewall feature, be sure the router meets the RAM and flash requirements. The best way to find the version needed for the IOS Firewall is to use the Software Advisor Tool in the following location (registered users only):

http://www.cisco.com/cgi-bin/Support/CompNav/Index.pl

The Software Advisor tool can be used to determine the appropriate Cisco IOS software image to download, based on feature set, release, and platform. When you use the Software

Advisor, search the feature list for "Context-Based Access Control (CBAC)". If you want to upgrade the software from your existing version keeping the same feature sets, you can use the "Compare the feature" option to find the desired version of IOS.

Unable to Connect (Inbound and Outbound) across CBAC

If you are unable to connect to the Internet or from the Internet to the internal network across a CBAC router, you need to first find out if there is any session created (upon seeing the first request packet the inspection engine creates a session). If the session is created, check the state of the session by executing **show ip inspect session** on the router. If there is no session, the packet is not even reaching the inspection engine. Among many, the following are some of the common causes of this problem:

- Packet failure to reach the router's incoming interface
- Misconfigured ACL
- Misconfigured NAT and routing
- IP Inspection not applied or applied in the wrong direction

Packet Failure to Reach the Router's Incoming Interface

If there are routing problems, or problems with Layer 2 between the host and the router, the packet may not reach to the router's incoming interface. Send a ping from the host to the router's incoming interface and see if there is any response. If the host is in the same subnet as the router's incoming interface, and you get the ping response, be sure to set up a default gateway on the host pointing to the router's incoming interface. If there is no ping reply, execute **show arp** on the router and see if the host's arp entry is there. If it is not there, be sure your host is not assigned a duplicate IP address in the network and troubleshoot the problem further on the switch or hub. You may be running into a bad interface, a bad cable, or misconfiguration on the switch.

If the sending host is in a different subnet (multiple hops away), send a ping to the router's incoming interface and see if there is any response. If there is no response, perform a **tracert** from the host and see where the packets are being dropped. Then troubleshoot the routing issue in that specific device. If you get a reply of the ping packets, be sure to open all the necessary ports for the other traffic there are problems with.

Without the ping test, if you want to see quickly if the packets are reaching the router's incoming interface or not, define an ACL with the log keyword to the end of the ACL. This will send the information about the traffic that is allowed or being dropped by the ACL to syslog. If there is no syslog message generated, the packets are not hitting the router at all. Example 5-17 shows the configuration required to see if the Telnet packets from host 10.1.1.10 are hitting the router's interface Ethernet 0 going to 20.1.1.1.

Example 5-17 *Configuration Required Troubleshooting Connectivity Problem*

```
Router(config)#access-list 101 permit tcp host 10.1.1.1 host 20.1.1.1 eq 23 log
Router(config)#access-list 101 permit ip any any
Router(config)#interface ethernet 0
Router(config-if)#ip access-group 101 in
```

Misconfigured ACL

The first packet that the client sends to create a connection must be permitted by both the incoming access list on the interface on which it arrives and the outgoing access list on the interface through which it leaves. CBAC opens channels for the packets only after the conversation initiation packet. If either access list denies the conversation initiation, CBAC does not create a conversation, and therefore won't create the temporary access list entries that permit the return traffic. The packets will be dropped. You can find out if the packet initiation is denied through an ACL with **debug ip packet detail ACL** command. The ACL in this command defines the source and destination addresses and ports of the initiation traffic. The goal is to see if this initiation is being denied because of misconfigured ACL, NAT, or routing problems.

Example 5-18 shows how to use **debug ip packet detail ACL**, to capture the debug output when host 10.1.1.1 is trying to send an initial packet for Telnet to the host 20.1.1.1.

Example 5-18 *Show How To Use the* **debug ip packet detail** *Command*

```
Router(config)# access-list 101 permit tcp host 10.1.1.1 host 20.1.1.1 eq 23
Router# debug ip packet detail 101
Router#
```

Misconfigured NAT and Routing

After you have verified that the packets are reaching to the router's interface and are not being dropped by the ACL, verify if you have configured a destination NAT. If so, verify if the NAT translation is being built up or not by executing **show ip nat translation**. If the proper translation is built up, be sure there is a route for the destination you are trying to reach by executing **show ip route destination_ip/network**. If you do not find a route, define one for the destination network. Note that the initial packet must leave the router before the inspection engine inspects and creates a session with SIS_OPENING. As discussed earlier, **debug ip packet detail ACL** can be used in conjunction with the **show** commands mentioned in this section to determine if the failure of the initial packet is caused either by the NAT or by routing. However, it is beyond the scope of this chapter to go through NAT or routing troubleshooting. However, the **debug ip nat** command can assist in getting details on why NAT is not working.

IP Inspection Applied In the Wrong Direction

The direction of inspection rule is a point of confusion for many who first configure CBAC because they think of a firewall as filtering traffic coming from an *outside* network to an *inside* network. So, the assumption is that the inspection should be applied to traffic coming from the untrusted side. The problem with this is that CBAC works in terms of *conversations,* not *packets*. So, if the conversations are initiated from inside (most of the time, this is the case), inspection must be applied to the outbound direction. Here is a useful rule of thumb: *Inspection is applied in the direction of conversation initiation and the extended ACL is applied on the opposite direction.*

UDP Inspection Is Not Configured

A DNS query works on protocol UDP and port number 53. Assume the DNS server for your corporation is located at the Internet service provider (ISP) network, which is on the unprotected side of the CBAC router. If one of your internal hosts on the protected side of the CBAC router tries to reach a website on the protected or unprotected side using a domain name, it will make a DNS query for name resolution to the IP address, before it can make the actual web connection. If you do not inspect UDP on the CBAC router, this name resolution will fail. This will cause the failure of the actual web request.

After going through the preceding troubleshooting steps, if you are still having issues, execute **show ip inspect session** again. If the session is there and the status that is shown is anything but SIS_OPEN, troubleshoot this further by checking the following:

- Return traffic might not be coming back to the router.
- ICMP traffic is not inspected.
- There is a problem with inspecting Single Channel Protocol.
- The required Multi-Channel Protocol is not inspected.
- IP URL Filtering might be blocking the connection.
- There is a redundancy or asymmetric routing problem.

Return Traffic Might Not Be Coming Back to the Router

With **show ip inspect session** command output, if you find that the session is being created but staying *half-open*, other devices along the path may be blocking the return traffic. There also may be issues with the route on the other destination device. If NAT is not working properly on the router, the destination device may not be able to respond back to the wrongly translated IP address of the source. As shown in Example 5-18, **debug ip packet detail ACL** can be used with the addition of the following line in the access-list 101 to find out if the return traffic is coming back to the router or not.

```
access-list 101 permit tcp host 20.1.1.1 eq 23 host 10.1.1.1
```

ICMP Traffic Is Not Inspected

Before version 12.2(11) YU & 12.2(15) T, there was no Internet Control Message Protocol (ICMP) inspection engine in CBAC for ICMP traffic. However, some ICMP packets are either necessary or really helpful on almost every real network. For example, for path MTU discovery, you need to allow ICMP **packet-too-big**, and for debugging connectivity issue across, you must allow **echo** and **echo reply**. However, keep in mind that some ICMP packets are dangerous, and allowing all ICMP packets always creates some level of security risk. So, if you are running a version older than 12.2(11) YU or 12.2 (15) T, allow the necessary ICMP packets for the return traffic on the incoming interface (outside) of the unprotected network. Example 5-19 shows commonly used ICMP services on the ACL applied as inbound on the outside interface.

Example 5-19 *Common ICMP Services Allowed on the Outside Interface of a CBAC Router*

```
Router(config)#access-list 100 permit icmp any any administratively-prohibited
Router(config)#access-list 100 permit icmp any any echo
Router(config)#access-list 100 permit icmp any any echo-reply
Router(config)#access-list 100 permit icmp any any packet-too-big
Router(config)#access-list 100 permit icmp any any time-exceeded
Router(config)#access-list 100 permit icmp any any traceroute
Router(config)#access-list 100 permit icmp any any unreachable
```

If you are running version 12.2(11) YU or 12.2 (15) T and above, you can configure inspection rules for ICMP inspection.

There Is a Problem with Inspecting Single Channel Protocol

For single channel protocols such as HTTP or SMTP, generic inspection (inspecting TCP) is sufficient. However, to achieve additional security against protocol violation, you have the option of inspecting with SMTP or HTTP. The big confusion comes when inspecting with HTTP. With HTTP inspection (if Java-list is not configured), by default Java filtering is turned on. So, connection requests for all the websites serving Java applets are denied by the CBAC. Hence, if you run into a problem with browsing certain sites, either remove inspection for HTTP or configure Java-list in conjunction with ACL to allow the trusted sites for Java applets.

Before 12.3(7) T, CBAC didn't have any option for inspecting ESMTP traffic. So, if you inspect SMTP, and your mail server runs ESMTP (for example, Microsoft Exchange Server), you will have problems getting e-mail. As work-arounds, either turn off SMTP inspection on the router or turn off ESMTP in the mail server as shown in the following link:

http://www.microsoft.com/exchange/en/55/help/default.asp?url=/exchange/en/55/help/documents/server/xog05031.htm

If you are running IOS version 12.3(7)T or above, and want to inspect ESMTP, refer to the following link for more details:

http://www.cisco.com/en/US/products/sw/iosswrel/ps5207/products_feature_guide09186a00801ed6ee.html

Required Multi-Channel Protocol is Not Inspected

If there are connectivity issues with multi-channel protocols such as FTP or H323 for example, make sure you are inspecting those specific protocols. In multi-channel protocols, the data channels are built up based on the negotiation that takes place using a control channel. So, the IOS firewall engine must inspect the control channel to get the necessary information from the negotiation that takes place to create openings on the ACL for the data channel. So, if you do not inspect the application layer protocol, the inspection engine for that protocol is not used. Instead, a generic inspection engine, such as TCP or UDP, is used, which does not go into the payload to get all the required information for the subsequent data channels once the control channel is built up. Hence the data channels fail. For FTP a typical symptom is this: when you execute **ls**, it hangs infinitely. If inspecting multi-channel protocol does not resolve the issues, then most likely there is a software bug, which can be confirmed by Cisco Support if presented with the **debug ip inspect multi_channel_protcol** (for example, FTP).

IP URL Filtering Blocking The Connection

If the IOS firewall is configured with an external URL filtering server, the URL server's policy has determined whether a connection is allowed or denied. So, if there is a configuration error in defining the policy, the connection across the IOS firewall router will fail. Therefore, you will need to recheck the URL server policy to be sure your URL server is not accidentally denying connections due to misconfiguration.

Redundancy or Asymmetric Routing Problems

IOS Firewall does not support router redundancy or load sharing among multiple routers; instead, it supports interface redundancy and load sharing. This means that if the request packet goes through router A, it must return back through router A. Otherwise, if CBAC is configured, router B drops the packets if router B receives them. If the packet leaves from router A serial interface 0 and returns on serial interface 1, if you have the same access-list 101 applied on both of the interfaces, the return packets will make it through and the connection will be established without any problem. This is because when CBAC creates a new channel, it installs the temporary access list entries on the interfaces used for the initial packet, but those same access lists may be installed on backup interfaces that provide additional paths to the same destinations. It is even possible to use CBAC with load sharing, if all the parallel interfaces are configured identically. If you configure the same access list and inspection parameters on two interfaces that are alternate paths to the same destination, connectivity should work. Remember to use the same access lists (with the same access list numbers) on both redundant interfaces. This works fine with dial backup for serial interface.

Performance Issues

If traffic or responses from the Command Line Interface (CLI) parser are slow, use the commands shown in Examples 5-20 and 5-21 to check if you are running short of memory and CPU.

Example 5-20 *Sample Output of CPU Utilization Under Normal Conditions*

```
Router#show processes cpu
CPU utilization for five seconds: 2%/0%; one minute: 1%; five minutes: 0%
 PID Runtime(ms)   Invoked      uSecs    5Sec    1Min    5Min TTY Process
   1           0         2          0   0.00%   0.00%   0.00%   0 Chunk Manager
   2          28     91967          0   0.00%   0.00%   0.00%   0 Load Meter
   3           0        12          0   0.00%   0.00%   0.00%  61 Modem Autoconfig
   4           0         1          0   0.00%   0.00%   0.00%   0 EDDRI_MAIN
   5      626536     68810       9105   0.00%   0.16%   0.20%   0 Check heaps
   6           0        50          0   0.00%   0.00%   0.00%   0 Pool Manager
--More—
Router#
```

Example 5-21 *Sample Output of Memory Utilization Under Normal Conditions*

```
Router#show processes memory
Total: 95974624, Used: 23276556, Free: 72698068
 PID TTY  Allocated      Freed    Holding    Getbufs    Retbufs Process
   0   0     211660      28936    6561888          0          0 *Init*
   0   0       1044  213092464       1044          0          0 *Sched*
   0   0  103793828  105060340   13875032    2973466          0 *Dead*
   1   0          0          0       6852          0          0 Chunk Manager
   2   0        188        188       3852          0          0 Load Meter
   3  61          0          0       6904          0          0 Modem Autoconfig
   4   0      65580          0      90432          0          0 EDDRI_MAIN
   5   0          0          0       6852          0          0 Check heaps
   6   0     126044      59592       7616      81604     105792 Pool Manager
--More—
Router#
```

If CPU utilization goes beyond 50%, investigate the issue further to see where the problem is. Find out if there were any changes to the CBAC configuration. If there were no configuration changes, your network may be under attack and running short of memory and CPU, as the router processes all the unnecessary packets. The best way to find that out is to analyze the syslog and see if there is an alert message from the router indicating that the router is going to aggressive mode and calming down. If you realize the system is under attack, it is best to block the traffic from the upstream router with the ACL and inform your ISP about the situation so that they can block the traffic. Because most of the time the traffic comes with spoofed random IP, the upstream router may be configured with rate limiting so that innocent users' traffic is not completely blocked. It is important to note that CBAC protects your internal network from the attack but at the cost of performance, and if an attack continues for a long time, the rate limiting on the upstream router may be applied as a work-around until the ISP identifies the source of the attack.

If you are not under attack and still having performance problems, check the following items to troubleshoot the issue:

- Timeouts for TCP, UDP, and DNS
- Short threshold values for half-open or new connections

- HTTP inspection dilemma
- Switching path
- Large ACL
- Reverse DNS and Identification Protocol (IDENT)
- The running of old code

Timeouts for TCP, UDP, and DNS

There are a number of timeouts in CBAC configuration. As the TCP is connection-oriented, it has a mechanism for tearing down the connections when the job is finis hed. So, leaving the TCP connection timeout values at the defaults (as shown in Table 5-3) is recommended unless otherwise required for certain applications.

However, UDP connections heavily rely on the CBAC timeout values, which are connectionless, and there is no mechanism to let the other party or the CBAC router know when the job is finished. Choosing an appropriate timeout value for UDP connections is very difficult. For UDP, generic UDP inspection simply creates a channel when it sees the first request packet from the client, and keeps that channel open until no traffic has been seen between the client and the server for a preset time. If you set the timeout for too short a time, you may kill certain types of connections prematurely. For example, a Network File System (NFS) may remain mounted across CBAC for a long time with no activity. As NFS is UDP based, the connection may time out prematurely due to a UDP session timeout on CBAC. Therefore, when NFS is called for on any activity, CBAC requires the rebuilding of the session. Performing NFS across CBAC or any firewall is strongly discouraged. And if you set the idle timeout for UDP too high, you may be accumulating a number of UDP sessions for nothing. The problem is even more serious when you have a DNS server on ISP and your client needs to make the entire DNS query to the ISP DNS server across the firewall. Luckily, the IOS Firewall has the option of setting up the timeout for DNS, which is much shorter than the generic UDP timeout.

Table 5-3 shows different default timeout values for TCP and UDP. With the commands listed in the table, it is possible to reset these timeout values.

Table 5-3 *Timeout Options Available in CBAC*

Timeout	Command	Default (in sec)
The length of time the software waits for a TCP session to reach the established state before dropping the session	**ip inspect tcp synwait-time** *seconds*	30
The length of time a TCP session will still be managed after the firewall detects a FIN-exchange	**ip inspect tcp finwait-time** *seconds*	5
The length of time a TCP session will still be managed after no activity (the TCP idle timeout)	**ip inspect tcp idle-time** *seconds*	3600

continues

Table 5-3 *Timeout Options Available in CBAC (Continued)*

Timeout	Command	Default (in sec)
The length of time a UDP session will still be managed after no activity (the UDP idle timeout)	**ip inspect udp idle-time** *seconds*	30
The length of time a DNS name lookup session will still be managed after no activity	**ip inspect dns-timeout** *seconds*	5

Short Threshold Values for Half-open and New Connections

It is extremely important to establish baselines for your network to find out what is normal before performing this function: manipulating different threshold values for the total number of half-open connections, or total new connection request rate. If you ambitiously set these threshold values too low, the router may go into aggressive mode and start dropping legitimate traffic. Because of this, you will not only experience packet drops, but the performance of the connections will be very poor. To prevent this, you must determine the values of these thresholds for your network.

HTTP Inspection Dilemma

If you have inspection turned on for HTTP, Java filtering is turned on by default as discussed before. HTTP inspection causes the packets to be inspected in strict order. So any out-of-order packets received are dropped, causing the packets to be retransmitted. This may cause a delay in downloading web pages. You can verify this by running the following debugs on the router:

```
debug ip inspect detailed
debug ip inspect tcp
debug ip inpsect http
```

When performance degrades due to out-of-order packets, you will receive a message as follows with the three debug commands listed previously:

```
Feb 17 17:37:59.428 CST: CBAC* sis 83207F08 L4 inspect result: DROP packet 833BE
CC4 (200.1.1.1:80) (20.1.1.1:4383) bytes 272 http
```

You can get around the problem in two ways: either turn off HTTP inspection or upgrade the code to version 12.3(5.13) or 12.3(5.13) T or above.

NOTE Generally per-packet load balancing increases chances of out-of-order packets. Hence, for better performance, install per-flow load balancing instead of per-packet load balancing.

Switching Path

CBAC can work on Process, Fast, or Cisco Express Forwarding (CEF) switching paths. However, CBAC works best with CEF. If there are performance issues with CBAC, first try turning off CBAC and verifying if the performance issue is caused by CBAC. If it is, turn on CBAC with process switching. This may slow down the packets, but it should work. Then turn on CEF or Fast switching and compare the performance. If CEF or Fast switching fails to provide better performance, the most likely cause is IOS software anomalies. For help with IOS software anomalies, consult with Cisco support.

Large ACL

ACL comprises multiple access controls elements (ACEs), and they are processed sequentially in top-down fashion. So it is very important to configure the entries that are most likely to be matched toward the top of the access list. The performance impact of an access list increases linearly with the increase in the number of ACEs. So, try summarizing the address ranges of the ACEs as much as possible. The smaller the list is, the lesser the CPU utilization and time to sequentially search for an entry. If you have a huge number of ACEs even after summarization, configure turbo ACL. Note that the turbo ACL feature is available on only 7200, 7500, and 12000 series routers. To turn on turbo ACL, simply execute the **access-list compiled** command after creating the ACL. The turbo ACL feature compiles the ACL ACEs into a set of special lookup tables while maintaining the first-match requirement. These tables allow for making permit or deny decisions quickly and consistently, which boosts performance dramatically. Keep in mind, however, the following caution: if you have less than five ACEs, a standard or extended ACL may perform better than turbo ACL. This is because, the turbo ACL compilation may take more CPU cycles than the CPU cycles gained with finding a faster match. Additionally, try to use netflow with ACL to boost the performance, because when net flow is enabled, only the first packet in a given flow goes through ACL checking. The rest of the packets bypass ACL checks. Netflow can be turned on in the Cisco router with the **ip route-cache flow** command under the interface configuration mode.

Reverse DNS and IDENT Protocols

If there is a problem in which users can connect to servers but have to wait a long before data comes back, something might be preventing the server from doing reverse DNS or IDENTD. To work around the DNS issue, be sure to allow UDP/53 to the DNS server from the destination server, provided the DNS server is behind the CBAC router. To get around the problem for IDENT protocol, be sure to allow TCP/113 through the CBAC router so that the server can communicate with the client on TCP/113.

Running Older Code

If you are running Cisco IOS version less than 12.2(8) T, you should seriously consider upgrading the code base, because a major performance initiative materialized from this specific version. Here are some of the changes that were made to improve the performance of CBAC:

- Allow users to dynamically change the size of the session hash table from 1K to 8K without reloading the router by using the **ip inspect hashtable** command. When a packet belonging to an existing session comes into the router, a hash table is used to map the packet to an existing firewall session. By increasing the size of the hash table, the number of sessions per hash bucket can be reduced, and consequently the search time for the session is greatly reduced. This improves the throughput performance of the base engine. You should increase the hash table size when the total number of sessions running through the CBAC router is approximately twice the current hash size; decrease the hash table size when the total number of sessions is reduced to approximately half the current hash size. Essentially, try to maintain a 1:1 ratio between the number of sessions and the size of the hash table.

- In versions prior to the performance improvement initiative, while processing a packet for connection setup and connection teardown of TCP connections, the base engine of CBAC "bumps up" several packets to the process-switching path. This drastically slows down their processing. Also, the base engine needs to process each packet again when it is bumped up into the process switching path. This whole process of punting packets back and forth degrades performance substantially. The new version prevents these restrictions by allowing only the first packet of any connection to be bumped up to the process-switching path, while the remaining packets are processed by the base engine in the fast path. Thus, the base engine is no longer slowed down by bumping up several packets or by processing packets twice.
- With the release of version 12.3(7) T, Cisco IOS Firewall Access Control Lists (ACL) bypass enhances the performance of Cisco IOS Firewall by removing multiple lookups on the return traffic passing through the router. Before this release, multiple checks are performed of each packet of the return traffic of an existing firewall flow: the input ACL search, the output ACL search, and the inspection session search. With updated code, a check is performed only once, and packets are marked if they belong to an existing firewall session before the input ACL search. This marking is used to skip the input and output dynamic ACL searches.

Intermittent Packet Drops

Intermittent packet drops can occur for various reasons. Go through the performance troubleshooting steps to be sure you are not hitting any performance issue. In addition, you may need to check the following to troubleshoot the intermittent packet drops issue:

- **Fragmentation issue**—If you are running a version of IOS code older than 12.3(8) T, you may run into issues with fragmentation. CBAC does not support IP fragments earlier than version 12.3(8) T, so packets may be dropped intermittently if they come out of order. To get around this problem, you may configure IP TCP adjust-mss under the interface facing towards the client, so that MTU negotiation can take place, and both client and server adjust their MTU to avoid the fragmentation.
- **URL filtering**—If you are running IP URL filtering, be sure that the policy defined in the URL server is not denying the packet.

IP URL Filtering Is Not Working

Troubleshooting IP URL filtering-related issues is fairly simple. With the help of **ip urlfilter audit-trail** command, to troubleshoot any issue you can turn on an audit trail for IP URL filtering and get all the required messages as shown in Table 5-4.

Table 5-4 *Audit Trail with URL Filtering*

Audit Trail	Description
`%URLF-3-SERVER_DOWN: Connection to the URL filter server 10.92.0.9 is down`	Router is unable to talk to the URL server.
`%URLF-3-ALLOW_MODE: Connection to all URL filter servers are down and ALLOW MODE is OFF`	Router is unable to talk to URL server but the system enters allow mode.
`%URLF-5-SERVER_UP: Connection to an URL filter server 10.92.0.9 is made, the system is returning from ALLOW MODE`	Router is able to talk to the URL server and it's in allow mode now.
`%URLF-4-URL_TOO_LONG: URL too long (more than 3072 bytes), possibly a fake packet?`	URL in a lookup request is too long; any URL longer than 3K is dropped.
`%URLF-4-MAX_REQ: The number of pending request exceeds the maximum limit <1000>`	The number of pending requests in the system exceeds the maximum limit and all further requests are dropped.
`%URLF-6-SITE_ALLOWED: Client 10.0.0.2:12543 accessed server 10.76.82.21:8080`	This message is logged for each request whose destination IP address is found in the cache. The URL is not logged because the IP address of the request is found in the cache.
`%URLF-4-SITE-BLOCKED: Access denied for the site 'www.sports.com'; client 10.54.192.6:34557 server 172.24.50.12:80`	A request finds a match against one of the blocked domains in the exclusive-domain list or the corresponding entry in the IP cache.
`%URLF-6-URL_ALLOWED: Access allowed for URL http://www.n2h2.com/; client 10.54.192.6:54123 server 192.168.0.1:80`	URL request that is allowed by a UFS. It includes the allowed URL, source IP address, source port number, destination IP address, and destination port number. Longer URLs will be truncated to 300 bytes and logged.
`%URLF-6-URL_BLOCKED: Access denied URL http://www.playstation.com; client 10.54.192.6:54678 server 172.19.14.2:80`	URL request that is blocked by a UFS. It includes the blocked URL, source IP address, source port number, destination IP address, and destination port number. Longer URLs are truncated to 300 bytes and then logged.

Case Studies

So far we have seen how CBAC with ACL can filter the traffic based on the IP address and port numbers. This section looks into a feature of IOS Firewall called auth-proxy that allows you to control the traffic based on the user name. This feature allows security administrators to apply specific security policies on a per-user basis. Users are authenticated and authorized according to their profiles in a Terminal Access Controller Access Control System (TACACS+) or Remote Authentication Dial-In User Service) RADIUS server.

How auth-proxy Works

Before getting into the details of the troubleshooting steps of auth-proxy, you must first understand how auth-proxy works. Figure 5-6 illustrates the mechanics of auth-proxy.

Figure 5-6 *Auth-proxy Operation*

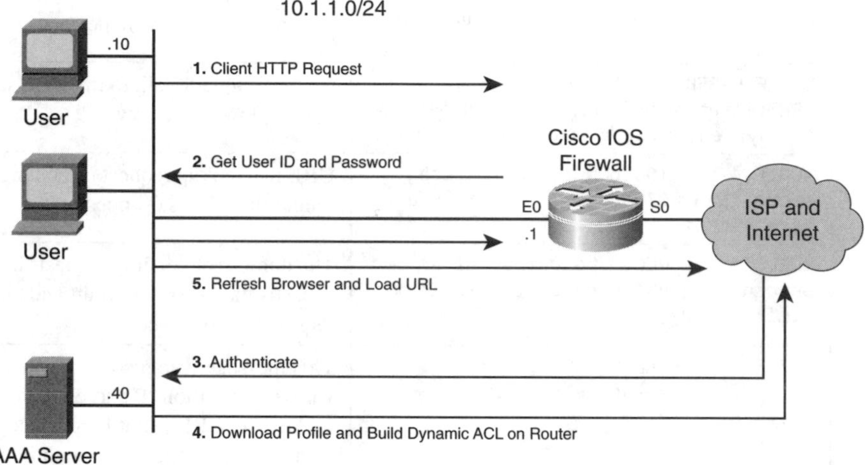

The following sequence describes the steps outlined in Figure 5-6:

1. The user initiates a HTTP (HTTPS/FTP/Telnet) connection going through the router. The router intercepts the request and starts auth-proxy. If the user has already been authenticated, the connection is completed with no further auth-proxy activity.
2. If there is no authentication info for this user, the user is prompted for username and password.
3. If the authentication succeeds, the user's authorization profile is downloaded from the Authentication, Authorization and Accounting (AAA) server, which contains an ACL that is then dynamically created by the router based on the source IP address of the client. This dynamic ACL is then stored in the hashed storage, which is called the Authorization cache.
4. In the final step, the Auth Proxy router refreshes the client's HTML request for reload and directs it to the target URL.

Method of Authentication

User authentication for auth-proxy can be performed using one of four methods: HTTP, Secure HTTP (HTTPS), Telnet, or FTP. HTTPS support for auth-proxy was first introduced in IOS version 12.2(11)YU, and was first integrated in version 12.2(15)T. However, FTP and Telnet support was introduced in IOS version 12.3(1). The mechanism of auth-proxy is the same regardless of methods for authentication being used. For HTTP, TELNET or FTP authentication, username and password goes in clear text from client to the router. If you want to encrypt the packets, you need to configure HTTPS. Ensure that the Cisco IOS image supports crypto (*k9) to be able to configure HTTPS.

Supported Platform

Auth-proxy is supported in many Cisco router platforms. Among them are Cisco 800 Series, Cisco 900 Series, Cisco 1700 Series, Cisco 2600 series, Cisco 3600 series, Cisco 3700, Cisco 7100, and Cisco 7200 series, Cisco 7500 Series, and Catalyst Series Routers.

Configuration Steps

The following steps walk you through the configuration of auth-proxy:

Step 1 Configure AAA (required) on the router:

```
Router#show running-configuration
aaa new-model
aaa authentication login default tacacs+ | radius
aaa authorization auth-proxy default tacacs+ | radius
tacacs-server host hostname | ip-address
tacacs-server key string
radius-server host hostname | ip-address
radius-server key string
```

Step 2 Configure the user's profile in the TACACS+ or RADIUS server. The output that follows is a sample profile output in TACACS+ in Cisco Secure ACS Unix. This same syntax can be mapped to Cisco Secure ACS on Windows. It is shown in Cisco Secure ACS Unix to show the syntax in the text.

```
default authorization = permit
key = cisco
user = newuser1 {
login = cleartext cisco
service = auth-proxy
{
priv-lvl=15
proxyacl#1="permit tcp any any eq 26"
proxyacl#2="permit icmp any host 60.0.0.2"
proxyacl#3="permit tcp any any eq smtp"
proxyacl#4="permit tcp any any eq telnet"
}
}
```

The RADIUS protocol has a similar profile:

```
user = proxy{
radius=Cisco {
check_items= {
2="proxy"
}
reply_attributes= {
9,1="auth-proxy:priv-lvl=15"
9,1="auth-proxy:proxyacl#1=permit icmp any any"
9,1="auth-proxy:proxyacl#2=permit tcp any any"
9,1="auth-proxy:proxyacl#3=permit udp any any"
}
}
}
```

Step 3 Configure the HTTP Server (required)

```
Router#show running-config
ip http server
/* Enables the HTTP server on the router.*/
ip http authentication aaa
/* Sets authentication to follow aaa rules  */
ip http access-class access-list-number
/* ACL to control access to HTTP Server */
```

Step 4 Configure the authentication proxy (required). First, you must turn on auth-proxy as follows:

```
Router#show running-config
....
! Sets the proxy idle timeout, def. 60 minutes.
ip auth-proxy auth-cache-time min
! Displays the name of the firewall router in the authentication proxy login
! page.
ip auth-proxy auth-proxy-banner

! Defines the AuthProxy rule. Only hosts matching the ACL will be
intercepted.
ip auth-proxy name auth-proxy-name http  [auth-cache-time min] [list
std-access-list]
! Apply auth-proxy on the interface.
interface type number
ip auth-proxy auth-proxy-name
```

A complete configuration of auth-proxy is shown in Example 5-22.

Example 5-22 *A Complete Auth-proxy Configuration on the Router*

```
Router#show running-config
! Removed irreverent configuration for simplicity.
!
! Define what needs to be be authenticated.
 aaa authentication login default group radius none
 aaa authorization exec default group radius none
 aaa authorization auth-proxy default group radius
! The following line will set up the banner.
 ip auth-proxy auth-proxy-banner
 !
! Set ACL entries to timeout after 10 minutes.
  ip auth-proxy auth-cache-time 10
 !
! Set the list name to be associated with interface.
  ip auth-proxy name my_auth_proxy_list http
 ip audit notify log
interface Ethernet0
ip address 10.1.1.1 255.255.255.0
!Apply the access list to the interface
  ip access-group 110 in
! Apply the auth-proxy list name.
  ip auth-proxy my_auth_proxy_list
 !
! Enable http server and authentication.
 ip http server
 ip http authentication aaa
 !
! This access list is used for auth-proxy. It's always a good
! idea to test the auth-proxy with just a single host instead before applying
! for all production traffic to minimize the downtime. In the following access-
! list 110, host 10.1.1.10 is denied access anything but the router's interface
! Ethernet 0 which ip address is 10.1.1.1. Rest of the traffic is allowed. This
! means, only traffic from 10.1.1.10 going through the router will be redirected
! to interface Ethernet 0, which ip address is 10.1.1.1 and then incepted and
! authenticated by the auth-proxy.
access-list 110 permit tcp host 10.1.1.10 host 10.1.1.1 eq www
access-list 110 deny ip host 10.1.1.10 any
access-list 110 permit ip any any
!
! Radius Server is defined by the following lines.
 radius-server host 10.1.1.40
 radius-server key cisco
Router#
```

Now that you are comfortable with the auth-proxy configuration, you are ready to walk though a detailed description of auth-proxy troubleshooting as presented in the section that follows.

Troubleshooting auth-proxy

Troubleshooting auth-proxy is fairly simple. Most of the problems that arise with auth-proxy are caused by misconfiguration and lack of understanding. Take steps to resolve the following questions to troubleshoot any auth-proxy-related issues.

Step 1 Are you sending HTTP/HTTPS/FTP/Telnet traffic across the router or to the interface?

Be sure you are sending initial traffic across the router, not to the router's directly connected interface towards the client. The first packet must be routed to another interface of the router for the router to trigger auth-proxy. If you do not see the User Name and Password prompt for the auth-proxy, you may be sending packets to the interface of the router instead of through the interface.

Step 2 Do you get the authentication prompt?

If you are sending the initial packets across the router and still don't get the authentication prompt, be sure you have applied the auth-proxy under the interface.

Step 3 Is the ACL allowing First Authentication Packet to the incoming interface ACL?

You must define an inbound ACL on the interface facing towards the client so that it denies all the traffic that you want to authenticate. However, the client's HTTP/HTTPS/FTP/Telnet traffic must be permitted to the interface itself. So, even though the client will attempt connection across the router, that connection will be redirected by the router to the interface where auth-proxy is configured. Hence, the ACL that is applied on the interface, where auth-proxy name is applied, should allow HTTP, HTTPS, Telnet, or FTP traffic to the interface IP address from the auth-proxy client. Otherwise, the connection request by the auth-proxy client across the router will be dropped by the ACL before triggering the auth-proxy. After authenticated and authorized, the downloadable ACL from the AAA server will decide which connections are allowed or denied by the router for the traffic that goes across the router.

Step 4 If Steps 1–3 are verified and you get the authentication prompt, but authentication fails, the problem is with authentication and or authorization (refer to Chapter 9, "Troubleshooting AAA on IOS Routers"). If you run **debug aaa authentication, debug aaa authorization,** and **debug radius** or **debug tacacs,** and if you are having AAA issues, Table 5-5 will help in identifying the cause of the problem.

Table 5-5 *Messages Returned by AAA* **debug** *Commands for User Authentication Failure*

Protocols Used	Messages shown with AAA debug	Reasons for Failure	What the User Sees
RADIUS and TACACS+	`AAA/AUTHEN (1587177845): status = ERROR`	RADIUS/ TACACS+ server is unreachable	`500 Internal Server Error`
RADIUS	`Access-Reject & status = FAIL`	Wrong Username/ password	`Authentication Failed`
TACACS+	`AUTHEN status = FAIL & status=FAIL`	Wrong Username/ password	`Authentication Failed`
TACACS+	`received author response status = FAIL & Post authorization status = FAIL`	Successful authentication but authorization fails	`Authentication Failed`
RADIUS/ TACACS+	`Debug shows the acl is downloaded but not getting applied due to bad format.`	ACL returns in invalid format	`Authentication Successful but user unable to pass traffic`
RADIUS	`auth-proxy:priv-lvl=1`	Priv-lvl 15 is not downloaded	`Authentication Failed`

If implemented appropriately, auth-proxy along with CBAC can be a very powerful firewall tool for your network security. The section that follows discusses some of the common questions and confusions regarding CBAC.

Common Problems and Resolutions

This section looks into some of commonly asked questions and confusions regarding CBAC in a question-and-answer format.

1 Is load balancing possible with CBAC?

Answer: Yes, if it is in the same router, but be sure to apply the same ACL on both the interfaces which participate in load-balancing the traffic.

2 With which features does the Cisco IOS Firewall not interoperate?

Answer: The Cisco IOS Firewall does not interoperate with the following features: TCP intercept Asymmetric routing, where ingress and egress are two different routers; Load-balancing, where ingress and egress are two different routers.

Layer 4 and Layer 7 inspection of fragmented packets is not supported.

The Cisco IOS Firewall operation with Server Load Balancing (SLB) has not been tested.

3 Does CBAC work with standard ACL on the opposite direction of the CBAC inspection rule?

Answer: No. Because the ACE in the ACL is created based on snm5-tuples which are based on Layer 4 information; you must have extended ACL configured so that ACE can be created by CBAC.

4 Does Cisco IOS Firewall work with fast switching?

Answer: Yes, the firewall works with all high-performance switching modes that the platform supports, including Cisco Express Forwarding (CEF), flow, fast and process switching modes.

5 Does the firewall work with Channelized T1 by applying distinct policies to different channel groups?

Answer: Yes. The same is true when distinct policies are applied to different Frame Relay subinterfaces.

6 Can non-IP protocols be routed while using Cisco IOS Firewall?

Answer: Yes, other protocols such as Internetwork Packet Exchange [IPX] and AppleTalk can function alongside the firewall technology, but the firewall will not inspect associated traffic.

Best Practices

This section looks into some of the best practices for the router CBAC is configured with.

- Basic Router Security
- Anti-spoofing Configuration

Basic Router Security

A router that's used as a firewall needs to be well secured itself. That means that nothing (services) unnecessary should be enabled. In addition, everything that can be password-protected should be password-protected. The following are some important guidelines for setting basic router security:

- **Services**—Any service that is enabled on the router has the potential to pose a security threat to the router. A determined, hostile party may find ways to misuse the enabled services to access the firewall router and exploit the resources of the router and the network. Here is a general rule of thumb: do not enable any local service (such as Simple Network Managing Protocol [SNMP] or Network Time Protocol [NTP]) that is not required. Local services such as Cisco Discovery Protocol (CDP) and NTP are on by default. So if you do not need these services, turn them off. To turn off CDP, enter the **no cdp run** global configuration command and to turn off NTP, enter the **ntp disable** interface configuration command on each interface that does not use NTP. If NTP is essential, configure it only on required interfaces to listen only to certain peers.

  For local services that are enabled, protect against misuse by configuring the services to communicate only with specific peers, and protect the router by configuring access lists to deny packets for the services at specific interfaces.

Disable minor services with **no service tcp-small-servers** and **no service udp-small-servers** global configuration commands unless otherwise needed.

- **Directed Broadcast**—Directed broadcasts can be misused to multiply the power of denial-of-service attacks, because every denial-of-service packet sent is broadcast to every host on a subnet. Furthermore, some hosts have other intrinsic security risks present when handling broadcasts.

  Directed broadcasts are rarely required by IP networks, hence directed broadcasts should be disabled for all applicable protocols on the CBAC router and on all your other routers in the network. To disable it, use the **no ip directed-broadcast** global configuration command.

- **Access Control and Password**—Configure access control before connecting a console port to the network in any way, including attaching a modem to the port. Be aware that a break on the console port may give complete control of the firewall to hackers, even with access control configured. In a non-AAA environment, configure **login** and **password** commands. If AAA is configured on the router, be sure to apply the authentication, authorization, and accounting for console port as well.

  Instead of using Telnet, try using Secure Shell (SSH) and control who can access the router. If you must use Telnet, apply access lists to limit who can use Telnet to access the router, and add password protection to all virtual terminal ports.

  For privileged access to the firewall, use the **enable secret** command rather than the **enable password** command.

- **Hiding Internal Network**—Configure the **no ip proxy-arp** command to prevent the internal addresses from being revealed. This is especially important if you do not already have NAT configured to prevent internal addresses from being revealed.

Anti-spoofing Configuration

The CBAC router should have anti-spoofing access lists. That means you should input access lists on all, or nearly all, interfaces, set up to reject any packet that has a source address that's not expected to be on that interface. For example, if the router is an Internet firewall, it should reject all packets coming from the Internet that claim to be from the private network. Similarly, it should reject all packets coming from the private network with source addresses that aren't part of the private network, because anti-spoofing is not optional in either direction.

Disable source routing. For IP, enter the **no ip source-route** global configuration command. Disabling source routing at all routers can help prevent spoofing.

Prevent the firewall from being used as a relay by configuring access lists on any asynchronous Telnet ports.

PART III

Troubleshooting Virtual Private Networks

Chapter 6 Troubleshooting IPSec VPNs on IOS Routers

Chapter 7 Troubleshooting IPSec VPN on PIX Firewalls

Chapter 8 Troubleshooting IPSec VPNs on VPN 3000 Series Concentrators

CHAPTER 6

Troubleshooting IPsec VPNs on IOS Routers

Virtual Private Networks (VPNs) have been evolving for several years, and by now have reached maturity. IPsec protocol has played a significant role in this evolution. In fact, IPsec has become the de facto standard for VPN implementation, and the majority of VPN implementations are on IPsec. This chapter focuses on the details of the IPsec protocol to give you a fundamental understanding of the protocol itself, and to give you a foundation for Chapters 7 and 8, "Troubleshooting IPsec VPN on PIX Firewalls" and "Troubleshooting IPsec VPNs on VPN 3000 Series Concentrators." The troubleshooting section of this chapter focuses primarily on IOS implementation, and toward the end of the chapter, the section entitled "Common Problems and Resolutions" discusses common IPsec interoperation issues, such as Network Address Translation (NAT), firewalls, and so on, which are primarily for IOS routers but also apply to other products.

Overview of IPsec Protocol

IPsec protocol provides the security for the unicast IP protocol traffic. Whether you implement site-to-site or remote access VPN, IPsec is used to protect information as it travels from one private network to another private network over a public network. IPsec consists of a suite of protocols that are defined in RFC 2401 as the following:

- **Security protocols**—Authentication header (AH) and encapsulation security payload (ESP)
- **Key management**—ISAKMP, IKE, SKEME
- **Algorithms**—for encryption and authentication

Before going into the details of security protocols and key management components, it is important to understand the encryption and authentication protocols which are discussed in the next section.

Encryption and Decryption

The term encryption is used to describe the transformation of plain text into a form that makes the original text incomprehensible to an unauthorized recipient that does not have a matching key to decode or decrypt the encrypted message. Decryption is the reverse of encryption, which means that decryption is the transformation of encrypted data back into plain text. A cipher is a cryptographic algorithm that is used for data encryption and decryption. One function is used for encryption and other function is used for decryption. You must use a key in addition to a cipher for encryption and decryption.

Encryption is used for data confidentiality, which is one of the most important requirements for any VPN implementation. An encryption/decryption algorithm built into IPsec makes IPsec a desirable protocol for IPsec implementation.

Cryptographic algorithms can be categorized as follows:

- Symmetric algorithms
- Asymmetric algorithms

Symmetric Algorithms

Symmetric cryptographic algorithms are based on the sender and receiver of the message knowing and using the same secret key. The sender uses a secret key to encrypt the message, and the receiver uses the same key to decrypt it. The main problem with using the symmetric key approach is finding a way to distribute the key without anyone else obtaining it. Anyone who overhears or intercepts the key in transit can later read and modify messages encrypted or authenticated using that key, and can forge new messages. DES, 3DES, and AES are popular symmetric encryption algorithms. A detailed explanation of these algorithms is beyond the scope of this book.

NOTE DES uses a 56-bit key and is not considered secure anymore; in 1999, the DES key was cracked in less than 24 hours by using an exhaustive key search. Triple DES (3DES) and AES are the recommended encryption algorithms as of this writing.

Asymmetric Algorithms

Asymmetric encryption algorithms, also known as public key algorithms, use separate keys—one for encryption and another for decryption. The encryption key is called the public key and can be made public. Only the private key that is used for decryption needs to be kept secret. Although the public and private keys are mathematically related, it is not feasible to derive one from the other. Anyone with a recipient's public key can encrypt a message, but the message can only be decrypted with a private key that only the recipient knows. Therefore, a secure communication channel to transmit the secret key is no longer required, as it is in the case of symmetric algorithms.

The initiator and responder communicate securely using public key encryption as follows:

1. Initiator and responder agree on a public key algorithm.
2. Responder sends initiator his public key and initiator sends responder her public key.

3 Initiator sends responder a message, encrypting the message using responder's public key.

4 Responder receives the message and decrypts initiator's message using his private key.

Remember that public key encryption is rarely used to encrypt messages because it is much slower than symmetric encryption. Public key encryption is used, however, to solve the problem of key distribution for symmetric key algorithms, which is, in turn, used to encrypt actual messages. Therefore, public key encryption is not meant to replace symmetric encryption, but can supplement it and make it more secure.

Digital Signatures

Another good use of public key encryption is for message authentication, also known as a digital signature.

Encrypting a message with a private key creates a digital signature, which is an electronic means of authentication and provides non-repudiation. Non-repudiation means that senders will not be able to deny that they sent messages. That is, a digital signature attests not only to the contents of a message, but also to the identity of the sender. Because it is usually inefficient to encrypt an actual message for authentication, a document hash known as a message digest is used. The basic idea behind a message digest is to take a variable-length message and convert it into a fixed-length compressed output called the message digest. Because the original message cannot be reconstructed from the message digest, the hash is labeled "one-way." An initiator and responder's communication using digital signature proceeds as follows:

1 Initiator computes a one-way hash of a document that she wishes to send responder.

2 Initiator encrypts the hash with her private key. The encrypted message digest becomes the digital signature.

3 Initiator sends the document along with the digital signature to responder.

4 Responder decrypts the digital signature using initiator's public key and also computes a one-way hash of the document received from initiator. If the two values match, responder can be sure that the document came from initiator and the document was not tampered with in transit. The slightest change in the document will cause the values to not match and will cause the authentication to fail.

When the message digest generated is encrypted using a key, it's called a keyed message digest. Another definition for a keyed message digest is message authentication code (HMAC).

Security Protocols

There are two security protocols of IPsec. AH and ESP provide the security services to the unicast IP packets. AH and ESP are discussed in detail in subsequent sections.

Authentication Header (AH)

AH provides connectionless integrity, data authentication, and optional replay protection, but it does not provide confidentiality.

AH is an IP protocol, identified by a value of 51 in the IP header. The Next header field indicates what follows the AH header. In transport mode, it will be the value of the upper layer protocol being protected (for example, UDP or TCP). In tunnel mode, this value is 4.

AH in transport mode is useful if the communication endpoints are also the IPsec endpoints. In tunnel mode, AH encapsulates the IP packet, and an additional IP header is added before the AH header. Although the tunnel mode of AH could be used to provide IPsec VPN end-to-end security, there is no data confidentiality in AH, therefore this mode is not very useful. AH is defined by RFC2402.

Encapsulating Security Header (ESP)

ESP provides confidentiality, data integrity, and optional data origin authentication and anti-replay services. It provides these services by encrypting the original payload and encapsulating the packet between a header and a trailer.

ESP is identified by a value of 50 in the IP header. The ESP header is inserted after the IP header and before the upper layer protocol header. The IP header itself could be a new IP header in tunnel mode or the original IP packet's header in transport mode.

ESP is defined by RFC2406.

Both AH and ESP can work in one of the two following modes:

- Transport mode
- Tunnel mode

Transport Mode

Transport mode is used when both communicating peers are hosts. It may also be applied when one peer is a host and the other is a gateway, if that gateway is acting as a host. For example, a router is sending syslog message traffic to a syslog server across the tunnel. For transport mode to work, you need to have routable IP addresses. Transport mode has an advantage of adding less overhead to the original packets.

Transport mode can be configured both with AH and ESP.

- **Transport mode—Authentication Header**—AH protocol protects the external IP header along with the data payload (see Figure 6-1). It protects all the fields in the header that are not mutable and do not change in transport. The AH header is placed between the IP header and ESP, if present, and other higher-layer protocols.

Figure 6-1 *Showing IP Packet in Transport Mode*

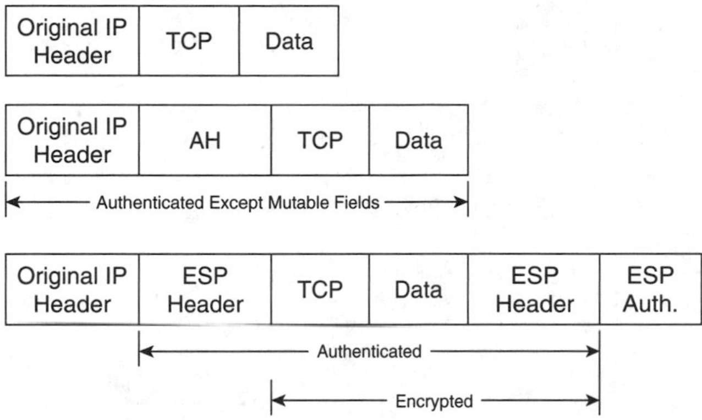

- **Transport mode—Encapsulating Security Payload**—In transport mode, the IP payload is encrypted and the original headers are left intact. The ESP header is inserted between the IP header and the upper-layer protocol header (see Figure 6-1). The upper-layer protocols are encrypted and authenticated along with the ESP header. ESP does not authenticate the IP header itself. Figure 6-1 shows an IP packet after applying ESP in transport mode.

Tunnel Mode

Tunnel mode is used between two gateways or between a host and a gateway, if that gateway is the conduit to the actual source or destination. In tunnel mode, the entire original IP packet is encrypted and becomes the payload of a new IP packet. So the original IP packets don't have to be routable to the Internet. The new IP header has the destination address of its IPsec peer. The biggest advantage of tunnel mode is that all the information from the original packet, including the headers, is protected. Tunnel mode protects against traffic analysis because, although the IPsec tunnel endpoints can be determined, the true source and destination endpoints cannot be determined because the information in the original IP header has been encrypted.

Just as in transport mode, tunnel mode may be configured both with AH and ESP.

- **Tunnel Mode with AH**—The entire original header is authenticated and the new IP header is protected in the same way as the IP header is protected in transport mode (see Figure 6-2).

Figure 6-2 *Showing IP Packet in Tunnel Mode*

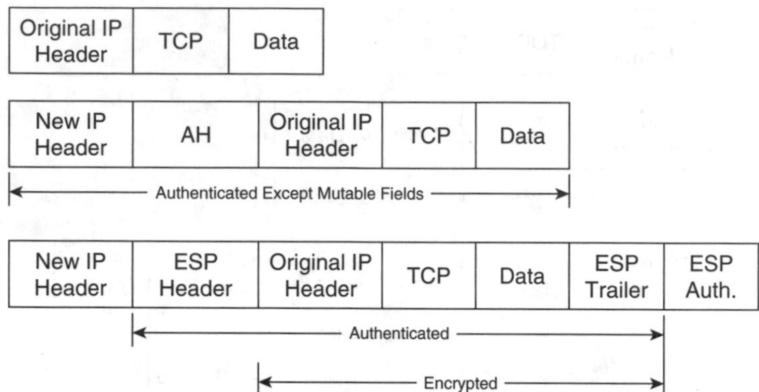

- **Tunnel Mode with ESP**—When ESP is used in tunnel mode, the original IP header is protected because the entire original IP datagram is encrypted (see Figure 6-2). With ESP authentication mechanism, the original IP datagram and the ESP header are included; however, the new IP header is not included in the authentication. When both authentication and encryption are selected, encryption is performed first, before authentication on the initiator. On the responder, authentication occurs before the decryption. One reason for this order of processing is that it facilitates rapid detection and rejection of replayed or bogus packets by the receiving node. Before decrypting the packet, the receiver can detect the problem and potentially reduce the impact of denial-of-service attacks.

Security Associations (SAs)

To have IPsec conversations, you first need to establish a security association. Each device must agree on the policies or rules of the conversation by negotiating these policies with their potential peers. SA is nothing but an instantiation of security policy for a given data flow within the IKE/IPsec environment. An SA is unidirectional, so it represents a unidirectional connection for the traffic. So, if you have traffic flowing in both directions, you need two security associations. For example, if there are two gateways, A and B, and if they need to send and receive traffic over the IPsec tunnel, both of the gateways need to have two SAs on each, one for incoming traffic and another one for outgoing traffic. If both AH and ESP are configured for a unidirectional traffic, two sets of security associations are created for the traffic.

An SA is uniquely identified by an IP destination address, a security protocol (AH or ESP) identifier, and a unique security parameter index (SPI) value. A SPI is a 32-bit number assigned to the initiator of the SA request by the receiving IPsec endpoint. Upon receiving a packet, the destination address, protocol, and SPI are used to determine the SA, which allows the receiving gateway to authenticate or decrypt the packet according to the security policy configured for that SA.

Internet Key Exchange Protocol (IKE) Protocol, which is discussed in greater detail in the sections that follow, is used to create and maintain an SA on both ends of the tunnel.

SA and Key Management with IKE Protocol

As mentioned previously, IKE stands for Internet Key Exchange Protocol, which is defined by RFC 2409. It is used primarily to exchange keying materials and for establishing security associations. It is possible to configure both keying materials and the security associations manually, but for large-scale deployment, this is not a very scalable solution. So, IKE is a *must* because it addresses this issue.

IKE is a two-phase protocol:

- IKE Phase 1
- IKE Phase 2

More detailed discussion follows in subsequent sections.

IKE Phase 1

The purpose of IKE phase 1 is to authenticate peers, establish a secure IKE SA, and generate keys for IPsec for the secure communication. This is accomplished with IPsec peers agreeing on IKE parameters, exchanging keying material, and authenticating each other.

IKE Phase 1 can function in one of the two modes to accomplish this task:

- Main mode negotiation
- Aggressive mode negotiation

Main Mode Negotiation

In Main mode negotiation, IPsec peers exchange a total of six messages—three messages in each direction. The first four messages are the same regardless of the types of authentication configured for Phase 1:

- Pre-shared keys
- Rivest, Shamir, Adleman (RSA) signatures
- RSA encrypted nonces

As the pre-shared keys and the RSA signatures are pre-dominantly used in the field for IPsec, these two authentication methods are explained in detail in this section.

Work through the following numbers and correlate them with packet numbers in Figure 6-3.

Figure 6-3 *IKE Phase 1 Negotiation with Pre-Shared Key in Main Mode*

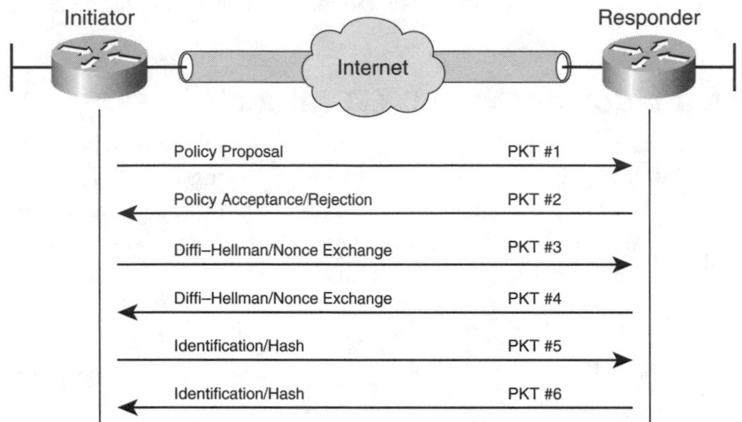

1. As shown in Figure 6-3, the first packet is sent by the initiator to the responder with the initiator cookie and the IKE policy proposal. Every policy configured on the initiator with the command **crypto isakmp policy** *policy_number* is sent to the Responder. The policy may contain parameters such as encryption algorithm, hash algorithm, authentication method, Diffie-Hellman group, and SA lifetime. These policy proposals are contained within an SA payload and its associated Proposal and Transform payloads.

2. Upon receiving the IKE packet 1 from the initiator, the responder examines the IKE policy information and attempts to find a match with its own locally configured IKE policies. Assuming the Responder finds a matching IKE policy, it responds with a message indicating acceptance of one of the initiator's policies. Again, this proposal is contained with an SA payload. The peers have now negotiated an IKE policy.

3. In the third packet, the initiator sends out Diffie-Hellman public values and nonces (random numbers) to the responder.

4. In the fourth packet, the Responder does the same thing as in the third packet. These values are exchanged in the KE and NONCE payloads, respectively. With these values and the private value, the Diffie-Hellman algorithm comes up with the same shared secret key on both sides of the tunnel.

   The two nonce values (initiator's and responder's), together with the pre-shared key, are then used to generate the first of four session key values (SKEYID).

   SKEYID is used, together with the shared secret key (from the Diffie-Hellman exchange) and other keying material, to derive three other session key values called SKEYID_d, SKEYID_a, and SKEYID_e. These session key values are used to derive keys for IPsec, authenticate other ISAKMP messages, and encrypt ISAKMP messages, respectively.

At this stage, an IKE policy has been agreed upon (first two messages), keying material has been exchanged (second two messages), and session key values have been calculated.

5 In the fifth packet, the initiator exchanges hash and identification values, contained in HASH and ID payloads, with the responder.

6 In the sixth packet, the responder does the same thing as the initiator. The peers then authenticate each other based on the hash values received. If the received hash value is the same as a hash value calculated locally, authentication succeeds.

Main mode negotiation with RSA signature (digital certificate) authentication is very similar to Main mode with pre-shared key authentication. The first four packets are exactly the same. The difference occurs with the fifth and the sixth packets. IKE peers use RSA signature authentication exchange identification, certificates, and signature. These elements are carried in the ID, CERT, and SIG payloads, respectively.

Aggressive Mode Negotiation

Unlike Main mode, Aggressive mode negotiation exchanges only three messages instead of six, so it is faster than Main mode, but slightly less secure because the ID payload is exchanged unencrypted.

Figure 6-4 illustrates aggressive mode using pre-shared key authentication.

Figure 6-4 *IKE Phase 1 Negotiation with Pre-Shared Key in Aggressive Mode*

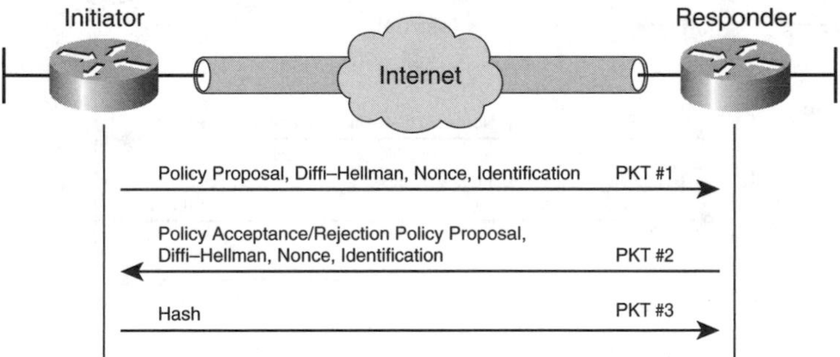

Based on Figure 6-4, work through the following packets to complete the Aggressive mode negotiation with pre-shared key:

1 In Aggressive mode with Pre-shared Key Authentication, initiator sends the first message with proposed IKE policies, its Diffie-Hellman public value, a nonce value, and identification. These are contained in the SA, KE, NONCE, and ID payloads, respectively. Note that all payloads exchanged during Aggressive mode perform the same function as in Main mode.

2. Upon receiving the first packet, the responder replies with a message containing the accepted IKE policy, its Diffie-Hellman public value, a nonce, a hash used by the initiator to authenticate the responder, and identification. These are contained in the SA, KE, HASH, and ID payloads.
3. In the third and final packet for phase 1 negotiation, the initiator sends a message consisting of a hash (used by the responder to authenticate the initiator). The hash is contained in a HASH payload.

If RSA signature is used instead of pre-shared key, the first packet consists of SA, KE, NONCE, and ID payloads. The second packet from the responder consists of SA, KE, NONCE, ID, CERT, and SIG payloads. Finally, the initiator sends a certificate and signature. These are contained in CERT and SIG payloads.

IKE Phase 2

Upon completion of Phase 1 with IKE SA established, Phase 2 begins to negotiate and establish IPsec SAs. Unlike Phase 1, Phase 2 can negotiate only one mode—Quick mode. The session key IDs (SKEYID_a and SKEYID_e) are used to protect Quick mode.

The router negotiates Quick mode with three messages between the initiator and the responder as shown in Figure 6-5.

Figure 6-5 *IKE Phase 2 Negotiation Using Quick Mode*

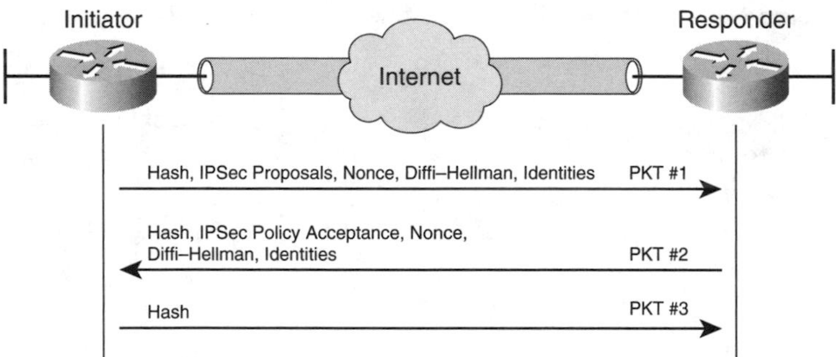

Work through the following numbers to correlate the message ID number shown in Figure 6-5:

1. The first message sent by the initiator to the responder contains a hash, IPsec proposals, a nonce, and optionally, another Diffie-Hellman public value, and identities. These elements are contained in **HASH, SA, NONCE, KE, and ID payloads**, respectively.
   a. The hash is used to authenticate the message to the responder.
   b. The IPsec proposals are used to specify security parameters, such as the security protocol (AH or ESP), encryption algorithm, hash algorithm, and IPsec tunnel

mode (transport or tunnel) to be used for the IPsec SA. These parameters are configured on routers using the **crypto ipsec transform-set** command.

c The nonce is used to protect against replay attacks. It is also used as additional keying material.

d The Diffie-Hellman public value is included in the message only if the initiator is configured for Perfect Forward Secrecy (PFS). Normally, keys used with IPsec SA are derived from keying material generated during IKE phase 1. This means that IPsec keys generated using PFS are more secure. PFS is configured using the **set pfs {group 1 | group 2}** command under the **crypto map**).

e Phase 2 ID payloads (identities) are used to exchange addresses, protocols, and ports for which this IPsec SA is being established. This is configured using a crypto access list.

2 In the second packet, the responder replies with a message containing a hash (used by the initiator to authenticate the responder), an IPsec proposal acceptance, a nonce value, and optionally, a Diffie-Hellman public value (if the responder supports PFS), and identities. These elements are again contained in HASH, SA, NONCE, KE, and ID payloads. The payloads in the message that the responder sends serve the same purpose as those sent by the initiator.

3 The initiator sends a third and final message. This contains a hash (HASH payload), and it acknowledges the responder's message and proves that the initiator is alive.

Diagnostic Commands and Tools

show and **debug** commands are your friends for troubleshooting IPsec VPN issues on Cisco Router. You can diagnose any problem if you know how to use these commands and interpret their output correctly. This part of the chapter introduces and examines the **show** and **debug** commands in detail and tells you how to use them properly.

show Commands

show commands are used to determine the status of the tunnel and the activities relating to the tunnel. These commands display very short, concise information about the state of the tunnel. Most of the time, if interpreted properly, knowing the state of the tunnel helps you with first-hand analysis, and guides you in the right direction with your troubleshooting steps. For example, with the **show crypto isakmp sa** command (discussed next), if you realize that Phase I is not in the **QM_IDLE** state, then you need only to run the **debug crypto isakmp** command.

show Command for Phase I

To find the state information of Phase I of IPsec tunnel negotiation, use the following command:

```
Router# show crypto isakmp sa [detail]
```

This command shows the Internet Security Association Management Protocol (ISAKMP) security associations built between peers. Example 6-1 shows ISAKMP SA between peer 20.1.1.1 and 30.1.1.1, which is in **QM_IDLE** state, which means that Main mode has been successfully completed.

Example 6-1 *Output for* **show crypto isakmp sa** *Command*

```
Router# show crypto isakmp sa
dst       src         state       conn-id     slot
30.1.1.1  20.1.1.1    QM_IDLE     1           0
```

The ISAKMP SA can be in several; states, depending on which state of the negotiation is taking place. Knowing these states is important, because based on this state information, you can figure out in which state Phase I negotiation is occurring. Tables 6-1, 6-2, and 6-3 show the states displayed in the **show crypto isakmp sa** command when main mode, aggressive modes, and quick modes are being negotiated or have been negotiated.

Table 6-1 *States Displayed in the* **show crypto isakmp sa** *Command When Main Mode Is Being Negotiated*

State	Descriptions
OAK_MM_NO_STATE	This is the initial state of Phase I establishment life cycle. However, Phase I should be in this state momentarily and you might not be able to view this state during the normal Phase I buildup process. If you see Phase I in this state for a longer time, this is an indication that a failure of tunnel establishment for Phase I has occurred.
OAK_MM_SA_SETUP	The peers have agreed on parameters for the ISAKMP SA. Phase I will be in this state after packet 1 and packet 2 exchange of the Main Mode negotiation.
OAK_MM_KEY_EXCH	The peers have exchanged Diffie-Hellman public keys and have generated a shared secret. The ISAKMP SA remains unauthenticated.
OAK_MM_KEY_AUTH	The ISAKMP SA has been authenticated. If the router initiated this exchange, this state transitions immediately to OAK_QM_IDLE, and a quick mode exchange begins.

Table 6-2 *States Displayed in the* **show crypto isakmp sa** *Command When Aggressive Mode Is Being Negotiated*

State	Description
OAK_AG_NO_STATE	This is the initial state of Phase I establishment life cycle. However, Phase I should be in this state momentarily and you might not be able to view this state during the normal Phase I buildup process. If you see Phase I in this state for longer time, this is an indication that a failure of tunnel establishment for Phase I has occurred.
OAK_AG_INIT_EXCH	The peers have performed the first exchange in aggressive mode, but the SA is not authenticated.
OAK_AG_AUTH	The ISAKMP SA has been authenticated. If the router initiated this exchange, this state transitions immediately to OAK_QM_IDLE, and a quick mode exchange begins.

Table 6-3 *States Displayed in the* **show crypto isakmp sa** *Command When Quick Mode Is Being Negotiated*

State	Description
OAK_QM_IDLE	The ISAKMP SA is idle. It remains authenticated with its peer and may be used for subsequent quick mode exchanges.

show Commands for Phase II

There are several **show** commands that can be used to find the IPsec counters to see if the packet is being encrypted, encapsulated, and sent or received correctly:

1 **show crypto ipsec sa** [peer *address*]

This command shows the output of IPsec SAs between two peers. The encrypted tunnel is built between 20.1.1.1 and 30.1.1.1 for traffic going between networks 10.1.1.0 and 10.1.2.0. You can see the two Encapsulating Security Payloads (ESPs) that SAs built inbound and outbound. The authentication header (AH) is not used because there are no AH SAs.

Example 6-2 shows the output of the **show crypto ipsec sa** command.

Example 6-2 *Sample Output for the* **show crypto ipsec sa** *Command*

```
Router# show crypto ipsec sa
interface: FastEthernet0
    Crypto map tag: test, local addr. 20.1.1.1
   local  ident (addr/mask/prot/port): (10.1.1.0/255.255.255.0/0/0)
   remote ident (addr/mask/prot/port): (10.1.2.0/255.255.255.0/0/0)
   current_peer: 30.1.1.1
     PERMIT, flags={origin_is_acl,}
    #pkts encaps: 7767918, #pkts encrypt: 7767918, #pkts digest 7767918
```

continues

Example 6-2 *Sample Output for the* **show crypto ipsec sa** *Command (Continued)*

```
    #pkts decaps: 7760382, #pkts decrypt: 7760382, #pkts verify 7760382
    #pkts compressed: 0, #pkts decompressed: 0
    #pkts not compressed: 0, #pkts compr. failed: 0,
    #pkts decompress failed: 0, #send errors 1, #recv errors 0
     local crypto endpt.: 20.1.1.1, remote crypto endpt.: 30.1.1.1
     path mtu 1500, media mtu 1500
     current outbound spi: 3D3
     inbound esp sas:
      spi: 0x136A010F(325714191)
        transform: esp-3des esp-md5-hmac ,
        in use settings ={Tunnel, }
        slot: 0, conn id: 3442, flow_id: 1443, crypto map: test
        sa timing: remaining key lifetime (k/sec): (4608000/52)
        IV size: 8 bytes
        replay detection support: Y
     inbound ah sas:
     inbound pcp sas:
inbound pcp sas:
outbound esp sas:
   spi: 0x3D3(979)
    transform: esp-3des esp-md5-hmac ,
    in use settings ={Tunnel, }
    slot: 0, conn id: 3443, flow_id: 1444, crypto map: test
    sa timing: remaining key lifetime (k/sec): (4608000/52)
    IV size: 8 bytes
    replay detection support: Y
outbound ah sas:
outbound pcp sas:
```

2 show crypto engine connections active

This command shows current active IPsec VPN connections and allows you to quickly check the packets are being encrypted or decrypted. Example 6-3 shows the output of **show crypto engine connection active**.

Example 6-3 *Output for the* **show crypto engine connection active** *Command*

```
Router# show crypto engine connection active
ID   Interface        IP-Address       State  Algorithm              Encrypt  Decrypt
 1   Ethernet0/3      209.165.200.227 set    HMAC_SHA+3DES_56_C          0        0
! The following two lines shows 19 packets encrypted and decrypted
2000 Ethernet0/3      209.165.200.227 set    HMAC_MD5+3DES_56_C          0       19
2001 Ethernet0/3      209.165.200.227 set    HMAC_MD5+3DES_56_C         19        0
Router#
```

3 show crypto engine connections dropped-packet

This command is used to find the dropped packets of an established IPsec tunnel. This is very useful because you know if you have performance issues, or suspect that the tunnel is dropping the packets.

show Commands for Interface Counters

In additiion to analyzing the counters of IPsec tunnel, you also need to analyze the counters of the interfaces to see if the packets are being forwarded or received on the interfaces, as shown in the following section:

1 **show ip access-lists** *<number>*

   The <number> should be the number of the access-list used in the crypto map. This ensures that the packet is included in the interesting traffic access-list.

2 **show interface** *<interface name>* **statistics**

   This command shows the number of packets that are processed and fast-switched.

3 **show interfaces** *<interface name>*

   This command shows dropped packets, and input and output queue sizes.

show Command for Verifying IPsec Configuration

If you have a tunnel establishment problem, you can use the following commands to verify the configuration on both peers of an IPsec tunnel:

- **Verifying Policy Configuration**—The following command shows the policy configured on the router. At least one of the policies must match between the two peers for a successful tunnel establishment:

  ```
  Router# show crypto isakmp policy
  ```

- **Verifying transform set configuration**—If the transform set does not match between peers, Phase II of tunnel establishment will fail. The following command allows you to verify the transform set configuration:

  ```
  Router# show crypto ipsec transform-set
  ```

- **Verifying if the crypto map is applied correctly**—If Phase II is failing, you must ensure that the crypto map is applied to the correct interface, and if the interesting traffic ACL includes the traffic to go through the tunnel. For this, execute the **show crypto map** command as shown in Example 6-4. This gives you the summary version of IPsec configuration for Phase II. To verify that the crypto map is applied to the proper interface, use the command shown in Example 6-4.

Example 6-4 *Showing the Output of the* **show crypto map** *Command*

```
Router# show crypto map
Crypto Map "mymap" 10 ipsec-isakmp
        Peer = 172.16.171.33
        Peer = 172.16.171.39
! Following line shows the interesting traffic for the VPN
        Extended IP access list 101
            access-list 101 permit ip 10.1.2.0 0.0.0.255 10.1.1.0 0.0.0.255
! This shows the peer of the IPSec tunnel
        Current peer: 172.16.171.33
```

continues

Example 6-4 *Showing the Output of the* **show crypto map** *Command (Continued)*

```
! Shows the lifetime of the Security Association
        Security association lifetime: 4608000 kilobytes/3600 seconds
        PFS (Y/N): N
! The transform set applied to the crypto map is shown below
        Transform sets={ myset, }
! Crypto map is applied to the Ethernet 0 interface.
        Interfaces using crypto map mymap:
                Ethernet0
Router#
```

- **Certificate Verification**—To verify the certificate on the router, use the following commands:

```
Router# show crypto key pubkey-chain
Router# show crypto key mypubkey
```

Commands for Tearing Down Tunnel

To tear down the SA for Phase II, you can use the following command on both sides:

```
Router# clear crypto sa
```

Then clear ISAKMP SA with the following command, which will tear down the ISAKMP SA:

```
Router# clear crypto isakmp
```

This should send out a "delete" message to the peer; however, this is an unacknowledged message, which could be lost.

debug Commands

After you identify the state of the tunnel with **show** commands, you may run the **debug** command to see why the tunnel is in a particular state. **debug** commands tell you precisely where the tunnel is broken. The three most important and mostly used **debug** commands are shown in Example 6-5.

Example 6-5 *Running the* **debug** *Commands for the IPsec Tunnel Buildup Process*

```
! The following command shows phase I information of an IPSec tunnel negotiation process
Router# debug crypto ISAKMP
! The following commands shows phase II debug information of IPSec tunnel negotiation
Router# debug crypto ipsec
! The following debug command shows additional details of the tunnel build up process
Router# debug crypto engine
! To see isakmp packets, look for UDP packets to and from port 500. This debug is useful
! to see if the ISAKMP packets are hitting the router.
Router# debug ip udp
```

Most of the time, you have to run the first three commands as shown in Example 6-5. The fourth debug command in the example is used only if you are unable to receive any IKE packets, but want to verify that the UDP/500 packets are reaching the router.

Configure millisecond timestamps to find the exact timing of the problem with the following commands:

```
Router(config)# service timestamps debug datetime msec
Router(config)# service timestamps log datetime msec
```

To find additional details of a particular packet, that is, if it has been forwarded or dropped, or if there is a crypto failure, run the following debug:

```
Router# debug ip packet [detail] <access-list-number>
```

You need to specify the access-list to capture the traffic you want.

NOTE Turn on Process switching to see the details with this **debug** command output.

CAUTION Be very careful when running the **debug ip packet detail** command in a busy system, as this command generates a lot of debug output. Be sure to restrict the amount of traffic with access-list.

Analysis of Problem Areas

The problem areas of IPsec are divided into the following categories based on their implementations:

- Basic LAN-to-LAN troubleshooting
- GRE over IPsec troubleshooting
- PKI-based troubleshooting
- Remote Access VPN troubleshooting

Basic LAN-to-LAN Troubleshooting

A basic LAN-to-LAN tunnel is the simplest form of IPsec tunnel in which private networks behind the tunnel end points communicate across the tunnel.

Because this is the simplest form of IPsec Tunnel, the troubleshooting steps that are described in the sections that follow form the foundation knowledge required for the subsequent sections of this book. Before going into the details of troubleshooting steps for a basic LAN-to-LAN tunnel, it's extremely important to understand a successful tunnel establishment process and understand the debug information. This section starts with this discussion. Then the section goes into the details of tunnel establishment failure issues, and issues with sending traffic across the tunnel. The following section is organized as follows:

- Successful LAN-to-LAN tunnel establishment process
- Tunnel establishment fails due to Phase I failure
- Tunnel establishment fails due to Phase II failure
- Tunnel is established but unable to pass any traffic

Successful LAN-to-LAN Tunnel Establishment Process

Before looking into the details of configuration and troubleshooting steps for a LAN-to-LAN tunnel, it is important to understand the sequence of events that occurs when traffic needs to pass through an IPsec tunnel in both inbound and outbound directions. The list that follows explains both inbound and outbound IPsec traffic through the router configured with IPsec:

- For outbound IPsec traffic (inside to outside)
  - **a** If using IPsec, check for the input access-list and then if allowed, decrypt the IPsec packets; otherwise drop the packets.
  - **b** Check the input access-list for decrypted traffic (Beginning with Version 12.3(8), this step is omitted).
  - **c** Check policy routing and then routing.
  - **d** Perform NAT and Crypto (check map and mark for encryption).
  - **e** Perform Outbound access control list (ACL) checking after Network Address Translation (NAT).
  - **f** If allowed and marked for encryption by the interesting traffic ACL, main/aggressive Mode starts to establish Phase I with a bidirectional IKE SA.
  - **g** Then Quick mode, which is Phase II negotiation, triggers and establishes IPsec SA, which is unidirectional; so it needs two SAs for both traffic directions.
  - **h** Then either with AH or ESP or both sides, send actual data over the tunnel.
- For Inbound IPsec traffic (Outside to Inside)

  The sequence of events is the same as for outbound except that NAT occurs before policy routing or routing.

Figure 6-6 shows a typical LAN-to-LAN tunnel setup. The configuration and troubleshooting for the remainder of this section is based on Figure 6-5.

Figure 6-6 *Basic LAN-to-LAN Tunnel Between the Dhaka and Doha Routers*

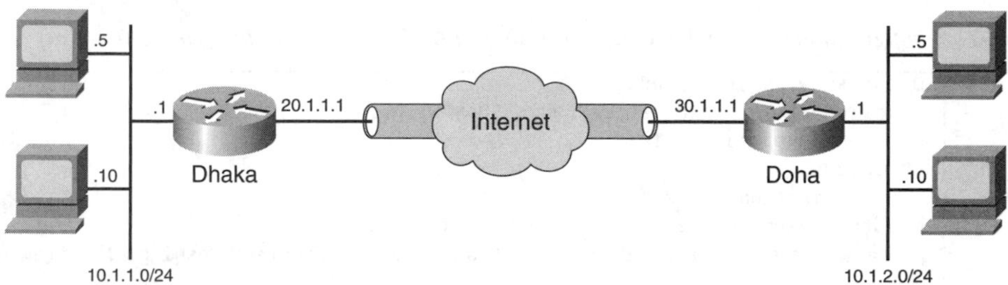

Example 6-6 shows the Dhaka router's basic LAN-to-LAN tunnel configuration. Note that Example 6-6 shows only the IPsec configuration; the irrelevant configuration has been removed for clarity.

Example 6-6 *Configuration of the Dhaka Router for LAN-to-LAN Tunnel Shown in Figure 6-6*

```
Dhaka# show running-config
! Define Phase 1 parameters under ISAKMP policy
crypto isakmp policy 10
 encryption 3des
 authentication pre-share
crypto isakmp key cisco123 address 30.1.1.1
! Transform-set defines IPSec encryption and authentication hashing algorithm for Phase
! II
crypto ipsec transform-set myset esp-3des esp-md5-hmac
!
! Apply the transform-set and the ACL, peers and so on under crypto map
crypto map to_Doha 10 ipsec-isakmp
 set peer 30.1.1.1
 set transform-set myset
 match address 101

! Interface that is connected to the private side of the network
interface Ethernet0/0
 ip address 10.1.1.1 255.255.255.0
!
! crypto map is then applied to an outbound interface
interface Ethernet1/0
 ip address 20.1.1.1 255.255.255.0
 crypto map to_Doha
!
ip classless
! The route must exist for the other side's private network which is 10.1.2.0/24. The
! following default route defines includes this network. Also make sure that the next hop
! is on the direction of outgoing interface where crypto map is applied.
ip route 0.0.0.0 0.0.0.0 20.1.1.100
! Access-list defines interesting VPN traffic
access-list 101 permit ip 10.1.1.0 0.0.0.255 10.1.2.0 0.0.0.255
Dhaka#
```

Example 6-7 shows the Doha router's basic LAN-to-LAN tunnel configuration.

Example 6-7 *Configuration of the Doha Router for LAN-to-LAN Tunnel Shown in Figure 6-6*

```
Doha# show running-config
! Define Phase 1 parameters under ISAKMP policy
crypto isakmp policy 10
 encr 3des
 authentication pre-share
crypto isakmp key cisco123 address 20.1.1.1
! Transform-set defines IPSec encryption and authentication hashing algorithm for Phase
! II
crypto ipsec transform-set myset esp-3des esp-md5-hmac
!
! Apply the transform-set and the ACL, peers and so on under crypto map
crypto map to_Dhaka 10 ipsec-isakmp
 set peer 20.1.1.1
 set transform-set myset
 match address 101

! Interface that is connected to the private side of the network
interface Ethernet0/0
 ip address 10.1.2.1 255.255.255.0
!
! crypto map is then applied to an outbound interface
interface Ethernet1/0
 ip address 30.1.1.1 255.255.255.0
 crypto map to_Dhaka
!
ip classless
! The route must exist for the other side's private network which is 10.1.2.0/24. The
! following default route defines includes this network. Also make sure that the next hop
! is on the direction of outgoing interface where crypto map is applied.
ip route 0.0.0.0 0.0.0.0 30.1.1.100
! Access-list defines interesting VPN traffic
access-list 101 permit ip 10.1.2.0 0.0.0.255 10.1.1.0 0.0.0.255
Doha#
```

Now, before going into the details of debug command output, go through a packet flow. Take an example based on the LAN-to-LAN tunnel that has just been configured. Assume that host 10.1.1.10 on the LAN segment of the Dhaka router wants to communicate with a host 10.1.2.10 that is on the LAN segment of the Doha router. Also, assume that the connection is initiated from Dhaka to Doha. The following sequence of events takes place:

1 Based on the route on Host with IP address 10.1.1.10, an IP packet is sent to the Dhaka router. Dhaka router will consult its routing table and based on its default route, it will forward the packet via the Ethernet 1/0 interface.

2 Before the packet is transmitted out of this interface, as there is a crypto-map applied, the Dhaka router will consult the SPD to see if there is a policy match for this packet (Source:10.1.1.10, Destination: 10.1.2.1). The SPD is built based on the

access-list defined for interesting traffic. As the access-list 101 includes the packet's source and destination address, the router will decide that the traffic needs to be IPsec protected.

3 The next step is to see if an IKE or IPsec SA is already established to the IPsec peer. Because this is the first packet to this destination, there will be no SA existing in the SADB. All packets that match this policy can be queued or dropped until the IKE and IPsec SA are established. IOS IPsec drops all packets while waiting for IKE and IPsec SAs to be established. That's why if you ping, you will first see some one- or two-packet loss.

4 IKE phase 1 negotiation is performed between the peers to establish the ISAKMP SA. The IKE phase negotiation is based on the ISAKMP policy. The establishment of ISAKMP can be verified with the **show crypto isakmp sa** command.

5 Upon successful establishment of ISAKMP SA (Phase I), IPsec SA negotiation takes place. This can be verified with the **show crypto ipsec sa** command.

6 After the IKE and IPsec SA are established, the original IP packet is encapsulated in IPsec tunnel mode using an ESP header, as this is what is configured in the transform-set. As Tunnel mode is used, a new IP header is added with the source IP address of 20.1.1.1 and destination IP address of 30.1.1.1. This packet is handed back to the usual IP forwarding routines to process the packet.

7 The encrypted IPsec packet arrives into the Doha router, and the presence of an IPsec header in the IP packet indicates that it must be decrypted on the Doha router.

8 The outer header destination address (30.1.1.1), the security protocol ESP, and the SPI in the ESP header are used as indexes into the SADB to find the SA for this packet.

9 Once there is a hit in the SADB, the packet is authenticated and then decrypted using the proper transforms.

10 Once the packet is decrypted, the 5-tuple check of the policy corresponding to the packet is checked. The 5-tuple is the source address of the inner IP header, destination address of the inner IP header, source port of the inner header, destination port of the inner header, and the IP protocol ID. Querying the SPD validates the 5-tuple. The lifetime counter in bytes is decremented and the anti-replay window is updated.

   The packet would have been dropped in the following cases:

   a The SA was not in the SADB.

   b The sequence number was on the left of the sliding window; therefore, the packet failed the replay check.

   c Authentication failed.

   d The length was incorrect.

   e The SA lifetime had expired.

11 If all goes well in the previous step, the packet is passed to the usual IP packet processing on the hub router.

Now that you understand the packet flows for the IPsec packet, it is time to explore the debug commands output to correlate the packet path as just discussed. Example 6-8 shows the debug output on the Dhaka router.

Example 6-8 *Dissection of Most Useful* **debug** *Commands Output*

```
Dhaka# show debug
Cryptographic Subsystem:
  Crypto ISAKMP debugging is on
  Crypto Engine debugging is on
  Crypto IPsec debugging is on

! Traffic is initiated from host 10.1.1.10 to host 10.1.2.10 which matches the ACL
! defined for interesting traffic.
    22:17:24.426: IPsec(sa_request): ,
! In the following line, local is the Dhaka router (Initiator) IP address, and remote is
! the Doha router's (Responder) IP address.
  (key eng. msg.) OUTBOUND local= 20.1.1.1, remote= 30.1.1.1,
! local proxy is source network behind the Initiator (Dhaka Router) and remote proxy is
! the Destination Network behind the Responder (Doha Router). This information is driven
! by the access-list defined for the crypto map.
    local_proxy= 10.1.1.0/255.255.255.0/0/0 (type=4),
    remote_proxy= 10.1.2.0/255.255.255.0/0/0 (type=4),
! This information is based on the transform-set defined
    protocol= ESP, transform= esp-3des esp-md5-hmac ,
  lifedur= 3600s and 4608000kb,
  spi= 0x4579753B(1165587771), conn_id= 0, keysize= 0, flags= 0x400A
! Main Mode exchange begins here. The first two packets negotiate phase I SA parameters
      ISAKMP: received ke message (1/1)
      ISAKMP: local port 500, remote port 500
      ISAKMP (0:1): Input = IKE_MESG_FROM_IPSec, IKE_SA_REQ_MM Old State =
           IKE_READY  New State = IKE_I_MM1
      ISAKMP (0:1): beginning Main Mode exchange
  22:17:24: ISAKMP (0:1): sending packet to 30.1.1.1(I)MM_NO_STATE
  22:17:24: ISAKMP (0:1): received packet from 30.1.1.1  (I) MM_NO_STATE
  22:17:24: ISAKMP (0:1): Input = IKE_MESG_FROM_PEER, IKE_MM_EXCH
  Old State = IKE_I_MM1  New State = IKE_I_MM2

22:17:24: ISAKMP (0:1): processing SA payload. message ID = 0
22:17:24: ISAKMP (0:1): processing vendor id payload
22:17:24: ISAKMP (0:1): Checking ISAKMP transform 1 against priority 10 policy
22:17:24: ISAKMP:       hash SHA
22:17:24: ISAKMP:       default group 1
22:17:24: ISAKMP:       auth pre-share
22:17:24: ISAKMP:       life type in seconds
22:17:24: ISAKMP:       life duration (VPI) of  0x0 0x1 0x51 0x80
22:17:24: ISAKMP (0:1): atts are acceptable. Next payload is 0
22:17:24: ISAKMP (0:1): Input = IKE_MESG_INTERNAL, IKE_PROCESS_MAIN_MODE
Old State = IKE_I_MM2  New State = IKE_I_MM2
```

Example 6-8 *Dissection of Most Useful* **debug** *Commands Output (Continued)*

```
! The policy 10 on this router and the atts offered by the other side matched
! Third and fourth packets completes Diffie-Hellman exchange
ISAKMP (0:1): sending packet to
30.1.1.1 (I) MM_SA_SETUP
ISAKMP (0:1): Input = IKE_MESG_INTERNAL,
 IKE_PROCESS_COMPLETE Old State = IKE_I_MM2  New State = IKE_I_MM3
ISAKMP (0:1): received packet from 30.1.1.1 (I) MM_SA_SETUP
ISAKMP (0:1): Input = IKE_MESG_FROM_PEER, IKE_MM_EXCH
Old State = IKE_I_MM3  New State = IKE_I_MM4
ISAKMP (0:1): processing KE payload. message ID = 0
ISAKMP (0:1): processing NONCE payload. message ID = 0
ISAKMP (0:1): found peer pre-shared key matching 209.165.201.4
ISAKMP (0:1): SKEYID state generated
ISAKMP (0:1): processing vendor id payload
! The fifth and sixth packets complete IKE authentication and Phase 1 SA is established
ISAKMP (0:1): SA is doing pre-shared key
authentication using id type ID_IPV4_ADDR
. . . . . .
ISAKMP (0:1): sending packet to 30.1.1.1
(I) MM_KEY_EXCH
ISAKMP (0:1): Input = IKE_MESG_INTERNAL,
IKE_PROCESS_COMPLETEOld State = IKE_I_MM4  New State = IKE_I_MM5
ISAKMP (0:1): received packet from 30.1.1.1 (I) MM_KEY_EXCH
ISAKMP (0:1): Input = IKE_MESG_FROM_PEER, IKE_MM_EXCH
Old State = IKE_I_MM5  New State = IKE_I_MM6
ISAKMP (0:1): processing ID payload. message ID = 0
ISAKMP (0:1): processing HASH payload. message ID = 0
ISAKMP (0:1): SA has been authenticated with 209.165.201.4
ISAKMP (0:1): Input = IKE_MESG_INTERNAL, IKE_PROCESS_COMPLETE
Old State = IKE_I_MM6  New State = IKE_P1_COMPLETE
!IKE Quick Mode IPSec SA Negotiations
! Begin Quick Mode exchange. The IPSec SA is negotiated in QM
ISAKMP (0:1): beginning Quick Mode exchange,
 M-ID of 843945273
ISAKMP (0:1): sending packet to 30.1.1.1 (I) QM_IDLE
ISAKMP (0:1): Node 843945273, Input = IKE_MESG_INTERNAL, IKE_INIT_QM Old State =
  IKE_QM_READY  New State = IKE_QM_I_QM1
ISAKMP (0:1): received packet from 30.1.1.1 (I) QM_IDLE
! IPSec SA proposal offered by far end will be checked against local crypto map
! configuration
ISAKMP (0:1): processing HASH payload. message ID = 843945273
ISAKMP (0:1): processing SA payload. message ID = 843945273
ISAKMP (0:1): Checking IPSec proposal 1
ISAKMP: transform 1, ESP_3DES
ISAKMP:   attributes in transform:
ISAKMP:      encaps is 1
ISAKMP:      SA life type in seconds
ISAKMP:      SA life duration (basic) of 3600
ISAKMP:      SA life type in kilobytes
ISAKMP:      SA life duration (VPI) of  0x0 0x46 0x50 0x0
```

continues

Example 6-8 *Dissection of Most Useful* **debug** *Commands Output (Continued)*

```
ISAKMP:      authenticator is HMAC-MD5
ISAKMP (0:1): atts are acceptable.
IPSec(validate_proposal_request): proposal part #1,
  (key eng. msg.) INBOUND local= 20.1.1.1, remote= 30.1.1.1,
    local_proxy= 10.1.1.0/255.255.255.0/0/0 (type=4),
    remote_proxy= 10.1.2.0/255.255.255.0/0/0 (type=4),
    protocol= ESP, transform= esp-3des esp-md5-hmac ,
    lifedur= 0s and 0kb,
    spi= 0x0(0), conn_id= 0, keysize= 0, flags= 0x2
! IKE Quick Mode SA Creation Phase
! Two IPSec SAs have been negotiated, an incoming SA with the SPI generated by initiator
! and an outbound SA with the SPIs proposed by the remote end
ISAKMP (0:1): Creating IPsec SAs
inbound SA from 30.1.1.1 to 20.1.1.1(proxy 10.1.2.0 to 10.1.1.0)
has spi 0x8EAB0B22 and conn_id 2000 and flags 2
 lifetime of 3600 seconds lifetime of 4608000 kilobytes
outbound SA from 20.1.1.1 to 30.1.1.1 (proxy 10.1.1.0 to 10.1.2.0)
has spi -1910720646 and conn_id 2001 and flags A
  lifetime of 3600 seconds lifetime of 4608000 kilobytes
! The IPsec SA info negotiated by IKE will be populated into router's SADB
22:17:25 : IPsec(key_engine): got a queue event...
22:17:25: IPsec(initialize_sas): ,
  (key eng. msg.) INBOUND local= 20.1.1.1, remote= 30.1.1.1,
    local_proxy= 10.1.1.0/255.255.255.0/0/0 (type=4),
    remote_proxy= 10.1.2.0/255.255.255.0/0/0 (type=4),
    protocol= ESP, transform= esp-3des esp-md5-hmac ,
    lifedur= 3600s and 4608000kb,
    spi= 0x4579753B(1165587771), conn_id= 2000, keysize= 0, flags=0x2
22:17:25: IPsec(initialize_sas): ,
  (key eng. msg.) OUTBOUND local= 20.1.1.1, remote= 30.1.1.1,
    local_proxy= 10.1.1.0/255.255.255.0/0/0 (type=4),
    remote_proxy= 10.1.2.0/255.255.255.0/0/0 (type=4),
    protocol= ESP, transform= esp-3des esp-md5-hmac ,
    lifedur= 3600s and 4608000kb,
    spi= 0x8E1CB77A(2384246650), conn_id= 2001, keysize= 0, flags= 0xA
! IKE Quick Mode Phase 2 is completed
! IPsec SA created in SADB,sent out last packet with commit bit set; IPsec tunnel
! established
IPsec(create_sa): sa created,
 (sa) sa_dest= 20.1.1.1,
 sa_prot= 50,
 sa_spi= 0x4579753B(1165587771),
 sa_trans= esp-3des esp-md5-hmac ,
 sa_conn_id= 2000
IPsec(create_sa): sa created,
 (sa) sa_dest= 30.1.1.1, sa_prot= 50, sa_spi= 0x8E1CB77A(2384246650),
 sa_trans= esp-3des esp-md5-hmac , sa_conn_id= 2001
ISAKMP (0:1): sending packet to 30.1.1.1 (I) QM_IDLE
ISAKMP (0:1): Node 843945273, Input = IKE_MESG_FROM_PEER, IKE_QM_EXCH
Old State = IKE_QM_I_QM1  New State = IKE_QM_PHASE2_COMPLETE
Dhaka#
```

Once you are comfortable with the packet paths, and can read and understand the debug output, go through the next few sections to find how to troubleshoot the IPsec VPN issues.

Tunnel Establishment Fails at Phase I

As discussed before, IPsec is established in two phases—Phase I and Phase II. So, the tunnel establishment might fail in either phase. You should execute **show** commands as discussed in the "Diagnostic Tools and Commands" section. First identify if it is a Phase I or Phase II failure. If the **show crypto isakmp sa** shows anything other than the **QM_IDLE** state as shown in Example 6-1, the problem is with Phase I. Run the debug commands as discussed in the "Diagnostic Tools and Commands" section and compare the output as shown in the preceding section for a successful tunnel negotiation. Work through the following steps to isolate any issues pertaining to Phase I tunnel establishment:

Step 1 Correct connectivity problems between the peers.

You must make sure that tunnel end points (Dhaka and Doha routers) can ping to each other's public interfaces where the crypto map is applied. If they are unable to ping to each other, make sure you have the route defined for both (usually the defined default gateway if these are gateway routers). Remember that some ISPs may block the ICMP packet. Therefore ping may fail even with the proper connectivity. For IPsec tunnel to establish, you must have UDP/500 (ISAKMP) open in both directions of tunnel end points. A quick way to verify that would be to use the **debug ip udp** command, which will show if the initiator or the responder is getting any ISAKMP request or response or not.

Step 2 Avoid configuration mismatches between the tunnel end points.

If the IP connectivity is tested and shown to be without problems, you must ensure the configuration on the tunnel end points. For Phase I, the ISAKMP policy must match, which gets exchanged in packet 1 and 2 of Phase I in Main Mode. Packet 1 sends all the configured ISAKMP proposals on the Initiator to the responder. Responder must match at least one ISKAMP policy as a whole to be able to successfully build up the Phase I. Packet 2 carries either a matching proposal or a failure message. If there is no match, the initiator tries the default policy of 65535, and if that does not match either, it fails ISAKMP negotiation. This occurrence outputs the debug message shown in Example 6-9, which shows the default policy on the router.

Example 6-9 *Sample Output of* **debug** *Commands when ISAKMP Fails with Policy Mismatch*

```
Dhaka# debug crypto isakmp
3d01h: ISAKMP (0:1): processing SA payload. message ID = 0
3d01h: ISAKMP (0:1): found peer pre-shared key matching 209.165.200.227
ISAKMP (0:1): Checking ISAKMP transform 1 against priority 1 policy
ISAKMP:       encryption 3DES-CBC
```

continues

Example 6-9 *Sample Output of* **debug** *Commands when ISAKMP Fails with Policy Mismatch (Continued)*

```
ISAKMP:       hash MD5
ISAKMP:       default group 1
ISAKMP:       auth pre-share
ISAKMP:       life type in seconds
ISAKMP:       life duration (VPI) of  0x0 0x1 0x51 0x80
ISAKMP (0:1): Hash algorithm offered does not match policy!
ISAKMP (0:1): atts are not acceptable. Next payload is 0
ISAKMP (0:1): Checking ISAKMP transform 1 against priority 65535 policy
ISAKMP:       encryption 3DES-CBC
ISAKMP:       hash MD5
ISAKMP:       default group 1
ISAKMP:       auth pre-share
ISAKMP:       life type in seconds
ISAKMP:       life duration (VPI) of  0x0 0x1 0x51 0x80
ISAKMP (0:1): Encryption algorithm offered does not match policy!
ISAKMP (0:1): atts are not acceptable. Next payload is 0
ISAKMP (0:1): no offers accepted!
ISAKMP (0:1): phase 1 SA not acceptable!
Router#
```

To verify the ISAKMP policy, you need to execute **show crypto isakmp policy** on both routers, and correct the policy mismatch issue. Be sure that at least one of the policies matches in its entirety.

Step 3 Check for IKE Packets on the Initiator with the **debug** command.

If you run **debug crypto isakmp**, you should see some IKE packets on the initiator. If there are no IKE packets, go through the following list to correct the problem:

— **Check to see if Internet Security Association Management Protocol (ISKAMP) is turned off**—ISAKMP is enabled by default on Cisco routers. If you turned it off, the ISKAMP packet would not be generated. The quickest way to verify this is by executing **show crypto isakmp sa** as shown below:

```
Dhaka# show crypto isakmp sa
ISAKMP is turned off
Dhaka#
```

To correct the problem, enable ISAKMP with the following command:

```
Dhaka(Config)# crypto isakmp enable
```

— **Find out if the Peer IP address configured correctly**—If the peer address is not configured correctly, or if the certificate is used but the router has not generated RSA keys, authenticated the CA, and obtained a certificate IKE, Phase I negotiation is not initiated and the following messages are displayed with the debug as shown in Example 6-10.

Example 6-10 *Peer Address Is Not Configured Correctly*

```
Dhaka# debug crypto isakmp
*Jul  5 22:44:45.760: ISAKMP: Looking for a matching key for 30.1.1.1 in default
*Jul  5 22:44:45.760: ISAKMP: Looking for a matching key for 30.1.1.1 in test
*Jul  5 22:44:45.760: ISAKMP (0:2): No pre-shared key with 30.1.1.1!
*Jul  5 22:44:45.760: ISAKMP (0:2): No Cert or pre-shared address key.
*Jul  5 22:44:45.760: ISAKMP (0:2): construct_initial_message: Can not start Mai
Dhaka#
```

— **Check and correct the Routing Problem On the Initiator**—If ISAKMP is turned on and you are still unable to see IKE packets, execute **show ip route host|network_address** to verify that the route not only exists for the tunnel end point, but also for the actual destination network through the same interface as the crypto map applied. Otherwise, IKE will not be triggered. Usually, routers have default routes for both the remote side private network and the remote tunnel IP address.

— **Verify Crypto Map and make sure it is applied on the correct interface**—If the crypto map is not applied, or applied on the wrong interface, ISAKMP will not be triggered, and therefore you will not see any IKE packets. The best way to find out if the crypto map is applied to the correct interface is to execute the **show crypto map tag crypto_map_name** command on both initiator and responder. The crypto map needs to be applied on the outgoing interface of the router. The outgoing interface is the interface to which the routing table is pointing to reach the remote side private network. Additionally, if you don't want to use the outside interface's IP as the local ID for VPN tunnel, use the command **crypto map <name> local-address <interface>**, to specify the correct interface. If there are physical and logical interfaces involved in carrying outgoing traffic, the crypto map should be applied to both; however, this restriction has been removed in the latest Cisco IOS. A misconfigured crypto map results in the error shown in Example 6-11.

Example 6-11 *Sample Output of IPsec* **debug** *Commands with the Crypto Map Applied on the Wrong Interface*

```
Router# show debug
Cryptographic Subsystem:
Crypto ISAKMP debugging is on
Crypto Engine debugging is on
Crypto IPsec debugging is on
. . .
! Following line is an indication that a wrong local IP address is selected.
IPsec(validate_proposal): invalid local address 209.165.201.4
ISAKMP (0:4): atts not acceptable. Next payload is 0
ISAKMP (0:4): phase 2 SA not acceptable!
Router#
```

- **Check to see if the Interesting Access-list is configured correctly**—The crypto access-list defines the interesting traffic—traffic that should go through the tunnel. If your VPN traffic is not included in the crypto ACL, IKE negotiation does not occur. Ideally, the crypto ACL on both sides of the tunnel should be mirror images of each other. For example, if you want to send traffic from 10.1.1.0 network behind the Dhaka router (Figure 6-6) to 10.1.2.0 network behind the Doha router, your access-list on the Dhaka router should be **access-list 101 permit ip 10.1.1.0 0.0.0.255 10.1.2.0 0.0.0.255** and the exact reflection of this ACL should be **access-list permit ip 10.1.2.0 0.0.0.255 10.1.1.0 0.0.0.255** on the Doha router. If the access-lists are not the reflection of each other, then you need to be sure that the responder has an ACL which is a superset of the ACL defined in the initiator. Otherwise, the tunnel establishment will fail. Here is an example to illustrate this point. Assume that Dhaka is the initiator, and Doha is the responder. If Dhaka has an ACL **access-list 101 permit ip 10.1.1.0 0.0.0.255 10.1.2.0 0.0.0.255** and Doha has a superset ACL of **access-list permit ip 10.1.0.0 0.0.255.255 10.1.0.0 0.0.255.255**, the tunnel will be established if Dhaka initiates the tunnel. However, if Doha initiates the tunnel, it will fail, because the ACL on Doha is beyond the scope of the ACL on Dhaka.

Step 4 Verify IKE packets on the responder with **debug** commands.

If Step 3 is verified successfully but Phase I is still not established, verify that the responder is seeing the IKE packets. The following list outlines some of the common steps to follow to prevent the responder from receiving the IKE packets:

- Perform Step 1 to ensure that the IP connectivity is established.
- Verify the peer IP address to ensure that the initiator is not sending IKE Phase I requests to the wrong IP.
- IKE Phase I and Phase II negotiation occurs using UDP/500. If there is a firewall between the tunnel end points, or if the responder has an incoming ACL on the interface where crypto map is applied, make sure that UDP/500 is allowed.

  See Example 6-12 for the debug messages that are shown on the Dhaka router, which initiated the IKE messages, and shows retransmit, which is an indication that the receiver, the Doha router, is not getting the traffic.

Example 6-12 *IKE Negotiation Messages on Initiator the Dhaka Router when ISKMP Is Blocked by a Firewall or by the Interface ACL on the Doha Router*

```
Dhaka# debug crypto isakmp
*Jul  5 22:50:42.144: ISAKMP (0:1): retransmitting phase 1 MM_NO_STATE...
*Jul  5 22:50:42.144: ISAKMP (0:1): incrementing error counter on sa: retransmit
  phase 1
*Jul  5 22:50:42.144: ISAKMP (0:1): retransmitting phase 1 MM_NO_STATE
*Jul  5 22:50:42.144: ISAKMP (0:1): sending packet to 30.1.1.1 my_port 500 peer_
  port 500 (I) MM_NO_STATE
*Jul  5 22:50:52.144: ISAKMP (0:1): retransmitting phase 1 MM_NO_STATE...
*Jul  5 22:50:52.144: ISAKMP (0:1): incrementing error counter on sa: retransmit
  phase 1
*Jul  5 22:50:52.144: ISAKMP (0:1): retransmitting phase 1 MM_NO_STATE
*Jul  5 22:50:52.144: ISAKMP (0:1): sending packet to 30.1.1.1 my_port 500 peer_
  port 500 (I) MM_NO_STATE
```

Open up UDP/500 on both the firewall (in both directions of traffic) and the inbound ACL on the interface where the crypto map is applied to resolve this issue.

Step 5 Avoid authentication failure.

Authentication failure is one of the many reasons IKE phase I establishment might fail. If the pre-shared key is used for authentication, you must ensure that you have defined the same pre-shared key on both peers; otherwise, the IKE Phase I will fail, resulting in the debug messages shown in Example 6-13.

Example 6-13 *Sample Output of the* **debug** *Commands Output with Pre-shared Key Mismatch*

```
Dhaka# debug crypto isakmp
ISAKMP (62): SKEYID state generated
ISAKMP (62); processing vendor id payload
ISAKMP (62): speaking to another IOS box!
ISAKMP: reserved not zero on ID payload!
! Following messages indicates an authentication failure
%CRYPTO-4-IKMP_BAD_MESSAGE: IKE message from 209.165.200.227
 failed its sanity check or is malformed
Router#
```

If the pre-shared key is not the same, correct the problem. If the pre-shared key is the same on both sides, remove and add the pre-shared key back again on the routers to see if the problem is corrected. If this also fails, there could be a bug. If you are using certificates for IKE authentication, refer to the section entitled "Public Key Infrastructure (PKI) Troubleshooting" for more details.

Tunnel Establishment Fails at Phase II

After Phase I is established, two peers negotiate with each other to create the IPsec SA. If Phase II negotiation fails, IPsec SA is not established. The following are some of the steps you can follow to troubleshoot Phase II failure:

Step 1 Check for IPsec transform set mismatches between peers.

If there is a mismatch on IPsec Transform set between the peers, quick mode negotiation fails. You need to verify IPsec SA negotiation with the **show crypto ipsec sa** command. Example 6-14 shows the output of **debug crypto isakmp** on the initiator router, which is failing in quick mode due to a transform set mismatch resulting in the **SA not acceptable** message.

Example 6-14 *IKE Quick Mode Fails with Transform Set Mismatch*

```
Dhaka# debug crypto isakmp
Dhaka# debug crypto ipsec
ISAKMP (0:2): Checking IPsec proposal 1
ISAKMP: transform 1, ESP_3DES
ISAKMP:   attributes in transform:
ISAKMP:      encaps is 1
ISAKMP:      SA life type in seconds
ISAKMP:      SA life duration (basic) of 3600
ISAKMP:      SA life type in kilobytes
ISAKMP:      SA life duration (VPI) of  0x0 0x46 0x50 0x0
! Transform set mismatch as shown in the following message
IPsec(validate_proposal): transform proposal (prot 3, trans 3, hmac_alg 0) not
  supported
ISAKMP (0:2): atts not acceptable. Next payload is 0
ISAKMP (0:2): SA not acceptable!
Dhaka#
```

Step 2 Resolve asymmetric crypto access-lists issues.

If the crypto map access-lists are not the mirror image of each other on both peers, Quick Mode might fail, or one side can initiate quick mode successfully, but the other side cannot. If you have the Dhaka router crypto access-list configured with source address 10.10.0.0/16 and destination address of 20.20.0.0/16, and the Doha router configured with source 20.20.20.0/24 and destination of 10.10.10.0/24, the Dhaka router cannot initiate successful quick mode because Dhaka's access-list address range is outside the scope of the address ranger on Doha's. Therefore, Doha rejects Dhaka's IPsec SA proposal. However, Doha can successfully initiate quick mode, as Dhaka's access-list addresses include addresses in Doha's. Example 6-15 shows the debug output of quick mode failure with asymmetric crypto access-lists.

Example 6-15 *Output of* **debug** *Commands When Configured with the Wrong Access List*

```
Dhaka# debug crypto isakmp
Dhaka# debug crypto ipsec
Cryptographic Subsystem:
Crypto ISAKMP debugging is on
Crypto Engine debugging is on
Crypto IPsec debugging is on
. . .
1w6d: IPSec(validate_proposal_request): proposal part #1,
  (key eng. msg.) INBOUND local= 209.165.201.4, remote= 209.165.200.227,
    local_proxy= 10.1.2.0/255.255.255.0/0/0 (type=4),
    remote_proxy= 10.1.1.0/255.255.255.0/0/0 (type=4),
    protocol= ESP, transform= esp-3des esp-md5-hmac ,
    lifedur= 0s and 0kb,
    spi= 0x0(0), conn_id= 0, keysize= 0, flags= 0x4
1w6d: IPsec(validate_transform_proposal): proxy identities not supported
1w6d: ISAKMP (0:2): IPSec policy invalidated proposal
1w6d: ISAKMP (0:2): phase 2 SA not acceptable!
```

Example 6-16 shows a properly configured mirror image access-list for two peers.

Example 6-16 *A Sample of a Properly Configured Reflected Access List*

```
Dhaka(config)# access-list 101 permit ip 10.10.10.0 0.0.0.255 20.20.20.0 0.0.0.255
Doha(config)# access-list 101 permit ip 20.20.20.0 0.0.0.255 10.10.10.0 0.0.0.255
```

Step 3 Avoid overlapping access-lists.

If you have multiple peers on a router, make sure that the matching address access lists for each of the peers are mutually exclusive of the matching address access lists for the other peers. If you don't do that, the router chooses the wrong crypto map to try to establish a tunnel with one of the other peers. See Example 6-17 for a sample output of this behavior.

Example 6-17 *Output of the IPsec* **debug** *Command Showing a Problem with Overlapping Access Lists*

```
Dhaka# debug crypto isakmp
Dhaka# debug crypto ipsec
! Only showing the relevant debugs output
IPsec(validate_proposal_request): proposal part #1,
  (key eng. msg.) INBOUND local= 209.165.200.227, remote= 209.165.202.149,
    local_proxy= 10.1.1.0/255.255.255.0/0/0 (type=4),
    remote_proxy= 10.1.2.0/255.255.255.0/0/0 (type=4),
    protocol= ESP, transform= esp-3des esp-md5-hmac ,
    lifedur= 0s and 0kb,
    spi= 0x0(0), conn_id= 0, keysize= 0, flags= 0x4
IPsec(validate_transform_proposal): peer address 209.165.202.149 not found
ISAKMP (0:2): IPsec policy invalidated proposal
ISAKMP (0:2): phase 2 SA not acceptable!
```

continues

Example 6-17 *Output of the IPsec* **debug** *Command Showing a Problem with Overlapping Access Lists (Continued)*

```
Access list for 209.165.201.4:
Access-list 100 permit ip 10.1.1.0 0.0.0.255 10.1.2.0 0.0.0.255
Access-list 100 permit ip 10.1.1.0 0.0.0.255 10.1.5.0 0.0.0.255
Access list for 209.165.202.149:
Access-list 110 permit ip 10.1.1.0 0.0.0.255 10.1.2.0 0.0.0.255
Dhaka#
```

After you go through Steps 1 through 3, make sure that Phase II is established executing the **show crypto ipsec sa** command, as shown in Example 6-2.

Tunnel Is Established but Unable To Pass Traffic

Even if a tunnel is established, as verified in the preceding section, traffic still might not be able to flow for several reasons. The following steps will help in troubleshooting the problem with data passing across the tunnel:

1 Routing issues

If either or both sides of encryption or decryption counters are not incrementing with **show crypto ipsec sa** command output, there might be an issue with routing. Be sure that you have a route defined for the remote side private network that is pointing to the gateway of the router through the interface where the crypto map is applied. To verify that the routing is taking place properly, you might want to run **debug ip packet <acl> detailed**. Example 6-18 shows how to run **debug ip packet <acl> detailed** for traffic originating from 10.1.1.10 behind the Dhaka router going to FTP server behind the Doha router, which has an IP address of 10.1.2.10 across the tunnel.

Example 6-18 *Illustration of How to Use the* **debug ip packet <acl> detailed** *Command*

```
Dhaka(config)# access-list 101 permit tcp host 10.1.1.10 host 10.1.2.10 eq 21
Dhaka(config)# access-list 101 permit tcp host 10.1.2.10 eq 21 host 10.1.1.10
Dhaka(config)# exit
Dhaka# debug ip packet 101 detail
```

Be sure to run in Process Switching so you can see the details of the packet. You will need to be careful when running this in a busy system.

2 Firewall issues

If there is any firewall between the tunnel endpoints, or if there is an access-list in the egress interface of tunnel end points, be sure to open up protocol AH (IP/51) and Encapsulating Security Payload (ESP) (IP/50). For ISAKMP, you need to open up port UDP/500. If NAT-T is configured, UDP/4500 port also needs to be open. For more discussion on this, refer to the section entitled, "Firewall with IPsec Issues" under "Common Problems and Resolutions."

3 Network Address Translation (NAT) issues

If you do not have a firewall blocking any of the necessary ports, check to see if there is any NAT device between the tunnel end points. You might also have NAT turned on at tunnel end points. To get around the problem, refer to the "NAT with IPsec Issues" subsection under the section entitled, "Common Problems and Resolutions."

4 Hardware Encryption card problem

If you are running the Hardware Encryption card, and you are having problems passing traffic across the tunnel, as a temporary work-around, you might want to turn off the Hardware Encryption card. If turning off the Hardware Encryption card resolves the issue, the problem could be with the hardware, or you might be running into a bug with the Hardware Encryption card on the code.

5 Interface problem

Different interfaces use different switching and encapsulation codes. If you are using serial, and it fails, try your setup on simple Ethernet or other interfaces.

6 Switching path problem

Different switching methods use completely different code paths with completely different sets of problems. If CEF switching does not work, try regular fast-switching or vice versa. Turn off fast-switching and see if the problem goes away. Even if the problem does not disappear with the "process switched," it is much easier to debug IPsec problems with process switching, as you can actually get some useful packet debugs. With switching path problems, you might run into issues such as packet drops, latency, and reliability problems.

GRE over IPsec

As mentioned at the beginning of this chapter, IPsec only encapsulates unicast IP traffic, which might be less than desirable in networks in which multicast or non-IP traffic needs to be transferred securely across the IPsec tunnel. With GRE over IPsec, this is possible. The following list outlines the reasons why GRE over IPsec is used:

- To pass multicast and broadcast traffic across the tunnel securely.
- To pass non-IP traffic (for instance, International Packet Exchange (IPX) across the tunnel securely.
- To have resiliency (high availability). For more details on this, refer to the section entitled, "Best Practices."
- To help in saving memory and CPU of the router. This is because, for every ACL entry, two IPsec SAs are created. Hence, if regular IPsec is configured, the number of ACLs to include the interesting traffic becomes high, which increases the number of IPsec SAs on the router. These ACEs can be replaced by a single ACL for GRE traffic, which ends up creating only two IPsec SAs. This saves memory on the router.

Configuration Steps

To integrate GRE over IPsec, you need to configure the tunnel interface on both sides, and force the private network to go through the tunnel using dynamic routing protocol (you also can use static routing if you desire). When the actual packet arrives at the router, the router forwards the packet to the tunnel interface, and then encapsulates the packet with a GRE header and tries to send the packet to the outgoing interface where a crypto map is configured. So, the crypto map is triggered and encapsulates the packet with an IPsec header, as the interesting traffic ACL includes the GRE source and destination addresses.

Example 6-19 shows a basic GRE over IPsec configuration on the Dhaka router, based on Figure 6-6. Basic LAN-to-LAN tunnel configuration on the Dhaka router as shown in Example 6-7 is replaced by the GRE over IPsec configuration as shown in the following example.

Example 6-19 *Dhaka Router Configuration for a Basic GRE Over IPsec*

```
Dhaka# show running-config
! Phase 1 policy is defined here for phase 1 of IPsec tunnel build up process
crypto isakmp policy 1
 encryption 3des
 authentication pre-share
crypto isakmp key cisco123 address 30.1.1.1
! Phase II attributed for IPsec tunnel is defined by transform-set
crypto ipsec transform-set myset esp-3des esp-md5-hmac
!
! Phase II information is applied to the crypto map
crypto map GRE_to_Doha 10 ipsec-isakmp
 set peer 30.1.1.1
 set transform-set myset
 match address 101
crypto map GRE local-address Ethernet 1/0
! Interface Ethernet 0/0 is connected to the private side of the network
interface Ethernet0/0
 ip address 10.1.1.1 255.255.255.0
!
! Tunnel Interface Creation & crypto map applied
interface Tunnel0
ip address 1.1.1.1 255.255.255.252
ip mtu 1440
tunnel source Ethernet 1/0
tunnel destination 30.1.1.1
! Crypto map is applied to the tunnel interface. This is required if you are running
! IOS version prior to 12.2(13)T. Beginning with IOS version 12.2(13)T, it is
! strongly discouraged to apply the crypto map under the tunnel interface; only
! crypto map on the physical interface is required.
crypto map GRE_to_Doha
! crypto map is then applied to an outbound interface
interface Ethernet1/0
 ip address 20.1.1.1 255.255.255.0
 crypto map GRE_to_Doha
!EIGRP turned to get GRE, and regular traffic updates to the routing table
router eigrp 10
network 1.1.1.0 0.0.0.3
network 10.1.1.0 0.0.0.255
no auto-summary
```

Example 6-19 *Dhaka Router Configuration for a Basic GRE Over IPsec (Continued)*

```
no eigrp log-neighbor-changes
ip classless
! The following default route will allow Dhaka router to the talk to the Doha Router
ip route 0.0.0.0 0.0.0.0 20.1.1.100
! Access-list defines GRE traffic as interesting traffic
access-list 101 permit gre host 20.1.1.1 host 30.1.1.1
Dhaka#
```

Troubleshooting Steps

You can run the **debug tunnel** command to troubleshoot the GRE tunnel issue. It is strongly recommended to ensure that you can build up the GRE tunnel over IP before you turn on IPsec for the GRE tunnel. While working with GRE over IPsec, remember the following points:

- If you are running an IOS version earlier than 12.2(13)T, you need to apply the **crypto map** on both the tunnel interfaces and the physical interfaces to correctly invoke switching paths to achieve IPsec. Beginning with IOS Version 12.2(13)T, or 12.3 and later, the configured IPsec crypto map needs to be applied to the physical interface only, and is no longer required to be applied on the GRE tunnel interface. You can still apply the crypto map on both physical and tunnel interfaces, but it is strongly recommended to apply the crypto map on the physical interface only.
- Specify GRE traffic as IPsec interesting traffic. On the Dhaka router, the interesting traffic for the GRE traffic should be defined with the following access-list:

  ```
  Dhaka(config)# access-list 101 permit gre host 20.1.1.1 host 30.1.1.1
  ```

  Make sure that the source and destination addresses are the source and destination addresses of the GRE tunnel interface. In this case, the source is 20.1.1.1, which is the actual physical interface IP address. The destination address is the remote peer IP address, which is 30.1.1.1.
- Static or Dynamic routing protocol needs to be configured for the remote private network pointing to the tunnel interface as next hop. GRE tunnel should be encrypted by the IPsec tunnel.
- Take appropriate precautions to avoid the recursive routing problem. Otherwise, the tunnel interface will flap (going up and down). This situation arises, when based on the routing table, the router sends the GRE packets to its own interface instead of sending them to the physical interface. The message you get on the router is as follows:

  ```
  Tunnel0 temporarily disabled due to recursive routing.
  ```

  Keep the following list in mind to avoid the recursive routing loop:

  — Use different routing protocols or separate routing protocol identifiers for GRE traffic and actual traffic.

- Keep tunnel IP address and actual IP network address ranges distinct.
- For the tunnel interface IP address, don't use unnumbered to loopback interface when the loopback's IP address resides in the ISP address space.
- Use static routes for the end point of GRE tunnel interfaces.
- Use route filtering so that the router does not point to the tunnel interface for its own routes.

Public Key Infrastructure (PKI) Troubleshooting

So far, this chapter has discussed IKE authentication using pre-shared keys. This section looks into some of the issues that you might run into when using digital certificates as a means of IKE authentication. The digital certificate is issued by a certificate authority (CA) server. The CA should issue the certificate at the time you install the device. It is not done for each IKE exchange. That is, after a device obtains a certificate, it does not need to contact the CA during the connection setup process unless you configure the device for Certificate Revocation List (CRL) Verification. This setup avoids the reliability problems associated with a centralized key server.

Configuration Steps

The Cisco Certificate Enrollment Protocol (CEP) manages the certificate life-cycle process. This protocol supports operations such as certificate enrollment, certificate revocation, and certificate access, allowing Cisco routers to participate within a public key infrastructure (PKI).

The general procedure has four steps as follows:

Step 1 The first step is to generate an RSA key pair on the router. The generated keys are saved in the private configuration in non-volatile random access memory (NVRAM). This private configuration is never displayed to the user or backed up to another device. A single CA must be defined for the router using its fully qualified domain name (FQDN) or IP address, the CA's HTTP common gateway interface (CGI) script path, and optionally, the certificate revocation list (CRL) query URL.

Step 2 The second step of the general procedure is to retrieve the CA certificate. To authenticate the certificate of another device, the router must query the CA to obtain the CA certificate containing the CA public key. Because the router has no means of validating the CA certificate automatically, the key should be authenticated manually by contacting the CA administrator and comparing the fingerprints of the certificate. The validated certificate is stored in the configuration, and the public key from the CA certificate is added to the RSA public key chain.

Step 3 The third step of the general procedure is to request that the CA generate a certificate for the key pair of the router by sending an enrollment request. A dialog is begun in which the user-defined certificate attributes are entered (a challenge password, a user addressable name, and optionally, the router serial number and IP addresses). The CA operator may cease to manually validate the request, and the fingerprints can be compared.

Step 4 The fourth and last step of the general procedure is to request receipt of the certificate. Because there might be a significant delay, the certificate is retrieved asynchronously.

Work through the following steps to enroll the certificate with the CA server:

Step 1 Define the hostname and domain-name.

This is required, because the router assigns FQDN to the RSA key and Certificates.

```
Router(config)# hostname Dhaka
Dhaka(config)# ip domain-name cisco.com
! Hence the fully qualified domain name is FQDN= Dhaka.cisco.com
Dhaka(config)#
```

Step 2 Set the router clock.

Step 3 Generate the RSA key pair.

RSA key pair is used to sign and encrypt IKE key management messages. By default, a general purpose RSA key pair is generated. You can specify that usage keys be generated, which will generate a separate RSA key pair for signing and encryption. The syntax for generating the RSA key pair is as follows:

```
crypto key generate rsa <general-keys> <usage-keys >  <word>
```

In the Dhaka router, the RSA key is generated as follows:

```
Dhaka(config)# crypto key generate rsa
The name for the keys will be: Dhaka.cisco.com
! The following message is because this RSA keys already exist on the router
% You already have RSA keys defined for Dhaka.cisco.com.
% Do you really want to replace them? [yes/no]: yes
Choose the size of the key modulus in the range of 360 to 2048 for your
  General Purpose Keys. Choosing a key modulus greater than 512 may take
    a few minutes.
! If you don't define the modulus, 512 will be used.
How many bits in the modulus [512]:
Generating RSA keys ...
[OK]

Dhaka(config)#
```

Step 4 Define the Certificate Authority (CA).

Define the communication parameters between the router and CA with the following parameters:

— **Define enrollment URL**—specifies the CA location. Enrollment URL is the minimum configuration requirement.

— **Define Registration Authority**—provides interface between CA and end device (router), and publishes a CRL. This is the default enrollment mode, even without RA mode specified.

— **Define Certificate Revocation List URL**—Specifies the URL of the CDP (CRL Distribution Point), and off-box cert retrieval location.

— **Define enrollment retry-count**—This defines how many times a router will resend a certificate request. Default is 10, range is 1 to 100.

— **Define enrollment retry period**—This is the wait period between certificate request retries in minutes. Default uses back-off.

The following configuration is a setup on the Dhaka router for the CA server located at 20.1.1.100:

```
Dhaka(config)# crypto ca identity vpn
Dhaka(ca-identity)# enrollment url http://20.1.1.100:80
Dhaka(ca-identity)# query url ldap://20.1.1.100
Dhaka(ca-identity)# enrollment retry count 20
Dhaka(ca-identity)# enrollment retry period 5
Dhaka(ca-identity)# enrollment mode ra
Dhaka(ca-identity)#
```

Step 5 Authenticate the CA.

You need to authenticate the CA to obtain the CA's self-signed certificate, which contains the CA's public key as follows for the Dhaka Router:

```
Dhaka(config)# crypto ca authenticate vpn
        Certificate has the following attributes:
! This finger prints should matched with the published finger print of the CA
! server
       Fingerprint: 1FCDG2C9 2DEDA6DC 4819D44C B4CFF5F2
       % Do you accept this certificate? [yes/no]: yes
Dhaka(config)#
```

Manually authenticate the CA's public key by comparing the CA's certificate fingerprint as shown previously.

Step 6 Enroll with the CA.

You need to enroll the router with the CA to obtain a signed certificate for each of the router's RSA key pairs. A general purpose RSA key which is generated by default has one RSA key pair and therefore will need one certificate. However, special usage RSA keys have two RSA key pairs and will need two certificates. The Dhaka router has generated a general purpose key, so it will get one certificate from the CA server:

```
Dhaka(config)# crypto ca enroll vpn
     % Start certificate enrollment ..
Dhaka(config)#
```

Troubleshooting Steps

The PKI problem can be categorized as follows:

- Certificate enrollment process failure
- Certificate enrollment is fine but IKE authentication still fails

More detailed discussions follow in the next sections.

Certificate Enrollment Process Failure

The certificate enrollment process may fail for two reasons, which are discussed in order:

1 Incorrect CA URL for CA Server

You need to know the correct enrollment URL from CA administration to authenticate the CA and register with the CA server. You also need to find out from CA administration if the registration authority (RA) is used. Also find out how many certificates you are supposed to obtain. For CA mode only, you get the CA root certificate and the router identity certificate. However, for RA mode, you get the CA root certificate, the RA signature certificate, the RA encryption certificate, and the router identity certificate.

Example 6-20 shows a sample URL for the Microsoft CA server.

Example 6-20 *URL (Identity) for Microsoft CA*

```
Dhaka(config)# crypto ca trustpoint DhakaPKI
Dhaka(ca-trustpoint)# enrollment mode ra
Dhaka(ca-trustpoint)# enrollment url http://10.1.1.10/certsrv/mscep/mscep.dll
Dhaka(ca-trustpoint)# crl query ldap://10.1.1.11
Dhaka(ca-trustpoint)#
```

Example 6-21 shows a sample URL for the Entrust CA server.

Example 6-21 *URL (Identity) for Entrust CA*

```
Dhaka(config)# crypto ca trustpoint DhakaPKI
Dhaka(ca-trustpoint)# enrollment mode ra
Dhaka(ca-trustpoint)# enrollment url http://10.1.1.12
Dhaka(ca-trustpoint)# crl query ldap://10.1.1.12
Dhaka(ca-trustpoint)#
```

Example 6-22 shows a sample URL for the Verisign CA server.

Example 6-22 *URL (Identity) for Verisign Testdrive CA*

```
Dhaka(config)# crypto ca trustpoint DhakaPKI
Dhaka(ca-trustpoint)# enrollment url http://testdriveIPsec.verisign.com
Dhaka(ca-trustpoint)# crl option
Dhaka(ca-trustpoint)#
```

2 HTTP (TCP/80 Port) is blocked between the router and the CA server

The CA or the registration authority (RA) server should be accessible (TCP/80) from the router. If there is any firewall blocking between the router and CA or RA server, the certificate enrollment process fails, resulting in the message shown in Example 6-23.

Example 6-23 *Sample Output When the Router Is Unable to Query the Servers*

```
Dhaka# debug crypto pki message
Dhaka# debug crypto pki transaction
CRYPTO_PKI: socket connect error
CRYPTO_PKI: 0, failed to open http connection
CRYPTO_PKI: 65535, failed to send out the pki message
!or
a Failed to query CA certificate message
Dhaka#
```

Certificate Enrollment Is Fine but IKE Authentication Still Fails

IKE authentication occurs on the fifth and sixth packets of IKE negotiation. In the fifth packet, the responder receives the ID payload, cert payload, and signature payload from the initiator. The responder verifies if the initiator's ISAKMP identity in the ID payload matches the identity in the certificate. It performs CRL checking, lifetime checking, and verifies the integrity of the certificate using the public key. It performs an IKE authentication integrity check by recalculating the hash in the signature payload.

Checking PKI enrollment and certificate lifetime required multiple commands, the user had to correlate output:

```
show crypto pki certificates
show crypto pki timers
show crypto pki trustpoints
```

Beginning with IOS Version 12.3(11)T, you can check configured trustpoints, enrollment status, and certificate lifetime with just the following command:

```
show crypto pki trustpoint status
```

In addition to **show** commands, you need to run the following **debug** commands to troubleshoot PKI problem:

```
debug crypto pki  messages
debug crypto pki  transactions
```

Example 6-24 shows the debug output of a successful IKE negotiation with a certificate on the responder (the Doha router).

Example 6-24 *A Successful Authentication on the Doha Router (Responder)*

```
Doha# debug crypto isakmp
Doha# debug crypto pki message
Doha# debug crypto pki transaction
ISAKMP (0:1): processing ID payload. message ID = 0
ISAKMP (0:1): processing CERT payload. message ID = 0
ISAKMP (0:1): processing a CT_X509_SIGNATURE cert
CRYPTO_PKI: status = 0: poll CRL ldap search: server=10.1.1.11, base=CN = CRL1, OU
  = dohavpn, O = cisco, C = bangladesh, attribute=: scope=2, filter=cn=CRL1
CRYPTO_PKI: ldap_bind() succeeded.
CRYPTO_PKI: set CRL update timer with delay: 66494
CRYPTO_PKI: the current router time: 10:00:28 UTC Apr 18 2004
CRYPTO_PKI: the last CRL update time: 03:28:42 UTC Apr 18 2004
CRYPTO_PKI: the next CRL update time: 04:28:42 UTC Apr 19 2004
CRYPTO_PKI: transaction GetCRL completed
CRYPTO_PKI: Certificate verified, chain status= 1
ISAKMP (0:1): OU = dohavpn
ISAKMP (0:1): processing SIG payload. message ID = 0
ISAKMP (1): sa->peer.name = , sa->peer_id.id.id_fqdn.fqdn = Doha.dohavpn.com
ISAKMP (0:1): SA has been authenticated with 20.1.1.1
Doha#
```

IKE with a digital signature may fail for one of the following reasons:

1. ISAKMP identity mismatch

   The router assigns an FQDN to the keys and certificates used by IPsec. During IKE or Phase 1 negotiation the router checks the FQDN in the certificate. Therefore you have to use **ISAKMP identity as hostname**, instead of address on both of the routers. You will see the following message if there is an ISAKMP identity mismatch:

   ```
   Dhaka#
   3d15h: ISAKMP (0:162): processing a CT_X509_SIGNATURE cert
   3d15h: %CRYPTO-6-IKMP_NO_ID_CERT_ADDR_MATCH: ID of
           30.1.1.1   (type 1) an certificate addr with 30.1.1.1
   Dhaka#
   ```

2 Time and Date Mismatch

If the date and time of the clock on the router does not fall between the start and end dates on the certificates and the next/last update of the CRL, the following errors will be seen during Phase 1 negotiation:

```
CRYPTO_PKI: New CRL Not Yet Valid
        (router time not synched to CA?)
         CRL published: 16:17:34 PST Jan 10 2002
```

During certificate authentication, you will see the following message:

```
% Error in receiving Certificate Authority certificate: status = FAIL,
  cert length = 0
```

Use the **show clock** command in conjunction with the **show crypto ca cert** command as shown in Example 6-25, and compare the output to verify the validity of the certificate.

Example 6-25 show crypto ca cert *Output*

```
Dhaka# show crypto ca cert
Certificate
  Status: Available
Certificate Serial Number: 3C9CC580
 Certificate Usage: General Purpose
  Issuer:
    OU = vpn
     O = cisco
     C = Bangladesh
 Subject:
! Following is a FQDN Name
   Name: Dhaka.dhakavpn.com
   OID.1.2.840.113549.1.9.2 =<16> Dhaka.dhakavpn.com
!  Distinguished Name (DN)
 OU = dhakavpn
     O = cisco
     C = Bangladesh
CRL Distribution Point:
  CN = CRL1, OU = dhakavpn, O = cisco, C = Bangladesh
! Following lines show the Certificate Lifetime. The start and end date should be
! within the time shown in the show clock output from the router.
Validity Date:
   start date: 19:29:42 UTC Mar 24 2004
   end   date: 19:59:42 UTC Mar 24 2006
  Associated Trustpoint: DhakaPKI

CA Certificate
...
RA KeyEncipher Certificate
...
RA Signature Certificate
...
Dhaka#
```

If the certificate start and end dates are correct, make sure the router time is correct. This can be verified with the **show clock** command. You can correct the time with the following command:

```
Dhaka# clock set 20:10:01 19 march 2005
```

3 Certificate lifetime issue

If the certificate lifetime expires, you need to re-enroll; otherwise, IKE negotiation fails. The re-enrollment process can be automated as shown in Example 6-26.

Example 6-26 *Turning on Auto-enrollment*

```
Dhaka(config)# crypto ca trustpoint DhakaPKI
Dhaka(ca-trustpoint)# enrollment url http://20.1.1.100
Dhaka(ca-trustpoint)# enrollment mode ra
Dhaka(ca-trustpoint)# crl query ldap://20.1.1.100
Dhaka(ca-trustpoint)# serial-number none
Dhaka(ca-trustpoint)# ip-address none
Dhaka(ca-trustpoint)# password revokeme
Dhaka(ca-trustpoint)# auto-enroll
```

4 The router does not have the CRL configured

If you do not specify the **CRL optional** command on the router, it will check for the CRL during Phase one negotiation. If the CRL is not present, you will see the following errors:

```
CRYPTO_PKI: status = 275: failed to insert CRL
```

To correct the problem, define the CRL as optional as shown below:

```
Dhaka(config)# crypto ca identity vpn
Dhaka(ca-identity)# crl optional
Dhaka(ca-identity)#
```

Remote Access Client VPN Connection

Remote Access VPN connections can be implemented with the IPsec protocol in conjunction with the AAA on the router. This section details the following topics:

- Configuration steps
- Troubleshooting steps

Configuration Steps

Figure 6-7 depicts a typical Remote Access VPN connection on the Dhaka router with DNS and WINS Server.

Figure 6-7 *A Basic Remote Access VPN Setup on Dhaka Router*

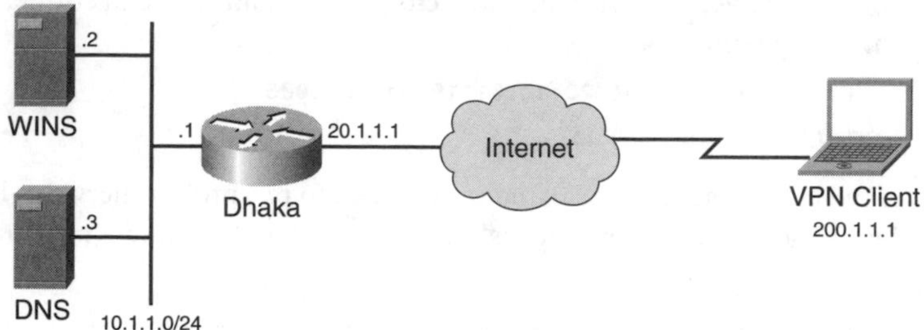

Example 6-27 shows a Remote Access VPN configuration on the Dhaka router with the comments followed by the commands.

Example 6-27 *Configuration of Remote Access VPN*

```
!aaa commands enable user Authentication and Group Authorization with the local user
! database
aaa new-model
aaa authentication login userauthen local
aaa authorization network groupauthor local
! This username and password should be used for Extended Authentication for the Remote
! Access VPN Connection
username cisco password 0 cisco123
!
! Phase 1 Policy with all parameters are defined here
crypto isakmp policy 3
 encr 3des
 authentication pre-share
 group 2
!
! The Group name and password will be used on the VPN Clients are vpnclient/cisco123.
! Mode-configuration parameters that will be passed to the VPN clients are defined
  here.
crypto isakmp client configuration group vpnclient
 key cisco123
 dns 10.1.1.3
 wins 10.1.1.2
 domain cisco.com
! IP address to the VPN client will be assigned by this pool
 pool ippool
! This access-list will define the traffic that needs to encrypted and encapsulated by
! the IPsec tunnel.
 acl 100
!  Phase 2 of the IPsec tunnel negotiation is defined with the following command
crypto IPsec transform-set myset esp-3des esp-sha-hmac
!
! A dynamic map is created to bind the transform set just created
crypto dynamic-map dynmap 10
 set transform-set myset
!
```

Example 6-27 *Configuration of Remote Access VPN (Continued)*

```
! This is the actual crypto map that will be applied to the interface. The following line
! turns on XAuth based on the AAA Authentication method defined in the beginning of the
! configuration using the local user database.
crypto map clientmap client authentication list userauthen
! The following line turns on authorization
crypto map clientmap isakmp authorization list groupauthor
! The following command tells the router to respond on the address assignment request
crypto map clientmap client configuration address respond
! Dynamic map that was created earlier is applied to the actual crypto map
crypto map clientmap 10 IPsec-isakmp dynamic dynmap
! This is the pool that was defined under the group configuration. The Pool is defined
! with the network 10.1.3.0/24 networks. Hence, when the VPN client tries to connect, it
! will be assigned one of the IP address listed in this pool.
ip local pool ippool 10.1.3.1 10.1.3.254
!
! This access-list is applied under the group configuration for split tunneling. As you
! can see from the following ACL, only traffic defined in this access-list will be
! encrypted and will go through the tunnel.
access-list 100 permit ip 10.1.1.0 0.0.0.255 10.1.3.0 0.0.0.255
!
!crypto map is then applied to outbound interface
interface FastEthernet1/0
 ip address 20.1.1.1 255.255.255.0
 crypto map clientmap
! rest of the irrelevant configuration is removed.
Dhaka#
```

Troubleshooting Steps

Troubleshooting a Remote Access VPN connection involves analyzing the log on both routers and on the VPN clients. Troubleshooting steps discussed for LAN-to-LAN are also applicable for the Remote Access VPN. This section examines a successful debug command output for a Remote Access VPN connection.

Example 6-28 shows a Phase I negotiation for a Remote Access VPN in Aggressive mode:

Example 6-28 *Phase I Establishment for Aggressive Mode*

```
Dhaka# debug crypto isakmp
Dhaka# debug crypto ipsec
! The following message indicates that this Router received an ISAKMP message from the
! VPN client on src port 500, dst port=500
ISAKMP (0:0): received packet from 200.1.1.1 (N) NEW SA
ISAKMP: local port 500, remote port 500
. . .
!Router is trying to match the received proposal # 1 with the configured proposal # 3
ISAKMP (0:10): Checking ISAKMP transform 1 against priority 3 policy
ISAKMP:      encryption 3DES-CBC
```

continues

Example 6-28 *Phase I Establishment for Aggressive Mode (Continued)*

```
ISAKMP:       hash SHA
ISAKMP:       default group 2
ISAKMP:       auth XAUTHInitPreShared
ISAKMP:       life type in seconds
ISAKMP:       life duration (VPI) of  0x0 0x20 0xC4 0x9B
!Received Proposal is acceptable as shown in the following line
ISAKMP (0:10): atts are acceptable. Next payload is 3
. . .
!Since VPN client does Aggressive Mode, the new state is IKE_R_AM_AAA_AWAIT
Old State = IKE_READY  New State = IKE_R_AM_AAA_AWAIT
Dhaka#
```

Example 6-29 shows x-auth completion on Phase I.

Example 6-29 *Showing X-Auth Completion for Remote Access VPN connection*

```
Dhaka#
! Router is requesting the VPN client for User Authentication as shown in the following
! line
ISAKMP (0:10): Need XAUTH
. . .
ISAKMP/xauth: request attribute XAUTH_TYPE_V2
ISAKMP/xauth: request attribute XAUTH_MESSAGE_V2
ISAKMP/xauth: request attribute XAUTH_USER_NAME_V2
ISAKMP/xauth: request attribute XAUTH_USER_PASSWORD_V2
! Router is receiving the X-Auth Attributes from the VPN Client
. . .
ISAKMP: Config payload REPLY
ISAKMP/xauth: reply attribute XAUTH_TYPE_V2 unexpected
ISAKMP/xauth: reply attribute XAUTH_USER_NAME_V2
ISAKMP/xauth: reply attribute XAUTH_USER_PASSWORD_V2
Dhaka#
```

Example 6-30 shows Mode Configuration for Phase I.

Example 6-30 *Showing Mode Configuration for Remote Access VPN Connection*

```
Dhaka#
! Received mode configuration request from the VPN client
ISAKMP (0:10): checking request:
ISAKMP:     IP4_ADDRESS
ISAKMP:     IP4_NETMASK
ISAKMP:     IP4_DNS
ISAKMP:     IP4_NBNS
ISAKMP:     ADDRESS_EXPIRY
ISAKMP:     APPLICATION_VERSION
! Unknown Attr: is not an Error. It just means that router does not support this mode-
! config. Attribute requested by the VPN clientc
ISAKMP:     UNKNOWN Unknown Attr: 0x7000
. . .
```

Example 6-30 *Showing Mode Configuration for Remote Access VPN Connection (Continued)*

```
! Router is sending the Mode-Configuration to the VPN client
ISAKMP: Sending private address: 10.1.3.1
ISAKMP: Unknown Attr: IP4_NETMASK (0x2)
ISAKMP: Sending IP4_DNS server address: 10.1.1.3
ISAKMP: Sending IP4_NBNS server address: 10.1.1.2
ISAKMP: Sending ADDRESS_EXPIRY seconds left to use the address: 86395
ISAKMP: Sending APPLICATION_VERSION string: Cisco Internetwork OperatingSystem
  Software
IOS (tm) 7200 Software (C7200-IK9S-M), Version 12.2(8)T,  RELEASE SOFTWARE (fc1)
ISAKMP: Unknown Attr: UNKNOWN (0x7000)
Dhaka#
```

Upon completion of Phase I negotiation, Phase II negotiation takes place as shown in Example 6-31.

Example 6-31 *IOS Showing Phase II negotiation of a Remote Access VPN Connection*

```
Dhaka#
!  Router is checking and validating the IPsec proposals
ISAKMP (0:11): Checking IPsec proposal 4
ISAKMP: transform 1, ESP_3DES
ISAKMP:   attributes in transform:
ISAKMP:      authenticator is HMAC-SHA
ISAKMP:      encaps is 1
ISAKMP:      SA life type in seconds
ISAKMP:      SA life duration (VPI) of  0x0 0x20 0xC4 0x9B
ISAKMP (0:11): atts are acceptable.
Dhaka#
. . .
! After validating the  phase II, the IPsec SAs are created; One SA for inbound traffic
! and the other SA for the outbound traffic
ISAKMP (0:11): Creating IPsec SAs
        inbound SA from 200.1.1.1 to 20.1.1.1
        (proxy 10.1.3.1 to 20.1.1.1)
        has spi 0x962A493B and conn_id 2000 and flags 4
        lifetime of 2147483 seconds
        outbound SA from 20.1.1.1   to 200.1.1.1   (proxy   20.1.1.1   to 10.1.3.1)
        has spi -2145675534 and conn_id 2001 and flags C
        lifetime of 2147483 seconds
Dhaka#
```

To analyze the log on the VPN Client software, click on **Log** from the VPN Client window. Then click on **Log Settings** and set the logging level to **High** for all the classes. Then you can bring up **Log Window** by clicking on **Log Window**.

Many troubleshooting techniques applied for the LAN-to-LAN tunnel also can be used for the Remote Access VPN connection. If Remote Access VPN connection fails, you need to analyze the debug on the Router, and the log on the Remote Access VPN client.

Following are some of the important points to keep in mind while troubleshooting Remote Access VPN connection:

- VPN clients only propose Diffie-Hellman Groups 2 and 5. Configure DH group 2 or 5 (not 1) on the router.
- Configure **isakmp identity hostname** if rsa-sig is used as an IKE authentication method.
- AAA authorization must be enabled on the router, so that the router can accept and send mode-configuration attributes.
- If VPN Clients are behind the NAT/PAT device, configure NAT-T or the IPsec over TCP feature.
- If NAT-T or IPsec over TCP is configured, be sure the firewall between the VPN Client and the router is allowing UDP/4500 or TCP/10000.

Case Studies

This case study section centers on Dynamic Multipoint VPN, which is a new feature introduced in IOS code to address the scalability issue for LAN-to-LAN tunnel with GRE and IPsec.

In the LAN-to-LAN troubleshooting section, you have seen how GRE over IPsec works and addresses some of the issues that Basic LAN-to-LAN has—unable to encrypt non-IP, multicast, and broadcast traffic.

In a large-scale VPN deployment, several spokes need to talk to each other. So, you have the option of building either a full mesh, or a hub and spoke network. Because full mesh does not scale very well, hub and spoke networks are mainly deployed, in which every spoke builds up the tunnel with the hub and communicates through the hub.

The problem with this deployment is that that the hub has to encrypt and decrypt the packet twice to pass one data stream between the spokes, which overburdens the hub's CPU. Also, in regard to configuration, for every spoke, the hub needs to have configuration so that spokes can build up the tunnel. If there are hundreds of spokes, the situation becomes quite complex, and sometimes impossible. Dynamic multipoint VPN comes to your rescue under this type of circumstance. With DMVPN set up, all the spokes build up the tunnel with only the hub using the Multipoint GRE interface, and with the help of NHRP, spokes dynamically learn about the peer's IP address and learn all the information necessary from the hub to build up the tunnel dynamically. DMVPN not only builds tunnels on demand, but also tears down tunnels dynamically. Hub configuration is reduced dramatically, and with the addition of new spokes, hub configuration does not have to be modified. A detailed discussion of DMVPN is beyond the scope of this book, so a brief discussion of its operation will have to suffice.

DMVPN Architecture

DMVPN relies on two proven Cisco technologies:

- Multipoint GRE Tunnel Interface (mGRE interface)
- Next Hop Resolution Protocol (NHRP)

Multipoint GRE Tunnel Interface (mGRE Interface)

This allows a single GRE interface to build multiple IPsec tunnels, and significantly simplifies the size and complexity of the configuration.

An mGRE interface has an IP address, a tunnel source interface, and a tunnel key as follows:

```
spoke-A# show running-config
! This is the physical interface that is used as source for the mGRE tunnel
interface Ethernet0
 ip address 172.17.16.1 255.255.255.0
! Following is a mGRE tunnel interface
interface Tunnel 0
 ip address 192.168.0.10 255.0.0.0
 tunnel source Ethernet0
 tunnel mode gre multipoint
 tunnel key 1
spoke-A#
```

The tunnel address is the IP address defined on the tunnel interface. The NBMA (Non-Broadcast Multiple Access) address is the IP address used as a tunnel source (or destination). Therefore in the preceding example, the **192.168.0.10** is spoke-A's tunnel address and **172.17.16.1** is spoke-A's NBMA address.

Unlike point-to-point GRE interface, mGRE interfaces do not have a tunnel destination defined. Because mGRE tunnels do not have a tunnel destination address, they need to rely on another protocol that tells mGRE tunnel interface the destination of the packets it sends out. Next Hop Resolution Protocol (NHRP) comes to rescue for mGRE tunnel interface to get the destination address dynamically, as discussed in the next section.

Next Hop Resolution Protocol (NHRP)

NHRP is a client/server model protocol which is defined by RFC2332. The hub is considered to be the **Next Hop Server (NHS)** and the spokes are considered to be the **Next Hop Client (NHC)**. The hub or the NHS maintains a NHRP cache just like ARP cache, for all the spokes Real IP (NBMA address) and the GRE tunnel interface IP address (VPN layer address).

The cache on the hub and spoke can be built up in one of the following ways:

- Manually add static entries
- Hub learns via registration requests by spoke
- Spokes learn via resolution requests—used for spoke-to-spoke communication only

Each spoke registers its real address (NBMA address) when it boots (it obtains it dynamically). The spokes send registration requests to the hub with their actual physical IP addresses, which are called NBMA addresses, along with the tunnel IP address (VPN layer address) with the cache timeout value. Upon receiving the registration requests, the hub caches the NHRP mapping in the NHRP cache database.

Spokes have a permanent IPsec tunnel to the hub, but not to the spokes. When a spoke needs to send a packet to a destination (private) subnet on another spoke, it queries the NHRP server for the real (outside) address of the destination spoke. Then the originating spoke can initiate a dynamic IPsec tunnel to the target spoke (because it knows the peer address). The spoke-to-spoke tunnel is built over the mGRE interface.

DMVPN was first introduced in 12.2(12)T. It is supported in 7204/6, 37xx, 26xx, 17xx. Only the latest T trains are supported on 9xx and 8xx routers as well.

DMVPN can be deployed in one of the following modes:

- **Hub and Spoke**—All traffic moves via the hub.
- **Spoke-to-Spoke**—Spoke-to-spoke traffic moves directly, bypassing the hub. Initial traffic during NHRP resolution and tunnel buildup phase still may go through the hub.

To understand both of these scenarios fully with DMVPN, go through the configuration discussed in the next section.

Configuration Steps

To illustrate both hub and spoke and spoke-to-spoke deployment of DMVPN network, you will be configuring the DMVPN based on Figure 6-8.

Figure 6-8 *DMVPN for Dynamic Spoke-to-spoke*

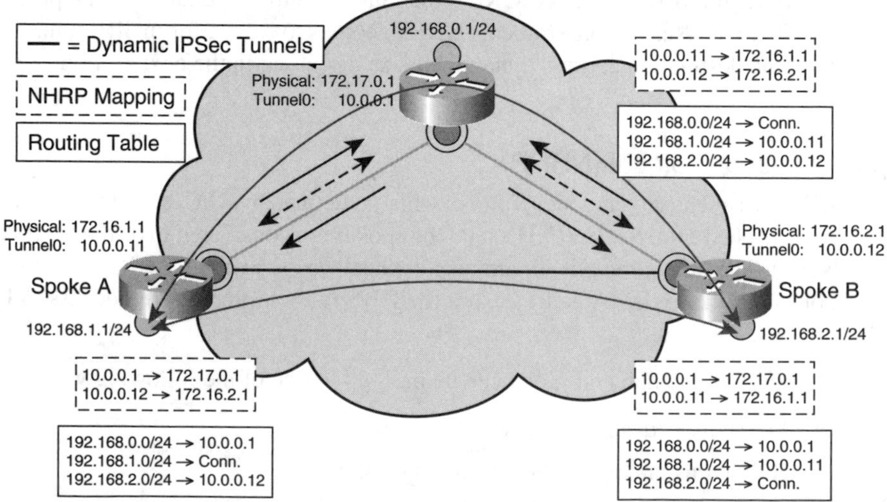

For hub and spoke on the hub you must create an mGRE tunnel interface, and on the spoke you can create a point-to-point tunnel interface or the mGRE interface. For spoke-to-spoke setup, you must use mGRE interface on the hub and the spokes. The configuration discussed will be using the mGRE interface on the hub and the spokes.

Work-through the following steps to configure hub and spoke and spoke-spoke tunnels in DMVPN network:

Step 1 Define Network ID under mGRE tunnel interface on the hub and the spokes.

To define network ID under the mGRE tunnel interface so that the mGRE tunnel interface can use NHRP, use the following command on hub and spokes:

```
ip nhrp network-id <id>
```

Here <id> is a unique number, and should be defined in the same way on the hub and all spokes.

Step 2 Configure spokes so that the initial NHRP cache can be built on the hub.

Initially, the hub has an empty cache unless you have the static NHRP mapping configured. On the other hand, the spoke has one static entry mapping with the hub's tunnel address to the hub's NBMA address as follows:

```
ip nhrp map 10.0.0.1 172.17.0.1
```

Be sure to configure the following to send the Multicast traffic to the hub from the spoke, so that dynamic routing protocols can communicate between the hub and spoke:

```
ip nhrp map multicast 172.17.0.1
```

Step 3 Configure the spokes to register to the hub.

For the spokes to register themselves to the hub, the hub must be declared as a Next Hop Server (NHS) as follows:

```
ip nhrp nhs 10.0.0.1
ip nhrp holdtime 3600
ip nhrp registration no-unique
```

The spokes control the cache on the hub. The spokes send **Registration-requests** to the hub, and the request contains the spoke's **Tunnel, NBMA** addresses, the **hold time,** and some flags. The hub creates an entry in its NHRP cache, and this entry will be valid for the duration of the hold time defined in the registration by the spoke.

Step 4 Configure the hub to send Multicast packets to the spokes.

The hub must send multicast traffic to all the spokes that registered to it for dynamic routing protocol. As the spoke's NBMA or the physical

IP address is not known, this must be done dynamically (this is introduced in IOS Version 12.2(13)T) with the following command under mGRE tunnel interface:

```
ip nhrp map multicast dynamic
```

Step 5 Configure the routing protocol on the hub and spokes.

Configure the spokes with dynamic routing protocol to advertise their private networks to the hub. You can use BGP, EIGRP, OSPF, RIP or ODR. It is strongly recommended to use EIGRP.

Step 6 Send Hello messages for dynamic routing protocol exchanges.

With the Tunnel defined, static NHRP entry to hub presence, and NHRP entry marked for multicast, spokes immediately send the Hellos to the Hub.

Upon receiving NHRP registrations from spokes, the hub inserts the NHRP information into the cache and marks it as "Multicast" because of the following configuration under mGRE tunnel interface:

```
ip nhrp map multicast dynamic
```

The hub sends Hellos to all the registered spokes simultaneously.

Step 7 Readjust the default bandwidth on the mGRE tunnel interface.

The default bandwidth of a GRE tunnel interface is 9 Kbps. This has no influence on the traffic, but EIGRP will take half of the interface bandwidth maximum (4.5 Kbps), which is too low. So adjust the bandwidth to 10000 Kbps with the following command:

```
Hub(config)# interface tunnel 0
Hub(config-if)# bandwidth 10000
Hub(config-if)#
```

Step 8 Turn off split-horizon on the hub.

To allow spoke-to-spoke communication via the hub (Hub and Spoke setup), turn off split-horizon on the hub with the following command:

```
Hub(config)#
Hub(config)# router eigrp 1
Hub(config-router)# no ip split-horizon eigrp 1
Hub(config-router)#
```

You must consider summarization, and be sure to set the bandwidth in the hub to **spoke direction**.

Step 9 Enable IPsec protection on mGRE tunnel interfaces.

Because the GRE tunnel is insecure, it must be protected with IPsec. DMVPN introduced tunnel protection. Work through the following step to enable IPsec on the tunnel interface:

(a) Define a transform set with the following command:

```
crypto ipsec transform-set ts esp-sha-hmac esp-3des
  mode transport
```

(b) Configure IPsec profile (this is replacement for the crypto map for DMVPN) with the following commands. IPsec Profile is just like the **crypto map** command without "set peer" and "match address," and this information is unknown until the registration process takes place for NHRP.

```
crypto ipsec profile prof
  set transform-set ts
```

(c) Apply the profile on the tunnel interface with the following command. Internally IOS will treat this as **crypto map** and will get the missing information (set peer and match address parameters from the NHRP cache). The following command must be applied on hub and spokes.

```
tunnel protection ipsec profile prof
```

So far based on the configuration, spoke-to-spoke can communicate with each other through the hub. If you want to enable direct spoke-to-spoke tunnel communication, you need to rely on the following:

- The routing table
- The NHRP table

To create a spoke–to-spoke tunnel, a spoke must learn a routing entry to the destination network (this is the private network of the other spoke). The **next hop** must be the spoke tunnel IP address. The spoke must learn the **NBMA address** of the **next hop**. The IPsec tunnel between the spokes is built only after that.

1 Route learning on the spokes

The routing protocol is always between the hub and the spokes (hub and spoke has neighbor relationships, not spoke-to-spoke). All the spokes learn the route of the private network of other spokes via the hub. For spoke-to-spoke to work correctly, the hub must preserve and advertise the private network's next hop as advertised by the spokes themselves (as the tunnel interface IP address). Different routing protocols behave differently in terms of preserving the next-hop information.

a RIP keeps the next-hop information by default. This can not be disabled.

b The next-hop preservation in EIGRP is not a default. It is turned on with the interface command.

```
no ip next-hop-self eigrp <as>
```

c Next hop preservation in BGP is a default. It can be disabled with the BGP command.

```
neighbor <n> next-hop-self
```

d In OSPF, next-hop preservation happens naturally except in point-to-multipoint mode.

2 NHRP learning on spokes

A spoke will send an NHRP resolution request to its NHS to learn an NBMA address. The queried address can be a network address. Ideally, the queried address should be a next-hop address. The NHS will respond with an NBMA address from its cache. The spoke will populate its cache with the answer. The resolution reply will have a lifetime set to the remaining lifetime in the hub cache. If the NHS does not have the entry in its cache, it returns an error and the spoke will install an entry pointing to the NHS.

During the learning process, the spoke will forward all the packets to its NHS, and this happens in process switching. As soon as the NHRP entry is created but NOT inserted in the cache, an IPsec tunnel will be negotiated. The NHRP entry will be inserted in the cache and used when the IPsec tunnel is actually ready The IPsec tunnel will disappear when the NHRP entry times out.

Example 6-32 shows the hub configuration of Figure 6-8.

Example 6-32 *Hub Configuration of DMVPN*

```
Hub# show running-config
crypto isakmp policy 1
 authentication pre-share
crypto isakmp key cisco47 address 0.0.0.0
!
crypto IPsec transform-set trans2 esp-des esp-md5-hmac
!
crypto ipsec profile vpnprof
 set transform-set trans2
!
interface Tunnel0
 bandwidth 1000
 ip address 10.0.0.1 255.255.255.0
 ip mtu 1416
 ip nhrp authentication donttell
 ip nhrp map multicast dynamic
 ip nhrp network-id 99
 ip nhrp holdtime 300
 no ip split-horizon eigrp 1
 no ip next-hop-self eigrp 1
```

Example 6-32 *Hub Configuration of DMVPN (Continued)*

```
 delay 1000
 tunnel source Ethernet0
 tunnel mode gre multipoint
 tunnel key 100000
 tunnel protection ipsec profile vpnprof
interface Ethernet0
 ip address 172.17.0.1 255.255.255.0
!
interface Ethernet1
 ip address 192.168.0.1 255.255.255.0
!
router eigrp 1
 network 10.0.0.0 0.0.0.255
 network 192.168.0.0 0.0.0.255
!
```

Example 6-33 shows spoke configuration.

Example 6-33 *Spoke Configuration of DMVPN Network*

```
Spoke-AA#show running-config
crypto isakmp policy 1
 authentication pre-share
crypto isakmp key cisco47 address 0.0.0.0
!
crypto IPsec transform-set trans2 esp-des esp-md5-hmac
!
crypto ipsec profile vpnprof
 set transform-set trans2
!
interface Tunnel0
 bandwidth 1000
 ip address 10.0.0.3 255.255.255.0
 ip mtu 1416
 ip nhrp authentication donttell
 ip nhrp map 10.0.0.1 172.17.0.1
 ip nhrp network-id 99
 ip nhrp holdtime 300
 ip nhrp nhs 10.0.0.1
 delay 1000
 tunnel source Ethernet0
 tunnel mode gre multipoint
 tunnel key 100000
 tunnel protection ipsec profile vpnprof
!
interface Ethernet0
 ip address dhcp hostname Spoke1
!
interface Ethernet1
 ip address 192.168.1.1 255.255.255.0
!
router eigrp 1
 network 10.0.0.0 0.0.0.255
 network 192.168.1.0 0.0.0.255
```

Troubleshooting DMVPN

Problems on the DMVPN network can categorized as follows:

- NHRP mapping problems
- Crypto socket creation problems
- Crypto VPN problems
- Dynamic routing protocol problems
- Problems with passing data across an established tunnel

Most of the problems that occur in these areas are caused by misconfiguration or a bug in the code. This section helps you identify and troubleshoot configuration-related issues. Most of the problem areas can be identified with show commands output. You might end up running **debug** commands to find additional details about the DMVPN problem.

NHRP Mapping Problem

NHRP (cache) Mapping problems can be identified by executing **show ip nhrp** command as shown in Example 6-34.

Example 6-34 *Showing the Successful Mappings of NHRP with* **show ip nhrp** *Command*

```
Hub1# show ip nhrp
! This is the first dynamic NHRP Mapping
! Tunnel0 is the interface of the NHRP cache entry that was created. 00:11:03 is the time
! since the NHRP entry was created.  00:04:52 is the time in which the positive and
! negative authoritative NBMA address will expire (hours:minutes:seconds). This value is
! based on the ip nhrp holdtime command.
10.0.0.11/32 via 10.0.0.11, Tunnel0 created 00:11:03, expire 00:04:52
! Type dynamic means NBMA address was obtained from NHRP Request packet. static—NBMA
! address means statically configured.
! The flag in the following shows Authoritative unique registered which means
! that the NHRP information was obtained from the Next Hop Server or router that
! maintains the NBMA-to-IP address mapping for a particular destination. Implicit—
! Indicates that the information was learned not from an NHRP request generated from the
! local router, but from an NHRP packet being forwarded or from an NHRP request being
! received by the local router. Negative caching indicates that the requested NBMA
! mapping could not be obtained.
  Type: dynamic, Flags: authoritative unique registered
! The following shows the NBMA (Nonbroadcast Multi-access Address). The address format is
! Appropriate for the type of network being used (for example, ATM, Ethernet, Switched
! Multimegabit Data Service (SMDS), or multipoint tunnel).
  NBMA address: 172.16.1.1
! This is the Second dynamic NHRP Mapping
10.0.0.12/32 via 10.0.0.12, Tunnel0 created 01:03:31, expire 00:05:46
  Type: dynamic, Flags: authoritative unique registered
  NBMA address: 172.16.2.1
. . .
Hub1#
```

If the NHRP does not work correctly, analyze the problem further with the **debug nhrp** command.

Following is a list of some of the important NHRP-related issues that you need to keep in mind:

- NHRP Key must match on all the spokes and the hub in the DMVPN network
- Go through the following list and be sure that you are not configuring something that is not supported. For example, on the cat6500 and 7600 series switch, the defining key is not supported. For more information, check the following URL: http://www.cisco.com/univercd/cc/td/doc/product/software/ios122/122newft/122t/122t13/ftgreips.htm#wp1069602

Crypto Socket Creation Problem

Crypto socket is a bridge between the NHRP and the IPsec crypto tunnel. If the crypto socket creation fails, the NHRP also will fail. Example 6-35 shows successful crypto socket creation.

Example 6-35 *Successful Crypto Socket Built Up*

```
Hub1# show crypto socket
! This is the first crypto socket.
Tu0 Peers (local/remote): 172.17.0.1/172.16.1.1
  Local Ident  (addr/mask/port/prot): (172.17.0.1/255.255.255.255/0/47)
  Remote Ident (addr/mask/port/prot): (172.16.1.1/255.255.255.255/0/47)
! Following two lines are indication of successful socket creation
  Socket State: Open
  Client: "TUNNEL SEC" (Client State: Active)
! This is the second socket
Tu0 Peers (local/remote): 172.17.0.1/172.16.2.1
  Local Ident  (addr/mask/port/prot): (172.17.0.1/255.255.255.255/0/47)
  Remote Ident (addr/mask/port/prot): (172.16.2.1/255.255.255.255/0/47)
  Socket State: Open
  Client: "TUNNEL SEC" (Client State: Active)
. . .
Crypto Sockets in Listen state:
1   TUNNEL SEC Profile: "vpnprof" Map-name "Tunnel0-head-0"
Hub1#
```

If you experience a problem with crypto socket creation, the only remedy as of the writing of this book is to reboot the router, which frees the stuck crypto socket. There is no CLI command to unstick a crypto socket.

Crypto VPN problem

To find out if IPsec is causing the problem, simply remove the **tunnel protection ipsec profile profile_name** command from the tunnel interface and see if everything works well. After removing this command, NHRP will go over IP instead of IPsec. If this test reveals an IPsec issue, troubleshoot it just as discussed in the "LAN-to-LAN" troubleshooting section.

Dynamic Routing Protocol Problem

Following is a list of dynamic routing protocols you can configure in the DMVPN network:

- Enhanced Interior Gateway Routing Protocol (EIGRP)

  Be sure that the following line is configured for the hub and spoke deployment:

  ```
  no ip split-horizon eigrp <as>
  no auto-summary
  ```

  If you have spoke-to-spoke deployment, configure the following command.

  ```
  no ip next-hop-self eigrp <as>
  ```

  You must be running Cisco IOS Version 12.3(1) to run the this command.

- Open Shortest Path First (OSPF)

  To use OSPF in the DMVPN network, configure the following commands:

  ```
  ip ospf network broadcast
  ip ospf priority (2(hub)|0(spoke))
  ```

- Border Gateway Protocol (BGP)

  If you configure BGP, you must configure the hub as the route reflector.

- Routing Information Protocol (RIP)

  If RIP is configured on the DMVPN network, configure the following under the RIP routing process:

  ```
  no ip split-horizon
  no auto-summary
  ```

It is strongly recommended that you configure EIGRP on the DMVPN network.

If you have problems with neighbor relationships with the dynamic routing protocol, pay close attention on the following:

- Make sure that on the hub router, you have the following command in the tunnel interface:

  ```
  ip nhrp map multicast dynamic
  ```

- You must avoid this configuration on the spoke; otherwise you might experience neighbor flaps. On the spoke you should have the following configured for the multicast:

  ```
  ip nhrp map multicast NBMA_Address (Physical_Interface)_Of_Hub
  ```

This is because the spokes do not have to send any multicast to other spokes; they have to send multicast to the hub to build up the neighbor relationship.

- On the spokes, you must not configure more than two multipoint GRE tunnels sharing the same source interface.

Passing Data Across an Established Tunnel Problem

If everything looks good, but you are unable to pass traffic, remember the following points:

- When the hub is behind the PAT device, there are no restrictions.
- If you are using IPsec Transport mode (highly recommended), two spokes *may* have the same pre-NAT (outside physical address) but *must* have unique post-NAT addresses. This means that two spoke routers behind the same NAT box must be translated to unique post-NAT IP addresses. Two spokes behind different NAT boxes may have the same pre-NAT IP address (of course they would have different post-NAT IP addresses).
- If you are using IPsec Tunnel mode, all spokes *must* have unique pre-NAT IP addresses, but *may* have the same post-NAT IP addresses. This means that two spokes behind different NAT boxes *must* have unique pre-NAT IP addresses. Two spokes behind the same NAT device (of course will have unique pre-NAT IP addresses), *may* have the same post-NAT IP address.
- You must turn on CEF switching.

Common Problems and Resolutions

Most of the issues discussed in this section cause problems during or after tunnel buildup. For instance, the tunnel might have been built up properly, but users might be unable to send data for one of the following reasons:

- NAT with IPsec Issues
- Firewall and IPsec issues
- MTU issues
- Split tunneling issues

NAT With IPsec Issues

NAT can interact or interfere with IPsec in the following ways:

- NAT in the tunnel end points
- NAT in the middle of an IPsec tunnel

NAT in the Tunnel End Points

There can be either a dynamic or static NAT entry configured on tunnel end points (routers). For IPsec to function correctly, be sure to configure NAT on the router to bypass the IPsec packets. Example 6-36 shows a sample output of bypassing dynamic NAT entries on the Dhaka router shown in Figure 6-6.

Example 6-36 *Sample Output of Bypassing Dynamic NAT Entries on Dhaka Router as Shown in Figure 6-6*

```
! The following line is perform PAT for the internet bound traffic for inside network
! 10.1.1.0/24
Dhaka(config)# ip nat inside source route-map nonat interface Ethernet1/0 overload
! Following deny statement on the ACL is to exclude the traffic from NAT/PAT. This is the
! traffic will go through the IPSec tunnel.
Dhaka(config)# access list 150 deny ip 10.1.1.0 0.0.0.255 10.1.2.0 0.0.0.255
! Rest of the traffic will be translated
Dhaka(config)# access list 150 permit ip 10.1.1.0 0.0.0.255 any
! Need to apply the ACL under the route map
Dhaka(config)# route-map nonat permit 10
Dhaka(config)# match ip address 150
Dhaka(config)#
```

Bypassing static NAT entries is a bit tricky. Static NAT entries can be bypassed using a loopback interface and policy routing for Cisco IOS images in versions earlier than 12.2.4T; starting from 12.2.4T, a route-map can be used with static NAT to bypass NAT.

Example 6-37 shows the configuration required to bypass static NAT on the Dhaka router.

Example 6-37 *Configuration Steps Required for Bypassing Static NAT Entries for Dhaka Router Shown in Figure 6-5*

```
Dhaka# show running-config
crypto map to_Doha 10 IPsec-isakmp
 set peer 30.1.1.1
 set transform-set myset
! This is the ACL that defines the traffic that needs to go through the IPsec tunnel.
! When configuring NAT, you need to bypass this traffic
 match address 101
! Create a loop back interface so that static NAT can be pointed here as outgoing
Interface loopback 0
 ip address 1.1.1.1 255.255.255.252
interface Ethernet1/0
 ip address 20.1.1.1 255.255.255.0
! This is the outgoing interface (facing towards the internet)
 ip nat outside
! Crypto map is applied here
 crypto map to_Doha
interface Ethernet0/0
 ip address 10.1.1.1 255.255.255.0
! This is the inside interface for the NAT
 ip nat inside
 ip route-cache policy
```

Example 6-37 *Configuration Steps Required for Bypassing Static NAT Entries for Dhaka Router Shown in Figure 6-5 (Continued)*

```
! This policy route will be triggered before NAT and the crypto which will take care of
! the bypassing of the IPSec traffic.
 ip policy route-map nonat
! ACL 1 defines what traffic needs to be NATed.
ip nat inside source list 1 interface Ethernet0/3 overload
! This is the static NAT
ip nat inside source static 10.1.1.12 20.1.1.20
! This access-list 1 is used in the NAT statement to traffic that traffic that needs to
! be translated
access list 1 permit 10.0.0.0 0.255.255.255
! This ACL is to define the IPSec interesting traffic
access list 101 permit ip 10.1.1.0 0.0.0.255 10.1.2.0 0.0.0.255
! This ACL is used in the route map to define the traffic that needs to bypass the NAT
access list 120 permit ip 10.1.1.0 0.0.0.255 10.1.2.0 0.0.0.255
! This route map is applied on the Ethernet 0/0 interface
route-map nonat permit 10
 match ip address 120
 set ip next-hop 1.1.1.2
Dhaka#
```

Example 6-38 shows how to bypass static NAT using route map on the Dhaka router shown in Figure 6-6.

Example 6-38 *Shows How to Bypass Static NAT Using Route Map on Dhaka Router Shown in Figure 6-6*

```
Dhaka# show running-config
crypto map to_Doha 10 IPsec-isakmp
 set peer 30.1.1.1
 set transform-set myset
 match address 101
interface Ethernet1/0
ip address 20.1.1.1 55.255.255.0
 ip nat outside
 crypto map to_Doha
interface Ethernet0/0
ip address 10.1.1.1 255.255.255.0
ip nat inside

ip nat inside source list 1 interface Ethernet0/3 overload
ip nat inside source static 10.1.1.1 20.1.1.20 route-map nonat
access-list 1 permit 10.1.1.0 255.255.255.0
access-list 101 permit ip 10.1.1.0 0.0.0.255 10.1.2.0 0.0.0.255
access-list 120 deny   ip 10.1.1.0 0.0.0.255 10.1.2.0 0.0.0.255
access-list 120 permit ip 10.1.1.0 0.0.0.255 any

route-map nonat permit 10
 match ip address 120
Dhaka#
```

NOTE Example 6-38 shows how to bypass static NAT, which is a better method than bypassing static NAT as shown in Example 6-37.

If NAT is broken, execute the following debug to troubleshoot NAT issues on the router.

```
show ip nat translation
debug ip nat
debug ip policy
```

NAT in the Middle

In many cases, VPN clients are behind NAT/PAT, a device that causes IPsec tunnel establishment failure. To work around this problem you can configure IPsec over NAT (NAT-T), which was first introduced in 12.2(15)T for IOS routers. The IPsec pass-through feature is supported on certain NAT/PAT devices; ISAKMP cookie and ESP Security Parameter Index (SPI) are used to build a translation table. NAT-T is turned on by default on Cisco IOS.

You should use ESP authentication rather than AH because NAT devices modify the outer IP header, which causes the AH integrity check to fail. Also, use Tunnel mode instead of Transport mode. More detailed discussions on the NAT with IPsec issues can be found in the following links:

http://www.cisco.com/en/US/products/sw/iosswrel/ps1839/products_feature_guide09186a0080110c03.html

http://www.cisco.com/en/US/products/sw/iosswrel/ps1839/products_feature_guide09186a00801541de.html

http://www.cisco.com/en/US/products/sw/iosswrel/ps1839/products_feature_guide09186a0080110bca.html

Firewall and IPsec Issues

In some situations, a firewall can play a role in IPsec implementation.

- Firewall in the middle

  If you have a firewall in the middle between two IPsec peers that are blocking ISAKMP (UDP/500), Phase 1 and 2 of IPsec tunnel establishment fails, because both Phases I and II of IPsec happen on UDP/500. If a UDP/500 port is open but IP/51 for AH and IP/50 for ESP are blocked by the firewall, the tunnel will be established with IKE and IPsec SA, but the data will not pass across the tunnel. So, in addition to opening UDP/500 port for ISAKMP, you also need to open up IP protocol 50 for ESP and IP Protocol 51 for AH.

Additionally, if you have NAT-T configured, you need to open up UDP/4500, and for IPsec over TCP you need to open up the TCP/10000 on the firewall.

- Firewall on the IPsec tunnel end points

  If you have an access list configured on the egress interface of the tunnel end points router, you need to open up all the ports in your access list as discussed in the previously listed item.

Maximum Transmission Unit (MTU) Issues

When sending IPsec traffic across the tunnel for both LAN-to-LAN and Remote Access VPN connections, MTU can cause problems. This is because IPsec adds additional overhead to the original packets. The problem is aggravated when you configure GRE over IPsec, as the GRE adds additional overhead to the original IP packets in addition to IPsec. The sizes of overhead vary depending on a number of variables, but usually a rough estimate for overhead when using configured IPsec tunnel mode is 60 bytes with ESP encryption and authentication. If transport mode is used, you can save 20 bytes, because no additional IP header is added to the packet. If you use GRE over IPsec, it adds an additional 24 bytes.

Large IPsec packets introduce the following two problems:

- If the large IPsec packet size is greater than the maximum MTU allowed on the interface where the crypto map is applied, and if the Do not Fragment (DF) bit is *not* set, the router will fragment the IPsec packet before it sends out to the receiving end.
- Path MTU Discovery (PMTUD) is a mechanism to detect the smallest MTU along the path for the packet flows from the sender to the receiver. If the DF bit is set, and packet size is greater than the size of the outgoing interface of a router, the router sends a Internet Control Message Protocol (ICMP message 3, code 4) reply to the sender asking for a reduction in the packet size. If the ICMP reply is blocked by a firewall, the sender never receives the reply, so the packet is dropped.

There are several ways to get around the MTU issue with IPsec:

- Reduce the MTU size on the end station (both sender and receiver). To do so, find the size of the packets allowed across the path with the help of the following test from the Windows command prompt:

  ```
  ping -l packet_size -F destination_ip_address
  ```

  If ICMP is blocked, this test fails.

- If you have a huge number of hosts, this may not be a viable solution, as you will be setting up MTU on all the hosts. In this circumstance, the best option is to use **ip tcp adjust-mss** on the ingress (Local LAN) interface as follows:

  ```
  ip tcp adjust-mss size
  ```

This command works only for the TCP connection. When the initial TCP connection is made, the router using the TCP connection instructs the end hosts to set the MTU to the number configured by the **ip tcp adjust-mss size** command.

- If you want PMTUD to work, allow an ICMP unreachable (type 3, code 4) message between the IPsec peers. If you have GRE over IPsec configured, you might want to configure the **tunnel path-mtu-discovery** command on the GRE tunnel interface to enable PMTUD on the GRE tunnel interface. The **tunnel path-mtu-discovery** command helps the GRE interface set its IP MTU dynamically, rather than statically with the ip mtu command. It is recommended that both commands be used for setting the MTU. The **ip mtu** command is used to provide room for the GRE and IPsec overhead relative to the local physical outgoing interface IP MTU. The **tunnel path-mtu-discovery** command allows the GRE tunnel IP MTU to be further reduced if there is a lower IP MTU link in the path between the IPsec peers.
- If PMTUD and the **ip tcp adjust-mss** fails, and you need to fragment the packets, you should fragment the packet on the Initiator Router before the encryption. With this, de-fragmentation takes place on the end hosts, not on the Responder router. More details on pre-fragmentation can be found at the following location: http://www.cisco.com/en/US/products/sw/iosswrel/ps1833/products_feature_guide09186a008009c92c.html
- If the DF bit is set and PMTUD is not working due to ICMP packets block, you should configure the router to clear the DF bit to avoid packet drops. In that way, at the cost of CPU overhead on the receiving end, you are ensuring that the packets are not dropped. For more details on this, refer to the following link: http://www.cisco.com/en/US/products/sw/iosswrel/ps1839/products_feature_guide09186a0080087ae1.html#wp1015359

For a detailed discussion on MTU, refer to the following link:

http://www.cisco.com/en/US/tech/tk827/tk369/technologies_white_paper09186a00800d6979.shtml

Split Tunneling Issues

If you have traffic that needs to go to the Internet or another network bypassing the tunnel, once the tunnel is established on the VPN Client, you need to configure a split tunnel. With split tunnels, you need to define the traffic that should go through the tunnel and the network that should bypass the tunnel. If split tunneling is configured incorrectly, you might not be able to access subnets outside the VPN tunnel. Example 6-39 shows an excerpt of how to enable split tunneling for the VPN connections. The **access list 101** command is associated with the group as configured in the **crypto isakmp client configuration group my-group** command. This allows the Cisco VPN client to bypass the tunnel to access other networks that are not defined in the access-list 101. The VPN client is assigned an IP address from a pool defined with network 10.1.3.0/24. Therefore, based on access-list 101, traffic flows encrypted between 10.1.3.0/24, which is the IPsec tunnel network and the 10.1.1.0/24, which is the inside network. The rest of the traffic goes unencrypted, bypassing the tunnel (for example, Internet-bound traffic).

Example 6-39 *Excerpt of Configuration for Split Tunneling on Router*

```
Dhaka# show running-config
!
! This group name is configured earlier for defining the mode-config parameters. You just
! need to add the acl 101 that you have defined for the traffic that needs to go through
! the IPsec tunnel.
crypto isakmp client configuration group my-group
 key hw-client password
 dns 10.1.1.3
 wins 10.1.1.2
 domain cisco.com
 pool dynpool
! Following line is an addition to existing group configuration for turning on split
! tunneling.
 acl 101
!
! The ACL must include the network that should go through the tunnel. Rest of the traffic
! from VPN clients not defined in this ACL will go in clear text.
access-list 101 permit ip 10.1.3.0 0.0.0.255 10.1.1.0 0.0.0.255
!
Dhaka#
```

Best Practices

High Availability in IPsec is very important for both LAN-to-LAN and Remote Access VPN connections. It is beyond the scope of this chapter to present every best practice for designing a robust IPsec VPN network (any design guide will do that). However, this section provides some detail on the features available that might assist you in configuring the resiliency for both LAN-to-LAN and Remote Access VPN connections.

Resiliency for IPsec can be obtained in either of the two following ways:

- Stateful failover
- Stateless failover

Stateful Failover

The Stateful failover feature is introduced in Versions 12.2S and 12.3(11)T. This feature enables a router to continue processing and forwarding packets after an outage for VPN traffic. The IPsec head end router maintains a full IPsec session and state information at a backup head end router to take over the active IPsec sessions should the primary head end router fail. With Stateless Failover (which is discussed in the following section), there is no way to maintain an IPsec session through a failed IPsec router. Sessions must time out and connectivity be re-established, causing network downtime.

IPsec Stateful Failover is implemented using the Stateful switchover (SSO) and Hot Standby Routing Protocol (HSRP) feature. HSRP provides network redundancy for IP networks, which means that HSRP monitors both the inside and outside interfaces so that if either interface goes down, the whole router is considered to be down and ownership of Internet Key Exchange (IKE) and IPsec security associations (SAs) is passed to the standby router (which transitions to the HSRP active state). SSO allows the active and standby routers to share IKE and IPsec state information so that each router has enough information to become the active router at any time. Before you configure Stateful Failover, you must ensure that you have the identical Hardware, the same software version, and the same configuration on both sides. Configuring stateful failover for IPsec involves configuring HSRP by assigning a virtual IP address, and enabling the SSO protocol for replicating the IKE and IPsec SA information.

For a more detailed information on this feature, refer to the following link:

http://www.cisco.com/univercd/cc/td/doc/product/software/ios123/123newft/123t/123t_11/gt_topht.htm

Stateless Failover

In Stateless Failover, the state information (IKE and IPsec SAs) are not replicated to the backup peer. So the remote peer must take the following two actions:

1. The peer must be able to detect a connectivity failure to take the actions.
2. Once connectivity failure is detected, the peer must take action to reconnect with another peer, which has connectivity to the same private network as the failed peer.

The Loss of IP connectivity could be caused by many variables, such as device failure, local link failure, or loss of connectivity to the service provider (SP), and so on. A more detailed discussion on how to achieve Stateless Failover on Cisco IOS Router is presented in next few sections.

Loss of Connection Detection Mechanism

Presently, Cisco IOS software offers the following mechanisms to detect the loss of IP connectivity for IPsec VPN implementation:

- IKE Keepalives
- Dead peer detection (DPD)
- Dynamic routing protocols
- GRE keepalives

1 IKE keepalive

The default lifetime for an IKE SA is 24 hours and for IPsec SA, it is 1 hour. So, if there is loss of IP connectivity, there is no standards-based mechanism for either type of SA to detect loss of this connectivity to a peer, except when the quick mode (QM) negotiation fails. This means that when using a default lifetime setting, an IPsec peer might be forwarding data into a "black hole" for up to an hour, before the QM timeout.

Another problem is that SA may become stalled or "dead" in the security association database (SADB). This occurs when a peer has lost connectivity and there is no mechanism to clear the SA out of the SADB until the lifetimes expire. The problem with this situation is that the "dead" peer tries to reestablish connectivity, and connection is refused because an SA already exists with that peer. IKE keepalives assist in the maintenance of the SADB to prevent this from occurring.

The keepalive packets by default are sent every ten seconds. This value is configurable. Once three packets are missed, the IPsec connection is considered down or "dead," and the old SA will be cleared.

To re-establish connectivity, the IPsec device must have at least two IPsec peers defined in its crypto map statement (see Example 6-40). The router tries the next peer sequentially until a connection is established or it runs out of peers, at which time it rolls back to the top of the list.

Keepalive is supported by IOS and PIX, and DPD was originally supported by a client. Now DPD is supported on all platforms.

Example 6-40 *IKE Keepalive Configuration*

```
Dhaka# show running-config
crypto isakmp policy 10
authentication pre-share
!
! IKE Keepalive is configured with the following command.
crypto isakmp keepalive 10
!
crypto isakmp key cisco1234 address 30.1.1.1
crypto isakmp key cisco1234 address 40.1.1.1
!
crypto ipsec transform-set strong esp-3des esp-sha-hmac
!
crypto map to_Doha 10 isakmp-ipsec
  set peer 30.1.1.1
  set peer 40.1.1.1
  set transform-set strong
  match address 101
!
interface Ethernet0/0
ip address 10.1.1.1 255.255.255.0
!
```

continues

Example 6-40 *IKE Keepalive Configuration (Continued)*

```
interface ethernet1/0
ip address 20.1.1.1 255.255.255.0
crypto map to_Doha
!
ip route  0.0.0.0 0.0.0.0 ethernet1/0
ip route 10.1.0.0 255.255.0.0 ethernet1/0
access-list 101 permit ip 10.1.1.0. 0.0.0.255 10.1.2.0 0.0.0.255
Dhaka#
```

2 Dead Peer Detection (DPD)

As discussed in the previous section, the major problem with original IKE keepalives is that they do not scale well in large hub-and-spoke networks, where the hub must process many keepalive messages from its various peers. Moreover, keepalive messages are tied to the IKE SA and consequently are handled at the process level, which causes performance degradation.

One way of addressing these performance issues is to reduce the number of keepalive messages exchanged without significantly increasing the failover time. DPD is based upon the ability to send a keepalive message only when necessary, because it tracks existing traffic and communication with the peer. A keepalive is not sent until a "worry state" has occurred, which is defined by each peer and is usually caused by lack of traffic from its peer. This means that the router does not have to inform another router that it is alive at every specified time interval. When the traffic needs to be sent out, and the pre-configure time has elapsed without any traffic, only then is the DPD message sent. This reduces the number of messages exchanged dramatically compared to the IKE keepalive.

Configuration for DPD is the same as for the IKE keepalive. It is important to note that it DPD feature was first introduced in Version 12.2(8) T.

Unlike keepalive, DPD works in both site-to-site deployments and Remote Access VPN Client deployments. Starting with release 3.6, the Cisco VPN (Unity) client supports stateless failover to multiple peers with DPD as long as you are using auto-initiation and stored password.

3 Dynamic Routing Protocol

In the GRE over IPsec deployment, the dynamic routing protocol can be used as a method to detect a dead peer. If the Hellos are missed, the neighbor goes down, causing routing to disappear. This helps routers to take alternate peers to send out the traffic.

4 GRE keepalive

In the GRE-over-IPsec deployment, IPsec tunnel failure can be detected based on the GRE keepalive. If the GRE keepalive is missed, the tunnel interface goes down, causing the alternate tunnel interface to process the traffic using alternate IPsec tunnel.

Stateless Failover Mechanism Options

Now that you are comfortable with the link failure detection mechanism, it is time to explore the various options available to be configured once the link failure occurs and is detected by one of the mechanisms discussed in the preceding section. This section explores some of the options that are available for reconnecting with the standby device when the link failure occurs.

Backup Peer for Basic LAN-to-LAN IPsec

With either IPsec keepalive or DPD configured, you can define multiple IPsec peers under the single crypto map. The first one in the list will be used to build up the IPsec tunnel. If the first one in the list fails, the second peer in the list will be tried. In Example 6-40 under **IKE Keepalive** in the previous section, the following configuration defines multiple peers under the same crypto map statement:

```
crypto map to_Doha 10 isakmp-ipsec
! With this configuration, Router will always try to build up the IPsec tunnel with peer
! 30.1.1.1. If this peer is down for any reason, peer 40.1.1.1 will be tried.
  set peer 30.1.1.1
  set peer 40.1.1.1
  set transform-set strong
  match address 101
```

Hot Standby Routing Protocol (HSRP) and Reverse Route Injection (RRI)

HSRP and RRI together can provide a robust resilience mechanism for hub and spoke connections. HSRP is used for IP redundancy to assist in failing over between two devices when an interface or link becomes unusable. HSRP tracks the state of the router's interfaces and IP connectivity, which provides a mechanism to switch between primary and secondary devices on a failure. HSRP has now been closely coupled with IPsec to track state changes and provide a better solution for stateless IPsec failover. It is now possible to use the HSRP Virtual IP Address (VIP) as a peer endpoint address. HSRP is an active-standby solution, which means that when the primary one is active, the secondary does not have any traffic passing through it. However, it is possible to have multiple active HSRP groups defined, thus allowing half the peers to be active on one device and the other half on the second device. A side benefit of HSRP is that the remote peer now has a much simpler configuration because only one peer needs to be defined—that of the HSRP VIP. In the event of a failure, all SAs must be re-established.

So, as you can see, HSRP provides the redundancy guarantee for spokes. However, this might create problems as well. When failover occurs, devices behind the head-end devices need to know which head-end currently owns the active SAs for IPsec traffic; otherwise, those devices may return the replies to the wrong routers. RRI was developed to correct the routing behavior of the upstream devices and to ensure that a return gets back to the active peer.

RRI allows for static routes to be automatically inserted into the routing process for those networks and hosts protected by a remote tunnel endpoint. These protected hosts and networks are known as remote proxy identities. Each route is created based on the remote proxy network and mask, with the next hop to this network being the remote tunnel endpoint. Using the remote VPN router as the next hop forces traffic through the crypto process to be encrypted. Once the static route is created on the VPN router, this information is then propagated to upstream devices, allowing them to determine which is the correct VPN router to receive returning traffic to maintain IPsec state flows. RRI works with both static and dynamic crypto maps.

In Figure 6-6, if you have two routers in parallel on the Doha site, and if you want to configure HSRP and RRI, both of the Doha routers must be configured in exactly the same way. The important configuration elements are the interface standby group information, interface crypto map command, crypto map, keepalives, and routing as shown in Example 6-41.

Example 6-41 *Configuration of Primary Router on the Doha Site*

```
Doha# show running-config
crypto isakmp policy 10
authentication pre-share
!
crypto isakmp key cisco1234 address 20.1.1.1
!
crypto isakmp keepalive 10
!
crypto ipsec transform-set strong esp-3des esp-sha-hmac
!
! Here you have just a single crypto map pointing to the VIP
crypto map to-Dhaka 10 ipsec-isakmp
   set peer 20.1.1.1
   set transform-set strong
   match address ipsec
   reverse-route
!
interface FastEthernet0/0
 ip address 30.1.1.1 255.255.255.0
 standby 1 ip 30.1.1.3
 standby 1 priority 100
 standby 1 preempt
 standby 1 name VPNHA
 standby 1 track FastEthernet0/1
 crypto map HQ-to-Remote redundancy VPNHA

interface FastEthernet0/1
ip address 10.1.2.1 255.255.255.0
!
router eigrp 100
  network 10.0.0.0
!
ip route 0.0.0.0  0.0.0.0 FastEthernet0/0
!
ip access-list extended ipsec
   permit ip 10.1.2.0 0.0.0.255 10.1.1.0 0.0.0.255
Doha#
```

The following is a listing of some important points about HSRP and RRI implementation:

- Although HSRP and RRI provide a mechanism to failover to a secondary device, keepalives are still required to track the state of each peer and to maintain the health of the SADB when a failure occurs. DPD is highly recommended for this solution.
- HSRP does not replicate IPsec state information to the standby router; new SAs need to be built with the secondary device.
- HSRP is limited to LAN-based media technology because of the way it broadcasts Hello packets between peers. This means that HSRP and crypto map together cannot be configured on the edge device, which has only WAN interfaces.
- RRI requires a link-state routing protocol (EIGRP or OSPF) to propagate the static routes, which are created each time a peer establishes an IPsec connection.
- HSRP and GRE do not work together when tying GRE to the same physical interface on which HSRP is running. The main issue is the way the HSRP VIP address is advertised.
- If there is a device behind the head-end boxes which does not support routing or can only have a single default route, such as a firewall, it is desirable to configure HSRP on both LAN interfaces.
- It is also important to set the preempt timers to the same value. These are new changes in HSRP code that prevent the original primary from taking back the connections once it comes back online, which causes the IPsec tunnels to be rebuilt for no reason.
- HSRP works for both site-to-site and remote access VPNs.

Generic Routing Encapsulation (GRE) Tunnels over IPsec

To attain redundancy with the GRE over IPsec, the remote peer of the IPsec tunnel should be configured with two GRE tunnels, one to the primary head-end VPN router and the other to the backup VPN router. Both GRE tunnels are secured with IPsec: each one has its own IKE SA and two IPsec SAs. Because GRE can carry multicast and broadcast traffic, it is possible and very desirable to configure a routing protocol for these virtual links. Once a routing protocol is configured, the failover mechanism comes automatically. The Hello or keepalive packets sent by the routing protocol over the GRE tunnels provide a mechanism to detect loss of connectivity. In other words, if the primary GRE tunnel is lost, the remote site detects this event by the loss of the routing protocol Hello packets. Once virtual-link loss is detected, the routing protocol chooses the next best path. For this case, the backup GRE tunnel is chosen.

Therefore, the second part of VPN resiliency is obtained by the automatic behavior of the routing protocol. Because the backup GRE tunnel is always up and secured (MM and QM have already been negotiated), the failover time is determined by the Hello packet mechanism and the convergence time of the routing protocol. Aside from providing a failover mechanism, GRE tunnels also provide the ability to encrypt multicast/broadcast packets and non-IP protocols. It is recommended to use EIGRP as a routing protocol because it performs better than OSPF for GRE over IPsec. In Figure 6-6, if you have another router in Doha, when one of the tunnels is down, packets flow through the other tunnel, so the Dhaka LAN still should be able to access resources to the Doha LAN.

Example 6-42 shows the configuration of Dhaka. This router is configured with GRE, EIGRP, and IPsec. Important configuration elements are the redundant peers and multiple crypto maps, GRE tunnel interfaces, the bandwidth setting on the backup GRE interface, the routing protocol, and multiple access control lists (ACLs) as shown in highlighted areas.

Example 6-42 *Configuration of GRE over IPsec for Dhaka*

```
Dhaka# show running-config
crypto isakmp policy 10
authentication pre-share
!
crypto isakmp key cisco1234 address 30.1.1.1
crypto isakmp key cisco1234 address 30.1.1.2
!
crypto ipsec transform-set strong esp-3des esp-sha-hmac
!
! Two crypto maps - one for the primary and other one for the secondary router.
crypto map to_Doha 10 ipsec-isakmp
   set peer 30.1.1.1
   set transform-set strong
   match address gre1
crypto map to_Doha 20 ipsec-isakmp
   set peer 30.1.1.2
   set transform-set strong
   match address gre2
!
interface Tunnel0
ip address 1.1.1.1 255.255.255.0
tunnel source Ethernet 1/0
tunnel destination 30.1.1.1
crypto map Remote-to-HQ
!
interface Tunnel1
ip address 10.4.2.1 255.255.255.0
bandwidth 5
tunnel source Ethernet 1/0
tunnel destination 30.1.1.2
crypto map to_Doha
!
interface Ethernet0/0
ip address 10.1.1.1 255.255.255.0
!
interface Ethernet 1/0
ip address 20.1.1.1 255.255.255.0
crypto map to_Doha
!
router eigrp 100
  network 10.0.0.0
```

Example 6-42 *Configuration of GRE over IPsec for Dhaka (Continued)*

```
  network 1.1.1.0
!
ip route 0.0.0.0  0.0.0.0 ethernet 1/0
!
ip access-list extended gre1
   permit gre host 20.1.1.1 host 30.1.1.1
!
ip access-list extended gre2
   permit gre host 20.1.1.1 host 30.1.1.2
Dhaka#
```

NOTE To control which tunnel should be primary and which one should be secondary, you can use delay, and the bandwidth command. If you do not specify any of these, the traffic will be load sharing on both tunnels, and they will act as backups for each other.

CHAPTER 7

Troubleshooting IPsec VPN on PIX Firewalls

Virtual Private Network (VPN) implementation on the PIX Firewall is very similar to the IOS Router with a few exceptions. This chapter examines the difference in detail and explores both LAN-to-LAN and Remote Access VPN implementations and troubleshooting using IP Security Protocol (IPsec) on the PIX Firewall. The discussion of this chapter is based on PIX Firewall version 7.0. The same code which runs on ASA 5500 Series Appliances has some additional VPN features (for example, secure sockets layer [SSL] VPN), and will not be discussed in this chapter, as these features are not available on the PIX firewall platforms. The case study section contains a new feature called *Hairpinning*, which allows the PIX firewall to act as a hub for both VPN clients and other VPN peers such as the IOS Router, PIX firewall, and so on.

Overview of IPsec Protocol

For a thorough overview of IPsec protocol, refer to Chapter 6, "Troubleshooting IPsec VPNs on IOS Routers." So that this chapter can focus on the IPsec VPN implementation and Troubleshooting on the PIX Firewall, the information from Chapter 6 is not repeated in this section.

Diagnostic Commands and Tools

Just as with Cisco IOS routers, the **show** and **debug** commands are invaluable on PIX Firewall to troubleshoot the IPsec issue. In this section, we work through some of the most important commands that you can use to troubleshoot any IPsec issue on the PIX firewall.

show Commands

IPsec depends on successful policy negotiation. Even though IPsec peers are negotiating Internet Key Exchange (IKE) and IPsec parameters, if the policies do not match, the negotiations will result in failure. You can troubleshoot IKE and IPsec by using the following **show** commands:

- **show crypto isakmp**—This command shows the state information of phase I of the two-phased IPsec tunnel negotiation. Example 7-1 shows all the options available with this command on version 7.0.

Example 7-1 **show crypto isakmp** *Command Arguments*

```
PIX-A# show crypto isakmp ?
  ipsec-over-tcp  Show IPsec over TCP data
  sa              Show ISAKMP sas
  stats           Show ISAKMP statistics
  |              Output modifiers
  <cr>
PIX-A#
```

Table 7-1 summarizes the meaning of different arguments with this command as shown in Example 7-1.

Table 7-1 **show crypto isakmp** *Command Arguments*

Command Arguments	Meaning of Arguments
IPsec-over-tcp stats	Shows various connection information of IPsec-over-TCP tunnel.
sa	Shows a summary of IKE Phase I SA state information. To see details, use the keyword **detail** after Security Association (**SA**) in the arguments.
stats	Provides various statistics of the Phase I SAs.

Example 7-2 shows the output of the **show crypto isakmp sa detail** command on the PIX firewall, which contains an established phase I of LAN-to-LAN VPN tunnel.

Example 7-2 **show crypto isakmp sa** *on PIX-A Firewall*

```
PIX-A# show crypto isakmp sa detail

   Active SA: 1
    Rekey SA: 0 (A tunnel will report 1 Active and 1 Rekey SA during rekey)
Total IKE SA: 1

1   IKE Peer: 172.16.172.163
    Type    : L2L              Role    : initiator
! MM_ACTIVE indicates a successful IKE Phase I
    Rekey   : no               State   : MM_ACTIVE
    Encrypt : 3des             Hash    : MD5
    Auth    : preshared        Lifetime: 43200
    Lifetime Remaining: 43177
PIX-A#
```

- **show crypto ipsec**—This command shows the state information of phase II for the IPsec tunnel. Example 7-3 shows the arguments available for the **show crypto ipsec** command and all the arguments available for this command.

Example 7-3 **show crypto ipsec** *Command Arguments*

```
PIX-A# show crypto ipsec ?

  df-bit         Show IPsec DF policy
  fragmentation  Show IPsec fragmentation policy
  sa             Show IPsec SAs
  stats          Show IPsec global statistics
PIX-A#
```

Table 7-2 summarizes the arguments available with the **show crypto ipsec** command.

Table 7-2 **show crypto ipsec** *Command Arguments*

Arguments	Meaning
df-bit	Shows the details of IPsec DF policy.
fragmentation	Shows details of IPsec fragmentation policy.
sa	Shows the phase II establishment, in addition to the counters for packets encryption and decryption of an IPsec tunnel. This information is very useful.
stats	Shows the statistics of the phase II connection information.

Example 7-4 shows the **show crypto ipsec sa** command output for a successful LAN-to-LAN tunnel.

Example 7-4 *Phase II SA Output With* **show crypto ipsec sa** *Command*

```
  PIX-A# show crypto ipsec sa
interface: outside
    Crypto map tag: mymap, local addr: 172.16.172.164

! Following are the networks defined to be protected by the LAN-to-LAN tunnel.
      local ident (addr/mask/prot/port): (192.168.1.0/255.255.255.0/0/0)
      remote ident (addr/mask/prot/port): (192.168.2.0/255.255.255.0/0/0)
      current_peer: 172.16.172.163

! Following two lines indicates that packets are encrypting and decrypting fine
! through the LAN-to-LAN tunnel.
      #pkts encaps: 4, #pkts encrypt: 4, #pkts digest: 4
      #pkts decaps: 4, #pkts decrypt: 4, #pkts verify: 4
      #pkts compressed: 0, #pkts decompressed: 0
      #pkts not compressed: 4, #pkts comp failed: 0, #pkts decomp failed: 0
      #send errors: 0, #recv errors: 0

      local crypto endpt.: 172.16.172.164, remote crypto endpt.: 172.16.172.163
```

continues

Example 7-4 *Phase II SA Output With* **show crypto ipsec sa** *Command (Continued)*

```
      path mtu 1500, ipsec overhead 60, media mtu 1500
      current outbound spi: 6BA480CE
! Following SA is for inbound connection
    inbound esp sas:
      spi: 0x2A29F111 (707391761)
         transform: esp-3des esp-md5-hmac
         in use settings ={L2L, Tunnel, }
         slot: 0, conn_id: 2, crypto-map: mymap
         sa timing: remaining key lifetime (kB/sec): (4274999/28244)
         IV size: 8 bytes
         replay detection support: Y
! Following SA is for outbound connection
    outbound esp sas:
      spi: 0x6BA480CE (1805942990)
         transform: esp-3des esp-md5-hmac
         in use settings ={L2L, Tunnel, }
         slot: 0, conn_id: 2, crypto-map: mymap
         sa timing: remaining key lifetime (kB/sec): (4274999/28241)
         IV size: 8 bytes
         replay detection support: Y
PIX-A#
```

- **show commands for configuration**—You can verify various configurations of IPsec with the command **show running-config** commands. The commands can be **isakmp**, **crypto**, and so on. Example 7-5 shows how to check the Internet Security Association and Key Management Protocol (ISAKMP) configuration.

Example 7-5 *The* **isakmp** *Configuration on the PIX Firewall*

```
PIX-A# show running-config isakmp | include 10
isakmp policy 10 authentication pre-share
isakmp policy 10 encryption 3des
isakmp policy 10 hash md5
isakmp policy 10 group 2
isakmp policy 10 lifetime 43200
PIX-A#
```

Various configuration checks pertaining to IPsec tunnel can be verified with different command options, which are explained in the chapter when the topic is relevant.

debug Commands

IPsec depends on successful policy negotiation. While IPsec peers are negotiating IKE and IPsec parameters, if the policies do not match, the negotiations will result in failure. You can troubleshoot IPsec by using the following commands:

- **debug crypto isakmp** *<1–255>*—Shows the detailed information on phase I in IPsec tunnel build-up process. The level of debug output ranges from 1 to 255, with 1 as the lowest and 255 as the highest.

- **debug crypto ipsec** <*1–255*>—Provides detailed information on the phase II negotiation of the IPsec tunnel build-up process. The level of debug output ranges from 1 to 255, with 1 as the lowest and 255 as the highest.
- **debug crypto engine** <*1–255*>—Shows debug messages for crypto engine-related error operations. The level of debug output ranges from 1 to 255, with 1 as the lowest and 255 as the highest.

From the debug error messages, you can determine what part of the negotiation is failing and correct the appropriate parameter. The amount of detail that you will get from the debug commands output depends on the level you set to run the debug commands. Table 7-3 summarizes different levels of debug commands and the amount of detail you will receive in the output of the debug commands.

Table 7-3 *Debug Level Explanation for IPsec*

Event Levels	Explanation
1-3 = WARNING and FAULT	Provides the highest-priority severity indicating a potentially serious problem, CRASH or non-recoverable error.
2 = INFORMATIONAL	Provides the lowest level of information. For example user connect/disconnect.
3-4 = INFORMATIONAL	Provides more information than Level 2. Level 3 provides information about Phase 1 and 2 completion. It also provides information about user connection failure. Level 4 provides more details on connect/disconnect of the VPN tunnel.
5-7 = DEBUG	Level 5 provides the lowest level of debugging information. More information is provided by 6 and 7.
8	High-Level Header Decode.
9	Low-Level Header Decode.
10	Hex Dump of Header.
11, 254, 255	Hex Dump of Packet. Debug level 254 specifies IKE packets decode. This displays a sniffer-like decoding of fields and values for each IKE packet. 255 specifies an IKE packet dump, which displays the octets within the packets.

NOTE Most of the IPsec problems can be diagnosed by running debug at level 5. Sometimes you may need to run the debug at level 7, but rarely will you need to run the debug at a level higher than 7. Debug Level 8-255 is used by the Cisco Developer for issues with the IPsec tunnel.

Categorization of Problem Areas

The problem areas of IPsec can be categorized based on their implementations as follows:

- LAN-to-LAN Troubleshooting
- Remote Access VPN Troubleshooting

LAN-to-LAN Troubleshooting

This section presents the configuration and troubleshooting steps of IPsec LAN-to-LAN VPN tunnel between two PIXen based on Figure 7-1.

Figure 7-1 *Typical LAN-to-LAN and Remote Access VPN Setup*

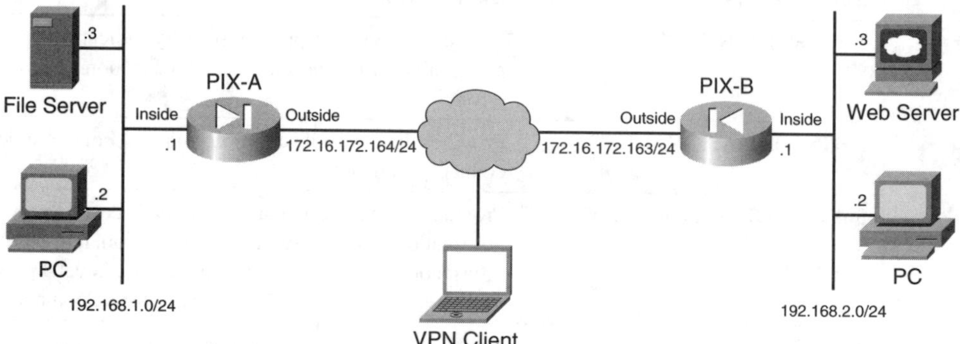

As shown in Figure 7-1, PIX-A and PIX-B are running PIX version 7.0 and are configured for a LAN-to-LAN tunnel. The troubleshooting steps that follow the configuration steps use the same setup as shown in Figure 7-1.

Configuration Steps

Work through the steps that follow to configure a basic LAN-to-LAN IPsec tunnel between two PIX firewalls:

Step 1 Configure the basic PIX firewall.

Before you attempt to configure LAN-to-LAN VPN tunnel, you need to configure the interface and the routing on the PIX firewall. Example 7-6 shows how to configure the outside interface of the PIX firewall and define the route. The same procedure can be used to configure the rest of the interfaces on the PIX firewall.

Example 7-6 *Configuring Interfaces on the PIX Firewall*

```
! From configuration mode, go under interface configuration mode.
PIX-A(config)# interface ethernet0
! Assign the IP address and subnet mask for the interface
PIX-A(config-if)# ip address 172.16.172.164 255.255.255.0
! Name the interface with the nameif command. If you define the name as outside
! interface, the security level is set to zero.
PIX-A(config-if)# nameif outside
!Set the speed and duplex with the following two lines.
PIX-A(config-if)# speed auto
PIX-A(config-if)# duplex full
! You can set the security level with the security-level command. The following line
! is not necessary if the interface is named as outside.
PIX-A(config-if)# security-level 0
! Enable the interface with the following command.
PIX-A(config-if)# no shutdown
! Define the default gateway or more specific static route for private network
! of the other side of the tunnel.
PIX-A(config-if)# route outside 0.0.0.0 0.0.0.0 172.16.172.1
PIX-A(config-if)#
```

Step 2 Configure ISAKMP policy and enable on the outside interface.

To configure ISAKMP policies, in global configuration mode, use the **isakmp policy** command with its various arguments. The syntax for ISAKMP policy commands is:

isakmp policy *priority* **attribute_name [attribute_value | integer]**

Example 7-7 shows how to configure the ISAKMP policy on the PIX firewall.

Example 7-7 *ISAKMP Policy Configuration on PIX Firewall*

```
! Set the authentication method as pre-shared key with the following command.
PIX-A(config)# isakmp policy 20 authentication pre-share
! Encryption key method is defined as 3DES with the following command.
PIX-A(config)# isakmp policy 20 encryption 3des
! Hashing algorithm is defined as MD5 for this example.
PIX-A(config)# isakmp policy 20 hash md5
! Set the Diffie-Hellman group 2 with the following command.
PIX-A(config)# isakmp policy 20 group 2
! The default timeout value is 28800 or 8 hours. Following command set up the
! timeout value to be 12 hours.
PIX-A(config)# isakmp policy 20 lifetime 43200
! Enable ISAKMP on the outside interface.
PIX-A(config)# isakmp enable outside
PIX-A(config)#
```

Step 3 Create a transform set.

A transform set combines an encryption method and an authentication method. During the IPsec security association negotiation with ISAKMP, the peers agree to use a particular transform set to protect a particular data flow. The transform set must be the same for both peers.

You can create multiple transform sets, and then specify one or more of these transform sets in a **crypto map** entry. PIX firewall uses the transform set information to protect the data flows for that crypto map entry access list. For more overview information, refer to the section in this chapter entitled "Creating a Transform Set" in "LAN-to-LAN Troubleshooting."

To configure a transform set, in global configuration mode, use the **crypto ipsec transform-set** command. The syntax is:

```
crypto ipsec transform-set transform-set-name encryption-method
  authentication-method
```

Example 7-8 configures a transform set with the name **myset**, esp-3des encryption, and esp-md5-hmac authentication.

Example 7-8 *Configuring Transform Set on the PIX Firewall*

```
PIX-A(config)# crypto ipsec transform set myset esp-3des esp-md5-hmac
PIX-A(config)#
```

Step 4 Configure an Access-list (ACL) to define Interesting Traffic for LAN-to-LAN IPsec tunnel.

The access-list in LAN-to-LAN IPsec tunnel is used to define the interesting traffic between the tunnel end points of the PIX firewalls that needs to be protected by the tunnel. To configure an ACL, use the following syntax:

```
access-list listname extended permit ip source-ipaddress source-netmask
  destination-ipaddress destination-netmask
```

Example 7-9 shows an access-list configuration (ACL 101) on PIX-A that protects the traffic between two private networks (between PIX-A and PIX-B). The source network for the access-list on PIX-A is 192.168.1.0/24 and destination network is 192.168.2.0/24.

Example 7-9 *Defining Interesting Traffic by Access List on PIX-A Firewall*

```
PIX-A(config)# access-list 101_extended permit ip 192.168.1.0 255.255.255.0
  192.168.2.0 255.255.255.0
PIX-A(config)#
```

You must configure a mirror image access-list on the other side of the tunnel (PIX-B) to define the interesting traffic for the IPsec tunnel as shown in Example 7-10.

Example 7-10 *Mirror Image ACL on PIX-B Firewall to Define IPsec LAN-to-LAN Tunnel Interesting Traffic*

```
PIX-B(config)# access-list 101_extended permit ip 192.168.2.0 255.255.255.0
  192.168.1.0 255.255.255.0
PIX-B(config)#
```

Note that this access-list is the mirror image of the ACL defined on PIX-A firewall.

Step 5 Define a tunnel group for a LAN-to-LAN tunnel.

A tunnel group is used to identify AAA servers, specify connection parameters, and define a default group policy. PIX Firewall stores tunnel groups internally. There are two default tunnel groups in the PIX firewall: **DefaultRAGroup**, which is the default IPsec remote-access tunnel group; and **DefaultL2Lgroup**, which is the default IPsec LAN-to-LAN tunnel group. You can change them but not delete them. To establish a basic LAN-to-LAN VPN connection, you must configure the following two attributes for a tunnel group:

(a) Set up the connection type to be IPsec_L2L (IPsec LAN-to-LAN tunnel) with the configuration shown in Example 7-11. Be sure to define the tunnel name with the peer's IP address. This is how the PIX firewall identifies the tunnel group for authentication.

Example 7-11 *Creating LAN-to-LAN VPN Tunnel-Group on PIX Firewall*

```
PIX-A(config)# Tunnel-Group 172.16.172.163 type IPsec_L2L
PIX-A(config)#
```

(b) Define the pre-shared key as shown in Example 7-12.

Example 7-12 *Configuration of the Pre-shared Key for LAN-to-LAN IPsec Tunnel*

```
PIX-A(config)# tunnel-group 172.16.172.163 ipsec-attributes
PIX-A(config-ipsec)# pre-shared-key cisco123
PIX-A(config)#
```

Step 6 Create a crypto map for a LAN-to-LAN tunnel.

The crypto map applied on the interface triggers the IPsec process. Several components are tied together with the **crypto map** command. As you can apply only one crypto map per interface, you must create the crypto map with the same name but different sequence number to provide different security for different subnets. Also, if you have different peers, you need to create multiple entries of the crypto map with different sequence numbers but with the same name.

Example 7-13 shows how to create a crypto map on PIX-A firewall for the LAN-to-LAN tunnel with PIX-B firewall.

Example 7-13 *Creating Crypto Map on the PIX-A Firewall for LAN-to-LAN Tunnel*

```
! Assign the access-list previously created to  the crypto map entry.
PIX-A(config)# crypto map mymap 10 match address 101
! Define the Peer IP address with the following command.
PIX-A(config)# crypto map mymap 10 set peer 172.16.172.163
! Apply the transform set to the crypto map. You can apply multiple transform
! sets to the same crypto map.
PIX-A(config)# crypto map mymap 10 set transform-set myset
PIX-A(config)#
```

Apply the crypto map to an interface. Once a crypto map is configured, you need to apply it on the outgoing interface of the packet destination. Applying a crypto map is supported on all interfaces of the PIX firewall. When you make any changes to the applied crypto map, PIX firewall automatically applies the changes to the running configuration. It drops any existing connections and reestablishes them after applying the new crypto map. The syntax for applying the crypto map is as follows:

```
crypto map map-name interface interface-name
```

Example 7-14 shows how to apply the crypto map on the outside interface of PIX firewall PIX-A.

Example 7-14 *Applying the Crypto Map on the Outside Interface of PIX-A*

```
PIX-A(config)# crypto map mymap interface outside
PIX-A(config)#
```

Step 7 Bypass the NAT translation for the IPsec VPN traffic.

If you have **nat-control** turned off on the PIX firewall, you do not need any special configuration to create the NAT exemption for the LAN-to-LAN VPN traffic unless you have NAT configured that translates the source network of the VPN traffic to a routable IP address. Under this circumstance, or when the **nat-control** is turned on, you must bypass the NAT for the private networks of the VPN traffic. You can understand this best by looking at an example. Assume that network 192.168.1.0/24 on PIX-A is translated to the interface IP address (172.16.172.164) for the Internet connection with the nat/global statement. With this setup, whether you have the **nat-control** turned on or off, you need to configure the NAT exemption to allow the LAN-to-LAN private network to bypass the NAT. This is because even if you have the **nat-control** off, PIX still performs the NAT translation if it is configured. When the **nat-control** is tuned on, PIX must perform the NAT translation, hence NAT exemption is a must for the VPN traffic. Example 7-15 shows how to configure the NAT exemption for the LAN-to-LAN VPN traffic.

Example 7-15 *Bypassing the LAN-to-LAN VPN Traffic Across the Tunnel*

```
PIX-A(config)# show running-config nat-control
! The following line indicates that the nat-control is turned off
no nat-control
! Now check to see if there is a NAT configured that may include the private
! network that needs to be protected by the IPSec tunnel
PIX-A(config)# show running-config nat
! The following line indicates the NAT is configured for the source network of
! the VPN traffic that needs to be protected by the tunnel.
nat (inside) 1 192.168.1.0 255.255.255.0
! The following command verifies the corresponding global stmt, which says all
! internet bound traffic uses the outside interface IP address.
PIX-A(config)# show running-config global
global (outside) 1 interface
! To bypass the LAN-to-LAN VPN traffic, create a new ACL or use the existing
! crypto ACL which is 101 on the PIX firewall with the source and destination
! addresses to be the private networks on both sides.
PIX-A(config)# access-list 110 extended permit ip 192.168.1.0 255.255.255.0
  192.168.2.0 255.255.255.0
! Apply the ACL with NAT statement to configure NAT exemption.
PIX-A(config)# nat (inside) 0 access-list 110
! Following line verifies the NAT configuration
PIX-A(config)# show running-config nat
nat (inside) 0 access-list 110
nat (inside) 1 192.168.1.0 255.255.255.0
! Following line verifies the ACL configuration
PIX-A(config)# show running-config access-list 110
access-list 110 extended permit ip 192.168.1.0 255.255.255.0 192.168.2.0
  255.255.255.0
PIX-A(config)#
```

Step 8 Allow the actual IPsec traffic through the tunnel.

You must allow the decrypted IPsec tunnel traffic with either the **sysopt** command or by creating an access-list to allow the private networks, and to apply the access-list on the outside interface as inbound. Example 7-16 shows how to allow the decrypted packets on the PIX outside interface by using the **sysopt** command or access-list.

Example 7-16 *Configuration to Bypass ACL Checks to Allow the Decrypted Traffic*

```
! Use the sysopt command in global configuration mode to have the PIX firewall
! to allow IPSec connections.
PIX-A(config)# sysopt connection permit-ipsec
! The following ACL substitute the sysopt command. The source address of the ACL
! is the network or addresses defined with IP address Pool.
PIX-A(config)# access-list 120 permit 192.168.2.0 255.255.255.0 192.168.1.0
  255.255.255.0
! Apply the access-list to the interface
PIX-A(config)# access-group 120 in interface outside
! Save your changes.
PIX-A(config)# write memory
PIX-A(config)#
```

Follow the preceding steps to configure PIX-B firewall. Example 7-17 shows the configuration that needs to be performed for LAN-to-LAN tunnel.

Example 7-17 *Configuration on the PIX-B Firewall for the LAN-to-LAN Tunnel*

```
! Following lines are for configuring interface
PIX-B(config)# interface ethernet0
PIX-B(config-if)# ip address 172.16.172.163 255.255.255.0
PIX-B(config-if)# nameif outside
PIX-B(config-if)# speed auto
PIX-B(config-if)# duplex full
PIX-B(config-if)# no shutdown
! Following lines are to define ISAKMP policy which should match to one of the policies
! defined on PIX-A
PIX-B(config)# isakmp policy 10 authentication pre-share
PIX-B(config)# isakmp policy 10 encryption 3des
PIX-B(config)# isakmp policy 10 hash md5
PIX-B(config)# isakmp policy 10 group 2
PIX-B(config)# isakmp policy 10 lifetime 43200
PIX-B(config)# isakmp enable outside
! Following line defines the transform-set
PIX-B(config)# crypto ipsec transform set myset esp-3des esp-md5-hmac
! Following line defines the ACL for the interesting traffic for LAN-to-LAN VPN
PIX-B(config)# access-list 101_list extended permit ip 192.168.2.0 255.255.255.0
  192.168.1.0 255.255.255.0
! Define the tunnel-group with the name to be the peer's IP address, i.e, PIX-A's outside
! interface IP address. The pre-shared-key has to match on both sides.
PIX-B(config)# tunnel-group 172.16.172.164 type IPSec_L2L
PIX-B(config)# tunnel-group 172.16.172.164 ipsec-attributes
PIX-B(config-ipsec)# pre-shared-key cisco123
! The following lines are used to configure the crypto map
PIX-B(config)# crypto map mymap 10 match address 101
PIX-B(config)# crypto map mymap 10 set peer anyhost 172.16.172.164
PIX-B(config)# crypto map mymap 10 set transform-set myset
PIX-B(config)# crypto map mymap interface outside
! Configure sysopt for IPSec to allow the decrypted traffic on the outside interface
PIX-B(config)# sysopt connection permit-ipsec
! For additional configuration on NAT and others, refer to the previous configuration
! steps for the PIX-A firewall
PIX-B(config)# write memory
PIX-B(config)#
```

Troubleshooting Steps

The LAN-to-LAN IPsec tunnel may fail to process traffic for several reasons. This section examines the details of all possible causes and how to resolve them. The troubleshooting IPsec LAN-to-LAN tunnel issues can classified as follows:

- Tunnel is not established: Phase I failure
- Tunnel is not established: Phase II failure
- Tunnel is established completely but unable to pass data

The sections that follow provide a detailed discussion of these topics.

Tunnel Is Not Established: Phase I Failure

If you are unable to pass any traffic across the LAN-to-LAN IPsec tunnel, you should first investigate the status of the tunnel state on both the Initiator and the Responder PIXen. You might experience tunnel establishment failure either in Phase I or Phase II. For successful tunnel establishment, you must have both Phase I And Phase II established. The **Show crypto isakmp sa** command allows you to view the status of the tunnel, and if it is MM_ACTIVE, this means that the Phase I is established, as shown in Example 7-18. PIX versions earlier than 7.0 shows **QM_IDLE** for phase I establishment.

Example 7-18 *A Successful Phase I Establishment on PIX Version 7.0 and Later*

```
PIX-A# show crypto isakmp sa

   Active SA: 1
    Rekey SA: 0 (A tunnel will report 1 Active and 1 Rekey SA during rekey)
Total IKE SA: 1

1   IKE Peer: 172.16.172.163
    Type    : L2L              Role    : initiator
! The following line shows MM_ACTIVE for the initiator state which is an indication that
! Phase I is established.
    Rekey   : no               State   : MM_ACTIVE
PIX-A#
```

If Phase II is established, **show crypto ipsec sa** will provide the details as shown in Example 7-19.

Example 7-19 *Phase II Establishment of Tunnel on PIX Version 7.0*

```
PIX-A# show crypto ipsec sa
interface: outside
! The following line shows the crypto map name and the peer IP address
    Crypto map tag: mymap, local addr: 172.16.172.164
! The following two lines show the private networks of both sides whose traffic
! will be protected by the IPSec tunnel.
      local ident (addr/mask/prot/port): (192.168.1.0/255.255.255.0/0/0)
      remote ident (addr/mask/prot/port): (192.168.2.0/255.255.255.0/0/0)
      current_peer: 172.16.172.163
! The following counters are extremely important to see if the tunnel is processing any
! traffic. Encaps indicates that this side is encrypting and sending the traffic fine to
! the other side. And decrypts counter indicates that the other side is sending the reply
! and this is able to decrypt the traffic.
      #pkts encaps: 4, #pkts encrypt: 4, #pkts digest: 4
      #pkts decaps: 4, #pkts decrypt: 4, #pkts verify: 4
      #pkts compressed: 0, #pkts decompressed: 0
      #pkts not compressed: 4, #pkts comp failed: 0, #pkts decomp failed: 0
      #send errors: 0, #recv errors: 0
```

continues

Example 7-19 *Phase II Establishment of Tunnel on PIX Version 7.0 (Continued)*

```
      local crypto endpt.: 172.16.172.164, remote crypto endpt.: 172.16.172.163

      path mtu 1500, ipsec overhead 60, media mtu 1500
      current outbound spi: 88BB86AD
! The following inbound SA has an SPI number indicating that this is established.
    inbound esp sas:
      spi: 0x1A280A9D (438831773)
         transform: esp-3des esp-md5-hmac
         in use settings ={L2L, Tunnel, }
         slot: 0, conn_id: 1, crypto-map: mymap
         sa timing: remaining key lifetime (kB/sec): (4274999/28776)
         IV size: 8 bytes
         replay detection support: Y
! The following outbound SA has an SPI number indicating that this is established.
    outbound esp sas:
      spi: 0x88BB86AD (2293991085)
         transform: esp-3des esp-md5-hmac
         in use settings ={L2L, Tunnel, }
         slot: 0, conn_id: 1, crypto-map: mymap
         sa timing: remaining key lifetime (kB/sec): (4274999/28774)
         IV size: 8 bytes
         replay detection support: Y

PIX-A#
```

Before exploring failure or possible causes of failure for Phase I and Phase II, it is worth dissecting the debug output of a successful LAN-to-LAN IPsec tunnel on the Initiator side, which is shown in Example 7-20.

Example 7-20 *Dissection of* **debug** *Commands for a Successful IPsec Tunnel*

```
PIX-A# debug crypto isakmp 7
PIX-A# debug crypto ipsec 7
! Usually level 5 will give you the details to troubleshoot most of the issues.
! Sometimes, you may run level 7. Rarely you may need to run level 255.
Jun 05 21:38:55 [IKEv1 DEBUG]: pitcher: received a key acquire message!
! The following line shows the initiation of the first packet for IPSec tunnel by the
! Initiator.
Jun 05 21:38:55 [IKEv1]: IP = 172.16.172.163, IKE Initiator: New Phase 1, Intf 2,
  IKE Peer 172.16.172.163  local Proxy Address 192.168.1.0, remote Proxy Address
  192.168.2.0,  Crypto map (mymap)
Jun 05 21:38:55 [IKEv1 DEBUG]: IP = 172.16.172.163, constructing ISA_SA for isakmp
Jun 05 21:38:55 [IKEv1 DEBUG]: IP = 172.16.172.163, constructing Fragmentation VID +
  extended capabilities payload
Jun 05 21:38:55 [IKEv1]: IP = 172.16.172.163, IKE DECODE SENDING Message (msgid=0)
  with payloads : HDR + SA (1) + VENDOR (13) + NONE (0) total length : 144
Jun 05 21:38:56 [IKEv1]: IP = 172.16.172.163, IKE DECODE RECEIVED Message (msgid=0)
  with payloads : HDR + SA (1) + VENDOR (13) + NONE (0) total length : 104
Jun 05 21:38:56 [IKEv1 DEBUG]: IP = 172.16.172.163, processing SA payload
! The following line indicates that IKE phase I policy is accepted by the other side
Jun 05 21:38:56 [IKEv1 DEBUG]: IP = 172.16.172.163, Oakley proposal is acceptable
```

Example 7-20 *Dissection of* **debug** *Commands for a Successful IPsec Tunnel (Continued)*

```
Jun 05 21:38:56 [IKEv1 DEBUG]: IP = 172.16.172.163, processing VID payload
Jun 05 21:38:56 [IKEv1 DEBUG]: IP = 172.16.172.163, Received Fragmentation VID
Jun 05 21:38:56 [IKEv1 DEBUG]: IP = 172.16.172.163, IKE Peer included IKE
  fragmentation capability flags:  Main Mode:        True  Aggressive Mode:  True
Jun 05 21:38:56 [IKEv1 DEBUG]: IP = 172.16.172.163, constructing ke payload
Jun 05 21:38:56 [IKEv1 DEBUG]: IP = 172.16.172.163, constructing nonce payload
Jun 05 21:38:56 [IKEv1 DEBUG]: IP = 172.16.172.163, constructing Cisco Unity VID
  payload
Jun 05 21:38:56 [IKEv1 DEBUG]: IP = 172.16.172.163, constructing xauth V6 VID payload
Jun 05 21:38:56 [IKEv1 DEBUG]: IP = 172.16.172.163, Send IOS VID
Jun 05 21:38:56 [IKEv1 DEBUG]: IP = 172.16.172.163, Constructing ASA spoofing IOS
  Vendor ID payload (version: 1.0.0, capabilities: 20000001)
Jun 05 21:38:56 [IKEv1 DEBUG]: IP = 172.16.172.163, constructing VID payload
Jun 05 21:38:56 [IKEv1 DEBUG]: IP = 172.16.172.163, Send Altiga/Cisco VPN3000/Cisco
  ASA GW VID
Jun 05 21:38:56 [IKEv1]: IP = 172.16.172.163, IKE DECODE SENDING Message (msgid=0)
  with payloads : HDR + KE (4) +
NONCE (10) + VENDOR (13) + VENDOR (13) + VENDOR (13) + VENDOR (13) + NONE (0) total
  length : 256
Jun 05 21:38:56 [IKEv1]: IP = 172.16.172.163, IKE DECODE RECEIVED Message (msgid=0)
  with payloads : HDR + KE (4) +
NONCE (10) + VENDOR (13) + VENDOR (13) + VENDOR (13) + VENDOR (13) + NONE (0) total
  length : 256
Jun 05 21:38:56 [IKEv1 DEBUG]: IP = 172.16.172.163, processing ke payload
Jun 05 21:38:56 [IKEv1 DEBUG]: IP = 172.16.172.163, processing ISA_KE
Jun 05 21:38:56 [IKEv1 DEBUG]: IP = 172.16.172.163, processing nonce payload
Jun 05 21:38:56 [IKEv1 DEBUG]: IP = 172.16.172.163, processing VID payload
Jun 05 21:38:56 [IKEv1 DEBUG]: IP = 172.16.172.163, Received Cisco Unity client VID
Jun 05 21:38:56 [IKEv1 DEBUG]: IP = 172.16.172.163, processing VID payload
Jun 05 21:38:56 [IKEv1 DEBUG]: IP = 172.16.172.163, Received xauth V6 VID
Jun 05 21:38:56 [IKEv1 DEBUG]: IP = 172.16.172.163, processing VID payload
Jun 05 21:38:56 [IKEv1 DEBUG]: IP = 172.16.172.163, Processing VPN3000/ASA spoofing
IOS Vendor ID payload (version: 1.0.0, capabilities: 20000001)
Jun 05 21:38:56 [IKEv1 DEBUG]: IP = 172.16.172.163, processing VID payload
Jun 05 21:38:56 [IKEv1 DEBUG]: IP = 172.16.172.163, Received Altiga/Cisco VPN3000/
  Cisco ASA GW VID
! The following shows that the tunnel group configuration is found. This is where the
! pre-shared key is defined.
Jun 05 21:38:56 [IKEv1]: IP = 172.16.172.163, Connection landed on tunnel_group
  172.16.172.163
Jun 05 21:38:56 [IKEv1 DEBUG]: Group = 172.16.172.163, IP = 172.16.172.163,
  Generating keys for Initiator...
Jun 05 21:38:56 [IKEv1 DEBUG]: Group = 172.16.172.163, IP = 172.16.172.163,
  constructing ID
Jun 05 21:38:56 [IKEv1 DEBUG]: Group = 172.16.172.163, IP = 172.16.172.163,
  construct hash payload
Jun 05 21:38:56 [IKEv1 DEBUG]: Group = 172.16.172.163, IP = 172.16.172.163,
  computing hash
Jun 05 21:38:56 [IKEv1 DEBUG]: IP = 172.16.172.163, Constructing IOS keep alive
  payload: proposal=32767/32767 sec.
Jun 05 21:38:56 [IKEv1 DEBUG]: Group = 172.16.172.163, IP = 172.16.172.163,
  constructing dpd vid payload
```

continues

Example 7-20 *Dissection of* **debug** *Commands for a Successful IPsec Tunnel (Continued)*

```
Jun 05 21:38:56 [IKEv1]: IP = 172.16.172.163, IKE DECODE SENDING Message (msgid=0)
  with payloads : HDR + ID (5) + HASH (8) +
IOS KEEPALIVE (14) + VENDOR (13) + NONE (0) total length : 92
Jun 05 21:38:56 [IKEv1]: IP = 172.16.172.163, IKE DECODE RECEIVED Message (msgid=0)
  with payloads : HDR + ID (5) + HASH (8) +
IOS KEEPALIVE (14) + VENDOR (13) + NONE (0) total length : 92
Jun 05 21:38:56 [IKEv1 DEBUG]: Group = 172.16.172.163, IP = 172.16.172.163,
  Processing ID
Jun 05 21:38:56 [IKEv1 DEBUG]: Group = 172.16.172.163, IP = 172.16.172.163,
  processing hash
Jun 05 21:38:56 [IKEv1 DEBUG]: Group = 172.16.172.163, IP = 172.16.172.163,
  computing hash
Jun 05 21:38:56 [IKEv1 DEBUG]: IP = 172.16.172.163, Processing IOS keep alive
  payload: proposal=32767/32767 sec.
Jun 05 21:38:56 [IKEv1 DEBUG]: Group = 172.16.172.163, IP = 172.16.172.163,
  processing VID payload
Jun 05 21:38:56 [IKEv1 DEBUG]: Group = 172.16.172.163, IP = 172.16.172.163, Received
  DPD VID
Jun 05 21:38:56 [IKEv1]: IP = 172.16.172.163, Connection landed on tunnel_group
  172.16.172.163
! Following line is an indication of phase I establishment and the beginning of phase II
! negotiation.
Jun 05 21:38:56 [IKEv1 DEBUG]: Group = 172.16.172.163, IP = 172.16.172.163, Oakley
  begin quick mode
! The following message affirms the phase I establishment
Jun 05 21:38:56 [IKEv1]: Group = 172.16.172.163, IP = 172.16.172.163, PHASE 1 COMPLETED
Jun 05 21:38:56 [IKEv1]: IP = 172.16.172.163, Keep-alive type for this connection: DPD
Jun 05 21:38:56 [IKEv1 DEBUG]: Group = 172.16.172.163, IP = 172.16.172.163, Starting
  phase 1 rekey timer: 41040000 (ms)
Jun 05 21:38:56 [IKEv1 DEBUG]: IKE got SPI from key engine: SPI = 0xbb5bb46c
Jun 05 21:38:56 [IKEv1 DEBUG]: Group = 172.16.172.163, IP = 172.16.172.163, oakley
  constructing quick mode
Jun 05 21:38:56 [IKEv1 DEBUG]: Group = 172.16.172.163, IP = 172.16.172.163,
  constructing blank hash
Jun 05 21:38:56 [IKEv1 DEBUG]: Group = 172.16.172.163, IP = 172.16.172.163,
  constructing ISA_SA for ipsec
Jun 05 21:38:56 [IKEv1 DEBUG]: Group = 172.16.172.163, IP = 172.16.172.163,
  constructing ipsec nonce payload
Jun 05 21:38:56 [IKEv1 DEBUG]: Group = 172.16.172.163, IP = 172.16.172.163,
  constructing proxy ID
! The following lines show the interesting traffic ACL getting exchanged. These ACL
! should be the mirror image of each other.
Jun 05 21:38:56 [IKEv1 DEBUG]: Group = 172.16.172.163, IP = 172.16.172.163,
  Transmitting Proxy Id:
  Local subnet:  192.168.1.0  mask 255.255.255.0 Protocol 0  Port 0
  Remote subnet: 192.168.2.0  Mask 255.255.255.0 Protocol 0  Port 0
Jun 05 21:38:56 [IKEv1 DEBUG]: Group = 172.16.172.163, IP = 172.16.172.163,
  constructing qm hash
Jun 05 21:38:56 [IKEv1]: IP = 172.16.172.163, IKE DECODE SENDING Message
  (msgid=529335a6) with payloads : HDR + HASH (8) + SA (1) + NONCE (10) + ID (5) +
  ID (5) + NOTIFY (11) + NONE (0) total length : 192
Jun 05 21:38:57 [IKEv1]: IP = 172.16.172.163, IKE DECODE RECEIVED Message
  (msgid=529335a6) with payloads : HDR + HASH (8) + SA (1) + NONCE (10) + ID (5) +
  ID (5) + NONE (0) total length : 164
```

Example 7-20 *Dissection of* **debug** *Commands for a Successful IPsec Tunnel (Continued)*

```
Jun 05 21:38:57 [IKEv1 DEBUG]: Group = 172.16.172.163, IP = 172.16.172.163,
  processing hash
Jun 05 21:38:57 [IKEv1 DEBUG]: Group = 172.16.172.163, IP = 172.16.172.163,
  processing SA payload
Jun 05 21:38:57 [IKEv1 DEBUG]: Group = 172.16.172.163, IP = 172.16.172.163,
  processing nonce payload
Jun 05 21:38:57 [IKEv1 DEBUG]: Group = 172.16.172.163, IP = 172.16.172.163,
  Processing ID
Jun 05 21:38:57 [IKEv1 DEBUG]: Group = 172.16.172.163, IP = 172.16.172.163,
  Processing ID
Jun 05 21:38:57 [IKEv1 DEBUG]: Group = 172.16.172.163, IP = 172.16.172.163, loading
  all IPSEC SAs
Jun 05 21:38:57 [IKEv1 DEBUG]: Group = 172.16.172.163, IP = 172.16.172.163,
  Generating Quick Mode Key!
Jun 05 21:38:57 [IKEv1 DEBUG]: Group = 172.16.172.163, IP = 172.16.172.163,
  Generating Quick Mode Key!
! The negotiation for phase II shows completed here.
Jun 05 21:38:57 [IKEv1]: Group = 172.16.172.163, IP = 172.16.172.163, Security
  negotiation complete for LAN-to-LAN
Group (172.16.172.163)  Initiator, Inbound SPI = 0xbb5bb46c, Outbound SPI = 0x7ea88a9e
Jun 05 21:38:57 [IKEv1 DEBUG]: Group = 172.16.172.163, IP = 172.16.172.163, oakley
  constructing final quick mode
Jun 05 21:38:57 [IKEv1]: IP = 172.16.172.163, IKE DECODE SENDING Message
  (msgid=529335a6) with payloads : HDR + HASH (8) +
NONE (0) total length : 72
Jun 05 21:38:57 [IKEv1 DEBUG]: IKE got a KEY_ADD msg for SA: SPI = 0x7ea88a9e
Jun 05 21:38:57 [IKEv1 DEBUG]: pitcher: rcv KEY_UPDATE, spi 0xbb5bb46c
Jun 05 21:38:57 [IKEv1]: Group = 172.16.172.163, IP = 172.16.172.163, Starting P2
Rekey timer to expire in 27360 seconds
! The following line confirms phase II completion, hence complete establishment of IPSec
! LAN-to-LAN tunnel.
Jun 05 21:38:57 [IKEv1]: Group = 172.16.172.163, IP = 172.16.172.163, PHASE 2
  COMPLETED (msgid=529335a6)

PIX-A#
```

Now that you are comfortable with the show and debug command output of a successful IPsec LAN-to-LAN tunnel, if your Phase I for tunnel build-up fails, work through the following steps to correct the problem:

Step 1 Check for connectivity problems.

If you have problems with phase I establishment, first be sure that you can ping the responder from the initiator, and vice versa. This will ensure that you have proper routing configured for the peer IP address. If the peer IP address is not reachable, then Phase I negotiation will not take place.

Step 2 Be sure you get IKE Packets in the Initiator Debug Output.

If all parameters are configured properly on the Initiator, you should see the IKE packets with the **debug crypto ISAKMP** command. If you do not see any debug output, then work through the following steps to correct the problem:

- **ISAKMP is turned off**—Unlike Cisco IOS router, ISAKMP is disabled by default on the PIX Firewall. So, if you do not turn it on, ISAKMP will not be triggered, and debug will not show any IKE packets. You can verify this by executing the command shown in Example 7-21. This example also shows how to enable ISAKMP on the interface.

Example 7-21 *Verifying and Correcting the Problem of ISAKMP Not Being Applied*

```
PIX-A(config)# show running-config isakmp | include enable
! As nothing is shown, ISAKMP is not turned on the interface. The following
! command shows how to turn on ISAKMP on the outside interface
PIX-A(config)# show running-config isakmp | include enable
! The following line indicates that ISAKMP is enabled on the outside interface.
isakmp enable outside
PIX-A(config)# exit
PIX-A#
```

- **Routing Problem on the Initiator**—If ISAKMP is enabled on the interface, but you still do not see the IKE packets on the initiator debug, you may have problems with routing on the initiator. You must have a route on the initiator (PIX-A) for the private network (192.168.2.0/24) of the responder (PIX-B), which is pointing towards the interface where ISAKMP is applied. This can be done either through a static route or default gateway. Example 7-22 shows how to verify whether the route exists on the routing table for the private network.

Example 7-22 *Verifying that a Route for the Private Network Exists Through Outside Interface for the Responder Private Network*

```
PIX-A(config)# show route
! The following default gateway is on the outside interface of the PIX firewall
! where ISAKMP is applied. This is how the private network that needs to be
! protected via tunnel can be reached. The requirement is that the private
! traffic that needs to be go through the tunnel needs to hit the interface (in
! this case outside interface) where the crypto map and ISAKMP is applied.
S    0.0.0.0 0.0.0.0 [1/0] via 172.16.172.1, outside
! The following two lines are for directly connected networks
C    172.16.172.0 255.255.255.0 is directly connected, outside
C    192.168.1.0 255.255.255.0 is directly connected, inside
PIX-A(config)#
```

- **Crypto Map is not applied or is applied to the wrong interface**—After verifying and fixing the routing problem on the initiator for the private network of the responder, if you are still unable to see IKE packets, be sure that you have crypto map applied to the outgoing interface. This is the interface through which the private network on the Responder will be reached by the initiator as per the routing table, even though the packet may not be able to reach due to the private address. However, sending the packet on the outgoing interface is required to trigger Phase II And Phase I of the PIX Firewall. If the crypto map is not applied, or applied on the wrong interface, Phase I will not come up as it is brought into action by the crypto map. Use the command shown in Example 7-23 to verify if and where the crypto map is applied.

Example 7-23 *Initiator (PIX-A) Properly Has the Crypto Map Applied on the Outside Interface of the PIX Firewall*

```
PIX-A# show running-config crypto map | include interface
crypto map mymap interface outside
PIX-A#
```

— **The incorrect interesting traffic access-list is configured**—The traffic that needs to go through the tunnel is defined by the access-list that is applied to the crypto map. So, if the access-list does not include the source or destination network that should go through the tunnel, the tunnel will not be triggered, even if everything else is configured correctly. Remember that this access-list needs to be configured as mirror images on the initiator and responder. Example 7-24 shows that the access-list is properly configured on the PIX-A.

Example 7-24 *Access-list Configured on the Initiator (PIX-A)*

```
PIX-A# show running-config crypto | include address
! Following line indicates access-list 101 is applied to crypto map
crypto map mymap 10 match address 101
PIX-A# show running-config access-list 101
! Following line shows the network for which ACL is configured that needs to be
! protected by the IPSec tunnel.
access-list 101 extended permit ip 192.168.1.0 255.255.255.0 192.168.2.0
  255.255.255.0
PIX-A#
```

— **Tunnel group is not configured, or is configured with the wrong peer IP address**—If you do not have the tunnel group configured on the initiator/responder, or it is configured with the wrong Peer IP address for the tunnel-group name, Phase I will not be established. Example 7-25 shows the debug message that appears on the initiator (PIX-A), when the tunnel group is not configured with the IP address of the peer (PIX-B).

Example 7-25 debug *Message on the Initiator when the Tunnel Group Is Not Configured*

```
PIX-A# show running-config tunnel-group
! Nothing shows, meaning no tunnel-group configured.
PIX-A# debug crypto isakmp 5
PIX-A# debug crypto ipsec 5
! Only showing the relevant information
06 03:09:59 [IKEv1 DEBUG]: IP = 172.16.172.163, Oakley proposal is acceptable
06 03:09:59 [IKEv1 DEBUG]: IP = 172.16.172.163, IKE Peer included IKE fragmentation
  capability flags:  Main Mode:        True  Aggressive Mode:  True
! The following line shows the tunnel-group not configured.
06 03:09:59 [IKEv1]: Group = 172.16.172.163, IP = 172.16.172.163, Can't find a valid
  tunnel group, aborting...!
PIX-A#
```

Step 3 Be sure the responder is receiving IKE packets.

If you see the IKE packets generated on the initiator, not on the responder, then the problem is that the responder is not receiving the IKE request. This can be caused by the following:

- **Connectivity issue**—Perform the ping test from both initiator and responder to each other and be sure they have the proper connectivity to each other.
- **Wrong peer IP address on the Initiator**—If you have the wrong peer, then the actual responder will not see the packet, as the initiator will be sending an IKE Phase I request to the wrong IP.
- **IKE Packets are blocked by the Firewall**—Phase I and phase II negotiation occurs using **UDP/500**. If there is a NAT device, and NAT-T is configured on the PIX firewall, the negotiation also takes place on **UDP/4500**. So, if there is a firewall between, be sure that both **UDP/4500** and **UDP/500** are allowed through the firewall.

Step 4 Check for policy mismatches.

If there is a mismatch in IKE policy, Phase I negotiation will fail. The initiator sends all the IKE policies configured along with the default one (65535). If the receiver is not configured with a matching policy, you will see an error message, as shown in Example 7-26 on the initiator, which is PIX-A.

Example 7-26 debug *Output of ISAKMP Failure Message on Initiator Due to Policy Mismatch*

```
PIX-A# debug crypto isakmp 5
PIX-A# debug crypto ipsec 5
Jun 05 23:50:50 [IKEv1]: IP = 172.16.172.163, IKE Initiator: New Phase 1, Intf 2,
  IKE Peer 172.16.172.163  local Proxy Address 192.168.1.0, remote Proxy Address
  192.168.2.0,  Crypto map (mymap)
! The following notification came from responder informing initiator that none
```

Example 7-26 debug *Output of ISAKMP Failure Message on Initiator Due to Policy Mismatch (Continued)*

```
! of the policies is acceptable that are sent by the initiator
Jun 05 23:50:50 [IKEv1]: IP = 172.16.172.163, Received an un-encrypted
  NO_PROPOSAL_CHOSEN notify message, dropping
Jun 05 23:50:50 [IKEv1]: IP = 172.16.172.163, Information Exchange processing failed
PIX-A#
```

The debug messages that appear due to policy mismatch on the responder, which is PIX-B, are shown in Example 7-27.

Example 7-27 debug *Output of ISAKMP Failure Message on Responder Due to Policy Mismatch*

```
PIX-B# debug crypto isakmp 5
PIX-B# debug crypto ipsec 5
! The following message clearly indicates the responder is not finding a similar
! policy sent by the Initiator.
Jun 05 23:55:26 [IKEv1 DEBUG]: IP = 172.16.172.164, All SA proposals found
  unacceptable
Jun 05 23:55:26 [IKEv1]: IP = 172.16.172.164, Error processing payload: Payload ID: 1
Jun 05 23:55:26 [IKEv1 DEBUG]: IP = 172.16.172.164, IKE MM Responder FSM error
  history (struct &0x1a07d68)  <state>, <event>:  MM_DONE, EV_ERROR-->MM_START,
  EV_RCV_MSG-->MM_START, EV_START_MM-->MM_START, EV_START_MM
PIX-B#
```

The solution is to compare the IKE policy configuration on both sides of the tunnel and configure a common ISAKMP policy on both peers. Example 7-28 shows the IKE policy configured on the initiator, PIX-A.

Example 7-28 *IKE Policy Configured on the Initiator, PIX-A*

```
PIX-A# show running-config isakmp
isakmp enable outside
! Policy 10 is configured on the initiator by administrator
isakmp policy 10 authentication pre-share
isakmp policy 10 encryption des
isakmp policy 10 hash md5
isakmp policy 10 group 2
isakmp policy 10 lifetime 43200
! Policy 65535 is a default policy.
isakmp policy 65535 authentication pre-share
! Encryption for 65535 policy is 3DES by default which is modified to DES
isakmp policy 65535 encryption des
isakmp policy 65535 hash sha
isakmp policy 65535 group 2
isakmp policy 65535 lifetime 86400
PIX-A#
```

Now look at the ISAKMP policy on the responder, PIX-B, as shown in Example 7-29.

Example 7-29 *Policy Configured on the Responder, PIX-B*

```
PIX-B# show running-config isakmp
isakmp enable outside
isakmp policy 10 authentication pre-share
! Encryption algorithm is 3DES but the initiator is using DES.
isakmp policy 10 encryption 3des
isakmp policy 10 hash md5
isakmp policy 10 group 2
isakmp policy 10 lifetime 43200
isakmp policy 65535 authentication pre-share
! Encryption algorithm for the default policy us is 3DES but the initiator is
! using DES.
isakmp policy 65535 encryption 3des
isakmp policy 65535 hash sha
isakmp policy 65535 group 2
isakmp policy 65535 lifetime 86400
PIX-B#
```

As you can see, both policies (including the default policy) mismatch on both sides for the encryption algorithm. To correct the problem, you need to match the encryption algorithm for at least one of the policies, as shown in Example 7-30 for PIX-A.

Example 7-30 *Correcting the Policy Configuration for Encryption Algorithm on Initiator, PIX-A*

```
PIX-A# configure terminal
! The following two lines define the encryption protocol with 3DES for both user
! defined policy 10, and the default policy 65535
PIX-A(config)# isakmp policy 10 encryption 3des
PIX-A(config)# isakmp policy 65535 encryption 3des
PIX-A(config)#
```

Step 5 Check for authentication failure.

If the ISAKMP policy matches on both sides, Phase I still might fail due to authentication failure. Authentication failure might occur if you have a pre-shared key mismatch on both sides of the tunnel. Example 7-31 shows the debug output with the failure message that displays to indicate that the pre-shared key mismatches. The same types of message also can be seen on the responder.

Example 7-31 *Sample Output of the* **debug** *Commands on Initiator with Pre-shared Key Mismatch*

```
PIX-A# debug crypto isakmp 5
PIX-A# debug crypto ipsec 5
! Only relevant message is presented
Jun 05 22:27:06 [IKEv1]: IP = 172.16.172.163, Connection landed on tunnel_group
  172.16.172.163
! The following message is an indication of pre-shared key mismatch
Jun 05 22:27:06 [IKEv1]: Group = 172.16.172.163, IP = 172.16.172.163, Received an
  un-encrypted PAYLOAD_MALFORMED notify message, dropping
```

Example 7-31 *Sample Output of the* **debug** *Commands on Initiator with Pre-shared Key Mismatch (Continued)*

```
! The following message affirms it again that it's a pre-shared key mismatch
! issue
Jun 05 22:27:06 [IKEv1]: Group = 172.16.172.163, IP = 172.16.172.163, Error, peer
  has indicated that something is wrong with our message.  This could indicate a
  pre-shared key mismatch.
Jun 05 22:27:06 [IKEv1]: Group = 172.16.172.163, IP = 172.16.172.163, Information
  Exchange processing failed
Jun 05 22:27:14 [IKEv1]: Group = 172.16.172.163, IP = 172.16.172.163, Duplicate
  Phase 1 packet detected.  Retransmitting last packet.
Jun 05 22:27:14 [IKEv1]: Group = 172.16.172.163, IP = 172.16.172.163, Duplicate
  Phase 1 packet detected.  Retransmitting last packet.
Jun 05 22:27:14 [IKEv1]: Group = 172.16.172.163, IP = 172.16.172.163, Duplicate
  Phase 1 packet detected.  Retransmitting last packet.
! Only shows the relevant information
PIX-A#
```

Identify the tunnel involved and re-enter the pre-shared key on both sides as in Example 7-32. This example shows how to define the pre-shared key on PIX-A. The same procedure can be used to define the pre-shared key on PIX-B.

Example 7-32 *Defining the Pre-Shared Key*

```
! Following line shows which tunnel you need to make changes.
PIX-A# show running-config tunnel
tunnel-group 172.16.172.163 type ipsec-l2l
tunnel-group 172.16.172.163 ipsec-attributes
 pre-shared-key *
PIX-A# configure terminal
! Following lines define pre-shared key
PIX-A(config)# tunnel-group 172.16.172.163 ipsec-attributes
PIX-A(config-ipsec)# pre-shared-key cisco123
PIX-A(config-ipsec)# end
PIX-A#
```

Tunnel Is Not Established: Phase II Failure

Once you use the **show crypto isakmp sa command** to verify that Phase I of the IPsec tunnel is shown MM_ACTIVE, you need to verify that the SAs are created for Phase II by using the **show crypto ipsec sa** command. If the SAs are not created, work through the following steps to resolve the problem:

Step 1 Watch for IPsec transform-set mismatches between peers.

If there is a mismatch on IPsec transform set between the peers, Quick Mode negotiation will fail. Example 7-33 shows the output of **debug crypto isakmp and debug crypto ipsec** on the initiator (PIX-A), which is failing on Quick Mode due to transform-set mismatch.

Example 7-33 *IKE Quick Mode Fails with Transform Set Mismatch*

```
PIX-A# debug crypto isakmp 5
PIX-A# debug crypto ipsec 5
! Only showing the relevant information.
! The following line shows the phase I is established
Jun 06 04:20:52 [IKEv1]: Group = 172.16.172.163, IP = 172.16.172.163, PHASE 1 COMPLETED
Jun 06 04:20:52 [IKEv1]: IP = 172.16.172.163, Keep-alive type for this connection: DPD
Jun 06 04:20:52 [IKEv1 DEBUG]: Group = 172.16.172.163, IP = 172.16.172.163, Starting
  phase 1 rekey timer: 41040000 (ms)
Jun 06 04:20:52 [IKEv1 DEBUG]: Group = 172.16.172.163, IP = 172.16.172.163,
  Transmitting Proxy Id:
  Local subnet:  192.168.1.0  mask 255.255.255.0 Protocol 0  Port 0
  Remote subnet: 192.168.2.0  Mask 255.255.255.0 Protocol 0  Port 0
! Following line is an indication that responder didn't like the transform-set
Jun 06 04:20:52 [IKEv1]: Group = 172.16.172.163, IP = 172.16.172.163, Received non-
  routine Notify message: No proposal chosen (14)
Jun 06 04:20:52 [IKEv1]: Group = 172.16.172.163, IP = 172.16.172.163, Connection
  terminated for peer 172.16.172.163.  Reason: Peer Terminate  Remote Proxy N/A,
  Local Proxy N/A
PIX-A#
```

Step 2 Be sure the crypto map access-lists are symmetrical.

If the crypto map access-list is not a mirror image on both peers, Phase II (Quick Mode) negotiation will fail. Example 7-34 shows the debug output with the message that you will see when the ACL is not the mirror-imaged r.

Example 7-34 *Output of* **debug** *Commands When the Wrong Access-list Is Configured*

```
PIX-A#debug crypto isakmp 5
PIX-A#debug crypto ipsec 5
! Only showing the relevant debug output
! Following line indicates a Phase I completion
Jun 09 18:16:15 [IKEv1]: Group = 172.16.172.163, IP = 172.16.172.163, PHASE 1 COMPLETED
Jun 09 18:16:15 [IKEv1]: IP = 172.16.172.163, Keep-alive type for this connection: DPD
Jun 09 18:16:15 [IKEv1 DEBUG]: Group = 172.16.172.163, IP = 172.16.172.163, Starting
  phase 1 rekey timer: 41040000 (ms)
! Proxy identities are sent to the other side based on the ACL defined for the crypto map
Jun 09 18:16:15 [IKEv1 DEBUG]: Group = 172.16.172.163, IP = 172.16.172.163,
  Transmitting Proxy Id:
  Local subnet:  192.168.1.0  mask 255.255.255.0 Protocol 0  Port 0
  Remote subnet: 192.168.2.0  Mask 255.255.255.0 Protocol 0  Port 0
! Following 2 lines indicates that responder doesn't have the mirror image of the ACL
Jun 09 18:16:16 [IKEv1]: Group = 172.16.172.163, IP = 172.16.172.163, Received non-
  routine Notify message: Invalid ID info (18)
Jun 09 18:16:16 [IKEv1]: Group = 172.16.172.163, IP = 172.16.172.163, Connection
  terminated for peer 172.16.172.163.  Reason: Peer Terminate  Remote Proxy N/A,
  Local Proxy N/A
PIX-A#
```

The debug message is very clear and indicates where the problem is on the responder PIX (PIX-B) as shown in Example 7-35. Because of this, it is important to analyze the debug on both sides of the tunnel.

Example 7-35 debug *Output on the Responder when ACL Is Not Mirror Image*

```
PIX-B(config)# debug crypto isakmp 5
PIX-B(config)# debug crypto ipsec 5
! Only showing the relevant debug information.
! Following line shown phase I is successful
Jun 09 18:20:53 [IKEv1]: Group = 172.16.172.164, IP = 172.16.172.164, PHASE 1 COMPLETED
Jun 09 18:20:53 [IKEv1]: IP = 172.16.172.164, Keep-alive type for this connection: DPD
Jun 09 18:20:53 [IKEv1 DEBUG]: Group = 172.16.172.164, IP = 172.16.172.164, Starting
  phase 1 rekey timer: 36720000 (ms)
Jun 09 18:20:53 [IKEv1]: Group = 172.16.172.164, IP = 172.16.172.164, Received
  remote IP Proxy Subnet data in ID Payload:   Address 192.168.1.0, Mask
  255.255.255.0, Protocol 0, Port 0
Jun 09 18:20:53 [IKEv1]: Group = 172.16.172.164, IP = 172.16.172.164, Received local
  IP Proxy Subnet data in ID Payload:   Address 192.168.2.0, Mask 255.255.255.0,
  Protocol 0, Port 0
Jun 09 18:20:53 [IKEv1]: QM IsRekeyed old sa not found by addr
Jun 09 18:20:53 [IKEv1]: Group = 172.16.172.164, IP = 172.16.172.164, Static Crypto
  Map check, checking map = mymap, seq = 10...
! Following line is an indication that you do not have the ACL mirror image
Jun 09 18:20:53 [IKEv1]: Group = 172.16.172.164, IP = 172.16.172.164, Static Crypto
  Map check, map = mymap, seq = 10, ACL does not match proxy IDs src:192.168.1.0
  dst:192.168.2.0
Jun 09 18:20:53 [IKEv1]: Group = 172.16.172.164, IP = 172.16.172.164, Tunnel
  rejected: Crypto Map Policy not found for Src:192.168.1.0, Dst: 192.168.2.0!
PIX-B(config)#
```

Example 7-36 shows a properly configured mirrored image on both PIX-A and PIX-B.

Example 7-36 *Properly Configured Mirrored Access-list on PIX-A and PIX-B*

```
! Following command will tell you the ACL applied to crypto map on PIX-A
PIX-A(config)# show running-config crypto map | include address
crypto map mymap 10 match address 101
! Find out the Access-list 101 with the following command
PIX-A(config)# show running-config access-list 101
access-list 101 extended permit ip 192.168.1.0 255.255.255.0 192.168.2.0 255.255.255.0
PIX-A(config)#
! Now verify the ACL applied to crypto map on PIX-B
PIX-B(config)# show running-config crypto map | include address
crypto map mymap 10 match address 101
! Find out the details of the ACL on the PIX-B.  From the following output, it
! shows the ACL is the same on both PIX-A and PIX-B, which is not correct.
PIX-B(config)# show running-config access-list 101
access-list 101 extended permit ip 192.168.1.0 255.255.255.0 192.168.2.0 255.255.255.0
! Now remove the access-list and correct the access-list with the following two
! lines.
PIX-B(config)# no access-list 101 extended permit ip 192.168.1.0 255.255.255.0
  192.168.2.0 255.255.255.0
PIX-B(config)# access-list 101 extended permit ip 192.168.2.0 255.255.255.0
  192.168.1.0 255.255.255.0
! Verify the access-list again
PIX-B(config)# show running-config access-list 101
access-list 101 extended permit ip 192.168.2.0 255.255.255.0 192.168.1.0 255.255.255.0
PIX-B(config)#
```

Step 3 Check the address ranges of the access lists.

If you have ACLs that are mirror images of each other with the exception that one is a superset of the other side, then one side will be able to initiate and successfully negotiate the tunnel, but the other side will not. An example illustrates this point. Assume that on a PIX-A firewall, you have a crypto access-list configured with a source address of 192.168.0.0/16 (instead of 192.168.1.0/24) and a destination address of 192.168.2.0/16, and on PIX-B the access-list is configured with a source of 192.168.2.0/24 and a destination of 192.168.1.0/24. With this configuration, PIX-A would not be able to initiate successful quick mode. This is because PIX-A's access-list address range is outside the scope of the address range on PIX-B's, and hence PIX-B would reject PIX-A's IPsec SA proposal. However, PIX-B would be able to successfully initiate Quick Mode, as PIX-A's access-list addresses include addresses in PIX-B's.

Step 4 Avoid overlapping access lists.

If you have multiple peers on a PIX firewall, be sure that the match address access lists for each of the peers are mutually exclusive of the match address access list for the other peers. If you do not do that, the PIX firewall will choose the wrong crypto map, and will try to establish a tunnel with one of the other peers.

Tunnel Is Established Completely But Cannot Pass Data

If you have verified that the tunnel is up, but counters for encrypting and decrypting the packets are not increasing, study this section for assistance in troubleshooting this issue.

- **Routing Issues**—If the encrypt or decrypt counters for packets are not incrementing when you execute **show crypto ipsec sa** on either side or both sides, it indicates that there might be an issue with routing. Be sure that you have a route defined for the remote side private network for each other on both PIXen. The route should point to the gateway of the router through the interface where the crypto map is applied. To verify that the routing is taking place properly, you can execute the **show route** command. Note that a specific route for the remote private network is not needed, if you have a default gateway through the interface (for example, outside interface) where the crypto map is applied.
- **Firewall Issues**—The most common mistake made by security administrators is the assumption that to establish the tunnel and send data across the tunnel, you just need to open only UDP/500 and UDP/4500 for NAT-T on the firewall. Although this assumption is correct for building up the IPsec tunnel, to allow actual data to flow through the tunnel, you need to allow ESP (IP/50) packets across the firewall between the IPsec tunnel end points. In addition to that, you either must configure **sysopt permit ipsec** or create an ACL to allow the actual traffic on the interface of the PIX firewall where the crypto map is applied. You can verify that the sysopt for IPsec is permitted with the command **show running-config sysopt | include ipsec**.

- **Translation Issues**—PIX version 7.0 has the option to turn on or off the NAT engine with the **nat-control** command. If you upgrade the PIX firewall from version 6.x and have the NAT configured, the nat-control is turned on by default. Therefore you will be required to configure the NAT. Otherwise, if you erase the configuration, and it starts from a new configuration, then nat-control is turned off by default. If you have the nat-control turned off, then you do not need to exempt the IPsec interesting traffic with the **nat 0 ACL** command. Otherwise, you will need to exempt the interesting traffic with the **nat 0 ACL** command. Example 7-37 illustrates some of the configuration options with and without nat-control turned on.

Example 7-37 *Using* **nat-control** *in the IPsec VPN Setup*

```
PIX-A# show running-config nat-control
! Following line indicates that the nat-control is turned off. So, with this
! setup, you do not need any additional configuration to bypass the NAT for the
! IPSEC traffic
no nat-control
PIX-A# configure terminal
! Following command turns on NAT-CONTROL, so to allow traffic across you need to
! perform NAT and configure NAT-exemption for VPN traffic.
PIX-A(config)# nat-control
! The following line verifies the nat-control is turned on
PIX-A(config)# show running-config nat-control
nat-control
PIX-A(config)#
! The following line creates the access-list to bypass the NAT rule for VPN
! traffic
PIX-A(config)# access-list nonat permit ip 192.168.1.0 255.255.255.0 192.168.2.0
  255.255.255.0
! The following line applies the ACL to the nat 0 statement on the inside
! interface to activate the NAT bypass for the VPN traffic.
PIX-A(config)# nat (inside) 0 access-list nonat
PIX-A(config)#
```

Remote Access VPN Troubleshooting

This section presents details on the configuration steps and troubleshooting steps required for Remote Access VPN Clients with the PIX firewall:

- Configuration steps
- Troubleshooting steps

Configuration Steps

Work through the following steps to configure Remote Access VPN on the PIX firewall using IPsec protocol:

Step 1 Configure the basic PIX firewall.

Before you attempt to configure Remote Access VPN, you need to configure the interface and the routing on the PIX firewall. Example 7-38 shows how to configure the outside interface of the PIX firewall and define the route. The same procedure can be used to configure the rest of the interfaces on PIX Firewall.

Example 7-38 *Configuring Interfaces on the PIX Firewall*

```
! From configuration mode, go under interface configuration mode.
PIX-A(config)# interface ethernet0
! Assign the IP address and subnet mask for the interface
PIX-A(config-if)# ip address 172.16.172.164 255.255.255.0
! Name the interface with the nameif command. If you define the name as outside
! interface, the security level is set to zero.
PIX-A(config-if)# nameif outside
!Set the speed and duplex with the following two lines.
PIX-A(config-if)# speed auto
PIX-A(config-if)# duplex full
! You can set the security level with the security-level command. The following line
! is not necessary if the interface is named as outside.
PIX-A(config-if)# security-level 0
! Enable the interface with the following command.
PIX-A(config-if)# no shutdown
! Define the default gateway or more specific static route.
PIX-A(config-if)# route outside 0.0.0.0 0.0.0.0 172.16.172.1
PIX-A(config-if)#
```

Step 2 Configure ISAKMP policy and enable on the outside interface.

To configure ISAKMP policies, in global configuration mode, use the **isakmp policy** command with its various arguments. The syntax for ISAKMP policy commands is:

isakmp policy *priority* **attribute_name [attribute_value | integer]**

Example 7-39 shows how to configure the ISAKMP policy on the PIX firewall.

Example 7-39 *ISAKMP Policy Configuration on PIX Firewall*

```
! Set the authentication method as pre-shared key with the following command.
PIX-A(config)# isakmp policy 20 authentication pre-share
! Encryption key method is defined as 3DES with the following command.
PIX-A(config)# isakmp policy 20 encryption 3des
! Hashing algorithm is defined as MD5 for this example.
PIX-A(config)# isakmp policy 20 hash md5
! Set the Diffie-Hellman group 2 with the following command.
PIX-A(config)# isakmp policy 20 group 2
! The default timeout value is 28800 or 8 hours. Following command set up the
! timeout value to be 12 hours.
PIX-A(config)# isakmp policy 20 lifetime 43200
! Enable ISAKMP on the outside interface.
PIX-A(config)# isakmp enable outside
PIX-A(config)#
```

Step 3 Configure an address pool to assign an IP address to the VPN client.

PIX Firewall requires a method for assigning IP addresses to users. A common method is to use address pools. The alternatives are having a Dynamic Host Configuration Protocol (DHCP) server assign an address or having an authentication, authorization and accounting (AAA) server assign them. To configure an address pool locally on the PIX firewall, use the **ip local pool** command. The syntax is:

```
ip local pool poolname first_address-last_address
```

Example 7-40 shows how to configure a local pool on the PIX firewall.

Example 7-40 *Configuring IP Pool on the PIX Firewall*

```
PIX-A(config)# ip local pool mypool 192.168.0.1-192.168.0.100
PIX-A(config)#
```

Step 4 Configure a user database on the PIX firewall.

To perform authentication for VPN Client users, known as X-Auth, you must create the users either locally on the PIX firewall or on an external AAA server. Example 7-41 shows a username creation with the username **cisco** and the password **cisco**.

Example 7-41 *Creating Users Locally on the PIX Firewall*

```
PIX-A(config)# username cisco password cisco
PIX-A(config)#
```

Step 5 Create a transform set.

A transform set combines an encryption method and an authentication method. During the IPsec security association negotiation with ISAKMP, the peers agree to use a particular transform set to protect a particular data flow. The transform set must be the same for both peers.

You can create multiple transform sets, and then specify one or more of these transform sets in a **crypto map** entry. PIX Firewall uses the transform set information to protect the data flows for that crypto map entry access list. For more overview information, refer to the section entitled "Creating a Transform Set" in the "LAN-to-LAN Troubleshooting" section of this chapter.

To configure a transform set, in global configuration mode, use the **crypto ipsec transform-set** command. The syntax is:

```
crypto ipsec transform-set transform-set-name encryption-method
  authentication-method
```

Example 7-42 configures a transform set with the name **myset**, esp-3des encryption, and esp-md5-hmac authentication.

Example 7-42 *Configuring Transform Set on the PIX Firewall*

```
PIX-A(config)# crypto ipsec transform set myset esp-3des esp-md5-hmac
PIX-A(config)#
```

Step 6 Define the Windows Internet Naming Service (WINS) and Domain Name System (DNS) Server IP address.

You can define the WINS and DNS Server IP address using group-policy. There is a default group-policy on the PIX firewall. Example 7-43 shows how to create group-policy for the WINS and DNS Server IP address.

Example 7-43 *Defining the WINS and DNS Server IP Address*

```
! Default group policy named DfltGrpPolicy can be verified with the following
! command
PIX-A(config)# show running-config all group-policy
group-policy DfltGrpPolicy internal
group-policy DfltGrpPolicy attributes
 banner none
! Rest of the output is removed.
! Define the Internal group with the following command
PIX-A(config)# group-policy mypolicy internal
! Define the WINS and DNS Server with the following three commands
PIX-A(config)# group-policy mypolicy attributes
PIX-A(config-group-policy)# dns-server value 172.16.172.165
PIX-A(config-group-policy)# wins-server value 172.16.172.166
PIX-A(config-group-policy)# exit
! Verify the configuration of DNS and WINS Server
PIX-A(config)# show run all group-policy mypolicy
group-policy mypolicy internal
group-policy mypolicy attributes
 wins-server value 172.16.172.166
 dns-server value 172.16.172.165
PIX-A(config)#
```

Apply the group-policy under tunnel-group with the next step.

Step 7 Define a tunnel group for Remote Access VPN.

A tunnel group is used define X-Auth, Group password, IP address pool, and so on. There are two default tunnel groups in the PIX firewall: **DefaultRAGroup**, which is the default IPsec remote-access tunnel group; and **DefaultL2Lgroup**, which is the default IPsec LAN-to-LAN tunnel group. You can change them but cannot delete them. To establish a basic Remote Access VPN connection, you must configure the following three attributes for a tunnel group:

(a) Set up the connection type to be IPsec_RA (IPsec remote access) with the configuration shown in Example 7-44.

Example 7-44 *Creating Remote Access VPN Tunnel-Group on PIX Firewall*

```
PIX-A(config)# tunnel-group mygroup type IPsec_RA
PIX-A(config)#
```

(b) Define an authentication method for user authentication (X-Auth), and address-pool under the **general-attributes** subcommand as shown in Example 7-45. Also apply the group-policy under the same tunnel-group.

Example 7-45 *Assigning Address Pool to the Tunnel Group*

```
PIX-A(config)# tunnel-group mygroup general-attributes
PIX-A(config-general)# address-pool mypool
! Apply the group-policy under tunnel group for Remote Access VPN
PIX-A(config-general)# default-group-policy mypolicy
PIX-A(config-general)#
```

(c) Define the group password with the pre-shared-key under the **ipsec-attributes** subcommand as shown in Example 7-46.

Example 7-46 *Configuring the Group Password*

```
PIX-A(config)# tunnel-group mygroup ipsec-attributes
PIX-A(config-ipsec)# pre-shared-key cisco123
PIX-A(config)# write memory
PIX-A(config)#
```

Step 8 Create a dynamic crypto map.

PIX Firewall uses dynamic crypto maps to define a policy template in which not all of the parameters have to be configured. For example, these dynamic crypto maps let the PIX firewall receive connections from VPN clients without known IP addresses. Add the transform-set to the dynamic crypto map statement. You need to enable Reverse Routing Injection (RRI), which lets the PIX firewall learn routing information for connected VPN clients. These static routes can be redistributed to the downstream routers using Routing Information Protocol (RIP) or Open Shortest Path First Protocol (OSPF). Example 7-47 shows how to create a dynamic crypto map on the PIX firewall.

Example 7-47 *Creating Dynamic Crypto Map on the PIX Firewall*

```
! Tie the transform-set created earlier to the dynamic crypto map with the
! following command.
PIX-A(config)# crypto dynamic-map mydyn 1 set transform-set myset
! Enable RRI, so the PIX firewall learns the client route as a static route so
! that they can be redistributed to other dynamic routing protocol.
PIX-A(config)# crypto dynamic-map mydyn 1 set reverse-route
PIX-A(config)#
```

Step 9 Create a crypto map entry to use the dynamic crypto map.

Next, create a crypto map entry that lets the PIX firewall use the dynamic crypto map to set the parameters of IPsec security associations. Example 7-48 shows how to create a crypto map to use the dynamic crypto map created earlier.

Example 7-48 *Configuration of Creating and Applying Crypto Map on Outside Interface*

```
! Create a crypto map that uses a dynamic crypto map previously configured with
! the following command.
PIX-A(config)# crypto map mymap 1 ipsec-isakmp dynamic mydyn
! Now apply the crypto map on the outside interface
PIX-A(config)# crypto map mymap interface outside
PIX-A(config)#
```

Step 10 Allow the sctual IPsec traffic through the tunnel.

You must allow the decrypted IPsec tunnel traffic either by using the **sysopt** command, or by creating an access-list to allow the private networks, and apply the access-list on the outside interface as inbound. Example 7-49 shows how to allow the decrypted packets on the PIX outside interface with the **sysopt** command or with an access-list.

Example 7-49 *Configuration to Bypass ACL Checks to Allow the Decrypted Traffic*

```
! Use the sysopt command in global configuration mode to have the PIX firewall
! to allow IPSec connections.
PIX-A(config)# sysopt connection permit-ipsec
! The following ACL substitute the sysopt command. The source address of the ACL
! is the network or addresses defined with IP address Pool.
PIX-A(config)# access-list 120 permit 192.168.0.0 255.255.255.0 any
! Apply the access-list to the interface
PIX-A(config)# access-group 120 in interface outside
! Save your changes.
PIX-A(config)# write memory
PIX-A(config)#
```

Troubleshooting Steps

Before getting into the details of the different issues that might occur when the VPN client is connecting to the PIX firewall, this section examines a successful debug message pertaining to IPsec. Example 7-50 shows the debug output at level 7 for a successful Remote Access VPN tunnel. Most of the time, you can run these debugs at level 5 and will be able to isolate the problem. The debug at level 7 will be rarely needed; however, in the interest of showing details on the packet flow, debug level 7 is used in Example 7-50.

Example 7-50 *Successful Tunnel Build-up for Remote Access VPN*

```
PIX-A#debug crypto isakmp 7
PIX-A#debug crypto ipsec 7
PIX-A#
! Following are the payloads received from the VPN Clients
```

Example 7-50 *Successful Tunnel Build-up for Remote Access VPN (Continued)*

```
Jun 08 04:47:51 [IKEv1 DEBUG]: IP = 10.1.1.50, processing SA payload
Jun 08 04:47:51 [IKEv1 DEBUG]: IP = 10.1.1.50, processing ke payload
Jun 08 04:47:51 [IKEv1 DEBUG]: IP = 10.1.1.50, processing ISA_KE
! Removed other payloads received from the VPN Clients
Jun 08 04:47:51 [IKEv1 DEBUG]: IP = 10.1.1.50, Received Cisco Unity client VID
! Following line shows the Remote Access VPN client request found the VPN group
Jun 08 04:47:51 [IKEv1]: IP = 10.1.1.50, Connection landed on tunnel_group mygroup
! Following line indicates staring of IKE SA negotiation is getting processed.
Jun 08 04:47:51 [IKEv1 DEBUG]: Group = mygroup, IP = 10.1.1.50, processing IKE SA
! Following line indicates policy is acceptable
Jun 08 04:47:51 [IKEv1 DEBUG]: Group = mygroup, IP = 10.1.1.50, IKE SA Proposal # 1,
  Transform # 10 acceptable  Matches global IKE entry # 1
! Following lines show ISA SA is being constructed
Jun 08 04:47:51 [IKEv1 DEBUG]: Group = mygroup, IP = 10.1.1.50, constructing ISA_SA
  for isakmp
Jun 08 04:47:51 [IKEv1 DEBUG]: Group = mygroup, IP = 10.1.1.50, constructing ke
  payload
Jun 08 04:47:51 [IKEv1 DEBUG]: Group = mygroup, IP = 10.1.1.50, constructing nonce
  payload
Jun 08 04:47:51 [IKEv1 DEBUG]: Group = mygroup, IP = 10.1.1.50, Generating keys for
  Responder...
! Removed other payloads from display
Jun 08 04:47:51 [IKEv1 DEBUG]: Group = mygroup, IP = 10.1.1.50, constructing xauth
  V6 VID payload
! Removed some other payloads from display
Jun 08 04:47:51 [IKEv1 DEBUG]: Group = mygroup, IP = 10.1.1.50, Send Altiga/Cisco
  VPN3000/Cisco ASA GW VID
Jun 08 04:47:51 [IKEv1]: IP = 10.1.1.50, IKE DECODE SENDING Message (msgid=0) with
  payloads : HDR + SA (1) + KE (4) + NONCE (10) + ID (5) + HASH (8) + VENDOR (13) +
  VENDOR (13) + VENDOR (13) + VENDOR (13) + VENDOR (13) + NONE (0) total length : 36
  9
Jun 08 04:47:51 [IKEv1]: IP = 10.1.1.50, IKE DECODE RECEIVED Message (msgid=0) with
  payloads : HDR + HASH (8) + NOTIFY (11) + VENDOR (13) + VENDOR (13) + NONE (0)
  total length : 116
Jun 08 04:47:51 [IKEv1 DEBUG]: Group = mygroup, IP = 10.1.1.50, processing hash
! Removed output from displaying
Jun 08 04:47:54 [IKEv1 DEBUG]: process_attr(): Enter!
! Mode-config is processing the reply attributes to the VPN client
Jun 08 04:47:54 [IKEv1 DEBUG]: Processing MODE_CFG Reply attributes.
! Following 4 lines indicate the DNS and WINS are not configured, hence showing "cleared"
Jun 08 04:47:54 [IKEv1 DEBUG]: Group = mygroup, Username = cisco, IP = 10.1.1.50,
  IKEGetUserAttributes: primary DNS = cleared
Jun 08 04:47:54 [IKEv1 DEBUG]: Group = mygroup, Username = cisco, IP = 10.1.1.50,
  IKEGetUserAttributes: secondary DNS = cleared
Jun 08 04:47:54 [IKEv1 DEBUG]: Group = mygroup, Username = cisco, IP = 10.1.1.50,
  IKEGetUserAttributes: primary WINS = cleared
Jun 08 04:47:54 [IKEv1 DEBUG]: Group = mygroup, Username = cisco, IP = 10.1.1.50,
  IKEGetUserAttributes: secondary WINS = cleared
Jun 08 04:47:54 [IKEv1 DEBUG]: Group = mygroup, Username = cisco, IP = 10.1.1.50,
  IKEGetUserAttributes: IP Compression = disabled
Jun 08 04:47:54 [IKEv1 DEBUG]: Group = mygroup, Username = cisco, IP = 10.1.1.50,
  IKEGetUserAttributes: Split Tunneling Policy = Disabled
! Following line indicates the X-Authentication is successful.
Jun 08 04:47:54 [IKEv1]: Group = mygroup, Username = cisco, IP = 10.1.1.50, User
  (cisco) authenticated.
```

continues

Example 7-50 *Successful Tunnel Build-up for Remote Access VPN (Continued)*

```
! Removed debug output from displaying
Jun 08 04:47:54 [IKEv1 DEBUG]: Processing cfg ACK attributes
Jun 08 04:47:54 [IKEv1]: IP = 10.1.1.50, IKE DECODE RECEIVED Message (msgid=64c2feef)
  with payloads : HDR + HASH (8) + ATTR (14) + NONE (0) total length : 197
Jun 08 04:47:54 [IKEv1 DEBUG]: process_attr(): Enter!
! Following attributes are request items from the VPN Clients.  Removed some of the
! attributes request from the debug output.
Jun 08 04:47:54 [IKEv1 DEBUG]: Processing cfg Request attributes
Jun 08 04:47:54 [IKEv1 DEBUG]: MODE_CFG: Received request for IPV4 address!
Jun 08 04:47:54 [IKEv1 DEBUG]: MODE_CFG: Received request for IPV4 net mask!
Jun 08 04:47:54 [IKEv1 DEBUG]: MODE_CFG: Received request for DNS server address!
Jun 08 04:47:54 [IKEv1 DEBUG]: MODE_CFG: Received request for WINS server address!
Jun 08 04:47:54 [IKEv1 DEBUG]: Group = mygroup, Username = cisco, IP = 10.1.1.50,
  constructing blank hash
Jun 08 04:47:54 [IKEv1 DEBUG]: Group = mygroup, Username = cisco, IP = 10.1.1.50,
  constructing qm hash
Jun 08 04:47:54 [IKEv1]: IP = 10.1.1.50, IKE DECODE SENDING Message (msgid=64c2feef)
  with payloads : HDR + HASH (8) + ATTR (14) + NONE (0) total length : 159
Jun 08 04:47:54 [IKEv1 DEBUG]: Group = mygroup, Username = cisco, IP = 10.1.1.50,
  Delay Quick Mode processing, Cert/Trans Exch/RM DSID in progress
Jun 08 04:47:54 [IKEv1 DEBUG]: Group = mygroup, Username = cisco, IP = 10.1.1.50,
  Resume Quick Mode processing, Cert/Trans Exch/RM DSID completed
! Following line indicates that Phase I of IPSec Remote Access VPN is completed.
Jun 08 04:47:54 [IKEv1]: Group = mygroup, Username = cisco, IP = 10.1.1.50, PHASE 1
  COMPLETED
! Following line indicates that this connection will use DPD for keep alive method.
Jun 08 04:47:54 [IKEv1]: IP = 10.1.1.50, Keep-alive type for this connection: DPD
Jun 08 04:47:54 [IKEv1 DEBUG]: Group = mygroup, Username = cisco, IP = 10.1.1.50,
  Starting phase 1 rekey timer: 41040000 (ms)
! Removed some debug output from this location
Jun 08 04:47:54 [IKEv1 DEBUG]: Group = mygroup, Username = cisco, IP = 10.1.1.50,
  Processing ID
! Remote Proxy is the VPN client IP address for Phase II which is shown in the line below
Jun 08 04:47:54 [IKEv1]: Group = mygroup, Username = cisco, IP = 10.1.1.50, Received
  remote Proxy Host data in ID Payload:  Address 192.168.0.1, Protocol 0, Port 0
Jun 08 04:47:54 [IKEv1 DEBUG]: Group = mygroup, Username = cisco, IP = 10.1.1.50,
  Processing ID
Jun 08 04:47:54 [IKEv1]: Group = mygroup, Username = cisco, IP = 10.1.1.50, Received
  local IP Proxy Subnet data in ID Payload:  Address 0.0.0.0, Mask 0.0.0.0, Protocol
  0, Port 0
Jun 08 04:47:54 [IKEv1]: QM IsRekeyed old sa not found by addr
Jun 08 04:47:54 [IKEv1]: Group = mygroup, Username = cisco, IP = 10.1.1.50, IKE
  Remote Peer configured for SA: mydyn
Jun 08 04:47:54 [IKEv1]: Group = mygroup, Username = cisco, IP = 10.1.1.50,
  processing IPSEC SA
! Following line shows there is a match for transform set between the client and the PIX
Jun 08 04:47:54 [IKEv1 DEBUG]: Group = mygroup, Username = cisco, IP = 10.1.1.50,
  IPSec SA Proposal # 11, Transform # 1 acceptable  Matches global IPsec SA entry # 1
Jun 08 04:47:54 [IKEv1]: Group = mygroup, Username = cisco, IP = 10.1.1.50, IKE:
  requesting SPI!
Jun 08 04:47:54 [IKEv1 DEBUG]: IKE got SPI from key engine: SPI = 0x3dbb59a3
Jun 08 04:47:54 [IKEv1 DEBUG]: Group = mygroup, Username = cisco, IP = 10.1.1.50,
  oakley constucting quick mode
Jun 08 04:47:54 [IKEv1 DEBUG]: Group = mygroup, Username = cisco, IP = 10.1.1.50,
  constructing blank hash
```

Example 7-50 *Successful Tunnel Build-up for Remote Access VPN (Continued)*

```
Jun 08 04:47:54 [IKEv1 DEBUG]: Group = mygroup, Username = cisco, IP = 10.1.1.50,
  constructing ISA_SA for ipsec
Jun 08 04:47:54 [IKEv1]: Group = mygroup, Username = cisco, IP = 10.1.1.50,
  Overriding Initiator's IPsec rekeying duration from 2147483 to 28800 seconds
Jun 08 04:47:54 [IKEv1 DEBUG]: Group = mygroup, Username = cisco, IP = 10.1.1.50,
  constructing ipsec nonce payload
Jun 08 04:47:54 [IKEv1 DEBUG]: Group = mygroup, Username = cisco, IP = 10.1.1.50,
  constructing proxy ID
! The local and Remote Proxy Identities for the VPN connection are shown in the
! following lines
Jun 08 04:47:54 [IKEv1 DEBUG]: Group = mygroup, Username = cisco, IP = 10.1.1.50,
  Transmitting Proxy Id:
  Remote host: 192.168.0.1  Protocol 0  Port 0
  Local subnet:  0.0.0.0  mask 0.0.0.0 Protocol 0  Port 0
! Timer negotiation for the tunnel
Jun 08 04:47:54 [IKEv1 DEBUG]: Group = mygroup, Username = cisco, IP = 10.1.1.50,
  Sending RESPONDER LIFETIME notification to Initiator
Jun 08 04:47:54 [IKEv1 DEBUG]: Group = mygroup, Username = cisco, IP = 10.1.1.50,
  constructing qm hash
Jun 08 04:47:54 [IKEv1]: IP = 10.1.1.50, IKE DECODE SENDING Message (msgid=cef83b87)
  with payloads : HDR + HASH (8) + SA (1) + NONCE (10) + ID (5) + ID (5) + NOTIFY
  (11) + NONE (0) total length : 176
Jun 08 04:47:54 [IKEv1]: IP = 10.1.1.50, IKE DECODE RECEIVED Message
  (msgid=cef83b87) with payloads : HDR + HASH (8) + NONE (0) total length : 48
Jun 08 04:47:54 [IKEv1 DEBUG]: Group = mygroup, Username = cisco, IP = 10.1.1.50,
  processing hash
Jun 08 04:47:54 [IKEv1 DEBUG]: Group = mygroup, Username = cisco, IP = 10.1.1.50,
  loading all IPSEC SAs
Jun 08 04:47:54 [IKEv1 DEBUG]: Group = mygroup, Username = cisco, IP = 10.1.1.50,
  Generating Quick Mode Key!
Jun 08 04:47:54 [IKEv1 DEBUG]: Group = mygroup, Username = cisco, IP = 10.1.1.50,
  Generating Quick Mode Key!
! Both inbound and outbound SAs are evident with the corresponding SPI numbers
Jun 08 04:47:54 [IKEv1]: Group = mygroup, Username = cisco, IP = 10.1.1.50, Security
  negotiation complete for User (cisco)  Responder, Inbound SPI = 0x3dbb59a3,
  Outbound SPI = 0xaaad36b4
Jun 08 04:47:54 [IKEv1 DEBUG]: IKE got a KEY_ADD msg for SA: SPI = 0xaaad36b4
Jun 08 04:47:54 [IKEv1 DEBUG]: pitcher: rcv KEY_UPDATE, spi 0x3dbb59a3
Jun 08 04:47:54 [IKEv1]: Group = mygroup, Username = cisco, IP = 10.1.1.50, Starting
  P2 Rekey timer to expire in 27360 seconds
! The VPN Client route is added to the PIX as shown in the following line
Jun 08 04:47:54 [IKEv1]: Group = mygroup, Username = cisco, IP = 10.1.1.50, Adding
  static route for client address: 192.168.0.1
! Following line indicates a successful phase II negotiation
Jun 08 04:47:54 [IKEv1]: Group = mygroup, Username = cisco, IP = 10.1.1.50, PHASE 2
  COMPLETED (msgid=cef83b87)
PIX-A#
```

The Remote Access VPN Client problems can be categorized as follows:

- Tunnel is not established
- Tunnel is established completely but is unable to pass data

The next sections present a detailed discussion of these topics.

Tunnel Is Not Established

After you become familiar with the debug output on PIX Firewall (see the preceding section), and the log output from VPN Client (see Chapter 8, "Troubleshooting IPsec VPNs on VPN 3000 Series Concentrators") for a successful Remote Access VPN client connection, work through the following steps if your VPN tunnel is not coming up. You can also refer to the section in this chapter entitled "LAN-to-LAN Troubleshooting" for additional details on the following steps:

Step 1 Enable ISAKMP on the interface.

Unlike the router, ISAKMP is not enabled by default on the PIX. Use the **isakmp enable** *<interface>* command to enable it on an interface of the PIX firewall.

Step 2 Look for an attributes mismatch between VPN Client and PIX.

VPN clients propose only DH groups 2 and 5. If you configure DH groups other than types 2 and 5, the VPN client cannot build up a tunnel with the PIX Firewall, and you will receive a message similar to that shown in Example 7-51.

Example 7-51 debug *Message when DH group 7 Is Configured*

```
PIX-A(config)# debug crypto ipsec 5
PIX-A(config)# debug crypto isakmp 5
! Based on the groupname client used is used to find the corresponding tunnel.
PIX-A(config)# Jun 08 07:46:23 [IKEv1]: IP = 10.1.1.50, Connection landed on
  tunnel_group mygroup
! Following line indicates that the Phase I proposal is not acceptable. DH group
! is one of the attributes of Phase I. PIX is configured with DH 7, but the
! client supports only DH 2 or DH 5
Jun 08 07:46:23 [IKEv1 DEBUG]: Group = mygroup, IP = 10.1.1.50, All SA proposals
  found unacceptable
Jun 08 07:46:23 [IKEv1]: IP = 10.1.1.50, All IKE SA proposals found unacceptable!
Jun 08 07:46:23 [IKEv1 DEBUG]: Group = mygroup, IP = 10.1.1.50, IKE AM Responder FSM
  error history (struct &0x194c0f8)  <state>, <event>:  AM_DONE, EV_ERROR-->
  AM_BLD_MSG2, EV_PROCESS_SA-->AM_BLD_MSG2, EV_GROUP_LOOKUP-->AM_BLD_MSG2,
  EV_PROCESS_MSG
PIX-A(config)#
```

Step 3 Look for group authentication failures.

IKE authentication can fail due to mismatches in group names or passwords. If you are using certificates and if rsa-sig is used as an IKE authentication method, configure **isakmp identity hostname**; otherwise, IKE authentication will fail. Example 7-52 shows the debug message indicating group password failure.

Example 7-52 debug *Output of Wrong Group Name or Password for VPN Client Connection*

```
PIX-A(config)# debug crypto isakmp 5
PIX-A(config)# debug crypto ipsec 5
PIX-A(config)# Jun 08 08:05:29 [IKEv1]: IP = 10.25.35.227, Connection landed on
  tunnel_group mygroup
```

Example 7-52 debug *Output of Wrong Group Name or Password for VPN Client Connection (Continued)*

```
Jun 08 08:05:29 [IKEv1 DEBUG]: Group = mygroup, IP = 10.25.35.227, IKE SA Proposal
  # 1, Transform # 10 acceptable  Matches global IKE entry # 1
Jun 08 08:05:30 [IKEv1]: Group = mygroup, IP = 10.25.35.227, Received an un-encrypted
  INVALID_HASH_INFO notify message, dropping
! Following line clearly indicates the it's a pre-shared-key mismatch problem.
! On the VPN client, modify the profile and define the proper group name.
Jun 08 08:05:30 [IKEv1]: Group = mygroup, IP = 10.25.35.227, Error, peer has indicated
  that something is wrong with our message.  This could indicate a pre-shared key
  mismatch.
Jun 08 08:05:30 [IKEv1]: Group = mygroup, IP = 10.25.35.227, Information Exchange
  processing failed
PIX-A(config)#
```

Step 4 Look for user authentication (Extended Authentication or X-Auth) failures.

In addition to group authentication, user authentication is required for a successful user authentication Remote Access VPN connection. X-Auth occurs between Phase I And Phase II of the IPsec tunnel establishment process. Note that a LAN-to-LAN tunnel does not require the X-Authentication. X-Auth can be performed either locally on the PIX Firewall or by an AAA server. So, if the authentication fails with the AAA Server, you may want to try authenticating the tunnel with the local user database. Example 7-53 shows the debug message that appears on the PIX firewall when the user authentication fails.

Example 7-53 debug *Output of Remote Access VPN with Either Bad Username or Password*

```
PIX-A(config)# debug crypto isakmp 5
PIX-A(config)# debug crypto ipsec 5
PIX-A(config)# Jun 08 08:14:01 [IKEv1]: IP = 10.25.35.227, Connection landed on
  tunnel_group mygroup
Jun 08 08:14:01 [IKEv1 DEBUG]: Group = mygroup, IP = 10.25.35.227, IKE SA Proposal
  # 1, Transform # 10 acceptable  Matches global IKE entry # 1
! Following line clearly indicates either a bad username or password.
Jun 08 08:14:15 [IKEv1]: Group = mygroup, Username = cisco, IP = 10.25.35.227, Remote
  peer has failed user authentication -  check configured username and password
PIX-A(config)#
```

Step 5 Enable mode config pushing.

Turning on authorization is a must for pushing (mode config pushing) the WINS or DNS information to the client. So, if PIX is unable to push the attributes, be sure that authorization is turned on.

Tunnel Is Established Completely But Unable to Pass Data

If the Remote Access VPN tunnel is established, but you cannot send any traffic across the tunnel, work through the following steps to correct the problem:

Step 1 Check for valid IP addresses.

If your IPsec tunnel is up, but unable to send any traffic across the tunnel, check to see if you are assigned a valid IP address. If you are not getting an IP address from the PIX, check to see how the PIX is configured to allocate an IP address. If the IP pool is defined locally on the PIX firewall, check to see if you are running short of IP addresses.

Step 2 Be sure IPsec traffic is allowed.

After IPsec tunnel traffic is decrypted, it has to go through the ACL check on the interface where the crypto map is (for example, outside interface) applied. To allow this traffic, you must either configure **sysopt connection permit-ipsec** to bypass the access-list, or you need to create an access-list on the interface as inbound to allow the IPsec traffic.

Step 3 Bypass the NAT if necessary.

For the Remote Access VPN client host to access the private network behind the PIX seamlessly, the NAT needs to be bypassed on the PIX firewall. If **nat-control** is turned on, you must bypass the NAT for the VPN traffic with the **NAT 0 access list** command. If **nat-control** is not turned on but the **nat** is configured on the inside interface that includes network address for the VPN traffic, you need to bypass the NAT in the same way as when the **nat-control** is turned on.

Step 4 Enable NAT-T or IPsec over TCP.

If your VPN client is behind a NAT/PAT device, be sure to turn on NAT-T or IPsec over TCP on both the PIX firewall and the VPN Client.

Step 5 Be sure the required ports are open.

If there is a firewall between the VPN client and the PIX firewall, be sure UDP/500, UDP/4500, TCP/10000, and ESP (IP/50) are open. If all other ports are open, but ESP is blocked, then even though the tunnel will be established, it will not be able to pass any traffic across the tunnel.

Case Studies

In the previous section, you have seen how to configure and troubleshoot both LAN-to-LAN and Remote Access VPN on the PIX firewall. In this section, you will examine a new feature in PIX version 7.0 called Hairpinning, which allows the PIX firewall to act as a hub for Remote Access VPN client and as a LAN-to-LAN peer. With Hairpinning, PIX allows the traffic to route back on the same interface it receives from. The case study is implemented based on Figure 7-1 and on the configurations that are performed in the previous sections from both LAN-to-LAN and Remote Access VPN client.

The goal of this case study is to ensure that the Remote Access VPN client laptop (see Figure 7-1) can make a VPN connection to PIX-A, and access the private network (192.168.1.0/24). Additionally, be sure this Remote Access VPN client can access the resources on PIX-B private network (192.168.2.0/24) also. This can be accomplished by creating a LAN-to-LAN between PIX-A and PIX-B for the VPN client.

Before you attempt to configure Hairpinning, you must ensure that both VPN client and LAN-to-LAN connections work independently. The configuration for Hairpinning involves reconfiguring hub PIX (PIX-A) and LAN-to-LAN peer (PIX-B). You do not need to make any configuration changes on the VPN client.

Work through the following steps to configure the Hub PIX (PIX-A):

Step 1 Review the configuration for both LAN-to-LAN and Remote Access VPN connection configurations on PIX-A. Example 7-54 shows the configuration you have built up so far on the PIX-A for both LAN-to-LAN and Remote Access VPN connection.

Example 7-54 *Current Configuration on the PIX-A for both LAN-to-LAN and Remote Access VPN Connections*

```
PIX-A# show running-config
! Showing only the LAN-to-LAN and Remote Access VPN connections on PIX-A
interface Ethernet0
 nameif outside
 security-level 0
 ip address 172.16.172.164 255.255.255.0
!
interface Ethernet1
 nameif inside
 security-level 100
 ip address 192.168.1.1 255.255.255.0
! The following access-list is used for LAN-to-LAN tunnel
access-list 101 extended permit ip 192.168.1.0 255.255.255.0 192.168.2.0
  255.255.255.0
! The following pool assigns the IP address to the VPN Client for the Remote
! Access VPN connection
ip local pool mypool 192.168.0.1-192.168.0.100
route outside 0.0.0.0 0.0.0.0 172.16.172.1 1
! The following lines are used to define the WINS and DNS Server IP
group-policy mypolicy internal
group-policy mypolicy attributes
 wins-server value 172.16.172.166
 dns-server value 172.16.172.165
! The following username is defined for the Remote Access VPN
username cisco password 3USUcOPFUiMCO4Jk encrypted
! The following transform set is used for both LAN-to-LAN and Remote Access VPN
! connections.
crypto ipsec transform-set myset esp-3des esp-md5-hmac
! This dynamic crypto map is for Remote Access VPN
crypto dynamic-map mydyn 1 set transform-set myset
crypto dynamic-map mydyn 1 set reverse-route
! The following lines are for LAN-to-LAN crypto map
crypto map mymap 10 match address 101
crypto map mymap 10 set peer 172.16.172.163
```

continues

Example 7-54 *Current Configuration on the PIX-A for both LAN-to-LAN and Remote Access VPN Connections (Continued)*

```
crypto map mymap 10 set transform-set myset
! The following crypto map is for Remote Access VPN
crypto map mymap 20 ipsec-isakmp dynamic mydyn
! Crypto map is applied with the following line on the outside interface.
crypto map mymap interface outside
! ISAKMP is applied on the outside interface
isakmp enable outside
! Following lines are for ISAKMP policy 10 (user defined)
isakmp policy 10 authentication pre-share
isakmp policy 10 encryption 3des
isakmp policy 10 hash md5
isakmp policy 10 group 2
isakmp policy 10 lifetime 43200
! ISAKMP policy 65535 is the default policy on PIX
isakmp policy 65535 authentication pre-share
isakmp policy 65535 encryption 3des
isakmp policy 65535 hash sha
isakmp policy 65535 group 2
isakmp policy 65535 lifetime 86400
! Tunnel-group name with the Peer IP address is for LAN-to-LAN tunnel
tunnel-group 172.16.172.163 type ipsec-l2l
tunnel-group 172.16.172.163 ipsec-attributes
 pre-shared-key *
! Tunnel-group name mygroup is the tunnel-group for Remote Access VPN
tunnel-group mygroup type ipsec-ra
tunnel-group mygroup general-attributes
 address-pool mypool
 default-group-policy mypolicy
tunnel-group mygroup ipsec-attributes
 pre-shared-key *
!
PIX-A#
```

Step 2 Modify access-list 101 to allow the IP local pool address for the LAN-to-LAN tunnel. This is shown in Example 7-55.

Example 7-55 *Access-list Modification on the Hub PIX (PIX-A)*

```
PIX-A# show running-config access-list 101
access-list 101 extended permit ip 192.168.1.0 255.255.255.0 192.168.2.0
  255.255.255.0
PIX-A# configure terminal
! The following line adds the IP local Pool address for the LAN-to-LAN tunnel,
! so that Remote Access VPN client can pass traffic through this LAN-to-LAN
! tunnel to the private network of the PIX-B firewall.
PIX-A(config)# access-list 101 extended permit ip 192.168.0.0 255.255.255.0
  192.168.2.0 255.255.255.0
PIX-A(config)# show running-config access-list 101
access-list 101 extended permit ip 192.168.1.0 255.255.255.0 192.168.2.0
  255.255.255.0
access-list 101 extended permit ip 192.168.0.0 255.255.255.0 192.168.2.0
  255.255.255.0
PIX-A(config)#
```

Step 3 Enable Hairpinning on the outside interface with the following command:

```
PIX-A(config)# same-security-traffic permit intra-interface
```

Work through the following steps to configure the LAN-to-LAN peer (PIX-B):

Step 1 Be sure that the PIX-B can establish a tunnel with the HUB PIX (PIX-A), and that their respective private networks can pass traffic through the tunnel.

Step 2 Add an access-list entry to access-list 101 to add the VPN client network as interesting traffic for VPN tunnel on PIX-B. The VPN client network is the IP pool defined on the PIX-A firewall for the VPN tunnel. For this setup, the IP pool defined on the PIX-A includes address 192.168.0.1-192.168.0.100. Example 7-56 shows the access-list configuration changes needed on PIX-B.

Example 7-56 *Access-list Configuration Changes Needed on PIX-B*

```
! Check the existing Access-list for the LAN-to-LAN tunnel
PIX-B(config)# show running-config access-list
access-list 101 extended permit ip 192.168.2.0 255.255.255.0 192.168.1.0
  255.255.255.0
! The following line adds network 192.168.0.0/24, which is for the VPN client
! network
PIX-B(config)# access-list 101 extended permit ip 192.168.2.0 255.255.255.0
  192.168.0.0 255.255.255.0
! Verify the access-list configuration on PIX-B
PIX-B(config)# show running-config access-list
access-list 101 extended permit ip 192.168.1.0 255.255.255.0 192.168.2.0
  255.255.255.0
access-list 101 extended permit ip 192.168.1.0 255.255.255.0 192.168.0.0
  255.255.255.0
PIX-B(config)#
```

No additional configuration is required on the VPN Client software.

Common Problems and Resolutions

There are several common issues that you might encounter with the tunnel build-up process or with sending data across the tunnel. These have been discussed in the preceding relevant troubleshooting sections. This section reiterates all the following common problems in more detail and provides solutions.

- NAT with IPsec issues
- Firewall and IPsec
- Maximum Transmission Unit (MTU) issues
- Split tunneling issues

NAT with IPsec Issues

NAT can interact or interfere with IPsec in two ways, which are discussed in detail in this section.

NAT in the tunnel End Point

If you have NAT configured on the tunnel end points (for example, on PIX-A or PIX-B or both), for IPsec to work properly, you must configure a NAT exemption. You would do so under the following circumstances:

- If the **nat-control** command is enabled—If the **nat-control** command is on, you must configure NAT; otherwise, PIX will not pass traffic. Under this configuration setup, you need to configure NAT because the traffic requires translation (usually Internet-bound traffic), and create a NAT exemption for the VPN traffic.
- If the **nat-control** command is disabled, but the PIX is configured with NAT—If the **nat-control** command is turned off, but you have NAT configured, which translates the source network of the VPN traffic, you need to create the NAT exemption to bypass the NAT for the VPN traffic.
- If the **nat-control** is disabled, and NAT is not configured—With this configuration setup, you do not need any configuration to bypass the NAT for the VPN traffic.

You can configure NAT exemption for both LAN-to-LAN and Remote Access VPN traffic. See the "Troubleshooting LAN-to-LAN" and "Troubleshooting Remote Access VPN" for configuration details.

In some special cases, you also may need to perform the translation for the VPN traffic. Examine an example that illustrates this point. Assume that the PIX-A in Figure 7-1 has a private network 192.168.1.0/24 network, and PIX-B has the same private network. If these private networks need to communicate with each other through VPN tunnel, you must translate either side to avoid the duplicate network problem. Assume that 192.168.1.0/24 on PIX-B is translated to 192.168.2.0/24 by static command. For a successful tunnel build-up, you must include the translated IP address in the interesting traffic ACL for crypto map.

NAT Device In the Middle of Tunnel End Points

If you have a NAT device between the IPsec peers (for both LAN-to-LAN) and remote access, regular IPsec may not work. For this circumstance, a few work-arounds are discussed in this section.

IPsec over NAT Transparency (NAT-T)

If you have a NAT device between a VPN client and a PIX firewall for Remote Access VPN, or between two PIXen in the case of a LAN-to-LAN VPN, you can configure NAT Transparency (NAT-T). NAT-T encapsulates IPsec traffic in UDP using port 4500, thereby providing NAT devices with port information. NAT-T auto-detects any NAT devices, and only encapsulates IPsec traffic when necessary. NAT-T is disabled by default on the PIX firewall. When you enable NAT-T, PIX Firewall automatically opens port 4500 on all IPsec-enabled interfaces. You can enable IPsec over NAT-T globally on the PIX firewall by using the command **isakmp nat-traversal** *natkeepalive*. If you want to set the **keepalive** value to one hour, you can use the following command:

```
PIX-A(config)# isakmp nat-traversal 3600
```

The default **keepalive** is 20 seconds. This keepalive is used to prevent the NAT device translation from timing out.

To configure NAT transparency, open the VPN Client by going to **Start > Programs > Cisco Systems VPN Client > VPN Client**. Select the profile, and click on **Modify**. Click on **Transport** and check the **Enable Transparent Tunneling** check box. Finally, choose **IPsec over UDP(NAT/PAT)** radio button.

IPsec over TCP

IPsec over TCP encapsulates both the ISAKMP and IPsec protocols within a TCP packet, and enables secure tunneling through both NAT and PAT devices and firewalls. This feature is disabled by default. It is important to note that IPsec over TCP does not work with proxy-based firewalls. This feature is available only for Remote Access VPN, not for LAN-to-LAN tunnel. The default port is TCP/10000.

To configure IPsec over TCP, you need to configure both the PIX and the VPN client software. On the PIX firewall, use the following command to turn on IPsec over TCP on the port you choose. Use the default port. You can leave the port off.

```
isakmp ipsec-over-tcp [port port 1...port0]
```

The following example shows how to set up IPsec over TCP on port 425:

```
PIX-A(config)# isakmp ipsec-over-tcp port 425
```

To configure IPsec over TCP, open VPN Client by going to **Start > Programs > Cisco Systems VPN Client > VPN Client**. Select the profile, and click on **Modify**. Click on **Transport** and check the **Enable Transparent Tunneling** check box. Finally, choose **IPsec over TCP** radio button, and define the port number you desire.

When to Use NAT-T or IPsec over TCP/UDP?

The PIX firewall can be configured simultaneously for standard IPsec, IPsec over TCP, NAT-Traversal, and IPsec over UDP. If you have all options configured, the following is the sequence of precedence:

1 IPsec over TCP

2 NAT transparency (NAT-T)

3 NAT over UDP

Following are the transparent tunneling options available for different types of VPN implementation:

- **For LAN-to-LAN tunnel**—You can configure regular IPsec, NAT-T, and IPsec over UDP for LAN-to-LAN VPN.
- **For Remote Access VPN**—You can configure all options: regular IPsec, NAT-T, and IPsec over UDP for Remote Access VPN implementation.
- **For Hardware Clients**—The VPN 3002 hardware client can connect using standard IPsec, IPsec over TCP, NAT-Traversal, or IPsec over UDP.

So, depending on the types of VPN implementation, you can configure all options available or a specific transparent tunneling option.

Firewall and IPsec

Just like the NAT, a firewall can play a role in IPsec implementation for both LAN-to-LAN and Remote Access VPN implementation.

- **Firewall in the middle**—If you have a firewall in the middle between 2 IPsec peers blocking ISAKMP (UDP/500), phase I of IPsec will fail, as both phases I and II of IPsec occur on UDP/500. If you have UDP/500 open but ESP blocked (IP/50) by the firewall, then even though the tunnel will be established with IKE and IPsec SA, data will not be able to pass across the tunnel. So, you need to open UDP/500 and ESP (IP/50). If you have configured IPsec over TCP, then you need to open TCP/10000 (by default) across the firewall. If NAT-T is configured, then the firewall needs to allow UDP/4500 packets. Otherwise, the tunnel will not be built up.
- **Firewall on the IPsec end point**—Unlike IOS router, you do not need to allow the UDP/500, UDP/4500, TCP/10000, or ESP packet on the outside interface of the PIX firewall to allow the peer to build up the tunnel with the PIX firewall. However, you need to allow the decrypted IPsec packet on the interface where the tunnel is terminated. To allow all IPsec decrypted traffic, configure **sysopt connection permit-ipsec** to bypass ACL checking. Otherwise, allow all those decrypted data packets using access-list.

Maximum Transmission Unit (MTU) Issues

When sending IPsec traffic across the tunnel for both LAN-to-LAN and Remote Access VPN, MTU can cause problems because of additional overhead on the packets imposed by IPsec. The sizes of overhead vary across several variables, but usually a rough estimate for overhead, when configured for IPsec tunnel mode, is 60 bytes with ESP encryption and authentication. If transport mode is used, you can save 20 bytes, as no additional IP header is added to the packet. The list that follows outlines two problems that large IPsec packets introduce:

- If the IPsec packet size is greater than the maximum MTU allowed on the interface where the crypto map is applied, and if "Do not Fragment (DF)" is set, then the PIX firewall will drop the packets.

- If the IPsec packet size is greater than the maximum MTU allowed on the interface where the crypto map is applied and if the DF is not set, PIX will fragment the packet, and will send it to the other side. Although this is better than dropping the packets, it poses some problems on the receiving device. The receiving device needs to defragment the packets, and if the fragmented packet comes out of order, this consumes resources unnecessarily, and can cause packet drops.

There are several ways to get around this problem:

- **Path MTU Discovery (PMTUD)**—PMTUD is a mechanism for detecting the smallest MTU along the path for the packet flows from the sender to the receiver. If the DF bit is set, and the packet size is greater than the size of the outgoing interface of the PIX firewall, the PIX will send an Internet Control Message Protocol (ICMP) (message 3, code 4) reply to the sender requesting notification of the packet size. If the TCP/IP stack of the sender supports PMTUD, and if the ICMP reply packets are not blocked by a firewall, the sender will re-adjust the MTU before sending out the packets. Otherwise, packets will be dropped. It is strongly recommended that you reduce the MTU size of the packet on the end devices. This way you can avoid doing the fragmentation on the network devices.
- **Reduce MTU size on End hosts**—As mentioned before, it is strongly recommended to reduce the MTU on the end hosts. If the PMTUD does not work, you need to set the MTU size on the end hosts manually. For LAN-to-LAN connections, set the MTU of the end host for the Network Interface Card (NIC) for TCP/IP stack. In case of Remote Access VPN, you have the option of setting the MTU with the "Set MTU" utility installed with the VPN client software. Before you try to adjust the MTU, find out what MTU size is allowed across the path. You can determine this with the **ping –l packet_size –F destination_ip_address** command in your Command prompt of end host, as shown in Example 7-57 (on Windows 2000 Professional):

Example 7-57 *Checking for MTU on Windows 2000 Professional*

```
D:\>ping -l 1450 -f www.xyz.com

Pinging www.xyz.com [10.1.1.100] with 1450 bytes of data:

Packet needs to be fragmented but DF set.
Packet needs to be fragmented but DF set.
Packet needs to be fragmented but DF set.
Packet needs to be fragmented but DF set.

Ping statistics for 10.1.1.100:
    Packets: Sent = 4, Received = 0, Lost = 4 (100% loss),
Approximate round trip times in milli-seconds:
    Minimum = 0ms, Maximum =  0ms, Average =  0ms

D:\>
```

Perform the ping test readjusting the size of packet until you get a reply on the ping. The size with which you get a ping reply is the MTU allowed along the path.

- **Dynamically adjust MTU on End Host with TCP protocol**—If you have a large number of hosts, and if the PMTUD doesn't work because ICMP packets are blocked along the path, setting the MTU on end host manually may not be a scalable solution. If so, you can adjust the MTU on end hosts with the **sysopt connection tcpmss** command on the PIX firewall. This command only works for TCP-based applications. PIX firewall has **sysopt** command for **tcpmss** turned on by default, and the **tcpmss** is set for 1380. This value is recommended, and will work under normal circumstances. If it doesn't work for you, you can re-adjust this value, but perform a test with the command shown in example 7-58. Example 7-58 shows how to check the MTU size of the interface, what value is set for **tcpmss** and how to reset this value.

Example 7-58 *Checking the MTU,* **tcpmss** *Value, and Resetting this Value on the PIX Firewall*

```
PIX-A(config)# show running-config mtu
! Following shows MTU on the interface is set to 1500 bytes. Any packet larger
! than 1500 bytes will be fragmented
mtu outside 1500
mtu inside 1500
PIX-A(config)# show running-config sysopt | include tcpmss
! The following line shows the tcpmss is set to 1380 bytes. This is the default
! recommended settings that is on by default on the PIX firewall. This is the
! value that will be suggested to end host by the PIX firewall.
sysopt connection tcpmss 1380
sysopt connection tcpmss minimum 0
! If there is another device between the PIX and the destination end host, and
! that device requires the packet size to be 1250, you can readjust the tcpmss
! with the following command.
PIX-A(config)# sysopt connection tcpmss 1250
! Verify the settings again
PIX-A(config)# show running-config sysopt | include tcpmss
sysopt connection tcpmss 1250
sysopt connection tcpmss minimum 0
PIX-A(config)#
```

For more details on MTU, refer to the following links:

http://www.cisco.com/en/US/tech/tk827/tk369/technologies_white_paper09186a00800d6979.shtml

http://www.cisco.com/en/US/partner/tech/tk870/tk877/tk880/technologies_tech_note09186a008011a218.shtml

http://www.cisco.com/en/US/partner/products/hw/routers/ps4081/products_tech_note09186a0080094268.shtml

Split Tunneling Issues

Split tunneling allows a Remote Access VPN client to conditionally direct packets over an IPsec tunnel in encrypted form or to a network interface in clear text form, depending on your need. With split tunneling enabled, traffic that is destined for the other side of the tunnel goes through the tunnel encrypted. Other traffic goes in clear text (for instance, Internet-bound traffic). Split tunneling also allows you to access the Local LAN (for example, printer, file server, and so on) while the tunnel is up.

To configure split tunneling, first set the rules for tunneling traffic by specifying the split-tunneling policy with the following command under group-policy:

```
split-tunnel-policy {tunnelall | tunnelspecified | excludespecified}
```

The default policy is to tunnel all traffic on the PIX firewall. Different options for split tunneling policy are explained as follows:

- **tunnelall**—This is the default option, and it dictates that the VPN client should send all traffic across the tunnel. Essentially, this option disables split tunneling. Remote users reach the Internet through the corporate network and do not have access to local networks. This is recommended when possible.
- **tunnelspecified**—This option allows you to define the traffic that needs to be encrypted and go through the tunnel. This is accomplished by creating an access-list and defining the networks that need to be encrypted and encapsulated by the tunnel. Data to all other addresses travels in the clear and is routed by the remote user's Internet service provider. If you need to configure this option, be sure to install a personal firewall or Host IPS software on the VPN client hosts.
- **excludespecified**—This option allows you to define a list of networks to which traffic goes in the clear. This feature is useful when you want to access devices on the local network, such as printers, while you are connected to the corporate network through a tunnel. This option is supported only on the Cisco VPN client. The list of networks for this option is defined by the access-list, and any traffic not defined by this access-list passes through the tunnel encrypted.

Work through the following steps to configure a split tunneling policy to tunnel only specified networks that are defined by access-list:

Step 1 Create an access-list to define the source and destination network that must go through the tunnel. The rest of the other traffic will be sent from the VPN client host in clear text (for example, Internet-bound traffic). Example 7-59 shows a standard access-list that includes network 192.168.1.0/24, and 192.168.2.0/24 for the VPN client traffic.

Example 7-59 *Creating a Standard Access-List that Defines the Network that Should Go Through the Remote Access VPN Connection*

```
! You must create a standard access-list for split tunneling
PIX-A(config)# access-list 1 permit 192.168.1.0 255.255.255.0
! The above access-list is for the network on PIX-A LAN side
! The following access-list is for the LAN network access on PIX-B if you have
! the Hairpinning configured as shown in the Case Study section.
PIX-A(config)# access-list 1 permit 192.168.2.0 255.255.255.0
! The following command verifies the configuration of access-list 1 that you
! have just created.
```

continues

Example 7-59 *Creating a Standard Access-List that Defines the Network that Should Go Through the Remote Access VPN Connection (Continued)*

```
PIX-A(config)# show running-config access-list 1
access-list 1 standard permit 192.168.1.0 255.255.255.0
access-list 1 standard permit 192.168.2.0 255.255.255.0
PIX-A(config)#
```

Step 2 Define the split-tunnel-policy and the network list under the group-policy that you have previously configured (the name of the policy is **mypolicy**). Example 7-60 shows how to apply the access-list and define the tunnel policy type.

Example 7-60 *Configuring Split-Tunnel-Policy and Appyling the Network List on PIX-A*

```
PIX-A(config)# group-policy mypolicy attributes
! Following command turns on split tunneling with tunnelspcified option
PIX-A(config-group-policy)# split-tunnel-policy tunnelspecified
! Following command applies the Split tunneling list 1 that you have created in
! the previous step.
PIX-A(config-group-policy)# split-tunnel-network-list value 1
PIX-A(config-group-policy)#
```

Once you build up the Remote Access VPN tunnel connection, right-click on the VPN Client icon at the bottom of the screen, and choose **Statistics** to bring up the VPN Client Statistics window. Look under **Route Details > Secured Routes**. If split tunneling is working, then you should only see 192.168.1.0/24 and 192.168.2.0/24 networks listed under **Secured Routes**. Only networks listed under **Secured Routes** will go through the tunnel.

Best Practices

High availability in IPsec is very important for both LAN-to-LAN and Remote Access IPsec VPN. There are several features available on PIX Firewall to provide resilience for site-to-site and Remote Access IPsec VPN connections. This section looks into all the features and available options on the PIX firewall to attain high availability for the VPN connection:

- Dead peer discovery (DPD)
- Reverse route injection (RRI)
- Stateful failover for VPN connections

A more detailed discussion follows in the next sections.

Dead Peer Discovery (DPD)

To achieve resiliency for IPsec connections, it is extremely important to monitor the continued presence of a remote peer and report its own presence to that peer. If the peer becomes unresponsive, the PIX firewall removes the connection. Enabling IKE keepalives prevents hung connections when the IKE peer loses connectivity. Dead Peer Discovery (DPD) helps to detect the connectivity loss very efficiently. DPD is based upon the ability to send a keepalive message only when necessary, because it tracks existing traffic and communications with the peer. A keepalive is not sent until a **worry state** has occurred, which is defined by each peer and is usually caused by lack of traffic from its peer. This is an intelligent way to reduce the number of messages and, most important, it will reduce the amount of overhead on the head-end device. DPD can be configured with **isakmp keepalive** command under **tunnel-group group_name ipsec-attributes**. DPD should be configured in conjunction with "Reverse Route Injection" and "Stateful Failover for VPN Connections," which are discussed in the following sections.

Reverse Route Injection (RRI)

Reverse Route Injection (RRI) lets the PIX firewall install the route for the connected peers/clients. For LAN-to-LAN connection, the route is installed based on the access-list defined for crypto map for interesting traffic. For Remote Access VPN, these routes are installed based on the address assigned to the client with AAA, IP Pools, or DHCP server. The route installed by RRI is a static route in the routing table of the PIX firewall, and can be redistributed to the downstream routers via RIP or OSPF protocols. This feature is extremely useful when a backup is in place, and when there are many changes on the remote peers. RRI can work in conjunction with the Stateful VPN Failover that is discussed in the next section to provide good resiliency for both LAN-to-LAN and Remote Access VPN connections.

To enable RRI, use **crypto map map-name seq-num set reverse-route** for both LAN-to-LAN and Remote Access VPN connections. RRI can also be configured for dynamic crypto maps.

Stateful Failover For VPN Connections

In version PIX 7.0, stateful failover is supported for IPsec, IPsec over NAT-T, IPsec over UDP and IPsec over TCP for Remote Access VPN connections. Stateful failover is also supported for IPsec, IPsec over NAT-T for LAN-to-LAN VPN connections. Certificates and RSA/DSA crypto keys created on the active unit will be replicated to the standby unit. For Remote Access VPN, DHCP leases are replicated. Hence, the Remote Access VPN client that uses DHCP-assigned IP address will be renewed automatically after failover. VPN stateful failover supports all common AAA servers: NT Domain, SDI, RADIUS, and so on. It is important to note that stateful failover for VPN connections is only supported in single routed mode, and not supported in multi-context or transparent firewall mode.

To enable stateful failover for VPN connection, configure LAN Base stateful failover as shown in Chapter 3, "Troubleshooting Cisco Secure PIX Firewalls," to enable stateful failover for the VPN connections. You do not need any special configuration for the VPN connections.

CHAPTER 8

Troubleshooting IPsec VPNs on VPN 3000 Series Concentrators

The VPN 3000 Concentrator series is the most popular and highly deployed VPN appliance in today's network primarily because of its Remote Access Client Virtual Private Network (VPN) connections. You can also build up LAN-to-LAN VPN tunnel with a wide variety of devices with VPN 3000 Series Concentrators. This chapter examines the troubleshooting aspect of the VPN 3000 Series Concentrator in greater detail. The Case Studies section contains the configuration and troubleshooting of SSL VPN in greater details based on the new version, 4.7. For a higher-level explanation of IPsec in general, refer to Chapter 6, "Troubleshooting IPsec VPNs on IOS Routers".

Diagnostic Commands and Tools

Troubleshooting IPsec VPN on the VPN 3000 Concentrator is very handy due to its useful debug and monitoring tools. This section discusses both of these tools in greater detail, and this discussion forms the foundation for the rest of the chapter.

Debug Tool

Event log is the debug tool in the VPN 3000 Concentrator, which is used to capture and view relevant debug messages for IPsec tunnel. Various event classes correspond to Internet Key Exchange (IKE), IPsec negotiation events, extended user authentication (x-auth) and Mode configuration (mode-config) information for VPN tunnel. If you are not yet sure what to look for, you can set all events classes to a specific severity level by going to **Configuration > System > Events > General**, which is good for a general view of the problem. Use syslog for bulk logging when you have a busy system with higher severities configured. Console logging is the most CPU-intensive, so be careful when turning on higher-level logging for all classes. Remember to turn logging back to defaults when you are finished collecting debug information.

Once you have some idea of the problem you are experiencing with the **General** events, enable more specific logging by using classes and going into **Configuration > System > Events > Classes**. Classes can be used to disable certain messages and for enabling a specific subset of event messages. Some of the most commonly used event classes are shown in Figure 8-1.

Figure 8-1 *Viewing the Debug in the Event Filter Window*

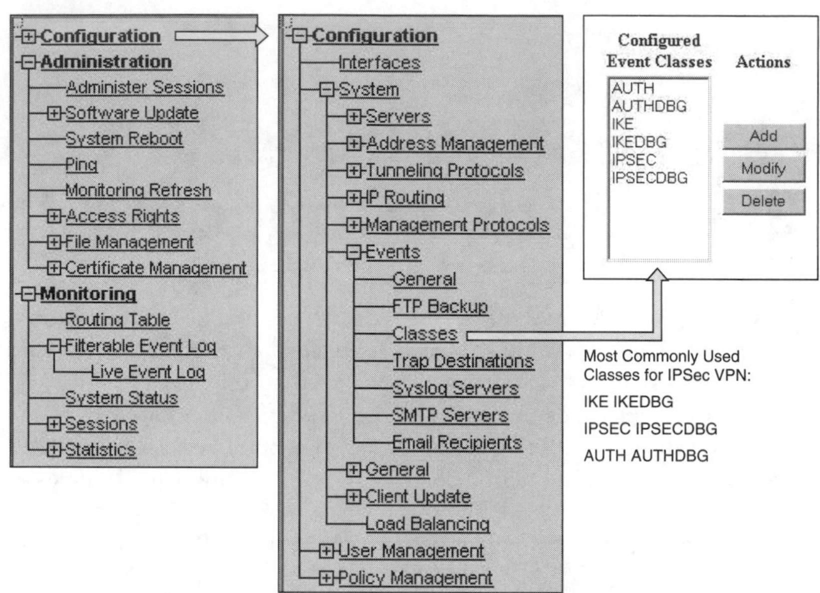

Configuring event classes and turning them on is a fairly simple process, and is the first step required to get the debug information. Once you log in to VPN concentrator using the browser, follow these steps to configure event classes:

Step 1 Browse to **Configuration>System>Events Classes** (see Figure 8-1).

Step 2 Select the **Class Name** you want to modify or click the **Add** button to add a new class.

Step 3 If you are adding a new class, in the new configuration window (see Figure 8-2), select **Event Class** from the Class Name drop-down.

Step 4 Check the **Enable** checkbox.

Step 5 Raise the severity level for **Events to Log** from 1-5 (Default) to 1-9, for Debug (consult with Table 8-1 for more details on severity level).

Step 6 Follow Steps 2 to 5 for all necessary classes.

Step 7 Be sure to click the **Save Needed** button.

Figure 8-2 shows the configuration of the event class **cert** with **Events to Log** set to 9 so that it will show the debug information of a certificate-related message.

Figure 8-2 *Configuration of An Event Class Cert*

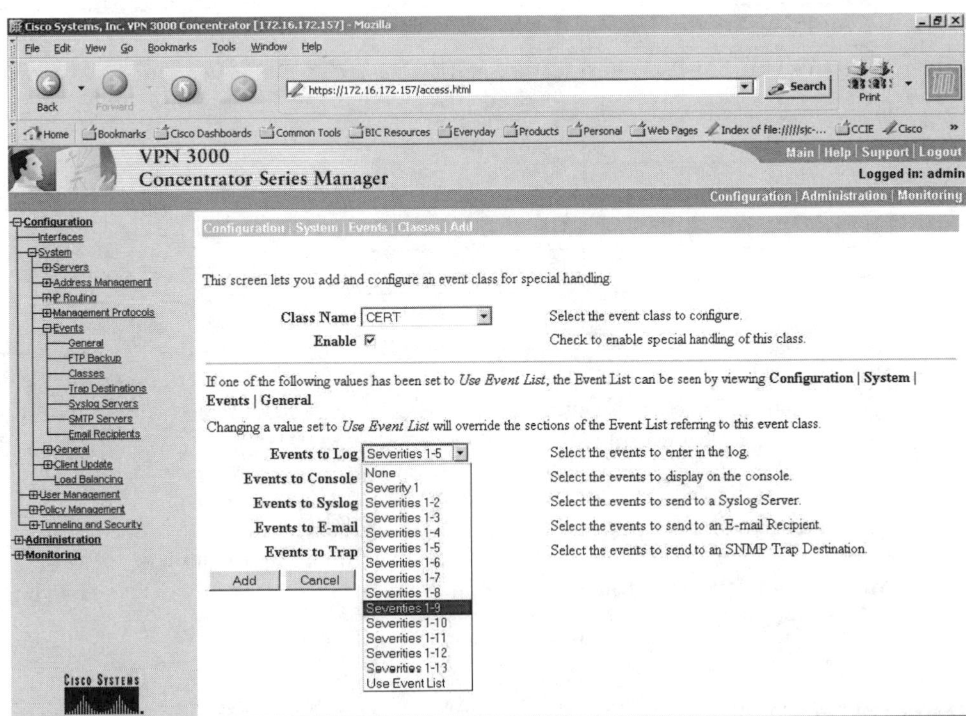

As you can see, you can control the number of messages you receive for a specific class based on the severity level, so it's important that you understand the meaning and level of detail you will receive based on the severity level. You will typically find yourself using severity level 1-9, as that is most appropriate for debugging. If you run into problems where packet level details are required by Cisco Developer, you may need to run it at severity level 1-13, because with a severity level of 10-13 you will see packet-level detail messages, which are usually analyzed by developers. Table 8-1 defines the various severity levels available for different classes.

Table 8-1 *Event Severity Level Explanation*

Event Levels	Explanation
1 = FAULT	The highest priority severity. Indicates a CRASH or non-recoverable error.
2–3 WARNING	Indicates a problem that may require user action. Level 2 indicates a pending CRASH or severe problem. Level 3 indicates a potentially serious problem.
4–6 INFORMATIONAL	Level 4 provides the lowest level of information. More information is provided by 5 and 6.

continues

Table 8-1 *Event Severity Level Explanation (Continued)*

Event Levels	Explanation
7–9 DEBUG	Level 7 provides the lowest level of debugging information. More information is provided by 8 and 9.
10	High-Level Header Decode.
11	Low-Level Header Decode.
12	Hex Dump of Header.
13	Hex Dump of Packet.

NOTE Raise the severity of classes to level 9 during troubleshooting and set it back to the default of (5) or uncheck the Enable button of classes when you are finished with troubleshooting. Level 10-13 is most useful with **Authdecode** and **RADIUS**.

Once you configure the event classes, the next and final step to view the log is to go to the Monitoring tab. See the following section, Monitoring Tool, for more details on how to view the event log.

Monitoring Tool

The Monitoring Tool produces results that are equivalent to the output of different **show** commands for an IPsec session on the router or PIX firewall. Additionally, this tool presents the debug level output for the classes configured in the previous section, and statistics pertaining to the VPN Concentrator itself. The Monitoring Tool produces statistics, which display, on various activities that are going through or to the Concentrator. These statistics are invaluable first-hand information to isolate the problem fairly quickly.

The most important information under the Monitoring section is the Event Log, which, as mentioned before, is equivalent to debug output on the router or PIX firewall. You can view the events for the event classes configured in the "Debug Tool" section in two ways: **Filterable Event Log** or **Live Event Log**. For the Live Event Log, you merely click on **Live Event Log** and messages will be displayed in real time. The Live Event Log window scrolls very quickly with huge amounts of events being generated by the Concentrator—events that pertain to the VPN tunnel build-up process. You may, therefore, find this **Live Event Log** useful only in a few circumstances, and only if you are very familiar with the packet flow of VPN tunnel build-up process. Quite often you may want to use the **Filterable Event Log** option to capture the debug for the following reasons:

- With Filterable Event Log, you can save the log into a text file so that you can analyze the log offline, search for a specific message of interest, or send it to Cisco support for in-depth analysis.

- You can apply a filter when getting the log, based on event class, client IP, and or based on Group Name, in the case of Remote Access Client. This eliminates many messages that you may not be interested in seeing and reduces the time required to analyze the log to a greater extent.
- Figure 8-3 shows how to use **Filterable Event Log** to display the debug output for IKE-related messages of a VPN tunnel build-up process.

Figure 8-3 *Viewing Debug Output for IKE in Event Log Window*

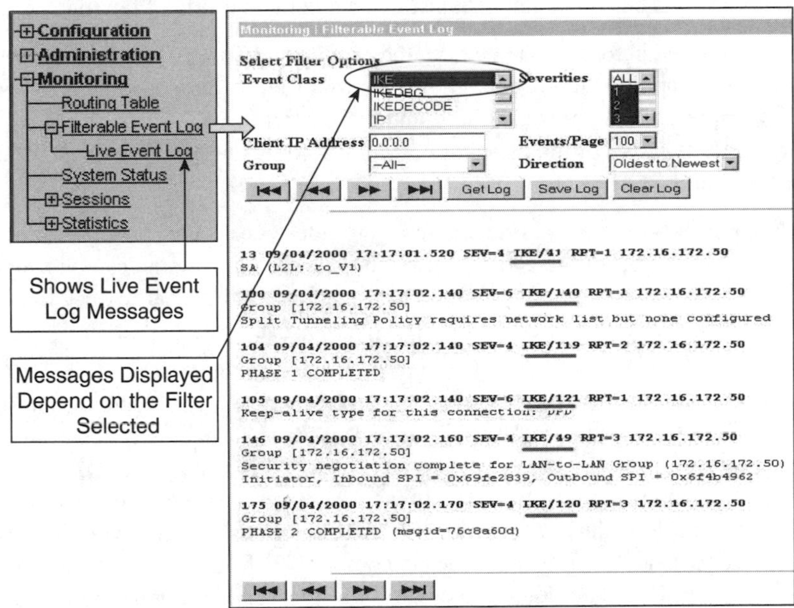

Capturing the debug for a failure of tunnel build-up process will not help unless you know how to properly read and interpret the log message that is being captured. Figure 8-4 is an attempt to show you how to read one of the lines taken from the event log shown in Figure 8-3 (the previous figure).

Figure 8-4 *Event Log: Message Header Explained*

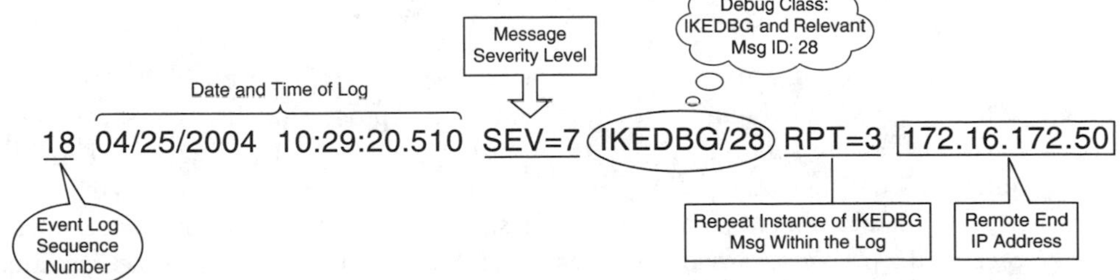

Whether you are troubleshooting LAN-to-LAN or Remote Access VPN, always analyze the log on both sides of the tunnel. In the case of LAN-to-LAN, you need to analyze the log messages of the other side (it can be another VPN Concentrator, IOS router, PIX firewall, and so on). In the case of Remote Access VPN, you need to get and analyze the VPN client logs (see the "VPN Client Log" section for details on this). Under some rare circumstances, you may be able to isolate the problem merely by looking at the log from one side of the IPsec tunnel. However, to isolate the issue efficiently and in a timely manner, analyzing the log on both sides of the tunnel end points is a must. There are numerous problems, which you might not be able to analyze just by analyzing one side of the log.

As mentioned before in this section, the Monitoring Tool produces some very valuable statistics in addition to the debug level log for different classes. Following is a list of some very important statistics available under the Monitoring tab that help in isolating the connectivity issues of the IPsec tunnel and in finding out statistics on the health of the VPN concentrator itself:

- **The Monitoring > Routing** Table provides you all the routing entries built up in the routing table of the concentrator. These are the first statistics you need to examine if you have problems building up the tunnel or sending traffic once the tunnel is up.
- Just as with **debug ip packet detail** on the router, you can turn on the event log with class **IPDBG** to see if the packet is hitting the concentrator. This is especially important when you have a routing problem in your LAN and need to see if the tunnel is not getting built up because the packet is not hitting the concentrator. Alternatively, for this you can rely on various stats under **Monitoring > Statistics > MIB-2 Stats**. For example, if interface stats **in** increases over the time of test, it ensures that packets are reaching the concentrator. The ARP table has the other very important stats for troubleshooting Layer 2 issues in your LAN before the packet goes through the IPsec tunnel. For example, if you create an IP pool of overlapping addresses with your private LAN, there is a very good chance that remote access client will not be able to send data due to ARP conflict; you can find that information by looking at the ARP table.
- **The Monitoring > System** Status gives information on the overall health of the VPN concentrator. If you ever run into a problem that requires analysis with a VPN performance issue, these are the statistics you need to look at.

Administer Sessions

You can use the **Administration > Administer Sessions** window on the VPN Concentrator to find out if the VPN tunnel is getting built up, and processing data across the tunnel by looking at counters for both **Bytes Tx** (Transmit), and **Bytes Rx** (Receive). This helps in quickly identifying if the problem is with the tunnel not coming up, or with the inability to pass any data across the tunnel. You can also find out which side of the tunnel device is causing the problem. The following example illustrates this point. Assume that in your

Concentrator, you see that **Bytes Tx** is incrementing over time, but **Bytes Rx** is staying at zero or at the same number over a period of time. You know that your Concentrator is processing and sending the data over the tunnel, but the other Concentrator may not be responding. The problem could be a drop in transit by another device that is sitting between the Concentrators. Or for some reason the other side of the VPN Concentrator could be failing to respond to your Concentrator. You can confirm what is actually happening by looking at the **Bytes Rx** and **Bytes Tx** counters. In theory, these two counters should be exactly opposite each other. The **Bytes Tx** of your side should be the **Bytes Rx** of the other side and vice versa, assuming there are no packet drops in transit. Merely by looking at these statistics, you can cut the scope of the problem analysis phase in half by ensuring that your Concentrator is not causing the problem. This means that you do not have to troubleshoot the Concentrator on your side. Figure 8-5 shows an IPsec LAN-to-LAN tunnel that has both **Bytes Tx** and **Bytes Rx** counters, which is an indication that the tunnel is processing data traffic properly.

Figure 8-5 *Administer Sessions Window Showing an IPsec LAN-to-LAN Tunnel*

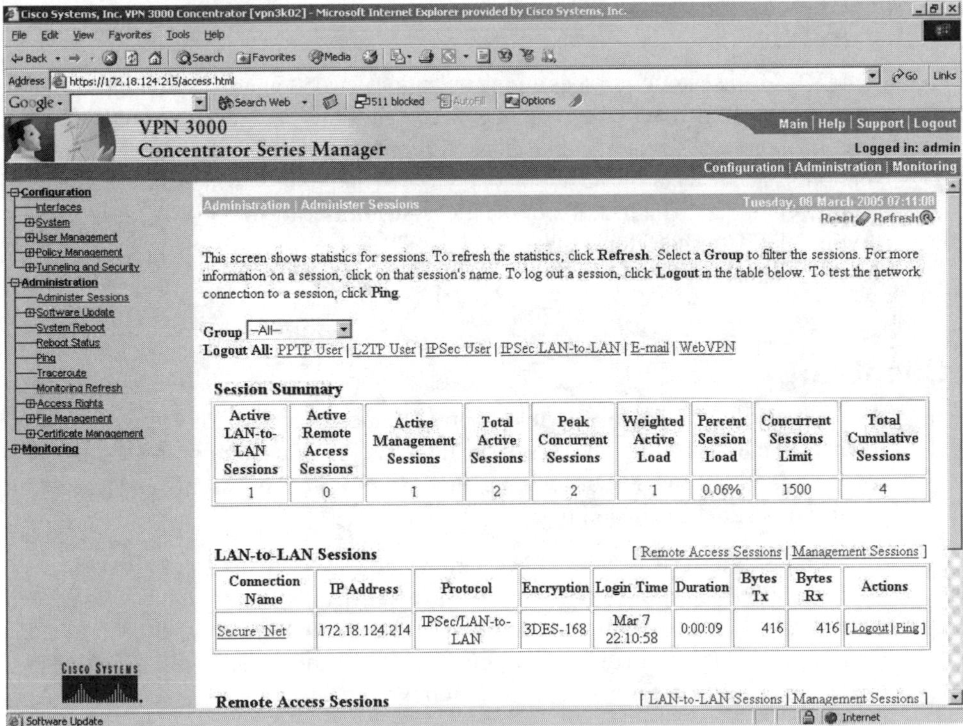

In addition to the tunnel statistics for troubleshooting, **Administer Sessions** windows also allow you to terminate any VPN session.

Configuration Files

The VPN Concentrator saves the current boot configuration file with both the name **CONFIG** and the previously running configuration as **CONFIG.BAK** in flash memory. The location of these files is **Administration > File Management**. These files can be used for troubleshooting, especially when you need to send these files to the Cisco Support Team or for offline analysis.

LED Indicators

Under normal operations, LED indicators on the VPN Concentrator are green. The usage gauge LEDs are normally blue. LEDs that are amber or off may indicate an error condition. NA means not applicable; that is, the LED does not have that state. If you have different LED colors, you might be experiencing hardware issues. Consult the Cisco Support Team for additional analysis.

Crash Dump File

If the VPN Concentrator crashes during operation, it saves internal system data in nonvolatile memory (NVRAM), and then automatically writes this data to a CRSHDUMP.TXT file in flash memory when it is rebooted. This file contains the crash date and time, software version, tasks, stack, registers, memory, buffers, and timers, which are helpful to Cisco support engineers. The location of the file is **Administration > File Management > Files**. If your VPN Concentrator crashes, send the CRSHDUMP.TXT file to the Cisco Support Team for analysis.

VPN Client Log

As mentioned before, while troubleshooting Remote Access VPN connection, you need to analyze the log from both sides of the tunnel: VPN Concentrator log and the VPN client log. Just as with the VPN Concentrator, the Cisco VPN client has monitoring capability and a fairly robust debug capability (called Log Viewer).

To open Log Viewer, open the VPN Client window by going to **Start > Programs > Cisco Systems VPN Client > VPN Client.** In the opened VPN Client, you can click on the **Log** tab or bring up a separate log window by clicking on **Log Window**. By default the logging is turned on, and you can disable it by clicking on **Disable**. Click on **Log Settings** to change the log level of different classes as shown in Figure 8-6.

It is recommended to turn all classes of the VPN client log to high and remember to disable event logging when you have finished troubleshooting.

Figure 8-6 *Turning on Debug Logging for Different Classes on VPN Client*

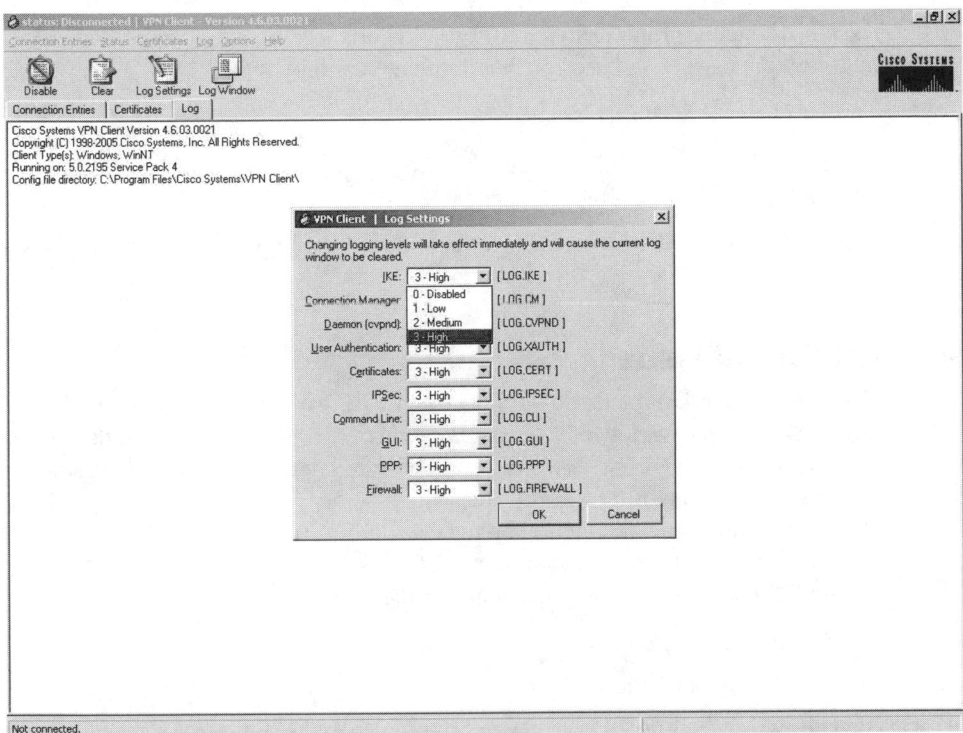

Table 8-2 shows how to read an IKE message collected from the Log Viewer.

Table 8-2 *Reading the IKE Message on the Log Viewer*

Time	Connection Name	Transmit Direction	IKE Message
01:38:02.570	Cisco VPN	- SENDING>>>>	ISAKMP OAK MM (SA)

Details on the VPN Client GUI Error Lookup Tool and location can be found at the following URL:

http://www.cisco.com/warp/public/471/vpn-clnt-err-dict.html

Log Viewer shows only the debug messages relating to the VPN tunnel. To view the statistics of the tunnel, for example, whether the packets are encrypted and decrypted or not, you need to right-click on the **VPN Client Icon > Statistics**. These statistics are important for troubleshooting any data packet transmission issue after the tunnel is built up.

Release notes of the VPN clients can be found in the following location:

http://www.cisco.com/univercd/cc/td/doc/product/vpn/client/index.htm

VPN client software can be downloaded from the following location:

http://www.cisco.com/cgi-bin/tablebuild.pl/vpnclient-3des

Analysis of Problem Areas

You can divide the problem areas of IPsec VPN on the VPN 3000 Series Concentrator into the following categories based on their implementations:

- LAN-to-LAN Tunnel Issues
- Remote access VPN Issues
- Digital Certificate Issues

Sections that follow discuss in detail the configuration and troubleshooting aspects of these topics.

LAN-to-LAN Tunnel Issues

As mentioned earlier, the Cisco VPN 3000 Series Concentrator can build LAN-to-LAN tunnels with a wide variety of Cisco and non-Cisco devices. It is beyond the scope of this text to discuss the configuration and troubleshooting details of all the devices with which the VPN Concentrator interoperates. Regardless of the types of devices that you have on the other side of the tunnel, configuration for LAN-to-LAN on the VPN Concentrator is the same. This section discusses how to configure a LAN-to-LAN between two Concentrators, which will lead to the discussion of some of the issues and how to resolve them:

- Configuration Steps
- Troubleshooting Steps

The following sections discuss the configuration and troubleshooting aspects of configuration and troubleshooting of LAN-to-LAN tunnel between two VPN 3000 series Concentrators.

Configuration Steps

LAN-to-LAN tunnel configuration involves configuring two tunnel end points (two concentrators for example) as peers of each other. This section explains the configuration required on one of the VPN Concentrators for a LAN-to-LAN tunnel. The same configuration with minor changes can be implemented on the other Concentrator. Work through the following steps to configure one of the VPN 3000 Concentrator for LAN-to-LAN tunnel:

Step 1 Go to **Configuration > Interfaces** and configure the IP addresses on both public and private interfaces. Also, be sure that a filter is applied for each interface. It is recommended to select the default filter for the respective interface (for example, apply the **Private Default)** filter on the Private interface).

Step 2 Browse to page **Configuration > System > IP Routing > Default Gateways** to set up a **Default Gateway** for the Concentrator and a **Tunnel Default Gateway** for the decrypted tunneled traffic.

Step 3 To define a more specific route for the private network on both sides of the tunnel, go under **Configuration > System > IP Routing > Static Routes** to define the routes.

Step 4 To define Network Lists for the interesting traffic that will go through the tunnel, go to **Configuration > Policy Management > Traffic Management > Network Lists**, and either **Add** or **Modify** the Network List for both the local side and the remote side. Remember that these network lists should be the mirror images of each other for both the Concentrators.

Step 5 If a certificate is used for IKE authentication, you need to install a certificate by going to **Administration > Certificate Management** (see the section in this chapter entitled "Digital Certificate Issues" for more details). If a pre-shared key is used, ignore this step.

Step 6 If you want to configure an IKE proposal (and do not want to use the default ones), you can go to **Configuration > Tunneling and Security > IPsec > IKE Proposals,** and **Add** or **Modify** the IKE proposal. Be sure that the IKE proposal is under **Active Proposals**.

Step 7 To define a custom IPsec Security Association (IPSEC SAs), go to **Configuration > Policy Management > Traffic Management > Security Associations**. Then either **Add** or **Modify** the IPsec SAs.

Step 8 Go to **Configuration > Tunneling and Security > IPsec > LAN-to-LAN** to add or modify a LAN-to-LAN connection. Use the parameters defined in Steps 4-7 to complete the LAN-to-LAN tunnel connection configuration.

For more details on configuration of VPN 3000 Concentrator refer to the following link:

http://www.cisco.com/en/US/products/hw/vpndevc/ps2284/prod_configuration_examples_list.html

Troubleshooting Steps

The problem areas of a LAN-to-LAN tunnel can be classified as follows:

- Tunnel not established
- Tunnel established but unable to send traffic
- Interpretability issues with other vendors

The sections that follow present detailed discussions of these topics.

Tunnel Not Established

If end users complain that they are unable to send any traffic across the tunnel, you should first check whether the LAN-to-LAN tunnel is established. You can verify this by going into **Administration > Administer Sessions** page and looking under **LAN-to-LAN Sessions**.

If you do not see any sessions, perform a ping on the other Concentrator's private interface IP address and see if you can ping and if the tunnel shows that it is established. If you still have issues, you need to troubleshoot the issue further with the steps outlined in this section. But, before you look into the possibilities of why the tunnel is not being built up, you need to understand the Event Log messages for a good LAN-to-LAN tunnel establishment process. Table 8-3 shows the highlights of the sequence of events involved in LAN-to-LAN tunnel establishment on both initiator and responder sides for Main Mode negotiation.

Table 8-3 *Event Log of Both Initiator and Responder for a Successful LAN-to-LAN Tunnel Phase I (Main Mode)*

Initiator	Pkt#	Responder
9 04/10/2005 22:48:24.280 SEV=8 IKEDBG/0 RPT=4 172.16.172.50 SENDING Message (msgid=0) with payloads : ! This is where the SA payload is sent ! by the Initiator HDR + SA (1) + NONE (0) ... total length : 84	1 → ← 2	1 04/10/2005 10:50:03.820 SEV=8 IKEDBG/0 RPT=1 172.16.172.119 SENDING Message (msgid=0) with payloads : ! This is where the SA payload is sent ! by the responder HDR + SA (1) + NONE (0) ... total length : 84
27 04/10/2005 22:48:24.490 SEV=8 IKEDBG/0 RPT=10 172.16.172.50 SENDING Message (msgid=0) with payloads : ! This is the 3rd packet and sent by ! the initiator with DH key and the ! Nounce HDR + KE (4) + NONCE (10) + VENDOR (13) + VENDOR (13) + VENDOR (13) + VENDOR (13) + NONE (0) ... total length : 256	3 → ← 4	10 04/10/2005 10:50:04.020 SEV=8 IKEDBG/0 RPT=7 172.16.172.119 SENDING Message (msgid=0) with payloads : ! This is the 4th packet sent by the ! Responder with DH key and the Nounce HDR + KE (4) + NONCE (10) + VENDOR (13) + VENDOR (13) + VENDOR (13) + VENDOR (13) + NONE (0) ... total length : 256
54 04/10/2005 22:48:24.700 SEV=8 IKEDBG/0 RPT=18 172.16.172.50 SENDING Message (msgid=0) with payloads : ! This is the ID payload and the 5th ! packet sent by the Initiator HDR + ID (5) + HASH (8) + IOS KEEPALIVE (14) + VENDOR (13) + NONE (0) ... total length : 92	5 → 6 ←	41 04/10/2005 10:50:04.240 SEV=8 IKEDBG/0 RPT=14 172.16.172.119 SENDING Message (msgid=0) with payloads : ! This is the ID payload and the 6th ! packet sent by the Responder HDR + ID (5) + HASH (8) + IOS KEEPALIVE (14) + VENDOR (13) + NONE (0) ... total length : 92

Table 8-4 shows the sequence of events for a LAN-to-LAN tunnel on both initiator and responder sides for Quick Mode negotiation (only highlights are shown).

Table 8-4 *Event Log of Both Initiator and Responder for a Successful LAN-to-LAN Tunnel Phase II (Quick Mode)*

Initiator	Pkt#	Responder
124 04/10/2005 22:48:24.800 SEV=8 IKEDBG/0 RPT=29 172.16.172.50 SENDING Message (msgid=70633ee2) with payloads : ! This is the IPSEC - Phase II proposal ! sent by the Initiator, and the first ! packet of Quick Mode negotiation. HDR + HASH (8) + SA (1) + NONCE (10) + ID (5) + ID (5) + NOTIFY (11) + NONE (0) ... total length : 180	1 → 2 ←	95 04/10/2005 10:50:04.450 SEV=8 IKEDBG/0 RPT=34 172.16.172.119 SENDING Message (msgid=70633ee2) with payloads : ! This is the 2nd packet by the ! Responder in response to the first ! packet by the Initiator HDR + HASH (8) + SA (1) + NONCE (10) + ID (5) + ID (5) + NONE (0) ... total length : 152

Table 8-4 *Event Log of Both Initiator and Responder for a Successful LAN-to-LAN Tunnel Phase II (Quick Mode) (Continued)*

Initiator	Pkt#	Responder
142 04/10/2005 22:48:24.820 SEV=8 IKEDBG/0 RPT=36 172.16.172.50 SENDING Message (msgid=70633ee2) with payloads : ! This is the 3rd and the final packet ! by the Initiator before the Quick ! Mode is established. HDR + HASH (8) + NONE (0) ... total length : 72	3 →	136 04/10/2005 10:50:04.470 SEV=8 IKEDBG/0 RPT=35 172.16.172.119 RECEIVED Message (msgid=70633ee2) with payloads : HDR + HASH (8) + NONE (0) ... total length : 48

Now that you have become familiar with the debug messages of a normal LAN-to-LAN tunnel build-up process on VPN 3000 series Concentrator, work through the following steps to troubleshoot the issue with the tunnel establishment process:

Step 1 Check the connectivity between the Concentrators.

On the VPN Concentrator, go to **Administration > Ping**, and ping to the public interface IP address of the other Concentrator, and see if you receive a response. If you do not receive a response, work through the following steps to correct the problem:

(a) Check to see if you have a default gateway set up for the Concentrator by going to **Configuration > System > IP Routing > Default Gateways**.

(b) Ping to the Gateway IP address, and see if you get any response. If the Gateway responds, the problem may be with a device in transit dropping the packet reaching to the other Concentrator.

(c) Perform Traceroute to the IP address of the other Concentrator by going into the **Administration > Traceroute** page on your VPN Concentrator and find out where the packets are being dropped.

(d) Your ISP may be blocking ICMP packets, and if so, you will not be able to ping. Under this circumstance, you can send a UDP probe instead of ICMP for the traceroute. This process is discussed in the steps that follow.

(e) If the ping and traceroute both succeed or both fail due to ISP blocking of the ICMP protocol, perform Traceroute using UDP probes on port 500 instead of ICMP pings by going into **Administration > Traceroute** page. This will ensure that the ISKMP is allowed across the path between VPN 3000 Concentrators. If traceroute fails, talk to your ISP to correct the problem.

Step 2 Check the configuration on both sides of the tunnel.

Once you verify the IP connectivity between the Concentrators, verify the configuration of both Concentrators to see if they match each other. Everything should match except the network lists, which should be mirror images of each other.

Step 3 Verify that the Network Lists are configured correctly.

The Network List defines the interesting traffic of the LAN-to-LAN tunnel. Therefore, if the source and destination of a packet do not match the network list, an IPsec tunnel will not be initiated. Hence, you must ensure that Network Lists are defined correctly on both Concentrators. Pay close attention when you pass NATed traffic across the tunnel. When you configure NAT on the Concentrator to translate the private network, be sure to define the NATed IP rather than the actual private IP of the network in the Network Lists. For instance, if you have 10.1.0.0 NATed to 20.1.0.0, your Network List should include 20.1.0.0 instead of 10.1.0.0 as interesting traffic. It is an absolute requirement for Network Lists to be mirror images of each other on both Concentrators, so verify this configuration.

Step 4 Analyze the IKE packets on both Concentrators.

Once you verify the configuration, you need to analyze the IKE messages on both sides to find out the cause of failure for tunnel establishment. See the section in this chapter entitled "Diagnostic Commands and Tools" for details and follow the procedure explained under the subsection entitled "Debug Tool" to enable severity level 1-9 for **IKE, IKEDBG, IPsec, IPsecDBG , AUTH,** and **AUTHDBG** event classes. **IKE** and **IKEDBG** show the phase I information, **IPsec** and **IPsecDBG** show phase II, and **AUTH/AUTHDBG** shows the authentication-related messages. You should see the IKE- and IPsec-related messages on both of the Concentrators.

Download the "VPN3000 Concentrator Event Information" file from the following location and look for the message from the index. As of writing this book, the latest file name is "**vpn3000events-4.7.Rel.zip**".

http://www.cisco.com/cgi-bin/tablebuild.pl/vpn3000-3des

Step 5 Check the Filter on the public interface to allow ISKMP (UDP/500) and ESP (IP/50).

If you don't see the IKE packets, and if you have a custom filter or a misconfigured public filter applied on the public interface, you need to check the filter to ensure that the filter is allowing *IPSEC-ESP In (forward/in)* rule. If you do not have this rule under **"Current Rules in Filter"**, you need to insert it there. Otherwise, the tunnel will not be established.

Step 6 Check Filter Configuration on the Public Interface.

If the firewall has the necessary ports open, check to see if the default public filter is applied on the public interface. If the filter is not applied, apply the filter, and if the filter is not the default public filter (but is a custom filter), be sure to allow **UDP/500** for **ISAKMP**, and **ESP** packets.

Tunnel is Established but Unable to Pass Traffic

If, over a period of time, the tunnel in the **Administration > Administer Sessions** page shows **Established** but the counters for **Bytes Tx** or **Bytes Rx** shows zero or the same number, then work through the following steps to troubleshoot the issue:

Step 1 Check the filter for the tunneled traffic.

If you have a filter for the tunneled traffic, choose **None**, and see if the traffic is flowing across the tunnel properly. To select **None** for the tunneled traffic filter, go to **Configuration > Tunneling and Security > IPsec > LAN-to-LAN**, and select your LAN-to-LAN Connection and click on **Modify**. On the next Window, select **None** for the **Filter**. If the traffic flows across the tunnel without problems, verify the Filter by going into **Configuration > Policy Management > Traffic Management > Assign Rules to Filter** for your specific filter rules. Check the rules being applied by going into **Configuration > Policy Management > Traffic Management > Rules > Modify**, and be sure the desired traffic is allowed by the rules.

Step 2 Check the routing issue.

If you have a routing issue, you might run into a problem with one side sending packets across the tunnel but the other side not responding. This can be verified by going to the **Administration > Administer Sessions** page. The **Bytes Tx** is for Transmit and **Bytes Rx** is for Receive. This problem might be caused by an overlap in the network. Take an example to illustrate this problem. Assume that you have a LAN-to-LAN tunnel between the central and remote site. Additionally, assume that your LAN segment for the remote site is 10.1.1.0/24, which overlaps with the LAN segment of the central site, which is 10.1.0.0/16. In this circumstance, if the Remote VPN Concentrator is the initiator of the tunnel, the tunnel will be built up, but the head end will be unable to route packets to the remote site with the default gateway. This is because you will have a more specific route for network 10.1.0.0/16 pointing to the 10.1.0.1 as the next hop, which is local to its network. So, to overcome this problem, in addition to your default gateway, you must have a more specific route for the 10.1.1.0/24 network pointing to the next hop, which is the default gateway for this Central side Concentrator.

Step 3 Check the Network Address Translation (NAT) issue.

When working with the IPsec tunnel, you can encounter two NAT issues—one when NAT is on the VPN Concentrator; and the other when NAT/PAT is between the Concentrators:

— **NAT On the VPN Concentrator**—Having NAT on the VPN Concentrator is required if you have the same network on the LAN sides of both Concentrators. For instance, if you have 10.1.0.0/24 network on both sides of the tunnel, you need to translate one side of the tunnel to some other network address, so that addresses are unique. It is recommended to perform the translation on the head end (central site). Also note that for outbound traffic, NAT is applied on the source address, and for inbound traffic NAT is applied on the destination address. The destination NAT (d-NAT) is not supported on the Concentrator as of the writing of this book. For more details on how to apply NAT for LAN-to-LAN tunnels, refer to the following link: http://www.cisco.com/univercd/cc/td/doc/product/vpn/vpn3000/4_7/config/polmgt.htm#wp1640172

You must be running VPN Concentrator version 3.6 to configure NAT for a LAN-to-LAN setup. More details on configuration can be found in the following location:

http://www.cisco.com/en/US/products/hw/vpndevc/ps2284/products_configuration_example09186a00801ae24c.shtml

— **NAT/PAT between the Concentrators**—If you have NAT/PAT configured between Concentrators, you must configure NAT-T (NAT-Transparency) on the VPN Concentrators so that the tunnel gets built up on UDP/4500. When the NAT-T is configured, both VPN Concentrators detect the presence of a NAT device, and tunnel negotiation takes place on UDP/4500. As the initial negotiation takes place using UDP/500, you need to open up UDP/500, UDP/4500, and ESP for successful tunnel establishment and for passing data traffic across the tunnel. For more details on this subject, go to the following links:

http://www.cisco.com/univercd/cc/td/doc/product/vpn/vpn3000/4_7/config/tunnel.htm#wp1029463

For NAT-T configuration details between a VPN client and Concentrator (the same method can be used for VPN Concentrator LAN-to-LAN tunnel), refer to the following link:

http://www.cisco.com/en/US/partner/products/hw/vpndevc/ps2284/products_tech_note09186a00800946af.shtml

Interpretability issues with other vendors

Troubleshooting interoperability issues that occur between Cisco devices and devices from other vendors can be tricky sometimes, but if the devices are configured correctly, many problems can be avoided without even running a debug. All the techniques discussed in the preceding section are applicable for troubleshooting VPN 3000 concentrators with other vendor devices. Following are two suggestions that will help in interoperating a VPN 3000 appliance with other vendors' devices:

- Start with configuring the two ends side-by-side with exact Matching policies (both phase I and Phase II). Table 8-5 lists the minimum required parameters for Phases I and II.

Table 8-5 *Required Parameters for Phase I and II*

Phase I Parameters	Phase II Parameters
IKE authentication method	IPsec mode (tunnel or transport)
Hash algorithm	Encryption algorithm
DH group	Authentication algorithm
ISAKMP SA lifetime	PFS group
Encryption algorithm	IPsec SA Lifetime
Matching pre-shared secret	Interesting traffic definition

- Turn off vendor-specific features such as Mode-config, x-Auth, IKE keepalive, Dead Peer Detection (DPD) and so on, and then build up the tunnel. Once the tunnel build-up is confirmed, start adding extra unique features that are supported by the concentrator.

Remote Access VPN Connection

As mentioned before in the "Diagnostic Commands and Tools" section, troubleshooting Remote Access VPN involves analyzing the logs on both the VPN client and the VPN Concentrator. This section looks at the configuration and troubleshooting details of Remote Access VPN implementation.

Configuration Steps

You need to configure both the VPN Concentrator and VPN Client for a successful Remote Access VPN connection. The next two sections explain this configuration in detail.

VPN Concentrator Configuration

Work through the following steps to configure a Remote Access VPN connection on the VPN Concentrator:

Step 1 Log in to the VPN Concentrator GUI, and verify that there are IP addresses assigned to the private (inside) and public (outside) interfaces. Also verify that there is a default gateway assigned so that the Concentrator can forward to the default gateway the packets for the destinations that it does not know about. In addition, be sure the private and public filters are applied to their respective interfaces.

Step 2 To assign an available range of IP addresses, go to **Configuration > System > Address Management > Pools > Add**. Specify a range of IP addresses that do not conflict with any other devices on the inside network.

Step 3 To instruct the VPN Concentrator to use the pool, go to **Configuration > System > Address Management > Assignment**, and check the **Use Address Pools** box.

Step 4 To enable split tunneling, define a network list under **Configuration > Policy Management > Traffic Management > Network Lists**. This list should contain the networks on which you want traffic to be encrypted. These are usually the internal subnets of the VPN 3000 Concentrator.

Step 5 To globally define the Domain Name System (DNS), NetBIOS Name Server (NBNS), Authentication, Authorization, and Accounting server (AAA), and so on, go to **Configuration > System > Servers**. Refer to Chapter 12, "Troubleshooting AAA on VPN 3000 Series Concentrator," for AAA implementation on VPN 3000 Concentrator.

Step 6 Define a Group name and password for the Remote Access VPN connection by going to **Configuration > User Management > Groups > Add**. Under the **Identity** tab, be sure to select **Internal** for Group Authentication.

Step 7 Under **General Tab**, be sure that **IPsec** is checked for **Tunneling Protocol**. You may also define the DNS and WINS Server per group or define Inherit from the Base Group.

Step 8 To use the globally defined DNS or WINS Server, click on the **IPsec** tab, and set the authentication to **Internal** locally for user authentication on the Concentrator.

Step 9 Next select the **Client Config** tab, and scroll down to **Split Tunneling Policy**. Ensure that the following option is selected: **Only tunnel networks in this list**. Next, go to the Split Tunneling Network List and select the previously defined Network List.

Step 10 Go to **Configuration > User Management > Users > Add**, and add a user to the previously defined group.

VPN Client Configuration

Work through the following steps to configure the VPN client profile:

Step 1 Open **Start > Programs > Cisco Systems VPN Client > VPN Client**.

Step 2 Click on **New to** create a new VPN Connection Entry.

Step 3 Define the **Connection Entry** and **Host** IP address for the VPN Concentrator.

Step 4 Under the **Authentication** tab, select **Group Authentication** and provide the **Group Name** and **Group Password**. If a certificate is used instead of **Group Authentication**, choose the **Certificate Authentication** Radio button. Refer to the section of this chapter entitled "Digital Certificate Issues" for details on **Certificate Authentication** on the VPN Client.

Step 5 Under **Transport** tab, check the **Enable Transparent Tunneling** check box. Choose **IPsec over UDP** or **IPsec over TCP** depending on your configuration on the VPN Concentrator and your NAT/PAT and Firewall setup. If local LAN access is needed so that you can still access the local LAN when you have the VPN tunnel established, check the **Allow Local LAN Access** check box.

Step 6 If you want to define Alternate VPN Concentrator's IP, click on the **Backup Servers** tab.

Troubleshooting Steps

Before looking at some possible reasons of tunnel failure, it is worth examining the debug of a successful Remote Access VPN tunnel build-up process. Remote Access VPN Client uses Aggressive Mode negotiation (three packets exchange instead of six packets for Main Mode in the case of LAN-to-LAN tunnels) to build up the tunnel with the VPN Concentrator. Example 8-1 shows the default event log on the VPN Concentrator for a successful phase I Aggressive Mode negotiation.

Example 8-1 *Default Event Log on VPN 3000 Concentrator for the Aggressive Mode Negotiation*

```
! Shows the VPN Client IP Address, mode supported, and Fragmentation Capabilities
1 06/20/2005 10:39:28.760 SEV=5 IKEDBG/64 RPT=7 172.16.172.119
IKE Peer included IKE fragmentation capability flags:
Main Mode:        False
Aggressive Mode:  True

! Shows the Group and User Authentication Status
3 06/20/2005 10:39:33.670 SEV=4 IKE/52 RPT=3 172.16.172.119
Group [mygroup] User [myuser]
User (myuser) authenticated.

! Provides the VPN Client OS and Client Version information
4 06/20/2005 10:39:33.700 SEV=5 IKE/184 RPT=3 172.16.172.119
Group [mygroup] User [myuser]
Client Type: WinNT
Client Application Version: 4.0.5 (B)

! Shows the connection Type
6 06/20/2005 10:39:34.560 SEV=4 AUTH/22 RPT=6 172.16.172.119
User [myuser] Group [mygroup] connected, Session Type: IPsec

! Shows the Aggressive Mode Status — Completed Successfully
7 06/20/2005 10:39:34.560 SEV=4 IKE/119 RPT=6 172.16.172.119
Group [mygroup] User [myuser]
PHASE 1 COMPLETED
```

Once phase 1 is established, phase 2 negotiation starts. A successful phase 2 (Quick Mode) is shown in example 8-2.

Example 8-2 *Default Event Messages For Working Client on VPN 3000 Concentrator with Quick Mode*

```
! Shows the IP address assigned by the VPN Concentrator to the VPN Client
8 06/20/2005 10:39:34.570 SEV=5 IKE/25 RPT=3 172.16.172.119
Group [mygroup] User [myuser]
Received remote Proxy Host data in ID Payload:
Address 10.1.1.40, Protocol 0, Port 0

! Local and Remote Proxies are the networks that will be encrypted by the IPSec
tunnel.
! All Zeros Indicate, all traffic will go through the tunnel, hence no Split
Tunneling
11 06/20/2005 10:39:34.570 SEV=5 IKE/34 RPT=4 172.16.172.119
Group [mygroup] User [myuser]
Received local IP Proxy Subnet data in ID Payload:
 Address 0.0.0.0, CAsk 0.0.0.0, Protocol 0, Port 0

! Shows the locally Matched IPsec SA
14 06/20/2005 10:39:34.570 SEV=5 IKE/66 RPT=4 172.16.172.119
Group [mygroup] User [myuser]
IKE Remote Peer configured for SA: ESP-3DES-MD5
```

Example 8-2 *Default Event Messages For Working Client on VPN 3000 Concentrator with Quick Mode (Continued)*

```
! Shows the negotiated Phase 2 Re-Key Interval
15 06/20/2005 10:39:34.570 SEV=5 IKE/75 RPT=3 172.16.172.119
Group [mygroup] User [myuser]
Overriding Initiator's IPsec rekeying duration from 2147483 to 28800 seconds

! Shows Inbound and Outbound SPIs
17 06/20/2005 10:39:34.580 SEV=4 IKE/49 RPT=6 172.16.172.119
Group [mygroup] User [myuser]
Security negotiation complete for User (myuser)
Responder, Inbound SPI = 0x1999168f, Outbound SPI = 0xa3bd8da1

! Shows User and Group—Quick Mode Completed Successfully
20 06/20/2005 10:39:34.580 SEV=4 IKE/120 RPT=6 172.16.172.119
Group [mygroup] User [myuser]
PHASE 2 COMPLETED (msgid=d2d8d26a)

! Finally shows that Network Access Control (NAC) is disabled
21 06/20/2005 10:39:34.580 SEV=4 NAC/27 RPT=3
NAC is disabled for peer - PUB_IP:172.16.172.119, PRV_IP:10.1.1.40
```

To analyze the Remote Access VPN establishment efficiently, and quickly, you must analyze the log on both the VPN 3000 Concentrator and the VPN Client. Example 8-3 shows the phase 1 establishment on the VPN Client using Aggressive mode.

Example 8-3 *Phase 1 Establishment for Aggressive Mode Negotiation on VPN Client*

```
! The following lines indicate that the VPN Client Environment is fine.
453     12:16:26.937  06/20/05  Sev=Info/4        CM/0x63100002
Begin connection process

! Following lines indicates that Microsoft IPsec server is stopped successfully
454     12:16:26.968  06/20/05  Sev=Info/4        CVPND/0xE3400001
Microsoft IPsec Policy Agent service stopped successfully

! Showing the Interface Used for the Connection
455     12:16:26.968  06/20/05  Sev=Info/4        CM/0x63100004
Establish secure connection using Ethernet
.
.
.
! Shows the VPN Concentrator IP address the VPN Client is trying to establish VPN
! connection
457     12:16:27.968  06/20/05  Sev=Info/6        IKE/0x6300003B
Attempting to establish a connection with 172.16.172.119.

! This is the 1st packet in Aggressive Mode sent by the VPN Client
458     12:16:27.968  06/20/05  Sev=Info/4        IKE/0x63000013
SENDING >>> ISAKMP OAK AG (SA, KE, NON, ID, VID(Xauth), VID(dpd), VID(Nat-T),
  VID(Frag), VID(Unity)) to 172.16.172.119

! Following line indicates that IPSec Driver has successfully started
459     12:16:27.968  06/20/05  Sev=Info/4        IPSEC/0x63700008
```

continues

Example 8-3 *Phase 1 Establishment for Aggressive Mode Negotiation on VPN Client (Continued)*

```
  IPsec driver successfully started

! Following is the 2nd message sent by the VPN VPN Concentrator, which is received
! by the VPN Client
463     12:16:28.125  06/20/05  Sev=Info/4        IKE/0x63000014
RECEIVING <<< ISAKMP OAK AG (SA, KE, NON, ID, HASH, VID(Unity), VID(Xauth),
  VID(dpd), VID(Frag), VID(?), VID(?)) from 172.16.172.119

! The following message shows that VPN Concentrator is Cisco-Unity compliant
464     12:16:28.125  06/20/05  Sev=Info/5        IKE/0x63000001
Peer is a Cisco-Unity compliant peer

! Shows that the Peer Supports Extended Authentication
465     12:16:28.125  06/20/05  Sev=Info/5        IKE/0x63000001
Peer supports XAUTH

! Shows that the Peer Supports Dead Peer Detection (DPD)
466     12:16:28.125  06/20/05  Sev=Info/5        IKE/0x63000001
Peer supports DPD

! IKE Packet Fragmentation is supported.
467     12:16:28.125  06/20/05  Sev=Info/5        IKE/0x63000001
Peer supports IKE fragmentation payloads

! The Peer Supports Delete with Reason Messages
468     12:16:28.125  06/20/05  Sev=Info/5        IKE/0x63000001
Peer supports DWR Code and DWR Text

! The 3rd message which is the final message in Aggressive mode is sent by the
VPN Client.
470     12:16:28.125  06/20/05  Sev=Info/4        IKE/0x63000013
SENDING >>> ISAKMP OAK AG *(HASH, NOTIFY:STATUS_INITIAL_CONTACT, VID(?),
  VID(Unity)) to 172.16.172.119

! UDP Port Number Used for IKE—Port 500 (Not NAT-T) as shown by the local and remote
! port which is 0x01F4 in Hex.
471     12:16:28.125  06/20/05  Sev=Info/4        IKE/0x63000083
IKE Port in use - Local Port =  0x01F4, Remote Port = 0x01F4

! The following line shows the IKE Aggressive Mode Complete
472     12:16:28.125  06/20/05  Sev=Info/4        CM/0x6310000E
Established Phase 1 SA. 1 Crypto Active IKE SA, 0 User Authenticated IKE SA in the
  system
```

In a Remote Access VPN connection, right after the phase 1 establishment, X-auth and mode configuration take place as shown in Example 8-4. This happens when the IP address assignment, DNS server IP address, and so on are assigned to the VPN Client.

Example 8-4 *X-Auth and Mode Configuration Messages After Phase 1 Establishment*

```
! Shows VPN client received Username/Password Prompt from VPN Concentrator
474     12:16:28.125  06/20/05  Sev=Info/4IKE/0x63000014
RECEIVING <<< ISAKMP OAK TRANS *(HASH, ATTR) from 172.16.172.119

! Username/Password prompt is presented to the user here
475     12:16:28.125  06/20/05  Sev=Info/4CM/0x63100015
Launch xAuth application

! Users entered username/password is sent to the VPN Concentrator
477     12:16:30.687  06/20/05  Sev=Info/4IKE/0x63000013
SENDING >>> ISAKMP OAK TRANS *(HASH, ATTR) to 172.16.172.119

! Received Authentication Acknowledgement from the VPN Concentrator
479     12:16:30.984  06/20/05  Sev=Info/4IKE/0x63000014
RECEIVING <<< ISAKMP OAK TRANS *(HASH, ATTR) from 172.16.172.119

! VPN Client is sending Authentication Acknowledgement back to the VPN Concentrator
480     12:16:30.984  06/20/05  Sev=Info/4IKE/0x63000013
SENDING >>> ISAKMP OAK TRANS *(HASH, ATTR) to 172.16.172.119

! Show user authentication is successful
481     12:16:30.984  06/20/05  Sev=Info/4CM/0x6310000E
Established Phase 1 SA.  1 Crypto Active IKE SA, 1 User Authenticated IKE SA in
  the system

! VPN Client is sending firewall status to the VPN Concentrator
483     12:16:31.000  06/20/05  Sev=Info/5IKE/0x6300005D
Firewall Policy: Product=Cisco Systems Integrated Client, Capability= (Centralized
  Protection Policy).

484     12:16:31.000  06/20/05  Sev=Info/4IKE/0x63000013
SENDING >>> ISAKMP OAK TRANS *(HASH, ATTR) to 172.16.172.119

! Receiving Mode Config Attributes from the VPN 3000 Concentrator
486     12:16:31.859  06/20/05  Sev=Info/4IKE/0x63000014
RECEIVING <<< ISAKMP OAK TRANS *(HASH, ATTR) from 172.16.172.119

! Tunnel Assigned IP Address from the VPN Concentrator to the VPN Client
487     12:16:31.859  06/20/05  Sev=Info/5IKE/0x63000010
MODE_CFG_REPLY: Attribute = INTERNAL_IPV4_ADDRESS: , value = 10.1.1.40

! Tunnel Assigned Subnet CAsk is shown below
488     12:16:31.859  06/20/05  Sev=Info/5IKE/0x63000010
MODE_CFG_REPLY: Attribute = INTERNAL_IPV4_NETCASK: , value = 255.255.255.0

! Following lines show if the Password Allowed to Be Stored Locally. Value 0x00000000
! means NO
489     12:16:31.859  06/20/05  Sev=Info/5IKE/0x6300000D
MODE_CFG_REPLY: Attribute = MODECFG_UNITY_SAVEPWD: , value = 0x00000000

! Number of Entries in the Split Tunnel List. In this log it shows 2.
490     12:16:31.859  06/20/05  Sev=Info/5IKE/0x6300000D
```

continues

Example 8-4 *X-Auth and Mode Configuration Messages After Phase 1 Establishment (Continued)*

```
MODE_CFG_REPLY: Attribute = MODECFG_UNITY_SPLIT_INCLUDE (# of split_nets), value =
  0x00000002

! Detail of all Networks in the Split List
491     12:16:31.859  06/20/05  Sev=Info/5IKE/0x6300000F
SPLIT_NET #1
        subnet = 10.1.1.0
        CAsk = 255.255.255.0
        protocol = 0
        src port = 0
        dest port=0

! Perfect Forward Secrecy (Disabled) as the value is set to 0x00000000
493     12:16:31.859  06/20/05  Sev=Info/5IKE/0x6300000D
MODE_CFG_REPLY: Attribute = MODECFG_UNITY_PFS: , value = 0x00000000

! Peer version information is shown here
494     12:16:31.859  06/20/05  Sev=Info/5IKE/0x6300000E
MODE_CFG_REPLY: Attribute = APPLICATION_VERSION, value = Cisco Systems, Inc./VPN
3000 Concentrator Version 4.7.Rel built by vmurphy on CAr 10 2005 12:35:39
```

After the successful X-Auth and mode-config of the VPN connection, phase 2 negotiation (Quick Mode) starts as shown in Example 8-5.

Example 8-5 *Shows a Successful Quick Mode Negotiation (Phase II) on VPN Client*

```
! Quick Mode Starts here. Sending Quick Mode Message 1
497     12:16:31.875  06/20/05  Sev=Info/4IKE/0x63000013
SENDING >>> ISAKMP OAK QM *(HASH, SA, NON, ID, ID) to 172.16.172.119

!  Received IKE Notify message from the VPN Concentrator
500     12:16:31.890  06/20/05  Sev=Info/4IKE/0x63000014
RECEIVING <<< ISAKMP OAK INFO *(HASH, NOTIFY:STATUS_RESP_LIFETIME) from
  172.16.172.119

! Received Quick Mode Message 2 from the VPN Concentrator
504     12:16:31.890  06/20/05  Sev=Info/4IKE/0x63000014
RECEIVING <<< ISAKMP OAK QM *(HASH, SA, NON, ID, ID, NOTIFY:STATUS_RESP_LIFETIME)
  from 172.16.172.119

! Sending Quick Mode Message 3 as shown below
506     12:16:31.890  06/20/05  Sev=Info/4IKE/0x63000013
SENDING >>> ISAKMP OAK QM *(HASH) to 172.16.172.119

507     12:16:31.890  06/20/05  Sev=Info/5IKE/0x63000059
! Loading SPIs here
Loading IPsec SA (MsgID=D335FB24 OUTBOUND SPI = 0x448FCE67 INBOUND SPI = 0x26DCA8D9)
! Non-VPN Routing Table
510     12:16:31.937  06/20/05  Sev=Info/5CVPND/0x63400013
    Destination          NetCAsk           Gateway         Interface       Metric
      0.0.0.0            0.0.0.0        172.16.172.119   172.16.172.119        20
     127.0.0.0          255.0.0.0        127.0.0.1        127.0.0.1             1
    172.16.172.119   255.255.255.255     127.0.0.1        127.0.0.1            20
```

Example 8-5 *Shows a Successful Quick Mode Negotiation (Phase II) on VPN Client (Continued)*

```
! Virtual Adapter Enabled with the Tunnel Assigned Address
511     12:16:32.562  06/20/05  Sev=Info/4CM/0x63100034
The Virtual Adapter was enabled:
        IP=10.1.1.40/255.255.255.0
        DNS=0.0.0.0,0.0.0.0
        WINS=0.0.0.0,0.0.0.0
        DoMain=
        Split DNS Names=

! Routing Table post VPN, Repeated for All Subnets in the Network List
512     12:16:32.562  06/20/05  Sev=Info/5CVPND/0x63400013
     Destination           NetCAsk          Gateway            Interface       Metric
       0.0.0.0             0.0.0.0        172.16.172.119     172.16.172.119      20
      10.1.1.0        255.255.255.0       10.1.1.40           10.1.1.40          10
     10.1.1.40        255.255.255.255     127.0.0.1          127.0.0.1           10
 10.255.255.255       255.255.255.255     10.1.1.40          10.1.1.40           10
     127.0.0.0            255.0.0.0       127.0.0.1          127.0.0.1            1
 172.16.172.119       255.255.255.255     127.0.0.1          127.0.0.1           20

! Virtual Adapter is Added
514     12:16:32.609  06/20/05  Sev=Info/6CM/0x63100036
The routing table was updated for the Virtual Adapter

! Locally Assigned and Tunnel Assigned Addresses
516     12:16:32.953  06/20/05  Sev=Info/4CM/0x63100038
Address watch added for 172.16.172.119.  Current hostname: rail, Current
  address(es): 10.1.1.40, 172.16.172.119.

! Tunnel Assigned Address to the Virtual Adapter
522     12:16:33.015  06/20/05  Sev=Info/4IPSEC/0x6370002E
Assigned VA private interface addr 10.1.1.40
```

After becoming comfortable with the sequence of events that takes place for a successful Remote Access VPN connection, examine the possible causes of tunnel failure as listed in the following sections:

- VPN Client cannot connect
- VPN Client can connect but Tunnel is not passing traffic
- VPN Client can connect but users cannot access Internet
- VPN Client can connect but users cannot access local LAN

Details on the above listed items follow in the following sections.

VPN Client Cannot Connect

Unlike LAN-to-LAN tunnel, with the Remote Access VPN, you can immediately determine if the tunnel is establishing or not. When the tunnel is successfully established, this message displays: "You are connected."

The Remote Access VPN tunnel establishment may fail for various reasons. Using a systematic approach is the best way to check various possibilities and correct them as you analyze the best approach to troubleshooting Remote Access VPN issues. Work through the following steps to correct the Remote Access VPN tunnel establishment failure:

Step 1 Check the connectivity between the VPN Client and the Concentrator.

From the VPN client PC, ping to the public interface IP addresses of the VPN Concentrator. If you cannot ping, work through the following steps to correct the problem:

(a) Be sure that the default gateway is defined on the VPN client host, and that the host can ping to the default gateway IP address.

(b) Go to the VPN Concentrator GUI, and verify that you have a default gateway defined for the Concentrator. If none is defined, define one. Otherwise, go to **Administration > Ping**, and ping to the default gateway of the Concentrator.

(c) If both the VPN Concentrator and VPN client can ping each other, then ensure that ISKMP packets are allowed by a firewall that is between them. This can be done by performing Traceroute using a UDP probe instead of the ICMP ping to the IP address of the other Concentrator. To perform this action, go to **Administration > Traceroute** page on your VPN Concentrator.

Step 2 Be sure that IKE packets are being exchanged between the VPN Client and the Concentrator.

Once connectivity is verified with the previous step, check the event logs on both VPN client and Concentrator. See the "Diagnostic Commands and Tools" section for details on how to use the Event Log features on both VPN Client and the Concentrator. If the IKE packets are being exchanged, you should see messages similar to the one shown in examples 8-6 on the VPN Client.

Example 8-6 *IKE Messages Shown on VPN Client*

```
121    20:04:56.778  06/20/05  Sev=Info/4IKE/0x63000013
SENDING >>> ISAKMP OAK INFO (NOTIFY:INVALID_HASH_INFO) to 172.16.172.119
135    20:12:54.580  06/20/05  Sev=Info/4IKE/0x63000014
RECEIVING <<< ISAKMP OAK AG (SA, KE, NON, ID, HASH, VID, VID, VID, VID) from
172.16.172.119
```

Example 8-7 shows the IKE packets seen on the VPN concentrator.

Example 8-7 *IKE Messages on VPN Concentrator*

```
1 04/07/2005 20:04:16.640 SEV=8 IKEDBG/0 RPT=2955 192.168.1.100
RECEIVED Message (msgid=0) with payloads : HDR + SA (1) + KE (4) + NONCE (10) + ID (5) +
VENDOR (13) + VENDOR (13) + VENDOR (13) + NONE (0) ... total length : 561
```

If you do not see the IKE packets on the VPN client, then the problem is on the VPN client. You may need to stop and restart the **cvpnd** service with **net stop cvpnd** and **net start cvpnd**, or you may need to reboot the VPN client PC. As a last resort you may end up re-installing the VPN client software. If you see the IKE packets on VPN client but do not see the IKE packets on the VPN 3000 Concentrator, go to the next step.

Step 3 Be sure the firewall between the VPN Client and Concentrator allows ISKMP (UDP/500) packets.

If you do not see the IKE packets on VPN 3000 Concentrator, check to see if you have a firewall between the VPN client and Concentrator. If you do, be sure that ISKMP (UDP/500) packets are allowed through the firewall. Otherwise, IKE packets will be dropped by the firewall. If you have a NAT device between the VPN client and Concentrator, and you have NAT-T configured, then you need to allow UDP/4500 for the NAT-T. If a firewall between blocks the UDP/500 packets, you will see the event log on VPN Client as shown in Example 8-8.

Example 8-8 *VPN Client Log When the NAT-T Fails Due to UDP/4500 Packets Block*

```
! Received Aggressive Mode Message 2
595    20:47:46.335  06/21/05  Sev=Info/4IKE/0x63000014
RECEIVING <<< ISAKMP OAK AG (SA, KE, NON, ID, HASH, VID(Unity), VID(Xauth), VID(dpd),
  VID(Nat-T), NAT-D, NAT-D, VID(Frag), VID(?), VID(?)) from 172.16.172.119
! Sending Aggressive Mode Message 3 to the VPN Concentrator. Here it shows NAT-T
! Negotiated UDP Port 4500
603    20:47:46.355  06/21/05  Sev=Info/4IKE/0x63000013
SENDING >>> ISAKMP OAK AG *(HASH, NOTIFY:STATUS_INITIAL_CONTACT, NAT-D, NAT-D,
  VID(?), VID(Unity)) to 172.16.172.119
! The Client Receives the Retransmissions
608    20:47:54.327  06/21/05  Sev=Info/5IKE/0x6300002F
Received ISAKMP packet: peer = 172.16.172.119
609    20:47:54.327  06/21/05  Sev=Info/4IKE/0x63000014
RECEIVING <<< ISAKMP OAK AG (Retransmission) from 172.16.172.119
! The Client Retransmits AM MSG 2
610    20:47:54.327  06/21/05  Sev=Info/4IKE/0x63000021
Retransmitting last packet

611    20:47:54.327  06/21/05  Sev=Info/4IKE/0x63000013
SENDING >>> ISAKMP OAK AG *(Retransmission) to 172.16.172.119
! The Client Receives the Unencrypted Delete Message
625    20:48:18.321  06/21/05  Sev=Warning/3IKE/0xA3000058
Received CAlformed message or negotiation no longer active (message id: 0xB7381790)
! The Client Sends It's Own Delete Message
636    20:49:18.007  06/21/05  Sev=Info/4IKE/0x63000013
SENDING >>> ISAKMP OAK INFO *(HASH, DWR) to 199.246.40.12
```

On the VPN Concentrator, you will not see any re-transmission. Instead, you will see the messages shown in Example 8-9.

Example 8-9 *VPN Concentrator Log When the NAT-T Fails Due to UDP/4500 Packets Block*

```
333 05/06/2005 09:55:03.860 SEV=7 IKEDBG/65 RPT=1 172.16.172.1190
Group [mygrou]
! FSM Error—Time Out Waiting for AM MSG 3 is shown below
IKE AM Responder FSM error history (struct &0x7ea8590)
<state>, <event>:
AM_DONE, EV_ERROR_CONT
AM_DONE, EV_ERROR
AM_WAIT_MSG3, EV_TIMEOUT
AM_WAIT_MSG3, NullEvent
! Sending a Delete MSG After the Time Out. You will not see Retransmissions. The
! Concentrator Resends AM MSG 2 Three Times at 8 Second Intervals
338 05/06/2005 09:55:03.860 SEV=8 IKEDBG/81 RPT=7 172.16.172.1190
SENDING Message (msgid=d0257b9c) with payloads :
HDR + HASH (8) + DELETE (12)
total length : 76
```

If IPsec over TCP is configured, the default port you need to allow is TCP/10000. If another port is used, you need to allow that specific port. Additionally, you need to allow ESP (IP/50) to enable the tunneled traffic.

Step 4 Be sure that the filter applied on the public interface allows ISKMP (UDP/500) and ESP (IP/50) traffic.

If the firewall has the necessary ports open, check to see that the filter is applied on the public interface of the concentrator. By default, the public filter allows all the necessary ports for the IKE message. However, if the filter is not public or if you have customized the filter, be sure to have the **IPSEC-ESP In (forward/in)** rule under **"Current Rules in Filter"** on your filter.

If NAT-T is configured, you must assign the **NAT-T In** and **NAT-T Out** rules to that filter, applied and active on the public interface.

Step 5 IKE Proposal Parameters mismatch between the VPN Client and VPN Concentrator.

In Aggressive Mode Message 1, the VPN client sends a list of supported proposals to the VPN Concentrator. On the concentrator, you need to have at least one of the proposals sent by the VPN client active. The concentrator will match based on order in the active proposal list. To verify the proposals on the VPN Concentrator, go to **Configuration > Tunneling and Security > IPsec > IKE Proposals**.

Step 6 Check for Group Authentication Failure.

Upon receiving the IKE proposal, the VPN concentrator first finds the group name and authenticates the group. Example 8-10 shows a successful group authentication in VPN 3000 Concentrator.

Example 8-10 *Successful Group Authentication on VPN 3000 Concentrator*

```
15 04/07/2005 20:04:16.640 SEV=9 IKEDBG/23 RPT=42 192.168.1.100
Starting group lookup for peer 192.168.1.100
39 04/12/2005 01:54:03.230 SEV=6 AUTH/41 RPT=26 192.168.1.100
! The following line shows the group authentication is successful.
Authentication successful: handle = 17, server = Internal, group = mygroup
40 04/07/2005 20:12:14.500 SEV=7 IKEDBG/0 RPT=2984 192.168.1.100
Group [mygroup]
Found Phase 1 Group (mygroup)
```

Table 8-6 shows some of the most common group-authentication problems and how to resolve them.

Table 8-6 *Common Group Authentication Issues and Resolution On VPN Concentrators*

Parameters MisMatch	Client Error Message	VPN Concentrator Error message	How to resolve
Group Name MisMatch	`GI VPN start callback failed "CM_PEER_NOT_RESPONDING" (16h).`	`No Group found Matching mygroupo for Pre-shared key peer 192.168.1.100`	Check group name. If missing configure it in VPN Concentrator, or if it exists, correct the group name in client configuration.
Group Password MisMatch	`Hash verification failed... May be configured with invalid group password.`	`Group [mygroup] Received non-routine Notify message: Invalid hash info (23)`	Correct the group password on the concentrator or specify it correctly on the VPN client.
Group Lock Configuration	`GI VPN start callback failed "CM_PEER_NOT_RESPONDING" (16h).`	`User (U1) not member of group (test_grp), authentication failed.`	If the Group Lock feature is enabled on the Group test_grp, then the User must be part of test_grp to connect.

Step 7 Verify that User Authentication (X-Auth) is successful.

Once group authentication is successful, user authentication occurs if it is configured on the VPN Concentrator. If the user authentication fails at this stage, the VPN tunnel will not be built up. Note that user authentication can be performed either locally on the VPN Concentrator or using an external AAA server. If the authentication is configured with an AAA Server, refer to Chapter 12, "Troubleshooting AAA on VPN 3000 Series Concentrator." If authentication is performed locally on the

VPN Concentrator, turn on **XAuth** Verbose level to high on the VPN Client and set the level of logging for **AUTH**, **AUTH**, and **AUTHDBG** to 1-9 following the procedure explained in the "Diagnostic Commands and Tools" section. The same section also explains how to interpret the event log message. Example 8-11 shows an example of a successful user authentication on the VPN 3000 Concentrators Event Log.

Example 8-11 *A Successful User Authentication Event Log on VPN Concentrator*

```
116 04/12/2005 02:08:52.970 SEV=6 AUTH/4 RPT=9 192.168.1.100
Authentication successful: handle = 19, server = Internal, user = vpn3k
165 04/12/2005 02:08:53.170 SEV=7 IKEDBG/14 RPT=20 192.168.1.100
Group [mygroup] User [vpn3k] Authentication configured for Internal
171 04/12/2005 02:08:53.170 SEV=4 IKE/52 RPT=9 192.168.1.100
Group [mygroup] User [vpn3k] User (vpn3k) authenticated.
```

Step 8 If authentication fails, be sure the appropriate authentication server is set by going into **Configuration > System > Servers > Authentication servers**. To ensure that the specific group configuration for the authentication server does not override the server configuration setup under System, go into **Configuration > User Management > Groups > Authentication Servers**, and check to see if the VPN Concentrator is configured correctly to assign the address.

If the VPN client can connect to the VPN Concentrator but is unable to get the IP address, check the log on both client and Concentrator to find the cause of the problem. Example 8-12 presents the Event Log on the VPN Concentrator that shows it is unable to assign the IP address to the VPN client.

Example 8-12 *Event Log on the VPN Concentrator Shows That it Is Unable to Assign an IP Address to the VPN Client*

```
! The following line indicates that VPN Concentrator is unable to allocate an IP
! address
Group [mygroup] User [U1] IKE received response of type [FAILED] to a request from
the IP address utility
. . .
204 04/11/2005 00:29:42.500 SEV=5 IKE/132 RPT=2 192.168.1.100
! The following line reaffirms that the obtaining of IP address is indeed
! unsuccessful.
Group [mygroup] User [U1] Cannot obtain an IP address for remote peer
```

Typically, the address assignment problem occurs due to misconfiguration. But there also can be other reasons for the VPN Concentrator being unable to assign an IP address to the VPN Client. The list that follows outlines procedures to deal with the most common problems:

— **Be sure that the IP address Pool is configured**—To allocate an IP address from a local pool, be sure that the pool is configured under **Configuration > System > Address Management > Pools**. Be sure that you have a correct pool defined, and if you do not, define one. On the other hand, if you want to assign the address from an AAA server, define the pool on the AAA server.

— **Be sure Method of Assignment is selected**—Merely defining a pool is sufficient unless you check the correct box under **Configuration > System > Address Management > Assignment** page. This is one of the most common mistakes an engineer makes.

— **Be sure you are not reaching to max of address from address pool**—If you are having address assignment issues with a specific client intermittently, or after a certain number of host connection, chances are that your Concentrator is hitting the max on the address pool. Consider redefining the address pool to add additional addresses to the pool.

Figure 8-7 shows how to create the IP address pool and apply it on a VPN 3000 Concentrator.

Figure 8-7 *Configuration for Creating an IP Pool*

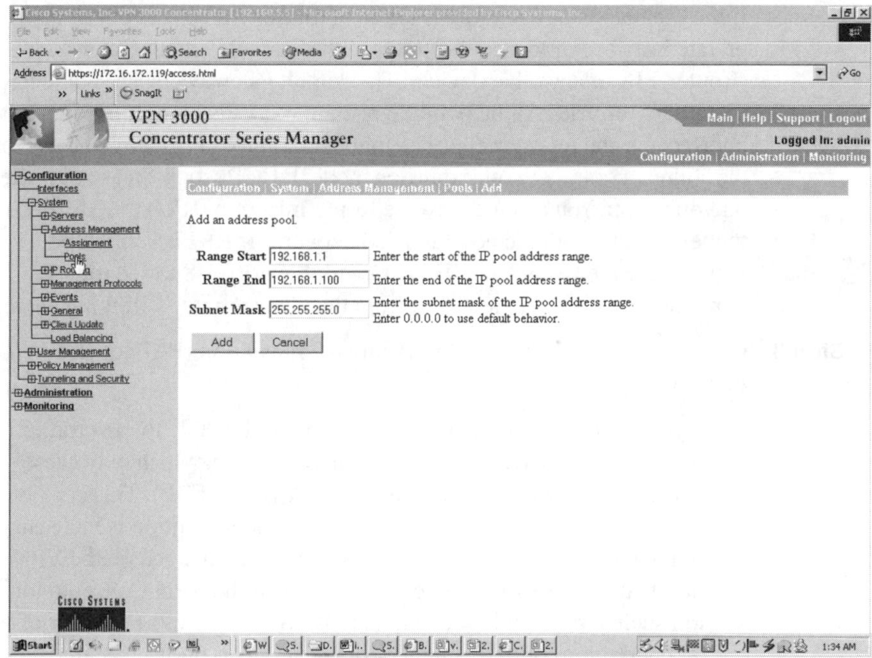

VPN Client can Connect but Tunnel Is Not Passing Traffic

If the VPN Client is able to connect but unable to pass any traffic, work through the steps that follow to isolate and resolve the problem:

Step 1 Check Routing for Issues on the VPN Client PC.

If the tunnel is up and you still cannot send any traffic across the tunnel (this can be verified by checking the number of encrypts/decrypt packets in both client and VPN concentrator session logs), then most likely the problem is with client routing. Traffic originating from the laptop will be sent to the NIC, not through the VPN tunnel, if these circumstances apply: first, you connected your laptop earlier to the corporate network that allocated an IP address from a 10.1.0.0 network; and second, when you connect from home, the VPN 3K assigns you an IP address from the 10.1.0.0 network. This problem is very prominent in Microsoft Windows 95/98/NT.

To solve the problem, release the Dynamic Host Configuration Protocol (DHCP) that learned the IP address that you learned while you were connected to the LAN. Also, be sure that the default gateway is set up correctly. For more details on this specific issue, refer to the following link:

http://www.cisco.com/en/US/partner/products/sw/secursw/ps2308/products_tech_note09186a00801b7615.shtml

Step 2 Check for Routing on the VPN 3000 Concentrator.

If the Tunnel default gateway is defined, traffic will be sent out of the private interface of the Concentrator to the Tunnel Default Gateway (Router, PIX or any other device). The default gateway device should have a route for tunneled traffic pointing back to the VPN Concentrator private interface for the return traffic. The tunneled route can be defined based on the address pools, network extension mode, DHCP scope, and so on, based on your setup. You can use Reverse Route Injection (RRI) to redistribute tunneled routes into the non-tunneled network. If RRI is configured, you can use the Event Class **IPDBG** with Severity 1-8 to see routes dynamically added and removed from the Concentrator's Routing Table.

Step 3 Check to see if you have a Port Address Translation (PAT) device in the middle.

Once you verify the routing issue, if you are still unable to pass traffic, check to see if you have a PAT device in the middle, which may cause problems with the Encapsulating Security Payload (**ESP**). This can be verified by checking to see if the number packet encryption is increasing and that the number of the packet decryption is unchanged on the VPN Client. On the VPN Concentrator, if you look at the VPN Concentrator session statistics, you will see that there is no change in the number of packet encryptions or to the number of packet decryptions (see under **Administration > Administer Sessions**). If you have a NAT/PAT device, configure for NAT Transparency (NAT-T) or IPsec over Transmission Control Protocol (TCP) or User Datagram Protocol (UDP) on both VPN 3000 Concentrator and on the VPN client as per the following link:

http://www.cisco.com/en/US/partner/products/hw/vpndevc/ps2284/products_tech_note09186a00800946af.shtml

On the VPN Concentrator, go to the **Client Config** tab of the Group to configure NAT-T or IPsec over TCP.

On the VPN Client Properties window, click on the **Transport** tab, and turn on NAT-T or IPSEC over TCP as shown in Figure 8-8.

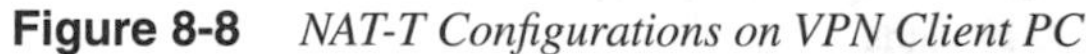

Figure 8-8 *NAT-T Configurations on VPN Client PC*

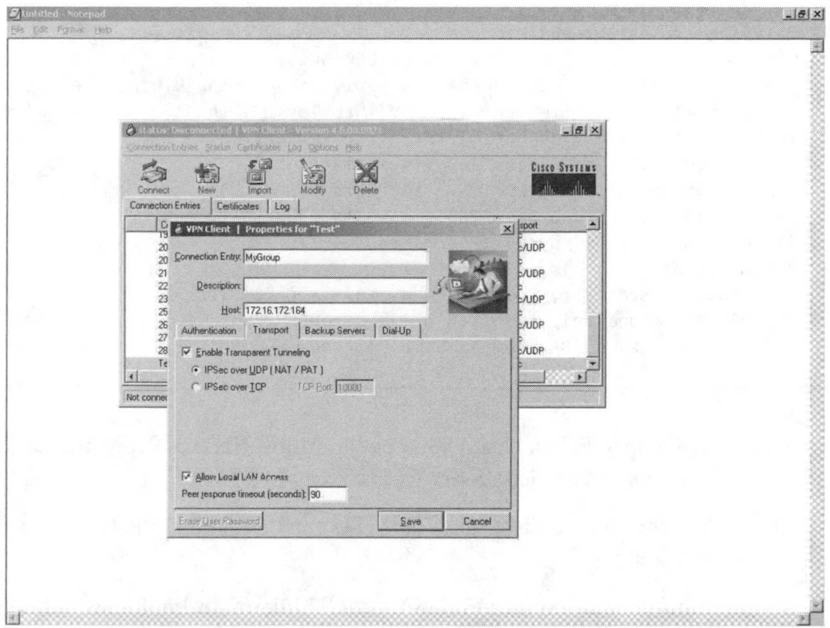

Step 4 Check maximum Transmission Unit (MTU) Issues.

If you have solved both the routing and PAT issues, and you can ping the resources in your corporate network, you still might be unable to use certain applications. If so, there is a very good chance that you are running into MTU issues across the path. You can verify this by pinging the application server with "–l" and "–f" options. **–l** is used to define the number of bytes and **–f** forces the packet not to be fragmented. Start with a 1500 bytes packet and reduce this number until you stop receiving the message "Packet needs to be fragmented but DF set," and get a ping reply.

Example 8-13 shows a sample ping test performed from a Windows machine to uncover any MTU issues.

Example 8-13 *Sample Test To Identify MTU Issues*

```
D:\>ping -f -l 1300 www.xyz.com
Pinging www.xyz.com [10.1.1.1] with 1300 bytes of data:
! The following lines indicate that 1300 bytes are too big along the path, so
! need to reset the MTU to some sCAller number on the VPN client.
Packet needs to be fragmented but DF set.
```

continues

Example 8-13 *Sample Test To Identify MTU Issues (Continued)*

```
Packet needs to be fragmented but DF set.
Packet needs to be fragmented but DF set.
Packet needs to be fragmented but DF set.
Ping statistics for 10.1.1.1:
    Packets: Sent = 4, Received = 0, Lost = 4 (100% loss),
ApproxiCAte round trip times in milli-seconds:
    Minimum = 0ms, CAximum =  0ms, Average =  0ms
D:\>ping -f -l 1250 www.xyz.com
Pinging www.xyz.com [10.1.1.1] with 1250 bytes of data:
! As the following lines indicate a reply, that means MTU can be set to this
! number minus 42 byeted for layer VII to layer IV header. So, ideally you
! should set the MTU on the client to be 1208 bytes.
Reply from 10.1.1.1: bytes=1250 time=51ms TTL=47
Reply from 10.1.1.1: bytes=1250 time=29ms TTL=47
Reply from 10.1.1.1: bytes=1250 time=32ms TTL=47
Reply from 10.1.1.1: bytes=1250 time=34ms TTL=47
Ping statistics for 10.1.1.1:
    Packets: Sent = 4, Received = 4, Lost = 0 (0% loss),
ApproxiCAte round trip times in milli-seconds:
    Minimum = 29ms, CAximum =  51ms, Average =  36ms
D:\>
```

To set up MTU on Cisco VPN client, follow **Start > Programs > Cisco Systems VPN Client > Set MTU**

A more detailed discussion on MTU can be found at the following location:

http://www.cisco.com/en/US/tech/tk827/tk369/technologies_white_paper09186a00800d6979.shtml

On the VPN 3000 Concentrator's public interface (where the VPN tunnel terminates), set the highest MTU value possible.

Step 5 Check for filters.

Three types of filters can affect the traffic going through the tunnel. These three filters are:

— Static filters applied to an interface

— Static filters applied to the user group

— Dynamic filters applied through the RADIUS Server

Work through the following steps to verify if the filter is causing the problem:

(a) Try to determine if traffic is indeed being dropped due to a filter by checking the counters on **Monitoring > Statistics > Filtering**.

If the **"Filtered"** counter increases over a period of time, there is a very good chance that traffic is being dropped by the filter.

(b) Next, verify if the rule you have defined for the filter is working the way you intended. You can verify this by changing the Action of the rule to **Drop and Log** or **Forward and Log** by going into **Configuration > Policy Management > Traffic Management > Rules > Add or Modify**. Then enable the **FilterDBG** Event Class to Severity to Log 1-9. This will allow traffic affected by the rule to be logged to Syslog or to the Event Log.

(c) Check the Dynamic filter assigned by the RADIUS Server to see the rules being applied to a dynamic filter. To do so, go to the **Monitoring > Dynamic Filters** page. You can find details on Dynamic Filters in the detail screen of a specific user session on the **Monitor > Session > Detail** screen. Analyze the dynamic filter applied for the specific user and make sure the filter is accurate. If the filter is applied incorrectly, correct the configuration on the RADIUS Server.

Step 6 Check for Microsoft networking issues.

If you have a problem specific to Microsoft networking through the VPN tunnel, refer to the following link:

http://www.cisco.com/en/US/products/sw/secursw/ps2308/products_tech_note09186a0080194b4a.shtml

VPN Client can connect but User Cannot Access the Internet

If you can access all resources on the private network of the other side of the tunnel (VPN 3000 Concentrator) but cannot access anything on the Internet, it could be because one of the following setups is not configured for tunneled traffic:

- **You are tunneling all traffic but do not have a Gateway on the VPN Concentrator for Internet-bound traffic**—On the VPN Concentrator, you can configure it to force all traffic to go through the tunnel from the VPN client. This ensures that the VPN client cannot make any connections to the Internet in clear text bypassing the IPsec tunnel. This provides extra security to the client while it is connected to the corporate network via tunnel. If you want the users from the VPN client under this setup to be able to connect to the Internet as well, you need to define a route for the Internet-bound traffic on the VPN Concentrator. The easiest solution is to define a tunnel default gateway to an Internal Router and have the internal router make the routing decision for the inside traffic versus Internet-bound traffic. The VPN Concentrator itself cannot be used to redirect the traffic on the public interface where the tunnel is terminated.

- **You do not have the Split tunneling configured**—If you do not want to send the Internet-bound traffic across the tunnel from the VPN Client, then be sure to configure split tunneling so that VPN client can make the connections to the Internet in clear text from the client PC itself. Note that with split tunneling, you are leaving the client PC vulnerable. Therefore, be sure to install a Personal Firewall or other host base Intrusion Detection Agent (for example CSAgent). To configure Split Tunneling, you first need to define a Network List that includes the networks that need to be tunneled. To define a network list, go to **Configuration > Policy Management > Traffic Management > Network Lists**. Then click on **Add** or **Modify**.

Once you have defined the Network List, you need to apply the Network List under the **Client Config** Tab of the **Group Setup** page. Under the **Client Config** tab, select only **tunnel networks in the list**. From the **Split Tunneling Network List** drop-down list, select the Network List defined earlier to allow going through the tunnel. No special configuration is required on the VPN Client.

VPN Client Can Connect But Users Cannot Access the Local LAN

If you cannot access any resources on the local LAN (for example, you are unable to print to the local printer) after building up the VPN tunnel, use the VPN client local LAN feature to allow local LAN traffic that is not encrypted. Go to the **Client Config** Tab of the Group Setup page. Under the **Client Config** tab, select the **Tunnel everything** button and check the **Allow the networks in list to bypass the tunnel** box. From the **Split Tunneling Network List**, select **VPN Client Local LAN (Default)**.

To turn on Local LAN access, on the VPN Client GUI, for the user profile, go under the **Transport** tab, and check **Allow Local LAN Access**.

Digital Certificate Issues

Digital Certificate can be used to authenticate peers for both LAN-to-LAN and Remote Access VPN connections. As the creation and usage of Certificate for peer authentication is very similar for both LAN-to-LAN and Remote Access VPN connections, this section describes the Digital Certificate implementation only for the Remote Access VPN connection. One important point to note is that when a digital certificate is used for the peer authentication, both Remote Access VPN and LAN-to-LAN connections perform Main Mode negotiation. As you have seen before, with the pre-shared key, however, although the LAN-to-LAN connection performs Main Mode negotiation, Remote Access VPN connection uses Aggressive Mode negotiation for phase I tunnel establishment. The sections that follow provide detailed information on these topics:

- Digital certificate on the VPN client
- Digital certificate on the VPN concentrator
- Troubleshooting steps

Digital Certificate on the VPN Client

Work through the following steps to configure a VPN client with the digital certificate:

Step 1 Enroll or import the CA root certificate and digital certificate for the VPN client connection entry by clicking on **Certificates > Enroll or Import** and refer to the following links:

http://www.cisco.com/univercd/cc/td/doc/product/vpn/client/4_6/ugwin/vc6.htm#wp1173362

http://www.cisco.com/en/US/partner/products/sw/secursw/ps2308/products_configuration_example09186a00801c8c41.shtml

Step 2 Under the **Certificate** Tab, Select **Verify**. This will check if the certificate has a complete chain and its validity dates are acceptable.

Step 3 Assign the certificate to the connection entry through the **Authentication** tab by selecting the **Certificate Authentication** radio button and selecting the certificate from the drop-down list of Certificate name.

Step 4 Optionally choose **Send CA Certificate Chain** option if you want to send the chain of the certificate to the Concentrator.

Digital Certificate on the VPN Concentrator

Just as with a VPN Client, you must import the CA root and digital certificate on the VPN Concentrator. Work through the following steps to import the CA root certificate and the digital certificate on the VPN Concentrator:

Step 1 On VPN 3000 Concentrator GUI, go to **Administration > Certificate Management**, and import/install the CA root certificate and the VPN Concentrator. Identity the certificate (Digital certificate) by using the instructions in the following links:

http://www.cisco.com/univercd/cc/td/doc/product/vpn/vpn3000/4_7/admon/certCAn.html

http://www.cisco.com/en/US/products/hw/vpndevc/ps2284/products_tech_note09186a00800946f1.shtml

http://cisco.com/en/US/products/hw/vpndevc/ps2284/products_tech_note09186a008044acb7.shtml

Step 2 Go to the **Administration > Certificate Management** page to verify both the root and the to identity the certificates and their validity. The concentrator does not allow the installation of an ID certificate that does not have a complete chain. Remember that the concentrator cannot install an ID cert that was not requested by the specific concentrator. Select the **View** option of the Identity (ID) certificate to verify its validity. If the certificate validity dates have expired, you will see a message that is similar to this: **The certificate is not yet valid**. Regenerate the certificate to correct the problem. Also be sure that the VPN Concentrator time is not off by much; otherwise, a valid certificate may be shown as invalid, as the VPN Concentrator time may not fall between the validity dates of the certificate.

Step 3 Go to **Configuration > Tunneling and Security > IPsec > IKE Proposals** on the VPN Concentrator GUI, and be sure that the **VPNClient-3DES-MD5-RSA** rule is under **ActiveProposals**. By default this is not under **Active Proposals**.

Step 4 Configure a custom or modified IPsec SA that will use the certificates that you have installed and verified by going to the **Configuration > Policy Management > Traffic Management > Security Associations > Add** page. The Issuer CN field designates the certificates in the SA configuration. The Negotiation Mode must be set to Main Mode. If the client does not have the full certificate chain installed you, may have to send the entire certificate chain. The IKE Proposal must support digital certificates.

Step 5 Group Matching is performed based on one or more fields in the incoming client certificate DN. If you are matching to a group from the OU field in the certificate, the defined group name must match the OU exactly. If you "Default to Group", that group must have an SA that supports certificates. Select the options by going into **Configuration > Policy Management > Group Matching > Policy**.

Step 6 The group that matches must have an IPsec SA assigned that supports certificates. You can also enable peer identity checking. Be sure that the configuration setting matches the certificates in use by the clients. To configure the group to use the certificate, go to **Configuration | User Management | Groups | Modify**, which will allow you to modify the group. Click on the **IPsec** tab, and select **IPsec SA** from the drop-down list that you have created earlier.

Troubleshooting Steps

As mentioned before, when a certificate is used for IKE phase I authentication, Main mode negotiation takes place between two IPsec peers for both LAN-to-LAN and Remote Access VPN connections. Before looking into the details of how to troubleshoot the IKE phase I negotiation when the Certificate is used, it is important to go through the event log on both the VPN Client and Concentrator and become absolutely comfortable with the sequence of events that takes place to isolate the problem with certification failure.

Example 8-14 shows the event log on the VPN Client with a successful phase 1 Main Mode negotiation.

Example 8-14 *Event Log for a Successful Phase I Main Mode Negotiation on VPN Client with Certificate for Authentication*

```
! Following message indicates that the tests for the Certificate Chain, its Validity
! dates and the Presence of the Private Key are successful.
850     16:03:23.964  05/28/05  Sev=Info/4CERT/0x63600013
Cert (cn=HTTS,ou=TAC,o=Cisco,l=San Jose,st=CA,c=US) verification succeeded.

! The VPN Client Sends Main Mode Message 1 with IKE Proposals that required certificate.
! If the VPN Concentrator doesn't have an Active IKE Proposal with Certificate
! Capability, the Negotiations Fails at this stage on the Concentrator.
857     16:03:25.105  05/28/05  Sev=Info/4IKE/0x63000013
SENDING >>> ISAKMP OAK MM (SA, VID(Xauth), VID(dpd), VID(Nat-T), VID(Frag),
VID(Unity)) to 172.16.172.157

! The VPN Client Receives Main Mode Message 2  from Concentrator indicating that the IKE
! Proposal Was OK.
862     16:03:25.198  05/28/05  Sev=Info/4IKE/0x63000014
RECEIVING <<< ISAKMP OAK MM (SA, VID(Frag)) from 172.16.172.157

! VPN Client is sending Main Mode Message 3
865     16:03:25.214  05/28/05  Sev=Info/4IKE/0x63000013
SENDING >>> ISAKMP OAK MM (KE, NON, VID(?), VID(Unity)) to 172.16.172.157

! The VPN Client receives Main Mode Message 4 containing the Cert Request
871     16:03:25.370  05/28/05  Sev=Info/4IKE/0x63000014
RECEIVING <<< ISAKMP OAK MM (KE, NON, CERT_REQ, CERT_REQ, CERT_REQ, CERT_REQ,
CERT_REQ, VID(Unity), VID(Xauth), VID(?), VID(?)) from 172.16.172.157

! The VPN Client sends Main Mode Message 5 with the Client Cert to the Concentrator.
875     16:03:25.511  05/28/05  Sev=Info/4IKE/0x63000013
SENDING >>> ISAKMP OAK MM *(ID, CERT, CERT_REQ, SIG, NOTIFY:STATUS_INITIAL_CONTACT)
to 172.16.172.157

! The VPN Client receives Main Mode Message 6 Containing the Concentrator Cert.
885     16:03:25.792  05/28/05  Sev=Info/4IKE/0x63000014
RECEIVING <<< ISAKMP OAK MM *(ID, CERT, SIG, VID(dpd)) from 172.16.172.157

! VPN Client validates the Concentrator Cert signed by the right Root certificate
and is
! ready to Start X-AUTH
886     16:03:25.886  05/28/05  Sev=Info/4CERT/0x63600013
Cert (cn=ID from Break,ou=TAC,o=Cisco,l=San Jose,st=CA,c=US) verification succeeded.

! Phase 1 SA is established here
889     16:03:25.886  05/28/05  Sev=Info/4CM/0x6310000E
Established Phase 1 SA.  1 Crypto Active IKE SA, 0 User Authenticated IKE SA in the
  system
```

Example 8-15 shows the corresponding event log on the VPN 3000 Concentrator with a successful phase 1 Main Mode negotiation.

Example 8-15 *Event Log for A Successful Phase I Main Mode Negotiation on Concentrator with Certificate for Authentication*

```
! Main Mode message 1 sent by the VPN Client with IKE proposals is received by the VPN
! Concentrator
12 05/16/2005 16:15:01.910 SEV=8 IKEDBG/81 RPT=19017 172.16.172.1570
RECEIVED Message (msgid=0) with payloads :
HDR + SA (1) + VENDOR (13) + VENDOR (13) + VENDOR (13) + VENDOR (13) + VENDOR
(13) + NONE (0)
total length : 1144

! As the Concentrator does not log sending Main Mode Message 2 unless there is a failure
! you do not see the MM Message 2. If there is misMatch on Active IKE Proposals, you will
! receive "All SA Proposals Found Unacceptable". As there is no message logged, this is
! an indication that IKE proposals are accepted by the VPN Concentrator.

! Main Mode message 3 is received on the Concentrator from the VPN Client. You May
! receive duplicate of this message in certain version of code, which you can ignore.
1305 05/16/2005 16:15:02.110 SEV=8 IKEDBG/81 RPT=19018 172.16.172.1570
RECEIVED Message (msgid=0) with payloads :
HDR + KE (4) + NONCE (10) + VENDOR (13) + VENDOR (13) + NONE (0)
total length : 224

! Following is the Main Mode Message 4 sent to the VPN Client Requesting for the
! Client Certificate.
1319 05/16/2005 16:01:37.690 SEV=9 IKEDBG/0 RPT=30523 172.16.172.1570
constructing certreq payload

1332 05/16/2005 16:01:37.710 SEV=8 IKEDBG/81 RPT=18861 172.16.172.1570
SENDING Message (msgid=0) with payloads :
HDR + KE (4) + NONCE (10)
total length : 961

! The following is Main Mode message 5 that the Concentrator Receives from the VPN client
! which contains the Client Cert and a Request for Concentrator's cert by the client
1334 05/16/2005 16:01:37.920 SEV=8 IKEDBG/81 RPT=18862 172.16.172.1570
RECEIVED Message (msgid=0) with payloads :
HDR + ID (5) + CERT (6) + CERT_REQ (7) + SIG (9) + NOTIFY (11) + NONE (0)
total length : 1555

! The VPN Concentrator first tries to Match a Group to the incoming client Cert
! based on the IP address.
1343 05/16/2005 16:01:37.930 SEV=9 IKEDBG/23 RPT=42 172.16.172.1570
Starting group lookup for peer 172.16.172.1570

! VPN Concentrator will be unable to find out the group based on the IP address of the
! client, which is expected, and you can ignore the following failure.
1344 05/16/2005 16:01:37.930 SEV=5 IKE/21 RPT=10 172.16.172.157
No Group found by Matching IP Address of Cert peer 172.16.172.157

! Now Concentrator will perform the group Match based on the Cert subject and DN. You
! need to raise the CERT class up to level 1-9 to see the following level of details.
```

Example 8-15 *Event Log for A Successful Phase I Main Mode Negotiation on Concentrator with Certificate for Authentication (Continued)*

```
1345 05/16/2005 16:01:37.930 SEV=9 CERT/107 RPT=5
Performing group Match for cert peer 172.16.172.157
using the following cert subject DN info:
OID: CountryName (26) value: US
OID: StateProvinceName (28) value: CA
OID: LocalityName (27) value: San Jose
OID: OrganizationName (30) value: Cisco
OID: OrganizationalUnitName (31) value: TAC
OID: CommonName (23) value: HTTS

1353 05/16/2005 16:01:37.930 SEV=9 CERT/108 RPT=5
Performing group Match for cert peer 172.16.172.1570
using the following cert issuer DN info:
OID: EmailAddress (13) value: xyz@cisco.com
OID: CountryName (26) value: US
OID: StateProvinceName (28) value: CA
OID: LocalityName (27) value: San Jose
OID: OrganizationName (30) value: Cisco
OID: OrganizationalUnitName (31) value: TAC
OID: CommonName (23) value: system

! Following three messages indicates the group Cisco is found based on issuer value
! O=Cisco.
1362 05/16/2005 16:01:37.930 SEV=9 CERT/109 RPT=5
Group Match component succeeded for cert peer 172.16.172.1570
OID (30) "CISCO" = "CISCO"

1364 05/16/2005 16:01:37.930 SEV=5 CERT/110 RPT=10
Group Match for cert peer 172.16.172.1570 succeeded using rule
issuer-o="cisco"

1365 05/16/2005 16:01:37.930 SEV=5 CERT/105 RPT=10
Group [Cisco] found for cert peer 172.16.172.157 by group Match rule
issuer-o="cisco"

! Finally, Group Cisco meets the Criteria
1367 05/16/2005 16:01:38.040 SEV=7 IKEDBG/80 RPT=42 172.16.172.1570
Group [Cisco]
Found Phase 1 Group (Cisco)

! Following message indicates the Concentrator finds the Client Certificate to be valid
! in terms of Dates and Certificate Authority (CA).
1376 05/16/2005 16:01:38.050 SEV=7 CERT/1 RPT=5
Certificate is valid: session = 9

! Certificate Revocation List (CRL) checking is done here.
1390 05/16/2005 16:01:38.050 SEV=5 CERT/116 RPT=5
Requesting CRL using HTTP. The HTTP URL is: http://xyz.com/CertEnroll/system.crl

! If you want to see the details of CRL http transaction, you need to use the CLIENT
! Event Class.
```

continues

Example 8-15 *Event Log for A Successful Phase I Main Mode Negotiation on Concentrator with Certificate for Authentication (Continued)*

```
1392 05/16/2005 16:01:38.060 SEV=7 CLIENT/28 RPT=1
CLIENT_InitiateRequest(718d9b8, 7)

1407 05/16/2005 16:01:38.210 SEV=9 CLIENT/23 RPT=1
Total HTTP data bytes received: 327

! The following message shows the CRL Check
1427 05/16/2005 16:01:38.210 SEV=7 CERT/2 RPT=5
Certificate has not been revoked: session = 9

! The Concentrator validates it's own Certificate as shown below.
1429 05/16/2005 16:01:38.220 SEV=5 IKE/79 RPT=8 172.16.172.1570
Group [Cisco]
Validation of certificate successful
(CN=HTTS, SN=44B4C7C8000000000030)

! All Client and Concentrator Certificate Processing is Successful—Sending Main Mode
! Message 6 as shown by the following lines.
1438 05/16/2005 16:01:38.240 SEV=8 IKEDBG/81 RPT=18863 172.16.172.1570
SENDING Message (msgid=0) with payloads :
HDR + ID (5) + CERT (6)
total length : 1549
```

Now that you are comfortable with the event log for a successful phase 1 negotiation of a Main Mode Remote Access VPN connection, work through the following steps to troubleshoot the digital certificate issues:

Step 1 If the VPN client does not send Main Mode Message 1, there is a problem with the certificate on the client. Check the validity dates, and make sure the personal certificate ties back to a trusted root. If the certificate is stored on the local system, ensure that it can be read by VPN client software.

Step 2 If the tunnel establishment fails in Main Mode Message 1 and 2, there may be a problem with active IKE proposals on the Concentrator. Be sure there is an active proposal that supports certificates.

Step 3 If the Concentrator does not receive Main Mode Message 5 from the VPN client, it could be because of IKE fragmentation. The certificate sent from the VPN client might be big enough to cause the packet to be fragmented.

Step 4 One of the following reasons could cause the Concentrator to receive the Main Mode message 5, but fails:

— **Group Matching**—Be sure your rules are defined properly so that the VPN Concentrator can perform group matching properly. Raise the CERT and IKEDBG Event Classes to level 1–9 to see group Matching information.

— **The group may not have the right IPsec SA associated with it**— You must have right IPsec SA associated with the group. The default logging gives you this information.

— **The Client certificate does not validate**—If the VPN client certificate does not validate, be sure the certificates matched to the group are from the same Root CA as the certificates from the VPN client. If there is a tiered CA structure, set the client to **Send CA Certificate Chain**. If the certificate fails due to certificate chain issues, you might receive the following message on VPN Concentrator:

```
Unable to complete certificate chain, reason = Incomplete
  certificate chain
```

— **CRL checking Failure**—Be sure the search strings and URLs are defined correctly. For LDAP, take a sniffer trace to analyze the response from the LDAP server. The **Cert** Event Class shows the DN you are sending. For http, the **Client** Event Class will add detail to the exchange. If the search is all right, be sure the cert has not been revoked (Cert Event Class can be used to find details).

— **After CRL checking, the concentrator validates its own certificate before sending it to the client**—If this validation fails, default logging provides you the information. To correct the problem, check and correct the time and date on the Concentrator.

Step 5 **Finally the Concentrator sends Main Mode Message 6 to the VPN Client**—This may fail at the VPN client primarily due to a chaining issue. Set the Certificate Transmission parameter in the IPsec SA to entire certificate chain for tiered CA structures.

Case Studies

This section discusses the new feature called Secure Socket Layer (SSL) VPN or Web VPN on the VPN Concentrator. SSL VPN provides remote access connectivity from almost any Internet-enabled location using a Web browser and its native SSL encryption. This section presents a general discussion, configuration steps and troubleshooting issues for different modes of operation for SSL VPN. SSL VPN can be operated in one of the three modes based on your corporation needs and requirements:

- **Clientless**—This mode of operation is for web-based applications (web server access with http/https), and file shares (CIFS). A standard browser acts as a VPN client in this mode, and the VPN Concentrator acts as a proxy.

- **Thin client**—This mode of operation is for fixed TCP port applications (such as e-mail/Telnet/ssh, terminal services, and so on). Any multi-channel protocol that requires port negotiation (FTP, for example) does not work with this mode. Java applet (generally less than 100K) is downloaded using a browser on a client PC which proxies TCP connections.
- **SSL VPN Client (SVC)**—A larger client (generally around 500K max) is delivered to the end user and the applications that can be accessed are very similar to those available via regular IPsec Remote Access VPN client. This client is delivered via a web page, and never needs to be manually distributed or installed.

The next few sections present more detailed discussions on all three modes of operation.

Clientless SSL VPN

As mentioned before, in Clientless SSL VPN mode of operation, a standard browser is used as a VPN client. There is no requirement to download any applet on the client PC, as the VPN Concentrator acts as a proxy in this mode. Clientless SSL VPN is supported for website access and web applications such as NT and Active Directory file sharing (CIFS). For websites, the URL is mangled to present to the end user. For NT and Active Directory file sharing, the application is translated to HTTP, and presents to users in HTML format. The sections that follow discuss the following topics:

- Configuration steps for basic SSL VPN connection
- Troubleshooting steps for Basic SSL VPN connection
- Configuration steps for web server access
- Troubleshooting steps for web server access
- Configuration steps for CIFS access
- Troubleshooting steps for CIFS access

Configuration Steps for Basic SSL VPN Connection

Work through the following steps to configure Basic SSL VPN Connection:

Step 1 Go to **Configuration > Interfaces > Ethernet2**, and check **Allow WebVPN HTTS sessions** to turn on **WebVPN**. If you want to allow the HTTPS web access to the VPN Concentrator for Management purpose, check **Allow Management HTTPS sessions**.

Step 2 Be sure **WebVPN** box is checked under **Tunneling Protocols when you go to** the **General** tab on the page **Configuration > User Management > Base Group**. You also can set this up in the specific group.

Step 3 To enable client authentication using digital certificates for both HTTPS administrative and WebVPN sessions, go to the **Configuration >**

Tunneling and Security > SSL > HTTPS page, and check **the Enable HTTPS** box, define the HTTPS port 443, and check **Client Authentication**. Note that WebVPN sessions require an active authorization server. By default **Client Authentication** is not checked.

Step 4 Go to the **Configuration > Tunneling and Security > SSL > Protocols** page and check at least one encryption protocol. The default is that all three protocol options are checked. It is recommended to set everything at the default.

Troubleshooting Steps for Basic SSL VPN Connection

When working with Basic SSL VPN Connection, you may encounter these problems, which are described in the sections that follow:

- Inability to establish SSL session with VPN 3000 Concentrator
- Inability to login to VPN 3000 Concentrator

Inability to Establish SSL Session with VPN 3000 Concentrator

Work through the following steps to troubleshoot the inability to establish an SSL session:

Step 1 To verify general connectivity, ping by name and IP address of the VPN Concentrator's from the client PC. If the ICMP is blocked between the client and the VPN Concentrator, try http or https on the public interface and see if you can connect.

Step 2 If one vendor's browser does not work, try a different browser and check to see if you get the web portal page.

Step 3 Be sure the interface you are connecting to is configured to support WebVPN Connections by going into the **Configuration > Interfaces > Ethernet2** page.

Step 4 Verify that the Interface you are connecting to has an SSL certificate and that the certificate is valid by going into **Administration > Certificate Management**. Look under the **SSL Certificates** section. View the certificate to see the details and validity of the certificate.

Step 5 Enable **Allow Management HTTPS Sessions** on the interface and try connecting to https://VPN_Concentrator_IP_Address/admin. This also will fail if the issue is with the certificate.

Step 6 Verify that the group the user is connecting to supports WebVPN.

Step 7 Verify the SSL/HTTPS configuration by verifying that the HTTPS is enabled, the port defined and authentication is turned on.

Step 8 Turn on **SSL** Event Class severities 1-9. This gives you general reason codes for the failure.

Step 9 Use an external sniffer to trace the network traffic. Verify that the three-way TCP handshakes complete successfully. If the TCP handshake completes, you should see an SSL handshake occur. The sniffer also helps you determine the cipher suites being negotiated and where in the session the establishment process is breaking.

Step 10 Verify that the cipher being offered by the client is supported by the configuration of the concentrator:

- Server Gated Cryptography (SGC) is not supported.
- Minimum 56 bit keys.
- Verify that the certificates you are using are valid; the smart card certificate can be read by the browser.
- Try using the self-signed concentrator certificates.

Step 11 If you still fail to create a HTTPS session to the concentrator, contact the Cisco Support Team.

Inability to Log in to VPN 3000 Concentrator

If you can get the Web VPN portal but cannot establish an SSL VPN connection because of login failure, work through the following steps to diagnose the problem:

Step 1 Enable logging for the **auth** and **webvpn** classes at severity levels 1–9, try to connect to the SSL VPN, and see if it shows any error.

Step 2 If you are using an external AAA server, verify that you have network connectivity to the AAA server.

Step 3 Verify that the client's browser is not configured to use a proxy server.

Step 4 Perform a test authentication to the external AAA server from the VPN 3000 Concentrator.

Configuration Steps for Web Server Access

To provide the links of the websites on the Web VPN portal after the user logs in, work through the following steps:

Step 1 Complete the configuration steps explained in the section entitled "**Configuration Steps for Basic SSL VPN Connection.**"

Step 2 Configure access to URLs in the **Configuration > Tunneling and Security > WebVPN > Servers and URLs** screen. To add a new URL for the website, click on **Add**. In the **Add** page, specify the **Name** as it should appear on the Web VPN portal page, **server type** (HTTP/HTTPS Server), and the **actual web site URL**.

NOTE Outlook Web Access (OWA) on the Microsoft Exchange Server can be accessed using the procedure previously explained, as OWA on Exchange Server works just like any other web application.

Troubleshooting Steps For Web Server Access

You might run into one of the following problems with web server access through SSL VPN connection:

- Web site does not display at all.
- Web site displays but incorrectly.

The sections that follow detail the troubleshooting of these two issues. But before you delve into those details, it is important to know how to turn on debug for website access issues on the VPN Concentrator. The next section discusses this topic.

Turning on WEBVPN Event Class for Logging

Work through the following steps to turn on debug and collect the log to troubleshoot issues pertaining to web access through SSL VPN tunnel:

Step 1 From VPN Concentrator GUI, go to the **Monitoring > WebVPN Logging** page, and turn on the logging by checking **Enable**. Be sure to define the username and path to capture the amount of information you desire.

Step 2 View or copy the log files from the **Administration > File Management** page. WebVPN Logging creates pairs of files; Mangled.xxx and Original.xxx. The Original file contains the request sent from the Concentrator to the Web Server and the response sent from the Web Server to the Concentrator. The Mangled file contains the response message sent from the Concentrator to the browser.

Inability to Browse to Website

If you cannot browse to a website, work through the following steps to troubleshoot the issue:

Step 1 Try to access the website directly (locally) without going through the SSL VPN connection.

Step 2 Be sure DNS Server is configured and functioning correctly on the VPN 3000 Concentrator by pinging to the website using the domain name from the **Administration > Ping** page. If you do not get a DNS response, check to be sure that the DNS server is defined correctly, by going to the following page: **Configuration > System > Servers > DNS**. Be sure that the DNS server IP address is defined correctly and **Enabled** is checked.

Step 3 Check to see if the Proxy server configuration is needed for website access. If so, from the VPN GUI, go to **Configuration > Tunneling and Security > WebVPN > HTTP/HTTPS Proxy** and define the proxy server.

Step 4 Go to **Configuration > System > Events > Classes > Add** and set the severities of **WEBVPN** Event Class to 1-8, which will display basic connectivity. Use the **WEBVPN** Logging tool or Sniffer trace to track down the failure.

Website Displays Incorrectly

Work through the following steps to troubleshoot issues with website displays:

Step 1 Try to access the website directly (locally) without going through the SSL VPN connection.

Step 2 Clear the browser's cache and retry with a new window.

Step 3 Be sure that there are no pop-up blockers enabled for the browser. Pop-up blockers can cause a page to be blocked, resulting in a blank page.

Step 4 Establish another WebVPN session using a different type of browser (for example, if Internet Explorer is not working, then try Mozilla or Netscape), and try accessing the website again.

Step 5 Verify proxy settings/requirements on the browser.

Step 6 Refer to the current VPN 3000 Concentrator version release notes, or the new version release notes, and check for any possible bug.

Step 7 If no known bug found is found, then enable **WEBVPN** logging and start the log right before the failed display with the procedure shown in the section entitled "Turning on WEBVPN Event Class For Logging."

Configuration Steps for CIFS Access

With SSL VPN, you can allow shared drives and folders to be navigated through a WebVPN session. Sharing and authentication rules defined on the server will be enforced. Work through the following steps to configure CIFS access on the VPN 3000 Concentrator:

Step 1 Complete the configuration steps explained in the section entitled "Configuration Steps for Basic SSL VPN Connection."

Step 2 On the VPN 3000 Concentrator GUI, go to the **Configuration > System > Servers > NBNS** page and define a WINS Server IP address, and turn it on by checking **Enabled**.

Step 3 Configure access to URLs in the **Configuration > Tunneling and Security > WebVPN > Servers and URLs** screen. To add a new URL for the file server, click on **Add.** In the **Add** page, specify the **Name** as it should appear on the Web VPN portal page, the **server type** (CIFS Server), and the **actual File Server location**.

Troubleshooting Steps for CIFS Access

Work through the following steps if you cannot browse to a file share:

Step 1 Check to see if you can locally access the CIFS without going through the SSL VPN.

Step 2 Verify the access method. Check to see if it is a configured server or if it is the user entering the server name or trying to browse the network.

Step 3 Verify that the access method desired is allowed from the group the user is mapped to.

Step 4 Make sure an NBNS server is defined and it is working. Go to **Configuration > System > Servers > NBNS** on VPN 3000 Concentrator GUI and be sure that the WINS server IP address is correct and that the **Enabled** box is checked.

Step 5 Verify that the resource you are trying to access is allowed.

Step 6 Keep in mind that when browsing to a non-shared service, you will still be prompted for a username and password. Hence, you need to determine if the failure is a login failure or access is not allowed for reading the file.

Thin Client

Not every application can be translated to the web format as discussed in the previous section. Hence, a thin client may be required to support additional applications that cannot be webified. Using a port-forwarding configuration, it is possible to access some common TCP-based applications. Port forwarding requires a very small application that runs on the end user's system, often in the form of Java or ActiveX. The client application is a port forwarder. It listens for connections on a port that is defined for each application. When packets come in on that port, they are tunneled inside of an SSL connection to the SSL VPN device, which unpacks them and forwards them to the real application server. To use the port forwarder, the end user simply points the application he wants to run at his own system rather than at the real application server. You can also think of this as a local proxy server that accepts connections on a local host address on the remote user's computer and proxies the traffic over the SSL VPN through the SSL VPN gateway to the destination server.

Port forwarding is an effective technique, but it also has some limitations. For port forwarding to work, the applications need to work well and predictably in their network connectivity patterns and requirements. ActiveX or Java applet support is required on the client machine, along with the permissions in the browser to run them.

Examples of applications that are not web-enabled but can be addressed with port forwarding are common mail protocols, including SMTP, POP3 and MAPI, and remote shell programs, such as Telnet.

The thin client is delivered via Java from the Concentrator to the client PC. A local thin client acts as a proxy and tunnels and forwards (most) TCP application traffic. Some system permissions may be required, particularly for hostname mapping. Port mapping works on TCP-based applications, with static ports.

The WebVPN user chooses this mode when downloading the Java Applet by clicking the **Start Application Access** option from the portal page or from the floating toolbar. The VPN 3000 Concentrator can be configured to automatically download the applet on the client PC.

The client PC should have Java Runtime Environment (JRE) 1.4.1 or greater. When the applet is downloaded to start Port Forwarding mode, the **hosts** file (available at C:\WINNT\system32\drivers\etc\hosts) is backed up as **"hosts.webvpn"**. Once the original file is backed up, the applet then adds a Mapping in the **hosts** file for each port forwarding entry configured in the port forwarding list that is assigned to the user.

The sections that follow cover the following topics:

- Configuration steps for port forwarding
- Java applet debugging
- Troubleshooting steps port forwarding
- Configuration steps for MAPI proxy
- Troubleshooting Steps for MAPI proxy
- Configuration steps for E-mail Proxy
- Troubleshooting steps for E-mail Proxy

Configuration Steps for Port Forwarding

Work through the following steps to configure port forwarding for a single channel TCP-based application:

Step 1 Complete the configuration steps explained in the "Configuration Steps for Basic SSL VPN Connection" section.

Step 2 Go to the **Configuration > User Management > Groups** to select your group. Click on the **WebVPN Port Forwarding** tab, then click on **Add** to add the port forwarding mapping for a single-channel TCP application. You need to define the Name and local/remote TCP Port. The local port can be any port between 1024 to 65535. The remote port is the actual Application port. The Remote Server IP address is the application server IP address. Port forwarding can be configured globally on the **Configuration > Tunneling and Security > WebVPN > Port Forwarding** page for all SSL VPN groups.

Step 3 Go to **Configuration > User Management > Groups > Modify** to edit group configuration. Under **WebVPN** tab, **Enable Port Forwarding**."

Java Applet Debugging

Before you delve into the details of troubleshooting steps for Port Forwarding and MAPI Proxy, you must know how to run Java Applet Debug, which is discussed in this section. Work through the following steps to enable the Java applet debugging:

Step 1 Open the **Control Panel**.

Step 2 Select **Java Plug-in**.

Step 3 Click the **Advanced** tab (this might vary based on the JRE version).

Step 4 For Java Runtime Parameters, make entries as shown in Figure 8-9:

```
-Dcisco.webvpndebug=n
```

Here, n = 0, 1, 2, 3 or 4

- 0 = debug messages are disabled
- 1 = errors and configuration messages
- 2 = warnings and status messages
- 3 = stats, data and stack dumps (to debug applet crashes)
- 4 = additional stack traces

A debug level of 2 should be sufficient to obtain useful debugging information for the Java applet.

Troubleshooting Steps for Port Forwarding

If a single-channel TCP application does not work over port forwarding, work through the following steps to correct the problem:

Step 1 Verify that the right version of JRE is installed on the client PC.

Figure 8-9 *Java Run-time Debug Settings*

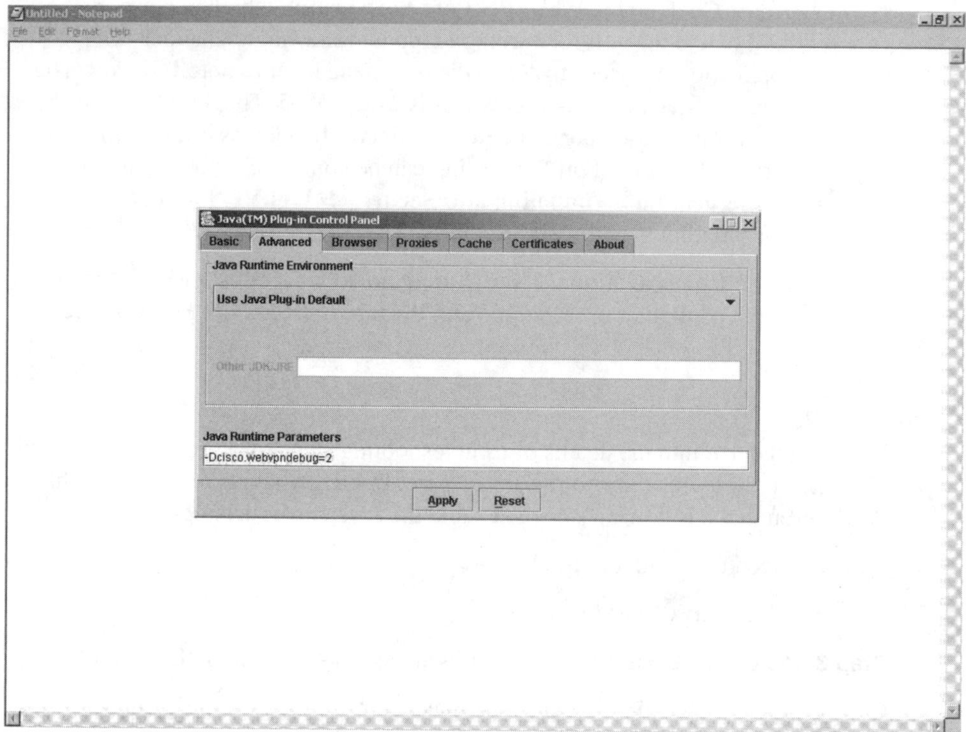

Step 2 From DOS, enter **netstat –a** to ensure that the right ports have been opened on the client PC.

Step 3 Verify that the hosts file has been modified correctly, if the name of the application server is defined. If the hosts file is not modified, ensure that you are not running into any write permission issues. Look at the following files on the c:\WINNT\system32\drivers\etc directory:

```
C:\WINNT\system32\drivers\etc>dir
 Volume in drive C is SYSTEM
 Volume Serial Number is E891-B6C4
 Directory of C:\WINNT\system32\drivers\etc

06/13/2005  10:53p      <DIR>          .
06/13/2005  10:53p      <DIR>          ..
06/13/2005  10:52p                16,000 hosts
02/25/2005  10:43a                740 hosts.webvpn
C:\WINNT\system32\drivers\etc>
```

The **hosts** file should contain the port forwarding mapping. The **hosts.webvpn** file is the original **hosts** file that will be restored when the Port Forwarding application is closed.

As an example, the **hosts** file should contain Port Forwarding address mappings that look like this:

```
127.0.0.2 TAC.cisco.com # added by WebVpnPortForward at Fri Feb 25
  10:43:20 EST 2005
127.0.0.2 HTTS # added by WebVpnPortForward at Fri Feb 25 10:43:20
  EST 2005
```

Improper termination might require you to restore the hosts file manually by renaming hosts.webvpn back to hosts. If the hosts file cannot be modified, the Application Access Applet will be populated with loopback interface addresses and port numbers.

Step 4 Verify that DNS is working correctly from the Concentrator.

Go to **Administration > Ping** and ping to the TCP application using the domain name. If with domain name you are unable to ping, but with IP address, you can ping, then the problem is with the DNS, and you need to check the DNS Server IP to make sure that one is defined and that it is a correct DNS Server.

Step 5 Verify that the right port numbers are defined on the Concentrator local Port that is local to the PC; Remote Port is the translated port through the applet.

Step 6 Get a sniffer trace from the private side of the concentrator, which will give details on communication information between the VPN Concentrator and the end application.

Step 7 Use the procedure discussed in the section entitled "Java Applet Debugging" to debug the applet-related issues.

Configuration Steps for MAPI Proxy

Even though MAPI Proxy uses a Port Forwarding mechanism to communicate with the Exchange server, you do not need to configure any port forwarding mapping on the VPN Concentrator. One very important requirement is that you must have connected your Outlook MAPI client to the Exchange server locally before you configure the VPN Concentrator for the MAPI Proxy. Work through the following steps to configure the MAPI Proxy:

Step 1 Connect your Outlook 2000 MAPI Client to the VPN Exchange server on your Local LAN. This will load all the mapping information to the registry of the client PC.

Step 2 Complete the configuration steps explained in the **"Configuration Steps for Basic SSL VPN Connection"** section.

Step 3 Go to the **Configuration > User Management > Groups > Modify** page to edit the group you have configured. Go to the **WebVPN** tab, and check **Enable Outlook/Exchange Proxy**.

Step 4 You do not need any other configuration on the Outlook2000 MAPI Client.

NOTE Outlook2000 MAPI client support was introduced in Version 4.1.5. Outlook2003 MAPI client is not supported in any version. However, you can use the Full Tunneling feature on Version 4.7, which does not rely on Port Forwarding.

Troubleshooting Steps for MAPI Proxy

Work though the following steps to troubleshoot the MAPI Proxy:

Step 1 Work through the troubleshooting steps as explained in the "Troubleshooting Steps for Single Channel TCP Application" section.

Step 2 You must have already successfully connected to the exchange server through LAN access. The Application Access Applet on the client PC will read Registry Keys populated during the LAN connection to the Exchange Server. Both Global Catalog Server and Exchange server can be detected through the registry entries.

Step 3 The Application Access Applet is populated with the server names determined from the following registry entries:

- HKCU\Software\Microsoft\Windows NT\CurrentVersion\Windows Messaging Subsystem\Profiles\<default profile>
- HKCU\Software\Microsoft\Windows Messaging Subsystem\Profiles\<default profile>
- Exchange server Key: 13dbb0c8aa05101a9bb000aa002fc45a\001e6602
- Global catalog server Key: dca740c8c042101ab4b908002b2fe182\001e6602

If either the Exchange Server or Global Catalog server is not found, MAPI Proxy will fail. Example 8-16 shows JAVA console output (refer to the section entitled "Java Applet Debugging" for details on how to turn on debug for Java Applet) when Exchange server is found but the Global Catalog server is not found.

Example 8-16 *Java Console Debug Output when Exchange Server Is Found But Global Catalog Server Is Not Found*

```
user diretory = C:\Documents and Settings\mygroup\
Looking for DLL: "C:\Documents and Settings\mygroup\WebVpnRegKey4-63-67-72-190.dll"
DLL exits? YES
System dir: C:\WINDOWS\System32
Windows dir: C:\WINDOWS
System dir: C:\WINDOWS\System32
Windows dir: C:\WINDOWS
WebVPN Service: debug level: 3
Default Exchange Profile:  Mygroup Exchange
Looking for exchange server in: Software\Microsoft\Windows NT\CurrentVersion\Windows
  Messaging Subsystem\Profiles\Mygroup Exchange\13dbb0c8aa05101a9bb000aa002fc45a
Exchange server: My-local-exchange Server
Looking for global catalog server in: Software\Microsoft\Windows NT\
  CurrentVersion\Windows Messaging Subsystem\Profiles\Mygroup Exchange\
  dca740c8c042101ab4b908002b2fe182
Registry error: Query value key failed
updateRegistry: orig value:
ncalrpc,ncacn_ip_tcp,ncacn_spx,ncacn_np,netbios,ncacn_vns_spp
updateRegistry: new value:
ncalrpc,ncacn_http,ncacn_ip_tcp,ncacn_spx,ncacn_np,netbios,ncacn_vns_spp
Found hosts file: C:\WINDOWS\System32\drivers\etc\hosts
Exchange = true
```

Step 4 Ensure that you have **Enable Outlook/Exchange Proxy** checked under the group setup.

Step 5 Ensure the DNS is working from the Concentrator.

Configuration Steps for E-mail Proxy

With the E-mail Proxy configuration (this is different than MAPI Proxy as discussed earlier), the Concentrator acts as a relay for secure e-mail protocols. Work through the following steps to configure E-mail Proxy:

Step 1 Go to **Configuration > Interfaces > Ethernet 2** to modify public interface settings. Under the **WebVPN** tab, check **Allow POP3S sessions**, **Allow ICAP4S sessions**, and **Allow SMTPS sessions**.

Step 2 Browse to **Configuration > Tunneling and Security > WebVPN > E-mil Proxy** page to define Authentication, mail server IP, and so on.

Step 3 Refer to the following link for additional details on VPN Concentrator and e-mail client configuration: http://www.cisco.com/univercd/cc/td/doc/product/vpn/vpn3000/4_7/config/enduser2.htm#wp1589079

Troubleshooting Steps for E-mail Proxy

Work through the following steps if the e-mail client is unable to send and receive e-mail:

Step 1 Be sure SMPTS, POP3s, or IMAP4S are open on the public interface.

Step 2 Be sure SSL is enabled for incoming and outgoing mail in the e-mail client.

Step 3 If the client is trying to use an incorrect port number or if SSL is not enabled on the client, there is no notification from the concentrator.

Step 4 Be sure that SSL is working between the VPN Client and the Concentrator.

Step 5 If the SSL connection is failing, you will see **SSL** events on the VPN Concentrator as follows:

```
71 06/02/2005 14:38:04.410 SEV=6 SSL/20 RPT=1 172.16.172.119 Received
  an SSL alert fatal/SSL_ALERT_UNKNOWN_CA.
72 06/02/2005 14:38:04.410 SEV=6 SSL/15 RPT=617 172.16.172.119 Socket
  is closing (context=0x6A0004): received alert. 73 06/02/2005
  14:38:04.410 SEV=5 EMAILPROXY/47 RPT=172.16.172.119
```

Step 6 Verify that the concentrator configuration is for Required Authentication.

Step 7 Verify the username and password that is set on the client with respect to the configuration on the concentrator.

Step 8 If piggyback authentication is configured, verify that the username/password format is correct as follows:

```
vpnusername:mailusername
vpnpassword:mailpassword
```

With Piggyback authentication, be sure the WebVPN session is up; otherwise, piggyback will not work.

It is important to note that Concentrator log messages generally will display what happens in the process but will not display failures in client-server authentication.

Step 9 Test the account locally, and then through the concentrator. Generally if SSL can come up and the account works, the E-mail Proxy should work fine.

Thick Client (SSL VPN Client)

Thick Client, or the SSL VPN Client, provides the full tunneling ability for the Remote Access VPN Connection on VPN Concentrator. Thick client, or the SSL VPN Client software (generally 500K max), is delivered via automatic download (Active X, Java, or EXE) to the user PC. This client is delivered via a web page (the device that the user is connecting to) and never needs to be manually distributed or installed. No reboot is required after the SSL VPN client is downloaded and installed. It provides similar access to traditional IPsec VPN client, but provides better accessibility over firewalls and NAT than the traditional IPsec VPN Client. SSL VPN Client usually requires administrative privileges for initial install, but in the absence of admin privileges, a stub-installer is used. The sections that follow discuss both the configuration and troubleshooting of SSL VPN Client implementation. The discussion is organized as follows:

- Configuration steps for SSL VPN client
- Troubleshooting steps for SSL VPN client

Configuration Steps for SSL VPN Client

Work through the following steps to configure the SSL VPN client configuration on the VPN 3000 Concentrator:

Step 1 Complete the configuration steps explained in the "Configuration Steps for Basic SSL VPN Connection" section.

Step 2 Go to **Configuration > User Management > Groups > Modify** to edit the group that you have configured for Basic SSL VPN connection. Under the **WebVPN** tab, check **Enable Cisco SSL VPN Client** to turn on the SSL VPN client option. The **Require Cisco SSL VPN Client** option is used if you want to allow the users to use only the SSL VPN client. If you do not want to remove the SSL VPN Client at the end of the session, check the **Keep Cisco SSL VPN Client** option.

Step 3 For IP address assignment, DNS/WINS Server address, and so on, follow the configuration steps explained in the section entitled "VPN Concentrator Configuration" under "Remote Access VPN Connection."

Troubleshooting Steps for SSL VPN Client (SVC)

The sections that follow examine the following issues that can arise with SSL VPN Client implementations:

- SSL VPN Client tunnel establishment
- SSL VPN Client installation

SSL VPN Client Establishment Issues

Before the VPN Concentrator can push the SSL VPN client software to the client PC, the tunnel must be established. Follow the configuration and troubleshooting steps in the section entitled "Basic SSL VPN Connection" to correct SSL VPN connection issues. Once the SSL VPN connection is established, the SSL VPN client software is downloaded and installed on the client PC. After that, SSL VPN client builds a full tunnel with the VPN Concentrator. If the SSL VPN Client installs correctly, usually you will not run into any tunnel establishment problems for the SSL VPN client. If you run into problems with the SSL VPN client installation, follow the steps outlined in the next section to correct the problem.

SSL VPN Client Installation Issues

If you can navigate to the WebVPN Portal page, but the client does not install, work through the following steps to fix the problem:

Step 1 Verify the group configuration for SSL VPN client.

Go to **Configuration > User Management > Groups > Modify** to verify that the group your user is in has **Enable Cisco SSL VPN Client** enabled.

Step 2 Check which account is being used and what rights it has.

You can do this by right-clicking on **My Computer** and going to Users and Groups. Select the **Users** by double-clicking on it, and then find out which group it is a member of. With Groups, Administrators, and Power Users, both ActiveX and Java are enabled by default. The Users group has more restrictions applied and only Java is allowed to run with default privileges.

Step 3 Verify the browser settings.

The following Internet Explorer settings are required for SSL VPN Client (SVC) Installation. Use these settings as a guideline for other browsers:

— To access and launch the executable page, enable the following parameters:

Scripting > Active scripting > Enable

Downloads > File download > Enable

— To launch ActiveX, enable the following parameters:

Scripting > Active scripting > Enable

ActiveX controls and plug-ins > Download signed ActiveX controls > Enable

ActiveX controls and plug-ins > Run ActiveX controls and plug-ins > Enable

— To launch Java using the Microsoft Virtual Machine, enable the following parameters:

Scripting > Active scripting > Enable

Scripting > Scripting of Java applets > Enable

ActiveX controls and plug-ins > Download signed ActiveX controls > Enable

Microsoft VM > Java permissions > High, medium or low safety

This information can be found from the following link:

http://www.cisco.com/univercd/cc/td/doc/product/vpn/ciscosec/csd/csd30/csdfaq.htm#wp1056392

Step 4 Add the VPN 3000 Concentrator to the trusted Zone list. This ensures that the security settings are set to low, which by default allows both ActiveX and Java to be run as described in the following Release note: http://www.cisco.com/en/US/partner/products/hw/vpndevc/ps2284/prod_release_note09186a0080405b6c.html#wp535991

You can go to **Configuration > System > Servers > Firewall** to add the VPN 3000 Concentrator to the trusted zone list.

Step 5 Check the version of Sun Java.

If Sun Java is being used, then ensure that there is a "Java Plug-In" option under the control panel and select this to check that your browser of choice is selected under the Browser Tab.

Step 6 Clear the browser cache and cookies.

Clear the browser cache and cookies, and be sure to restart the browser.

Step 7 Try a different browser vendor.

If one browser vendor does not work, try a different browser vendor.

Step 8 Try a different website.

If one site does not work, try to access a different website that you know uses ActiveX or JAVA.

Step 9 Verify the proxy settings.

SSL VPN Client can read and work only with Microsoft Internet Explorer proxy settings as of the writing of this book.

Step 10 Analyze the client PC environment.

If you still have issues, the application and system event logs on the client PC might not be indicating failures. In this case, use the **WINMSD.exe** file to generate a full dump of the client PC, and look at the **SetupApi.log** file to look at specific install issues that may exist.

Common Problems and Resolutions

This section discusses some of the common problems and resolution with VPN 3000 series Concentrator.

1 Is Outlook Web Access (OWA) 2003 or Exchange 2003 supported on SSL VPN?

   Answer: Support for Outlook Web Access (OWA) 2003 and Exchange 2003 Server are as follows:

   — OWA 2003 is supported in Version 4.1.7.

   — Outlook thick client connecting to an Exchange 2003 server using Exchange (MAPI) is not supported until full tunneling (Version 4.7).

   — Outlook thick client e-mail is supported using the Port Forwarding client as long as the e-mail client is not Outlook 2003. Outlook 2003 will be supported with WebVPN Version 4.7 and the full tunneling feature.

   — The use of OWA2003 with S/MIME has not been specifically tested with Version 4.7; however, this is not an issue with the full tunneling support in Version 4.7.

2 My VPN Client with IPSEC over TCP is not working on Windows XP SP2. What should I do?

   Answer: If your IPSEC over TCP VPN is not working on Windows XP running SP2, then you need to add a rule in the Microsoft firewall to allow UDP/62515. You can do this either through the Microsoft Firewall GUI by adding an Exception rule or you can do it by entering the following command from a DOS prompt:

```
netsh fi add port UDP 62515 "Cisco VPN Service" enable all
```

   To verify if the built-in firewall that comes with XP SP2 is causing the VPN client connection problem for IPsec over TCP, disable the Windows Firewall.

   If the VPN connection comes up successfully, refer to the following link:

   http://support.microsoft.com/?id=884020%3Ehttp://support.microsoft.com/?id=884020

   Programs that connect to IP addresses that are in the loopback address range may not work as you expect in Windows XP Service Pack 2. This problem occurs if the program connects to a loopback address other than 127.0.0.1. Windows XP Service Pack 2 (SP2) prevents connections to all IP addresses that are in the loopback address range except for 127.0.0.1.

3 What are the functions of UDP ports 625xx on VPN Client PC?

   Answer: The ports are used for the VPN Client communication between the actual shim/Deterministic NDIS Extender (DNE) and the TCP/IP stack of the PC. For example, port 62515 is used by the VPN Client for sending information to the VPN Client log.

4 How can I collect full memory dumps on Windows Operating Systems?

Answer: Work through the following steps to collect the full memory dump on Windows XP (other Windows Operating Systems can use a similar procedure):

Step 1 Go to the **Start > Settings > Control Panel > System > Advanced** Tab.

Step 2 Then click the **Settings** button under the **Startup and Recovery** section.

Step 3 Under **Write Debugging Information**, select **Complete memory dump**.

5 What should I do if I receive the message "VPN Sub-System Not Available" after upgrading VPN Client on some XP Machines?

Answer: This error message indicates that some service is causing the VPN client not to respond in a timely fashion to the GUI. To work around this problem, work through the following steps:

Step 1 Stop and start the **cvpnd** service. This can be done through the services control panel, or through command prompt, by typing the following two commands:

```
net stop cvpnd
net start cvpnd
```

Step 2 If the installation never worked before, reinstall the VPN Client software, which requires a reboot. This should resolve the problem.

6 Is there a limit to the number of Cisco Secure Desktop (CSD) locations that can be defined?

Answer: No, there is no limit.

7 Can the files that are created within the CSD vault be saved onto the guest PC, external media, or shared network folders?

Answer: Following is a list of different media that can or cannot be used to save the files created in CSD vault:

- **Guest PC**—Files that are created within the CSD vault cannot be saved to the Guest PC. One caution to this is that certain e-mail applications such as Outlook, Outlook Express, Eudora, and Lotus Notes operate as they would on the client PC. These applications are not generally found in public domain PCs.
- **External media such as USB fob, floppies, and so on**—Files created within CSD vault can be saved onto an external media such as USB fob, floppy, and so on. However, the data is encrypted and will be removed once the vault is uninstalled, and will not be visible if the key is removed.
- **Shared network folders**—Files created within CSD vault can be saved into the shared network folders that exist as part of the Network Neighborhood on the client PC. Then they will also appear on the Secure Desktop Network Neighborhood.

8 When a file is created or amended within the Secure Desktop space, can it be saved to a Network Neighborhood if a network connection via SSL or IPSEC exists?

Answer: Yes.

9 When is the keystroke logger initiated?

Answer: It is initiated at the creation of the secure desktop space. Note that this requires that the user has admin privileges to operate.

10 Does the keystroke logger produce events in the VPN 3000 Concentrator logs?

Answer: No.

11 When specifying a valid antivirus package, how does the concentrator verify the date? Does it just verify that a valid antivirus product is installed regardless of its being up-to-date?

Answer: With Cisco Secure Desktop (SSL VPN) in Version 4.7, the verification is performed by checking when it was last updated (in terms of days). For IPsec and NAC (Version 4.7), this is done using Cisco Trust Agent and all of the regularly available functionality with NAC.

12 Even if ActiveX and Java are disabled, can I execute the CSD installation via browser?

Answer: Yes, if both Active X and Java are not detected on the client PC, then a full .exe package (instful.exe) will be downloaded onto the PC to be executed by the user for installation of the CSD package.

13 Is there any restriction of Sun JVM for Cisco Secure Desktop and SSL VPN Client?

Answer: No there are no restrictions for Cisco Secure Desktop or the SSL VPN Client. However, it is advisable to use a Sun JVM of greater than 1.5.x.

14 Does the Cisco Security Agent (CSA) Version 4.5 inter-operate with CSD and SVC?

Answer: Yes it does. CSA Version 4.5 now supports and is fully compatible with both CSD and SVC. Initial implementations of CSA earlier than Version 4.5 build 550 required that CSA services were stopped using the **`net stop csagent`** command or removed completely (if earlier than Version 4.5). These issues have now been resolved in the Version 4.5 release.

15 What should I do if I get CSD fails with "error initializing Main application window" and "HTTP 404 Not Found (/CACHE/sdesktop/install/css/Main.css)" Errors?

Answer: Be sure that the CPU does not spike to 100 percent. If so, close down all other foreground and background applications that are running. Also, check to ensure that the Kernel Driver **"twingostoragedriver"** is present on the PC. To perform this task, right-click on **My Computer**, and select **Manage**, which will bring up the **Computer Management** window. In the **Computer Management** window, go to **Computer Management (Local) > System Tools > System Information > Software**

Environment > Drivers. If the driver is not present, re-install CSD while all other applications are closed down to ensure that there are sufficient resources to allocate to this task.

16 If ActiveX and Java are disabled, how can I execute SVC installation via browser?

Answer: If both Active X and Java fail to be detected on the client PC, the user will simply be directed to the WebVPN portal page only if the **"Require Cisco SSL VPN Client"** option under the WebVPN parameters for the group of interest is not checked. If this option is checked, the redirect to the WebVPN portal page will not occur. There is no option to download an install package for the SSL VPN Client. Remember, however, that there is an **sslclient-win-1.0.0.x.zip** file that contains a pre-install package to install the SVC Agent service (using Admin privileges) onto a client PC. This install procedure is detailed in the release notes. Once installed, this allows for the full SSL VPN Client package to be downloaded and installed while in non-admin mode using the ActiveX/Java download mechanism which needs to be enabled on the client PC.

17 What privileges are required to be present within Internet Explorer (IE) to allow for ActiveX to function for SSL VPN client installation?

Answer: If you have a **"Guest"** account created on a client PC, it is important to determine which group that **"Guest"** account is associated with. This can be achieved by right-clicking on **"My Computer"** and selecting **Manage > Local users and Groups > Users > Select a user**. Double-click and find out what group that user is a member of. The list includes Administrators, Power Users, and Users. The Users group does not allow ActiveX to function, whereas the others do.

18 Is there anything that can be done to check the platform before the VPN is established or even before authentication for the SSL VPN tunnel?

Answer: Yes, use Cisco Secure Desktop with the registry, file/hash, or digital certificate to make this determination.

19 Does Installation of the SVC work with Microsoft Java Virtual Machine (MS JVM)?

Answer: Yes, but remember that Microsoft will not support this past December 31, 2007, and in fact this can no longer be downloaded from the Microsoft website. Refer to the following link for details: http://www.microsoft.com/mscorp/java/

20 Which Operating Systems SVC Client is supported?

Answer: Only Windows 2000 and XP are supported because only those Windows operating systems permit the installation of a network driver without rebooting.

21 Is RADIUS with Expiry and MS IAS Supported with the SSL VPN Client?

Answer: No. RADIUS with expiry is not supported for SSL VPN.

22 Are any FAQs maintained on CCO for VPN 3000 and Secure Desktop?

Answer: Yes, refer to the following locations:

http://www.cisco.com/warp/customer/471/vpn_3000_faq.shtml

http://www.cisco.com/univercd/cc/td/doc/product/vpn/ciscosec/csd/csd30/csdfaq.htm

Best Practices

This section explores the features that you can use on the VPN 3000 series concentrator to avoid experiencing a single point of failure for both LAN-to-LAN and Remote Access Client tunnels. In today's network, resiliency with the VPN connection is very crucial. The VPN 3000 Concentrator includes three features that ensure high availability. The following sections delve into the details of these three features.

- Redundancy using VRRP
- Redundancy and load sharing using clustering
- Redundancy using IPsec backup servers

Redundancy Using VRRP

As the name implies, the Virtual Router Redundancy Protocol (VRRP) provides redundancy for VPN connection to the Concentrator. When you have two or more Concentrators sitting in parallel in your network, you can configure VRRP so that a user can access to the VPN even if one VPN Concentrator is out of service because of a system crash, power failure, hardware failure, physical interface failure, or system shutdown or reboot. In VRRP implementation, Redundant VPN Concentrators are identified by group, a single Master is chosen for the group, and one or more VPN concentrators can be backups of the group's Master. The Master communicates its state to the backup devices, and if the Master fails to communicate its status, VRRP tries each backup in order of precedence. Then the responding backup assumes the role of Master.

In the case of IPsec LAN-to-LAN connections, switchover is fully automatic. This means that when the tunnel is dropped, a new tunnel is re-established automatically and this process is transparent to the LAN-to-LAN users. But, for Remote Access VPN clients, when users are disconnected from the failing system, users are notified of the disruption and can reconnect without changing any connection parameters. Typically switchover occurs within 3 to 10 seconds.

Following are some important points to remember when implementing VRRP in your VPN 3000 series Concentrators deployment:

- When the Master is restored, there is no auto switchover to back the Concentrator. This is done manually.
- The failover is not stateful, so the tunnel must be rebuilt, and the traffic must be retransmitted.

- VRRP is not a load-sharing mechanism; it's a standby mechanism and cannot be used with clustering.
- If either the public or private interfaces of the Master system go down, the other interfaces shut down automatically and the backup VPN device takes over. The backup VPN device takes over only when it stops receiving VRRP messages on *both* the public and private interfaces.
- Some failures might not be detected by VRRP. For example, if a Cisco Catalyst switch is between the Master and backup devices that connect to each other, and if you shut down the switch port, this does not bring down the link layer. Therefore, the VPN concentrator does not detect the interface as DOWN (this can be verified in **Configuration > Interfaces** screen). The VPN Concentrator therefore continues sending messages to the backup device. In this case, because the backup device is still receiving VRRP messages on at least one interface, it does not take over as the Master.
- When a Cisco switch is configured that is connected to primary and secondary concentrators, port fast must be turned on to eliminate the inherent delays with Spanning Tree Protocol (STP) that in turn cause a delay in recognizing that a backup VPN Concentrator has taken over as the Master. With port fast, this delay can be reduced to 15 seconds. For details on how to configure port fast, refer to the following link: http://www.cisco.com/warp/public/473/12.html

The following procedure shows how to configure VRRP on the Master and backup systems:

Step 1 Go to **Configuration > System > IP Routing > Redundancy**.

Step 2 Check **Enable VRRP** check box to turn VRRP.

Step 3 Leave the **Group ID** at its default, which is 1. You can specify anything between 1 and 255.

Step 4 Enter a Group Password (maximum of 8 characters) in the **Group Password** field.

Step 5 From the drop-down list of **Role**, select **Master** or **Backups** based on which Concentrator you are configuring.

Step 6 The **Advertisement Interval** is 1 second by default. You can specify up to 255 seconds.

Step 7 Under **Group Shared Addresses**, define both the Private and Public interface IP address. The Public interface IP address will be used by the VPN Client or LAN-to-LAN peer to build up the tunnel. The Private Shared address will be used by the local LAN host of this VPN Concentrator. Figure 8-10 shows a configuration example of turning on VRRF on the Master Concentrator with private shared IP address of 10.1.1.1 and public interface shared IP address of 20.1.1.1.

Step 8 Click **Apply** and save the configuration.

Step 9 Follow steps 1 through 8 for all the concentrators that are participating in the VRRP.

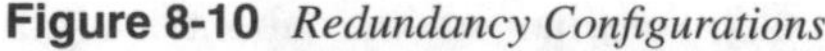

Figure 8-10 *Redundancy Configurations*

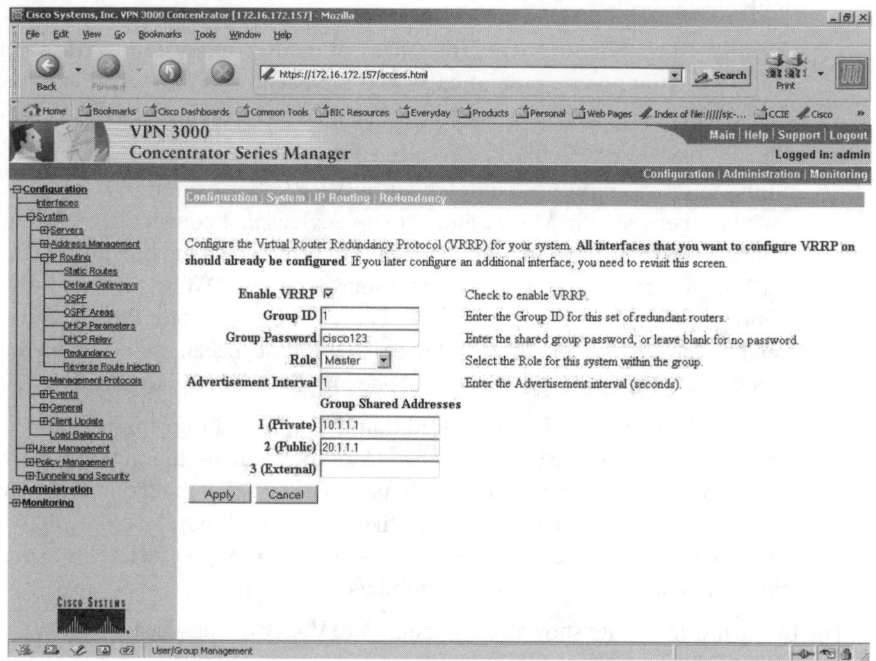

As mentioned before, VRRP is used for high availability not for load sharing. For redundancy and load sharing for VPN Client, you must use clustering, which is discussed next. It is important to note that you must not configure VRRP with Clustering. If both Load Sharing and Redundancy are required for Remote Access VPN, configure Clustering only.

Redundancy and Load Sharing Using Clustering

Clustering provides a robust redundancy mechanism by way of load sharing for a Remote Access VPN Client. If you have two or more VPN concentrators sharing the same private network, you should consider configuring clustering, which will give you both load sharing and backup features. When you have all the VPN concentrators up and load sharing is configured, load balancing directs session traffic to the least loaded device. In this way, load balancing distributes the load among all devices. It makes efficient use of system resources and provides increased performance and high availability.

Logically two or more concentrators are on the same LAN and public networks are grouped together into a virtual cluster to implement load sharing. All the concentrators in the virtual cluster carry session loads; however, one VPN concentrator in the virtual cluster acts as the *virtual cluster Master that* directs incoming calls to the other concentrators, called *secondary devices.* The virtual cluster Master monitors all devices in the cluster, tracks how busy each is, and distributes the session load accordingly.

The role of virtual cluster Master is not tied to a physical device; it can shift among devices. Selection of a virtual cluster Master is interesting. If the devices in the virtual cluster are powered up at different times, the first device powered up assumes the role of the virtual cluster Master, and the remainder become secondary devices. If all the devices in the virtual cluster are powered up at the same time, the highest-priority device becomes the virtual cluster Master. However, in these circumstances, if more than one device has the same highest priority, the one with the lowest IP address becomes the virtual cluster Master. When the Master fails, one of the secondary devices becomes Master based on priority, and if the devices are at the same priority level, then the decision will be based on the lowest IP address.

As priority plays an important role, it is very important that you assign the proper priority to devices. If your network has different models of VPN Concentrators, the rule of thumb is to choose the device with the greatest load capacity to be the virtual cluster Master. Therefore, assign the highest priority. Table 8-7 shows recommended priorities that are based on different models of hardware capacity. However, if you have the same models of VPN 3000 concentrators, use configure priority 10 for all the devices to shorten the decision-making time to select the virtual cluster Master.

Table 8-7 *Priority Suggestions for VPN Concentrators*

VPN Concentrator Model	Priority Default
3005	1
3015	3
3030	5
3060	7
3080	9

The virtual cluster appears to outside clients as a single *virtual cluster IP address*. This IP address is not tied to a specific physical device. It belongs to the current virtual cluster Master; hence, it is virtual. A VPN client attempting to establish a connection connects first to this virtual cluster IP address. The virtual cluster Master then sends back to the client the public IP address of the least-loaded available host in the cluster. In a second transaction (transparent to the user), the client connects directly to that host. In this way, the virtual cluster Master directs traffic evenly and efficiently across resources.

If a machine in the cluster fails, the terminated sessions can immediately reconnect to the virtual cluster IP address. The virtual cluster Master then directs these connections to another active device in the cluster. Should the virtual cluster Master itself fail, a secondary device in the cluster immediately and automatically takes over as the new virtual session Master. Even if several devices in the cluster fail, users can continue to connect to the cluster as long as any one device in the cluster is up and available.

NOTE Load balancing works only for remote access VPNs with Cisco VPN Client Release 3.0 and later, or Cisco VPN 3002 Hardware Client Release 3.5 and later. All other clients, including LAN-to-LAN connections, can connect to the VPN concentrator on which load balancing is enabled, but they cannot participate in load balancing. Clustering can only be used as an alternative to VRRP. It is not possible to use both options simultaneously.

Work through the following procedure to configure clustering:

Step 1 Identify the filters that you have applied on the interfaces by browsing to **Configuration > Interfaces** window.

Step 2 Open the **Configuration > Policy Management > Traffic Management > Filters** window.

Step 3 Select the filter you have applied to the **Private interface** from **Filter list**.

Step 4 Click on **Assign Rules to Filter** to open the **Configuration > Policy Management > Traffic Management > Assign Rules to Filter** window.

Step 5 Make sure that **VCA In (forward/in)** and **VCA Out (forward/out)** are in the **Current Rules in Filter** list. If they are not in this list, add them and then click **Done**.

Step 6 Follow steps 1 through 4 for the Public interface as well. Click the **Save Needed** icon to save your edits.

Step 7 Open the **Configuration > System > Load Balancing** window to enable and configure load balancing as shown in Figure 8-11.

Step 8 Enter an IP address in the **VPN Virtual Cluster IP Address** box from the Public interface IP address network. This is the address VPN Client uses to connect.

Step 9 In the **VPN Virtual Cluster UDP Port**, keep the default port unless another application is using this port in your network.

Step 10 Check the **Encryption** check box to enable encryption for the communication among the clustering devices.

Step 11 If you have **Encryption** checked, specify an **IPsec Shared Secret** that is common among the Concentrators in the virtual cluster group.

Step 12 Check **WebVPN Redirect via DNS** if you want to enable DNS redirection instead of IP Address redirection for WebVPN sessions.

Step 13 Under **Device Configuration**, check the **Load Balancing Enable** check box to include this VPN Concentrator in the virtual cluster.

Step 14 For **Priority**, enter a value between 1–10 (refer to Table 8-7 to make this decision).

Step 15 In the **NAT Assigned IP Address** text box, enter the translated (public) IP address if this device is behind a NAT device and the IP of this box is translated by the NAT devices. Otherwise, leave it at the default, which is 0.0.0.0.

Step 16 Click **Apply** and finally **Save** to complete the configuration of one of the concentrator participants of the virtual cluster.

Figure 8-11 *Sample Configuration of cluster on a Concentrator*

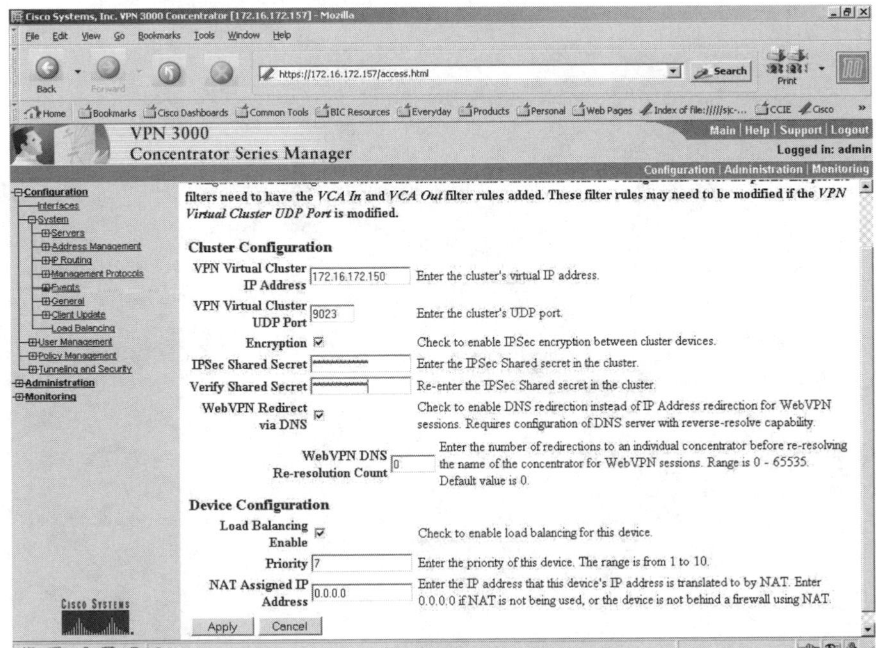

Follow steps 1 through 16 to configure the remainder of the concentrators participating in clustering.

Redundancy Using IPsec Backup Servers

If you do not want to configure VRRP, or a cluster for Remote Access VPN redundancy, you can accomplish this by configuring the IPsec Backup Servers. You can configure a backup server in either of the two ways:

- **Manually on the VPN Client**—You can add multiple host names or IP addresses of VPN Concentrators or clusters per connection on Remote Access VPN Client. To do that, click on **Backup Servers** tab and then **Add**, which will allow you to define the VPN Concentrator or the cluster's name or IP address. Be sure to check **Enable Backup Servers**. On the VPN Concentrator, be sure that you configure **User Client Configured List** for **IPsec Backup Servers** under **Client Config** tab of group configuration under **Configuration | User Management | Groups | Modify**.
- **Automatically Push from the VPN Concentrator**—You can configure group profiles on VPN Concentrator so that VPN Concentrator will push the IPsec Backup Servers list to the VPN Client after the successful connection establishment. To perform this task, go to **Configuration > User Management > Groups > Modify** to edit the group. Then go under **Client Config** tab, and select **Use List Below** for the **IPsec Backup Servers**. Be sure to define the list of the Backup Concentrators in the box provided.

Part IV

Troubleshooting Network Access Control

Chapter 9 Troubleshooting AAA on IOS Routers

Chapter 10 Troubleshooting AAA on PIX Firewalls and FWSM

Chapter 11 Troubleshooting AAA on the Switches

Chapter 12 Troubleshooting AAA on VPN 3000 Series Concentrator

Chapter 13 Troubleshooting Cisco Secure ACS on Windows

CHAPTER 9

Troubleshooting AAA on IOS Routers

AAA, which stands for Authentication, Authorization, and Accounting, is an integral part of security functionality on the Cisco IOS Router. As the name implies, authentication verifies who the users are, authorization allows or denies what users can do after authentication, and accounting logs user activity. Because this chapter launches the discussion of Network Access Control, a detailed explanation of AAA architecture is included, as is the protocol involved with it. This discussion forms the foundation knowledge required for understanding this chapter and the following AAA chapters on Switch, Private Internet Exchange (PIX) Firewall, and the Virtual Private Network (VPN) Concentrator. AAA protocol implements the client-server model. This chapter examines the client side of the equation on the router. The chapter concludes with the best practices.

Overview of Authentication, Authorization, and Accounting (AAA)

AAA is an architectural framework, which provides three independent security functions to many Cisco devices such as Cisco routers, PIX firewalls, and switches:

- **Authentication**—Authentication provides a method to identify users before giving access to the requested services or network resources. When the user makes a connection request to the device or through the device, the user is challenged for the username and password, and either is then authenticated or denied.
- **Authorization**—Authorization controls access to network resources after the user is authenticated. Different users have different privileges, and different resources or information have different levels of confidentiality. Therefore, assigning resources based on the resource security and user privilege is an important aspect of access control. Authorization enables system administrators to accomplish this task. AAA authorization works by assembling a set of attributes that describe what the user is authorized to perform. Remote security servers, such as Remote Authentication Dial-In User Service (RADIUS) and Terminal Access Controller Access Control System (TACACS+), authorize users for specific rights by associating attribute-value (AV) pairs, which define those rights, with the appropriate user. Authorization can also be used to assign static IP addresses or to download the access control list (ACL), and so on. Note that authorization without authentication is meaningless.

- **Accounting**—Provides the method for collecting and sending security server information used for billing, auditing, and reporting. Examples of information collected by accounting include user identities, start and stop times, executed commands (such as Point-to-Point Protocol [PPP]), number of packets, and number of bytes. Accounting enables tracking of the services users are accessing and of the amount of network resources they are consuming.

AAA Architecture

There are three main components of the AAA framework, as shown in Figure 9-1.

Figure 9-1 *Basic AAA Architecture*

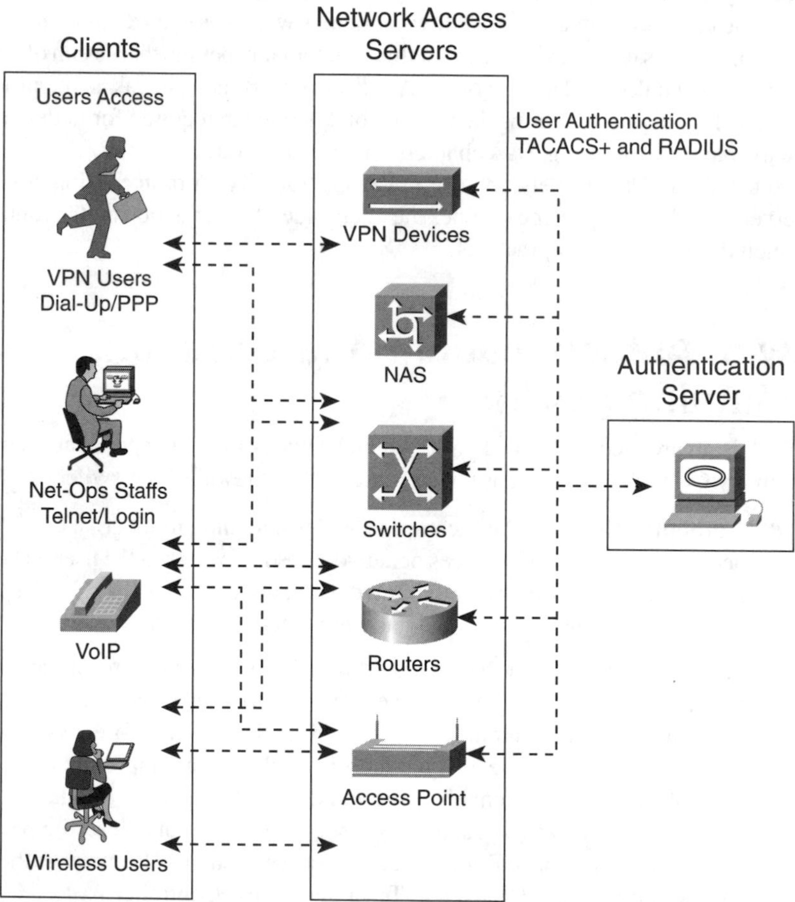

- **Client**—This is the user client PC or laptop from which users try to access resources.
- **Network Access Server (NAS) or AAA Client**—The client makes a connection to NAS either to configure it (for device management) or to access network resources through it (for example, Virtual Private Network setup for accessing the network

resources of a local-area network [LAN] segment behind the NAS). The communication between the client and the NAS depends on the application. For instance, if the intention is to manage the NAS, then options available are Telnet, Secure Shell (SSH), and console. Examples of NAS or AAA clients include routers, switches, virtual private network (VPN) concentrators, and PIX firewalls.

- **Authentication Server**—The actual user profile resides at the authentication server when a built-in local user database is used. The Authentication Server can be integrated with various external user databases such as Microsoft Active Directory, Novell NDS (Netscape Directory Server), and so on. If the authentication server is integrated, the user profiles reside on the external user databases. When the client tries to access the network resources to log in to the NAS, NAS forwards that request to the Authentication Server. The NAS itself can act as the Authentication Server, but it is not very scalable. Examples of authentication servers include Cisco Secure Access Control Server (CSACS) on Windows (see Chapter 13, "Troubleshooting Cisco Secure ACS on Windows"), Cisco Secure Unix, and Cisco Access Registrar. The communication between the NAS and the AAA server requires special protocols, which leads to the next topic in the chapter.

AAA Communication Protocols

Several protocols are used in AAA communications between the NAS and Authentication Server including TACACS+, RADIUS, Kerberos, TACACS, and XTACACS. As TACACS+ and RADIUS are highly used protocols for AAA, we will discuss only these two protocols in the following section in greater details.

TACACS+

TACACS+ protocol was developed by Cisco Systems, Inc. as an extension of the original TACACS/XTACACS protocol specification (RFC 1492). TACACS+ comprises three components:

- Protocol with a frame format that uses TCP/49
- Authentication server
- AAA Client (NAS)

There are several reasons why Transmission Control Protocol (TCP) is used for TACACS+ protocols. Here are some of them, as per TACACS+ specifications:

- TCP offers a connection-oriented transport, whereas User Datagram Protocol (UDP) offers best effort delivery.
- TCP provides a separate acknowledgment that a request has been received.
- TCP provides an immediate indication of an unavailable server.
- By using TCP keepalives, you can detect server crashes out-of-band with actual requests.
- TCP is more scalable than UDP.

One of the unique and most important features of TACACS+ protocol is that it encrypts the entire packet communicated between the NAS and the AAA server. Hence, TACACS+ is a protocol of choice for device management. On the other hand, RADIUS encrypts only the password, but RADIUS protocol is the RFC standard. In addition, UDP has become highly reliable in today's network because of the upper-layer retries. Hence, RADIUS is the protocol of choice for Network Access Control-related implementations such as X-Auth for a VPN connection and PPP authentication for dial-in users.

TACACS+ Operation for Authentication

TACACS+ uses three different packet exchanges between the NAS and Authentication server for completing authentication.

- **START**—First packet sent by NAS to TACACS+ service
- **REPLY**—Sent by TACACS+ service to NAS
- **CONTINUE**—Sent by NAS to carry follow-up information

The following steps take place between the user, NAS, and the Authentication server as shown in Figure 9-2.

Figure 9-2 *TACACS+ AAA Packet Flows*

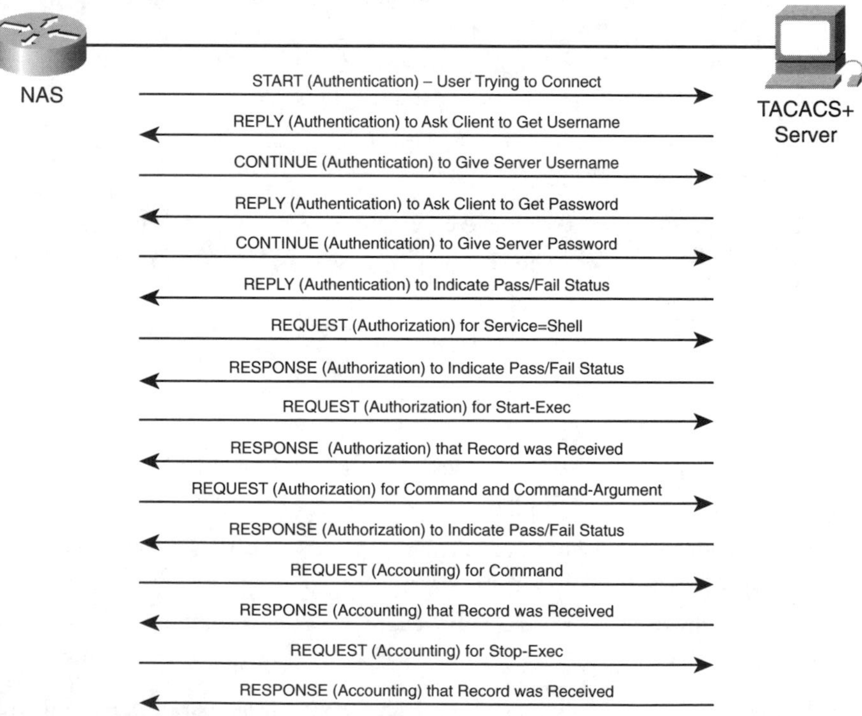

Step 1 When the connection is initiated by the client to the NAS, NAS initiates the START packet to the TACACS+ service to obtain a username prompt.

Step 2 TACACS+ service sends a REPLY packet in return to NAS asking for a username, which is then displayed to the user.

Step 3 The user enters a username, and the network access server sends a CONTINUE packet to TACACS+ service with the user name information that it just received from the client.

Step 4 TACACS+ service sends a second REPLY asking for a user password, which is then forwarded by the NAS to the user.

Step 5 The user enters a password, and the password is then sent to the TACACS+ service with a CONTINUE packet.

Step 6 TACACS+ service makes the decision whether to allow or deny the request and sends one of the responses shown in Table 9-1 in REPLY packet.

NOTE START and CONTINUE packets are always sent by the NAS, and REPLY is the only packet sent by the TACACS+ service to exchange the authentication information and the decision about users' authentication.

Table 9-1 *The Response and Meaning of the Response for Authentication from the TACACS+ Server*

Response	Description
ACCEPT	The user is authenticated and service may begin at this stage. If, however, NAS is configured to require authorization, authorization starts at this time.
REJECT	The user has failed to authenticate, either because of a wrong username or password.
ERROR	An error occurred some time during authentication phase. Error condition may occur due to shared secret key mismatch, no existent AAA client on the TACACS+ daemon, or because of some other protocol violation. If an ERROR response is received, the network access server typically tries an alternative method for authentication if configured.

TACACS+ Operation for Authorization

If configured, authorization starts immediately after the authentication succeeds. Because TACACS+ supports the independent AAA architecture, Authentication and Authorization responses are handled in separate packets. This makes TACACS+ more desirable than RADIUS for device management when command authorization is required. This is because RADIUS handles both Authentication and Authorization replies in the same packet. Without successful user authentication, authorization will not be triggered. TACACS+ completes authorization with the following two packets as shown in Figure 9-2:

- REQUEST packet—Always sent by NAS
- RESPONSE packet—Always sent by the TACACS+ service

The following sequence of events takes place for authorization:

1. Following authentication, the authorization process starts with NAS sending an authorization REQUEST packet to the TACACS+ server. This packet may contain information about the privileges (0-15) or the service (EXEC or PPP) needed for the client to access the network resources or the device.
2. The TACACS+ server then responds with one of the messages shown in Table 9-2.

Table 9-2 *The Response and Meaning of the Response for Authorization from the TACACS+ Server*

Response	Description
FAIL	Services or Privileges requested by the NAS for the client are not authorized.
PASS_ADD	This is a successful authorization message, which tells the NAS to authorize the arguments it sent via REQUEST packet and also authorize additional arguments that the TACACS+ Server added to the RESPONSE packet (in addition to what's requested).
PASS_REPL	This is a successful authorization message just like PASS_ADD. Here, however, the TACACS+ server is asking the NAS to replace the arguments that it sent with the REQUEST packet with the argument that the Server authorizes in the RESPONSE packet.
ERROR	Error condition during authorization phase. For details refer to Table 9-1.
FOLLOW	With this message, the TACACS+ server recommends to NAS that it contact another TACACS+ server. It is up to NAS, however, to entertain the suggestion. The suggestion for the alternate TACACS+ server comes in the REPLY packet.

TACACS+ Operation for Accounting

TACACS+ accounting works very much like authorization in TACACS+ protocol. Just as with authorization, TACACS+ uses REQUEST and RESPONSE packets to exchange the information that needs to be logged for billing and auditing. Accounting in TACACS+ starts with NAS sending a REQUEST packet that contains one of the accounting records shown in Table 9-3.

Table 9-3 *Accounting Records Go into the REQUEST Packet for Accounting*

Accounting Records	Description
START Record	This indicates to the TACACS+ server that the service is about to begin.
STOP Record	This indicates to the TACACS+ server that the service is about to stop.
CONTINUE Record	This provides the TACACS+ server updated information. This is sent while the service is in progress. A record being both Start and Continue is an indication that the Update record is a duplicate of the original Start record.

Upon receiving the REQUEST packet, the TACACS+ server sends a REPLY packet to the NAS with one of the status messages shown in Table 9-4.

Table 9-4 *Status in the REPLY Packet from TACACS+ Server to NAS*

Status	Description
SUCCESS	TACACS+ has received the ACCOUNTING packet successfully.
ERROR	AAA failed to write the information to the database.
FOLLOW	TACACS+ Server suggests that the NAS send the accounting record to another TACACS+ server. Details on the alternate server information are in the REPLY packet; however, it is up to NAS to adhere to the request.

RADIUS

RADIUS was developed by Livingston Enterprises, Inc. RADIUS Authentication and Authorization is defined by RFC 2865, and RADIUS accounting is defined by RFC 2866. The maximum packet length is 4096 bytes, and each value can have a maximum length of 253 bytes. As with TACACS+, RADIUS comprises three components:

- Protocol with a frame format that uses UDP/1812 (authentication and authorization) and UDP/1813 (for accounting). UDP/1645 is also used for authentication and authorization, and UDP/1646 for accounting.
- Authentication Server
- AAA Client (NAS)

Though TCP is a reliable protocol and works very well for TACACS+, UDP is effective and very useful for RADIUS protocol. The following are some of the advantages of using UDP for RADIUS protocol:

- If the request to a primary authentication server fails, a secondary server must be queried.
- The timing requirements of this particular protocol are significantly different than TCP provides.

- The stateless nature of this protocol simplifies the use of UDP.
- UDP simplifies the server implementation.

The following are some of the weaknesses of the RADIUS protocol:

- Unlike TACACS+, RADIUS does not encrypt the whole body with an MD5 hashing algorithm. It encrypts only the end user password in the RADIUS packet.
- RADIUS does not support the independent AAA architecture as Authentication and Authorization responses are included in a single packet. This makes it less than desirable for device management when command authorization is required.

RADIUS Operation for Authentication and Authorization

RADIUS uses four packets to complete authentication and authorization between the NAS and the AAA Server. When the user wants to connect to the network using NAS, NAS collects and forwards the following information in an ACCESS-REQUEST packet as shown in Figures 9-3 through 9-5:

- Username
- User password in encrypted format
- NAS IP address and the port
- Type of service user wants

NOTE Note that this is different than TACACS+, because in the case of TACACS+ this username and password challenge comes from the AAA server. In RADIUS, this information is collected by the NAS, before making the Access-Request to the AAA Server.

Figure 9-3 *RADIUS Authentication and Authorization Packet Flows*

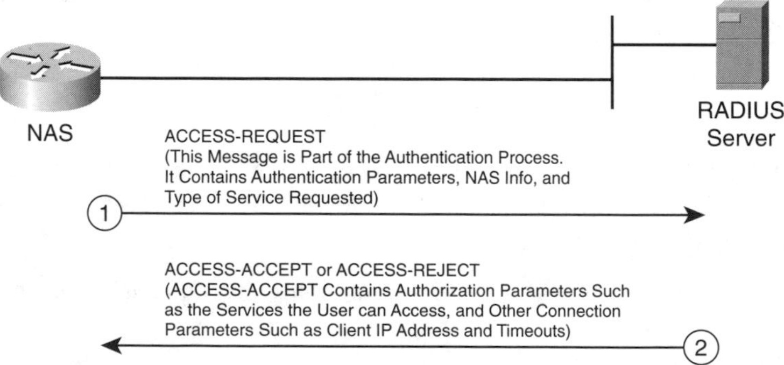

Figure 9-4 *RADIUS Authentication and Authorization Packet Flows (Continued)*

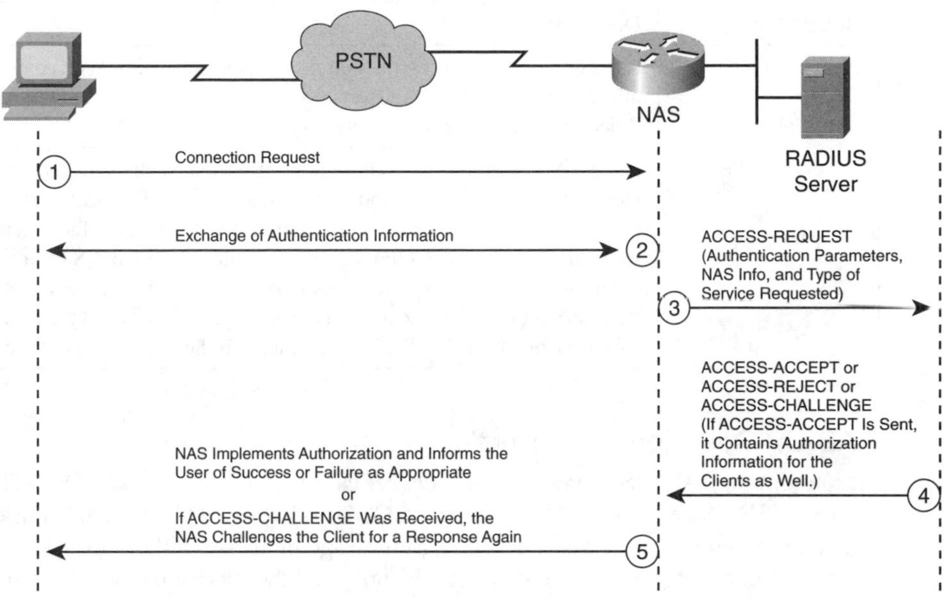

Figure 9-5 *RADIUS Authentication and Authorization Packet Flows (Continued)*

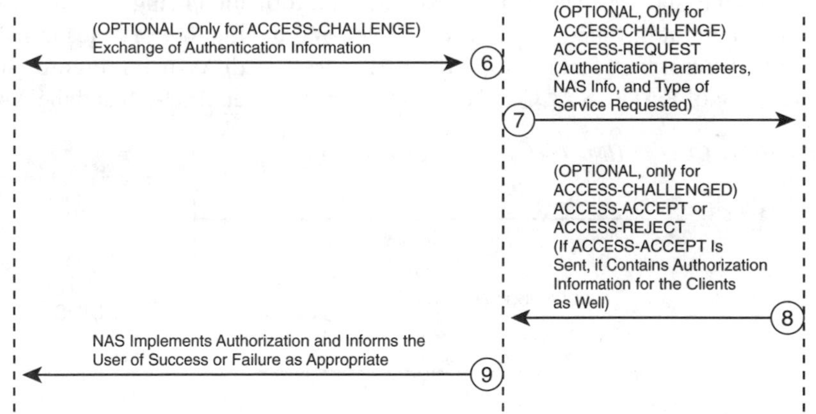

The RADIUS Server responds to NAS with one of the messages shown in Table 9-5.

Table 9-5 *AAA Server Responses from the AAA Server*

Response	Description
Access-Accept	If the user is successfully authenticated by the AAA server, this message is sent to the NAS, which also contains Attribute Value (AV) pairs for the user to be applied on the NAS, such as downloadable access control list (ACL), static IP address, DNS server IP, and Windows Internet Name Service (WINS) Server IP.

continues

Table 9-5 *AAA Server Responses from the AAA Server (Continued)*

Response	Description
Access-Reject	If the user authentication fails on the AAA server, the AAA Server sends this message to NAS. AAA server may send text messages in the Access-Reject message to present to the user.
Access-Challenge	If the AAA server needs additional information, such as the user's password for Challenge Handshake Authentication Protocol (CHAP), it uses the Access-Challenge message to inform the NAS, which then is forwarded to the client. On receiving the information, the NAS forwards the information (in this case user's password) to the AAA server in the ACCESS-REQUEST packet. This message continues until the ACCESS-ACCEPT or ACCESS-REJECT is sent from the AAA server to the NAS.

RADIUS Operation for Accounting

Accounting in RADIUS works with ACCOUNTING-REQUEST and ACCOUNTING-RESPONSE packets. The NAS sends an ACCOUNTING-REQUEST packet at the beginning or end of a user session. The Start message in the ACCOUNTING-REQUEST packet contains information about a user's identity and the service being offered to users. When the user session is over, the NAS sends another ACCESS-REQUEST packet to the AAA Server with a Stop message informing the server of the type of service that was delivered to the user. There may be additional information being sent from the NAS, such as the amount of time the user is connected and the number of bytes transferred. This information is sent from NAS to the AAA server with AV pairs. Figure 9-6 shows the exchange of RADIUS ACCOUNTING packets between the NAS and the AAA server.

Figure 9-6 *RADIUS ACCOUNTING Packet Flows (Continued)*

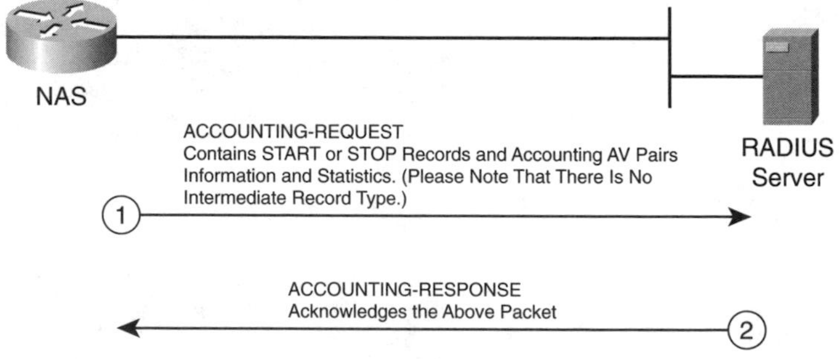

Difference between RADIUS and TACACS+

To decide which protocol to use for which features, it is important to note the difference between the TACACS+ and RADIUS protocols. Table 9-6 summarizes the differences between these two very important protocols for AAA implementation.

Table 9-6 *RADIUS versus TACACS+*

RADIUS	TACACS+
RADIUS uses UDP.	TACACS+ uses TCP.
RADIUS encrypts only the password in the ACCESS-REQUEST packet. Less secure.	TACACS+ encrypts the entire body of the packet. More secure.
RADIUS combines authentication and authorization.	TACACS+ uses the AAA architecture, which separates authentication, authorization, and accounting.
Industry standard (created by Livingston).	Cisco proprietary.
RADIUS does not support ARA access, Net BIOS Frame Protocol Control protocol, NASI, and X.25 PAD connections.	TACACS+ offers multi-protocol support.
RADIUS does not allow user control of which commands can be executed on a router.	TACACS+ provides two ways to control the authorization of router commands: per user or per group.

AAA can complement many security features provided by the router. The following is a list of all the features in which AAA complements the router with additional security. These features are discussed in detail in the section entitled "Analysis of Problem Areas."

- Router management.
- Point-to-Point Protocol (PPP) authentication for async dial-in, ISDN, and so on.
- AAA and pre-shared keys for Secure Internet Protocol (IPsec).
- Extended authentication (X-Auth) for IPsec.
- AAA and auth-proxy.
- AAA and lock and key.
- AAA for Virtual Private Dial-up Network (VPDN).
- Network Admission Control (NAC).

Diagnostic Commands and Tools

The **show** and **debug** commands are very important for troubleshooting AAA issues on the router.

show Commands

The **show** commands in AAA on the router are mainly used to view the status of a user authentication success or failure, and to find the status of the NAS-to-AAA-server connection. The following are some of the important **show** commands that can be used with the **debug** commands described in the following sections.

- **show aaa servers**—To display information about the number of packets sent to and received from AAA servers. This command was first introduced in IOS version 12.2(6) T and integrated in IOS version 12.3(7) T.
- **show tacacs**—To display statistics for a TACACS+ server. This command was first introduced in IOS version 11.2.
- **show radius statistics**—To display the RADIUS statistics for accounting and authentication packets. This command was first introduced in IOS version 12.1(3) T.
- **show users [all]**—To display information about the active lines on the router. This was first introduced in IOS version 10.0.
- **show aaa user {all |** *unique_id***}**—To display attributes related to an AAA session of a single user or all users. This command was first introduced in IOS version 12.2(4) T.

debug Commands

Using AAA **debug** commands is by far the most useful and easiest way to isolate a problem pertaining to AAA. There are specific commands for specific issues. For instance, if you run into problems with authentication, there is the option to run the basic **debug** command to see the authentication-related message.

The following three commands are extensively used to isolate issues with AAA:

- **debug aaa authentication**—Mainly used for troubleshooting AAA authentication problem.
- **debug aaa authorization**—Used to view the success or failure of authorization messages.
- **debug aaa accounting**—Used to see the debug message related to accounting issues.

Example 9-1 shows a sample output of AAA.

Example 9-1 *Sample* **debug** *Output of AAA Commands*

```
Router#debug aaa authentication
Router#debug aaa authorization
Router#debug aaa accounting
Oct 17 02:45:30.110: AAA/BIND(0000002D): Bind i/f
Oct 17 02:45:30.114: AAA/ACCT/EVENT/(0000002D): CALL START
Oct 17 02:45:30.114: Getting session id for NET(0000002D) : db=821C0394
Oct 17 02:45:30.114: AAA/ACCT(00000000): add node, session 16
Oct 17 02:45:30.114: AAA/ACCT/NET(0000002D): add, count 1
Oct 17 02:45:30.114: Getting session id for NONE(0000002D) : db=821C0394
Oct 17 02:45:30.114: AAA/AUTHEN/LOGIN (0000002D): Pick method list 'default'
Oct 17 02:45:36.274: AAA/AUTHOR (0000002D): Method list id=0 not configured. Ski
p author
Router#
```

To see the communication details between the NAS and AAA server for either TACACS+ or RADIUS, run either **debug tacacs** or **debug RADIUS** which will show debug information pertaining to the protocol.

Example 9-2 shows the sample output of TACACS+ debug message.

Example 9-2 *Sample Debug Output of* **tacacs+** *Commands*

```
Router#debug tacacs+
Oct 17 02:48:43.238: TPLUS: Queuing AAA Authentication request 46 for processing
Oct 17 02:48:43.238: TPLUS: processing authentication start request id 46
Oct 17 02:48:43.238: TPLUS: Authentication start packet created for 46()
Oct 17 02:48:43.242: TPLUS: Using server 171.69.89.217
Oct 17 02:48:43.242: TPLUS(0000002E)/0/NB_WAIT/8226E298: Started 5 sec timeout
Oct 17 02:48:43.246: TPLUS(0000002E)/0/NB_WAIT: socket event 2
Oct 17 02:48:43.246: TPLUS(0000002E)/0/NB_WAIT: wrote entire 37 bytes request
Oct 17 02:48:43.246: TPLUS(0000002E)/0/READ: socket event 1
Oct 17 02:48:43.250: TPLUS(0000002E)/0/READ: Would block while reading
Oct 17 02:48:43.650: TPLUS(0000002E)/0/READ: socket event 1
Oct 17 02:48:43.654: TPLUS(0000002E)/0/READ: read entire 12 header bytes (expect
 16 bytes data)
Oct 17 02:48:43.654: TPLUS(0000002E)/0/READ: socket event 1
Oct 17 02:48:43.654: TPLUS(0000002E)/0/READ: read entire 28 bytes response
Oct 17 02:48:43.654: TPLUS(0000002E)/0/8226E298: Processing the reply packet
Oct 17 02:48:43.654: TPLUS: Received authen response status GET_USER (7)
Oct 17 02:48:45.538: TPLUS: Queuing AAA Authentication request 46 for processing
Oct 17 02:48:45.538: TPLUS: processing authentication continue request id 46
Oct 17 02:48:45.542: TPLUS: Authentication continue packet generated for 46
Oct 17 02:48:45.542: TPLUS(0000002E)/0/WRITE/821C0790: Started 5 sec timeout
Oct 17 02:48:45.542: TPLUS(0000002E)/0/WRITE: wrote entire 22 bytes request
Oct 17 02:48:45.966: TPLUS(0000002E)/0/READ: socket event 1
Oct 17 02:48:45.966: TPLUS(0000002E)/0/READ: read entire 12 header bytes (expect
 16 bytes data)
Oct 17 02:48:45.966: TPLUS(0000002E)/0/READ: socket event 1
Oct 17 02:48:45.970: TPLUS(0000002E)/0/READ: read entire 28 bytes response
Oct 17 02:48:45.970: TPLUS(0000002E)/0/821C0790: Processing the reply packet
Oct 17 02:48:45.970: TPLUS: Received authen response status GET_PASSWORD (8)
Oct 17 02:48:49.526: TPLUS: Queuing AAA Authentication request 46 for processing
Oct 17 02:48:49.530: TPLUS: processing authentication continue request id 46
Oct 17 02:48:49.530: TPLUS: Authentication continue packet generated for 46
Oct 17 02:48:49.530: TPLUS(0000002E)/0/WRITE/821C0790: Started 5 sec timeout
Oct 17 02:48:49.530: TPLUS(0000002E)/0/WRITE: wrote entire 25 bytes request
Oct 17 02:48:50.010: TPLUS(0000002E)/0/READ: socket event 1
Oct 17 02:48:50.010: TPLUS(0000002E)/0/READ: read entire 12 header bytes (expect
 6 bytes data)
Oct 17 02:48:50.010: TPLUS(0000002E)/0/READ: socket event 1
Oct 17 02:48:50.010: TPLUS(0000002E)/0/READ: read entire 18 bytes response
Oct 17 02:48:50.010: TPLUS(0000002E)/0/821C0790: Processing the reply packet
Oct 17 02:48:50.010: TPLUS: Received authen response status PASS (2)
Router#
```

NOTE When AAA debug is running in conjunction with TACACS+ or RADIUS, separate the debug by looking for TPLUS, AAA, and RADIUS. This helps in understanding which part you are having problems with.

Troubleshooting PPP authentication issues requires you to run the **debug ppp authentication** and **debug ppp negotiation** commands, which provide details on PPP-related items. The command **debug condition user** *username* sets conditional debugging for a specific user and generates output debugs related to the user. This command is helpful in an enterprise environment for troubleshooting.

Analysis of Problem Areas

The problem areas of AAA on an IOS router can be categorized as follows based on their implementations:

- Router management troubleshooting
- Dial-up networking troubleshooting
- X-Auth troubleshooting for IPsec
- Auth-proxy troubleshooting

Router Management Troubleshooting

There are two access modes available on the router: character mode or shell exec mode and PPP mode. PPP mode is used for dial-up networking, which is discussed later in this chapter. Shell exec mode is used for router management. As discussed before, TACACS+ protocol is more flexible for router management and provides more granular control. This section examines configuration and troubleshooting in more detail and describes TACACS+ implementation for router management.

Login Authentication

This section looks into the process of turning on user login authentication on the router followed by a discussion of troubleshooting.

Configuration Steps

To turn on login authentication (for console, vty line access) follow these steps:

Step 1 Turning on AAA Process

The first step for configuring authentication is to turn on AAA under global configuration mode by executing the command shown in Example 9-3.

Example 9-3 *Turning on AAA on the Router*

```
Router(config)#aaa new-model
Router(config)#
```

Step 2 Create a local user database.

If there is a small number of users who should have access to the router, you can create the users on the router. A local user database is also recommended to configure for backup methods. Example 9-4 shows that the username Cisco is created in the local database, which may be used for backup when the AAA server is down. Note that a simple unencrypted password is used here for simplicity. We highly recommend using the encryption form for the password with the command **username cisco 7 password**.

Example 9-4 *Creating a Local User*

```
Router(config)#username Cisco pass Cisco
Router(config)#
```

Step 3 Configure AAA server communication parameters on the router.

If you have many users and want to centralize management of users, configure AAA server communication parameters on the router. Example 9-5 shows a router configured with 2 TACACS+ servers. 10.1.1.1 is the primary server because it is entered first in the configuration.

Example 9-5 *Defining TACACS+ Server with Backup*

```
Router(config)#tacacs-server host 10.1.1.1 key Cisco
Router(config)#tacacs-server host 20.1.1.1 key cisco
Router(config)#tacacs-server host 20.1.1.1 timeout 30
Router(config)#
```

By default, if the primary server is down or reports an error condition after three tries for five seconds each try, the router sends the authentication request to the second server, in this case, 20.1.1.1. Note that the timeout for the backup server is changed from 5 seconds to 30 seconds in the example. The number of tries may be changed from three as well if desired. Another way of defining the same set of servers is shown in Example 9-6, in which group options for AAA servers are used.

Example 9-6 *Defining TACACS+ Server with Backup*

```
Router(config)#aaa group server tacacs+ MYTACACS
Router(config-sg-tacacs+)#server 10.1.1.1
Router(config-sg-tacacs+)#server 20.1.1.1
Router(config-sg-tacacs+)#exit
Router(config)#tacacs-server key cisco
```

Step 4 Configure AAA client (router) parameters on the AAA server.

For the router to communicate with the AAA server, the NAS (router) must be defined as an AAA client on the AAA server. For this configuration, use the Cisco Secure ACS on Windows as discussed in Chapter 13, "Troubleshooting Cisco Secure ACS on Windows." To configure the AAA client, log in to the ACS browser GUI interface. From the navigation menu, click on **NAS Configuration**, click on **NDG Name** (if configured), then click on **Add AAA client**, which will bring up a window for AAA client definition. Important parameters are **NAS IP, Shared Secret,** and the Selection of the Protocol to be used. For this example, select TACACS+ for the protocol. Once AAA client is defined, you *must* click the **Submit+Restart** button for changes to take effect and to go into the Windows Registry.

Step 5 Create a user on the AAA Server.

Log in to ACS Windows, browse to User setup, and define a user. You need only define the password and map the user to an unconfigured group of ACS.

Step 6 Define the method list for AAA authentication.

Tell the router what to authenticate and how, which is done by configuring the method list. The method list defines the types of authentication that should be performed (for example, login versus PPP or enable authentication). It also defines the types of protocols to be used (TACACS+, local, RADIUS, and so on), and the order in which they should be used. Multiple authentication methods can be configured in the method list as a fall-back mechanism, but only one method will be tried at any one time. Method name is any arbitrary name. It must be applied to a specific interface before any of the defined authentication methods will be performed. However, a default method list is automatically applied to all interfaces. Otherwise, a named method list is explicitly defined. The syntax for defining authentication is as follows:

```
Router(config)#aaa authentication <service> {default | list-name}
  method1 [method2...]
```

Three parameters are required to be configured for authentication. First is the service. There are several options available for service, as shown in Example 9-7.

Example 9-7 *Services Available for Authentication*

```
Router(config)#aaa authentication ?
  arap             Set authentication lists for arap.
  attempts         Set the maximum number of authentication attempts
  banner           Message to use when starting login/authentication.
  enable           Set authentication list for enable.
  fail-message     Message to use for failed login/authentication.
  login            Set authentication lists for logins.
  password-prompt  Text to use when prompting for a password
  ppp              Set authentication lists for ppp.
  sgbp             Set authentication lists for sgbp.
  username-prompt  Text to use when prompting for a username
Router(config)#
```

The most commonly used services are **login**, **enable**, and **PPP**. The example uses login service. The second parameter that must be configured is the name of the method list. Then the actual methods must be configured in sequential order. Example 9-8 shows a method list configured for service login. The name of the method is **mylist**, and it is configured for TACACS+ and local method for authentication. So, if the TACACS+ server is down or reports an error condition, then try the local user database.

Example 9-8 *Sample Output of Defining the Method List*

```
Router(config)#aaa authentication login mylist group MYTACACS local
Router(config)#
```

Step 7 Apply the method list to a interface.

Once a method list is defined successfully, you must apply the method under the interface or line, or authentication will not be triggered. The exception is the default method list. Note that if there are both a default method list and a named method list configured, and the named list is applied to the interface or line, the name list takes precedence over the default method list. Example 9-9 shows that method list mylist created in Example 9-8 is applied under line vty 0 4.

Example 9-9 *Method List* **mylist** *Being Applied*

```
Router(config)#line vty 0 4
Router(config-line)#login authentication mylist
Router(config-line)#
```

Troubleshooting Steps

If the AAA server is configured for authentication and authentication is failing, we suggest using the local user database for authentication. This will help determine if the issue is with the NAS or with the AAA server. If local user authentication fails, you may isolate the problem with the **debug aaa authentication** command and by using the questions that follow:

Step 1 Is it just a single user failing?

If there are just one or two users failing, the user might be entering either the wrong username or password. To find the cause, search for the string **user not found** or **password validation** in the **"debug aaa authentication"** output.

Step 2 Is there multiple user failure?

If there is multiple user failure, there may be misconfiguration on the router. Execute the **show run** command to verify the config and make sure that you have the **aaa authentication login/ppp default method_lists** command turned on. Then run **debug aaa authentication** if needed to isolate the issue further.

Step 3 Is authentication working for Telnet but not for the console?

If you can authenticate via Telnet but not via console, then you may have not applied the method name under line console. Execute **login authentication listname** under **line con 0**.

If local user is working, and AAA server is failing the authentication, you may run the **test** command on the router as shown in Example 9-10 to simulate simple authentication steps to troubleshoot the issue further. In this example, because the RADIUS server is not defined in the configuration, the output shows there is no authoritative response from the server.

Example 9-10 *Test User Authentication from the Router*

```
Router#test aaa authentication group radius user_name user_password legacy
Attempting authentication test to server-group radius using radius
No authoritative response from any server.
Router#
```

Most of the time, AAA server-based authentication can be isolated with the **debug aaa authentication** and **debug tacacs/radius** commands, on the router. Sometimes, however, you also may need to analyze the log on the AAA server to isolate a possible misconfiguration on the server. The following discussion shows how to troubleshoot authentication failure that is caused by various reasons.

Before we look at some of the possible causes of authentication failure, let's take a look at the successful authentication debug as shown in Example 9-11.

Example 9-11 **debug** *Output of Successful User Authentication with TACACS+*

```
Router#
1w0d: TAC+: send AUTHEN/START packet ver=192 id=753768982
1w0d: TAC+: Using default tacacs server-group "tacacs+" list.
1w0d: TAC+: Opening TCP/IP to 10.48.66.102/49 timeout=5
! Router connected to the TACACS+ Server
1w0d: TAC+: Opened TCP/IP handle 0x81F639C4 to 10.48.66.102/49
1w0d: TAC+: 10.48.66.102 (753768982) AUTHEN/START/LOGIN/ASCII queued
1w0d: TAC+: (753768982) AUTHEN/START/LOGIN/ASCII processed
1w0d: TAC+: ver=192 id=753768982 received AUTHEN status = GETUSER
! Enter Username
1w0d: TAC+: send AUTHEN/CONT packet id=753768982
1w0d: TAC+: 10.48.66.102 (753768982) AUTHEN/CONT queued
1w0d: TAC+: (753768982) AUTHEN/CONT processed
1w0d: TAC+: ver=192 id=753768982 received AUTHEN status = GETPASS
! Enter Password
1w0d: TAC+: send AUTHEN/CONT packet id=753768982
1w0d: TAC+: 10.48.66.102 (753768982) AUTHEN/CONT queued
1w0d: TAC+: (753768982) AUTHEN/CONT processed
! User is successfully authenticated
1w0d: TAC+: ver=192 id=753768982 received AUTHEN status = PASS
1w0d: TAC+: Closing TCP/IP 0x81F639C4 connection to 10.48.66.102/49
Router#
```

- **NAS does not have the AAA Server configuration**—If there are multiple user failures, investigate if you accidentally have removed the AAA server entry from the NAS. A quick way to find this out is by executing the command **show running-config | include tacacs**. If you do not have the TACACS+ server defined, define one and see if the issue is resolved.
- **AAA Server does not have the NAS configured as AAA client**—You may have AAA Server definition on the NAS (router), but if you do not have the NAS (router) defined as an AAA client on the AAA Server, the server drops the authentication request. Sometimes, you may run into this issue even if you define NAS as your AAA client if the source IP address of the TACACS+ packet changes. Under this circumstance, end users will sometimes be able to authenticate, and at other times, the authentication will fail. This is because if there are multiple paths to the AAA server from NAS, the TACACS+ packet may have different source IP addresses at different times, because the packet may leave from the router through different interfaces. To get around this problem, the best practice is to define a loopback interface on the NAS (router) and force the TACACS+ packet to source always from the loopback interface. This can be achieved with the **ip tacacs source-interface Loopback 0** global configuration command on the router. In this command, assume Loopback 0 is created, so that TACACS+ packet always sources from this interface. Even though it is strongly recommended to use a loopback interface under this type of redundant path scenario, you can force the TACACS+ packet to use one of the physical interfaces of the redundant path as the source IP address. Then on the AAA server, define this interface (either the loopback or the physical interface for TACACS+ source IP) as the AAA client in the AAA client table. Otherwise, you must define all interface IP addresses that the router may use to source the TACACS+ packet.
- **Shared secret key mismatch between the NAS and the server**—The shared secret key is used to encrypt the packet with an MD5 hashing algorithm. If there is a shared secret key mismatch, CS ACS will not trust the NAS. Therefore, it will fail the authentication unless the backup method is configured. On the NAS with **debug tacacs**, the error condition will be reported and on the ACS Failed Attempt log, you will see clearly the Shared secret key mismatch problem.
- **Connection problem between the NAS and AAA server**—If there is a connectivity problem between the NAS and the AAA server, all the users will fail. If you run **debug tacacs**, you will see the "Destination unreachable" message. Run a ping test from the router to the AAA server and see if you can ping. If ping is successful, be sure the outgoing/incoming interface on the router does not have an ACL that may be blocking the TACACS+ (TCP/49) traffic. Also, be sure that there is no Layer 2 or Layer 3 firewall between the NAS and AAA server that may be blocking the communication. A personal firewall or HOST IDS on the AAA server may block the port as well. So, be sure you create the necessary exception. Also, be sure service for TACACS+ is running on the AAA server.
- **User does not exist on the server**—If user fails with **status = FAIL** in the **debug aaa authentication & debug tacacs**, investigate the issue on the CS ACS Server. First

look at the Failed Attempt under **Reports and Activity** and see why the user is failing. Most of the time, this will reveal the reason for the failure. However, to find additional details, you may want to investigate the **auth.log** after turning on FULL logging, which collects debug information on the CS ACS Server. More details on this can be found in Chapter 13, "Troubleshooting Cisco Secure ACS on Windows." In the **auth.log** file of CS ACS, search the file by the username you get from Failed Attempts log and see if the user is tagged as an **unknown** user. This happens when the user does not exist on the CS ACS local database. If the user does not exist on the external user database or CS ACS is not configured with an external user database, you will see the fail message in the **auth.log** file.

- **User password invalid**—If the user enters the wrong password, or the password that is configured is not supported, you may receive a "CS Password Invalid message" on the **"Failed Attempt"** log under **"Reports and Activity"** of the CS ACS server. On the router debug, you will receive **status = FAIL**.
- **NAS filter**—If you have a network access server (NAS) filter configured for the group to which the user is mapped, make sure the authentication request is not blocked by the NAS filter. Note that the NAS filter works with authentication, not with authorization. Hence, if the NAS filter is configured incorrectly on the CS ACS server, the authentication request will not be processed at all. On the router debug you will receive **status = FAIL**, but on the ACS under the Failed Attempt log, you should see the message related to the NAS filter. If you look at the **TCS.log** file, which is part of **package.cab** (more on this in Chapter 13, "Troubleshooting Cisco Secure ACS on Windows"), you will see the user request will come in, but will not be forwarded to the authentication service for further processing. This can be verified by looking at the auth.log where the user request cannot be found.
- **Exec authorization**—On the NAS (router), if you have exec authorization turned on, but you do not have **Shell(exec)** checked and **"Privilege level"** defined under the User/Group setting, authentication will fail. On the router, you will receive a **status = FAIL** message.

Enable Password Authentication

Once the users log in to the router, they can get to the enable mode by entering the enable password. However, sharing the same enable password is unwise for security reasons. Instead, assigning enable passwords based on the individual user name provides more control for access control. In addition to what's configured in the preceding section, Example 9-12 shows the additional configuration required on the router to turn on enable password authentication by the Cisco Secure ACS Server.

Example 9-12 *Configurations Required for Enable Authentication*

```
Router(config)#aaa authentication enable default group MYTACACS enable
Router(config)#
```

In this example, enable authentication is performed against the TACACS+ server, and if the TACACS+ server is unavailable, the router's enable password is configured as a back door. This enable password should not be shared with everyone. Also, note that unless the AAA server is down, you cannot get into the enable mode just by entering the enable password.

Figure 9-7 shows the configuration required on the Cisco Secure ACS server for enable authentication.

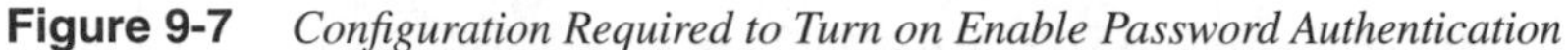

Figure 9-7 *Configuration Required to Turn on Enable Password Authentication*

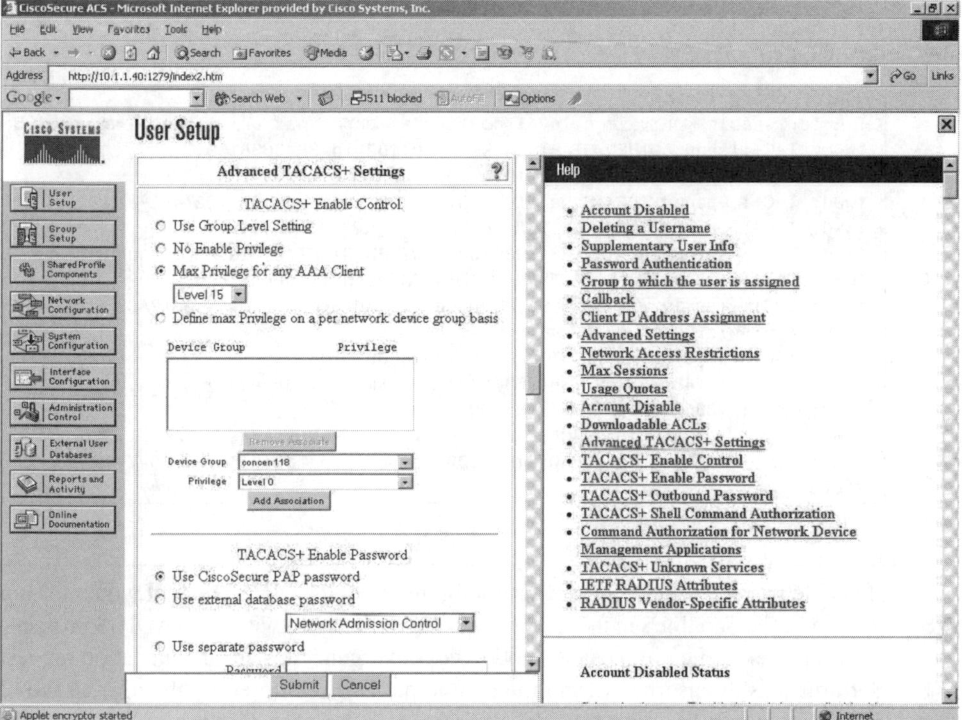

In Figure 9-7, "Max Privilege for any AAA Client" is set to "15" and Under the "TACACS+ Enable Passwords" section. "Use Cisco Secure PAP password" is checked. This means the user can use the same password as login for enable authentication, and will have privilege level 15 access to the privilege mode on the router. If you want, you can define a separate password for enable authentication than login.

The troubleshooting steps for enabling password authentication are almost the same as those discussed in the Login Authentication section. Additional information that's important and specific to enable password authentication follows:

- If the "No enable Privilege" is set without defining a privilege for the user on Cisco Secure ACS, you will see the message on the user station as shown in Example 9-13.
- The CS ACS Failed Attempt will report "CS password invalid."

Example 9-13 *Test Run Failure for the Enable Password*

```
Username: cisco
Password: <user password on ACS>
Router>enable
Password: <enable/user password on ACS>
% Error in authentication.
Router>
```

- On the router, if you run **debug tacacs**, you will see a message similar to that shown in Example 9-14.

Example 9-14 debug tacacs *Output for Enable Password Authentication*

```
Router#debug tacacs
! Enter enable <privilege level configured under max privilege level on ACS>
1w0d: TAC+: send AUTHEN/START packet ver=192 id=3843638108
1w0d: TAC+: Opening TCP/IP to 10.48.66.102/49 timeout=5
1w0d: TAC+: Opened TCP/IP handle 0x81F2A0D0 to 10.48.66.102/49
1w0d: TAC+: Opened 10.48.66.102 index=1
1w0d: TAC+: 10.48.66.102 (3843638108) AUTHEN/START/LOGIN/ASCII queued
1w0d: TAC+: (3843638108) AUTHEN/START/LOGIN/ASCII processed
1w0d: TAC+: ver=192 id=3843638108 received AUTHEN status = GETPASS
! Enter enable Password
1w0d: TAC+: send AUTHEN/CONT packet id=3843638108
1w0d: TAC+: 10.48.66.102 (3843638108) AUTHEN/CONT queued
1w0d: TAC+: (3843638108) AUTHEN/CONT processed
1w0d: TAC+: ver=192 id=3843638108 received AUTHEN status = FAIL | PASS
1w0d: TAC+: Closing TCP/IP 0x81F2A0D0 connection to 10.48.66.102/49
Router#
```

NOTE If enable password authentication is configured with RADIUS protocol, you must configure the username **$enable$** in the ACS server. This is because with the RADIUS protocol, when the user tries to enter into enable mode, the router generates an authentication request with **$enable$** as the username, and the enable password entered by the user as the enable password. When this request arrives at the CS ACS server, it checks enable password for user $enable$. Hence, if user **$enable$** is not defined with a common password shared by all users with same privilege level, enable authentication will fail with the following message displayed: "External DB user invalid or bad password" in the Failed Attempt log.

Exec Authorization

Exec authorization is used to assign the privilege level to a user either by the AAA server or by the router itself. If configured locally on the router, this privilege level also determines what commands the user may execute. By default, there are three privilege levels on the router.

- privilege level 1 = non-privileged (prompt is router>), the default level for logging in.

- privilege level 15 = privileged (prompt is router#), the level after going into enable mode.
- privilege level 0 = seldom used (prompt is router>), but includes 5 commands: **disable**, **enable**, **exit**, **help**, and **logout**.
- Levels 2–14 are not used in a default configuration, but commands that are normally at level 15 can be moved down to one of those levels, and commands that are normally at level 1 can be moved up to one of those levels.

Example 9-15 shows the configuration in which **snmp-server** commands are moved down from privilege level 15 (the default) to privilege level 7. The **ping** command is moved up from privilege level 1 to privilege level 7. When user **backup** is authenticated, that user is assigned privilege level 7 by the server and a **show privilege** command displays "Current privilege level is 7." The user can ping and perform snmp-server configuration in configuration mode.

Example 9-15 *Authorization* **exec** *Command*

```
Router#
aaa new-model
aaa authentication login default group tacacs+|radius local
aaa authorization exec default group tacacs+ |radius local
username backup privilege 7 password 0 backup
tacacs-server host 10.1.1.40
tacacs-server key cisco
radius-server host 10.1.1.40
radius-server key cisco
privilege configure level 7 snmp-server host
privilege configure level 7 snmp-server enable
privilege configure level 7 snmp-server
privilege exec level 7 ping
privilege exec level 7 configure terminal
privilege exec level 7 configure
Router#
```

As a logged-in user, to determine the privilege level, use the **show privilege** command. To determine what commands are available at a particular privilege level for the version of Cisco IOS software that you are using, type a question mark (**?**) at the command line when logged in at that privilege level.

As you can see, if set locally on the router, command authorization relies heavily on the privilege level assigned to the user. However, this can be accomplished with command authorization (instead of relying on the privilege level only) with TACACS+ server. Note that RADIUS does not have command authorization capability. Unlike local privilege-level based authorization, which is based on the router, authorization with external AAA server scales very well. The following section explains how to accomplish the authorization with CS ACS Server.

The following are the configuration steps required on the CS ACS on Windows for TACACS+ exec authorization:

Step 1 Enter the username and password.

Step 2 In Group Settings, make sure **shell/exec** is checked, and that **7** has been entered in the privilege level box.

The following are the configuration steps required for the Radius Authorization.

Step 1 Enter the username and password.

Step 2 In the Group Settings for IETF, optionally check the box **[006] Service-Type**, and select **NAS Prompt** from the drop-down list.

Step 3 In the **Cisco IOS/PIX RADIUS Attributes** area, check the **[009\001] cisco-av-pair box**, and in the rectangular box underneath, enter **shell:priv-lvl=7.**

With exec authorization enabled on the router, when the user uses Telnet or Console to access the router, the user is taken directly to the privilege mode based on the privilege level defined either locally on the router or CS ACS server. Example 9-16 illustrates this behavior for user "Cisco," who is taken directly to the router's privilege mode after Telnet login authentication.

Example 9-16 *Sample Telnet Login Session When Exec Authorization Is Configured*

```
User Access Verification

Username: Cisco
Password:

Router#
```

Before getting into issues that might arise when exec authorization is configured, let's examine a good authentication with exec authorization debug output. Example 9-17 shows **debug tacacs+** on the router for a successful user authentication when exec authorization is turned on as shown in Example 9-17.

Example 9-17 **debug tacacs+** *Output of Successful User Authentication with Exec Authorization Turned on*

```
Router#debug tacacs
1w0d: TAC+: send AUTHEN/START packet ver=192 id=2766506766
1w0d: TAC+: Using default tacacs server-group "tacacs+" list.
1w0d: TAC+: Opening TCP/IP to 10.48.66.102/49 timeout=5
1w0d: TAC+: Opened TCP/IP handle 0x821E4F30 to 10.48.66.102/49
1w0d: TAC+: 10.48.66.102 (2766506766) AUTHEN/START/LOGIN/ASCII queued
1w0d: TAC+: (2766506766) AUTHEN/START/LOGIN/ASCII processed
! Here Router is asking user to Enter Username
1w0d: TAC+: ver=192 id=2766506766 received AUTHEN status = GETUSER
```

Example 9-17 **debug tacacs+** *Output of Successful User Authentication with Exec Authorization Turned on (Continued)*

```
1w0d: TAC+: send AUTHEN/CONT packet id=2766506766
1w0d: TAC+: 10.48.66.102 (2766506766) AUTHEN/CONT queued
1w0d: TAC+: (2766506766) AUTHEN/CONT processed
! Here Router is asking user to enter Password
1w0d: TAC+: ver=192 id=2766506766 received AUTHEN status = GETPASS
1w0d: TAC+: send AUTHEN/CONT packet id=2766506766
1w0d: TAC+: 10.48.66.102 (2766506766) AUTHEN/CONT queued
1w0d: TAC+: (2766506766) AUTHEN/CONT processed
! Authentication status shows Pass here
1w0d: TAC+: ver=192 id=2766506766 received AUTHEN status = PASS
1w0d: TAC+: Closing TCP/IP 0x821E4F30 connection to 10.48.66.102/49
1w0d: TAC+: using previously set server 10.48.66.102 from group tacacs+
1w0d: TAC+: Opening TCP/IP to 10.48.66.102/49 timeout=5
1w0d: TAC+: Opened TCP/IP handle 0x81EFB590 to 10.48.66.102/49
1w0d: TAC+: Opened 10.48.66.102 index=1
! Authorization starts here
1w0d: TAC+: 10.48.66.102 (2142041245) AUTHOR/START queued
1w0d: TAC+: (2142041245) AUTHOR/START processed
! Authorization Pass as shown in the status
1w0d: TAC+: (2142041245): received author response status = PASS_ADD
1w0d: TAC+: Closing TCP/IP 0x81EFB590 connection to 10.48.66.102/49
! Privilege level 7 is getting assigned by the AAA server
1w0d: TAC+: Received Attribute "priv-lvl=7"
```

The following are some of the common mistakes that you may encounter with the exec authorization:

- **Exec Authorization is not turned on**—If you do not have the exec authorization turned on, of course the privilege level will not be assigned to the user. So, you may not get the expected behavior.
- **Exec is not checked on the ACS Server**—If you have the exec configured on the NAS but not on the server, authentication will fail for the user.
- **Privilege level is not configured on the ACS Server**—Along with having the exec enabled on the Server, you must also configure the privilege level in the group for the users; otherwise, authentication may fail.

Command Authorization

You can control the commands the user may execute with command authorization. In addition to configuration for authentication, Example 9-18 shows the configuration needed on the router to turn on command authorization.

Example 9-18 *Turning on AAA Command Authorization*

```
!The following commands turn on command authorization for level 1
Router(config)#aaa authorization commands 1 default group tacacs none
!The following command turn on authorization for level 15
```

continues

Example 9-18 *Turning on AAA Command Authorization (Continued)*

```
Router(config)#aaa authorization commands 15 default group tacacs none
!The following command turn on command authorization for config commands
Router(config)#aaa authorization config-commands
Router(config)#
```

On the ACS Server for command authorization, configure one of the following options except the first—none:

- **None**—No authorization for shell commands.
- **Assign a Shell Command Authorization Set for any network device**—One shell command authorization set is assigned, and it applies to all network devices.
- **Assign a Shell Command Authorization Set on a per Network Device Group Basis**—Enables you to associate particular shell command authorization sets to be effective on particular NDGs.
- **Per Group Command Authorization**—Enables you to permit or deny specific Cisco IOS commands and arguments at the group level.

You may also configure the Shared Profile component for command authorization. Work through the steps that follow to configure command authorization on the CS ACS under the group that allows the user to execute only the **show users** command and to deny the rest of the commands:

Step 1 In Group Setup, under **Shell Command Authorization Set**, click the **Per Group Command Authorization** button.

Step 2 For Unmatched Cisco IOS commands, click the **Deny** button.

Step 3 Check the **Command** check box, and in the text box underneath, define **show**.

Step 4 In the **Arguments** box, type the argument **users**.

Step 5 For Unlisted arguments, click the **Deny** button.

Step 6 Finally click on Submit and Restart.

Example 9-19 shows a successful authorization debug command.

Example 9-19 **debug** *Output of Successful Command Authorization*

```
Router#debug aaa authorization
Router#debug tacacs
!After the user authentication, user tries to execute show users command, as configured
!in aaa authorization commands 1 default group tacacs+ none.
*Mar 15 18:21:32: AAA/AUTHOR/CMD: tty3 (4185871454) user='Cisco'
*Mar 15 18:21:32: tty3 AAA/AUTHOR/CMD (4185871454): send AV service=shell
*Mar 15 18:21:32: tty3 AAA/AUTHOR/CMD (4185871454): send AV cmd=show
*Mar 15 18:21:32: tty3 AAA/AUTHOR/CMD (4185871454): send AV cmd-arg=users
*Mar 15 18:21:32: tty3 AAA/AUTHOR/CMD (4185871454): send AV cmd-arg=
*Mar 15 18:21:32: tty3 AAA/AUTHOR/CMD (4185871454): found list "default"
```

Example 9-19 debug *Output of Successful Command Authorization (Continued)*

```
*Mar 15 18:21:32: tty3 AAA/AUTHOR/CMD (4185871454): Method=tacacs+ (tacacs+)
*Mar 15 18:21:32: AAA/AUTHOR/TAC+: (4185871454): user=Cisco
*Mar 15 18:21:32: AAA/AUTHOR/TAC+: (4185871454): send AV service=shell
*Mar 15 18:21:32: AAA/AUTHOR/TAC+: (4185871454): send AV cmd=show
*Mar 15 18:21:32: AAA/AUTHOR/TAC+: (4185871454): send AV cmd-arg=users
*Mar 15 18:21:32: AAA/AUTHOR/TAC+: (4185871454): send AV cmd-arg=
*Mar 15 18:21:32: TAC+: using previously set server 172.18.124.113 from group
tacacs+
*Mar 15 18:21:32: TAC+: Opening TCP/IP to 172.18.124.113/49 timeout=5
*Mar 15 18:21:32: TAC+: Opened TCP/IP handle 0x54F26C to 172.18.124.113/49
*Mar 15 18:21:32: TAC+: Opened 172.18.124.113 index=1
*Mar 15 18:21:32: TAC+: 172.18.124.113 (4185871454) AUTHOR/START queued
*Mar 15 18:21:33: TAC+: (4185871454) AUTHOR/START processed
*Mar 15 18:21:33: TAC+: (4185871454): received author response status = PASS_ADD
*Mar 15 18:21:33: TAC+: Closing TCP/IP 0x54F26C connection to 172.18.124.113/49
*Mar 15 18:21:33: AAA/AUTHOR (4185871454): Post authorization status = PASS_ADD
Router#
```

Some of the issues that might arise with the command authorization are as follows:

- **Command Authorization not turned on for the correct privilege**—If the user gets privilege level 10 from the AAA server, but the router has only AAA command authorization turned on for levels 1 and 15, the user will not be authorized for commands on the router. To fix this problem, turn on command authorization for level 10 with command **aaa authorization commands 10 default group tacacs none**.
- **Cannot command authorize the config commands**—If you are missing **aaa authorization config-commands** from the router configuration, the configuration mode command will not be authorized.
- **Misconfiguration on the AAA server**—If you have the group profile configured incorrectly on the AAA server, the command authorization will fail. One such misconfiguration example is not defining the commands and arguments on the AAA server for the group profile as it is parsed by the router. Defining **show run** in the group profile will not work, but **show running-config** will work because that's the full form of the **show** command. This is how it is parsed and sent to the AAA server by the router. So, make sure to define the commands in the group profile with full form as it is parsed by the router.

Accounting

To capture user activity and send it to the AAA server, configure AAA accounting on the router as shown in Example 9-20.

Example 9-20 *Turning on Accounting for Telnet and Console*

```
!The following command will turn on Exec accounting to capture the telnet/console
session
Router(config)#aaa accounting exec default start-stop
!System accounting provides information about all system-level events
```

continues

Example 9-20 *Turning on Accounting for Telnet and Console (Continued)*

```
Router(config)#aaa accounting system default start-stop
!The following Command accounting provides information about the EXEC shell commands for
!a specified privilege level that are being executed on a network access server. Each
!command accounting record includes a list of the commands executed for that privilege
!level, as well as the date and time each command was executed, and the user who executed
!it.
Router(config)#aaa accounting commands 1 default start-stop
Router(config)#aaa accounting commands 15 default start-stop
```

Dialup Networking Troubleshooting

While TACACS+ protocol is more flexible for router management, RADIUS is more suitable for dialup networking. This section examines configuration and troubleshooting in more detail and describes RADIUS implementation for dialup networking.

Authentication and Authorization for Dialup Networking

There are two ways the users can dial into the router: using character mode or packet mode. When users dial in with character mode, it is a non-PPP session, just like a hyperterminal dial into the router. This is also called shell mode. In this mode, the user lands on the router itself. With packet mode, users will use dialup networking and log in to the network. In this case, PPP is transparent to the user. When using character mode, configure the router so that users will be challenged for username and password to log in. Example 9-21 shows the configuration needed on the router for PPP authentication and authorization.

Example 9-21 *The Configuration for Dial Access to an Async Link*

```
Dhaka#show running-config
Building configuration...
Current configuration:
!
version 12.2
service timestamps debug datetime localtime
service timestamps log uptime
no service password-encryption
!
hostname Dhaka
!
aaa new-model
!Define the following line for character mode authentication, like telnet, console
!etc for router management
aaa authentication login default group radius local
!The following line is for packet mode authentication (for dialup network). As the
!method name is default, it will be applied automatically to async and ISDN interface.
aaa authentication ppp default group radius local
```

Example 9-21 *The Configuration for Dial Access to an Async Link (Continued)*

```
!The following statement turns on authorization for packed mode (for dial up
!network). This is needed  for assigning IP address, DNS Server IP, WINS IP etc. from
!the AAA Server.
aaa authorization network default group radius local
enable password cisco%tac!123
!
interface Ethernet0
ip address 10.1.1.10 255.255.255.0
no ip directed-broadcast
no ip mroute-cache
!
interface Group-Async1
!You must assign an IP-address to the async interface otherwise, you may run into
!routing problem. Here using the same ip address as the Etherenet0 interface.
ip unnumbered Ethernet0
no ip directed-broadcast
encapsulation ppp
no ip mroute-cache
async mode interactive
! The following command assigns IP address dynamically using the pool name default
!which is configured below.
peer default ip address pool default
no cdp enable
!Following line turns on PPP authentication. Here for simplicity pap is used. In the
!production network, it is recommended to use chap pap.
ppp authentication pap chap
!Grouping line 1-16
group-range 1 16
!For this test setup, only one ip address is defined in the local pool. In production
!network, you will have the range of ip address.
ip local pool default 10.1.1.30
!This is the default gateway for the router.
ip default-gateway 10.1.1.1
ip classless
ip route 0.0.0.0 0.0.0.0 10.1.1.1
!
!The following extended access-list is defined on the router, but not applied to any
!specific interface. As a reply attribute of authorization packet, this ACL name may be
!downloaded from the AAA server, which then will be applied for the specific user. The
!source address in the ACL is directly reflected up the pool address defined, from which
!users IP address will be assigned. In this example, as 10.1.1.30 is the only ip defined
!in the pool, this ip address is allowed to a host 10.1.1.35.
ip access-list extended dial_access
permit ip host 10.1.1.30 host 10.1.1.35
dialer-list 1 protocol ip permit
no cdp run
!
```

continues

Example 9-21 *The Configuration for Dial Access to an Async Link (Continued)*

```
radius-server host 10.1.1.40 auth-port 1645 acct-port 1646 key ciscohtts123
!
line con 0
exec-timeout 0 0
password cisco$ard^54
transport input none
line 1 16
autoselect during-login
autoselect ppp
!This statement is needed if user connects to the network in character mode and you
!want the user to user to do PPP automatically.
autocommand ppp
script dialer callback
modem InOut
transport input all
line aux 0
transport input all
line vty 0 4
exec-timeout 0 0
password cisco^rea%345
!
end
Dhaka#
```

Example 9-22 shows the debug output of successful authentication and authorization.

Example 9-22 *The* **debug** *Output When the Authentication Is Successful*

```
Dhaka#debug radius
Dhaka#debug aaa authentication
Dhaka#debug aaa authorization
Dhaka#debug ppp authentication
Dhaka#debug aaa per-user
Dhaka#debug ppp negotiation
Dhaka#show debug
General OS:
  AAA Authentication debugging is on
  AAA Authorization debugging is on
  AAA Per-user attributes debugging is on
PPP:
  PPP authentication debugging is on
  PPP protocol negotiation debugging is on
Radius protocol debugging is on
Dhaka#
Jul 20 08:29:44.006: %LINK-3-UPDOWN: Interface Async1, changed state to up
As61 PPP: Using dialer call direction
As61 PPP: Treating connection as a callin
As61 PPP: Authorization required
As61 PAP: I AUTH-REQ id 0 len 15 from "cisco"
As61 PAP: Authenticating peer cisco
AAA/AUTHEN/PPP (00000061): Pick method list 'default'
```

Example 9-22 *The* **debug** *Output When the Authentication Is Successful (Continued)*

```
As61 PPP: Sent PAP LOGIN Request
RADIUS(00000061): Storing nasport 1 in rad_db
RADIUS: Pick NAS IP for uid=97 tableid=0 cfg_addr=0.0.0.0 best_addr=10.1.1.10
RADIUS/ENCODE(00000061): acct_session_id: 97
RADIUS(00000061): sending
RADIUS(00000061): Send Access-Request to 10.1.1.40:1645 id 67, len 96
RADIUS:  authenticator C1 54 19 75 55 B5 B1 96 - 73 26 D1 EF 43 83 0A DA
RADIUS:  Framed-Protocol      [7]   6   PPP                      [1]
RADIUS:  User-Name            [1]   6   "cisco"
RADIUS:  User-Password        [2]   18  *
RADIUS:  Calling-Station-Id   [31]  7   "async"
RADIUS:  Vendor, Cisco        [26]  15
RADIUS:   cisco-nas-port      [2]   9   "Async1"
RADIUS:  NAS-Port             [5]   6   1
RADIUS:  NAS-Port-Type        [61]  6   Async                    [0]
RADIUS:  Service-Type         [6]   6   Framed                   [2]
RADIUS:  NAS-IP-Address       [4]   6   10.1.1.10
RADIUS: Received from id 21645/67 10.1.1.40:1645, Access-Accept, len 38
RADIUS:  authenticator 1B F4 44 9E C4 98 38 AC - C4 DC 24 74 78 20 79 D3
RADIUS:  Service-Type         [6]   6   Framed                   [2]
RADIUS:  Framed-Protocol      [7]   6   PPP                      [1]
RADIUS:  Framed-IP-Address    [8]   6   255.255.255.255
RADIUS(00000061): Received from id 21645/67
As61 PPP: Received LOGIN Response PASS
Dhaka#
```

With the authorization turned on, you can download information from the CS ACS. The sections that follow describe that information.

Downloading ACL per User Basis Using Filter-id

You can restrict what the user can do by using an ACL in two ways: using a filter ID, or using attribute value (AV) pairs. This section examines the configuration needed both on the router and the ACS Server to download the ACL name with filter-id.

Example 9-23 shows the configuration needed on the router for the task.

Example 9-23 *Configuration Needed to Download the ACL Name and Applied on the Router for User Access*

```
Dhaka(config)# aaa authorization network default group radius
Dhaka(config)# ip access-list extended dial_access
Dhaka(config-ext-nacl)# permit ip host 10.1.1.30 host 10.1.1.35
```

Figure 9-8 shows that the access-list name that is defined on the router is defined in the Internet Engineering Task Force (IETF) RADIUS attribute 11.

Figure 9-8 *Filter ID Definition for Radius*

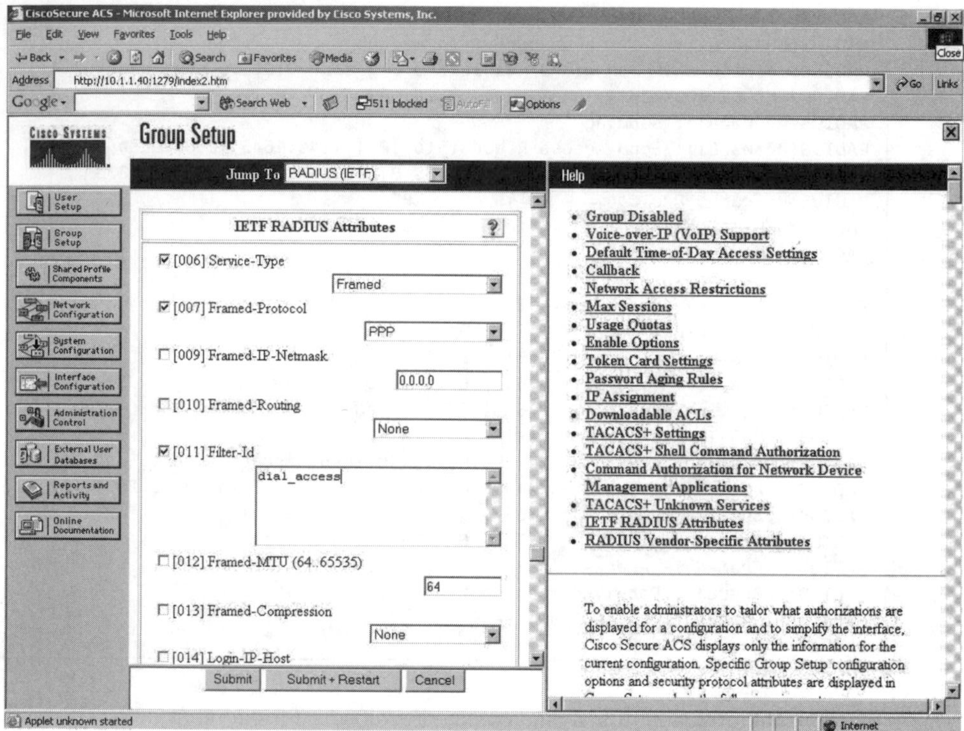

Example 9-24 shows the ACL name downloaded to the NAS.

Example 9-24 *The ACL Being Downloaded from ACS*

```
Dhaka#debug aaa authentication
Dhaka#debug aaa authorization
Dhaka#debug ppp authentication
Dhaka#debug aaa per-user
Dhaka#debug ppp negotiation
Dhaka#show debug
General OS:
  AAA Authentication debugging is on
  AAA Authorization debugging is on
  AAA Per-user attributes debugging is on
PPP:
  PPP authentication debugging is on
  PPP protocol negotiation debugging is on
Dhaka#
*Mar 10 22:36:47.640: As1 AAA/AUTHOR/IPCP: Start. Her address 0.0.0.0, we want
10.1.1.30
*Mar 10 22:36:47.644: As1 AAA/AUTHOR/IPCP: Processing AV service=ppp
*Mar 10 22:36:47.644: As1 AAA/AUTHOR/IPCP: Processing AV inacl=dial_access
*Mar 10 22:36:47.648: As1 AAA/AUTHOR/IPCP: Authorization succeeded
*Mar 10 22:36:47.648: As1 AAA/AUTHOR/IPCP: Done. Her address 0.0.0.0, we want
10.1.1.30
```

Example 9-24 *The ACL Being Downloaded from ACS (Continued)*

```
*Mar 10 22:36:47.652: As1 IPCP: O CONFNAK [ACKrcvd] id 3 len 10
*Mar 10 22:36:47.656: As1 IPCP: Address 10.1.1.30 (0x0306AB44C936)
*Mar 10 22:36:47.996: As1 IPCP: I CONFREQ [ACKrcvd] id 4 len 10
*Mar 10 22:36:48.000: As1 IPCP: Address 10.1.1.30 (0x0306AB44C936)
*Mar 10 22:36:48.004: As1 AAA/AUTHOR/IPCP: Start. Her address 10.1.1.30, we
want 10.1.1.30
*Mar 10 22:36:48.012: AAA/AUTHOR/IPCP As1 (2638016128): Port='Async1' list='' se
rvice=NET
*Mar 10 22:36:48.012: AAA/AUTHOR/IPCP: As1 (2638016128) user='filterin'
*Mar 10 22:36:48.016: AAA/AUTHOR/IPCP: As1 (2638016128) send AV service=ppp
*Mar 10 22:36:48.016: AAA/AUTHOR/IPCP: As1 (2638016128) send AV protocol=ip
*Mar 10 22:36:48.020: AAA/AUTHOR/IPCP: As1 (2638016128) send AV addr*10.1.1.30
*Mar 10 22:36:48.020: AAA/AUTHOR/IPCP (2638016128) found list "default"
*Mar 10 22:36:48.024: AAA/AUTHOR/IPCP: As1 (2638016128) Method=RADIUS
*Mar 10 22:36:48.028: RADIUS: allowing negotiated framed address 10.1.1.30
*Mar 10 22:36:48.032: AAA/AUTHOR (2638016128): Post authorization status = PASS_
REPL
*Mar 10 22:36:48.036: As1 AAA/AUTHOR/IPCP: Processing AV service=ppp
!Access-list name dial_access is downloaded from the AAA Server
*Mar 10 22:36:48.040: As1 AAA/AUTHOR/IPCP: Processing AV inacl=dial_access
*Mar 10 22:36:48.040: As1 AAA/AUTHOR/IPCP: Processing AV addr=10.1.1.30
*Mar 10 22:36:48.044: As1 AAA/AUTHOR/IPCP: Authorization succeeded
*Mar 10 22:36:48.044: As1 AAA/AUTHOR/IPCP: Done. Her address 10.1.1.30, we
want 10.1.1.30
*Mar 10 22:36:48.048: As1 IPCP: O CONFACK [ACKrcvd] id 4 len 10
*Mar 10 22:36:48.052: As1 IPCP: Address 10.1.1.30 (0x0306AB44C936)
*Mar 10 22:36:48.056: As1 IPCP: State is Open
*Mar 10 22:36:48.064: As1 AAA/AUTHOR/PER-USER: Event IP_UP
*Mar 10 22:36:48.064: As1 AAA/AUTHOR: IP_UP
*Mar 10 22:36:48.068: As1 AAA/PER-USER: processing author params.
*Mar 10 22:36:48.072: As1 AAA/AUTHOR: Parse 'interface Async1'
*Mar 10 22:36:48.192: As1 AAA/AUTHOR: Parse returned ok (0)
!here the ACL is getting applied to the interface
*Mar 10 22:36:48.192: As1 AAA/AUTHOR: Parse 'IP access-group dial_access in'
*Mar 10 22:36:48.336: As1 AAA/AUTHOR: Parse returned ok (0)
*Mar 10 22:36:48.340: As1 AAA/AUTHOR: enqueue peruser IP txt=interface Async1
no IP access-group dial_access in
*Mar 10 22:36:48.344: As1 IPCP: Install route to 10.1.1.30
Dhaka#
```

This can be verified by executing the command shown in Example 9-25.

Example 9-25 *The Async Interface Status*

```
Dhaka# show ip interface async 1
Async1 is up, line protocol is up
Interface is unnumbered. Using address of Ethernet0 (10.1.1.10)
Broadcast address is 255.255.255.255
Peer address is 10.1.1.30
MTU is 1500 bytes
Helper address is not set
Directed broadcast forwarding is disabled
```

continues

Example 9-25 *The Async Interface Status (Continued)*

```
Outgoing access list is not set
!This is where you can confirm access list "dial_access" being applied.
Inbound access list is dial_access, default is not set
Proxy ARP is enabled
Security level is default
Split horizon is enabled
ICMP redirects are always sent
ICMP unreachables are always sent
ICMP mask replies are never sent
IP fast switching is disabled
IP fast switching on the same interface is disabled
IP Null turbo vector
IP multicast fast switching is disabled
IP multicast distributed fast switching is disabled
IP route-cache flags are None
Router Discovery is disabled
IP output packet accounting is disabled
IP access violation accounting is disabled
TCP/IP header compression is disabled
RTP/IP header compression is disabled
Probe proxy name replies are disabled
Policy routing is disabled
Network address translation is disabled
Web Cache Redirect is disabled
BGP Policy Mapping is disabled
Dhaka#
```

Downloading ACL/ROUTES, WINS, and DNS IP Using AV Pair

The IETF draft standard specifies a method for communicating vendor-specific information between the NAS and the RADIUS server by using the vendor-specific attribute (attribute 26). Cisco's vendor-ID is 9, and the supported option has vendor-type 1, which is named "cisco-avpair." The format of AV pair is as follows:

```
protocol: attribute sep value *
```

"Protocol" is a value of the Cisco "protocol" attribute for a particular type of authorization. "Attribute" and "value" is an appropriate attribute-value (AV) pair defined in the Cisco TACACS+ specification. The following are some AV pairs:

```
cisco-avpair= "ip:addr-pool=first"
cisco-avpair= "shell:priv-lvl=15"
Cisco:Avpair="ip:route#1=15.15.15.16 255.255.255.255 12.12.12.13"
Cisco:Avpair="ip:inacl#1=permit icmp 1.1.1.0 0.0.0.255 9.9.9.0 0.0.0.255"
Cisco:Avpair="ip:dns-server=10.1.1.1"
Cisco:Avpair="ip:wins-server=20.1.1.1"
```

An example illustrates how to configure ACL on CS ACS, which is then downloaded to NAS (router) using Cisco RADIUS AV pair. Follow this same method to configure and download other attributes such as route, dns-server, etc., to the NAS with AV pair. The difference between this filter-id and AV pair implementation for downloading attributes is that with filter-id, you must define the ACL on the router, whereas with AV pair you can define the ACL on the CS ACS server and download to the router. In both cases, you must have authorization enabled on the router. As part of the authorization reply packet from the CS ACS server, the ACL will be downloaded and installed on the router configuration for the user. Figure 9-9 shows the configuration on the ACS.

Figure 9-9 *The ACL Definition in the AV Pair*

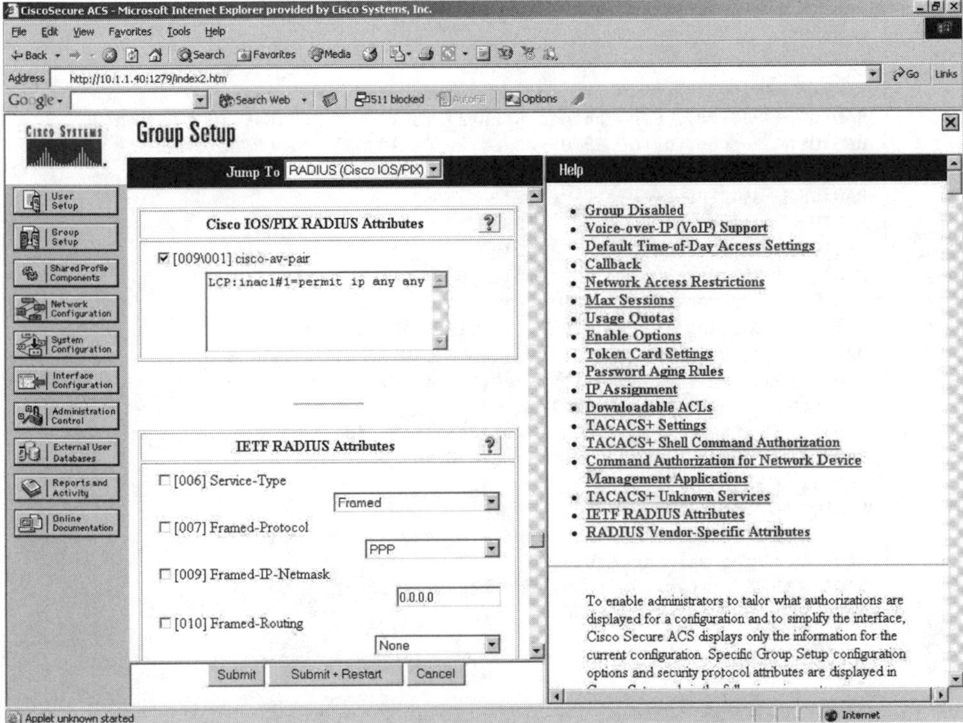

Troubleshooting steps for PPP authentication are very similar to the login authentication that was discussed in the Login Authentication section. So, for details, refer to the "Troubleshooting Steps" under the "Login Authentication" in the Router Management section. Be aware of the following issues that are specific to dialup networking:

- **RADIUS Server Unreachable**—If the RADIUS server is unreachable, you will receive the debug message shown in Example 9-26.

Example 9-26 *Radius Server Unreachable in the* **debug**

```
Dhaka#debug radius
Dhaka#debug aaa authentication
Dhaka#debug aaa authorization
Dhaka#debug ppp authentication
Dhaka#debug aaa per-user
Dhaka#show debug
```

continues

Example 9-26 *Radius Server Unreachable in the* **debug** *(Continued)*

```
General OS:
  AAA Authentication debugging is on
  AAA Authorization debugging is on
  AAA Per-user attributes debugging is on
PPP:
  PPP authentication debugging is on
Radius protocol debugging is on
Dhaka#

AAA/AUTHEN/LOGIN (0000002D): Pick method list 'default'
RADIUS(0000002D): Send Access-Request to 10.1.1.40:1645 id 16, len 90
RADIUS:  authenticator EF 8F 65 E1 E8 C2 16 59 - 82 53 0E B7 6E 0B 26 08
RADIUS:  User-Name           [1]   6   "cisco"
RADIUS:  User-Password       [2]   18  *
RADIUS:  Vendor, Cisco       [26]  13
RADIUS:   cisco-nas-port     [2]   7   "tty63"
RADIUS:  NAS-Port            [5]   6   63
RADIUS:  NAS-Port-Type       [61]  6   Virtual                   [5]
RADIUS:  Calling-Station-Id  [31]  15  "10.1.10.20"
RADIUS:  NAS-IP-Address      [4]   6   10.1.1.1
!When you have communication problem with the server, you will receive many
!retransmit like the one below.
RADIUS: Retransmit to (10.1.1.40:1645,1646) for id 21645/16
RADIUS(0000002D): Retransmit id 21645/16
!Finally it will give up.
RADIUS: Tried all servers.
RADIUS: No valid server found. Trying any viable server
RADIUS: Tried all servers.
RADIUS/DECODE: parse response no app start; FAIL
RADIUS/DECODE: parse response; FAIL
Dhaka#
```

- **Wrong Password**—If the user enters the wrong password, you will see debug messages as shown in Example 9-27.

Example 9-27 *User Authentication Failing Due to a Bad Password*

```
Dhaka#debug radius
Dhaka#debug aaa authentication
Dhaka#debug aaa authorization
Dhaka#debug ppp authentication
Dhaka#debug aaa per-user
Dhaka#show debug
General OS:
  AAA Authentication debugging is on
  AAA Authorization debugging is on
  AAA Per-user attributes debugging is on
PPP:
  PPP authentication debugging is on
Radius protocol debugging is on
Dhaka#
```

Example 9-27 *User Authentication Failing Due to a Bad Password (Continued)*

```
RADIUS(0000008D): Send Access-Request to 10.1.1.40:1645 id 114, len 96
RADIUS:  authenticator 2E 41 E3 D9 80 F1 EB BD - BE 3A 0F 35 13 14 23 37
RADIUS:  Framed-Protocol     [7]   6   PPP                         [1]
RADIUS:  User-Name           [1]   6   "cisco"
RADIUS:  User-Password       [2]   18  *
RADIUS:  Calling-Station-Id  [31]  7   "async"
RADIUS:  Vendor, Cisco       [26]  15
RADIUS:   cisco-nas-port     [2]   9   "Async1"
RADIUS:  NAS-Port            [5]   6   1
RADIUS:  NAS-Port-Type       [61]  6   Async                       [0]
RADIUS:  Service-Type        [6]   6   Framed                      [2]
RADIUS:  NAS-IP-Address      [4]   6   10.1.1.1
RADIUS: Received from id 21645/114 10.1.1.40:1645, Access-Reject, len 32
RADIUS:  authenticator 73 09 AC 01 71 BB 3C D3 - 0D 7B 28 44 65 2A BA 08
RADIUS:  Reply-Message       [18]  12
RADIUS:   52 65 6A 65 63 74 65 64 0A 0D                    [Rejected??]
RADIUS(0000008D): Received from id 21645/114
RADIUS/DECODE: Reply-Message fragments, 10, total 10 bytes
As61 PPP: Received LOGIN Response FAIL
As61 PAP: O AUTH-NAK id 1 len 26 msg is "Authentication failed"
Dhaka#
```

- **Token password is failing authentication**—If you are using OTP, be sure to resynchronize the passcode if needed. Also, be sure to configure the PAP authentication on both the client and the NAS, because that's the only password OTP supports.
- **User account password or profile expired**—If Example 9-27 confirms the failure due to bad password, look at the **auth.log** file on CS ACS, and for RADIUS, search for the expiration in the profile, such as: **Password-Expiration = "24 Jan 2004"**.
- **Mismatch authentication type**—If there is a mismatch on authentication type between the NAS and the client, the authentication will fail. For example, if the client is configured to use CHAP (Challenge Handshake Authentication Protocol) only, and NAS is configured with PAP only, authentication will fail.
- **User workstation configured incorrectly**—If the user workstation misconfiguration is related to password type, you may run into password failure problems. Review the user dialup networking setup, and check for the setup for the parameter such as **Requires encrypted password** for Windows 95 and 98 client. For Windows NT client, in the Dial-Up Networking window, select the connection name, and then **select File > Properties**. Select **Accept any authentication including clear text** to accept both PAP and CHAP passwords. However, if the **Accept only encrypted authentication** box is checked, the PC accepts only CHAP authentication under the **Security Tab**. For Windows 2000, in Network and Dial-Up Connections, select the **connection name**, and then select **Properties**. On the Security tab, check the settings in the **Advanced > Settings > Allow these protocols** area and check **PAP, CHAP**, or **MS-CHAP**.

- **External user database does not support PPP authentication type**—CS ACS can be integrated with various external user databases, such as Novel NDS, Microsoft Active Directory (AD), and so on. These databases do not support all authentication types. For instance Microsoft AD does not support CHAP; instead, it supports MS-CHAP. So, if the NAS and client are configured with CHAP only, the external user database, Microsoft AD, will cause the authentication to fail. This failure information can be found in the auth.log file in CS ACS.
- **User exceeded the maximum number of concurrent sessions**—If the max session is configured and the user reaches the maximum number of concurrent sessions, the user authentication will fail. To fix the problem, for RADIUS, look for this AVP: **Maximum-Channels**. Adjust the value as appropriate.
- **Service definition for authorization**—If you are missing **service=ppp** and related AVPs (**protocol=ip** and **protocol=lcp**), your authorization will fail. So be sure to configure these values on the Group Profile.
- **AVPs are downloaded to NAS but not being applied**—If for **debug aaa authorization** and **debug radius** you see the attributes are downloaded to the router but not being applied, you do not have the aaa authorization turned on for PPP on the router. To fix the problem, turn on authorization with command **aaa authorization network default group radius** on the NAS.
- **Incorrect reply attributes from ACS server**

  Example 9-28 shows an example of a wrong reply attribute debug.

Example 9-28 debug *Output for a Wrong Reply Attribute Scenario*

```
Dhaka#debug radius
Dhaka#debug aaa authentication
Dhaka#debug aaa authorization
Dhaka#debug ppp authentication
Dhaka#debug aaa per-user
Dhaka#show debug
General OS:
  AAA Authentication debugging is on
  AAA Authorization debugging is on
  AAA Per-user attributes debugging is on
PPP:
  PPP authentication debugging is on
Radius protocol debugging is on
Dhaka#
*Apr  5 23:12:28.228: AAA/AUTHOR/EXEC: Authorization FAILED
*Apr  5 23:12:30.228: AAA/MEMORY: free_user (0x612311BC) user='rad_dial' ruser=''
port='tty4' rem_addr='408/3241933' authen_type=ASCII service=LOGIN priv=1
*Apr  5 23:12:30.936: %ISDN-6-DISCONNECT: Interface Serial0:0  disconnected from
unknown, call lasted 61 seconds
*Apr  5 23:12:30.980: %LINK-3-UPDOWN: Interface Serial0:0, changed state to down
Dhaka#
```

To fix the problem, configure RADIUS AVP as follows:

```
Frame-Protocol=ppp, Service Type is Framed.
```

Accounting for Dialup Networking

Network accounting provides information for all PPP, SLIP, or ARAP sessions, including packet and byte counts. On the router, network accounting can be turned on with the following command:

```
aaa accounting network default start-stop group radius
```

X-Auth Troubleshooting for IPsec

The Extended Authentication (X-Auth) feature allows the user of the IPsec client to perform user authentication and group authentication. Because group authentication is common for all users of the same group, this per-user basis authentication provides one extra layer of authentication to provide additional security in collaboration with TACACS+ or RADIUS protocols. Extended authentication is negotiated between the Internet Key Exchange (IKE) phase 1 and IKE phase 2. X-Auth was introduced in 12.1(1) T. However, it was not supported in 12.1(1) mainline. Due to some issues with older versions, using 12.1(3) T and above is recommended.

Router IPsec configuration remains as it is. Example 9-29 shows that additional configuration needed to turn on AAA authentication.

Example 9-29 *Configuration Required to Turn on AAA Authentication for X-Auth*

```
Dhaka# configure terminal
Dhaka(config)# aaa new-model
Dhaka(config)# aaa authentication login default local
Dhaka(config)# aaa authentication login xauth_list group tacacs+
Dhaka(config)# crypto map test client authentication list xauth_list
Dhaka(config)# tacacs-server host 10.1.1.40 key cisco123
Dhaka#
```

On CS ACS, all you need is a username and password to have a valid user defined. Troubleshooting x-auth on the router is the same as shown in the Login Authentication section, so the same steps are not duplicated here.

Auth-proxy Troubleshooting

Auth-proxy is discussed in greater detail in the "Case Studies" section of Chapter 5, "Troubleshooting an IOS Firewall." The troubleshooting is very similar to that discussed in the preceding section. For auth-proxy, the priv level must be 15 for this to work properly. So, be sure to turn on exec authorization and auth-proxy authorization, and set the priv-level to 15.

Case Studies

In this case study, VPDN is configured so that a user dials into the L2TP Access Concentrator (LAC), and based on the domain name, two things happen: a VPDN tunnel is created to the L2TP Network Server (LNS), and the actual user is authenticated by the Radius Server on the LNS side. This case study is based on Figure 9-10.

Figure 9-10 *Basic VPDN Setup*

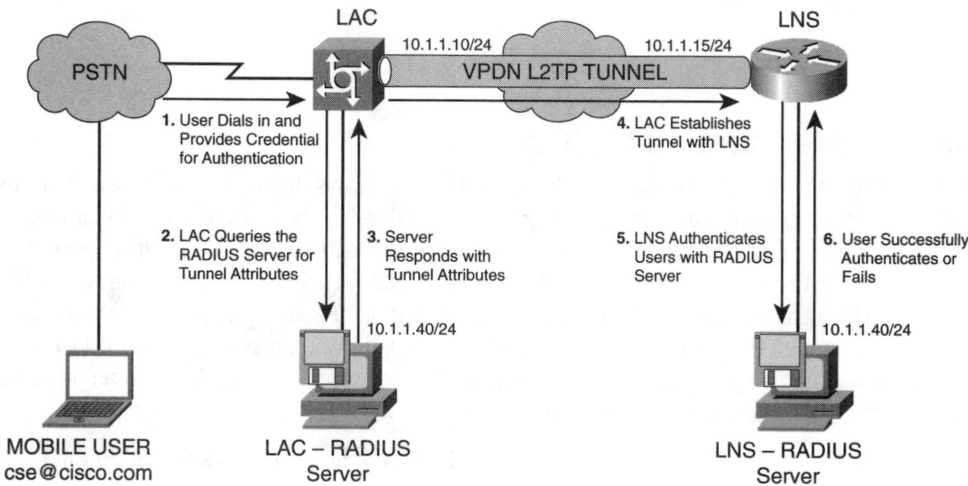

Router Configuration

As shown in Figure 9-10, there are two routers (LAC and LNS) involved for a successful VPDN implementation. In this section, work through the configuration of these two routers.

LAC Configuration

LAC configuration involves turning on VPDN, and configuring AAA for domain name authentication. Example 9-30 shows the configuration of the LAC with an explanation.

Example 9-30 *Configuration of the LAC Router*

```
LAC# show running-config
Building configuration...
Current configuration:
!
version 12.2
service timestamps debug datetime
service timestamps log uptime
no service password-encryption
!
```

Example 9-30 *Configuration of the LAC Router (Continued)*

```
hostname LAC
!
!AAA commands needed to authenticate the user and obtain
!VPDN tunnel information. Don't forget to turn on the authorization for PPP
aaa new-model
aaa authentication login default group local
aaa authentication ppp default if-needed group radius
aaa authorization network default group radius
aaa accounting exec default start-stop group radius
aaa accounting network default start-stop group radius
enable password cisco^%we@sd
!
!The following line is for router management, not significance for VPDN.
!For simplicity, cisco123 is used as password, use strong password for
!production router.
username cisco password 0 cisco123
ip subnet-zero
no ip domain-lookup
!
!The following line turns on VPDN on the router.
vpdn enable
!
!Following line is needed to make VPDN tunnel authorization to be performed based on the
!domain name. Note that the default is DNIS.
vpdn search-order domain
!
interface Ethernet0
 ip address 10.1.1.10 255.255.255.0
 no ip directed-broadcast
!
interface Async1
 ip unnumbered Ethernet0
 no ip directed-broadcast
 ip tcp header-compression passive
 encapsulation ppp
 async mode dedicated
 peer default ip address pool async
 no cdp enable
 ppp authentication chap
!
interface Group-Async1
 physical-layer async
 no ip address
 no ip directed-broadcast
!
ip local pool default 10.1.5.5 10.1.5.50
ip local pool async 10.1.10.1 10.1.10.5
ip classless
ip route 0.0.0.0 0.0.0.0 10.1.1.1
!
```

continues

Example 9-30 *Configuration of the LAC Router (Continued)*

```
!Define the RADIUS server with the following command. Use strong password here. For
!simplicity, used ciscohtts123 in this example
radius-server host 10.1.1.40 auth-port 1645 acct-port 1646 key ciscohtts123
!
line con 0
 transport input none
line 1
 session-timeout 20
 exec-timeout 0 0
 password cisco123
 autoselect during-login
 autoselect ppp
 modem InOut
 transport preferred none
 transport output none
 stopbits 1
 speed 38400
 flowcontrol hardware
line 2 16
 modem InOut
 transport input all
 speed 38400
 flowcontrol hardware
line aux 0
line vty 0 4
 password cisco123
!
end
LAC#
```

Example 9-31 shows the configuration of the HomeGateway.

Example 9-31 *Configuration of LNS Router*

```
LNS# show running-config
Building configuration...
Current configuration:
!
version 12.2
service timestamps debug datetime
service timestamps log uptime
no service password-encryption
!
hostname LNS
!You must make sure to turn on PPP Authorization along with other authentication
!commands.
aaa new-model
aaa authentication login default group local
aaa authentication ppp default group radius local
aaa authorization network default group radius local
aaa accounting exec default start-stop group radius
aaa accounting network default start-stop group radius
```

Example 9-31 *Configuration of LNS Router (Continued)*

```
enable password cisco^%we@sd
!
username cisco password 0 cisco123
ip subnet-zero
no ip domain-lookup
!User the_LNS is used to authenticate the tunnel. The password used here must match the
!vpdn:l2tp-tunnel-password configured in the LAC RADIUS server.
username LNS password 0 DHAKA
!Enable VPDN on the LNS.
vpdn enable
!VPDN group for connection from the LAC.
vpdn-group 1
!This command specifies that the router uses virtual-template 1 for tunnel-id DOHA
!(which matches the tunnel-id configured in the LAC RADIUS server).
accept dialin l2tp virtual-template 1 remote DOHA
!The username used to authenticate this tunnel is the_LNS (configured above).
local name the_LNS
!
interface Ethernet0
 ip address 10.1.1.15 255.255.255.0
 no ip directed-broadcast
!
!Virtual-template that is used for the incoming connection.
interface Virtual-Template1
 ip unnumbered Ethernet0
 no ip directed-broadcast
 peer default ip address pool default
 ppp authentication chap
!
interface Async1
 ip unnumbered Ethernet0
 no ip directed-broadcast
 encapsulation ppp
 async mode interactive
 peer default ip address pool async
 ppp authentication chap
!
ip local pool default 10.1.6.1 10.1.6.5
ip local pool async 10.1.12.100 10.1.12.110
ip classless
ip route 0.0.0.0 0.0.0.0 10.1.1.1
!
!RADIUS server host and key information is defined with the following line. It's
!recommended to define a strong key
radius-server host 10.1.1.40 auth-port 1645 acct-port 1646 key ciscohtts123
!
line con 0
 transport input none
line 1
 session-timeout 20
 exec-timeout 5 0
```

continues

Example 9-31 *Configuration of LNS Router (Continued)*

```
 password ww
 autoselect during-login
 autoselect ppp
 modem InOut
 transport input all
 escape-character BREAK
 stopbits 1
 speed 38400
 flowcontrol hardware
line 2 8
line aux 0
line vty 0 4
 password ww
!
end
LNS#
```

Once both LAC and LNS configuration is complete, proceed with the RADIUS Server as described in the following section.

RADIUS Server Configuration

In this case study, Cisco Secure ACS Windows is used as a RADIUS Server. This section explains the configuration required on both the LAC and LNS side RADIUS section.

LAC RADIUS Configuration

The LAC router strips off the username and sends the domain name to the LAC RADIUS Server as part of the authentication/authorization request. So the LAC RADIUS Server needs to configure the domain name as a username along with the tunnel attributes. Work through the following steps to complete this task:

Step 1 From left Navigation, click on **Network Configuration** and set up the LAC Network Access Server (NAS) as the AAA client to use **RADIUS (Cisco IOS/PIX)**.

Step 2 Configure the user 'cisco.com' with the password **cisco** for both plain and CHAP. This is the username that is used for the tunnel attributes.

Step 3 Click on the **Group Setting** button in the left navigation bar. Select the group the user belongs to and click **Edit Settings**. Scroll down to the **IETF RADIUS** section and select Attribute 6 **Service-Type** as **Outbound** (see Figure 9-11). *If all checkable options do not appear, go into* ***Interface Configuration*** *and check the various boxes to make them appear in the group area.*

Figure 9-11 *LAC RADIUS Server Configuration for Tunnel Attributes*

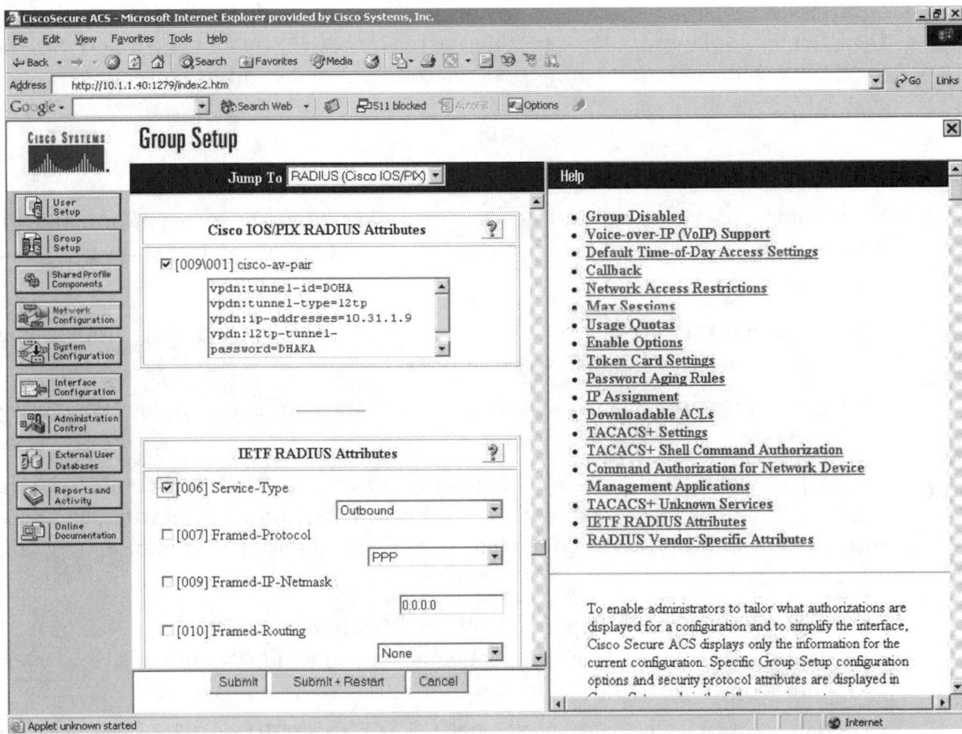

Step 4 In the Cisco IOS/PIX RADIUS attributes section at the bottom, check the box for **009\001 cisco-av-pair**, and type all the attributes as shown in Figure 9-11.

LNS RADIUS Configuration

Actual user authentication occurs at the LNS RADIUS Server. Complete the following steps to configure the LNS RADIUS Server:

Step 1 Configure the user id **cse@cisco.com** and input any password for plain and CHAP.

Step 2 Click on the **Group Setup** button in the left bar. Select the Group the user belongs to and click **Edit Settings**.

Step 3 In the section for Internet Engineering Task Force (IETF) RADIUS Attributes, select **Service-type (attribute 6) = Framed** and **Framed-Protocol (attribute 7) = PPP** from the drop-down menu. Note that you must also click the check box located next to the selected attributes **Service-Type** and **Framed-Protocol**.

If you follow the steps for LAC, LNS, and RADIUS Servers configuration for the corresponding sites, you may not run into any issues with this VPDN implementation. However, most of the problems arise during run time, so it's extremely important to become familiar with the troubleshooting steps as explained in the following section.

Troubleshooting Steps

Show commands are extremely important to display the VPDN tunnel information to verify if your configuration is working correctly or not. The following two **show** commands are used frequently:

- **show vpdn tunnel**—Displays information about all active Layer 2 forwarding and L2TP tunnels in summary-style format.
- **show caller ip**—Displays a summary of caller information for the IP address you provide.

Once a problem is identified with the **show** command, run the **debug** command to find out details. Along with **debug aaa authentication|authorization|accounting**, and **debug radius**, the following list of commands will assist you in troubleshooting the VPDN issues:

- **debug vtemplate**—Displays cloning information for a virtual access interface, from the time it is cloned from a virtual template to the time the virtual access interface comes down when the call ends.
- **debug vpdn error**—Displays errors that prevent a PPP tunnel from being established, or errors that cause an established tunnel to be closed.
- **debug vpdn events**—Displays messages about events that are part of normal PPP tunnel establishment or shutdown.
- **debug vpdn l2x-errors**—Displays Layer 2 protocol errors that prevent Layer 2 establishment or prevent its normal operation.
- **debug vpdn l2x-events**—Displays messages about events that are part of normal PPP tunnel establishment or shutdown for Layer 2.
- **debug vpdn l2tp-sequencing**—Displays messages about L2TP.

If you are having problems with successful VPDN connections, analyze the debug output on both LAC and LNS routers. The following two sections demonstrate that analysis.

LAC Router Troubleshooting

Before looking at some of problems that you may encounter on the LAC, look at the debug as shown in Example 9-32 when the VPDN works.

Example 9-32 debug *Output from the LAC When VPDN Works*

```
LAC# show debug
General OS:
  AAA Authentication debugging is on
  AAA Authorization debugging is on
  AAA Accounting debugging is on
VPN:
  L2X protocol events debugging is on
  L2X protocol errors debugging is on
  VPDN events debugging is on
  VPDN errors debugging is on
  L2TP data sequencing debugging is on
VTEMPLATE:
  Virtual Template debugging is on
Radius protocol debugging is on
LAC#
Mar  9 12:22:16: As1 AAA/AUTHOR/FSM: (0):
    LCP succeeds trivially
2d18h: %LINK-3-UPDOWN: Interface Async1, changed state to up
Mar  9 12:22:17: As1 VPDN: Looking for tunnel -- cisco.com --
Mar  9 12:22:17: AAA: parse name=Async1 idb type=10 tty=1
Mar  9 12:22:17: AAA: name=Async1 flags=0x11 type=4 shelf=0 slot=0
    adapter=0 port=1 channel=0
Mar  9 12:22:17: AAA/AUTHEN: create_user (0x25BA84)
    user='cisco.com' ruser='' port='Async1' rem_addr=''
    authen_type=NONE service=LOGIN priv=0
Mar 9 12:22:17: AAA/AUTHOR/VPDN (6239469): Port='Async1' list='default' service=NET
Mar  9 12:22:17: AAA/AUTHOR/VPDN:  (6239469) user='cisco.com'
Mar  9 12:22:17: AAA/AUTHOR/VPDN:  (6239469) send AV service=ppp
Mar  9 12:22:17: AAA/AUTHOR/VPDN:  (6239469) send AV protocol=vpdn
Mar  9 12:22:17: AAA/AUTHOR/VPDN (6239469) found list "default"
Mar  9 12:22:17: AAA/AUTHOR/VPDN:  (6239469) Method=RADIUS
Mar  9 12:22:17: RADIUS: authenticating to get author data
Mar  9 12:22:17: RADIUS: ustruct sharecount=2
!Sending the initial request packet to the RADIUS Server
Mar  9 12:22:17: RADIUS: Initial Transmit Async1 id 66
    10.1.1.40:1645, Access-Request, len 77
Mar  9 12:22:17:          Attribute 4 6 0A1F0106
Mar  9 12:22:17:          Attribute 5 6 00000001
Mar  9 12:22:17:          Attribute 61 6 00000000
Mar  9 12:22:17:          Attribute 1 15 7274702E
Mar  9 12:22:17:          Attribute 2 18 6AB5A2B0
Mar  9 12:22:17:          Attribute 6 6 00000005
!Access received from the RADIUS Server
Mar  9 12:22:17: RADIUS: Received from id 66
    10.1.1.40:1645, Access-Accept, len 158
Mar  9 12:22:17:          Attribute 6 6 00000005
Mar  9 12:22:17:          Attribute 26 28 0000000901167670
Mar  9 12:22:17:          Attribute 26 29 0000000901177670
Mar  9 12:22:17:          Attribute 26 36 00000009011E7670
Mar  9 12:22:17:          Attribute 26 39 0000000901217670
Mar  9 12:22:17: RADIUS: saved authorization data for user 25BA84 at 24C488
!RADIUS server supplies the VPDN tunnel attributes as shown by the following four lines.
```

continues

Example 9-32 debug *Output from the LAC When VPDN Works (Continued)*

```
Mar  9 12:22:17: RADIUS: cisco AVPair "vpdn:tunnel-id=DOHA"
Mar  9 12:22:17: RADIUS: cisco AVPair "vpdn:tunnel-type=l2tp"
Mar  9 12:22:17: RADIUS: cisco AVPair "vpdn:ip-addresses=10.1.1.15,"
Mar  9 12:22:17: RADIUS: cisco AVPair "vpdn:l2tp-tunnel-password=DHAKA"
Mar  9 12:22:17: AAA/AUTHOR (6239469): Post authorization status = PASS_ADD
Mar  9 12:22:17: AAA/AUTHOR/VPDN: Processing AV service=ppp
Mar  9 12:22:17: AAA/AUTHOR/VPDN: Processing AV protocol=vpdn
Mar  9 12:22:17: AAA/AUTHOR/VPDN: Processing AV tunnel-id=DOHA
Mar  9 12:22:17: AAA/AUTHOR/VPDN: Processing AV tunnel-type=l2tp
Mar  9 12:22:17: AAA/AUTHOR/VPDN: Processing AV ip-addresses=10.1.1.15,
Mar  9 12:22:17: AAA/AUTHOR/VPDN: Processing AV l2tp-tunnel-password=DHAKA
Mar  9 12:22:17: As1 VPDN: Get tunnel info for cisco.com with LAC DOHA, IP 10.1.1.15
Mar  9 12:22:17: AAA/AUTHEN: free_user (0x25BA84)
    user='cisco.com' ruser='' port='Async1' rem_addr=''
    authen_type=NONE service=LOGIN priv=0
!The following line shows the LNS ip address which is 10.1.1.15
Mar  9 12:22:17: As1 VPDN: Forward to address 10.1.1.15
Mar  9 12:22:17: As1 VPDN: Forwarding...
Mar  9 12:22:17: AAA: parse name=Async1 idb
    type=10 tty=1
Mar  9 12:22:17: AAA: name=Async1 flags=0x11 type=4
    shelf=0 slot=0 adapter=0 port=1 channel=0
Mar  9 12:22:17: AAA/AUTHEN: create_user (0xB7918)
    user='cse@cisco.com' ruser='' port='Async1'
    rem_addr='async' authen_type=CHAP service=PPP priv=1
Mar  9 12:22:17: As1 VPDN: Bind interface direction=1
Mar  9 12:22:17: Tnl/Cl 51/1 L2TP: Session FS enabled
Mar  9 12:22:17: Tnl/Cl 51/1 L2TP: Session state change from idle to wait-for-tunnel
Mar  9 12:22:17: As1 51/1 L2TP: Create session
Mar  9 12:22:17: Tnl 51 L2TP: SM State idle
Mar  9 12:22:17: Tnl 51 L2TP: O SCCRQ
Mar  9 12:22:17: Tnl 51 L2TP: Tunnel state change from idle to wait-ctl-reply
Mar  9 12:22:17: Tnl 51 L2TP: SM State wait-ctl-reply
!Following line shows username is forwarded to LNS
Mar  9 12:22:17: As1 VPDN: cse@cisco.com is forwarded
Mar  9 12:22:17: Tnl 51 L2TP: I SCCRP from the_LNS
!Tunnel authentication is show successful here by the following three lines.
Mar  9 12:22:17: Tnl 51 L2TP: Got a challenge from remote peer, the_LNS
Mar  9 12:22:17: Tnl 51 L2TP: Got a response from remote peer, the_LNS
Mar  9 12:22:17: Tnl 51 L2TP: Tunnel Authentication success
Mar  9 12:22:17: Tnl 51 L2TP: Tunnel state change from
    wait-ctl-reply to established
Mar  9 12:22:17: Tnl 51 L2TP: O SCCCN  to the_LNS tnlid 38
Mar  9 12:22:17: Tnl 51 L2TP: SM State established
Mar  9 12:22:17: As1 51/1 L2TP: O ICRQ to the_LNS 38/0
Mar  9 12:22:17: As1 51/1 L2TP: Session state change from
    wait-for-tunnel to wait-reply
Mar  9 12:22:17: As1 51/1 L2TP: O ICCN to the_LNS 38/1
Mar  9 12:22:17: As1 51/1 L2TP: Session state change from
    wait-reply to established
2d18h: %LINEPROTO-5-UPDOWN: Line protocol on Interface
    Async1, changed state to up
LAC#
```

The following is a list of common problems you may encounter with VPDN on the LAC router. Examples shown for every problem are generated with the same debug as shown in Example 9-31.

- **Wrong domain name in the username**—If the user name comes in with the wrong domain name, the RADIUS Server will cause the domain name authentication to fail. In Example 9-33, the debug shows that the user comes in as cse@xyz.com instead of cse@cisco.com, hence the LAC RADIUS Server does not recognize this domain.

Example 9-33 *Wrong Domain Name Fails on the LAC Router*

```
LAC#
Mar  9 12:50:48: RADIUS: Received from id 86 10.1.1.40:1645, Access-Reject, len 46
Mar  9 12:50:48:         Attribute 18 26 41757468
Mar  9 12:50:48: RADIUS: failed to get authorization data: authen status = 2
%VPDN-6-AUTHORFAIL: L2F NAS LAC, AAA authorization failure for As1 user cse@xyz.com
LAC#
```

- **Invalid Tunnel IP from the RADIUS Server**—If the user profile on CS ACS is configured for the domain name with the wrong tunnel IP address, the LAC router will get the wrong tunnel IP. Therefore, the user attempts to establish a session that will fail with the debug message shown in Example 9-34.

Example 9-34 **debug** *Output on the LAC Router When CS ACS Provides Wrong Tunnel IP*

```
LAC#
Mar  9 12:55:45: As1 VPDN: Forward to address 1.1.1.1
Mar  9 12:55:45: As1 VPDN: Forwarding...
Mar  9 12:55:45: Tnl 56 L2TP: Tunnel state change from idle to wait-ctl-reply
Mar 9 13:32:46: As1 56/1 L2TP: Discarding data packet because tunnel is not open
LAC#
```

- **Tunnel Password Mismatch**—The tunnel password that is provided by the LAC RADIUS Server to the LAC router should match the LNS router password. If they do not match, debug messages as shown in Example 9-35 will result.

Example 9-35 **debug** *Message When There Is Tunnel Password Mismatch between the LAC and LNS*

```
LAC#
Mar  9 12:57:37: Tnl 59 L2TP: Tunnel Authentication fails for the_LNS
Mar  9 12:57:37: Tnl 59 L2TP: Expected E530DA13B826685C678589250C0BF525
Mar  9 12:57:37: Tnl 59 L2TP: Got E09D90E8A91CF1014C91D56F65BDD052
Mar  9 12:57:37: Tnl 59 L2TP: O StopCCN to the_LNS tnlid 44
Mar  9 12:57:37: Tnl 59 L2TP: Tunnel state change from wait-ctl-reply to shutting-
down
Mar  9 12:57:37: Tnl 59 L2TP: Shutdown tunnel
LAC#
```

LNS Router Troubleshooting

Just as with the LAC router, it is worth going through a good debug output on the LNS router. Example 9-36 shows a good debug from the LNS when the VPDN works.

Example 9-36 debug *Output of LNS Router When VPDN Works*

```
LNS# show debug
General OS:
  AAA Authentication debugging is on
  AAA Authorization debugging is on
  AAA Accounting debugging is on
VPN:
  L2X protocol events debugging is on
  L2X protocol errors debugging is on
  VPDN events debugging is on
  VPDN errors debugging is on
  L2TP data sequencing debugging is on
VTEMPLATE:
  Virtual Template debugging is on
Radius protocol debugging is on
LNS#
Mar  9 12:22:16: L2TP: I SCCRQ from DOHA tnl 51
!The following line shows tunnel created for the LAC
Mar  9 12:22:16: Tnl 38 L2TP: New tunnel created for
    remote DOHA, address 10.1.1.10
Mar  9 12:22:16: Tnl 38 L2TP: Got a challenge in SCCRQ, DOHA
Mar  9 12:22:16: Tnl 38 L2TP: O SCCRP  to DOHA tnlid 51
Mar  9 12:22:16: Tnl 38 L2TP: Tunnel state change from idle to wait-ctl-reply
Mar  9 12:22:16: Tnl 38 L2TP: I SCCCN from DOHA tnl 51
Mar  9 12:22:16: Tnl 38 L2TP: Got a Challenge Response in SCCCN from DOHA
!Tunnel authentication is successful
Mar  9 12:22:16: Tnl 38 L2TP: Tunnel Authentication success
Mar  9 12:22:16: Tnl 38 L2TP: Tunnel state change from wait-ctl-reply to established
Mar  9 12:22:16: Tnl 38 L2TP: SM State established
Mar  9 12:22:17: Tnl 38 L2TP: I ICRQ from DOHA tnl 51
Mar  9 12:22:17: Tnl/Cl 38/1 L2TP: Session FS enabled
Mar  9 12:22:17: Tnl/Cl 38/1 L2TP: Session state change
    from idle to wait-for-tunnel
Mar  9 12:22:17: Tnl/Cl 38/1 L2TP: New session created
Mar  9 12:22:17: Tnl/Cl 38/1 L2TP: O ICRP to DOHA 51/1
Mar  9 12:22:17: Tnl/Cl 38/1 L2TP: Session state change
    from wait-for-tunnel to wait-connect
Mar  9 12:22:17: Tnl/Cl 38/1 L2TP: I ICCN from DOHA tnl 51, cl 1
Mar  9 12:22:17: Tnl/Cl 38/1 L2TP: Session state change
    from wait-connect to established
Mar  9 12:22:17: Vi1 VTEMPLATE: Reuse Vi1, recycle queue size 0
Mar  9 12:22:17: Vi1 VTEMPLATE: Hardware address 00e0.1e68.942c
!Following three lines shows using Virtual-template 1 for this user.
Mar  9 12:22:17: Vi1 VPDN: Virtual interface created for cse@cisco.com
Mar  9 12:22:17: Vi1 VPDN: Set to Async interface
Mar  9 12:22:17: Vi1 VPDN: Clone from Vtemplate 1 filterPPP=0 blocking
Mar  9 12:22:17: Vi1 VTEMPLATE: Has a new cloneblk vtemplate, now it has vtemplate
Mar  9 12:22:17: Vi1 VTEMPLATE: ************* CLONE
    VACCESS1 *****************
```

Example 9-36 debug *Output of LNS Router When VPDN Works (Continued)*

```
Mar  9 12:22:17: Vi1 VTEMPLATE: Clone from Virtual-Template1
interface Virtual-Access1
default ip address
no ip address
encap ppp
ip unnum eth 0
no ip directed-broadcast
peer default ip address pool default
ppp authen chap
end

Mar  9 12:22:18: cse@cisco.com 38/1 L2TP: Session
    with no hwidb
02:23:59: %LINK-3-UPDOWN: Interface Virtual-Access1,
    changed state to up
Mar  9 12:22:19: Vi1 AAA/AUTHOR/FSM: (0): LCP succeeds
    trivially
Mar  9 12:22:19: Vi1 VPDN: Bind interface direction=2
Mar  9 12:22:19: Vi1 VPDN: PPP LCP accepted rcv CONFACK
Mar  9 12:22:19: Vi1 VPDN: PPP LCP accepted sent CONFACK
Mar  9 12:22:19: Vi1 L2X: Discarding packet because of
    no mid/session
Mar  9 12:22:19: AAA: parse name=Virtual-Access1 idb type=21 tty=-1
Mar  9 12:22:19: AAA: name=Virtual-Access1 flags=0x11
    type=5 shelf=0 slot=0 adapter=0 port=1 channel=0
Mar  9 12:22:19: AAA/AUTHEN: create_user (0x2462A0)
    user='cse@cisco.com' ruser='' port='Virtual-Access1'
    rem_addr='' authen_type=CHAP service=PPP priv=1
Mar  9 12:22:19: AAA/AUTHEN/START (2229277178):
    port='Virtual-Access1' list='' action=LOGIN
    service=PPP
Mar  9 12:22:19: AAA/AUTHEN/START (2229277178):
    using "default" list
Mar  9 12:22:19: AAA/AUTHEN/START (2229277178):
    Method=RADIUS
Mar  9 12:22:19: RADIUS: ustruct sharecount=1
!Access-request packet is sending to the RADIUS Server
Mar  9 12:22:19: RADIUS: Initial Transmit Virtual-Access1
    id 78 171.68.120.194:1645, Access-Request, len 92
Mar  9 12:22:19:        Attribute 4 6 0A1F0109
Mar  9 12:22:19:        Attribute 5 6 00000001
Mar  9 12:22:19:        Attribute 61 6 00000005
Mar  9 12:22:19:        Attribute 1 23 6464756E
Mar  9 12:22:19:        Attribute 3 19 34A66389
Mar  9 12:22:19:        Attribute 6 6 00000002
Mar  9 12:22:19:        Attribute 7 6 00000001
Mar  9 12:22:19: RADIUS: Received from id 78
!Access-Accept received as shown here
    171.68.120.194:1645, Access-Accept, len 32
Mar  9 12:22:19:        Attribute 6 6 00000002
Mar  9 12:22:19:        Attribute 7 6 00000001
Mar  9 12:22:19: AAA/AUTHEN (2229277178): status = PASS
```

continues

Example 9-36 debug *Output of LNS Router When VPDN Works (Continued)*

```
Mar  9 12:22:19: Vi1 AAA/AUTHOR/LCP: Authorize LCP
Mar  9 12:22:19: AAA/AUTHOR/LCP Vi1 (1756915964):
    Port='Virtual-Access1' list='' service=NET
Mar  9 12:22:19: AAA/AUTHOR/LCP: Vi1 (1756915964)
    user='cse@cisco.com'
Mar  9 12:22:19: AAA/AUTHOR/LCP: Vi1 (1756915964)
    send AV service=ppp
Mar  9 12:22:19: AAA/AUTHOR/LCP: Vi1 (1756915964)
    send AV protocol=lcp
Mar  9 12:22:19: AAA/AUTHOR/LCP (1756915964) found
    list "default"
Mar  9 12:22:19: AAA/AUTHOR/LCP: Vi1 (1756915964)
    Method=RADIUS
Mar  9 12:22:19: AAA/AUTHOR (1756915964): Post
    authorization status = PASS_REPL
Mar  9 12:22:19: Vi1 AAA/AUTHOR/LCP: Processing
    AV service=ppp
Mar  9 12:22:19: AAA/ACCT/NET/START User
    cse@cisco.com, Port Virtual-Access1, List ""
Mar  9 12:22:19: AAA/ACCT/NET: Found list "default"
Mar  9 12:22:19: Vi1 AAA/AUTHOR/FSM: (0): Can we
    start IPCP?
Mar  9 12:22:19: AAA/AUTHOR/FSM Vi1 (1311872588):
    Port='Virtual-Access1' list='' service=NET
Mar  9 12:22:19: AAA/AUTHOR/FSM: Vi1 (1311872588)
    user='cse@cisco.com'
Mar  9 12:22:19: AAA/AUTHOR/FSM: Vi1 (1311872588)
    send AV service=ppp
Mar  9 12:22:19: AAA/AUTHOR/FSM: Vi1 (1311872588)
    send AV protocol=ip
Mar  9 12:22:19: AAA/AUTHOR/FSM (1311872588)
    found list "default"
Mar  9 12:22:19: AAA/AUTHOR/FSM: Vi1 (1311872588)
    Method=RADIUS
Mar  9 12:22:19: AAA/AUTHOR (1311872588): Post
    authorization status = PASS_REPL
Mar  9 12:22:19: Vi1 AAA/AUTHOR/FSM: We can start
    IPCP
Mar  9 12:22:19: RADIUS: ustruct sharecount=2
Mar  9 12:22:19: RADIUS: Initial Transmit Virtual-Access1
    id 79 171.68.120.194:1646, Accounting-Request, len 101
Mar  9 12:22:19:         Attribute 4 6 0A1F0109
Mar  9 12:22:19:         Attribute 5 6 00000001
Mar  9 12:22:19:         Attribute 61 6 00000005
Mar  9 12:22:19:         Attribute 1 23 6464756E
Mar  9 12:22:19:         Attribute 40 6 00000001
Mar  9 12:22:19:         Attribute 45 6 00000001
Mar  9 12:22:19:         Attribute 6 6 00000002
Mar  9 12:22:19:         Attribute 44 10 30303030
Mar  9 12:22:19:         Attribute 7 6 00000001
Mar  9 12:22:19:         Attribute 41 6 00000000
```

Example 9-36 debug *Output of LNS Router When VPDN Works (Continued)*

```
Mar  9 12:22:19: Vi1 AAA/AUTHOR/IPCP: Start.  Her
    address 0.0.0.0, we want 0.0.0.0
Mar  9 12:22:19: Vi1 AAA/AUTHOR/IPCP: Processing
    AV service=ppp
!The authorization is shown to be successful
Mar  9 12:22:19: Vi1 AAA/AUTHOR/IPCP: Authorization
    succeeded
Mar  9 12:22:19: Vi1 AAA/AUTHOR/IPCP: Done.  Her
    address 0.0.0.0, we want 0.0.0.0
Mar  9 12:22:19: RADIUS: Received from id 79
    171.68.120.194:1646, Accounting-response,
    len 20
Mar  9 12:22:19: Vi1 AAA/AUTHOR/IPCP: Start.
    Her address 0.0.0.0, we want 10.1.6.1
Mar  9 12:22:19: Vi1 AAA/AUTHOR/IPCP: Processing
    AV service=ppp
Mar  9 12:22:19: Vi1 AAA/AUTHOR/IPCP: Authorization
    succeeded
Mar  9 12:22:19: Vi1 AAA/AUTHOR/IPCP: Done.
    Her address 0.0.0.0, we want 10.1.6.1
Mar  9 12:22:19: Vi1 AAA/AUTHOR/IPCP: Start.
    Her address 10.1.6.1, we want 10.1.6.1
Mar  9 12:22:19: AAA/AUTHOR/IPCP Vi1 (2909132255):
    Port='Virtual-Access1' list='' service=NET
Mar  9 12:22:19: AAA/AUTHOR/IPCP: Vi1 (2909132255)
    user='cse@cisco.com'
Mar  9 12:22:19: AAA/AUTHOR/IPCP: Vi1 (2909132255)
    send AV service=ppp
Mar  9 12:22:19: AAA/AUTHOR/IPCP: Vi1 (2909132255)
    send AV protocol=ip
Mar  9 12:22:19: AAA/AUTHOR/IPCP: Vi1 (2909132255)
    send AV addr*10.1.6.1
Mar  9 12:22:19: AAA/AUTHOR/IPCP (2909132255)
    found list "default"
Mar  9 12:22:19: AAA/AUTHOR/IPCP: Vi1 (2909132255)
    Method=RADIUS
Mar  9 12:22:19: AAA/AUTHOR (2909132255): Post
    authorization status = PASS_REPL
Mar  9 12:22:19: Vi1 AAA/AUTHOR/IPCP: Reject
    10.1.6.1, using 10.1.6.1
Mar  9 12:22:19: Vi1 AAA/AUTHOR/IPCP: Processing
    AV service=ppp
Mar  9 12:22:19: Vi1 AAA/AUTHOR/IPCP: Processing
    AV addr*10.1.6.1
Mar  9 12:22:19: Vi1 AAA/AUTHOR/IPCP: Authorization
    succeeded
Mar  9 12:22:19: Vi1 AAA/AUTHOR/IPCP: Done.
    Her address 10.1.6.1, we want 10.1.6.1
02:24:00: %LINEPROTO-5-UPDOWN: Line protocol on
    Interface Virtual-Access1, changed state to up
LNS#
```

The following is a list of problems that you may encounter on the LNS side for VPDN:

- **Tunnel ID for LAC is missing or misconfigured**—You must ensure that the proper Tunnel ID is configured for LAC. In this case study, you must have already configured **"accept dialing l2tp virtual-template 1 remote DOHA"** on the LNS; otherwise, you will receive a debug message as shown in Example 9-37.

Example 9-37 debug *Message When Tunnel ID is Misconfigured or Not Configured*

```
LNS#
Mar  9 13:45:32: L2TP: I SCCRQ from DOHA tnl 62
Mar  9 13:45:32: L2X: Never heard of DOHA
Mar  9 13:45:32: L2TP: Could not find info block for DOHA
LNS#
```

- **Tunnel password mismatch**—If there is a password mismatch between the LAC and LNS, you will get the same message as you did for the LAC router as shown in Example 9-34.
- **Actual user authentication failure**—Actual user authentication occurs at the LNS router. Hence, if the LNS RADIUS Server is not configured with the proper username and password, then although the VPDN tunnel may become built up, the user will still not be able to access network resources.

This troubleshooting concludes the case study on VPDN. In the next section, we examine some of the common problems and resolutions.

Common Problems and Resolutions

This section discusses some of common problems you may encounter and how to resolve them when you configure AAA on the Cisco IOS Routers.

1. Why are users who have a privilege level less than 15 unable to view the complete running configuration, but able to see the complete startup configuration on the Cisco IOS Router?

   Answer: When configuring access to the router by privilege levels, you face the common issue that the **show running** or **writes terminal** command is configured at or below the user's privilege level. But, when the user executes the command, the configuration appears to be blank. This is actually by design, as explained in the paragraphs that follow.

   The **write terminal/show running-config** command shows a blank configuration. This command displays all the commands that the current user is permitted to modify (in other words, all the commands at or below the user's current privilege level). The command should not display commands above the user's current privilege level because of security considerations. If it did display the commands, commands like **snmp-server community** could be used to modify the current configuration of the router and gain complete access to the router.

The **show config/show start-up config** command displays a full configuration but does not truly show the actual configuration. Instead, the command simply prints out the contents of non-volatile random access memory (NVRAM), which happens to be the configuration of the router at the time the user executes a **write memory** command.

2 Why am I unable to authorize my console port?

Answer: Console port authorization was introduced from version 12.0(6) T and is off by default to lessen the likelihood of accidentally being locked out of the router. If a user has physical access to the router via the console, console port authorization is not extremely effective. Console port authorization can be turned on under line con 0 with the hidden command **aaa authorization console**. Example 9-38 shows an error message that displays when you are attempting to turn on exec authorization for console without configuring aaa authorization by using the aaa authorization console command.

Example 9-38 *Sample Output from Router When Attempting to Turn on Authorization Without Using the aaa Authorization Console Command Globally*

```
User Access Verification

Username: user15
Password:

c2621#
c2621#conf t
Enter configuration commands, one per line. End with CNTL/Z.
c2621(config)#line con 0
c2621(config-line)# authorization exec default
%Authorization without the global command 'aaa authorization console' is useless
c2621(config-line)#
```

3 How can I send an accounting record to multiple AAA servers?

Answer: You must configure broadcast in the following command:

```
aaa accounting {network | exec | commands (level) | connection |
  system | commands (level) | auth-proxy | resource} {default |
  (namedlist)} {start-stop | stop-only | none | wait-start} [broadcast]
```

4 Can I configure RADIUS and TACACS+ protocol for authentication on the same router with the same or two different AAA servers?

Answer: Yes, but it is possible for two different types of access modes. For instance, you can configure RADIUS for console port access, and TACACS+ for Telnet access.

You must define at least one named method list, and the other one can be left as default. It is a common practice to configure RADIUS for dialup connections, and TACACS+ for router management. If you configure RADIUS and TACACS+ for two different services (LOGIN and PPP), you can define both method names as default.

5 Is it possible to authenticate users with RADIUS protocol, but authorize them with TACACS+ protocol?

Answer: Yes, it is possible. You need to define RADIUS protocol for authentication and TACACS+ protocol for authorization in the method list. This works, because TACACS+, unlike RADIUS protocol, handles authorization in a separate packet than authentication.

6 Can you define *none* as the authentication or authorization method?

Answer: Yes, it is possible. This effectively bypasses the authentication/authorization if defined as a method. The *None* method is mainly used as the primary method in the console port to avoid authentication when the default login method is defined for Telnet access. This is also used as the last backup method to avoid a possible deadlock situation if all available methods are unavailable to process the authentication and authorization requests.

Best Practices

This section looks into some of the important issues for improving performance and avoiding a lockout situation. The following is a list of some good practices to achieve this:

- Always configure Fall Back Authentication Method so that you can avoid a lockout situation if the authentication server is unavailable.
- Save the good running configuration of the router to NVRAM with the **write memory** command before starting AAA configuration. Once AAA is configured, make sure it works as expected before writing it into NVRAM. This way, you can **reload** the router if you are locked out due to misconfiguration.
- Unless it is absolutely needed, do not configure authorization for the console. Also, try to avoid authentication for your console with the authentication server, rather than configuring local user databases.
- Unless you have multiple AAA servers, and you have a network latency issue, do not increase the timeout for the AAA server from the default 5 seconds to a higher number.
- Avoid sending AAA requests over wide-area network (WAN) links, or slow links unless it is required, because this may slow down the performance.

- Source the RADIUS/TACACS+ packets from a specific interface, so that the AAA server always trusts the NAS because the packet will always be sourcing from one interface. Using a loop back interface is preferred because that provides high availability.
- Configure dead-time for RADIUS to improve the performance, if you have a backup RADIUS Server configured.

CHAPTER 10

Troubleshooting AAA on PIX Firewalls and FWSM

The AAA implementation on PIX firewalls and Firewall Services Modules (FWSMs) is very similar to that on routers with very few exceptions. As of writing this text, the current version of PIX is 7.x, and the current version of FWSM is 2.3.x. The discussion in this chapter is based on PIX Version 7.x. Hence some of the features discussed in this chapter may not be supported on the FWSM Version 2.3.x, which is based on PIX code base 6.3.x. This difference will be pointed out throughout the chapter. The primary focus of this chapter is troubleshooting techniques on AAA, which is the same on both PIX and FWSM. The Case Study section of this chapter examines the feature called Virtual HTTP or Virtual Telnet that addresses some of the problems posed by the Cut-Thru Proxy. Finally, the chapter concludes with Best Practices.

Overview of Authentication, Authorization, and Accounting (AAA)

A thorough understanding of AAA architecture and two commonly used protocols (RADIUS and TACACS+) that support this architecture is a must. You need this knowledge to understand and troubleshoot AAA issues on the PIX firewall. Refer to Chapter 9, "Troubleshooting AAA on IOS Routers" under the section of the same title for details on this. The discussion in this chapter focuses on the perimeter of the PIX and FWSM domain.

PIX Firewall can be configured to support AAA for one of the following purposes:

- **To manage administrative users**—These users connect to the firewall to make configuration changes or to monitor activity through the console, Telnet, Secure Shell (SSH), or the PIX Device Manager (PDM)/Adaptive Security Device Manager (ASDM) application.
- **To manage Cut-Thru Proxy users**—The users of the Cut-Thru Proxy are the end users who make connections across the firewall. When the user first initiates a connection, the firewall intercepts the connection with an authentication challenge. If the user is successfully authenticated, that connection is allowed and with the cut-through proxy feature, the future connections are allowed without any additional interception.
- **To mange VPN users (VPN is not supported on FWSM)**—The users of the Remote Access VPN connection perform extended authentication (X-Auth) in addition to the group authentication.

For the administrative, Cut-Through Proxy, and VPN users the following security services are available using AAA framework:

- **Authentication**—Authentication involves identification of the user.
- **Authorization**—Authorization involves what the user does. Although authentication is valid without authorization, authorization is not valid without authentication.
- **Accounting**—Accounting involves actions the user took after login to the firewall or through the firewall.

More details discussion follow in the next few sections on AAA.

Authentication

A firewall can authenticate a user based on a generic password only, against its local user database, or against an external database server (for example, Cisco Secure ACS Server). Support for different authentication methods is based on the connections types. For example, administrative users' authentication can be done merely by requiring a password, whereas the cut-through proxy authentication requires either a local user or an external database where username and password can be configured.

For administrative users, when users log into a firewall, they are assigned a privilege level from 1 to 15. Note that privilege level 0 is available, but is not assigned to the administrative users. When users log in with just the password configured on the firewall, a default user name enable_1 is used and the user gets privilege level 1. However, when successfully entering into enable mode, that user gets privilege level 15.

NOTE For SSH connection, if only a password is configured on the firewall for login, use **pix** as the username and **password** for login. If Telnet is used for authentication, use only the **password** for the Telnet login. For PDM/ASDM, leave the username field blank and use the **password** as configured on the PIX firewall.

To authenticate users based on an individual username (instead of default username enable_1), you can configure either a LOCAL user database or external server for authentication. You can assign different privilege levels to the user and control what commands users may be able to execute after login to the firewall. Privilege level is discussed in the "Authorization" section, which is discussed in the coming section.

For Cut-Through Proxy and Remote Access VPN connections, user authentication must be performed either by the LOCAL user database or by the external AAA server.

NOTE Local User Authentication support was first introduced in PIX Firewall version 6.2.

Prior to version 7.0, PIX firewall authentication protocol support is limited to the local user database, TACACS+, and RADIUS protocol. The PIX Firewall Version 7.0 introduced few new client APIs that are used for different types of authentication servers.

Table 10-1 summarizes AAA support for different protocols based on PIX Firewall Version 7.0.

Table 10-1 *Support of AAA for Different Protocol Types*

Protocol	Authentication	Authorization	Accounting
Internal server	Yes	Yes	No
RADIUS	Yes	Yes	Yes
TACACS+	Yes	Yes	Yes
SDI	Yes	No	No
NT	Yes	No	No
Kerberos	Yes	No	No
LDAP	No	Yes	No

As you can see in Table 10-1, authentication is supported by different protocols with the exception of the LDAP database. Authentication for administrative users for PIX management, Remote Access VPN connection, and Cut-Through Proxy connections are not supported by every protocol. Table 10-2 shows the authentication support by different protocols based on PIX Version 7.0.

Table 10-2 *Authentication Support for Different Authentication Methods Based on Version 7.0*

Authentication of	LOCAL	RADIUS	TACACS	SDI	NT	Kerberos	LDAP
VPN users	Yes	Yes	Yes	Yes	Yes	Yes	No
Administrators	Yes	Yes	Yes	No	No	No	No
Cut-Through	Yes	Yes	Yes	No	No	No	No

We recommend strongly that you configure a fallback method so that you are not completely locked out from the PIX firewall if the AAA server is unavailable. AAA fallback was first introduced in PIX Firewall Version 6.3.4. This feature provides the ability for authentication and authorization requests to fall back on the local user database when the AAA server is unreachable. Fallback is available only with the LOCAL user database for firewall management connection (both authentication and authorization), and Remote Access VPN connection (only authentication).

You can configure fallback authentication for the authentication to login to PIX firewall with the following command:

```
[no] aaa authentication [serial|enable|telnet|ssh|http] console server-tag [LOCAL]
```

The LOCAL user database can be used as a fallback method for authentication for the Remote Access VPN connection. The syntax for configuring the LOCAL user database as a fallback method for Remote Access VPN connection is as follows:

```
[no] crypto map name set client authentication server-tag [LOCAL]
```

Authorization

On the firewall, authorization for different types of connections has different meanings. For example, authorization for an administrative session means being able to control what commands users can execute after login to the firewall, and authorization for Cut-Through Proxy controls what resources users can access after the authentication. For VPN Connection, authorization may control what traffic should be encapsulated and protected by the tunnel by using the split tunneling concept. Table 10-3 shows the authorization support by different protocols based on PIX version 7.0

Table 10-3 *Authorization Support by Different Protocols on Version 7.0*

Authorization of	LOCAL	RADIUS	TACACS	SDI	NT	Kerberos	LDAP
VPN Users	Yes	Yes	No	No	No	No	Yes
Administrators	Yes	No	Yes	No	No	No	No
Cut-Through	No	Yes	Yes	No	No	No	No

Use of Authorization for different connection types is explained in the following sections:

- Authorization for an administrative session
- Authorization for cut-through proxy
- Authorization for VPN connection (X-Auth)

Authorization for an Administrative Session

Command authorization allows the firewall to control commands performed on the firewall by the users. Command Authorization is possible only when using a local user database or TACACS+ server (not with RADIUS). This feature is first introduced in PIX Version 6.2. Table 10-3 summarizes the support for authorization on different connections using various protocols on Version 7.0.

Command Authorization is performed based on the privilege level (0-15) if a local user database is used. Every administrative user is assigned a privilege level (1-15). Level 0 is not assigned to any administrative user. Every command on the firewall has a privilege level assigned to it. Levels 0 and 15 are default levels. Level 15 has every command available, but level 0 has a limited number of commands available.

Privilege levels for users are compared with the level of the command executed by users. If the privilege level of the command is at lower level or at the same level as the privilege level of a user, the command will be allowed; otherwise, the command will be denied. For example, if the user is at level 2 and the command you are executing is at privilege level 0, then the command execution will be allowed on the firewall.

As mentioned before, each firewall command has a privilege level associated with it. Some commands with arguments can be used in several different modes. Each of these is considered a separate command, having a unique privilege level. Therefore, the privilege levels are assigned according to the command arguments and the mode in which it is used.

Privilege level for the user is assigned by enable authentication. If the local regular enable password is used for authentication, the enable password can be configured locally with different privilege levels. If authentication is performed based on the RADIUS protocol, the enable password is the same as the login password, and all users are assigned privilege level 15. Therefore, authorization for an administrative session is not possible with the RADIUS server. If TACACS+ is used, the enable password can be configured the same as the login password, and the different privilege level (1-15) can be configured for the users. That privilege level can be used for command authorization. Additionally, the TACACS+ server can be configured to perform command authorization more flexibly than the local user database.

If an external AAA server is used, multiple AAA servers can be defined if one is unreachable. Beginning with PIX Version 6.3.4, in the backup method, LOCAL user database can be used in case all AAA servers are unreachable for command authorization.

NOTE For administrative users using a local user database on the firewall, command authorization is done by privilege level only. When TACACS+ is used, the command authorization can be done using a combination of both privilege level and individual command definition, which provides more flexibility.

Authorization for Cut-Through Proxy Authorization for cut-through proxy is not possible with the local user database—it is only possible with the TACACS+ and RADIUS protocols. With the cut-through proxy authorization, you can control what resources the end users can access after authentication. RADIUS protocol emulates authorization with the help of ACL. But the TACACS+ protocol performs authorization with command parsing and with the help of ACL.

Authorization for VPN Connection (X-Auth)

Authorization for Remote Access VPN connection is used to assign the DNS/WINS IP addresses and to download the ACL from the AAA Server using TACACS+ or the RADIUS protocol for the split tunneling. Local user database authorization is also possible in addition to the RADIUS and TACACS+ protocols, and LDAP server.

Accounting

The accounting for firewall administrative sessions is available only through syslog server in versions earlier than PIX Firewall Version 7.x. By default, all the syslog message IDs that are required for accounting are enabled. However, if you have edited the default Syslog ID settings, you need to ensure that the syslog Message IDs shown in Table 10-4 are enabled for the accounting for the administrative session.

Table 10-4 *The Syslog Message ID Needs To Be Turned on for Administrative Session to PIX Firewall*

Syslog Message ID	Description
611101 (6)	Successful user authentication
611102 (6)	Failed user authentication
111008 (5)	User executed the command text
111009 (6)	User executed the command show text
611103 (5)	User logged out
502103 (5)	User changed privilege levels

Beginning with PIX 7.x, accounting packets can be generated and sent to the one or more AAA servers for the administrative session. This provides the ability to generate accounting records for tracking administrative access to PIX Firewall, and for tracking all configuration changes that are made during an administrative session.

Accounting records will not be generated for a command if the users execute the command at a higher level than the level at which it is configured on the PIX firewall.

Accounting for cut-through proxy and remote access VPN connection is possible with TACACS+ and RADIUS protocols. Accounting for both of these types of connections can log the connection activities to the AAA server. Table 10-5 summarizes accounting support by different methods on various protocols based on PIX Firewall Version 7.0.

Table 10-5 *Accounting Support for Different Methods by Different Protocols on PIX Version 7.0.*

Accounting of	LOCAL	RADIUS	TACACS	SDI	NT	Kerberos	LDAP
VPN Connection	No	Yes	Yes	No	No	No	No
Administrative connections	No	Yes	Yes	No	No	No	No
Cut-Through Proxy	No	Yes	Yes	No	No	No	No

More details on AAA can be found from the following release note at this URL:

http://www.cisco.com/univercd/cc/td/doc/product/iaabu/pix/pix_sw/v_53/relnotes/index.htm

You can find out the features introduced on different releases of PIX Firewall Version 6.3.x in the following location:

http://www.cisco.com/univercd/cc/td/doc/product/iaabu/pix/pix_sw/v_63/63rnotes/index.htm

PIX 7.0 version features can be found in the following location:

http://www.cisco.com/univercd/cc/td/doc/product/iaabu/pix/pix_sw/v_70/70_rn/index.htm

Diagnostic Commands and Tools

There are several tools and commands available to troubleshoot issues pertaining to AAA on the PIX firewall and FWSM firewall. Among these tools and commands, **show** and **debug** commands are among the most useful. This section discusses in detail how to use these commands and tools efficiently.

show commands

show commands for AAA on PIX Firewall are used to determine the statistics of the AAA server and other AAA-related issues. This section discusses some **show** commands that are used often and provides information relevant to good troubleshooting.

```
show/clear aaa-server
```

Table 10-6 lists commands that are used to display the server statistics, and it lists the meanings of those commands.

Table 10-6 *Command Syntax for Server Statistics*

Command	Action
`show aaa-server <groupname> host <hostname>`	Display server statistics for the indicated server.
`show aaa-server <groupname>`	Display statistics for all servers in the indicated server group.
`show aaa-server`	Display statistics for all aaa-servers across all groups.
`show aaa-server protocol <radius| kerberos| tacacs+| ldap| nt_domain| rsa_ace>`	Display statistics for all aaa-servers of the identified protocols.
`clear aaa-server statistics <groupname> host <hostname>`	Clear the statistics for all servers in the indicated server group.
`clear aaa-server statistics <groupname>`	Clear the statistics associated with the indicated server.
`clear aaa-server statistics`	Clear the statistics for all aaa-servers across all groups.
`clear aaa-server statistics protocol <radius| kerberos| tacacs+| ldap| nt_domain| rsa_ace>`	Clear the statistics for all aaa-servers of the identified protocols.

Example 10-1 shows the server statistics.

Example 10-1 *Displaying Server Statistics*

```
PIX(config)# show aaa-server group1 host 192.168.1.5
Server Group:          group1
Server Protocol:       RADIUS
Server Address:      192.168.1.5
Server port:         1645
Server status:      ACTIVE/FAILED. Last transaction (success) at 11:10:08 UTC  Fri
Aug 22
Average round trip time4ms
Number of requests              20
Number of retransmissions       1
Number of accepts               16
Number of rejects               4
Number of challenges            5
Number of malformed responses   0
Number of bad authenticators    0
Number of pending requests      0
Number of timeouts              0
Number of unrecognized responses  0
```

debug Commands

AAA **debug** commands are by far the most useful and easiest way to isolate a problem pertaining to AAA. There are specific commands for specific issues. For instance, if you have a problem with authentication, you have the option to run debug only to see the authentication-related message. Following is a list of debug commands available on PIX Firewall to diagnose issues pertaining to AAA.

- **debug radius**—This command provides the RADIUS protocol communication information between the PIX firewall and RADIUS Server. The complete syntax of the command is as follows:

  ```
  [no|show] debug radius <session|decode|all|user <username>>
  ```

- **debug tacacs**—Just as with the RADIUS debug, this command shows the details of the TACACS protocol between the communications of PIX firewall and AAA server. The syntax of the command is as follows:

  ```
  [no|show] debug tacacs <session|user <username>>
  ```

- **debug sdi | ntdomain | Kerberos | ldap**—To get the debug information pertaining to SDI, ntdomain, Kerberos, or Lightweight Directory Access Protocol (LDAP) server, we can run this debug command. This is useful when there is an issue with PIX Firewall and the communication of these servers. Following is the syntax for running the debug for a different authentication server:

  ```
  [no|show] debug sdi|ntdomain|Kerberos|ldap <1-255>
  ```

- **debug aaa**—This command is used to see the AAA interaction between the client and the PIX firewall. The syntax of the command is as follows:

```
[no|show] debug aaa <authentication|authorization|accounting|internal|vpn
  <1-255>>
```

All of the options except VPN support only one level (For example, **debug aaa** authentication, debug aaa authorization, and so on). So even if you define any level between 1 and 255, it will not make any difference. The **debug aaa vpn** command will accept levels 1-255. However, there are only five meaningful levels, which are described in Table 10-7.

Table 10-7 *Different Levels That Can Be Used With the* **debug aaa vpn** *Command on a Firewall*

Debug Level	Description
1	Shows error conditions. You should not see any output at this level under normal conditions.
2	Shows warnings, infrequent, but non-routine occurrences
3	High level subsystem trace information
4	Same as level 3, but with more verbose
5	Same as level 4, but more verbose
6–255	Same as level 5

Syslog

PIX Firewall has extensive syslog capability. To troubleshoot any issue on the PIX firewall, you will find that Syslog is an important piece that is almost always required. Syslog information can be sent into multiple locations—a console, monitor (for Telnet), buffer, or external syslog server. To troubleshoot AAA issues specifically on the PIX firewall after turning the debug on, you must also turn on the syslog to the debug level. Enabling it in this way captures the debug output into syslog. It is recommended to turn on debug to buffer instead of the console or monitor (for Telnet). If the issue requires extensive syslog information, it is best to configure a syslog for the external syslog server. Example 10-2 shows how to turn on the debug level syslog and send the output to different storage areas, such as the external syslog server, buffer, and so on.

Example 10-2 *Configuration To Turn on* **debug** *Logging For Various Locations*

```
PIX# configure terminal
! Turn on the timestamp for the logging
PIX(config)# logging timestamp
! The following command will increase the queue size to be 8192 K. 512 K is the
  default
PIX(config)# logging queue 8192
! Following command will turn on debug level logging for buffer
PIX(config)# logging buffered debugging
```

continues

Example 10-2 *Configuration To Turn on* **debug** *Logging For Various Locations (Continued)*

```
! It is strongly recommended to turn off console logging on a busy firewall. You can turn
! off the console logging with the following command
PIX(config)# no logging console
! If you want to see the debug on the telnet or ssh screen instead of buffer, turn the
! debug on for monitor with the following command. It is recommended to avoid running
! debug level logging for monitor
PIX(config)# logging monitor debugging
!Following configuration is to send syslog in debug mode to 192.168.1.70
PIX(config)# logging host inside 192.168.1.70
PIX(config)# logging trap debugging
! Finally you must turn on logging with the following command.
PIX(config)# logging enable
!To view the syslog messages, you need to execute the following command
PIX(config)# show logging
PIX(config)#
```

Other Useful Tools

Problems with AAA occur either on the firewall or on the AAA server itself. To troubleshoot problems on the AAA server side, you need to analyze the log on the AAA server itself. For example, if authentication is failing and PIX configuration is not at fault and you are unable to diagnose the issue with the **debug** commands and the syslog, you should analyze the log on the AAA server. If Cisco Secure ACS is used for AAA, analyze the **package.cab** file (refer to Chapter 13, "Troubleshooting Cisco Secure ACS on Windows") to find the cause of the problem.

If neither the firewall log nor the AAA server log provides the information required to get to the root cause of the problem, you can capture sniffer traces between the client and the firewall and the sniffer traces between the firewall and the AAA server. Remember that you should not define the key if the TACACS+ protocol is used to see the packet traces in clear text between the firewall and the AAA server. If the RADIUS protocol is used, then you can sniff and analyze the packets between the firewall and the RADIUS server without any problem.

Problem Areas Analysis

The problem areas of AAA on PIX firewall and FWSM can be categorized as follows based on their implementations:

- Firewall management with AAA troubleshooting
- Cut-Through Proxy with AAA troubleshooting
- Extended authentication (X-Auth) for IPsec VPN with AAA troubleshooting

The sections that follow discuss these problem areas.

Firewall Management with AAA Troubleshooting

You can connect to the PIX firewall in several ways to configure or monitor the PIX firewall. You can get CLI access to the PIX firewall for configuration and monitoring purpose in the following ways:

- **Using Console**—Console port is ready to be used on the PIX firewall as soon as you power on the PIX firewall. You do not need any configuration on the PIX firewall.
- **Using Telnet**—If you want to remotely manage the PIX firewall using Telnet, you can do so on all interfaces except the outside interface. For Telnet access to the outside interface, you must configure IPsec to include IP traffic that is generated by the PIX firewall, and enable Telnet on the outside interface.
- **Using SSH**—SSH can be configured instead of Telnet for secured access to the PIX firewall. We recommend that you manage PIX firewall with SSH instead of Telnet. Additionally, managing PIX Firewall from an outside network with Telnet is not possible, as Telnet is not allowed to the outside interface. Although it is possible to get around the problem by terminating a VPN tunnel on the outside interface, SSH is the preferred method to manage the PIX firewall from the outside.
- **Using Telnet over IPsec**—As mentioned before, Telnet is not allowed to the outside interface of the PIX firewall because of security reasons. So if you really need to Telnet to the outside interface, the only way to accomplish that is by creating an IPsec tunnel to the outside interface and then allowing the Telnet to the outside interface.
- **PDM/ASDM/Firewall MC/Security Monitor**—Connection between the Management Software (PDM/ASDM/Firewall MC) and the Monitoring Software (Security Monitor) takes place using HTTPS (http/SSL). You need to configure a web server and generate a certificate to allow the HTTPS connection to the firewall.

Once the connection parameters are configured on the firewall, you can add security to the connection by configuring AAA, which provides per-user control for the connections. This section presents the configuration and troubleshooting setup as follows:

- Login authentication issues
- Enable authentication issues
- Authorization issues
- Accounting issues

Login Authentication Issues

This section delves into the details of both login authentication and troubleshooting. Before you attempt to enable authentication, you should configure the authentication and be sure that it works with the basic login credentials without configuring AAA. This section explains the following topics in detail:

- Configuring basic authentication with different communication methods on the Firewall

- Configuring local user database authentication
- Configuring external AAA server authentication
- Configuring a fallback method for authentication
- Troubleshooting login authentication

Configuring Basic Authentication with Different Communication Methods on the Firewall

Before you configure local user database or AAA for login authentication on the PIX firewall, be sure that you can connect to the PIX firewall with the Basic Login credentials. For login and enable authentication, you can use **passwd** to configure login password, and **enable password** to configure enable authentication. The following list of configuration methods on the PIX Firewall details the configuration for basic authentication for these different connection methods:

- **Basic Authentication for Telnet on the PIX firewall**—To turn on Telnet on the PIX firewall, you must use the **telnet** command. Example 10-3 shows how to turn on **telnet** on the PIX firewall for 192.168.1.0 network to the inside interface of the PIX firewall.

Example 10-3 *Shows How to Configure Telnet Access to the PIX Firewall*

```
PIX# configure terminal
! Set login password with the following command. If you want to set encrypted
! password you must provide 16 bytes string.
PIX(config)# passwd cisco12345678912 encrypted
! The following command will set up the enable password on the PIX firewall.
PIX(config)# enable password cisco76687463274 encrypted
! The following command allows 192.168.1.0 network to be able to telnet to the
! inside interface on the PIX firewall
PIX(config)# telnet 192.168.1.0 255.255.255.0 inside
! Following command is used to verify that the telnet is enabled.
PIX(config)# show running-config telnet
192.168.1.0 255.255.255.0 inside
PIX(config)#
```

- **Basic Authentication for SSH connection on the PIX firewall**—SSH requires that an RSA key be created on the PIX firewall. To create an RSA key, you must have Data Encryption Standard (DES) or 3DES features turned on (this can be verified with the **show version** command). If you do not have the DES/3DES feature enabled, you need to send an e-mail to licensing@cisco.com with your **show version** output and request for a DES/3DES **activation key**. Then you can insert the key into the PIX with the activation-key command. Use **crypto key generate rsa general-keys** to generate the RSA key on the PIX Firewall, and execute the **SSH** command to allow the addresses that can SSH into the PIX Firewall. Example 10-4 shows a sample configuration for turning on SSH on the PIX firewall.

Example 10-4 *Sample Configuration SSH on the PIX Firewall*

```
PIX# configure terminal
! Set login password with the following command. If you want to set encrypted
! password you must provide 16 bytes string.
PIX(config)# passwd cisco12345678912 encrypted
! The following command will set up the enable password on the PIX firewall.
PIX(config)# enable password cisco76687463274 encrypted
! Following two lines are needed to generate the RSA key
PIX(config)# hostname PIX
PIX(config)# domain-name cisco.com
! The following command will remove the existing key from the PIX.
PIX(config)# crypto key zeroize rsa
! Generate the key with the following command
PIX(config)# crypto key generate rsa general-keys
! Save the RSA key with the following command
PIX(config)# write memory
! Turn on and allow the SSH connection from 192.168.1.0/24 network with the
! following commands
PIX(config)# ssh 192.168.1.0 255.255.255.0 inside
PIX(config)# ssh timeout 60
PIX(config)# exit
! Save the configuration with the following command
PIX# write memory
PIX#
```

After successful configuration of SSH on the PIX firewall, you may use an SSH client (for example, **putty.exe**, which can be downloaded freely from the Internet by searching with the string "**putty.exe**") to connect to the PIX firewall. If the firewall gives you the option of accepting a certificate, then the PIX firewall is configured correctly for SSH. When asking for a username, enter **pix** as username and for the password enter the password configured on the PIX firewall. For enable access, just enter the enable password configured on the PIX.

- **Basic Authentication for VPN connection to allow Telnet to the outside interface of the PIX firewall with Basic Authentication**—You need to configure Remote Access VPN using IPsec protocol to allow the Telnet access from outside to the **outside** interface of the PIX firewall. Refer to Chapter 7, "Troubleshooting IPsec VPN on PIX Firewalls" for details on Remote Access VPN configuration using IPsec. Then, following the procedure explained earlier under "Basic Authentication for Telnet on the PIX Firewall," allow the Telnet access to the IP address assigned by the PIX to the VPN client. As the IP address is assigned from the pool, we recommend that you add the pool with the Telnet command to allow access. Here is an example to illustrate the point. Assume that you have an IP Pool defined for the VPN traffic with network address 192.168.1.0, so that the VPN client will get one of the IP addresses from this pool (It could be any IP address from the pool). Therefore, you need to include this network with the **telnet** command as follows:

```
PIX(config)# telnet 192.16.1.0 255.255.255.0 outside
```

- **Basic Authentication for PDM/ASDM/Firewall MC/Security Monitor Access (HTTPS)**—For PDM/ASDM/Firewall MC/Security Monitor access, you need to configure a web server on the firewall and generate a certificate for the HTTPS connection. Example 10-5 shows how to configure HTTPS on the firewall.

Example 10-5 *Configuring HTTPS on the PIX Firewall*

```
PIX# configure terminal
! Turn on the web server with the following command.
PIX(config)# http server enable
! Allow the network that can connect to the web server using ASDM/Firewall MC or
! Security Monitor
PIX(config)# http 192.168.1.0 255.255.255.0 inside
PIX(config)# exit
! Save the configuration with the following command
PIX# write memory
PIX#
```

Regardless of the type of method you choose to connect to the PIX firewall for management purposes, it is strongly recommended that you control access to the PIX with AAA as covered in the section that follows.

Configuring Local User Database Authentication

If you want to configure per user authentication for login, you have the option to configure this per-user authentication with the local user database on the PIX firewall.

Work through the following steps for configuring local user database authentication:

Step 1 Configure local user database with the username command as follows:

```
PIX(config)# username superuser password cisco privilege 15
PIX(config)# username basicuser password cisco123 privilege 5
PIX(config)#
```

Step 2 By default, the local user database is configured on the PIX firewall and identified as **LOCAL**. Verify the statistics of the local user database with the following command:

```
PIX(config)# show aaa-server LOCAL
```

Step 3 Turn on Authentication for different connection types (Telnet, SSH, console and so on) to use the LOCAL user database with the following command:

```
PIX(config)# aaa authentication {serial | enable | telnet | ssh | http}
  console server-tag [ LOCAL ]
```

For example,if you want to turn on SSH authentication to use local user database, you can use the following command:

```
PIX(config)# aaa authentication ssh console LOCAL
```

With the above configuration, you can log in to PIX using the **SSH** protocol with username as **superuser** and **basicuser**.

Configuring External AAA Server Authentication

As mentioned before, the local user database is not very scalable when there are a large number of users to manage. Therefore, you must use an external AAA server for the central point of user management. Configuring an external AAA server-based authentication for login requires configuring both an AAA server and the PIX firewall. Work through to following steps to accomplish this task:

Step 1 Configure AAA Server for user setup and AAA client configuration.

Before you turn on AAA for the login on the PIX firewall, you must configure the AAA server. The term Cisco Secure Access Control Server (CS ACS) is used throughout this chapter for the AAA server. Work through the following steps to configure the Cisco Secure ACS Server:

(a) **Define the PIX firewall as an AAA Client**—The PIX firewall must be defined as an AAA client on the AAA server for the PIX to be able to connect to the AAA server to send authentication requests. On CS ACS, go to **Network Configuration > Click on Network Device Group** (if NDG is configured) **> Add Entry>** Give an AAA client name for PIX, define the **IP address** of the PIX, and the shared secret key. For **Authenticating Using,** select **TACACS+ (Cisco IOS)** for TACACS+ or **RADIUS (Cisco IOS/PIX)** for RADIUS authentication.

(b) **Create Users**—Go under **User Setup** and add a user. You do not need a special configuration for simple login authentication. Assign the user to a specific group.

Step 2 Define communication parameters for the AAA server on the PIX firewall.

To define the AAA server, you need to define the type of protocol you want to use (RADIUS or TACACS+), the IP address of the AAA server, and optionally a shared secret key. We recommend strongly that you use the complex shared secret key for better security. See Example 10-6 for both RADIUS and TACACS+ server definitions on the PIX firewall.

Example 10-6 *Defining AAA Server*

```
! Following two lines define a AAA server with TACACS+ protocol. Note that
! MY_TACACS is the tag for the AAA server and has to be match (case sensitive)
! on both lines.
PIX(config)# aaa-server AuthTacacs protocol tacacs+
PIX(config)# aaa-server AuthTacacs host 192.168.1.5 cisco timeout 5
```

continues

Example 10-6 *Defining AAA Server (Continued)*

```
! The following two lines define a AAA server with RADIUS protocol
PIX(config)# aaa-server AuthRadius protocol radius
PIX(config)# aaa-server AuthRadius host 192.168.1.10 cisco timeout 5
PIX(config) exit
PIX#
```

Step 3 Turn on AAA for Login Authentication.

Commands for turning on authentication are slightly different for different methods of login to the PIX firewall. For example, to enable authentication for SSH using TACACS+ protocol, use the following command:

```
PIX(config)# aaa authentication ssh console AuthTacacs
```

To use the RADIUS server, use the following command:

```
PIX(config)# aaa authentication ssh console AuthRadius
```

When users use SSH to access the PIX with the preceding command turned on, they are prompted for username and password, which is defined on the AAA server. It is important to note that **console** is the keyword that tells the PIX that authentication is for an administrative connection. Console authentication is turned on by the keyword **serial**.

CAUTION While adding authentication statements, always have a connection open to the PIX in the event that backing out the commands is necessary. Additionally, do not save the configuration unless you thoroughly test your AAA configuration so that if you are locked out, you need only perform a reboot to return your original configuration.

Configuring Fallback Method for Authentication

Beginning with PIX version 6.3.4, you can configure a local user database as a fallback method in case the AAA server is unavailable. Fallback method is available to use only with the local user database.

To configure fallback, you need to combine the procedure for authentication using both the AAA server and the local user database. For example, to turn on fallback for SSH connection to the firewall, use the following command:

```
PIX(config)# aaa authentication ssh console AuthTacacs LOCAL
```

With the preceding configuration, if the TACACS+ server is unavailable, the local user database will be used for SSH authentication. Note that if multiple TACACS+ servers are defined with the **AuthTacacs** server tag, the firewall will try all TACACS+ servers in the list before it uses the local user database.

If a fallback method is used, you need to configure the AAA server that is used as a primary method for authentication with proper parameters on the firewall. For example, if the fallback method is used, you might not want to increase the maximum failed attempts to a high number, because that could delay the authentication if the AAA server is down. Following is a list of options available for configuring different parameters for the AAA server:

- **Max-failed-attempts**—This is the maximum number of AAA requests attempted to each server within an AAA server group. The parameter must be within [1-5] inclusive. The default value is 3.

  ```
  PIX(config)# [no] aaa-server AAA-Server-Tag max-failed-attempts number
  ```

- **Deadtime**—Deadtime is the number of timeout minutes for declaring an AAA server group as unresponsive. The parameter must be within [0-1440] inclusive. The default value is 10.

  ```
  PIX(config)# [no] aaa-server AAA-Server-Tag deadtime minutes
  ```

NOTE The AAA fallback is available only for administrative session traffic authentication and command authorization, not for cut-through proxy or x-auth traffic.

Troubleshooting Login Authentication

Before delving into the details of troubleshooting authentication problem for SSH, Telnet and other types of connections, it is worth of going through a debug output for a successful user authentication, which is shown in Example 10-7.

Example 10-7 *Successful User Authentication for SSH Session with Output from the* **debug aaa authentication** *and* **debug tacacs** *Commands*

```
PIX(config)# logging console debugging
PIX(config)# debug aaa authentication
PIX(config)# debug tacacs
! Following lines show the SSH connection is allowed and username prompt is sent to the
! user
PIX# Jul 25 2005 02:23:49 : %PIX-6-609001: Built local-host outside:10.25.136.50
Jul 25 2005 02:23:49 : %PIX-6-609001: Built local-host NP Identity
  Ifc:172.16.172.164
Jul 25 2005 02:23:49 : %PIX-6-302013: Built inbound TCP connection 5849 for
  outside:10.25.136.50/3455 (10.25.136.50/3455) to NP Identity Ifc:172.16.172.164/
  22 (172.16.172.164/22)
Jul 25 2005 02:23:49 : %PIX-7-710001: TCP access requested from 10.25.136.50/3455
  to outside:172.16.172.164/ssh
Jul 25 2005 02:23:49 : %PIX-7-710002: TCP access permitted from 10.25.136.50/3455
  to outside:172.16.172.164/ssh
PIX-A#
! Username and the password information is received and sent to the AAA server
PIX-A# JReceived response from kodom, session id 2147485136
```

continues

Example 10-7 *Successful User Authentication for SSH Session with Output from the* **debug aaa authentication** *and* **debug tacacs** *Commands (Continued)*

```
Making authentication request for host 171.69.89.217, user kodom, session id:
  2147485136
mk_pkt - type: 0x1, session_id: 2147485136
ul user: kodom
 Tacacs packet sent
Sending TACACS Start message. Session id: 2147485136, seq no:1
 Received TACACS packet. Session id:537906095  seq no:2
! Asking for the password from the user
25 tacp_procpkt_authen: GETPASS
Authen Message: Password:
Processing challenge for user kodom, session id: 2147485136, challenge: Password:
Received response from kodom, session id 2147485136
Making authentication request for host 171.69.89.217, user kodom, session id:
2147485136
mk_pkt - type: 0x1, session_id: 2147485136
mkpkt_continue - response: ***
 Tacacs packet sent
Sending TACACS Continue message. Session id: 2147485136, seq no:3
Received TACACS packet. Session id:537906095  seq no:4
! The following line indicates the successful user authentication
tacp_procpkt_authen: PASS
TACACS Session finished. Session id: 2147485136, seq no: 3
2005 02:24:03 : %PIX-6-609001: Built local-host outside:171.69.89.217
Jul 25 2005 02:24:03 : %PIX-6-302013: Built outbound TCP connection 5850 for
  outside:171.69.89.217/49 (171.69.89.217/49) to NP Identity Ifc:172.16.172.164/
  1374 (172.16.172.164/1374)
Jul 25 2005 02:24:03 : %PIX-6-109005: Authentication succeeded for user 'kodom' from
  10.25.136.50/0 to 172.16.172.164/22 on interface outside
! Shows the login is permitted to the PIX
Jul 25 2005 02:24:03 : %PIX-6-605005: Login permitted from 10.25.136.50/3455 to
  outside:172.16.172.164/ssh for user "kodom"
Jul 25 2005 02:24:03 : %PIX-6-302014: Teardown TCP connection 5850 for
  outside:171.69.89.217/49 to NP Identity Ifc:172.16.172.164/1374 duration 0:00:00
  bytes 108 TCP FINs
Jul 25 2005 02:24:03 : %PIX-6-609002: Teardown local-host outside:171.69.89.217
  duration 0:00:00
PIX#
```

Work through the following steps to troubleshoot authentications problem with login:

Step 1 Turn off AAA for login.

If the login is not working for SSH, console, PDM/ASDM, Firewall MC and so on, when AAA is configured, turn off AAA and configure the Basic Login credential to ensure that the problem is not with the connection method configured. For example, if SSH is configured with AAA on the PIX, turn off AAA for SSH and check to see if you can log in with the basic login credentials. Your host IP address might not be configured as the allowed host. If not, you might get the following message in the syslog:

```
315001: Denied SSH session from 50.1.1.1 on interface outside
```

Then find out if the 50.1.1.1 address is allowed on the PIX with the following command:

```
PIX# show ssh
192.168.1.0 255.255.255.0 inside
PIX#
```

As you can see, 192.168.1.0 is the only network allowed from which you can use SSH to log in to the PIX firewall. To add the 50.1.1.1 address for an SSH connection, you can use the following command:

```
PIX# configure terminal
PIX(config)# ssh 50.1.1.1 255.255.255.255 outside
PIX(config)# exit
PIX#
```

Step 2 Check for a bad Username/Password on the AAA Server.

If the authentication is working with basic login credentials, turn AAA back on, and check to see if the user is entering the correct username and password. Example 10-8 shows an example of authentication failure either because of the wrong username or a bad password.

Example 10-8 *Authentication Failure for SSH Connection*

```
PIX# debug aaa authentication
PIX# debug tacacs
Sending TACACS Continue message. Session id: 2147485138, seq no:3
! A failed message indicates either username or password is not correct.
Received TACACS packet. Session id:1969178652  seq no:4
tacp_procpkt_authen: FAIL
TACACS Session finished. Session id: 2147485138, seq no: 3
25 2005 06:11:03 : %PIX-6-609001: Built local-host outside:171.69.89.217
PIX#
```

Step 3 The AAA server is not responding.

Authentication might fail if the AAA server is down, which will result in the messages shown in Example 10-9.

Example 10-9 *Error Message Received in the Syslog When the AAA Server Is Down*

```
PIX# debug aaa authentication
PIX# debug tacacs
JReceived response from kodom, session id 2147485144
Making authentication request for host 171.69.89.217, user kodom, session id:
  2147485144
umk_pkt - type: 0x1, session_id: 2147485144
 user: kodom
1  Tacacs packet sent
2Sending TACACS Start message. Session id: 2147485144, seq no:1
! Following message indicates PIX is unable to make authentication request to
! the AAA server.
```

continues

Example 10-9 *Error Message Received in the Syslog When the AAA Server Is Down (Continued)*

```
TACACS Request timed out
Received response from kodom, session id 2147485144
Making authentication request for host 171.69.89.217, user kodom, session id:
  2147485144
PIX#
```

Step 4 Configure Network Access Restrictions on the AAA server.

Network Access Restrictions (NAR) is a filtering mechanism on the AAA server that takes place during the authentication. Nothing special needs to be configured on the firewall. On the AAA server, for example on Cisco Secure ACS, you can configure NAS (PIX, routers and so on) to allow or deny users from accessing the NAS. Set this up under Group Settings as either **Denied Calling/Point of Access Locations** or **Permitted Calling/Point of Access**. If the authentication is failing even after defining the correct username and password, ensure that authentication is not failing due to NAR configuration on the AAA server.

Enable Authentication

This section explains how to configure and troubleshoot Enable authentication with various methods.

Configuring Enable Authentication

Enable password authentication can be performed one of the following ways:

1 Enable Authentication with Enable Password.

By default, enable password is *none* (meaning no password is required) on the firewall, and has a privilege level of 15. So if you do not have any configuration for the enable authentication, the enable password *none* is used, unless you define one or more enable passwords. You can assign different privilege levels (1-15) to the enable password.

When the users enter into enable mode with a specific level (for example enable 10) the enable password configured for that specific level must be used. For example, if enable password is configured on the firewall with the **enable password cisco level 10** command, then the user must enter into the enable mode with the **Firewall> enable 10** command, not with the **Firewall> enable** command. Be sure to create an enable password with privilege level 15.

Following is the syntax to define enable password on the firewall:

```
PIX(config)# enable password password [level level] [encrypted]
```

To remove enable password, use the following command:

```
PIX(config)# no enable password level level
```

2 Enable authentication with the local user database.

If you perform login authentication with the local user database, then be sure to assign a privilege level to the user. The same password and the privilege level will be provided to the user for enable access. If you perform login authentication with the AAA server, but enable authentication with the local user database, then be sure to configure the same username defined on the AAA server and assign a password for the user that will be used for enable access. This password can be different than the login password defined on the AAA server. A user can be created with a different privilege level with the following command:

```
PIX(config)# username {name} {nopassword | password password [encrypted]}
  [privilege priv_level]}
```

To remove the user, use the following command:

```
PIX(config)# no username [name]
```

To turn on authentication for the enable authentication with the local user database, use the following command:

```
PIX(config)# aaa authentication enable console LOCAL
```

3 Enable authentication with the external AAA server.

If the enable authentication is performed using RADIUS protocol, the enable password is the same as the login password, and the privilege level 15 is assigned for all users. In essence, enable authentication with the RADIUS protocol does not add any additional security for the enable access.

To configure enable authentication with the RADIUS protocol, use the following command:

```
PIX(config)# aaa authentication enable console AuthRadius
```

Here the **AuthRadius** is the radius server tag.

We recommend strongly that you configure enable authentication with TACACS+ protocol. As with TACACS+, you can define a separate enable password, assign privilege levels to the user, and control what commands users can execute in a more granular fashion than for a local user database. You must configure both TACACS+ server and the firewall to configure enable authentication.

On the firewall, you need the following command to turn on enable authentication with TACACS+ protocol:

```
PIX(config)# aaa authentication enable console AuthTacacs
```

Work through the following steps to configure the Cisco Secure ACS server for the enable password configuration:

a On CS ACS GUI, go to **Interface Configuration > Advanced TACACS+ Settings**. Check **Advanced TACACS+ Features in Advanced Configuration Options** and click Submit. This makes the Advanced TACACS+ Settings visible under the user configuration.

b Go to **User Setup**, then either create a new user or edit an exiting user. In the User Setup page, check the radio button for **Max Privilege for any AAA Client**, and select the level to 15 from the drop-down box next to it under **Advanced TACACS+ Settings**. Also under **TACACS+ Enable Password**, choose the password you want to use for enable password. Then click **Submit**.

Note Unlike working with a router, you cannot take the user directly to the privilege mode based on the privilege level. The privilege level is assigned based on the enable privilege level. So, the user always will be taken to the user mode and based on the enable level, will be assigned to a certain level.

4 Use the fallback method for enable authentication.

Just as with authentication, if you want to use the local user database as a fallback method for enable authentication, use the following command:

```
PIX(config)# aaa authentication enable console AuthTacacs LOCAL
```

If the AAA server is unavailable, you can gain access to the enable mode with the password defined for the user you have used to login to the PIX. So it is critical that you configure at least one user with privilege level 15 and turn on the fallback method for the login authentication also.

Troubleshooting Enable Authentication

Troubleshooting steps for enable password authentication are almost same as those discussed for Login Authentication. Example 10-10 shows a successful enable password authentication with TACACS+ protocol:

Example 10-10 *Successful User Authentication with TACACS+ Protocol*

```
PIX# debug aaa authentication
PIX# debug tacacs
! By now the user authentication is successful, hence rest of the debug output if for
! enable authentication only.
PIX# Jmk_pkt - type: 0x1, session_id: 2147485158
 user: kodom
 Tacacs packet sent
Sending TACACS Start message. Session id: 2147485158, seq no:1
Received TACACS packet. Session id:1036787635  seq no:2
tacp_procpkt_authen: GETPASS
Authen Message: Password:
! Same username as login is used with the enable password defined for the user
uProcessing challenge for user kodom, session id: 2147485158, challenge: Password:
mk_pkt - type: 0x1, session_id: 2147485158
mkpkt_continue - response: ***
 Tacacs packet sent
Sending TACACS Continue message. Session id: 2147485158, seq no:3
```

Example 10-10 *Successful User Authentication with TACACS+ Protocol (Continued)*

```
Received TACACS packet. Session id:1036787635  seq no:4
! Shows successful enable password authentication
tacp_procpkt_authen: PASS
TACACS Session finished. Session id: 2147485158, seq no: 3
1 25 2005 07:01:31 : %PIX-6-609001: Built local-host outside:171.69.89.217
PIX#
```

Additional information that is important and specific to enable password authentication is as follows:

- Under **Advanced TACACS+ Settings** of User Profile, or under **Enable Option** of Group profile, be sure **"No enable Privilege"** is not checked. You must assign privilege level 15. Otherwise, enable authentication will fail.
- If login is done externally with an AAA server but enable authentication is performed locally, be sure the user name matches between the AAA server and the local user database.
- If a separate password is used for enable authentication, be sure you are entering the password correctly. If the external database is configured on the Cisco Secure ACS server for enable password, change it to use the same password as login to see if the external server is causing the problem. If you find it is an external database issue, investigate the issue on the AAA server (refer to Chapter 13, "Troubleshooting Cisco Secure ACS on Windows" for details).
- If enable password is configured locally with different privileges, be sure that you are authenticating enable password with that specific privilege level. For example, if the enable password is at level 10, configure, then be sure to go into enable mode by typing **enable 10** not just **enable**.

Command Authorization

With the blessings of privilege levels, you can control the commands users can execute on the firewall after the enable authentication with the local user database. If TACACS+ is used, more granular command authorization is possible with the TACACS+ server. This section explains how to control command authorization for different methods of authentication for enable access:

- Command Authorization based on Enable Password Privilege level
- Command Authorization using local user database
- Command Authorization using an external AAA server

Command Authorization Based on Enable Password Privilege Level

As discussed before, you can configure multiple enable passwords with different privilege levels locally. Every command on the PIX firewall has a privilege level assigned. If you authenticate enable access with a password that has the same or higher privilege level than the level of the command, that command will be allowed. For example, if your enable password is defined as cisco3, which has level 3, you can execute every command that is at level 0. You must have the authorization turned on to use a local user database with the following command to control the command execution; otherwise, you will be able to execute all commands regardless of the privilege level assigned to you.

Command Authorization Using Local User Database

Command authorization done locally on PIX Firewall is based on privilege level. There are 16 privilege levels in PIX Firewall. Two of them are set to the defaults 0 and 15. Anything from 1 to 14 has the same sets of commands that the privilege level 0 has. Every command has a predefined privilege level and most of them are at level 15. However, it is possible to change the command privilege level from higher to lower. For instance, **show running-config** is a level 15 command, and it is possible to bring this down to level 10. So, a user with level 10 or above can execute this command. Users with levels lower than 10 will not be able to execute a level 10 command. Example 10-11 walks you through the privilege level concept and different commands available with local database command authorization. The example also shows how to turn on command authorization with the following command:

```
PIX(config)# aaa authorization command LOCAL
```

Example 10-11 *Privilege Level Command Execution and How to Turn on Command Authorization Based on the Privilege Level*

```
PIX# configure terminal
! Create a user with privilege level 15 named superuser
PIX(config)# username superuser password cisco123 privilege 15
! If you want some users to be able to execute subset of all the commands available on
! the PIX, you must create user in a lower level than 15. User alice is created with the
! privilege level 10 below.
PIX(config)# username alice password cisco privilege 10
! As most of the commands are at level 15 by default, you have to move some commands down
! to level 10 so that "alice" can issue them. In this instance, you want your level 10
! user to be able to issue the show clock command, but not to reconfigure the clock.
PIX(config)# privilege show level 10 command clock
! You must also allow the users to be able to logout even if the user is at level 1. As
! the level 10 should be able to execute any commands available between level 0-9, it
! makes sense to assign this command to level 1.
PIX(config)# privilege configure level 1 command logout
! You will need the user to be able to issue the enable command (the user will be in
! level 1 when attempting this).
PIX(config)# privilege configure level 1 mode enable command enable
! By moving the disable command to level 1, any user between levels 2-15 can get out of
! enable mode.
PIX(config)# privilege configure level 1 command disable
! With the above setup if the user alice telnets in and go into enable mode with the same
! password, then alice with the assigned to privilege 10 which will have same command
! access as level 1.
```

Example 10-11 *Privilege Level Command Execution and How to Turn on Command Authorization Based on the Privilege Level (Continued)*

```
PIX# show curpriv
Username : alice
Current privilege level : 10
Current Mode/s : P_PRIV
! At this point, open up another telnet and login to the PIX with superuser that has
! privilege level 15 so that you can use that window for configuration changes and
! modification.
PIX# show curpriv
Username : superuser
Current Privilege level : 15
Current Mode/s : P PRIV
! Once logged in with superuser and verifying the privilege level, turn on command
! Authorization as follows.
PIX(config)# aaa authorization command LOCAL
! On the other window login to the PIX with username alice that has privilege level 10
! and execute show xlate that should fail. Show clock should be successful.
PIX# show clock
19:18:53.026 UTC Sun Jan 9 2005
PIX# show xlate
Command authorization failed
PIX#
```

Command Authorization Using an External AAA Server

Command Authorization with the local user database is not scalable. Hence, with a larger user database, you should consider implementing command authorization using an external AAA server. Command Authorization is possible with TACACS+ protocol but not with the RADIUS protocol.

Command authorization by TACACS+ is based on submitting the entire command expression to a TACACS+ server for authorization before execution. While this section deals only with command authorization for a TACACS+ server, a local user database as discussed in the preceding section will be used as a fallback method. Note that fallback using a local user database is possible only with PIX Version 6.3.4 and above.

Configuring command authorization with the external TACACS+ server is a two-step process: configuring the TACACS+ server, and configuring PIX Firewall.

Work through the steps that follow to configure an ACS in Windows for command authorization:

Step 1 Authentication must be working before performing command authorization. To perform command authorization with CS ACS, go to **Interface Configuration > TACACS+ (Cisco)**. Check **Shell (exec) for user and/or group** and click **Submit**. This will make the shell command authorization settings visible under the user (or group) configuration.

Step 2 Go to **User Setup** and create a user who has permission to execute any commands on the firewall. For example, give this username **superuser, and** assign this user to a group name.

Step 3 Go to **Group Setup,** and select the group name where username **superuser** is assigned from the drop-down box and click on **Edit Settings**.

Step 4 In the Group Setting page, **permit** unmatched Cisco IOS commands.

Step 5 For the other users, select **Group Settings**, find the desired group from the drop-down box, and click **Edit Settings**.

Step 6 Go to **Shell Command Authorization Set**, check the **Command** button, and enter **login**. Select **Permit**, under **Unlisted Arguments**. Repeat these processes for the **logout, enable**, and **disable** commands.

Step 7 Go to **Shell Command Authorization Set**, check the **Command** button, and enter **show**. Under **Arguments** enter **permit clock**, and select **deny** for Unlisted Arguments. Refer to Figure 10-1 for the configurations of steps 4 and 5.

Step 8 Click **Submit**.

Figure 10-1 *Command Authorization Setup on the ACS Server*

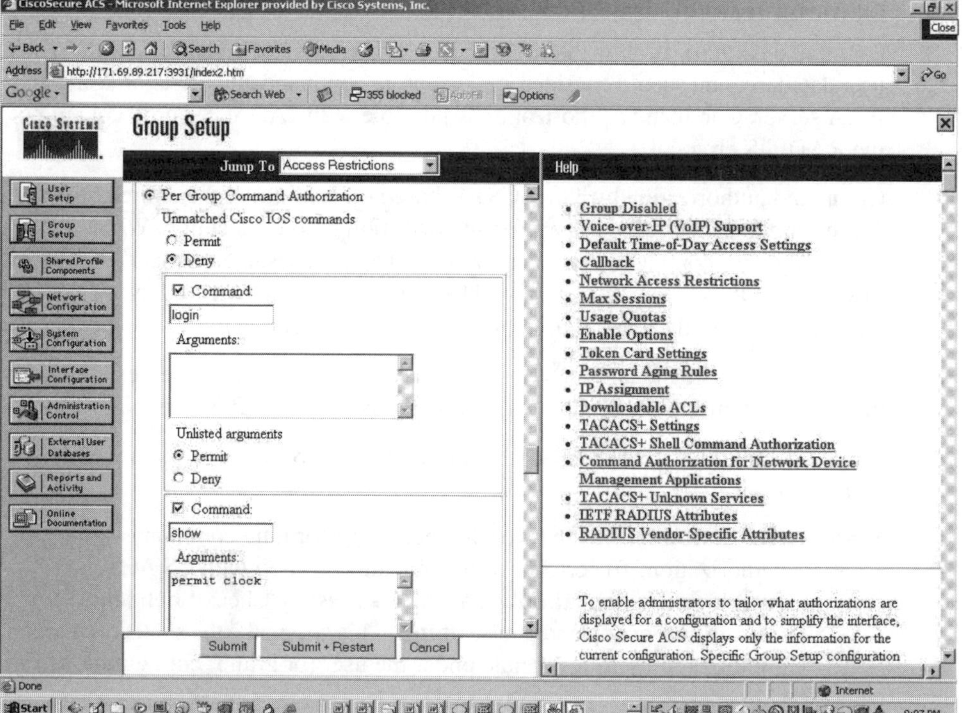

Once you are finished with the Cisco Secure ACS server configuration, you need to configure PIX Firewall for command authorization. Example 10-12 shows the configuration needed on the PIX firewall to turn on command authorization.

Example 10-12 *AAA Configuration Needed for the Authorization with TACACS+ Server and Local User Database as a Fallback Method*

```
PIX# configure terminal
! Assuming that the AAA-server is configured with AAA server name tag TACSERVER,
! following statements will enable telnet and enable authentication with tacacs+ server,
! and Local user database is configured as backup.
PIX(config)# aaa authentication telnet console TACSERVER LOCAL
PIX(config)# aaa authentication enable console TACSERVER LOCAL
! Following line will turn on authorization with tacacs+ server and local user database
! as fall-back method.
PIX(config)# aaa authorization command TACSERVER LOCAL
PIX(config)#
```

Troubleshooting Steps

To troubleshoot command authorization, run the following commands:

```
PIX# debug aaa authorization
PIX# debug tacacs
```

Before you look at some of the possible causes of failure, go through Example 10-13 for a successful command authorization using tacacs+ protocol:

Example 10-13 *Command Authorization in Action for Administrative Session*

```
PIX# debug aaa authorization
PIX# debug tacacs
Jul 25 2005 07:09:36 : %PIX-7-111009: User 'kodom' executed cmd: show running-config
Jmk_pkt - type: 0x2, session_id: 2147485175
mkpkt - authorize user: kodom
! Configure terminal is what entered in PIX CLI, and they are sent to the AAA server with
! command "configure" and argument "terminal" as you can see in the following lines.
cmd=configure
ucmd-arg=terminal  Tacacs packet sent
Sending TACACS Authorization message. Session id: 2147485175, seq no:1
Received TACACS packet. Session id:243213034  seq no:2
! Following two lines indicate success of command authorization
tacp_procpkt_author: PASS_ADD
tacp_procpkt_author: PASS_REPL
TACACS Session finished. Session id: 2147485175, seq no: 1
l 25 2005 07:09:40 : %PIX-6-609001: Built local-host outside:171.69.89.217
Jul 25 2005 07:09:40 : %PIX-6-302013: Built outbound TCP connection 5918 for
  outside:171.69.89.217/49 (171.69.89.217/49) to NP Identity Ifc:172.16.172.164/
  1425 (172.16.172.164/1425)
Jul 25 2005 07:09:40 : %PIX-5-111007: Begin configuration: console reading from
  terminal
Jul 25 2005 07:09:40 : %PIX-5-111008: User 'kodom' executed the 'configure terminal'
  command.
PIX#
```

Command authorization might not work due to one or more of the following reasons:

- If the authorization does not work at all, be sure that authorization is turned on with the following command:

```
aaa authorization command TACSERVER LOCAL
```

- If authorization is performed with the local user database, be sure that the command is at the same or at a lower privilege level than the user's privilege. Otherwise, you need to log in as admin user with privilege level 15 to bring the privilege level down to the user level.
- If authorization is turned on with the TACACS+ protocol, run **debug aaa authorization** and **debug tacacs** to find out how the command is sent out to the AAA server. Revise the AAA server group profile configuration to ensure that the command and arguments are match the permit as you see it in the debug on the PIX firewall.
- If expected permit commands are denied, and vice versa, revise the logic of the commands, and correct if needed.

Accounting

Beginning with PIX Version 7.0, Accounting for firewall administrative sessions is possible. Previously it was only available with the syslog. To enable accounting for a special connection type, use the following command:

```
Firewall(config)# [no] aaa accounting http | serial | telnet | ssh | enable console
  AAA-Server-Tag
```

You can enable accounting for capturing and sending the command executed on the firewall with the following command:

```
Firewall(config)# [no] aaa accounting command [privilege level] AAA-Server-Tag
```

Refer to Table 10-8 for an explanation of the arguments of the accounting command.

Table 10-8 *Keywords for the AAA Accounting Command Shown for Admin Session*

Keywords	Meaning
AAA-Server-Tag	This is the AAA sever name tag.
Accounting	Enable or disable accounting services.
http	Enable or disable the generation of accounting records for HTTP connection.
Serial	Enable or disable the generation of accounting records for console session.
telnet	Enable or disable the generation of accounting records for Telnet connection.
SSH	Enable or disable the generation of accounting records for SSH connection.
Enable	Enable or disable the generation of accounting records for enable authentication.

Table 10-8 *Keywords for the AAA Accounting Command Shown for Admin Session (Continued)*

Keywords	Meaning
Console	Indicates that accounting records will be generated for administrative session via different connection types.
Command	Enable or disable the generation of accounting records to record each command that is entered on the firewall.
Privilege Level	If specified, the privilege level indicates the minimum level that must be associated with a command to generate an accounting record. The default privilege level is 0, which means that every command executed on the firewall will generate accounting records.

If you are having problem with accounting, run the following debug commands on the PIX firewall:

```
PIX# debug aaa accounting
PIX# debug radius
```

or,

```
PIX# debug tacacs
```

Information can be shown either on the console or syslog. If Cisco Secure ACS is used as an external AAA server, you can view accounting records by clicking the **Reports and Activity** button. Then click **TACACS+ Accounting** or **RADIUS Accounting**. All accounting reports are in comma-separated value (.csv) format and can be displayed in a web browser.

Cut-Through Proxy Authentication

You can configure the firewall to force the users to authenticate before connections are permitted. After successful user authentication, the user's authentication status is cached to permit subsequent connections from the same IP address from where the initial connection authenticated user initiated. The firewall functions as an authentication proxy for the subsequent connections. Subsequent connections simply "cut through" the firewall very efficiently. That's why this feature is called Cut-Through Proxy.

While firewall can intercept all types of IP traffic, it can authenticate only the FTP, Telnet, SSH, HTTP, and HTTPS protocols traffic because of the authentication scheme available for these protocols.

Note that Figure 10-2 will be used for the remainder of the chapter as the AAA for Management and Cut-Through Proxy.

If the cut-through proxy authentication is enabled on the firewall, when the user connections go through the firewall, they are intercepted by AAA, and the firewall presents a username/password prompt. How a user provides a username and password differs as follows:

- **For Telnet/SSH**—The user sees a username prompt, and then a request for a password. If authentication (and authorization) is successful at the firewall, the user is prompted for username and password by the destination host beyond. With Telnet/SSH, the username/password needs to be entered twice—once for the firewall, and once for the end host.

Figure 10-2 *A Typical Setup for AAA for Management and Cut-Through Proxy Setup*

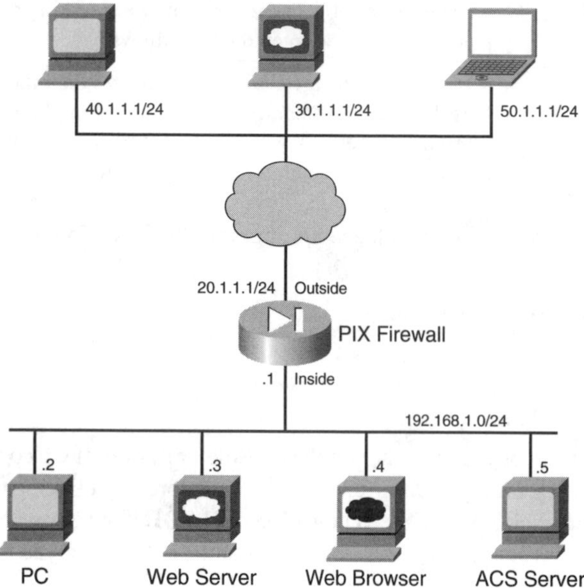

- **For FTP**—The user sees a username prompt first and then the password. The user needs to enter **local_username@remote_username** for **username** and **local_password@remote_password** for **password**. The firewall sends the **local_username** and **local_password** to the AAA server and authenticates the user. If authentication (and authorization) is successful at the firewall, the **remote_username** and **remote_password** are passed to the destination FTP server beyond. With FTP, you have the option to enter the username/password once.
- **For HTTP/HTTPS**—The user sees a window displayed in the browser requesting username and password. If authentication (and authorization) is successful, the user arrives at the destination website beyond.

Authentication for Cut-Through Proxy

Cut-Through Proxy authentication can be performed by either of the following methods:

- Cut-Through Proxy Authentication with Local User Database
- Cut-Through Proxy Authentication Using TACACS+/RADIUS Protocol

The sections that follow go through the configuration of these two methods, followed by the troubleshooting steps for Cut-Through Proxy Authentication.

Cut-Through Proxy Authentication with Local User Database

To configure cut-through proxy with the local user database, you need to configure the local user database with the following command on the firewall:

```
PIX(config)# username {name} {nopassword | password password [encrypted]}
  [privilege priv_level]}
```

To remove a user, use the following command:

```
PIX(config)# no username [name]
```

You can turn on the authentication for the connections going across the firewall with one of the following ways:

1 Using the include/exclude option

The matching criteria are added to the firewall configuration using an include statement which will trigger the authentication. Exclude is used to exclude the traffic from exemption of cut-through proxy authentication. Use the following syntax to turn on authentication for different types of connection using a LOCAL user database:

```
Firewall(config)# aaa authentication {include | exclude} service if_name
  local_ip local_mask [foreign_ip foreign_mask] server_tag
```

The service can be http/https/telnet/ssh/ftp. It is possible to define these services as tcp/80, tcp/443, tcp/23, tcp/21, and so on. However, remember that not every protocol has native support for interactive authentication capability. For instance, you can define a service as tcp/25 for SMTP, but as the SMTP does not have the interactive native support for an authentication scheme, the packet for the mail traffic will simply be dropped, unless you authenticate from the mail server, and PIX caches the user information for the mail server IP. This can be accomplished with Virtual Telnet, which is discussed in detail in the Case Studies section of this chapter.

if_name in the command indicates the location from which the traffic will be initiated and intercepted by the firewall. **Local_ip** and **local_mask** indicate the source IP address of the packet, and the **foreign_ip** and **foreign_mask** define the destination address and mask of the traffic. For the inbound traffic, if you have the static defined for the destination IP address, the **foreign_ip** is the actual server IP on the inside network, not the translated IP that is seen on outside for a specific server or network. For example, if the server on the inside has an IP address of 10.1.1.50, which is translated with an external IP address of 200.1.1.50, then you should use the untranslated address 10.1.1.50, not the translated address 200.1.1.5 in the AAA statement, when you turn on authentication, authorization or accounting.

server_tag for the local user database is always **LOCAL**, and this is configured within the software.

Example 10-14 shows how to turn on authentication for both inbound and outbound traffic using the local user database.

Example 10-14 *Turning on Cut-Through Proxy Authentication With Include/Exclude Option Using Local User Database*

```
! Configure local user database with the following command first. Simple username
! and unsecure password is used for demonstration purpose only. You should choose
! secure password and different username
Firewall(config)# username cisco password cisco privilege 15
! The following static is for destination address translation for the inbound
! traffic, and source address translation for the outbound traffic.
Firewall(config)# static (inside,outside) 200.1.1.0 10.1.1.0 netmask 255.255.255.0
! Following command will turn on cut-through proxy authentication for all inbound
! TCP traffic
Firewall(config)# aaa authentication include tcp/0 outside 0.0.0.0 0.0.0.0 0.0.0.0
  0.0.0.0 LOCAL
! Following statement will exclude exemption for cut-through proxy for only for
! server 10.1.1.100 that is on inside. Note carefully that even though the
! translated IP address for the 10.1.1.100 is 200.1.1.100, this translated IP is
! not used.
Firewall(config)# aaa authentication exclude tcp/0 outside 0.0.0.0 0.0.0.0
  10.1.1.100 255.255.255.255 LOCAL
! The following command enables cut-through proxy authentication for the outbound
! http traffic.
Firewall(config)# aaa authentication include http inside 0.0.0.0 0.0.0.0 0.0.0.0
  0.0.0.0 LOCAL
Firewall(config)#
```

2 Using access-list

With the include/exclude option, you can turn on cut-through proxy authentication that is based only on source and destination IP and the service type. However, this does not allow authenticating the traffic based on source/destination port information. With access-list, you have this flexibility. Using ACL, you can define your traffic based on 5-tuples: source and destination address and port, and the service type. Then apply the ACL with the authentication statement by using the following command:

```
Firewall(config)# aaa authentication match acl_name if_name server_tag
```

Example 10-15 shows how to turn on cut-through proxy authentication using ACL.

Example 10-15 *Turning on Cut-Through Proxy Authentication with ACL Option Using Local User Database*

```
! Configure local user database and the statics using the following commands
Firewall(config)# username cisco password cisco privilege 15
Firewall(config)# static (inside,outside) 200.1.1.0 10.1.1.0 netmask 255.255.255.0
! Define two ACLs - one for inbound traffic and one for outbound traffic Proxy
! authentication
Firewall(config)# access-list inbound deny tcp any host 10.1.1.100
Firewall(config)# access-list inbound permit ip any any
Firewall(config)# access-list outbound permit tcp any any eq www
! Now apply both of the ACLs with the following two statements to turn on cut-
! through proxy authentication for traffic in both direction that meet the ACL
! criteria.
Firewall(config)# aaa authentication match inbound outside LOCAL
Firewall(config)# aaa authentication match outbound inside LOCAL
Firewall(config)#
```

A local user database is not scalable for a large network. An external AAA server must be configured to address the scalability issue, which we discuss next.

Cut-Through Proxy Authentication Using RADIUS or TACACS+ Protocol

The configuration on the firewall to turn on cut-through proxy authentication is very similar to that of a local user database, which is discussed in the preceding section. The only exception is the server-group—instead of using **LOCAL**, a server group for either RADIUS or TACACS+ protocol must be defined.

Before you attempt any configuration on the firewall for cut-through proxy, we recommend strongly that you configure the AAA server first.

Work through the following steps to configure the Cisco Secure ACS Server so that Firewall can use it for authentication purposes:

Step 1 Log in to the CS ACS GUI

Step 2 Define Firewall as an NAS on the CS ACS Server. To accomplish this, go to **Network Configuration**, click on the **Network Device Group** (if the Network Device Group option is turned on), then click on **Add Entry** for adding an AAA client. In the **Add AAA Client** window, define the **AAA Client Hostname**, **AAA Client IP Address**, and the **Key** that will be defined on the Firewall for authentication. Select **TACACS+ (Cisco IOS)** or **RADIUS (Cisco IOS/PIX)** protocol from the drop-down list of **Authenticate Using** drop-down box. If you want to use both TACACS+ and RADIUS protocol, be sure to use a different name for the AAA clients.

Step 3 Go to **User Setup** and add a user. Map the user to a specific group on the Cisco Secure ACS Server.

Step 4 Edit the group that the users are mapped to by going to **Group Setup**. For the TACACS+ protocol, you do not need any special settings for the group. However, if you use RADIUS protocol, check the **[006] Service-Type** check box under **IETF RADIUS Attributes** and select **Login** from the drop-down box next to it.

Step 5 Click on the **Submit+Restart button**.

Once AAA server configuration is complete, work through the following steps to configure firewall:

Step 1 Define the AAA server.

You need to define communication parameters for the AAA server to configure on the firewall. First, define the server tag name and identify TACACS+ or RADIUS protocol with the following commands:

```
Firewall(config)# aaa-server AuthTacacs protocol tacacs+
Firewall(config)# aaa-server AuthRadius protocol radius
```

Once the name is defined and you have chosen a specific protocol, define the communication details such as IP address and shared secret key of the AAA server by using the following command:

```
Firewall(config)# aaa-server AuthTacacs (inside) host 192.168.1.5 cisco
Firewall(config)# aaa-server AuthRadius (inside) host 192.168.1.5 cisco
```

Step 2 Turn on cut-through proxy Authentication.

Just as with the local user database, the cut-through proxy authentication can be turned on either with the include/exclude option or with the access-list option. Example 10-16 shows how to turn on authentication for both inbound and outbound traffic using the TACACS+ protocol.

Example 10-16 *Turning on Cut-Through Proxy Authentication with Include/Exclude Option Using TACACS+ Protocol*

```
! The following static is for destination address translation for the inbound
! traffic, and source address translation for the outbound traffic.
Firewall(config)# static (inside,outside) 200.1.1.0 10.1.1.0 netmask 255.255.255.0
! Following command will turn on cut-through proxy authentication for all inbound
! TCP traffic
Firewall(config)# aaa authentication include tcp/0 outside 0.0.0.0 0.0.0.0 0.0.0.0
  0.0.0.0 AuthTacacs
! Following statement will exclude exemption for cut-through proxy for only for
! server 10.1.1.100 that is on inside. Note carefully that even though the
! translated IP address for the 10.1.1.100 is 200.1.1.100, this translated IP is
! not used.
Firewall(config)# aaa authentication exclude tcp/0 outside 0.0.0.0 0.0.0.0
  10.1.1.100 255.255.255.255 AuthTacacs
! The following command enables cut-through proxy authentication for the outbound
! http traffic.
Firewall(config)# aaa authentication include http inside 0.0.0.0 0.0.0.0 0.0.0.0
  0.0.0.0 AuthTacacs
Firewall(config)#
```

If you want to accomplish the task shown in Example 10-17 with the access-list, follow the procedure it demonstrates.

Example 10-17 *Turning on Cut-Through Proxy Authentication with ACL Option Using RADIUS Protocol*

```
Firewall(config)# static (inside,outside) 200.1.1.0 10.1.1.0 netmask 255.255.255.0
! Define two ACLs - one for inbound traffic and one for outbound traffic Proxy
! Authentication
Firewall(config)# access-list inbound deny tcp any host 10.1.1.100
Firewall(config)# access-list inbound permit ip any any
Firewall(config)# access-list outbound permit tcp any any eq www
! Now apply both of the ACLs with the following two statements to turn on cut-
! through proxy authentication for traffic in both direction that meet the ACL
! criteria.
Firewall(config)# aaa authentication match inbound outside AuthRadius
Firewall(config)# aaa authentication match outbound inside AuthRadius
Firewall(config)#
```

Troubleshooting Cut-Through Proxy Authentication

You must ensure that the connection across the firewall works before turning on cut-through proxy authentication. Once cut-through proxy authentication is turned on and if authentication fails, you need to enable logging with debug level turned on (see the "Syslog" subsection under the section entitled "Diagnostic Commands and Tools"). You need to run **debug aaa authentication**, and **debug radius** or **debug tacacs** to find out the details on authentication failure for the cut-through proxy authentication. If the syslog does not provide the cause of failure, you need to analyze the log on the AAA server. For details on how to analyze the log on the CS ACS server, refer to Chapter 13, "Troubleshooting Cisco Secure ACS on Windows."

Before delving into the details of the different issues with cut-through proxy authentication, this section first examines the look of a successful cut-through proxy authentication in the syslog. Example 10-18 shows a successful cut-through proxy authentication for inbound traffic authentication using TACACS+ protocol initiating the packet from 50.1.1.1 to inside 192.168.1.2 (20.1.1.102) and vice versa (see Figure 10-2).

Example 10-18 *Successful Authentication for TACACS+ (Inbound)*

```
PIX# logging monitor debug
Jul 25 2005 07:33:51 : %PIX-6-609001: Built local-host outside:50.1.1.1
Jul 25 2005 07:33:51 : %PIX-6-609001: Built local-host inside:192.168.1.2
Jul 25 2005 07:33:51 : %PIX-6-302013: Built inbound TCP connection 5947 for
  outside:50.1.1.1/11003 (50.1.1.1/11003) to inside:192.168.1.2/23 (192.168.1.2/23)
Jul 25 2005 07:33:51 : %PIX-6-109001: Auth start for user '???' from 50.1.1.1/11003
  to 192.168.1.2/23
Jul 25 2005 07:33:55 : %PIX-6-609001: Built local-host outside:171.69.89.217
Jul 25 2005 07:33:55 : %PIX-6-302013: Built outbound TCP connection 5949 for
  outside:171.69.89.217/49 (171.69.89.217/49) to NP Identity Ifc:172.16.172.164/
  1428 (172.16.172.164/1428)
Jul 25 2005 07:33:57 : %PIX-2-109011: Authen Session Start: user 'kodom', sid 34
! Following message indicates successful user authentication.
Jul 25 2005 07:33:57 : %PIX-6-109005: Authentication succeeded for user 'kodom' from
  50.1.1.1/11003 to 192.168.1.2/23 on interface outside
Jul 25 2005 07:33:57 : %PIX-6-302014: Teardown TCP connection 5949 for
  outside:171.69.89.217/49 to NP Identity Ifc:172.16.172.164/1428 duration 0:00:01
  bytes 107 TCP FINs
PIX#
```

For additional details of a successful cut-through proxy authentication, refer to Example 10-19.

Example 10-19 *Successful Cut-Through Proxy Authentication with Debug AAA Authentication And Debug Tacacs*

```
PIX# debug aaa authentication
PIX# debug tacacs
JReceived response from , session id 2147485179
Making authentication request for host 171.69.89.217, user , session id: 2147485179
! Username challenged sent to the end user
Processing challenge for user , session id: 2147485179, challenge: Please enter your
username and password:
Username:
```

continues

Example 10-19 *Successful Cut-Through Proxy Authentication with Debug AAA Authentication And Debug Tacacs (Continued)*

```
ul 25 2005 07:39:59 : %PIX-6-302013: Built inbound TCP connection 5960 for
  outside:50.1.1.1/11004 (50.1.1.1/11004) to inside:192.168.1.2/23 (192.168.1.2/23)
Jul 25 2005 07:39:59 : %PIX-6-109001: Auth start for user '???' from 50.1.1.1/11004
  to 192.168.1.2/23
Jul 25 2005 07:40:00 : %PIX-7-711002: Task ran for 130 msecs, process = dbgtrace
JReceived response from kodom, session id 2147485179
Making authentication request for host 171.69.89.217, user kodom, session id:
  2147485179
mk_pkt - type: 0x1, session_id: 2147485179
 user: kodom
 Tacacs packet sent
! Sending the start packet to the AAA server
Sending TACACS Start message. Session id: 2147485179, seq no:1
Received TACACS packet. Session id:1683598253  seq no:2
! Getting password here.
tacp_procpkt_authen: GETPASS
Authen Message: Password:
Processing challenge for user kodom, session id: 2147485179, challenge: Password:
ul 25 2005 07:40:03 : %PIX-6-609001: Built local-host outside:171.69.89.217
Jul 25 2005 07:40:03 : %PIX-6-302013: Built outbound TCP connection 5962 for
  outside:171.69.89.217/49 (171.69.89.217/49) to NP Identity Ifc:172.16.172.164/
  1429 (172.16.172.164/1429)
Received response from kodom, session id 2147485179
JuMaking authentication request for host 171.69.89.217, user kodom, session id:
  2147485179
mk_pkt - type: 0x1, session_id: 2147485179
mkpkt_continue - response: ***
 Tacacs packet sent
Sending TACACS Continue message. Session id: 2147485179, seq no:3
Received TACACS packet. Session id:1683598253  seq no:4
! Following message indicates a successful cut-through proxy authentication
tacp_procpkt_authen: PASS
user: kodom authenticated, session id: 2147485179
TACACS Session finished. Session id: 2147485179, seq no: 3
l 25 2005 07:40:07 : %PIX-2-109011: Authen Session Start: user 'kodom', sid 35
Jul 25 2005 07:40:07 : %PIX-6-109005: Authentication succeeded for user 'kodom' from
  50.1.1.1/11004 to 192.168.1.2/23 on interface outside
Jul 25 2005 07:40:07 : %PIX-6-302014: Teardown TCP connection 5962 for
  outside:171.69.89.217/49 to NP Identity Ifc:172.16.172.164/1429 duration 0:00:04
  bytes 107 TCP FINs
PIX#
```

Following is a list of some possible causes of cut-through proxy authentication problems:

- **Incorrect username or bad password**—User authentication might fail due to an incorrect username or bad password. In either case, the user will see the following message after getting three opportunities to enter the username and password.

  ```
  Error: Max number of tries exceeded.
  ```

  Example 10-20 shows syslog for authentication failure with TACACS+ protocol for inbound traffic.

Example 10-20 *Syslog Message for Bad Authentication (Username or Password) – TACACS+ (Inbound)*

```
PIX(config)# logging monitor debugging
PIX-A# Jul 25 2005 07:48:16 : %PIX-6-302013: Built inbound TCP connection 5981 for
  outside:50.1.1.1/11006 (50.1.1.1/11006) to inside:192.168.1.2/23 (192.168.1.2/23)
Jul 25 2005 07:48:16 : %PIX-6-109001: Auth start for user '???' from 50.1.1.1/11006
  to 192.168.1.2/23
Jul 25 2005 07:48:20 : %PIX-6-609001: Built local-host outside:171.69.89.217
Jul 25 2005 07:48:20 : %PIX-6-302013: Built outbound TCP connection 5983 for
  outside:171.69.89.217/49 (171.69.89.217/49) to NP Identity Ifc:172.16.172.164/
  1433 (172.16.172.164/1433)
Jul 25 2005 07:48:24 : %PIX-6-302014: Teardown TCP connection 5983 for
  outside:171.69.89.217/49 to NP Identity Ifc:172.16.172.164/1433 duration 0:00:03
  bytes 108 TCP FINs
Jul 25 2005 07:48:30 : %PIX-6-609001: Built local-host outside:171.69.89.217
Jul 25 2005 07:48:30 : %PIX-6-302013: Built outbound TCP connection 5984 for
  outside:171.69.89.217/49 (171.69.89.217/49) to NP Identity Ifc:172.16.172.164/
  1434 (172.16.172.164/1434)
Jul 25 2005 07:48:32 : %PIX-6-302014: Teardown TCP connection 5984 for
  outside:171.69.89.217/49 to NP Identity Ifc:172.16.172.164/1434 duration 0:00:01
  bytes 107 TCP FINs
Jul 25 2005 07:48:39 : %PIX-6-609001: Built local-host outside:171.69.89.217
Jul 25 2005 07:48:39 : %PIX-6-302013: Built outbound TCP connection 5985 for
  outside:171.69.89.217/49 (171.69.89.217/49) to NP Identity Ifc:172.16.172.164/
  1435 (172.16.172.164/1435)
! Following failed message indicates a failure with either username/password.
Jul 25 2005 07:48:41 : %PIX-6-109006: Authentication failed for user 'kodom' from
  50.1.1.1/11006 to 192.168.1.2/23 on interface outside
Jul 25 2005 07:48:41 : %PIX-6-302014: Teardown TCP connection 5985 for
  outside:171.69.89.217/49 to NP Identity Ifc:172.16.172.164/1435 duration 0:00:01
  bytes 109 TCP FINs
Jul 25 2005 07:48:42 : %PIX-6-302014: Teardown TCP connection 5981 for outside:50.1.1.1/
  11006 to inside:192.168.1.2/23 duration 0:00:25 bytes 374 TCP FINs
PIX#
```

- **Communication Problem between PIX and AAA Server**—Several conditions might be considered communication problems between the PIX and AAA Server:
  - PIX may not have proper routing. Execute ping from the PIX to verify.
  - PIX has connectivity, but TACACS+ or RADIUS protocols might be blocked by a firewall between PIX and the AAA server.
  - The shared secret might be a mismatch between the PIX and AAA Server.
  - PIX might not be defined as the AAA client on the AAA Server.

  Under any of these circumstances, PIX might be unable to send the authentication information to the AAA server, and this will result in authentication failure. The user sees a username, then a password, then **RADIUS server failed**, and then finally **Error: Max number of tries exceeded.** See Example 10-21 to see the syslog message when TACACS+ is used for inbound authentication, and the authentication fails.

Example 10-21 *Syslog Message When PIX Has Communication Problem with AAA Server*

```
PIX(config)# logging monitor debug
PIX-A# Jul 25 2005 07:55:12 : %PIX-6-302013: Built inbound TCP connection 5987 for
  outside:50.1.1.1/11007 (50.1.1.1/11007) to inside:192.168.1.2/23 (192.168.1.2/23)
Jul 25 2005 07:55:12 : %PIX-6-109001: Auth start for user '???' from 50.1.1.1/11007
  to 192.168.1.2/23
Jul 25 2005 07:55:16 : %PIX-6-609001: Built local-host outside:171.69.89.217
Jul 25 2005 07:55:16 : %PIX-6-302013: Built outbound TCP connection 5989 for
  outside:171.69.89.217/49 (171.69.89.217/49) to NP Identity Ifc:172.16.172.164/
  1436 (172.16.172.164/1436)
Jul 25 2005 07:55:16 : %PIX-6-302014: Teardown TCP connection 5989 for
  outside:171.69.89.217/49 to NP Identity Ifc:172.16.172.164/1436 duration 0:00:00
  bytes 0 TCP Reset-O
! Following message indicates server is unavailable
Jul 25 2005 07:55:16 : %PIX-6-109002: Auth from 50.1.1.1/11007 to 192.168.1.2/23
  failed (server 171.69.89.217 failed) on interface outside
Jul 25 2005 07:55:16 : %PIX-6-609001: Built local-host outside:171.69.89.217
Jul 25 2005 07:55:16 : %PIX-6-302013: Built outbound TCP connection 5990 for
  outside:171.69.89.217/49 (171.69.89.217/49) to NP Identity Ifc:172.16.172.164/
  1437 (172.16.172.164/1437)
PIX#
```

- **User's Account Locked Out**—If you configure a lockout feature on the AAA server after a certain number of failed authentication attempts, the user account will be locked out. Hence, subsequent authentication requests will fail. Re-enable the user account so that it can authenticate.
- **User reached the MAX session limit**—If you have a session limit configured on the AAA server, be sure that you do not exit more often than the number of times that is configured for simultaneous authentication for a specific user or a group.
- **User Reaches the Proxy Limit**—If you have too many simultaneous connection requests, you may run short of the proxy limit, which is by default 16. So, if a user makes 17 connection requests at the same time across the firewall, one connection will not be authenticated and the connection will be dropped. You can disable proxies by using the **disable** parameter. To return to the default proxy-limit value (16), use the **no** form of this command.

```
aaa proxy-limit proxy_limit
aaa proxy-limit disable
no aaa proxy-limit
```

Authorization for Cut-Through Proxy

To control the resources users may access once they are authenticated, you need to implement authorization. On the other hand, if you want to allow authenticated users to perform all operations, then authentication is sufficient. Authorization can be performed either with the TACACS+ or RADIUS protocol. Even though a PIX firewall supports a local user database for cut-through proxy authentication, it does not support authorization.

Authorization for a cut-through proxy is implemented differently using TACACS+ and RADIUS protocols due to the different nature of the protocols.

Authentication and authorization are performed separately in TACACS+, whereas in RADIUS both authentication and authorization are performed together. Therefore, command authorization is possible with TACACS+, but not with RADIUS.

When an end user who is going through the firewall tries to Telnet/FTP/HTTP/HTTPS to an IP address of a server, the packets are intercepted and authenticated, and then the Telnet/FTP/HTTP/HTTPS are sent to the AAA server as commands, and the IP address after that goes as arguments to the TACACS+ server for the command authorization. For example, if the user enters **http 192.168.1.105** on the browser, after successful user authentication, if the authorization is turned on for HTTP traffic for the specific destination, the firewall will send http as a command and **192.168.1.105** as an argument to the TACACS+ server for command authorization.

Authorization can be performed for any type of pass-through IP traffic across the firewall. For example, if you want to authorize the SMTP mail traffic, you can perform authentication from the main server using Telnet/FTP/HTTP/HTTPS, which will cause the firewall to cache the IP address of the mail server. Then, if the authorization is turned on for the mail server using tcp/25 as the service, mail traffic will be authorized. On the TACACS+ server, you need to ensure that tcp/25 is configured as the command and the destination IP address (not the mail server IP address) is configured as argument.

If you want to have more granular control with authorization, configure an access-list on the firewall and then download the name of the access-list from the TACACS+ server. Support for ACL for command authorization is introduced in PIX Firewall Version 5.2.

Authorization with RADIUS protocol for the pass-through traffic is only possible via ACL, which will be discussed in the coming section.

NOTE To implement authorization for HTTP in an enterprise network, use URL filtering software such as Websense, N2H2, and so on. AAA Authorization implementation for HTTP authorization is limited based on the IP address not on the DNS, or other important criteria that these URL filtering servers offer.

Configuration steps for the cut-through proxy authorization are discussed in next two sections.

Configuring Cut-through Proxy Authorization using the TACACS+ Protocol

The cut-through proxy authorization configuration discussed in this section is based on Figure 10-2.

Configuring cut-through proxy authorization using the TACACS+ protocol is a two-step process: configuring user and group profiles with command authorization on the TACACS+ server, and enabling authorization on the firewall. For this configuration, Cisco Secure ACS on Windows is used. It supports the TACACS+ protocol.

Work through the steps that follow to configure the Group Profile on the ACS on Windows for Authorization. To illustrate this better, assume that you want the user to be able to use Telnet to access 20.1.1.100, use FTP to access 20.1.1.101, and use HTTP to access any website.

Step 1 Assume that PIX already was added as NAS during authentication configuration earlier on the CS ACS using TACACS+.

Step 2 Select **Group Setup** from the Navigation bar on the left side, choose the **Group** on the next window, and click on **Edit**. This is the group to which the end users belong that need to be authenticated by the firewall.

Step 3 On the Group Setup page, Choose **TACACS+** from the **Jump To** drop-down box. That will take you to the TACACS+ configuration section of the page.

Step 4 Check **Shell Exec**, and under Shell Command Authorization Set, choose the **Per Group Command Authorization** button.

Step 5 Click **Deny unmatched IOS commands**.

Step 6 Check the **Command** check box. In the text box next to the **command** check box, enter **telnet** as the command, and in the **Arguments:** rectangle box, enter **permit 20.1.1.100** as argument. Finally, choose **Deny** for **Unlisted arguments**.

Step 7 Click on the **Submit + Restart** button to restart the CS ACS services.

Step 8 To allow the FTP access to 20.1.1.101, follow steps 6 and 7. Instead of using **telnet** as a command, use **ftp**, and for argument use **20.1.1.101**.

Step 9 To allow HTTP access to all sites, in the command text box, enter **http**, leave the **arguments** rectangle box **blank**, and for the **Unlisted arguments**, choose **permit**.

Step 10 Finally, click the **Submit+Restart** button.

Step 11 If you want to have more granular control using an access-list, define an ACL on the PIX firewall but do not apply this ACL on any interface. Check the **Access control list** box, and fill in the number (for example, access-list 115 is defined)

Step 12 Click the **Submit+Restart** button.

When you are finished with the CS ACS configuration, the next step is to enable authorization on the firewall as shown in Example 10-22.

Example 10-22 *Turning on Authorization for Cut-Through Proxy*

```
PIX# configure terminal
! Following three lines will turn on authorization for inbound traffic (telnet/http/ftp)
! using TACACS+ protocol. This is the only syntax available prior to PIX firewall version
! 5.2. The same syntax can be used on the latest version of PIX as well.
PIX(config)# aaa authorization include telnet outside 0.0.0.0 0.0.0.0 0.0.0.0
  0.0.0.0 AuthInbound
PIX(config)# aaa authorization include http outside 0.0.0.0 0.0.0.0 0.0.0.0 0.0.0.0
  AuthInbound
PIX(config)# aaa authorization include ftp outside 0.0.0.0 0.0.0.0 0.0.0.0 0.0.0.0
  AuthInbound
! If you are running PIX version 5.2 and above, it is strongly recommended to use the
! following syntax. The same ACL 101 that was created for earlier can be applied for the
! authorization as well. Hence, you just need to turn on authorization with the ACL 101
! earlier created to turn on authorization for cut-through proxy.
PIX(config)# aaa authorization match 101 outside AuthInbound
! If you want to have more granular control for instance you want to control the traffic
! based on 5-tuple of the connection - source/destination port, source/destination IP
! address and the protocol. Define ACL 115 with along with the authorization line defined
! earlier.  Do not apply the ACL on any interface.
PIX(config)# access-list 115 permit tcp any host 50.1.1.1 eq telnet
PIX(config)# access-list 115 permit tcp any host 50.1.1.1 eq www
PIX(config)# access-list 115 permit tcp any host 50.1.1.1 eq ftp
PIX(config)# access-list 115 deny tcp any host 30.1.1.1 eq www
PIX(config)# access-list 115 deny tcp any host 30.1.1.1 eq ftp
PIX(config)# access-list 115 deny tcp any host 30.1.1.1 eq telnet
PIX(config)# exit
PIX#
```

CAUTION In Example 10-22, both ways to enable authorization for cut-through proxy are shown. Use either method, but not both. Otherwise, undesirable results will occur.

Troubleshooting Cut-Through Proxy Authorization using the TACACS+ Protocol

Most authorization problems for the cut-through proxy using the TACACS+ protocol arise because of a lack of understanding and misconfiguration. Careful review of the configuration of both the firewall and the AAA server can eliminate many problems. However, logs and debug commands available on the firewall, and the log on the Cisco Secure ACS software, can help you to nail down any problem. It's important to learn how to use the log and the **debug/show** command efficiently. It is equally important to be extremely familiar with the AAA server log. Refer to Chapter 13, "Troubleshooting Cisco Secure ACS on Windows" for details on how to use the logging capability on Cisco Secure on Windows software.

By now, you should be familiar with how to turn on the syslog in the debug level. Therefore, go through the debug level log for a successful user authorization session and become comfortable with it, so that you can easily identify a deviation when authorization does not work under a specific condition. Example 10-23 shows syslog when user authentication and authorization is successful.

Example 10-23 *Syslog for a Successful Authentication and Authorization Using the TACACS+ Protocol*

```
PIX(config)# logging monitor debugging
Jul 25 2005 08:10:32 : %PIX-6-302013: Built inbound TCP connection 5995 for
  outside:50.1.1.1/11008 (50.1.1.1/11008) to inside:192.168.1.2/23 (192.168.1.2/23)
Jul 25 2005 08:10:32 : %PIX-6-109001: Auth start for user '???' from 50.1.1.1/11008
  to 192.168.1.2/23
Jul 25 2005 08:10:35 : %PIX-6-609001: Built local-host outside:171.69.89.217
Jul 25 2005 08:10:35 : %PIX-6-302013: Built outbound TCP connection 5997 for
  outside:171.69.89.217/49 (171.69.89.217/49) to NP Identity Ifc:172.16.172.164/
  1440 (172.16.172.164/1440)
Jul 25 2005 08:10:37 : %PIX-2-109011: Authen Session Start: user 'kodom', sid 36
! Following line indicates authentication is successful
Jul 25 2005 08:10:37 : %PIX-6-109005: Authentication succeeded for user 'kodom' from
  50.1.1.1/11008 to 192.168.1.2/23 on interface outside
Jul 25 2005 08:10:37 : %PIX-6-302013: Built outbound TCP connection 5998 for
  outside:171.69.89.217/49 (171.69.89.217/49) to NP Identity Ifc:172.16.172.164/
  1441 (172.16.172.164/1441)
Jul 25 2005 08:10:37 : %PIX-6-302014: Teardown TCP connection 5997 for
  outside:171.69.89.217/49 to NP Identity Ifc:172.16.172.164/1440 duration 0:00:02
  bytes 107 TCP FINs
Jul 25 2005 08:10:37 : %PIX-6-302013: Built outbound TCP connection 5999 for
  outside:171.69.89.217/49 (171.69.89.217/49) to NP Identity Ifc:172.16.172.164/
  1442 (172.16.172.164/1442)
Jul 25 2005 08:10:37 : %PIX-6-302014: Teardown TCP connection 5998 for
  outside:171.69.89.217/49 to NP Identity Ifc:172.16.172.164/1441 duration 0:00:00
  bytes 87 TCP FINs
! Following line indicates authorization is successful
Jul 25 2005 08:10:37 : %PIX-6-109007: Authorization permitted for user 'kodom' from
  50.1.1.1/11008 to 192.168.1.2/23 on interface outside
Jul 25 2005 08:10:37 : %PIX-6-302014: Teardown TCP connection 5999 for
  outside:171.69.89.217/49 to NP Identity Ifc:172.16.172.164/1442 duration 0:00:00
  bytes 101 TCP FINs
PIX#
```

Now that you are familiar with a successful user authentication and authorization, go through Example 10-24, which shows an example of user authorization failure with TACACS+ protocol, but of successful authentication.

Example 10-24 *Syslog for Successful Authentication with Authorization Failure Using the TACACS+ Protocol*

```
PIX(config)# logging monitor debugging
Jul 25 2005 08:15:47 : %PIX-6-302013: Built inbound TCP connection 6009 for
  outside:50.1.1.1/11009 (50.1.1.1/11009) to inside:192.168.1.2/23 (192.168.1.2/23)
Jul 25 2005 08:15:47 : %PIX-6-109001: Auth start for user '???' from 50.1.1.1/11009
  to 192.168.1.2/23
Jul 25 2005 08:15:50 : %PIX-6-609001: Built local-host outside:171.69.89.217
Jul 25 2005 08:15:50 : %PIX-6-302013: Built outbound TCP connection 6011 for
  outside:171.69.89.217/49 (171.69.89.217/49) to NP Identity Ifc:172.16.172.164/
  1443 (172.16.172.164/1443)
Jul 25 2005 08:15:53 : %PIX-2-109011: Authen Session Start: user 'kodom', sid 37
! Authentication is successful.
Jul 25 2005 08:15:53 : %PIX-6-109005: Authentication succeeded for user 'kodom' from
  50.1.1.1/11009 to 192.168.1.2/23 on interface outside
```

Example 10-24 *Syslog for Successful Authentication with Authorization Failure Using the TACACS+ Protocol (Continued)*

```
Jul 25 2005 08:15:53 : %PIX-6-302013: Built outbound TCP connection 6012 for
  outside:171.69.89.217/49 (171.69.89.217/49) to NP Identity Ifc:172.16.172.164/
  1444 (172.16.172.164/1444)
Jul 25 2005 08:15:53 : %PIX-6-302014: Teardown TCP connection 6011 for
  outside:171.69.89.217/49 to NP Identity Ifc:172.16.172.164/1443 duration 0:00:03
  bytes 107 TCP FINs
Jul 25 2005 08:15:53 : %PIX-6-302013: Built outbound TCP connection 6013 for
  outside:171.69.89.217/49 (171.69.89.217/49) to NP Identity Ifc:172.16.172.164/
  1445 (172.16.172.164/1445)
Jul 25 2005 08:15:53 : %PIX-6-302014: Teardown TCP connection 6012 for
  outside:171.69.89.217/49 to NP Identity Ifc:172.16.172.164/1444 duration 0:00:00
  bytes 87 TCP FINs
! Authorization is failing for telnet session.
Jul 25 2005 08:15:53 : %PIX-6-109008: Authorization denied for user 'kodom' from
  50.1.1.1/11009 to 192.168.1.2/23 on interface outside
Jul 25 2005 08:15:53 : %PIX-6-302014: Teardown TCP connection 6013 for
  outside:171.69.89.217/49 to NP Identity Ifc:172.16.172.164/1445 duration 0:00:00
  bytes 101 TCP FINs
Jul 25 2005 08:15:54 : %PIX-6-302014: Teardown TCP connection 6009 for
  outside:50.1.1.1/11009 to inside:192.168.1.2/23 duration 0:00:06 bytes 170 TCP
  FINs (kodom)
PIX#
```

The log in Example 10-24 shows that authorization failed for the specific IP and port on the outside interface of the firewall. To understand why, analyze the log on the AAA server. For your setup, you are using Cisco Secure ACS as an AAA server. So, go under "Reports and Activity" and then "Failed Attempt," and find out how the commands are parsing to the AAA server from the firewall. Get the syntax from there and apply the same command and argument on the Group setup.

Following are some important points to check to ensure that authorization is configured correctly:

- Verify that **Shell/Exec** is turned on under the **TACACS+ Settings** of the Group profile to which the user belongs.
- Check that the ACL tag defined on the TACACS+ server matches the one defined on the PIX firewall.
- Ensure that traffic is allowed on the ACL that is defined on the PIX firewall, and that the tag is downloaded to the PIX firewall.
- Define the complete syntax of the commands when defining command authorization. If authorization fails, look under the **Reports and Activity** section for the failed attempt and find out how the commands are sent to the Cisco Secure ACS server. Based on this information, be sure to permit the commands and the arguments.
- Configure the authorization to intercept the traffic for authorization on the PIX firewall. Otherwise, the authorization may be skipped.
- For the inbound cut-through proxy, define the local IP address as the destination, not the translated IP in the include/exclude statement.
- Define the authorization traffic for authentication, because authorization traffic will be denied if authentication is not performed on the traffic.

Configuring Cut-through Proxy Authorization using the RADIUS Protocol

As the RADIUS protocol cannot perform command authorization, it must rely on the access-list to control the traffic going across the firewall. Whereas the TACACS+ protocol can implement authorization using an access-list in addition to command authorization, ACL usage for controlling traffic is very limited; only downloading the ACL name/number is possible. ACL usage to control the traffic using the RADIUS protocol is very flexible. In addition to having the ability to download the ACL name from the RADIUS server, it is also possible to define and download the contents of the ACL using the RADIUS protocol. The following list explains methods available to implement authorization with ACL using the RADIUS protocol:

- Downloading the name of the ACL from RADIUS Server
- Defining access-lists on the firewall without applying any interface
- Defining the ACL number under the user profile on the RADIUS server
- Upon successful authentication, downloading the number from the AAA server to activate the ACL for controlling users' access to different network resources.

NOTE Unlike TACACS+, you do not need to enable authorization on the firewall to download the ACL from the RADIUS Server. This is because the ACL name or the content of the ACL is downloaded from the RADIUS Server as part of the Access Accept packet of the RADIUS Protocol. There is no need to turn on authorization.

On the Cisco Secure ACS Server, access-list name or number can be defined in one of the two following ways.

- **Using vendor-specific Attribute**—Beginning with PIX Firewall Version 5.2, you can define the ACL using the vendor-specific attribute. A vendor-specific attribute for the ACL can be set under the Group setup by checking the box **009\001 AV_Pair (vendor-specific),** and defining **acl=115** in the Cisco/RADIUS rectangular box.
- **Using Standard IETF attribute**—Beginning with PIX Version 6.0.1, the ACL name/number can be defined using a standard Internet Engineering Task Force (IETF) RADIUS attribute 11 (Filter-Id).

  Access-list 115 needs to be defined on the firewall.
- Downloading the contents of the ACL from the RADIUS Server

  If you have a large number of ACLs to manage for different users, the number of ACLs can outgrow the capacity of the memory of the firewall. In addition, if you have more than one firewall using the same policy to control the traffic, every firewall must be locally configured with the same ACL. So the authorization implementation defining the ACL on the firewall may not be scalable. To address this issue, you can define the ACL content on the

AAA server and then download the ACL based on user authentication to one, or more than one, firewall. You must be running PIX Firewall Version 6.2 or above to implement this feature.

NOTE Downloading contents of the ACL from the AAA server is not possible with the TACACS+ protocol. With TACACS+, only downloading the ACL name or number is possible, as discussed before.

You can define the ACL on the Cisco Secure ACS server in one of the following ways:

- Using a Vendor-Specific Attribute

  You can use a Cisco vendor-specific attribute to define the ACL that may be downloaded to the firewall. To set this up on the CS ACS Server, edit the group to which the users belong, and go under **RADIUS (Cisco IOS/PIX)** settings. Choose the **[009\001] cisco-av-pair** check box, and define the contents of the ACL that is displayed in a rectangular box, as shown in Figure 10-3, to allow only Telnet access and deny all other traffic.

  ```
  ip:inacl#=permit tcp any any eq telnet
  ip:inacl#=deny ip any any
  ```

  Finally click the **Submit + Restart** button.

- Using Shared Profile Components

  If you have multiple groups that require the same ACL to be applied, defining the same ACL for different groups is not a very scalable solution. Beginning with Cisco Secure ACS 3.0, you can configure a Shared Profile Component, which is a template for the ACL that can be applied to different user groups.

NOTE Configuring a Shared Profile component may not be possible with RADIUS servers from other vendors. Defining a Shared Profile Component is possible only if you are running Cisco Secure ACS version 3.0 and above.

Before you can configure a Shared Profile Component on the CS ACS, you must enable that option. Go to the **Interface Configuration > Advance Options** page. Then check either the **User-Level Downloadable ACLs** or **Group-Level Downloadable ACLs** checkbox or both checkboxes, based on your requirements. Finally, click on **Submit**.

Figure 10-3 *Defining ACL Using the Cisco IOS/PIX RADIUS Attribute.*

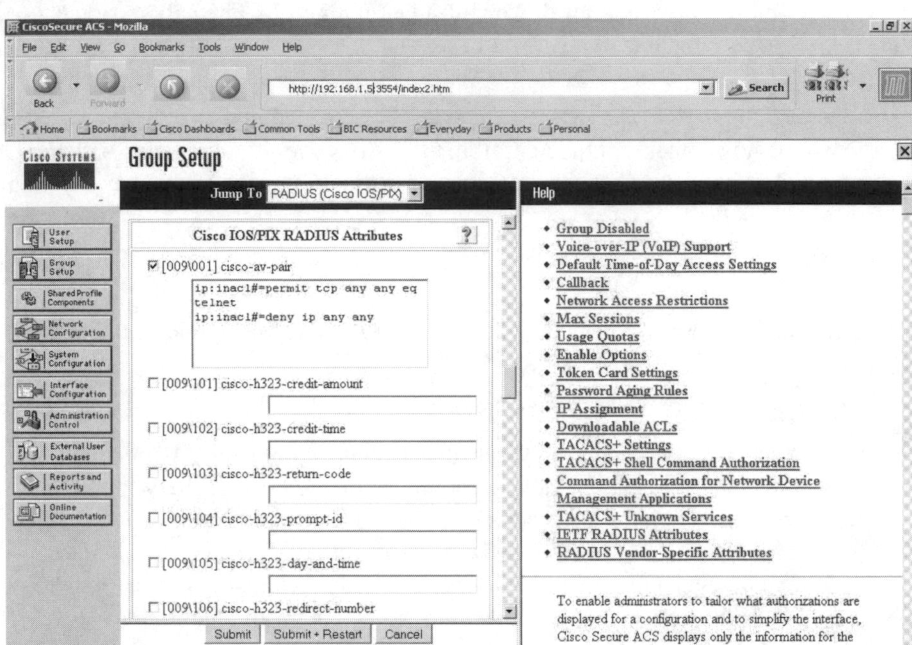

Next you need to define the **Shared Profile Component** (ACL template), which can be mapped to different groups. To accomplish this task, click on **Shared Profile Components,** then **Downloadable IP ACLs,** and then **Add**. This will display the **Downloadable IP ACLs** window, where you need to define the **Name** and, optionally, **Description**. To define ACL contents for this ACL, click on **Add**, which will bring up the **Downloadable IP ACL Content** page (see Figure 10-4), where you need to provide a **Name**. In the **ACL Definitions** rectangle box, define the actual ACE in the ACL which follows the same syntax as the extended ACL of the firewall. For example, to allow only Telnet traffic, the syntax for the **ACL Definitions** will resemble the following:

```
Permit tcp any any eq telnet
```

Click the **Submit** button of the **Downloadable IP ACL Content** page, which will bring you back to the **Downloadable IP ACLs** page. Here be sure that the newly created **ACL Contents** selects the proper firewall (NAS) for the **Network Access Filtering.** If you choose not to filter it based on a specific firewall, choose **All-AAA-Clients,** which is selected by default.

Figure 10-4 *Shared Profile Components for Downloadable IP ACL Configuration*

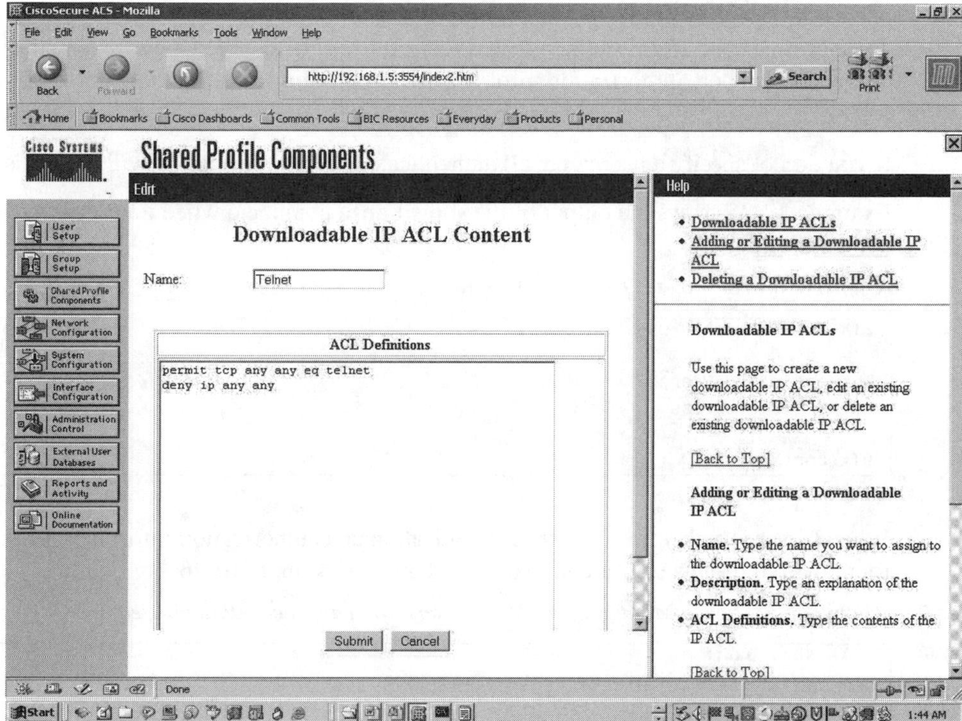

Once the downloadable IP ACL is configured, you can apply this to as many users' groups as you want. To apply Downloadable IP ACL, go to **Group Setup >**. Select the Group, and then click on **Edit Settings,** which will display the **Group Setup** page. In the **Group Setup** page, from the **Jump To** drop-down box, choose **Downloadable ACLs,** which will take you to the **Downloadable ACLs** settings. Check the **Assign IP ACL:** checkbox, and from the drop-down box next to it, choose the Downloadable IP ACL name you have just created. Then click the **Submit+Restart** button.

- **Firewall Configuration**—If you have configured the **access-group** command to apply ACLs to interfaces, be sure to use the **per-user-override** keyword. Otherwise, traffic for a user session must be permitted by both the interface ACL and the user-specific ACL. With the **per-user-override** keyword, the user-specific ACL determines what is permitted, not the interface ACL. The complete syntax for thc acccss-group with the **per-user-override** argument is as follows:

```
access-group access-list {in | out} interface interface_name
  [per-user-override]
```

Troubleshooting Cut-Through Proxy Authorization using the RADIUS Protocol

To determine the currently authenticated users, the host IP to which they are bound, and any cached IP and port authorization information, use the **show uauth** command as follows:

```
PIX# show uauth [username]
```

If you do not specify a username, all authenticated users' information will be displayed.

Example 10-25 shows the output of the **show uauth** command when no user is authenticated.

Example 10-25 *Output of the* **show uauth** *Command With No Users Authentication*

```
PIX(config)# show uauth
                        Current    Most Seen
Authenticated Users       0          0
Authen In Progress        0          1

PIX(config)#
```

When a user is authenticated, user authentication and authorization information can be found with the **show uauth** command, as shown in Example 10-26.

Example 10-26 *Output of the* **show uauth** *Command When Users Are Authenticated/Authorized*

```
PIX# show uauth
                        Current    Most Seen
Authenticated Users       1          1
Authen In Progress        2          3
user 'kodom' at 192.168.2.2, authorized to:
   port 192.168.1.2/telnet
   absolute   timeout: 0:05:00
   inactivity timeout: 0:00:00
PIX-A# Jul 25 2005 09:03:19 : %PIX-7-111009: User 'enable_3' executed cmd: show uauth

PIX#
```

Once you verify the user authentication, the next step is to verify whether the ACL tag is downloaded correctly to the PIX firewall. If PIX is configured with an ACL (not applied to any interface) and if the ACL tag is downloaded from the AAA server upon successful user authentication, the ACL should be applied for the authenticated users. This can be verified with the command shown in Example 10-27.

Example 10-27 **show access-list** *Command Output After Successful Download of ACL Name/Number for Allowing Telnet*

```
PIX# show access-list
access-list AAA-user-cse; 2 elements
access-list AAA-user-cse permit tcp any any eq telnet (hitcnt=1)
access-list AAA-user-cse deny ip any any (hitcnt=0)
PIX#
```

If the ACL content is downloaded from the RADIUS Server, the downloaded ACL looks like that shown in Example 10-28.

Example 10-28 *Output of the* **show access-list** *Command When the Content of the ACL Is Downloaded to the PIX from the RADIUS Server*

```
PIX# show access-list
access-list #ACSACL#-PIX-cse_access_list-3cff1bb3; 2 elements
access-list #ACSACL#-PIX-cse_access_list-3cff1bb3
   permit tcp any any eq telnet (hitcnt=1)
access-list #ACSACL#-PIX-cse_access_list-3cff1bb3
   deny ip any any (hitcnt=0)
111009: User 'enable_15' executed cmd: show access-list
PIX#
```

If the **show uauth** or **show access-list** command does not show you the output as expected, you can run the debug and analyze the log to see the reason for failure on the PIX firewall as on the Cisco Secure ACS Server.

Example 10-29 shows the syslog for user authentication for only Telnet access and denial of other traffic when ACL content is downloaded from the CS ACS to the PIX firewall.

Example 10-29 *PIX Debugs for a Valid Authentication and Downloaded Access List*

```
PIX# show log
. . . . . .
 305011: Built dynamic TCP translation from inside:
  192.168.1.2/11063 to outside:40.1.1.1/1049
109001: Auth start for user '???' from 192.168.1.2/11063
   to 40.1.1.1/23
109011: Authen Session Start: user 'cse', sid 10
109005: Authentication succeeded for user 'cse'
   from 192.168.1.2/11063
   to 40.1.1.1/23 on interface inside

302013: Built outbound TCP connection 123 for outside:
   40.1.1.1/23 (40.1.1.1/23) to inside:
   192.168.1.2/11063 (20.1.1.1/1049) (cse)
. . . . . .
PIX#
```

Following are some of the causes for an authorization failure with the RADIUS protocol for a cut-through proxy connection:

- **Override keyword is missing from the access-group statement**—If you have an access-group applied on the interface, you need to ensure that you have the override optional argument configured in the access-group statement. Otherwise, traffic must be allowed by both interface ACL and per-user ACL configured on the PIX firewall. The syntax for the access-group statement is as follows:

```
access-group access-list {in | out} interface interface_name
  [per-user-override]
```

- **There is a mismatched ACL Name/Number between the PIX and CS ACS**—If you have configured the access-list on the PIX firewall, or the ACL name is defined on the AAA server, ensure that the names match each other. The name is case sensitive. Otherwise, the proper ACL will not be applied for the user traffic, which might result in unexpected behavior.

Accounting for Cut-Through Proxy

You can use the following syntax to configure accounting for cut-through proxy connection:

```
[no] aaa accounting {include | exclude} service  interface-name local-ip local-mask
  foreign-ip foreign-mask server-tag
```

For example, to turn on accounting for all inbound traffic, you may execute the following command:

```
PIX(config)# aaa accounting include any outside 0.0.0.0 0.0.0.0 0.0.0.0 0.0.0.0
  AuthInbound
```

However, it is recommended to use the following syntax to configure cut-through proxy accounting:

```
PIX(config)# [no] aaa accounting match acl-name  interface-name server-tag
```

The following command shows how to turn on accounting for all inbound traffic using ACL.

```
PIX(config)# access-list 150 permit ip any any
PIX(config)# aaa accounting match 150 outside AuthRadius
```

If the accounting does not work as expected, you need to analyze the log on both the PIX firewall and on the AAA server. You need to first examine the debug output of the following command to see if the PIX is generating the accounting packets correctly or not:

```
PIX# debug aaa accounting
```

Additionally, to see the interaction of accounting records from the PIX firewall to AAA server, you can use either of the following commands depending on the type of protocols you are using:

```
PIX# debug radius
PIX# debug tacacs
```

If the accounting appears to be working correctly on the PIX firewall, you can analyze the log on the AAA server to see if the problem is with the AAA server. If Cisco Secure ACS is used for AAA, refer to "Troubleshooting Cisco Secure ACS on Windows" for additional details.

Extended Authentication (X-Auth) Issues for Remote Access VPN Connection

Extended Authentication (X-Auth) is an enhancement of IKE version 1 for a Remote Access VPN connection that allows performing both user and group authentication. When X-Auth is configured on the PIX firewall (FWSM does not support VPN), users are prompted to enter username and password, which is either locally stored in the PIX firewall or in any external database, such as Cisco Secure ACS, ACE Server, NT domain and so on. Extended authentication is performed after IKE phase 1 and before phase 2. In phase 1, group authentication takes place, then X-Auth is performed. Right after X-Auth, if authentication is successful, mode configuration takes place, where PIX Firewall pushes configuration parameters for VPN clients, such as DNS Server IP, WINS Server IP, and so on.

Beginning with PIX Firewall Version 5.2, X-Auth includes support for access-list which allows you to control what traffic needs to be encrypted and what traffic should be transmitted in clear text. The minimum VPN client version requirement is 2.5. This feature is called split-tunneling. If you have a requirement to allow the VPN client to connect to the internal network of the VPN Gateway using the secured tunnel, but want the rest of the traffic to go to the Internet in clear text from the VPN client, you need to configure split-tunneling.

Beginning with PIX Firewall Version 6.2, the download of access-control lists (ACLs) from an AAA server to the PIX firewall is supported. This enables the configuration of a per-user ACL on an AAA server to provide per-user ACL authorization. It is then downloadable through the AAA server to the PIX firewall. This feature is supported for RADIUS servers only, not with TACACS+ servers.

Configuration Steps

With PIX Firewall versions earlier than 7.0, to apply x-auth, use the following command:

```
[no] crypto map map-name client [token] authentication aaa-server-name [LOCAL]
```

With **username**, you can define local users on the PIX firewall. To use the local user database, use the key word **LOCAL**. Otherwise, define a AAA server and assign the same name defined in the preceding command.

Beginning with PIX Version 7.0, you can define attributes for users who are locally created on the PIX firewall.

Work through the steps that follow to configure the X-Auth for PIX Version 7.0 and above.

Step 1 Create the local user database and define the attributes for the user as shown in Example 10-30.

Example 10-30 *Creating a Local User Database*

```
PIX(config)# username laurie nopassword privilege 15
PIX(config)# username laurie attributes
! DefaultGroupPolicy will be applied to this user
PIX(config-username)# vpn-group-policy DefaultGroupPolicy
! Following are to set up the timeout values
PIX(config-username)# vpn-idle-timeout 10
PIX(config-username)# vpn-session-timeout 120
! This user will create IPSec tunnel
PIX(config-username)# vpn-tunnel-protocol  IPsec
```

continues

Example 10-30 *Creating a Local User Database (Continued)*

```
PIX(config-username)# exit
PIX(config)# exit
PIX#
```

To remove all attributes for a specific user, use the following command:

```
PIX(config)# no username laurie attributes
```

To remove a specific user, use the following command:

```
PIX(config)# no username laurie
```

To clear the username database from the firewall, use the following command:

```
PIX(config)# clear config username
username cisco1 password jmINXNH6p1BxUppp encrypted privilege 15
PIX#
```

Step 2 Create a new tunnel group that supports IPsec remote access tunnels as shown in Example 10-31. Here you can specify whether you want to use the local user database or the external AAA server. Be sure that the external AAA server is configured before you attempt to define an AAA server.

Example 10-31 *Creating a Tunnel Group of IPsec Remote Access*

```
PIX(config)# tunnel-group tungrp1 type ipsec-ra
! Now enter the general-attributes mode to define the AAA server.
PIX(config)# tunnel-group tungrp1 general-attributes
! The following lines will turn on both authentication and authorization using
! local user database.
PIX(config-general)# authentication-server-group LOCAL
PIX(config-general)# authorization-server-group LOCAL
! Instead of using local user database, if you want to use RADIUS protocol, use
! the following commands to turn on authentication/authorization and accounting.
! Note that for authentication and authorization using RADIUS protocol is done
! in the same packet. So no need to have the authorization statement to turn on
! authorization. Authentication statement is sufficient.
PIX(config-general)# authentication-server-group AuthRadius
PIX(config-general)# accounting-server-group AuthRadius
PIX(config-general)# exit
! If you want to assign IPSec specific attribute you can execute the following
! command which will provide you with the IPSec related attributes.
PIX(config)# tunnel-group tungrp1 ipsec-attributes
PIX(config-ipsec)#
```

Now to remove all general attributes for this tunnel group:

```
PIX(config)# no tunnel-group tungrp1 general-attributes
```

To remove our tunnel-group specifically by name:

```
PIX(config)# clear config tunnel-group tungrp1
```

To clear the tunnel-group database:

```
PIX(config)# clear config tunnel-group
```

Step 3 For accounting to work correctly, configure the following two commands:

```
PIX(config)# sysopt connection permit-ipsec
PIX(config)# sysopt ipsec pl-compatible
```

Troubleshooting Techniques

Troubleshooting AAA for the Remote Access VPN is very similar to of the troubleshooting described in the sections entitled "Firewall Management with AAA Troubleshooting" and "Cut-Through Proxy with AAA Troubleshooting," with some exceptions. As the connection type is VPN using IPsec, in addition to AAA troubleshooting, you also need to troubleshoot the VPN problem. To debug Remote Access VPN, you may want to refer to Chapter 7, "Troubleshooting IPsec VPN on PIX Firewalls." Following are the two commands that you need to use to troubleshoot IPsec VPN issues:

```
PIX# debug crypto ipsec 5
PIX# debug crypto isakmp 5
PIX# debug crypto engine 5
PIX#
```

To troubleshoot AAA issues for the VPN connection, look at the log on VPN Client **Log Window**, debug on the PIX firewall, and the log on the AAA server.

To turn on logging to the debug level on the VPN client, go to **Start > Programs > Cisco Systems VPN Client > VPN Client**. Then click on **Log Settings** and set **User Authentication** log to **High**. It is recommended that you also set all other classes to high if the tunnel is failed and you are uncertain about the reason of failure. Refer to Chapter 7, "Troubleshooting IPsec VPN on PIX Firewalls."

To turn on debug level syslogging, refer to the "syslog" subsection of section entitled "Diagnostic Commands and Tools" in this chapter. Run the following command to get details about AAA problems:

```
PIX# debug aaa authentication
PIX# debug aaa authorization
PIX# debug aaa accounting
PIX# debug aaa vpn 5
PIX# debug radius
```

If you have authentication problems with the external RADIUS server, you might want to turn on local user database authentication to eliminate the possibility that the external AAA server is causing the problem.

If local user database authentication works well, you need to analyze the log on the AAA sever. For Cisco Secure ACS troubleshooting, you need to analyze the **package.cab** file, which is discussed in Chapter 13, "Troubleshooting Cisco Secure ACS on Windows."

Case Studies

As discussed earlier, only Telnet/SSH/FTP/HTTP/HTTPS protocols have the option to provide the interactive authentication method, hence implementing the cut-through proxy is possible. However, for a mail server, an IP phone or printer does not have the options to provide the interactive authentication prompt. Under this circumstance, if authentication is not required, it is best is to configure AAA Exemption for these devices. However, if authentication is required for these devices, then to work around the problem posed by cut-through proxy authentication, Virtual Telnet or HTTP might be required. This case study section explores these options in detail and shows you how to get around some of the unique problems posed by the cut-through proxy configuration on the firewall.

Case Study 1: AAA Exemption

If authentication is not required, and you want avoid the problem with cut-through proxy authentications for the applications that do not have the capability to present interactive authentication prompts, you can use either of the following options as described in the sections that follow:

- IP Exemption
- MAC Exemption

IP Exemption

If you know the source and or the destination IP address of the devices for which you want to bypass authentication, you can use IP exemption.

You can exempt the IP from authentication and authorization in two ways, as shown in Example 10-32.

Example 10-32 *Configuration for IP Exemption on the Firewall*

```
! Following shows one of the two ways how to exempt IP from authentication and
! authorization.
Firewall(config)# aaa authentication exclude telnet outside 192.168.1.2
  255.255.255.255
30.1.1.1 255.255.255.255 AuthTacacs
Firewall(config)# aaa authorization exclude telnet outside 192.168.1.2
  255.255.255.255
30.1.1.1 255.255.255.255 AuthTacacs
! Following lines shows rest of the other telnet traffic will be intercepted for the
! authentication and authorization.
Firewall(config)# aaa authentication include telnet outside 0.0.0.0 0.0.0.0 0.0.0.0
  0.0.0.0 AuthTacacs
Firewall(config)# aaa authorization include telnet outside 0.0.0.0 0.0.0.0 0.0.0.0
  0.0.0.0 AuthTacacs
! The same task can be accomplished by access-list as well as shown in the following
! lines. Make sure not to configure both option as that will cause firewall to behave
```

Example 10-32 *Configuration for IP Exemption on the Firewall (Continued)*

```
! very unpredictable manner.
Firewall(config)# access-list 101 deny tcp host 30.1.1.1 host 192.168.1.2 eq telnet
Firewall(config)# access-list 101 permit tcp any any eq telnet
Firewall(config)# aaa authentication match 101 outside AuthTacacs
Firewall(config)# aaa authorization match 101 outside AuthTacacs
Firewall(config)#
```

NOTE If you exempt an IP from authentication, you also must exempt the same IP from authorization if authorization is enabled; otherwise, packets will be dropped by the authorization.

MAC Exemption

IP Exemption works well if the devices behind the firewall have the static IP address. However, if the devices are assigned IP addresses dynamically, the IP Exemption does not work. This is where MAC Exemption is required. This feature is first introduced in PIX Version 6.3.

In MAC Exemption, both the IP address and MAC address of the traffic are checked to avoid the security risk of allowing a spoofed MAC address traffic to bypass authentication. If a firewall receives the first request for connection from a specific MAC address, the MAC will not exist in the cache of **uauth** table, which can be viewed by using the **show uauth** command on the firewall. Hence cut-through proxy authentication will be prompted. If subsequent connections are coming from the same MAC and the IP address, the connections will be bypassed from authentication. However, if the packet comes from the same MAC but a different IP address, authentication will be required.

Both authentication and authorization are bypassed if MAC Exemption is turned on. You can define the addresses that should bypass the authentication with the following command:

```
PIX(config)# [no] mac-list id deny|permit mac macmask
```

After a mac-list is defined, you can use the following command to turn on MAC Exemption:

```
PIX(config)# [no] aaa mac-exempt match id
```

You can view the mac-list with the following command:

```
PIX# show running-config mac-list [id]
```

To clear the mac-list, you can use the following command:

```
PIX(config)# clear configure mac-list [id]
```

Table 10-9 shows the meaning of arguments for the preceding commands.

Table 10-9 **mac-list** *and* **mac-exempt** *Command Arguments*

Arguments	Meaning
Id	MAC access list number.
Deny	Traffic matching deny is not included in the MAC list and is subjected to both authentication and authorization.
Permit	Traffic matching permit is included in the MAC list and is exempt from authentication and authorization.
Mac	Source MAC address in **aabbcc.ddeeff.gghhii** form.
Macmask	Applies the netmask to mac, which is a string of 1's followed by 0's in the form **aabbcc.ddeeff.gghhii**, and allows the grouping of MAC addresses.
Show	Provides the MAC-list in the privilege mode.
Clear	Removes the **mac-list** command statements along with the rest of the AAA configuration.

Example 10-33 shows how to configure a MAC access list.

Example 10-33 *MAC Access List Configuration*

```
PIX(config)# mac-list adc permit 00a0.c95d.0282 ffff.ffff.ffff
PIX(config)# mac-list adc deny 00a1.c95d.0282 ffff.ffff.ffff
PIX(config)# mac-list ac permit 0050.54ff.0000 ffff.ffff.0000
PIX(config)# mac-list ac deny 0061.54ff.b440 ffff.ffff.ffff
PIX(config)# mac-list ac deny 0072.54ff.b440 ffff.ffff.ffff
!Following show command shows the mac-list configuration
PIX(config)# show running-config mac-list
mac-list adc permit 00a0.c95d.0282 ffff.ffff.ffff
mac-list adc deny 00a1.c95d.0282 ffff.ffff.ffff
mac-list ac permit 0050.54ff.0000 ffff.ffff.0000
mac-list ac deny 0061.54ff.b440 ffff.ffff.ffff
mac-list ac deny 0072.54ff.b440 ffff.ffff.ffff
!Following command bind the ac mac-list to the aaa mac-exempt
PIX(config)# aaa mac-exempt match ac
PIX(config)#
```

AAA Exemption with IP or MAC should be configured only when you want to bypass the authentication for certain IP or MAC addresses that do not support interactive authentication prompts. However, if the cut-through proxy authentication is required for these devices, then you need to configure Virtual Telnet on the firewall, which is discussed next.

Case Study 2: Virtual Telnet

Virtual Telnet can be used to address one of the following issues:

- To use Next PIN or New PIN mode with an SDI server

- To authenticate uncommon protocols (For example SMTP)
- To authorize uncommon protocols (For example SMTP)

This section examines both configuration and troubleshooting of Virtual Telnets.

Configuring Virtual Telnet

Inbound virtual Telnet is implemented based on Figure 10-2. Authenticating mail inbound is not a good idea, as there is no interactive window displayed for mail to be sent inbound. Using the AAA Exemption is a better choice as discussed in the preceding section. However, if you really want to authenticate the mail traffic, you can accomplish that with the command shown in Example 10-34. The same implementation can be used for other uncommon protocols that do not have interactive authentication, such as TFTP.

Example 10-34 *Configuration Needed for Inbound Mail Traffic Authentication*

```
PIX# configure terminal
! The following statement is required for authenticating the mail traffic.
PIX(config)# aaa authentication include tcp/25 outside 0.0.0.0 0.0.0.0 0.0.0.0
  0.0.0.0 AuthTacacs
! The following statement is needed to turn on authorization.
PIX(config)# aaa authorization include tcp/25 outside 0.0.0.0 0.0.0.0 0.0.0.0
  0.0.0.0 AuthTacacs
! The above two lines can be substituted by creating ACL and applying it with AAA as
! shown below.
PIX(config)# access-list 101 permit tcp any any eq smtp
PIX(config)# aaa authentication match 101 outside AuthTacacs
PIX(config)# aaa authorization match 101 outside AuthTacacs
! Following command is needed to turn on Virtual telnet on IP address 20.1.1.3. You need
! to make sure to create a static for this IP address for the inbound traffic. Also make
! sure to create the static for the actual destination.
PIX(config)# virtual telnet 20.1.1.3
! Following line is to create the static translation for Virtual IP address 20.1.1.3
PIX(config)# static (inside,outside) 20.1.1.3 192.168.1.103 netmask 255.255.255.255 0 0
! Following line is to create the static for the actual mail server
PIX(config)# static (inside,outside) 20.1.1.102 192.168.1.2 netmask 255.255.255.255 0 0
! Following access-list is to include Virtual server IP address for telnet for cut-thru
! proxy authentication
PIX(config)# access-list 110 permit tcp any host 20.1.1.3 eq telnet
! Following line is to configure cut-through proxy authentication for the mail server.
PIX(config)# access-list 110 permit tcp any tcp host 20.1.1.102 eq smtp
PIX(config)# access-group 110 interface outside in
PIX(config)#
```

Use the following procedure to configure the Cisco Secure ACS Server for the mail authentication:

Step 1 On CS ACS GUI, click on **Group Setup**, select the group to edit.

Step 2 On the Group Setup page, under **TACACS+ Settings**, check the **Shell (exec)**.

Step 3 Under **Shell Command Authorization Set,** select the **Per Group Command Authorization** radio button.

Step 4 For **Unmatched Cisco IOS commands** select the **Deny** radio button.

Step 5 Check the **Command** box, and enter **telnet** as the command. Leave the **argument** rectangle **blank**, and choose **Unlisted Arguments** as **Permit**.

Step 6 Finally, click the **Submit+Restart button**.

With the preceding configuration, users first need to use Telnet to access the Virtual IP address from outside. This will authenticate the user, and caches the authentication based on source IP address. Then the user can send mail traffic. If authorization is turned on, you need to create the access-list on the PIX firewall and define this ACL number to the Group Profile under **TACACS+ Settings**. You need to check the **Access control list** checkbox and in the textbox next to it, put the ACL tag configured on the PIX firewall.

To authenticate outbound mail traffic, the procedure is the same. You do not however, need to configure static for the Virtual IP address for the Telnet.

NOTE After successful user authentication, Virtual Telnet caches the user authentication and authorization information, which can be viewed with the **show uauth** command. This allows anyone from the authenticated host to bypass the authentication/authorization. To prevent this, if you want to clear the cache in the **uauth** table of the firewall after you finish your task, you need to Telnet to the virtual Telnet IP address again. This toggles the session off.

Troubleshooting Virtual Telnet

Troubleshooting Virtual Telnet is the same process as for the cut-through proxy authentication. Most of the problems pertaining to Virtual Telnet arise from the misconfiguration of the Virtual Telnet IP address. Following are some of the most important points you need to keep in mind when configuring Virtual Telnet:

- For the inbound traffic, the virtual Telnet IP address must be a routable IP which is reachable from the end-user PC. For outbound traffic, the address can be a private address if it is reachable from the end user PC.
- For inbound traffic, the virtual IP address must have an internal private address. For outbound traffic, translation is not required for the virtual IP address.
- For both inbound/outbound traffic, virtual IP addresses must be included for AAA authentication.
- A virtual IP address must be unique, which means that this address should not be used for any host in the network.
- The virtual IP address for Telnet should not be the same as the virtual HTTP address, as discussed in the next case study.

Case Study 3: Virtual HTTP

Virtual HTTP is needed for the following reasons:

- To avoid multiple authentications while visiting different sites
- To avoid authentication failure if the web server requires a second authentication (double authentication)
- To work with New PIN Mode for the web traffic, you must configure Virtual Telnet along with Virtual HTTP

If the web server requires user authentication in addition to a cut-through proxy authentication on the PIX firewall, you might consider configuring Virtual HTTP. Otherwise, the browser cache could cause problems with web server authentication.

The configuration for Virtual Telnet is very similar to that of Virtual HTTP except for the protocol type. With virtual Telnet, you use Telnet protocol, and for virtual HTTP, the HTTP protocol is used.

Following is the command needed to implement virtual HTTP:

```
virtual http #.#.#.# warn
```

Note the following important points:

- When the user tries to go outside the PIX, authentication is required. If the warn parameter is present, the user receives a redirect message.
- The authentication is good for the length of time in the uauth.
- Do not set the **timeout uauth** command duration to 0 seconds with virtual HTTP. This blocks HTTP connections to the real web server.
- The virtual HTTP IP address must be unique and can not be in use anywhere else in the network.
- If the ACL is applied on the inside interface, you must allow the access to the IP address on port 80 or 443.
- The virtual HTTP and virtual Telnet IP addresses must be included in the **aaa authentication** statements. In this example, specifying 0.0.0.0 does include these addresses.

Example 10-35 shows the configuration required to turn on virtual HTTP.

Example 10-35 *Virtual HTTP Configuration on the PIX Firewall*

```
PIX# configure terminal
PIX(config)# virtual http 192.168.1.40
PIX(config)#
```

When the user from 192.168.1.4 points the browser at 30.1.1.1, the following message is displayed to the user:

```
Enter username for PIX (IDXXX) at 192.168.1.40
```

After authentication, the traffic is redirected to 30.1.1.1.

Common Problems and Resolutions

This section works through some frequently asked questions and answers.

1 Can I implement cut-through proxy authentication behind a PAT device?

Answer: After successful user authentication, authentication information is cached on the PIX firewall based on the source IP address. Hence, so long as the authentication information does not timeout, the subsequent authentication will not be prompted for the username/password. If all devices are behind a PAT device, the source IP address for all devices will be the same, but source ports will be different. As the cut-through proxy cache is based on source IP address, not the source port, if one of the devices authenticates, the rest of the devices will not be authenticated, as the source IPs for all devices are the same. To work around this problem, you may set the uauth absolute timeout to zero, which effectively will disable the caching of user credentials. Therefore, users will be prompted for authentication even if they are using the same source IP address. However, disabling the uauth cache can create a problem for users browsing the web. If the traffic to be authenticated is only by Telnet and FTP, setting the uauth timeout to zero solves the problem, and all users can be authenticated for each connection, including those users sharing the same source IP.

2 When configuring http console authentication on the PIX to go to TACACS+ or RADIUS, is there a way to keep it from sending more than one authentication request when a user logs into PDM(PIX Device Manager)/ASDM (ASA Device Manager)? Sending more than one authentication request causes user authentication problems with a One Time Password database such as SDI.

Answer: PIX firewall does not support one-time passwords for **http console authentication**. Each HTTP connection to the PIX is authenticated with the AAA server. When PDM starts up, it makes multiple connections to the PIX to get the configuration and other information.

3 Can the same address be used for both virtual Telnet and HTTP server?

Answer: No, you cannot use the same address for both virtual Telnet and virtual HTTP.

4 Should I Telnet directly to the virtual Telnet server IP and get authenticated, or should I Telnet to something beyond PIX, so that PIX will redirect to the virtual Telnet IP address?

Answer: With virtual Telnet, you should always Telnet to the virtual Telnet IP. That is the only way it works. Redirection is not involved with virtual Telnet. You redirect only with virtual HTTP.

5 Do next pin and new pin modes work only with Telnet on a PIX firewall?

Answer: No. They also work with virtual HTTP. But, you need to be sure to configure virtual Telnet in addition to virtual HTTP.

6 What is the configuration recommendation for the HTTP next token?

Answer: Following are some configuration recommendations for http next token:

— Do not configure both virtual HTTP and virtual Telnet at the same time. Configure and test each one separately. First enable virtual HTTP and test basic authentication using a browser (not next token mode). If virtual HTTP is working, configure and test virtual Telnet using a Telnet client—clear uauth—then simply Telnet to the virtual address and authenticate. Once they are both working, then test next token / new pin using a browser.

— Choose a unique address for each virtual server. Each address should be routable from the clients to the PIX and should not be in use by any devices on the network. Do not choose the same address for virtual HTTP and virtual Telnet; two separate addresses are required.

7 When was the fallback method to use the LOCAL user database introduced?

Answer: The fallback method to use the LOCAL database in case the AAA server is unavailable was introduced in PIX Firewall Version 6.3.4.

8 Is accounting supported for GRE traffic?

Answer: Yes, from Version 6.3.4 GRE accounting is supported.

9 Is cut-thru proxy supported based on source port? Or is it based on source IP only?

Answer: It is based on source IP only.

10 Can I customize the prompt to show to users for Cut-Through Proxy Authentication? Can I also provide feedback on the successful or failed authentication?

Answer: You can customize the prompt the user sees when trying to make connections across the PIX Firewall. Customizations of prompt options are as follows: You can change the prompt that the user first sees with cut-through proxy by using the **auth-prompt** command as follows:

```
auth-prompt prompt PIX515B
```

With this command, users going through the PIX see the prompt **PIX515B**.

If you want to provide feedback on a successful or failed authentication, you can use the following commands:

```
auth-prompt accept "GOOD_AUTHENTICATION"
auth-prompt reject "BAD_AUTHENTICATION"
```

Then users see the messages shown in Example 10-36 concerning authentication status on a failed/successful login.

Example 10-36 *Message That Appears to Client with Successful/Failure of User Authentication*

```
PIX515B
Username: junk
Password:
"BAD_AUTHENTICATION"

PIX515B
Username: cse
Password:
"GOOD_AUTHENTICATION"
```

11 Can I configure Per-User Idle and Absolute Timeouts for Cut-through Proxy Authentication?

Answer: The PIX **timeout uauth** command controls how often re-authentication is required. If TACACS+ authentication/authorization is on, this is controlled on a per-user basis.

To configure timeout and idle timeout on the ACS Server using TACACS+, follow these steps:

Step 1 On CS ACS GUI, from left Menu navigation, click on **Group Setup**, choose the **Group**, and click on **Edit**.

Step 2 On the Group Configuration page, select **TACACS+** from the **Jump To** drop-down menu.

Step 3 Check the **Shell (Exec)** box.

Step 4 Check **Idle time** and enter a value of **2**.

Step 5 Check the **Timeout** box and enter a value of **1**.

Step 6 Click the **Submit+Restart** button.

NOTE You must have the authorization turned on for timeout and idle timeout to work properly.

Best Practices

This section presents some of the important methods for improving performance and avoiding a lockout situation. Following is the list of such some good practices:

- If you are running PIX Version 6.3.4 or later, be sure to create a local user and configure a local user database as a fallback, just in case there is a communication problem between the PIX and AAA server.

- When TACACS+ is configured with authorization for pass-through traffic, be sure not to enable accounting for all traffic. Otherwise, PIX will generate many accounting records for a single PIX Firewall.
- When configuring cut-through proxy for HTTP(S), be sure not to set the absolute timeout to zero. This is because, for loading a single HTTP page, the browser might need to make multiple connections to the web server. If the absolute timeout is set to zero, for every request to load a single web page, you need to enter authentication information multiple times. For FTP and Telnet, this is not an issue.
- If you have a backup RADIUS Server configured, configure dead-time for RADIUS to improve the performance.
- If you have a web server that requires authentication in addition to cut-thru proxy authentication by the PIX firewall, always configure virtual Telnet and virtual HTTP on the PIX firewall. Additionally, virtual Telnet should be used when you need to authenticate/authorize the port that cannot be used as a service for authentication (HTTP/HTTPS/Telnet/FTP can be used as service). One such protocol is SMTP (TCP/25), so if you need SMTP authentication by the PIX firewall, you need to configure virtual Telnet.
- Do not configure console authentication for PIX Device Manager (PDM) with a One-time Token card (for example, SDI), because when PDM starts up, it makes multiple connections to the PIX to get the configuration and other information, and for each HTTP/HTTPS connection to the PIX, the user is authenticated with the AAA server. Because the one-time password changes at certain time intervals, first one or two connections will successfully authenticate, but subsequent connection authentication will fail.

CHAPTER 11

Troubleshooting AAA on the Switches

Recently, Authentication, Authorization, and Accounting (AAA) implementation on the switch has become extensive and popular due to the enrichment and growth of the 802.1x protocol and Cisco's initiative on Identity-based Network Services (IBNSs). Authenticating the device has become increasingly important for security administrators, and this need is addressed by the IBNS initiative. This chapter examines AAA implementation and troubleshooting with a focus on these two areas—device management and port authentication on Cisco switches.

Overview of AAA

AAA is implemented on the switch for two purposes:

- Switch Management
- Identity-based Network Services (IBNSs)

Switch Management

Just like routers, switches can be configured for AAA implementation for management purposes. The configuration may differ based on which mode is running (Native IOS or Hybrid). The primary focus of this chapter is the Hybrid mode (Cat OS), as the Native IOS AAA implementation on the switch is the same as Router IOS (see Chapter 9, "Troubleshooting AAA on IOS Routers," for details for device management purpose).

Identity-Based Network Services (IBNSs)

Identity-based Network Services (IBNSs), a Cisco initiative, is a superset of IEEE 802.1x functionality. IBNS is a systems framework for delivering local-area network (LAN) authentication, a part of which is using 802.1x. 802.1 x works in link layer (Layer 2) of the OSI model.

Figure 11-1 shows a typical IBNS network in which phones, laptops, and desktop computers may be connected to the switch ports, and some or all of the ports on the switch may be running dot1x authentication. If the IBNS is implemented on the switch port, devices must be authenticated before receiving connectivity.

Figure 11-1 *Typical Setup of IBNS in Switch Environment*

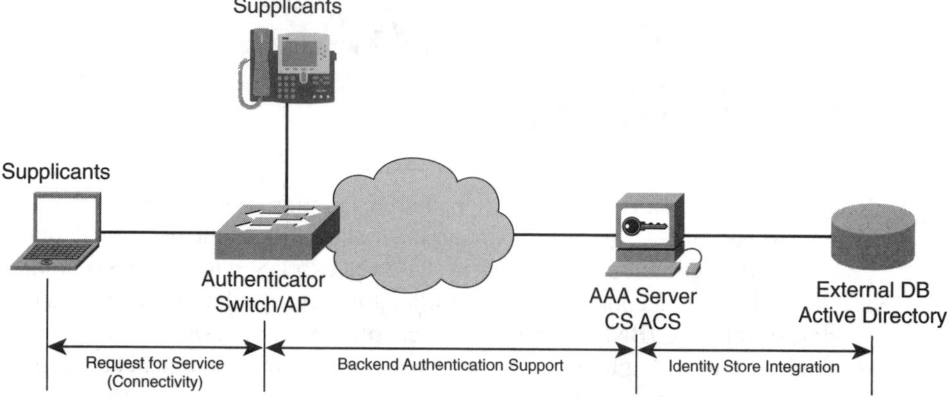

IBNS is built upon three main components: IEEE 802.1x Framework, Extensible Authentication Protocol (EAP), and Remote Authentication Dial-In User Service (RADIUS) protocol. Although EAP is used for actual authentication, EAP encapsulation over LANs (EOPL), which is defined by the IEEE 802.1x standard and RADIUS protocol, is used as the transport medium for carrying EAP packets between the Supplicant and the Authentication Server. So, to understand the IBNS concept completely, you need to understand all three components that are the building blocks of the IBNS technology solution as explained in the sections that follow.

IEEE 802.1x Framework

IEEE 802.1x (also known as dot1x) is a standard set by the IEEE 802.1 working group. It's a framework designed to address and provide port-based access control using authentication. The 802.1x authenticates network clients using information unique to the client and with credentials known only to the client. This service is called port-level authentication because, for security reasons, it is offered to a single endpoint for a given physical port. The 802.1x framework defines the following three roles in the authentication process as depicted in Figure 11-2:

- **Supplicant**—The endpoint that is seeking network access is known as the *supplicant*. The supplicant may be an end user device or a standalone device, such as an IP phone. The device must be running 802.1x-compliant software.
- **Authenticator**—The device to which the supplicant directly connects and through which the supplicant obtains network access permission is known as the *authenticator*. The authenticator performs the following operations:
  - Requests identity information (credentials) from the supplicant

— Verifies credentials using the RADIUS server

— Relays a response to the supplicant.

— Encapsulates and decapsulates the EAP frames and interacts with the RADIUS server as an AAA client.

- **Authentication server**—Performs the actual authentication of the supplicant. The authentication server is a RADIUS server that validates the identity of the supplicant and notifies the switch whether or not the supplicant is authorized to access the LAN and switch services. The authentication server can also send information to the switch about the Virtual Local Area Network (VLAN) that is assigned to the user.

Figure 11-2 *802.1x Authentication Sequence*

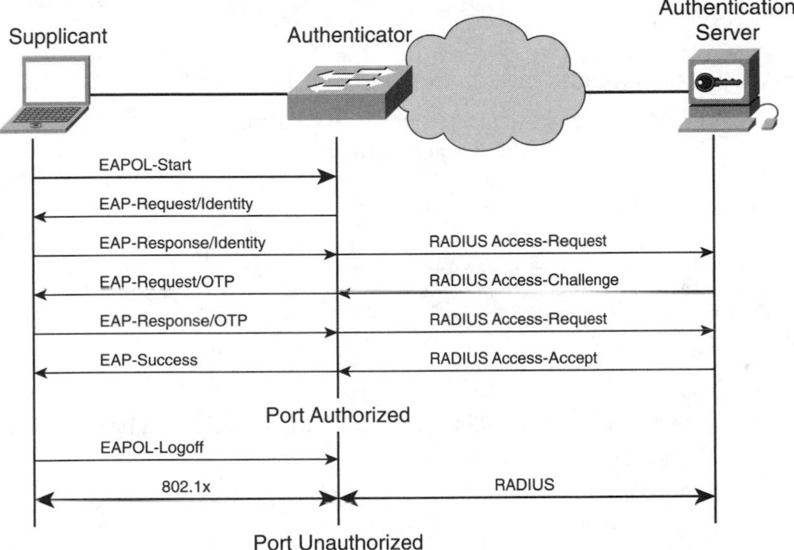

In Table 11-1, the terminology for different components is mapped to AAA terms for your understanding.

Table 11-1 *IEEE 802.1x Terminology Mapped to AAA Terminology*

IEEE Terms	AAA Terms
Supplicant	Client
Authenticator	Network Access Device
Authentication Server	AAA/RADIUS Server

The authentication process, which consists of exchanges of Extensible Authentication Protocol (EAP) messages, occurs between the supplicant and the authentication server. The authenticator acts as a transparent relay (middleman) for this exchange and as a point of enforcement for any policy configuration instructions the authentication server may send back as a result of the authentication process.

The IEEE 802.1x specification defines a new link layer protocol, 802.1x, which is used for communications between the supplicant and the authenticator. Communications between the supplicant and authentication server also leverage the RADIUS protocol carried over standard UDP.

Figure 11-3 shows a dot1x frame that contains the EAP information.

Figure 11-3 *dot1x Frame Format*

Ethernet Header	802.1x Header	EAP Payload

EAP encapsulation over LANs (EAPOL)

EAP over LAN carries EAP packets between the supplicant and the authenticator (switch). Figure 11-4 shows the EAPOL frame format.

Figure 11-4 *EAPOL Frame Format*

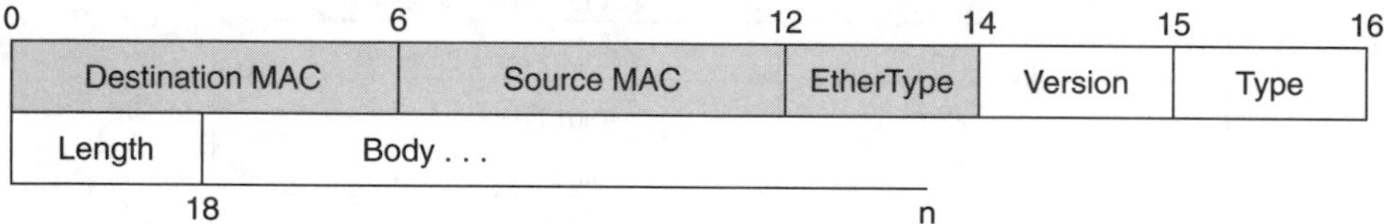

Depending on the functions being performed, the EAPOL can be one of the following types:

- EAPOL-Start
- EAPOL-Logoff
- EAP-Packet
- EAPOL-Key
- EAPOL-Encapsulated-ASF-Alert

At this point you can explore the basic operation of the 802.1x framework as explained in the following section.

Standard 802.1x Operation

When 802.1x is enabled on a switch port, the port is set to an unauthorized mode, allowing only EAPOL traffic to pass through the switch port (see Figure 11-5).

Figure 11-5 *Standard 802.1x Operation*

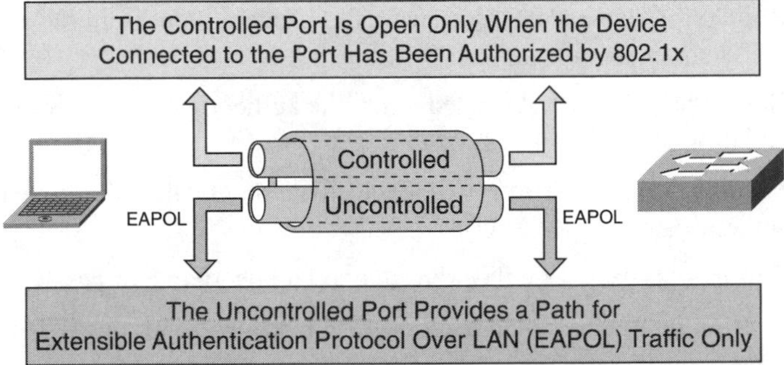
The Controlled Port Is Open Only When the Device Connected to the Port Has Been Authorized by 802.1x
Controlled
Uncontrolled
EAPOL
EAPOL
The Uncontrolled Port Provides a Path for Extensible Authentication Protocol Over LAN (EAPOL) Traffic Only

Because of the default operation of 802.1x, the Media Access Control (MAC) address of a machine is unknown until a supplicant transmits EAPOL frames, or until the port is authorized after successful authentication.

As Figure 11-5 shows, only EAPOL traffic can be processed by a switch port before it is authenticated via 802.1x. Once a port is authorized, only one MAC address can send traffic into the network. Any other MAC address on the wire is a security violation on the port. This operation ensures the validity of the authenticated session.

The IEEE 802.1x standard defines a client/server access control and authentication protocol that restricts unauthorized devices from connecting to a LAN through publicly accessible ports. The 802.1x protocol controls network access by creating two distinct virtual access points at each port. One access point is an uncontrolled port; the other is a controlled port. All traffic through the single port is available to both access points. 802.1x authenticates each user device that is connected to a switch port. It can assign the port to a VLAN before making available any services that are offered by the switch or the LAN. Until a device is authenticated, 802.1x access controls restrict traffic through the port to which the device is connected; only EAPOL traffic is permitted. After authentication is completed, enterprise traffic is allowed through the port.

Extensible Authentication Protocol (EAP)

EAP was initially developed for Point-to-Point Protocol (PPP) authentication. It is a flexible protocol used to carry arbitrary authentication information. It typically rides on top of another protocol such as 802.1x or RADIUS, as Figure 11-3 shows. This protocol is defined by RFC 2284 and 3748 (3748 made 2284 obsolete). Figure 11-6 shows the format of an EAP frame.

Figure 11-6 *EAP Frame Format*

0	8	16 31
Code	Identifier	Length
Data . . .		

In Figure 11-6, the code can be any of the following four values:

- **Request**—This code is used when the packet is sent from the authenticator (switch) to the authentication server.
- **Response**—This code is used when the authentication server responds back to the authenticator with success or failure.
- **Success**—When the user is successfully authenticated, this code is used to inform the authenticator.
- **Failure**—If the user fails either due to bad username or password, this code is used.

The identifier is used to match responses with requests, and format of the data field is determined by the code field.

The following is a list of authentication methods used with EAP:

- **Challenge-response-based**
  - **EAP-MD5**—Uses MD5 based challenge-response for authentication.
  - **LEAP**—Uses username/password authentication.
  - **EAP-MSCHAPv2**—Uses username/password MSCHAPv2 challenge-response authentication.
- **Cryptographic-based**
  - **EAP-TLS**—Uses x.509 v3 PKI certificates and the TLS mechanism for authentication. (TLS stands for Transport Layer Security.)
- **Tunneling methods**
  - **PEAP**—Protected EAP tunnel mode EAP encapsulator; tunnels other EAP types in an encrypted tunnel, much like Web-based SSL.
  - **EAP-TTLS**—Other EAP methods over an extended EAP-TLS encrypted tunnel.
  - **EAP-FAST**—Recent tunneling method designed to avoid the requirement of certificates for deployment.
- **Other**
  - **EAP-GTC**—Generic token and OTP authentication.

EAP implementation in the Microsoft environment is well explained in the following link: http://msdn.microsoft.com/library/default.asp?url=/library/en-us/eap/eap/about_extensible_authentication_protocol.asp

RADIUS IN 802.1x

Just as dot1x carries the EAP packet between the supplicant to the authenticator, RADIUS carries the EAP packet between the authenticator to the authentication server. The IEEE

802.1X RADIUS Usage Guidelines are defined by RFC 3580. Figure 11-7 shows a RADIUS packet with the EAP packet in it.

Figure 11-7 *Format of a RADIUS Packet with dot1x*

IP Header	UDP Header	RADIUS Header	EAP Payload

RADIUS may carry policy instructions back to the authenticator in the form of Attribute Value (AV) pairs to the switch as shown in Figure 11-8.

Figure 11-8 *Format of a RADIUS Packet with AV Pairs with dot1x*

IP Header	UDP Header	RADIUS Header	EAP Payload	AV Pairs

What Is Authenticated

In 802.1x framework, both user and machine may be authenticated if configured. To understand how that may affect the Windows login procedure, examine the sequence of events that happens when Windows 2000 or XP boots up with user and machine authentication turned on:

1. Power On.
2. Load NDIS Drivers.
3. 802.1x Machine Auth.

   This step is skipped if machine authentication is turned off. Note that this step occurs before receiving the DHCP IP address. So, if the machine authentication fails, the machine doesn't receive the IP address.
4. Dynamic Host Configuration Protocol (DHCP).
5. Setup secure channel to Domain Controller (DC).
6. Download applicable domain-configured Computer Group Policy Objects (GPOs).
7. Apply Computer Group Policy Objects.
8. Present the Graphical Identification and Authentication (GINA) (**Ctrl-Alt-Del**) login to the end user.

   Windows Domain Authentication occurs.

   At this stage, 802.1x user authentication occurs when the user credentials are provided either in the form of a username/password or through a certificate.

   If user authentication fails, even though the machine authentication succeeds, actual user traffic will not be allowed. The only traffic allowed is through the secured tunnel to the domain controller to perform the 802.1x user authentication.

9 Machine queries the DHCP server to get the IP address, default gateways, and so on, using DHCP.

Note this is the second DHCP query after user authentication. In this step, the IP address can be assigned based on the VLAN assignment.

Machine Authentication

Microsoft introduced machine authentication to allow the supplicant to authenticate at boot time using the identity and credentials of the computer, so that the client could establish the required secure channel to update and participate in the domain GPO model. Machine authentication allows the computer to authenticate itself to the network using 802.1x, just after a PC loads device drivers at boot time. At boot time, the Windows OS uses machine authentication to authenticate using 802.1x, and to subsequently communicate with Windows domain controllers to pull down machine group policies. This alleviates the problem of domain GPOs being broken by the introduction of 802.1x. The identity that is used is the actual name of the computer as it exists in the active directory. The credentials used to authenticate the computer can be password-based or PKI certificate-based, depending on the EAP type used. Protected Extensible Authentication Protocol (PEAP) with EAP-Microsoft Challenge Handshake Authentication Protocol version 2 (MSCHAPv2) can perform machine authentication using the machine password, which is known to each machine and to the active directory. PEAP with EAP-TLS and EAP-TLS can perform machine authentication using a machine certificate.

NOTE It is not mandatory to configure machine authentication with AD. But if you don't configure machine authentication, it breaks group and system policies.

Authorization

Authorization provides the ability to enforce policies on identities. The most basic authorization in 802.1x, and IBNS is the ability to allow or disallow access to the network at the link layer by applying Dynamic VLAN assignment based on the identity or a group of identities. In addition, MAC-based filtering is also possible to provide more granular control.

Accounting

802.1x and RADIUS Accounting are similar to other accounting and tracking mechanisms that already exist using RADIUS, with the additional capability of operating through 802.1x as an L2 transport. Accounting and tracking information can include basic billing, usage, and various events related to any 802.1x ports.

The combination of 802.1x with RADIUS Accounting enhances the overall value of IBNS by providing the additional capabilities for network session awareness and the notion of an authenticated identity into an enterprise management infrastructure.

RADIUS Accounting Session Start/Stop Records

Accounting start records are sent only at the notification of an authenticated session. Accounting takes place after a RADIUS-Accept packet is sent by an authentication server toward an authenticator, and an EAPOL-Success frame is sent by an authenticator toward a supplicant. Start records for accounting are thus sent under the following conditions:

- When an 802.1x authentication succeeds
- When an 802.1x re-authentication succeeds

NOTE When re-authentication succeeds, this changes the value of Attribute [40] (Acct-Status-Type) for all Cisco Catalyst switches. Instead of the value of this AV pair being Start, it becomes Interim Update. For more information on AV pairs, see the sections that follow.

Accounting stop records are sent under multiple conditions. More conditions can affect the determination of the end of a session than the beginning of a session, and the reliance on lower layer protocols (such as 802.1x). Accounting stop records are sent once the following conditions are met:

- **Explicit session termination**—EAPOL-Logoff processing of an authenticated session. Note that an EAPOL-Logoff frame originated by a supplicant in this condition must be received by a switch to successfully terminate the session and process a stop record.
- **Implicit session termination**—This can occur when a link-down event occurs on an 802.1x-enabled switch port, which includes one of the following scenarios:
  - Reboot of PC or supplicant
  - Switch port is administratively shut down
  - Cable is unplugged

NOTE RADIUS Accounting stop records are not sent when a switch reloads for any reason. They are also not sent when 802.1x fails authentication or re-authentication.

RADIUS Accounting and Attribute-Value Pairs

RADIUS Accounting leverages information contained in start and stop records. The information contained in these packets is in the form of AV pairs. RADIUS Accounting contains AV pairs that provide information about an authenticated session that can be further used by the ACS or any network system. In addition to authentication and authorization, RADIUS was originally extended to provide a technique for collecting accounting information specific to end user communication sessions and storing it on an accounting server. If an 802.1x authenticator is configured and enabled for RADIUS Accounting, it forwards start records to the accounting server as soon as a connection is established, and then collects information about the session. When the session is terminated, the authenticator sends a stop record to the server indicating that the session is over. Both start and stop records are acknowledged by the RADIUS server.

Extension of IEEE 802.1x Standard by Cisco IBNS Initiative

Cisco supports the IEEE 802.1x standard completely and offers some important extensions with the help of RADIUS Authentication, Authorization, and Accounting. Some of these important features are explained in the following sections.

802.1x with VLAN Assignment

With the standard 802.1x implementation, authenticated users are placed in the preconfigured VLAN assigned to the port. Cisco IBNS offers the capability to dynamically assign VLANs to ports based on user identity. This feature lets you maintain a username-to-VLAN association with a RADIUS server. After successful 802.1x authentication, the RADIUS server sends the VLAN to the switch for a specific user or device, and the switch configures the attached port for the specified VLAN. Thus, 802.1x-authenticated ports are assigned to a VLAN based on the identity of the user or the device. In Native IOS, switches must be configured for RADIUS authorization, but in Cat OS, RADIUS authorization configuration is not required. RADIUS authentication is sufficient to apply the dynamically downloaded VLAN to the switch port.

802.1x with Port Security

Single host mode is the default for 802.1x implementation on the access port of the switch. So, after the supplicant is successfully authenticated, the MAC is known to the switch. Hence, additional devices trying to connect will result in port violation.

802.1x with Voice VLAN ID

Based on the default operation of 802.1x as explained in the section entitled "Standard 802.1x Operation," traffic from a single host is allowed on the wire. Thus, voice traffic would be not allowed, and this would break the deployment of IP phones. Cisco now allows voice traffic from an auxiliary VLAN without 802.1x authentication when the switch recognizes via CDP that a Cisco phone is attached to the port. This operation is designed to allow CDP from an IP phone, regardless of the 802.1x state on a port. This has changed the default operation of 802.1x on any Multi-VLAN Access Port (MVAP). CDP packets now are allowed to enter a switch port, regardless of the 802.1x state of the port. CDP frames are sent untagged by an IP Phone and arrive at a switch in the access VLAN. So, like EAPOL, CDP frames are then passed on for normal processing on the uncontrolled port.

802.1x Guest VLAN

Devices in the network that do not have the 802.1x client cannot authenticate on the switch; hence, these devices are assigned to the guest VLAN, if a guest VLAN is configured on the switch ports where these devices are connected. Examples of such devices are printers, IP phones, and so on. This feature also helps organizations migrate toward 802.1x implementations by allowing network access to devices that are not yet enabled for 802.1x. With this feature enabled, users trying to connect to the network that do not have an 802.1x-compatible device are placed in the guest VLAN.

High Availability for 802.1x

For modular switches (Cat 6500 series switches for example), this feature offers synchronization of run-time 802.1x port security information between active and standby supervisors. This maintains the state information of the port security, if the active supervisor engine fails, on the secondary engine.

802.1x with ACL Assignment

Based on 802.1x user's authentication, it is possible to dynamically assign an access control policy to an interface on the switch. You can use this feature to restrict users to certain segments of the network, limit access to sensitive servers, or even restrict the protocols and applications used. This feature is available on the selective switch, and requires RADIUS authorization to be turned on.

Access Restrictions for 802.1x

You can accomplish additional access restrictions with the flexibility of Access Restriction configuration on the CS ACS server. Following is the list of various methods available for the access restrictions:

- Time-of-day and day-of-week restrictions
- Network Access Server (NAS) IP filtering, which restricts user and port access based on the NAS IP address
- MAC address filtering, which restricts device authentication based on the MAC address

Diagnostic Commands and Tools

It is important to become familiar with and use the diagnostic commands on the switch to troubleshoot the AAA implementation on the switch. The following sections describe how to utilize the **show** and **debug** commands for switch management and port authentication.

Switch Management

If a switch is in Native IOS, and is configured for AAA, the **show** and **debug** commands are the same as those shown in AAA implementation on the IOS router in Chapter 9, "Troubleshooting AAA on IOS Routers." Therefore, the discussion is skipped here. However, for hybrid mode in which the switch is running the Cat OS, **show** commands are used primarily to verify the configuration. Example 11-1 shows the output of the **show authentication** output with local and enable password authentication turned on.

Example 11-1 show authentication *Command Output*

```
CAT6509-Hybrid> (enable) show authentication

Login Authentication:  Console Session    Telnet Session     Http Session
---------------------  ---------------    ---------------    ---------------
tacacs                 disabled           disabled           disabled
radius                 disabled           disabled           disabled
kerberos               disabled           disabled           disabled
!The following line shows that local authentication is turned on for all types of access
!for login authentication
local                  enabled(primary)   enabled(primary)   enabled(primary)
attempt limit          3                  3                  -
lockout timeout (sec)  disabled           disabled           -

Enable Authentication: Console Session    Telnet Session     Http Session
---------------------  ---------------    ---------------    ---------------
tacacs                 disabled           disabled           disabled
radius                 disabled           disabled           disabled
kerberos               disabled           disabled           disabled
!The following line shows enable authentication is turned on to use local user database
!for all methods
local                  enabled(primary)   enabled(primary)   enabled(primary)
attempt limit          3                  3                  -
lockout timeout (sec)  disabled           disabled           -
CAT6509-Hybrid> (enable)
```

The **show localusers** command is used to verify the creation of local user accounts. It also shows the privilege level as illustrated in Example 11-2.

Example 11-2 show localusers *Command Output*

```
CAT6509-Hybrid> (enable) set localuser user cisco password cisco123 privilege 15
Adde
d local user picard.
CAT6509-Hybrid > (enable) show localusers
Local User Authentication: disabled
Username                        Privilege Level
---------                        -------------
cisco                             15
CAT6509-Hybrid> (enable)
```

To verify the Terminal Access Controller Access Control System (TACACS+) configuration, you can execute the command shown in Example 11-3.

Example 11-3 show tacacs *Command Output*

```
CAT6509-Hybrid> (enable) show tacacs
Login Authentication:  Console Session   Telnet Session
---------------------  ----------------  ----------------
tacacs                 disabled          disabled
radius                 disabled          disabled
local                  enabled(primary)  enabled(primary)

Enable Authentication: Console Session   Telnet Session
---------------------- ----------------- ----------------
tacacs                 disabled          disabled
radius                 disabled          disabled
local                  enabled(primary)  enabled(primary)
Tacacs key:
Tacacs login attempts: 3
Tacacs timeout: 5 seconds
Tacacs direct request: disabled
Tacacs-Server                              Status
----------------------------------------   -------
10.1.1.1
10.1.1.2                                  primary
10.1.1.3
CAT6509-Hybrid> (enable)
```

Just like **show tacacs** output, **show radius** provides the configuration for radius protocol. Example 11-4 shows the output of radius server configuration.

Example 11-4 show radius *Command Output*

```
CAT6509-Hybrid> (enable) show radius
Login Authentication:  Console Session   Telnet Session
---------------------  ----------------  ----------------
tacacs                 disabled          disabled
radius                 disabled          disabled
local                  enabled(primary)  enabled(primary)
Enable Authentication: Console Session   Telnet Session
---------------------- ----------------- ----------------
```

continues

Example 11-4 show radius *Command Output (Continued)*

```
tacacs                   disabled          disabled
radius                   disabled          disabled
local                    enabled(primary)  enabled(primary)

Radius Deadtime:                0 minutes
Radius Key:
Radius Retransmit:              2
Radius Timeout:                 5 seconds

Radius-Server                   Status   Auth-port
-----------------------------   -------  -----------
20.1.1.1                     primary  1812
CAT6509-Hybrid> (enable)
```

show authorization is used to verify the TACACS+ authorization configuration, as Example 11-5 illustrates.

Example 11-5 show authorization *Command Output*

```
CAT6509-Hybrid> (enable) show authorization
Telnet:
-------
            Primary   Fallback
            -------   --------
exec:       tacacs+    deny
enable:     tacacs+    deny
commands:
 config:    tacacs+    deny
 all:       -          -

Console:
--------
            Primary   Fallback
            -------   --------
exec:       tacacs+    deny
enable:     tacacs+    deny
commands:
 config:    tacacs+    deny
 all:       -          -
CAT6509-Hybrid> (enable)
```

Example 11-6 shows how to verify the configuration:

Example 11-6 show accounting *Command Output*

```
CAT6509-Hybrid> (enable) show accounting
Event     Method  Mode
-----     ------- ----
exec:     tacacs+ stop-only
connect:  tacacs+ stop-only
system:   tacacs+ stop-only
```

Example 11-6 **show accounting** *Command Output (Continued)*

```
commands:
config:    -        -
all:       tacacs+ stop-only
TACACS+ Suppress for no username: enabled
Update Frequency: periodic, Interval = 120

Accounting information:
-----------------------
Active Accounted actions on tty0, User (null) Priv 0
Active Accounted actions on tty288091924, User (null) Priv 0
Overall Accounting Traffic:
           Starts   Stops  Active
           -----    -----  ------
Exec           0       0       0
Connect        0       0       0
Command        0       0       0
System         1       0       0
CAT6509-Hybrid> (enable)
```

As we have seen so far, the **show** commands are primarily used for the configuration verifications. The **set trace** command on the switch is similar to **debug** commands on the router, which are very useful in troubleshooting AAA-related issues. However, before enabling debugging on the catalyst, analyze the AAA server logs to find the reasons for failure. This is easier and less disruptive to the switch. The following is the general form of the **debug** command on the switch:

```
set trace tacacs | radius | kerberos 4
```

To turn off debugging, you need to execute the following command:

```
set trace tacacs | radius | kerberos 0
```

Identity-Based Network Services (IBNSs)

The **show** commands shown in the preceding section should be used in conjunction with the specific **show** commands that will be discussed in this section to troubleshoot port authentication issue. On Native IOS, to display various statistics pertaining to the dot1x, you can use the following command:

```
show dot1x [all] | [interface interface-id] | [statistics [interface interface-id]]
  [ | {begin | exclude | include} expression]
```

To display the 802.1x administrative and operational status for the switch, use the **show dot1x all** privileged EXEC command (see Example 11-7). To display the 802.1x administrative and operational status for a specific interface, use the **show dot1x interface** *interface-id* privileged EXEC command (see example 11-8). **show dot1x,** as Example 11-7 shows, reveals if the dot1x is globally enabled or not.

Example 11-7 show dot1x all *Command Output*

```
Switch# show dot1x
! Shows that authentication control is enabled.
Sysauthcontrol                     = Enabled
Dot1x Protocol Version             = 1
Dot1x Oper Controlled Directions   = Both
Dot1x Admin Controlled Directions = Both

Switch# show dot1x all
Dot1x Info for interface FastEthernet0/3
----------------------------------------------------
Supplicant MAC 00d0.b71b.35de
   AuthSM State      = CONNECTING
   BendSM State      = IDLE
! Following line indicates that Supplicant is not authenticated yet
PortStatus         = UNAUTHORIZED
MaxReq             = 2
HostMode           = Single
Port Control       = Auto
QuietPeriod        = 60 Seconds
Re-authentication = Disabled
ReAuthPeriod       = 3600 Seconds
ServerTimeout      = 30 Seconds
SuppTimeout        = 30 Seconds
TxPeriod           = 30 Seconds
Guest-Vlan         = 0
Dot1x Info for interface FastEthernet0/7
----------------------------------------------------
!Following line indicates that Supplicant is not authenticated yet
PortStatus         = UNAUTHORIZED
MaxReq             = 2
!Following line indicates that port is configured for multihost mode. So, a single MAC
!is not locked for the port after successful authentication. This is one of the options
!to get around the problem with hub environment where multiple hosts are possible to be
!connected.
HostMode           = Multi
Port Control       = Auto
QuietPeriod        = 60 Seconds
Re-authentication = Disabled
ReAuthPeriod       = 3600 Seconds
ServerTimeout      = 30 Seconds
SuppTimeout        = 30 Seconds
TxPeriod           = 30 Seconds
Guest-Vlan         = 0
Switch#
```

Example 11-8 show dot1x interface fastethernet0/3 *Command Output*

```
Switch# show dot1x interface fastethernet 0/3
Supplicant MAC 00d0.b71b.35de
   AuthSM State      = AUTHENTICATED
   BendSM State      = IDLE
```

Example 11-8 show dot1x interface fastethernet0/3 *Command Output (Continued)*

```
!This indicates that the authentication is successful
PortStatus         = AUTHORIZED
MaxReq             = 2
!The hostmode is set to single, which means only authenticated MAC address is allowed to
!this port.  Other machines connected via hub or phone will be considered as security
!violation.
HostMode           = Single
Port Control       = Auto
!Following are various times relating to dot1x operations
QuietPeriod        = 60 Seconds
Re-authentication = Disabled
ReAuthPeriod       = 3600 Seconds
ServerTimeout      = 30 Seconds
SuppTimeout        = 30 Seconds
TxPeriod           = 30 Seconds
Guest-Vlan         = 0
Switch#
```

To display 802.1x statistics for all interfaces, you can use the **show dot1x all statistics** privileged EXEC command. To display 802.1x statistics for a specific interface, use the **show dot1x statistics interface** *interface-id* privileged EXEC command, as Example 11-9 shows.

Example 11-9 show dot1x statistics interface fastethernet 0/3 *Command Output*

```
Switch# show dot1x statistics interface fastethernet 0/3
PortStatistics Parameters for Dot1x
--------------------------------------------
TxReqId = 15    TxReq = 0       TxTotal = 15
RxStart = 4     RxLogoff = 0    RxRespId = 1    RxResp = 1
RxInvalid = 0   RxLenErr = 0    RxTotal= 6
RxVersion = 1   LastRxSrcMac 00d0.b71b.35de
Switch#
```

Table 11-2 explains all the statistical output shown in Example 11-9.

Table 11-2 show dot1x statistics *Field Descriptions*

Field	Description
TxReqId	Number of Extensible Authentication Protocol (EAP)-request/identity frames that have been sent
TxReq	Number of EAP-request frames (other than request/identity frames) that have been sent
TxTotal	Number of Extensible Authentication Protocol over LAN (EAPOL) frames of any type that have been sent
RxStart	Number of valid EAPOL-start frames that have been received

continues

Table 11-2 **show dot1x statistics** *Field Descriptions (Continued)*

Field	Description
RxLogoff	Number of EAPOL-logoff frames that have been received
RxRespId	Number of EAP-response/identity frames that have been received
RxResp	Number of valid EAP-response frames (other than response/identity frames) that have been received
RxInvalid	Number of EAPOL frames that have been received and have an unrecognized frame type
RxLenErr	Number of EAPOL frames that have been received in which the packet body length field is invalid
RxTotal	Number of valid EAPOL frames of any type that have been received
RxVersion	Received packets in the 802.1x version 1 format
LastRxSrcMac	Source MAC address carried in the most recently received EAPOL frame

To check to which VLAN the port belongs, **show vlan brief** can be used as shown in Example 11-10.

Example 11-10 **show vlan brief** *Command Output*

```
switch# show vlan brief
VLAN Name                             Status    Ports
---- -------------------------------- --------- -------------------------------
1    default                          active    Fa0/1, Fa0/13, Fa0/14, Fa0/15
                                                Fa0/16, Fa0/17, Fa0/18, Fa0/19
                                                Fa0/21, Fa0/22, Fa0/23, Gi0/1
                                                Gi0/2
2    ACS                              active    Fa0/24
10   Cisco                            active    Fa0/2, Fa0/3, Fa0/4, Fa0/5
                                                Fa0/6, Fa0/7, Fa0/8, Fa0/9
                                                Fa0/10, Fa0/11, Fa0/12
99   Guest                            active    Fa0/20
100  Machine                          active
Switch#
```

Categorization of Problem Areas

The problem areas of an AAA implementation on a switch may be categorized as follows:

- Switch management troubleshooting
- Identity-based Network Services (IBNSs) troubleshooting

Switch Management Troubleshooting

TACACS+ Protocol is more desirable for configuring AAA for switch management, although RADIUS and Kerberos are the other two options available. The local user database is primarily used for console authentication or as a fall-back method for Telnet or SSH access to the switch. The primary focus of this section is on configuring and troubleshooting AAA implementation using TACACS+ along with the local user database.

Table 11-3 shows AAA features introduced on different versions of the switch code.

Table 11-3 *AAA Features Available Based on CatOS Release*

AAA Method	CatOS 2.2–5.1	CatOS 5.1–5.4.1	CatOS 5.4.1–7.5.1	CatOS 7.5.1 and later
TACACS+ Authentication	Yes	Yes	Yes	Yes
RADIUS Authentication	No	Yes	Yes	Yes
Kerberos Authentication	No	No	Yes	Yes
Local Username Authentication/ Authorization	No	No	No	Yes
TACACS+ Command Authorization	No	No	Yes	Yes
TACACS+ Exec Authorization	No	No	Yes	Yes
RADIUS Exec Authorization	No	No	Yes	Yes
Accounting - TACACS+/RADIUS	No	No	Yes	Yes
TACACS+ Enable Authorization	Yes	Yes	Yes	Yes
RADIUS Enable Authorization	No	Yes	Yes	Yes
TACACS+ Enable Authorization	No	No	Yes	Yes

Login Authentication

This section steps through the configuration and discusses some of the common issues that you may encounter, and how to troubleshoot them.

Configuration Steps

To configure AAA authentication, perform the following tasks:

Step 1 Create local user database

If you are running CatOS version 7.5.1 or above, configure the local user database as follows:

Example 11-11 *Sample Output of Local User Database*

```
Switch> (enable) set localuser user admin password powerpass privilege 15
Switch> (enable) set localuser user basic password nonenable
```

It is important to note that there are only two privilege levels (0 and 15) for the authentication of local users as shown in example 11-12, where admin has a privilege level 15 (enable access privilege), but the user basic has privilege level 0, which is exec privilege. So, when admin uses Telnet or console, it can get to the enable mode but the username basic will be in the user mode. User basic needs to know the enable password to reach the enable mode, which can be configured with the set, **enable** password command. The local user database can be configured as the only user authentication method, or it can be configured as a backup for the external AAA server authentication so that users are not locked out.

Step 2 Turn on and verify the local authentication as a fallback (back door) or only method for authentication, as Example 11-12 shows.

Example 11-12 *Turning on Local User Authentication*

```
Switch> (enable) set authentication login local enable
Switch> (enable) show aaa authentication
Switch> (enable)
```

Step 3 Define the TACACS+ server and shared secret key on switch.

Configure the communication parameters between the switch and AAA server (TACACS+ or RADIUS) by providing the IP address and the shared secret key (optional) for encryption, as Example 11-13 shows.

Example 11-13 *Configuration Required for Communicating with AAA Server*

```
Switch> (enable) set tacacs server 10.1.1.40
Switch> (enable) set tacacs key cisco
Switch> (enable)
```

Step 4 Define the AAA client on the AAA Server.

Configure switch as an AAA client on the Cisco Secure ACS by browsing to **Network Configuration > Add AAA client > Add Entry** (Define Switch IP address and shared secret key) **> Stop/Restart the service**.

Note that the Switch IP address and shared secret key must be defined on the switch.

Step 5 Create the user database on the Cisco Secure.

After login to Cisco Secure ACS, go to **User Setup > Create a user with username and password > Map the user to a group on ACS unconfigured**. No special parameters need to be defined for simple user authentication to the switch.

Step 6 Turn on TACACS+ authentication, as Example 11-14 shows.

Example 11-14 *Turning on TACACS+ Authentication on the Switch*

```
Switch> (enable) set authentication login tacacs enable
Switch> (enable)
```

Troubleshooting Steps

Troubleshooting authentication needs to be done on both switches, and on the TACACS+ server side. It is, however, recommended to troubleshoot the AAA issue for the switch with the CS ACS server itself. You can turn on debug with the **set trace tacacs 4** on the switch. It is worth examining a successful authentication debug on the switch before you go through some of the common issues that you may encounter. Example 11-15 walks through the debug output on the switch.

Example 11-15 *The debug Output for Successful User Authentication with TACACS+ protocol*

```
Switch> (enable) set trace tacacs 4
AAA/AUTHEN: update_user user='' ruser='(null)' port='telnet146'
rem_addr='10.1.1.20' authen_type=1 service=LOGIN priv=12005 Mar 26 22:10:08.510
AAA/AUTHEN/START (0): port='telnet146' list='(null)' action=LOGIN service=LOGIN
TAC+: send AUTHEN/START packet ver=192 id=224470576
! Opening connection with tacacs+ server
TAC+: Opening TCP/IP connection to 10.1.1.40
TAC+: ver=192 id=224470576 received AUTHEN status = GETUSER2005 Mar 26 22:10:09.
520
! Getting username input from the user
AAA/AUTHEN (224470576): status = GETUSER
User Access Verification

Username:
2005 Mar 26 22:10:16.590
! Got the username administrator
AAA/AUTHEN: update_user user='administrator' ruser='(null)' port='telnet146' rem
_addr='10.1.1.20' authen_type=1 service=LOGIN priv=12005 Mar 26 22:10:16.590
AAA/AUTHEN/CONT (224470576): continue_login2005 Mar 26 22:10:16.590
AAA/AUTHEN (224470576): status = GETUSER
TAC+: send AUTHEN/CONT packet id=224470576
! Here asking for the password
TAC+: ver=192 id=224470576 received AUTHEN status = GETPASS
2005 Mar 26 22:10:17.090
AAA/AUTHEN (224470576): status = GETPASSPassword:
2005 Mar 26 22:10:19.980 AAA/AUTHEN/CONT (224470576): continue_login
2005 Mar 26 22:10:19.980 AAA/AUTHEN (224470576): status = GETPASS
TAC+: send AUTHEN/CONT packet id=224470576
! Here shows authentication successful
TAC+: ver=192 id=224470576 received AUTHEN status = PASS
2005 Mar 26 22:10:20.480 AAA/AUTHEN (224470576): status = PASS
Switch> (enable)
```

Now take a look at some of the common problems you may encounter with the TACACS+ authentication.

- **TACACS+ server is unreachable or mismatch in the shared secret key**—If the TACACS+ server is unreachable or the shared secret key is mismatched between the TACACS+ server and the switch, an error message will be reported, as in Example 11-16. If an alternate method (for example, local user database) is configured as a backup method, the switch will try to authenticate the user with the backup method.

Example 11-16 *The ERROR Message When TACACS+ Server Is Unreachable*

```
2005 Mar 29 15:29:22.430
AAA/AUTHEN: update_user user='' ruser='(null)' port='telnet146' rem_addr='10.25.
35.229' authen_type=1 service=LOGIN priv=12005 Mar 29 15:29:22.430
AAA/AUTHEN/START (0): port='telnet146' list='(null)' action=LOGIN service=LOGIN
TAC+: send AUTHEN/START packet ver=192 id=340001563
TAC+: no tacacs server definedTACACS: Unable to contact Server
!The following line shows the ERROR message when TACACS+ server is unreachable
2005 Mar 29 15:29:22.430 AAA/AUTHEN (340001563): status = ERROR
2005 Mar 29 15:29:22.430 AAA/AUTHEN/START (340001563): failed to authenticate
2005 Mar 29 15:29:22.430 %AAA: enable: Internal error.
Trying Local Login Authentication
```

- **Bad Username or Password**—If the username or password is invalid, then authentication will fail. This is different than an error message, as we have seen earlier. For example, as with bad username or password, the backup method is not tried. Example 11-17 shows the debug output for a bad username or password authentication.

Example 11-17 *Debug Output for AAA When Bad Username or Password Is Entered*

```
2005 Mar 29 15:39:14.490 AAA/AUTHEN: update_user user='' ruser='(null)'
port='telnet146' rem_addr='10.1.1.20' authen_type=1 service=LOGIN priv=1
2005 Mar 29 15:39:14.490 AAA/AUTHEN/START (0): port='telnet146' list='(null)'
action=LOGIN service=LOGIN
TAC+: send AUTHEN/START packet ver=192 id=599265646
TAC+: Opening TCP/IP connection to 10.1.1.40
TAC+: ver=192 id=599265646 received AUTHEN status = GETUSER
2005 Mar 29 15:39:15.490 AAA/AUTHEN (599265646): status = GETUSER
User Access Verification

Username:
2005 Mar 29 15:39:17.800 AAA/AUTHEN: update_user user='admin123' ruser='(null)'
port='telnet146' rem_addr='10.25.35.229' authen_type=1 service=LOGIN priv=1
2005 Mar 29 15:39:17.800 AAA/AUTHEN/CONT (599265646): continue_login
2005 Mar 29 15:39:17.800 AAA/AUTHEN (599265646): status = GETUSER
TAC+: send AUTHEN/CONT packet id=599265646
TAC+: ver=192 id=599265646 received AUTHEN status = GETPASS
2005 Mar 29 15:39:18.300 AAA/AUTHEN (599265646): status = GETPASSPassword:
2005 Mar 29 15:39:20.890 AAA/AUTHEN/CONT (599265646): continue_login
2005 Mar 29 15:39:20.890 AAA/AUTHEN (599265646): status = GETPASS
TAC+: send AUTHEN/CONT packet id=599265646
!The FAIL message indicates the either bad username or password invalid.
TAC+: ver=192 id=599265646 received AUTHEN status = FAIL
2005 Mar 29 15:39:21.400

AAA/AUTHEN (599265646): status = FAIL
% Authentication failed.
2005 Mar 29 15:39:21.400
```

Enable Password Authentication

To authenticate enable access to the switch after the user logs into the switch, set this up on the switch and on the Cisco Secure ACS Server.

Configuration Steps

The following steps are required on the switch:

Step 1 Turn on enable password authentication with local user database. This means that the enable access for the user will be authenticated with the enable password defined on the switch. If TACACS+ is configured as a primary method for authentication, then enable password will be used in case the TACACS+ server is unreachable. Example 11-18 shows how to turn on enable authentication with a local user database.

Example 11-18 *Turning on Enable Authentication with a Local User Database on Switch*

```
Switch> (enable) set authentication enable local enable
Switch (enable) set enable
Enter old password:
Enter new password: cisco
Retype new password: cisco
Password changed.
Switch (enable)
```

Step 2 Configure Enable parameters for users and groups on CS ACS.

Turn on **Advanced TACACS+ Features** by browsing to **Interface Configuration** and selecting **TACACS+ (Cisco IOS)**. Then check **Advanced TACACS+ Features** under **Advanced Configuration Options** setting. Click **Submit**. Under the **Enable Options** of **User/group setup**, deselect **No Enable Privilege** and select the desired enable privilege level either based on AAA client or Network Device Group (NDG).

To authenticate the enable password with a separate password other than the login password, you can go to the **TACACS+ Enable Password** section of user setup and set up a password that differs from the user's actual login password.

Step 3 Configure TACACS+ for enable password authentication as shown in Example 11-19.

Example 11-19 *Configuration to Turn on Enable Authentication*

```
Switch (enable) set authentication enable tacacs enable
Switch (enable)
```

Troubleshooting Steps

Troubleshooting steps for the Enable password authentication are the same as for login authentication. Following are some of the important points to be aware of when using enable password authentication:

- **Enable Authentication is not turned on on the switch**—Turn on enable authentication on the switch to use the TACACS+ server. By default, enable authentication with the enable password is turned on. If the TACACS+ server is down, enable password is used as a backup if the enable login with enable password is enabled.

- **Enable Password is not defined on the CS ACS**—When configuring a user profile, either use the same password as the login or define a separate password for enable access under the "TACACS+ Enable Password" section. Also, you must define "Max Privilege for any AAA Client" under "Advanced TACACS+ Settings."

Authorization

Authorization comes after successful user authentication. There are two ways to perform authorization. The following sections explain how to perform the configuration and how to troubleshoot.

Configuration Steps

Two types of authorization can be configured on the switch. The first is TACACS+ Exec Authorization:

- **TACACS+ Exec Authorization**—Just as with a router, it's possible to send the authorization request for the enable access before the switch allows the users to log in so that the user doesn't need to enter the enable password to get to the enable mode (the user will be taken directly to the enable mode). This applies to both the console and the Telnet session. Example 11-20 shows how to turn on exec authorization using TACACS+ protocol.

Example 11-20 *Turning on Exec Authorization*

```
Switch (enable) set authorization exec enable tacacs+ none both
Switch (enable)
```

You must configure shell/exec for the user profile under TACACS+ server.

This is especially useful when you want to bypass the enable password authentication either locally or via the AAA server. It is also useful if you want to prevent users, such as PPP users, from logging into the switch without shell/exec service configured on the server. PPP users will get the following message:

```
Exec mode authorization failed.
```

In addition to permitting/denying exec mode for users, users can be forced into enable mode when entering by having privilege level 15 assigned on the server. It is important to note that this feature is available on version 5.5(3), 6.1(1), and above.

As stated previously, two types of authorization can be configured on the switch. The second is TACACS+ Command Authorization, which is discussed next:

- **TACACS+ Command Authorization**—Command authorization is also possible on the switch just as it is with routers. Example 11-21 shows the configuration required for command authorization using TACACS+. In the event that the TACACS+ server is down, authentication is configured as none. Both keywords signify that command authorization is turned on for both console and Telnet sessions.

Example 11-21 *Configuration Required for Command Authorization*

```
Switch (enable) set authorization commands enable config tacacs none both
Switch (enable)
```

Once you turn on command authorization on the switch, you must configure the TACACS+ server for the command authorization to allow set port enable 2/8.

Troubleshooting Steps

Troubleshooting steps for authorization are the same as for authentication. If authorization fails, you must turn on the **set trace tacacs 4** command to see the debug on the switch. You also need to analyze the log of the AAA server. This section explains the problems you may encounter specifically with the authorization configured on the switch:

- **User is not taken directly to the Enable Mode**—On the switch, the **authorization exec** command must be turned on. Also, you must ensure that your switch version supports the privilege level download feature from the AAA server you are running, so that you can be taken directly to the enable mode after authentication. (See Table 11-3 for the version information of the TACACS+ Exec Authorization feature.) On the CS ACS, you must have the Exec turned on for the user/group profile with privilege level set to greater than 1.
- **Command Authorization is not working**—First you need to be sure that the authorization is turned on either for exec or commands. Then check the configuration of the CS ACS to see if the system is properly configured for the commands. Run the trace command to identify the commands that are being parsed by the CS ACS server. Finally, match the command authorization syntax defined on the CS ACS server.

Accounting

Accounting can be turned on for authentication and for authorization. The section that follows has configuration and troubleshooting steps for accounting.

Configuration Steps

To turn on accounting on the switch with TACACS+ protocol, use the following options:

- To collect exec level log (for instance, user getting switch prompt), execute **set accounting exec enable start-stop tacacs+**.

- To collect the information about connection/disconnection information (for example, users' disconnection out of the switch), configure **set accounting connect enable start-stop tacacs+**.
- To capture system-related messages (for instance, a reboot of the switch), turn on **set accounting system enable start-stop tacacs+**.
- To capture which commands users are executing on the switch, issue the following command: **set accounting commands enable all start-stop tacacs+**.
- To remind the server of a task (for example, to update records once every minute to make sure a user is still logged in), configure **set accounting update periodic 1**.

Troubleshooting Steps

Accounting problems arise mostly if certain attributes are not being logged to the CS ACS server. For this, turn on trace to see what information is being sent as a form of accounting to the CS ACS server. Examining the log on the CS ACS server will reveal if the problem lies there or not.

Identity-Based Network Services (IBNSs)

Turning on dot1x protocol on the switch port also enables user authentication and machine authentication for the Microsoft Windows Networking environment. You can avoid machine authentication, but when using Microsoft AD, it's not recommended, as this may break the GPO model for AD.

Here are some important points to note when turning on machine authentication:

- The computer must be a member of the domain.
- If using TLS, the computer must obtain a certificate, either through auto-enrollment (see the case study) or manually.
- If using PEAP or TLS, be sure that the certificate of the certificate authority (CA) is in the local machine store; typically, it is added if the CA is up when the machine is added to the domain. If not, you can force the certificate to be in the local machine store via auto-enrollment (see the "Case Studies" section).
- Click the check box for the **Authenticate as Computer** option.

There are two ways to turn on machine authentication:

- **Machine Auth Using PEAP**—Uses account information for the computer created at the time the machine is added to the domain. Hence, the computer *must* be a member of the domain. If doing mutual authentication, the computer *must* trust the signing CA of the RADIUS server's certificate.

- **Machine authentication using EAP-TLS**—Authenticates the computer using certificates. The computer *must* have a valid certificate. If doing mutual authentication, the computer *must* trust the signing CA of the RADIUS server's certificate. The easiest way to implement machine authentication is by using MS-CA and Windows GPOs. This may require a DHCP lease renewal after authentication.

  Machine authentication using EAP-TLS is not automatic and must be scripted or done manually.

Configuration Steps

You need to configure several devices for successful PEAP Machine Authentication.

Installation of Certificate

The following are the certificates required for Machine Authentication with PEAP:

- On the supplicant, install a machine certificate from Active Directory (AD) (refer to the case study), and the CA Root Certificate as shown in the "Case Studies" section. The CA used is Microsoft Enterprise CA Server.
- On the ACS, install ACS Server certificate, and the CA root certificate. The procedures are shown in the "Case Studies" section.

Configuration of Authenticator (Switch)

On the Authenticator (Switch) follow these steps for Hybrid mode (Cat OS):

Step 1 Define Global Commands as shown in Example 11-22.

Example 11-22 *Global Commands Required Turning on dot1x*

```
Switch#
!RADIUS configuration
set radius server <ip_address> auth-port 1812 primary
set radius key <key>

!Global 802.1x configuration
set dot1x system-auth-control enable
set dot1x quiet-period 10 (default: 30)
set dot1x tx-period 10 (default: 30)
set dot1x supp-timeout 5 (default: 30)
set dot1x server-timeout 5 (default: 30)
set dot1x max-req 4 (default: 2)
set dot1x re-authperiod

!Global 802.1x Guest VLAN (CatOS 7.6+)
set dot1x guest-vlan <vlan>
```

Step 2 Define per-port commands on the switch as shown in Example 11-23.

Example 11-23 *Per-Port command to Turn on dot1x*

```
Switch#
!Port Level 802.1x configuration
set port dot1x <mod/port> port-control auto
set port dot1x <mod/port> port-control force-authorized
set port dot1x <mod/port> multiple-host enable/disable
set port dot1x <mod/port> re-authentication enable/disable

!Port Level 802.1x Guest VLAN (CatOS 8.3+)
set port dot1x <mod/port> guest-vlan {vlan | none}
```

The following configuration is needed on the Native IOS:

Step 3 The Global Commands needed are shown in Example 11-24.

Example 11-24 *Global Configuration needed with Native IOS*

```
Switch#
!RADIUS configuration
radius-server host <ip_address>
radius-server key <key>
aaa new-model
aaa authentication dot1x default group radius
aaa authorization default group radius
aaa authorization config-commands

!802.1x Global Commands
dot1x system-auth-control
dot1x max-req
dot1x timeout quiet-period
dot1x timeout tx-period
dot1x timeout re-authperiod
dot1x re-authentication
IOS Commands based on Per-Port are shown below for Native IOS
Switch#
!IOS Per-port configuration
dot1x port-control auto

!IOS Per-port Guest VLAN
dot1x guest-vlan <vlan>
Switch#
```

Configuration of Supplicant

The following steps are used to configure supplicant:

Step 1 Open **Network Connections**.

Step 2 Right-click **Local Area Connection** and then click **Properties**.

Step 3 Click **Authentication**, and then check **Enable IEEE 802.1x authentication** for this network. For EAP type, select **PEAP**, check **Authenticate as computer when Computer Information is Available.**

Step 4 Click **PEAP Properties**. On the next window under When Connecting, select **Validate Server Certificate.** Under Trusted Root Certificate Authorities, check the **Root CA** you have installed on the client. Under Select Authentication Method, choose **Secure Password (EAP-MSCHAP v2)**. Click on **Configure** and choose **Automatically Use my Windows Logon name and password (and domain if any)**.

Configuration of ACS Server

The following are step-by-step procedures for ACS configuration for the PEAP Authentication:

Step 1 Install the ACS Server Certificate and the CA Server Certificate on the ACS Server (refer to the "Case Studies" section towards the end of this chapter).

Step 2 Log in to ACS, and then browse to **Network Configuration**. Click **Add Entry**.

Step 3 Enter a Network Device Group Name and click **Submit**.

Step 4 Click on the new created Network Device Group and click on **Add Entry**.

Step 5 Fill in the switch name, IP address, and key (shared secret you've entered on switch). Also, under Authenticate Using, select **RADIUS** (Cisco Aironet) which includes RADIUS Internet Engineering Task Force (IETF) attributes.

Step 6 Click on the **Submit+ Restart** button.

Step 7 Click on **External User Database > Database Configuration > Windows Database > Configure**.

Step 8 In the "Windows User Database Configuration" page under the Configure Domain List, move **Domains** from Available Domains to Domain List.

Step 9 In the same pages as Step 8, under the Windows EAP Settings, enter a check to indicate if the password change inside PEAP is allowed. This setting does *not* apply to PEAP-GTC. Note that you should *not* change the **machine authentication name prefix**. Currently MS uses **host/** to distinguish between user and machine authentication.

Step 10 Click **Submit**.

Step 11 Click on **External User Database > Unknown User Policy.** Check the **Check the following external user databases** button and move the **Windows Database** to right under **Selected Databases**.

Step 12 Click **Submit**.

Step 13 Select **Group Setup > Default Group** and click on **Edit Settings**.

Step 14 Scroll down to Radius IETF Attributes and check **Attribute 27** (Session Timeout). Set it to 60 seconds.

Step 15 Click on **Submit** and then **Restart**.

Step 16 Go to System Configuration> Global Authentication Setup.

Step 17 Select which EAP authentication will be enabled. (for example, PEAP-MS-CHAPv2 is selected.)

Step 18 Click **Submit** and then **Restart**.

Authorization

Dynamic VLAN can be assigned to the port after successful user authentication. This is accomplished with an IETF RADIUS AV pair. If the switch is running Native IOS, configure authorization with **aaa authorization network default group radius** to apply the dynamic VLAN downloaded from CS ACS. However, if you are running Cat OS, then you do not have to turn on authorization; authentication is sufficient. Following is the list of AV pairs used for configuring user or group profiles on CS ACS to assign dynamic VLAN to the port where the supplicant is connected:

- [64] Tunnel-Type—"VLAN" (13)
- [65] Tunnel-Medium-Type—"802" (6)
- [81] Tunnel-Private-Group-ID—<*VLAN name*>

On CS ACS, if you do not see these attributes under user or group profile, then browse to **Interface Configuration > RADIUS (IETF)** and select the attributes in the previous list for a user or group or for both. Then go under the user or group setup and define the attributes as listed previously. For attribute [81] Tunnel-Private-Group-ID—<*VLAN name*>, you must define a VLAN name, not the VLAN ID. On the switch, you must have the same name with a VLAN ID tied to it.

Troubleshooting Steps

The following troubleshooting steps may help you in isolating a dot1x implementation on the switch.

On the Windows Client

To get the debug level logging, follow these steps on the Windows client:

Step 1 Choose **Start > Run**, and then type **cmd** in the text box, which will cause a **DOS** prompt to display.

Step 2 Enter **netsh ras set tracing * enabled** to turn on debugging.

Step 3 Run the Authentication test.

Step 4 Analyze the debug messages on the client.

The debug information on the client will go into different directories depending on whether you are using Windows XP or Windows 2000. For Windows XP, the debug information will go into **<installation drive>:\WINDOWS\tracing**. For Windows 2000, it will go to **<installation drive>:\WINNT\tracing**.

Step 5 Table 11-4 shows files and what goes into those files.

Table 11-4 *Files in the Tracing Directory and Information That Goes into Those Files*

Files Name	Description
RASTLS.LOG	MS-PEAP phase 1—TLS
CISCOEAPPEAP.LOG	Cisco-PEAP phase 1—TLS
RASCHAP.LOG	MS-PEAP phase 2—MS-CHAP
EAPOL.LOG	Whole EAP communication

Step 6 After you finish with the test, be sure to turn off tracing by using this command—**netsh ras set tracing * disable.**

Step 7 Analyze the client logs to be sure that the EAP packet is sending the proper credentials to the switch.

Step 8 If an error condition is reported, go through the client settings to ensure that all the authentication types and parameters are set up correctly.

Step 9 Once the client log indicates that everything is set up correctly, and EAP packets are forwarding the information to the Authenticator, the next step is to look at the Authenticator debug.

For more details on how to analyze the client log, refer to:

http://www.microsoft.com/technet/prodtechnol/winxppro/maintain/wifitrbl.mspx

On the Authenticator (Switch) Side

On the switch you can run debug commands to see the EAPOL packet exchange between the client and the switch. The debug command to capture the information on the Catalyst OS is **set tracing dot1x <0-15>**. Note that 15 is a full debug, including packet dump. Be sure to turn it off once you are finished.

In Native IOS, the command to turn on debug is **debug dot1x <backend | fesm | besm | CR>**, which turns on debugging for the authenticator process. To capture the debug output of the communication between the Authenticator (Switch) and the AAA Server, run the AAA-related debug command, which was discussed in the "Diagnostic Commands and Tools" section of this chapter for Cat OS. For Native IOS, refer to Chapter 9, "Troubleshooting AAA on IOS Routers."

Example 11-25 shows a successful authenticated debug output on the switch.

Example 11-25 *Successful* **debug** *Output Session When PEAP or EAP-TLS Is Used*

```
2005 Mar 29 00:52:13 %PAGP-5-PORTTOSTP:Port 2/2 joined bridge port 2/2
! Authentication is starting here..
2005 Mar 29 00:53:05 %SECURITY-7-
DOT1X_AUTHENTICATOR_STATE:DOT1X: authenticator state for port 2/
2 is AUTHENTICATING
2005 Mar 29 00:53:05 %SECURITY-7-
DOT1X_BACKEND_STATE:DOT1X: backend state for port 2/2 is RESPONSE
2005 Mar 29 00:53:06 %SECURITY-7-
DOT1X_BACKEND_STATE:DOT1X: backend state for port 2/2 is REQUEST
2005 Mar 29 00:53:08 %SECURITY-7-
DOT1X_BACKEND_STATE:DOT1X: backend state for port 2/2 is RESPONSE
2005 Mar 29 00:53:08 %SECURITY-7-
DOT1X_BACKEND_STATE:DOT1X: backend state for port 2/2 is REQUEST
2005 Mar 29 00:53:09 %SECURITY-7-
DOT1X_BACKEND_STATE:DOT1X: backend state for port 2/2 is RESPONSE
2005 Mar 29 00:53:09 %SECURITY-7-
DOT1X_BACKEND_STATE:DOT1X: backend state for port 2/2 is REQUEST
2005 Mar 29 00:53:09 %SECURITY-7-
DOT1X_BACKEND_STATE:DOT1X: backend state for port 2/2 is RESPONSE
2005 Mar 29 00:53:10 %SECURITY-7-
DOT1X_BACKEND_STATE:DOT1X: backend state for port 2/2 is REQUEST
2005 Mar 29 00:53:10 %SECURITY-7-
DOT1X_BACKEND_STATE:DOT1X: backend state for port 2/2 is RESPONSE
2005 Mar 29 00:53:11 %SECURITY-7-
DOT1X_BACKEND_STATE:DOT1X: backend state for port 2/2 is REQUEST
2005 Mar 29 00:53:11 %SECURITY-7-
DOT1X_BACKEND_STATE:DOT1X: backend state for port 2/2 is RESPONSE
2005 Mar 29 00:53:12 %SECURITY-7-
DOT1X_BACKEND_STATE:DOT1X: backend state for port 2/2 is REQUEST
2005 Mar 29 00:53:12 %SECURITY-7-
DOT1X_BACKEND_STATE:DOT1X: backend state for port 2/2 is RESPONSE
2005 Mar 29 00:53:13 %SECURITY-7-
DOT1X_BACKEND_STATE:DOT1X: backend state for port 2/2 is SUCCESS
2005 Mar 29 00:53:13 %SECURITY-7-
DOT1X_BACKEND_STATE:DOT1X: backend state for port 2/2 is FINISHED
2005 Mar 29 00:53:13 %SECURITY-5-
DOT1X_AUTHENTICATION_SUCCESS:Authentication successful for port 2/2
!Port is successfully authorized here, which means actual traffic from supplicant may
!flow now
2005 Mar 29 00:53:14 %SECURITY-5-DOT1X_PORT_AUTHORIZED:DOT1X: port 2/2 authorized
2005 Mar 29 00:53:14 %SECURITY-7-
DOT1X_AUTHENTICATOR_STATE:DOT1X: authenticator state for port 2/
2 is AUTHENTICATED
```

On the Authentication Server Side

The AAA server, for instance Cisco Secure ACS on Windows, has an extensive logging facility, which allows you to analyze the failure by the server or an external user database. For more details about server-side troubleshooting, refer to Chapter 13, "Troubleshooting Cisco Secure ACS on Windows," in particular the section on "CS ACS with Active Directory Integration." In summary, you need to go under **Reports and Activity** and then to **Failed Attempt**. For a more detailed analysis of the log, analyze the **auth.log** file, which is explained in detail in Chapter 13. Example 11-26 shows the **RDS.log** file logging output.

Example 11-26 *RDS.log for Successful Authentication When PEAP/EAP-TLS Is Used*

```
! Following shows the packets and RADIUS attributes received from the Switch
Request from host 10.1.1.1:1812 code=1, id=245, length=99 on port 2341
    [001] User-Name   value:  eaptls@acs.cisco
    [004] NAS-IP-Address     value:  10.1.1.1
    [012] Framed-MTU   value:  1000
    [079] EAP-Message   value:  .....eaptls@acs.cisco
    [080] Message-Authenticator
       value:  6A 0A E3 64 4C D3 19 F2 AB 66 BB 0E 78 B5 CD 1A
ExtensionPoint: Initiating scan of configured extension points...
ExtensionPoint: Supplier [Cisco Aironet] not associated with vendor [RADIUS (IETF)
], skipping...
ExtensionPoint: Calling [AuthenticationExtension] for Supplier [Cisco Generic EAP]
ExtensionPoint: [GenericEAP.dll->AuthenticationExtension] returned [11 -
 challenge]
! EXTRA STUFF REMOVED

Request from host 10.1.1.1:1812 code=1, id=251, length=112 on port 2341
    [001] User-Name   value:  eaptls@acs.cisco
    [004] NAS-IP-Address     value:  10.1.1.1
    [012] Framed-MTU   value:  1000
    [024] State        value:  CISCO-EAP-CHALLENGE=0.202.77.6
    [079] EAP-Message  value:  .\Q....
    [080] Message-Authenticator
       value:  78 7F 6F 6E E2 65 D7 47 87 78 34 C0 3D FB 52 1A
ExtensionPoint: Initiating scan of configured extension points...
ExtensionPoint: Supplier [Cisco Aironet] not associated with vendor [RADIUS (IETF)
], skipping...
ExtensionPoint: Calling [AuthenticationExtension] for Supplier [Cisco Generic EAP]
ExtensionPoint: [GenericEAP.dll->AuthenticationExtension] returned [4 -
 accept_continue]
ExtensionPoint: Start of Attribute Set
    [079] EAP-Message  value:  .a..
    [026] Vendor-Specific vsa id: 311
          [016] MS-MPPE-Send-Key
        value:  ).5.__~._Lá_2ûQ.à.._.>¢m_Æ_ä_#"....å.T_,__M_...¿_.
    [026] Vendor-Specific vsa id: 311
          [017] MS-MPPE-Recv-
Key    value:  #Hï$N=XÄ._..u_ì.Uá_8.Éí ...ñ¬_..._..__»__xë
ExtensionPoint: End of Attribute Set
```

continues

Example 11-26 *RDS.log for Successful Authentication When PEAP/EAP-TLS Is Used (Continued)*

```
AuthorExtensionPoint: Initiating scan of configured extension points...
AuthorExtensionPoint: Supplier [Cisco Aironet] not associated with vendor [RADIUS
(IETF)], skipping...
AuthorExtensionPoint: Supplier [Cisco Downloadable ACLs] not associated with vendo
r [RADIUS (IETF)], skip
ping...
! The following lines are the RADIUS response packet with AV pair after successful
! authentication
Sending response code 2, id 251 to 10.1.1.1 on port 2341

    [064] Tunnel-Type   value:  [T1] 13

    [081] Tunnel-Private-Group-ID    value:  [T1] 2

    [008] Framed-IP-Address    value:  255.255.255.255

    [079] EAP-Message  value:  .a..

    [026] Vendor-Specific vsa id: 311

          [016] MS-MPPE-Send-key
        value:  ).5.__~._Lá_2ûQ.à.._.>¢m_Æ_ä_#"....å.T_,__M_...¿_.

    [026] Vendor-Specific vsa id: 311

          [017] MS-MPPE-Recv-Key
        value:  #Hï$N=XÄ._..u_ì.Uá_8.Éí ...ñ¬_..._..___(_»__xë
```

Case Studies

This section walks through all the certificate generation and installation procedures needed for successful PEAP implementation.

Configuring Automatic Client Enrollment on AD and Installing a Machine Certificate on a Windows Client

The following steps describe how to enable automatic client certificate enrollment.

Step 1 On Domain Controller select **Start>Programs>Administrative Tools>Active Directory Users and Computers**.

Step 2 Right-click the domain's name and select **Properties**.

Step 3 Go to the Group **Policy** tab, select the **Default Domain Policy**, and click the **Edit** button as shown in Figure 11-9.

Figure 11-9 *Domain Policy on the CA Server Environment*

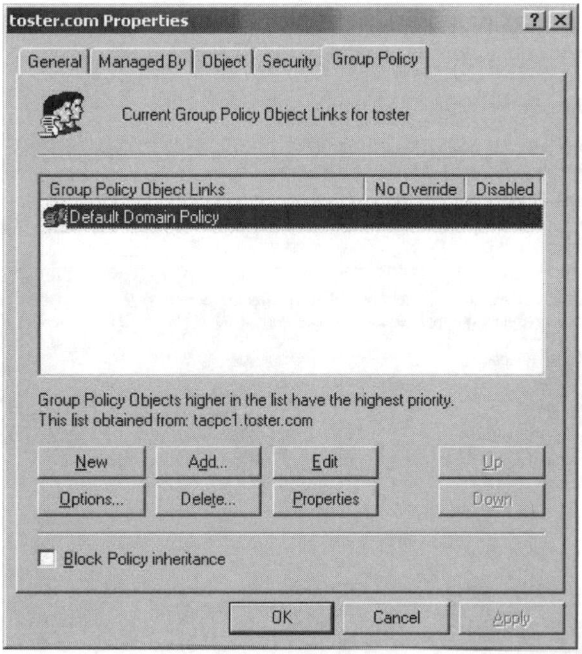

toster.com Properties

General | Managed By | Object | Security | Group Policy

Current Group Policy Object Links for toster

Group Policy Object Links	No Override	Disabled
Default Domain Policy		

Group Policy Objects higher in the list have the highest priority.
This list obtained from: tacpc1.toster.com

New | Add... | Edit | Up
Options... | Delete... | Properties | Down

Block Policy inheritance

OK | Cancel | Apply

Step 4 Go to **Computer Configuration> Windows Settings> Security Settings> Public Key Policies> Automatic Certificate Request Settings** as shown in Figure 11-10.

Figure 11-10 *Group Policy on the CA Server*

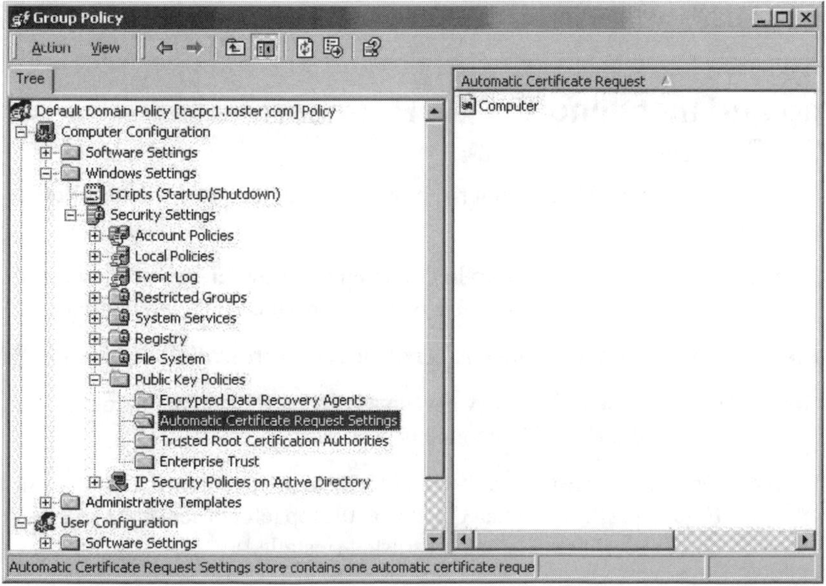

Step 5 Right-click and select a **New>Automatic Certificate Request**.

Step 6 Select a **Computer** certificate template as shown in Figure 11-11. Then select the desired CA and press **Finish**.

Figure 11-11 *Certificate Template on the CA Server*

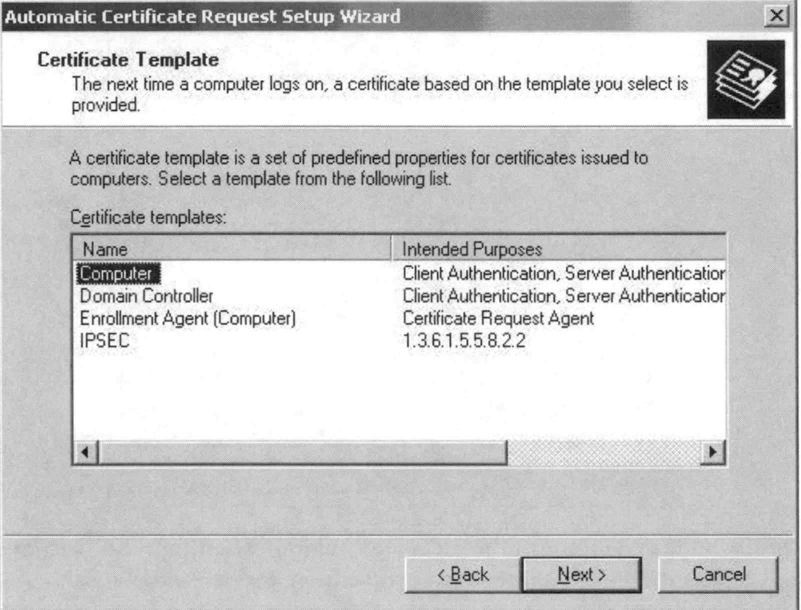

Step 7 From now on, any computer that will join the domain will automatically get a certificate.

Generating and Installing the CA Root Certificate on the ACS Server

On the local ACS machine, point the browser at the Microsoft certification authority server as follows:

Step 1 If you are configured to log in, open the browser, browse to ***http://IP-address-of-Root-CA/certsrv***, and provide all the credentials.

Step 2 Choose **Retrieve the CA certificate or certification revocation list**.

Step 3 Click on **Download CA certificate** and save it on the local machine. Make sure Base 64 encoded is selected.

Step 4 Open the certificate and click on **Install Certificate** as shown in Figure 11-12. Note that the icon at the top left corner of the screen shows that the certificate is not yet trusted (installed).

Figure 11-12 *CA Root Certificate*

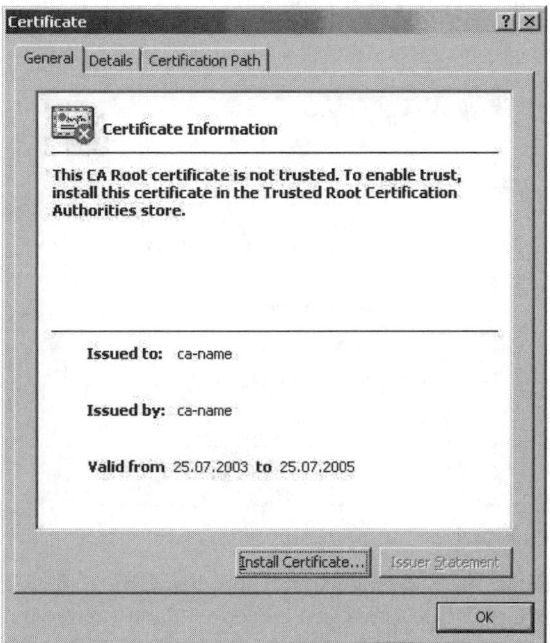

Step 5 Install the certificate in Local Computer/Trusted Root Certificate Authorities. Click **Next** and select **Place all certificates in the following store** and click **Browse** as shown in Figure 11-13.

Figure 11-13 *Selecting Cert Storage for CA Cert*

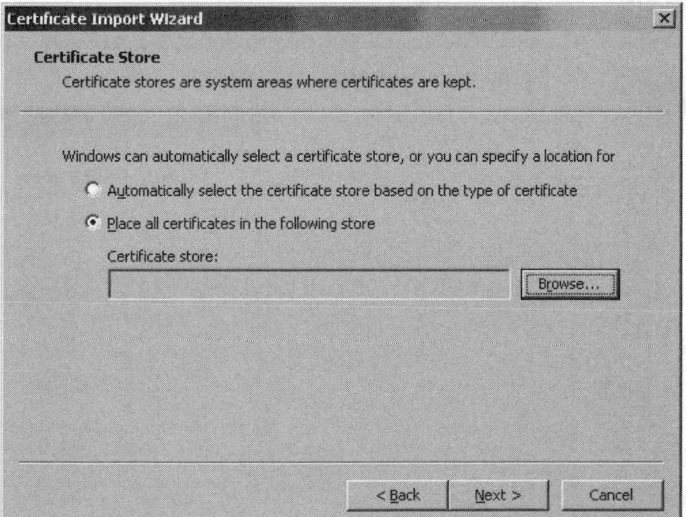

Step 6 Check **Show physical stores** and select under **Trusted Root Certificate Authorities** and **Local Computer**. Click **OK** as shown in Figure 11-14.

Figure 11-14 *Choosing Local Computer for CA Cert*

Step 7 Click **Finish**.

Step 8 Log in to ACS. Go to **System Configuration > ACS Certificate Setup > Edit Certificate Trust List** and check the trusted root certificate you've just installed as shown in Figure 11-15. Click **Submit** and restart ACS under **System Configuration > Service Control > Restart**.

Figure 11-15 *Editing CA Cert Trust List*

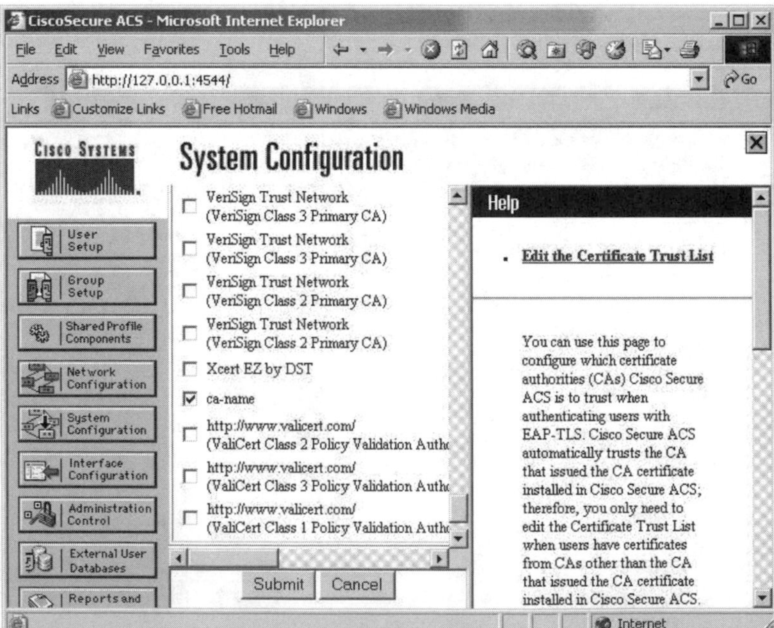

Generating and Installing an ACS Server Certificate on the ACS Server

Follow the steps below to generate and install the ACS server certificate:

Step 1 Go to **System Configuration → ACS Certificate Setup → Generate Certificate Signing Request**. This displays a Signing Request Form as shown in Figure 11-16.

Step 2 In the Signing Request Form, fill in all the fields, and click **Submit.** This gives you the cipher text you need to copy and paste into the Signing Request to the CA sever, as discussed in step 3.

Step 3 Open a browser, and point to http://MS_Certificate_Server_IP/certsrv, which will bring up a signing Request Page. Choose **Request a Certificate.** In the next screen, choose **Advanced request → Click on Next → Choose Submit Certificate Request using a base 64 encoded PKCS#10**. Then click **Next**, which will bring the page shown in Figure 11-16. Enter the Cipher text generated in Step 2 and select Web Server Certificate template.

Figure 11-16 *Signing Request Form for Entering the Cipher Text Generated on ACS*

Step 4 Once you click **Submit**, you see a window similar to that shown in Figure 11-17. (If the auto-enrollment on the CA server is turned on, you will get this window. Otherwise, browse back to the CA Server as http://MS_CA_Server_IP/certsrv and change this option to **Check on a Pending Certificate**.)

Figure 11-17 *ACS Server Certificate Approval Screen*

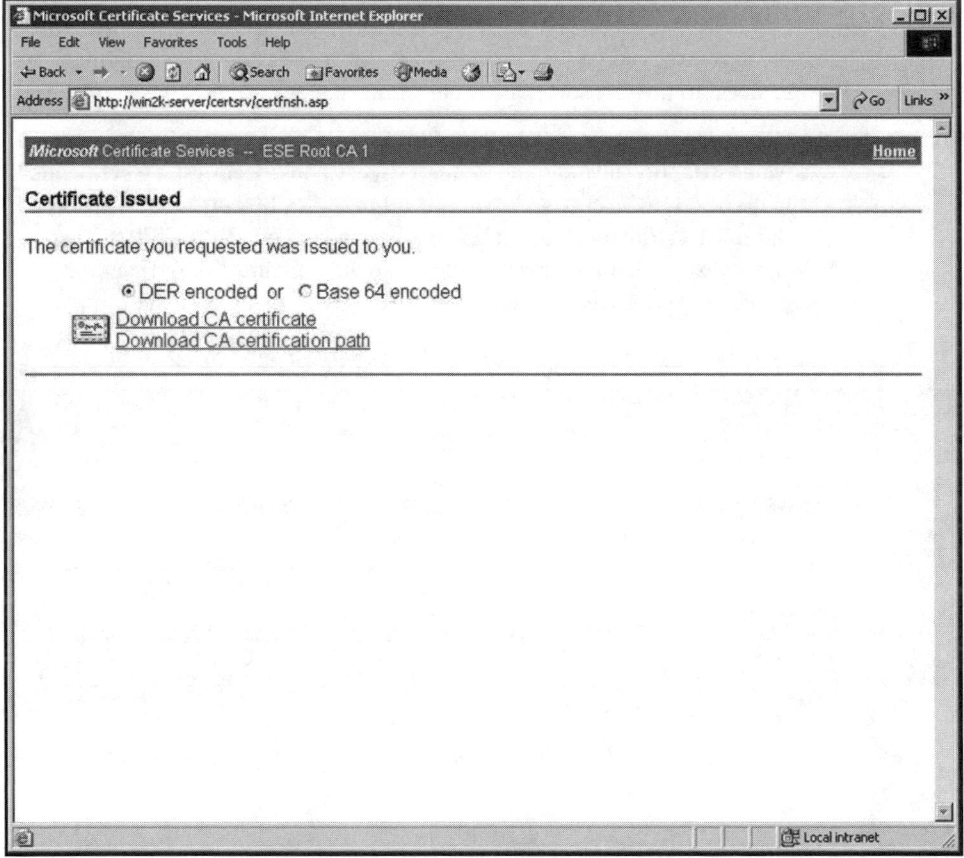

Step 5 Choose **Base 64 encoded** and download the CA certificate. The file type needs to have a **.cer** extension. The file can be stored anywhere.

Step 6 To install the server certificate that is downloaded in Step 5, go to ACS GUI, then browse to **System Configuration > ACS Certificate Setup > Install ACS Certificate**. Then you will see the screen shown in Figure 11-18.

Step 7 In the form shown in Figure 11-19, choose **Read Certificate from file** and specify the name and location of the file downloaded earlier. Then click **Submit**, which displays another window, as shown in Figure 11-19.

Figure 11-18 *ACS Server Cert Installation Screen*

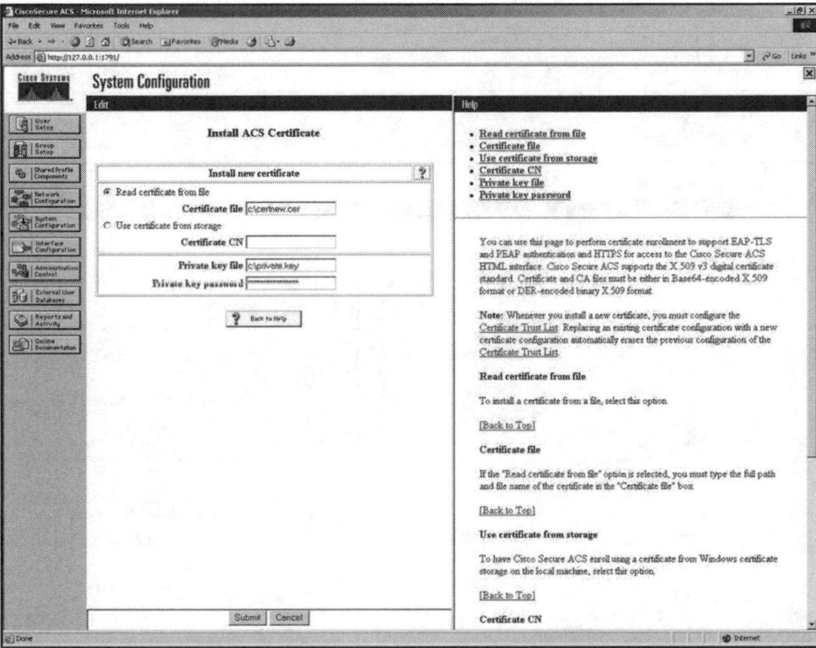

Figure 11-19 *ACS Server Cert Installation Screen*

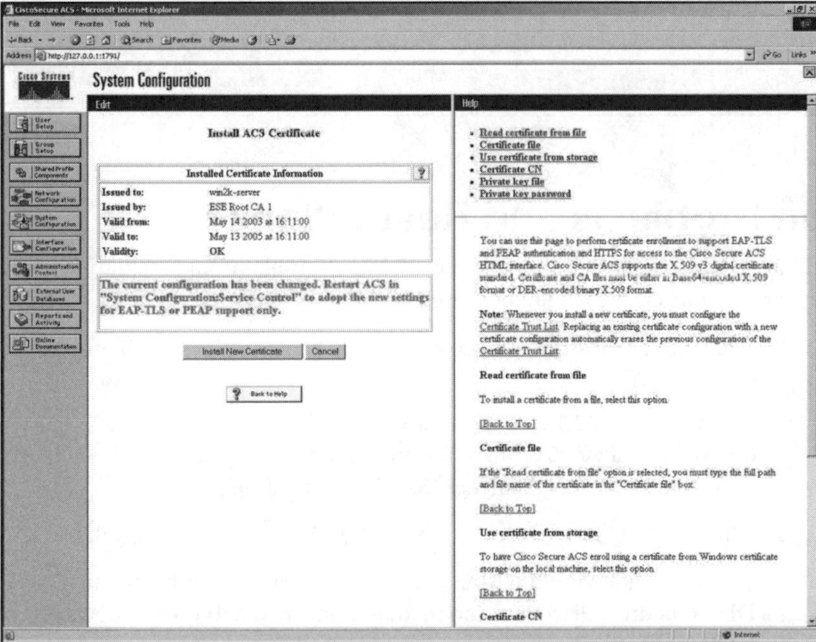

Step 8 Turn on Authentication parameters at **System Configuration > Global Authentication Setup** as shown in Figure 11-20.

Figure 11-20 *Global Authentication Setup*

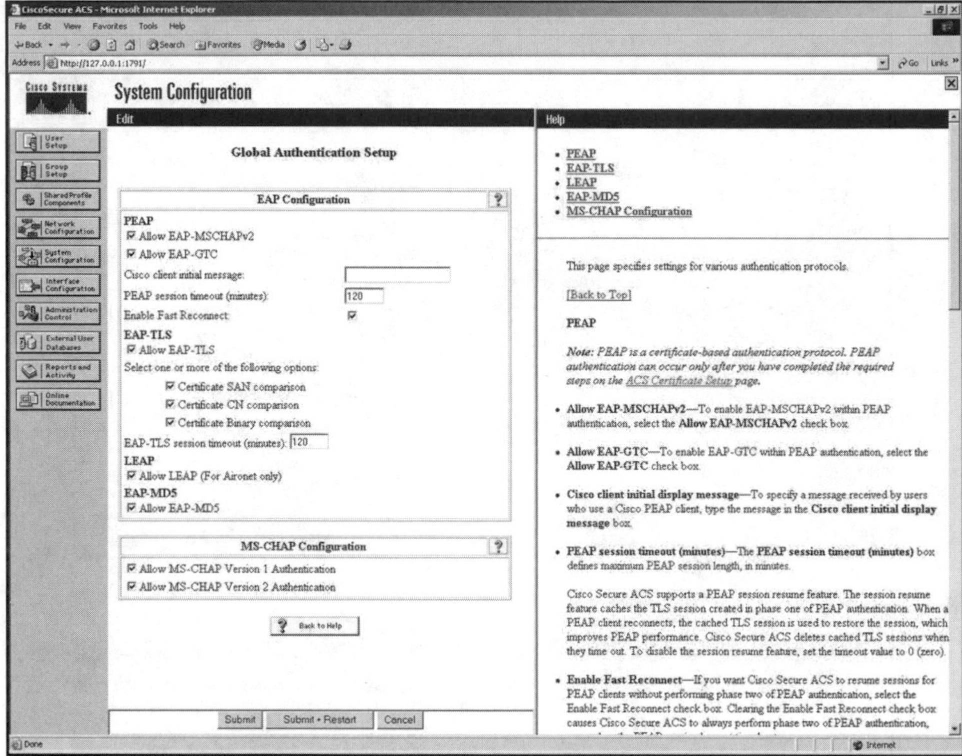

Common Problems and Resolutions

This section examines some commonly found problems and resolutions with the dot1x implementations, which are not discussed in the preceding sections.

1 Are there any restrictions on the types of ports on the switch on which 802.1x can be configured?

Answer: Yes. 802.1x can be configured only on standard Layer 2 access ports. 802.1x cannot be configured on a Trunk port, Private VLAN Trunk (PVLAN) port, EtherChannel port, or Switch Port Analyzer (SPAN) destination port.

2 Why does my DHCP time out when 802.1x is configured on the switch?

Answer: With wired interfaces a successful 802.1x authentication *does not* force a DHCP address discovery (no media-connect signal) on Windows XP before Service Pack 1a. This produces a problem, as DHCP starts once the interface comes up. Hence if 802.1x authentications take too long, DHCP may time out. So, even though the switch port is in Authorized state, the supplicant will not have any IP address.

3 How do you address the DHCP timeout (DHCP-Timeout at 62 Sec) with 802.1x?

Answer: Using Machine authentication allows the Supplicant to obtain an IP address. For a fix by the patch, you need to have the following service or the previously listed service packs on Windows XP and 2000 operating systems:

- **Windows XP**—Service Pack 1a + KB 826942
- **Windows 2000**—Service Pack 4

Updated supplicants trigger DHCP IP address renewal. Successful authentication causes a client to ping the default gateway (three times) with a sub-second timeout. Lack of echo reply triggers a DHCP IP renew. Successful echo reply leaves IP as is. A pre-renewal ping prevents lost connections when the subnet stays the same but the client may be WLAN roaming.

4 Does 802.1x work when Wake on LAN (WoL) is used to turn on computers remotely or to install applications and patches?

Answer: Cisco IBNS supports WoL functionality through the 802.1x with the Wake On LAN feature, which lets you perform automated tasks, such as overnight software upgrades or system backups.

The 802.1x specification supports WoL with the definition of unidirectional controlled ports, which can be configured to allow only outbound frames to be transmitted in the pre-authenticated state. You can send a WoL magic packet to a host connected to a unidirectional controlled port in the sleep standby (S2) state to wake it to a normal operational state.

If the supplicant on the workstation is configured to automatically authenticate when prompted, it can then authenticate to the switch port. If the authentication is successful, the switch applies any policies received from the RADIUS server and puts the port into a normal forwarding state.

5 Is the host MAC currently sent back to a RADIUS server?

Answer: Yes, the MAC address of the supplicant is returned to the RADIUS server in the Calling Line Station Identifier (CLSID) RADIUS attribute. The supplicant MAC address can be used to make policy decisions, such as restricting access (even to otherwise validated identities), or logged for auditing purposes.

6 What are my options for authenticating printers with 802.1x?

Answer: One option is running with port security instead of 802.1x. Another option is to assign unauthenticated printers to the guest VLAN.

7 What are the options when clients go into hibernation, Wake on LAN (WoL), or sleep mode?

Answer: When a host is in hibernation or sleep mode, the network interface tends to be inactive. For WoL to work, the client platform must support the WoL specification for standby mode and be able to listen for the WoL magic packet while in standby. Check the host platform documentation to determine if this feature is supported. Cisco provides WoL support on the authenticator with the 802.1x with Wake on LAN feature.

8 During normal 802.1x operation, if a supplicant responds with an incorrect login or password, does it fail authentication and get placed into a guest VLAN?

Answer: The port is placed in the Held state as a result of unsuccessful 802.1x authentication. The port is not placed into a guest VLAN in this case.

9 What is the Held state, as indicated on my switch when I enter the **show port dot1x** or **show dot1x** commands?

Answer: After the first failed authentication, the supplicant triggers a quiet period on the authenticator. The quiet period is a configurable interval that is set to 60 seconds, by default. During the quiet period, the authenticator, which controls the ports on the switch, ignores all frames from the supplicant on that port. Ideally, the quiet period is the same on the supplicant and authenticator and neither communicates until the quiet period is over. This can help prevent brute force authentication attacks or denial of service (DoS) attacks on a switch or WLAN access point.

10 During the quiet period, is the host allowed on the network?

Answer: No.

11 With 802.1x, can I restrict a specific port to a single MAC address?

Answer: Yes; this is known as single-host mode, which is the default on Cisco devices.

12 How does a RADIUS server know if a user is still connected after authentication?

Answer: This requires RADIUS accounting support on the switch.

13 Does a Cisco Catalyst switch support 802.1x user authentication with a VLAN assignment and MAC address authentication at the same time?

Answer: Cisco Catalyst switches support 802.1x user authentication. MAC address authentication is more of an authorization issue. If a switch port is configured to run as an 802.1x authenticator, then the switch port is logically down before authentication, so the MAC address is not known. Successful 802.1x authentication has to happen for the MAC address to be learned. To make this work better, run port security in addition to 802.1x.

14 In an environment with a large number of active VLANs using Dynamic VLAN assignment, would all the switches have to be set up with VLAN information for every VLAN they handle?

Answer: They would not, because VLAN assignment can be performed by name. This means that the switches do not need to be manually configured to trunk every individual VLAN into every area of the network. You just need to configure the VLAN name itself, which can be any unique alphanumeric value within a specific VTP domain.

Best Practices

For the seamless function of AAA and dot1x implementation on the switch, implement the following best practices.

For Switch Management

Follow the suggestion as outlined in the list that follows for secured switch management with AAA:

- Always configure a fallback method to avoid the lockout problem when AAA is configured for switch management.
- Use SSH rather than Telnet whenever possible and configure AAA for SSH.
- Use **ip permit** command to control Telnet access (**set ip permit enable telnet** and **set ip permit** *range mask* | *host*).
- Configure the switch to source TACACS+ or radius packet from the same interface or IP address.
- Do not enable console authentication to use an external AAA server unless otherwise required.

For Identity-Based Network Services (IBNSs)

This section delves into some of the unique design problems you may run into, and how to resolve the issues by implementing of IBNS.

- If you have devices in the network that do not have 802.1x supplicants, you should either configure a guest VLAN or implement port security on the switch ports where these devices are connected. Another option is to configure a multi-host mode, but avoiding multi-host mode configuration is strongly recommended due to lack of port security.
- If you have multiple devices connected to the 802.1x-enabled switch port via a hub or IP Phone, configure multiple-authentication mode instead of multiple-host mode. Because multi-host mode does not provide the security on the port, multiple authentication does provide security based on the MAC address.
- For IP Phone deployment, configure switch access ports as Multi-VLAN Access Ports (MVAPs), and implement 802.1x port authentication. To configure MVAP, you need to configure 2 VLANs for a single port: one is an access VLAN for regular traffic, and the other one is Voice VLAN ID (VVID) for Voice Over IP traffic. This is preferred over a Guest VLAN or multi-host VLAN.

CHAPTER 12

Troubleshooting AAA on VPN 3000 Series Concentrator

IP Security Virtual Private Network (IPsec VPN) is discussed in greater detail in Chapter 8, "Troubleshooting IPsec VPNs on VPN 3000 Series Concentrators," and Authentication, Authorizing, and Accounting (AAA) implementation on IOS Routers is discussed in Chapter 9, "Troubleshooting AAA on IOS Routers." With the knowledge you gained about AAA from Chapter 9, you can successfully explore this chapter's presentation of AAA implementation on the VPN 3000 series concentrators to fill out the picture presented in Chapter 8. This chapter discusses AAA in the context of IPsec only for the VPN connection, and it discusses how AAA can be used to manage the VPN 3000 series concentrators. Troubleshooting steps are examined throughout the chapter, which concludes with Best Practices.

AAA Implementation on the Concentrator

As mentioned in the introduction, AAA can be implemented on a VPN 3000 Concentrator for two purposes:

- VPN concentrator management
- Tunnel group and user authentication (X-Auth)

The sections that follow describe each of these purposes in detail.

VPN Concentrator Management

Just as with other Cisco devices such as router, Private Internet Exchange (PIX), etc., the VPN concentrator can be managed using TACACS+ (Terminal Access Controller Access Control System) protocols. The authorization feature allows the VPN 3000 Concentrator to download certain privilege levels from the AAA Server.

Tunnel Group and User Authentication

Both Tunnel Group and User can be authenticated with the RADIUS server or locally on the VPN 3000 Concentrators for IPsec VPN connection. You can also authenticate the Tunnel Group on the VPN 3000 Concentrators, and perform user authentication on the

RADIUS server or vice versa. So, it's important to understand the sequence of events that occurs on the VPN 3000 Concentrator for Tunnel Group and user authentication when the VPN client connects to the VPN 3000 Concentrator. The following steps outline the sequence of events:

1 At Phase I of the IPsec tunnel negotiation of the Remote Access VPN connection request, the VPN client sends the group name (also called tunnel group) and password to the VPN 3000 Concentrator. If the group is configured internally, the VPN 3000 Concentrator validates the group name/password against its internal database. If the group is configured externally, the VPN 3000 Concentrator tries to authenticate the group name and password against an external server, for example, Cisco Secure Access Control Server (CS ACS), Microsoft Active Directory (Microsoft AD) and so on. If the group name and password are invalid, you receive this error message: Unable to negotiate IPsec. You can see the error in the event log with debug (1-9) turned on for AUTH, AUTHDBG, AUTHDECODE, IPSEC, IPSECDBG, and IPSECDECODE.

2 If the group name is valid, the Group is authenticated via RADIUS if the password for the Group is stored on the RADIUS Server. The RADIUS server can return many attributes for the group or none at all. At a minimum, the RADIUS server should return the Cisco/Altiga attribute "IPsec Authentication = RADIUS" to tell the concentrator how to authenticate the user. If not, the base group's IPsec Authentication method should be set to "RADIUS." Otherwise, the local user authentication on the VPN 3000 Concentrator will occur.

3 Once the group is authenticated and gets attributes from the Radius Server, the VPN client is asked to enter a username and password. If the group is authenticated locally, the concentrator obtains configuration information such as whether the user should be authenticated against the internal or external database. If authentication was accomplished through the RADIUS server, the concentrator gets this information as a reply attribute. In either case, if the group attribute indicates that the user should be authenticated against an internal server, the concentrator will see if the user is defined internally and will try to authenticate. If the user's authenticity is to be tested against an external server, the concentrator forwards that user's name and password information to the external database, such as a Cisco Secure ACS as configured on the concentrator.

4 If the user is authenticated via RADIUS, the RADIUS server can return many attributes for the user or none at all. If the RADIUS server returns the attribute CLASS (standard RADIUS attribute #25), the VPN 3000 Concentrator uses that attribute as a group name and moves to Step 6, or else it goes to Step 7.

5 If the authentication method in the group is set to NONE, the client machine is not prompted to enter its username and password, and the client machine can establish a tunnel via group name and password only.

6 (Optional) If the user is part of another group, this group is authenticated next. If the user does not belong to another group or the tunnel group, the user defaults to the base group and this step does *not* occur.

7 The tunnel group from Step 1 is authenticated again. (This is done in case the Group Lock feature is being used. This feature is available in version 2.1 or later.) If the Group Lock feature is turned on in the tunnel group and user belongs to a different group, then authentication fails at this stage.

8 If the user is successfully authenticated, the concentrator pushes down the mode configuration to the client machine. Mode configuration includes network lists, banners, assignment of IP addresses, and so on. If the client connection hangs at this point with just "Negotiating IPsec policy" and never establishes a connection, you need to check these logs: IKE, IKEDBG, IKEDECODE (debug should be 1-9). If everything goes well, you should receive this message: "Your Link is now secure."

Once the VPN 3000 Concentrator has authenticated the user and group(s), it must organize the attributes it has received. The VPN Concentrator uses the attributes in the following order of preference, no matter if the authentication was done internally or externally:

1 **User attributes**—These take precedence over all others.

2 **Group attributes**—Any attributes missing from the user attributes are filled in by the group attributes. Any attributes that are the same are overridden by the user attributes.

3 **Tunnel Group attributes**—Any attributes missing from the user or group attributes are filled in by the tunnel group attributes. Any attributes that are the same are overridden by the user attributes.

4 **Base Group attributes**—Any attributes missing from the user, group, or tunnel group attributes are filled in by the base group attributes.

Diagnostic Commands and Tools

To set up debugging for authentication troubleshooting, follow these steps:

Step 1 Browse to **Configuration > System > Events > General**, and check **Save Log on Wrap**.

Step 2 To configure a class to monitor in the logs, under **Configuration > System > Events > Classes > Add**, select a class name, make sure the class is enabled, and set severity to log at 1-13 (to capture all events). You can set this a bit lower (1-9 is sufficient in most cases), if you want less verbosity. If you are using a syslog server and would like the debugs to go there for collection, you can set the syslog value at 1-13. The default level is 1-5, which might not indicate all the events leading to an error or problem.

Step 3 For authentication troubleshooting, follow Step 2 for classes: AUTH, AUTHDBG, and AUTHDECODE. It might also be beneficial to see IPsec-related messages, and IPSEC, IPSECDBG, and IPSECDECODE classes.

Step 4 To view logs while events are occurring, go to **Monitoring > Live Event Log**.

Step 5 To view logs that were generated after the event, either go to **Administration > File Management > Files** to view older log files (for example, after a crash) or go to **Monitoring > Filterable Event Log**.

Step 6 To scroll though all the log events on one page, it is better to click on **Get Log**, under **Monitoring > Filterable Event Log.** Also, to move the log off the VPN 3000 Concentrator for off-line analysis, press **Ctrl+A**, and **Ctrl+C** on the keyboard to copy the log from the "**Get Log**" popup window and paste it with Ctrl+V into a notepad.

Analysis of Problem Areas

The problems of AAA implementation on VPN 3000 may be categorized as follows:

- VPN concentrator management troubleshooting
- Group/user authentication (x-auth) troubleshooting

VPN Concentrator Management Troubleshooting

Only TACACS+ protocol is supported for VPN concentrator management. To control the user who manages the concentrator from the GUI, there must be a concentrator running version 3.0 or above and Cisco Secure ACS 2.4 and above.

Configuration Steps

Configuring the VPN 3000 Concentrator for authentication and authorization with TACACS+ server is a two-step process:

- Configuration on the Cisco Secure ACS server
- Configuration on the VPN 3000 Concentrator

The following sections explain the steps required to configure TACACS+ for VPN Concentrator Management.

Configuration on the Cisco Secure ACS

Cisco Secure ACS configuration involves defining VPN 3000 Concentrator as an AAA client under the Network Configuration, and defining user profiles. User profiles can be defined either locally on the CS ACS database, or can be configured in external user databases. Refer to Chapter 13, "Troubleshooting Cisco Secure ACS on Windows," for additional detail on external user database integration with CS ACS. The following steps explain how to configure the VPN 3000 Concentrator as an AAA client, and how to create the user profiles locally on the CS ACS:

Step 1 Click **Network Configuration** in the left Navigation panel. Under **AAA Clients** click **Add Entry**.

Step 2 On the next screen, fill out the form to add the VPN 3000 Concentrator as the TACACS client. Define a shared secret, and be sure to enter the same secret on the VPN 3000 Concentrator. Select **Authenticate using = TACACS+ (Cisco IOS)**.

Step 3 Click on the **Submit + Restart** button.

Step 4 Define a user account that can be used for TACACS+ authentication by the VPN 3000 Concentrator. To do so, click **User Setup** in the left panel. Add the name of the user (the user is admin), and click **Add/Edit**. The username does not have to be defined as "admin"; it can be any other name.

Step 5 On the next screen, define the password, and map this user to a specific group. In this example, the user "admin" is mapped to the group, Group 10.

Step 6 Click **Submit**.

Step 7 Click **Group Setup** in the left panel. From the drop-down menu, select your group (Group 10 in this example) and click **Edit Settings**.

Step 8 On the next screen, be sure that the following attributes are selected under TACACS+ Settings: **Shell (exec)** and **Privilege level = 15** as shown in Figure 12-1.

Figure 12-1 *Group Setup with Shell Exec Turned On and Privilege Level Set to 15*

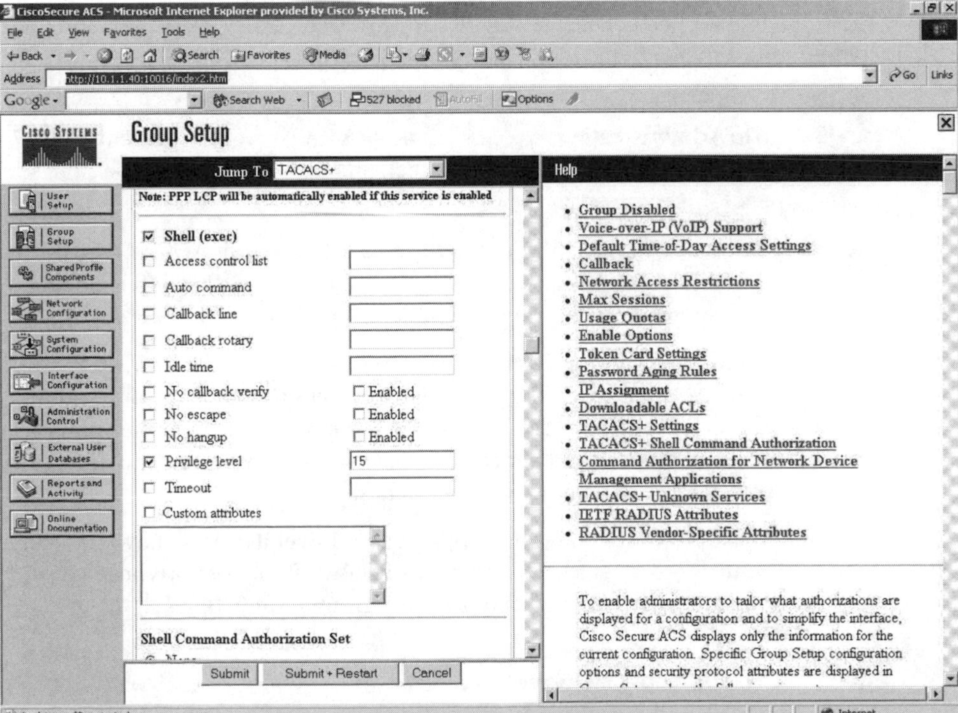

Step 9 Click the **Submit + Restart** button.

Configuration on the VPN 3000 Concentrator

Once CS ACS is configured, configure the VPN 3000 Concentrator to forward the authentication request to the CS ACS server for authentication. Once you turn on TACACS+ for authentication, you can no longer log in to the VPN 3000 Concentrator from the GUI using the local administrative accounts and passwords (admin, config, isp, etc.). However, the access rights for the accounts that are locally defined on the VPN 3000 Concentrator are used to define the privileges a particular TACACS+ user receives when logging in, based on the privilege level defined for the user on the TACACS+ server. So, if you have privilege levels defined for the user profile on the TACACS+ server, after user authentication, the privilege level is downloaded to the VPN 3000 Concentrator. This downloaded privilege level needs to be matched with at least one "AAA Access Level" on the locally configured administrative accounts. Otherwise, authentication fails.

If the corresponding "AAA Access Level" is defined, this externally configured user account will have the same permission as the configured access right for this specific access level. For example, to permit a user to modify the configuration, but not read/write files, assign the user a privilege level of 12 on the TACACS+ server (pick any number between 1 and 15). Then, on the VPN 3000 Concentrator, pick one of the other locally configured administrators. Next, set its AAA Access Level to 12, and set the permissions on this user to be able to modify the configuration, but not to read/write files. Because of the matching privilege/access level, the user gets those permissions when logging in.

The following section details the step-by-step procedure for VPN 3000 Concentrator configurations to assign the user a privilege level of 15:

Step 1 To add an entry for the TACACS Server in the VPN 3000 Concentrator, go to **Administration > Access Rights > AAA Servers > Authentication** in the navigation tree in the left panel, and then click **Add** in the right panel.

Step 2 On the next screen, fill out the form as follows with ACS Server IP address: the shared secret key should be the same as that defined on the ACS Server, and the rest of the fields should be left at their defaults.

Step 3 To modify the Admin Account on the Concentrator for TACACS Authentication, go to **Administration > Access Rights > Administrators** and click **Modify** for the user "admin" to modify the properties of this user. You may select other administrator accounts to define the **AAA Access Level** and **activate** the account.

Step 4 On the next screen, set the **AAA Access Level** as 15 as shown in Figure 12-2. This level has to be matched with the user privilege level defined on the CS ACS servers for the group profile to which the users belong.

Step 5 Click on **Apply** and **Save** as needed.

Figure 12-2 *Defining AAA Access Level to 15 for One Administrative User on VPN 3000 Concentrator*

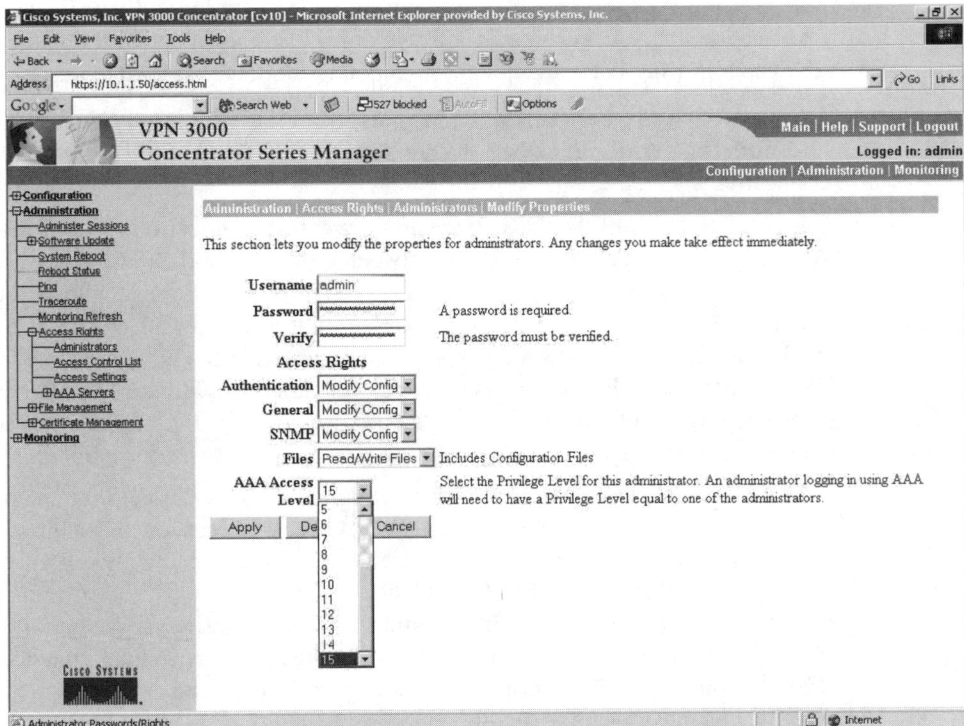

TIP While turning on AAA for administration purposes on the VPN 3000 Concentrator, it is very important to keep the session from timing out. The default idle timeout for the session is 600 seconds. So, it is recommended to increase this timeout value to 1800 seconds on the **Administration > Access Rights > Access Settings** screen. Once you perform the test with the authentication server, open a new Web browser window, log in, and be sure the user login and authorization are working as expected before logging out of the current session. Once you are comfortable with the setting, you can change the idle session timeout to default or to any value.

Troubleshooting Steps

Once you are finished with the configuration, do not log out from the session without performing the following test:

Step 1 To test the authentication, go to **Administration > Access Rights > AAA Servers > Authentication**. Select your server, and then click **Test**.

Step 2 Your authentication should be successful.

If the authentication fails, turn on logging as discussed in the "Diagnostic Commands and Tools" section. Also, on the CS ACS server under Reports and Activity, look at the active Failed Attempts file. For more details, you may also look at the **auth.log** file on the CS ACS. The following list outlines some common issues that you need to be aware of:

- **IP connectivity issue**—Perform a ping test from the VPN 3000 Concentrator (**Administration | Ping**) to the AAA server to be sure you don't have a problem with connectivity.
- **TACACS+ (TCP/49) traffic is blocked between the concentrator and the CS ACS server**—If you have a firewall between the VPN 3000 Concentrator and the CS ACS server, be sure to open TCP/49 in both directions. For example, if you have a VPN 3000 Concentrator on the DMZ interface of the PIX firewall, and CS ACS server on the inside interface network, you must have an ACL on the DMZ interface to allow the TCP packets with source port any and destination port 49. If the TACACS+ packet is blocked by the PIX firewall, when you perform the Authentication Server Test, you will see this message: **Authentication Error: No active server found**.
- **TACACS+ packet is blocked by filter**—If your TACACS+ server is on the public interface network, then you must allow the TACACS+ packets on the public interface filter. If you do not have both in and out rules for public filters to allow TACACS+ packets, the authentication will fail and display this message while performing the Authentication Server Test: **Authentication Error: No active server found**. To resolve this problem, create an **in** rule with a source port any and a destination port TCP/49. Then create an **out** rule with source port TCP/49 and destination port any. Finally, you must assign these rules to the public interface filter.
- **Shared secret key mismatch**—You must be sure that the shared secret keys defined on VPN concentrator and the ACS Server match; otherwise, ACS will not trust VPN 3000 Concentrator and will therefore reject authentication.
- **Wrong username or password**—You must ensure that you are entering the right username and password for authentication. Keep in mind that the username and password are case sensitive.
- **Misconfigured user/group profile on CS ACS server**—Be sure that on the CS ACS server, in the User or Group profile under "TACACS+ Settings" you have **Shell (exec)** checked and the appropriate **Privilege level** is set.
- **Misconfigured AAA access level on VPN 3000 Concentrator**—Be sure the Privilege level defined for the TACACS+ users matches the **AAA access level** set for at least one administrator account. Otherwise, authorization will fail, and therefore the user will be unable to log in to the VPN 3000 Concentrator.

Group/User Authentication (X-Auth) Troubleshooting

For Remote Access VPN, the VPN 3000 Concentrator can be configured to authenticate groups and users. Although user authentication is optional (strongly recommended), group authentication is mandatory. Both group and user authentication can be performed locally on the VPN 3000 Concentrator or on an external user database such as RADIUS Server. The following are the different combinations of group and user authentication locally or with the RADIUS Server:

- Both group and user authentications are performed locally on the VPN 3000 Concentrator.
- Group authentication is done locally and no user authentication is done.
- Group authentication is done locally on the VPN 3000 Concentrator, and user authentication is done with the RADIUS Server.
- Group authentication is done with a RADIUS server, and user authentication is done locally.
- Both group and user authentication are performed with a RADIUS Server.
- The user is locked to a specific group.

CS ACS is used as a RADIUS server with VPN 3000 Concentrator to configure the above scenarios as follows.

Both Group and User Authentication Are Performed Locally on the VPN 3000 Concentrator

To authenticate both groups and users locally on the VPN 3000 Concentrator, you must configure both users and groups locally. Then point both user and group authentication to LOCAL as per the following steps:

Step 1 Go to **Configuration > System > Servers > Authentication** and click **Add**. For the Server Type, select **Internal**, and then click **Add**.

Step 2 Go to **Configuration > System > Pools** and click **Add**. In the new window, define the range of IP addresses and the netmask.

Step 3 Go to **Configuration > System > Address Management** and check the option you want. To use the address defined in step 2, check the **Use Address Pools** box.

Step 4 Go to **Configuration > User Management > Groups**, click **Add**, and configure the parameters for group identity, DNS, and authentication.

Step 5 On the **Identity** tab, set the following parameters.

```
Group Name (case sensitive)
Password (case sensitive)
Type = Internal
```

Step 6 On the **General** tab, set the following parameters:

```
Primary DNS
Secondary DNS
Primary WINS
Secondary WINS
```

Note The IP addresses of the two WINS servers are passed to the VPN Client upon connection.

Step 7 On the **IPsec** tab, set the following parameter:

```
Authentication=Internal
```

Step 8 When you have configured these parameters, click **Add**.

Group Authentication Is Done Locally and No User Authentication Is Done

The configuration for this setup is almost identical to that described in the preceding section with one exception: In Step 7, select **None** instead of **Internal** for **Authentication.**

Group Authentication Is Done Locally on VPN 3000 Concentrator and User Authentication Is Done with RADIUS Server

The configuration steps for this setup are very similar to those described in the section entitled "Both Group and User Authentications are Performed Locally on the VPN 3000 Concentrator" with the following exceptions:

Step 1 Go to **Configuration > System > Servers > Authentication** and click **Add**. For the Server Type, select **Internal**, and then click **Add**.

Step 2 To configure the CS ACS RADIUS Server, go to **Configuration > System > Servers > Authentication**, and click **Add**. Then configure the following parameters:

```
Server Type: Select RADIUS.
Authentication Server: Enter the IP address or host name of the RADIUS
server.
Server Secret: Enter the exact same string as that on the RADIUS server.
```

Step 3 When you have configured these parameters, click **Add**.

Step 4 Go to **Configuration > System > Address Management** and check the **Use Address from Authentication Server** option to assign the address from CS ACS server.

Step 5 Go to **Configuration > User Management > Groups**, click **Add**, and configure the parameters for group identity, DNS, and authentication.

Step 6 On the Identity tab, set the following parameters:

```
Group Name (case sensitive)
Password (case sensitive)
Type = Internal
```

Step 7 On the **General** tab, set the following parameters:

```
Primary DNS
Secondary DNS
```

```
Primary WINS
Secondary WINS
```

Step 8 On the **IPsec** tab, set the following parameter:

```
Authentication=Radius
```

Step 9 When you have configured these parameters, click **Add**.

With VPN Concentrator release 3.0 and later, you can configure individual CS ACS RADIUS servers for individual groups, as opposed to having one ACS RADIUS server that is defined globally and used by all groups. Any groups that do not have individual ACS RADIUS servers configured use the ACS server that is defined globally.

You can also choose to define individual ACS RADIUS servers for each group. To do this, go to **Configuration > User Management > Groups**, highlight a group, and choose **Modify Auth Server**.

Follow these steps to configure the CS ACS RADIUS server to communicate with the VPN 3000 Concentrator:

Step 1 Add the VPN 3000 Concentrator as a Network Access Server (NAS) on the CS ACS RADIUS server under the Network Configuration section.

```
Add the IP address of the VPN 3000 Concentrator in the NAS IP Address box.
Add the same key you defined earlier on the VPN 3000 Concentrator in the
Key box.
From the Authenticate Using: drop-down menu, select RADIUS (Cisco VPN
3000).
```

Step 2 Click the **Submit + Restart** button.

Step 3 Go to user setup, set up the user, and map the user to a specific group.

Step 4 Once finished with this configuration, go back to Test Authentication on the VPN Concentrator for the Authentication server and perform the authentication with the user you have just created.

Group Authentication Is Done with a RADIUS Server and User Authentication Is Done Locally

This is not a very common setup, but it is possible to authenticate the group with a RADIUS server, and authenticate users locally. Upon completion of group authentication, CS ACS replies with the authentication type to Internal to the VPN 3000 concentrator. So, the group name for the VPN 3000 Concentrator needs to be defined as username on the CS ACS server. This still requires that the names of the groups be configured on the VPN 3000 Concentrator, but the group type is configured as "External."

- External Groups can return Cisco/Altiga attributes if the RADIUS server supports Vendor Specific Attributes (VSAs).

- Any Cisco/Altiga attributes *not* returned by RADIUS default to the values in the Base Group.
- If the RADIUS server does *not* support VSAs, *all* attributes default to the Base Group attributes.

NOTE A VPN 3000 Concentrator Group name is treated just like a user on the CS ACS server. This username needs to be mapped to a CS ACS group name that is not the same as the VPN 3000 Concentrator Group name.

Work through the following steps to configure the VPN 3000 Concentrator:

Step 1 Go to **Configuration > System > Servers > Authentication** and click **Add**. For the Server Type, select **Internal**, and then click **Add**.

Step 2 To add the CS ACS RADIUS Server, go to **Configuration > System > Servers > Authentication**, and click **Add**. Then configure the following parameters:

```
Server Type: Select RADIUS.
Authentication Server: Enter the IP address or host name of the RADIUS server.
Server Secret: Enter the exact same string as that on the RADIUS server.
```

Step 3 When you have configured these parameters, click **Add**.

Step 4 Go to **Configuration > System > Pools** and click **Add**. In the new window, define the range of IP addresses and the netmask.

Step 5 Go to **Configuration > System > Address Management** and check the option you want. To use the address defined in step 2, check the **Use Address Pools** box.

Step 6 Go to **Configuration > User Management > Groups**, click **Add**, and configure the **Identity** tab, and set the following parameters:

```
Group Name (Case Sensitive)
Password (case sensitive)
Type = External
```

This is the same group name and password you must define when you create a user on the CS ACS RADIUS server for this group name and password.

Step 7 When you have configured these parameters, click **Add**.

Follow these steps to configure the CS ACS RADIUS server to communicate with the VPN 3000 Concentrator:

Step 1 Add the VPN 3000 Concentrator as a Network Access Server (NAS) on the CS ACS RADIUS server under the Network Configuration section.

```
Add the IP address of the VPN 3000 Concentrator in the NAS IP Address box.
Add the same key you defined earlier on the VPN 3000 Concentrator in the
Key box.
From the Authenticate Using: drop-down menu, select RADIUS (Cisco VPN
3000).
```

Step 2 Click **Submit + Restart** button.

Step 3 Go to **Interface Configuration > RADIUS (Cisco VPN 3000 Concentrator)** and check for both user and group, attribute "**[026/3076/013] CVPN3000-IPsec-Authentication**," to be sure it appears under both user and group configuration.

Step 4 Go to user setup. Create a user with the same name as the VPN Group name that is defined on the VPN 3000 Concentrator. Map this user into a CS ACS group.

Step 5 Either on the CS ACS user or group profile, check the **[3076\013] CVPN3000-IPsec-Authentication** attribute under **Cisco VPN 3000 Concentrator RADIUS Attributes,** and select **Internal** from the drop-down list.

Step 6 Once finished with this configuration, go back to Test Authentication on the VPN 3000 Concentrator for the Authentication server and perform the authentication with the user you have just created. Remember this username is the same name as the group name that was configured on the VPN 3000 Concentrator.

Both Group and User Authentications Are Performed with the RADIUS Server

If you want to authenticate both group and user with the CS ACS RADIUS server, follow the steps below to configure the VPN 3000 Concentrator:

Step 1 To add the CS ACS RADIUS Server, go to **Configuration > System > Servers > Authentication**, and click **Add**. Then configure the following parameters:

```
Server Type: Select RADIUS.
Authentication Server: Enter the IP address or host name of the RADIUS
server.
Server Secret: Enter the exact same string as that on the RADIUS server.
```

Step 2 When you have configured these parameters, click **Add**.

Step 3 Go to **Configuration > System > Address Management** and check the **Use Address from Authentication Server** option to assign the address from CS ACS server.

Step 4 Go to **Configuration > User Management > Groups**, click **Add**, and configure the parameters for group identity, DNS, and authentication.

Step 5 On the **Identity** tab, set the following parameters.

```
Group Name (case sensitive)
Password (case sensitive)
Type = External
```

Step 6 On the **General** tab, leave the DNS and WINS server IP fields blank. This will be defined on the CS ACS server under user/group profile.

Step 7 On the **IPsec** tab, set the following parameter:

```
Authentication=RADIUS
```

Step 8 When you have configured these parameters, click **Add**.

Follow these steps to configure the CS ACS RADIUS server to communicate with the VPN 3000 Concentrator:

Step 1 Add the VPN 3000 Concentrator as a network access server (NAS) on the CS ACS RADIUS server under the Network Configuration section.

```
Add the IP address of the VPN 3000 Concentrator in the NAS IP Address box.
Add the same key you defined earlier on the VPN 3000 Concentrator in the
Key box.
From the Authenticate Using: drop-down menu, select RADIUS (Cisco VPN 3000).
```

Step 2 Click **Submit + Restart** button.

Step 3 Go to **Interface Configuration > RADIUS (Cisco VPN 3000 Concentrator)** and check for both user and group, attribute **[026/3076/013] CVPN3000-IPsec-Authentication**, to be sure it appears under both the user and group configuration. In addition, do the same for the **Primary and Secondary DNS and WINS servers** attribute.

Step 4 Go to user setup. Create a user with the same name as the VPN Group name defined on the VPN 3000 Concentrator. Map this user into a CS ACS group.

Step 5 Either on the CS ACS user or group profile, check the **[3076\013] CVPN3000-IPsec-Authentication** attribute under **Cisco VPN 3000 Concentrator RADIUS Attributes**, and select **RADIUS** from the drop-down list.

Step 6 Create an actual user profile for Remote Access VPN for user authentication, and map the user to a group. Either on the group or user profile, define the WINS and DNS servers' IP address (both primary and secondary) under the **Cisco VPN 3000 Concentrator RADIUS Attributes**.

Step 7 Once finished with this configuration, go back to Test Authentication on the VPN 3000 Concentrator for the Authentication server and perform the authentication that you have just created with both user and group. Remember this username is the same name as the group name configured on the VPN 3000 Concentrator.

User Is Locked to a Specific Group

The configuration on the VPN 3000 Concentrator is similar to a standard configuration as discussed earlier with various scenarios. The ability to lock users into a group defined on the VPN 3000 Concentrator is enabled by defining a return attribute in the RADIUS user profile. This attribute contains the VPN 3000 Concentrator group name that you want the user to be locked into. This attribute is the Class attribute (IETF RADIUS attribute number 25), and has to be returned to the VPN Concentrator in the following format:

OU=*groupname;*

Here *groupname* is the name of the group on the VPN 3000 Concentrator that the user locks into. *OU* has to be in capital letters, and there must be a semicolon at the end.

Assume that the VPN Client software is distributed to all users with an existing connection profile using a *groupname* of Common_Group and password **cisco123**. Each user has a discrete username/password (in the example, the username/password is cisco/cisco). When the user's name is sent to the RADIUS server, the RADIUS server sends down information on the *real group* that the user is to be in. In the example, it is **Secured_Group**.

By doing this, you can completely control the group assignment on the RADIUS server and keep the assignment transparent to the users. If the RADIUS server does not assign a group to the user, the user remains in the Common_Group group, and because the Common_Group group has very restrictive filters, the user cannot pass any traffic. If the RADIUS server does assign a group to the user, the user inherits the attributes, including the less-restrictive filters that are particular to the group. In the example, you would apply a filter to group "**Secured_Group**" on the VPN Concentrator to permit all traffic.

Here is additional configuration that is needed on the VPN 3000 Concentrator for the Group Lock to work:

Step 1 Define a filter that drops access to everything in the internal network. This is applied to the group "Common_Group," so that even if the users can authenticate into this group and stay in it, they are still not able to access anything.

Step 2 Under **Configuration > Policy Management > Traffic Management > Rules**, add a rule called **Drop All** and leave everything at the defaults.

Step 3 Under **Configuration > Policy Management > Traffic Management > Filters**, create a filter called **Drop All** and leave everything at the defaults. Add the Drop All rule to it.

Step 4 Under **Configuration > User Management > Groups**, add a group called **Common_Group**. This is the group that all users have pre-configured in the VPN Client. They authenticate into this group initially, and then are locked into a different group after user authentication. Define the group just like any other VPN group by defining the password, specifying the authentication type (such as RADIUS or Internal authentication) and so on. Make sure you add the Drop All filter (that you just created) under the **General** tab. To use RADIUS authentication for users in this group, set the group's Type (under the Identity tab) to **Internal** and Authentication (under the IPsec tab) to **RADIUS**. Make sure the Group Lock feature is not checked for this group. Note that even if you do not define a Drop All filter, make sure there is at least one filter defined here.

Step 5 Define the user's ultimate destination group (the example is "Secured_Group"), and apply a filter.

NOTE You must define a filter here. If you do not want to block any traffic for these users, create an "Allow All" filter and apply the "Any In" and "Any Out" rules to it. You must define a filter of some kind to pass traffic. To use RADIUS authentication for users in this group, set the group's Type (under the Identity tab) to **Internal** and Authentication (under the IPsec tab) to **RADIUS**. Be sure the Group Lock feature is not checked for this group.

Dynamic Filters on the VPN 3000 Concentrator

The VPN 3000 Concentrator allows you to define remote access user filters on an external RADIUS server, such as Cisco Secure ACS, rather than on the VPN 3000 Concentrator. Using an external RADIUS server allows centralized filter management and greater scalability. Also, configuring filters in this way allows you to assign filters to a particular tunnel group or a particular user.

These filters are called *dynamic filters* because they remain in place only for the duration of the session to which they apply. When a user authenticates via RADIUS, the VPN 3000 Concentrator downloads the filter associated with the user and applies it for the duration of the connection. When the connection finishes, the filter drops.

Configure this feature on the RADIUS server, not on the VPN 3000 Concentrator. (The filters you configure on the VPN 3000 Concentrator are *static*.)

You can configure a dynamic filter on either a user or a group. If both user dynamic filters and group dynamic filters apply to a single connection, the user filters take precedence. If both dynamic filters and static filters apply to the same connection, the dynamic filters take precedence. The order of precedence is:

- Dynamic user filter
- Dynamic group filter
- Static user filter
- Static group filter

NOTE If you encounter problems using this feature, debug by tracking the FILTERDBG event class. If you are concerned about filter syntax errors, track events with severity level 6. The error log shows how the VPN Concentrator parses the filter. To view the actual filtering, track events with severity level 9; in this case, be sure to define the filter using the keyword "log."

If you want to see the currently loaded dynamic filter, you may browse to **Monitoring > Dynamic Filters Screen**.

This screen shows a list of the unique dynamic filters currently in use on the VPN 3000 Concentrator. Select a filter to view its associated rules in the text box below the list of dynamic filters. The syntax of each rule is as follows:

```
[Prefix] [Action] [Protocol] [Source] [Source Wildcard Mask] [Destination]
[Destination Wildcard Mask] [Established] [Log] [Operator] [Port]:
```

Table 12-1 shows the meaning of the fields that make up the Dynamic Filters.

Table 12-1 *Meaning of Fields for Dynamic Filters*

Field	Description
Prefix	Unique identifier for the AV pair. For example: ip:inacl#1=. This field appears only when the filter has been sent as an AV pair.
Action	Action to perform if rule matches: deny, permit.
Protocol	Number or name of an IP protocol. Either an integer in the range 0-255 or one of the following keywords: icmp, igmp, ip, tcp, udp.
Source	Network or host from which the packet is sent, specified as an IP address, a hostname, or the keyword "any". If specified as an IP address, the source wildcard mask must follow.
Source Wildcard Mask	The wildcard mask to be applied to the source address.
Destination	Network or host to which the packet is sent, specified as an IP address, a hostname, or the keyword "any". If specified as an IP address, the source wildcard mask must follow.
Destination Wildcard Mask	The wildcard mask to be applied to the destination address.
Log	Generates a FILTER log message. You must use this keyword to generate events of severity level 9.
Operator	Logic operators: greater than, less than, equal to, not equal to.
Port	The number of a TCP or UDP port: in the range 0-65535.

Configuration of Dynamic Filters on CiscoSecure ACS

You can configure dynamic filters on any RADIUS server by using the Cisco vendor-specific RADIUS attribute (26/9/1) AV-Pair to define and transmit attribute/value pairs. In configuring the feature, refer to Table 12-2 for a list of tokens that the VPN Concentrator supports.

Table 12-2 *VPN Concentrator-Supported Tokens*

Token	Syntax Field	Description
ip:inacl#*Num*=	N/A (Identifier)	(Where *Num* is a unique integer.) Starts all AV pair access control lists.
Deny	Action	Denies action. (Default.)
Permit	Action	Allows action.
Icmp	Protocol	Internet Control Message Protocol (ICMP).
1	Protocol	Internet Control Message Protocol (ICMP).
IP	Protocol	Internet Protocol (IP).
0	Protocol	Internet Protocol (IP).
TCP	Protocol	Transmission Control Protocol (TCP).
6	Protocol	Transmission Control Protocol (TCP).
UDP	Protocol	User Datagram Protocol (UDP).
17	Protocol	User Datagram Protocol (UDP).
any	Hostname	Rule applies to any host.
host	Hostname	Any alphanumeric string that denotes a hostname.
log	Log	When the event is hit, a filter log message appears. (This is the same as permit and log or deny and log.)
lt	Operator	Less than value.
gt	Operator	Greater than value.
eq	Operator	Equal to value.
neq	Operator	Not equal to value.
range	Operator	Inclusive range. Should be followed by two values.

You can configure Cisco Secure ACS by using either of the following screens:

- Using Cisco IOS/PIX RADIUS attributes
- Using Downloadable PIX/IP ACLs

Using Cisco IOS/PIX RADIUS Attributes

When you define VPN 3000 Concentrator on the CS ACS under AAA client configuration, be sure to choose the **RADIUS (Cisco IOS/PIX)** dictionary. In the user/group configuration, under "Cisco IOS/PIX RADIUS Attributes," check "**[009\001] cisco-av-pair**" box, and define the ACL shown in Example 12-1 in the rectangle text box.

Example 12-1 *ACL Needed To Be Created on ACS*

```
ip:inacl#1=permit ip 10.1.1.0 0.0.0.255 host 20.1.1.1
ip:inacl#2=permit ip 10.1.1.0 0.0.0.255 30.1.1.0 0.0.0.255
ip:inacl#3=deny ip 10.1.1.0 0.0.0.255 30.1.1.0 0.0.0.255 log
ip:inacl#4=permit TCP any host 20.1.1.100 eq 80
ip:inacl#5=permit TCP any host HOST12 neq 80
```

Figure 12-3 shows the mapping of ACL that is outlined in Example 12-5.

Figure 12-3 *Screenshot of ACL Definition for Filter Using Cisco AV Pair on a CS ACS Server*

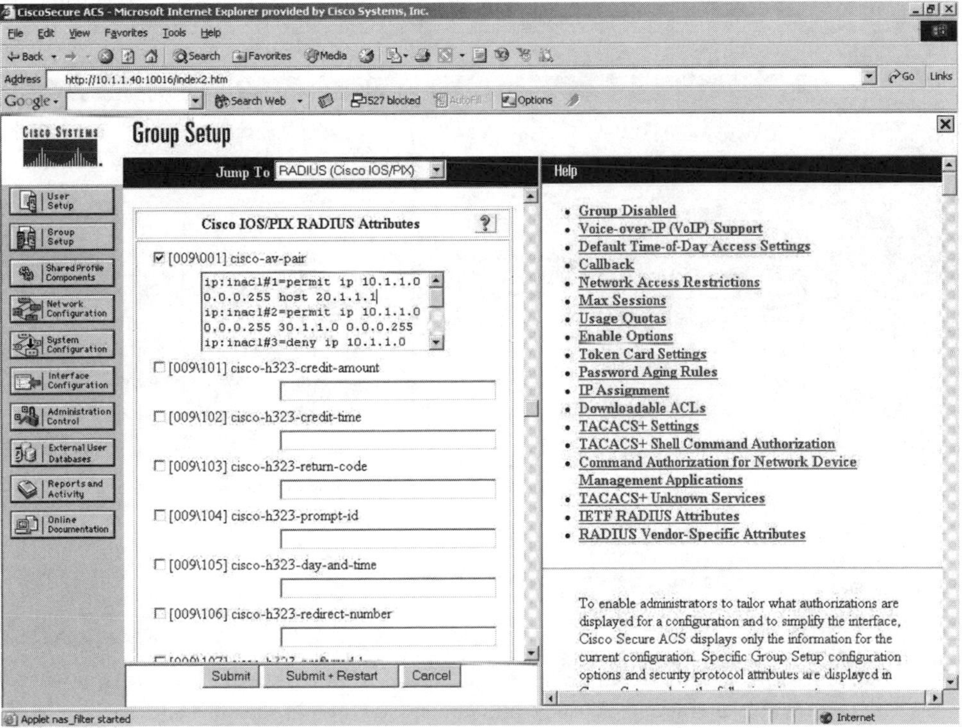

Using Downloadable PIX/IP ACLs

As mentioned earlier, you can use a per user or per group downloadable ACL using the shared profile component on the CS ACS. For Shared Profile components, the syntax for downloadable ACLs is shown in Example 12-2.

Example 12-2 *Downloadable ACL Syntax for Shared Profile Components on CS ACS*

```
ip:inacl#1=permit ip 10.1.1.0 0.0.0.255 host 20.1.1.1
ip:inacl#2=permit ip 10.1.1.0 0.0.0.255 30.1.1.0 0.0.0.255
ip:inacl#3=deny ip 10.1.1.0 0.0.0.255 30.1.1.0 0.0.0.255 log
ip:inacl#4=permit TCP any host 20.1.1.100 eq 80
ip:inacl#5=permit TCP any host HOST12 neq 80
```

Figure 12-4 shows the mapping of the downloadable ACL.

Figure 12-4 *VPN Connection Filter Using Downloadable ACL Using Shared Profile Components*

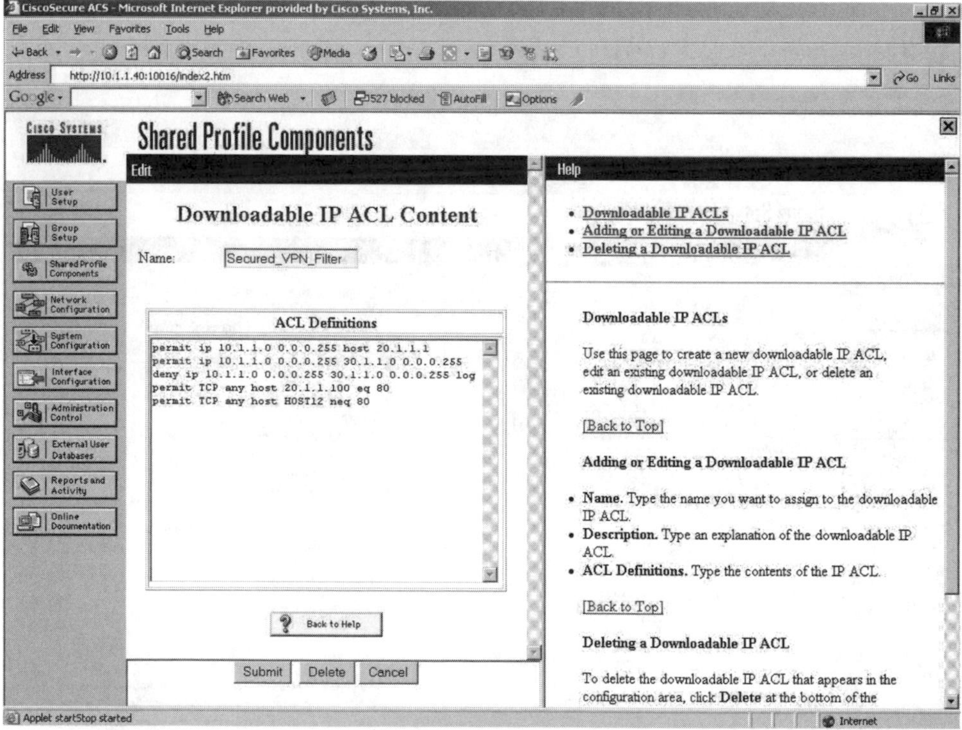

Once the Shared Profile Component for Downloadable IP ACL is created, it needs to be mapped either in a group or user profile under the **Downloadable ACLs** section by checking the **Assign IP ACL** box and selecting the Shared Profile created for Downloadable IP ACL. If you do not see the **Downloadable ACLs** option in the group or user profiles, enable this by going to **Interface Configuration > Advanced Options**. Check **User-Level Downloadable ACLs** or **Group-Level Downloadable ACLs**. Define CS ACS as the RADIUS server on the VPN 3000 Concentrator.

Troubleshooting Steps

The troubleshooting steps and issues discussed in the subsection of "Troubleshooting Steps" under "VPN Concentrator Management Troubleshooting" apply to the troubleshooting steps of this section as well. You need to analyze the ACS Server and the VPN Concentrator log to troubleshoot any failure with authentication. The following are some commonly known reasons for failure:

- **Authentication failure due to wrong groupname**—If your client sends the wrong groupname, you will see a message such as **Remote peer no longer responding** in the VPN client. In the concentrator you may receive the log shown in Example 12-3.

Example 12-3 *Failure with Wrong Group Name*

```
6 03/14/2005 22:23:10.540 SEV=4 IKE/22 RPT=2 10.25.35.228
No Group found matching Common_Group1 for Pre-shared key peer 10.1.1.100
```

- **Authentication failure due to the wrong group password**—On the client, you may receive **Failed to establish secure connection to the security gateway**. In the VPN log, you might see a log similar to that shown in Example 12-4.

Example 12-4 *Failure Due to Wrong Group Password*

```
256 03/14/2005 22:42:02.780 SEV=8 IKEDBG/81 RPT=71 10.1.1.100
RECEIVED Message (msgid=0) with payloads :
HDR + NOTIFY (11) + NONE (0)
total length : 40

258 03/14/2005 22:42:02.780 SEV=4 IKE/0 RPT=16 10.1.1.100
Group [Common_Group]
received an unencrypted packet when crypto active!! Dropping packet.
```

- **Authentication failure due to wrong username or password**—On the client, you may receive this message: **User authentication failed** after giving three options to enter the correct password, but on the concentrator you would receive the log shown in Example 12-5.

Example 12-5 *Failure Due to Wrong User Name*

```
582 03/14/2005 22:31:52.440 SEV=8 AUTHDBG/58 RPT=19
AUTH_Callback(7af0440, 0, 0)

583 03/14/2005 22:31:52.440 SEV=3 AUTH/5 RPT=24 10.1.1.100
Authentication rejected: Reason = Unspecified
handle = 125, server = 10.1.1.40, user = cisco123, domain = <not specified>
```

- **Authentication failure due to group lock**—If the Group Lock feature is enabled on the Group—Common_Group, the user must be part of Common_Group to connect. If the user belongs to a different group such as "Secured_Group," "cisco123" would not connect because it is part of the group named Secure_Group and not part of the group named Common_Group. Authentication would fail with the same message as shown in Example 12-6.

Example 12-6 *Authentication Failure Due to Group Lock*

```
585 03/14/2005 22:32:50.441 SEV=4 IKE/60 RPT=25 10.1.1.100
User [ cisco123 ]
User (cisco123) not member of group (Common_Group), authentication failed.
```

This Troubleshooting section concludes the "Analysis of Problem Areas" section. The next section discusses a case study for the password expiry feature with Windows NT/2000 domain controller integrated with CS ACS.

Case Studies

In this case study, we explore how to configure the password expiry feature with Cisco Secure ACS integrated with the Active Directory for VPN 3000 Concentrator. In this case study, assume that the CS ACS is sitting outside the concentrator, so a filter needs to allow UDP/1645 and UDP/1646 traffic for RADIUS to function correctly.

VPN 3000 Concentrator Configuration

Assume that everything other than Password expiry feature and the VPN 3000 Concentrator have been configured and that the VPN client was connecting without problems before configuring the password expiry feature.

Group Configuration on the VPN 3000 Concentrator

Follow the steps outlined here to configure the group:

Step 1 To configure the group to accept the NT Password Expiration Parameters from the RADIUS Server, go to **Configuration > User Management > Groups**, select your group from the list, and click **Modify Group**. The example that follows shows how to modify a group named ipsecgroup.

Step 2 Go to the **IPsec** tab and make sure that **RADIUS with Expiry** is selected for the **Authentication** attribute.

Step 3 To enable this feature on the VPN 3002 Hardware Clients, go to the HW Client tab, be sure that Require Interactive Hardware Client Authentication is enabled, and then click **Apply**.

Defining the CS ACS RADIUS Server on VPN 3000 Concentrator

Follow the steps outlined here to configure the Radius Server on the VPN Concentrator:

Step 1 To configure the CS ACS RADIUS server settings on the concentrator, go to **Configuration > System > Servers > Authentication > Add**.

Step 2 On the **Add** screen, type in the values that correspond to the CS ACS RADIUS server and click **Add**. In your setup, you are using the following values:

```
Server Type: RADIUS
Authentication Server: 10.1.1.40
Server Port = 0 (for default of 1645)
Timeout = 4
Reties = 2
Server Secret = cisco123
Verify: cisco123
```

CS ACS Windows Configuration

Follow these steps to complete the configuration on the CS ACS Side:

AAA Client Definition for VPN 3000 Concentrator

Step 1 Log in to CS ACS GUI and click **Network Configuration** in the left panel. Under AAA Clients, click **Add Entry**.

Step 2 On the Add AAA Client screen, type the appropriate values to add the concentrator as the RADIUS (Cisco VPN 3000) client, and then click the **Submit + Restart** button.

Step 3 An entry for your 3000 Concentrator displays under the AAA Clients section.

Configuring the Unknown User Policy for Windows NT/2000 Domain Authentication

To configure User Authentication on the RADIUS server as a part of the Unknown User Policy, follow these steps:

Step 1 Click **External User Database** in the left panel, and then click the link for **Database Configuration**.

Step 2 Under External User Database Configuration, click **Windows NT/2000**.

Step 3 On the Database Configuration Creation screen, click **Create New Configuration**.

Step 4 When prompted, type a name for the NT/2000 Authentication and click **Submit**.

Step 5 Click **Configure** to configure the Domain Name for User Authentication.

Step 6 Select your Windows/NT domain from the **Available Domains**, then click the **right-arrow** button to add it to the Domain List. Under MS-CHAP Settings, ensure that the options for **Permit password changes using MS-CHAP version 1** and **version 2** are selected. Click **Submit** when you are finished.

Step 7 Click **External User Database** in the left panel, and then click the link for **Database Group Mappings**. You should see an entry for your previously configured external database.

Step 8 On the Domain Configurations screen, click **New configuration** to add the domain configurations.

Step 9 Select your domain from the list of Detected Domains and click **Submit**.

Step 10 Click on your domain name to configure the group mappings.

Step 11 Click **Add mapping** to define the group mappings.

Step 12 On the Create New Group Mapping screen, map the group on the NT/Windows domain to a group on the CS ACS RADIUS server, and then click **Submit**.

Step 13 Click **External User Database** in the left panel; then click the link for **Unknown User Policy**. Be sure that the option for **Check the following external user database** is selected. Click the **right-arrow** button to move the previously configured external database from the list of **External Databases** to the list of **Selected Databases**.

Testing the NT/RADIUS Password Expiration Feature

Before testing the password expiry, work through the steps that follow to be sure configuration is working for regular test authentication:

Step 1 Go to **Configuration > System > Servers > Authentication**. Select your **RADIUS server** and click **Test**.

Step 2 When prompted, type your **NT/Windows domain user name** and **password**, and then click **OK**.

Step 3 If your authentication is set up properly, you should get a message stating Authentication Successful.

Step 4 If you receive any message other than that shown in the preceding step, there is some configuration or connection problem. Repeat the configuration and testing steps outlined in this document to ensure that all settings were made properly. Also check the IP connectivity between your devices.

Now perform the actual test for password expiry as follows:

Step 1 If the user is already defined on the domain server, modify the properties so that the user is prompted to change the password at the next login. Go to the **Account** tab of the user's properties dialog box, and select the option for **User must change password at next logon**. Then click **OK**.

Step 2 Launch the VPN client, and then try to establish the tunnel to the concentrator.

Step 3 During User Authentication, you should be prompted to change the password.

Common Problems and Resolutions

This section examines some of the commonly found problems and resolutions with the AAA implementation on the VPN 3000 Concentrator, which are not discussed in the preceding sections.

1. Is it possible to have multiple primary Security Dynamics Incorporated (SDI) servers?

   Answer: The VPN 3000 Concentrators are able to download the secret file of only one node at a time. In SDI Version pre-5.0, you can add multiple SDI servers, but they must all share the same node secret file. (Think of it as the primary and backup servers.) In SDI Version 5.0, you can enter only the one primary SDI server (the backup servers are listed in the node secret file) and replica servers.

2. How can I view the user information in the internal user database? It is not visible when I look in the config file.

   Answer: To view users and passwords, go to **Administration > Access Rights > Access Settings**, select **Config File Encryption=None**, and save the config. You should be able to search for the specific user.

3. How many users can the internal database store?

   Answer: The number of users is version-dependent and specified in the **Configuration > User Management** section of the User Guide for your VPN 3000 Concentrator release. A total of 100 users or groups (the sum of users and groups must equal 100 or less) is possible in VPN 3000 Releases 2.2 through 2.5.2. In VPN 3000 Releases 3.0 and later, the number for the 3005 and 3015 Concentrators remains at 100. For the VPN 3030 and 3020 Concentrator, the number is 500. For the VPN 3060 or 3080 Concentrators, the number is 1000. Also, using an external authentication server improves scalability and manageability.

4 Can I use TACACS+ for administrative authentication? What should I keep in mind while I use it?

Answer: Yes, starting in VPN 3000 Concentrator Release 3.0, you can use a TACACS+ for administrative authentication. After you configure TACACS+, make sure you test authentication before you log out. Improper configuration of TACACS+ can lock you out and rectifying the problem requires a console port login in order to disable TACACS+.

5 What do I do when the administrative password is forgotten?

Answer: In versions 2.5.1 and later, connect a PC to the VPN 3000 Concentrator's console port using a straight-through RS-232 serial cable with the PC set for:

- 9600 bits per second
- Eogjt data bits
- No parity
- One stop bit
- Hardware flow control on
- VT100 emulation

Reboot the VPN Concentrator. After the diagnostic check is complete, a line of three dots (...) appears on the console. Press **CTRL-C** within three seconds after these dots appear. A menu displays that lets you reset the system passwords to their defaults.

6 What is the purpose of the group name and group password?

Answer: The group name and group password are used to create a hash which is then used to create a security association.

7 What authentication mechanisms and systems does the Cisco VPN 3000 Concentrator Series support for client PCs?

Answer: AD, NT Domain, RADIUS or RADIUS proxy, RSA Security SecurID (SDI), Digital Certificates, and internal authentication are supported.

Best Practices

The following is the list of best practices to implement for the seamless functioning of AAA implementation on the VPN 3000 series Concentrator:

- If TACACS+ is implemented on the VPN 3000 Concentrator for administration purposes, be sure that you can console into the VPN 3000 Concentrator with the admin user name and password. This is important because it is the only fallback method available if the TACACS+ server is down, or either the VPN 3000 Concentrator or CS ACS is misconfigured.

- Increase the session timeout while configuring TACACS+ for GUI administration authentication. Also, be sure not to close the current session without making sure the authentication works with the Authentication server Test button. It is also highly recommended to open another browser session to perform the login and make sure everything works as expected before closing the current session.
- Use HTTPS (secure HTTPS) instead of HTTP for management purposes.
- Restrict who can access the VPN 3000 Concentrator. By default everything is allowed. To restrict access to specific hosts or networks, go to the **Administration > Access Rights > Access Control List Screen** and define the host or network address with a mask. Also select the Group name of the admin who can access the VPN 3000 Concentrator from the specific host or network defined in this step.

CHAPTER 13

Troubleshooting Cisco Secure ACS on Windows

Cisco Secure Access Control Server, which is known as CS ACS, fills the server-side requirement of the Authentication, Authorization, and Accounting (AAA) client server equation. For many security administrators, the robust and powerful AAA engine, along with CS ACS's ability to flexibly integrate with a number of external user databases, makes the CS ACS software the first and sometimes only choice for an AAA server-side solution. This chapter explores CS ACS in detail and walks you through troubleshooting steps. The chapter focuses on the approach required to troubleshoot any issue efficiently, either with the CS ACS software itself or with the whole AAA process.

Overview of CS ACS

Before delving into the details of how an AAA request from a network access server (NAS) is processed by CS ACS, you need a good understanding of all the components that bring the Cisco Secure ACS into existence.

CS ACS Architecture

As shown in Figure 13-1, Cisco Secure ACS comprises a number of services.

- **CSAdmin**—This service provides the Web interface for administration of Cisco Secure ACS. Although it is possible, and sometimes desirable, to use the Command Line Interface (CLI) for CS ACS configuration, the Graphical User Interface (GUI) is a must because certain attributes may not be configured via CLI. In addition, with the GUI, the administrator has little or no chance to insert bad data, which could lead to database corruption, because the GUI has a sanity check mechanism for user data insertion. The web server used by CS ACS is Cisco proprietary and uses TCP/2002 rather than the standard port 80. Therefore, another web server may be running on the CS ACS server, but this is not recommended because of the security risk and other possible interference.

Figure 13-1 *Diagram of the Relationship Among Cisco Secure ACS Services*

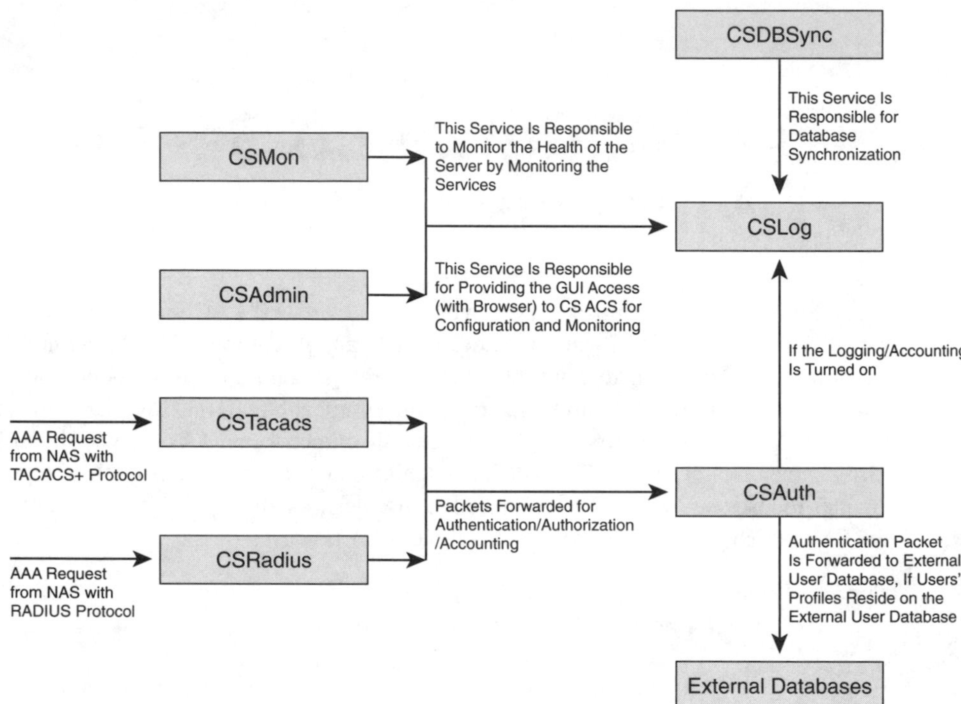

Because CSAdmin service is coded as multi-threaded, it is possible to open multiple sessions from different locations to the CS ACS Server for configuration purposes, but CS ACS does not allow making the same profile or attribute changes by multiple administrators at the same time. For instance, group 200 may not be modified by two administrators at the same time. You need to create an admin account to allow remote access to CS ACS from another machine; you do not need the admin account, however, if you access it from the CS ACS server itself. To bring up the CS ACS GUI from a host other than CS ACS, point to the following location:

```
http://<ip_address_of_CS ACS_server>:2002
```

All the services except CSAdmin can be stopped and restarted from the GUI (**System > Service Control>Stop/Restart**). CSAdmin can be controlled via a Windows Services applet, which can be opened by browsing to **Start > Programs > Administrative Tools > Services applet**.

- **CSAuth**—CSAuth is the heart of CS ACS server, which processes the authentication and authorization requests from the NAS. It also manages the Cisco Secure CS ACS database.
- **CSDBSync**—CSDBSync is the database synchronization service, which allows the CS ACS database to be in sync with third-party relational database management system (RDBMS) systems. This feature is very useful when an organization has multiple data feed locations.

- **CSLog**—This is a logging service for audit-trailing, accounting of authentication, and authorization packets. CSLog collects data from the CSTacacs or CSRadius packet and CSAuth, and then scrubs the data so that data can be stored into comma-separated value (CSV) files or forwarded to an Open DataBase Connectivity (ODBC)-compliant database.
- **CSMon**—CSMon service is responsible for the monitoring, recording, and notification of Cisco Secure CS ACS performance, and includes automatic response to some scenarios. For instance, if either Terminal Access Controller Access Control System (TACACS+) or Remote Authentication Dial-In User Service (RADIUS) service dies, CS ACS by default restarts all the services, unless otherwise configured. Monitoring includes monitoring the overall status of Cisco Secure ACS and the system on which it is running. CSMon actively monitors three basic sets of system parameters:
  - **Generic host system state**—monitors disk space, processor utilization, and memory utilization.
  - **Application-specific performance**—periodically performs a test login each minute using a special built-in test account by default.
  - **System resource consumption by Cisco Secure ACS**—CSMon periodically monitors and records the usage by Cisco Secure ACS of a small set of key system resources. Handles counts, memory utilization, processor utilization, thread used, and failed log-on attempts, and compares these to predetermined thresholds for indications of atypical behavior.

  CSMon works with CSAuth to keep track of user accounts that are disabled for exceeding their failed attempts count maximum. If configured, CSMon provides immediate warning of brute force attacks by alerting the administrator that a large number of accounts have been disabled.

  By default CSMon records exception events in logs both in the CSV file and Windows Event Log that you can use to diagnose problems. Optionally you can configure event notification via e-mail so that notification for exception events and outcomes includes the current state of Cisco Secure ACS at the time of the message transmission. The default notification method is simple mail-transfer protocol (SMTP) e-mail, but you can create scripts to enable other methods. However, if the event is a failure, CSMon takes the actions that are hard-coded when the triggering event is detected. Running the CSSupport utility, which captures most of the parameters dealing with the state of the system at the time of the event, is one such example. If the event is a warning event, it is logged, the administrator is notified if it is configured, and no further action is taken. After a sequence of re-tries, CSMon also attempts to fix the cause of the failure and individual service restarts. It is possible to integrate custom-defined action with CSMon service, so that a user-defined action can be taken based on specific events.

- **CSTacacs**—The CSTacacs service is the communication bridge between the NAS and the CSAuth service. This service listens on TCP/49 for any connection from NAS. For security reasons, the NAS identity (IP) must be defined as an AAA client with a shared secret key, so that CS ACS accepts only a valid NAS.
- **CSRadius**—CSRadius service serves the same purpose as CSTacacs service, except that it serves the RADIUS protocol. CSRadius service listens on UDP/1645 and UDP/1812 for authentication and authorization packets. For accounting, it listens on both UDP/1646 and UDP/1813 so that NAS can communicate on either port. However, it is recommended to use UDP/1812 and 1813 because UDP/1645 and 1646 are standard ports for other applications.

The Cisco Secure ACS information is located in the following Windows Registry key as shown in Figure 13-2:

```
HKEY_LOCAL_MACHINE\SOFTWARE\CISCO
```

Figure 13-2 *Cisco Secure ACS Registries Location*

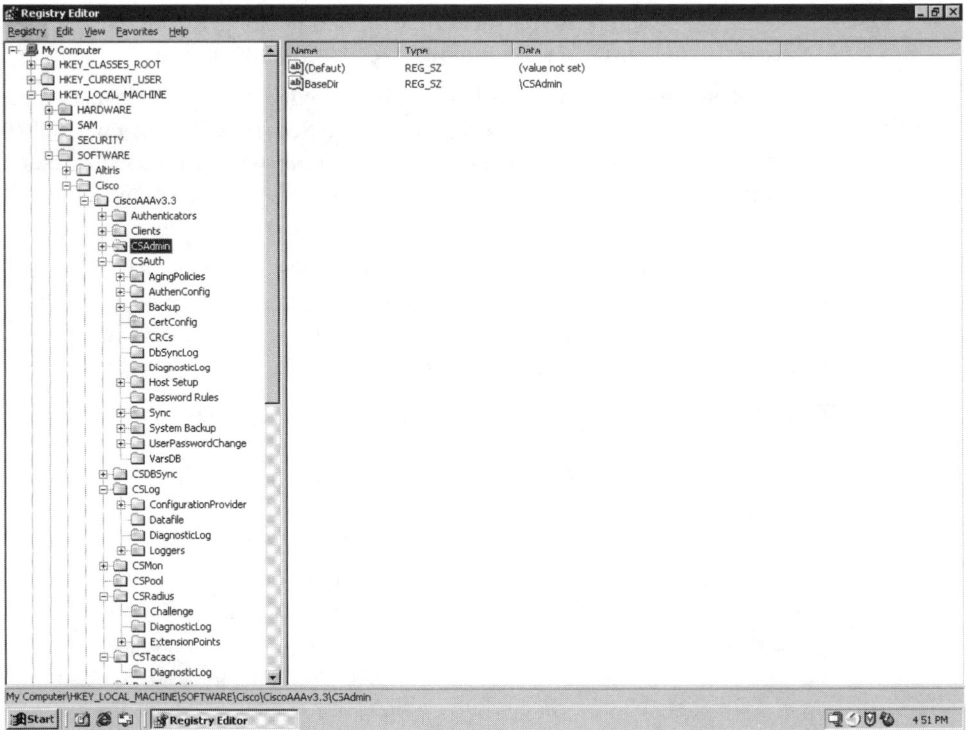

You can get to the screen shown in Figure 13-2 by browsing **Start>Run>Type** and entering "regedit" in the text box. Do not make any changes to Windows Registry settings related to CS ACS unless advised by a Cisco representative, as you may inadvertently corrupt your application. This chapter explains where the Registry entry should be added or modified.

The Life of an AAA Packet in CS ACS

This section builds on the knowledge that you have gained from the preceding section, to examine the life of an AAA packet within CS ACS when it hits the CS ACS server. When the packet reaches the CS ACS, the following events occur:

1. NAS interacts with CS ACS Server using CSTacacs or CSRadius Services. So, CSTacacs or CSRadius service receives the packet from the NAS.
2. Then NAS checking is performed with the IP address and shared secret and if successful, then CSTacacs or CSRadius performs the Network Access Restrictions (NAR) checking. If CSTacacs or CSRadius decides that it is a valid packet and passes the NAR test, the packet goes to the CSAuth Service.
3. The CSAuth checks the Proxy Distribution table and finds out if there is any matching string for the username in the Character String Column of the Proxy Distribution Table. If there is a match, and AAA proxy information is defined, then the authentication request is forwarded to the appropriate AAA server, and CS ACS at this stage acts as a middle man for AAA services. However, if there is no matching string found, ACS Local database performs the AAA services as described in the next step.
4. The CSAuth service looks up the user's information in its own internal database and if the user exists, it either allows or denies access based on password and other parameters. This status information, and any authorization parameters, are sent to the CSTacacs or CSRadius service, which then forwards the status information to the NAS.
5. If the user does not exist in the CS ACS local database, CS ACS marks that user as unknown and checks for an unknown user policy. If the unknown user policy is to fail the user, CS ACS fails the user. Otherwise, if external database is configured, CS ACS forwards that information to the configured external user database. Cisco Secure CS ACS tries each external user database until the user succeeds or fails.
6. If the authentication is successful, the user information goes into the cache of CS ACS, which has a pointer for using the external user database. This user is known as a dynamic user.
7. The next time the dynamic user tries to authenticate, Cisco Secure ACS authenticates the user against the database that was successful the first time. These cached user entries are used to speed up the authentication process. Dynamic users are treated in the same way as known users.
8. If the unknown user fails authentication with all configured external databases, the user is not added to the Cisco Secure user database and the authentication fails.
9. When a user is authenticated, Cisco Secure ACS obtains a set of authorizations from the user profile and the group to which the user is assigned. This information is stored with the username in the Cisco Secure user database. Some of the authorizations included are the services to which the user is entitled, such as IP over Point-to-Point Protocol (PPP), IP pools from which to draw an IP address, access lists, and password-aging information.

10 The authorizations, with the approval of authentication, are then passed to the CSTacacs or CSRadius modules to be forwarded to the requesting device.

11 If configured on the NAS, accounting starts right after the successful user authentication. Accounting can be configured for authorization as well. A **START** record from NAS is sent which follows the same paths as authentication requests on CS ACS with the addition of **CSLog** service involvement. For instance, if the radius protocol is used, packets go through **CSRadius** service first, then **CSAuth**. **CSAuth** then forwards the packet to the **CSLog** service. **CSLog** service decides if the accounting requests should be forwarded to another AAA server based on the Proxy Distribution Table, or should be processed locally. Additionally, if ODBC logging is configured for accounting, the packet is forwarded to the ODBC database. The same path is followed for the **STOP** record from the NAS, which completes the accounting record for a specific session.

CS ACS can integrate with a number of external user databases. Table 13-1 shows the components that are needed to integrate with those external user databases.

Table 13-1 *Components Needed to Integrate with External Databases*

External Database	What CS ACS Uses to Communicate to the External Database
NT/2K & Generic LDAP	CS ACS and OS contain all the files needed. No extra files required.
Novell Netware Directory Service (NDS)	NDS client.
ODBC	Windows ODBC and third party ODBC driver.
Token Server	Client software provided by vendor.
Radius Token Server	Use RADIUS interface.

CS ACS can be integrated with many external user databases; however, not every database supports every authentication protocol. Table 13-2 shows the protocols supported for specific databases.

Table 13-2 *Protocols Supported on Various Databases*

	ASCII	PAP	CHAP	ARAP	MS CHAP v.1	MS CHAP v.2	LEAP	EAP-MD5	EAP-TLS
CS ACS Local Database	Yes	Yes	Yes	Yes	Yes	Yes	Yes	Yes	Yes
Windows SAM	Yes	Yes	No	No	Yes	Yes	Yes	No	No
Windows AD	Yes	Yes	No	No	Yes	Yes	Yes	No	Yes
Novell NDS	Yes	Yes	No	No	No	No	No	No	No
LDAP	Yes	Yes	No	No	No	No	No	No	Yes

Table 13-2 *Protocols Supported on Various Databases (Continued)*

	ASCII	PAP	CHAP	ARAP	MS CHAP v.1	MS CHAP v.2	LEAP	EAP-MD5	EAP-TLS
ODBC	Yes	Yes	Yes	Yes	Yes	Yes	Yes	No	No
LEAP Proxy RADIUS	No	No	No	No	Yes	No	Yes	No	No
Active Card	Yes	Yes	No	No	No	No	No	No	No
Crypto Card	Yes	Yes	No	No	No	No	No	No	No
RADIUS Token Server	Yes	Yes	No	No	No	No	No	No	No
VASCO	Yes	Yes	No	No	No	No	No	No	No
Axent	Yes	Yes	No	No	No	No	No	No	No
RSA	Yes	Yes	No	No	No	No	No	No	No
SafeWord	Yes	Yes	No	No	No	No	No	No	No

Diagnostic Commands and Tools

Cisco Secure ACS has extensive logging capability that allows an administrator to troubleshoot any issue pertaining to CS ACS Server itself (for example, replication) or an AAA requests problem (for example, an authentication problem) from NAS. This section explores these tools and how to use them efficiently.

Reports and Activity (Real-time Troubleshooting)

The **Failed Attempts** log under the **Reports and Activity** from the GUI is the quickest and best way to find out the reasons for authentication failure. **Failed Attempts** logs are turned on by default. However, if you want to add additional fields to the Default, you may by browsing to **System Configuration > Logging > CSV Failed Attempts**. In the **CSV Failed Attempts File Configuration** page, move desired attributes from **Attributes** to **Logged Attributes**. Then click on **Submit**. These additional attributes are shown under **Reports and Activity**. Occasionally, you might need to look at the **Passed Authentications** to troubleshoot authorization or NAS Access Restriction (NAR) issues. By default, the **Passed Authentication** log is not turned on. To turn it on, go to **System Configuration > Logging > CSV Passed Authentications,** and check **Log to CSV Passed Authentications report** under **Enable Logging**. There are other logs available for different services. For instance, for replication issues, there is a corresponding CSV file called **Database Replication** under **Reports and Activity**.

Radtest and Tactest

These tools are available to simulate AAA requests from the CS ACS server itself, which eliminates any possibilities of NAS configuration issues. This is especially important for troubleshooting the authentication issues with external user database authentication, for example, Microsoft Active Directory (AD) or Secure ID server. These tools are installed as part of CS ACS installation and located at **C:\Program Files\CiscoSecure ACS v3.3\Utils>**. More details on how to run these tools can be found at the following location: http://www.cisco.com/en/US/products/sw/secursw/ps2086/products_tech_note09186a00800afec1.shtml#auth_of

Package.cab File

Package.cab is the result of execution of the CSSupport utility, which includes all the log files for every service that we have discussed in the section entitled "CS ACS Architecture." Before running the CSSupport utility as shown in the paragraphs that follow, to capture the debug level logging, be sure to collect the "FULL" logging (on CS ACS, **System Configuration > Service Control > Level of detail > Choose FULL > Restart**). This is shown in Figure 13-3. Also be sure to check Manage Directory and set the appropriate option.

Figure 13-3 *Turning on Full Logging on CS ACS*

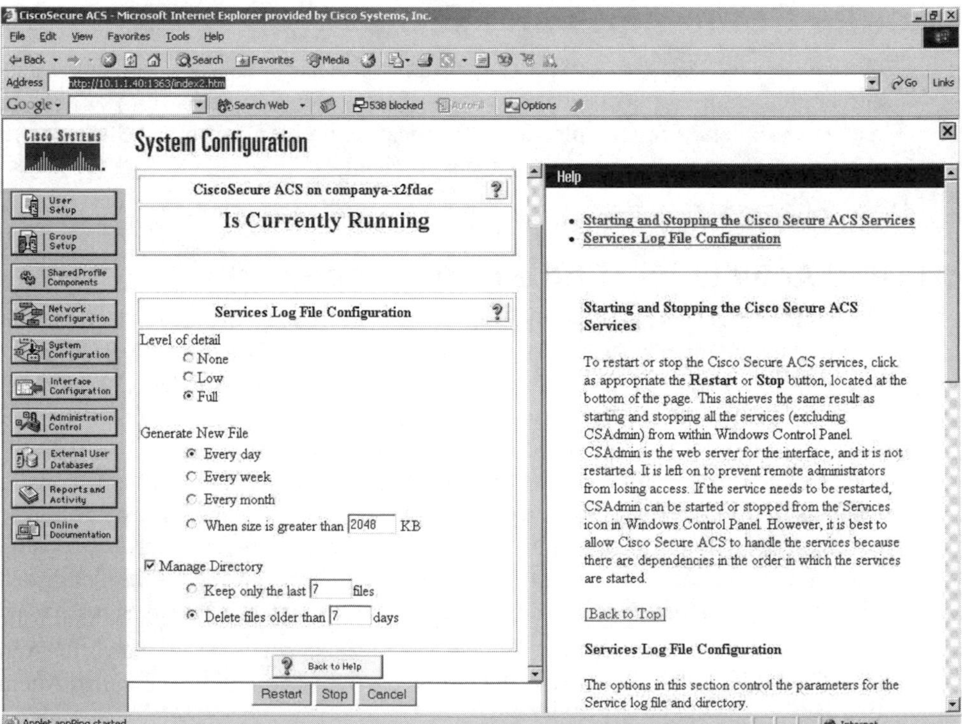

Once you set up the logging level to "FULL", run a few tests that are sure to fail and then run cssupport.exe as shown below:

```
C:\Program Files\CiscoSecure ACS v3.3\utils\CSSupport.exe
```

The Package.cab file contains a good deal of meaningful information, but the amount of information may be overwhelming. So, being able to read the file efficiently is a key to success in isolating issues from the Package.cab file logs. Before getting into any more detail, you need to understand what goes into the makings of the package.cab file. Figure 13-4 shows the unzipped version of package.cab with a listing of files (icons are arranged by type).

Figure 13-4 *Listing of Files in package.cab*

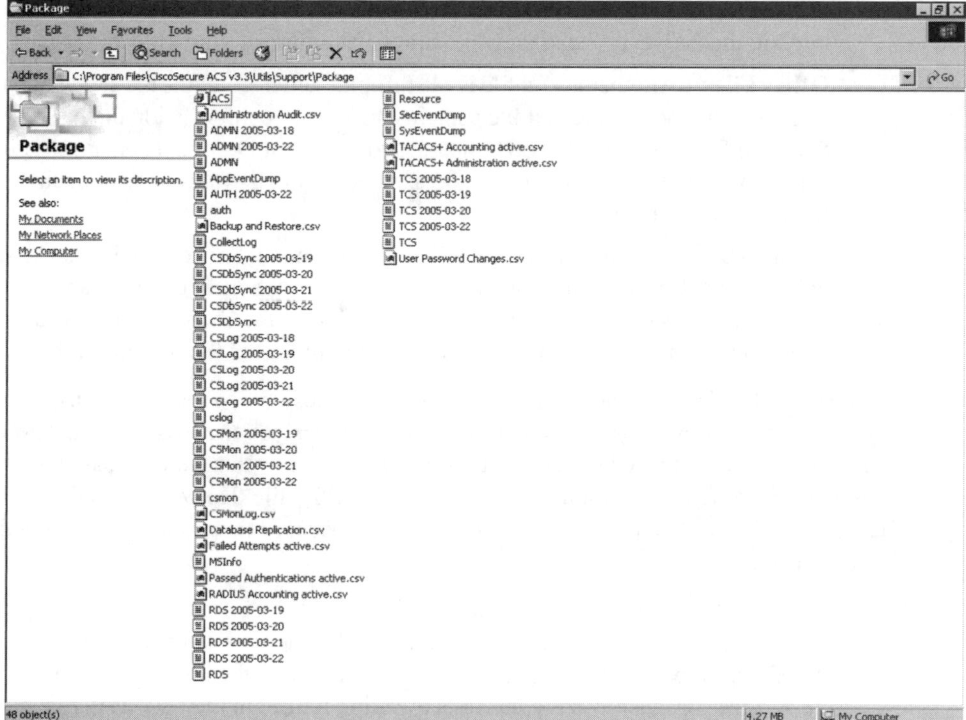

The following are short descriptions of the files of package.cab:

- **CSV Files**—CSV files contain the information about Audit log, Accounting, and Failed and Passed Authentication. Most of the files contain statistics, but to troubleshoot issues, Failed and Passed Authentication files are often used in conjunction with the log files that are discussed in the paragraphs that follow. The CSV files are created every day. Each file name without the date is the Active file. So, Failed Attempts active.csv is the active file, which stores the Failed Attempts information from the NAS.

- **Log Files**—Every service discussed in the "CS ACS Architecture" section of this chapter has a corresponding log file. These files contain extensive logs about each and every service. For instance, auth.log contains all the current log information of CSAuth service. Just like CSV files, log files are created every day and the active log file is the one without the date in its name.
- **User Database Files**—Three files go into making the CS ACS database. These files are **user.dat**, **user.idx**, and **varsdb.mdb**. You should *not* manipulate these files. Unless otherwise requested by Cisco, capturing these files is not necessary when running the CSSupport.exe utility.
- **Registry File**—ACS.reg contains the Registry information of the CS ACS Server. Substantial CS ACS configuration (for example, NAS) goes into the Windows Registry. So, reading this file may be required for some troubleshooting. Do not import this file into another server; instead, open it with a text editor of your choice.
- **Other Files**—Another useful file is MSInfo.txt, which contains the server and the OS information. The resource.txt file contains the resource information on the server, and SecEventDump.txt, AppEventDump.txt, and SysEventDump.txt contain an additional event dump on the server that may be used occasionally to troubleshoot any issues with the server itself.

As mentioned before, reading these files efficiently to isolate the problem is a key to success in troubleshooting CS ACS. To illustrate how to analyze the files, examine an example. The example assumes that a regular login authentication by the CS ACS Server is failing. The NAS debug does not give any conclusive output that indicates the reason for the failure.

To analyze this, first look at the Failed Attempts active.csv file to see why the user is failing. Quite often the information obtained from this file gives you the reason, so that no further analysis is needed; however, that's not always the case. For this example, assume that you have no conclusive reason for failure from the CSV file. However, you do have the username. The next step is to analyze the auth.log, because that contains more detailed information.

So, you search the username in the auth.log file. In this case, unfortunately, you receive no results from the search based on that username. So there must be a problem. It could be that CSTacacs service cannot process and forward the authentication request to the CSAuth service. Because you see the authentication failure in the Failed Attempts log, the authentication request must be reaching the CS ACS, and the first service that receives that packet is the CSTacacs, as the communication protocol configured between NAS and CS ACS is TACACS+. So, you need to analyze the TCS.log file, which contains all the activities that CSTacacs performs. As expected, you see the user request coming from the NAS. However, the user request is not being forwarded to the CSAuth service. After a little investigation, we find that NAR is configured for this user and, hence, packets are being dropped by the CSTacacs service; therefore, they are not being forwarded to the CSAuth service. Hence, you do not see the user in the auth.log. For every AAA request failure, you must look at the Failed Attempt first, and then search for the username in the auth.log. If an additional detail is needed, you need to analyze either the TCS.log or the RDS.log. Note that both CSTacacs and CSRadius form the communication bridge between the NAS and CS ACS, and CSAuth is the communication bridge between the CSTacacs/CSRadius and any external user databases such as Active Directory, NDS, and so on.

Categorization of Problem Areas

The problem areas of CS ACS can be categorized as follows:

- Installation and upgrade issues
- CS ACS with Active Directory integration
- CS ACS with Novell NDS integration
- CS ACS with ACE Server (Secure ID [SDI]) integration
- Replication issues
- Network access restrictions (NAR) issues
- Downloadable ACL issues

Installation and Upgrade Issues

If you follow the procedure properly, installation or upgrade is a fairly easy process for both CS ACS on Windows and CS ACS Appliance. This section examines the installation and upgrade procedure, important issues to be aware of, things that may go wrong, and how to resolve the problems.

CS ACS on Windows Platform

Depending on the version of CS ACS that needs to be installed, check the following documentation to make sure all the minimum requirements for the Operating System version, Service Packs (SPs), and so on, are met. Otherwise, abnormal failure might occur that might not be diagnosed or supported by Cisco TAC unless the documented minimum requirement is fulfilled.

http://www.cisco.com/warp/public/480/csnt.html

Installation steps are intuitive, and therefore they are not covered here.

Upgrading from an older to a new version is a little more complex than installing a new version. However, if you work through the following steps carefully, you can minimize the chance of upgrade failure substantially:

Step 1 Review the prerequisites for installation of the version that you are trying to upgrade. If you must perform an incremental upgrade, for instance, from CS ACS 2.3 on NT platform to CS ACS 3.3 on Win 2K platform, define the strategy.

Step 2 Back up the database using C:\Program Files\CiscoSecure ACS v3.3\Utils>**CSUtil -b** (full backup including NAS information) and C:\Program Files\CiscoSecure ACS v3.3\Utils>**CSUtil -d** (partial backup, only users/groups information) options, and save the files offline in a different location.

Step 3 Run the **setup.exe** file of the new version.

Step 4 If the standard upgrade procedure in Step 3 fails, run the uninstall shield or uninstaller from the control panel, and choose the option during uninstall to keep the old database. Then install the new version. These procedures should find the information saved by the uninstall procedure and import it.

Step 5 If Step 4 fails, chances are very high that your Registry has been corrupted. If so, uninstall the CS ACS completely, and run the **clean.exe** files, which come in the CS ACS CD. These files will clean up the Registry. Then proceed with the installation. In the newer version (for instance, CS ACS 3.3), the Clean utility comes as **setup.exe** within the **Clean** directory, which is in the **ACS Utilities\Support** directory of the installation CD.

Step 6 If all the services started on the newer version, import the **dump.txt** that you have created in Step 2 with the **csutil -d** option, which contains only the user and group information. You still need to define the NASs. If there is a small number of NASs, this may work.

Step 7 If you have a large number of NASs, build another server with a version that runs the old version of code and import the database that is created in Step 2 with the **csutil -b** option, which includes the whole database that has the NAS information in it. Then follow Steps 2–6.

You should be aware of the following important facts if you are trying to upgrade one of the older CS ACS versions or from the trial version:

- The minimum CS ACS version requirement to run on the Windows platform is CS ACS 2.5.
- If you are upgrading CS ACS from 2.3 on a Windows NT platform to CS ACS 3.3 on the Windows 2000 platform, be sure to upgrade to CS ACS 2.6 on the NT platform first, and be sure the database upgraded and data migrated properly. As CS ACS 2.6 can run on Windows 2000, upgrade the OS of your CS ACS server to Windows 2000 after ensuring that the service packs and other prerequisites are fulfilled, and, finally, upgrade to the target version of CS ACS, which is CS ACS 3.3.
- If you are running a trial version, to migrate that version to production, just upgrade or install the production CS ACS version on top of the trial version. For example, you can install the CS ACS 3.1 production version over the CS ACS 2.6 trial version, or install the CS ACS 3.3 production version over the CS ACS 3.3 trial version.

CS ACS installation or upgrade may fail for the following reasons:

- Running an unsupported version of OS, service pack (SP), or browser.
- CS ACS services are crashing.

  If you are running a supported browser and service pack but CS ACS is still crashing, upgrade to the latest build of the CS ACS release that you are running. There may be a bug that has been fixed in the latest build of that release. If you are running the latest release, provide Cisco TAC with the package.cab file or, at least, run **drwtsn32** in a DOS prompt, with the following box checked: Dump Symbol Table.

CS ACS with Active Directory Integration

To integrate with the Active Directory, Cisco Secure ACS can be installed in one of the following modes:

- **Standalone Server**—If CS ACS is installed on a standalone server, CS ACS can authenticate Windows users only against the local SAM database.
- **Domain Controller**—If CS ACS is installed on a Primary Domain Controller (PDC) or Backup Domain Controller (BDC), it will be able to authenticate Windows users who are defined in any trusted domain.
- **Member Server**—CS ACS on a member server will also authenticate users defined in any trusted domains. However, lack of permissions could cause issues with domain lists, authentication, and Remote Access Service (RAS) flag fetching.

Cisco Secure ACS services run under the local system account on the server. The local system account has almost the same privileges as the administrator.

When a new external WindowsNT/2000 database is defined on CS ACS, CS ACS fetches the list of domains trusted by the domain of the computer where the server is installed. CS ACS fetches the list of trusted domains only to populate it to Java control. The user can add domains manually as well. CS ACS uses the list of enumerated domains to determine the order in which they will be checked when an external authentication is presented.

When a new mapping between Windows NT/2000 user groups and Cisco Secure ACS user group is defined, CS ACS obtains and displays the list of the user groups defined in the selected Windows domain.

When a windows user is being authenticated, CS ACS uses Microsoft's Network Logon on behalf of the user to verify the user's credentials. This is a noninteractive login, as opposed to a desktop login.

CS ACS fetches the following information about that user:

- List of user groups to which the user belongs.
- Callback flag.

Values are set on the MS user definition page, which includes Admin set phone #, and user set (send by the client during authentication).

- Dialin permission (RAS flag).
- Password status.
- Microsoft Point-to-Point Encryption (MPPE) keys (there are two, a 56-bit and 128-bit key).

Until CS ACS version 3.0, there were no "hooks" into the Security Accounts Manager (SAM) database to change the password through CS ACS. CS ACS 3.0 uses an API to change MS-CHAP passwords, but the MS-CHAPv2 protocol must be supported end-to-end.

Table 13-3 shows the trust relationship for CS ACS with the domain controller when the CS ACS is on the member server of Domain A.

Table 13-3 *Trust Relationship of CS ACS and Windows Domain Controller When CS ACS Is on a Member Server of Domain A*

Task	Trust Direction	Description
Fetch list of domains trusted by Domain A.	A trusts other domains.	The list includes domains trusted by A.
Fetch list of user groups from a trusted Domain B.	B trusts A.	CS ACS reads information (accesses resources) on Domain B.
Authenticate a user with account on Domain B.	A trusts B.	CS ACS performs the network logon with user name. The user with an account on Domain B is going to access a computer in Domain A.
Fetch information (callback, and so on) on user with account on Domain B.	B trusts A.	CS ACS reads information (accesses resources) on Domain B.
Change password of a user with account on Domain B (CS ACS v3.0).	B trusts A.	CS ACS changes information (Access ressources) on Domain B.

Configuration Steps

The following steps are required to integrate CS ACS with the domain controller:

On the domain controller serving the CS ACS server follow these steps:

Step 1 Create a user.

Step 2 Make the user hard to hack by giving it a very long, complicated password.

Step 3 Make the user a member of the Domain Administrator group.

Step 4 Make the user a member of the Administrators group.

On the Windows 2000 server running CS ACS, follow these steps:

Step 1 Add a new user to the proper local group. Go to **Start > Settings > Control Panel > Administrative Tools > Computer Management**. Open **Local Users and Groups** and then **Groups**. Double-click the **Administrators** group. Click **Add**. Choose the domain from the **Look in** box. Double-click the user created earlier to add it. Click **OK**.

Step 2 Give the new user special rights on CS ACS server. Go to **Start > Settings > Control Panel > Administrative Tools > Local Security Policy > Local Policies**. Open **User Rights Assignment**. Double-click on **Act as part of the operating system**. Click **Add**. Choose the domain from the **Look in** box. Double-click the user created earlier to add it. Click **OK**. Double-click **Log on as a service**. Click **Add**. Choose the domain from the **Look in** box. Double-click the user created earlier to add it. Click **OK**.

Step 3 Set the CS ACS services to run as the created user. Open **Start > Settings > Control Panel > Administrative Tools > Services**. Double-click the **CSADMIN** entry. Click the **Log On** tab. Click **This Account** and then the **Browse** button. Choose the domain, and double-click the user created earlier. Click **OK**. Repeat for the remainder of the CS services.

Step 4 Wait for Windows to apply the security policy changes, or reboot the server. If you rebooted the server, skip the rest of these instructions. Otherwise, stop and then start the **CSADMIN** service. Open the CS ACS GUI. Click on **System Config**. Click on **Service Control**. Click **Restart**.

NOTE If the Domain Security Policy is set to override settings for "Act as part of the operating system" and "Log on as a service" rights, the user rights changes listed in the previous steps also need to be made there.

Troubleshooting Steps

This section discusses some of the common issues that you may run into when integrating with Active Directory.

Windows Group to CS ACS Group Mapping Problems

During Configuring of Group mapping, the user sees a pop-up window. If you are having problems with Group mapping, you may see the following message:

```
Failed to enumerate Windows groups. If you are using AD consult the installation
guide for information
```

Possible causes of the problems are as follows:

- **CS ACS services do not have privileges to execute the NetGroupEnum function**—Refer to Configuration steps discussed for "CS ACS with Active Directory Integration" in the preceding section to correct the permission issue.
- **NetBIOS over Transmission Control Protocol (TCP) is not enabled**—NetBIOS over TCP must be enabled; otherwise, group mapping will fail.
- **Domain Name System (DNS) is not working correctly**—You may try to reregister DNS with commands: "ipconfig/flushdns" then "ipconfig/registerdns" at the DOS prompt.
- **Remote Procedure Call (RPC) is not working correctly (for example, after applying the blaster patch)**—In that case, consult with Microsoft.
- **Domain Controller (DCs) are not time-synchronized**—Run the command net time /Domain: <DomainName> to synchronize time.
- **Different service packs**—If you run different SPs on different DCs, you may run into this problem. Apply the same patch to fix the problem.
- **NetLogon Services are not running**—NetLogon Services must up and running on all DCs.
- **Check that no firewall (FW) packet filters are installed**—If there is a packet-filtering firewall installed, be sure to select **Yes** on DNS properties to "allow dynamic updates".

CS ACS Maps User to Wrong Group of CS ACS (Default Group)

After successful user authentication based on the group mapping configuration, the user is mapped to a specific CS ACS group. The following list summarizes some of the reasons why the user may be mapped to the wrong CS ACS group:

- **Misconfiguration of group mapping**—If the user belongs to both group X and group Y, CS ACS assigns the user according to the order in which the user was configured.
- **Service accounts under which CS ACS services are running do not have permission to validate groups for another user**—Log in as user, under the CS ACS services that are running. Check if you have access to get the groups of another user.

CS ACS with Novell NDS Integration

This section works through the configuration steps that lead in turn to sections that cover troubleshooting steps.

Configuration Steps

Use the following steps to configure an NDS database with CS ACS on Windows.

Step 1 Consult with your Novell NetWare administrator to get administrator context information for CS ACS and the names of the Tree, Container, and Context details.

Step 2 On CS ACS, click on **External User Databases > Database Configuration > Novell NDS > Configure**.

Step 3 In the **Novell NDS** configuration window, enter a name for the configuration. This is for information purposes only.

Step 4 Enter the **Tree name**.

Step 5 Enter the full **Context List**, with items separated by dots(.). You can enter more than one context list. If you do, separate the lists with a comma and space. For example, if your Organization is Corporation, your Organization Name is Chicago, and you want to enter two Context names, Marketing and Engineering, you would enter**: Engineering.Chicago. Corporation**, **Marketing.Chicago.Corporation**. You do not need to add users in the Context List.

Step 6 Click **Submit**. Changes take effect immediately; you do not need to restart the Cisco Secure ACS.

Caution If you click **Delete**, your NDS database is deleted.

Step 7 Then perform the Group Mappings (between the Novell NDS Database Groups and CS ACS Groups) by browsing to **External User Databases > Database Group Mappings > Novell NDS.**

Step 8 Finally, configure the unknown user policy by selecting **Check the following external user databases** and moving the **Novell NDS** database from the **External Databases** to the **Selected Databases** text box on the **External User Databases > Unknown User Policy** page.

Troubleshooting Steps

You can isolate any problem that you may have with the troubleshooting steps in the sections that follow.

Novell Client Is Not Installed

You must install the Novell client on the CS ACS server, so that CS ACS can talk to the Novell NDS database. If you do not have the Novell client installed on the CS ACS, and you try to configure Novell NDS database settings from the **External User Database > Database Configuration > Novel NDS**, you will receive an error message similar to the following:

```
An error has occurred while processing the External Database Configuration Page
because of an internal error..
```

Revise the Configuration on CS ACS

Most of the time, the Novell NDS authentication failure is caused by misconfiguration. Therefore, check to see if the tree name, context, and container name are all specified correctly. Start with one container in which users are present; later more containers can be added if needed.

Check Admin Username

Check the admin username to be sure it is correct, and that you have defined a fully qualified path. For example, instead of admin, define admin.cisco, as the latter is a fully qualified name.

Example 13-1 shows the incorrect provision of admin credentials.

Example 13-1 *Incorrect Admin Credentials*

```
AUTH 03/22/2005 10:40:21 I 0360 0676 External DB [NDSAuth.dll]: Tree 224462640 could
not log in with admin credentials supplied
```

Perform Group Mapping

Performing Group Mapping is an excellent test to ensure the admin context can connect and pull the group information from the Novell NDS database. Therefore, if you are unable to map groups, the admin user does not have permission to list the groups. Under that circumstance, check that the admin can list users in the other domain. One way to verify that is as follows: on the CS ACS Server, using Nwadmin, examine the groups from the other domain. If you cannot do so, consult with the Novell administrator.

Authentication Failure with a Bad Password

Before looking at authentication that has failed either due to the wrong username or a bad password, it's extremely important to understand and be familiar with the sequence of events that occur within CS ACS with Novell NDS authentication. Therefore, closely observe the successful user authentication log shown in Example 13-2.

Example 13-2 *Successful User Authentication Against NDS Database*

```
AUTH 03/22/2005 12:20:56 I 5081 1764 Start RQ1026, client 2 (127.0.0.1)
! As the user doesn't exist on the local database, CS ACS is tagging this as unknown user
AUTH 03/22/2005 12:20:56 I 4683 1764 Attempting authentication for Unknown User
'cisco'
! The following two lines indicate that Novell NDS is configured to this user
! authentication. This is being done by selecting Novell NDS database for Unknown User
! Policy
AUTH 03/22/2005 12:20:56 I 1280 1764 ReadSupplierRegistry: Novell NDS loaded
```

Example 13-2 *Successful User Authentication Against NDS Database (Continued)*

```
AUTH 03/22/2005 12:20:56 I 0863 1764 pvAuthenticateUser: authenticate 'cisco'
against Novell NDS
! Following lines indicate that CS ACS is trying to lock a thread for this user
! Authentication.
AUTH 03/22/2005 12:20:56 I 0360 1764 External DB [NDSAuth.dll]: User cisco waiting
for lock
AUTH 03/22/2005 12:20:56 I 0360 1764 External DB [NDSAuth.dll]: User cisco waiting
in lock
! A new thread is getting initialized here for the user authentication under ndstest
tree
AUTH 03/22/2005 12:20:56 I 0360 1764 External DB [NDSAuth.dll]: Initializing thread
0 for tree ndstest
AUTH 03/22/2005 12:20:56 I 0360 0472 External DB [NDSAuth.dll]: Starting Thread 0
! The following two lines indicate that the user authentication is under works
AUTH 03/22/2005 12:20:56 I 0360 0472 External DB [NDSAuth.dll]: Thread 0 for tree
ndstest Waiting for work
AUTH 03/22/2005 12:20:56 I 0360 0472 External DB [NDSAuth.dll]: Thread 0 for tree
ndstest Got work
! This is where the user is authenticated.
AUTH 03/22/2005 12:20:56 I 0360 0472 External DB [NDSAuth.dll]: Authenticated
cisco.OU=SJ.TESTING.LAB, Response 0
AUTH 03/22/2005 12:20:56 I 0360 1764 External DB [NDSAuth.dll]: Back from Wait for
user cisco with code 0
AUTH 03/22/2005 12:20:56 I 0360 1764 External DB [NDSAuth.dll]: Response 0 from
successful Tree ndstest
AUTH 03/22/2005 12:20:56 I 0360 0472 External DB [NDSAuth.dll]: Response 0 from Tree
ndstest
AUTH 03/22/2005 12:20:56 I 0360 0472 External DB [NDSAuth.dll]: Thread 0 for tree
ndstest Waiting for work
! Following three lines indicates that the group mappings between Novell NDS and CS ACS
! are successful. Third line in particular indicates that user is mapped to CS ACS Group
! number 150.
AUTH 03/22/2005 12:20:56 I 0360 1764 External DB [NDSAuth.dll]: Added
'sj_acs.SJ.testing.LAB' to Group List for user: cisco.OU=SJ.TESTING.LAB
AUTH 03/22/2005 12:20:56 I 0360 1764 External DB [NDSAuth.dll]: There were 1 Groups
for this user: cisco.OU=SJ.TESTING.LAB
AUTH 03/22/2005 12:20:56 I 0360 1764 External DB [NDSAuth.dll]: User cisco
authenticated into group 150
AUTH 03/22/2005 12:20:56 I 0360 1764 External DB [NDSAuth.dll]: User cisco out from lock
AUTH 03/22/2005 12:20:56 I 3421 1764 User cisco password type changed
AUTH 03/22/2005 12:20:56 I 1586 1764 User cisco feature flags changed
AUTH 03/22/2005 12:20:56 I 1586 1764 User cisco feature flags changed
AUTH 03/22/2005 12:20:56 I 5081 1764 Done RQ1026, client 2, status 0
```

As mentioned before, it is extremely important to understand the sequence of events that occur with a successful user authentication as shown in Example 13-2, before you can analyze and find the cause of failure for a bad user password. With the knowledge gained from Example 13-2, examine example 13-3, which shows failed authentication due to a bad password.

Example 13-3 *Shows a Failed Authentication Attempt Due to Bad Password to NDS Database*

```
AUTH 08/13/2003 14:11:47 I 0276 2212 External DB [NDSAuth.dll]: User cisco waiting
for lock
AUTH 08/13/2003 14:11:47 I 0276 2212 External DB [NDSAuth.dll]: User cisco waiting
in lock
AUTH 08/13/2003 14:11:47 I 0276 2212 External DB [NDSAuth.dll]: Initializing thread
0 for tree ndstest
AUTH 08/13/2003 14:11:47 I 0276 1968 External DB [NDSAuth.dll]: Thread 0 for tree
ndstest Got work
AUTH 08/13/2003 14:11:50 I 0276 1968 External DB [NDSAuth.dll]: Response 1 from Tree
ndstest
AUTH 08/13/2003 14:11:50 I 0276 1968 External DB [NDSAuth.dll]: Thread 0 for tree
ndstest Waiting for work
! In the following line, code 102 indicates that authentication fails due to bad
username
! or wrong password.
AUTH 08/13/2003 14:11:53 I 0276 2212 External DB [NDSAuth.dll]: Back from Wait for
user cisco with code 102
! Then eventually it times out trying.
AUTH 08/13/2003 14:11:53 I 0276 2212 External DB [NDSAuth.dll]: Timeout trying User
cisco
AUTH 08/13/2003 14:11:53 I 0276 2212 External DB [NDSAuth.dll]: User cisco out from
lock
```

Authentication Failure When the User Does Not Exist

If the user does not exist on the Novell NDS database or the user enters the wrong username, the authentication will fail, giving the same error code as a bad password (error code 102). Example 13-4 shows the output when the user does not exist on the database.

Example 13-4 *Failed Authentication Due to Unknown User*

```
AUTH 08/13/2003 14:13:24 I 0276 2212 External DB [NDSAuth.dll]: User cisco123
waiting for lock
AUTH 08/13/2003 14:13:24 I 0276 2212 External DB [NDSAuth.dll]: User cisco123
waiting in lock
AUTH 08/13/2003 14:13:24 I 0276 2212 External DB [NDSAuth.dll]: Initializing thread
0 for tree ndstest
AUTH 08/13/2003 14:13:24 I 0276 1968 External DB [NDSAuth.dll]: Thread 0 for tree
ndstest Got work
AUTH 08/13/2003 14:13:24 I 0276 1968 External DB [NDSAuth.dll]: Response 1 from Tree
ndstest
AUTH 08/13/2003 14:13:24 I 0276 1968 External DB [NDSAuth.dll]: Thread 0 for tree
ndstest Waiting for work
AUTH 08/13/2003 14:13:26 I 5094 2220     Worker 3 processing message 275.
AUTH 08/13/2003 14:13:26 I 5081 2220 Start RQ1012, client 27 (127.0.0.1)
AUTH 08/13/2003 14:13:26 I 5081 2220 Done RQ1012, client 27, status 0
AUTH 08/13/2003 14:13:26 I 5094 2220     Worker 3 processing message 276.
AUTH 08/13/2003 14:13:26 I 5081 2220 Start RQ1031, client 27 (127.0.0.1)
AUTH 08/13/2003 14:13:26 I 5081 2220 Done RQ1031, client 27, status 0
! In the following line, the code 102 is an indication that user authentication failed
! either due to bad username or wrong password.
AUTH 08/13/2003 14:13:30 I 0276 2212 External DB [NDSAuth.dll]: Back from Wait for
user cisco123 with code 102
```

Example 13-4 *Failed Authentication Due to Unknown User (Continued)*

```
! Eventually will timeout
AUTH 08/13/2003 14:13:30 I 0276 2212 External DB [NDSAuth.dll]: Timeout trying User
cisco123
AUTH 08/13/2003 14:13:30 I 0276 2212 External DB [NDSAuth.dll]: User cisco123 out
from lock
AUTH 08/13/2003 14:13:30 I 0276 2212 External DB [NTAuthenDLL.dll]: Starting
authentication for user [cisco123]
! Following lines indicate that NT/2K domain is also configured next in order, so
! attempting authentication to NT/2K domain as well and eventually fails.
AUTH 08/13/2003 14:13:30 I 0276 2212 External DB [NTAuthenDLL.dll]: Attempting NT/
2000 authentication
AUTH 08/13/2003 14:13:30 E 0276 2212 External DB [NTAuthenDLL.dll]: NT/2000
authentication FAILED (error 1326L)
AUTH 08/13/2003 14:13:30 I 1547 2212 Unknown User 'cisco123' was not authenticated
```

Wrong Group Mapping

After successful user authentication, the user is mapped to a specific CS ACS group. Two things determine which CS ACS group the user is mapped to: the Novell NDS group or groups the user belongs to, and the CS ACS group mapping configuration under the External Database Configuration page. If there are problems with proper group assignment by CS ACS after successful Novell NDS user authentication, analyze the **auth.log** file to find out which NDS database groups a specific user belongs to, and if the same group or groups are mapped to the desired CS ACS group. Examine the following example. Assume that the user belongs to all the following groups and maps to the CS ACS Group 10:

- superuser.xyz
- http_only.xyz
- http_ftp.xyz
- http_netmeeting.xyz

Analyze the log as shown in Example 13-5.

Example 13-5 *Sample Output: User Saad Belongs to Multiple Groups That Do Not Match with the Group Mapped to CS ACS*

```
AUTH 10/13/2004 10:20:49 I 0259 1340 External DB [NDSAuth.dll]: Initializing
thread 0 for tree XYZ
AUTH 10/13/2004 10:20:49 I 0259 0676 External DB [NDSAuth.dll]: Thread 0 for
tree XYZ Got work
AUTH 10/13/2004 10:20:52 A 0259 0676 External DB [NDSAuth.dll]: Login
Attempt: Context 'MKT.DH.XYZ' User 'saad.MKT.DH.XYZ'
Password 'saad' result 0
AUTH 10/13/2004 10:20:52 I 0259 0676 External DB [NDSAuth.dll]:
Authenticated saad.MKT.DH.XYZ, Response 0
AUTH 10/13/2004 10:20:52 I 0259 1340 External DB [NDSAuth.dll]: Back from
Wait for user saad with code 0
AUTH 10/13/2004 10:20:52 I 0259 1340 External DB [NDSAuth.dll]: Response 0
from successful Tree XYZ
```

continues

Example 13-5 *Sample Output: User Saad Belongs to Multiple Groups That Do Not Match with the Group Mapped to CS ACS (Continued)*

```
AUTH 10/13/2004 10:20:52 I 0259 0676 External DB [NDSAuth.dll]: Response 0
from Tree XYZ
AUTH 10/13/2004 10:20:52 I 0259 0676 External DB [NDSAuth.dll]: Thread 0 for
tree XYZ Waiting for work
AUTH 10/13/2004 10:20:52 I 0259 1340 External DB [NDSAuth.dll]: Added
'Everyone.MKT.DH.XYZ' to Group List for user:
saad.MKT.DH.XYZ
AUTH 10/13/2004 10:20:52 I 0259 1340 External DB [NDSAuth.dll]: Added
'http netmeeting.XYZ' to Group List for user:
saad.MKT.DH.XYZ
AUTH 10/13/2004 10:20:52 I 0259 1340 External DB [NDSAuth.dll]: There were 2
Groups for this user: saad.MKT.DH.XYZ
AUTH 10/13/2004 10:20:52 I 0259 1340 External DB [NDSAuth.dll]: User saad
authenticated into group 0
```

So, from Example 13-5, you see that user saad belongs to NDS groups "Everyone.MKT. DH.XYZ" and "http_netmeeting.XYZ". Thus, the user does *not* meet the requirements to be mapped to group 10 on CS ACS, as both of the groups are not mapped on the CS ACS to group 10. As any unmatched group defaults to the CS ACS Default Group, saad is mapped to Group 0. So, the user must belong to *all* the NDS groups in the mapping, to be mapped into the configured CS ACS group, not just one.

On CS ACS to map this user into group 10, you need a map, which has one of the following combinations of NDS groups:

- Everyone.MKT.DH.XYZ
- http_netmeeting.XYZ
- Everyone.MKT.DH.XYZ' and 'AAA_http netmeeting.XYZ'

It does not matter if a user also belongs in other NDS groups, in addition to those listed in the mapping, but the user must belong in all the NDS groups listed in a mapping to be mapped to a proper CS ACS group.

CS ACS with ACE Server (Secure ID [SDI]) Integration

Cisco Secure ACS can integrate with a few token servers, but this chapter discusses only the ACE server. The ACE server is also known as the SDI server, so both names will be used interchangeably throughout this chapter. Because the implementation of other token servers is very similar to the implementation of the ACE server, the discussion of ACS integration with ACE is applicable for the other token servers as well. The SDI server can be installed on the same machine on which Cisco Secure ACS is running, or on a separate machine. ACE client software is required on the system running Cisco Secure ACS software.

Installation and Configuration Steps

Use the following steps to install and configure CS ACS with SDI Software

Step 1 Install the ACE server as per ACE direction.

Step 2 Bring the ACE server into host configuration mode (run sdadmin).

Step 3 Be sure you have configured the hostname/ip-address of Cisco Secure ACS system as a client in the ACE server setup. This can be verified under **Client > Edit Client** from ACE Server Host configuration window. For CS ACS Windows client, encryption should be Data Encryption Standard (DES), because the client is Windows, and you have to choose **Net OS Client**. When you click the **User Activations** tab, you must see the **SDI user** under **Directly Activated Lists**.

Step 4 Be sure the user is activated on the client—the client is the system on which Cisco Secure ACS is installed. This can be verified under **Users > Edit Users > Client Activations**. In this window you will see a list of available clients. Choose the right one and move them under **Clients Directly Activated On**.

Step 5 Be sure the CS ACS client and the SDI server can perform forward and reverse lookups of each other (that is, ping by name or IP).

Step 6 Copy the SDI server's **sdconf.rec** to the CS ACS client; this can reside anywhere on the CS ACS client.

Step 7 The installation of the ACE client on Windows may differ slightly by version. Run **agent.exe** to initiate the installation process of the ACE client. During installation, when asked to install **Network Access Protection Software**, answer **No**, and leave the **root certificate** box blank. Then go to **Next**. When prompted, specify the path to the **sdconf.rec** file, including the file name.

Step 8 After the client installation and reboot, go to Windows **Control Panel > SDI Agent > Test Authentication with Ace Server > Ace/Server Test Directly** and enter the **username**, **code**, and **card** configured on the Ace server to perform an authentication test and check the communication between the SDI client and the server. If this test does not work, it means the SDI client is not communicating with the SDI server. It also means the CS ACS Windows will not be able to communicate with the SDI Server. This is because CS ACS uses an SDI client interface to communicate with the SDI server.

Step 9 Then install **CS ACS** on Windows as usual.

Step 10 From **Navigation**, go to **External User Databases > Database Configurations > Configure**. ACS should be able to find the SDI Dynamic Linked Library (DLL).

Step 11 Go back to **External User Databases.** Click on **Unknown User Policy** and check the **second radio button.** Then move the SDI database from External Databases to Selected databases.

Step 12 Go back to **External User Databases** and click on **Database Group Mapping > SDI Database > Cisco Secure ACS group** to pick the group that will be mapped to SDI group.

Step 13 Go to Group setup and edit the settings for the group that was mapped to SDI. In this case, it is **Default Group**. Add appropriate attributes for TACACS+ & RADIUS depending on what kind of service the user will use (either Shell or PPP).

Troubleshooting Steps

Use the following step-by-step procedures to troubleshoot the SDI issues with CS ACS:

Step 1 First, authenticate the user with the ACE test agent.

Step 2 If this works, confirm that the card is synchronized with the database. Be sure to use DES encryption on the SDI server when the card is initialized. Choosing SDI will not work.

Step 3 If this does not work, resynchronize from the Token menu in host configuration mode. Click on **Token > Edit Token**, and then choose the token that you want to resynchronize. You will have a menu to resynchronize.

Step 4 Next, bring up the activity monitor (**Report > Log Monitor > Activity Monitor**) on the ACE server while attempting Telnet authentication to a device.

Step 5 Then check to see if there are any errors on the activity monitor on the ACE server.

Step 6 If the ACE server works, but there is a problem with the dial users, check the settings on the network access servers (NASs) to be sure that Password Authentication Protocol (PAP) is configured. Then try connecting as a non-SDI user.

Step 7 If that works, connecting as an SDI user should work. Put the username in the username tab and the passcode in the password tab on Dial-up Networking.

Step 8 If the client from where you are dialing is configured to bring up the post terminal screen after dialing, then be sure the following AAA statement is on the NAS:

```
aaa authentication ppp default if-needed    tacacs+/Radius
```

The key is to use **>if-needed>**. This means that if the user is already authenticated by the following AAA statement:

```
aaa authentication login default tacacs+/radius
```

then you do not have to authenticate the user again when doing PPP. This also applies when using the normal PAP password.

Here are some common problems that you might face with SDI and CS ACS integration:

- **The ACE log displays the message "Passcode accepted", but the user still fails**—Check the CS ACS Failed Attempts log to determine the cause of the problem. The failure could be due to authorization issues.
- **The ACE log displays the message "Access Denied, passcode incorrect"**—This is an ACE problem with the passcode. During this time, the CS ACS Failed Attempts log shows either the message **External DB auth failed** or **External DB user invalid** or **bad password**.
- **The ACE log displays the message "User not in database"**—Check the ACE database. During this time, the CS ACS Failed Attempts log shows either the message **External DB auth failed** or **External DB user invalid or bad password**.
- **The ACE log displays the message "User not on agent host"**—This is an ACE configuration problem. To solve this problem, configure the user on the agent host.
- **The CS ACS log displays the message "External database not operational"**—If the ACE log does not show any attempts, confirm the operation with the ACE client test authentication and check to be sure that the ACE/server authentication engine is running.
- **The CS ACS log displays the message "CS user unknown" or "Cached token rejected/expired" with nothing in the ACE log**—If the network device is sending a Challenge Handshake Authentication Protocol (CHAP) request and the CS ACS does not have an enumerated ACE user with a separate CHAP password, CS ACS does not send the user to ACE because token-only authentication requires PAP.

Replication Issues

Replication allows the CS ACS Server to maintain distributed databases. This helps the NAS to improve fault tolerance (by providing a backup server) or to improve performance (by sharing throughput across several servers). Replication can be configured as a straightforward master-to-slave relationship, or as a pipeline, or even as a tree in which each slave automatically replicates to its children upon receipt of replicated data from its parent.

Configuration

Replication is configured by the GUI. The GUI is used on both the master and slave to configure both ends of the replication.

The following are the steps required for replication on the master (IP Address 10.1.1.1) and the slave (IP address 30.1.1.1). Use the following steps to configure the master CS ACS:

Step 1 Log in to the primary CS ACS server GUI.

Step 2 Turn on **Distributed System Settings** and enable **Cisco Secure Database Replication** options—found under **Interface Configuration->Advanced Options**.

Step 3 In the **Network Configuration** section, add each secondary server to the AAA Servers table as shown in Figure 13-5. The Traffic Type should be left defaulting to *inbound/outbound* unless there is a good reason to do otherwise.

Figure 13-5 *Slave CS ACS Server Entry Configuration on the Primary CS ACS Server*

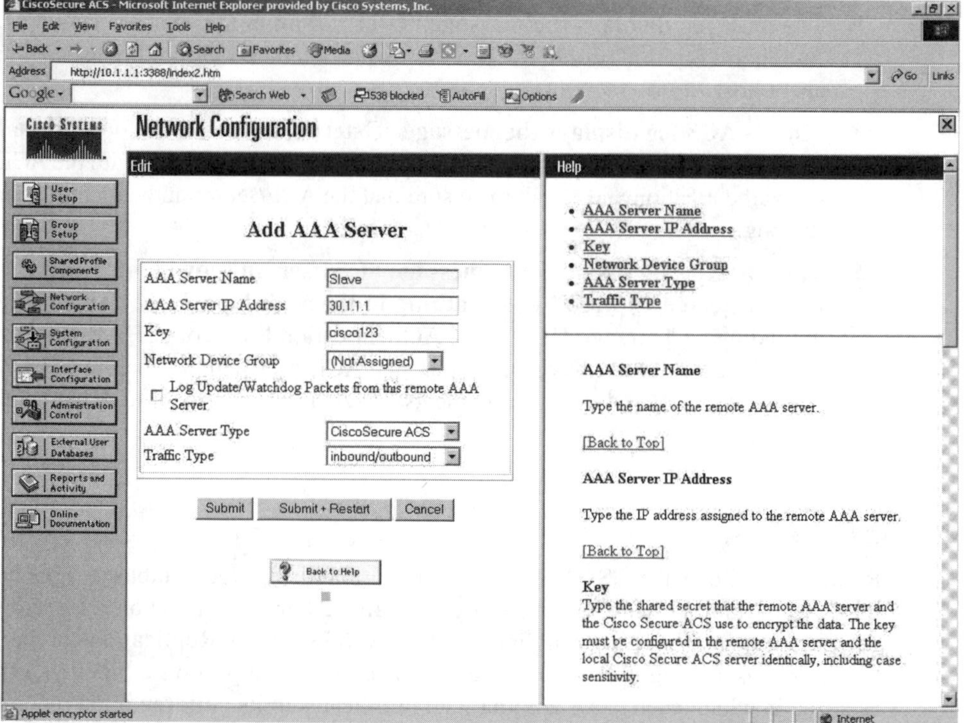

Step 4 In the navigation bar, click **System Configuration.** Then click **Cisco Secure Database Replication**, which brings up the **Database Replication Setup** page.

Step 5 Select the **Send** check box for each database component to send to the secondary server as shown in Figure 13-6.

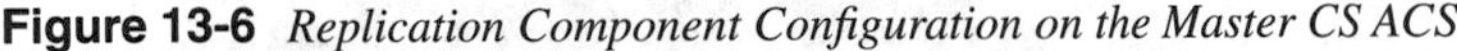

Figure 13-6 *Replication Component Configuration on the Master CS ACS*

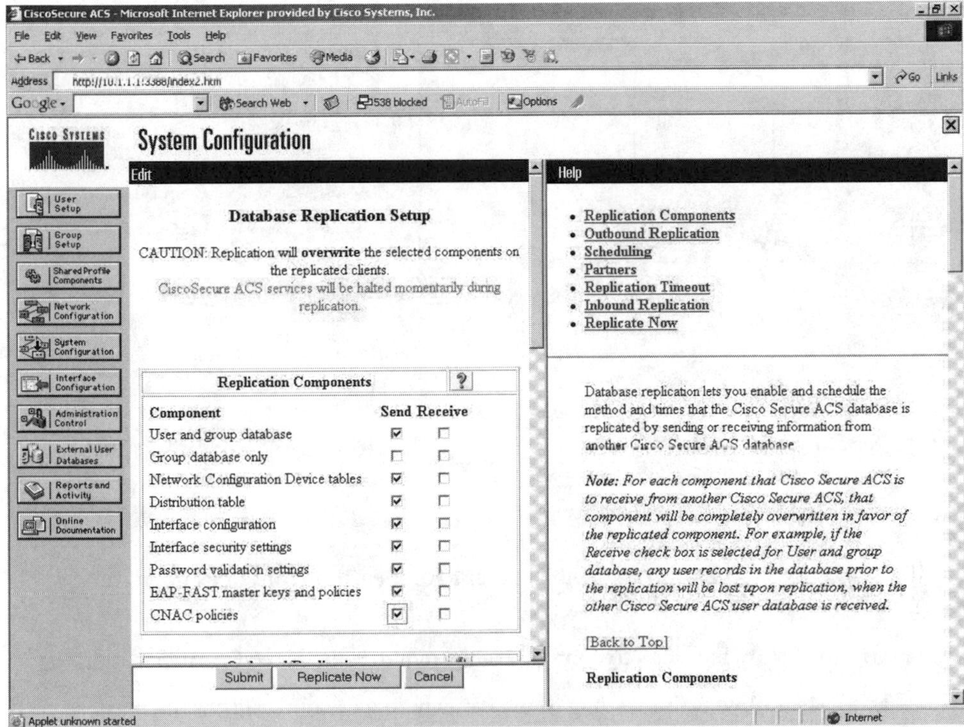

Step 6 Select a scheduling option from one of the four options: **Manually**, **Automatically Triggered Cascade, Every X Minutes,** or **At Specific times**. To set up Auto Replication, you *must not* select **manually,** and the **Scheduling Option** must be set up on Master, not on the slave.

Step 7 Under the **Replication Partners**, add the **secondary CS ACS server** to the Replication Partner column as shown in Figure 13-7.

Figure 13-7 *Replication Partner Configuration on Master*

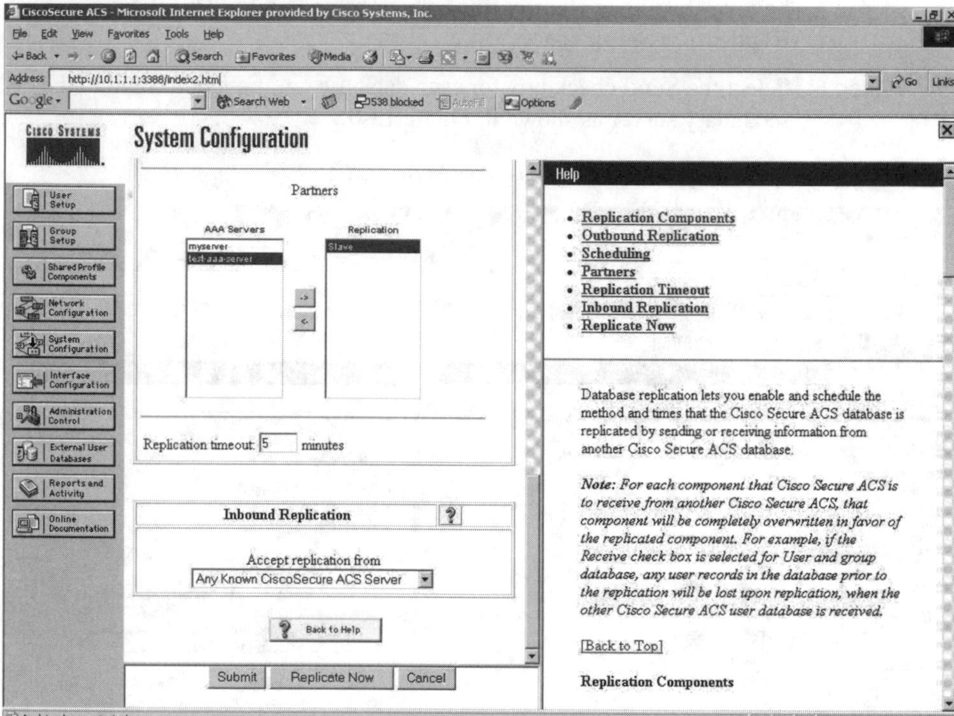

Step 8 Click **Submit.** Note that **Accept Replication from** does not have any meaning on the master.

Use the following steps to configure steps required the slave CS ACS server:

Step 1 Follow the preceding Steps 1-4, which were outlined for the master server.

Step 2 Click the **Receive** check box for each database component to be received from a primary server as shown in Figure 13-8.

Step 3 Leave the Scheduling Option set to **Manually**.

Step 4 Do not add the primary server to the **Replication Partner** column, under the Replication Partners; the replication partner column should be blank as shown in Figure 13-9.

Figure 13-8 *Replication Components Configuration on the Slave*

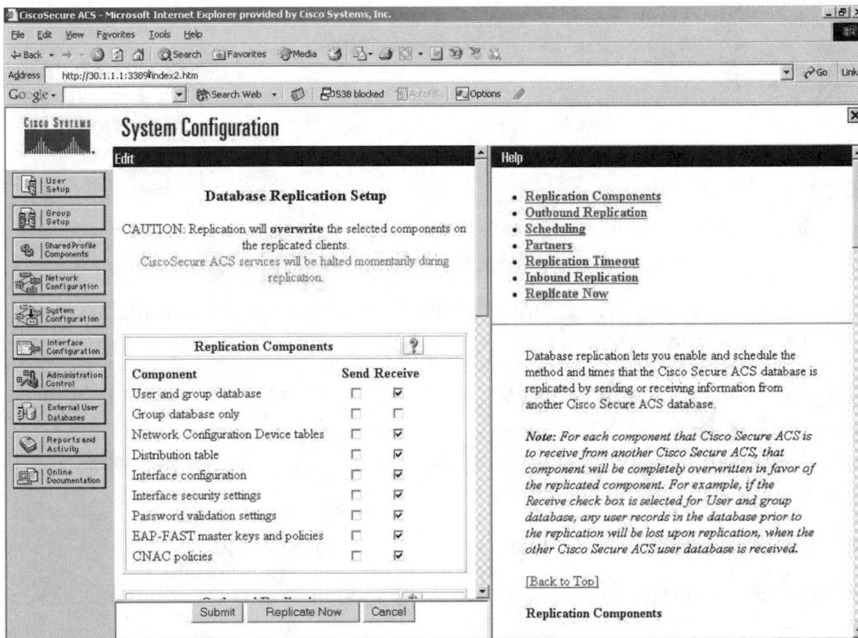

Figure 13-9 *Replication Partners Configuration on the Slave*

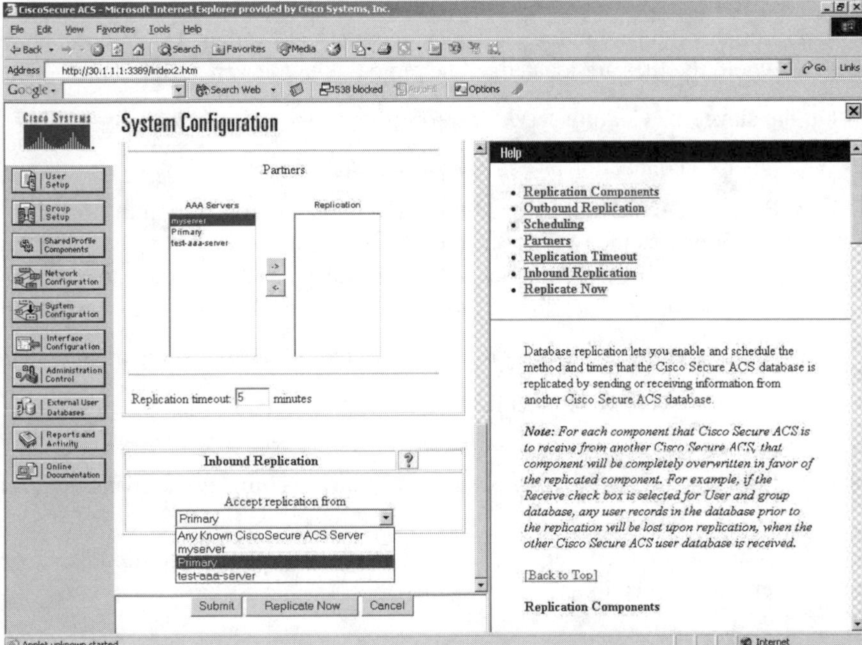

Step 5 From the **Accept Replication From** drop-down list, select **Master Server**. If you have more than one Master server, select **Any Known Cisco Secure ACS for Windows 2000/NT Server**.

Step 6 Click **Submit**.

Troubleshooting Steps

Before getting into the details of some of the common problems that you might face with replication, it is useful to examine the internal workings of replication.

On the master, a dedicated thread within the CSAuth service continually monitors the time and controls the outbound replication when due. The following actions are performed:

1. Lockout and wait for any open transactions to complete (authentication's and admin's updates).
2. Dump the required **registry keys** and copy/compress required files to a temporary location.
3. Release lockouts, allowing normal service to resume.

For each child replication partner, CSAuth then performs the following tasks:

1. Connects to remote CSAuth server.
2. Exchanges version and component specifications.
3. Copies permitted files onto remote AAA server.
4. Initiates replication take-up on the remote AAA server. This request also specifies where the files are located on the remote AAA server.

On the slave, the CSAuth service performs the following task:

1. Opens a connection as per any client request.
2. Responds to the master's request for version and replication information checks by verifying that the two servers are running the same software version. The master will have sent a list of components it is allowed to send. The slave then removes any components it is not allowed to receive. The resultant list is returned to the master.
3. Performs remote file copy operations as the master transmits the replication set.

When the slave receives the replication take-up command from the master, it performs the following:

1. Lockout and wait for any open transactions to complete (authentications and administrator updates).
2. Load the required Registry keys. Uncompress and save required files from the temporary location.

3 Release lockouts, allowing normal service to resume.

4 Restart any services as configured in the Registry (default CSRadius and CSTacacs).

5 Kick the replication thread so that if so configured, "cascade" replication occurs.

To view the actions performed by the CSAuth service for replication as described in the previous steps, analyze the **auth.log** file. The replication CSV file gives a summary version of the status of replication. Therefore, to troubleshoot the replication issues, first look at the CSV file, which is under **Reports & Activity,** or in the logs directory of the CS ACS installation. If the problem cannot be resolved with the CSV file, you can analyze the **auth.log** (...\csauth\logs\auth.log), which shows details of failure (be sure to turn logging to FULL).

To see only the replication log on auth.log file, search for string "**dbreplicate(out)**" on the master and "**dbreplicate(in)**" on the slave server. Example 13-6 shows the output of auth.log file on the Master Server.

Example 13-6 *Replication Only Log on the Master Server*

```
DBReplicate(OUT) attempting to exchange sync info with host acs1
DBReplicate(OUT) attempting to tx files to host acs1
DBReplicate(OUT) - one or more files could not be sent to acs1
DBReplicate(OUT) to host acs1 was denied
Etc.
```

The following are some of the issues that you might encounter, and their resolutions.

- **Compatible version numbers**—Both ends of a replication *must* be running the same version. However, they may be running different builds of the same version, that is, 2.3(1.24) and 2.3(1.29). This has caused a few problems in clients replicating from 2.3 betas to 2.3 FCS systems due a change in Registry encryption. This might be rectified in the future but is worth bearing in mind.
- **Master being rejected by the slave**—The slave AAA server may reject connection attempts from the master due to the master PC having several network adapter cards. This is because the slave can see the IP address of the wrong card, that is, it does not see the one configured in its network configuration. Either the second card can be removed, or another dummy AAA server (with the second IP address) can be added.
- **Secret value/shared key problems**—Both AAA servers must share the same secret key.
- **Proxy entries on slave overwritten**—If you use replication to update several distributed masters, each with its own proxy distribution table, you might see that the slave will keep on losing its proxy table. This is a misconfiguration, and can be resolved by unchecking the component **Distribution Table** on the tx/rx list.

- **Replication timeout**—After issuing the replication take-up request, the master waits up to 5 minutes before assuming that the slave died and reporting it as such. Should the slave be configured so that it uses RDBMS synchronization, it is possible that a large number of transactions could block the slave from accepting the replication before the master gives up. Try to avoid this type of setting.
- **Master CS ACS entry is missing on the slave server**—In the auth.log file of the secondary server, you may see the following message:

  ```
  Worker 2 message from unknown host x.x.x.x - closing conn 41
  ```

  So, on the slave, configure the master CS ACS entry.
- **CS ACS's own server entry is missing from the server list**—When CS ACS is installed, its own entry is created as an AAA server. If you remove that, you may run into problems with the CS ACS replication, and the auth.log could display the following message:

  ```
  "ERROR  Inbound database replication aborted - check IP address for this AAA
  Server"
  ```

  This appears when the AAA server's list does not contain the CS ACS machine itself. You need to investigate further the Registry of both master and slave. After checking the Registry of both master and slave, you might find that the slave machine on the AAA Servers list has only the master configured and does not have its own definition. On the slave CS ACS, only MASTER (Master CS ACS) is configured as an AAA server (type=1) as shown in Example 13-7.

Example 13-7 *Registry on the Slave Server*

```
[HKEY_LOCAL_MACHINE\SOFTWARE\Cisco\CiscoAAAv3.1\Hosts\MASTER]
"key"=hex:36,2e,70,77,e6,24,01,37,73,59,da,d9,b3,61,1d,d9,de,47,79,e2,28,b4,cd,\
  27,42,11,7d,a4,c9,6e,bd,85
"vendor"=dword:ffffffff
"protocol"=dword:00000063
"type"=dword:00000001
"direction"=dword:00000003
"acct Packet Filter"=dword:00000005
"network device group"=dword:00000006
"ip"=hex(7):31,00,37,00,32,00,2e,00,32,00,35,00,2e,00,35,00,37,00,2e,00,39,00,\
  31,00,00,00,00,00
"lastModified"=hex:50,7c,26,f8,fb,0d,c3,01
```

On the master server, there are two AAA servers configured : MASTER(the Master itself) and SLAVE(the Slave CS ACS) as shown in Example 13-8.

Example 13-8 *Registries of the CS ACS Servers*

```
[HKEY_LOCAL_MACHINE\SOFTWARE\Cisco\CiscoAAAv3.1\Hosts\CPFACS01]
"key"=hex:eb,e5,07,d8,98,ad,fe,5b,f2,88,81,e8,83,1f,e0,00,36,d6,57,03,f7,fd,dc,\
  5b,61,89,6a,a6,a8,78,b9,5b
"vendor"=dword:ffffffff
```

Example 13-8 *Registries of the CS ACS Servers (Continued)*

```
"protocol"=dword:00000063
"type"=dword:00000001
"direction"=dword:00000003
"acct Packet Filter"=dword:00000005
"network device group"=dword:00000000
"ip"=hex(7):31,00,37,00,32,00,2e,00,32,00,35,00,2e,00,35,00,37,00,2e,00,39,00,\
  31,00,00,00,00,00
"lastModified"=hex:80,06,62,dd,e5,07,c3,01

[HKEY_LOCAL_MACHINE\SOFTWARE\Cisco\CiscoAAAv3.1\Hosts\HQACS02]
"key"-hex:58,a5,28,70,6e,50,f6,80,64,7c,fe,1f,70,c1,b1,bb,8d,d7,0f,1f,7a,11,ac,\
  64,86,b3,4a,c9,a5,37,db,a4
"vendor"=dword:fffffff
"protocol"=dword:00000063
"type"=dword:00000001
"direction"=dword:00000003
"acct Packet Filter"=dword:00000005
"network device group"=dword:00000006
"ip"=hex(7):31,00,37,00,32,00,2e,00,32,00,35,00,2e,00,35,00,37,00,2e,00,39,00,\
  32,00,00,00,00,00
"lastModified"=hex:c0,be,de,ab,fb,0d,c3,01
```

Add a profile of the slave CS ACS to the slave CS ACS AAA Server's list to fix the problem.

- **Bi-directional replication between two CS ACS Servers**—Bi-directional replication is not supported. If you configure the bi-directional replication, you will see messages like the one in Example 13-9 in the auth.log file and the replication will fail. So avoid configuring bidirectional replication.

Example 13-9 *Auth.log Output for Bidirectional Replication*

```
03/22/2005      21:26:19        ERROR   Inbound database replication from ACS
'dumb' denied
03/22/2005      21:36:36        INFO    Outbound replication cycle starting...
03/22/2005      21:36:42        ERROR   ACS 'dumb' has denied replication request
```

- **NAT or Firewall device between the replication partners**—If there is a Network Address Translation (NAT) or firewall device between the replication partners, you may see the following message on the auth.log

  ```
  denied - shared secret mismatch
  ```

  From CS ACS version 3.1 and above, the IP address is embedded in the data and used as part of the server verification process. Hence, if the NAT device changes the source IP of the server, replication no longer works. To get around the problem, you may want to configure the firewall or NAT device so that it keeps the same source IP address. In addition to taking care of the NAT issue, be sure to allow TCP/2000 for the communication to take place.

- **Replication is not working for some components**—A master CS ACS has a **dirty** flag for each replication component. If no data changes on the master between replication cycles, nothing is replicated. To see which components are being replicated, be sure that **user.dat, user.idx,** and **varsdb.mdb** are being transmitted. The users are listed in **user.dat**. The advanced settings for users and groups are in **varsdb.mdb**.
- **Slave server does not have enough space**—If you have a **10-MB** database that needs to be replicated to a slave CS ACS, there must be enough space to hold the compressed file set, you need space in temp during de-compress, and you need space for uncompressed files. For a **10-MB** database, **50-MB** should be comfortable.

Network Access Restrictions (NARs) Issues

Network Access Restrictions (NARs) allow you to define additional authorization conditions that must be met before a user can gain access to the network. Even though it is an authorization condition, NAR is indeed an authentication process.

Cisco Secure ACS supports two basic types of network access restrictions:

- IP-based restrictions in which the originating request relates to an existing IP address
- Non-IP-based filters for all other cases in which the automatic number identification (ANI) may be used

A non-IP-based NAR is a list of permitted or denied "calling"/"point of access" locations that you can employ in restricting an AAA client when you do not have an IP-based connection established. The non-IP-based NAR generally uses the calling line ID (CLI) number and the Dialed Number Identification Service (DNIS) number.

Configuration Steps

To illustrate the functionality of NAR, consider the following example. Table 13-4 shows how users belonging to a default group can connect via Router1. Users in Group1 can connect only via AP11 and Group2 users get access via Router2 and AP11.

Table 13-4 *Configuration Metric*

Group	User	Router1	Router2	AP11
Default	Laci	Pass	Fail	Fail
Group1	Magi	Fail	Fail	Pass
Group2	Torri	Fail	Pass	Pass

This can be accomplished in several ways: using per "User defined Network Access Restriction" and using "Shared Profile Component for NAR", whereas all NAR is applied on Group-Settings.

The following are the configuration steps for NAR:

Step 1 Define Router1, Router2, and AP11 as AAA client under AAA client, if not defined already.

Step 2 Define users listed in Table 13-4 and map them to corresponding groups.

Step 3 Go to each group's settings and under **Access Restrictions**, define the parameters as shown in Figure 13-10 for all three devices such as Default Group, which allows only Router1.

Figure 13-10 *NAR Configuration for Group*

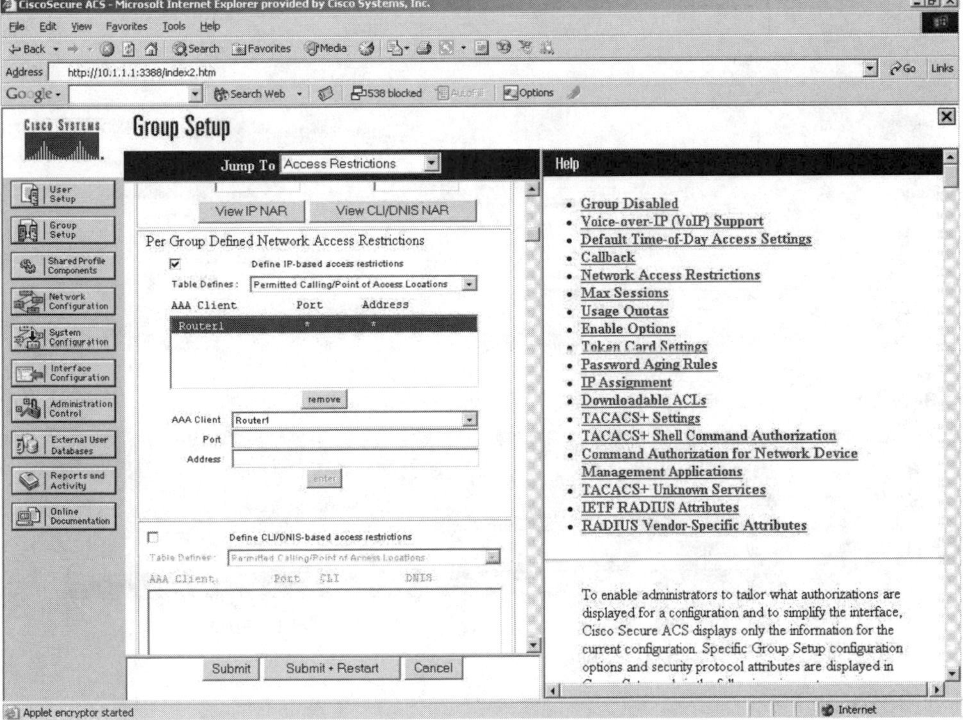

Step 4 If Shared Profile components is the component that is used instead, then from Navigation, click on **Shared Profile Component**, and define three NARs: NAR-AP, NAR-router1, and NAR-router2 in a manner similar to that shown in Figure 13-11 for Router1. The name of the NAR is NAR-router1.

Step 5 Now apply the NAR defined in Step 4 on all three groups under network access restrictions in a manner similar to that shown in Figure 13-12, which is configured for Default Group.

Figure 13-11 *Shared Profile Component for NAR*

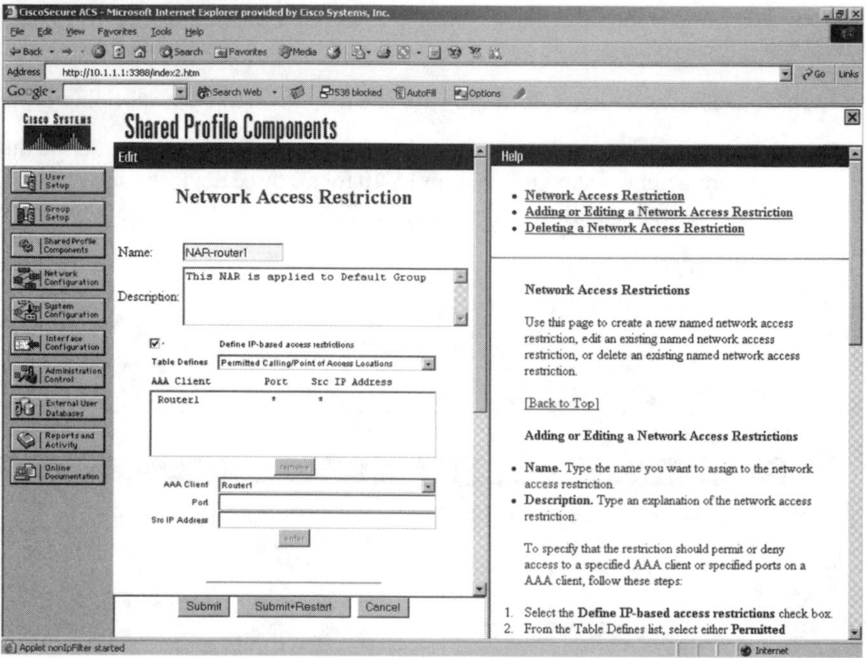

Figure 13-12 *NAR Applied on Default Group*

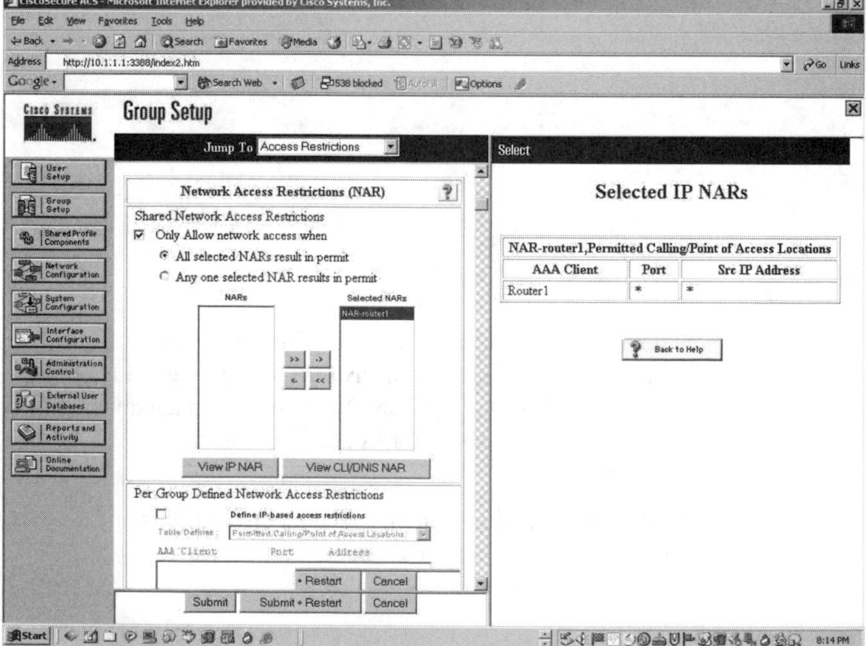

NOTE This setup can also be extended to use Network Device Groups (NDG). Configuration steps are exactly the same, but instead of selecting NAS, select NDG.

Troubleshooting Steps

The best way to troubleshoot the NAR issues is to use Failed Attempts or Passed Authentications reports to understand why access was or was not granted to a certain user. Usually, the caller ID, network access server (NAS) port, and NAS IP address fields are available and can be used to debug the session. When the reason for acceptance or denial is unclear, you can add the Filter Information field to these reports (both to Failed Attempts and Passed Authentications). This field will provide additional data. However, remember that you must use the Shared Profile Component (SPC) NARs configuration to get this additional information. With traditional NARs, it is hard to find the cause of acceptance or denial, as the first message (No Filter Activated) always appears regardless of the results. For additional details, look at the **RDS.log** or **TCS.log** and see how the packet is coming to the CS ACS Server from NAS and if it is getting forwarded to the **CSAuth** service, which shows the information on **auth.log**.

Example 13-10 shows the auth.log file for successful authentication.

Example 13-10 *Snippet of auth.log File Shows NAR Passing*

```
03/22/2005,18:41:21,Authen OK,laci,Default Group,10.0.0.2,66,10.0.0.171,,,,,,All
Access Filters Passed.,,router1,,,No,laci,cisco,,,

03/22/2005,18:42:08,Authen OK,torri,Group 2,10.0.0.2,66,10.0.0.172,,,,,,Access
Filter NAR-router2 from Group 2 permitted on Filter Line: 'router2 (Port=*) (IP=*)'.
This is sufficient to satisfy an 'Any Selected' SPC NAR
config.,,router2,,,No,torri,cisco,,,

03/22/2005,18:42:59,Authen OK,magi,Group 1,0040.9638.8e9a,99,10.0.0.1,,,,,,All
Access Filters Passed.,,ap11,,,No,magi,cisco,,,

03/22/2005,18:43:10,Authen OK,torri,Group 2,0040.9638.8e9a,99,10.0.0.1,,,,,,Access
Filter NAR-AP from Group 2 permitted on Filter Line: 'ap11 (Port=*) (CLI=*)
(DNIS=*)'. This is sufficient to satisfy an 'Any Selected' SPC NAR
config.,,ap11,,,No,torri,cisco,,,
```

Example 13-11 shows the auth.log file for unsuccessful authentication.

Example 13-11 *Snippet of auth.log File Shows NAR Failing*

```
03/22/2005,18:41:39,Authen failed,magi,Group 1,10.0.0.2,User Access
Filtered,,,66,10.0.0.171,Access Filter NAR-AP from Group 1 denied on Filter Line:
'* (Port=*) (IP=*)'. This is sufficient to reject an 'All Selected' SPC NAR
config.,,,,,,,,router1,,,,No,magi,cisco,,,

03/22/2005,18:41:44,Authen failed,torri,Group 2,10.0.0.2,User Access
Filtered,,,66,10.0.0.171,No Access Filters
Passed.,,,,,,,,router1,,,,No,torri,cisco,,,

03/22/2005,18:41:57,Authen failed,laci,Default Group,10.0.0.2,User Access
Filtered,,,66,10.0.0.172,Access Filter NAR-router1 from Default Group Did not permit
any criteria. This is sufficient to reject an 'All Selected' SPC NAR
config.,,,,,,,,router2,,,,No,laci,cisco,,,
```

continues

Example 13-11 *Snippet of auth.log File Shows NAR Failing (Continued)*

```
03/22/2005,18:42:03,Authen failed,magi,Group 1,10.0.0.2,User Access
Filtered,,,66,10.0.0.172,Access Filter NAR-AP from Group 1 denied on Filter Line:
'* (Port=*) (IP=*)'. This is sufficient to reject an 'All Selected' SPC NAR
config.,,,,,,,,router2,,,,No,magi,cisco,,,

03/22/2005,18:42:45,Authen failed,laci,Default Group,0040.9638.8e9a,User Access
Filtered,,,97,10.0.0.1,Access Filter NAR-router1 from Default Group denied on Filter
Line: '* (Port=*) (CLI=*) (DNIS=*)'. This is sufficient to reject an 'All Selected'
SPC NAR config.,,,,,,,,ap11,,,,No,laci,cisco,,,
```

The following link contains some interesting and useful discussion about NAR and how to troubleshoot it efficiently:

http://www.cisco.com/en/US/products/sw/secursw/ps2086/products_white_paper09186a00801a8fd0.shtml

Downloadable ACL Issues

You can download ACL from the CS ACS Server to NAS to control which resources the user can access after getting access to the network. There are three ways to configure this, as described in the sections that follow.

Downloading ACL per User Basis Using Filter-id

With this option, you need to define the ACL in the NAS, and on the CS ACS server, and you need to define the name of the ACL using the Internet Engineering Task Force (IETF) RADIUS attribute 11 as shown in Figure 13-13.

Figure 13-13 *ACL Named Defined with IETF Radius Attribute*

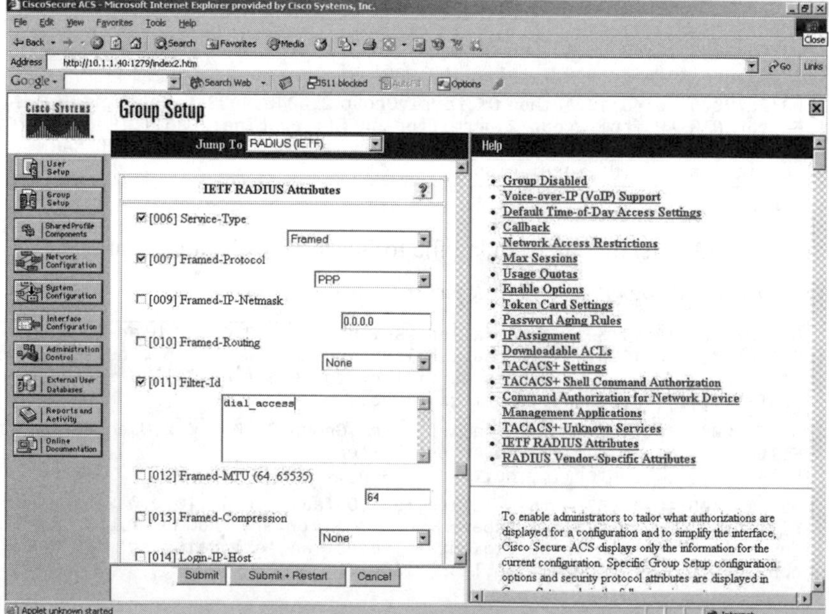

Using Cisco AV-Pair

On the NAS, you must have authorization turned on; otherwise, the AV pair will not be applied on the NAS. On CS ACS, you need to configure this under Group Profile. Click on **Group Setup > Select a Group** from drop-down, and then click on **Edit Settings**. In the Group Setup page, select **Cisco IOS/PIX RADIUS** from the **Jump To** drop-down. Then check "[009\001] cisco-av-pair" box, and define your ACL in the rectangle text box underneath as shown in Figure 13-14.

Figure 13-14 *ACL Defined Using Cisco AV Pair*

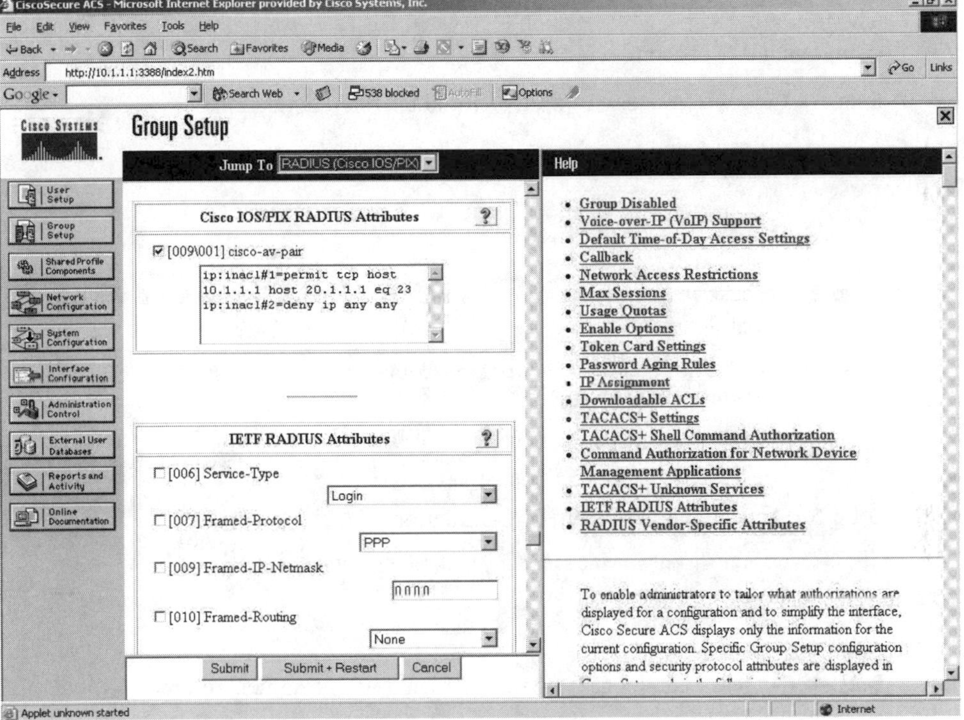

NOTE The variable x (ip:inacl#<x> . . .) must be defined with different numbers (for example 1, 2, 3 and so on) if multiple ACL entries are defined in the ACL. This ensures the order of the ACE in the ACL when downloaded to the NAS. If the same number is used for variable x for multiple ACL entries, then it may work, but the order of ACL entries will not be maintained, which may cause unexpected problems.

Using Shared Profile Components

If you are running CS ACS 3.0 and 3.1, under the Shared Profile component, the only option available to download ACL is for the PIX Firewall, which is called "Downloadable PIX

ACL." From CS ACS version 3.2 and above, "Downloadable IP ACL" is available under "Shared Profile Components", which is supported by PIX firewall, VPN Concentrator 4.0 code and above, and IOS version 12.3T and above.

The following sequence of events occurs if ACLs via Shared Profile Components are used:

1 The first stage is to download the name and version of the ACL where the device validates it against the local ACL cache.

2 In the second stage, the device (if needed) requests the ACL content, where CS ACS uses **inacl** for downloading the ACL.

The following step-by-step example shows the user fred when the Shared Profile component ACL is configured.

Step 1 Access a request from PIX (initial user authentication).

```
User-Name[1] = "fred"
User-Password[2] = <whatever>
...
<Other attributes>
...
```

Step 2 Access an acceptance from CS ACS (authentication response and ACL set assignment).

```
AV-Pair[26/9/1] ="ACS:CiscoSecure-Defined-ACL=#ACSACL#-myAcl-
1e45bc4890fa12b2
...
<Other attributes>
...
```

Step 3 Access a request from PIX (initiation of ACL download).

```
User-Name = "#ACSACL#-myAcl-1e45bc4890fa12b2"
...
<Other attributes>
...
```

Step 4 Access a challenge from CS ACS (first ACL fragment returned—more to follow).

```
State[24] = "TBD"
AV-Pair[26/9/1] = "ip:inacl#1 = permit tcp any anyestablished"
AV-Pair[26/9/1] = "ip:inacl#2 = permit ip any any"
...
<ACLs 3..59>
...
AV-Pair[26/9/1] = "ip:inacl#60 = deny icmp 2.2.2.0 0.0.0.255
9.9.9.00.0.0.255"
```

Troubleshooting Steps

Most of the time, downloadable ACL issues arise from mis-configuration either on the NAS or on the CS ACS server. So, first you must always perform a sanity check on the configuration, if there is any issue with downloadable ACL. Analyze **auth.log** and **RDS.log** files to find out what information CS ACS is sending to the NAS as reply attributes for authorization. Then look at the debug information on the NAS to see if the NAS understands the ACL that CS ACS is sending. Keep the following points in mind when you configure downloadable ACL:

1 Perform a sanity check on the configuration both on the NAS and CS ACS server.

2 Be sure to have the authorization turned on for the NAS; otherwise, even though CS ACS sends the ACL name or the ACL itself, NAS will not install it. In the authorization debug, you will see that ACL is downloading from CS ACS, but when you execute **show access-list** command, you will not see the ACL being installed.

3 If using filter ID to download only the ACL name to NAS, be sure that ACL is defined locally on the NAS first. Then be sure that the name of the ACL matches on both CS ACS and the NAS. Note that name is case sensitive.

4 When an AV pair is used to download ACL, be sure to define the ACL entries with different numbers to maintain the order of ACL entries.

Case Studies

This case study examines the csutil.exe, a very useful utility that comes with the CS ACS software. Csutil.exe is in the following location:

<ACS_install_directory>\utils\

For example, C:\Program Files\CiscoSecure ACS v3.2\utils\

The command syntax is as follows:

```
CSUtil.exe [-q] [-c] [-d] [-g] [-i filename] [[-p] -l filename] [-e - number] [-b
filename] [-r filename] [-f] [-n] [-u] [-y] [-listUDV] [-addUDV slotfilename] [-
delUDV slot]
```

To run this utility, some options require you to stop the services. To do this, use the **net stop** command. Example 13-12 shows the **CSAuth** service stopped with the **net stop** command.

Example 13-12 *Stopping the CSAuth Service*

```
C:\> net stop CSAuth
The CSAuth service is stopping.
The CSAuth service was stopped successfully.

C:\>
```

Csutil.exe has many options/arguments for different purposes. Table 13-5 summarizes the options.

Table 13-5 *Options Available for the csutil.exe Utility*

Arguments	Descriptions
-b	Back up system to a named file
-d	Export internal data to named file
-g	Export group information
-I	Import user or NAS information
-l	Load internal data from a named file
-n	Create/initialize the ACS database
-q	Run csutil.exe in quiet mode
-r	Restore system from a named file
-u	Export user information

Back Up and Restore the CS ACS Database

Database backup and restore can be accomplished from the GUI and by browsing to the System Configuration option. However, due to csadmin failure, GUI access may be unavailable. Besides, if performing backup/restore requires an external script, using csutil.exe is very handy. When performing the backup function, services will automatically be stopped, which means no user authentication occurs during the backup. You are prompted for confirmation. You may use the quiet mode to bypass this confirmation. The backup will contain the following information:

- User and group information
- System configuration

If a component of the backup is empty, a Backup Failed notice will be displayed for that component only. To uninstall or upgrade, copy the backup file to a safe location; otherwise it will be removed. The command syntax for database backup is as follows:

```
C:\Program Files\CiscoSecure ACS v3.2\csutil -b filename
```

Example 13-13 shows the sample output of a database backup.

Example 13-13 *Sample Run of Database Backup*

```
C:\Program Files\CiscoSecure ACS v3.3\Utils>csutil -b backup.dat
CSUtil v3.3(2.2), Copyright 1997-2004, Cisco Systems Inc
All running services will be stopped and re-started automatically.
Are you sure you want to proceed? (Y or N)(Y)
Done
C:\Program Files\CiscoSecure ACS v3.3\Utils>
```

If you restore the CS ACS database, services will automatically be stopped. You can restore user and group information or system configuration or both. Note that you can restore data only to the same version of CS ACS as the backup file, which means that this is not a system upgrade path. The following is the syntax used for database restore:

```
C:\> csutil -r [users|config | all] filename
```

Example 13-14 shows an example of database restore.

Example 13-14 *Sample Run of Database Restore*

```
C:\Program Files\CiscoSecure ACS v3.3\Utils>csutil -r all backup.dat
CSUtil v3.3(2.2), Copyright 1997-2004, Cisco Systems Inc
Reloading a system backup will overwrite ALL current configuration information
All Running services will be stopped and re-started automatically.
Are you sure you want to proceed? (Y or N)(Y)
CSBackupRestore(IN) file C:\Program Files\CiscoSecure ACS v3.3\Utils\System Back
up\CRL Reg.RDF not received, skipping..
Done
C:\Program Files\CiscoSecure ACS v3.3\Utils>
```

Creating a Dump Text File

A dump text file contains only the user and group information. This is useful for troubleshooting user profile issues. Cisco support may be able to load a dump file from your dump file to view user configuration to troubleshoot any possible configuration issue. Before creating a dump file, you need to manually stop the CSAuth service with the following command:

```
C:\> net stop CSAuth
```

Note that no user authentication takes place while the service is stopped. You must start the service manually with **net start CSAuth** once you are finished creating the dump. Command syntax to create dump file is as follows:

```
csutil -d filename
```

Example 13-15 shows a sample run of the creation of a dump file.

Example 13-15 *A Sample Run of Dump Text File Creation*

```
C:\Program Files\CiscoSecure ACS v3.3\Utils>net stop CSAuth
The CSAuth service is stopping.
The CSAuth service was stopped successfully.


C:\Program Files\CiscoSecure ACS v3.3\Utils>csutil -d dump.txt
CSUtil v3.3(2.2), Copyright 1997-2004, Cisco Systems Inc
Done

C:\Program Files\CiscoSecure ACS v3.3\Utils>
```

To load the dump file into CS ACS, first stop the **CSAuth** service, which means that user authentication will be stopped during that time. Loading a dump file will replace existing data. You can use the **-p** option to reset password aging counters. The syntax to use for loading the dump file is as follows:

```
csutil -p -l filename
```

Example 13-16 shows a sample run of a creation of a dump.txt file.

Example 13-16 *Sample Run of Dump.txt File Creation*

```
C:\Program Files\CiscoSecure ACS v3.3\Utils>net stop CSAuth
The CSAuth service is stopping.
The CSAuth service was stopped successfully.


C:\Program Files\CiscoSecure ACS v3.3\Utils>csutil -p -l dump.txt
CSUtil v3.3(2.2), Copyright 1997-2004, Cisco Systems Inc
Loading a database dump file will overwrite the existing database.
Are you sure you want to proceed? (Y or N)Y

Initializing database...
Loading database from file...
Password aging counters will be reset
Done

C:\Program Files\CiscoSecure ACS v3.3\Utils>
```

User/NAS Import Options

This feature allows changes either online or offline, and allows updating of the CS ACS database with a colon-delimited file. The following are the actions available for user and NAS:

- Users: add, change, and delete
- NAS: add and delete

You must restart **CSRadius** and **CSTacacs** for changes to take effect.

The following are some of the important points about importing:

- The first line must contain ONLINE or OFFLINE.

  This determines if the CSAuth service needs to be stopped during this process.

- CSUtils cannot distinguish between multiple instances of an external database.

  CSUtil will use the first instance of an external database.

Import User Information

You can add users to the existing database with the entry shown in Example 13-17. This entry adds the user Joe to group 2 in the CS ACS database. It also points authentication for this user to the internal CS ACS database with a password of **my1Password**.

Example 13-17 *Adding a User to CS ACS*

```
ADD:Joe:PROFILE:2:CSDB:my1Password
```

To change the CS ACS profile for Joe, use the command shown in Example 13-18. This entry updates Joe to group 3 and points the password to the NT domain database.

Example 13-18 *Updating a User to CS ACS*

```
UPDATE:Joe:PROFILE:3:EXT_NT
```

The DELETE entry can be used to delete users as shown in Example 13-19.

Example 13-19 *Deleting a User from CS ACS*

```
DELETE:Joe
```

Import NAS Information

Use the entry shown in Example 13-20 to add an NAS to the CS ACS database. This entry adds the router named router1, using the shared secret of my1NAS. This NAS will use RADIUS.

Example 13-20 *Adding NAS*

```
ADD_NAS:router1:IP:10.10.10.10:KEY:my1NAS:VENDER:"RADIUS (Cisco IOS/PIX)"
```

If you need to delete a specific NAS, use the command shown in Example 13-21, which deletes NAS router1.

Example 13-21 *How to Delete a Specific NAS*

```
DEL_NAS:router1
```

You can also choose to run all the previously shown procedures using a single text file. Example 13-22 shows a sample text file that contains multiple actions for different users.

Example 13-22 *import.txt File Whose Content Can Be Imported Once*

```
OFFLINE
ADD:user01:CSDB:userpassword:PROFILE:1
ADD:user02:EXT_NT:PROFILE:2
ADD:chapuser:CSDB:hello:CHAP:chappw:PROFILE:3
ADD:mary:EXT_NT:CHAP:achappassword
ADD:joe:EXT_SDI
ADD:user4:CSDB:user4password
ADD:user5:CSDB_UNIX:unixpassword
UPDATE:user9:PROFILE:10
DELETE:user10
ADD_NAS:router1:IP:10.10.10.10:KEY:my1NAS:VENDOR:"TACACS+ (Cisco
IOS)":NDG:"California"
DEL_NAS:router2
```

Compact User Database

When you delete a user from the CS ACS database, the record is marked as deleted. You might need to compact the database to actually remove the "deleted records". Compacting the database addresses this issue. When you compact a database, it first dumps the data, then creates a new database, and finally imports all the data that was dumped earlier. The following is the syntax for compacting a database:

```
csutil.exe  -q -d -n -l
```

Example 13-23 shows the sample of database compact run.

Example 13-23 *Sample Database Compact Command*

```
C:\Program Files\CiscoSecure ACS v3.3\Utils>net stop CSAuth
The CSAuth service is stopping.
The CSAuth service was stopped successfully.

C:\Program Files\CiscoSecure ACS v3.3\Utils>csutil -q -d -n -l
CSUtil v3.3(2.2), Copyright 1997-2004, Cisco Systems Inc
Done

Initializing database....
Done

Initializing database...
Loading database from dump.txt...
Done

C:\Program Files\CiscoSecure ACS v3.3\Utils>
```

Export User and Group Information

Export User and Group Information may be useful for troubleshooting the configuration issue by Cisco support. You will need to stop CSAuth before exporting this information.

To export user information to users.txt, enter the following command:

```
csutil.exe -u
```

To export group information to groups.txt, enter the following command:

```
csutil.exe -g
```

Other features of CSUtil.exe include the following:

- Export Registry information to setup.txt.
- Decode CS ACS internal error codes.
- Recalculate Cyclic Redundancy Check (CRC) values for manually copied files.
- Import user-defined RADIUS vendors and VSA sets.

Common Problems and Resolutions

This section examines some of the commonly encountered problems that were not discussed earlier.

1 I am getting "Crypto Error" while trying to install/upgrade CS ACS. How do I fix this?

Answer: Use an administrator account when performing the installation.

Rename the **pdh.dll** file in the system32 directory.

The problem lies in MS CryptoAPI settings. If you remove or customize Internet Explorer or install any security patches, the IE updates and security updates often distribute modified CryptoAPI files. Installing these can sometimes break existing CryptoAPI clients. You might also receive this error message if the CS ACS services are being run as another user (or were installed as another user) or if the file permissions to the CryptoAPI data do not permit access. If nothing has changed on IE, follow these steps:

1 Uninstall CS ACS.

2 Search the Documents and Settings folder for any files with **CiscoSecure ACS** in the file name; they will be in a user's **Application Data\Microsoft\Crypto\RSA folder**.

3 If found, delete the CS ACS file.

4 Search the Registry for a key named **CiscoSecure ACS v2.0 Container**.

5 If found, delete the key. This removes any existing CiscoSecure CryptoAPI references. Now try to reinstall.

Uninstalling CS ACS manually:

1 Under **HKEY_LOCAL_MACHINE\SOFTWARE\CISCO**, delete the **Cisco\CiscoAAAvX** Registry tree.

2 From the same location, delete the directory.

3 Then go to Services applet and make sure none of the seven services for CS ACS are listed there.

4 If the services are installed and show up in the service list, there are entries in the Registry for them. Search the Registry for **Cisco** and selectively delete the keys and values.

2 What can I do when my Registry of CS ACS is corrupted?

Answer: It is a good idea to back up the Registry of Windows when it is clean, before even installing the CS ACS software, so that it can be imported back if the Registry is corrupted and the CS ACS needs to be reinstalled.

Execute the **clean.exe** utility on the CS ACS CD.

3 What can I do when I get the following error when upgrading from an older to a newer version?

"The old installation folder appears to be locked by another application:
c:\Program Files\CiscoSecureACSv3.X
Please close any applications that are using any files or directories in this folder and re-run setup."

Answer: Get a **dump.txt**, uninstall, reinstall, and reconfigure NAS only if you have a small number of NASs. If you have a large number of NASs, this may not work.

Reboot the server to ensure that it is not locked up by other applications.

Are there any shared directories on the CS ACS machine?

If you are installing remotely via either VNC or "Terminal Services" or "Remote Desktop", try installing locally.

If you *must* install remotely, try installing by using **Control Panel > Add/Remove Programs** (then browse to setup.exe). This helps occasionally when using a terminal service connection.

If the problem still persists, download the **Filemon** utility from the following location and run it while the installation is getting the error.

http://www.sysinternals.com/ntw2k/source/filemon.shtml

Filemon captures all file activity and shows the error code, so you can see which particular file is causing trouble with the install shield. You may also find out which process is locking the file by using the **Handle** tool that can be downloaded from the following location.

http://www.sysinternals.com/ntw2k/freeware/handle.shtml

Killing the process and deleting the file may resolve the issue.

You may want to turn on the **Manage Log Directory** option under **System Config > Service Control** and **System Config > Logging > <all CSV logs>**. During an upgrade under some circumstances, this may fix the message stating that the folder is locked.

4 I am trying to upgrade a CS ACS that is installed under D: drive, but am having problems with space issues under C:. Why?

Answer: When performing a clean install, the Installation Wizard gives you the option of choosing the location in which you want to install the CS ACS software. However, this option is not available for upgrades. For example, when you try to upgrade by running the new version of CS ACS setup.exe, the Installation Wizard drops the new version on the C: drive. So, whenever the installation process finds a previous configuration and prompts the user to keep the existing database and configuration, you do not have the option of selecting an installation location. Whenever the installation process is clean and the user is not prompted to keep the existing database and configuration, you will have the option of selecting a different installation location. This might create a problem if the C: drive is low in space. To get around the problem, the only option available is to create more disk space on the C: drive.

5 What's the minimum CS ACS version requirement for MS-CHAP v2 support?

Answer: The minimum requirement is version CS ACS 3.0.

6 Is it possible to force the user to provide login credentials when trying to launch the CS ACS Windows Admin GUI from the CS ACS Server itself locally?

Answer: Yes, it is possible. If you have **allowAutoLocalLogin** set to 1 in the Registry, you do not need to provide login credentials. So to force the user to provide login credentials if accessing CS ACS locally, change value for **allowAutoLocalLogin** to 0. To find out this key, you can search using this keyword.

7 If I lose the admin password to get into the GUI, how can I recover it?

Answer: By default, the CS ACS does not require you to provide login credentials if you are accessing it locally from the CS ACS server itself. However, if you force local login by un-checking the **Allow automatic local login** check box under **Administration Control > Session Policy** (this essentially sets the **allowAutoLocalLogin** in the Registry to 0 as discussed in question 6), and you lose the admin password, the best solution is to set the **allowAutoLocalLogin** to **1**. Then you can log in to the CS ACS locally from the server and add or modify administrators. The Registry location for the **allowAutoLocalLogin** is as follows:

```
HKEY_LOCAL_MACHINE\SOFTWARE\Cisco\CiscoAAAv3.3\CSAdmin\Security
```

8 Under the **Security** key, you can modify **allowAutoLocalLogin** by right-clicking and choosing **modify**. How can I set up a default NAS so that I do not have to create multiple AAA clients on CS ACS for every NAS that uses the same shared secret key?

Answer: You can add a default NAS in the NAS configuration area by leaving the host name and IP address blank. Put in only the key. Click **Submit**, and you will see NAS **others** and ***.*.*.***. Note that this works only for TACACS+, not RADIUS.

9 Which registries pertain to the CS ACS Server?

Answer: HKEY_local_machine\software\cisco\CiscoAAAv3.x and HKEY_local_machine\software\cisco\CiscoSecureACSv3.x

10 I want to use TACACS+ for router management and one RADIUS for dial on the same CS ACS Server. Is it possible? How?

Answer: Yes, it is possible. Just configure the NAS method lists for login authentication with TACACS+ and PPP authentication with RADIUS. On CS ACS, just define two AAA clients with the same IP, different names and different protocols (TACACS+ and RADIUS).

11 How do I capture debugs for Cisco to use to troubleshoot my issue?

Answer: On CS ACS GUI, select **System configuration > Service control** and **set logging to FULL**. Then in the section underneath, select **Manage Logs** so that they do not grow out of control. Then wait until AAA fails again and the logs on the server are collected by running **cssupport.exe** from the command-line. This is found in the utils directory in the Cisco Secure ACS directory.

12 How do I find the exact release of Cisco Secure ACS?

Answer: There are two ways of checking:

First, when you bring up the browser, look for the following at the bottom of the page:

```
CiscoSecure ACS
!The following line indicates the release
Release 3.3(2) Build 2
Copyright ©2004 Cisco Systems, Inc.
```

The second way is to bring up a DOS prompt on the CiscoSecure ACS machine and run the following:

```
C:\Program Files\CiscoSecure ACS v3.3\Utils>CSUtil.exe
CSUtil v3.3(2.2), Copyright 1997-2004, Cisco Systems Inc

Usage: [-q] [-b <backup filename> ] [-c] [-d] [-e <number>] [-g] [-i <file>]
     [[-p] -l <file>] [-n] [-r <all¦users¦config> <backup file> ] [-s] [-u] [-y]
! Rest of the output it removed as irrelevant for this question.
C:\Program Files\CiscoSecure ACS v3.3\Utils>
```

The second option is better.

13 Can ACE server (SDI) and Cisco Secure ACS be installed on the same system?

Answer: Yes there is no problem with running both Cisco Secure ACS and the ACE server (SDI) on the same machine.

14 Do I need to have the SDI client installed?

Answer: When using the SDI database as an external database, it is necessary to install SDI ACE client on the same machine on which Cisco Secure ACS is running. Also note that it is a good practice to install SDI before installing Cisco Secure ACS.

15 Can we send accounting information to another system and also have a copy on the local system?

Answer: Yes this is possible and it is configured under **System configuration: Logging.**

16 Can CS ACS act as a proxy server to other servers?

Answer: Yes, CS ACS can receive authentication requests from the network access servers (NASs) and forward them to other servers. You need to define the other servers by going to the **Network Configuration > AAA Servers** section on the source. The source server is defined as a TACACS+ or RADIUS NAS on the target. Once those are defined, configure the Distributed System Settings in the source Network Configuration to define the proxy parameters.

17 What kind of web server and database does CS ACS use? Who provides patches for those two components?

Answer: CS ACS has its own proprietary database, which spreads over to multiple files. The CS ACS web server is also Cisco proprietary. If any vulnerability is found, Cisco provides the patches because, unlike other software, those components are Cisco proprietary.

18 How do I back up CS ACS?

Answer: You can back up CS ACS through the GUI using the System Configuration tab, or you can use the command-line interface (CLI). If you use the GUI, there is a backup of the users, groups, and Registry settings. If you use the CLI, to back up users and group information, use **$BASE\utils\csutil –d**. To back up users, groups and Registry settings, use **$BASE\utils\csutil -b**.

19 Can I use the backup utility on one CS ACS and then restore the information on another server?

Answer: No, the backup utility is intended to save the user, group, and Registry information from one CS ACS box and restore it to the same CS ACS box running the same version of software. If there is a need to clone a CS ACS box, replication is available instead.

If you need to copy only users and groups from one server to another, use the **csutil -d** command. The resulting dump text (.txt) file is then copied to the target box, and you can use the **csutil -n -l** command to initialize the database and import the users and groups.

20 Is domain stripping supported with CS ACS?

Answer: Yes, CS ACS does support domain stripping. This is useful when there is a combination of Virtual Private Dialup Network (VPDN) and non-VPDN users.

Domain stripping is also useful when the external NT database is used for authentication. The first time the users log in, the username is populated automatically in CS ACS. Since a user may come in as "DOMAIN_X\user" or as "user," names may appear in the CS ACS as "DOMAIN_X\user" or as "user," resulting in both entries in the database. The duplicate entries can be avoided by using domain stripping, wherein the prefix domain with the delimiter "\" can be erased to have a consistent database. You can set this up by going to **Network Configuration > Proxy Distribution Table**.

21 After successful installation of CS ACS, services are running. However, when I try to bring up the GUI, I get this error: "Invalid administration control." What should I do?

Answer: If you have proxy server configured on the browser, you will see this message. To work around the problem, disable the proxy server completely.

22 What is the limit of NASs that can be supported by CiscoSecure ACS for Windows?

Answer: There is no limit. The number simply depends on the number that the Windows Registry can hold, as the NAS information goes to Windows Registry. It is estimated that the Windows Registry can hold thousands of NASs. Note that, unlike users or groups information, NAS information does not go the CS ACS database.

23 Where does the CS ACS copy the configuration of the old CS ACS and how can that be useful if the upgrade fails?

Answer: When upgrade is performed from one version to another. The previous CS ACS version configuration is copied to the following hidden folder:

```
%systemroot%\Program Files\CiscoSecure ACS Configuration
```

If you run into a problem with an upgrade, the system can be purged of all information, such as the Registry, folders and so on. If you leave the saved configuration folder, the next installation will find this information and will try to import the configuration from the old settings. This may come to your rescue when an upgrade fails due to file permission problems and so on. So, you must not remove this folder.

24 How can I disable the users' option to change the password by using Telnet to access the router?

Answer: You can change the password after using Telnet to access the router and click **Enter** without entering any password. This behavior can be prevented with the following setting on CS ACS.

Step 1 Back up the local Registry.

Step 2 Go to Registry key

```
HKEY_LOCAL_MACHINE\SOFTWARE\Cisco\CiscoAAAv<your_version>\CSTacacs.
```

Step 3 Add a Registry value by highlighting **CSTacacs**, right-clicking and selecting **NEW-DWORD**.

Step 4 When the new key appears on the right-hand side of the window, type **disablechangepassword** into the new key window.

Step 5 The default value for the new key is 0, which allows users to change the password. Right-click on the new key, select **Modify**, and then change the key value to **1** to disable the ability to change the password.

Step 6 After adding this new key, restart the **CSTacacs** and **CSAuth services**.

25 When was PPTP (Point-to-Point Tunneling Protocol) with MPPE (Microsoft Point to Point Encryption) keying support introduced to Cisco Secure ACS for Windows?

Answer: This was introduced on CS ACS version 2.6.

26 How can I import a large number of NASs?

Answer: The procedure to bulk import NASs is similar to the import of users. The following flat-file is an example:

```
ONLINE
ADD_NAS:sam_i_am:IP:10.31.1.51:KEY:cisco:VENDOR:CISCO_T+
ADD_NAS:son_of_sam:IP:10.31.1.52:KEY:cisco:VENDOR:CISCO_R
```

The NASs may also be imported into a particular Network Device Group. The following flat-file is an example:

```
ADD_NAS:koala:IP:10.31.1.53:KEY:cisco:VENDOR:CISCO_R:NDG:my_ndg
```

27 What databases are supported for the synchronization?

Answer: CSV files and any ODBC-compliant database such as Oracle and MS SQL are supported.

28 With Cisco Secure you can force users to change their passwords after a given time period. Can you do this when you are using the Windows NT database for authentication?

Answer: This feature is available in all versions when you are using the Cisco Secure database for authentication. From version 3.0, support of Microsoft Challenge Handshake Authentication Protocol (MS-CHAP) Version 2 and MS-CHAP Password Aging is available. This works with the Microsoft Dial-Up Networking client, the Cisco VPN Client (versions 3.0 and later), and any desktop client that supports MS-CHAP. This feature prompts you to change your password after a login attempt when the password has expired. The MS-CHAP-based password-aging feature supports users who authenticate with a Windows user database and is offered in addition to password aging supported by the Cisco Secure ACS user database. This feature has been added in CS ACS 3.0, but it also requires device/client support. Cisco Systems is gradually adding such device/client support to various hardware.

29 How can users change their own passwords?

Answer: Users can be notified of expiring Cisco Secure ACS database passwords on dial connections if the Cisco Secure Authentication Agent is on the PC. You can also use User Changeable Password (UCP) software, which runs with Microsoft IIS, once the users are in the network. When the users are on the network, they can point their browsers to the system where User Control Point (UCP) is installed and change their passwords.

30 My CS ACS "Logged in Users" report works with some devices, but not with others. What is the problem?

Answer: For the "Logged in Users" report to work (and this also applies to most other features involving sessions), packets should include at least the following fields:

- Authentication Request packet

  nas-ip-address
  nas-port

- Accounting Start packet

  nas-ip-address
  nas-port
  session-id
  framed-ip-address

- Accounting Stop packet

  nas-ip-address
  nas-port
  session-id
  framed-ip-address

Attributes (such as nas-port and nas-ip-address) that appear in multiple packets should contain the same value in all packets.

If a connection is so brief that there is little time between the start and stop packets (for example, HTTP through the PIX), then the report entitled "Logged-in Users" will not work either.

CS ACS versions 3.0 and later allow the device to send either nas-port or nas-port-id.

31 How are user passwords stored in CS ACS?

Answer: Passwords are encrypted using the Crypto API Microsoft Base Cryptographic Provider v1.0. This offers either 56-bit or 128-bit encryption, depending on how the server is set up. The default cipher will be RC4.

32 Can I change the default port for RADIUS and TACACS+ protocols on CS ACS?

Answer: Yes, you can, but it is strongly discouraged. RADIUS Protocol listens on UDP/1645 and UDP/1812 for Authentication & Authorization and UDP/1646 and UDP/1813 for accounting. The location for ports for RADIUS is as follows:

```
HKEY_LOCAL_MACHINE\SOFTWARE\Cisco\CiscoAAAv3.3\CSRadius
"AuthenticationPort"=dword:1812
"AccountingPort"=dword:1813
This can also be changed in the newer version:
HKEY_LOCAL_MACHINE\SOFTWARE\Cisco\CiscoAAAv3.3\CSRadius
AccountingPort = 1646
AccountingPortNew = 1813
AuthenticationPort = 1645
AuthenticationPortNew = 1812
```

You can change any of the values previously listed. TACACS+ protocol on CS ACS listens by default on TCP/49. You can change the TACACS+ port by editing attribute values of the proper key in the Windows Registry:

```
HKEY_LOCAL_MACHINE\SOFTWARE\Cisco\CiscoAAAv3.3\CSTacacs
"Port"=dword:59
```

As mentioned before, it is strongly discouraged to change these default ports to something else.

33 I am unable to delete the users and some users seem to belong to multiple groups. How may I get around the problem?

Answer: Open up DOS prompt of CS ACS Server and type **$BASE\utils\csutil -q -d -n -l dump.txt**. Here "$BASE" is the directory where the software was installed. Issuing this command causes the database to be unloaded and reloaded to clear up the counters. Before performing this task, we strongly recommend that you back up the CS ACS database.

34 I cannot start services for RADIUS after re-installing the software a few times. The event error says that service was terminated with "service specific error 11".

Answer: Here are some possible reasons for encountering the problem:

- The most common problems occur when you run Windows with an unsupported service pack or there is software contention with another application. Check installation guide and the release notes for the supported OS and service pack.
- To check for port conflicts, go to the command line of the server and type **netstat -an | findstr 1645** and **netstat -an | findstr 1646** to see if any other

service is using these User Data Protocol (UDP) ports. If another service is using these ports, you will see something similar to the following:

```
UDP 0.0.0.0:1645 *:*
UDP 0.0.0.0:1646 *:*
```

- Microsoft Server services may not have been started. To check this, go to **Control Panel > Services** and ensure that the Server service options for **Started** and **Automatic** are selected.

35 When accessing CS ACS GUI through a firewall, the address for the server in the URL field changes from a global IP address to a local address. Why does this happen?

Answer: The global IP address does not change when you change to subsequent pages after the initial login from version CS ACS 3.0.

36 Can a user be in more than one group at a time?

Answer: No, a user cannot be in more than one group at a time.

37 Are the dynamically mapped users stored in cache replicated?

Answer: Yes. Dynamically mapped users are stored in cache in the same way as internal users. Those dynamic users simply never refer to the password fields and the group can be dynamic (mapped by the external authenticator). CS ACS replicates the group/user database with both internal and external users at the same time. You cannot do one type without the other, as replication simply performs remote file copies from master to slave.

Best Practices

The following are best practices for the CS ACS Server:

- Before CS ACS installation, back up the Windows Registries, so that if a new installation of CS ACS or upgrade is needed, and if the Registries are corrupted, you can restore the Registries without re-imaging the operating system.
- Before performing any upgrade, always back up the database either via Web or using CLI (csutil). Also perform regular scheduled backups depending on how often you make changes.
- Unless it is absolutely necessary, do not install any web server, FTP server, and so on, which may introduce vulnerabilities to the server. Follow the Windows Operating System (Windows OS) Security Guidelines to harden the Windows OS before installing CS ACS.
- To attain maximum availability, configure replication and schedule replication at least once in a day (the scheduling depends on how many changes are made to the server).

- Protect the CS ACS Server from malicious viruses or worms by using Enterprise Anti-Virus Software and host-based IDSs (CSA Agent for example) and Personal Firewall.
- If you have a small LAN environment, then put the CS ACS on your internal LAN and protect it from outside access by using a firewall and the NAS. For high availability, configure database replication to a secondary CS ACS as a backup. However, if you have a large enterprise network, which is geographically dispersed, where access servers may be located in different parts of a city, in different cities, or on different continents, a central ACS may work if network latency is not an issue. But connection reliability over long distances may cause problems. In this case, local ACS installations may be preferable to a central server. If you want to maintain the same database for all the CS ACS servers, database replication or synchronization from a central server may be necessary. Using external user databases such as Microsoft Active Directory (AD) or Lightweight Directory Access Protocol (LDAP) for authentication may complicate this even more. Additional security measures may be required to protect the network and user information being forwarded across the WAN. In this case, the addition of an encrypted connection between regions would be required.
- When replication is performed, the services are stopped on the server. Therefore, the server does not perform authentication. To eliminate this downtime, it is always a good idea to configure on the authentication device for failover. To clarify this, assume that you have one CS ACS in the U.S. replicating to a second CS ACS in Canada. Configuring the authenticating devices to try the U.S. and then Canada may not be the best plan. You might consider installing a second local server (in the U.S.) and replicating from the U.S. master to the U.S. slave. The U.S. slave could then replicate to the Canada slave.

PART V

Troubleshooting Intrusion Prevention Systems

Chapter 14 Troubleshooting Cisco Intrusion Prevention System

Chapter 15 Troubleshooting IDSM-2 Blade on Switch

Chapter 16 Troubleshooting Cisco IDS Network Module (NM-CIDS)

Chapter 17 Troubleshooting CiscoWorks Common Services

Chapter 18 Troubleshooting IDM and IDS/IPC Management Console (IDS/IPC MC)

Chapter 19 Troubleshooting Firewall MC

Chapter 20 Troubleshooting Router MC

Chapter 21 Troubleshooting Cisco Security Agent Management Console (CSA MC) and CSA Agent

Chapter 22 Troubleshooting IEV and Security Monitors

CHAPTER 14

Troubleshooting Cisco Intrusion Prevention System

Cisco Secure Intrusion Prevention System (IPS) comprises three main components: first, the IPS Sensor, which is the sniffing or inline component of Cisco Intrusion Prevention System; second, a management section of IPS (IPS MC, for example), which will be discussed in Chapter 18, "Troubleshooting IDM and IDS/IPS Management Console (IDS/IPS MC);" and third, a reporting tool (for example, a Security Monitor, which is discussed in Chapter 22, "Troubleshooting IEV and Security Monitors"). This chapter focuses on how to troubleshoot issues with IPS software on the sensor. As IPS software implementation is the same on all platforms (Sensor Appliance, IDSM-2 blade (IDSM stands for intrusion detection system module), NM (Network Module)-CIDS blade, and ASA-SSM (Security Services Module)), troubleshooting software issues on IPS software are the same across these platforms.

First, the chapter discusses the building blocks of IPS and some high-level details of IPS operation, and then it discusses troubleshooting tools and techniques. Once you understand the level of detail required to use the tools and apply techniques, you will see the main problem area categories and how to troubleshoot them efficiently and quickly. The chapter finishes with a detailed case study on different capturing techniques on various switches that are needed for IPS to function correctly, and concludes with a section on Best Practices.

Overview of IPS Sensor Software

Troubleshooting IPS issues demands that you understand the underlying architecture of IPS Software. This not only helps you feel comfortable with the product, but helps you to be a very efficient and confident troubleshooter, qualities that can distinguish you from others. To begin becoming an effective troubleshooter, you need to start with the software building blocks, which are the foundation of IPS software. Sections that follow discuss the following Sensor software topics:

- IPS deployment architecture
- IPS sensor software building blocks
- Communication protocols

- Modes of sensor operation
- Hardware and interfaces supported

IPS Deployment Architecture

As mentioned before, there are primarily three components of an IPS deployment for a single sensor as depicted in Figure 14-1.

Figure 14-1 *A Typical IPS Deployment in the Network*

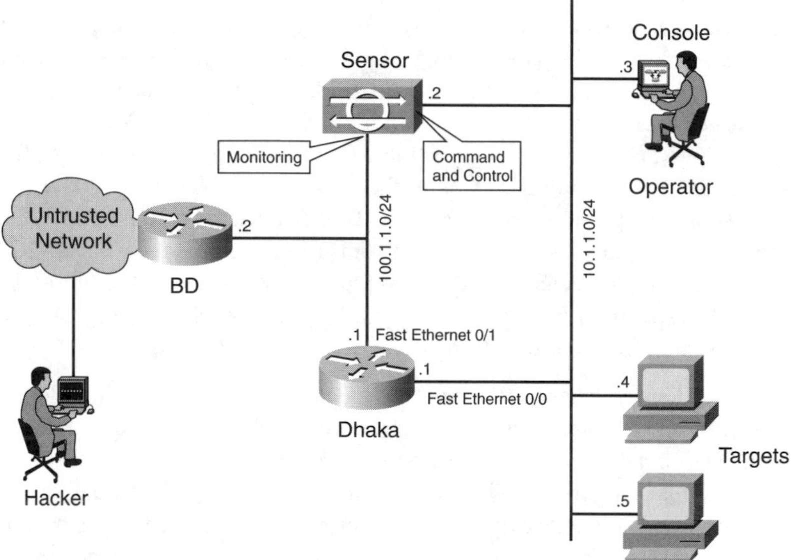

Typically more than one sensor is managed by a single IPS MC and by the Security Monitor. The three main components of an IPS deployment are as follows:

- **Sensor**—A sensor can be an Appliance (IDS 42xx series), IDSM-2 blade, NM-CIDS module, or ASA-SSM module. You can deploy the sensor in Inline mode or Promiscuous mode. In Inline mode, the traffic is redirected through the sensor, and in Promiscuous mode, the traffic is sniffed to the sensor. The sensor will be discussed thoroughly in this chapter.
- **Management Console**—A management console for the sensor is used to configure and deploy the sensor software to the sensor. IPS Device Manager (IDM), an integral part of the sensor software, can be used to configure and upgrade the software on the sensor. If you want to manage more than one sensor, you can use the IPS MC, which is discussed thoroughly in Chapter 18. IPS MC communicates with sensor using SSH and SSL. More details on the communication protocol used between IPS MC (or IDM) and the sensor are discussed in the "Communication Protocol" section.

- **Monitoring Device**—A monitoring device is used to pull the events from the sensor, which then displays the events in real time. You can also correlate events, and generate static reports as you need. Several monitoring devices support pulling events from the sensor. Security Monitor is one such monitoring device, which is discussed in detail in Chapter 22, "Troubleshooting IEV and Security Monitors."

Although it's extremely important to understand all three components of the IPS Architecture, the sensor is the core of everything. To understand the sensor in depth, you need to comprehend the IPS Software building blocks.

IPS Software Building Blocks

There are several interoperating applications—processes that go into making IPS software on the Linux platform. These applications and processes are described as follows:

- MainApp
- AnalysisEngine
- Command Line Interface (CLI)

The applications that make up the sensor can be verified by using the **show version** output.

MainApp

This application initializes the sensor, starts and stops other applications, and performs upgrades. Following are some of the components of the MainApp application:

- **ctlTransSource (Control Transaction server)**—This allows sensors to communicate control transactions with each other. Sensor currently provides **Network Access Controller** master blocking sensor capability with this application.
- **Event Store**—This is an indexed store used to store IPS events (error, status, and alert system messages) that is accessible through the CLI, IDM, Adaptive Security Device Manager (ASDM), or Remote Data Exchange Protocol (RDEP).
- **InterfaceApp**—This handles bypass and physical settings and defines paired interfaces. Physical settings are speed, duplex, and administrative state.
- **LogApp**—This component writes all the application's log messages to the log file and the application's error messages to the Event Store.
- **Network Access Controller (NAC)**—This manages remote network devices (firewalls, routers, and switches) to provide blocking capabilities when an alert event has occurred. Network Access Controller creates and applies access control lists (ACLs) on the controlled network device or uses the **shun** command on the firewalls (PIX and FWSM).

- **NotificationApp**—Sends Simple Network Management Protocol (SNMP) traps when triggered by alert, status, and error events. **NotificationApp** uses the public domain SNMP agent. SNMP GETs provide information about the general health of the sensor.
- **Web Server**—This application is the sensor's web server, which is capable of both HTTP and HTTPS communications. The web server uses several servlets (idm, event-server, transaction-server and iplog-server) to perform their respected tasks as follows:
  - **idm** (Intrusion Detection Device Manager) servlet provides the IDM web-based management interface.
  - **event-server** servlet is used to serve events to external management applications such as Security Monitor.
  - **transaction-server** allows external management applications such as the IDS MC to initiate control transactions with the sensor. Control transactions are used to configure and control sensors.
  - **iplog-server** is used to serve IP logs to external systems such as Security Monitor.
- **AuthenticationApp**—This application configures and manages authentication on the sensor. It verifies that users are authorized to perform Command Line Interface (CLI), IDM, ASDM, or RDEP actions.

AnalysisEngine

This application is the actual sensing engine. The AnalysisEngine performs packet capture, processes the signature and alarm channel configurations, and generates alert events based on its configuration and the IP traffic. The AnalysisEngine stores its events in the Event Store.

CLI

This application is the calling line ID (CLI) shell application that is started when you log in to the sensor through Telnet or SSH. All accounts created through the CLI will use the CLI as their shell (except the service account—only one service account is allowed). Which CLI commands are allowed depends on the privilege of the user.

Communication Protocols

There are several communication protocols used on the sensor. These protocols enable Sensor's processes to communicate with each other and external management devices to communicate with sensors. Following are three types of communication methods:

- **Inter-process Communication**—Within Sensor, all applications use an interprocess communication application programming interface (API) called **IDAPI** to handle internal communications and to interact with each other—for example, after

AnalysisEngine captures and analyzes the network traffic on its interfaces. When a signature is matched, **AnalysisEngine** generates an alert, which is stored in the Event Store. The communication between the **AnalysisEngine** and the Event Store uses **IDAPI**.

- **External Communication with Management Console**—Management Console, such as IPS MC, communicates with Sensor using SSH protocol when it initially pulls the sensor's configuration. Configuration and Sensor software upgrade is pushed by IPS MC using the RDEP2 or Cisco Intrusion Detection Event Exchange (CIDEE), which uses HTTP over SSL. RDEP2 is discussed in detail in this section. IDM, which is an integral part of the IPS software, uses HTTPS (HTTP over SSL).
- **External communication with Reporting devices**—An IPS Reporting tool such as Security Monitor communicates with sensors using a protocol called RDEP2 or CIDEE. RDEP2 uses the industry standards HTTP, Transaction Layer Security (TLS) and Secure Sockets Layer (SSL) and Extensible Markup Language (XML) to provide a standardized interface between RDEP2 agents (between the Security Monitor as client and the sensor as Server). CIDEE specifies the extensions to Security Device Event Exchange (SDEE) that are used by the Cisco IPS. SDEE is a product-independent standard for communicating security device events. SDEE is an enhancement to the current version of RDEP2 that adds extensibility features that are needed for communicating events generated by various types of security devices. RDEP2, SDEE, and CIDEE are discussed next.
- **RDEP2**—RDEP2 is a communication protocol used to exchange IPS event, IP log, configuration, and control messages between IPS clients (for example, Security Monitor) and IPS servers (for example, Sensor). RDEP2 communications consist of request and response messages. RDEP2 clients initiate request messages to RDEP2 servers. RDEP2 servers respond to request messages with response messages.

  RDEP2 defines three classes of request/response messages: event, IP log, and transaction messages. Event messages include IPS alert, status, and error messages. Clients use IP log requests to retrieve IP log data from servers. Transaction messages are used to configure and control IPS servers.

  RDEP2 uses HTTP, TLS and SSL and XML to provide a standardized interface between RDEP2 monitoring tool (Security Monitor) and the IPS sensor. RDEP2 uses HTTP message formats and message exchange protocol to exchange messages between the monitoring device and the sensor.

  IPS sensors can accept connections from one to ten RDEP2 clients (Security Monitor) simultaneously. Clients selectively retrieve data by time range, type of event (alert, error, or status message), and level (alert = high, medium, low, or informational; error = high, medium, or low). Events are retrieved by a query (a single bulk get), a subscription (a real-time persistent connection), or both. Communications are secured by TLS or SSL. The monitoring application sends an RDEP2 event request to the sensor's web server, which passes it to the event server. The event server queries the event store through Intrusion Detection Application Programming Interface (IDAPI), and then returns the result. For retrieving events, the sensor is backward-compatible to RDEP, even though the new standard for retrieval is RDEP2. It is strongly recommended to use RDEP2 to retrieve events and send configuration changes for IPS 5.0.

IPS MC also sends configuration changes to the sensor through RDEP2. The IPS MC sends an RDEP2 control transaction to the sensor's web server, which passes it to the control transaction server. The control transaction server passes the control transaction through IDAPI to the appropriate application, waits for the application's response, and then returns the result.

- **SDEE**—SDEE, developed by Cisco Systems, Inc., is a product-independent standard for communicating security device events. SDEE is an enhancement to the current version of RDEP2 that adds extensibility features that are needed for communicating events generated by various types of security devices.

  Systems that use SDEE to communicate events to clients are referred to as SDEE providers. SDEE specifies that events can be transported using the HTTP or HTTP over SSL and TLS protocols. When HTTP or HTTPS is used, SDEE providers act as HTTP servers, whereas SDEE clients are the initiators of HTTP requests.

- **CIDEE**—CIDEE specifies the extensions to SDEE that are used by the Cisco IPS. The CIDEE standard specifies all possible extensions that are supported by IPS. Specific systems may implement a subset of CIDEE extensions. However, any extension that is designated as being required *must* be supported by all systems. CIDEE supports the following events:

  — **<evError>**—This is used for error events. Error events are generated by the CIDEE provider when the provider detects an error or warning condition. The <evError> event contains an error code and textual description of the error.

  — **<evStatus>**—This is used for status message events. Status message events are generated by CIDEE providers to indicate that something of potential interest occurred on the host. Different types of status messages can be reported in the status event—one message per event. Each type of status message contains a set of data elements that are specific to the type of occurrence that the status message is describing. The information in many of the status messages might be useful for audit purposes. Errors and warnings are not considered status information and are reported using <evError> rather than <evStatus>.

  — **<evShunRqst>**—This is used for a block request event. It is generated to indicate that a block action is to be initiated by the service that handles network blocking.

- **IDIOM—**IDIOM is a data format standard that defines the event messages that are reported by the IPS, in addition to the operational messages that are used to configure and control intrusion detection systems. These messages consist of XML documents that conform to the IDIOM XML schema.
- **IDCONF**—IPS 5.0 manages its configuration using XML documents. IDCONF specifies the XML schema including IPS 5.0 control transactions. The IDCONF schema does not specify the contents of the configuration documents, but rather the framework and building blocks from which the configuration documents are developed. It provides mechanisms that let the IPS managers and CLI ignore features that are not configurable by certain platforms or functions through the use of the feature-supported attribute. IDCONF messages are exchanged over RDEP2 and are wrapped inside IDIOM request and response messages. IDIOM, for the most part, has been superseded by IDCONF, SDEE, and CIDEE.

Modes of Sensor Operation

Starting from IPS version 5.0, Sensor can function in one of the following modes:

- Inline
- Inline bypass
- Promiscuous
- Combined

Modes are described in the sections that follow.

Inline Mode

Running Inline mode puts the IPS sensor directly into the traffic flow. Because an inline IPS sensor sits in the path of traffic flow, it stops attacks by dropping malicious traffic before it reaches the intended target, thus providing a protective service. Not only is the inline device processing information on Layers 3 and 4, but it is also analyzing the contents and payload of the packets for more sophisticated embedded attacks (Layers 3 to 7). This deeper analysis lets the system identify and stop or block attacks that normally would pass through a traditional firewall device.

In Inline mode, a packet comes in through the first interface of the pair of the sensor and out the second interface of the pair. The packet is sent to the second interface of the pair unless that packet is being denied or modified by a signature. You can configure ASA-SSM to operate inline even though it has only one sensing interface.

In Inline mode, in addition to **Blocking**, and TCP reset, which are available in Promiscuous mode, additional action types include the following:

- **request-block-connection**—Request SHUN of connection

- **request-block-host**—Request SHUN of attacker host
- **deny-attacker-inline**—Do not transmit packets with source address of attacker
- **deny-packet-inline**—Do not transmit the single packet causing alert
- **deny-connection-inline**—Do not transmit packets on this TCP connection
- **log-attacker-packets**—Activate packet logging for attacker address
- **log-victim-packets**—Activate packet logging for victim address
- **log-pair-packets**—Activate packet logging for attacker/victim address pair
- **reset-tcp-connection**—Send TCP RST packets to terminate connection
- **produce-alert**—Write evIdsAlert to EventStore
- **produce-verbose-alert**—Write evIdsAlert to EventStore with triggerPacket
- **request-snmp-trap**—Write evIdsAlert to EventStore with SNMP request in AlarmTraits

NOTE Even though you can run IPS 5.0 software on IDS-4210, and Cisco IDS Network Module (NM-CIDS), these two sensors do not operate in Inline mode.

Inline Bypass Mode

Because the traffic is passing through the sensor in Inline mode, it is a point of failure for the network behind it. To mitigate this risk, a software driver-level Bypass mode option is available. The Bypass mode will unconditionally copy packets from one interface to the other. The Bypass has an Automatic mode that will activate it during sensorApp configuration operations, or if sensorApp is unresponsive. Automatic bypass mode is turned on by default, which is the recommended configuration. However, if you want to turn Bypass on permanently, there is a serious security consequence, as all the packets will bypass IPS processing subsystems.

NOTE Bypass mode functions only when the operating system is running. If the sensor is powered off or shut down, Bypass mode does not work—traffic is not passed to the sensor.

Promiscuous Mode

Packets do not flow through the IPS in Promiscuous mode. The sensor analyzes a copy of the monitored traffic rather than the actual redirected packet. The advantage of operating in Promiscuous mode is that the IPS does not affect the packet flow. The disadvantage of operating in Promiscuous mode, however, is that the IPS cannot stop malicious traffic from reaching its intended target for certain types of attacks, such as atomic attacks (single-packet attacks). The response actions implemented by promiscuous IPS devices are post-event responses and often require assistance from other networking devices, for example, the **Blocking** feature. **TCP reset** is another action type in Promiscuous mode, but not a guaranteed mechanism to stop attacks. Although such response actions can prevent some classes of attacks, for atomic attacks, the single packet has the chance of reaching the target system before the promiscuous-based sensor can apply an ACL modification on a managed device (such as a firewall, switch, or router) or perform TCP reset on the connection.

Combined Modes

Sensor platforms with three or more interfaces can combine both Inline and Promiscuous traffic input, or with four or more interfaces, you can have two separate inline feeds. The combinations are flexible; the only rule is that Inline mode takes two interfaces. Note that if you have the same traffic coming in on multiple interfaces, irregular results will ensue. You might see duplicate non-TCP alarms, or with TCP you might get many 13xx alarms or TCP stream collisions resulting in no alarm.

Hardware and Interfaces Supported

It is important to know which sensors support IPS version 5.0. Table 14-1 summarizes all the sensors that support IPS 5.0. This information is taken from the following link, so refer to this link for additional details:

Table 14-1 *Supported Sensors for Version IPS 5.0*

Model Name	Part Number	Optional Interfaces
IDS-4210	IDS-4210 IDS-4210-K9 IDS-4210-NFR	— — —
IDS-4215	IDS-4215-K9 IDS-4215-4FE-K9	IDS-4FE-INT= —
IDS-4235	IDS-4235-K9	IDS-4FE-INT=
IDS-4250	IDS-4250-TX-K9 IDS-4250-SX-K9 IDS-4250-XL-K9	IDS-4FE-INT=, IDS-4250-SX-INT=, IDS-XL-INT= IDS-XL-INT= —
IPS-4240	IPS-4240-K9	—

continues

Table 14-1 *Supported Sensors for Version IPS 5.0 (Continued)*

Model Name	Part Number	Optional Interfaces
IPS-4255	IPS-4255-K9	—
ASA-SSM-10	ASA-SSM-AIP-10-K9	—
ASA-SSM-20	ASA-SSM-AIP-20-K9	—
IDSM-2	WS-SVC-IDSM2-K9	—
NM-CIDS	NM-CIDS-K9	—

Many times, knowing and using the proper interfaces for different purposes is a challenge, and the source of many problems with IPS operation. Table 14-2 summarizes all the available interfaces that are supported on sensors. This information is taken from the following location:

http://www.cisco.com/univercd/cc/td/doc/product/iaabu/csids/csids11/hwguide/hwintro.htm#wp490986

Table 14-2 *Interface Support for Appliances and Modules Running IPS 5.0*

Base Chassis	Added PCI Cards	Interfaces Supporting Inline	Possible Port Combinations	Interfaces Not Supporting Inline
IDS-4210	—	None	N/A	All
IDS-4215	—	None	N/A	All
IDS-4215	4FE	FastEthernet0/1 4FE FastEthernet1/0 FastEthernet1/1 FastEthernet1/2 FastEthernet1/3	1/0<->1/1 1/0<->1/2 1/0<->1/3 1/1<->1/2 1/1<->1/3 1/2<->1/3 0/1<->1/0 0/1<->1/1 0/1<->1/2 0/1<->1/3	FastEthernet0/0
IDS-4235	—	None	N/A	All
IDS-4235	4FE	4FE FastEthernet1/0 FastEthernet1/1 FastEthernet1/2 FastEthernet1/3	1/0<->1/1 1/0<->1/2 1/0<->1/3 1/1<->1/2 1/1<->1/3 1/2<->1/3	GigabitEthernet0/0 GigabitEthernet0/1
IDS-4250	—	None	N/A	All

Table 14-2 *Interface Support for Appliances and Modules Running IPS 5.0 (Continued)*

Base Chassis	Added PCI Cards	Interfaces Supporting Inline	Possible Port Combinations	Interfaces Not Supporting Inline
IDS-4250	4FE	4FE FastEthernet1/0 FastEthernet1/1 FastEthernet1/2 FastEthernet1/3	1/0<->1/1 1/0<->1/2 1/0<->1/3 1/1<->1/2 1/1<->1/3 1/2<->1/3	GigabitEthernet0/0 GigabitEthernet0/1
IDS-4250	SX	None	N/A	All
IDS-4250	XL	2 SX of the XL GigabitEthernet2/0 GigabitEthernet2/1	2/0<->2/1	GigabitEthernet0/0 GigabitEthernet0/1
IDSM-2	—	port 7 and 8 GigabitEthernet0/7 GigabitEthernet0/8	0/7<->0/8	GigabitEthernet0/2
IPS-4240	—	4 onboard GE GigabitEthernet0/0 GigabitEthernet0/1 GigabitEthernet0/2 GigabitEthernet0/3	0/0<->0/1 0/0<->0/2 0/0<->0/3 0/1<->0/2 0/1<->0/3 0/2<->0/3	Management0/0
IPS-4255	—	4 onboard GE GigabitEthernet0/0 GigabitEthernet0/1 GigabitEthernet0/2 GigabitEthernet0/3	0/0<->0/1 0/0<->0/2 0/0<->0/3 0/1<->0/2 0/1<->0/3 0/2<->0/3	Management0/0
NM-CIDS	—	None	N/A	All
ASA-SSM-10	—	GigabitEthernet0/1	By security context	GigabitEthernet0/0
ASA-SSM-20	—	GigabitEthernet0/1	By security context	GigabitEthernet0/0

Diagnostic Commands and Tools

Diagnostic commands and tools are very easy to use on Sensor. These commands and tools provide much meaningful information on the sensor for troubleshooting issues that range from easy to complex. In the following section, you work with some of the most important commands for troubleshooting any sensor-related issue. It is important to become familiar with these commands.

show Commands

show commands in Sensor are used to find out the statistics and state information of the sensor applications, configurations, version, and so on. These commands are very useful tools and quite handy for troubleshooting sensor issues. Some of the most frequently show commands are as follows outlined in the sections that follow.

show version

The **show version** command provides the information about different applications that go into making the sensor. It's important that all these applications are running for the sensor to function completely. If one of the applications dies, the output of this command will provide this information. Additionally, the **show version** command also provides the information of the latest version the sensor is running, disk and memory usage, and upgrade history, as shown in Example 14-1.

Example 14-1 show version *Output from IPS 5.x Sensor*

```
sensor# show version
Application Partition:

Cisco Intrusion Prevention System, Version 5.0(1)S149.0

OS Version 2.4.26-IDS-smp-bigphys
Platform: IDS-4235
! The following line shows the serial number of the sensor
Serial Number: CGTWJ11
! The following line shows this sensor is not licensed
No license present
Sensor up-time is 24 days.
Using 782422016 out of 923549696 bytes of available memory (84% usage)
system is using 17.3M out of 29.0M bytes of available disk space (59% usage)
application-data is using 31.2M out of 174.7M bytes of available disk space (19%
  usage)
boot is using 40.5M out of 75.9M bytes o.f available disk space (56% usage)
application-log is using 530.5M out of 2.8G bytes of available disk space (20% usage)
! It is expected that CLI process will not be running.  However, the other two
! processes must be running for the proper functioning of the sensor.

MainApp          2005_Mar_04_14.23   (Release)   2005-03-04T14:35:11-0600   Running
AnalysisEngine   2005_Mar_04_14.23   (Release)   2005-03-04T14:35:11-0600   Running
CLI              2005_Mar_04_14.23   (Release)   2005-03-04T14:35:11-0600

Upgrade History:

  IDS-K9-maj-5.0-1-   22:16:00 UTC Thu Mar 04 2004

Recovery Partition Version 1.1 - 5.0(1)S149

sensor#
```

show configuration

The **show configuration** command is used to check the current configuration of the sensor. To get the specific information from the sensor configuration, use the pipe (|) with **begin, exclude or include** to filter the information that you want to get. For instance if you want to see the allowed hosts configured on the sensor, execute the command shown in Example 14-2.

Example 14-2 show configuration *Command Displaying Only the Allowed Host Configuration*

```
sensor# show configuration | include access-list
accessList ipAddress 10.0.0.0 netmask 255.0.0.0
accessList ipAddress 172.16.0.0 netmask 255.255.0.0
sensor#
```

show events

The **show events** command is one of the most useful commands for troubleshooting issues on a sensor, in particular, alarm-related issues. Without any other arguments, this command displays alarms and errors in real time. However, to retrieve from the database the alarms or errors that were stored in the past, there are different arguments, which are found by executing the **show events ?** command on the sensor. Example 14-3 shows the events written to the sensor database for the past 30 minutes.

Example 14-3 *Output for* **show events** *Command for Past 30 Minutes*

```
sensor# show events past 00:30:00

evStatus: eventId=1111026292731744312 vendor=Cisco
  originator:
    hostId: sensor
    appName: mainApp
    appInstanceId: 4255
  time: 2005/04/10 00:02:07 2005/04/09 16:02:07 UTC
  controlTransaction: command=getVersion successful=true
    description: Control transaction response.
    requestor:
      user: cids
      application:
        hostId: 10.1.1.50
        appName: -cidcli
        appInstanceId: 5589
--MORE—
Sensor#
```

To clear the events from the EventStore, execute the **clear events** command.

show statistics *service*

The **show statistics** *service* command is used to view statistics for the designated service. These statistics are useful in identifying problems pertaining to the designated services.

Example 14-4 shows the list of available services and the statistics that can be obtained using this command.

Example 14-4 *Available Services and Statistics that Can Be Obtained with* **show statistics** *Command*

```
sensor# show statistics ?
analysis-engine        Display analysis engine statistics.
authentication         Display authentication statistics.
denied-attackers       Display denied attacker statistics.
event-server           Display event server statistics.
event-store            Display event store statistics.
host                   Display host statistics.
logger                 Display logger statistics.
network-access         Display network access controller statistics.
notification           Display notification statistics.
sdee-server            Display SDEE server statistics.
transaction-server     Display transaction server statistics.
transaction-source     Display transaction source statistics.
virtual-sensor         Display virtual sensor statistics.
web-server             Display web server statistics.
sensor# show statistics
```

Example 14-5 shows the statistics of Authentication application.

Example 14-5 *Statistics of Authentication Application*

```
sensor# show statistics authentication
General
   totalAuthenticationAttempts = 37
   failedAuthenticationAttempts = 0
sensor#
```

While troubleshooting issues with any of the applications, it's important to clear the counters of the application to see the statistics for a specific time interval. Example 14-6 shows the statistics of the authentication application and how to clear the statistics with the **clear** option on the **show statistics** command.

Example 14-6 *Clearing Statistics of Authentication Application*

```
sensor# show statistics authentication clear
General
   totalAuthenticationAttempts = 37
   failedAuthenticationAttempts = 0
! The above command shows the statistics of the authentication application and also
! clear the counters at the same time. The following command output verifies that
! the counters are reset to zero.
sensor# show statistics authentication
General
   totalAuthenticationAttempts = 0
   failedAuthenticationAttempts = 0
sensor#
```

show interfaces

The most useful information of the output of the show interfaces command enables you to identify different interfaces, their status, and counter information. Example 14-7 shows the output of show interface command for Command and Control interface.

Example 14-7 **show interfaces** *Command Output from IPS 5.x*

```
sensor# show interfaces gigabitEthernet0/1
MAC statistics from interface GigabitEthernet0/1
! Media Type TX indicates that this is a Command and Control Interface
   Media Type = TX
! You need to ensure that the Link Status shows up
   Link Status = Up
   Link Speed = Auto_100
   Link Duplex = Auto_Full
! You should see packets and bytes received on this interface if there is any
! activity
   Total Packets Received = 5662817
   Total Bytes Received = 438650587
   Total Multicast Packets Received = 12
   Total Receive Errors = 0
   Total Receive FIFO Overruns = 0
   Total Packets Transmitted = 506540
   Total Bytes Transmitted = 125982450
   Total Transmit Errors = 0
   Total Transmit FIFO Overruns = 0
sensor#
```

show tech-support

The **show tech-support** command captures all status and configuration information on the sensor. The command allows the information to be transferred to a remote system. The output can be very large, approximately 1 MB. The output includes the current configuration, version information, and **cidDump** (the following section contains more information on this topic) information. **show tech-support** can be obtained from the sensor for troubleshooting purposes either via the CLI or by using IDM. With CLI, after logging into sensor using an admin account, you can execute the following command to get the tech-support information

```
show tech-support [page] [password] [destination-url destination-url]
```

Example 14-8 shows how to generate and place the tech-support output of the sensor into an FTP server using the relative path of user **csidsuser**.

Example 14-8 *Generating and Transferring the* **show tech-support** *File to the Relative Directory of User in FTP Server*

```
sensor# show tech-support destination-url ftp://csidsuser@10.1.1.40/reports/
  sensorReport.html
password:*******
```

Example 14-9 shows how to transfer the tech-support output to the user absolute directory path.

Example 14-9 *Generating and Transferring the* **show tech-support** *File to the Absolute Directory of User in FTP Server*

```
sensor# show tech-support destination-url
ftp://csidsuser@10.1.1.40//absolute/reports/sensorReport.html
password:*******
```

You can view the **show tech-support** output page by page with the following command:

```
Sensor# show tech-support page
```

The system information appears on the screen, one page at a time. Press the spacebar to view the next page or press **Ctrl-C** to return to the prompt.

To leave passwords and other security information in the output of the **show tech-support**, use the following command:

```
Sensor# show tech-support password
```

You can also generate the **tech-support** file from the sensor using IDM. To do that, click on **Monitoring > Support Information > System Information** within IDM.

cidDump Script

If you cannot log in to the sensor with the administrator account to the CLI or IDM, you will not be able to collect the **show tech-support** output. But, with the **service** account, you can log in to the sensor and collect the **cidDump**.

Work through the following steps to run the **cidDump** script:

Step 1 Log in to the sensor service account.

Step 2 Switch the **service** user to root with the **"su – "** command using the service account password.

Step 3 Type the **/usr/cids/idsRoot/bin/cidDump** command. This will generate the cidDump.html file.

Step 4 Compress the resulting **/usr/cids/idsRoot/log/cidDump.html** file with the following command:

```
gzip /usr/cids/idsRoot/log/cidDump.html
```

Step 5 You can analyze this resulting HTML file offline or send it to the Cisco Support team for an in-depth analysis.

tcpdump command

tcpdump is the command available on Linux shell. This allows you to see if the interfaces of the sensor are receiving the traffic. This can also be used for signature fidelity issues, or to validate a false positive or false negative traffic. The output of the **tcpdump** can be analyzed by another sensor using **tcpdump** or a pcap decoder such as Ethereal. Example 14-10 shows and explains how to use the **tcpdump** command on the sensor after logging in with the **service** account.

Example 14-10 *Using* **tcpdump** *on the Sensor After Logging in With Service Account*

```
login: service
Password:
Last login: Wed Aug  4 20:25:50 from 10.21.88.88
***NOTICE***
! Output removed
bash-2.05a$ su -
Password:
[root@sensor root]#
! Execute command ifconfig -a to identify the sniffing interface. The sniffing
! interface does not have an IP address bound to it.
! Following line shows Sensor is capturing GigabitEthernet0/0 interface traffic
! which is the sniffing interface
-bash-2.05b#tcpdump -i ge0_0
-bash-2.05b#
! Following line shows how to capture and save the traffic into a pcap file format
! so that you can read it offline by another Sensor or network analyzer. The filter
! in the following line can be replaced by any filtering criteria, for example src
! for source address.
-bash-2.05b# tcpdump -i ge0_0 -w myFileName.pcap [filter]
! Once you are done with capturing, you need to execute the following
Ctrl + C
! Once the pcap file is generated, you can read it either via a packet capture
! software (for example Ethereal) or you can use tcpdump to open it up on the same
! or different sensor as follows.
-bash-2.05b#tcpdump -r myFilename.pcap
```

More details about the tcpdump can be found from the following location:

http://www.ethereal.com/docs/man-pages/tcpdump.8.html

http://www.tcpdump.org/tcpdump_man.html

iplog

iplog can be used instead of **tcpdump**, and **iplog** has several advantages. If you need to capture binary traffic over a period of time for a specific signature, **tcpdump** is not a very useful tool, as **tcpdump** is for real-time traffic. The **iplog** file captures the binary packets, and these binary packets are written in a common format most commonly referred to as the **libpcap** format, and as **tcpdump** files. The **libpcap** format files can be read by most sniffer programs (for example, Ethereal). The IP Log data is stored in a sort of circular logging buffer, which means that when the buffer is full, the oldest IP log data is overwritten by the newest IP Log data. More details on **iplog** can be found at the following location:

http://www.cisco.com/univercd/cc/td/doc/product/iaabu/csids/csids11/cliguide/cliiplog.htm

packet Command

You can display or capture live traffic from an interface and have the live traffic or a previously captured file to display on the screen. Storage is available for one local file only; subsequent capture requests overwrite an existing file. The size of the storage file varies depending on the platform. Even though capturing live traffic off the interface does not disrupt any of the functionality of the sensor, it can cause significant performance degradation. Example 14-11 summarizes the usage of the **packet** command.

Example 14-11 *Using the* **packet** *Command on the Sensor*

```
! To display the live traffic on the Sensor, log in to the sensor using an account with
! administrator or operator privileges.  Following command shows how to display the
! live traffic on the interface GigabitEthernet0/1
sensor# packet display GigabitEthernet0/1
! You can use the expression option to limit what you display, for example, only TCP
! packets.
sensor# packet display GigabitEthernet0/1 verbose expression ip proto \\tcp
! To display information about the packet file execute the following command.
sensor# packet display file-info
! Instead of using the display, you can capture the live traffic and save it into a
! file which can be displayed later with the display argument. Only one capture is
! possible at a time.
! To capture the live traffic on the interface GigabitEthernet0/1 execute the
! following command
sensor# packet capture GigabitEthernet0/1
! To view this captured file, you can use the display argument as follows.
sensor# packet display packet-file
! packet-file can be transferred to an FTP or SCP server for offline analysis
sensor# copy packet-file scp://cisco@10.1.1.100/analysis/
! If you want to erase the packet-file, use the following command.
sensor# erase packet-file
sensor#
```

Classification of Problem Areas

Sensor function problem areas can be classified as follows:

- Initial setup issues
- User management issues
- Software installation and upgrade issues

- Licensing issues
- Communication issues
- Issues with receiving events on monitoring device
- Blocking issues
- TCP reset issues
- Inline IPS issues

Initial Setup Issues

On a fresh installation, you must log in to the sensor using console or through a serial terminal using **cisco/cisco** as username/password. If you are prompted to change the password, that means that this is the first time you are accessing the sensor, because the password change option is given only during the first time you log in after the installation or re-image of the Sensor software. You must choose a strong password that is at least eight characters long, and is not a dictionary word.

When you log in to the sensor, first you should initialize the sensor with the **setup** command, which will allow you to enable the Command and Control port and assign the IP address and default gateway for the sensor, so that it can be managed remotely.

Work through the following steps to initialize the sensor:

Step 1 Enter the **setup** command. The System Configuration Dialog, which is interactive, displays. The default settings are displayed as shown in Example 14-12.

Example 14-12 *Initializing the Sensor with the* **setup** *Command*

```
Sensor# setup
--System Configuration Dialog--
At any point you may enter a question mark '?' for help.
Use ctrl-c to abort configuration dialog at any prompt.
Default Settings are in square brackets '[]'.
Current Configuration:
networkParams
ipAddress
netmask
defaultGateway
hostname
telnetOption
accessList
exit
Initial Configuration Tasks
timeParams
summerTimeParams
active-selection
exit
exit
```

continues

Example 14-12 *Initializing the Sensor with the* **setup** *Command (Continued)*

```
service webServer
general
ports
exit
exit
```

Step 2 Press the spacebar to get to the following question:

```
Continue with configuration dialog? [yes]:
```

Press the spacebar to show one page at a time. Press **Enter** to show one line at a time.

Step 3 Enter **yes** to continue.

Step 4 Enter the **hostname**. The default **hostname** is **sensor.**

Step 5 Enter the **IP address, netmask**, and the **default gateway**.

Step 6 Enter the **Telnet server status**. You can disable or enable Telnet services. The default is disabled.

Step 7 Enter the **web server port**. The web server port is the TCP port used by the web server (1 to 65535). The default is 443. Note that if you change the web server port, you must specify the port in the URL address of your browser when you connect to IPS Device Manager (IDM) in the format **https://Sensor_IP:port**. For example, if the sensor's IP address is 10.1.1.150, you can invoke the IDM with the **https://10.1.1.150**.

Step 8 Configure the network access list as follows:

(a) When asked, "Modify current access list?", enter **yes** and then Press **Enter** as shown in Example 14-13 to delete or add entry to the ACL.

Example 14-13 *Partial Output of the* **setup** *Command to Add/Delete the ACL*

```
Modify current access list?[no]: yes
Current access list entries:
  [1] 10.0.0.0/8
  [2] 20.1.1.0/24
  [3] 171.0.0.0/8
  [4] 172.0.0.0/8
! Choice 2 will delete 20.1.1.0/24 from the ACL
Delete: 2
! Hitting Return without specifying anything will skip the Delete option and take you
! to permit option
Delete:
! Following line will allow 30.1.1.0/24
Permit: 30.1.1.0/24
! Do not specify anything to skip the Permit option
Permit:
Modify system clock settings?[no]:yes
```

(b) Repeat these steps until you have entered all the networks you want to add to the access list.

Step 9 Modify the system clock settings as follows:

(a) Enter **yes** to modify the system clock settings as shown in Example 14-13.

(b) Enter **yes** if you want to use NTP.

(c) Enter **yes** to modify summertime settings. Note that summertime is also known as Daylight Saving Time (DST). If your location does not use summertime, go to Step o.

(d) Enter recurring, date, or disable to specify how you want to configure summertime settings. The default is recurring.

(e) If you entered **recurring**, enter the month you want to start summertime settings. The default is apr. The valid entries are jan, feb, mar, apr, may, jun, jul, aug, sep, oct, nov, and dec.

(f) Enter the week you want to start summertime settings. The default is first. The valid entries are first, second, third, fourth, fifth, and last.

(g) Enter the day you want to start summertime settings. The default is sun. The valid entries are sun, mon, tue, wed, thu, fri, and sat.

(h) Enter the time you want to start summertime settings. The default is 02:00:00. Note that the default recurring summertime parameters are correct for time zones in the United States. The default values specify a start time of 2 a.m. on the first Sunday in April, and a stop time of 2 a.m. on the fourth Sunday in October. The default summertime offset is 60 minutes.

(i) Enter the month you want summertime settings to end. The default is oct. The valid settings are jan, feb, mar, apr, may, jun, jul, aug, sep, oct, nov, and dec.

(j) Enter the week you want the summertime settings to end. The default is last. The valid entries are first, second, third, fourth, fifth, and last.

(k) Enter the day you want the summertime settings to end. The default is sun. The valid entries are sun, mon, tue, wed, thu, fri, and sat.

(l) Enter the time you want summertime settings to end. The default is 02:00:00.

(m) Enter the DST zone. The zone name is a character string up to 128 characters long.

(n) Enter the summertime offset. The default is 60. Specify the summertime offset from UTC in minutes (negative numbers represent time zones west of the Prime Meridian).

(o) Enter **yes** to modify the system time zone.

(p) Enter the standard time zone name. The zone name is a character string up to 128 characters long.

(q) Enter the standard time offset. The default is 60. Your configuration appears with the following options:

```
[0] Go to the command prompt without saving this config.
[1] Return back to the setup without saving this config.
[2] Save this configuration and exit setup.
```

Step 10 Enter **2** to save the configuration.

User Management Issues

Based on different privilege levels, you can create users, delete them, change their privileges, or change their passwords. There are four levels of privileges available for users on Sensor: administrator, operator, service, and viewer. This section discusses how to create or modify user accounts. It also discusses details of the **service** account, a special account for password recovery and the troubleshooting that is necessary under special circumstances.

Creation and Modification of User Profiles

You can use the **username** command to add or delete users. Additionally, you can change the password or change the privilege levels of users with the **username** command. Example 14-14 shows how to create users, delete users, or change the user profiles.

Example 14-14 *Creating and Deleting Users on the Sensor*

```
! You need to login to Sensor with administrator user name. The following lines
! adding users with the administrator privilege
sensor# configure terminal
sensor(config)# username csids privilege administrator
Enter Login Password: *****
Re-enter Login Password: *****
```

Example 14-14 *Creating and Deleting Users on the Sensor (Continued)*

```
! If you do not specify a privilege level for the user, the user is assigned the
! default viewer privilege. You can verify if the user is added by executing show
! users all after exiting from configuration mode
! If you want to remove the user just created, you can use the no form of the username
! command as shown in the following line.
sensor(config)# no username csids
! If you want to change the password of the administrator, you can use the password
! command as shown in the following lines
sensor# configure terminal
sensor(config)# password
Enter Old Login Password: ************
Enter New Login Password: ************
Re-enter New Login Password: ************
sensor(config)#
! If you want to change the password of another user, you must login to the Sensor
! with dministrator privilege, and change the password as follows. In the following
! example tester password is reset.
sensor# configure terminal
sensor(config)# password tester
Enter New Login Password: ******
Re-enter New Login Password: ******
! If you need to change the privileges of a user, you need to use the privilege
! command.
! Following lines shows how to change the user tester from viewer to administrator.
sensor# show users all
    CLI ID   User         Privilege
*   7309     cisco        administrator
             service      service
             tester       viewer
sensor# configure terminal
sensor14(config)# privilege user tester administrator
Warning: The privilege change does not apply to current CLI sessions. It will be
 applied to subsequent logins.
sensor(config)# exit
sensor# show users all
    CLI ID   User         Privilege
*   7309     cisco        administrator
             service      service
             tester       administrator
sensor#
! If you want to assign service privileges to an existing user, you must first remove
! the user and add it with service privileges. You cannot use the privilege command
! to accomplish this.
sensor#
```

Creating the Service Account

A **service** account is a special user account that is used under rare circumstances to recover user passwords or troubleshoot issues such as a sensor crash. In Sensor, it is possible to assign the same privilege to more than one user, with the exception of the

service privilege. You can have only one **service** account on the sensor. To create the service account, you need to follow the same procedure as explained in Example 14-14. You need to be sure that you are adding a user with a **service** privilege level. It is important to note that if you want to assign **service** privileges to an existing user, you must first remove the user and add it with service privileges. You cannot use the **privilege** command to accomplish this.

After the creation of the **service** account, login to Sensor with this account and you will see the messages as shown in Example 14-15.

Example 14-15 *Sample Run of Service Account Login*

```
login: service
Password:
Last login: Fri Nov  5 16:49:11 from 171.69.89.219
***NOTICE***
This product contains cryptographic features and is subject to United States
and local country laws governing import, export, transfer and use. Delivery
of Cisco cryptographic products does not imply third-party authority to import,
export, distribute or use encryption. Importers, exporters, distributors and
users are responsible for compliance with U.S. and local country laws. By using
this product you agree to comply with applicable laws and regulations. If you
are unable to comply with U.S. and local laws, return this product immediately.

A summary of U.S. laws governing Cisco cryptographic products may be found at:
http://www.cisco.com/wwl/export/crypto

If you require further assistance please contact us by sending email to
export@cisco.com.
Press Enter to continue

************************ WARNING ************************
UNAUTHORIZED ACCESS TO THIS NETWORK DEVICE IS PROHIBITED.
This account is intended to be used for support and
troubleshooting purposes only. Unauthorized modifications
are not supported and will require this device to be
re-imaged to guarantee proper operation.
*********************************************************
bash-2.05a$
```

CAUTION It's extremely important that you do not make any changes to the configuration of the sensor using the service account, except under the direction of Cisco Support. Modification of the configuration must be done at your own risk and is not supported by Cisco Systems, Inc.

Software Installation and Upgrade Issues

This section focuses primarily on the upgrade issues of the IDS 42xx series Sensor Appliances. Module software installation and upgrade issues are discussed in their respective chapters. For example, installation and upgrade issues for IDSM-2 are thoroughly discussed in Chapter 15, "Troubleshooting IDSM-2 Blades on Switch." Installing and upgrading to IPS version 5.0 is used as an example throughout this section. This section discusses the following items in details in:

- Obtaining sensor software
- IPS software image naming conventions
- Installing or re-imaging the ips appliances system image
  - Using CD-ROM
  - Using Trivial File Transfer Protocol (TFTP) server
- Disaster recovery plan
  - Recovering the application partition
  - Upgrading the recovery partition image
- Upgrading major/minor software or service pack/signature update
- Upgrading to IPS 5.0

Obtaining Sensor Software

There are two main ways to procure different types of IDS/IPS Sensor software: using a CD or downloading from the Cisco.com web site. System image is the only software image available on the CD (you will get the base software of IDS/IPS Sensor when you purchase the Sensor). You can order the CD from the following location: www.cisco.com/upgrade. However, all types of IDS/IPS Sensor software images (for example System image, service packs, signature upgrade, and so on) are downloadable from the Cisco.com web site. Before you are presented with the software download location, it is important that you take care of the following two issues:

- **Applying for Cryptographic Access**—To download IDS/IPS Sensor software, you must have a Cisco.com user account with cryptographic access. To apply for cryptographic access with your Cisco.com (this account needs to have **a smartnet** contract) account, go to the following site and select the product for which you want cryptographic access and submit the request:

  http://www.cisco.com/pcgi-bin/Software/Crypto/crypto_main.pl

  If you do not have a Cisco.com user account, apply for it at the following location:

  http://tools.cisco.com/RPF/register/register.do

- **Active Update Notification**—Subscribe to the mailing list of "Active Update Notification" for information about the latest update software from the following location:

  http://www.cisco.com/cgi-bin/front.x/ipsalerts/ipsalertsHome.pl

  You need to fill out a form that can be found at the "Active Update Notifications <http://www.cisco.com/offer/newsletter/123668_4/>" link under "Active Updates" on the right side of the page of the preceding link.

Now that you are ready with a Cisco.com user account with cryptographic capabilities, you can download all types of IDS/IPS Sensor software from the following location:

http://www.cisco.com/kobayashi/sw-center/ciscosecure/ids/crypto/

IPS Software Image Naming Conventions

If you have visited the link for IDS/IPS Sensor Software provided in the preceding section, you might already have realized how many different types of IDS/IPS Sensor software you need to deal with. Hence, having a clear understanding of the IDS/IPS software naming convention is extremely important. The naming convention of the IDS/IPS Sensor software may be categorized as follows:

- Platform-dependent image
- Platform-independent image

A more thorough discussion on naming conventions for both types of images is as follows.

Platform-Dependent Image

Following is a list of platform-dependent images available on different sensors:

- **System image file (For all platforms)**—The system image includes the combined recovery and application image used to re-image an entire sensor.
- **Recovery partition image file**—A recovery partition image file is a partition on the sensor that contains a full IPS application image to be used for recovery.
- **Maintenance partition image file (IDSM-2 only)**—A maintenance partition image file is a full IPS image that can be used to re-image the maintenance partition of the IDSM-2.
- **Recovery and Upgrade CD (All Sensors that have CD-ROM drives)**—This is a CD image for recovery or upgrade of an appliance that has a CD-ROM drive.
- **Boot Loader (For NM-CIDS only)**—This is used for re-imaging NM-CIDS.
- **Helper image (For NM-CIDS only)**—This is used to re-image a NM-CIDS hard disk drive.

Table 14-3 describes the platform-dependent releases.

Table 14-3 *Platform-Dependent Releases*

Release	Target Frequency	Identifier	Supported Platform	Example File Name
System image	Annually	sys	All	IPS-4255-K9-sys-1.1-a-5.0-2.img
Recovery partition image file	Annually	r	All Appliances	IPS-K9-r-1.1-a-5.0-2.pkg
Maintenance partition image	Annually	mp	IDSM-2 only	c6svc-mp.2-1-2.bin.gz
Recovery and upgrade CD	Annually or as needed	cd	All appliances with a CD-ROM drive	N/A
Boot loader	As needed	boot	NM-CIDS	servicesengine-boot-1.0-17-1_dev.bin
Helper image	As needed	helper	NM-CIDS	NM-CIDS-K9-helper-1.0-1.bin

Platform-Independent Image

Some platform-independent Sensor update files are base files, some are cumulative, and yet others are incremental. Knowing which Sensor software type is base, cumulative, or incremental, and their dependencies on each other, is extremely important. Following is an attempt to explain this level of detail:

- **Major version**—A major version upgrade contains new functionality or an architectural change in the product. For example, the IPS 5.0 base version release includes everything since the previous major release (the minor version features, service pack fixes, and signature updates) plus any new changes. Major upgrade 5.0(1) requires 4.1. The 5.0(1) major upgrade is used only to upgrade 4.1 sensors to 5.0(1). If you are reinstalling 5.0(1) on a sensor that already has 5.0(1) installed, use the system image or recovery procedures rather than the major upgrade.
- **Minor version**—A minor version upgrade is incremental to the major version. Minor version upgrades are also base versions for service packs. The first minor version upgrade for 5.0 is 5.1(1). Minor version upgrades are released for minor enhancements to the product. Minor version upgrades contain all previous minor features, service pack fixes, and signature updates since the last major version, and the new minor features being released. The minor upgrade requires the major version.
- **Service pack**—Service packs are cumulative following a base version release (minor or major). Service packs are used for the release of defect fixes with no new

enhancements. Service packs contain all the service pack fixes and signature updates since the last base version (minor or major) and the new defect fixes being released.

- **Signature Update**—Signature updates are cumulative and increment by one with each new release (for example, S45, S46, S47). Signature updates include every signature since the initial signature release (S1) in addition to the new signatures being released.
- **Patch release**—Patch releases are for interim fixes.
- **Recovery Package**—As of the writing of this book, r 1.1 is the latest recovery image. This can be revised to r 1.2 if it is necessary to release a new recovery package that contains the same underlying application image. If there are defect fixes for the installer, for example, the underlying application version may still be 5.0(1), but the recovery partition image will be r 1.2.

Except for the Signature update file, the rest of the other IDS Sensor software update uses the format: **IPS-update_type-x.y-z-.pkg**. Following is the explanation of the image version format:

- **update_type**—**update_type** can be **maj** for Major version, **min** is for Minor version, and so on
- **x**—represents Major version
- **y**—represents Minor version
- **z**—represents Service Pack level

The signature file follows the following format to name its file: **IPS-sig-Sx-minreq-5.0-1.pkg**. Here **sig** is the update type, **Sx** is the signature level, and **minreq** defines the minimum software requirement before applying this signature. In this case, the minimum requirement is version 5.0-1. Table 14-4 summarizes different platform-independent software updates.

Table 14-4 *Platform-Independent Release Examples*

Release	Target Frequency	Identifier	Example File Name
Signature update	Weekly	sig	IPS-sig-S70-minreq-5.0-1.pkg
Service pack	Semi-annually or as needed	sp	IPS-K9-sp-5.0-2.pkg
Minor version	Annually	min	IPS-K9-min-5.1-1.pkg
Major version	Annually	maj	IPS-K9-maj-5.0-1.pkg
Patch release	As needed	patch	IPS-K9-patch-5.0-1pl.pkg
Recovery package	Annually or as needed	r	IPS-K9-r-1.1-a-5.0-1.pkg

Even though you become comfortable with the naming conventions and understand how to select and apply the software on the Sensor, it is strongly recommended to read the Readme file of the corresponding Sensor software.

Installing or Re-imaging the IPS Appliances System Image

As mentioned before, the system image is used to recover the whole sensor (both Maintenance and Application partitions). If you have a sensor with both application and maintenance partitions corrupted, then you need to re-image the sensor with the system image. Starting from version 5.0, the system image is the same for the appliance and the blades on the switch, router, and ASA. This section explains how to perform the installation or the upgrade of the Sensor Appliances. Depending on the model, you need to upgrade the sensor using either of the following two methods:

- Using a CD-ROM
- Using TFTP Server

Details on re-imaging using both methods follow.

Using a CD-ROM

You can use the recovery/upgrade CD on appliances that have a CD-ROM, such as the IDS-4210, IDS-4235, and IDS-4250. The recovery/upgrade CD re-images both the recovery and application partitions. Work through the following steps to re-image the Sensor Appliance which has the CD-ROM drive:

Step 1 Insert the recovery/upgrade CD into the CD-ROM drive.

Step 2 Power off the IDS appliance and then power it back on. The boot menu appears, which lists important notices and boot options.

Step 3 Type **k** if you are installing from a keyboard, or type **s** if you are installing from a serial connection.

A blue screen is displayed for several minutes without any status messages while the files are being copied from the CD to your appliance.

Step 4 When you are finished with the installation, log in to the appliance by using a serial connection or with a monitor and keyboard. The default username and password is cisco/cisco.

Step 5 When you are prompted, change the password. The passwords must be at least eight characters long and be strong, that is, they should not be dictionary words.

Step 6 When you are in the sensor prompt, type the **setup** command to initialize the appliance.

This procedure almost always works, but, if for some reason the sensor does not boot from the upgrade CD-ROM, use the steps that follow to troubleshoot this issue:

Step 1 Connect the sensor either with a keyboard and monitor, or through the serial port using a terminal server or laplink cable and PC. If connected through the serial port, console redirection must be enabled in the BIOS to change BIOS settings.

Step 2 Reboot the sensor.

Step 3 Use the arrow keys to select the **Boot** menu.

Step 4 Navigate to the **Boot Device Priority** option, again using the arrow keys, and press **Enter**.

Step 5 Change the boot order by selecting a drive using the arrow keys, and pressing + or – to move the drive up or down in the list respectively. Boot order should be: [Removable Devices], [ATAPI CD-ROM Drive], [Hard Drive] ...

Step 6 Click **ESC** to exit the Boot Device Priority submenu.

Step 7 Use the arrow keys to navigate to the Exit menu.

Step 8 Select **Exit Saving Changes** and click **Enter**.

Step 9 Select **Yes** in the Setup Confirmation window, and click **Enter**.

Step 10 The system will reboot.

Using TFTP Server

Some of the IPS Appliances, IDS-4215, IPS-4240, or IPS-4255 System Image, must be installed/re-imaged by using the ROMMON. This involves a TFTP server on which the image file is downloaded and then transferred from that to the sensor's compact flash. To install or re-image the sensor using the TFTP server, follow these steps:

Step 1 Download the IPS system image file (for example IPS-4240-K9-sys-1.1-a-5.0-1.img) to the tftp root directory of a TFTP server from your IPS from the following location:

http://www.cisco.com/cgi-bin/tablebuild.pl/ips5-system

Step 2 IDS-4215 must be running BIOS version 5.1.7 or later and ROMMON version 1.4 or later to install system image 5.0-1 or 5.0-2. If IDS-4215 does not have the correct BIOS and ROMMON versions, you must upgrade the BIOS and ROMMON before re-imaging (see Example 14-16 for details on upgrading BIOS and ROMMON). This problem is specific only to IDS-4215, not IPS-4240 and IPS-4255

Step 3 Boot IPS Sensor.

Step 4 Enter **CTRL-R** (for IDS-4215) or Press **Break or Esc** (for IPS-4240, and IPS-4255) within five seconds at the following prompt while the system is booting:

```
Evaluating Run Options...
```

Step 5 Check the current network settings with the following command:

```
rommon> set
```

Step 6 Use Table 14-5 to assign different network parameters. Note that not all values listed in Table 14-5 are required to establish network connectivity. The address, server, gateway, and image values are required.

Table 14-5 *Commands That Can Be Entered in ROMMON of Sensor*

Commands in ROMMON	Meaning of the commands
ADDRESS=*IP_address*	Address—Local IP address of the sensor
CONFIG=*name*	Config—Application configuration file path/name
GATEWAY=*IP_address*	Gateway—Gateway IP address used by the sensor
IMAGE=*name*	Image—System image file path/name
PORT=*name*	Port—Ethernet interface port used for sensor management
SERVER=*IP_address*	Server—TFTP server IP address where the application image is stored
VLAN=*ID_number*	VLAN—VLAN ID number (leave as 0)

Step 7 If needed, change the interface used for the TFTP download with the following command:

```
rommon> PORT=interface_name
```

The default interface used for TFTP downloads is Management0/0, which corresponds to the MGMT interface of IPS-4240. For IDS-4215, Ports 0 (monitoring port) and 1 (command and control port) are labeled on the back of the chassis. If you want to use default setting, you do not need to use the **port** command to set up the port.

Step 8 Assign an IP address for the local port on IPS. This IP address should be the same IP address that you used for the Command and Control interface under the normal mode of operations.

```
rommon> ADDRESS=ip_address
```

Step 9 Assign the TFTP server IP address with the following command:

```
rommon> SERVER=ip_address
```

Step 10 Assign the gateway IP address if the TFTP server is more than one hop away with the following command:

```
rommon> GATEWAY=ip_address
```

Step 11 Verify that you have access to the TFTP server by pinging it from your local Ethernet port with one of the following commands:

```
rommon> ping server_ip_address
rommon> ping server
```

Step 12 Define the path and filename on the TFTP file server from which you are downloading the image using the following command:

```
rommon> IMAGE=path/file_name
```

An example on a UNIX platform is as follows:

```
rommon> IMAGE=/system_images/IPS-4240-K9-sys-1.1-a-5.0-2.img
```

Note that the path is relative to the UNIX TFTP server's default tftpboot directory. Images located in the default tftpboot directory do not have any directory names or slashes in the IMAGE specification.

An example on the Windows platform is as follows:

```
rommon> IMAGE=C:\system_images\IPS-4240-K9-sys-1.1-a-5.0-2.img
```

Step 13 Type **set** and press **Enter** to verify the network settings.

Step 14 You can use the **sync** command to store these settings in NVRAM so they are maintained across boots. Otherwise, you must type this information each time you want to boot an image from ROMMON.

Step 15 Download and install the system image with the following command:

```
rommon> tftp
```

CAUTION To avoid corrupting the system image, do not remove power from IPS-4240 while the system image is being installed.

Example 14-16 *Upgrading the IDS-4215 BIOS and ROMMON*

```
! Download the BIOS ROMMON upgrade utility (IDS-4215-bios-5.1.7-rom-1.4.bin) to the
! TFTP root directory of a TFTP server that is accessible from IDS-4215 from location:
! http://www.cisco.com/cgi-bin/tablebuild.pl/ips5-firmware
! Boot IDS-4215. While rebooting, IDS-4215 runs the BIOS POST. After the completion
! of POST, the console displays the message: Evaluating Run Options ...for about ! 5
seconds.
Press Ctrl-R while this message is displayed to display the ROMMON menu.
! Specify an IP address for the local port on IDS-4215
rommon> address ip_address
! Specify the TFTP server IP address
rommon> server ip_address
! Specify the gateway IP address
rommon> gateway ip_address
! Verify that you have access to the TFTP server by pinging it from the local Ethernet
! port
rommon> ping server_ip_address
rommon> ping server
```

Example 14-16 *Upgrading the IDS-4215 BIOS and ROMMON (Continued)*

```
! Specify the filename on the TFTP file server from which you are downloading the
! image
rommon> file filename
! For example
rommon> file IDS-4215-bios-5.1.7-rom-1.4.bin
! Download and run the update utility
rommon> tftp
! Type y at the upgrade prompt and the update is executed.
IDS-4215 reboots when the update is complete.
! Do not remove power to IDS-4215 during the update process, otherwise the upgrade
! can get corrupted.
```

If you run into a problem with TFTP upgrade, check the following items to resolve the issue:

- If the TFTP server is in a different network than the sensor, make sure TFTP traffic is not blocked by a firewall or any network device with an Access Control List (ACL).
- Be sure to tie the IP address to the proper interface of the sensor, and be sure the interface is connected to the network. If you encounter a layer II issue, check the cable and check the port on the switch to be sure that it's up.
- Note that the image name is case-sensitive. So pay extra attention when defining the image name properly.
- Choose the proper system image, as they are named with specific platform. For example IPS-4215-K9-sys-1.1-a-5.0-2.img is for IPS-4215 and should not be used to upgrade IPS-4255.
- Some TFTP servers limit the maximum file size that can be transferred to approximately 32 MB. Therefore, it is recommended to use the following tftp server:
  - For Windows, use Tftpd32 version 2.0, from the following location: http://tftpd32.jounin.net/
  - For UNIX, use Tftp-hpa series, from the following location: http://www.kernel.org/pub/software/network/tftp/
- Turn on logging on the TFTP server and be sure you see the request coming from Sensor.
- Make sure that the TFTP is set to Send and Receive both permissions. Additionally, be sure the TFTP server root directory allows Read permission.

Disaster Recovery Plan

For high availability, it's extremely important to have a Disaster Recovery Plan (DRP) for your sensor. You must ensure that if the Application image is corrupted, you can recover it easily from the Recovery Partition. Also, be sure that you have the latest version installed on the Recovery partition. Following are the important action items that are necessary for the seamless operation of IPS Sensor.

- Recovering the application partition
- Upgrading the recovery partition image
- Recovering a lost password
- Recovering a working configuration

The last two bullet items are discussed thoroughly in the section entitled "Preventive Maintenance" under the "Best Practices" section. This section explains the how to recover an application partition from the recovery partition, and how to upgrade the recovery partition to the latest version so that the sensor can be upgraded to the latest version if the application partition fails.

Recovering the Application Partition

If the application partition, which is used under normal operation by the sensor, becomes corrupted, you can use either the system image to re-image the sensor (as described in the preceding section), or recover it from the recovery partition. If the recovery partition also is corrupted, then re-imaging the sensor with the System Image is the only option. Otherwise, the best approach is to use the recovery partition to recover the sensor. This is extremely useful if the sensor is installed in a remote location and you do not have physical access to the sensor. This is because the IP address, netmask, access lists, time zone, and offset are saved and applied to the re-imaged application partition. So, after the recovery process, you can remotely SSH to the sensor with the default username and password (cisco/cisco) and initialize the sensor again with the **setup** command. You cannot use Telnet until you initialize the sensor because Telnet is disabled by default.

Work through the following steps to recover the sensor from the recovery partition:

Step 1 Log in to the CLI of the sensor via SSH or Telnet using an account with administrator privileges.

Step 2 Enter configuration mode with the following command:

```
sensor# configure terminal
```

Step 3 Recover the application partition image with the following command:

```
sensor(config)# recover application-partition
Warning: Executing this command will stop all applications and re-image
the node to
version 5.0(0.27)S91(0.27). All configuration changes except for
network settings will be
reset to default.
Continue with recovery? []:
```

Step 4 Type **yes** to continue.

Shutdown begins immediately after you execute the **recover** command. Shutdown can take a while, and you will still have access to the CLI, but access will be terminated without warning.

Step 5 Once the application partition is re-imaged using the image stored on the recovery partition, log back in to the sensor using SSH and execute the **setup** command to initialize the sensor.

NOTE If for some reason, you cannot access the CLI to execute the **recover application-partition** command, you can reboot the sensor and select the option from the boot menu during the bootup process. This lets you boot to the recovery partition and re-image the application partition. Executing the **recovery** command in this way requires console or keyboard and monitor access to the sensor, which is possible on the appliances and NM-CIDS, but not on the IDSM-2 or ASA-SSM.

As you can see, Application Partition, using this procedure, uses the image stored in Recovery Partition. So, to install the most up-to-date version of the image on the application partition using Maintenance Partition, it is strongly recommended that you upgrade your recovery partition to the most recent version, as soon as it becomes available for download from Cisco.com. This is covered in the next section on how to upgrade the recovery partition.

Upgrading the Recovery Partition Image

As mentioned before, it is strongly recommended to upgrade the image on the recovery partition with the latest version so that it is ready if you need to recover the application partition on your appliance. It is important to understand that recovery partition images are generated for major and minor software releases and only in rare situations for service packs or signature updates.

Work through the following steps to perform the upgrade on the recovery partition from the application partition:

Step 1 Log in to Sensor CLI using SSH or Telnet with administrator privilege, execute **show version**, and be sure that you are running IPS version 5.0(1) or later.

Step 2 Download the recovery partition image file (IPS-K9-r-1.1-a-5.0-2.pkg) to an FTP, SCP, HTTP, or HTTPS server that is accessible from your sensor from the following location: http://www.cisco.com/cgi-bin/tablebuild.pl/ips5-system

Step 3 Enter configuration mode with the following command:

```
sensor# configure terminal
```

Step 4 Initiate the upgrade process with the following command:

```
sensor(config)# upgrade scp://user@server_ipaddress//upgrade_path/
  IPS-K9-r-1.1-a-5.0-2.pkg
```

To use FTP, use the following command:

```
sensor(config)# upgrade ftp://user@server_ipaddress//upgrade_path/
  IPS-K9-r-1.1-a-5.0-2.pkg
```

Step 5 Type the server password when prompted.

Step 6 The upgrade process begins.

NOTE Always read the Readme file which is located at the same place on Cisco.com as the actual image. The preceding procedure is taken from the Readme file. If there are any changes in upgrade procedure, the most accurate and up-to-date information can be found in the Readme file.

Upgrading Major/Minor Software or Service Pack/Signature Update

The upgrade process for the Major/Minor Software or Service Pack/Signature is the same for all platforms. There are several ways you can upgrade the sensor as follows:

- Automatic upgrade using the CLI of the sensor
- Manual upgrade using CLI of the sensor
- Upgrade using IDM or IPS MC (See Chapter 18 for more details.)

This section explains how to perform the Manual and Automatic upgrade using CLI on the sensor.

Automatic Upgrade Using the CLI of the Sensor

The auto update feature automatically upgrades the sensor based on a pre-configured time. You can configure the sensor to look for new upgrade files in your upgrade directory of FTP or SCP server automatically. Hence, you must download the software upgrade from Cisco.com and copy it to the upgrade directory of FTP or SCP server before the sensor can poll for automatic upgrades.

Work through the following steps to schedule automatic upgrades on the sensor using CLI:

Step 1 Log in to the CLI of Sensor through SSH or Telnet using an account with administrator privileges.

Step 2 Enable the auto-upgrade feature on the sensor with the following command:

```
sensor# configure terminal
sensor(config)# service host
sensor(config-hos)# auto-upgrade-option enabled
```

Step 3 Specify the scheduling:

For calendar scheduling, which starts upgrades at specific times on specific day, use the following commands:

```
sensor(config-hos-ena)# schedule-option calendar-schedule
sensor(config-hos-ena-cal# days-of-week sunday
sensor(config-hos-ena-cal# times-of-day 12:00:00
```

For periodic scheduling, which starts upgrades at specific periodic intervals, use the following commands:

```
sensor(config-hos-ena)# schedule-option periodic-schedule
sensor(config-hos-ena-per)# interval 24
sensor(config-hos-ena-per)# start-time 13:00:00
```

Step 4 Specify the IP address of the file server (this can be an FTP or SCP server) with the following commands:

```
sensor(config-hos-ena-per)# exit
sensor(config-hos-ena)# ip-address 10.1.1.100
```

Step 5 Specify the directory where the upgrade files are located on the file server (FTP or SCP server) with the following command:

```
sensor(config-hos-ena)# directory /download/update
```

Step 6 Specify the username for authentication on the file server (FTP/SCP):

```
sensor(config-hos-ena)# user-name cisco
```

Step 7 Specify the password of the user with the following command:

```
sensor(config-hos-ena)# password
Enter password[]: ******
Re-enter password: ******
```

Step 8 Specify the file server protocol:

To use FTP server, use the following command:

```
sensor(config-hos-ena)# file-copy-protocol ftp
```

To use SCP, use the following command:

```
sensor(config-hos-ena)# file-copy-protocol scp
```

To add the host when SCP is used, use the following command to add the SCP server to the trusted-host list:

```
sensor(config-hos-ena)# exit
sensor(config-hos)# exit
Apply Changes:?[yes]:
sensor(config)# ssh host-key 10.1.1.100
MD5 fingerprint is F3:10:3E:BA:1E:AB:88:F8:F5:56:D3:A6:63:42:1C:11
Bubble Babble is xucis-hehon-kizog-nedeg-zunom-kolyn-syzec-zasyk-
   symuf-rykum-sexyx
Would you like to add this to the known hosts table for this host?[yes]
Sensor(config)#
```

When the sensor is underused, it is strongly recommended to schedule the timing to be automatic, such as at midnight or during the weekend. Other than that, the troubleshooting is centered on the communication issues between the sensor and the FTP or SCP server, which is discussed thoroughly in the next section, on manual upgrade.

Manual Upgrade With the CLI of the Sensor

You must have the IPS subscription license to update your sensor (see the "Licensing Issues" section for more details). The upgrade procedure is the same for Major/Minor version, or Service Pack or signature upgrade. The procedure that follows explains how to upgrade a signature (IPS-sig-S169-minreq-5.0-1.pkg) update. The same procedure can be used to upgrade the sensor for Major/Minor version and Service Pack:

Step 1 Log in to the Sensor CLI using Administrator account.

Step 2 Back up a working copy of your sensor as explained in the "Best Practices" section of this chapter.

Step 3 Execute **show version** on the sensor and get the current version Sensor is running.

Step 4 Go to the following site to get the Readme file of the version of Signature upgrade file: http://www.cisco.com/cgi-bin/tablebuild.pl/ips5-sigup

Read through the Readme file and determine the minimum version requirement. Another way to verify the version requirement is to look at the name of the signature file. For this example, use the IPS-sig-S169-minreq-5.0-1.pkg file. As the name implies, the minimum requirement for upgrading this signature is that you are running 5.0(1) or 5.0(2).

Step 5 Download the binary file IPS-sig-S169-minreq-5.0-1.pkg to an ftp, scp, http, or https server on your network from:

http://www.cisco.com/cgi-bin/tablebuild.pl/ips5-sigup

You must preserve the original file name.

Step 6 Type the following command to enter Configuration mode:

```
Sensor#configure terminal
```

Step 7 Initiate the upgrade process by executing the following command:

```
upgrade [URL]/IPS-sig-S169-minreq-5.0-1.pkg
```

Here, the [URL] is the uniform resource locator pointing to where the signature update package is located. For example, to retrieve the update via FTP, type the following:

```
Sensor(config)#upgrade ftp://<username>@<ip-address>//<directory>/IPS-
  sig-S169-minreq-5.0-1.pkg
```

The available transport methods are: SCP, FTP, HTTP, or HTTPS.

Step 8 Enter the appropriate password when prompted.

Step 9 To complete the upgrade, type **yes** when prompted.

To uninstall the version S169 signature update on a 5.0(1) or 5.0(2) sensor and return the sensor to its previous state, follow these steps:

Step 1 Log in to the CLI using an account with administrator privileges.

Step 2 Type the following command to enter configuration mode:

```
Sensor# configure terminal
```

Step 3 Type the following command to start the downgrade:

```
Sensor(config)# downgrade
```

Sometimes, manual upgrade using Sensor CLI does not work due to FTP transfer problems. To work around that problem, transfer the file to the sensor manually, and then upgrade from the sensor itself. You might have to do this under some circumstances. Work through the following steps to accomplish this task:

Step 1 Log in using the "service" account (and do not "su" to root); the prompt will look like:

```
bash-2.05a$
```

Step 2 Connect to the FTP server with the following command:

```
bash-2.05a$ ftp ftp_server_address
```

Step 3 Set up the ftp client to use a "binary" mode to get the file using the following command:

```
ftp> bin
```

Step 4 Be sure that the update file is in the FTP server using the following command:

```
ftp> ls
```

Step 5 Retrieve the file (you may Copy and Paste the filename from the previous output from **ls** command):

```
ftp> get upgrade_file
```

Step 6 Close the FTP connection and quit from FTP client with the following commands:

```
ftp> close
ftp> quit
```

Step 7 Be sure the file is transferred to the sensor with the following command:

```
bash-2.05a$ ls
```

You should see the upgrade file that you downloaded from the ftp server.

Step 8 Log out of the service account:

```
bash-2.05a$ exit
```

Step 9 Log in to Sensor using administrator account.

Step 10 Enter configuration mode with the following command:

```
sensor# configure terminal
```

Step 11 Download the key from the sensor itself by specifying its own IP address with the following command:

```
sensor(config)# ssh host-key [sensor_ip_address]
```

Type **yes** to accept the key

Step 12 Apply the upgrade with the following command:

```
sensor(config)# upgrade scp://
User: service_account_user_name
Server's IP Address: sensor_ip_address
Port[22]:
File name: upgrade_file
Password: **********
Warning: Executing this command will apply a signature update to the
application
partition.
Continue with upgrade? : yes

sensor(config)#
```

If you run into a problem with the manual upgrade, go through the following list to troubleshoot the issue:

- **Check the connectivity problem**—Be sure your sensor can ftp or ssh or Telnet on port 80/443 from the sensor to the FTP, SCP server, or HTT/HTTPS server. This can be done from the sensor after logging into the service account. If you have connectivity problems, be sure that you do not have a firewall between the sensor and the FTP or SCP or HTTP/HTTPS server that might be blocking the necessary port. If SCP is used, be sure to add the SCP server in the trusted host of the sensor with the **ssh host-key** command.

- **Be careful with file naming**—When downloading the update file from the Cisco.com web site, be sure that the file name is not changed. Some browsers might add an extra extension to the file, so be careful about that. The file is case-sensitive, so be sure to compare the name of the file after you download from Cisco.com.
- **Check that the file path is correct**—If the correct path of the file is not specified, the sensor will be unable to pull the file. Use the following syntax for proper directory path:
  - For FTP server, use the following syntax:

    ```
    ftp:[//[username@] location]/relativeDirectory]/filename
    ftp:[//[username@]location]//absoluteDirectory]/filename
    ```
  - For SCP, use the following syntax:

    ```
    scp:[//[username@] location]/relativeDirectory]/filename
    scp:[//[username@]location]//absoluteDirectory]/filename
    ```
  - For http, use the following syntax:

    ```
    http:[[/[username@]location]/directory]/filename
    ```
  - For https, use the following syntax:

    ```
    https:[[/[username@]location]/directory]/filename
    ```
- **Settings for FTP server**—If FTP server is used, try to avoid using an anonymous user for upgrades. Also, remove any extra banners and allow the passive FTP.
- **Avoid busy hours for upgrade**—Try to avoid upgrading during the busy hours when Sensor processes a lot of traffic. Otherwise, Sensor might become unresponsive. If you have to perform the upgrade, then be sure to shut down the sensing interface or unplug the cable from the sensing interface. When the upgrade is completed, connect the cable back on the sensing interface or bring the sensing interface up.
- **Do not reboot the sensor**—Depending on the traffic load or amount of configuration, Sensor might appear unresponsive for a long time during the upgrade or downgrade process. Be patient, and do not reboot the sensor; otherwise, Sensor might become corrupted, and re-imaging will be only option left.

Upgrading to IPS 5.0

There are two ways to upgrade your sensor to IPS 5.0:

- Using a system image
- Using a major software update

More details on these methods follow.

Using System Image

If you use the system image to re-image the sensor completely, then you will lose all the configurations. There is no way that you can use the old configuration. There is no external tool that converts the IDS 4.x version configuration to the IPS 5.x version configuration. The only advantage with re-imaging the sensor is that you do not need to upgrade your sensor to a specific version before upgrading to 5.x. As of the writing of this book, the latest version of system file for IPS is 5.0(2), which can be downloaded from the following location:

http://www.cisco.com/cgi-bin/tablebuild.pl/ips5-system

If you have a CD-ROM on the sensor and if your contract entitles you to do so, you can order the CD from the following location:

www.cisco.com/upgrade

The procedure for re-imaging the system image of the sensor is explained in the section entitled "Installing or Re-imaging the IPS Appliances System Image."

Using a Major Software Update

To maintain the configuration of the sensor (this is the preferred method), use the major software update to upgrade your sensor to IPS 5.x. All the older versions of IDS need to be upgraded to 4.1 with the latest signature upgrade; otherwise, the major version upgrade will fail.

As of the writing of this book, the major upgrade file required to upgrade the version to IPS 5.0 is IPS-K9-maj-5.0-1-S149.rpm.pkg (version 5.0.1), which can be downloaded from the following location:

http://www.cisco.com/cgi-bin/tablebuild.pl/ips5

The procedure for the upgrade can be found in the Readme file. Refer to "Upgrading Major/Minor Software or Service pack/Signature Update" for additional details.

For a seamless upgrade to IPS version 5.0, keep the following important points in mind:

- Back up the running configuration and the **show version** output so you may downgrade if required and still have a working configuration.
- You cannot use the **downgrade** command to downgrade from 5.0(1) to 4.x; rather you need to re-image the sensor with a system file.
- If you have 4.0 installed on your sensor, you must upgrade to 4.1, then upgrade to 5.0.
- Upgrading from 4.1 to 5.0 converts the sensor configuration to IPS 5.0 format. The upgrade might stop if it comes across a value that it cannot translate. If this occurs, the resulting error message provides enough information to adjust the parameter to an acceptable value. After editing the configuration, try the upgrade again.

- In 4.*x*, custom signature IDs start at 20000. Any custom signatures that you have created in 4.*x* are converted to the 5.0 custom signature ranges, which begin at 60000.
- In 4.*x*, there is a parameter that lets you enable and disable signatures. In 5.0, there is a similar parameter, but there is also a parameter that lets you retire and unretire signatures. When you upgrade to 5.0, some signatures will be marked as enabled; however, they might also have been retired in 5.0, and therefore the enabled setting would be ignored. You must manually unretire the signature to ensure that it is enabled.
- In 5.0, you receive messages indicating that you need to install a license. The sensor functions properly without a license, but you need a license to install signature updates. The following section describes the procedure.

Licensing Issues

The IPS software requires you to have a subscription license to process signature updates. This is a new feature on version IPS 5.0. Earlier versions do not require this license. On IPS 5.0, without the license, the sensor will function correctly; however, you will not be able to upgrade a new signature without a license. Sections that follow explain how to procure the license key from Cisco.com and install it on the sensor.

How Do I Know if I have A Valid License?

You can view the status of the IPS subscription license key in two ways:

- Using CLI
- Using IDM

Using CLI

When you log in to Sensor using SSH or Telnet, the banner displays the licensing information. For example, if your sensor is not licensed, you will see the following message:

```
***LICENSE NOTICE***
There is no license key installed on the system.
Please go to http://www.cisco.com/go/license to obtain a new license or install a
  license.
```

You can also find out the license information by using the **show version** command as shown in Example 14-1. In the **show version** output, the sensor will display the following line if your sensor is not licensed:

```
No license present
```

Using IDM

Just as with CLI, when you log in to IDM, a dialog box informs you of your license status. It will tell you whether you have a trial, invalid, or expired license key. With no license key, an invalid license key, or an expired license key, you can continue to use IDM and the sensor, but you cannot download signature updates.

You can also find the IPS license information on IDM by clicking **Configuration > Licensing.**

How to Procure The License Key From Cisco.com

You can procure the license in two ways: via e-mail or by using IDM. When you use IDM, you can make the license request directly to the Cisco.com licensing server (IDM has this information built in) to pull the license key and install it at the same time. For that, you must have connectivity from the sensor to the Internet. However, to get the license key separately and then install it either via CLI or IDM, go to the following site:

http://www.cisco.com/go/license

You must know your IPS device serial number to obtain a license key. You can find the IPS device serial number IDM by clicking **Configuration > Licensing** or obtain it through the CLI by using the **show version** command.

Follow the steps to get the license key via e-mail:

Step 1 Go to www.cisco.com/go/license.

Step 2 Fill in the required fields. The most important piece of information is the correct IPS device serial number because the license key only functions on the device with that number.

Step 3 Your Cisco IPS Signature Subscription Service license key will be sent by e-mail to the e-mail address you specified. If you want to license the sensor using IDM, save the license file to a hard drive or to a network drive that is accessible by the client that is running the Device Manager.

Step 4 To license the sensor using CLI, transfer this license key to the sensor, a process which is discussed in the next section.

NOTE To obtain a license, you must have a Cisco Service for IPS contract. Contact your reseller, Cisco service or product sales to purchase a contract. You can install the first few signature updates for 5.0 without a license. This gives you time to get your sensor licensed. If you are unable to get your sensor licensed because of confusion with your contract, you can obtain a 60-day trial license that supports signature updates that require licensing.

Licensing the Sensor

There are two ways to license the sensor:

- Using IDM
- Using CLI

Using IDM

To install the sensor license, follow these steps:

Step 1 Click **Configuration > Licensing**. The Licensing panel displays.

Step 2 Choose the method for delivering the license. Select **Cisco Connection Online** to obtain the license from Cisco.com. The Device Manager contacts the license server on Cisco.com and sends the server the serial number to obtain the license key. This is the default method.

Step 3 If you have already received the license via e-mail, check the **License file** box, and click on **Browse Local** to upload the file from your local hard disk of your PC.

Step 4 Click **Update License**.

Step 5 The Licensing dialog box appears. Click **Yes** to continue.

Step 6 Click **OK**.

Using CLI

Once you get the license via e-mail as explained in the section entitled "How to Procure The License Key From Cisco.com," licensing Sensor requires you to transfer the license key to Sensor. Work through the following steps to license the sensor with SCP using CLI:

Step 1 Save the license key to a system that has a web server, FTP server, or SCP server.

Step 2 Log in to the sensor using an account with administrator privileges, and copy the license key to the sensor with the following command:

```
sensor# copy scp://user@10.89.147.3://tftpboot/dev.lic license-key
Password: *******
```

Step 3 Verify that the sensor is licensed with the **show version** command as shown in Example 14-17:

Example 14-17 *Shows the Sensor Is Licensed with the* **show version** *Command*

```
sensor# show version
Application Partition:

Cisco Intrusion Prevention System, Version 5.0(1)S149.0
```

continues

Example 14-17 *Shows the Sensor Is Licensed with the* **show version** *Command (Continued)*

```
OS Version 2.4.26-IDS-smp-bigphys
Platform: IPS-4255-K9
Serial Number: JAB0815R0JS
! The following line shows that the license is still valid
Licensed, expires: 19-Dec-2005 UTC
Sensor up-time is 2 days.
Using 706699264 out of 3974291456 bytes of available memory (17% usage)
system is using 17.3M out of 29.0M bytes of available disk space (59% usage)
application-data is using 36.5M out of 166.8M bytes of available disk space (23%
  usage)
boot is using 39.4M out of 68.6M bytes of available disk space (61% usage)

MainApp         2005_Feb_18_03.00  (Release)  2005-02-18T03:13:47-0600  Running
AnalysisEngine  2005_Feb_15_03.00  (QATest)   2005-02-15T12:59:35-0600  Running
CLI              2005_Feb_18_03.00  (Release)  2005-02-18T03:13:47-0600


Upgrade History:

            IDS-K9-maj-5.0-1-   14:16:00 UTC Thu Mar 04 2004

Recovery Partition Version 1.1 - 5.0(1)S149

sensor#
```

Step 4 Copy your license key from the sensor to a server to keep a backup copy of the license with the following command:

```
sensor# copy license-key scp://user@10.1.1.100://tftpboot/user.lic
Password: *******
sensor#
```

Communication Issues

You can connect to the sensor in a number of ways: Telnet, SSH, IDS MC (or IDM), Security Monitor and so on. The sections that follow discuss some of the connectivity issues:

- Basic connectivity issues
- Connectivity issues between IPS sensor and IPS MC or IDM
- Connectivity issues between IPS Sensor and security monitor

Basic Connectivity Issues

There might be several reasons why you cannot connect to the sensor either via Telnet or SSH. Work through the following steps to troubleshoot the connectivity issue to the sensor:

Step 1 Ping to the sensor and see if you can ping to the Command and Control interface of the sensor.

Step 2 If you cannot ping, log in to the sensor CLI through a console, terminal, or module session.

Step 3 Be sure that the sensor's management interface is enabled:

```
sensor# show interfaces
Interface Statistics
   Total Packets Received = 0
   Total Bytes Received = 0
   Missed Packet Percentage = 0
   Current Bypass Mode = Auto_off
MAC statistics from interface GigabitEthernet0/1
! The following line indicates that Media Type is backplane which is an
! indication that this is not Command & Control port
   Media Type = backplane
   Missed Packet Percentage = 0
   Inline Mode = Unpaired
   Pair Status = N/A
   Link Status = Up
   Link Speed = Auto_1000
   Link Duplex = Auto_Full
   Total Packets Received = 0
   Total Bytes Received = 0
   Total Multicast Packets Received = 0
   Total Broadcast Packets Received = 0
   Total Jumbo Packets Received = 0
   Total Undersize Packets Received = 0
   Total Receive Errors = 0
   Total Receive FIFO Overruns = 0
   Total Packets Transmitted = 0
   Total Bytes Transmitted = 0
   Total Multicast Packets Transmitted = 0
   Total Broadcast Packets Transmitted = 0
   Total Jumbo Packets Transmitted = 0
   Total Undersize Packets Transmitted = 0
   Total Transmit Errors = 0
   Total Transmit FIFO Overruns = 0
MAC statistics from interface GigabitEthernet0/0
! The following line indicates the Media Type TX which means this is a
! Command and Control Port
   Media Type = TX
   Link Status = Up
   Link Speed = Auto_100
   Link Duplex = Auto_Full
   Total Packets Received = 1822323
```

```
   Total Bytes Received = 131098876
   Total Multicast Packets Received = 20
   Total Receive Errors = 0
   Total Receive FIFO Overruns = 0
   Total Packets Transmitted = 219260
   Total Bytes Transmitted = 103668610
   Total Transmit Errors = 0
   Total Transmit FIFO Overruns = 0
sensor#
```

The management interface is the interface in the list with the status line **Media Type = TX**. If the Link Status is **Down**, go to Step 3. If the Link Status is **Up**, go to Step 5.

Step 4 Duplicate IP Address Shuts Interface Down

If another host in the network using the same IP address as the sensor comes up on the same network at the same time, the interface shuts down. Linux prevents the command and control interface from activating if it detects an address conflict with another host.

Step 5 Be sure the sensor's cabling is correct.

Step 6 Be sure the sensor's IP address is unique and correct with the **setup** command.

```
sensor# setup
--- System Configuration Dialog ---

At any point you may enter a question mark '?' for help.
User ctrl-c to abort configuration dialog at any prompt.
Default settings are in square brackets '[]'.

Current Configuration:

service host
network-settings
host-ip 10.89.130.108/23,10.89.130.1
host-name sensor
telnet-option enabled
access-list 0.0.0.0/0
ftp-timeout 300
no login-banner-text
exit
--MORE--
```

If the management interface detects that another device on the network has the same IP address, it will not come up. So, change the IP address, subnet mask, and default gateway of the sensor.

Step 7 Be sure that the management port is connected to an active port.

If the Command and Control port is not connected to an active port, the management interface will not come up on the sensor.

Step 8 Be sure that the IP address of the workstation that is trying to connect to the sensor is permitted in the sensor's access list:

```
sensor# setup
--- System Configuration Dialog ---

At any point you may enter a question mark '?' for help.
User ctrl-c to abort configuration dialog at any prompt.
Default settings are in square brackets '[]'.

Current Configuration:

service host
network-settings
host-ip 10.89.130.108/23,10.89.130.1
host-name sensor
telnet-option enabled
access-list 0.0.0.0/0
ftp-timeout 300
no login-banner-text
exit
--MORE—
Sensor#
```

If the workstation's network address is permitted in the sensor's access list, go to Step 6.

Step 9 Add a permit entry for the workstation's network address, save the configuration, and try to connect again. You can run the **setup** command to add addition, IP address, or network address on the sensor. Or, you can follow Example 14-18 to add permit to the access-list on the Sensor:

Example 14-18 *Verifying the Access List and Permitting or Denying on the ACL on Sensor*

```
! View the current access-list configuration on the Sensor.
sensor# show configuration | include access-list
access-list 10.0.0.0/8
access-list 64.0.0.0/8
sensor#
! Verify that the client IP address is listed in the allowed networks. If it is not,
! add it with the following commands.
sensor# configure terminal
sensor(config)# service host
sensor(config-hos)# network-settings
sensor(config-hos-net)# access-list 171.69.70.0/24
```

continues

Example 14-18 *Verifying the Access List and Permitting or Denying on the ACL on Sensor (Continued)*

```
! Now verify the settings
sensor(config-hos-net)# show settings
   network-settings
   -----------------------------------------------
      host-ip: 10.89.149.238/25,10.89.149.254 default: 10.1.9.201/24,10.1.9.1
      host-name: qsensor-238 default: sensor
      telnet-option: enabled default: disabled
      access-list (min: 0, max: 512, current: 3)
      -----------------------------------------------
         network-address: 10.0.0.0/8
         -----------------------------------------------
         network-address: 64.0.0.0/8
         -----------------------------------------------
         network-address: 171.69.70.0/24
         -----------------------------------------------
      -----------------------------------------------
      ftp-timeout: 300 seconds <defaulted>
      login-banner-text:  <defaulted>
   -----------------------------------------------
sensor(config-hos-net)#
```

Step 10 Be sure that the network configuration allows the workstation to connect to the sensor.

If the sensor is protected behind a firewall and the workstation is in front of the firewall, be sure that the firewall is configured to allow the workstation to access the sensor. Or, if the workstation is behind a firewall that is performing network address translation on the workstation's IP address, and the sensor is in front of the firewall, be sure that the sensor's access list contains a permit entry for the workstation's translated address.

Step 11 You can connect and you are getting login prompt but authentication fails.

Check to see if logins to the account have been disabled due to the failed login limit being reached. The sensor provides the configuration option to limit the number of consecutive failed login attempts. Once this limit is reached the account becomes locked until it is administratively unlocked. This option is disabled by default. It can be enabled in the CLI. To determine if a failed login attempt limit is enabled, enter the authentication service configuration mode and use the **show settings** command. If the **attemptLimit** is greater than zero, the failed login attempt limit is set to this value. Set the **attemptLimit** value to zero to disable this account-locking feature. This feature is required to satisfy the government's Common Criteria for security devices. To check the failed login count, log into the service account—if possible. From the service account shell, run the command **pam_tally.** The output shows the number of failed login attempts for each account. To reset the count, run **pam_tally—reset**. This command will reset the failed login counts.

Connectivity Issues Between IPS Sensor and IPS MC or IDM

If you have problems with importing the sensor's configuration or pushing the configuration or signature upgrade, work through the following steps to troubleshoot the issue:

Step 1 Go through the "Basic Connectivity Issues" section to ensure the basic network connectivity between the IDM or IPS MC.

Step 2 For IPS MC or the IDM to function correctly, ensure that TCP/22 (SSH) and TCP/443 (SSL) are not blocked by any network devices between the sensor and the IPS MC.

Step 3 Log in to IPS Sensor and execute the **show version** command. Ensure that **MainApp** is running; otherwise, IPS MC or IDM will not be able to connect to the IPS Sensor.

Step 4 If the **MainApp** is shown not running, upgrade to the latest version of Sensor, and reboot the sensor. If the problem persists, get the **show tech-support** output and send the output file to the developer for root cause analysis.

Connectivity Issues Between IPS Sensor and Security Monitor

Security Monitor is used as a reporting tool for the IPS events. Work through the following steps to troubleshoot issues with connecting the Security Monitor with IPS Sensor:

Step 1 In the Security Monitor go to **Monitor > Connections** and verify that the connection status is shown as TLS-Connected for the sensor that is experiencing connectivity problems. If you have any other status, go to the next step.

Step 2 Go through the **Basic Connectivity Issues** section to ensure the basic connectivity.

Step 3 Try to access the Event-Server using the browser with the following address:

https://<sensor's IP address>/cgi-bin/event-server

If the event-server is not accessible, then log in to the sensor and execute **show version** to ensure that **MainApp** is running, as the **web server** is part of **MainApp**. Upgrade to the latest version of IPS Sensor. If that does not resolve the problem, reboot the sensor. If you still have issues, look for any possible bugs on the sensor and on the Security Monitor.

Step 4 If the **MainApp** is running, use any network devices between IPS Sensor and Security Monitor to ensure that tcp/22 (for SSH) and tcp/443 (SSL) are open.

Issues with Receiving Events on Monitoring Device

If you are unable to receive any events on the Monitoring device (for example, on the Security Monitor), the cause of the problem might be either on a sensor or monitoring device. This section goes delves into troubleshooting steps for situations in which you are not able to generate events on the sensor itself. Troubleshooting the "not showing events" problem on the Security Monitor is discussed in detail in Chapter 22, "Troubleshooting Security Monitors." There might be several reasons why Sensor might not be generating events. These are the most important reasons:

- Sensorapp is not running
- Physical Connectivity, SPAN, or VACL Port Issues
- Unable to see alerts

The sections that follow explain the preceding bulleted items in detail. But first ensure that the Sensor is indeed not generating any events by using the **show events** command as shown in Example 14-19.

Example 14-19 *Checking To See if the Events Are Generated on the Sensor in Last 30 Minutes*

```
Sensor# show events past 00:30:00
evAlert: eventId=1047568419898617804 severity=informational
originator:
hostId: sj_4250_40
appName: sensorApp
appInstanceId: 1006
time: 2003/04/21 16:12:14 2003/04/21 16:12:14 PST
interfaceGroup: 0
vlan: 0
signature: sigId=2151 sigName=Large ICMP subSigId=0 version=S37
participants:
attack:
attacker: proxy=false
addr: locality=OUT 172.16.171.13
victim:
addr: locality=OUT 171.69.89.32
Sensor#
```

SensorApp Is Not Running

The **SensorApp** is the sensing process, which is part of **AnalysisEngine**, and it must always be running to receive any alerts. Work through the following steps to troubleshoot the **SensorApp** not running issue:

Step 1 Log in to the sensor either via SSH or Telnet.

Step 2 Find out the status of the **AnalysisEngine** service with the show version output as shown in Example 14-20.

Example 14-20 *show version Output Showing the AnalysisEngine Is Not Running*

```
sensor# show version
Application Partition:

Cisco Intrusion Prevention System, Version 5.0(1)S149.0

OS Version 2.4.26-IDS-smp-bigphys
Platform: IDS-4235
Serial Number: CGTWJ11
Trial license, expires: 27-Apr-2006 UTC
Sensor up-time is 3 days.
Using 247812096 out of 923549696 bytes of available memory (26% usage)
system is using 17.3M out of 29.0M bytes of available disk space (59% usage)
application-data is using 31.9M out of 174.7M bytes of available disk space (19%
  usage)
boot is using 40.5M out of 75.9M bytes of available disk space (56% usage)
application-log is using 531.2M out of 2.8G bytes of available disk space (20% usage)


MainApp          2005_Mar_04_14.23   (Release)   2005-03-04T14:35:11-0600   Running
! The following line shows the AnalysisEngine is not running. Hence SensorApp is not
! running
AnalysisEngine    2005_Mar_04_14.23   (Release)   2005-03-04T14:35:11-0600   Not
  Running
CLI              2005_Mar_04_14.23   (Release)   2005-03-04T14:35:11-0600

Upgrade History:

  IDS-K9-maj-5.0-1-   22:16:00 UTC Thu Mar 04 2004

Recovery Partition Version 1.1 - 5.0(1)S149

sensor#
```

Step 3 If the **AnalysisEngine** is not running, look for any errors pertaining to **AnalysisEngine**, as shown in Example 14-21.

Example 14-21 *Analysis Engine Error, Which Shows the Last Restart Was on March 20, 2005*

```
sensor# show events error fatal past 08:30:00 | include AnalysisEngine
evError: eventId=1077219258696330005 severity=warning

originator:
hostId: sensor
appName: sensorApp
appInstanceId: 1045
time: 2005/03/20 10:35:00 2005/03/20 10:35:00 UTC
errorMessage: name=errUnclassified Generating new Analysis Engine configuration
  file.
Sensor#
```

Step 4 As a first step to resolve the issue that the **SensorApp is** not running, check to see if a large number of signatures are set to **ipLogging**. If so, disable **ipLogging,** and check to see if this resolves the issue.

Step 5 If you still have problems, reboot the sensor to solve the problem.

Step 6 Check to see if you are running the latest version of Sensor. If not, go to the IPS Software download center on Cisco.com and go through the Readme file of the latest version. Check to see if there is any bug being reported pertaining to **AnalysisEngine**.

Step 7 Upgrade to the latest version of IPS software and see if the problem disappears.

Step 8 If the **AnalysisEngine** is not coming up even after you have completed the previous steps, get the **show tech-support** (**coredump** included) output and contact Cisco TAC support for further analysis.

Physical Connectivity, SPAN, or VACL Port Issues

If the sniffing port is not connected to a switch analyzer port (SPAN) or VACL (VACL stands for VLAN ACL) destination port correctly, or if you have misconfiguration on the switch, you will have problems getting the packets from the switch. Work through the following steps to troubleshoot issues pertaining to receiving traffic from the switch or the hub:

Step 1 Sniffing Interface Connected to the wrong port on the Switch

The Command and Control port is used to send the alarms to the Security Monitor, and the sniffing interface is used to capture the traffic feed from the switch. So, if you choose the wrong interface for the wrong task, for example, you connect the Command and Control port to the sniffing or VACL destination port on the switch, and you will not get the traffic feed, hence no alarm. Be sure that interfaces are up and counters are increasing by executing the **show interface** command as shown in Example 14-22. In this example, **Media Type = backplane** indicates a sniffing port.

Example 14-22 *A Working Sensing Interface*

```
sensor# show interfaces
Interface Statistics
   Total Packets Received = 0
   Total Bytes Received = 0
   Missed Packet Percentage = 0
   Current Bypass Mode = Auto_off
MAC statistics from interface GigabitEthernet0/1
! The following line indicates that GigabitEthernet0/1 interface is the sniffing
! interface. This interface should to be connected to the SPAN or the VACL destination
! port
```

Example 14-22 *A Working Sensing Interface (Continued)*

```
   Media Type = backplane
   Missed Packet Percentage = 0
   Inline Mode = Unpaired
   Pair Status = N/A
   Link Status = Up
   Link Speed = Auto_1000
   Link Duplex = Auto_Full
   Total Packets Received = 0
   Total Bytes Received = 0
   Total Multicast Packets Received = 0
   Total Broadcast Packets Received = 0
   Total Jumbo Packets Received = 0
   Total Undersize Packets Received = 0
   Total Receive Errors = 0
   Total Receive FIFO Overruns = 0
   Total Packets Transmitted = 0
   Total Bytes Transmitted = 0
   Total Multicast Packets Transmitted = 0
   Total Broadcast Packets Transmitted = 0
   Total Jumbo Packets Transmitted = 0
   Total Undersize Packets Transmitted = 0
   Total Transmit Errors = 0
   Total Transmit FIFO Overruns = 0
MAC statistics from interface GigabitEthernet0/0
! The media type TX indicates that this is the Command and Control port
   Media Type = TX
   Link Status = Up
   Link Speed = Auto_100
   Link Duplex = Auto_Full
   Total Packets Received = 1830137
   Total Bytes Received = 131624465
   Total Multicast Packets Received = 20
   Total Receive Errors = 0
   Total Receive FIFO Overruns = 0
   Total Packets Transmitted = 220052
   Total Bytes Transmitted = 103796666
   Total Transmit Errors = 0
   Total Transmit FIFO Overruns = 0
Sensor#
```

Check to see that the sensing port is connected to the correct span port or the VACL destination port on the switch.

Step 2 If the Link Status in Example 14-22 shows down, work through the following steps to correct the problem:

(a) Be sure that the sensor's sniffing interface is enabled and receiving traffic. You can use the setup command or follow Example 14-23 to enable the sniffing interface on the sensor.

Example 14-23 *Checking and Enabling the Sensing Interface*

```
sensor# configure terminal
sensor(config)# service interface
sensor(config-int)# physical-interfaces gigabitEthernet0/0
! The following command shows the configuration for the sniffing interface
sensor(config-int-phy)# show settings
   <protected entry>
   name: GigabitEthernet0/0
   -----------------------------------------------
      media-type: tx <protected>
      description:  <defaulted>
! The following line shows the admin-state is disabled administratively.
      admin-state: disabled default: disabled
      duplex: auto <defaulted>
      speed: auto <defaulted>
      alt-tcp-reset-interface
      -----------------------------------------------
         none
         -----------------------------------------------
         -----------------------------------------------
      -----------------------------------------------
   -----------------------------------------------
! The following line shows how to enable the sniffing interface
sensor(config-int-phy)# admin-state enabled
! Check the configuration settings again to see if the admin-state is enabled
sensor(config-int-phy)# show settings
   <protected entry>
   name: GigabitEthernet0/0
   -----------------------------------------------
      media-type: tx <protected>
      description:  <defaulted>
! Following line indicates the admin-state is enabled
      admin-state: enabled default: disabled
      duplex: auto <defaulted>
      speed: auto <defaulted>
      alt-tcp-reset-interface
      -----------------------------------------------
         none
         -----------------------------------------------
         -----------------------------------------------
      -----------------------------------------------
   -----------------------------------------------
sensor(config-int-phy)# exit
sensor(config-int)# exit
Apply Changes:?[yes]:
sensor(config)# exit
! Check to see if the sensing interface is shown UP or Down.
sensor# show interfaces gigabitEthernet0/0
! Extra lines are removed
   Media Type = TX
! Following line shows the link status is Up
   Link Status = Up
! Extra lines are removed
sensor#
```

(b) If the sniffing interface is up, but the link status is still shown as down, be sure a working cable is connected properly to the sensing port with the switch.

(c) Check the switch configuration, identify the SPAN or VACL destination port, and connect the sensor's sniffing port to this port.

Step 3 Check to see if the SPAN or VACL configuration is configured correctly.

If, over a period of time, the sniffing interface is connected to the switch port, and is shown as up in the interface statistics, but the counters for incoming packets are not incrementing, or are staying at zero, then most likely the problem is an incorrect configuration of SPAN or VACL on the switch. Check to see if the SPAN or VACL destination port on the switch is up, sending traffic, and configured correctly.

Unable to See Alerts

If you do not see any events generated with the **show events** command on the sensor, work through the following steps to troubleshoot the problem:

Step 1 Check to see if the virtual-sensor statistics is showing any alerts, as shown in Example 14-24.

Example 14-24 *Verifying that Alerts Are Being Generated on the Sensor*

```
Sensor#show statistics virtual-sensor
SigEvent Preliminary Stage Statistics
    Number of Alerts received = 0
    Number of Alerts Consumed by AlertInterval = 0
    Number of Alerts Consumed by Event Count = 0
    Number of FireOnce First Alerts = 0
    Number of FireOnce Intermediate Alerts = 0
    Number of Summary First Alerts  = 0
    Number of Summary Intermediate Alerts  = 0
    Number of Regular Summary Final Alerts  = 0
    Number of Global Summary Final Alerts  = 0
   Number of Alerts Output for further processing = 0alertDetails: Traffic Source: int0
Sensor#
```

Step 2 Be sure that the signature is enabled and not retired, as shown in Example 14-25.

Example 14-25 *Signature Is Enabled and Is Not Retired*

```
sensor# configure terminal
sensor(config)# service signature-definition sig0
sensor(config-sig)# signatures 1300 0
sensor(config-sig-sig)# status
```

continues

Example 14-25 *Signature Is Enabled and Is Not Retired (Continued)*

```
sensor(config-sig-sig-sta)# show settings
   status
   -----------------------------------------------
! The following line indicates that the signature is enabled.
      enabled: true <defaulted>
! The following line indicates that the signature is not retired.
      retired: false <defaulted>
   -----------------------------------------------
Sensor#
```

Step 3 Be sure that you have Produce Alert configured as an action.

If you have **Produce Alert** configured as event-action, but add another event-action later and do not add Produce Alert to the new configuration, alerts will not be sent to the Event Store. Every time you configure a signature, the new configuration overwrites the old one, so be sure you have configured all the event actions you want for each signature, as shown in Example 14-26.

Example 14-26 *Configuring And Checking Event Action Type Produce Alert*

```
sensor# configure terminal
sensor(config)# service signature-definition sig0
sensor(config-sig)# signatures 1300 0
sensor(config-sig-sig)# engine normalizer
! Make sure to define multiple event-action with pipe
sensor(config-sig-sig-nor)# event-action produce-alert|deny-connection-inline
sensor(config-sig-sig-nor)# show settings
   normalizer
   -----------------------------------------------
! Event-action types are shown as configured earlier
      event-action: produce-alert default: produce-alert|deny-connection-inline
      edit-default-sigs-only
      -----------------------------------------------
sensor#
```

Step 4 Be sure the sensor is receiving packets from the network.

Go through section entitled "Physical Connectivity, SPAN, or VACL Port Issue" for guidance on troubleshooting issues pertaining to the fact that the sensor is not able to receive any packets from the switch.

Step 5 Be sure that there is no filter that is applied to the sensor that could be blocking the events.

If you do not see the events, you need to be sure that you do not have the attacker address configured as filtering to eliminate the false positive. It is not very uncommon to define a filter for *ALL* signatures accidentally. The best way to find out if you have a filter in place is to execute this command on the sensor: **show configuration | include EventFilter**. If there is any filter for *ALL* then you will see a line similar to the following:

```
EventFilter
Filters DestAddrs * Exception False SIGID * SourceAddrs * SubSig *
```

From the IDM on the sensor (https://sensorip), go to **Configuration > Event Action Rules > Event Action Filters** and analyze all the filters defined, and either edit or remove the incorrect filters.

Blocking Issues

In addition to events logging, the sensor can be configured to take actions in response to malicious activities against your network. If you are running Promiscuous mode, there are two options available on sensor software for taking actions against malicious activities: Blocking and **tcp reset**. Inline mode has two more option types in addition to these two options.

Network Access Controller (NAC), the blocking application on the sensor, starts and stops blocks on routers, switches, PIX Firewalls, Firewall Services Module (FWSM), and ASA. Network Access Controller blocks the IP address on the devices it is managing. It sends the same block to all the devices it is managing, including any other master blocking sensors. Network Access Controller monitors the time for the block and removes the block after the time has expired.

As most blocking-related issues arise because of lack of understanding, lack of planning, and misconfiguration, this section presents everything you need to be aware of, works through the configuration, and concludes with troubleshooting. Following is a list of items discussed in this section:

- Types of blocking
- ACL or VACL considerations on the managed devices
- Supported managed devices and versions
- Proper planning for blocking
- Master Blocking Sensor (MBS)
- Configuration steps for blocking
- Configuring steps for the Master Blocking Sensor (MBS)
- Troubleshooting steps for blocking

A thorough discussion follows section by section, based on the preceding list.

Types of Blocking

Not every managed device supports all types of blocking that can be performed by the sensor. So it is important to understand the different types of blocking that the sensor can perform and how each type of managed device works with these types. Following is a list of three types of blocks that are supported by the sensor:

- **Host block**—Blocks all traffic from a given IP address. So it works based on source IP address. Cisco Secure firewalls (PIX, FWSM, and ASA series) perform **Host block** even if they are configured for **Connection block**.
- **Connection block**—Blocks traffic from a given source IP address/port to a given destination IP address/destination port for a specific protocol. So it relies on 5-tuples (Source and Destination IP addresses and ports, and the protocol). As mentioned before, connection blocks are not supported on Cisco Secure firewalls. Firewalls only support **host blocks** with additional connection information. Understand that multiple connection blocks from the same source IP address to either a different destination IP address or destination port automatically switch the block from a connection block to a host block.
- **Network block**—Blocks all traffic from a given network. It is possible to initiate host and connection blocks manually or automatically when a signature is triggered, but network blocks can only be initiated manually.

NOTE Blocking is a different feature altogether than the sensor's ability to drop packets in Inline mode when **deny packet inline, deny connection inline, and deny attacker inline** action types are configured. So, do not confuse these actions with **Blocking**.

ACL or VACL Consideration on the Managed Devices

On Cisco routers and Catalyst 6500 series switches, Network Access Controller creates blocks by applying ACLs or VACLs. ACLs and VACLs permit or deny passage of data packets through interface ports or VLANs. Each ACL or VACL contains permit and deny conditions that apply to IP addresses. The PIX Firewall, FWSM, and ASA do not use ACLs or VACLs. The built-in **shun/no shun** command is used. As the implementation of ACL and VACL is very similar for blocking performed by Sensor, the discussion focuses only on ACL, which is also appropriate for VACL. Several ACLs are used with the blocking. Hence it's critical to understand use of these ACLs:

- **Two ACLs used by Network Access Controller**—NAC uses two ACLs to manage devices. Only one is active at any one time. It uses the offline ACL name to build the new ACL, and then applies it to the interface.
- **Pre-Block ACL**—The Pre-Block ACL is mainly used for permitting the networks or hosts that you do not want the sensor to ever block. When a packet is checked against the ACL, the first line that is matched determines the action. If the first line matched is a permit line from the Pre-Block ACL, the packet is permitted even though there might be a deny line (from an automatic block) listed later in the ACL. The Pre-Block ACL can override the deny lines resulting from the blocks. To modify the Pre-Block

ACL on the router, you need to disable blocking from the sensor, make the changes on the ACL, and then re-enable the blocking on the sensor.

- **Post-Block ACL**—The Post-Block ACL is best used for additional blocking or permitting that you want to occur on the same interface or direction. If you have an existing ACL on the interface or direction that the sensor will manage, that existing ACL can be used as a Post-Block ACL. If you do not have a Post-Block ACL, the sensor inserts a **permit ip any any** at the end of the new ACL. If you need to modify the Post-Block ACL on the router, you need to disable blocking from the sensor, make the changes on the ACL, and then re-enable the blocking on the sensor.

You need to create and save Pre-Block and Post-Block ACLs in your router configuration. These ACLs must be extended IP ACLs, either named or numbered. See your router documentation for more information on creating ACLs.

Enter the names of these ACLs that are already configured on your router in the Pre-Block ACL and Post-Block ACL fields on the sensor. When the sensor starts up, it reads the contents of the two ACLs. It creates a third ACL (the active ACL of two ACLs used by NAC to manage blocking) with the following entries:

- A **permit** line for the sensor's IP address
- Copies of all configuration lines of the Pre-Block ACL
- A **deny** line for each address being blocked by the sensor
- Copies of all configuration lines of the Post-Block ACL
- If the Post-Block ACL is not configured, then add **permit ip any any** to allow the rest of the traffic. In the case of VACL and IDSM-2, the last statement is **permit ip any any capture**, with **capture** argument appended.
- The sensor applies the new ACL to the interface and direction that you designate. When the new ACL is applied to an interface or direction of the router, it removes the application of any other ACL to that interface or direction.

NOTE The Pre-Block or Post-Block ACL names are not used when Sensor creates and names the third ACL and applies it on the managed device.

Supported Managed Devices and Versions

Network Access Controller supports up to 250 devices in any combination by default. As not every network device and version of the device can be configured to be a managed device, it is important to know which devices and versions can be used as managed devices. Following is a list of such versions and devices:

- Routers using Cisco IOS 11.2 or later (using ACLs) include, Cisco 1600 series router, Cisco 1700 series router, Cisco 2500 series router, Cisco 2600 series router, Cisco 2800 series router, Cisco 3600 series router, Cisco 3800 series router, Cisco 7200 series router, and Cisco 7500 series router.

- Catalyst 5000 switches with Route Switch Module (RSM) with IOS 11.2(9)P or later (Using ACLs).
- Catalyst 6500 switches and 7600 routers with IOS 12.1(13)E or later (using ACLs).
- Catalyst 6500 switches and 7600 routers with Catalyst software version 7.5(1) or later (Using VACLs), which include Supervisor Engine 1A with Policy Feature Card (PFC), Supervisor Engine 1A with Multilayer Switching Feature Card (MSFC)1, Supervisor Engine 1A with MFSC2, Supervisor Engine 2 with MSFC2, and Supervisor Engine 720 with MSFC3. It is important to note that VACL blocking is supported on the Supervisor Engine and ACL blocking is supported on the MSFC.
- PIX Firewall with version 6.0 or later (**shun** command) which includes all platforms 501, 506E, 515E, 525, and 535.
- ASA with version 7.0 or later (With **shun** command), which includes platforms ASA-5510, ASA-5520, and ASA-5540.
- FWSM 1.1 or later (With **shun** command). If ASA or FWSM is configured in multi-mode, blocking is not supported for the admin context. Blocking is only supported in single mode and in multi-mode customer context.

So, as you can see, you can configure blocking using either ACLs, VACLS, or the **shun** command, depending on the types of platforms used as managed devices.

Proper Planning for Blocking

Implementing the blocking feature requires proper planning, as there are serious consequences in terms of blocking legitimate traffic. You can disrupt the network by blocking routing protocol traffic and experience other problems. With proper planning, you can implement blocking without any trouble. Following is a list that will assist you in the planning required to implement the blocking feature:

- Obtain a clear understanding of the network topology, and be absolutely sure about the devices which should be managed by the sensor for blocking.
- Find out the network or host addresses that should never be blocked. One such example is the sensor's IP address itself.
- From the administrators responsible for each device, obtain the usernames, passwords, enable passwords, and connection types (Telnet or SSH) needed to log into each device. If possible, get permission to access the managed devices.
- Be absolutely sure that you know the interface names of the managed device and the directions in which Sensor should apply the blocking.
- Understand which interfaces should and should not be blocked and in which direction (in or out). You do not want to accidentally shut down an entire network.
- Carefully define the network or host address that should never be blocked with the Pre-Block ACL or VACL. For additional blocking, use Post-Block ACL or VACL if needed. Get their names as they appear on the managed devices.

- Do not configure multiple sensors to control blocking on the same device. If multiple sensors are needed, configure one sensor as the master blocking sensor to manage the devices, and the other sensors can forward their block requests to the master blocking sensor. This brings up the discussion that follows on Master Blocking Sensor.

Master Blocking Sensor (MBS)

If you are monitoring more than one network by using multiple sensors, and if more than one sensor needs to initiate blocking to the same managed device, serious disruption to the traffic might occur. Hence, only one sensor must control the blocking for the managed devices. This is the role of the master blocking sensor (MBS). In this case, the MBS should be configured to control blocking for all managed devices. The non-MBS, also known as the blocking forwarding sensor, should be configured not to control blocking for a managed device, but rather to communicate its blocks to the MBS sensor.

You do not need any special configuration on the MBS to designate it to be an MBS. Most of the configuration is done on the blocking forwarding sensor, which forwards the block request to the MBS. You can configure one MBS to forward block requests to another MBS. But, you need to be extremely careful with a circular block that might occur if misconfigured. For example, assume that SensorA is configured as MBS for SensorB and SensorB is also configured as MBS for SensorA. Both SensorA and SensorB will forward the block request to each other, causing a circular block. With two sensors this can be easily avoided by merely configuring one for the MBS and one for the other sensor which is also acting as MBS for some other sensor (for example SensorC). But, if you have a complex setup with a number of sensors acting as MBS for non-MBS sensors in addition to the MBS Sensor, extra caution is warranted.

Configuration Steps for Blocking

Work through the following steps to configure blocking on the IOS router:

Step 1 Configure user profiles on the sensor so that Sensor can log in to the managed device. The user profile contains user id, password, and enable password information. If the username or password is not needed to log in to the device, you do not need to set a value for it. You must create a user profile before configuring the blocking device. Example 14-27 shows how to create a user profile on the sensor for the router.

Example 14-27 *Setting up User Profiles on the Sensor*

```
! Log in to the Sensor's CLI using an account with administrator privileges and enter
! network access mode
sensor# configure terminal
sensor(config)# service network-access
! Create the user profile name
sensor(config-net)# user-profiles ROUTER_PROFILE
! Type the username for that user profile
```

continues

Example 14-27 *Setting up User Profiles on the Sensor (Continued)*

```
sensor(config-net-use)# username cisco
! Specify the password for the user
sensor(config-net-use)# password
Enter password[]: ********
Re-enter password:********

! Specify the enable password for the user
sensor(config-net-use)# enable-password
Enter enable-password[]: ********
Re-enter enable-password ********
! Verify the user profile settings
sensor(config-net-use)# show settings
   profile-name: ROUTER_PROFILE
   -----------------------------------------------
      enable-password: <hidden>
      password: <hidden>
      username: cisco default:
   -----------------------------------------------
sensor(config-net-use)#
! Exit network access submode
sensor(config-net-use)# exit
sensor(config-net)# exit
Apply Changes:?[yes]:
! Press Enter to apply the changes or type no to discard them.
Sensor#
```

Step 2 If a managed device is configured with SSH, execute the following command on the sensor for each managed device to add them as trusted hosts. Otherwise, skip this step.

```
Sensor# configure terminal
sensor(config)# ssh host-key <device's IP address>
```

Step 3 Enter the network access submode of the sensor as follows:

```
sensor# configure terminal
sensor(config)# service network-access
```

Step 4 Set the IP address for the router controlled by Network Access Controller and define the user profile name as follows:

```
sensor(config-net)# router-devices ip_address
sensor(config-net-rou)# profile-name user_profile_name
```

It is important to note that Network Access Controller accepts any command you type. So be sure that you type the correct profile name.

Step 5 Define a communication method with the following command to access the sensor:

```
sensor(config-net-rou)# communication [telnet | ssh-des | sh-3des]
```

If no communication is specified, SSH 3DES is used.

Step 6 If a NAT device is used between the sensor and the managed device, specify the sensor's NAT address with the following command:

```
sensor(config-net-rou)# nat-address nat_address
```

Step 7 Set the interface name and direction with the following command:

```
sensor(config-net-rou)# block-interfaces interface_name [in | out]
```

The name of the interface must either be the complete name of the interface or an abbreviation that the router recognizes with the **interface** command.

Step 8 Optionally, add the pre-ACL name as follows:

```
sensor(config-net-rou-blo)# pre-acl-name pre_acl_name
```

Step 9 Optionally, add the post-ACL name as follows:

```
sensor(config-net-rou-blo)# post-acl-name post_acl_name
```

Step 10 Exit the network access submode as follows:

```
sensor(config-net-rou-blo)# exit
sensor(config-net-rou)# exit
sensor(config-net)# exit
sensor(config)# exit
Apply Changes:?[yes]:
```

Step 11 Press **Enter** to apply the changes or type **no** to discard them.

Step 12 Execute **show settings** to verify the correctness of the NAC configuration.

Blocking configuration for Native IOS on the switch or the MSFC uses the same procedure as blocking configuration for IOS on the router. The configuration for the VACL on the Hybrid mode is very similar to the configuration of IOS router, with the exceptions of the syntax. Example 14-28 shows the Blocking configuration for the CatOS (hybrid mode).

Example 14-28 *Blocking Configuration on the Sensor for CatOS on Switch 6500 and 7600 Series Router*

```
! Log in to the CLI using an account with administrator privileges and enter. Enter
! network access submode.
sensor# configure terminal
sensor(config)# service network-access
! Set the IP address for the router controlled by Network Access Controller
sensor(config-net)# cat6k-devices ip_address
! Type the user profile name that you created in Configuring User Profiles.
sensor(config-net-cat)# profile-name user_profile_name
! Network Access Controller accepts anything you type. It does not check to see if
! the logical device exists. Designate the method used to access the sensor.
sensor(config-net-cat)# communication [telnet | ssh-des/ | sh-3des]
```

continues

Example 14-28 *Blocking Configuration on the Sensor for CatOS on Switch 6500 and 7600 Series Router (Continued)*

```
! If unspecified, SSH 3DES is used. If you are using DES or 3DES, you must use the
! command ssh host-key ip_address to accept the key or Network Access Controller
! cannot connect to the device.  Specify the sensor's NAT address.
sensor(config-net-cat)# nat-address nat_address
! Specify the VLAN number.
sensor(config-net-cat)# block-vlans vlan_number
! (Optional) Add the pre-VACL name
sensor(config-net-cat-blo)# pre-vacl-name pre_vacl_name
! (Optional) Add the post-VACL name.
sensor(config-net-cat-blo)# post-vacl-name post_vacl_name
! Exit network access submode
sensor(config-net-cat-blo)# exit
sensor(config-net-cat)# exit
sensor(config-net)# exit
sensor(config)# exit
Apply Changes:?[yes]:
! Press Enter to apply the changes or type no to discard them.
Sensor#
```

Blocking is performed differently on the firewalls, as discussed before. Example 14-29 shows the configuration steps required to configure Blocking on Sensor for Cisco firewalls.

Example 14-29 *Configuration Steps Required to Configure Blocking on Cisco Firewalls*

```
! Log in to the Sensor's CLI using an account with administrator privileges and enter
! network access submode
sensor# configure terminal
sensor(config)# service network-access
! Set the IP address for the firewall controlled by Network Access Controller
sensor(config-net)# firewall-devices ip_address
! Type the user profile name that you created in Configuring User Profiles.
sensor(config-net-fir)# profile-name user_profile_name
! Network Access Controller accepts anything you type. It does not check to see if
! the logical device exists. Designate the method used to access the sensor.
sensor(config-net-fir)# communication [telnet | ssh-des | sh-3des]
! If unspecified, SSH 3DES is used. If you are using DES or 3DES, you must use the
! command ssh host-key ip_address to accept the key or Network Access Controller
! cannot connect to the device.

! Specify the sensor's NAT address
sensor(config-net-fir)# nat-address nat_address
! Exit network access submode.
sensor(config-net-fir)# exit
sensor(config-net)# exit
sensor(config)# exit
Apply Changes:?[yes]:
! Press Enter to apply the changes or type no to discard them.
Sensor#
```

Configuring Steps for the Master Blocking Sensor (MBS)

Work through the following steps to configure Master Blocking Sensor (MBS):

Step 1 Open two Telnet or SSH sessions, and log in to the sensor using an account with administrator privileges on both the master blocking sensor and the blocking forwarding sensor.

Step 2 On the Master Blocking Sensor, check to see if it requires TLS and what port is used with following commands:

```
MBS# configure terminal
MBS(config)# service web-server
MBS(config-web)# show settings
! The following line indicates that TLS is required to connect to this MBS
   enable-tls: true <defaulted>
   port: 443 <defaulted>
   server-id: HTTP/1.1 compliant <defaulted>
MBS(config-web)#
```

Configure TLS if necessary.

Step 3 Get the fingerprints of the Master Blocking Sensor's host certificate with the command **show tls fingerprint.**

Step 4 On the blocking forwarding sensor, configure it to accept the X.509 certificate of the Master Blocking Sensor (MBS) by using the following command:

```
sensor(config-web)# exit
sensor(config)# tls trusted-host ip-address mbs_ip_address port
 port_number
```

If, for example, 10.1.1.50 is the address of the master blocking sensor and its web server is listening on port 443, execute the following command on the blocking forwarding sensor:

```
sensor(config)# tls trusted-host ip-address 10.1.1.50 port 443
Certificate MD5 fingerprint is
F4:4A:14:BA:84:F4:51:D0:A4:E2:15:38:7E:77:96:D8Certificate SHA1
  fingerprint is
84:09:B6:85:C5:43:60:5B:37:1E:6D:31:6A:30:5F:7E:4D:4D:E8:B2
Would you like to add this to the trusted certificate table for this
  host?[yes]:
```

You are prompted to accept the certificate based on the certificate's fingerprint. Compare this fingerprint with the one collected from Step 3. If it matches, type **yes** or click the **Return** button.

Step 5 Enter **network access mode**, then go under **general** submode and define the MBS information with the commands shown in Example 14-30:

Example 14-30 *Defining Master Blocking Sensor Configuration on the Blocking Forwarding Sensor*

```
sensor(config)# service network-access
sensor(config-net)# general
! The following line defines the MBS's IP address
sensor(config-net-gen)# master-blocking-sensors mbs_ip_address
! Specify the username for an administrative account on the master blocking sensor
sensor(config-net-gen-mas)# username username
! Specify the password for the user
sensor(config-net-gen-mas)# password
Enter password []: *****
Re-enter mbs-password []: *****
sensor(config-net-gen-mas)#
! Specify the port number for the host's HTTP communications.
sensor(config-net-gen-mas)# port port_number
! The default is 80/443 if not specified.
! Set the status of whether or not the host uses TLS/SSL
sensor(config-net-gen-mas)# tls [true | false]
sensor(config-net-gen-mas)
! If you set the value to true, you need to use the command tls trusted-host
! ip-address
! mbs_ip_address.
! Exit network access submode
sensor(config-net-gen-mas)# exit
sensor(config-net-gen)# exit
sensor(config-net)# exit
sensor(config)# exit
Apply Changes:?[yes]:
! Press Enter to apply the changes or type no to discard them.
Sensor#
```

Step 6 On the master blocking sensor, add the block forwarding sensor's IP address to the access list.

Step 7 As shown in Example 14-31, initiate a manual block from the blocking forwarding sensor to a bogus host IP address to make sure the master blocking sensor is initializing blocks:

Example 14-31 *Initiating Manual Blocking from the Blocking Forwarding Sensor*

```
sensor# configure terminal
sensor(config)# service network-access
sensor(config-net)# general
sensor(config-net-gen)# block-hosts 10.10.10.100
! Exit network access general submode
sensor(config-net-gen)# exit
sensor(config-net)# exit
Apply Changes:? [yes]:
! Press Enter to apply the changes or type no to discard them.
! Verify that the block shows up in the Network Access Controller's statistics
sensor# show statistics network-access
Current Configuration
   AllowSensorShun = false
```

Example 14-31 *Initiating Manual Blocking from the Blocking Forwarding Sensor (Continued)*

```
   ShunMaxEntries = 100
State
   ShunEnable = true
   ShunnedAddr
      Host
         IP = 10.10.10.100
         ShunMinutes =
Sensor#
```

Step 8 Log in to the Master Blocking Sensor host's CLI and, using the **show statistics network-access** command, verify that the block also shows up in the master blocking sensor Network Access Controller's statistics, as shown in Example 14-32.

Example 14-32 *Verifying the Statistics on the MBS*

```
MBS# show statistics network-access
Current Configuration
   AllowSensorShun = false
   ShunMaxEntries = 250
   MasterBlockingSensor
      SensorIp = 10.1.1.100
      SensorPort = 443
      UseTls = 1
State
   ShunEnable = true
   ShunnedAddr
      Host
! This is Manual Blocking that is initiated from the forwarding sensor. This
! indicates that blocking forwarding sensor is appropriately forwarding the block
! request.
         IP = 10.10.10.100
         ShunMinutes = 60
         MinutesRemaining = 59
MBS#
```

Step 9 Log in to the managed devices and execute **show access-list** on IOS or **show shun** on PIX OS to verify if the blocking takes place.

CAUTION Only one sensor should control all blocking interfaces on a device.

Troubleshooting Steps for Blocking

Several factors might cause blocking to work incorrectly on the sensor. As a fact-finding step, it is imperative to verify that blocking is functioning. The sections that follow discuss blocking verifications procedure followed by the possible causes of blocking failure along with steps to solve the problems. The sections that follow cover the following topics:

- Verifying that blocking is functioning correctly
- Network Access Controller (NAC) is not running
- Sensor is unable to connect to the managed devices
- Blocking is not occurring for a specific signature
- Master blocking is not working

Verifying that Blocking is Functioning Correctly

After you configure blocking, you should first check to see that the blocking is working properly. This will ensure that blocking will work at the time of the attack. Checking is accomplished by initiating the sending of a manual block to a bogus host and then checking to see if deny entries exist for the blocked addresses in the router's ACL or, in the case of PIX firewall, checking to see if the shun is created for the bogus IP address.

You can initiate the manual block as shown in Example 14-33.

Example 14-33 *Initiating a Manual Block to a Bogus IP Address to the Sensor*

```
! Enter Network Access Controller general sub mode with the following commands
sensor# configure terminal
sensor(config)# service network-access
sensor(config-net)# general
! Start the manual block of the bogus host IP address
sensor(config-net-gen)# block-hosts 10.1.1.0
! Exit general sub mode
sensor(config-net-gen)# exit
sensor(config-net)# exit
Apply Changes:? [yes]:
! Press Enter to apply the changes or type no to discard them.
! If you want to remove manual block, you can execute the following command
sensor(config-net-gen)# no block-hosts 10.1.1.0
sensor(config-net-gen)#
```

If your managed device is a router, use Telnet to access the router and execute a **show access-list** command. If the blocking is working correctly, you should see that the bogus IP address is being denied.

If your managed device is a PIX firewall or FWSM, execute **show shun** and it will show that the bogus IP address is being shunned.

NOTE You can also perform a manual block from IDM by clicking **Monitoring > Active Host Blocks.**

If your network is under attack, and if you want to verify that the blocking is working on the sensor, you can execute the **show event | include sig_id** command, which will display the event that is triggered for the attack. If the field for "shun" is set to true for this attack event, look at the time on the field. If the field is set to **False** or does not exist, then the sensor is not even attempting to block for that alert. Once you have verified the alert as the field for shun set to true, look at the time on the field. Then execute **show event nac <time> <date>**, but replace the time and date with the time and date just before when your alarm fired, so that you can capture the details of the NAC event that was fired. Now, you can go to the managed devices and check to see if the ACL is applied on the routers and switches, and if the shun command is applied on the PIX firewall or FWSM.

Network Access Controller (NAC) is not running

If the blocking fails with the test described in the preceding section, you should first be sure that the Network Access Controller, which is responsible for blocking, is running. To verify if Network Access Controller is running, you can execute the show **version command** on the Sensor CLI. In IDS version 4.x, you will see a separate process for NAC, but in version IPS 5.x, Network Access Controller (NAC) is part of MainApp. So, if MainApp is not running, the Network Access Controller cannot run. Example 14-34 shows a sample output of **show version** that shows that MainApp is not running.

Example 14-34 *MainApp Is not Running in* **show version** *Output*

```
sensor# show version
Application Partition:

Cisco Intrusion Prevention System, Version 5.0(1.1)S152.0

OS Version 2.4.26-IDS-smp-bigphys
Platform: IPS-4255-K9
Serial Number: JAB0815R017
No license present
Sensor up-time is 3 days.
Using 734863360 out of 3974291456 bytes of available memory (18% usage)
system is using 17.3M out of 29.0M bytes of available disk space (59% usage)
application-data is using 35.6M out of 166.8M bytes of available disk space (23% usage)
boot is using 40.5M out of 68.6M bytes of available disk space (62% usage)
! The following line shows the MainApp is not running, which means NAC is also not
! running
MainApp          2005_Mar_04_14.23   (Release) 2005-03-04T14:35:11-0600 Not Running
AnalysisEngine   2005_Mar_18_12.53   (Release) 2005-03-18T13:03:21-0600 Running
CLI              2005_Mar_04_14.23   (Release) 2005-03-04T14:35:11-0600

Upgrade History:

  IDS-K9-sp-5.0-1.1-   12:53:00 UTC Fri Mar 18 2005

Recovery Partition Version 1.1 - 5.0(1.1)

sensor#
```

The preceding example shows that MainApp is Not Running. This usually happens if you run into software corruption or bugs. If you are not already running the latest version, a quick remedy would be to upgrade the latest version of the code on the sensor from the following location:

http://www.cisco.com/univercd/cc/td/doc/product/iaabu/csids/csids11/cliguide/cliobtsw.htm#wp1034270

It is also advisable to read the Readme file of the latest version of Sensor to see if there is any bug related to NAC that is fixed on the latest version of code. If upgrade does not resolve the issue, consult with Cisco Support for further diagnosis of the problem before you proceed with re-imaging the sensor.

Sensor is Unable to Connect to the Managed Devices

If you followed the steps in the preceding section, you verified that MainApp (NAC) is running. Next you need to verify that the sensor can connect to the managed devices. There are two ways to verify this. Work through the steps that follow to verify whether the sensor is connecting to the managed devices:

Step 1 Verify that Network Access Controller Connections are Active

Execute the **show statistics network-access** command to verify that the state is **Active** as shown in Example 14-35. If the State is not **Active** in the Network Access Controller statistics, there is a problem with connecting to the managed devices.

Example 14-35 *State Is Active for Network Access Control*

```
sensor# show statistics network-access  | include State
State
      State = Active
sensor#
```

If you have more than one managed device configured and you need to identify a specific device that is having connectivity problems, it is advisable to find out if there is any problem with any of the managed devices of the preceding example. If there is, then you might want to execute the **show statistics network-access** command without the additional filter, as shown in Example 14-36.

Example 14-36 *The Statistics Details of Network Access Control*

```
sensor# show statistics network-access
Current Configuration
   LogAllBlockEventsAndSensors = true
   EnableNvramWrite = false
   EnableAclLogging = false
   AllowSensorBlock = false
```

Example 14-36 *The Statistics Details of Network Access Control (Continued)*

```
   BlockMaxEntries = 250
   MaxDeviceInterfaces = 250
   NetDevice
      Type = Cisco
      IP = 10.89.147.54
      NATAddr = 0.0.0.0
      Communications = telnet
      BlockInterface
         InterfaceName = fa0/0
         InterfaceDirection = in
State
   BlockEnable = true
   NetDevice
      IP = 10.89.147.54
      AclSupport = uses Named ACLs
      Version = 12.2
      State = Active
sensor#
```

Step 2 If the Network Access Controller is not connecting, you can look for recurring errors with the following command:

show events error *hh:mm:ss month day year* | **include : nac**

Example 14-37 shows a recurring error since May 01, 2005, as the sensor is unable to connect to the managed device.

Example 14-37 *Recurring Error When the Sensor Is Unable to Connect to the Managed Device*

```
sensor# show events error 00:00:00 May 01 2005 | include : nac
evError: eventId=1111046752731786193 severity=error vendor=Cisco
  originator:
    hostId: sensor13
    appName: nac
    appInstanceId: 301
  time: 2005/05/04 17:38:47 2005/05/04 09:38:47 UTC
! The following message appears multiple times and indicates that the Sensor is
! unable to connect to the managed device.
  errorMessage: name=errSystemError Unable to execute a host block [171.69.75.13]
    because all of the devices are not reachable


evError: eventId=1111046752731786197 severity=error vendor=Cisco
  originator:
    hostId: sensor13
    appName: nac
    appInstanceId: 301
  time: 2005/05/04 17:38:47 2005/05/04 09:38:47 UTC
  errorMessage: name=errSystemError Unable to execute a host block [171.69.75.13]
    because all of the devices are not reachable
! Rest of the output is removed
Sensor#
```

If the previous steps reveal that the problem is with the connectivity between the sensor and the managed devices, work through the following steps to troubleshoot connectivity issues:

Step 3 Make sure the configuration settings (the username, password, and IP address) for each device are correct. Example 14-38 shows how to verify the settings:

Example 14-38 *Verifying the NAC Configuration*

```
sensor# configure terminal
sensor (config)# service network-access
sensor(config-net)# show settings
   general
   -----------------------------------------------
      log-all-block-events-and-errors: true <defaulted>
      enable-nvram-write: false <defaulted>
      enable-acl-logging: false <defaulted>
      allow-sensor-block: false <defaulted>
      block-enable: true <defaulted>
      block-max-entries: 250 <defaulted>
      max-interfaces: 250 <defaulted>
      master-blocking-sensors (min: 0, max: 100, current: 0)
      -----------------------------------------------
      -----------------------------------------------
      never-block-hosts (min: 0, max: 250, current: 0)
      -----------------------------------------------
      -----------------------------------------------
      never-block-networks (min: 0, max: 250, current: 0)
      -----------------------------------------------
      -----------------------------------------------
      block-hosts (min: 0, max: 250, current: 0)
      -----------------------------------------------
      -----------------------------------------------
      block-networks (min: 0, max: 250, current: 0)
      -----------------------------------------------
      -----------------------------------------------
   -----------------------------------------------
   user-profiles (min: 0, max: 250, current: 1)
   -----------------------------------------------
      profile-name: r7200
      -----------------------------------------------
         enable-password: <hidden>
         password: <hidden>
         username: netrangr default:
      -----------------------------------------------
   -----------------------------------------------
   cat6k-devices (min: 0, max: 250, current: 0)
   -----------------------------------------------
   -----------------------------------------------
   router-devices (min: 0, max: 250, current: 1)
   -----------------------------------------------
      ip-address: 10.89.147.54
      -----------------------------------------------
```

Example 14-38 *Verifying the NAC Configuration (Continued)*

```
        communication: telnet default: ssh-3des
        nat-address: 0.0.0.0 <defaulted>
        profile-name: r7200
        block-interfaces (min: 0, max: 100, current: 1)
        ---------------------------------------------
           interface-name: fa0/0
           direction: in
           ---------------------------------------------
              pre-acl-name:  <defaulted>
              post-acl-name:  <defaulted>
           ---------------------------------------------
        ---------------------------------------------
     ---------------------------------------------
   ---------------------------------------------
   firewall-devices (min: 0, max: 250, current: 0)
   ---------------------------------------------
   ---------------------------------------------
sensor(config-net)#
```

Step 4 Check to see if the sensor is blocking itself as shown in Example 14-39.

Example 14-39 *Shows How to Check to See if the Sensor Is Configured to Block Itself*

```
sensor# configure terminal
sensor(config)# service network-access
! Enter general submode
sensor(config-net)# general
! Configure the sensor to block itself
sensor(config-net-gen)# allow-sensor-block true
! By default, this value is false. Verify the settings
sensor(config-net-gen)# show settings
   general
   ---------------------------------------------
      log-all-block-events-and-errors: true <defaulted>
      enable-nvram-write: false <defaulted>
      enable-acl-logging: false <defaulted>
! As shown in the following line, default is False, but Sensor blocking is set to True
      allow-sensor-block: true default: false
      block-enable: true default: true
      block-max-entries: 100 default: 250
--MORE--
Sensor#
```

If the preceding example reveals that you are indeed blocking the sensor itself, this might cause the sensor to be unable to connect to the managed device. On the Cisco Router or on switches, you can work around this problem, but on the Cisco firewall, sensor blocking must be set to False with the following command:

```
sensor(config-net-gen)# allow-sensor-block false
```

Step 5 If the configuration looks good after you have followed the previous step, log in to the service account on the sensor and manually connect to the device to ensure that you have used the correct username, password, and enable password, and to ensure that the device is reachable from the sensor.

(a) Log in to the service account on the sensor.

(b) Use Telnet or SSH to access the managed device with the login ID and password that you have defined for the NAC configuration on the Sensor.

(c) If you cannot connect, check the managed device configuration to make sure that Telnet or SSH is allowed from the sensor.

(d) If you can connect to the managed devices but cannot log in, you need to troubleshoot the issue on the managed device for the login.

(e) If you cannot log in to the managed device from the service account, the NAC on the sensor will also be unable to log in to the managed device. So be sure that you can Telnet or SSH into the Managed device to log in and make configuration changes.

(f) If you use Telnet and cannot get the login prompt, go to Step 3 for additional troubleshooting. If you use SSH, go to Step 4. If Telnet and SSH both return the login prompt, and you cannot log in, then go to Step 5.

Step 6 If you cannot Telnet from the service account of the sensor, work through the following steps to troubleshoot the issue:

(a) Telnet to the managed device from another host in the network and see if you get the Telnet login prompt.

(b) If you are not getting a Telnet prompt, the incoming interface ACL probably is blocking all Telnet, or the managed device is not configured for Telnet login at all. However, if you are getting a Telnet login prompt from another host, the probable cause of the problem is that Sensor is not allowed to the managed device.

(c) If the managed device is a router, be sure that the sensor's IP address is allowed on the incoming interface ACL (if ACL is applied) and also allowed on the ACL that is applied as the access-class under line vty 0 4.

(d) If the managed device is a PIX firewall or FWSM, execute the **show telnet** command and be sure that the Sensor IP address is allowed. If the Sensor IP address is not allowed, add the sensor IP address as one of the allowed IPs for Telnet.

(e) If the managed device is a switch, be sure the ACL is allowing the Sensor's IP address.

Step 7 If you are using SSH to connect to the managed devices, be sure that the managed device supports SSH 1.5. The sensor does not support SSH 2.0. Work through the following steps to troubleshoot the SSH issue:

(a) Try to connect to the managed devices using another machine in the network with an SSH client.

(b) If you cannot get any login prompt, the problem might be with the ACL dropping the SSH packets. Also, you might have not have configured SSH on the managed device.

(c) Depending on whether you are using SSH-DES or SSH-3DES as the communication protocol for the network device, you need to configure it on the sensor and also with the command shown in Example 14-40:

Example 14-40 *Downloading the Public Key from the PIX Firewall*

```
sensor# configure terminal
! Enable SSH with the following command.
sensor(config)# ssh host 10.1.1.100
! Type yes when prompted to accept the device.
MD5 fingerprint is 70:33:DC:DB:DD:85:CE:C9:02:D4:D0:30:D2:B3:49:E5
Bubble Babble is xitak-ducun-muteg-lilos-luhok-vuzut-kyhop-dibul-mehur-vebak-texex
Would you like to add this to the known hosts table for this host?[yes]:
sensor(config)# exit
sensor#
```

(d) If the public key from the managed device is not downloaded, or if it is downloaded but becomes corrupted, you will receive the message similar to the ones shown in example 14-41. To resolve the issue, regenerate the RSA key on the managed device (in this case PIX firewall) and then download the key as per Example 14-42.

Example 14-41 debug *Messages Shown on the PIX Firewall When the Public Key Is Not Downloaded to the Sensor*

```
PIX# debug ssh
2933: SSH0: send SSH message: outdata is NULL
2934: SSH0: receive SSH message: 83 (83)
2935: SSH0: client version is - SSH-1.5-OpenSSH_3.7.1p2
2936: SSH0: begin server key generation
2937: SSH0: complete server key generation, elapsed time = 780 ms
2938: SSH0: declare what cipher(s) we support: 0x00 0x00 0x00 0x0c
2939: SSH0: send SSH message: SSH_SMSG_PUBLIC_KEY (2)
2940: SSH0: SSH_SMSG_PUBLIC_KEY message sent
2941: SSH0: TCP read failed, error code = 0x86300003 "TCP connection closed"
2942: SSH0: receive SSH message: [no message ID: variable *data is NULL]
2943: SSH0: Session disconnected by SSH server - error 0x03 "TCP connection closed"
PIX#
```

(e) To resolve the issue, regenerate the RSA key on the managed device (in this case PIX firewall) as shown in Example 14-42, and then download the key as per Example 14-40.

Example 14-42 *Removing and Regenerating A Key on the PIX Firewall*

```
PIX(config)# ca zeroize rsa
PIX(config)# ca generate rsa key 1024
PIX(config)# ca save all
```

(f) If the SSH is getting a login prompt but is unable to log in to the sensor from the service account of the sensor, go to the next step.

Step 8 If the SSH or Telnet presents a login prompt and you cannot log in, troubleshoot the issue on the managed devices themselves. If AAA is used for authentication, on the router, run **debug aaa authentication**, on the switch run **set trace tacacs/radius 4**, and on the PIX set **debug** level logging and analyze the debug output to see why the authentication is failing. The username and password that will be used for the sensor to log in must have a high enough privilege to write an access-list to the managed device.

Step 9 Verify the Interfaces and Directions on the Network Device

To verify that each interface and direction on each controlled device is correct, you can send a manual block to a bogus host and then check to see if deny entries exist for the blocked addresses in the managed device's ACL. You can either execute the **show running-config** or the **show access-list** command to verify whether the manual blocking is applied on the managed devices, such as on routers. On the PIX firewall, you can verify this by executing the **show ssh** command.

Blocking is Not Occurring for a Specific Signature

If blocking is not working for a specific signature, from IDM or IPS MC, edit the signature and check if the event action is set to block the host. If it is not, correct action needs to be set. Example 14-43 shows how to set the event action to block, and how to verify the settings.

Example 14-43 *Configuration and Verifications of the Blocking Configuration for a Signature*

```
sensor# configure terminal
sensor(config)# service signature-definition sig0
sensor(config-sig)#
! Make sure the event action is set to block the host:
! If you want to receive alerts, you must always add produce-alert any time you
! configure the event actions.
sensor(config-sig)# signatures 1300 0
sensor(config-sig-sig)# engine normalizer
sensor(config-sig-sig-nor)# event-action produce-alert|request-block-host
sensor(config-sig-sig-nor)# show settings
   normalizer
   -----------------------------------------------
      event-action: produce-alert|request-block-host default: produce-alert|deny
-connection-inline
      edit-default-sigs-only
      -----------------------------------------------
         default-signatures-only
         -----------------------------------------------
            specify-service-ports
            -----------------------------------------------
               no
               -----------------------------------------------
               -----------------------------------------------
            -----------------------------------------------
            specify-tcp-max-mss
            -----------------------------------------------
               no
               -----------------------------------------------
               -----------------------------------------------
            -----------------------------------------------
            specify-tcp-min-mss
            -----------------------------------------------
               no
               -----------------------------------------------
               -----------------------------------------------
--MORE--
! Exit signature definition submode
sensor(config-sig-sig-nor)# exit
sensor(config-sig-sig)# exit
sensor(config-sig)# exit
Apply Changes:?[yes]:
Sensor#
```

NOTE If you want to receive alerts, you must always add **produce-alert** any time you configure the event actions.

Master Blocking is Not Working

Troubleshooting for Master Blocking Sensor is very similar to blocking sensor troubleshooting. Hence the discussion in the preceding sections also applies to the master blocking sensor. This section explains additional specifics pertaining to the master blocking sensor which should be used in addition to the blocking troubleshooting.

To verify that a master blocking sensor is set up properly, or to troubleshoot a master blocking sensor that is not set up properly, you can use the **show statistics network-access** command. Be sure that the forwarding sensor is set up as a TLS trusted host if the remote master blocking sensor is using TLS for web access.

To verify a sensor's master blocking sensor configuration, follow these steps:

Step 1 View the Network Access Controller's statistics on the sensor that is configured to forward the blocking to the master blocking sensor, and verify that the master blocking sensor entries are in the statistics as shown in Example 14-44.

Example 14-44 *Network Access Statistics on the Sensor Forwarding Blocking Request*

```
sensor# show statistics network-access
Current Configuration
   AllowSensorShun = false
   ShunMaxEntries = 250
   MasterBlockingSensor
      SensorIp = 10.89.149.46
      SensorPort = 443
      UseTls = 1
State
   ShunEnable = true
   ShunnedAddr
      Host
         IP = 122.122.122.44
         ShunMinutes = 60
         MinutesRemaining = 59
Sensor#
```

Step 2 If the master blocking sensor does not show up in the statistics, you need to add it (see the Configuration section for more details).

TCP Reset Issues

TCP reset is another response that the IPS sensor can provide to an event in both Inline and Promiscuous mode. Work through the following steps to troubleshoot the issues pertaining to TCP reset on the IPS sensor:

Step 1 Be sure that the TCP reset is working

You can verify that the TCP reset is working or not by executing **show events alert** as shown in Example 14-45.

Example 14-45 *The Output of the* **show events alert** *Command*

```
sensor# show events alert
evAlert: eventId=1047575239898467370 severity=medium
originator:
hostId: sj_4250_40
appName: sensorApp
appInstanceId: 1004
signature: sigId=20000 sigName=STRING.TCP subSigId=0 version=Unknown
addr: locality=OUT 172.16.171.19
port: 32771
victim:
addr: locality=OUT 172.16.171.13 port: 23
actions:
! Following line indicates that the TCP reset sent is set to TRUE
tcpResetSent: true
sensor#
```

Step 2 Be sure that the correct alarms are being generated as shown in Example 14-45. If the correct alarm is not being generated, the most probable cause of the problem is that the signature is not enabled. Enable the specific signature to resolve the problem.

Step 3 Be sure that TCP resets are being sent with the help of the **tcpdump** command, as shown in Example 14-46.

Example 14-46 *TCP Reset Is Working*

```
root# tcpdump -i eth0 src host 172.16.171.19
tcpdump: WARNING: eth0: no IPv4 address assigned
tcpdump: listening on eth0
13:58:03.823929 172.16.171.19.32770 > 172.16.171.13.telnet: R 79:79(0) ack 62 win 0
13:58:03.823930 172.16.171.19.32770 > 172.16.171.13.telnet: R 80:80(0) ack 62 win 0
13:58:03.823930 172.16.171.19.32770 > 172.16.171.13.telnet: R 80:80(0) ack 62 win 0
13:58:03.823930 172.16.171.19.32770 > 172.16.171.13.telnet: R 80:80(0) ack 62 win 0
```

Step 4 TCP Reset is not occurring for a signature.

If the reset is not occurring for a specific signature, it is most likely that the TCP reset is not being set for the signature. Configure event-action to be TCP reset as shown in Example 14-47.

Example 14-47 *Checking if TCP Reset Is Configured and Configuring TCP Reset for a Specific Signature*

```
sensor# configure terminal
sensor(config)# service signature-definition sig0
sensor(config-sig)# signatures 1000 0
sensor(config-sig-sig)# engine atomic-ip
sensor(config-sig-sig-ato)# event-action reset-tcp-connection|produc-alert
sensor(config-sig-sig-ato)# show settings
   atomic-ip
```

continues

Example 14-47 *Checking if TCP Reset Is Configured and Configuring TCP Reset for a Specific Signature (Continued)*

```
    -----------------------------------------------
       event-action: produce-alert|reset-tcp-connection default: produce-alert
       fragment-status: any <defaulted>
       specify-l4-protocol
       -----------------------------------------------
          no
          -----------------------------------------------
          -----------------------------------------------
       -----------------------------------------------
       specify-ip-payload-length
       -----------------------------------------------
          no
          -----------------------------------------------
          -----------------------------------------------
       -----------------------------------------------
       specify-ip-header-length
       -----------------------------------------------
          no
          -----------------------------------------------
          -----------------------------------------------
       -----------------------------------------------
       specify-ip-tos
       -----------------------------------------------
--MORE--
sensor(config-sig-sig-ato)# exit
sensor(config-sig-sig)# exit
sensor(config-sig)# exit
Apply Changes:?[yes]:
```

Step 5 If the reset is not working for any signature, but the signature event-action is configured for TCP reset, be sure the switch is allowing incoming TCP reset packets from the sensor on the port where the sniffing port is connected. (Refer to the "Case Studies" section of this chapter for additional details.)

Step 6 Some switches do not allow incoming packets on SPAN destination ports. This is necessary if you wish to use TCP Reset. The third interface on the IDS-4250-XL *and* IDSM-2 can allow you to work around this problem by having a non-SPAN port send the TCP RST packets. However, be sure that the reset port is connected to the same switch as the sniffing ports of the XL card. If the sniffing ports are access ports (single VLAN), the reset port should be configured to be in the same VLAN. Note that if the 2 XL ports are access ports for different VLANs, the reset port can only be configured for one of these VLANs; use dot1q trunk ports to overcome this limitation. If the sniffing ports are Dot1q trunk ports (multi-VLAN), the sniffing ports and reset ports all must have the same Native VLAN, and the reset port must trunk all of the VLANs being trunked by both sniffing ports.

Inline IPS Issues

This section presents configuration steps and troubleshooting steps with the Inline IPS Sensor mode.

Configuration Steps

To configure Inline mode for an IPS Sensor, you must configure the switch and the sensor. You can either use CLI or IDM/IPS MC to configure Inline mode on the sensor. It is advisable to configure the switch first and then the sensor. In this section, you will use IDSM-2 for the Inline mode configuration. However, the configuration steps for the Sensor Appliance are the same. The only difference is that the port used for different VLANs for the IDSM-2 is within the switch itself. For Sensor appliances, these ports are the physical ports. This section explains how to configure the following switch running Catalyst software, in addition to Cisco IOS software and the sensor itself.

- Switch configuration running Catalyst software
- Switch configuration running Cisco IOS software
- IPS sensor configuration

Switch Configuration Running Catalyst Software

Configure IDSM-2 monitoring ports as trunk ports for inline operation for Catalyst software 8.4(1) or later with Supervisor Engine 1a, Supervisor Engine 2, Supervisor Engine 32, or Supervisor Engine 720. Because the native VLAN is the same as the sole VLAN being trunked, the traffic is not 802.1q encapsulated.

CAUTION The default configuration for IDSM-2 ports 7 and 8 is to trunk all VLANs 1 to 4094. If you clear the IDSM-2 configuration (**clear configuration** *module_number*), IDSM-2 will be trunking all VLANs. If the IDSM-2 interfaces are configured for inline, spanning tree loops will likely be created and a storm will occur. A storm occurs when numerous packets loop and never reach their destinations.

To configure the monitoring ports on IDSM-2 for inline mode, work through the following steps:

Step 1 Log in to the console of the switch.

Step 2 Enter privileged mode with the following command:

```
cat6k> enable
```

Step 3 Set the native VLAN for each IDSM-2 monitoring port with the following command:

```
cat6k (enable)> set vlan vlan_number slot_number/port_number
```

As an example, the following two lines show that sniffing ports 5/7 and 5/8 are mapped to VLANs 500 and 550 respectively.

```
cat6k (enable)> set vlan 500 5/7
cat6k (enable)> set vlan 550 5/8
```

Note that for the IDSM-2 blade, the sniffing ports are slot/7 and slot/8. If you connect your Sensor Appliance to the switch, you need to map these connected ports to the respective VLANs. Although for IDSM-2, the ports are fixed based on the slot number where the blade is inserted, Sensor sniffing interfaces can be connected to any ports you choose.

Step 4 Clear all VLANs from each IDSM-2 monitoring port except for the native VLAN on each port (500 for port 7 and 550 on port 8) using the following command:

```
cat6k (enable)> clear trunk slot_number/port_number vlan_range
```

For this specific example, use the following commands to clear the trunk for all other VLANs except the native ones for the respected ports:

```
cat6k (enable)> clear trunk 5/7 1-499,501-4094
cat6k (enable)> clear trunk 5/8 1-549,551-4094
```

Step 5 Enable Bpdu spantree filtering on the IDSM-2 monitoring ports using the following command:

```
cat6k (enable)> set spantree bpdu-filter 5/7-8 enable
```

Switch Configuration Running Cisco IOS Software

Configure the IDSM-2 (if Sensor, use the sensing ports connected to the switch) monitoring ports as access ports for inline operation. Note that Etherchannelling inline IDSM-2 is not yet supported in Cisco IOS. Cisco IOS software 12.2(18) SXE with Supervisor Engine 720 supports only one IDSM-2 inline between two VLANs.

Work through the following steps to configure VLANs for the Inline mode:

Step 1 Log in to the switch console.

Step 2 Enter configuration mode using the following command:

```
router# configure terminal
```

Step 3 Create two VLANs, one for each side of the inline IDSM-2 with the following commands:

```
router(config)# vlan vlan_number
router(config)# name vlan_name
router(config)# exit
router# exit
```

Step 4 If you have not done so already, configure an IOS access port for each interface on each inline VLAN:

(a) Enter global configuration mode with the following command:

```
router# configure terminal
```

(b) Select the IOS interface to be configured with the following command:

```
router(config)# interface interface_name
```

(c) Enter a description so that you know what the interface is for:

```
router(config-if)# description description
```

(d) Configure the interface as a Layer 2 switch port:

```
router(config-if)# switchport
```

(e) Configure the access mode VLAN:

```
router(config-if)# switchport access vlan vlan_number
```

(f) Configure the interface/port to be an access port:

```
router(config-if)# switchport mode access
```

(g) Exit global configuration mode:

```
router(config-if)# exit
router# exit
```

Step 5 Configure one IDSM-2 data port to be on each of the two VLANs you created in Step 3.

```
router# configure terminal
router(config)# intrusion-detection module slot_number data-port
  data_port_number
access-vlan vlan_number
router(config)# exit
```

Step 6 Verify the configuration with the following steps. In these examples, the IDSM-2 in slot 5 is inline between VLANs 500 and 550. The IDSM-2 data port 1 is on VLAN 500 and data port 2 is on VLAN 550

(a) Verify the IDSM-2 intrusion detection settings:

```
router# show run | include intrusion-detection
intrusion-detection module 5 management-port access-vlan 100
intrusion-detection module 5 data-port 1 access-vlan 500
intrusion-detection module 5 data-port 2 access-vlan 550
router#
```

(b) Verify that the IDSM-2 data port 1 is an access port on VLAN 500:

```
router# show intrusion-detection module slot_number data-port
  data_port_number state
```

For this example, use the following command:

```
router# show intrusion-detection module 5 data-port 1 state
Intrusion-detection module 5 data-port 1:

Switchport: Enabled
Administrative Mode: static access
Operational Mode: static access
Administrative Trunking Encapsulation: dot1q Operational Trunking
Encapsulation:
native Negotiation of Trunking: Off Access Mode VLAN: 500 (inline-vlan-1)
  Trunking
Native Mode VLAN: 1 (default) Trunking VLANs Enabled: NONE Pruning VLANs
  Enabled:
2-1001 Vlans allowed on trunk:500 Vlans allowed and active in management
  domain: 500
Vlans in spanning tree forwarding state and not pruned: 500
Administrative Capture Mode: Disabled
Administrative Capture Allowed-vlans: <empty>
```

(c) Verify the VLAN number:

```
router# show vlan id vlan_number
```

For this specific example use the following command:

```
router# show vlan id 500
VLAN Name                             Status    Ports
------- -------------------------- --------- -----------------------
500  engineering                      active    Gi3/2, Gi13/d1

VLAN Type  SAID      MTU   Parent RingNo BridgeNo Stp  BrdgMode Trans1 Trans2
------- ---- ---------- ----- ------ ------ -------- ---- -------- ---
500  enet  100661  1500  -      -      -        -    -        0      0

Remote SPAN VLAN
----------------
Disabled

Primary Secondary Type              Ports
------- --------- ---------------- -------------------------------
router#
```

IPS Sensor Configuration

Once you have finished with switch configuration, the next step is to configure the sensor (in this case IDSM-2 blade) for Inline mode. Work through the following configuration steps to accomplish this task:

Step 1 Log in to the CLI using an account with administrator privileges.

Step 2 Enter interface submode:

```
sensor# configure terminal
sensor(config)# service interface
```

Step 3 Name the inline pair:

```
sensor(config-int)# inline-interfaces PAIR_ENGINEERING
```

Step 4 Configure the two interfaces into a pair:

```
sensor(config-int-inl)# interface1 GigabitEthernet0/7
sensor(config-int-inl)# interface2 GigabitEthernet0/8
```

Step 5 Add a description of the interface pair:

```
sensor(config-int-inl)# description PAIR_ENGINEERING = Gig0/7 & Gig0/8
```

Step 6 Verify the settings:

```
sensor(config-int-inl)# show settings
   name: PAIR_ENGINEERING
   -----------------------------------------------
      description: PAIR_ENGINEERING = Gig0/7 & Gig0/8 default:
      interface1: GigabitEthernet0/7
      interface2: GigabitEthernet0/8
   -----------------------------------------------
```

Step 7 Exit inline interfaces submode:

```
sensor(config-int-inl)# exit
sensor(config-int)# exit
Apply Changes:?[yes]:
```

Step 8 Press **Enter** to apply the changes, or type no to discard them.

Step 9 Enter analysis engine mode to assign the interfaces to the virtual sensor:

```
sensor# configure terminal
ssensor(config)# service analysis-engine
sensor(config-ana)# virtual-sensor vs0
sensor(config-ana-vir)# logical-interface PAIR_ENGINEERING
```

Step 10 Exit analysis engine mode:

```
sensor(config-ana-vir)# exit
sensor(config-ana)# exit
```

```
sensor(config)#
Apply Changes:?[yes]:
```

Step 11 Press **Enter** to apply the changes or type no to discard them.

Troubleshooting Steps

Troubleshooting connectivity issues, signature generation issues, TCP Reset issues, blocking issues, and so on that were discussed for Promiscuous mode are the same for Inline mode. This section explains some of the problems that you might encounter with the Inline mode only:

- **Misconfiguration of the switch**—If the switch VLANs are not configured correctly, traffic might not be going through the sensor. This will result in the traffic not being analyzed.
- **Promiscuous Mode**—Before deploying the sensor using Inline mode, it is strongly recommended that you run the sensor in Promiscuous mode to determine the amount of traffic and events that are being generated. This can be useful to eliminate the false positive or false negative. Keep in mind that Inline mode will have more performance impact than the Promiscuous mode. So, you should rate the sensor accordingly.
- **Bypass Mode**—If you have packet drops, or the performance degrades to an unacceptable level, analyze the statistics using the **show statistics virtual-sensor** command. Enable the bypass mode so that you know whether there is a hardware or software issue. If with bypass mode, you are having performance or packet drops issues, you are running into a hardware problem. Otherwise, you are dealing with a software issue, in particular **AnalysisEngine**. So, search for a possible bug on Cisco.com (using the bug tool kit, at: http://www.cisco.com/cgi-bin/Support/Bugtool/home.pl) or upgrade to the latest version of IPS Sensor. To enable bypass mode, see Example 14-48:

Example 14-48 *Configuring Bypass Mode on the Sensor Running Inline Mode*

```
sensor# configure terminal
sensor(config)# service interface
sensor(config-int)# bypass-mode on
sensor1-23(config-int)# exit
Apply Changes:?[yes]:
Warning: Setting bypass-mode to on caused all intrusion-prevention packet inspection
  to be disabled.
sensor1-23(config)# exit
sensor1-23#
```

Remember that if you set the bypass-mode, the **AnalysisEngine** is bypassed completely; hence the sensor does not enforce any security. So be sure to change the bypass-mode back to **auto** once troubleshooting is performed, or turn on Promiscuous mode if Inline mode drops packets or causes performance problems that are unacceptable. This will give Cisco Systems, Inc. time to perform analysis and come up with a permanent fix.

Case Studies

This section provides some case studies that explain different methods of capturing traffic for IPS Sensor and IDSM-2 blade using different devices. A proper implementation of the traffic capturing technique is a very important and is an essential component of CS IPS operations and functions. Several devices are available to capture the traffic for IPS Sensor as detailed in the list and sections that follow:

- Capturing IPS traffic with a hub
- Capturing IPS traffic with SPAN
- Capturing IPS traffic with remote SPAN (RSPAN)
- Capturing IPS traffic with VACL
- Capturing IPS traffic with RSPAN and VACL
- Capturing IPS traffic with MLS IP IDS

Capturing IPS Traffic with a Hub

A hub is a single broadcast and collision domain, which means that any port connected to it will be able to see all traffic sent by any ports connected to it. Hence, hub deployment is simple and easy, as there is no configuration involved. All you need to do is plug into the hub the sensing interface of the sensor along with all other devices. This type of setup is very useful for learning purposes in an isolated lab environment. For IPS, the hub supports the TCP reset functionality of the sensor, as receiving input packet from the sensor is not an issue for the hub ports.

The biggest drawback with a hub is that it is a single collision domain, which results in poor network performance. For a larger deployment, a hub does not scale well, as it is a single broadcast domain.

If for any reason, the sensor is unable to sniff the packets, make sure that the hub port, cable and sensor Sniffing ports are in working condition. Be sure that your link light is green and blinking.

Capturing IPS Traffic with SPAN

As stated earlier, SPAN stands for Switch Port Analyzer. SPAN copies all packets from source VLANS or ports to a destination port. It is supported across most Cisco switches. However, different switches have different limitations on the use of SPAN, including the number of SPAN destination ports.

NOTE Some switches do not allow incoming packets on a SPAN destination port. However, allowing incoming packets on the SPN destination port is necessary if you wish to use a sniffing port as the TCP Reset port.

SPAN Terminology

To understand how SPAN works, and how to configure SPAN correctly, you need to understand different terminologies for SPAN. The following discussion is based on the Figure 14-2.

Figure 14-2 *SPAN Terminology*

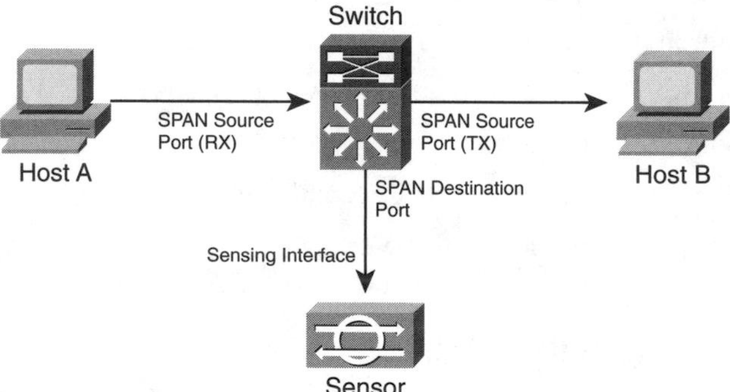

- **Ingress Traffic**—Traffic that is entering into the switch is called Ingress Traffic.
- **Egress Traffic**—Traffic that is leaving from the switch is called Egress Traffic.
- **SPAN Source port or VLAN**—SPAN source port can be the incoming port for the Ingress or outgoing port for the Egress traffic. SPAN Source Ports or VLANs are configured as either Rx (for Ingress traffic), Tx (for Egress traffic), or both (Ingress and Egress traffic on a port)
- **SPAN Destination Port**—Spanned traffic is transmitted to this port. This is where the IPS Sensor is connected.

SPAN Traffic Types

Following is a list of some of SPAN traffic types that can be configured on the switch when configuring SPAN:

- **Receive SPAN (Rx)**—The Rx SPAN session monitors all traffic inbound to a source port or VLAN, before modification or processing is performed by the switch. With Rx type, you must configure rx on both ports traffic traverses. For example, to capture the traffic in Figure 14-2 from Host A to Host B, configure Rx SPAN on both ports of the switch.

- **Transmit SPAN (Tx)**—The Tx SPAN session monitors all traffic outbound from a source port or VLAN, after modification and processing is performed on the switch. To capture the traffic in Figure 14-2 from Host A to Host B, configure both ports for Host A and Host B to be Tx SPAN.
- **Transmit and Receive SPAN (Both)**—With transmit and receive (both SPAN types), configure just one port instead of two to get the packet for both directions. In Figure 14-2, you just need to configure either switch port for Host A or Host B port as both to get a copy of the traffic that flows through the switch. If both ports are configured, then Sensor might get duplicate copies of packets.

SPAN on Catalyst 2900/3500XL

This section explains how to configure SPAN on Catalyst 2900/3500XL switches, and addresses some of the limitations of SPAN configuration.

Configuration Steps

You can configure SPAN with the **port monitor** *interface* command under the monitor command. Example 14-49 shows how to configure SPAN fa0/1-fa0/2 ports to port fa0/3.

Example 14-49 *SPAN Configuration*

```
c3524(config-if)#interface fa0/3
c3524(config-if)#port monitor fa0/1
c3524(config-if)#port monitor fa0/2
c3524(config-if)#^Z
c3524#show port monitor
Monitor Port             Port Being Monitored
---------------------    --------------------
FastEthernet0/24         FastEthernet0/1
FastEthernet0/24         FastEthernet0/2
C3524#
```

Limitations

Some of the characteristics and limitations of SPAN on 2900/3500XL switches are as follows:

- **Monitored ports must be on same VLAN**—You must have monitored and monitor interface on the same VLAN; otherwise, you will not be able to configure SPAN. Example 14-50 shows a message that will appear if the monitored and monitor ports are in different VLANs.

Example 14-50 *The Message that Is Shown when Monitored and Monitor Interfaces Are Not on the Same VLAN.*

```
c3524(config)#int fa0/3
c3524(config-if)#port monitor fa0/5
FastEthernet0/3 and FastEthernet0/5 are in different vlan
c3524(config-if)#
```

- **Unable to modify monitored ports**—If a port is configured to be monitored for SPAN, you cannot make any changes to the port unless you remove it from monitoring. If you attempt to make any change that is monitored, you will receive a message similar to that shown in Example 14-51.

Example 14-51 *Message Shown on the Switch When Attempting to Make Changes on the Monitored Port*

```
c3524(config)#int fa0/1
c3524(config-if)#switchport access vlan 2
FastEthernet0/1 is being monitored
C3524(config-if)#
```

- **Unable to Monitor a source VLAN**— You can only SPAN the source port, not VLAN. The **port monitor vlan** command is only used for monitoring management traffic destined to the IP address that is configured as VLAN 1 on the switch. Example 14-52 shows that a message appears on the switch if you try to configure a different VLAN other than for management VLAN.

Example 14-52 *Message That Appears on the Switch When a Different VLAN Is Assigned*

```
c3524(config)#int fa0/3
c3524(config-if)#port monitor vlan ?
  <1-1001>  VLAN interface number

c3524(config-if)#port monitor vlan 2
                                   ^
% Invalid input detected at '^' marker.

c3524(config-if)#port monitor vlan 1
c3524(config-if)#
```

- **Accidentally monitor all ports**—If you accidentally configure the **port monitor** command without specifying a specific port, all ports on the same VLAN of the monitor port will be spanned, which might create undesired results.
- Monitor Port must be configured as Static Access, not multi-VLAN.
- SPAN should not monitor Private VLAN Edge ports.
- If a monitored port is a VLAN trunk, only the specific VLAN that the Monitor port belongs to will be monitored.
- There is no limit on the number of SPAN sessions.

- RSPAN (Remote SPAN) is not supported.
- IPS TCP Resets do not work on most images. Learning cannot be disabled. There have been reports of some older images working, but that is not something you can count on.

SPAN on Catalyst 2950, 3550 and 3750

Although catalyst 2950/3550 and 3750 switches can monitor incoming (Rx) traffic on range of ports or VLANs, these switches can monitor outgoing (Tx) traffic on a single port only. Traffic routed from one VLAN to another is *not* captured as incoming (Rx) traffic. Whereas Catalyst 3750 and 3550 support two separate SPAN sessions, with separate or overlapping source ports or VLANs, Catalyst 2950 supports only one SPAN session.

Both switched and routed interfaces may be configured as source and destination ports. Remote SPAN (RSPAN) is supported on Catalyst 2950, 3550, and 3750 switches. Source port types include FastEthernet, GigabitEthernet, EtherChannel, and VLANs. Multiple SPAN sessions can monitor the same source ports. However, a SPAN source port cannot be configured as a SPAN destination port.

Unlike Catalyst 2900/3500XL, source ports can be in the same or different VLANs. Remember that the SPAN destination ports must be physical ports.

NOTE You must be running 12.1(12C)EA1 on Catalyst 3550, and 12.1(13)EA1 on 2950 to support IPS TCP Reset functionality.

Configuration Steps

You can configure SPAN using the **monitor session** command on Catalysts 2950, 3550, or 3750. This section presents some examples of SPAN configuration.

Example 14-53 shows the SPAN configuration for SPAN source interfaces (FastEthernet 0/1 and 0/2) and SPAN destination interface FastEthernet 0/3.

Example 14-53 *SPAN Configuration with Source Interfaces*

```
c3550(config)# monitor session 1 source ?
  interface  SPAN source interface
  remote     SPAN source Remote
  vlan       SPAN source VLAN

c3550(config)#monitor session 1 source interface fa0/1 - 2 rx
c3550(config)#monitor session 1 destination interface fa0/3
```

NOTE Only an Rx SPAN session can have multiple source ports. Note that the spaces in syntax when specifying multiple interfaces can be dash (–) or comma (,).

Example 14-54 shows the SPAN configuration with SPAN source VLANs.

Example 14-54 *SPAN Configuration with Source VLANs*

```
c3550(config)# monitor session 1 source vlan 1 - 5 rx
c3550(config)#monitor session 1 destination interface fa0/3
```

NOTE Only an Rx SPAN session can have multiple source VLANs. Note that the spaces in syntax when specifying multiple interfaces can be dash (—) or comma (,).

To allow the TCP reset feature on the sniffing port of the switch, define ingress VLAN with the "ingress VLAN" argument. Example 14-55 shows the configuration of a switch port that is required for TCP Resets.

Example 14-55 *TCP Reset Configuration on the Sniffing Port of the Switch*

```
c3550(config)#monitor session 1 source vlan 1 - 5 rx
c3550(config)#monitor session 1 destination interface fa0/3 ingress vlan 1
```

NOTE The Catalyst 2950/3550 will allow you to configure a single VLAN to receive untagged TCP Reset packets. TCP Reset support is configured through the "ingress VLAN" keywords. Only one VLAN is permitted. In Example 14-55, TCP reset will be performed only if the attackers are on VLAN 1. If the attack or target is on VLAN 2-5, TCP reset will not work.

Catalysts 3550 and 3750 support two monitor sessions as shown in Example 14-56; however, 2950 supports one monitor session.

Example 14-56 *Configuration of SPAN on 3550*

```
c3550(config)#monitor session 1 source interface fa0/1 - 3 rx
c3550(config)#monitor session 2 source interface fa0/3 , fa0/13 rx
c3550(config)#monitor session 1 destination interface fa0/5
c3550(config)#monitor session 2 destination interface fa0/10
```

NOTE Source ports or VLANs can be separated or overlapping, as shown in Example 14-57. SPAN source interface FastEthernet 0/3 is overlapping.

If you intend to monitor a VLAN trunk port, and wish to filter one or more of the VLANs on that trunk, you can follow Example 14-57. This example monitors only VLANs 5 and 100-200 on the trunk.

Example 14-57 *VLAN Filtering with SPAN Configuration*

```
c3550(config)# monitor session 1 source interface gigabit0/1
c3550(config)# monitor session 1 filter vlan 5 , 100 - 200
c3550(config)# monitor session 1 destination interface fa0/5
```

If the monitor session destination port is a trunk, you should also use keyword **encapsulation dot1q** as shown in Example 14-58. If you do not, packets will be sent on the interface in native format.

Example 14-58 *Configuration for Trunking on Destination SPAN Port*

```
c3550(config)# monitor session 1 destination interface fa0/5 encapsulation dot1q
```

Example 14-59 shows how to verify the configuration.

Example 14-59 *Verifying the SPAN Configuration*

```
c3550# show monitor session 1
Session 1
---------
 Type        : Local Session
Source Ports:
    RX Only:       None
    TX Only:       None
    Both:          None
Source VLANs:
    RX Only:       1-3
    TX Only:       None
    Both:          None
Source RSPAN VLAN: None
Destination Ports: Fa0/5
    Encapsulation: Native
Reflector Port:    None
Filter VLANs:      None
Dest RSPAN VLAN:   None
```

Limitations

Following are some of the limitations of using SPAN on Catalyst 2950, 3550 and 3750:

- Only RX SPAN sessions can have multiple source ports. Tx or both cannot have more than one session, as shown in Example 14-60.

Example 14-60 *RX SPAN Sessions Having Multiple Source Ports*

```
c3550(config)# monitor session 1 source interface fa0/1 , fa0/2 tx
% This platform allows a maximum of 1 TX monitor interface(s)
c3550(config)# monitor session 1 source interface fa0/1 , fa0/2 both
% This platform allows a maximum of 1 TX monitor interface(s)
c3550(config)# monitor session 1 source interface fa0/1 , fa0/2 rx
c3550(config)#
```

- It cannot monitor outgoing (TX or Both) traffic on VLANs, as shown in Example 14-61.

Example 14-61 *The Switch Cannot Monitor Outgoing Traffic on VLANs*

```
c3550(config)# monitor session 1 source vlan 100 tx
                                                 ^

% Invalid input detected at '^' marker.

c3550(config)# monitor session 1 source vlan 100 ?
  ,    Specify another range of VLANs
  -    Specify a range of VLANs
  rx  Monitor received traffic only
c3550(config)#
```

- Destination ports do not participate in the Spanning Tree or other L2 protocols such as CDP, VTP, and so on. Destination ports also do not learn addresses. VLAN changes to destination ports will not take place until you disable the destination port.

SPAN on Catalyst 4000/6000 with Cat OS

Catalyst 4000/6000 switches running Catalyst OS can be configured to monitor Rx, Tx, and both traffic types for source ports and VLANs. Whereas Catalyst 4000 supports up to 5 SPAN sessions, Catalyst 6000 supports 2 Rx or Both, and 4 Tx sessions. Following are some of the important points to keep in mind when configuring SPAN:

- To support RSPAN (Remote SPAN), you must run 6.3(1) or later on Catalyst 4000, and version 5.3 or later on Catalyst 6000 series switches.
- To support IPS TCP Reset functionality, you need to enable **inpkts**, which is disabled by default. This requires Cat OS 5.2 or higher.
- **inpkts** enabled can potentially cause spanning tree loops if another switch is mistakenly connected to the SPAN destination port.
- Learning is enabled by default, but should be disabled to support TCP Reset. Otherwise, an interruption in traffic might be experienced for the server receiving the reset. Recent versions of Cisco IPS no longer have this restriction because a random MAC address is used when sending the RST. However, it is still recommended to disable learning.

Configuration Steps

To configure SPAN on the Catalyst 6000 series switch, use the following syntax:

```
set span {src_mod/src_ports | src_vlans | sc0} {dest_mod/dest_port} [rx | tx | both]
  [inpkts {enable | disable}] [learning {enable | disable}] [multicast {enable |
  disable}] [filter vlans...] [create]
```

The syntax for the SPAN on Cat4k is as follows:

```
set span {src_mod/src_ports | src_vlan} dest_mod/dest_port [rx | tx | both] [filter
  vlan] [inpkts {enable | disable}] [learning {enable | disable}] [create]
```

Use the **create** keyword with different destination ports to create multiple SPAN sessions. If the **create** keyword is not used, and a SPAN session exists with the same destination port, the existing session will be replaced. If the destination port is different, a new session will be created.

To create a simple SPAN session with source port 2/1 and destination port 4/5, use the following command:

```
c6500 (enable) set span 2/1 4/5
```

The following command will configure SPAN for source VLAN 100 and destination 4/5.

```
c6500 (enable) set span 100 4/5
```

If TCP reset is required on the SPAN destination port, enable **inpkts** with the following command:

```
c6500 (enable) set span 136 3/5 inpkts enable learning disable
```

To filter certain VLANs, use the **filter** keyword as follows:

```
c6500 (enable) set span 3/15 4/5 filter 125,150
```

The following command shows how to remove a SPAN session on the cat6000 switch.

```
c6500 (enable) set span disable 3/5
```

SPAN on Catalyst 4000/6000 with Native IOS

Just as with Catalyst OS, Catalyst 4000/6000 switches running Native IOS can be configured to monitor Rx, Tx, and both traffic types for source ports and VLANs. Although it is possible to mix source interfaces and source VLANs in a single SPAN session, it is not possible to mix source VLANs with filter VLANs in a single SPAN session. The Layer 2 ports (configured with **switchport** command) and Layer 3 ports (without **switchport** command) can both be configured as SPAN source or destination ports.

Catalyst 4000 supports up to six SPAN sessions (a session configured with both is considered to be two sessions). Catalyst 6000 running Native IOS supports only two SPAN sessions. It supports 64 SPAN destination interfaces. With SPAN source interfaces, the Cat6k supports 1 egress and 64 ingress interfaces. Source interfaces do not need to belong to the same VLAN.

NOTE Catalyst 6000 running Native IOS supports RSPAN (Remote SPAN), but Catalyst 4000 running Native IOS does not support RSPAN. However, neither switch running Native IOS supports IPS TCP Reset functionality with current versions.

Configuration Steps

The syntax for configuring Catalyst 6000 series switches is as follows:

```
monitor session session_number source {{single_interface | interface_list |
  interface_range | mixed_interface_list | single_vlan | vlan_list | vlan_range |
  mixed_vlan_list} [rx | tx | both]} | {remote vlan rspan_vlan_ID}}
monitor session session_number destination {single_interface | interface_list |
  interface_range | mixed_interface_list} | {remote vlan rspan_vlan_ID}}
```

To configure SPAN on the Catalyst 4000 series switch, use the following syntax:

```
[no] monitor session {session_number} {source {interface type/num} | {vlan vlan_ID}}
  [, | - | rx | tx | both]
[no] monitor session {session_number} {destination {interface type/num} }
```

Example 14-62 shows a simple SPAN configuration based on the source port.

Example 14-62 *Sample SPAN Configuration Based on the Source Port*

```
c4500(config)#monitor session 1 source interface fastEthernet 3/3
c4500(config)#monitor session 1 destination interface fastethernet 3/4
c4500# show monitor
Session 1
---------
Type              : Local Session
Source Ports      :
    Both          : Fa3/3
Destination Ports : Fa3/4
    Encapsulation : Native
          Ingress : Disabled
C4500#
```

Example 14-63 shows the configuration of SPAN based on the source VLAN.

Example 14-63 *SPAN Configuration Based on the Source VLAN*

```
c6500(config)# monitor session 1 source vlan 1 - 100 both
c6500(config)# monitor session 1 destination interface FastEthernet 3/4
c6500# show monitor
Session 1
---------
Type              : Local Session
Source VLANs      :
    Both          : 1-100
Destination Ports : Fa3/4
C6500#
```

Example 14-64 shows only the monitor VLAN 100 on a trunk source port.

Example 14-64 *SPAN Configurations for Filtering Based on VLAN*

```
c6500(config)# monitor session 1 source interface GigabitEthernet 3/1
c6500(config)# monitor session 1 filter vlan 100
c6500(config)# monitor session 1 destination interface GigabitEthernet 3/2
c6500# show monitor session 1
```

Example 14-64 *SPAN Configurations for Filtering Based on VLAN (Continued)*

```
Session 1
---------
Type              : Local Session
Source Ports      :
    Both          : Gi3/1
Destination Ports : Gi3/2
Filter VLANs      : 100
C6500#
```

The following command will remove a SPAN session:

```
c4500(config)# no monitor session 1
```

Capturing IPS Traffic with Remote SPAN (RSPAN)

RSPAN has all the features of SPAN plus support for the source ports and the destination ports that are distributed across multiple switches. RSPAN therefore allows remote monitoring of multiple switches across your network.

The traffic for each RSPAN session is carried over a user-specified RSPAN VLAN that is dedicated for that RSPAN session in all participating switches. The SPAN traffic from the sources, which cannot be in the RSPAN VLAN, is switched to the RSPAN VLAN and is forwarded to the destination ports that are configured in the RSPAN VLAN. The traffic type for the sources (ingress, egress, or both) in an RSPAN session can be different in the different source switches but is the same for all the sources in each source switch for each RSPAN session. Do not configure any ports in an RSPAN VLAN except those that are selected to carry the RSPAN traffic. Learning is disabled on the RSPAN VLAN.

Hardware Requirements

The requirements for the RSPAN supervisor engine are as follows:

- **For source switches**—The Catalyst 6500 series switch with any of the following:
  - Supervisor Engine 1A and Policy Feature Card (PFC): WS-X6K-SUP1A-PFC.
  - Supervisor Engine 1A, PFC, and Multilayer Switch Feature Card (MSFC): WS-X6K-SUP1A-MSFC.
  - Supervisor Engine 1A, PFC, and MSFC2: WS-X6K-S1A-MSFC2.
  - Supervisor Engine 2 and PFC2: WS-X6K-S2-PFC2.
  - Supervisor Engine 1A, PFC, and MSFC2: WS-X6K-S1A-MSFC2.
  - Supervisor Engine 720 with the following onboard components: Policy Feature Card 3A (PFC3A/PFC3B/PFC3BXL), Multilayer Switch Feature Card 3 (MSFC3), and integrated 720-Gbps switch fabric: WS-SUP720.
  - Supervisor Engine 32, PFC3B/PFC3BXL, and MSFC2A: WS-SUP32-GE-3B.

- **For destination or intermediate switches**—Any Cisco switch supporting RSPAN VLAN.
- No third-party or other Cisco switches can be placed in the end-to-end path for RSPAN traffic.

Configuration Steps

Work through the following steps to configure RSPAN for capturing traffic from multiple switches and for monitoring the traffic on the switch port that you choose:

Step 1 Select an RSPAN VLAN for the RSPAN session that does not exist in any of the switches that will participate in RSPAN. With VTP enabled in the network, you can create the RSPAN VLAN in one switch, and VTP propagates it to the other switches in the VTP domain. Use VTP pruning to get an efficient flow of RSPAN traffic, or manually delete the RSPAN VLAN from all trunks that do not need to carry the RSPAN traffic. Example 14-65 shows how to set VLAN 500 as an RSPAN VLAN and verify the configuration.

Example 14-65 *Setting RSPAN VLAN for an RSPAN Session on CatOS*

```
Console> (enable) set vlan 200 rspan
vlan 200 configuration successful
Console> (enable)
Console> (enable) show vlan
! display truncated
VLAN DynCreated  RSPAN
---- ---------- --------
1    static     disabled
200  static     enabled
Console> (enable)
```

Step 2 Configure RSPAN source ports and VLANs for the RSPAN session. Example 14-66 shows how to configure RSPAN source port and VLAN.

Example 14-66 *Configuring Source Port and VLAN for the RSPAN Session*

```
Console> (enable)
! The following line shows how to specify ports 5/1 and 5/2 as the ingress source
! ports for RSPAN VLAN 200
Console> (enable) set rspan source 5/1-2 200 rx
Rspan Type       : Source
Destination      : -
Rspan Vlan       : 200
Admin Source     : Port 5/1-2
Oper Source      : None
Direction        : receive
Incoming Packets: -
Learning         : -
Multicast        : enabled
Filter           : -
```

Example 14-66 *Configuring Source Port and VLAN for the RSPAN Session (Continued)*

```
Console> (enable)
! The following line shows how to specify VLAN 100 as a source VLAN for RSPAN VLAN 200.
! Selecting the optional rx keyword makes all the ports in the VLAN ingress ports.
Console> (enable) set rspan source 100 200 rx
Rspan Type        : Source
Destination       : -
Rspan Vlan        : 200
Admin Source      : VLAN 100
Oper Source       : None
Direction         : receive
Incoming Packets: -
Learning          : -
Multicast         : enabled
Filter            : -
Console> (enable)
```

Step 3 Configure the RSPAN destination ports on the switch you choose. Example 14-67 shows how to configure an RSPAN destination port as RSPAN VLAN to be the source, and the port where the IPS Sensor is connected to be the RSPAN destination port.

Example 14-67 *Configuring RSPAN Destination Port*

```
Console> (enable) set rspan destination 6/1 200
Rspan Type        : Destination
Destination       : Port 6/1
Rspan Vlan        : 200
Admin Source      : -
Oper Source       : -
Direction         : -
Incoming Packets: disabled
Learning          : enabled
Multicast         : -
Filter            : -
Console> (enable)
```

Here RSPAN VLAN 200 is configured as the source, and port 6/1 is configured as the destination port of the RSPAN session.

Step 4 To disable RSPAN sessions, use the following command:

```
set rspan disable source all
```

Capturing IPS Traffic with VACL

VLAN ACL (VACL) specifies the traffic to be captured for a single port or VLAN. The VACL Capture copies filtered packets from source VLANS to a destination port. It is supported only on Catalyst 6000, with either Cat OS or Native IOS. It offloads processing from the supervisor engine to the Policy Feature Card (PFC), which is required when using this feature. The PFC is included with the Sup1A, Sup2, and Sup720.

Here are some important facts about VACL:

- Traffic matching the filter is copied to the Capture Ports.
- There is no limit on number of Capture Ports.
- The Capture Port must be in the forwarding state.
- Capture Ports do not transmit out all traffic that is captured. They only transmit traffic in the VLAN to which the Capture Port belongs. To capture traffic belonging to multiple VLANs, the Capture Port needs to be configured as a trunk.
- VACL can be applied to all packets, whether routed or switched, and can be configured on any VLAN.
- All packets entering a VLAN are checked against VACL, regardless of direction.
- VACLs can be applied to certain wide area network (WAN) interfaces (requires IOS 12.1(13) E). This is supported on Packet of SONET (POS), ATM, and serial interfaces.
- VACLs and Catalyst 6000 switches with an IOS Firewall (CBAC) *cannot* be configured on the same interfaces. When CBAC is needed, consider using **mls ip ids** instead.
- Be aware that VACLs apply to all traffic on a VLAN, not just traffic being captured. This can potentially interrupt traffic with a poorly written VACL.
- TCP Resets are supported. However, if the Capture Destination port is a trunk, the resets will not function properly (TCP Reset can only occur on a single VLAN). IDS 4.0 corrects this limitation.
- VACL Capture requires CatOS 5.3 or IOS 12.1(8a)EX.

VACL configuration on Catalyst Switch running CatOS and Native IOS are discussed in the sections entitled "VACL Configuration on Switch running CatOS" and "VACL Configuration on Switch running Native IOS" sections in Chapter 15, "Troubleshooting IDSM-2 Blade on Switch" respectively. Hence the same information is not repeated in this section.

Capturing IPS Traffic with RSPAN and VACL

You can use a combination of RSPAN and VACL features to capture and send the traffic to a SPAN destination across multiple switches.

For more details on RSPAN implementation with VACL, refer to the following link:

http://www.cisco.com/en/US/products/hw/switches/ps708/products_data_sheet09186a008017b753.html

Capturing IPS Traffic with MLS IP IDS

On Catalyst 6000 switches with IOS Firewall (CBAC), VACL Capture no longer functions, and an alternate capture method is needed. Using the **mls ip ids** command is a good option. This uses an Access Control List (ACL) to define interesting traffic, and then the traffic is captured by applying the command **mls ip ids** to VLAN interfaces. When monitoring multiple VLANs or interfaces, apply the command to each interface to see both sides of traffic flow. Doing so provides capabilities similar to VACL Capture.

Refer to Chapter 15, "Troubleshooting IDSM-2 Blades on Switch" under the sections entitled "MLS IP IDS Configuration on Switch running CatOS" and "MLS IP IDS Configuration on Switch running CatOS" for the MLS IP IDS configuration on the Catalyst switch running CatOS and Native IOS, respectively.

Common Problems and Their Resolution

This section discusses some commonly asked questions and answers on IPS Sensor.

1 I lost my password? How may I recover it?

   Answer: You can use service account to reset other account passwords. Log in as the service account, su to root, then enter passwd (user) to reset a user's password.

   Alternatively, if you have lost the service account password, then log in using an administrative account (cisco for example), and then delete and re-create the service account.

   However, if you have lost all the administrative account passwords and the service account password, the only recourse is to re-image the sensor.

   On a 4215, 4210, 4220, 4230, 4235 and 4250, you can connect to the serial console, reboot the sensor, and then when the Grub menu appears, select **Cisco IPS Recovery** (choice 1 on the Grub menu). When this process completes, all of your sensor data will be lost, and sensor will be restored back to default, except network settings (for example IP address, default gateway, and so on). All user accounts will be deleted, and you can log in to sensor with default username and password (cisco/cisco).

2 Does IPS 5.0 support AAA (TACACS+ or RADIUS)?

   Answer: AAA is not supported on Sensor version 5.0, which is the latest version of Sensor as of writing this book.

3 Why do I want to recover my sensor from Recovering Partition instead of using a CD?

   Answer: There are benefits to recovering from Recovery Partition instead of using CD:

   - With Recovery Partition, the network settings such as IP address, default gateway, and allowed hosts information is retained on the sensor. As IP address and allowed host info are retained, you can perform this recovery process remotely.
   - Another benefit is that the actual recovery (recover application partition) takes much less time than a CD recovery. This is because the CD recovery has to create both the Application Partition and the Recovery Partition.

4 Will I lose my configuration in particular signature tunings when a new signature update is applied to the sensor?

Answer: When a signature update is applied on a sensor, the new signatures are automatically merged into the existing settings on the sensor. The default settings for the existing signatures are updated in the same manner.

5 How can I know which signature belongs to which signature update level?

Answer: You can go to the following site, which groups the signature name based on the signature update file: http://www.cisco.com/cgi-bin/front.x/csec/idsHome.pl

6 Is ftp timeout configurable on the sensor?

Answer: Yes, it is configurable, but only from IPS version 5.0.

7 Can the sensor read and detect an encrypted attack?

Answer: It depends on whether the attack is in the data or in the protocol set up. If it is in the data (hence encrypted), the sensor will not see it, and so it will not be able to analyze it. However, if the violation occurs in the protocol setup, the sensor detects it and will take the action as configured. For example, IPS is able to detect SPAM on SMTP but unable to detect a word in the e-mail attachment.

8 Does Blocking have a time limit?

Answer: Yes, all blocking can be specified with a time limit, except for permanent blocks, which are in effect as long as they are configured.

9 Is it possible to block hosts for different lengths of time depending on the alarm?

Answer: This is not possible with automatic blocks that are performed by the sensor, but, with manual blocks it is possible. So, a possible solution is to configure the automatic blocks for a certain time, and then perform a manual block based on an alarm for which you specify the time. You can set a manual block for a much longer time period.

10 Is it possible to block a single connection on the PIX Firewall?

Answer: No, you cannot block a single connection on the PIX Firewall. Although, for automatic block, the sensor sends source/destination IP addresses, and source/destination ports to the PIX firewall, it is *not* a connection block, rather a source IP address block. The PIX blocks all packets originating from that IP address. The additional information is used by the PIX firewall to connection maintenance, for example, to remove the initial connection entry that was built up before the blocking is applied to the PIX. If this connection is not removed from the connection table and does not time out before block is removed or times out, then it is theoretically possible that the attacker can continue the attack on the original connection. Removing this connection from the connection table ensures that the original connection cannot be used to continue the attack after the block is removed.

For manual blocks, by default, the sensor sends only the source IP only to the PIX. Although additional information can be specified, the PIX still treats this as a host shun. This is because PIX itself does not support (using the shun command) the blocking of a single connection. The PIX shun command always blocks the source address regardless of whether or not the additional connection information is provided.

11 Does Blocking work on PIX with the Fail Over set up?

Answer: Yes it does, if Telnet is used as the communication protocol between the sensor and the PIX firewall. This is limited to the inside interface, as Telnetting to an outside interface is not possible because of the design of the PIX. If ssh is used as the communication protocol, then blocking will not work when the PIX failover. This is because the SSH key generated on the Primary/Active unit is different than on the Secondary unit.

12 I am sniffing the network segment that is on the outside of the PIX firewall, which is configured for NAT or PAT. Blocking is configured on the sensor to apply the shun command on the PIX with the attack detection. Is there any issue?

Answer: Yes, there is. To understand this issue, think about the following example. Assume that the PIX is configured with NAT or PAT for the outbound connection from the inside network, and an inside host is unintentionally attacking the outside network. The sensor will see the translated IP address of the inside host as an attacker (as the sensor is sniffing the outside interface network). If blocking is activated, it will send the shun command for the translated IP address, and this is inaccurate. If PAT is configured, the whole network on the inside of the PIX firewall will be blocked with the shun command, as the PAT address is the same for the whole inside network. The work-around is to sniff the inside network.

13 For how long will the shun command be on the PIX Firewall? Can I re-adjust the timer for blocking (shunning) on the PIX?

Answer: If blocking is configured manually on the PIX, the shun command will be on the PIX until it is removed. However, if it is dynamically applied by the sensor, then it will be on the PIX until it is removed or reboots or the timer expires.

With dynamic blocking done by Sensor, you can re-adjust the timeout value on the Sensor itself.

14 Is blocking performed in global or interface mode on the PIX firewall?

Answer: Blocking is an interface-based mechanism on the PIX or FWSM firewall. Though blocking is configured or applied in global mode on the PIX, it works on the interface where the attacker is attacking the network. For instance, if the attacker is coming from the outside interface network of the PIX, blocking will be applied to the outside interface as an input filter. Remember that this does not stop someone on the inside network from going to this host, but does prevent it from getting back in.

15 Is Blocking possible on the Firewall Services Module (FWSM)?

Answer: Blocking is fully supported on FWSM by the IPS version 5.0 and above.

16 How do I configure blocking with Hot Standby Router Protocol (HSRP) setup between two routers, or MSFCs on a switch?

Answer: When you configure HSRP between two active routers or MSFCs, Routers/MSFCs have their own IP addresses assigned to their physical interfaces, and the only address that is shared between the routers/MSFCs is the virtual HSRP IP address. Remember that the Virtual HSRP IP address is not an IP address of a complete physical interface; instead, it is part of the physical interface configuration. Because it is part of the physical interface configuration, you cannot apply an ACL using the HSRP interface IP address. Rather, you have to apply the ACL to the physical interface on which the HSRP is configured. So for blocking to work, the sensor has to manage both routers/MSFCs using their independent physical addresses, not the HSRP address, and it must apply the ACL to each router's physical interface on which the HSRP is configured.

17 In Promiscuous mode, why does the IPS sensor send 100 resets to both client and server?

Answer: The sensor will intentionally send 100 resets to the client and 100 resets to the server. This is because there might be a situation in which the client and server can respond to each other faster than the sensor can analyze and respond with the TCP reset packets in Promiscuous mode.

Because the server responds to the attack packet, the TCP sequence number will increase to some unknown value. Hence, if Sensor only sends one reset with the original sequence numbers, the reset would be ignored because the session would already have moved past those sequence numbers. So instead of sending one reset packet, Sensor takes 100 guesses in each direction (1 guess uses the original sequence numbers) to try to reset the connection. In most cases this works, and the sensor can reset the connection. In some cases when the client and server are near each other on the network, the session might proceed quickly enough that none of the 100 guesses would match appropriately, and the connection would continue without being reset. Hence, TCP resets are not guaranteed to work. However, in most real-world scenarios, in which the client and server are separate networks (usually the Internet), the TCP resets works well.

In Inline mode of IPS, Sensor can control when packets flow between the client and server. So the sensor needs to send only one TCP reset packet and it is known to be the correct sequence number. There is a chance that the TCP resets might get lost in transit, hence the deny-connection-inline action option is available that is new for Inline mode. You can configure the sensor to not only send the TCP reset packets, but also to deny any future packets on that connection. This way, if the resets are dropped, or the client/server intentionally ignores the resets, the sensor would still drop any additional packets and force the client/server to eventually time out and drop the connection.

18 In Inline mode, is it possible or recommended to tune the signature for TCP reset or blocking?

Answer: You can configure the signature for TCP reset or for Blocking just as you do in Promiscuous mode, although TCP reset implementation is different, and you should check the previous answer for details). However, the real advantage with inline is that you can also configure it for denyPacket or denyConnection actions. If all actions are configured, then all actions will take place. The trigger packet will be denied along with the rest of the packets in the connection and the TCP Reset will be sent. The deny keeps the attack from completing, while the TCP Reset lets the client and server know that the connection should be torn down. Without the TCP Reset the client and server will continue trying to send the packets, "thinking" they were merely lost in transit, but with the reset, the client and server tear down the connection. It is up to you whether or not to use TCP Reset in conjunction with denyPacket/denyConnection. DenyPacket/denyConnection works fine without TCP Reset, but it is not recommended to use only TCP Reset without denyPacket/denyConnection on an inline sensor because the deny actions do a better job of stopping the attack.

It is also possible to configure blocking in Inline mode. There is no general recommendation on whether you should configure blocking in Inline mode or not. It depends completely on specific scenarios. Assume that there are 3 different Internet connections to your network, and you have a sensor on each connection. If one sensor detects an attack and denyAttacker action is used, then that attacker IP can not enter the network through that one Internet connection in which that one sensor sits, but can still access the network from the other two Internet connections.

If the sensor were to do Blocking in addition to the denyAttacker, then the sensor could perform shunning on three firewalls of all three connections to block the attacker address. That way, the attacker would be blocked on all three Internet connections instead of just the one the sensor is on. Or you might have the sensor deployed in just one segment, but you want to block the ip from other segments as well. In that case, blocking must be used on the router between the segments, or better yet, on the switch where the actual machines are connected. If there is only one Internet connection and only one Internet address would be blocked, then denying just on the sensor might be enough without blocking on other devices. This would reduce the amount configuration on both the blocking device on the sensor and managed devices. Additionally, this would not place extra stress on the possibly low-end router being used for the Internet connection. So, deciding whether to configure Blocking or not depends completely on how your network topology is set up, and where the sensor is deployed.

Best Practices

For seamless operation and deployment of IPS Sensor in your network, you should take some proactive actions and do proper planning before IPS Sensor deployment. This section alerts you to some of the important issues that will make your IPS deployment and operations problem free.

Preventive Maintenance

Recovering IPS in the time of failure is crucial. Take the following preventive steps, so that you will be capable of recovering IPS in the event of failure.

Creation of Service Account

A **service** account is a special user account that gives you access to the Linux shell and eventually root access of the sensor. If you lost all other users' passwords, you could reset them using the **service** account. Additionally, the **service** account can be used to log in to the sensor to collect additional data for problem analysis. If you have not created the **service** account or if you have lost the password of the **service** account, along with the **administrator** account password of the sensor, then the only work-around is to re-image the sensor. More details on how to create a service account can be found under the "User Management Issues" section of this chapter.

Back up a Good Configuration

There are three ways you can back up the current configuration of the sensor:

- **Back up locally on the sensor**—It is extremely useful to keep a good working configuration before making any changes to the current configuration. This is extremely convenient because you can both erase the current configuration with the backup configuration or merge it.
- **Backup in Remote Server**—This is important at the time of a crash. You can recover the sensor from a crash. You can also copy a working copy of the sensor to multiple sensors that need the same configuration.
- **Using IPS MC**—If IPS Sensor is managed by IPS MC, you have a working configuration copy on the local database of IPS MC.

Sections that follow discuss the configuration steps required to use the backup configuration of the sensor both locally and to a remote server.

Backup Locally on the Sensor

Work through the following steps to back up the configuration of the Sensor:

Step 1 Log into the Sensor using an account with **administrator** privileges.

Step 2 Save the current configuration in a backup file with the following command:

```
sensor# copy current-config backup-config
```

Step 3 After you copy the current configuration to a backup file, ensure that the configuration is saved to the backup file correctly with the following command:

```
sensor# more backup-config
```

Step 4 You can merge the backup configuration with the current configuration with the following command:

```
sensor# copy backup-config current-config
```

Step 5 To overwrite the current configuration with the backup configuration use the following command:

```
sensor# copy /erase backup-config current-config
```

Step 6 You can erase both the backup and current configuration with the following command:

```
sensor# erase current-config
```

Backup in Remote Server

You can use FTP/SCP/HTTP/HTTPS servers as remote servers to back up and restore the Sensor configuration. Work through the following steps using FTP to back up and restore the sensor's configuration:

Step 1 Log in to the sensor using an account with administrator privileges.

Step 2 To back up the current configuration to the remote server, use the following command:

```
sensor# copy current-config
  ftp://admin_user@10.1.1.100//tftpboot/update/sensor100.cfg
Password: ********
```

Step 3 To restore the configuration file that you copied to the remote server use the following command:

```
sensor# copy ftp://admin_user@10.1.1.100//tftpboot/update/
  sensor100.cfg current-config
Password: ********
Warning: Copying over the current configuration may leave the box in an
  unstable state.
Would you like to copy current-config to backup-config before
  proceeding? [yes]:
Sensor#
```

Step 4 To erase the current configuration with the backup configuration from the ftp server, use the following command:

```
sensor# copy /erase ftp://admin_user@10.1.1.100//tftpboot/update/
  sensor100.cfg current-config
Password: ********
Warning: Copying over the current configuration may leave the box in an
  unstable state.
Would you like to copy current-config to backup-config before
  proceeding? [yes]
Sensor#
```

Recommendation on Connecting Sensor to the Network

The proper placement of the sensor in the network dictates the performance and functionality of the sensor. In this section, you are presented with some recommendations on where to connect the Sensing and Command and Control interfaces in Promiscuous mode.

Recommendation on Connecting the Sniffing Interface of the Sensor to the Network

The location at which you connect your sensor's sniffing interface to the network depends on how much traffic you want to analyze. A general recommendation is to monitor the internal connections of the firewall. This way you will not spend time filtering through alarms for packets that are already stopped by the firewall. If you are interested in understanding the attacks coming to your network before they are filtered by the firewall, connect the sniffing interface on the outside of the firewall. But, this should be done if you have enough human time and proper tools to go through the log. Otherwise, having an overwhelming amount of log information to analyze might be the cause of a legitimate attack going unanalyzed or unmitigated for longer than it should.

Rating IPS Sensor

Just as with any other network devices such as switches, routers, and firewalls, you must rate the IPS sensor higher than the normal traffic that is captured using the sniffing interface. This way the IPS sensor can keep up with usage spikes in the network.

Recommendation on Connecting Command and Control Interface

It is recommended to connect the Command and Control interface to either a specific network for configuring and managing your security devices (often known as the out of band secure management network), or at a minimum, to a VLAN that is used only for managing your security devices. If you are using a VLAN, then the Command and Control interface of the Sensor, interface of your IPS MC and the Security Monitor, and a firewall interface and other security devices, should be placed in this VLAN. You may then route to other VLANs in your network through your firewall to further protect this VLAN. Connections to and from your security devices should be over encrypted connections. The Cisco IPS comes loaded and running with SSH for CLI access, and TLS/SSL for access to its web server.

Recommendation on Settings of Signature on Sensor

The signature on the Cisco Sensor comes with preset severity levels. A general rule of thumb is to begin by using the default severities and see what alarms are detected on your network. Begin by looking at the high-level alarms and determine the cause of the alarm.

The NSDB (Network Security Database) is a good reference for more information about an alarm. The NSDB is installed on the sensors and the IPS MC as part of the signature update process. The NSDB also can be found at the following link:

http://www.cisco.com/cgi-bin/front.x/csec/idsHome.pl

If you see alarms that upon analysis are determined to be normal traffic, then you need to either filter the alarms for the particular address set, or lower the severity of the alarm, or even disable the alarm. Filtering or disabling the alarms will prevent you from having to spend time on these alarms in the future. If an alarm is legitimate, then you will need to determine if your system is vulnerable (refer to the NSDB for information on vulnerable machines). If the machine is not vulnerable, then consider also filtering this alarm. If the machine is vulnerable, you will need to see if the system has been compromised and take appropriate steps. Once the high- severity alarms have been analyzed, determine whether or not you want any automatic actions to occur for these alarms in the future. Available action includes resetting the TCP connection, blocking the source IP address, or logging the packets to and from the source address of the alarm in Promiscuous mode. In Inline mode, the sensor can drop the packet or the connection immediately, along with TCP reset and blocking.

Once you have gone through the high alarms, try to go through the medium-severity alarms following the same procedure. Continue to do the same thing with low-severity and information alarms.

Recommendation on Inline-Mode Deployment

Before deploying your Sensor in Inline mode, it is recommended that you run the Sensor in Promiscuous mode to understand and tune the signature. Once, you have reached an acceptable level of false positive, you can turn on Inline mode on the sensor. Be sure that you have the Bypass mode turned on when the sensor is deployed in Inline mode. Otherwise, if the sensor fails, all traffic going through the sensor will be affected.

CHAPTER 15

Troubleshooting IDSM-2 Blade on Switch

The Intrusion Detection Services Module 2 (IDSM-2) is part of a family of new generation service modules for the Catalyst 6500. The IDSM-2 provides high performance intrusion detection and prevention services from within the Catalyst 6500 chassis, using the same code base found in the Cisco IDS/IPS standalone appliances. Because the IDSM-2 module uses the same code base as the IDS/IPS Appliances, and IDS/IPS Sensor Troubleshooting is discussed thoroughly in Chapter 14, "Troubleshooting Cisco Intrusion Prevention System," the same information is not repeated in this chapter. You are strongly encouraged to go through Chapter 14 thoroughly for IDS/IPS sensor operations and troubleshooting. This chapter examines the configuration and troubleshooting which are unique to IDSM-2 blade.

Overview of IDSM-2 Blade on the Switch

The IDSM-2 blade provides up to 600 Mbps of Intrusion Detection and Intrusion Prevention services. Just like IDS/IPS Appliance, IDSM-2 module can operate in either Promiscuous or Inline Mode (see Chapter 14 for more details). The only difference between the IDS/IPS Appliance and the IDSM-2 blade is that in version 5.0, IDS/IPS Appliance can operate in both the Inline and the Promiscuous modes, but the IDSM-2 blade can operate either one or the other. This is because the IDSM-2 module has only two sniffing interfaces, so it cannot be configured for both Inline and Promiscuous mode; it requires at least three interfaces to configure both Promiscuous and Inline mode. For the same reason, you cannot configure multiple Inline pairs on IDSM-2, which is possible on IDS/IPS Appliance. This section covers the following items that are used for the seamless operation of IDSM-2 blade:

- Software and hardware requirements
- Slot assignment on the switch
- Front Panel indicator lights and how to use them
- Installing an IDSM-2 blade on the switch
- Removing an IDSM-2 blade from the switch
- Ports supported on an IDSM-2 blade

Software and Hardware Requirements

There are specific hardware and software requirements on the Catalyst switch for IDSM-2 support, as follows:

- Catalyst software release 7.5(1) or later with Supervisor Engine 1A with Multilayer Switch Feature Card 2 (MSFC2)
- Catalyst software release 7.5(1) or later with Supervisor Engine 2 with MSFC2 or PFC2
- Cisco IOS software release 12.2(14)SY with Supervisor Engine 2 with MSFC2
- Cisco IOS software release 12.1(19)E or later with Supervisor Engine 2 with MSFC2
- Cisco IOS software release 12.1(19)E1 or later with Supervisor Engine 1A with MSFC2
- Cisco IOS software release 12.2(14)SX1 with Supervisor Engine 720
- Cisco IDS/IPS software release 4.0 or later
- Any Catalyst 6500 series switch chassis or 7600 router

You can use "Software Advisor" from the following link to find out the supported versions of the Catalyst 6500 switches:

http://www.cisco.com/kobayashi/support/tac/tools.shtml#software

Slot Assignment on the Switch

Before you select a slot on the switch, you must understand some of the restrictions for assigning the appropriate slot for the IDSM-2 module on the switch. The following list will help in determining how to select the appropriate slot for the IDSM-2 blade:

- **Catalyst 6503**—A 3-slot chassis that reserves one slot for the Supervisor and offers two line card slots for other modules. The first slot is reserved for either the Supervisor 2 or Supervisor 720.
- **Catalyst 6006 and 6506**—A 6-slot chassis that reserves one slot for the Supervisor and offers five line card slots for other modules. If a Supervisor 2 is used, then Slot 1 is reserved for its use. If a Supervisor 720 is used, then either slot 5 or 6 must be used for this Supervisor.
- **Catalyst 6509**—A 9-slot chassis that reserves one slot for the Supervisor and offers eight line card slots for other modules. If a Supervisor 2 is used, then Slot 1 is reserved for its use. If a Supervisor 720 is used, then either slot 5 or 6 must be used for this Supervisor.
- **Catalyst 6509-NEBS-A**—A 9-slot chassis that reserves one slot for the Supervisor and offers eight line card slots for other modules. If a Supervisor 2 is used, then Slot 1 is reserved for its use. If a Supervisor 720 is used, then either slot 5 or 6 must be used for this Supervisor.

- **Catalyst 6513**—A 13-slot chassis that reserves one slot for the Supervisor and offers 12 line card slots for other modules. If a Supervisor 2 is used, then Slot 1 is reserved for its use. If a Supervisor 720 is used, then either slot 7 or 8 must be used for this Supervisor.

The IDSM-2 can reside in any slot that is not reserved for the Supervisor. The IDSM-2 has been tested to work with the Supervisor 1A (with MSFC2), the Supervisor 2, and the Supervisor 720.

NOTE Cisco supports only eight IDSM-2s per chassis.

Front Panel Indicator Lights and How to Use Them

The IDSM-2 has a status indicator and a Shutdown button. Locating and understanding the meaning of different light colors is very important. Table 15-1 explains them.

Table 15-1 *IDSM-2 States as Indicated by the Status Indicator*

Color	Description
Green	All diagnostics tests pass, so IDSM-2 is operational.
Red	A diagnostic other than an individual port test failed.
Amber	The IDSM-2 is running through its boot and self-test diagnostics sequence, or the IDSM-2 is disabled, or the IDSM-2 is in the shutdown state.
Off	The IDSM-2 power is off.

Installing the IDSM-2 Blade on the Switch

All Catalyst 6500 series switches support hot swapping, which lets you install, remove, replace, and rearrange modules without turning off the system power. When the system detects that a module has been installed or removed, it runs diagnostic and discovery routines, acknowledges the presence or absence of the module, and resumes system operation with no operator intervention.

To install the IDSM-2 in the Catalyst 6500 series switch, follow these steps:

Step 1 Choose a slot on the Catalyst 6500 switch for the IDSM-2 blade. Note that the supervisor engine must be installed in slot 1; a redundant supervisor engine can be installed in slot 2. If a redundant supervisor engine is not required, slots 2 through 9 (slots 2 through 6 on the 6-slot chassis and slots 2 through 11 on the 13-slot chassis) are available for modules.

Step 2 Hold the IDSM-2 with one hand, and place your other hand under the IDSM-2 carrier to support it.

Step 3 Verify that you have correctly installed the IDSM-2 and can bring it online by executing the command **show module** on the switch.

Removing the IDSM-2 Blade from the Switch

You must first shut down the IDSM-2 before removing it from a Catalyst 6500 series switch. Removing the module without going through a shutdown may damage your module, or corrupt your IDS/IPS Operating System on the module. Work through the following procedure to remove the IDSM-2 blade from the Catalyst 6500 series switch:

Step 1 Shut down the IDSM-2 blade by one of the following methods:

- Log in to the IDSM-2 and execute the **reset powerdown** command to shut down IDSM-2 blade.
- To shut down the module from CatOS, execute the **set module shutdown module_number** command.
- If you are running Native IOS on the switch and want to shut down the IDSM-2 module, execute **hw-module module module_number shutdown** command.
- As a last resort, you can press the **Shutdown** button on the IDSM-2 blade itself. Shutdown may take several minutes.

Step 2 Verify that the IDSM-2 blade shuts down by executing the **show module** command on the switch. Do not remove the IDSM-2 until the status indicator is amber or off.

Step 3 Carefully pull the IDSM-2 straight out of the slot, keeping your other hand under the carrier to guide it.

Ports Supported on IDSM-2 Blade

Eight ports appear to the switch for each IDSM-2 blade. This can be verified by executing command **show port IDSM_Module_Slot_Number** in CatOS. Example 15-1 shows eight ports on the module on CatOS:

Example 15-1 *Ports Appearing on the Switch Running CatOS*

```
Console> (enable) show port 2
* = Configured MAC Address
Port Name Status Vlan Duplex Speed Type
----- ------------------ ---------- ---------- ------ ----- ------------
! Port 2/1 is the TCP reset interface. This interface should be in the same VLAN as the
! sniffing interface
2/1 connected trunk full 1000 Intrusion Detection
! Port 2/2 is the Command and Control Interface
2/2 connected 251 full 1000 Intrusion Detection
2/3 disable 1 full 1000 Intrusion Detection
2/4 disable 1 full 1000 Intrusion Detection
2/5 disable 1 full 1000 Intrusion Detection
2/6 disable 1 full 1000 Intrusion Detection
```

Example 15-1 *Ports Appearing on the Switch Running CatOS (Continued)*

```
! Ports 2/7 and 2/8 are the Sniffing Interfaces
2/7 monitor trunk full 1000 Intrusion Detection
2/8 connected trunk full 1000 Intrusion Detection
Console> (enable)
```

The IDSM-2 module uses the following four IP ports:

- **Command and control port**—IDSM-2 uses GigabitEthernet0/2 interface as the command and control port that contains the IP address. If you are running CatOS, this is identified as port slot/2. In Example 15-1, 2/2 is the command and control port for the blade seated in slot 2. If you are running Native IOS, this port is identified as a management port, which is internally mapped to slot/2 port. Hence, on the 6K, set this port to a VLAN appropriate to the IP address you give the sensor. Try to avoid using VLAN 1, which is the default.
- **Capture/Sniffing Ports**—The module has two sniffing ports that are seen by the switch as ports 7 and 8. In Example 15-1, these ports are 2/7 and 2/8. If you are running Native IOS, these ports are identified as data-port 1 and 2. Data-port 1 is internally mapped to slot/7, and data-port 2 is mapped to slot/8 on the Native IOS switch. On the IDSM-2 blade, these ports are identified as GigabitEthernet0/7 and GigabitEthernet0/8 respectively. If you are using Inline mode, these two ports should be in two different VLANs. In Promiscuous mode, you can use either Switched Port Analyzer (SPAN) or Virtual Access Control List (VACL) to direct traffic to these ports. As the ports are Gigabit ports, and IDSM-2 blade cannot handle more than 600 mbps traffic, it is not necessary to use both ports in Promiscuous mode.
- **Reset Port**—In CatOS, port slot/1 is used for reset. Remember that the reset port must be assigned to the same VLAN as the sniffing port(s) to perform the TCP resets.

Diagnostic Commands and Tools

The **show** commands are very useful in troubleshooting issues on the switch side. You use different commands to accomplish the same task on CatOS and Native IOS. Some commands are common in both modes. All the **show** commands in different modes are explained as follows.

show Commands in Both Modes

Following is the list of common switch commands available on both CatOS and Native IOS for getting different statistical and configuration information on the switch:

- **show module**—Provides information on whether the module is up and functioning correctly.
- **show version**—Provides the version of CatOS or the Native IOS running on the switch.

show Commands in CatOS

Following is a list of commands specific to CatOS that are used to obtain specific details about the port and other relevant information on the switch for the IDSM-2 blade:

- **show port** *module_number*—Shows the ports of a specific module and provides the statistics of the ports. Also verifies which VLAN the port of the module belongs to.
- **show trunk**—When you use the **show trunk** command without specifying a module or port number, the command displays only the actively trunking ports. This command is useful to find out if the trunk is working properly for span ports (slot/7 and slot/8) of IDSM-2 blade.
- **show span** [**all**]—This command displays information about the current SPAN configuration. To see both local and remote SPAN configuration information, use this command with the **all** argument. Use this command to determine if SPAN is configured correctly on the switch for IDSM-2 blade.
- **show security acl**—Use this command to display the contents of the VACL that are currently configured or that are last committed to nonvolatile random-access memory (NVRAM) and hardware.
- **show test** *module_number*—Shows the test result of a module. The output of this command verifies the test results and checks for software corruption on the IDSM-2 module.

show Commands in Native IOS

Following is a list of commands available on the Native IOS that are used to obtain different stats and configuration information on the switch pertaining to IDSM-2 blade:

- **show intrusion-detection module** *module_number* **management-port {state|traffic}**—Use this command to obtain the statistics of the command and control port for the IDSM-2 blade on the switch.
- **show intrusion-detection module** *module_number* **data-port {1|2} {state|traffic}**—Use this command to obtain the statistics of the data-ports of the IDSM-2 blade on the switch.
- **show monitor session**—Use this command to display information about the Encapsulated Remote SPAN (ERSPAN), SPAN, and RSPAN sessions on the switch.
- **show vlan access-map** [*map-name*]—To display the contents of a VLAN-access map, use the **show vlan access-map** command. Use this command to verify the VACL configuration for the IDSM-2 blade.
- **show vlan filter**—To display information about the VLAN filter, use the **show vlan filter** command. This is useful to verify the VACL configuration on the switch for the IDSM-2 blade.

Common Problems and Resolutions

IDSM-2 uses the same code base as the sensor appliances. Hence, the common issues and resolutions are the same for IDSM-2 blade as the sensor appliances, with few exceptions. Chapter 14 explains the configuration and troubleshooting aspects on the Appliance and other platforms. Hence, for IDS/IPS, software-related troubleshooting is not explained again in this section. However, some aspects of troubleshooting are unique to IDSM-2, which is the focus of this chapter as follows:

- Hardware issues
- Communication issues with IDSM-2 command and control port
- Issues with not getting traffic from the switch in Promiscuous mode
- Issues with Inline mode
- Not generating events issues
- TCP reset issues
- Software installation and upgrade issues

Hardware Issues

After you insert the IDSM-2 blade into one of the slots on the switch, first be sure that the module is up and running correctly. Verification and troubleshooting steps are identical, but the commands are different on Native IOS and CatOS. The sections that follow explain how to troubleshoot the hardware issues on the Catalyst switch:

- IDSM-2 HW Issue on Native IOS
- IDSM-2 HW Issue on CatOS

IDSM-2 Hardware Issues on Native IOS

After installing the module, first check the status of the module. If you find any problem with the module, follow the steps in the troubleshooting section to rectify the problem.

Verify Hardware Operation

Execute the **show module** command on the switch that is running Native IOS to obtain the status of the module as shown in Example 15-2.

Example 15-2 show module *Command Output*

```
cat6506#show module
Mod Ports Card Type                              Model              Serial No.
--- ----- -------------------------------------- ------------------ -----------
  3   48  48 port 10/100 mb RJ45                 WS-X6348-RJ-45     SAL062100V7
  4    6  Firewall Module                        WS-SVC-FWM-1       SAD08450149
! The following line indicates that the IDSM-2 blade is in slot 5
```

continues

Example 15-2 show module *Command Output (Continued)*

```
  5    8  Intrusion Detection System            WS-SVC-IDSM-2      SAD074101MV
  6    2  Supervisor Engine 720 (Active)        WS-SUP720-3B       SAD082104HE

Mod MAC addresses                       Hw    Fw           Sw           Status
--- ---------------------------------- ------ ------------ ------------ -------
  3  0009.1267.27d8 to 0009.1267.2807   6.1   5.4(2)       8.3(0.110)TE Ok
  4  0003.e471.b758 to 0003.e471.b75f   3.0   7.2(1)       2.3(2)       Ok
! The following line indicates that the version of IDS sensor software is 5.0(2). It also
! shows that the status of the blade is OK.
  5  0003.feac.cb4a to 0003.feac.cb51   4.0   7.2(1)       5.0(2)       Ok
  6  000f.9093.cfd4 to 000f.9093.cfd7   4.0   8.1(3)       12.2(17d)SXB Ok

Mod Sub-Module                  Model              Serial        Hw     Status
--- --------------------------- ------------------ ------------ ------- -------
  3 Inline Power Module         WS-F6K-PWR                       1.0    Ok
! The following line is an indication of the presence of the IDSM-2 daughter card
! as a sub-module. This sub-module works to accelerates performance on the IDSM-2.
! The status of this IDSM-2 sub-module shows OK.
  5 IDS 2 accelerator board     WS-SVC-IDSUPG      ADEI32603225  2.2    Ok
  6 Policy Feature Card 3       WS-F6K-PFC3B       SAD082306Y9   1.0    Ok
  6 MSFC3 Daughterboard         WS-SUP720          SAD081805U0   2.1    Ok

Mod Online Diag Status
--- -------------------
  3 Pass
  4 Pass
! The Online Diag Status shows for slot 5 is Pass. This is where the IDSM-2 blade is
! inserted
  5 Pass
  6 Pass
cat6506#
```

The output in Example 15-2 shows that the IDSM-2 module is in a Catalyst 6506 chassis (with Supervisor 720 in slot 6) in slot 5. To obtain the same details as those contained in Example 15-2 for only the IDSM-2 blade, which is in slot 5 for Example 15-2, you can execute the command **show module 5**.

NOTE The status should read **ok.** If it reads **other**, the IDSM-2 is not yet online. It may take five minutes or more to bring the module online through the switch.

Troubleshooting Steps

If the IDSM-2 module is not coming on line and shows status as **other, unknown, faulty, errdisable, power-deny,** or **power-bad** in the output of the **show module** command, or if an amber or red status displays on the LED, work through the following steps to troubleshoot the issue:

Step 1 Be sure that you are running the supported HW and software on the switch for the IDSM-2 blade. If the IDSM-2 module is not supported in the software you are currently running, download the required software from the Cisco IOS Software Center at the following link: http://www.cisco.com/tacpage/sw-center/sw-ios.shtml

Refer to the following link for the supported software switch version: http://www.cisco.com/univercd/cc/td/doc/product/iaabu/csids/csids11/hwguide/hwIDSM-2.htm#wp712716

Step 2 If the status is **power-deny**, the switch does not have enough power available to power this module. Issue the **show power** command to confirm whether enough power is available. Refer to the Troubleshooting **C6KPWR-4-POWRDENIED: insufficient power, module in slot x power denied Error Messages** section in the following link: http://www.cisco.com/en/US/products/hw/switches/ps700/products_tech_note09186a00801751d7.shtml#subtopic4b

Step 3 If the status is **power-bad**, the switch is able to see a card, but unable to allocate power. This is possible if the Supervisor Engine is not able to access the Serial Programmable Read Only Memory (SPROM) contents on the module to determine the identification of the line card. You can issue the **show idprom module** *slot* command to verify if the SPROM is readable. If SPROM is not accessible, you can reset the module.

Step 4 Be sure the module is properly seated and is screwed down completely. If the module still does not come online, issue the global configuration command **diagnostic level complete** to ensure that the diagnostic is enabled, and then issue the **hw-module module** *slot number* **reset** command. If the module still does not come on line, inspect the backplane connector on the module to be sure it is not damaged. If there is no visual damage, try the module in another slot or a different chassis. Also, inspect for bent pins on the slot connector on the backplane. You may want to use a flashlight when inspecting the connector pins on the chassis backplane.

Step 5 Issue the **show diagnostics module** *slot number* command to identify any hardware failures on the module. You need to have complete diagnostics enabled by issuing the global configuration command **diagnostic level complete** for the switch to be able to perform diagnostics on the module. If you have minimal diagnostics enabled and you change to complete diagnostics, the module needs to reset for the switch to perform the full diagnostics. In the same output that is shown in Example 15-3, the **show diagnostics module** command is issued, but the output is inconclusive, as many of the tests have not been performed in minimal mode. The output shows how to turn on the diagnostic level and then issue the **show diagnostics module** command again to see the complete results, as shown in Example 15-3.

Example 15-3 *Turning on the Complete Level Logging for the IDSM-2 Module*

```
cat6506# configure terminal
Enter configuration commands, one per line.  End with CNTL/Z.
! The following command enables complete diagnostics.
This command is hidden
cat6506(config)#diagnostic level complete
! If you are running 12.2(14)SX on sup 720 for example use the following command
Cat6506(config)# diagnostic bootup level complete
cat6506(config)#end
cat6506#
6d05h: %SYS-5-CONFIG_I: Configured from console by console
! Reset the module with the following command
cat6506#hw-module module 5 reset
Device BOOT variable for reset = <empty>
Warning: Device list is not verified.

Proceed with reload of module?[confirm]
% reset issued for module 5
cat6506#
6d05h: SP: The PC in slot 5 is shutting down. Please wait ...
6d05h: SP: PC shutdown completed for module 5
6d05h: %C6KPWR-SP-4-DISABLED: power to module in slot 5 set off (Reset)
! The following line indicates a complete diagnostic test is in action
6d06h: %DIAG-SP-6-RUN_COMPLETE: Module 5: Running Complete Diagnostics...
! The following line shows the module passed the online diagnostics
6d06h: %DIAG-SP-6-DIAG_OK: Module 5: Passed Online Diagnostics
6d06h: %FABRIC-SP-5-LINECARDMODE_BUS_FORCED: The switching mode of module in slot 5
is forced to bus-mode.
6d06h: %OIR-SP-6-INSCARD: Card inserted in slot 5, interfaces are now online
cat6506#
! Following shows the complete diagnostics test results.
cat6506#show diagnostic module 5

! This line indicates the complete level diagnostic is turned on
Current bootup diagnostic level: complete

        Module 5:
! The following line shows the module pass the test
          Overall Diagnostic Result for Module 5 : PASS
          Diagnostic level at card bootup: complete
! A dot means pass, F means Fail and U means its not tested
          Test results: (. = Pass, F = Fail, U = Untested)
```

Example 15-3 *Turning on the Complete Level Logging for the IDSM-2 Module (Continued)*

```
                1) TestPortASICLoopback:

                  Port  1  2  3  4
                  ----------------
                        .  .  .  .


                2) TestPCLoopback:

                  Port  1  2  3  4
                  ----------------
                        .  .  .  .


                3) TestNetflowInlineRewrite:

                  Port  1  2  3  4
                  ----------------
                        .  .  .  .

cat6506#
```

Step 6 IDSM-2 hard drive has been working for too long and has stopped functioning.

If the IDSM-2 drive is in constant use for extended periods of time (2 weeks plus), you might encounter multiple problems: inability to log in, I/O errors to the console when doing read/write operations (**ls** command), and commands not executing properly (cannot find the PATH to the executable). The switch might report that the module is OK, but attempts to log in to the service account and execute commands will reveal that the problem exists. The latest version (for example, 4.1[4] and above) alleviates the problem, but this is something that you may need to check.

Step 7 If you still have issues, collect the **show tech-support** and **show logging** commands output, and look for any error or other types of messages related to the IDSM-2 blade to troubleshoot further.

IDSM-2 HW Issue on CatOS

Troubleshooting hardware issues with the IDSM-2 blade is very similar to the Native IOS mode. But, the syntax for **show** and **debug** commands are different. The sections that follow explain the verification of the hardware operation of the module, along with troubleshooting steps.

Verify Hardware Operation

Execute the **show module** command on the switch running CatOS to find out the status of the module as shown in Example 15-4.

Example 15-4 show module *Command Output*

```
cat6k> (enable) show module
Mod Slot Ports Module-Type               Model               Sub Status
--- ---- ----- ------------------------- ------------------- --- --------
1   1    2     1000BaseX Supervisor      WS-X6K-SUP1A-2GE    yes ok
15  1    1     Multilayer Switch Feature WS-F6K-MSFC         no  ok
2   2    48    10/100/1000BaseT Ethernet WS-X6548-GE-TX      no  ok
3   3    16    1000BaseX Ethernet        WS-X6516A-GBIC      no  ok
! The following line shows the IDSM-2 blade and the status shows OK.
4   4    8     Intrusion Detection Mod   WS-SVC-IDSM-2        yes ok

Mod Module-Name          Serial-Num
--- ------------------- -----------
1                        SAD041308AN
15                       SAD04120BRB
2                        SAD073906RC
3                        SAL0751QYN0
4                        SAD062004LV

Mod MAC-Address(es)                        Hw     Fw         Sw
--- -------------------------------------- ------ ---------- ---------------
1   00-d0-c0-cc-0e-d2 to 00-d0-c0-cc-0e-d3 3.1    5.3.1      8.4(1)
    00-d0-c0-cc-0e-d0 to 00-d0-c0-cc-0e-d1
    00-30-71-34-10-00 to 00-30-71-34-13-ff
15  00-30-7b-91-77-b0 to 00-30-7b-91-77-ef 1.4    12.1(23)E2 12.1(23)E2
2   00-0d-29-f6-01-98 to 00-0d-29-f6-01-c7 5.0    7.2(1)     8.4(1)
3   00-0e-83-af-15-48 to 00-0e-83-af-15-57 1.0    7.2(1)     8.4(1)
! This line shows the version information of the IDSM-2 and the sup
4   00-e0-b0-ff-3b-80 to 00-e0-b0-ff-3b-87 0.102  7.2(1)  5.0(2)

Mod Sub-Type                Sub-Model          Sub-Serial  Sub-Hw Sub-Sw
--- ----------------------- ------------------ ----------- ------ ------
1   L3 Switching Engine     WS-F6K-PFC         SAD041303G6 1.1
! The following line indicates the presence of acceleration card
4   IDS 2 accelerator board WS-SVC-IDSUPG      .           2.0
cat6k> (enable)
```

The next section explains how to perform troubleshooting steps if the module status is other than **OK**.

Troubleshooting Steps

After inserting IDSM-2 blade, execute the **show module** command and check to see the status of the module. Also observe the light on the blade. If the **show module** command shows a status other than **OK** (the switch does not recognize the IDSM-2 blade) or the IDSM-2 blade LED status is not green, work through the following steps to troubleshoot the issue:

Step 1 If you run an unsupported CatOS version that runs on the Supervisor module for the IDSM-2 module, the switch may not be able to recognize the module. Execute the **show version** command on the switch and refer to the following link to verify whether the hardware and software are supported for the IDSM-2 blade: http://www.cisco.com/univercd/cc/td/doc/product/iaabu/csids/csids11/hwguide/hwIDSM-2.htm#wp712716

Step 2 If the status indicator is off on IDSM-2, turn the power on to IDSM-2 with the following command:

```
cat6k> (enable) set module power up module_number
```

Step 3 If the IDSM-2 blade is disabled, enable it with the following command:

```
cat6k> (enable) set module enable module_number
```

Step 4 If the IDSM-2 module is still not coming up, reset the module with the following command:

```
cat6k> (enable) reset module_number
```

Step 5 The module may not come up if there is not sufficient power in the chassis. Issue the **show module** command to see the status of the module. If it indicates **power-deny**, it is most likely not a hardware issue but a power budget issue. Issue the **show environment power** command to check the redundancy mode of the power supply. If you use 1 + 1 redundancy, you have these two choices:

- Install two higher wattage power supplies if you still want 1+1 redundancy.
- Change the mode of power redundancy to **combined**. This means that the available power is now the sum of the two power supplies installed in the system. If you lose one of the power supplies, however, some of the modules may shut down because one of the power supplies would not be able to supply power on its own.

Refer to the following link for additional details on power management: http://www.cisco.com/en/US/partner/products/hw/switches/ps700/products_tech_note09186a008015bfa8.shtml

Step 6 If the IDSM-2 blade is improperly seated, the blade may not come on line. Turn off the switch and remove the module. Inspect for bent pins on the slot connector on the backplane. You may want to use a flashlight when inspecting the connector pins on the chassis backplane. Try to reseat it. Be sure that the screws on both sides are tightened, and confirm that the line card is inserted tightly into the chassis. Turn on power for the chassis and observe the status. In some cases, a badly seated card can cause symptoms that appear to be a hardware failure. A badly seated card may cause traffic corruption on the backplane. This might result in various problems occurring in the Catalyst chassis. For example, if one module corrupts traffic on the Catalyst backplane, this might cause the self-test to fail for both itself and other modules. Reseating all the cards can resolve this, and allow the self-tests to pass.

Step 7 Put the IDSM-2 module in a different slot to ensure that the slot in the chassis is not causing the problem.

Step 8 After reseating the IDSM-2 module, and putting that in a different slot, if the module status still shows anything other than OK, run a diagnostic test to eliminate the possibility of HW failure with the **show test** *mod* command. The **show test** command will show you a **diaglevel** entry. If this **diaglevel** is set to **bypass** or **minimal,** you can change this by issuing the **set test diaglevel complete** command, and resetting the module so that the self-test occurs. The **set test diaglevel complete** command executes all self-tests available, whereas the minimal and bypass options skip some or all of the tests. If you see an F in the output of the **show test** command, this indicates that this part might be suffering from a hardware failure. It's important to note that the **STATUS** LED should flash orange once and stay orange during diagnostic boot tests. It turns green when the module is operational (online).

Step 9 If the **port status** reads **fail**, be sure IDSM-2 is firmly connected in the switch.

Step 10 If the **hdd status** reads **fail**, you must re-image the application partition.

Step 11 If the diagnostics test turns out to be **OK**, and you are still having issues with the IDSM-2 blade, review Error Messages in the **show logging buffer -1023** command output and **show log** command output around the time you encountered the module failure.

Use the Error Message Decoder, which can be found in the following link, to help decipher the output of any messages:

http://www.cisco.com/cgi-bin/Support/Errordecoder/index.cgi

In addition to reviewing the error messages, it is a good idea to use the Bug Toolkit, at the following link:

http://www.cisco.com/cgi-bin/Support/Bugtool/launch_bugtool.pl

The **show version** command will provide the software version information to help you run a bug search. For example, if you identify an exception in the **show log** command output, use the Bug Toolkit to search for bugs on your Catalyst platform, software version, and the exception from the **show log**.

Communication Issues with IDSM-2 Command and Control Port

IDSM-2 module's port 2 is used as a command and control interface. If you have the module in slot 5, the port number for command and control is 5/2. To use Telnet or SSH to access the IDSM-2 blade, you must have this command and control port to connect to the rest of your network. If the IDSM-2 is managed by the IDS/IPS MC or IDM, and if the reporting tool (for example, Security Monitor) needs to pull the event, this interface must be enabled and must have connectivity to your network. This interface is also used for blocking. To establish the connectivity for the IDSM-2 blade to the rest of your network, put the Command and Control port of IDSM-2 in a VLAN that has connectivity to the rest of your network. By default, this interface is part of VLAN 1 on the switch. The sections that follow discuss how to configure the Command and Control port and how to troubleshoot it should a problem arise.

Configuration Steps

First, you need to map the Command and Control port to a specific VLAN, and second, you need to enable the Command and Control port on the IDSM-2 blade. The sections that follow cover these two topics:

- Switch configuration
- IDSM-2 blade configuration

Switch Configuration

Depending on whether you are running Native IOS or CatOS, use different syntax to assign the Command and Control port to a specific VLAN on the switch so that the IDS Management software or the Monitoring software can access the IDSM-2 blade. This is explained in the following list:

- **Assigning Command and Control port to a VLAN on CatOS**—The command and control port must be assigned to a VLAN from which it can be accessed by external management clients (for example, IDS MC or Security Monitor). If an appropriate VLAN does not exist, you can create it with the following command:

  ```
  set vtp domain name
  set vlan vlan number
  clear vlan vlan_number
  ```

  Now, add the Command and Control port (slot#/2) to the VLAN that you have just created with the following command:

  ```
  set vlan vlan number slot/port
  ```

  For example, to create a VLAN 150 and assign the Command and Control port of the IDSM-2 module that is on slot 5, you need the following configuration on the switch:

  ```
  set vtp domain cisco
  set vlan 150
  clear vlan 150
  set vlan 150 5/2
  ```

- **Assigning a Command and Control port to a VLAN on Native IOS**—You can use the following command to create a VLAN and assign the management port to the VLAN:

```
vtp domain name
vlan vlan_number
state active
intrusion-detection module module_number management-port access-vlan number
For example, if you want to create VLAN 150 and assign the Command and Control
port to VLAN 150 on Native IOS:
vtp domain cisco
vlan 150
state active
intrusion-detection module 5 management-port access-vlan 150
```

IDSM-2 Configuration

Following the switch configuration, you need to log in to the IDSM-2 blade with the **session** command as shown in Example 15-5, or use Telnet to access it from the switch by typing the address 127.0.0.x1, where x is the slot number where the IDSM-2 blade is inserted.

Example 15-5 *How to Session into the Blade*

```
cat6506# session slot 5 processor 1
The default escape character is Ctrl-^, then x.
You can also type 'exit' at the remote prompt to end the session
Trying 127.0.0.51 ... Open

! When you login the first time, you need to use cisco/cisco for username/password. Then
! you will be prompted for the new password. In this example, the initial password is
! already changed; hence you don't see the password change prompt.
login: cisco
Password:
Last login: Mon May  9 03:09:11 from 127.0.0.61
***NOTICE***
This product contains cryptographic features and is subject to United States
and local country laws governing import, export, transfer and use. Delivery
of Cisco cryptographic products does not imply third-party authority to import,
export, distribute or use encryption. Importers, exporters, distributors and
users are responsible for compliance with U.S. and local country laws. By using
this product you agree to comply with applicable laws and regulations. If you
are unable to comply with U.S. and local laws, return this product immediately.

A summary of U.S. laws governing Cisco cryptographic products may be found at:
http://www.cisco.com/wwl/export/crypto/tool/stqrg.html

If you require further assistance please contact us by sending email to
export@cisco.com.
sensor#
```

Once you are in the IDSM-2 CLI, you can enable and configure the Command and Control interface along with other initial setup requirements using the **setup** command.

Example 15-6 shows how to enable and configure the Command and Control port using the **setup** command.

Example 15-6 **setup** *Command Output*

```
Continue with configuration dialog?[yes]: yes
Enter host name[sensor]: IDSM-2
! The following line assigns the Command and Control port
Enter IP address[10.1.1.2]: 192.168.1.2
Enter netmask[255.255.255.0]: 255.255.255.0
! Following line assigns the default gateway for the IDSM-2 blade
Enter default gateway[10.1.1.1]: 192.168.1.1
Enter telnet-server status[disabled]: enable
Enter web-server port[443]:
```

With this setup, you can log in to IDSM-2 blade using IDM, or you can connect from IDS/IPS MC.

Troubleshooting Steps

Once you have gone through the configuration steps that are outlined in the preceding sections, you should be able to connect to the IDSM-2 blade's Command and Control port using IDM, SSH, IDS/IPS MC, and so on. If you cannot do so, work through the following steps to troubleshoot the issue:

Step 1 Check the Command and Control port statistics on the switch.

Run the following command to find out if the 5-minute output rate is increasing:

```
Cat6509# show intrusion-detection module 4 management-port traffic
```

Example 15-7 shows the traffic flow for Command and Control interface on Native IOS:

Example 15-7 *Finding Out If the Traffic Is Sent to the Command and Control Port of IDSM-2 Blade*

```
Cat6506# show intrusion-detection module 5 management-port traffic
Intrusion-detection module 5 management-port:
! Make sure the line shows the Command & Control port UP
Specified interface is up (connected)line protocol is up
Hardware is C6k 1000Mb 802.3, address is 000e.3879.4961 (bia 000e.3879.4961)
MTU 1500 bytes, BW 1000000 Kbit, DLY 10 usec,
reliability 255/255, txload 1/255, rxload 1/255
Encapsulation ARPA, loopback not set
Keepalive set (10 sec)
Unknown duplex, Unknown Speed, media type is unknown
output flow-control is unsupported, input flow-control is unsupported, 1000Mb/s
input flow-control is off, output flow-control is off
Last input never, output 00:00:48, output hang never
Last clearing of "show interface" counters never
```

continues

Example 15-7 *Finding Out If the Traffic Is Sent to the Command and Control Port of IDSM-2 Blade (Continued)*

```
Input queue: 0/2000/0/0 (size/max/drops/flushes); Total output drops: 0
Queueing strategy: fifo
Output queue: 0/40 (size/max)
! Make sure the following rate number increases
5 minute input rate 200 bits/sec, 10 packets/sec
5 minute output rate 300 bits/sec, 5 packets/sec
Cat6506#
```

If the 5-minute output rate is not increasing, the switch is not sending the IDSM traffic at all. Check that your VLANs are correct and that there is not a misconfiguration. Example 15-8 shows how to obtain the state information of the management port on the switch.

Example 15-8 *State Information of the Management Port*

```
Cat6506-A# show intrusion-detection module 5 management-port state
Intrusion-detection module 5 management-port:
Switchport: Enabled
Administrative Mode: dynamic desirable
Operational Mode: static access
Administrative Trunking Encapsulation: negotiate
Operational Trunking Encapsulation: native
Negotiation of Trunking: On
! The port is part of VLAN 150
Access Mode VLAN: 150 (default)
Trunking Native Mode VLAN: 150 (default)
Trunking VLANs Enabled: ALL
Pruning VLANs Enabled: 1-249,251-1001
Vlans allowed on trunk:150
Vlans allowed and active in management domain:150
Vlans in spanning tree forwarding state and not pruned: 150
Access Vlan = 150
Cat6506#
```

If you are running CatOS, execute **show vlan vlan_number** and **show port module_number/2** to determine the statistics and VLAN configuration of the Command and Control port.

Step 2 Check to see if the Command and Control port is enabled on the IDSM-2 blade. Verify that by executing the command shown in Example 15-9.

Example 15-9 *Verification of Command and Control Interface on the IDSM-2 Blade*

```
IDSM-2# show interfaces gigabitEthernet0/2
MAC statistics from interface GigabitEthernet0/2
   Media Type = backplane
! The link status should show up
   Link Status = Up
   Link Speed = Auto_1000
   Link Duplex = Auto_Full
! Make sure following two lines show some positive number and should increment
```

Example 15-9 *Verification of Command and Control Interface on the IDSM-2 Blade (Continued)*

```
! over time
   Total Packets Received = 410270
   Total Bytes Received = 33465114
   Total Multicast Packets Received = 1
   Total Receive Errors = 0
   Total Receive FIFO Overruns = 0
   Total Packets Transmitted = 64400
   Total Bytes Transmitted = 6813106
   Total Transmit Errors = 0
   Total Transmit FIFO Overruns = 0
IDSM-2#
```

If the Command and Control interface shows that the Command and Control port is down, run the **setup** command to enable the Command and Control port.

Step 3 Wrong VLAN number and VLAN routing issues.

Be sure that the Command and Control ports are in the correct VLAN. If the management software or the Security Monitor is in a different VLAN, be sure you have the Inter-VLAN routing configured. For example, if you have Command and Control interface on VLAN 150, and the Management software server is on VLAN 160, then you must have routing between VLAN 150 and 160.

Failing to Get Traffic from the Switch with Promiscuous Mode

There are two ports on the IDSM-2 blade that can be used to capture the traffic for analysis. On the switch side, you need to configure to send the packets to the IDSM-2 blade, and on the IDSM-2 blade, you must ensure that these sniffing ports are enabled and running. The sections that follow explain how to configure and troubleshoot the issues when IDSM-2 is running in Promiscuous mode.

Configuration Steps

The Promiscuous mode configuration for IDSM-2 involves configuring the switch to redirect the packets to the IDSM-2 blade, and on IDSM-2 to receive the packets from the switch. There are multiple options available to redirect the packets from the switch to the IDSM-2 blade:

- SPAN Configuration on Switch running Native IOS
- VACL Configuration on Switch running Native IOS
- Multilayer Switching (MLS) IP IDS Configuration on Switch running Native IOS
- SPAN Configuration on Switch running CatOS

- VACL Configuration on Switch running CatOS
- MLS IP IDS Configuration on Switch running CatOS
- IDSM-2 Blade Configuration

SPAN Configuration on Switch Running Native IOS

Work through the following steps to configure SPAN on the switch running Native IOS:

Step 1 Log in to the switch and enter into global configuration mode:

```
Cat6506# configure terminal
```

Step 2 Configure the source interfaces for the monitor session with the following command:

```
Cat6506(config)# monitor session (session_number) source interface
interface/port_number [, | - | rx | tx | both]
```

The following command captures the traffic in both directions on interface GigabitEthernet2/10:

```
Cat6506(config)# monitor session 1 source interface GigabitEthernet2/10
both
```

You can also source the VLAN with the following command:

```
Cat6506(config)# monitor session (session_number) source vlan
vlan_number [, | - | rx | tx | both]
```

Step 3 Configure the IDSM-2 data port (port 1 or 2 or both) as a SPAN destination with the following command:

```
monitor session (session_number) destination intrusion-detection-module
module_number data-port data_port_number
```

The following command defines data-port 1 as the destination port for SPAN:

```
Cat6506(config)# monitor session 1 destination intrusion-detection-
module 5 data-port 1
```

To disable the monitor session, use the **no monitor session session_number** command.

Step 4 To filter the SPAN session so that only certain VLANs are seen from switch port trunks, use the following command:

```
monitor session (session_number) {filter vlan {vlan_ID} [, | - ]}
```

The following command shows that the switch will span only VLAN 140 traffic on port GigabitEthernet2/10, and forward to the IDSM-2 blade.

```
Cat6506(config)# monitor session 1 filter vlan 140
```

Step 5 Exit configuration mode and monitor the sessions using the following command:

```
show monitor session session_number
```

Example 15-10 *Output of the* **show monitor** *command*

```
Cat6506# show monitor session 1
    Session 1
    ---------
    Type                    : Local Session
    Source Ports            :
        Both                : Gi2/10
    Destination Ports       : intrusion-detection-module 5 data-port 1
Cat6506#
```

Step 6 Configuring a Source Port/VLAN

You must define a source port or VLAN to capture the traffic that you want to send to the IDSM-2 module. You can use the following syntax to configure the source port or VLAN:

```
monitor session session source {{interface type} | {{vlan type} [rx |
tx | both]} | {remote vlan rspan-vlan-id}}
```

VACL Configuration on Switch Running Native IOS

If you do not want to configure SPAN as described in the previous section, use the steps that follow to configure the switch using Native IOS mode (for the 7600 and 6500 running native mode):

Step 1 Verify that the IOS version supports the IDSM-2.

Step 2 Place the Management Interface on the IDSM-2 into a VLAN with the following command:

```
intrusion-detection module module_number management-port access-vlan
number
```

Step 3 The command that follows shows how to assign the management interface to VLAN 120:

```
cat6506(config)#intrusion-detection module 5 management-port access-
vlan 120
```

Step 4 Create an ACL that will match the traffic that you want to send (capture) to the blade. In the example that follows, you want to match all Web traffic destined to the 10.1.1.0 network and send it to the IDSM. All other traffic should be passed normally. If access-list 151 is not created, all other traffic will be dropped.

```
cat6506(config)#access-list 150 permit tcp any 10.1.1.0 0.0.0.255
eq 80
cat6506(config)#access-list 151 permit ip any any
```

Step 5 Configure the router to capture the traffic in access-list 150 and pass the traffic in access-list 151, using a VLAN access-map as shown in Example 15-11:

Example 15-11 *Configuring ACL to Define Interesting Traffic to be Captured*

```
cat6506(config)#vlan access-map IDSM-2 10
cat6506(config-access-map)#match ip address 150
cat6506(config-access-map)#action forward capture
cat6506(config-access-map)#vlan access-map IDSM-2 20
cat6506(config-access-map)#match ip address 151
cat6506(config-access-map)#action forward
```

Step 6 Instruct the switch on which VLANs should be applied to the ACLs created earlier using the **vlan filter** command as follows:

```
vlan filter map_name vlan-list vlan_list
```

The example that follows shows VLANs 1-10, 36, and 124 tied to the access-list.

```
cat6506(config)#vlan filter IDSM-2 vlan-list 1-10,36,124
```

Step 7 Configure the IDSM-2 to receive capture packets on the specified VLANs. This tells the IDSM-2's sensing port to add these VLANs to the trunk with the following command:

```
intrusion-detection module module_number data-port data_port_number
capture allowed-vlan capture_vlans
```

Following is an example:

```
cat6506(config)#intrusion-detection module 5 data-port 1 capture
allowed-vlan 1-10,36,124
```

Step 8 Finally, you must enable the IDSM-2's sensing port to receive packets by using the command:

```
intrusion-detection module module_number data-port data_port_number
capture
```

Following is an example of how to use the command:

```
cat6506(config)#intrusion-detection module 5 data-port 1 capture
```

Example 15-12 shows the complete configuration that is configured with the previous steps.

Example 15-12 *Complete Configuration with VACL on Native IOS*

```
intrusion-detection module 6 management-port access-vlan 36
intrusion-detection module 6 data-port 1 capture
intrusion-detection module 6 data-port 1 capture allowed-vlan 1-10,36,124
!
vlan access-map IDSM-2 10
```

Example 15-12 *Complete Configuration with VACL on Native IOS (Continued)*

```
match ip address 150
action forward capture
vlan access-map IDSM-2 20
match ip address 151
action forward
!
vlan filter IDSM-2 vlan-list 1-10,36,124
!
access-list 150 permit tcp any 10.1.1.0 0.0.0.255
access-list 151 permit ip any any
```

NOTE If more than one module is inserted into the chassis, you might want to segregate which traffic goes to which module. This is done by limiting the VLANs specified in Step 5 with the **intrusion-detection module** statement. You should not do this by restricting the VLANS in the **vlan filter** command. All traffic to be sent to any IDSM-2 must be marked to be captured using the **vlan access-map** AND **vlan filter**, and then traffic is limited by VLAN when sent to the module. Note that the **vlan filter** matches on the ingress VLAN the packets that come in on it. If it fails, delete it all and re-enter it.

MLS IP IDS Configuration on Switch Running Native IOS

When you are using ports as router interfaces rather than switch ports, you cannot apply a VACL, as there is no VLAN. You can use the **mls ip ids** command to designate which packets will be captured. Packets that are permitted by the ACL will be captured. Those denied by the ACL will not be captured. The permit/deny parameter does not affect whether a packet is forwarded to destination ports. Packets coming into that router interface are checked against the IPS ACL to determine if they should be captured.

Work through the following steps to configure **mls ip ids** command to capture IDS traffic:

Step 1 Go into the global configuration mode as follows:

```
Cat6k# configure terminal
```

Step 2 Configure an ACL to designate which packets will be captured with the following command:

```
Cat6k(config)# ip access-list extended MY_ACL
```

Step 3 Select the interface that carries the packets to be captured:

```
Cat6k(config)# interface interface_name
```

Step 4 Specify the capture VLANs with the following command:

```
Cat6k(config)# intrusion-detection module module_number data-port
data_port_number capture allowed-vlan capture_vlans
```

The following command captures VLAN 150 traffic and sends it to the data-port 1:

```
Cat6k(config)# intrusion-detection module 5 data-port 1 capture
allowed-vlan 150
```

Step 5 Apply the ACL created in Step 2 to the interface selected in Step 3:

```
Cat6k(config-if)# mls ip ids MY_ACL
```

NOTE For IDSM-2 to capture all packets marked by the **mls ip ids** command, data port 1 or data port 2 of IDSM-2 must be a member of all VLANs to which those packets are routed.

SPAN Configuration on Switch Running CatOS

To configure a SPAN session in CatOS, the SPAN source port or source VLAN and the SPAN destination port must be identified. Then for the SPAN source port or VLAN, the direction of spanned traffic must be defined (that is, receive traffic only, transmit traffic only, or both receive and transmit traffic). The syntax for the SPAN configuration in CatOS is as follows:

```
set span {src_mod/src_ports | src_vlans | sc0} {dest_mod/dest_port}[rx | tx | both]
[inpkts {enable | disable}] [learning {enable | disable}][multicast {enable |
disable}][filter vlans...] [create]
```

The destination port can either be slot/7 or slot/8. If the IDSM-2 is seated in slot 5, the destination SPAN port will be port 4/7 or 4/8. Example 15-13 shows the setting up of a SPAN session to destination port 5/7.

Example 15-13 *A Simple SPAN Session Based on Source Port*

```
Console> (enable) set span 3/12 5/7
Enabled monitoring of Port 3/12 transmit/receive traffic by Port 5/7
```

This example simply sets up port 3/12 as the SPAN source port and port 5/7 as the SPAN destination port. This form of the command creates a SPAN session that sends a copy of both Receive and Transmit traffic. This assumes that the IDSM-2 is in slot 5.

Example 15-14 shows how to send a copy of transmit-only traffic from VLAN 100 to the SPAN destination port 5/7 (assuming the IDSM-2 is in slot 5).

Example 15-14 *Simple SPAN Session Based on Source VLAN*

```
Console> (enable) set span 100 5/7 tx
SPAN destination port incoming packets enabled.
Enabled monitoring of VLAN 100 transmit traffic by Port 5/7
Console> (enable)
```

After you configure the SPAN on CatOS, to verify SPAN configuration on CatOS, use the command shown in Example 15-15.

Example 15-15 *The SPAN Sessions on CatOS*

```
cat6k> (enable) show span

Destination      : Port 5/7
Admin Source     : VLAN 100
Oper Source      : Port 3/12
Direction        : receive
Incoming Packets: disabled
Learning         : enabled
Multicast        : enabled
Filter           : -

Session Number  : 1

Total local span sessions:  1
cat6k> (enable)
```

To disable the SPAN session that is sending traffic to IDSM-2, use the command shown in Example 15-16:

Example 15-16 *Disabling a SPAN Session*

```
cat6k> (enable) set span disable session 1
This command will disable your span session.
Do you want to continue (y/n) [n]? y
Disabled Port 13/7 to monitor receive traffic of VLAN 650
cat6k> (enable)
```

NOTE Both ports slot/7 and slot/8 can be used to capture traffic. However, in the 5.0 release, the total amount of traffic is limited to a maximum of about 600 Mbps, regardless of which combinations of ports are used. As there is no advantage to using both ports to capture traffic over using just a single port, we recommend using just a single port. If both ports slot/7 and slot/8 are used to capture traffic, these ports should be configured to monitor different VLANs. Otherwise, the capture traffic will be duplicated.

VACL Configuration on Switch Running CatOS

If you decide to configure VACL instead of SPAN, work through the following steps to configure VACL:

Step 1 Configure the VACL to define which traffic you want to capture with the following command:

```
set security acl ip acl_name permit ip [permit (...) | deny (...)]
capture
```

Only permitted traffic can be captured. To permit traffic but not capture it, do not use the **capture** keyword. The following example captures all http traffic destined to host 10.1.1.1:

```
Console> (enable) set security acl ip filter_http permit ip any host
10.1.1.1 capture
filter_http editbuffer modified. Use 'commit' command to apply changes.
Console> (enable)
```

The **capture** keyword at the end of the statement is used to indicate that this classified traffic should be directed to the port that is configured as the capture port.

Step 2 Commit the VACL defined in the previous step to hardware. This process writes the VACL into Ternary Content Addressable Memory (TCAMs) on the PFC. TCAMs are a specialized piece of memory designed to provide high-speed lookups of their contents. The command to commit a VACL to memory is as follows:

```
Console> (enable) commit security acl filter_http
ACL commit in progress.
ACL filter_http successfully committed.
Console> (enable)
```

Step 3 Map the VACL to the specific port (or VLAN) where the traffic is to be inspected. The following command maps the VACL to VLAN 55:

```
Console> (enable) commit security acl map filter_http 55
Mapping in progress.
VLAN 55 successfully mapped to ACL filter_http.
Console> (enable)
```

Step 4 Finally, define the capture port (either slot/7 or slot/8). The following command shows how to define the capture port (in this case 5/7, as the IDSM-2 module is slot 7).

```
Console> (enable) set security acl capture-ports 5/7
Successfully set the following ports to capture ACL traffic:.
5/7
Console> (enable)
```

Step 5 By default, the capture port is a trunk for all VLANs. So, to restrict the traffic for a specific VLAN, clear and reset the trunk. For example, capture port 7 could be set to be a trunk for only VLANs 2-5 using the following CatOS commands:

```
Console> (enable) clear trunk 5/7 1-4096
Console> (enable) set trunk 5/7 2-5
```

The process is now complete, and all traffic sourced from any host destined to host 10.1.1.1 in VLAN 55 will be copied and forwarded to the IDSM-2 (assuming in this example it is in slot 5) for monitoring.

MLS IP IDS Configuration on a Switch Running CatOS

If you are running the Cisco IOS Firewall on the MSFC, you cannot use VACLs to capture traffic for IDSM-2. This is because you cannot apply VACLs to a VLAN in which you have applied an IP inspect rule for the Cisco IOS Firewall. However, you can use the **mls ip ids** command to designate which packets need to be captured. Packets that are permitted by the ACL are captured. Those denied by the ACL are not captured. The permit/deny parameter does not affect whether a packet is forwarded to destination ports. Packets coming into that router interface are checked against the IPS ACL to determine if they should be captured. The **mls ip ids** command is applied as part of the MSFC configuration instead of the supervisor configuration. The **mls ip ids** command only captures incoming traffic. You will need to use the **mls ip ids** command on both the client-side router interface and server-side router interface, so that both directions of the connection will be captured.

Work through the following configuration to use the **mls ip ids** command to capture IPS traffic:

Step 1 Log in to the MSFC and configure an ACL to designate which packets will be captured with the following command:

```
msfc(config)# ip access-list extended word
```

Step 2 Select the interface that carries the packets to be captured with the following command:

```
msfc(config)# interface interface_name
```

Step 3 Apply the ACL created in Step 1 to the interface selected in Step 2:

```
msfc(config-if)# mls ip ids word
```

Step 4 Exit from MSFC to go to the switch.

Step 5 Add the IDSM-2 monitoring port (port 7 or 8) to the VACL capture list with the following command:

```
cat6k> (enable) set security acl capture module_number/port_number
```

NOTE For IDSM-2 to capture all packets marked by the **mls ip ids** command, port 7 or 8 of IDSM-2 must be members of all VLANs to which those packets are routed.

IDSM-2 Blade Configuration

Once you configure the switch to send the packets to the sniffing interface of the IDSM-2 blade, you need to enable the sniffing port on the IDSM-2 blade. The best way to enable the sniffing port is to run the setup and add the sniffing port for Promiscuous mode as shown in Example 15-17.

Example 15-17 *Enabling a Sniffing Port When Running Promiscuous Mode*

```
IDSM-2#setup
! The additional output has been removed. Only the relevant information on how to enable
! the sniffing interfaces are added here
Add Promiscuous interfaces?[no]:
Interface[]: GigabitEthernet0/7
Interface[]: GigabitEthernet0/8
Interface[]:
Add Inline pairs?[no]:
No changes were made to the configuration.
IDSM-2#
```

Troubleshooting Steps

Work through the following steps to troubleshoot the issue if the IDSM-2 is not receiving the traffic from the switch:

Step 1 Verify on the switch whether the switch is sending any traffic to the data port with the command as shown in Example 15-18:

Example 15-18 *The Output of the Data-port 1 Running Native IOS on the Switch*

```
Cat6506#show intrusion-detection module 5 data-port 1 traffic
Intrusion-detection module 5 data-port 1:

Specified interface is up line protocol is up (monitoring)
  Hardware is C6k 1000Mb 802.3, address is 0003.feac.cb50 (bia 0003.feac.cb50)
  MTU 1500 bytes, BW 1000000 Kbit, DLY 10 usec,
     reliability 255/255, txload 1/255, rxload 1/255
  Encapsulation ARPA, loopback not set
  Keepalive set (10 sec)
  Full-duplex, 1000Mb/s
  input flow-control is off, output flow-control is unsupported
  Last input 00:00:31, output 2d21h, output hang never
  Last clearing of "show interface" counters never
  Input queue: 0/2000/0/0 (size/max/drops/flushes); Total output drops: 0
  Queueing strategy: fifo
  Output queue: 0/40 (size/max)
! You need to make sure these counters are increasing
  5 minute input rate 1000 bits/sec, 40 packets/sec
  5 minute output rate 1000 bits/sec, 20 packets/sec
     4993 packets input, 1929584 bytes, 0 no buffer
     Received 4993 broadcasts, 0 runts, 0 giants, 0 throttles
     0 input errors, 0 CRC, 0 frame, 0 overrun, 0 ignored
     0 input packets with dribble condition detected
     526773 packets output, 90662579 bytes, 0 underruns
     0 output errors, 0 collisions, 3 interface resets
     0 babbles, 0 late collision, 0 deferred
     0 lost carrier, 0 no carrier
     0 output buffer failures, 0 output buffers swapped out
cat6506#
```

This should show a 5-minute output rate increasing. If it does not, the switch is not sending the IDSM traffic at all. Check that your VLANs are correct and that there is no misconfiguration.

Step 2 Check to see if the switch SPAN/VACL misconfigured.

Revise the switch configuration again and verify that the switch is configured correctly to forward the traffic to the data port of the IDSM-2 blade. Check to see if the Remote SPAN (RSPAN) that is needed by SPAN is configured (refer to Chapter 14, "Troubleshooting Cisco Intrusion Prevention System" for more details). Also be sure to use **mls ip ids** if and when needed, instead of VACL.

Step 3 Be sure that the sensor's sniffing interface is enabled and receiving traffic.

If the switch configuration is correct and sending traffic to the IDSM-2 blade, Be sure the sniffing port on the IDSM-2 blade is enabled. From the command line of the IDSM-2, execute a **show interfaces** command and be sure that the sniffing ports are receiving packets, as shown in Example 15-19.

Example 15-19 *The* **show interfaces** *Output on IDSM-2.*

```
sensor1-23# show interfaces
Interface Statistics
! Some additional output is removed
MAC statistics from interface GigabitEthernet0/7
   Media Type = backplane
   Missed Packet Percentage = 0
! Make sure the link status is up
   Link Status = Up
   Link Speed = Auto_1000
   Link Duplex = Auto_Full
! Make sure you are receiving traffic and it's increasing
   Total Packets Received = 527406
   Total Bytes Received = 90737051
   Total Multicast Packets Received = 81228
   Total Broadcast Packets Received = 25554
   Total Jumbo Packets Received = 0
   Total Undersize Packets Received = 0
   Total Receive Errors = 0
   Total Receive FIFO Overruns = 0
   Total Packets Transmitted = 5003
   Total Bytes Transmitted = 1933687
   Total Multicast Packets Transmitted = 5003
   Total Broadcast Packets Transmitted = 0
   Total Jumbo Packets Transmitted = 0
   Total Undersize Packets Transmitted = 0
   Total Transmit Errors = 0
   Total Transmit FIFO Overruns = 0
MAC statistics from interface GigabitEthernet0/8
   Media Type = backplane
! Output is removed
  Total Transmit FIFO Overruns = 0
IDSM-2#
```

You should see that traffic is being received.

Step 4 If you do not see any packets in the previous step, it is likely that the traffic is not spanned correctly, or that the interface on the IDSM-2 is down. In that case, revise your switch configuration. Also, use the **show interface** command to check that the interface of the sniffing ports (Gig 0/7 and/or Gig 0/8) is up.

Step 5 Allow all VLANs (1-4094) on the list of allowed VLANs to be captured by the IDSM-2 data port to see if routing between VLANs is preventing the traffic from being captured. VLAN routing can affect VACL capture. For the routed traffic, the capture ports transmit the packets only after they are Layer 3 switched. The packets are transmitted out of a port only if the output VLAN of the Layer 3-switched flow is the same as the capture port VLAN. For example, assume that you have flows from VLAN 10 to VLAN 20, and you add a VACL on one of the VLANs permitting these flows. Then you specify a capture port. This traffic is transmitted from the capture port only if it belongs to VLAN 20, or if the port is a trunk carrying VLAN 20. If the capture port is in VLAN 10, it does not transmit any traffic. Whether a capture port transmits the traffic or not is independent of the VLAN on which you placed the VACL.

If you want to capture the traffic from one VLAN going to many VLANs, the capture port has to be a trunk carrying all the output VLANs.

For the bridged traffic, because all the traffic remains in the same VLAN, ensure that the capture port is in the same VLAN as the bridged traffic.

Step 6 Configure VACL capture or span/monitor to a sniffer machine so that another machine (non-IDSM-2) gets the traffic. Look at the traffic arriving on that machine to see if it's getting the traffic. This will independently verify if it's a switch or an IDSM-2 issue.

Step 7 Loose ribbon cable on IDSM-2.

If the IDSM-2 is producing alerts and stops suddenly, this could be because the ribbon cable between the XL (Falcon) Card and the Komodo+ motherboard has become loose. For additional details refer to Partner Field Notice 52816, at the following link: http://www.cisco.com/en/US/partner/products/sw/securesw/ps2113/products_field_notice09186a0080234f9c.shtml

This could be observed after a module has been moved or shipped.

Issues with Inline Mode

The configuration steps on the IDSM-2 are the same for Inline as in Appliance, which is explained in detail in Chapter 14. So, the same information will not be repeated here.

However, as the switch has only two sniffing ports, only one Inline pair configuration is possible. For the same reason, you cannot configure both Inline and Promiscuous mode.

Not Generating Events Issues

If the IDSM-2 is receiving the traffic, which is verified but unable to generate any events, work through the following steps to troubleshoot this issue:

Step 1 Check to see if you are getting events. Verify if you are not receiving any events on the IDSM-2 blade by executing the following command:

```
sensor# show events past 00:30:00
```

This will show all the events in the past 30 minutes.

Step 2 IDSM is getting traffic but is not triggering any events.

If you are receiving the traffic to match the triggering criteria for the signature, you may not receive any events even though the IDSM-2 may be functioning as it is configured to. To test whether the IDSM-2 is functioning properly or not, you can enable the ICMP signatures and send ping across the sensing interface to see if there are any event triggers.

Step 3 The sensing interfaces on the IDSM could be down. Ensure that they are up and that they are assigned to an interface group.

Step 4 The IDS/IPS receives events for a while. But then it stops receiving traffic.

Even though the switch is sending traffic, the virtual sensor may not be processing the traffic. This can be verified by using the **show statistics virtual-sensor** command. This can be because of the sensorApp loop when IP logging on a dual processor. To work around the problem, work through the steps that follow for the IDSM-2 to operate in single mode:

(a) Log in to the service account and become root.

(b) Stop the cids applications by using the command "**/etc/init.d/cids stop**."

(c) Edit the **mainApp.conf** configuration file: "vi /usr/cids/idsRoot/etc/mainApp.conf"

(d) Add the following lines after the AnalysisEngine section:

Arg01=-t

Arg02=single

(e) Start the cids applications by using the command "**/etc/init.d/cids start**."

Step 5 A filter is blocking the events.

Be sure there is no filter that is applied to the sensor that could be blocking the events. If a filter is applied and you execute a **show conf**, you will see the following:

```
EventFilter
Filters DestAddrs * Exception False SIGID * SourceAddrs * SubSig *
```

From the IDM on the sensor (https://sensorip), log in, and go to **Configuration>Sensing Engine>Alarm Channel Configuration>Event filters** and delete any event filters that you see. These could be filtering out your events.

TCP Reset Issues

TCP reset concept, configuration, and troubleshooting are identical on the IDSM-2 blade and on Appliance. So, the same discussion is not repeated in this section. However, some specific issues are unique to IDSM-2 blade.

Unlike Sensor Appliances, IDSM-2 has a separate interface for TCP reset. Port 1 is used as the TCP reset interface. The IDSM-2 has a specific TCP reset interface because it cannot send TCP resets on its sensing ports.

If you have reset problems with the IDSM-2, try the following:

- If the sensing ports are access ports (a single VLAN), you need to configure the reset port to be in the same VLAN.
- If the sensing ports are dot1q trunk ports (multi-VLAN), the sensing ports and reset port all must have the same native VLAN, and the reset port must trunk all the VLANs being trunked by both the sensing ports.

Case Study

This section examines the following four case studies, which deal with the installation and upgrade of IDSM-2 software:

- How to re-image the IDSM-2 with system image
- How to upgrade the maintenance partition
- How to upgrade the signature/service packs/minor/major software upgrades
- How to upgrade the IDSM-2 blade from IDSM 4.x to 5.x

How to Re-image the IDSM-2 with System Image

If your application partition in the sensor is corrupted or if you need to recover the password, use the System Image to completely re-image the IDSM-2 sensor. Re-imaging

System Image will reformat the storage media and load both a new application image and a new recovery image. The current sensor configuration and all log files will be lost. Hence, the System Image file should not be used to upgrade the current software. For example, 5.0(2) System Image should not be used to upgrade the current software version to 5.0(2) if you want to maintain your current configuration settings. To upgrade from 5.0(1), use the 5.0(2) Service Pack file.

As of the writing of this book, the latest service pack is 5.0(2), and the system file is also 5.0(2). So, if you intend to upgrade to the latest service pack, you should not use the System Image; instead, use the service pack. Also, to upgrade your IDSM-2 blade from 4.x to IPS 5.x, install the 5.0(1) Major Update file, followed by the 5.0(2) Service Pack file, which is explained in the next case study.

The 5.0(1) Major Update file and 5.0(2) Service Pack file can both be found at the following URL:

http://www.cisco.com/cgi-bin/tablebuild.pl/ips5

In this case study, we explain the procedure for upgrading the system file. Work through the following steps to re-image IDSM-2 with a switch that runs Native IOS or CatOS. As discussed before, it's important to understand that all information in the application will be lost when you use the following procedure:

Step 1 Download the system file from the following location and put this in an FTP server:

http://www.cisco.com/cgi-bin/tablebuild.pl/ips5-cat6500-IDSM-2-sys

Step 2 Boot the IDSM-2 to the Maintenance Partition. To do this, in Native IOS, execute switch command **hw-module module** *x* **reset cf:1** where *x* stands for the slot number and **cf** stands for **compact flash**. If a problem is encountered using **cf:1**, try **hdd:2** as an alternative. Example 15-20 shows how to reset the module to maintenance partition.

Example 15-20 *Resetting the Module to Maintenance Partition*

```
Cat6506# hw-module module 5 reset cf:1
Device BOOT variable for reset =
Warning: Device list is not verified.
Proceed with reload of module? [confirm]y
% reset issued for module 5
!Rest of the output is suppressed.
Cat6506#
```

If you are running CatOS on the switch, use the switch command **reset** *x* **hdd:2**. If a problem is encountered using **hdd:2**, try to use **cf:1** as an alternative.

Step 3 Check that the IDSM-2 comes on line with the use of the switch command **show module** *x*. Be sure that the IDSM-2 software version has **m** located at the end and that the status is **OK**.

Step 4 Connect to the IDSM-2 now that it has booted up into the maintenance partition. Use the switch command **session slot** *x* **processor 1**. Use the username/password of **guest/cisco**.

```
Cat6506#session slot 5 processor 1
The default escape character is Ctrl-^, then x.
You can also type 'exit' at the remote prompt to end the session
Trying 127.0.0.51 ... Open
Cisco Maintenance image
login: guest
Password:
Maintenance image version: 1.3(2)
guest@idsm2.localdomain#
```

In CatOS, connect to the IDSM-2 in the maintenance partition using switch command **session** *x* and use the username/password of **guest/cisco**.

Step 5 Be sure that the IDSM-2 has IP connectivity to the FTP server. Use the command **ping** *ip_address* to verify the connectivity.

Step 6 If the IDSM-2 has IP connectivity, proceed to Step 12. Otherwise go to the next step.

Step 7 Be sure that the Command and Control Interface is configured properly on the switch. Use the command **show run | inc intrusion-detection** as shown in Example 15-21.

Example 15-21 *Verifying Whether the Command and Control Interface Is Configured Correctly on Native IOS*

```
cat6506#show run ¦ include intrusion-detection
intrusion-detection module 5 management-port access-vlan 150
cat6506#
```

If you are running CatOS, be sure that the Command and Control Interface is configured properly on the switch using the command **show port status** *x*/**2** as shown in Example 15-22.

Example 15-22 *Verifying that the Command and Control Interface Is Configured Correctly on CatOS*

```
Cat6509> (enable)show port status 5/2
Port  Name                 Status     Vlan       Duplex Speed Type
----- -------------------- ---------- ---------- ------ ----- ------------
 5/2                       connected  150          full  1000 Intrusion De
Cat6509> (enable)
```

Step 8 Be sure that the communication parameters are configured properly on the IDSM-2 Maintenance Partition executing the command **show ip**.

```
guest@idsm2 -sv-rack.localdomain#show ip
IP address      : 20.1.1.20
```

```
Subnet Mask      : 255.255.255.0
IP Broadcast     : 20.1.1.254
DNS Name         : idsm2.localdomain
Default Gateway  : 20.1.1.1
Nameserver(s)    :
guest@idsm2-sv-rack.localdomain#
```

Step 9 If none of the parameters are set, or if some of them need to be changed, clear them all. Use the command **clear ip**.

```
guest@idsm2.localdomain#clear ip
guest@localhost.localdomain#show ip
IP address       : 0.0.0.0
Subnet Mask      : 0.0.0.0
IP Broadcast     : 0.0.0.0
DNS Name         : localhost.localdomain
Default Gateway  : 0.0.0.0
Nameserver(s)    :
guest@idsm2-sv-rack.localdomain#
```

Step 10 Configure all the parameters to establish IP connectivity from the module to the rest of the network, as shown in Example 15-23.

Example 15-23 *Configuration Steps Required for the Maintenance Partition on IDSM-2 Module*

```
! Configure the IP address and mask information on the IDSM-2 Maintenance
! Partition. Use the command ip address ip_address netmask .
guest@localhost.localdomain#ip address 10.1.1.10 255.255.255.0
! Configure the default gateway on the IDSM-2 Maintenance Partition. Use the
! command ip gateway gateway-address .
guest@localhost.localdomain#ip gateway 10.1.1.1
! Configure the hostname on the IDSM-2 Maintenance Partition. Use the command ip
! host hostname . Although this is not necessary, it does help to identify the
! device since this also sets the prompt.
guest@localhost.localdomain#ip host idsm2
guest@idsm2.localdomain#
! You might possibly need to configure your broadcast address explicitly. Use
! the command ip broadcast broadcast-address . The default setting usually
! suffices.
guest@idsm2.localdomain#ip broadcast 10.1.1.254
guest@idsm2.localdomain#
```

Step 11 Check the IP Connectivity again and be sure you are able to ping to the FTP server.

Step 12 Re-image the IDSM-2 Application Partition. Use the command **upgrade** *ftp-url* **--install**.

```
guest@idsm2.localdomain# upgrade ftp://cisco@10.1.1.40//tftpboot/ WS-
SVC-idsm2 Downloading the image. This may take several minutes...
Password for cisco@10.1.1.40:
```

```
500 'SIZE WS-SVC-idsm2-K9-sys-1.1-a-5.0-2.bin.gz': command not
understood.
ftp://cisco@10.1.1.40//tftpboot/ WS-SVC-idsm2-K9-sys-1.1-a-5.0-
2.bin.gz
 (unknown size)/tmp/upgrade.gz          [|]    65259K
66825226 bytes transferred in 71.40 sec (913.99k/sec)
Upgrade file ftp://cisco@10.1.1.40//tftpboot/ WS-SVC-idsm2-K9-sys-1.1-
a-5.0-2.bin.gz is downloaded.
Upgrading will wipe out the contents on the hard disk.
Do you want to proceed installing it [y|N]: y
Proceeding with upgrade. Please do not interrupt.
If the upgrade is interrupted or fails, boot into
Maintenance image again and restart upgrade.
Creating IDS application image file...
Initializing the hard disk...
Applying the image, this process may take several minutes...
Performing post install, please wait...
Application image upgrade complete. You can boot the image now.
guest@idsm2.localdomain#
```

Step 13 Verify the boot device variable setting for the IDSM-2 with the **show bootvar device module x** command and boot the Application Partition using the Native IOS switch command **hw-module module x reset hdd:1** as shown in Example 15-24.

Example 15-24 *Resetting the Module to Application Partition on Native IOS*

```
Cat6506#show bootvar device module 5
[mod:5 ]:
Cat6506# hw-module module 5 reset hdd:1
Device BOOT variable for reset =
Warning: Device list is not verified.
Proceed with reload of module? [Confirm]y
% reset issued for module 5
!Output is suppressed.
Cat6506#
```

In CatOS, boot the IDSM-2 to the Application Partition. Use the switch command **reset** *x* **hdd:1**. Alternatively, you can use the **reset** command on the IDSM-2 if the boot device variable is set correctly.

Step 14 This step is an alternative to the previous step. To reset the IDSM-2 via the Maintenance Partition CLI, use the command **reset** as follows:

```
guest@idsm2.localdomain#reset
!Output is suppressed.
```

Step 15 Check that the IDSM-2 comes online. Use the switch command **show module** *x*. Be sure that the IDSM-2 software version is an application partition version, for example, 5.0(2), and that the status is OK.

Step 16 Connect to the IDSM-2 now that it has booted up into the application partition. Use the switch command **session slot** *x* **processor 1**. Use the username/password of **cisco/cisco** as shown in Example 15-25.

Example 15-25 *How to Session into the Application Partition*

```
Cat6506#session slot 5 processor 1
The default escape character is Ctrl-^, then x.
You can also type 'exit' at the remote prompt to end the session
Trying 127.0.0.51 ... Open
login: cisco
Password:
You are required to change your password immediately (password aged)
Changing password for cisco
(current) UNIX password:
New password:
Retype new password:
! Output is suppressed.
Cat6506#
```

If you are running CatOS, connect to the IDSM-2 using command **session** *x*. The username/password is the **cisco/cisco**.

Step 17 Configure the IDSM-2 using the **setup** command.

How to Upgrade the Maintenance Partition

The Maintenance Partition is used to re-image the Application Partition as you have seen in the preceding section. As of the writing of this book, the latest version of the Maintenance Partition is **c6svc-mp.2-1-2.bin.gz**. This and the new version of the image can be found at the following location:

http://www.cisco.com/cgi-bin/tablebuild.pl/cat6000-serv-maint

Work through the following steps to upgrade the Maintenance Partition on the IDSM-2 blade:

Step 1 Download the IDSM-2 maintenance partition file from the following location(**c6svc-mp.2-1-2.bin.gz**) to the FTP root directory of a FTP server that is accessible from your IDSM-2:

http://www.cisco.com/cgi-bin/tablebuild.pl/cat6000-serv-maint

Step 2 Session into the Application Partition with **session** *slot_number* if you are running CatOS. If you are running Native IOS, you can log in to Application partition; you can use the **session slot** *slot_number* **processor 1** command.

Step 3 Once you are in Application Partition of IDSM-2 blade, enter into the configuration mode with **configure terminal** command.

Step 4 Upgrade the maintenance partition:

```
IDSM-2# upgrade ftp://user@ftp_server_IP_address/directory_path/c6svc-mp.2-1-1.bin.gz
```

Step 5 You are asked to enter the password to log in to the FTP server and whether you want to continue. Enter the password and type **y** to continue.

Step 6 The maintenance partition file is upgraded.

How to Upgrade the Signature/Service Packs/Minor/Major Software Upgrade

You must have a valid maintenance contract for each IDSM-2 blade to receive and use software upgrades, including signature updates from Cisco.com. Beginning with IPS 5.0, an IPS Subscription Service License is required to install signature updates. As the license is tied to the serial number, you can move the IDSM-2 blade to a different chassis, and you do not need any additional license.

You can request an IPS Subscription Service License for all sensors covered by a maintenance contract at this URL:

http://www.cisco.com/go/license

To manage your maintenance contracts, use the Service Contract Center found at this URL:

http://www.cisco.com/cgi-bin/front.x/scccibdispatch?AppName=ContractAgent

With the initial release of 5.0, the first several signature updates will be released without the license enforcement to allow you time to get your maintenance contracts in order and your sensors licensed.

The upgrading procedure for the Signature, Service Packs, and minor or major releases is the same on the IDSM-2. The procedure that follows discusses the signature upgrade procedure, which also can be used for upgrading the Service Packs/Minor/Major software.

Before installing a new signature update, it is highly recommended that you back up your configuration file to a remote system. Refer to the following link on how to perform a backup using the **copy** command:

http://www.cisco.com/univercd/cc/td/doc/product/iaabu/csids/csids11/cmdref/crcmds.htm#wp458440

CAUTION Do not reboot the sensor during the installation process. Doing so will leave the IDSM-2 blade in an unknown state and may require that the IDSM-2 be re-imaged.

The procedure explained in the following steps is taken from the ReadMe file of the signature upgrade of Signature S155. To install the version S155 signature update on a 5.0(1) or 5.0(2) IDSM-2, follow these steps:

Step 1 Download the binary file IPS-sig-S166-minreq-5.0-1.pkg to an FTP, SCP, HTTP, or HTTPS server on your network from:

http://www.cisco.com/cgi-bin/tablebuild.pl/ips5-sigup

You must be sure to preserve the original file name.

For the Service Packs, minor and major releases, go to the following link:

http://www.cisco.com/cgi-bin/tablebuild.pl/ips5

Step 2 Log in to the IPS CLI using an account with administrator privileges.

Step 3 Type the following command to enter Configuration mode:

```
IDSM-2# configure terminal
```

Step 4 Execute the **upgrade** command by typing the following:

```
upgrade [URL]/IPS-sig-S166-minreq-5.0-1.pkg
```

Where the [URL] is a uniform resource locator pointing to where the signature update package is located. For example, to retrieve the update via FTP, type the following:

```
IDSM-2(config)#upgrade ftp://<username>@<ip-address>//<directory>/IPS-
sig-S166-minreq-5.0-1.pkg
```

The available transport methods are: SCP, FTP, HTTP, or HTTPS.

Step 5 Enter the required password when prompted.

Step 6 To complete the upgrade, type **yes** when prompted.

To uninstall the version S166 signature update on a 5.0(1) or 5.0(2) sensor and return the sensor to its previous state, follow these steps:

Step 1 Log in to the CLI using an account with administrator privileges.

Step 2 Type the following command to enter Configuration mode:

```
IDSM-2#configure terminal
```

Step 3 Type the following command to start the downgrade:

```
IDSM-2(config)#downgrade
```

NOTE The downgrade may take a long time to complete depending on the configuration of the sensor and the amount of traffic the sensor is processing. Do not reboot the sensor while the signature update is occurring, as the sensor may be left in an unknown state requiring the sensor to be re-imaged. For the major upgrade, you cannot downgrade to the earlier version. For example, you cannot downgrade from 5.0(1) to the 4.x version.

How to Upgrade the IDSM-2 Blade from IDSM 4.x to 5.x

Your IDSM-2 blade must be upgraded to the version 4.1(1) S47 or later before you can apply the 5.0(1) S149 major (**IPS-K9-maj-5.0-1-S149.rpm.pkg**) update.

To determine the current sensor version, log in to the CLI and type the **show version** command.

Before you upgrade your IDSM-2 blade to Cisco IPS version 5.0, be sure you have installed Maintenance version 2.1(2) on IDSM-2 (refer to section **How to upgrade the Maintenance Partition** for more details for upgrading Maintenance Partition).

All custom signatures will be renumbered to the 60,000 range in a 4.X to 5.X conversion. After 5.0 has been installed, you cannot **downgrade** to 4.1 using the **downgrade** command. You must reinstall 4.1 from a System Image or a CD. This results in the loss of any configuration settings.

Common Problems and Resolutions

This section examines two commonly encountered issues with IDSM-2.

1 Can I connect a serial cable to IDSM-2 blade?

Answer: You can connect a serial cable directly to the serial console port on IDSM-2. This lets you bypass the switch and module network interfaces. This is especially important if you cannot session into the IDSM-2 blade from the switch due to IDSM-2 crash.

Work through the following steps to connect a serial cable to IDSM-2:

Step 1 Locate the two RJ-45 ports on IDSM-2.

You can find them approximately in the center of the motherboard. If you are facing the module faceplate, the RJ-45 port on the right is the serial console port.

Step 2 Connect a straight-through cable to the right port on IDSM-2, and then connect the other end of the cable to a terminal server port.

Step 3 Configure the terminal server port to 19200 baud, 8 bits, no parity.

You can now log directly in to IDSM-2.

Note Connecting a serial cable to IDSM-2 works only if there is no module located above IDSM-2 in the switch chassis. This is because the cable has to come out through the front of the chassis.

2 Is it possible to use both Inline and Promiscuous mode at the same time?

Answer: As there are only two interfaces for sniffing (port mod/7 and mod/8), you can either configure Inline or Promiscuous mode.

3 Should I configure VACL or SPAN? Which one is preferred?

Answer: A common question asked when implementing the IDSM-2 is whether to use the SPAN or VACL Capture method of copying and forwarding traffic. The answer is "It depends." Normally, the preferred method is to use VACL Capture because it performs the following functions:

- Filters out specific traffic that should be inspected by the IDSM-2.
- Reduces the amount of unnecessary traffic that the IDSM-2 needs to process.
- Compares the limit of 2 receive SPAN sessions or 4 Tx sessions per Catalyst 6500 chassis with the ability to define a VACL capture across 4096 VLANs (each with a capture port). This means that the VACL option provides more flexibility in copying and sending traffic from more ports and/or VLANs.

However, there are times when SPAN might be more applicable, as creating a SPAN session is easier and is only a one-stage configuration process (two for Supervisor IOS). Ultimately, you choose what is more practical and appropriate for your setup.

4 How can I configure time on the IDSM-2 module?

Answer: While the IDS Sensor Appliance can be configured to use either its internal clock or Network Time Protocol (NTP), the module can be configured to use either the switch's time or NTP only. The module cannot be configured to use an internal clock. Therefore, there is no option to set the clock time in the module's CLI. By default, the module is configured to use the switch's time. So be sure that the time zone and summertime settings are correct on both the switch and the module, and that the clock setting is correct on the switch.

5 How can I recover other users' passwords if Administrator Username/Password is known?

Answer: If a password for an administrator account is known, you can reset the other user passwords. For example, if you have two users configured on the IDSM-2 named cisco and admin, and you lost the password for the user cisco, you can log in to IDSM-2 using the username admin and reset the password as shown in Example 15-26:

Example 15-26 *Resetting the Other User Password When Admin Username/Password Is Known*

```
IDSM-2# configure terminal
! Remove the usernames that you have lost password
IDSM-2(config)#no username cisco
! Define the username with the new password
```

continues

Example 15-26 *Resetting the Other User Password When Admin Username/Password Is Known (Continued)*

```
IDSM-2(config)#username cisco priv admin password 123cisco123
IDSM-2(config)#exit
IDSM-2#exit

[Connection to 127.0.0.51 closed by foreign host]
! Login back to the IDSM-2 to check to see if newly created password is accepted
Cat6506#session slot 5 processor 1
The default escape character is Ctrl-^, then x.
You can also type 'exit' at the remote prompt to end the session
Trying 127.0.0.51 ... Open
login: cisco
Password:
! Output is suppressed.
IDSM-2#
```

6 How can I recover other users' passwords if Service Username/Password is known?

Answer: If you lose all other passwords (including the administrator password), you can reset these lost passwords if you know the service account. For example, assume you have three usernames: cisco, admin, and service. Assume also that you have lost passwords for both cisco and admin. Use the commands shown in Example 15-27 to reset both the cisco and admin users' passwords.

Example 15-27 *Getting into the Service Account to Reset Users' Passwords on IDSM-2*

```
Cat6506#session slot 6 processor 1
The default escape character is Ctrl-^, then x.
You can also type 'exit' at the remote prompt to end the session
Trying 127.0.0.51 ... Open
login: service
Password:
! Output is suppressed.
! Get into root using the same password as service account
bash-2.05a$ su root
Password:
! Resetting the cisco user password
[root@idsm2 service]#passwd cisco
Changing password for user cisco.
New password:
Retype new password:
passwd: all authentication tokens updated successfully.
! Resetting the admin user password
[root@idsm2 service]#passwd admin
Changing password for user cisco.
New password:
Retype new password:
passwd: all authentication tokens updated successfully.
[root@idsm2 service]# exit
bash-2.05a$ exit
logout
```

Example 15-27 *Getting into the Service Account to Reset Users' Passwords on IDSM-2 (Continued)*

```
[Connection to 127.0.0.51 closed by foreign host]
! Log back in and see if you can login using the reset password
Cat6506#session slot 6 processor 1
The default escape character is Ctrl-^, then x.
You can also type 'exit' at the remote prompt to end the session
Trying 127.0.0.51 ... Open
login: cisco
Password:
! Output is suppressed.
IDSM-2#
```

NOTE The root password is the same as the service account's password.

Best Practices

Best Practices for IDS/IPS Sensor that are discussed in Chapter 14, apply to the IDSM-2 blade as well. In addition to the best practices listed there, here are some recommendations for implementing IDSM-2:

- Use VACL instead of SPAN when possible to filter out unnecessary traffic.
- Assign a Command and Control interface to a secured VLAN that is isolated from the rest of the network so that the security policy may be applied to the VLAN to secure the IDSM-2 blade.
- Be mindful of the amount of traffic spanning to the IDSM-2 blade. If the traffic volume crosses the limit that the IDSM-2 blade can handle, the IDSM-2 may become unresponsive or crash.
- Implement AAA on the switch so that IDSM-2 access can be limited for certain users using authorization configuration.

CHAPTER 16

Troubleshooting Cisco IDS Network Module (NM-CIDS)

Intrusion Prevention Systems (IPS) on routers come in two flavors: integrated IPS features, and external network modules called NM-CIDS. As the NM-CIDS uses the same code base as IPS Sensor, all the troubleshooting techniques pertaining to Sensor discussed in Chapter 14, "Troubleshooting Cisco Intrusion Prevention System," are applied here with some minor exceptions (for example, the inline feature of IPS that is supported on IPS Sensor is not supported on NM-CIDS). Hence, this chapter does not repeat the troubleshooting information on IPS operations that are performed on NM-CIDS. Instead the chapter focuses on configuration and troubleshooting of the Cisco IOS Router and NM-CIDS configuration issues. The chapter concludes with Best Practices specifically for NM-CIDS.

Overview of NM-CIDS on the Router

The IDS Network Module (NM-CIDS-K9) that may be installed in a Cisco 2600XM, 2691, 2800, 3660, or 3700 Series chassis can provide up to 45 MBps of full-featured intrusion protection services within the router. The NM-CIDS provides the ability to inspect all traffic traversing the router, to identify unauthorized or malicious activity such as hacker attacks, worms, or denial-of-service attacks, and to terminate this illegitimate traffic to suppress or contain threats. The NM-CIDS leverages the current Cisco IPS sensor technology to expand the IPS support into the branch office routers. Through collaboration with IPsec VPN and Generic Routing Encapsulation (GRE) traffic, this NM-CIDS can allow decryption, tunnel termination, and traffic inspection at the first point of entry into the network—an industry first. Only one NM-CIDS is supported in a given router, but it is not restricted to a specific NM-CIDS slot within the router. Figure 16-1 shows a typical NM-CIDS network setup.

This section discusses the following items pertaining to NM-CIDS in details.

- Software and hardware requirements
- Front panel indicator lights and how to use them
- Slot assignment on the router
- Installing NM-CIDS blade on the router
- Removing NM-CIDS blade from the router
- Ports supported on NM-CIDS

The sections that follow present details on these topics.

Figure 16-1 *NM-CIDS Network Setup*

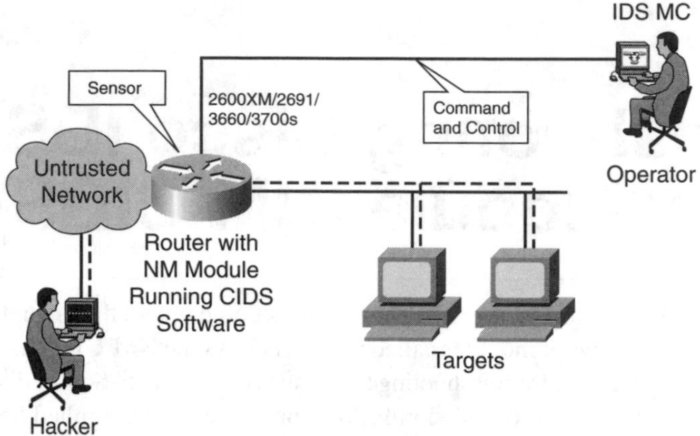

Software and Hardware Requirements

There are specific hardware and software requirements on the router to support NM-CIDS. You must be running one of the IOS versions to insert and use NM-CIDS:

- Cisco IOS software version 12.2(15)ZJ or later
- Cisco IOS software version 12.3(4)T or later

NOTE You must be running IDS software version 4.1 or later on the NM-CIDS.

The few routers that support NM-CIDS are listed in Table 16-1.

Table 16-1 *List of Supported/Unsupported Hardware Platforms (Routers)*

Routers	NM-CIDS
Cisco 2600 series	No
Cisco 2600XM series	Yes
Cisco 2691	Yes
Cisco 3620	No
Cisco 3631	No
Cisco 3640, Cisco 3640A	No
Cisco 3660	Yes
Cisco 3725	Yes
Cisco 3745	Yes
2811, 2821 2851, 3825, and 3845	Yes

Front Panel Indicator Lights and How to Use Them

The NM-IDS has a status indicator and a Shutdown button. Locating different indicators and understanding their meaning is necessary for troubleshooting the hardware and for operational issues. Table 16-2 summarizes the purpose of different indicators that are on the front panel of the NM-CIDS.

Table 16-2 *NM-IDS States as Indicated by the Status Indicator*

Indicators	Description
ACT	There is activity on the fast Ethernet connection.
DISK	There is activity on the IDS hard drive.
EN	NM-CIDS has passed a self-test and is available to the router.
LINK	The Fast Ethernet connection is available to the NM-CIDS.
PWR	Power is available to the NM-CIDS.

Slot Assignment on the Router

The NM-CIDS can be inserted in any available slot on the router, if you have the supported hardware (router) and the IOS software version. Only one NM-CIDS is supported per chassis on the supported router.

Installing NM-CIDS Blade on the Router

You must install the NM-CIDS offline in Cisco 2650XM, 2651XM, and 2961 series routers. To avoid damaging the NM-CIDS, you must turn *off* electrical power and disconnect network cables before you insert the NM-CIDS into a chassis slot or remove the NM-CIDS from a chassis slot.

Cisco 3660 and Cisco 3700 series routers allow you to replace NM-CIDS without switching off the router or affecting the operation of other interfaces. Online insertion and removal (OIR) provides uninterrupted operation to network users, maintains routing information, and ensures session preservation.

Removing NM-CIDS Blade from the Router

The same rule for inserting the NM-CIDS into the router applies for removing the NM-CIDS. Additionally, you must shut down the NM-CIDS before removing it. This is because, unlike other network modules, the NM-CIDS uses a hard-disk drive. Online removal of hard-disk drives without proper shutdown can result in file system corruption and might render the hard-disk drive unusable. The operating system on the NM-CIDS must be shut down in an orderly fashion before it is removed. You can use **service-module ids-sensor slot/0 shutdown** command to shut the module down from the router.

Ports Supported on NM-CIDS

To understand the interfaces supported on the NM-CIDS, look at the high-level hardware architecture of NM-CIDS as depicted in Figure 16-2.

Figure 16-2 *NM-CIDS Hardware Architecture*

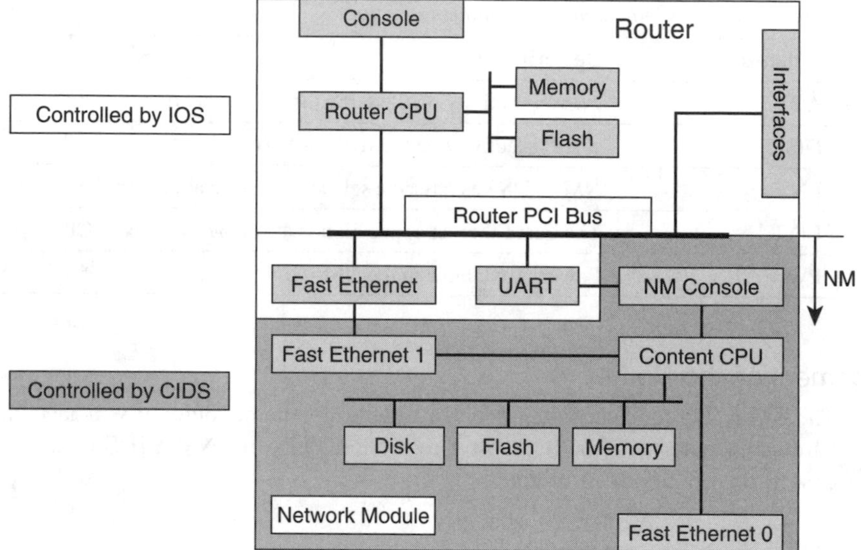

NM-CIDS uses three interfaces to perform the IDS/IPS functions of monitoring and Command and Control (see Figure 16-2) as follows:

- **Command and Control port**—There is one external Fast Ethernet interface on the NM-CIDS that can be used as the Command and Control port. This interface can be connected to a switch, to a hub, or directly to a workstation with IPS management software (for example, IPS MC). As this port is used for blocking, if you want to apply blocking on the same router in which the NM-CIDS is seated, you must ensure that this interface has connectivity with the router. Remember that even though NM-CIDS is seated in the same router (as an external host), this external interface on the NM-CIDS is external to the router.
- **Monitoring Interface**—An internal Fast Ethernet (FE) interface connects to the internal PCI bus on the router's backplane to provide monitoring capability. This internal FE interface provides a 100 Mbps full-duplex interface between the router and NM-CIDS. The IDS Network Module receives a copy of each packet that is to be inspected from the router's Peripheral Component Interconnect (PCI) bus to this internal Fast Ethernet interface. The packets are passed through the internal monitoring interface for classification and processing. The router-side interface for the internal Ethernet segment is known as "*interface IDS-Sensor*" in the Cisco IOS software. This is the only interface associated with the IPS that is visible in the output

of the **show interfaces** command. The router-side internal interface is connected to the router PCI backplane. This interface is used for TCP reset.

- **Console Port**—Unlike standard IDS or IPS Appliance, the NM-CIDS does not have an external console port. The internal Universal Asynchronous Receiver/Transmitter (UART) interface is used to provide the console access. Console access to the NM-CIDS is enabled when you issue a **service-module IDS-sensor <slot>/0 session** command from the IOS command line interface (CLI), or when you initiate a Telnet connection as explained later in this document. The lack of an external console port means that the initial configuration of the Cisco IPS is possible only through the router.

Diagnostic Commands and Tools

Show commands are very useful in troubleshooting issues on the router side. Some of the most important commands are briefly discussed as follows:

- **show version**—Displays the software version information on the router. This verifies whether you are running the supported version on IOS code on the router to support NM-CIDS.
- **show running-config**—Provides the current configuration of the router. You can find out the NM-CIDS related information (for example, the interface configuration) from the output of the **show running-config**. For example, to find out the interface name of the NM_CIDS, execute **show running-config | include IDS**.
- **show diag**—Provides the diagnostics information on the router about NM-CIDS.
- **show controller or show interface**—Verifies the IDS interface.

Common Problems and Resolutions

As mentioned before, this chapter does not detail the troubleshooting of IDS/IPS functionality or the feature of the NM-CIDS. Chapter 14, "Troubleshooting Cisco Intrusion Prevention System," explains the configuration and troubleshooting aspects on the Appliance and other platforms. Hence, IDS/IPS software-related troubleshooting is not explained again in this section. However, the aspects of troubleshooting that are unique to the NM-CIDS are the focus of this section. They are outlined as follows:

- Hardware issues
- NM-CIDS Console access issues
- Communication issues with NM-CIDS command and control port
- Issues with not receiving traffic from the router using the sniffing port
- Managing NM-CIDS from IOS router
- Software installation and upgrade issues

Hardware Issues

After you insert the NM-CIDS into one of the slots on the router, first be sure that the NM-CIDS is recognized by the router. You can execute **show running-config | include IDS**, or **show interfaces | include IDS**, or **show ip interface brief | include IDS** as shown in Example 16-1. Execute these commands to identify the interface name, which can be used to identify the slot number where the NM-CIDS is inserted on the router.

Example 16-1 *Identifying the Slot Number Where NM-CIDS Is Seated*

```
3725-ids#show running-config | include IDS
! This is the Fast Ethernet interface on the router side for IDS.
interface IDS-Sensor1/0
! Following can be used to find out the status of the interface.
3725-ids#show interfaces | include IDS
IDS-Sensor1/0 is up, line protocol is up
! If you want to find out additional details like IP address, use the following
! command
3725-ids#show ip interface brief | include IDS
IDS-Sensor1/0              1.1.1.1         YES TFTP   up                    up
3725-ids#
```

Example 16-1 shows that the interface name is IDS-Sensor1/0, which is an indication that the NM-CIDS is inserted into slot 1 on the router. Now that you know the slot number for NM-CIDS, execute **show diag slot_number** command as shown in Example 16-2 to obtain detailed information about the NM-CIDS.

Example 16-2 **show diag output** *for NM-CIDS on the Router*

```
3725-ids#show diag 1
3725 Backplane EEPROM:
        PCB Serial Number          : JAE073617MX
        Processor type             : 61
        Top Assy. Part Number      : 800-16147-02
        Board Revision             : C0
        Fab Part Number            : 28-4226-06
        Deviation Number           : 65535-65535
        Manufacturing Test Data    : FF FF FF FF FF FF FF FF
        RMA Number                 : 255-255-255-255
        RMA Test History           : FF
        RMA History                : FF
        Chassis Serial Number      : JMX0742L3AQ
        Chassis MAC Address        : 0007.b35b.ef40
        MAC Address block size     : 48
        Field Diagnostics Data     : FF FF FF FF FF FF FF FF
        Hardware Revision          : 0.1
        Number of Slots            : 2
        EEPROM format version 4
        EEPROM contents (hex):
          0x00: 04 FF C1 8B 4A 41 45 30 37 33 36 31 37 4D 58 09
          0x10: 61 40 02 59 C0 46 03 20 00 3F 13 02 42 43 30 85
          0x20: 1C 10 82 06 80 FF FF FF FF C4 08 FF FF FF FF FF
          0x30: FF FF FF 81 FF FF FF FF 03 FF 04 FF C2 8B 4A 4D
```

Example 16-2 **show diag output** *for NM-CIDS on the Router (Continued)*

```
          0x40: 58 30 37 34 32 4C 33 41 51 C3 06 00 07 B3 5B EF
          0x50: 40 43 00 30 C5 08 FF FF FF FF FF FF FF FF 41 00
          0x60: 01 01 02 FF FF FF FF FF FF FF FF FF FF FF FF FF
          0x70: FF FF FF FF FF FF FF FF FF FF FF FF FF FF FF FF
Slot 1:
! The following line shows Line card type and number of ports available.
        IDS Sensor Port adapter, 1 port
! The system has identified the NM-CIDS module port adapter.
        Port adapter is analyzed
! Elapsed time since insertion. If unknown, you can ignore it.
        Port adapter insertion time unknown
        EEPROM contents at hardware discovery:
! Hardware version number of the NM-CIDS.
        Hardware Revision          : 1.0
        Top Assy. Part Number      : 800-23372-01
        Board Revision             : A0
        Deviation Number           : 0-0
        Fab Version                : 02
! Serial number of the printed circuit board.
        PCB Serial Number          : FOC071617YB
        RMA Test History           : 00
! Return material authorization number, which is an administrative number assigned
! if the NM-CIDS needs to be returned for repair.
        RMA Number                 : 0-0-0-0
! Counter that indicates how many times the NM-CIDS has been returned and repaired.
        RMA History                : 00
! Part number of the NM-CIDS.
        Fab Part Number            : 28-5683-02
        Manufacturing Test Data    : 00 00 00 00 00 00 00 00
        Field Diagnostics Data     : 00 00 00 00 00 00 00 00
        Product (FRU) Number       : NM-CIDS
        EEPROM format version 4
        EEPROM contents (hex):
          0x00: 04 FF 40 04 25 41 01 00 C0 46 03 20 00 5B 4C 01
          0x10: 42 41 30 80 00 00 00 00 02 02 C1 8B 46 4F 43 30
          0x20: 37 31 36 31 37 59 42 03 00 81 00 00 00 00 04 00
          0x30: 85 1C 16 33 02 C4 08 00 00 00 00 00 00 00 00 C5
          0x40: 08 00 00 00 00 00 00 00 00 FF FF FF FF FF FF FF
          0x50: FF FF FF FF FF FF FF FF FF FF FF FF FF FF FF FF
          0x60: FF FF FF FF FF FF FF FF FF FF FF FF FF FF FF FF
          0x70: FF FF FF FF FF FF FF FF FF FF FF FF FF FF FF FF

        20GB IDE Disc Daughter Card
        Hardware Revision          : 1.0
        Top Assy. Part Number      : 800-20520-01
! Revision number (signifying a minor revision) of the NM-CIDS.
        Board Revision             : A0
! Revision number (signifying a minor deviation) of the NM-CIDS.
        Deviation Number           : 0-0
        Fab Version                : 01
        PCB Serial Number          : FOC07160HNW
```

continues

Example 16-2 show diag output *for NM-CIDS on the Router (Continued)*

```
        RMA Test History        : 00
        RMA Number              : 0-0-0-0
        RMA History             : 00
        Fab Part Number         : 28-5685-01
        Manufacturing Test Data : 00 00 00 00 00 00 00 00
        Field Diagnostics Data  : 00 00 00 00 00 00 00 00

! Version number of the EEPROM format.
        EEPROM format version 4
! Dumps of EEPROM programmed data.
        EEPROM contents (hex):
          0x00: 04 FF 40 03 83 41 01 00 C0 46 03 20 00 50 28 01
          0x10: 42 41 30 80 00 00 00 00 02 01 C1 8B 46 4F 43 30
          0x20: 37 31 36 30 48 4E 57 03 00 81 00 00 00 00 04 00
          0x30: 85 1C 16 35 01 C4 08 00 00 00 00 00 00 00 00 C5
          0x40: 08 00 00 00 00 00 00 00 00 FF FF FF FF FF FF FF
          0x50: FF FF FF FF FF FF FF FF FF FF FF FF FF FF FF FF
          0x60: FF FF FF FF FF FF FF FF FF FF FF FF FF FF FF FF
          0x70: FF FF FF FF FF FF FF FF FF FF FF FF FF FF FF FF

3725-ids#
```

You can also use **show controllers IDS-Sensor 1/0** to obtain more detail about the interface.

If output in Example 16-1 shows that NM-CIDS interfaces are not recognized, work through the following steps to troubleshoot the issue:

Step 1 Be sure that you are running the supported HW and software on the router for NM-CIDS. Refer to the "Installing NM-CIDS" of the corresponding IPS version for the NM-CIDS to identify the supported hardware and software version. For example, to determine the hardware and software requirements for IPS 5.0, refer to the following link: http://www.cisco.com/univercd/cc/td/doc/product/iaabu/csids/csids11/hwguide/hwnmcids.htm

Step 2 Reseat the NM-CIDS into a different slot on the router to be sure that the initial slot was not faulty.

Step 3 Check the status light of the NM-CIDS and be sure the appropriate light is lit. Refer to Table 16-2 for details.

Step 4 If the reseating does not help, get the **show tech-support** and **show logging** commands output, and look for any error or other types of messages related to the NM-CIDS to troubleshoot further.

Step 5 If all efforts fail to uncover the problem, the NM-CIDS is probably having a hardware (HW) failure. If so, contact the Cisco Support center for a hardware replacement.

NM-CIDS Console Access Issues

Unlike the IDS/IPS Appliances, the NM-CIDS does not have the dedicated console port. Therefore, for the initial configuration, you must session into NM-CIDS from the router where it is seated. Before you can session to the NM-CIDS you must assign an **IP address** to the **IDS-Sensor** interface, which is discussed in the next section.

Assigning IP Address to the IDS-Sensor Interface on the Router

Before you can assign an IP address, you need to identify the **IDS-Sensor** interface on the router. When assigning an IP address to **IDS-Sensor**, do not assign a routable IP address directly. It is strongly recommended to create a loopback interface with a non-routable IP address, and assign the loopback interface IP to the **IDS-Sensor** interface to prevent the sniffing interface of the NM-CIDS from attack.

Work through the steps that follow to assign the **IP address** to NM-CIDS:

Step 1 Find out which **IDS-Sensor** interface is visible to the router as shown in Example 16-1. This interface is used for sniffing packets for NM-CIDS. Without assigning an IP address to this interface, you cannot session into the NM-CIDS from the router.

Step 2 Create a loopback interface and assign an IP address as shown in Example 16-3.

Example 16-3 *Creating a Loopback Interface on the Router*

```
3725-ids#configure terminal
Enter configuration commands, one per line.  End with CNTL/Z.
3725-ids(config)#interface loopback 0
3725-ids(config-if)#ip address 1.1.1.1 255.255.255.0
3725-ids(config-if)#no shutdown
3725-ids(config-if)#
```

Step 3 Assign an unnumbered loopback interface (the loopback interface that you have just created in Step 2) to the **IDS-Sensor** interface that you have identified in Step 1. Then activate the interface with the **no shutdown** command, as shown in Example 16-4.

Example 16-4 *Unnumbered Loopback 0 Interface Being Applied Under IDS-Sensor Interface 1/0*

```
3725-ids#configure terminal
Enter configuration commands, one per line.  End with CNTL/Z.
3725-ids(config)#interface IDS-Sensor 1/0
3725-ids(config-if)#ip unnumbered loopback 0
3725-ids(config-if)#no shutdown
3725-ids(config-if)#
*Jan  2 23:04:27.454: %LINK-3-UPDOWN: Interface IDS-Sensor1/0, changed state to up
*Jan  2 23:04:28.454: %LINEPROTO-5-UPDOWN: Line protocol on Interface IDS-Sensor1/0,
  changed state to up
```

continues

Example 16-4 *Unnumbered Loopback 0 Interface Being Applied Under IDS-Sensor Interface 1/0 (Continued)*

```
*Jan  2 23:04:33.726: %LINEPROTO-5-UPDOWN: Line protocol on Interface IDS-Sensor1/0,
  changed state to down
*Jan  2 23:04:43.726: %LINEPROTO-5-UPDOWN: Line protocol on Interface IDS-Sensor1/0,
  changed state to up
3725-ids(config-if)#end
3725-ids#write memory
Building configuration
[OK]
3725-ids#
```

Step 4 Finally, verify that the IDS-Sensor interface is up and assigned with an IP address from the loopback interface as shown in Example 16-5.

Example 16-5 *IDS-Sensor Interface Is up and Assigned the IP Address by Loopback Interface*

```
3725-ids#show ip interface brief | include IDS
IDS-Sensor1/0          1.1.1.1         YES TFTP   up                    up
3725-ids#
```

Once you configure the **IDS-Sensor** interface with an IP address, and verify that it is up, the next step is to access the NM-CIDS with the **service-module ids-module** *slot_number*/**0** **session** command on the router, which is discussed in the next section.

Connecting to NM-CIDS

You can connect to NM-CIDS in the following two ways:

- Using **service-module** command
- Using Telnet

More details on the above items follow.

Using the **service-module** Command

You can connect to the NM-CIDS with the **service-module** command with the **session** argument that starts a reverse Telnet connection using the IP address of the **IDS-Sensor** interface. This allows you to connect to the IDS as shown in Example 16-6.

Example 16-6 *User's Session into the IDS Assuming the Blade Is Slot 1*

```
3725-ids#service-module IDS-Sensor 1/0 session
Trying 1.1.1.1, 2033 ... Open

User Access Verification
! The default user id and password is cisco/cisco for the initial login. This sample
! output is taken after the initial password is setup.  If initially, you log in to
! the NM-CIDS, it will present you with the password change sequence.
```

Example 16-6 *User's Session into the IDS Assuming the Blade Is Slot 1 (Continued)*

```
login: cisco
Password:
***NOTICE***
This product contains cryptographic features and is subject to United States
and local country laws governing import, export, transfer and use. Delivery
Of Cisco cryptographic products does not imply third-party authority to import,
Export, distribute or use encryption. Importers, exporters, distributors and
users are responsible for compliance with U.S. and local country laws. By using
this product you agree to comply with applicable laws and regulations. If you
are unable to comply with U.S. and local laws, return this product immediately.
A summary of U.S. laws governing Cisco cryptographic products may be found at:
http://www.cisco.com/wwl/export/crypto
If you require further assistance please contact us by sending email to
export@cisco.com.
Sensor#
```

Using Telnet

You can console directly to the NM-CIDS sensor by using Telnet to access the router's interface IP address with the reverse Telnet port number from a remote host. You can find out the port number for the NM-CIDS with formula slot_number * 32 + 2001. For example, if the NM-CIDS is inserted into slot 1, then you can Telnet remotely to the console of the NM-IDS with reverse Telnet port number 2033 (1 * 32 + 2001 = 2033).

Another way to determine the reverse Telnet port number is to use the **service-module** command, as shown in Example 16-7.

Example 16-7 *Finding out the Reverse Telnet Port Number and the Statistics from the NM-CIDS*

```
3725-ids#service-module IDS-Sensor 1/0 status
Service Module is Cisco IDS-Sensor1/0
! Following line indicates that reverse telnet is performed on line 33
Service Module supports session via TTY line 33
Service Module is in Steady state
Getting status from the Service Module, please wait..
! Following information is retrieved from the module
Cisco Systems Intrusion Detection System Network Module
  Software version:  4.1(0.4)S42(0.4)
  Model:             NM-CIDS
  Memory:            513220 KB


3725-ids#
```

Once the port number is identified through either method that was just discussed, use Telnet to access one of the interface IP addresses that you can reach from your host with the reverse Telnet port number as follows:

```
3745-ids# telnet 172.16.171.30 2033
```

NOTE Remember that you do not need to use Telnet to access the loopback interface (that is assigned for the IDS-Sensor interface) IP address with reverse Telnet port number. You can use Telnet to access any interface that is reachable from the host.

Disconnecting from NM-CIDS

While you are working with NM-CIDS using the **service-module** command with the **session** argument, you might want to switch back and forth to configure both the router and NM-CIDS. To accomplish that, you need to know how to suspend a session to return to the router. Once you have finished with the configuration of NM-CIDS and the router, you might want to close the session to the NM-CIDS completely, so that you do not leave NM-CIDS vulnerable. The following sections discuss in detail how to suspend and close down the session to NM-CIDS.

Suspending a Session and Returning to the Router

When you are finished with a session, you need to return to the router to establish the association between a session (the IDS application) and the router interfaces that you want to monitor.

To toggle between connections in a Telnet session, follow these steps:

Step 1 Hold **CTRL-Shift** simultaneously, and press **6**. Release all keys, and press **x**. This command takes you from a session prompt to a router prompt, and vice versa.

Step 2 Type the following at the prompt:

```
Router# disconnect
```

Step 3 Press **Enter** when prompted as follows:

```
Closing connection to 10.16.0.0 [confirm] <Enter>
```

Telnet clients vary. In some cases, you might have to press **CTRL-6 + x**. The control character is specified as ^^, CTRL-^, or ASCII value 30 (hex 1E).

CAUTION Failing to close a session properly makes it possible for others to exploit a connection that is still in place. Remember to type **exit** at the Router# prompt to close the Cisco IOS session completely. The following section describes how to close an open session.

Closing an Open Session

If you use the Telnet **disconnect** command to leave the session, the session remains running, and an open session can be exploited by someone wanting to take advantage of a connection that is still in place. To close on open session to the NM-CIDS, follow these steps:

Step 1 Exit the session by using the following command:

```
sensor# exit
```

Step 2 Suspend and close the session to the NM-CIDS by holding **CTRL-Shift** and pressing **6**. Finally, release all keys, and press **x.**

Step 3 Disconnect from the router by using the following command:

```
3725-ids# disconnect
```

Step 4 Press **Enter** to confirm the disconnection:

```
3725-ids# Closing connection to 10.16.0.0 [confirm] <Enter>
```

Step 5 Exit the session:

```
3725-ids#exit
```

Troubleshooting Console Access Issues

If you cannot use Console to access the sensor with the **service-module** command from the router or remotely with reverse Telnet, work through the following steps to correct the problem:

Step 1 Make sure the IDS-Sensor interface has an IP address and shows as UP.

Step 2 Execute the **service-module IDS-Sensor 1/0 status** command, and be sure you get the information NM-CIDS. If the NM-CIDS shows something similar to the information shown in Example 16-8, you might want to reset the NM-CIDS with the command shown in Example 16-9.

Example 16-8 *Verifying the Status of the NM-CIDS*

```
3725-ids#service-module IDS-Sensor 1/0 status
Service Module is Cisco IDS-Sensor1/0
Service Module supports session via TTY line 33
Service Module is in Steady state
Getting status from the Service Module, please wait..
STartIng IDS ApplIcatIon
3725-ids#service-module IDS-Sensor 1/0 reset
Use reset only to recover from shutdown or failed state
Warning: May lose data on the hard disc!
Do you want to reset?[confirm]
Trying to reset Service Module IDS-Sensor1/0.
3725-ids#
```

Step 3 If you have AAA authentication turned on for Telnet, then understand that the first username/password is from the router itself. Therefore, you need to enter the Telnet username and password, even if you session into the NM-CIDS from the router itself. This is because the session on a router opens a reverse Telnet session across the backplane to NM-CIDS. If you have the authentication turned on (with AAA) for the Telnet session on the router, then when you session into the NM-CIDS, you will be prompted for Telnet login credentials, which have been defined using AAA server, or locally on the router. Then you will be prompted to enter the login credentials for the NM-CIDS. If this is the first time you are sessioning into NM-CIDS, you need to enter cisco/cisco as the username/password, which will give you the option of changing your password to the username "cisco". You must change the password before you can access the NM-CIDS.

Step 4 If you have the access-class defined with an ACL to block the IP address, then you need to allow the IP address of the IDS-Sensor interface to be able to session into or reverse-Telnet into the NM-CIDS.

Step 5 Be sure the NM-CIDS allows the IP address of the NM-CIDS IDS-Sensor, so that you can session into the NM-CIDS.

Another way that you can connect to the NM-CIDS is by using the Command and Control interface of the NM-CIDS. As mentioned before, this is the only Fast Ethernet interface that is visible on the front panel of the NM-CIDS. However, to use the Command and Control interface to Telnet or SSH, you must assign an IP address and initialize the interface, which brings up the next discussion.

Communication Issues with NM-CIDS Command and Control Port

This section presents the configuration and troubleshooting steps for the Command and Control interface of the NM-CIDS.

- Configuration steps
- Troubleshooting steps

The sections that follow present more details on both configuration and troubleshooting.

Configuration Steps

Once you are in the NM-CIDS CLI, you can configure the initial setup using the **setup** command. This process will allow you to bring the NM-IDS online with IP addresses for its Command and Control interface. So, a management station for IDM and IDS MC can be used to manage the NM-IDS. The same IP can be used to pull all events into the Security Monitor. An example of the **setup** command and output is shown in Example 16-9.

Example 16-9 *How to Set Up the IP Address on the Command and Control Interface Using the* **setup** *Command*

```
sensor# setup
    --- System Configuration Dialog ---
At any point you may enter a question mark '?' for help.
User ctrl-c to abort configuration dialog at any prompt.
Default settings are in square brackets '[]'.
Current Configuration:
! Only showing the relevant information
Continue with configuration dialog?[yes]:
Enter host name[sensor]:NMCIDS
Enter IP interface[10.1.1.10/24,10.1.1.1]:20.1.1.10/24,20.1.1.1
Enter telnet-server status[disabled]:enabled
Enter web-server port[443]:
Modify current access list?[no]: yes
Current access list entries:
  [1] 20.0.0.0/8
  [2] 1.1.1.0/24
Delete:
NMCIDS#
```

At the completion of this process, the CLI will display the entered configuration and prompt you to confirm if the configuration should be saved and if NM-CIDS should be rebooted as follows:

```
Use this configuration?[yes]: yes
Configuration Saved.
Warning: The node must be rebooted for the changes to go into effect.
Continue with reboot? [yes]:
```

Enter **yes** for both **use this configuration** and **Continue with reboot**.

Troubleshooting Steps

If you cannot connect to the Command and Control interface of the NM-CIDS, work through the following steps to correct the problem:

Step 1 Ping to the default gateway of the NM-CIDS and be sure you can ping. If you cannot ping, be sure that the interface is connected to the switch or hub and that the link light is correct, and be sure that you do not have a duplicate IP addresses in the network.

Step 2 Be sure that the access-list is modified to allow the hosts or network addresses from where you need to Telnet or SSH to the NM-CIDS.

Step 3 Be sure that the switch or the hub has the proper routing configured for the Command and Control interface network to the rest of the network so that your host knows how to reach the Command and Control interface via Telnet or SSH.

Step 4 Be sure that the firewall is not filtering the traffic between the host and the NM-CIDS Command and Control interface.

Issues with Not Receiving Traffic from the Router Using the Sniffing Port

To forward a copy of the traffic to the NM-CIDS from the router, you must configure the **IDS-Sensor** interface as shown in Example 16-4. Additionally, you must configure monitored interfaces of the router to capture the packets. This section looks at the configuration and troubleshooting aspects of forwarding copies of traffic to the NM-CIDS.

- Configuration steps
- Troubleshooting steps

Configuration Steps

To start capturing traffic, you need to enable the desired interfaces (including subinterfaces) on the router for packet monitoring. You can select any number of interfaces or subinterfaces to be monitored. The packets sent and received on these interfaces are forwarded to the NM-CIDS for inspection. The enabling and disabling of the interfaces is configured through the router CLI (Cisco IOS).

Work through the steps that follow to configure packet capturing:

Step 1 Turn on CEF switching on the router, which is a *must* for redirecting traffic to NM-CIDS from the router as shown in Example 16-10.

Example 16-10 *Turning on CEF Switching*

```
3725-ids# configuration terminal
! CEF can be turned on with the following command
3725-ids(config)# ip cef
3725-ids(config)# exit
3725-ids#
```

Step 2 Identify the interfaces or subinterfaces on which you want the traffic to be captured with the help of the **show ip interface brief** command on the router. You can capture traffic from more than one interface/subinterface.

Step 3 Configure the command required to start monitoring the traffic. Example 16-11 shows that monitoring is enabled only on the Fast Ethernet 0/0 interface.

Step 4 Repeat the previous step for each interface or subinterface that you want to monitor.

Example 16-11 *Capturing Traffic on Fast Ethernet 0/0 Interface*

```
3725-ids# configure terminal
! Go into the interface mode where you want the traffic to be captured
3725-ids(config)# interface FastEthernet0/0
! Following command will copy network traffic to the NM-CIDS.
3725-ids(config-if)# ids-service-module monitoring
! Use the command no ids-service-module monitoring to turn off monitoring.
! Exit interface mode:
3725-ids(config-if)# end
3725-ids#
```

Step 5 You can verify whether the monitoring is working with the **show interfaces IDS-Sensor 1/0** command on the NM-CIDS. The interface should show as **up** and the counters should show as incrementing with time.

Troubleshooting Steps

If NM-CIDS is unable to receive any packets from the router, work through the following steps:

Step 1 Identify the interface and be sure the output counters increment over the period of time as shown in Example 16-12.

Example 16-12 *Interfaces Counters for IDS-Sensor Interface on the Router*

```
3725-ids#show interfaces IDS-Sensor 1/0
IDS-Sensor1/0 is up, line protocol is up
  Hardware is I82559FE, address is 0007.b35b.ef50 (bia 0007.b35b.ef50)
  Interface is unnumbered. Using address of Loopback0 (1.1.1.1)
  MTU 1500 bytes, BW 100000 Kbit, DLY 100 usec,
     reliability 255/255, txload 1/255, rxload 1/255
  Encapsulation ARPA, loopback not set
  Keepalive set (10 sec)
  ARP type: ARPA, ARP Timeout 04:00:00
  Last input 00:00:00, output 00:00:00, output hang never
  Last clearing of "show interface" counters never
  Input queue: 0/75/0/0 (size/max/drops/flushes); Total output drops: 0
  Queueing strategy: fifo
  Output queue: 0/60 (size/max)
  5 minute input rate 0 bits/sec, 0 packets/sec
! You can quickly find out if the interface is sending any traffic in last 5
! minutes or 5 seconds. Counter 0 is an indication that you need more
! investigation and observe this counter for longer period.
  5 minute output rate 25 bits/sec, 5 packets/sec
     5395 packets input, 350902 bytes, 0 no buffer
     Received 0 broadcasts, 0 runts, 0 giants, 0 throttles
     0 input errors, 0 CRC, 0 frame, 0 overrun, 0 ignored
     0 input packets with dribble condition detected
```

continues

Example 16-12 *Interfaces Counters for IDS-Sensor Interface on the Router (Continued)*

```
! Make sure output packets increment over period of time. Other counters
! increments over period of time in higher rate is an indication of problem.
     24113 packets output, 2267534 bytes, 0 underruns
     0 output errors, 0 collisions, 4 interface resets
     0 babbles, 0 late collision, 0 deferred
     0 lost carrier, 0 no carrier
     0 output buffer failures, 0 output buffers swapped out
3725-ids#
```

Step 2 If the output for the IDS-Sensor interface counter is not incrementing, check to see if the monitored interfaces are dropping the packets by the access-list.

Step 3 If there is no access-list on the monitored interface of the router, be sure that switching for Cisco Express Forwarding (CEF) is turned on in the router as shown by the commands in Example 16-13.

Example 16-13 *Verifying Whether the CEF Switching Is Turned On*

```
3725-ids#show running-config | include cef
ip cef
3725-ids#
```

Step 4 If the IDS-Sensor interface shows that it is forwarding the traffic to the NM-CIDS, but if you are still not getting any events, use the **show interface** command to ensure that the sensing interface of NM-CIDS is receiving the packets. If the NM-CIDS sensing interface does not show the counters incrementing over a period of time, or if the counters remain at zero, then reseat the NM-CIDS and see if that corrects the problem.

Step 5 If the sensing interface of the NM-CIDS is receiving traffic, troubleshoot the problem with information in Chapter 14, "Troubleshooting Cisco Intrusion Prevention System."

Managing NM-CIDS from an IOS Router

Although most of the commands to manage NM-CIDS are in the NM-CIDS itself, there are some handy commands available on the router itself that are used to manage the IDS blade on the router efficiently. The Cisco IOS provides the following command arguments to control the NM-CIDS: **shutdown**, **reload**, and **reset**:

- **Shutdown**—To bring NM-CIDS down gracefully, execute the following command:

```
3725-ids# service-module ids-sensor 1/0 shutdown
```

Be sure to execute a **shutdown** command before you remove the hard-disk drive from the NM-CIDS. Failing to do so can lead to the loss of data or the corruption of the hard-disk drive.

- **Reload**—This option performs a graceful halt and reboot of the operating system on NM-CIDS with the following command:

```
3725-ids# service-module ids-sensor 1/0 reload
```

- **Reset**—This command is used to recover from a shutdown as shown in Example 16-14.

Example 16-14 *Performing Reset of the Module*

```
3725-ids# service-module ids-sensor 1/0 reset
Use reset only to recover from shutdown or failed state
Warning: May lose data on the hard disc!
Do you want to reset?[confirm]
3725-ids#
```

Hard-disk drive data loss only occurs if you issue the **reset** command without first shutting down the NM-CIDS. You can use the **reset** command safely in other situations.

- **Status**—This option provides information on the status of the NM-CIDS as shown in Example 16-15.

Example 16-15 *Sample Output of the* **status** *Command*

```
3725-ids# service-module ids-sensor1/0 status
Service Module is Cisco IDS-Sensor1/0
! Shows the reverse telnet port information
Service Module supports session via TTY line 33
! The following line shows the module is in good state
Service Module is in Steady state
Getting status from the Service Module, please wait..
! Following output shows the details of the NM-CIDS
Service Module Version information received,
Major ver = 1, Minor ver= 1
Cisco Systems Intrusion Detection System Network Module
Software version: 4.1(1)S42(0.3)
Model: NM-CIDS
Memory: 254676 KB
3725-ids#
```

Software Installation and Upgrade Issues

There are several images available for NM-CIDS:

- **Boot loader image**—This image is required to load the helper image, which is required to re-image system image on NM-CIDS on version 4.1.

- **Helper Image**—The helper image is used to help loading the system image on the application partition of NM-CIDS. This image is no longer required on IPS version 5.x.
- **System Image**—This is the actual system image file for the application partition that can be used to re-image the application partition of NM-CIDS. As of writing this boot, the latest version of system image is **IPS-NM-CIDS-K9-sys-1.1-a-5.0-1.img–System**.
- **Major/Minor/Signature software upgrade files**—These files can be upgraded from the Application partition itself.

Remember the following important steps when upgrading from 4.1 to version 5.0:

- The 5.0(1) major upgrade, when applied to NM-CIDS, upgrades the bootloader to 1.0.17-1. Hence, instead of installing the system image, use the **upgrade** command to upgrade from 4.x to 5.0 using the major upgrade file (**IPS-K9-maj-5.0-1-S149.rpm.pkg**). Refer to Chapter 14, "Troubleshooting Cisco Intrusion Prevention System," for more details on how to upgrade the major release.
- To re-image the IPS 5.0 version from 4.1, you must upgrade the boot loader image (servicesengine-boot-1.0-17-1_dev.bin) first by booting to the old helper file where there is an option to update the boot loader in the helper menu. Refer to the "Common Problems and Resolutions" section of this chapter for a procedure to re-image the application. The procedure for the boot loader is very similar.
- The newer version of bootloader no longer requires a helper image to upgrade to IPS Version 5.0.

This is the location for different image files for NM-CIDS:

http://www.cisco.com/kobayashi/sw-center/ciscosecure/ids/crypto/

Case Studies

As mentioned before, Cisco Express Forwarding (CEF) switching is required on the router to forward the traffic to the NM-CIDS. Therefore it is important to understand how packets are processed when CEF is configured with various other features and services on the router. Once you build this knowledge, you need to know at which point the router forwards the packets to the NM-CIDS, so that you know which packets are forwarded and how they are forwarded to the NM-CIDS for various features. The goal of this case study is to examine this traffic forwarding technique to the NM-CIDS in detail, so that you know what to expect in terms of packets captured by the NM-CIDS.

CEF Forwarding Path

A packet goes through the following path when CEF is configured with other features on the router:

7 IOS IPS for atomic signatures

8. Inbound Access-list (ACL)
9. Decryption for VPN traffic (if the packet is decrypted, then it goes back to Step 1, or else it goes to Step 4)
10. Authentication proxy (Auth-proxy)
11. Network Address Translation (NAT) outside to inside
12. Forwarding Information Base (FIB) lookup
13. Output IPS check for atomic signatures
14. NAT inside to outside
15. Outbound Access-list (ACL)
16. Context-Based Access Control (CBAC)
17. Encryption for VPN traffic
18. Packet out

IPS Insertion Points

Now that you are familiar with the CEF packet path, it is time to understand the insertion points that are used to forward a copy of the packet to the NM-CIDS. An insertion point is the point in the CEF forwarding path from where a copy of the packet is sent to the NM-CIDS. For NM-CIDS, with CEF configured, a router is required to have at least two insertion points: one before FIB lookup, and one after the FIB lookup (FIB lookup is at Step 6 in the CEF forwarding path). These insertion points give desired results for NAT, IPsec, ACL, and so on, which are discussed next.

Network Address Translation (NAT)

The signature engines of NM-CIDS maintain the TCP session states for every TCP connection it monitors. The engines need to see packets in both directions to analyze the TCP session correctly. The source and destination IP addresses of the bi-directional packets have to be consistent. But, when Network Address Translation (NAT) is configured, the source and destination IP addresses are changed depending on the configuration. However, as the inserting point for packet forwarding is selected right before and after Step 6 of "CEF Forwarding Path," the Outside to Inside NAT (destination address translation) takes place (at Step 5) before the packets are forwarded to the NM-CIDS. And after the packets are forwarded to NM-CIDS, the inside to outside (Source Address Translation) NAT takes place at Step 8. This gives a consistent bi-directional state of the TCP packets for the NM-CIDS. This also helps in performing the blocking based on the actual source address, and translated destination address, as these addresses will be seen by the NM-CIDS in the packets.

Encryption

The NM-CIDS cannot interpret encrypted packets for any possible attacks. So if a router receives an encrypted packet and if the router is the termination point for the packet, it first decrypts the packet before sending it to the NM-CIDS as mentioned in Step 3 of the "CEF Forwarding Path" section.

Similarly, if the router needs to encrypt a packet before sending it, then it sends it to the NM-CIDS before it encrypts. In "CEF Forwarding Path," this takes place at Step 11, and the traffic is forwarded immediately before or after Step 6.

If the router is merely forwarding an encrypted packet (that is, the router is neither encrypting nor decrypting the packet), it sends the packet as is (without decryption) to the NM-CIDS. Although NM-CIDS can analyze the packet as a TCP/UDP packet, it is not able to analyze the contents of the packet, as encrypted.

Access List Check

The IOS performs an input-ACL check on a packet before it processes the packet for NAT or encryption. As explained earlier, the NM-CIDS monitors the packet after the NAT and decryption is processed. Therefore if the packet is dropped by the inbound ACL, it is not forwarded to the NM-CIDS. The IOS router performs an outbound ACL check after the packet is forwarded to the NM-CIDS. So the packet will be forwarded to the NM-CIDS even if the output ACL drops the packet. As described in the section entitled "CEF Forwarding Path," the insertion point is right before and after Step 6, and the inbound checking is performed at Step 2, but the outbound ACL checking is performed at Step 9.

IP Multicast, UDP Flooding, IP Broadcast

If the router is configured for IP Multicast, User Datagram Protocol (UDP) flooding or IP Broadcast, a packet received on the input interface is forwarded on two or more output interfaces. In this situation, if the input interface is configured for IPS monitoring, the packet will be sent to the NM-CIDS. However, if only the output interfaces are configured for monitoring, the packet will not be forwarded to the NM-CIDS.

Generic Routing Encapsulation (GRE) Tunnels

The NM-CIDS does not analyze GRE encapsulated packets. So if a GRE packet is received, and the incoming interface is enabled for IPS monitoring, the packet *will* not be forwarded to the NM-CIDS for monitoring. However, if a packet is encapsulated by the router into a

GRE tunnel, and the incoming interface is enabled for IPS monitoring, the packet (before encapsulation) will be sent to the NM-CIDS.

Address Resolution Protocol (ARP) Packets

Address Resolution Protocol (ARP) packets are handled at Layer 2 and are not forwarded to the NM-CIDS.

Packets Dropped by the IOS

The IP stack of the router verifies the integrity of the packets before forwarding the packets to NM-CIDS. The router will drop a packet if some of the fields in the packet are incorrect or unexpected. Following is a list of such cases in which the router drops the packets and they are not be forwarded to the NM-CIDS:

- Bad IP version.
- Incorrect IP option field.
- Bad header length. Total length is greater than 1546 bytes or less than 20 bytes.
- IP cyclic redundancy check (CRC) failure.
- Time to Live (TTL) is less than or equal to 1 (in this case, the packet is consumed by the router).

In these cases, an Internet Control Message Protocol (ICMP) message is sent back (indicating the reason for the drop).

Forwarding the Packets to the IDS at a Rate Higher Than the Internal Interface Can Handle

The internal interface between the router and the NM-CIDS is a 100 MBps back-to-back Ethernet port. So if the monitoring traffic exceeds 100 MBps, the router will not be able to forward that traffic. There is no guarantee of which packets would be sent and which would be dropped. This might interfere with the ability of the IPS to reassemble the TCP data stream, possibly preventing it from triggering an alarm.

The NM-CIDS is designed to monitor up to 45 MBps of traffic. So when the traffic approaches 100 MBps, in most cases the NM-CIDS itself will miss signatures.

Common Problems and Resolutions

This section examines two commonly seen issues with NM-CIDS operations.

Re-imaging the NM-CIDS Application Partition

You can use the helper image file to re-image the application partition on the NM-CIDS using TFTP server. This section presents the steps to perform the re-image, and to troubleshoot any issues pertaining to the re-image process as follows:

- Performing the re-image of application partition
- Troubleshooting steps

Performing the Re-image of Application Partition

The re-image of the application partition involves booting the sensor into boot-loader. You then load the helper image, which is used to load the actual application image.

Work through the following steps to perform this task:

Step 1 Obtain the helper image file from the following location: http://www.cisco.com/kobayashi/sw-center/ciscosecure/ids/crypto/

Step 2 Install a Trivial File Transfer Protocol (TFTP) server in a machine on your network.

Step 3 Put the IDS/IPS helper image file (example of helper image is NM-CIDS-K9-helper-1.0-1.bin) on the TFTP server root directory.

Step 4 Session in to the NM-CIDS with the following command to verify that NM-CIDS is working efficiently.

```
Router# service-module IDS-Sensor slot_number/0 session
```

Step 5 Suspend the session by pressing **Shift-CTRL-6 x**. You will see the router# prompt. If you do not see this prompt, try **Ctrl-6 x**.

Step 6 Reset the NM-CIDS with the following command:

```
Router# service-module IDS-Sensor slot_number/0 reset
```

When you are prompted to confirm the **reset** command, press **Enter** to confirm.

Step 7 Immediately after that, resume the suspended session by pressing **Enter**.

Step 8 After displaying its version, the bootloader displays the following prompt for 15 seconds:

```
Please enter '***' to change boot configuration:
```

If you type *** during the 15-second delay (or if there is no default boot device configured) you will enter the bootloader CLI.

Step 9 After sessioning in to the NM-CIDS, you will see the bootloader CLI prompt as follows:

```
ServicesEngine boot-loader>
```

Step 10 Set up the bootloader network parameters as shown in Example 16-16. You have to configure the bootloader only once.

Example 16-16 *The Bootloader Configuration*

```
ServicesEngine boot-loader> config
! Assign the IP address same as the Command and Control interface IP address.
! This is the same address that you have assigned to the Fast Ethernet interface
! which is visible from the front panel of the NM-CIDS
IP Address [10.1.1.60] >
! Assign the subnet mask for the IP address that you have assigned in the
! previous line
Subnet mask [255.255.255.0] >
! Specify the TFTP server IP address where the helper image is installed.
TFTP server [10.1.1.1] >
! Specify the default gateway IP address. This is very important if the TFTP
! server is more than one hop away.
Gateway [10.1.1.1] >
! Specify the helper image file name that you have installed on the TFTP server
Default Helper-file [mohawk_helper] >
! By default the interface that you have defined IP address for is external. So,
! select this default value. Just hit Return.
Ethernet interface [external] >
! The default boot device is disk. So, just hit Return
Default Boot [disk] >
ServicesEngine boot-loader>
```

Step 11 Once all the parameters are defined, load the helper image on NM-CIDS with the **boot helper** command as shown in Example 16-17.

Example 16-17 *Loading a Boot Helper Image*

```
ServicesEngine boot-loader> boot helper
Probing...EEPRO100Found Intel EtherExpressPro100 at x00000000 ROM
address 0x 00000000
Ethernet addr: 01:23:45:67:89:AB
Me: 10.1.2.3, Server: 10.1.2.5, Gateway: 10.1.2.254
Loading NM-CIDS-K9-helper-1.0-1.bin
```

NOTE To boot a helper image different from the one you configured as your default helper, type the command **boot helper** *name*.

After the helper image is loaded, the bootloader checks that it downloaded correctly. The bootloader will not run a helper if it is received incorrectly or it is not signed by Cisco. The following message indicates the helper is valid: **Image signature verified successfully.**

The Helper utility is launched as shown in Example 16-18.

Example 16-18 *Helper Utility Screen*

```
Cisco Systems, Inc.
Services engine helper utility for NM-CIDS
Version 1.0(1) [200305011547]
—-
Main menu
1 - Download application image and write to HDD
2 - Download bootloader and write to flash
3 - Display software version on HDD
4 - Display total RAM size
5 - Change file transfer method (currently secure shell)
Change file transfer method (currently secure shell)
r - Exit and reset Services Engine
h - Exit and shutdown Services Engine
Selection [1234rh]:
```

Work through the steps that follow to complete the rest of the steps:

Step 1 From the selection menu, type **5** to set the transfer method. Type **1** to choose Secure Shell, or choose **2** to choose TFTP. Use **r** to return to the Main Menu.

Step 2 Type **1** from the Selection Menu to start the re-imaging of the hard-disk of the NM-CIDS. If SSH is chosen, enter the username and SSH server IP address. If TFTP is chosen, just type the TFTP server IP address.

Step 3 Type the full pathname of the recovery image: /path /NM-CIDS.

Step 4 Type **y** to continue and you will see a message similar to that shown in Example 16-19.

Example 16-19 *Message Shown After Clicking Yes*

```
Ready to begin
Are you sure? y/n
You receive the following message:
The authenticity of host 10.1.2.10 (10.1.2.10) can't be
established. RSA key fingerprint is
7b:90:3b:16:5f:a1:34:92:ff:94:54:19:82:dc:73:ba.
Are you sure you want to continue connecting (yes/no)?
```

Type **yes**. Then, if SSH is used, specify the server password.

Step 5 Reboot the NM-CIDS as shown in Example 16-20.

Step 6 After sessioning into it, initialize the NM-CIDS with the **setup** command.

Example 16-20 *Message Shown When Rebooting the NM-CIDS*

```
Selection [1234rh]: r
About to exit and reset Services Engine.
Are you sure? [y/N]
```

Troubleshooting Steps

There can be primarily two problems you may encounter with the re-image process:

- **Unable to access to boot-loader**—You must issue a **service-module IDS-Sensor <slot>/0 reset** command instead of a **service-module IDS-Sensor <slot>/0 reload** command. The **reload** argument sends a message to the NM-CIDS asking it to reboot itself. If the NM-CIDS is in an unresponsive state, reload may fail. The **reset** command forces a hardware reset of the NM-CIDS. Before trying to access boot-loader, check to see if the NM-CIDS is in good state with **service-module IDS-Sensor <slot>/0 status**.
- **Unable to load helper image**—The bootloader brings up the external interface and locates the TFTP server host. This process may take some time. Press **p** to see a printout of the ARP table. You should see ARP entries for the NM-CIDS, TFTP server, and the Default Gateway. If this process takes too long and nothing changes for a long time, you may have network configuration or connectivity problems. When the TFTP load actually begins, a spinning character is displayed to indicate that packets are arriving from the TFTP server.

Configuring Time on the NM-CIDS

To correctly analyze the events after an attack, NM-CIDS must have the correct time stamp; otherwise, you cannot analyze correctly. The NM-CIDS gets its time from the Cisco router in which it is installed. As the routers do not have a battery, they cannot preserve a time setting when they are powered off. You must set the router's clock each time you power up or reset the router. Therefore, the best solution is to configure the router to use Network Time Protocol (NTP) server to provide time. NTP can be configured either on the NM-CIDS itself or on the router on which NM-CIDS is installed.

Default Behavior for Time Setting on NM-CIDS

By default, the NM-CIDS automatically synchronizes its clock with the clock in the router chassis in which it is installed. Note that only the Greenwich Mean Time (GMT) is synchronized between the router and the NM-CIDS, not the time zone and summertime settings.

CAUTION Be sure to set the time zone and summertime settings on both the router and the NM-CIDS; otherwise the local time for the NM-CIDS will be incorrect.

Using Network Time Protocol (NTP) Server

Instead having the NM-CIDS get its time from the router, you can configure your NM-CIDS to get its time from an NTP time synchronization source, such as a Cisco router. Refer to the following link for configuring a Cisco Router to be an NTP Server: http://www.cisco.com/en/US/products/sw/secursw/ps2113/products_installation_and_configuration_guide_chapter09186a008035809d.html#wp87016

You will need the NTP server IP address, the NTP key ID, and the NTP key value. You can configure the NM-CIDS to use NTP during initialization or you can set up NTP later. You can configure the sensor to use an NTP server as its time source. Refer to the following link:

http://www.cisco.com/en/US/products/sw/secursw/ps2113/products_installation_and_configuration_guide_chapter09186a008035809d.html#wp86931

It is recommended to use an NTP time synchronization source.

Best Practices

Best Practices for IPS Sensor that are discussed in Chapter 14, "Troubleshooting Cisco Intrusion Prevention System," also apply for NM-CIDS. In addition to that, here are some recommendations to keep in mind when you are implementing NM-CIDS:

- You must have the CEF switching turned on the IOS router.
- You must not configure NM-CIDS and integrated IDS/IPS feature on the IOS router.
- Do not configure traffic monitoring on the interfaces that are not required. Remember that the monitoring is applied in inbound and outbound directions.
- Be sure that the NM-CIDS interface is configured with an IP address that is not routable. It is also recommended to configure a loopback and apply that as an unassigned interface under the NM-CIDS interface.

- For Blocking, you must have a route for Command and Control (C & C) interface to the managed devices (Router, PIX, and so on).
- Baseline CPU and memory utilization before and after turning on NM-CIDS.
- Block unnecessary traffic using an ACL on the interface of the router, instead of relying on the NM-CIDS to save CPU cycles and memory utilization of the router.
- Implement AAA on the router so that NM-CIDS access can be limited for certain users using authorization configuration.

CHAPTER 17

Troubleshooting CiscoWorks Common Services

VPN/Security Management Solution (VMS) is a suite of Cisco Management Framework (CMF) technologies. CiscoWorks Common Services provides a common environment for Client Applications (Management Consoles known as MCs) for Intrusion Prevention System (IPS), firewalls, routers, and so on for configuration and reporting purposes. This chapter delves into troubleshooting issues that crop up when using CiscoWorks Common Services.

Overview of CiscoWorks Common Services

CiscoWorks Common Services provides a Web interface for the configuring and monitoring of different management consoles (MCs) for different network devices. Because CiscoWorks Common Services provides the underlying framework for client applications (MCs) to function correctly, CiscoWorks Common Services must be installed before any client applications. Client applications such as Firewall MC, IDS/IPS MC, etc., integrate with CiscoWorks Common Services and use its management functions.

Communication Architecture

The CiscoWorks Common Services Desktop can be accessed using one of the supported Web browsers by pointing to the IP address of the CiscoWorks Common Services server with two specific default ports (1741 and 1742). In normal mode, http is used as a transport protocol and 1741 is used as a transport port. However if SSL is turned on, https is used instead of http, and 1742 is used as a port instead of 1741. However, you can change the web server with the procedure explained in the following link:

http://www.cisco.com/univercd/cc/td/doc/product/rtrmgmt/cw2000/cw2000_d/comser22/usrguide/cmsrvall/desktop.htm#1044656

To launch CiscoWorks Common Services, on the browser type:

http://server_name(or ip):1741

NOTE If you enter http://server_name (or ip):port_number/login.html in your Web browser, the CiscoWorks Server will not launch. Hence, do not bookmark the CiscoWorks URL with the login.html.

User Management on CiscoWorks Common Services

User management on Common Services is very flexible with Services Roles and Privileges as follows:

- **Role**—Is a set of privileges.
- **Privileges**—Are the applications, features, and actions a user can access and use.

Common Services has five built-in roles with pre-defined privileges as shown in Table 17-1.

Table 17-1 *Default Roles and Privileges on Common Services*

Application	System Admin	Network Admin	Network Operator	Approver	Help Desk
Licensing	X	X			
Compact	X	X			
Backup	X	X			
Restore	X	X			
Preferences	X	X			
Checkpoint	X	X			
ACS/CMF Server	X	X			
Logging	X	X	X		
Edit User	X				

CiscoWorks Common Services supports the following database for authentication:

- CiscoWorks Local
- TACACS+
- IBM Secureway Directory
- KerberosLogin
- Local NT System
- MS Active Directory
- Netscape Directory
- RADIUS

For both authentication and authorization, CiscoWorks Common Services can be configured in one of these two modes:

- **Local**—–This is the default mode when you install CiscoWorks Common Services.
- **Cisco Secure ACS**—To use this mode, you must have a Cisco Secure ACS server installed on your network.

For additional details on this, refer to the following link:

http://www.cisco.com/univercd/cc/td/doc/product/rtrmgmt/cw2000/cw2000_d/comser22/usrguide/cmsrvmcs/sysadmin.htm

Diagnostic Commands and Tools

CiscoWorks Common Services has an extensive debug utility for diagnosing problems related to Common Services or any management console. The name of the utility is **MDCSUPPORT**. This utility collects registry information, log files, configuration settings, and host environment information, and any other relevant data, into a deliverable Zip file to support the MDCs that have been installed.

The **MDCSupport.exe** utility is a console application, which takes one optional command line argument, which is the output path/location of where the Zip file should be located. If no arguments are specified, the output goes to **<CoreRoot>\etc**. Otherwise, the output goes to the directory that is specified by the argument.

How to Collect mdcsupport on a Windows Platform

Work through the steps that follow to collect the mdcsupport file on Windows platform:

Step 1 Open the MS-DOS command prompt window by going to **Start> Run** > Enter **cmd** and clicking **OK**.

Step 2 The command prompt window opens. Enter **MDCSupport** at the prompt. Then press **Enter**.

Step 3 The **MDCSupport** utility creates a **.zip** (**MDCSupportInformation.zip**) file that contains your CiscoWorks Common Services configuration data and log files. The default directory of the **.zip** file is **\CSCOpx\MDC\etc**

NOTE **MDCSupportInformation.zip** is created by default in the **\CSCOpx\MDC\etc** directory. To change the location of the **.zip** file, enter **MDCSupport drive:\path** at the command prompt.

Categorization and Explanation of MDCSupport-Created Log Files

The best way to analyze the **MDCSupportInformation.zip** file is to open it by double-clicking it, and then sorting the files by size and examining the bigger files first. However, it is important to understand which files are responsible for which task, so that you can discover the problem on a specific component of the software more quickly.

Hence the sections that follow discuss different files that go into the making of the **MDCSupportInformation.zip** file:

- **Installation log**—After you unzip the **MDCSupportInformation.zip** file, the installation log files are located on the base directory. For example if you unzip the file in **D:\drive,** then these log files can be found in **D:\MDCSupportInformation** directory. The names of the installation log files are in the format of **Ciscoworks_setupxxx** (for example, the name of the first installation log file is **Ciscoworks_setup001**). These files are created on the root directory of the drive where the Windows 2000 Operating System is installed.
- **D:\MDCSupportInformation\PROGRA~1\CSCOpx\MDC directory**—In this directory, you will see Apache and other logs, and the tomcat directory.
- **D:\MDCSupportInformation\PROGRA~1\CSCOpx\MDC\apache directory**—This directory contains the configuration and log information about the Apache web server. Configuration information goes to the **conf** directory and log goes to **logs** directory. So, if you have issues with connecting to the CiscoWorks Common Services using a browser, always analyze the files in the **logs** directory. This is one of the two web servers for CiscoWorks Common Services. It works in conjunction with Tomcat (the second web server) for Java Servlet execution. If you want to find connection information between the Apache and the Tomcat web server, look at the connector log, which is **mod_jk.log**.
- **D:\MDCSupportInformation\PROGRA~1\CSCOpx\MDC\tomcat directory**—This directory contains **conf, logs,** and **mdc** directories. Of all three, the **log** directory contains the most important information for isolating a problem. In that directory, search for "exception" errors in the **stderr.log**, and search for "error" in the **stdout.log** file.
- **D:\MDCSupportInformation\PROGRA~1\CSCOpx\MDC\log directory**—This directory contains audit logs and Common Services log files.
- **D:\MDCSupportInformation\PROGRA~1\CSCOpx\MDC\etc directory**—This directory contains an extensive diagnostic log. In this directory **MDCSupport.log** contains a log of what has been collected by the **MDCSupport** utility, and any errors that have been encountered. **mdcsupporttemp** directory contains information about different management console (MCs), which are discussed in their respective chapters. Application and System Event Logs are also part of the same directory.

Following is the summary of what is collected by the MDCSupport tool:

- Database files.
- Configuration files and **MDCSupport** log file.
- Apache configuration and log files.
- Tomcat configuration and log files.
- Installation, audit, and operation log files.

- The CiscoWorks Common Services Registry subtree ([HKEY_LOCAL_MACHINE][SOFTWARE][Cisco][MDC]).
- Windows System Event and Application Event log files.
- Host environment information (operating system version and installed service packs, amount of RAM, disk space on all volumes, computer name, and virtual memory size).
- Process information.

Categorization of Problem Areas

Problem areas of VMS can be categorized as follows:

- Licensing issues
- Installation issues
- User management issues
- Database management issues

Licensing Issues

This section presents some of the most common licensing issues related to the CiscoWorks VPN/Security Management Solution (VMS) bundle.

Before you delve into further details, it is useful to review some of the licensing options you have on the VMS:

- **VMS Evaluation License**—This is a trial license, which expires in 90 days.
- **VMS Basic License**—This type of license supports up to five devices. This number restriction is only for the Management Consoles, not for CSA Agent. There is no license limitation on the number of CSA agents that can be managed if the agents are purchased separately.
- **VMS Restricted License**—This type of license supports up to 20 devices. Again, there is no license limitation on the number of CSA agents that can be managed, as they are purchased separately.
- **VMS Unrestricted License**—This type of license allows use of the product on a Windows or Solaris server for any number of devices.

VMS has two types of license keys that require registration with Cisco Systems and installation on the VMS server. These two types of license keys are:

- **The Management Center for Cisco Security Agent (CSA MC) key**—This key enables one CSA MC and three CSA server agents on the CiscoWorks Common Services server. Other agents are purchased and licensed separately.
- **Common services key**—This key enables all the other Management and Monitoring Center software in VMS. This key defines the number of hardware devices that can be managed.

Support of different licenses and installation methods is summarized in Table 17-2.

Table 17-2 *Support of Different Licenses on VMS*

License	VMS Basic	VMS Restricted	VMS Unrestricted	VMS Evaluation	Updating from a Previous VMS 2.x Version
Number of devices supported	5 device keys for Common Services	20 device keys for Common Services	Unlimited device keys for Common Services	Operates for 90 days	A previous VMS 2.0, 2.1 or 2.2 Common Services key will continue working with future VMS 2.x updates
CSA Support	Management of an unlimited number of CSA agents. Agents are purchased and licensed separately	Management of an unlimited number of CSA agents. Agents are purchased and licensed separately	Management of an unlimited number of CSA agents. Agents are purchased and licensed separately	N/A	N/A
Part Numbers	CWVMS-2.2-B-SR-K9 and bundled with various hardware bundles	CWVMS-2.2-WINR-K9 CWVMS-2.2-WUPGR-K9	CWVMS-2.2-UR-K9 CWVMS-2.2-UPGUR-K9	N/A	CWVMS-DEC03URMR-K9 CWVMS-DEC03RMR-K9
Registration for Common Services License Key	Not required	Refer to Registration for CiscoWorks Common Services	Registration for CiscoWorks Common Services	Not required	Not required. Use existing key from VMS 2.x
Installing the Common Services License Key	Refer to Installing the licensing key for VMS Common Services Key file name is VMS-SAMPLER.LIC and is located on the CD under license directory	Refer to Installing/ Upgrading the License Key for CiscoWorks Common Services	Refer to Installing/ Upgrading the License Key for CiscoWorks Common Services	Refer to Installing/ Upgrading the License Key for CiscoWorks Common Services	Refer to Installing/ Upgrading the License Key for CiscoWorks Common Services

Table 17-2 *Support of Different Licenses on VMS (Continued)*

License	VMS Basic	VMS Restricted	VMS Unrestricted	VMS Evaluation	Updating from a Previous VMS 2.x Version
Registration for CSA MC License Key	Not required	Refer to Registration for the Management Center for Cisco Security Agents	Refer to Registration for the Management Center for Cisco Security Agents	Not required	Refer to Registration for the Management Center for Cisco Security Agents
Installing CSA MC License Key	Refer to Installing the licensing key for the Management Center for Cisco Security Agents Key file name is CSAMC.LIC and is located on the CD under license directory	Refer to Installing the License Key for the Management Center for Cisco Security Agents	Refer to Installing the License Key for the Management Center for Cisco Security Agents	Refer to Installing the License Key for the Management Center for Cisco Security Agents	Refer to Installing the License Key for the Management Center for Cisco Security Agents

The sections that follow contain the registration and installation process of different licenses as described in Table 17-2.

Registration for CiscoWorks Common Services

If you have the VMS Basic CD, you do not need to register. You can find the license key file in the license directory of the VMS Basic CD. The name of the license key file is **SAMPLER.LIC**.

However, the VMS Restricted and Unrestricted software requires registration on a Cisco Web site. The Common Services component within VMS installs a 90-day unrestricted license by default. The license expires after 90 days and the product will no longer function. It is highly recommended that you register and install a production license immediately.

To obtain a production license for your Common Services software, register your software at one of the following Web sites. You will need to provide the Product Authorization Key (PAK), which is printed on a label affixed to the VMS Management and Monitoring Centers (VMMC) sub-box.

If you are a registered user of Cisco.com, use this Web site: http://www.cisco.com/cgi-bin/Software/FormManager/formgenerator.pl

If you are not a registered user of Cisco.com, use this Web site: http://www.cisco.com/pcgi-bin/Software/FormManager/formgenerator.pl

The production license will be sent to the e-mail address that you provided during registration process. Retain this license with your CiscoWorks Common Services software records.

Installing/Upgrading the License Key for CiscoWorks Common Services

After you obtain the production license via e-mail, work through the following steps to license your software or upgrade it from trial to production version:

Step 1 Copy the new license file to the CiscoWorks Common Services server. Note the name of the file and the directory location of the file.

Step 2 From the CiscoWorks server menu, select **VPN/Security Management Solution > Administration > Common Services > Licensing Information**. The License Information dialog box displays. The license type, number of devices supported by the license, and the expiration date of the license display under License Information. Note that the **VPN/Security Management Solution** drawer is available only if Management Center (MC) applications are installed on your server.

Step 3 To update your license, follow these steps:

- Enter the path to the new license file in the Filename field, or click **Select** to locate the new file that was noted in Step 1. Do not add the CSA license file by mistake. This will result in an error message suggesting a corrupt license. Then follow these steps: Click **Update**. After the system verifies the license file, a message indicates the status of the license update. To close the message box, click **OK**. The updated licensing information displays under License Information.

Registration for the Management Center for Cisco Security Agents (CSA MC)

In addition to registering for the VMS Common Services, you also need to register on the Cisco Web site for the Cisco Security Agent (CSA) software.

Web registration is not required if you have the VMS 2.2 kit that includes the VMS 2.2 update 1 (see the label on the VMMC CD—these kits are shipped after January 2004). Registration is also not required if you have the VMS Basic CD.

Older VMS 2.2 kits that shipped before January 2004 require registration for the CSA management console and three server agents that are included with VMS.

If you are a registered user of Cisco.com, use this Web site: http://www.cisco.com/cgi-bin/Software/FormManager/formgenerator.pl

If you are not a registered user of Cisco.com, use this Web site: http://www.cisco.com/pcgi-bin/Software/FormManager/formgenerator.pl

Installing the License Key for the Management Center for Cisco Security Agents (CSA MC)

You must install the CSA MC license before the CSA Agent license installation. Following are the two ways you can install the CSA MC license:

- **During installation**—During the installation, you are prompted to copy the license into the CSA MC directory. If you choose **Yes**, you can browse to the license file on the system (or in an accessible file share), save it, and continue the installation. So, once you get the license key file from Cisco, you need to save the file on the same server as CiscoWorks Common Services, or to a shared drive that the CiscoWorks server can access. Alternatively, you can choose **No** when prompted and copy the license when the installation has completed and the system is rebooted.
- **After installation**—To install the license file after CSA MC installation, go to **VPN/Security Management Solution > Management Center > Security Agents (V4.5) > Maintenance > License Information**. The License Information screen displays. You can browse to the license file by clicking the **Browse** button. Once the license file is located, click the **Upload** button to copy the file into the CSA MC directory. Ensure that you select the **CSA license file** and not the Common Services license file. You need to have the license file copied on the client PC from where you are accessing the CiscoWorks Common Services server.

Common Licensing Issues and Work-Arounds

Troubleshooting steps are explained in detail in Chapter 18, "Troubleshooting IDM and an IDS/IPS Management Console (IDS/IPS MC)" under the section entitled "IDS MC Licensing Issues," and therefore the details are not discussed thoroughly in this chapter. Following is a summary of the discussion covered in Chapter 18:

- **Corrupted or expired license**—There can be primarily two issues with licenses for CiscoWorks Common Services; the license is either corrupted or expired. In either case, you must get a new license from Cisco by sending an e-mail to licensing@cisco.com.
- **Terminal services issue**—You might receive installation errors with terminal services enabled (remote admin mode) for CiscoWorks or license errors while accessing VMS. To resolve these issues, disable Terminal Services before installing VMS.

Installation Issues

It is beyond the scope of this section to discuss all the details of installation procedures. This information can be found from the following location:

http://www.cisco.com/univercd/cc/td/doc/product/rtrmgmt/cw2000/cw2000_d/comser22/ig_wincv/instl.htm

This section summarizes the major points and then discusses installation troubleshooting.

The following is the minimum hardware requirement for Common Services:

- Pentium III minimum 1 GHz
- Windows 2000 Server
- Win2k Service Pack 2
- New Technology File System (NTFS) (recommended)
- 1 gigabyte physical RAM
- 2 gigabytes minimum available hard drive space

It is strongly recommended not to install CiscoWorks Common Services on any of the following:

- Primary domain controller
- Backup domain controller
- Terminal Server (If you require a Terminal Server, make sure to turn it off at the time of installation. Once the installation of CiscoWorks common services and other MCs is complete, you can turn this back on.)

The following are the prerequisites for Common Services installation:

- Minimum hardware.
- Target partition-formatted NTFS (recommended).
- Being logged into Windows as a local administrator.
- Required Microsoft components installed (Service packs, and so on).
- Removal of all software that uses conflicting ports (for example, HTTP, FTP, etc).
- Disabling of any hardware-specific services during installation. For example, disable any unnecessary COMPAQ services.
- Disabling of anti-virus software during time of installation.

Installation Steps

Work through the following steps to install the CiscoWorks Common Services:

Step 1 Place the CD in the drive.

Step 2 After Install starts, accept the licensing agreement.

Step 3 Install in the default directory on the NTFS drive of your choice **C:\Program Files\CSCOpx**.

Step 4 Locate the license file and provide it when asked.

Step 5 Enter the Windows administrator password and confirm the password.

Step 6 Default values for the Lock Manager (LM) and Frame Management System (FMS or database) are displayed. *Do not* change these port numbers unless another service on the system conflicts with them. The LM default port is 1272 and FMS is 9652.

Step 7 Enter the information such as HTTPS port (usually TCP/443), e-mail address of the system admin, and SMTP server information used by the Apache web server.

Generate a certificate with generation input and remember the information in the fields on this page. Input will be used to generate the local security certificate. Fields included are: Country code, State name, Company name, Organization name, Domain name, Certificate password.

Step 8 Then create a shortcut option display.

Change the passwords as needed: Causer (internal admin user, not visible, use random); Admin (admin); Guest (blank); CMF Database (random).

Step 9 Finally, you will be asked to restart the computer.

After the server is rebooted, you can point your browser as follows: **http://server_name:1741**

You can log in to Common Services by entering **admin** in the **Name** field. If you have not changed the default password during installation, type **admin** in the password field. Click **Connect** or press **Enter**.

Troubleshooting Installation Problems

Most of the installation-related issues are reported to the console at the time of the installation. Additional information can be found from the installation log, which is discussed under the "Diagnostic Commands and Tools" section. Following is a list of probable causes of installation failure:

- **Not logged in as administrator**—If you are not logged in to Windows with administrator privileges, you will receive this message during installation: "CiscoWorks Common Services installation cannot proceed because you are not logged in as an administrator." To resolve this issue, log in to Windows with local administrator privileges and try installing again.

- **Installation file corruption**—When you download the CiscoWorks Common Services software from the Cisco Web site, a transmission error can occur for various reasons. You will get message such as these: "Decompression failed on *file*. The error was for *error code per CompressGet;*" or "General file transmission error. Please check your target location and try again. Error number: *error code;*" or "Severe: Cannot run the dependency handler." In all cases, to resolve the issue, download the software again from the Cisco Web site.
- **File-write operation failure**—If a file-write operation failed, you will receive this message during installation: "Unable to write *infoFile* or Unable to create *infoFile*." Under this circumstance, run the file system checking utility, and then repeat the installation. Verify that you have write permission to the destination directory and windows TEMP directory; then repeat the installation. The environment variable %TEMP% provides the location on TEMP directory.
- **File-open operation failure**—If the file-open operation fails, it will result in "OpenFile failed: *pathname*" message. Run the file system checking utility, then repeat the installation. Verify whether you have read permission on *pathname*, and then repeat the installation.
- **Unable to stop the service**—During installation, one or more services might not be stopped by the installer, resulting in this message: "Cannot stop service *servicename*." Under this circumstance, select **Control Panel > Services** and stop the service *servicename* manually; then proceed with (un)installing.
- **Windows failed to load Dynamic Link Library (DLL)**—DLL is supposed to be available at any time for any process. Otherwise, installation will fail with either of these messages: "UseDLL failed for *dll*"; or "*function* failed: DLL function not found." Check permissions on the system32 directory under %WINDIR%. If *dll* is secure.dll or r_inst.dll, check the product installation media for errors or reinstall Windows.
- **Setting file permission failure**—If you are not logged in as administrator, or if you are installing on a FAT file system, CiscoWorks Common Services cannot provide file security, and the following error message will display during installation: "ProtectFile failed: *file*: error. WWW admin security may be incomplete."
- **Database corruption**—If the existing database file is broken, or if the previous version of CiscoWorks Common Services is destroyed, you will see this message: "Launch of isql script failed." Usually this problem occurs during reinstallation. Under this circumstance, you might need to contact the Cisco Support Team for consultation on whether the database recovery is possible.
- **DNS issues**—If you do not have the DNS name resolution for the server where you are installing the CiscoWorks Common Services or have problems with DNS resolution, you can still proceed with the CiscoWorks Common Services installation. However, you must correct the DNS problem before running the software. DNS might fail for a number of reasons, among which these three are important: the DNS server is not working, DNS is slow, or the host name of this server is not defined in DNS server.

- **Lack of space in the TEMP directory**—The installer requires temporary workspace. You have less than 8 MB of free space on *drive*. Please free up some space and try again. There is not enough drive space for temporary installation files. Make more drive space available (%TEMP%), then rerun installation.
- **Trying to install on Primary Domain Controller (PDC) or Backup Domain Controller (BDC)**—Installing CiscoWorks Common Services is not supported either on PDC or BDC. You must install it on a standalone server.
- **Installing in the wrong directory**—If you try to install CiscoWorks Common Services in a root directory (for example c:\> or d:\>), the installation will fail. You need to create a directory off the root to proceed with the installation.

User Management Issues

CiscoWorks Common Services provides the flexibility to change the user password and allows you to create or delete users. The following are some of tasks you can perform:

- **Changing Admin Password**—Select **Server Configuration > Setup > Security > Modify My Profile** in the navigation tree to change the admin password. Type a new password in the **Local Password** and **Confirm Password** fields. Finally, click **Modify**.
- **Modifying or Deleting a Guest Account**—Select **Server Configuration > Setup > Security > Modify/Delete Users** in the navigation tree. Then Select the **Guest** account and click **Delete** twice to delete the account.

Several user databases can be used to authenticate and authorize the user who needs to access the CiscoWorks Common Services using a browser. These databases are considered external databases to CiscoWorks Common Services. One of the most popular of these databases is Cisco Secure Access Control Server (CS ACS). In the "Case Studies" section of this chapter, we will explore how to configure the CiscoWorks Common Services with the CS ACS server for user authentication when accessing the CiscoWorks Common Services.

Database Management Issues

This section examines how to run a backup and a restore on a CiscoWorks Common Services server for disaster recovery, or just to back up the data from one server to the other.

Depending on the configuration of the server, you might need to back up one or more of the following databases:

- CiscoWorks Common Servers database containing the user information created in Common Services for login purpose.
- Management Console database (Sybase).
- CSA MC database, which is handled differently and is totally independent of the other MC database.

The sections that follow explain how to back up the CiscoWorks Common Services databases. The other components of database backup and restore procedures are explained in their corresponding chapters.

CiscoWorks Common Services Backup

You can schedule automatic database backup or choose an immediate backup of the CiscoWorks Common Services database. Database options work within the current version only and do not support other versions. Work through the following steps to configure automatic backup:

Step 1 Select **Server Configuration > Administration > Database Management > Schedule Backup**. The Set Backup Schedule dialog box displays.

Step 2 Enter the following information:

— **Backup Directory**—Location of the backup directory. It is recommended that your target location be on a different partition than where CiscoWorks is installed.

— **Generations**—Number of database backup copies to retain. The system keeps only the number of copies you specify.

— **Time**—From the drop-down lists, select the time for the backup to occur. Use a 24-hour format.

— **Frequency**—Select the backup schedule:

(a) Daily—The database is backed up every day at the time specified.

(b) Weekly—The database is backed up once a week on the day and time specified. Select the day of the week from the drop-down list.

(c) Monthly—The database is backed up once a month on the day and time specified. Select the day of the month from the drop-down list.

Click **Finish**. The Schedule Backup message verifies your schedule and provides the location of backup log files.

The database backup file name structure is as follows:

/generationNumber/suite/directory/filename

An explanation of the meaning of each field follows::

- **generationNumber**—Number of backups. For example, 1, 2, and 3, with 3 being the latest database backup.

- **Suite**—Application or suite. CiscoWorks server suite is **cmf**. Other optional suites are supported.
- **Directory**—What is being stored. Directories include databases and any suite applications.
- **Filename**—File that has been backed up. Files include database (.db), log (.log), version (DbVersion.txt), manifest (.txt), tar (.tar), and data files (datafiles.txt).

You can back up data on demand instead of waiting for the next scheduled backup by using this option. We recommend that your target location be on a different hard disk or partition than where CiscoWorks is installed. Database options work within the current version only and do not support other versions.

Follow these procedures to perform on-demand backup:

Step 1 Select **Server Configuration > Administration > Database Management > Back Up Data Now**. The Back up Data Now dialog box displays.

Step 2 Enter the pathname of the target directory.

Step 3 To begin the backup, click **Finish**. This process could take some time to complete.

CiscoWorks Common Services Restore

You can restore your database by running a script from the command line. Database options work within the current version only and do not support other versions.

NOTE If you restore the database when CiscoWorks server is enable for Secure Sockets Layer (SSL), the backed up Server Certificate and Private Key will also be restored. Your existing Certificate and Private Key will be overwritten. Restoring the database from a backup permanently replaces your database with the backed up version.

Work through the following steps on Windows platform to restore the CiscoWorks Common Services database:

Step 1 At the command line, make sure you have the correct permissions.

Step 2 Stop all processes: **net stop crmdmgtd**

Step 3 Restore the database: **%NMSROOT%\bin\perl %NMSROOT%\bin\restorebackup.pl [-force] [-s suite] [-gen generationNumber] -d backup directory**, where **%NMSROOT%** is the CiscoWorks installation directory.

Step 4 To restore the most recent version, enter the following command: **%NMSROOT%\bin\restorebackup.pl -d drive:\var\backup\%NMSROOT%\log\restorebackup.log**

Step 5 Restart the system: **net start crmdmgtd**

Case Studies

This case study goes through the configuration of User Authentication for managing Common Services using a Local database and an AAA Server.

Work through the following steps to authenticate the user against the local database:

Step 1 Select **Server Configuration>Setup>Security>Select Login Module**.

Step 2 Click **CiscoWorks Local** in the available module field. Then click **Next**.

Step 3 Click **False** in the debug field unless additional debug log files are needed.

Step 4 Click **Finish**.

The next time a user logs in, Common Services local login module will be used.

If you decide at this time to perform user authentication using a TACACS+ server, work through the following steps:

Step 1 Select **Server Configuration>Setup>Security>Select Login Module**.

Step 2 Select TACACS+ for Login Module.

Step 3 Click Next.

Step 4 Specify the IP address and the Key for the TACACS+ server. For Login fallback options, select the second radio button to enable the admin user to log in the event when TACACS+ server is unreachable.

Step 5 Click Finish.

It is important to synchronize to authentication server to use the AAA server for user authentication. Work through the following steps to perform this task:

Step 1 Go to **VPN/Security Management Solution > Administration > Common Services > Configuration > AAA Server**.

Step 2 Click the **Synchronize** button. This will clear the previous server information.

Step 3 Select the ACS option under "AAA Server Info." AAA server details will be populated automatically from the previous AAA server definition. Under Login, define Administrator Name and password along with the Shared Secret Key.

Then either click on **Finish** to save the configuration, or optionally, if you want to perform authorization for different MCs, then on the same page, click on **Register**. Then move **Available Application** to **Selected Application**. Then click **OK**. This will push the Authorization parameters for the MCs selected to the AAA server so that authorization can be turned on by CS ACS.

The following are the configuration steps required on the Cisco Secure ACS server for CiscoWorks Common Services Authentication:

Step 1 On CS ACS GUI, go to **Administration Control > Add Administrator**. Create an administrator account for Common Services. This administrator account is used by the CiscoWorks Common Services to complete the registration process, which is required to turn on authorization for different MCs.

Step 2 Configure CiscoWorks Common Services as an AAA client on the CS ACS Server by going to the **NAS Configuration** page on CS ACS GUI.

Step 3 Add a user account and map these users to their corresponding groups.

Step 4 Edit the group to which the users belong, and select the authorization parameter for the corresponding MCs.

Common Problems and Resolutions

This section deals with some of the problems commonly encountered with Common Services and their resolutions. For additional FAQ, refer to the following link:

http://www.cisco.com/univercd/cc/td/doc/product/rtrmgmt/cw2000/cw2000_d/comser22/usrguide/cmsrvall/diagnos.htm#wp1014270

1. What is the Positioning with the VMS Basic License?

   Answer: A VMS Basic kit is bundled with selected Cisco Security Devices. The VMS 2.2 Basic License offers the same functionality as the VMS 2.2 Restricted licensed software. The VMS Basic kit includes functionality to manage firewalls, routers VPNs, NIDS, and CSA.

   However, the VMS Basic kit differs from the VMS restricted license in the following areas:

   — The basic license does not provide the use of RME and VPN Monitor components.

   — The basic license is limited to the management of five devices. Note however, that the customer may manage an unlimited number of Cisco Security Agents that are licensed and purchased separately.

   — There is no registration required for VMS Basic. The license keys for Common Services, the Management Center for CSA, and the three CSA server agents to protect VMS are on the CD. Look in the license directory on the VMS Basic CD for two license files. Follow the previous instructions to add the licenses. Registration will be required if the customer has purchased additional CSA agents.

If you need support for 6 to 20 devices, the VMS restricted license is recommended. If you need to support more than 20 devices, or need to install on Solaris, the VMS Unrestricted License is recommended. Further information is available at www.cisco.com/go/vms.

2 Can I Extend the 90-day Evaluation License?

Answer: No, you cannot extend use of the evaluation license without re-installing the software. The purpose of providing the evaluation license is to evaluate the product in a lab environment (not in production) and get enough time to purchase and register the production license. You will need a license key that has been purchased to be installed on the CiscoWorks Server to continue using the software without re-installation.

3 How are the devices counted for VMS Basic and VMS Restricted Licenses?

Answer: The VMS Restricted License provides management for 20 devices (firewalls, IDSs, and routers) in total. For example, 5 PIX firewalls, 7 Cisco IOS routers, and 8 IDS sensors, or any other combination totaling 20 can be supported with this license. For VMS Basic, the total number of devices supported is five. Note, however, that you can manage an unlimited number of Cisco Security Agents, as Agents are licensed and purchased separately.

4 Where is the 90-day Evaluation License located?

When you install Common services v2.2, you are prompted for the license key, and the directory should automatically point to the default location. If you click on the **Browse** button and look in that directory, you will find a file that ends in **.lic**. Just select that file. If you have already performed the installation without adding the license, you can find it in the **<home>/CSCOpx/MDC/etc** directory.

5 I have lost my password for CiscoWorks Common Services. How can I recover my password?

Answer: All the CiscoWorks Common Services local user names and encrypted passwords including **admin** and **guest** are stored in **cwpass** file under the following directory:

C:\program files\CSCOpx\lib\classpath\com\cisco\nm\cmf\servlet

The original password file which contains **admin/admin** can be found at **cwpass** file under the following directory:

C:\program files\CSCOpx\lib\classpath\com\cisco\nm\cmf\servlet\orig directory.

If you want to reset both **admin** and **guest** user passwords, replace the whole **cwpass** file from "C:\program files\CSCOpx\lib\classpath\com\cisco\nm\cmf\servlet\orig" directory to "C:\program files\CSCOpx\lib\classpath\com\cisco\nm\cmf\servlet\"

If you merely want to change the **admin** password, then you can replace the line in **cwpass** beginning with admin with admin:0DPiKuNIrrVmD8IUCuw1hQxNqZc=::::F::.

Then **stop** and **start** the Daemon Manager Service.

6 During installation, which passwords are for the CiscoWorks Common Services user accounts and which are for Windows NT/2000 accounts?

Answer: The **administrator** account at the beginning of installation is the Windows NT/2000 administrator account for your CiscoWorks Common Service server.

causer account is an NT/2000 account to run the desktop services by CiscoWorks Common Services.

guest and **admin** accounts are both CiscoWorks Common Services accounts.

All database password accounts are database accounts that are used only by CiscoWorks Common services internally.

7 Can I back up CiscoWorks Common services information only excluding the MCs?

Answer: Yes, you can. Go to backup utility under **Server Configuration > Administration >** under Database Management to perform this task. This will back up CiscoWorks Common Service user data and Cisco Works-specific data and will not back up MC data.

8 Does CiscoWorks Common Services work in multi-homed server?

Answer: A multi-homed machine is a machine that has multiple NIC cards, each configured with different IP addresses. To run CiscoWorks Common Services on a multi-homed machine, there are two requirements.

- First, all IP addresses must be configured in DNS.
- Second, because of restrictions with Common Object Request Broker Architecture (CORBA), only one IP address can be used by the client/browser to access the server. You must select one IP address as the external address, with which the client will log in to the CiscoWorks server.

To select an IP address, modify the gatekeeper file located in NMSROOT\lib\vbroker\gatekeeper.cfg. Replace every instance of external-IP-address with the external IP address you choose, and remove the number character (#) character, from the following:

- #vbroker.gatekeeper.backcompat.callback.host=external-IP-address
- #vbroker.se.exterior.host=external-IP-address
- #vbroker.se.iiop_tp.host=external-IP-address
- #vbroker.se.interior.host=external-IP-address

After modifying the gatekeeper file, restart the Daemon Manager by entering:

net stop crmdmgtd

net start crmdmgtd

9 Are there any interoperability issues with CiscoWorks Common Services web server when another web server is installed on the same server where CiscoWorks Common Services is installed?

Answer: If the web sever uses port 80, then there should be no issues. However, as the sensor pulls the signature or service pack upgrades from IDS MC using SSL (TCP/443), this causes port conflicts with a different web server if it is running SSL. Hence, the author recommends not installing any other web server on the server on which CiscoWorks Common Services is installed.

10 How can I turn on SSL?

Answer: You can turn on SSL either via the Web or via CLI.

In the CiscoWorks desktop, select **Server Configuration > Administration > Security Management > Enable/Disable SSL**.

The Configure SSL window appears in the right frame. Click the Enable button.

You can turn SSL using CLI as well. Navigate to the directory *NMSROOT*\lib\web. Enter **<NMSROOT>\bin\perl ConfigSSL.pl –enable**. Then press **Enter**. Then stop and start the services with the following two commands:

net stop crmdmgtd

net start crmdmgtd

11 Where is the Compact Database log?

Answer: There should be logging information in: **$NMSROOT\MDC\tomcat\vms\maas**

12 Where can I find the debug information when I switch to TACACS+ with Debug set to True?

Answer: Debugging information is not shown in the Graphical User Interface (GUI), but can be found in the following locations:

— On Unix server, the debug information can be found in "$NMSROOT/objects/jrun/jsm-cw2000/logs/stdout.log"

— On Windows 2000, the debug can be found in "%NMSROOT%\lib\jrun\jsm-cw2000\logs\stdout.log"

13 Can I install Cisco Secure ACS and CiscoWorks Common Services in the same server?

Answer: This is not a supported configuration.

14 How do I replace a corrupted license?

Answer: Go to the CMF Desktop, and click on **VPN/Security ManagementSolution > Administration > Licensing Information**. Then choose the new license file and click **Update**.

Licenses are rarely corrupted; however, if it happens, send e-mail to licensing@cisco.com.

15 Can two different versions of Java Runtime Environment (JRE) exist on the same server?

Answer: Yes, two different version of JRE (for example JRE 1.4.1 and 1.3.1) can be installed on the same client PC. Sometimes, this is required for running two different applications or the same application with two different versions.

For all the applications to be accessed properly, do the following: In Internet Explorer (IE), go to **Tools > Internet Options > Advanced > Under Java (Sun)**, and uncheck the box marked **Use Java 2 v1.4.1_03 <applet>**.

Best Practices

Some of the best practices for managing the Common Services securely and efficiently are as follows:

- Install Common Services on its own partition.
- Use strong and separate passwords for Window Administrator and CiscoWorks Common Services.
- Avoid creating network shares on the CiscoWorks Common Services Server.
- Disable unnecessary accounts.
- Secure the Registry of the Windows platform.
- Apply all hot fixes and patches as soon as they are available.
- Disable unused and unneeded services.
- Disable all protocols except TCP/IP.
- Monitor the activities of your system regularly with Auditing/Reporting Tools. Cisco Security Agent (CSA) Management Console (MC), which is a component of VMS bundle, can be installed to monitor the stopping of malicious activity on the server.
- Limit physical access to the server. This is extremely important, as with physical access, CiscoWorks Common Services server function can be disrupted very badly.

CHAPTER 18

Troubleshooting IDM and IDS/IPS Management Console (IDS/IPS MC)

To take advantage of the full functionality intrusion detection system (IDS/IPS) sensors, you need two pieces of software: a management utility for configuring the sensor, and a reporting utility for viewing alarms generated by the sensor. The IDS/IPS sensors come loaded with an Intrusion Detection Manager (IDM) for configuration. For alarm viewing, the Intrusion Detection Event Viewer (IEV) can be downloaded free of charge (IEV is discussed in detail in Chapter 22, "Troubleshooting IEV and Security Monitors"). In summary, IDM is the management piece, and IEV is the reporting tool for small deployment (typically 1-2 sensors). As with IDM, you can configure only one sensor; however, this does not scale very well for large deployments. Hence, IDS/IPS Management Console (IDS/IPS MC), which is a component of VPN and Security Management Solution (VMS), is used to manage multiple sensors, and Security Monitor is used as a reporting tool for multiple sensors (IEV can be used for up to 5 sensors). This chapter delves into the details of both the management utility and comprehensive troubleshooting steps for IDM and the IDS/IPS MC on Windows platform.

Overview of IDM and IDS/IPS Management Console (IDS/IPS MC)

IDM (Intrusion Detection Manager) is a Web-based utility for configuring the sensors. IDM is included as part of the sensor software and can be accessed through the sensor's web server. IDM can be used only to configure the sensor on which it is running.

IEV (Intrusion Detection Event Viewer) is a Windows program that you can download free from Cisco.com and install on your own desktop. You then need to configure it to connect to the sensor and pull alarms from the sensor. IEV is limited to pulling events from five sensors, so it is only suitable for small installations (see Chapter 22, "Troubleshooting IEV and Security Monitors" for more details on IEV).

For larger deployments (more than five sensors) we recommend purchasing VPN and Security Management Solution (VMS). VMS contains two utilities used for managing and monitoring IDS/IPS sensors:

- **IDS/IPS Management Console (IDS/IPS MC)**—A Web-based configuration tool designed for configuration of multiple sensors.

- **Security Monitor (SecMon)**—A Web-based alarm viewing tool used for monitoring large numbers of sensors (see Chapter 22, "Troubleshooting IEV and Security Monitor" for troubleshooting Security Monitor).

IDS/IPS MC and Security Monitor Processes

A set of processes manage the tasks that IDS/IPS MC and Security Monitor perform. If one of those processes is not running, the function they are responsible for will not work. If there are some problems in running the application, it is always a good practice to check that all those processes are running. The following list outlines the processes and their main functions:

- **IDS_Analyzer**—Processes event rules and requests user-specified notifications when appropriate.
- **IDS_Backup**—Is responsible for the IDS/IPS MC and SecMon backup and restore processes.
- **IDS_DbAdminAnalyzer** —Periodically checks the database rules created and starts the execution if the triggering conditions are met.
- **IDS_DeployDaemon**—Manages the configuration deployment.
- **IDS_EvsServer**—Is the daemon for the Event viewer.
- **IDS_Notifier**— Receives notification requests (script, e-mail, or console) from other subsystems and performs the requested notifications.
- **IDS_Receiver**—Receives events and syslog and stores them in the database.
- **IDS_ReportScheduler**—Generates schedules reports.

If any of those processes is not running, the task that the process controls will not work. To check the status of the processes and start them, go to **Server Configuration > Administration > Process Management**. From there you can view the status of the processes, stop the processes, or start stopped processes. All the processes that start with **"IDS_"** are related to the Security Monitor or IDS/IPS MC.

As mentioned before, IDS/IPS MC is used to manage single or multiple sensors on different sensor platforms. It is important to understand and be aware of the versions of sensor supported by different IDS/IPS MC versions. Refer to the following link to find out the devices and sensor versions that are supported by different versions of IDS/IPS MC:

http://www.cisco.com/en/US/products/sw/cscowork/ps3990/products_device_support_tables_list.html

Communication Architecture

IDS/IPS MC uses both SSH (secure shell) and HTTPS (SSL) protocols to communicate with an IDS/IPS sensor to perform its task. Following is the list of functions it performs with the help of SSH and HTTPS:

- **Importing the configuration of a sensor**—When IDS/IPS MC imports the configuration from a sensor, it logs in to the sensor using SSH. Then the actual configuration of the sensor is transferred using RDEP protocol, which uses HTTPS (HTTP/SSL).

- **Deploying the configuration to a sensor**—The deployment of configuration uses different protocols in different versions. Before IDS/IPS MC 2.0, the deployment of the configuration to the sensor is performed using SSH. Basically IDS/IPS MC types the command using an SSH connection to the sensor, which is a very time-consuming process. Starting with IDS/IPS MC version 2.0, the changes of the configuration are pushed to the sensor using RDEP (HTTP/SSL), which is much more efficient.
- **Upgrading the signature or service packs to the sensor**—Upgrade of signature or service packs require both SSH and HTTPS. Command execution by IDS/IPS MC to the sensor is performed using SSH, and the actual signature or service packs are transferred to the sensor using HTTPS (HTTP/SSL).

So all communication takes place between IDS/IPS MC and the sensor using both SSH and SSL. Hence, it is extremely important to open these protocols in both directions if there is a firewall between IDS/IPS MC and the sensor.

Diagnostic Commands and Tools

Most of the problems that arise with IDS/IPS MC involve importing sensors, sensor upgrades, and configuration deployments to the sensor. This section explains various logs available to troubleshoot any of these issues with IDS/IPS MC.

Audit Reports

Audit Reports provide much useful information about the IDS/IPS MC server. So, if there is any problem, either with a specific subsystem or with the IDS/IPS MC server itself, first look for information in the Audit reports. Among all the templates under **Reports**, the most important one is **Audit Log Report**, which provides information that is broad in scope about any abnormal behavior of functions on IDS/IPS MC. So to find out the cause of any problem with the functionality of IDS/IPS MC, this is the first report you must generate and view on the IDS/IPS MC. In addition, this report leads you in the right direction for generating additional reports, such as specific subsystem reports. To generate an **Audit Log Report**, within the IDS/IPS MC, click the **Reports** tab and choose **Definitions.** Click, for example, **create** of the type **Audit log report** for the last day. Select **all** for event security and choose all the options available, and click **next**. Run this report immediately. Then, either view the report on the IDS/IPS MC itself or export it for offline analysis. More details on audit reports can be found from the following location:

http://www.cisco.com/univercd/cc/td/doc/product/rtrmgmt/cw2000/mgt_ids/idsmc20/ug/ch009.htm

MDCSupport File

If you want to have the comprehensive log to troubleshoot any issue on IDS/IPS MC, you must generate an MDCSupport file. Sections that follow describe how to collect the MDCSupport file.

How to Collect MDCSupport on a Windows Platform

Work through the steps that follow to collect the MDCSupport file on a Windows platform:

Step 1 Open the MS-DOS command prompt window through **Start> Run** >. Then enter **cmd** and click **OK**.

Step 2 The command prompt window opens. Enter **MDCSupport** at the prompt. Then press **Enter**.

Step 3 The **MDCSupport** utility creates a .zip file that contains your CiscoWorks Common Services configuration data and log files. The default directory of the .zip file is **/CSCOpx/MDC/etc**.

NOTE **MDCSupportInformation.zip** is created by default in the **/CSCOpx/MDC/etc** directory. To change the location of .zip file, enter **MDCSupport drive:\path** at the command prompt.

What to Look for and What Is Important in the MDCSupport File

Problems with the IDS/IPS MC are often unknown, and the MDCSupport file contains many files. Therefore, to identify the problem effectively, it is best to start by opening the file with WinZip, and then analyzing the file by sorting the files within the MDCSupport Zip file by file size. The largest file will always contain the most comprehensive information, so start by analyzing the largest file first. For example, if you sort by file size and see a very large **IDSDbAdminAnalyzer**, open it to look for errors. This file contains information on database transactions run on the IDS/IPS MC. You might get errors such as the following:

```
[04/06/2005 11:54:20] Looking at rule ID: 1
Exception in SystemContext - ASA Error -158: Value 72247 out of range for destination
[04/06/2005 11:54:20] Rule checker error:
[04/06/2005 11:54:20] com.cisco.nm.mdc.ids.common.exceptions.MdcException: ASA
Error -158: Value 72247 out of range for destination - com.sybase.jdbc2.jdbc
.SybSQLException: ASA Error -158: Value 72247 out of range for destination
[04/06/2005 11:54:20] Reached error toleration limit
```

This indicates that there may be a problem with the database index. Once you identify the problem, this can be followed up with the Cisco Support team for confirmation or for a possible fix.

Knowing the types of logs that go into different log files that are part of the package.cab file helps you analyze the log files of the package.cab file faster. Hence the list of different types of files with their contents are listed as follows:

- ***.evt files**—Files with the .evt extension contain information about Windows Event Log. These files display the errors Windows is encountering with the IDS/IPS MC and CiscoWorks. You have to load these files with the Event Viewer on a Windows system to view their output.
- **\apache\logs\error.log**—This log file contains information about errors on the web server for CiscoWorks. This is useful for troubleshooting issues with accessing the Web interface to CiscoWorks.
- **Ciscoworks_setup00X.log**—This file results from CiscoWorks installer output. It includes detailed information about the installation and any error messages for problems that occur at the time of installation. The best way to analyze this file is to open it and search by the key word "error" to see what problems may have occurred during the installation. You may have several of these files included in the Zip file depending on the number of times the software has been installed and re-installed.
- **stderr.log & stdout.log**—Process-related failures within IDS/IPS MC go into these files, so you must analyze these files. The following is an example of a database connection problem as reported by the stdout.log file:

```
Exception in SystemContext - IDSSystem unable to create SQL Statement: null
Database Connection creation failed!, err = JZ00L: Login failed. Examine the
SQLWarnings chained to this exception for the reason(s).
Detail - JZ006: Caught IOException: java.io.IOException: JZ0EM: End of data.
An error occurred while trying to add a message to the Audit Log, message
was IDSSystem unable to create SQL Statement: null
SQL Error is null
```

- **AuditLogFirst.log, AuditLogLast.log**—These are very important files and need to be analyzed thoroughly. The files display audit log information as discussed earlier in this section. Among many other things, this file shows if IDS/IPS MC has trouble pushing a signature update out, and will give you the specific details about the error message. For example, following is the message shown in the audit log when the signature upgrade job hangs on the IDS/IPS MC:

```
4644,'2005-04-06
16:06:15.703',0,0,3,11500,1004,1,3,0,'SYSTEM','sensor14: Error
while pushing files to the sensor java.lang.Exception: An exception
occurred during deploy, detail=The UI sensor version 4.1(4)S132 does
not match the real sensor version 4.1(4)S133',''
```

  Here you can see that the message clearly states that the IDS/IPS MC and sensor are not in agreement with the version that the IDS/IPS sensor is running; hence, the upgrade job hangs.

Enable Additional Debugging on IDS/IPS MC

Most of the issues with the IDS/IPS MC can be resolved with MDCSupport file. However, in some rare circumstances, getting to the root cause of the problem may not be possible without additional debug information. This information is usually analyzed by the Cisco developer. Work through the steps that follow to enable debugging on IDS/IPS MC:

Step 1 On the GUI, go to **Server Configuration > Administration > Process Management,** and stop the **IDS/_DeployDaemon** process.

Step 2 Back up the **DeploymentConfig.xml** file under **Program Files/CSCOpx/MDC/etc/ids/xml** into a location different from the installation base directory.

Step 3 Edit the **DeploymentConfig.xml** file with Notepad. In the **DeploymentConfig.xml** file change "**<DebugEnabled>false <DebugEnabled>**" to "**<DebugEnabled>true<DebugEnabled>**," and under **<CliLog>** change "**<Enabled>false<Enabled>**" to "**<Enabled>true<Enabled>**".

Step 4 On the GUI, go to **Server Configuration > Administration > Process Management,** and start the **IDS_DeployDaemon** process.

Import/Sigupdate will have debug messages in **/log/IDS_SensorInterfaceDebug.log** and deploy will have debug messages in the **IDS_DeploymentDebug.log** file. Also, collect the file **cli-log** in c or d:/documents and settings/(default user or username)/cli-log. More log files will be created under user's temp directory (**show temp**, from cmd line will report the exact temp directory) in Windows and under **/var/tmp** in Solaris.

NOTE When you are finished with debugging, reset the value for DebugEnabled and CliLog back to **false** and the value for CleanupTempFiles to **true**. These settings ensure that the log files do not become too large or consume large amounts of disk space.

Analysis of Problem Areas

After you install and initialize (with the **setup** command on the sensor) the sensor, the preliminary configuration of the sensor can be performed with IDM. By default the IDM is installed and turned on in the sensor. So, to access the sensor using IDM, you need only to open a supported version of the browser and point to the sensor's IP address as https://sensor_ip. As mentioned before, IDM can be used either as a primary management tool for the sensor (it can manage only one sensor) or for preliminary configuration, so that IDS/IPS MC can import the sensor configuration. Because IDM code runs on the sensor itself, most of the problems involve the IDM being unable to launch the IDM using a Web browser. This section explores the possible causes of not being able to launch IDM and goes into the details of IDS/IPS MC troubleshooting by covering the following topics:

- Important procedures and techniques
- Inability to access sensor using IDM

- IDS/IPS MC installation and upgrade issues
- IDS/IPS MC licensing issues
- Issues with importing sensors with IDS/IPS MC
- Signature or service pack upgrade issues with IDS/IPS MC
- Configuration deployment issues with IDS/IPS MC
- Database maintenance (pruning) issues with IDS/IPS MC

Important Procedures and Techniques

This section discusses some of the important procedures and techniques, which are essential for troubleshooting issues with importing a sensor, upgrading a signature or service packs, or deploying a configuration.

Verifying Allowed Hosts on the Sensor

Before you attempt to import the configuration from the sensor into IDS/IPS MC, your IDS/IPS MC must be one of the allowed hosts on the sensor. You can configure trusted hosts in two ways. Before you attempt to add the IDS/IPS MC network or host as a trusted host on the sensor, check to see if it is in the trusted list as shown in Example 18-1.

Example 18-1 *Network Lists that Are in the Sensor*

```
sensor# show configuration | include access
accessList ipAddress 171.0.0.0 netmask 255.0.0.0
accessList ipAddress 172.16.0.0 netmask 255.255.0.0
accessList ipAddress 10.0.0.0 netmask 255.0.0.0
accessList ipAddress 20.1.1.0 netmask 255.255.255.0
sensor#
```

Another way to verify allowed hosts (access-list) configuration is shown in Example 18-2.

Example 18-2 *Network List Configured on the Sensor*

```
sensor# configure terminal
sensor(config)# service host
!The following line is allowed only on version IDS 4.x
sensor(config-Host)# networkParams
!If you are running IPS 5.0 the above line should be replaced by the line below. The show
!settings output is from the IPS 5.0
sensor(config-Host)# network-settings
sensor(config-Host-net)# show settings
   network-settings
   -----------------------------------------------
      host-ip: 172.16.171.13/26,172.16.171.1 default: 10.1.9.201/24,10.1.9.1
      host-name: sensor13 default: sensor
      telnet-option: enabled default: disabled
```

continues

Example 18-2 *Network List Configured on the Sensor (Continued)*

```
!The following are the lists of network that are allowed to the sensor
      access-list (min: 0, max: 512, current: 3)
      -----------------------------------------------
         network-address: 10.0.0.0/8
         -----------------------------------------------
         network-address: 171.0.0.0/8
         -----------------------------------------------
         network-address: 172.0.0.0/8
         -----------------------------------------------
      -----------------------------------------------
      ftp-timeout: 300 seconds <defaulted>
      login-banner-text:  <defaulted>
   -----------------------------------------------
sensor(config-hos-net)#
```

If the desired host or network is not listed in the allowed host table, add in the sensor with the procedure described in the next sections.

Adding Allowed Hosts on the Sensor

The following are two ways to add trusted hosts on the sensor:

- Add an allowed host by running the **setup** command on the sensor.
- Add an allowed host manually on the sensor.

Adding an Allowed Host By Running **setup** Command on a Sensor

You can add the trusted hosts by running the **setup** command on the sensor as shown in Example 18-3.

Example 18-3 *Adding a Trusted Host Using the* **setup** *Command*

```
sensor# setup


    --- System Configuration Dialog ---

At any point you may enter a question mark '?' for help.
User ctrl-c to abort configuration dialog at any prompt.
Default settings are in square brackets '[]'.


Current Configuration:


networkParams
ipAddress 172.16.171.14
```

Example 18-3 *Adding a Trusted Host Using the* **setup** *Command (Continued)*

```
netmask 255.255.255.192
defaultGateway 172.16.171.1
hostname sensor14
telnetOption enabled
!These are the hosts allowed in the current configuration
accessList ipAddress 171.0.0.0 netmask 255.0.0.0
accessList ipAddress 171.69.0.0 netmask 255.255.0.0
accessList ipAddress 172.16.0.0 netmask 255.255.0.0
exit
timeParams
offset -480
standardTimeZoneName PDT
summerTimeParams
active-selection recurringParams
recurringParams
summerTimeZoneName PDT
exit
exit
exit
service webServer
general
ports 443
exit
exit


Current time: Mon Nov 15 16:02:12 2004


Setup Configuration last modified: Mon Nov 15 14:21:22 2004


Continue with configuration dialog?[yes]:
Enter host name[sensor14]:
Enter IP address[172.16.171.14]:
Enter netmask[255.255.255.192]:
Enter default gateway[172.16.171.1]:
Enter telnet-server status[enabled]:
Enter web-server port[443]:
!This is where you have the option to choose if you want to add additional allowed hosts
!to the ACL of the sensor
Modify current access list?[no]: yes
Current access list entries:
  [1] 171.0.0.0 255.0.0.0
  [2] 171.69.0.0 255.255.0.0
  [3] 172.16.0.0 255.255.0.0
Delete: 2
Delete:
! You are adding all hosts from 10.0.0.0 network to be able to connect to the sensor with
! the following line
```

continues

Example 18-3 *Adding a Trusted Host Using the* **setup** *Command (Continued)*

```
Permit: 10.0.0.0 255.0.0.0
!In the following line, you are leaving it blank and hit Enter which indicates that you
!have no more hosts to add
Permit:
Modify system clock settings?[no]:

The following configuration was entered.

networkParams
ipAddress 172.16.171.14
netmask 255.255.255.192
defaultGateway 172.16.171.1
hostname sensor14
telnetOption enabled
accessList ipAddress 171.0.0.0 netmask 255.0.0.0
accessList ipAddress 172.16.0.0 netmask 255.255.0.0
accessList ipAddress 10.0.0.0 netmask 255.0.0.0
exit
timeParams
offset -480
standardTimeZoneName PDT
summerTimeParams
active-selection recurringParams
recurringParams
summerTimeZoneName PDT
exit
exit
exit
service webServer
general
ports 443
exit
exit

[0] Go to the command prompt without saving this config.
[1] Return back to the setup without saving this config.
[2] Save this configuration and exit setup.

Enter your selection[2]:
Configuration Saved.
*16:04:23 PDT Mon Nov 15 2004
Modify system date and time?[no]:
sensor#
```

Adding an Allowed Host Manually on a Sensor

You can add the trusted hosts on the sensor using CLI. Example 18-4 shows how to add the trusted host.

Example 18-4 *Adding a Trusted Host Manually*

```
sensor# configure terminal
sensor(config)# service Host
sensor(config-Host)# networkParams
sensor(config-Host-net)# accessList ipAddress 20.1.1.0 netmask 255.255.255.0
sensor(config-Host-net)# exit
sensor(config-Host)# exit
Apply Changes:?[yes]:
sensor(config)# exit
sensor#
```

NOTE Make sure that the assigned ipAddress correlates to the netmask. A good example of an ipAddress is 10.1.1.0 255.255.255.0, and a bad example is 10.1.1.1 255.255.255.0.

Verifying the SSH and SSL Connection Between IDS/IPS MC and a Sensor

From the MC, open a command shell and change to {INSTALL_DIR}/CSCOpx/MDC/bin/ids directory.

Try **plink -ssh username@sensorIP.**

It should prompt you for the sensor's password.
Enter the password.

It may prompt you to accept a changed or new SSH fingerprint. Answer Yes.

You should now have a CLI prompt. Enter **show version.**
All the processes except CLI should report "Running". Exit.

Resolving SSH and SSL Connection Problems Between IDS/IPS MC and a Sensor

If IDS/IPS MC and the sensor are in two different networks, be sure that the network devices between IDS/IPS MC and the sensor are allowing SSH (TCP/22) and SSL (TCP/443) traffic in both directions. If both IDS/IPS MC and the sensor are in the same network, be sure that there is no Layer 2 firewall. If there is, open the ports (TCP/22, TCP/443) that are necessary for communication in both directions between the IDS/IPS MC and the sensor. Open a DOS prompt on the IDS/IPS MC, and try to connect to the sensor using plink -ssh username@ip_address_of_sensor, which will ensure that the communication is good between the IDS/IPS MC and the sensor.

Verifying If the Sensor Processes Are Running

To verify if all the processes are running on the sensor, use SSH or Telnet to access the sensor and execute **show version**. Example 18-5 shows the **show version** output on IDS/IPS sensor 4.x.

Example 18-5 *Output of* **show version** *Command from IDS/IPS Sensor 4.x*

```
sensor# show version
Application Partition:

Cisco Systems Intrusion Detection Sensor, Version 4.1(4)S145

OS Version 2.4.18-5smpbigphys
Platform: IDS-4250
Sensor up-time is 9 days.
Using 1123102720 out of 1980493824 bytes of available memory (56% usage)
Using 3.6G out of 15G bytes of available disk space (26% usage)


MainApp            2004_Apr_15_15.03  (Eng4e)    2004-09-09T15:08:54-0500  Running
AnalysisEngine     2004_Apr_15_15.03  (Eng4e)    2004-09-09T15:08:54-0500  Running
Authentication     2004_Apr_15_15.03  (Eng4e)    2004-09-09T15:08:54-0500  Running
Logger             2004_Apr_15_15.03  (Eng4e)    2004-09-09T15:08:54-0500  Running
NetworkAccess      2004_Apr_15_15.03  (Eng4e)    2004-09-09T15:08:54-0500  Running
TransactionSource  2004_Apr_15_15.03  (Eng4e)    2004-09-09T15:08:54-0500  Running
WebServer          2004_Apr_15_15.03  (Eng4e)    2004-09-09T15:08:54-0500  Running
CLI                2004_Apr_15_15.03  (Release)  2004-04-15T15:11:59-0500

Upgrade History:

  IDS-sig-4.1-4-S145.rpm.pkg   01:18:11 UTC Fri Feb 18 2005

Recovery Partition Version 1.2 - 4.1(1)S47


sensor#
```

Example 18-6 shows the output of the **show version** command, which shows all the processes are running on IPS version 5.0.

Example 18-6 *Output of* **show version** *Command from IDS/IPS Sensor 5.x*

```
sensor# show version
Application Partition:

Cisco Intrusion Prevention System, Version 5.0(1)S149.0

OS Version 2.4.26-IDS-smp-bigphys
Platform: IDS-4235
Serial Number: CGTWJ11
No license present
Sensor up-time is 16 days.
Using 780869632 out of 923549696 bytes of available memory (84% usage)
system is using 17.3M out of 29.0M bytes of available disk space (59% usage)
```

Example 18-6 *Output of* **show version** *Command from IDS/IPS Sensor 5.x (Continued)*

```
application-data is using 31.2M out of 174.7M bytes of available disk space (19%
usage)
boot is using 40.5M out of 75.9M bytes of available disk space (56% usage)
application-log is using 530.5M out of 2.8G bytes of available disk space (20% usage)


MainApp           2005_Mar_04_14.23  (Release)  2005-03-04T14:35:11-0600  Running
AnalysisEngine    2005_Mar_04_14.23  (Release)  2005-03-04T14:35:11-0600  Running
CLI               2005_Mar_04_14.23  (Release)  2005-03-04T14:35:11-0600

Upgrade History:

  IDS-K9-maj-5.0-1-   22:16:00 UTC Thu Mar 04 2004

Recovery Partition Version 1.1 - 5.0(1)S149

sensor#
```

Verifying That the Service Pack or Signature Level Sensor Is Running

After connecting to the sensor, you can execute **show version command** and look under the **Upgrade History:** to get the actual version information of the sensor. In Example 18-6, the sensor is shown to be running version 5.0(1) signature 149.

Verifying the Service Pack or Signature Level on IDS/IPS MC

If you are running IDS/IPS MC version 2.0 or above, you can find out the latest signature or service pack applied to the IDS/IPS MC by looking at the bottom of the first page of IDS/IPS MC. Before IDS/IPS MC version 2.0 or above, this information is not available. The only way to find the latest signature or service pack on the earlier version is by adding a dummy sensor on the IDS/IPS MC. Even on version 2.0 or above, though, you can find the latest version of the signature or service packs. To find the exact version of signature that the sensor is running (this may be a lower version than the latest version that IDS/IPS MC has), add a dummy sensor on the IDS/IPS MC. To determine the current version for IDS/IPS MC (in a version earlier than 2.0), work through the following steps:

Step 1 Go to the Device page and try to add one sensor (it can also be a non-existing sensor). Do not choose the **autodiscovery** option.

Step 2 In the second screen of the wizard, you will be asked to select the version of the sensor you want to add. The latest versions you see in this screen are the versions that are known to the IDS/IPS MC. Figure 18-1 shows how to find the version information with a dummy sensor.

Figure 18-1 *Checking the Version Information*

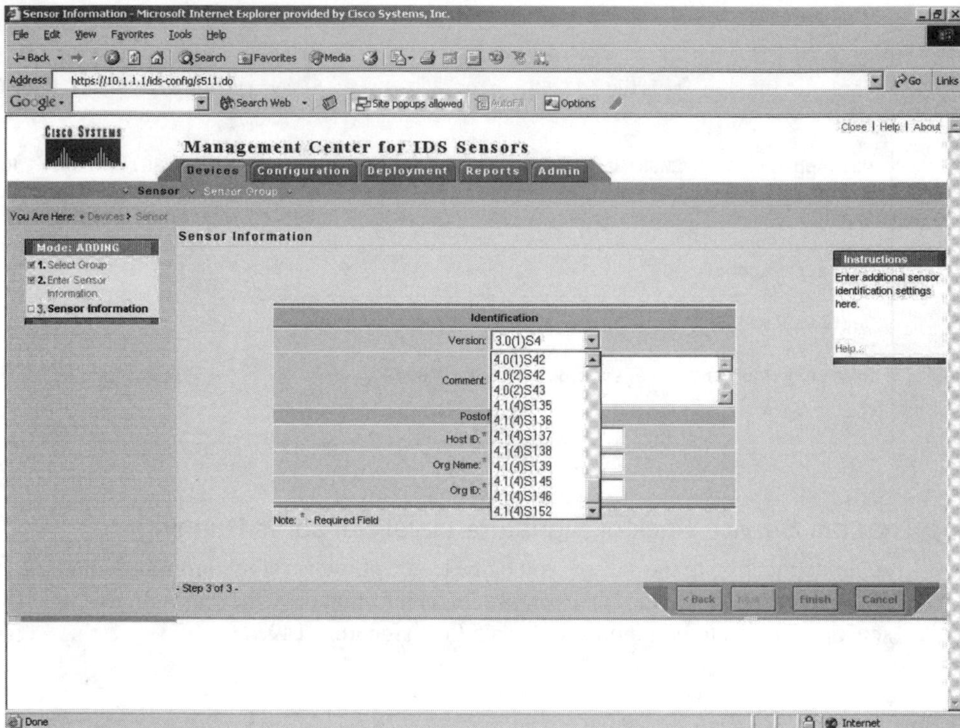

Step 3 You do not need to finish adding the sensor and can just click **Cancel**.

NOTE The IDS/IPS MC upgrade is not cumulative as it is on the sensor. You need to apply all the signature upgrades to the server for the signature to be recognized. It is not possible to downgrade the IDS/IPS MC server.

Verifying That the IDS/IPS MC (Apache) Certificate Is Valid

For successful secured communication between IDS/IPS MC and the sensor, the Apache certificate must be valid on the IDS/IPS MC. You can verify this by using the following procedure:

Step 1 Open a DOS command prompt.

Step 2 Change the directory to **ssl** by executing the following command:

```
C:\>cd Program Files\CSCOpx\MDC\Apache\conf\ssl
```

Step 3 Type the command **keytool –printcert –file server.cert.** This command provides the Apache Certificate details, including when it will expire. Note that part of the VMS installation creates an Apache certificate that expires in one year. Example 18-7 shows a certificate that does not expire until March 17, 2009.

Example 18-7 *The Certificate Does Not Expire Until March 17, 2009*

```
C:\cd Program Files\CSCOpx\MDC\Apache\conf\ssl>keytool -printcert -file server.cert
Owner: CN=wk2
Issuer: CN=Cisco Security Agent Root CA
Serial number: 4059c5a0
Valid from: Thu Mar 18 09:52:02 CST 2004 until: Tue Mar 17 09:52:02 CST 2009
Certificate fingerprints:
MD5:  7E:02:00:F3:43:57:3B:B3:F0:16:C1:F6:B3:77:F2:9F
SHA1:42:8A:6A:54:16:6E:7A:13:F6:82:F5:97:72:D6:D6:F5:DD:D1:E2:04
C:\cd Program Files\CSCOpx\MDC\Apache\conf\ssl>
```

Regenerating IDS/IPS MC (Apache) Certificate

If you have an expired certificated or corrupted certificate that is verified by the procedure explained in the preceding section, you can regenerate the Apache certificate using the following procedure:

Step 1 Stop the **CiscoWorks** Daemon Manager.

Step 2 Open a DOS command prompt.

Step 3 Type the command **cd install-dir/CSCOpx/MDC/Apache.**

Step 4 If you want to generate a certificate that has a validity period of longer than one year, edit the file **gencert.bat** and change the value **365** located at the end of the file to a larger value. For example, 3650 is about 10 years.

Step 5 Type the command **gencert**. This command creates a new certificate.

Step 6 Start the **CiscoWorks** Daemon Manager.

Resolving Issues with the IDS/IPS Sensor Being Unable to Get the Certificate

After you regenerate the certificate, it is important to refresh the trusted host. In addition, if the sensor is unable to get the certificate from IDS/IPS MC, work through the steps that follow to resolve this issue:

Step 1 Remove the existing certificate of IDS/IPS MC by using the following commands:

```
sensor# configure terminal
sensor(config)# no tls trusted-host ip-address [ip address of vms
server]
```

Step 2 Add the IDS/IPS MC by using the following command:

```
sensor(config)# tls trusted-host ip-address [ip address of vms server]
```

Step 3 If the previous two steps do not resolve the issue, log in to the service account, and 'su -' to the root. The procedure for creating a "service" account is explained in the section entitled "Creating a Service Account" under "Manually Updating the Signature Level on a Sensor." Then log in to the sensor with the "service" account and change to login as root. Then execute the commands shown in Example 18-8.

Example 18-8 *Procedure for Removing the Certificate to Resolve the Trusted Host Issue*

```
-bash-2.05b$ su -
Password:
-bash-2.05b# /etc/init.d/cids stop
Shutting down CIDS:
Remove cidmodcap:
Remove cidmodcap node:
-bash-2.05b# cd /usr/cids/idsRoot/etc/cert
-bash-2.05b# mv mytestca.cer mytestca.save
-bash-2.05b# rm -f *.cer
-bash-2.05b# mv mytestca.save mytestca.cer
-bash-2.05b# cd ..
-bash-2.05b# rm -f curTrustedCertificatesConfig.xml
-bash-2.05b# /etc/init.d/cids start
Checking kernel allocated memory: [  OK  ]
Load cidmodcap:
Create node:
Starting CIDS:
-bash-2.05b#
```

Step 4 After making the changes, reboot the sensor to be safe.

Step 5 Once the sensor is backed up, log in with the "Admin" account and add a trusted host as explained in Step 2.

Changing the VMS Server IP Address

Work through the steps that follow if you have changed the IP address of the VMS Server:

Step 1 Stop the service daemon manager.

Step 2 Use Notepad to open install-dir\MDC\etc\ids\xml\SystemConfig.xml.

Step 3 Change the <HostIP> value to the new IP address.

Step 4 Save the modified file.

Step 5 Copy the modified file to install-dir\MDC\Tomcat\vms\ids-config\web-inf\classes\com\cisco\nm\mdc\ids\common\SystemConfig.xml and install-dir\MDC\Tomcat\vms\ids-monitor\web-inf\classes\com\cisco\nm\mdc\ids\common\SystemConfig.xml.

Step 6 Use Notepad to open install dir\PostOffice\etc\routes.

Step 7 Change the host name and IP address to the new values.

Step 8 Save the modified file.

Step 9 Start the service daemon manager.

Manually Updating the Signature Level on the Sensor

In some rare circumstances, IDS/IPS MC upgrade may fail, so you might need to upgrade the signature or service packs of the sensor manually. To perform the manual upgrade, create a service account to transfer the upgrade file to the sensor from an FTP server, then run the upgrade command from the sensor itself.

Creating a Service Account

Work through the steps that follow to create the service account:

Step 1 Log in to the sensor using an "admin" account, and the prompt will look like following:

```
sensor#
```

Step 2 Enter into the configuration with thc following command:

```
sensor# configure terminal
```

Step 3 Create a user (this user name does not have to be service) with the service privilege by using the following command:

```
sensor(config)# username service privilege service password xxx
```

NOTE Only one service account can be configured on a sensor. The root user will have the same password as the service account.

Update Locally Over ftp/scp

Use the following technique if you cannot update the signature from the network (if it is failing). This technique downloads the update to the sensor and then upgrades from the local file system.

Step 1 If you do not have one, create a service account (refer to the previous section for instructions on creating a service account).

Step 2 Log in using the "service" account (and do not "su" to root). The prompt will look like:

```
bash-2.05a$
```

Step 3 Connect to the FTP server:

```
bash-2.05a$ ftp ftp_server_address
```

Step 4 Set up an FTP client to use a "binary" mode to get the file:

```
ftp> bin
```

Step 5 Check that the file is in the FTP server:

```
ftp> ls
227 Entering Passive Mode .
125 Data connection already open; Transfer starting.
-rwxrwxrwx 1 owner group 13280279 Aug 28 14:44 IDS-K9-min-4.1-1-S47.rpm.pkg
-rwxrwxrwx 1 owner group 2061291 Aug 28 14:47 IDS-sig-4.0-2-S47.rpm.pkg
-rwxrwxrwx 1 owner group 2120589 Oct 20 18:26 IDS-sig-4.1-1-S53.rpm.pkg
-rwxrwxrwx 1 owner group 2124411 Oct 20 19:43 IDS-sig-4.1-1-S54.rpm.pkg
226 Transfer complete.
```

Step 6 Retrieve the file (you may copy and paste the file name from the previous output):

```
ftp> get upgrade_file
```

Step 7 Close the FTP connection and quit from FTP client:

```
ftp> close
ftp> quit
```

Step 8 Check that the file is there. You should see the upgrade file that you downloaded from the FTP server.

```
bash-2.05a$ ls
```

Step 9 Log out of the service account.

```
bash-2.05a$ exit
```

Step 10 "Copy" the file from the server itself over scp. This will ensure that no network settings could be affecting the upgrade.

Step 11 Log in using the "cisco" account; the prompt will look like:

```
sensor#
```

Step 12 Enter configure terminal mode:

```
sensor# configure terminal
```

Step 13 Create the key:

```
sensor(config)# ssh host-key [sensor_ip_address]
```

Step 14 Type "**yes**" to accept the key.

Step 15 Apply the upgrade as follows:

```
sensor(config)# upgrade scp://
User: service_account_user_name
```

```
Server's IP Address: sensor_ip_address
Port[22]:
File name: upgrade_file
Password: **********
Warning: Executing this command will apply a signature update to the
application
partition.
Continue with upgrade? : yes
```

Unable to Access the Sensor Using IDM

If you are unable to access the sensor to configure it using IDM (by Web browser) follow these steps to troubleshoot problem:

Step 1 Ping to sensor's IP address fails.

If the ping to the sensor fails, check the network configuration. Run the **setup** command on the sensor to be sure the sensor's IP address and gateway are set correctly. Also be sure there are no routers, switches, or firewalls configured to interface with the sensor that may be blocking the traffic. If the network configuration is correct, verify that the sensor does not have an IP address conflict with another host on the network. Linux automatically prevents the command and control Ethernet port from activating if it detects an address conflict with another host. To check this, run the **show interfaces** command from the command line interface (CLI). The output should be **"command-control interface is up."** If the output is **"command-control interface is down,"** then there is a hardware issue, a cabling issue, or an IP address conflict.

Step 2 Ping succeeds, but SSH fails to connect or connection is refused.

Be sure the sensor's access list is configured to accept the user's address. This will have to be done from the CLI (run **setup**). If the access list is correct, be sure the sensor's SSH or Telnet and web server ports are open in the firewall.

Step 3 Sensor can be accessed via SSH but not via the Web browser.

If the sensor can be accessed through SSH, verify that you are accessing the correct port on the sensor (that is, http versus https). This can be verified by logging into the CLI and showing settings for the web server service.

Step 4 Access to the right port and right IP is still being refused.

If you are correctly addressing the sensor, verify that the web server is still running by using the **show version** CLI command. If the web server is no longer running, look for a bug on Cisco.com for the specific version you are running. If an upgrade is available for the sensor, proceed with the upgrade. If the issue persists, run **show tech-support** and send the output file to Cisco Support. Restart the sensor.

Step 5 Web server process is running, but you are still unable to connect.

If CLI indicates that the web server is still running, verify that the firewall has an open port for the sensor.

Step 6 You can connect and are getting a login prompt but authentication fails.

Check to see if logins to the account have been disabled due to the failed login limit being reached. The sensor provides the configuration option to limit the number of consecutive failed login attempts. Once this limit is reached, the account becomes locked until it is administratively unlocked. This option is disabled by default. It can be enabled in the CLI. To determine if a failed login attempt limit is enabled, enter the authentication service configuration mode and use the command **show settings**. If the **attemptLimit** is greater than zero, then the failed login attempt limit is set to this value. Set the **attemptLimit** value to zero to disable this account locking feature. This feature is required to satisfy the government's Common Criteria for security devices. To check the failed login count, log into the service account—if possible. From the service account shell, run the command **pam_tally**. The output shows the number of failed login attempts for each account. To reset the count, run **pam_tally --reset.** This command will reset the failed login counts.

IDS/IPS MC Installation and Upgrade Issues

IDS/IPS MC is installed as a component on top of Common Services. You must have the Common Services installed before you proceed with the IDS/IPS MC installation.

The installation procedure for the different versions of IDS/IPS MC are listed in the following link and are not discussed here.

> http://www.cisco.com/en/US/products/sw/cscowork/ps3990/prod_installation_guides_list.html

Here are some issues that you may experience while installing the IDS/IPS MC:

- **Installing IDS/IPS MC without administrator rights**—You must install IDS/IPS MC with a user who has administrator rights. We highly recommend that you install all the VMS components using the same user who has administrator rights.
- **Terminal services are running during installation**—Because of interoperability issues, you must not be running Terminal services during IDS/IPS MC installation. We recommend disabling it during installation or upgrading IDS/IPS MC.
- **Using special characters for passwords**—During the installation we recommend not using special characters for the different passwords. This causes confusion and installation failure.
- **No Domain Name System (DNS) record for the VMS Server**—You must have a DNS record for the IP address of the VMS server with the name of the VMS Server.

If you do not have the DNS Server configured for the IP address, be sure to modify your **hosts** file on the VMS server and on the client PC where you access the VMS Server. If you do not have the DNS record, you may be able to get to the login page, but may not be able to log in, because the web server points the link of subsequent pages to the name, not to the IP address.

- **Corrupt IDS/IPS MC software or corrupt installation**—If you have corrupt IDS/IPS MC software or if the software installation is corrupted, you might receive one of the following messages:
  - Unable to retrieve package name (idsmdc_c).
  - Unable to retrieve package version (idsmdc_c).
  - Unable to register IDS/IPS MC Resource with CiscoWorks Common Services Client Registrar.
  - Unable to initialize IDS/IPS MC Configuration Manager Database.

  To resolve the issue, download the IDS/IPS MC from the Cisco Web site, and reinstall the IDS/IPS MC.

- **Process dies or hangs**—Go to **Server Configuration > Administration > Process Management > Process Status** and be sure all the processes are running as shown in Table 18-1. If any of the processes dies, restart the service.

Table 18-1 *Processes That Must Be Running for IDS/IPS MC*

Processes	Description
Apache	Checks that the web server is running properly
ASANYs_SqlCoreDB	Checks that the SQL database is running properly
Daframework	Checks that the device agent is running properly
Fms	Checks that the database is running properly
IDS_Analyzer	Checks that the service that processes event rules and requests user-specified notifications when appropriate is running properly
IDS_Backup	Checks that the service that backs up and restores the IDS/IPS MC and Security Monitor database is running properly
IDS_DbAdminAnalyzer	Checks that the service that periodically applies active database rules to the current state of the server is running properly.
IDS_DeployDaemon	Checks that the service that manages all configuration deployments is running properly
IDS_EvsServer	Checks that the service that manages most Event Viewer data processing is running properly
IDS_Notifier	Checks that the service that receives notification requests (script, e-mail, and/or console) from other subsystems and performs the requested notification is running properly

continues

Table 18-1 *Processes That Must Be Running for IDS/IPS MC (Continued)*

Processes	Description
IDS_Receiver	Checks that the service that receives IDS/IPS and syslog events and stores them in the database is running properly
IDS_ReportScheduler	Checks that the service that generates all scheduled reports is running properly
JRunProxyServer (Windows only)	Checks that the Java servlet engine is running properly
Lm	Checks that the FMS database lock manager is running properly
NRPostOfficeD	Checks that the post office service, which enables communication to IDS/IPS sensors, is running properly
WebServer	Checks that the Apache web server is running properly

IDS/IPS MC Licensing Issues

You must have a valid IDS/IPS MC license in addition to the common services license for IDS/IPS MC to function fully (note that both licenses can be in the same file). You may experience two issues with IDS/IPS MC trial or purchased license file:

- Corrupted license
- Expired license

Corrupted License

VMS or IDS/IPS MC license files may be corrupted either at the time of generation by Cisco Systems, Inc. licensing department or in transfer vie e-mail. In either case, if the license is corrupted, you need to get another license by sending an e-mail to licensing@cisco.com.

Sometimes, the VMS server gives false messages while importing a valid license file. So, it is extremely important to verify that the license file is indeed corrupted. The only way this can be verified is by uploading the license file to a known working VMS server. The Cisco support team can verify this for you. However, if the license happens to be good for a known working VMS server, then you might be running into one of the following issues for which you are getting the corrupted license message:

- **Running terminal services**—If you are running terminal service on the VMS Server while importing the license, it will give you a false message, such as Invalid License. This is because there are known incompatibilities between Sybase SQL Anywhere and Windows Terminal Services. Sybase SQL Anywhere is used by CiscoWorks Common Services. Details about the problem are available on the Microsoft Web site:

  http://www.microsoft.com/windows2000/docs/W2kTSApCmpt.doc

  Under this circumstance, disable the terminal service and then import the license.

- **Database corruption or database not running**—You might get a license corruption message if either the VMS or IDS/IPS MC database is corrupted or not running. If so, you must be sure that the IDS/IPS MC or VMS server database is running properly.

Determining If a License Is Expired

There is another licensing issue on IDS/IPS MC that you might run into—the expired license. The expired license needs to be replaced with a valid license. A trial license should not be replaced by another trial license. To determine the status of the license, go to **VPN/Security Management Solution > Administration > Common Services > Licensing Information**. Click on **Select** and choose the license file from your PC. Click on **Upload**. If you have an expired license, you will see the message as shown in Figure 18-2.

Figure 18-2 *Error Message Seen with an Expired License*

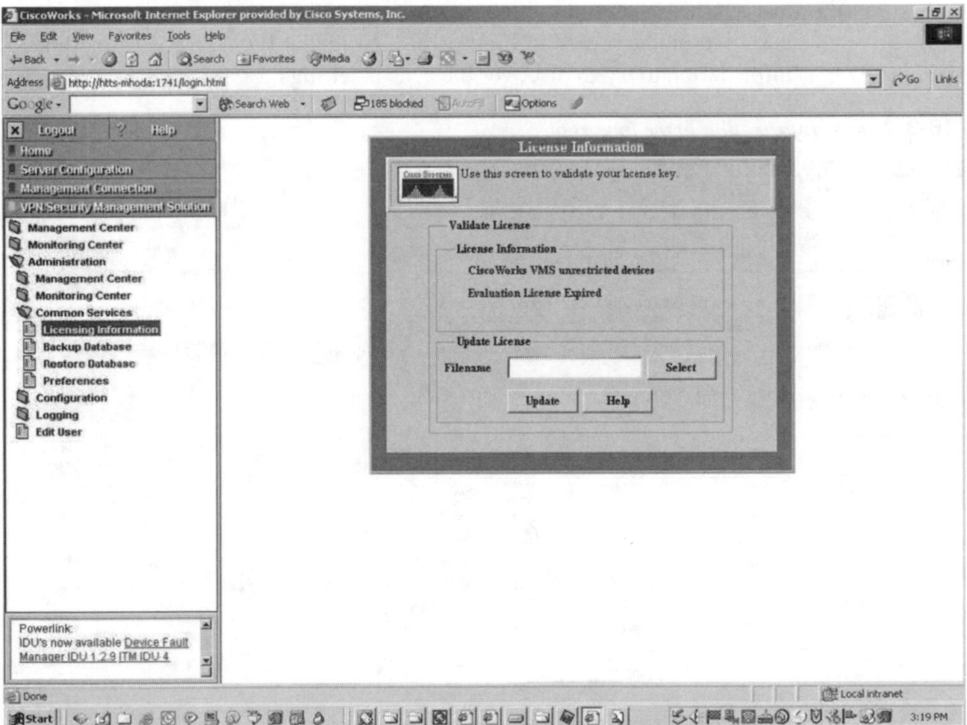

Importing Sensor Issues with IDS/IPS MC

IDS/IPS MC must add the sensor before you can configure it. This section examines the configuration steps on the IDS/IPS MC to add the sensor and troubleshooting steps, should you run into import problems.

Configuration Steps

Work through the steps that follow to configure IDS/IPS MC to import the configuration from the sensor:

Step 1 Open IDS/IPS MC.

Step 2 If you decide to create a device group, click on the **Devices tab**. Click on **Group Option** and click the **Create Subgroup** button. Provide a Group name and description and click OK.

Step 3 Click the **Devices tab** and the **Sensor** option.

Step 4 From the **Group pull down box**, select the group you just created.

Step 5 Click **Add** to launch the **Add Sensor Wizard** to add a new IDS/IPS sensor to that group.

Step 6 Fill out the sensor identification information. It should be similar to what is shown on the screen in Figure 18-3. Note that IDS/IPS MC uses this information to try to discover the sensor settings.

Figure 18-3 *Sensor Information in the Import on Sensor*

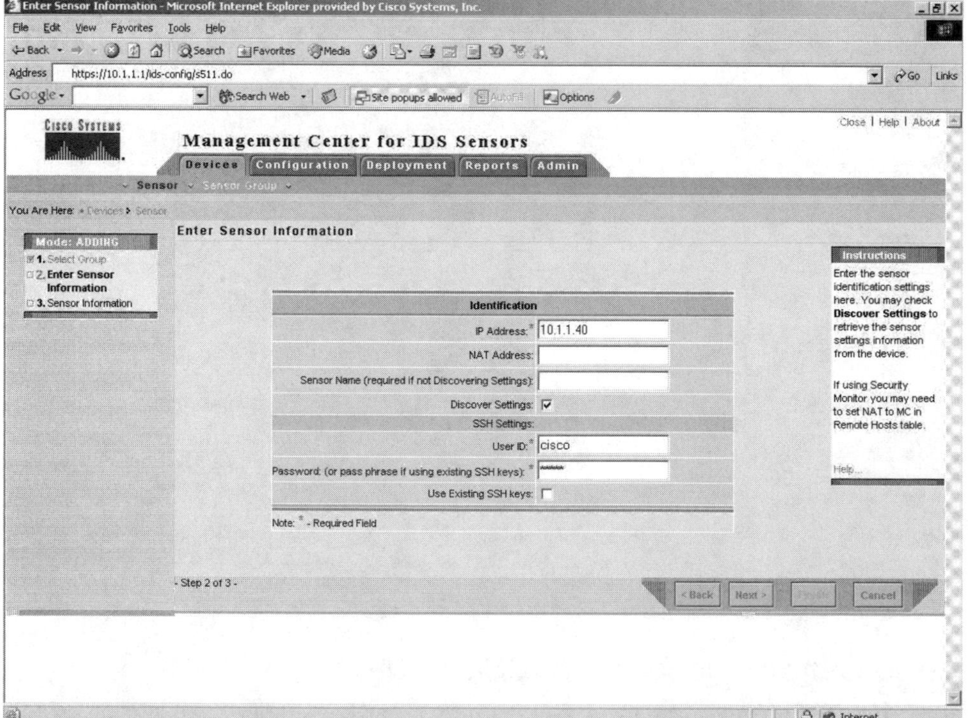

cisco is the username for this setup. You may have a different username, but be sure that the user has administrator privileges. The password here is **ciscotac123**. Be sure you do *not* check the SSH keys check box.

Step 7 Click **Next** when ready. Since the IDS/IPS MC is set up to discover sensor settings, you should automatically see the version field populated.

Step 8 When everything looks satisfactory, click **Finish** to import your sensor. You should now see your sensor in the list.

More details on how to add a sensor can be found at the following link:

http://www.cisco.com/univercd/cc/td/doc/product/rtrmgmt/cw2000/mgt_ids/idsmc20/ug/ch04.htm

Troubleshooting Steps

If you are unable to import the sensor configuration, work through the steps that follow to isolate and resolve the issue:

Step 1 Be sure that the IDS/IPS MC machine can access the IDS/IPS sensor using SSH.

The IDS/IPS MC communicates with the IDS/IPS sensor over SSH (22) and HTTPS (443). Be sure that both ports can communicate. Verify this with the procedure in the section entitled "Verifying the SSH and SSL Connection Between IDS/IPS MC and a Sensor" under "Important Procedures and Techniques." If you run into a problem with the SSH and or SSL connection with the sensor, follow the procedure entitled "Resolving SSH and SSL Connection Problems Between IDS/IPS MC and a Sensor" in the same section.

Step 2 Be sure all the sensor services are running.

All the processes must be running on the sensor for successful import of the sensor by the IDS/IPS MC. To verify if all the processes are running, execute the show version command (refer to "Verifying If the Sensor Process Are Running"). All the processes must have "running" status except the last process, which is the CLI process. If these are not all running, this will cause the import to fail. You can restart the services by logging into the service account and issuing /etc/init.d/cids restart. Unless you are experiencing a bug in the code, the service should restart.

Step 3 Be sure that the IDS/IPS sensor version is supported by the IDS/IPS MC.

There are many versions of IDS/IPS MC and the related sensors. You must ensure that the IDS/IPS Sensor version is supported by the IDS/IPS MC. To find out which IDS/IPS sensor versions are supported by different versions of IDS/IPS MC, refer to the following link: http://www.cisco.com/en/US/products/sw/cscowork/ps3990/products_device_support_tables_list. html

Step 4 Be sure you have exactly the same signature or service pack level on the IDS/IPS MC and on the sensor.

You must have the same service pack or signature levels on both the IDS/IPS MC and sensor. So, it is important to verify the version of IDS/IPS MC and sensor you are running. (Refer to the sections entitled "Verifying That the Service Pack or Signature Level Sensor Is Running" and "Verifying the Service Pack or Signature Level On IDS/IPS MC" under the "Important Procedures and Techniques" section.) Software versions must match exactly. For example, if you run version 4.1(4) S105 on the IDS/IPS sensor, you need to ensure that you apply IDS/IPS-sig-4.1-4-S105.zip to IDS/IPS MC. There is a common misconception that if you have a higher version of signature on the IDS/IPS MC, you can import the sensor that is running a lower version. This is untrue. Actually, the version needs to match to the signature level exactly for the import to work. For example, if you have IDS/IPS MC version 4.1(4)s120, you cannot import a sensor running 4.1(4)s105 unless the IDS/IPS MC is also running the same version, which is 4.1(4)s105. If you try to import the sensor configuration of a different version, it will warn you and will abort the import. If your IDS/IPS MC does not have the same signature or service pack level, you can download the latest signature from the following link:

http://www.cisco.com/cgi-bin/tablebuild.pl/idsmc-ids4-sigup

Step 5 Be sure that the username and password for the IDS/IPS sensor are correct.

When adding a sensor, you must enter the username and password that is defined on the sensor for the IDS/IPS MC to be able to import the configuration from the sensor. You can execute the **show users** command on the sensor to identify the users who are defined on the sensor.

Step 6 Be sure the SSL certificate on the IDS/IPS MC has not expired.

If the SSL certificate on the IDS/IPS MC expires, you will not be able to import the configuration from sensor. You can verify if the certificate is expired with the **keytool** tool. (Refer to the section entitled "Verifying If the IDS/IPS MC (Apache) Certificate Is Valid" under "Important Procedures and Techniques.") If your certificate has expired, refer to "Regenerating IDS/IPS MC (Apache) Certificate" under "Important Procedures and Techniques" to generate the certificate.

Step 7 If everything else fails, a reboot may be required for the server to resolve this import issue.

Signature or Service Pack Upgrade Issues with IDS/IPS MC

You can upgrade the sensor with a signature or service pack with the IDS/IPS MC. The sensor can be upgraded manually from the CLI as well (see "Manually Updating the

Signature Level on the Sensor" under the section entitled "Important Procedures and Techniques"). If you decide to upgrade the sensor manually (which is not a very common practice), IDS/IPS MC can be upgraded itself.

The sections that follow discuss the upgrade procedure and troubleshooting steps.

Upgrade Procedure

Before proceeding with the upgrade it is recommended that you read the "ReadMe" file for the corresponding signature or service pack upgrade files. As an alternative, you can read the information on Cisco.com to find the details of the upgrade procedure and additional details specific to the upgrade file. This section explains the generic step-by-step procedure on how to perform the upgrade from IDS/IPS MC 2.x:

Step 1 Download the signature or service pack update file (**.zip** extension) to the **<install-dir>/MDC/etc/ids/updates** directory on the IDS/IPS MC server from the following location:

http://www.cisco.com/cgi-bin/tablebuild.pl/mgmt-ctr-ids

Step 2 Open IDS/IPS MC from the CiscoWorks2000 Server desktop.

Step 3 Go to the **Configuration > Updates** page.

Step 4 Click on the **Update Network IDS/IPS Signature** link and then click the **Submit** button.

Step 5 On the **Update Network IDS/IPS Signatures** page, select the appropriate **Update File** from the drop-down list and then click the **Apply** button.

Step 6 In the next window, check the sensor or sensors that you want to upgrade. If you only want to upgrade the IDS/IPS MC, you do not have to select any sensor. Click the **Next** button.

Step 7 In the next window, you can either choose to run the upgrade with the **Immediate** option or can schedule the upgrade to run later with the **Scheduled** option. This **Scheduled** option is only available on IDS/IPS MC version 2.0.

Step 8 Click **Next**, and then **Finish**.

With IDS/IPS MC version 2.x, you can download the signature or service update file directly from Cisco.com with appropriate login credentials. Alternatively, you can download the file into a central local server and configure IDS/IPS MC in your network to pull the file from the local server automatically. Both these configuration options are available under **Admin > System Configuration > Automatic Signature download**.

By default, there is a maximum of 10 threads for performing an upgrade at one time by IDS/IPS MC. IDS/IPS MC takes a list of sensors and splits them between the 10 threads. So, if 30 sensors are selected for upgrade, each thread gets 3 sensors. IDS/IPS MC starts all threads and waits until they are all finished. Each thread gets the first sensor of the three selected sensors and starts the upgrade process. For every sensor upgrade, IDS/IPS MC logs in to the sensor and determines its version, and then logs out. IDS/IPS MC then decides if it needs to proceed with the upgrade. If IDS/IPS MC decides that the sensor needs to be upgraded, IDS/IPS MC executes the command over an SSH connection to the sensor, as shown in Example 18-9.

Example 18-9 *Commands Executed by the IDS/IPS MC to Sensor for Upgrading Signature*

```
sensor# configure terminal
sesnor(config)# tls trusted-host ip-address <ipaddress of MC> port <https port of
MC apache>
yes
sensor(config)# upgrade https://<ip address of MC>/vms/sensorupdate/IDS-sig-4.1-4-
S97.rpm.pkg
Yes
sensor(config)# exit
sensor# exit
```

If the update fails, IDS/IPS MC tries to upgrade all over again, up to three times. If the sensor hangs at any point (no response), IDS/IPS MC waits 30 minutes before declaring **update failed**.

Troubleshooting Steps

After initiating the signature or service pack upgrade process, it is important to verify that the update has been applied successfully to the sensor. There are two ways to accomplish this:

- Log in to the sensor and execute **show version** to verify what version the sensor is upgraded to.
- Run an **Audit Log Report** (see "**Audit Reports**" under the section entitled "**Diagnostic Commands and Tools**") in IDS/IPS MC and check to see if the IDS/IPS upgrade is successful.

Before delving into the details of the troubleshooting steps, go through the Audit log report as shown in Example 18-10 for a successful signature upgrade only to the IDS/IPS MC server itself.

Example 18-10 *Audit Reports for IDS/IPS MC Upgrade*

```
2004-01-31 13:39:45 PST 0.0.0.0 Shared service processes Common Java System Services
information INTERNAL Signatures for the Host Based IDS have been added to the
Signature Registry.
! This is the message indicating that IDS MC signature upgrade 4.1(3)S61 is being
applied
2004-01-31 13:39:45 PST 0.0.0.0 Shared service processes Common Java System Services
information INTERNAL Signatures for Sensor version 4.1(3)S61 have been added to the
Signature Registry.
2004-01-31 13:39:33 PST 0.0.0.0 Shared service processes Common Java System Services
information INTERNAL The update for version 4.1(3)S61 has processes Services
completed.
```

Example 18-10 *Audit Reports for IDS/IPS MC Upgrade (Continued)*

```
! The following line confirms the signature upgrade addition to the IDS MC.
2004-01-31 13:39:33 PST 0.0.0.0 Shared service processes Common Java System Services
information INTERNAL The meta-data provided in the Signature Update for version
4.1(3)S61 has been added to the system.
2004-01-31 13:39:15 PST 0.0.0.0 Shared service processes Common Java System Services
information INTERNAL A sensor update for version 4.1(3)S61 has started.
```

Example 18-11 shows a sample **Audit Log** when sensor is upgrade is requested from IDS/IPS MC.

Example 18-11 *Audit Reports for Sensor Upgrade b IDS/IPS MC Upgrade*

```
2004-01-31 13:54:20PST 0.0.0.0 Shared service processes Common Java System Services
information INTERNAL The update for version 4.1(3)S61 has completed.
2004-01-31 13:54:19 PST 0.0.0.0 Shared service processes Common Java System Services
information admin Changes for Sensor vpn-ids saved and lock released.
2004-01-31 13:54:17 PST 0.0.0.0 Shared service processes Common Java System Services
information INTERNAL The signature with the id of 5322.0 has been moved to a
different micro-engine because of a version change. The micro-engine parameter
tunings for this signature have been removed since they are not compatible with the
new micro-engine.
2004-01-31 13:54:12 PST 0.0.0.0 Shared service processes Common Java System Services
information INTERNAL The sensor inet-ids has been updated and its configuration
modified to match the update.
2004-01-31 13:54:11 PST 0.0.0.0 Shared service processes Common Java System Services
information admin Changes for Sensor inet-ids saved and lock released.
2004-01-31 13:54:06 PST 0.0.0.0 Shared service processes Common Java System Services
information INTERNAL The update process has completed for the sensor named vpn-ids.
2004-01-31 13:54:06 PST 0.0.0.0 Shared service processes Common Java System Services
information INTERNAL The update of sensor vpn-ids completed successfully.
2004-01-31 13:54:01 PST 0.0.0.0 Shared service processes Common Java System Services
information INTERNAL The update process has completed for the sensor named inet-ids.
2004-01-31 13:54:01 PST 0.0.0.0 Shared service processes Common Java System Services
information INTERNAL The update of sensor inet-ids completed successfully.
2004-01-31 13:53:54 PST 0.0.0.0 Shared service processes Common Java System Services
information INTERNAL The update was transferred to the sensor named vpn-ids.
2004-01-31 13:53:54 PST 0.0.0.0 Shared service processes Common Java System Services
information INTERNAL The transfer of the update to sensor vpn-ids succeeded.
2004-01-31 13:53:54 PST 0.0.0.0 Shared service processes Common Java System Services
information INTERNAL The transfer of the update to sensor inet-ids succeeded.
2004-01-31 13:53:54 PST 0.0.0.0 Shared service processes Common Java System Services
information INTERNAL The update was transferred to the sensor named inet-ids.
2004-01-31 13:53:53 PST 0.0.0.0 Shared service processes Common Java System Services
information INTERNAL Update of sensor vpn-ids started.
2004-01-31 13:53:53 PST 0.0.0.0 Shared service processes Common Java System Services
information INTERNAL Update of sensor inet-ids started.
2004-01-31 13:53:49 PST 0.0.0.0 Shared service processes Sensor Version Import
information vpn-ids.OrganizationName:Successfully imported sensor version from the
sensor
2004-01-31 13:53:40 PST 0.0.0.0 Shared service processes Sensor Version Import
information inet-ids.OrganizationName: Successfully imported sensor version from
the sensor
2004-01-31 13:53:35 PST 0.0.0.0 Shared service processes Common Java System Services
information INTERNAL A sensor update for version 4.1(3)S61 has started.
```

Once you become familiar with the successful signature or service pack upgrade audit log, work through the following steps to troubleshoot any issues with signature or service pack upgrade failure:

Step 1 Make sure the sensor and IDS/IPS MC fulfills the minimum software version requirements.

To be able to upgrade to the version you desire on the sensor or IDS/IPS MC, ensure that you have the minimum version required for the upgrade. This information can be found from the corresponding ReadMe file of the signature or the service packs file.

Step 2 Be sure the necessary ports are open for IDS/IPS MC to IDS/IPS communication.

The VMS server will ssh to the sensor on port 22, and then the IDS/IPS will pull the signature update down from the IDS/IPS MC via port 443, so be sure both ports are open between the two systems. If they are not, the job will hang. This can be verified with the procedure explained in the section entitled "Verifying SSH and SSL Connection between IDS/IPS MC and the Sensor" under the "Important Procedures and Techniques" section. If you run into a problem with SSH and or SSL connection with the sensor, follow the procedure entitled "Resolving SSH and SSL Connection Problems Between IDS/IPS MC And Sensor" in the same section.

Step 3 Be sure the filenames that you downloaded have not changed since downloading.

Be sure not to change the name of the files you downloaded from **www.cisco.com** and added to the **~CSCPpx/mdc/etc/ids/updates** directory. The files in this directory should be Zip files. The Zip files contain the **.rpm.pkg** files that will be sent to the sensor. You should not edit the filenames or contents. You can download the zip files from the following location:

http://www.cisco.com/pcgi-bin/tablebuild.pl/mgmt-ctr-ids-ids4updates

Step 4 Be sure the time on the sensor and the IDS/IPS MC is in sync.

Check the IDS/IPS sensor's time by issuing **show clock detail** from the command line. Also note the VMS server's current time. The times need to be the same for the update to occur correctly.

Step 5 Be sure the sensor's processes are all running.

If all the process are not running, you may see the following error message in the audit log:

```
Sensor xxx: Signature Update Process
The update of the sensor xxx failed during the update script process,
msg=An error occurred while trying to determine the sensor version.
Detail = Error occurred while communicating with xxx.xx.x.x: Connection
```

```
refused: connect An error occurred while running the update script on
the sensor named xxx. Detail = The update of the sensor xxx failed during
the update script process, msg=An error occurred while trying to
determine the sensor version. Detail = Error occurred while
communicating with xxx.xx.x.x: Connection refused: connect
```

Check to see that the necessary processes are running on the sensor. You can do this by logging into the sensor via CLI and issuing a **show version** command. You should see the processes below listed in the "Running" state. (See the section entitled "Verifying if the Sensor Processes Are Running" under "Important Procedures and Techniques"). If the processes are not running, or you cannot log in at all, try logging into the service account (if you have created one) and manually restarting the services.

Step 6 Be sure the Apache certificate is valid

The IDS/IPS MC (Apache) certificate must be valid for the successful secured communication between IDS/IPS MC and sensor. You can verify the certificate with the procedure explained in the section entitled "Verifying That the IDS/IPS MC (Apache) Certificate Is Valid" under "Important Procedures and Techniques." If the certificate is invalid, you can correct the problem by regenerating the certificate. (See the section entitled "Regenerating IDS/IPS MC (Apache) Certificate" under "Important Procedures and Techniques."

Step 7 Be sure that the VMS server is listed as trusted in the configuration of the IDS/IPS sensor.

Execute **show tls trusted-hosts** on the sensor and see if the IP address of your VMS server is listed in the output. If it is not listed, that means that the sensor is unable to get the certificate from the VMS server. The solution is explained in the next step. If you run into this problem, you will see errors such as that shown in **AuditLogFirst.log** file:

```
58639,2004-12-21 08:05:52.183,0,0,2,21000,1002,21005,2,21004,,'RDEP
Collector (th-sns-3) parsed an evError: errSystemError
MainApplication::processExecUpgradeCtlTrans errSystemError The host is
not trusted. Add the host to the system''s trusted TLS certificates.'
```

Step 8 Be sure the ids sensor is getting the certificate.

If you change the IP address of the VMS server, or regenerate the Apache certificate, you may have difficulties in getting a new updated certificate. To resolve the certificate issue, follow the procedure explained in "Resolving Issues With IDS/IPS Sensor Being Unable To Get The Certificate" under the "Important Procedures and Techniques" section.

Step 9 Be sure the IDS/IPS MC version settings for the sensor are in sync with the sensor version.

Be sure that the IDS/IPS MC configuration for the sensor is in sync with the sensor's actual version. You also need to make sure they are in the same signature level. If the sensor version is out of sync with what IDS/IPS MC expects, the upgrade will fail. For example, if you import a sensor and then upgrade the sensor's signature pack manually, the IDS/IPS MC will fail when it tries to update it further. To re-sync the version number of the sensor with IDS/IPS MC 2.0, simply select your sensor in the table of contents and then go to Configuration-Settings-Identification, and you will see what version the IDS/IPS MC thinks that the sensor currently has. Click the **Query sensor** button to update the IDS/IPS MC with the current IDS/IPS version information.

Step 10 Try re-importing the sensor into IDS/IPS MC.

Sometimes it becomes necessary to delete the sensor from the IDS/IPS MC configuration, and then re-import the sensor to resolve the signature or a service pack upgrade issue.

Step 11 Be sure the correct certificate is selected on the VMS server.

In version IDS/IPS MC 2.0 or 2.0.1, be sure you have not configured VMS to use the "CiscoWorks certificate" for communications as opposed to the default "Common Services Certificate" under **VPN/Security Management Solution > Administration > Configuration > Certificate**. To work around this problem, select **Common Services Certificate** instead of **CiscoWorks certificate**. This is a problem only on IDS/IPS MC 2.0 or 2.0.1 with IDS/IPS 4.x sensors.

Step 12 Be sure the VMS server has only one network card.

A multi-homed machine has multiple Network Interface Card (NIC), each configured with different IP addresses. To run CiscoWorks Common Services on a multi-homed machine, there are two requirements.

— First, all IP addresses must be configured in DNS.

— Second, because of restrictions with CORBA, only one IP address can be used by the client or browser to access the server. You must select one IP address as the external address, with which the client will log in to the CiscoWorks server.

To select an IP address, modify the gatekeeper file located in NMSROOT\lib\vbroker\gatekeeper.cfg. Replace every instance of external-IP-address with the external IP address you choose, and remove the "#" character, from the following:

— #vbroker.gatekeeper.backcompat.callback.host=external-IP-address

— #vbroker.se.exterior.host=external-IP-address

— #vbroker.se.iiop_tp.host=external-IP-address

— #vbroker.se.interior.host=external-IP-address

After modifying the gatekeeper file, restart the Daemon Manager by entering:

```
net start crmdmgtd
```

Step 13 Be sure the VMS server IP address is unchanged.

Ensure that the IP address of the VMS server running IDS/IPS MC has not changed since it was installed. IDS/IPS MC issues the **upgrade** command to the sensor and indicates where the update package exists. The old IP address is issued unless IDS/IPS MC is modified with the new IP address information (see "Changing the VMS Server IP Address" under the section entitled "Important Procedures and Techniques").

Step 14 Take corrective action if a signature update has failed, leaving the virtualSensor.xml file incomplete.

If a signature update is made to the sensor but the sensor did not apply the update completely, the Audit log will report an error message similar to the following:

```
"Error while pushing files to the sensor...an exception occurred during
deploy...Signature Conversion failed, Signature (xxx) from SensorConfig
is not a custom signature and is not found in the sensor XML..."
```

This indicates that a signature upgrade failed for some reason, and that you will have to re-apply the signature update. Verify if you are having this problem by looking at the **/usr/cids/idsRoot/etc/VS-Config/virtualSensor.xml** file. This file shows all the signatures that are configured on the sensor. You can **grep** this file for signature (for example "S146") to match against the latest signature showing with **show version** output. If you find that a sensor is running S146, yet there are missing S146 signatures, you should downgrade the sensor with the **downgrade** command, and then re-apply the signature update; or you can upgrade to a more recent signature version and it will overwrite the missing values.

Step 15 Update from two digit signature pack to three digits (for example S91->S127).

At the time of writing this book, up to version IDS/IPS MC 2.0, IDS/IPS MC cannot push down the update from a two-digit signature pack to a three-digit one. The solution is to manually update the signature level of the IDS/IPS sensor (see "Manually Updating the Signature Level on the Sensor" under the section entitled "Important Procedures and Techniques") and then re-import the sensor into IDS/IPS MC.

Step 16 Be sure the signature pack is available on the IDS/IPS MC.

To send the signature update to the sensor, that particular signature update must be available on the IDS/IPS MC. Check to be sure that the signature update is installed on the IDS/IPS MC. Otherwise it cannot be pushed to the sensor.

Step 17 Check the Network Address Translation (NAT) between the IDS/IPS MC and the sensor.

If you are running Network Address Translation (NAT) between the IDS/IPS MC and the IDS/IPS sensor, ensure that IDS/IPS MC Version 1.2.3 or later is installed with the latest patch.

Step 18 Check to see if the connection between IDS/IPS MC and the sensor is slow.

If the link between IDS/IPS MC and the IDS/IPS sensor is slow, ensure that IDS/IPS MC is running version 1.2 or later. In earlier versions of IDS/IPS MC, an update to an IDS/IPS sensor must be transferred within 30 minutes or the update fails. If desired, you can edit **.../CSOCpx/MDC/Tomcat/vms/ids-config/WEB-INF/classes/com/cisco/nm/mdc/ids/common/sigupdate/updateinfo.xml** file and change the **TransferTimeout** from the default as shown in Example 18-12 to your desired value.

Example 18-12 *Timeout Value in updateinfo.xml File*

```
!30 minutes for each update try

<TransferTimeout>1800</TransferTimeout>
!Retry update 3 times
<TransferTries>3</TransferTries>
!Wait 30 seconds before trying update again
<TransferWaitBetweenTries>30</TransferWaitBetweenTries>
!3.x only
<SP_UpdateScriptTimeout>1800</SP_UpdateScriptTimeout>
!3.x only
<SU_UpdateScriptTimeout>600</SU_UpdateScriptTimeout>
!Max number of concurrent updates to do
<MaxThreads>10</MaxThreads>
!after actual "upgrade https…" is done, how long between !tries to see if what
version of !sensor is
<CheckUpdate>120</CheckUpdate>
```

Be sure not to set a timeout for too long a period. If the timeout is too long, the update process may take a long time, and if there is a failure, the IDS/IPS MC will not be able to start another signature update until the timeout period is completely finished.

Step 19 Check for IDS/IPS MC Database connection problems.

If you experience issues with the database connection, you may be unable to upgrade the IDS/IPS sensor or the IDS/IPS MC itself, and you may be unable to access many components within IDS/IPS MC. Ensure that IDS/IPS MC version 1.2.3 or later is installed with the latest patch.

Configuration Deployment Issues with IDS/IPS MC

There are several XML files (for example virtualSensor.xml, analysisEngine.xml, and Hosts.xml, etc.) that the IDS/IPS MC imports from the sensor to build the configuration of the sensor in IDS/IPS MC. Once you make any changes on the sensor, depending on the version of IDS/IPS MC you are running, deployment of the configuration is performed in different ways. This is explained in the following section:

- **Pre-version IDS/IPS MC 2.x behavior**—Before IDS/IPS MC version 2.x, the sensor configured is deployed using SSH. IDS/IPS MC uses the CLI processor to push the configuration changes over the SSH connection command-by-command on the CLI parser of the sensor. It is as if you are manually typing the commands after making the SSH connection. For this reason, the processing time with configuration deployment with earlier versions were very long.
- **IDS/IPS MC Version 2.x**—With version IDS/IPS MC 2.x, the configuration deployment method has changed. Now, IDS/IPS MC makes the changes, generates all the necessary XML files with the changes made, and then imports the XML files from the sensor to compare them with the IDS/IPS MC local file using the MD5 hashing algorithm. Because of the changes in IDS/IPS MC local XML files, this hashing algorithm result will be different. At this point, instead of sending the commands to the CLI parser of the sensor using SSH, IDS/IPS MC pushes all the XML files to the sensor to overwrite the existing ones with these modified XML files created by IDS/IPS MC.

Even though the configuration deployment process is different behind the scenes, the configuration and troubleshooting steps are the same on different versions, as discussed in the section that follows.

Configuration Steps

After the sensor is imported to the IDS/IPS MC, you may make the necessary changes to the sensor configuration on IDS/IPS MC and then generate the configuration before pushing it to the sensor. To do so, work through the following steps:

Step 1 Make changes to a sensor by going to **Configuration->Settings**, and choosing your sensor under **Object Selector**. Then make the changes you desire. For example, choose a signature (SigID 2000 is "ICMP Echo Request") for testing purposes.

Step 2 Check the box next to the signature and click **Edit**, make changes, and then click **OK**.

Step 3 Go to the tab entitled **Configuration->Pending** to save the pending configuration. Choose your sensor (if it is there) and click the check box next to its name. Then click **Save**.

Step 4 Go to the **Deployment** tab and choose the **Generate Option**. Click the check box next to the name of the sensor you wish to change and click **Generate**. It will present a pop-up window. Click **OK** to proceed, then **Close** to close the window.

Step 5 Go to the **Deployment** tab and choose **Approve**. If your sensor is listed there, click the check box next to its name and click **Approve**.

Step 6 Go to the **Deployment** tab and choose **Deploy** and then **Submit**. Choose your sensor from the list and click **Deploy**. Choose your configuration and click Next. Then click **Next** for an immediate deploy, and click **Finish**.

Step 7 To quickly check to see if and when the deployment is successful, go to the **Configuration > History** page. In IDS/IPS MC version 2.x, you can also click the **Real time progress Viewer** icon (it is a page with a small red 'x' in the upper-right corner of the screen, next to **Actions and Notifications**).

NOTE A deployment to multiple sensors may take several minutes depending on the version you are running. If you are running a version earlier than IDS/IPS MC 2.x, it might take an hour or more. So, it is extremely important that you do not reset or stress the IDS/IPS MC server, and the sensor.

Troubleshooting Steps

After pushing out the configuration changes to the sensor from IDS/IPS MC, the next step is to ensure that the configuration changes applied to the sensor are successful. You can verify this in three ways (not all versions have all three options):

- **Using Progress Viewer**—After a deployment job is requested, click the **Real time progress Viewer** icon (it is a page with a small red 'x' in the upper-right corner of the screen, next to "Actions and Notifications." Wait about four minutes for the sensor to show up at the top of the list; the configuration change status should appear. Click **Refresh** to refresh the screen. This option is only available on IDS/IPS MC 2.x. If the deployment fails, click the check box next to the sensor and click **Show message**. The message will contain some details on failure.

- **Using the History page**—This option is available on all versions of IDS/IPS MC. Check the status of the deployment by going to **Configuration > History.** From this page, you can find out the status of individual sensors.
- **Using the Configuration Deployment report**—If you have many sensors deployed, it is better to generate a **Configuration Deployment** report. This feature is available on all IDS/IPS MC versions. You can generate this report by going to **Reports > Definitions > Create > Detailed Sensor Configuration Deployment Report > Next > Next > Run Now.** This is the simplest form of the report generation process. There are other options available with this process.

Once you have identified a problem with Configuration deployment by using one of the previously listed methods listed, the next step is to analyze the problem through generating the following necessary log files:

- **Using Progress Viewer**—As discussed before, using Progress Viewer, you can check not only the status of the deployment, but can get the details on the reasons for the failure. If the deployment fails, click the check box next to the sensor and click **Show message**. The message will contain details on the reasons for the failure.
- **Using Audit Log**—You can generate an Audit Log to find additional details on deployment as discussed in the "Diagnostic Commands and Tools" section. To generate an audit log report, click the **Reports** tab and then **Definitions**. Press the **Create** button and choose **Audit Log Report**, then **Next**. Choose all the options on this screen and click **Next**. Then click **Run Now** under Finish Options and click **Finish**. Once this report is completed, it will show up under **Reports** and **Completed**. Give it several minutes to complete. Once it is done, you can view the report or send it offline.

Using the points you learned in the previous discussion, you can delve into the details of some probable causes of deployment failure:

- **Required Process not running on IDS/IPS MC**—You might run into a problem when you have no sensors in Deployment selection even though you have made changes to the sensor configuration. This may happen if the **IDS_DeployDaemon** process is not running. Because, when a deployment is started, this daemon checks the devices that have pending configuration changes to be deployed and shows them in the Deployment page. If this daemon is not running, this task is not performed, so no devices are shown, even if there are changes waiting to be deployed. To resolve this problem, start the process by going to **Server Configuration > Administration > Process Management > Process start** and start the process.
- **Version Mismatch between IDS/IPS MC and a sensor**—Usually you should not run into this problem, unless you manually upgraded the sensor after the sensor configuration was imported. To verify the version information of the sensor, execute the **show version** command on the sensor. Then on the IDS/IPS MC, select the sensor

from the **Object Selector**, then go to **Configuration > Settings > Identification,** and look for version information. If the version does not match, then click **Query Sensor** on the same page to retrieve the current sensor version information. And then click the **Apply** button to save the changes. If the **Query Sensor** fails, most likely the problem is that you have applied the signature or service pack upgrade on the sensor only. Therefore, to match the sensor upgrade, you must upgrade your IDS/IPS MC to the corresponding version as well. Then perform the query again.

- **XML file corrupted—VirtualSensor.xml** on the sensor file may become corrupted due to failure of signature or service pack upgrade. If it is, your configuration deployment will fail as well. If you check the output of the **show messages** button on the **Progress Viewer** page within IDS/IPS MC, it might say the following:

```
A signature update failed, leaving the virtualSensor.xml file incomplete
"Error while pushing files to the sensor...an exception occurred during
deploy...Signature Conversion failed, Signature (xxx) from SensorConfig
is not a custom signature and is not found in the sensor XML..."
```

To resolve this issue, re-apply the signature update and then deploy the configuration.

Database Maintenance (Pruning) Issues

Both IDS/IPS MC and Security Monitor share the same database, Sybase for Audit Log, NIDS, CSA, and firewall logs. If the Security Monitor is installed on the same server as IDS/IPS MC, it is very important to manage the database for the logs, so that it does not outgrow the capacity of the server. The method used for database maintenance is called Pruning. Pruning, and database maintenance in general, is discussed in greater detail in Chapter 22, "Troubleshooting IEV and Security Monitors." So, those topics will not be covered in this chapter. However, this section discusses the configuration for Pruning, which is specific to IDS/IPS MC only. On IDS/IPS MC version 1.x, the default Pruning is accomplished by executing scripts, which have changed in version 2.x. There are three default Pruning rules in IDS/IPS MC version 1.x: IDS/IPS Events, Syslog Events, and Audit Logs. These rules can be edited and are found under **Admin > Database Rules**. Note that the same default Pruning rules are configured as the default for the Security Monitor on 1.x. In reality, the IDS/IPS Log and Syslog are received inserted into the database by the Security Monitor, and IDS/IPS MC only inserts the Audit Log to the database. So, in version IDS/IPS MC 2.x, the options available for modification are for Audit Log and Progress Viewer under **Admin > Database Management > Database > Pruning Configuration**.

Case Study

This case study examines the configuration required for shunning on the sensor by IDS/IPS MC based on Figure 18-4. Our assumption is that the IDS/IPS sensor is imported to the IDS/IPS MC and all the connectivity is established among IDS/IPS MC, IDS/IPS sensor, and the routers (managed device).

Figure 18-4 *Sensor Setup in the Network*

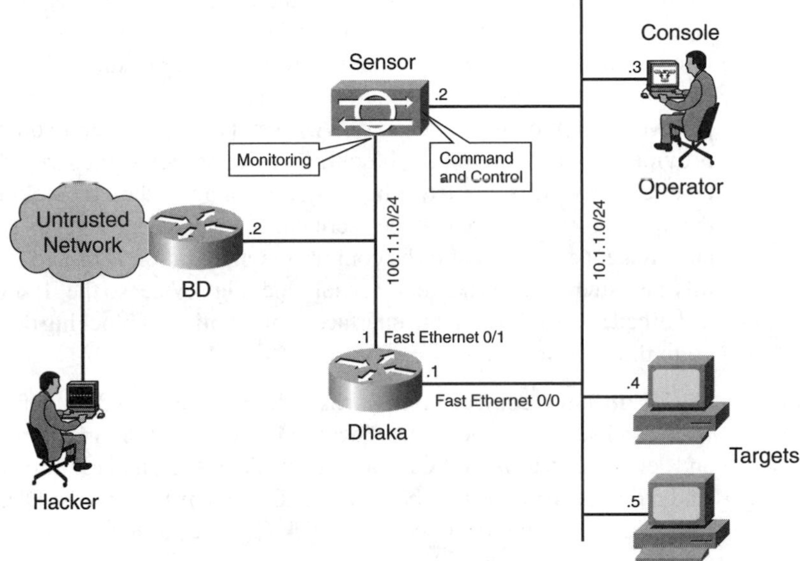

Work through the following procedures to configure shunning.

Step 1 At the VMS server console, select **VPN/Security Management Solution > Management Center > IDS/IPS Sensors.**

Step 2 Select the **Configuration** tab, select your sensor from Object Selector, and click **Settings**.

Step 3 To add a new signature, select **Signatures**, click **Custom**, and then click **Add**.

Step 4 Enter the new **Signature Name**, and then select the **Engine** (in this case, **STRING.TCP**) from the drop-down list.

Step 5 You can customize the available parameters by checking the appropriate radio button and clicking **Edit**. For this case study, edit the **ServicePorts** parameter to 23 (for Telnet). Also, edit the **RegexString** parameter to add the value **hackattempt**. When this is complete, click **OK** to continue.

Step 6 To edit the signature's severity and actions, or to Enable/Disable the signature, click the name of the signature.

Step 7 For this case study, change the severity to **High** and select the action as **Block Host**. Click **OK** to continue. The **Block Host** blocks attacking IP hosts or IP subnets and the **Block Connection** blocks TCP or UDP ports (based on attacking TCP or UDP connections).

Step 8 To configure the Blocking Device, select **Blocking > Blocking Devices** from the Object Selector (the menu on the left side of the screen), and click **Add** to enter all the required information. The minimum required information is marked with asterisks: Device Type, IP Address, Password, and Interfaces. If AAA is configured on the blocking device, then enable password is optional. However, if AAA is not configured and you just provide the password on the blocking device screen (no username), enable password is a must. When AAA is configured on a blocking device, you must ensure that the username has a privilege level of 15 and can create the access-list if the command authorization is turned on. In this case study, the Dhaka router is our blocking device, so the IP address is defined as 10.1.1.1. For the interface configuration of blocking devices, go to the next step.

Step 9 Click **Edit Interfaces**, and then click **Add**. In the new window, define the Blocking Interface Name, select **Blocking Direction (inbound/outbound)**, and define the **Pre-block ACL** and or **Post-block ACL** name. For this case study, **FastEthernet 0/1** in the **inbound** direction is used on the Dhaka router for a blocking interface. Then click **OK** to continue.

Step 10 Click **OK** twice to complete the configuration of the blocking device.

Step 11 To configure Blocking Properties, select **Blocking > Blocking Properties**. The Length of the automatic block is 30 minutes by default, which can be modified. In this case, it is changed to **10 minutes**. You may need to check the **Override** check box to be able to make the change. Click **Apply** to continue.

Step 12 Select **Configuration** from the main menu, then select **Pending**. Check the pending configuration to ensure it is correct, and click **Save**.

Step 13 To push the configuration changes to the sensor, generate and then deploy the changes by selecting **Deployment > Generate** and click **Apply**.

Step 14 Select **Deployment > Deploy**, and then click **Submit**.

Step 15 Check the check box next to your sensor, and then click **Deploy**.

Step 16 Check the check box for the job in the queue, and then click **Next** to continue.

Step 17 Enter the job name and schedule the job as Immediate. Then click **Finish**.

Step 18 Select **Deployment > Deploy > Pending**. Wait a few minutes until all the pending jobs have been completed. The queue should then be empty.

Step 19 To confirm the deployment, select **Configuration > History**. Ensure the status of the configuration is displayed as **Deployed**. This means that the sensor configuration has been updated successfully.

Launch the Attack and Blocking

To verify that the blocking process is working correctly, launch a test attack and check the results. Before launching the attack, work through the following procedure:

Step 1 Select **VPN/Security Management Solution > Monitoring Center > Security Monitor**.

Step 2 Choose **Monitor** from the main menu, click **Events** and then click **Launch Event Viewer**.

Step 3 Use Telnet to access the Dhaka router, as that is the blocking device in this case study (see Figure 18-4 for the location of Dhaka router), and verify that the sensor can communicate with the blocking device (in this case the Dhaka router). To verify the communication, execute the commands on the Dhaka router as shown in Example 18-13.

Example 18-13 *Verification of the Communication Between the Sensor and the Managed Router*

```
Dhaka# show user
   Line       User       Host(s)              Idle       Location
*  0 con 0                idle                 00:00:00
 226 vty 0                idle                 00:00:17 10.1.1.2
Dhaka#show access-list
Extended IP access list IDS_Ethernet1_in_0
10 permit ip host 10.1.1.4 any
20 permit ip any any (20 matches)
Dhaka#
```

Step 4 To simulate an attack, use Telnet from the BD router to the Dhaka router, type **hackattempt**, then hit **<Enter>**. As this **hackattempt** string goes over the Telnet connection, the IDS/IPS sensor will sniff that and will trigger the signature that was created earlier using the IDS/IPS MC. Because the action configured is **Blocking-Host**, your Telnet session will be reset and will be blocked for 10 minutes. Example 18-14 shows the Telnet session disconnection.

Example 18-14 *Telnet Session Disconnection Due to Shunning*

```
BD# telnet 100.1.1.1
Trying 100.1.1.1 ... Open
User Access Verification
Password:
Dhaka> enable
Password:
Dhaka#hackattempt
!--- Host 100.1.1.2 has been blocked due to the
!--- signature "hackattempt" being triggered.
[Connection to 100.1.1.1 lost]
```

Step 5 Now use Telnet to access the Dhaka router from another host and enter the command **show access-list** to see the dynamical ACL pushed by the sensor as shown in Example 18-15.

Example 18-15 *The Output of* **show access-list** *After the Attack*

```
Dhaka#show access-list
Extended IP access list IDS_Ethernet1_in_1
10 permit ip host 10.1.1.4 any
!You will see a temporary entry has been added to
!the access list to block the router from which you connected via Telnet previously.
20 deny ip host 100.1.1.2 any (37 matches)
    30 permit ip any any
```

Troubleshooting Steps

Work through the following procedure to troubleshoot issues with shunning:

Step 1 In the IDS/IPS MC, select **Reports > Generate**. Depending on the problem type, further detail can be found in one of the seven available reports.

At the sensor CLI, enter the command **show statistics networkaccess** and check the output to ensure that the "state" is active as shown in Example 18-16.

Example 18-16 *The Statistics of the Networkaccess Service*

```
sensor# show statistics networkAccess
Current Configuration
   AllowSensorShun = false
   ShunMaxEntries = 100
   NetDevice
      Type = Cisco
      IP = 10.1.1.1
      NATAddr = 0.0.0.0
      Communications = telnet
      ShunInterface
         InterfaceName = FastEthernet0/1
         InterfaceDirection = in
State
   ShunEnable = true
   NetDevice
      IP = 10.1.1.1
      AclSupport = uses Named ACLs
      State = Active
   ShunnedAddr
      Host
         IP = 100.1.1.2
         ShunMinutes = 10
         MinutesRemaining = 8
sensor#
```

Step 2 If the **State** does not show **Active**, be sure the communication parameter shows that the correct protocol is being used, such as Telnet or Secure Shell (SSH) with 3DES. If the configuration looks fine on the sensor based on Example 18-16, you can try ssh or Telnet to get into the blocking device after logging into sensor using **service** account. This will help verify that the issue is with the sensor or the blocking device. If it is an issue on the blocking device, troubleshoot the issue with AAA or SSH (if configured) to find out why login is failing with the blocking device.

Common Problems and Resolutions

This section delves into some of commonly seen problems that you may experience and ways to resolve them.

1 How can I upgrade my IDS/IPS sensor using IDS/IPS MC from version 3.x to 4.x?

Answer: Refer to the following link for a detailed procedure: http://www.cisco.com/en/US/products/sw/cscowork/ps3990/products_user_guide_chapter09186a008018d985.html#894197

2 Is IPS 5.0 version on sensor supported by IDS/IPS MC?

Answer: Yes, IPS 5.0 is supported on version IDS/IPS MC version 2.1. For additional details, refer to the following link:

http://www.cisco.com/univercd/cc/td/doc/product/rtrmgmt/cw2000/mgt_ids/idsmc21/index.htm.

3 Can I change the IP address of the VMS server running IDS/IPS MC?

Answer: Yes you can, but this is not recommended by Cisco Systems, Inc. Refer to "Changing the VMS Server IP Address" under the section entitled "Important Procedures and Techniques." You must also be sure to allow this host or network address of the VMS server to the allowed host table of the sensor (see "Adding Allowed Hosts on the Sensor" under the "Important Procedures and Techniques" section).

4 How can I validate the Apache Certificate? If the certificate is bad or expired, can I regenerate it?

Answer: Yes, you can verify the validity of the Apache certificate and can regenerate it if invalid. For verification, refer to "Verifying That the IDS/IPS MC (Apache) Certificate Is Valid" and for regeneration of the certificate refer to "Regenerating IDS/IPS MC (Apache) Certificate" under the section entitled "Important Procedures and Techniques."

5 How can I delete pending jobs in IDS/IPS MC?

Answer: First make sure whether you have pending job or not by going to the **Admin > System Configuration > View Current Locks**. To delete the pending job, go to the **Configuration tab > Pending**, and check the relevant jobs and click the **Delete** button.

6 Where does IDS/IPS MC store configuration files?

Answer: Configuration goes into the following locations:

— Database.

— <installdir >/mdc/etc/ids/xml/SystemConfig.xml.

— <installdir>/mdc/tomcat/vms/ids-monitor/web-inf/classes/com/cisco/nm/mdc/ids/common/SystemConfig.xml.

— <installdir>/mdc/tomcat/vms/ids-config/web-inf/classes/com/cisco/nm/mdc/ids/common/SystemConfig.xml.

The content of **SystemConfig.xml** files in the three different locations are exactly the same and are changed at install/uninstall time.

The sensor configuration files generated by IDS/IPS MC are temporarily stored in **C:\Document and Settings\username\Local Settings\Temp\deploy\sensors**. The format of the sensor directory name is **ipAddress-xxxx.tmp**, where **ipAddress** is the sensor's IP address, and **xxxx** is a unique number. These files are generated at the start of deployment and removed at the end of deployment. However, if you want IDS/IPS MC to leave files after deployment, you can change the **<CleanupTempFiles>true</CleanupTempFiles>** to **<CleanupTempFiles>false</CleanupTempFiles>** in the **<INSTALL_DIR>/MDC/etc/ids/xml/DeploymentConfig.xml** file. You must restart the **IDS_DeployDaemon** for this change to take effect. Note that this also leaves imported config files from the sensor.

7 How does the IDS/IPS MC push the configuration to the sensor?

Answer: If you are running sensor version 4.x and above and IDS/IPS MC 1.x, then IDS/IPS MC connects with the sensor using SSH and then sends the configuration command by command to the CLI of the sensor to write the configuration. However, if you are running version IDS/IPS MC 2.x, then the IDS/IPS MC creates the configuration file (xml format) and pushes the configuration file to the sensor using RDEP communication protocol (SSL/TLS). Because of this, in IDS/IPS MC 2.x configuration deployment is much faster.

8 What is the severity mapping between IDS/IPS MC and sensor?

Answer: The following is the severity mapping between the IDS/IPS MC and sensor (as of the writing this book. In the future this may change):

— 1 = Info

— 2 = Low

— 3 = Medium

— 4 = High

9 Can Sybase Database be installed and run on a separate machine for reporting, to ease DBA support such as database (DB) backups?

Answer: Yes, you can install Sybase database for IDS/IPS MC/Security Monitor on a different mounted drive. RAID disks are a better choice. Everything becomes

Input/Output (I/O) bound in high volumes. You can schedule a prune and load the pruned data into another database (Sybase, Oracle, etc.). You can also do a backup and load the IDS/IPS database into a Sybase installed on a different machine. This requires you to purchase an additional license for Sybase. The Security Monitor application uses the Sybase database shipped with VMS. There is no plugable replacement. To use the data on another database, you must somehow replicate it to that database. You can use the command line tools or any other means to do so.

10 What is the Overwrite button used for in the Advanced > Not Supported window?

Answer: The Overwrite button is used to overwrite the settings inherited from the parents. The button is not used to overwrite the setting on the sensor. What is added in the window is just added at the end of the configuration file.

11 If I edit the configuration file in the IDS/IPS MC going to Advanced > Not Supported Window, how does the IDS/IPS MC parser treat the changes?

Answer: This window is used for adding configurations not supported by IDS/IPS MC. The configuration you add here will be appended to the end of the file in the sensor. If the configuration entered is already present in the configuration, the sensor will have this information twice, and the last entry will be taken from the daemon.

12 There is a check box on IDS/IPS MC for the sensor identification page that says Use Existing Keys. What does this do and why would I want to use it?

Answer: If you want tighter security on your system, you can check this option of the sensor identification page on IDS/IPS MC. Normally with SSH, you can use the standard username and password for the connection. You can also use pre-shared keys that are set up on the sensor and on the MC. This check box allows you to use existing pre-shared keys from the IDS/IPS MC server memory. For more details look at the section entitled "Using SSH in IDS/IPS MC and Security Monitor" in the following link: http://www.cisco.com/univercd/cc/td/doc/product/rtrmgmt/cw2000/mgt_ids/idsmc20/ug/ch04.htm

13 Can you back up IDS/IPS MC and restore it on a different machine with a different hostname or IP address?

Answer: Yes, you can.

14 What applications have interoperability issues with VMS/IDS/IPS MC?

Answer: Microsoft IIS Web Server and Microsoft Terminal Services have interoperability issues with VMS/IDS/IPS MC.

15 How can I eliminate the two windows that pop up once I click on every window after enabling SSL?

Answer: Go to **Server configuration > Administration > Security Management > Create Self Signed Certificates**. Use the same IP address or name you will use to access the server. Then go to **VPN/Security Management Solution > Administration > Configuration > Certificate** and set it to use the CiscoWorks certificate. Then, restart the Daemon Manager and the browser. You will not be prompted for the certificate any more. It is however important to note that in IDS/IPS MC 2.0 and 2.0.1, using a CiscoWorks certificate causes signature update failure. So, it is better to avoid this in IDS/IPS MC version 2.0 and 2.0.1.

16 Does VMS support access through a Web proxy server?

Answer: This is not officially listed as supported, but it works.

17 Where can I download the latest versions and patches for IDS/IPS MC?

Answer: You must have cisco.com login privileges and can download the software from the following location: http://www.cisco.com/pcgi-bin/tablebuild.pl/mgmt-ctr-ids-app.

18 Where can I download the latest IDS/IPS sensor updates?

Answer: The latest IDS/IPS sensor updates are available in the following location: http://www.cisco.com/pcgi-bin/tablebuild.pl/mgmt-ctr-ids-ids4updates

Updates are for the following:

— Update IDS/IPS sensors using IDS/IPS MC.

— Update IDS/IPS MC.

— Update Security Monitor.

> **Note** IDS/IPS MC updates the Security Monitor automatically if it resides on the same server.

19 How can I receive e-mail notifications when a new IDS/IPS sensor update is available?

Answer: You can receive e-mail notifications for new updates and the latest product news by subscribing at:

http://www.cisco.com/univercd/cc/td/doc/product/iaabu/csids/csids11/5020_02.htm#wp1068414

20 Are both IDS/IPS sensor versions 3.x and 4.x supported by the IDS/IPS MC?

Answer: Yes, IDS/IPS MC version 1.1 supports both IDS/IPS sensor Version 3, which uses PostOffice Protocol and the newer Version 4.x, which supports Remote Data Exchange Protocol (RDEP) sensors.

21 What IDS/IPS sensor hardware and software versions does IDS/IPS MC support?

Answer: Refer to the following link for the updated version of sensor versions supported by IDS/IPS MC: http://www.cisco.com/en/US/products/sw/cscowork/ps3992/products_device_support_tables_list.html.

22 Can I import IOS IPS configuration into the IDS/IPS MC?

Answer: If you are running the IPS feature on the Cisco IOS Router and IDS/IPS MC version less than 2.0, then this is not possible. However, you can manage IOS IPS configuration with IDS/IPS MC 2.0.

23 I am managing my sensor using CSPM. How can I migrate to IDS/IPS MC?

Answer: You cannot migrate the CSPM database to IDS/IPS MC. However, you can import the configuration from the sensor to the IDS/IPS MC.

Best Practices

This section examines some of the important issues to improve the performance and avoid a lockout situation. The following is the list of such some good practices:

- Always apply upgrades to the latest version of IDS/IPS MC and apply the new patches available on the Cisco Web site.
- If you have more than one sensor to manage and get events, we recommend installing IDS/IPS MC and Security Monitor on a separate server. If you have a huge number of sensors, depending on number of events you are getting, you may consider installing the Security Monitor on multiple servers for load sharing purposes.
- Be sure to install VMS on a dedicated server, as it has its own web server and database server, which may cause resource conflict issues if other applications are installed. Be sure to fulfill the minimum requirements for running the VMS server. As performance is dependent on the configuration of hardware, not VMS software, it is always recommended to have a fast, powerful server.
- It is recommended to secure the VMS server with Cisco's Security Agent (CSA). CSA is Cisco's host-based IDS/IPS software. If you have CSA MC installed with the Common Services, the agent is installed for the server to protect VMS automatically. If you do not have the CSA MC installed, be sure to install at least the headless CSA Agent to protect the VMS Server itself from attacks.
- If the VMS is in a different network (VLAN) than the sensor, be sure the network devices between the management server and the sensor allow SSH (TCP/22) SSL (TCP/443) in both directions.
- Be sure to schedule for archiving and deleting the alarms to avoid filling the VMS database, as the more alarms stored in the database, the longer it will take your viewer to load the alarms for viewing.
- Do not install VMS on Primary/Backup Domain Controller, IIS web Server, Terminal Server, IEV, and CSPM.
- Be sure not to use domain or local admin user name and password when installing the VMS. Rather, create another user who has local administrator privilege.

CHAPTER **19**

Troubleshooting Firewall MC

Firewall MC is a software component that runs on Common Services to provide management for PIX firewall and FWSM configuration. As of writing this book, the latest version of PIX Firewall is Version 7.0, for which the Firewall MC is not developed. Hence, the discussion of this chapter is on Firewall MC Version 1.3.x on the Windows platform, which is used to manage PIX firewall Version 6.3.x and earlier, and FWSM. However, discussion in this chapter on Firewall MC can be used for configuring and troubleshooting of the new version of Firewall MC as well, which will support PIX Version 7.0. with some exceptions.

Overview of Firewall MC

Unlike the command line interface or the PIX device manager (PDM), the Firewall MC is a policy-based tool targeted for managing multiple firewalls in a large enterprise environment.

Firewall MC Processes

There are several processes that perform different tasks on Firewall MC. If one of these processes is not running, the function that it is responsible for will not work. If there are problems in running the application, it is always a good practice to check that all these processes are running. The processes and their main functions are the following:

- **Apache**—This is the web server process. Be sure that the web server is running properly.
- **ASANYs_SqlCoreDB**—This a SQL database. For the Firewall MC to function properly, be sure this is running properly.
- **Tomcat**—Be sure that the Java servlets that make up the Firewall MC and Auto Update Server (AUS) user interface are running properly.

If any of these processes are not running, the tasks they control will not run. To check the status of the processes and start them, go to **Server Configuration > Administration > Process Management**. From there you can view the status of the processes, stop the processes, or start stopped processes.

As mentioned before, Firewall MC is used to manage single or multiple firewalls on a variety of firewall platforms. It is important to understand and be aware of the versions of firewall supported by different Firewall MC Versions. Refer to the following link (Release notes) for a list of firewall versions that are supported by Firewall MC Version 1.3.3:

http://www.cisco.com/univercd/cc/td/doc/product/rtrmgmt/cw2000/mgt_pix/fwmc133/dvice133.htm

Communication Architecture

Firewall MC uses HTTPS (HTTP/SSL) protocol to communicate with Firewall to perform different tasks. Following is the list of functions Firewall MC performs with the help of the HTTPS protocol:

- **Importing Configuration of Firewall**—Firewall MC communicates with the firewalls using the HTTPS protocol to import the configuration. Firewall needs to be enabled with a web server, and an SSL certificate must be generated for secure http communication.
- **Deployment Configuration of the Firewall**—Firewall MC deploys configuration to the Firewall using the HTTPS protocol.
- **Communication with Auto-update Server**—When configuration is pushed to the Auto-update server from the Firewall MC, it uses the HTTPS protocol. When the firewall pulls the image or the configuration files, it also uses the HTTPS protocol.

So, as you can see, all communications that take place among firewalls, Firewall MC, and the Auto-update server use the HTTPS (http/SSL) protocol.

Diagnostic Commands and Tools

There is extensive debug capability for troubleshooting issues with the Firewall MC. This section gives you details on how to use this capability efficiently.

Collecting the Debug Information (Diagnostics)

If you encounter problems while working with Firewall MC, You can view this debug information in two ways: by using a GUI and by using CLI.

Using GUI

You can view the debug log messages in the Common Services user interface, by selecting **VPN Security Management Solution > Admin > Logging > Operation**. This is useful for viewing the information in real time without having console access to the Firewall MC server. However, to analyze the log offline or to send this information to the Cisco support center for additional analysis, you may want to follow the procedure described in the following section.

Using CLI

As mentioned earlier, to analyze the log offline or to provide the debug to Cisco Support team, you can use a command line utility included in CiscoWorks Common Services. This is called **MDCSupport.exe**. This utility collects configuration and system information in a .zip file called **MDCSupportInformation.zip**. To run this utility, simply open a DOS prompt on the Firewall MC server, and type **MDCSupport**. If you do not specify a location, the **MDCSupportInformation.zip** file is created in the default location: the **c:\>Program Files\CSCOpx\MDC\etc** directory. If you have installed the CiscoWorks Common Services in a different location, the file will be generated under that directory instead of c:\.

What Does the CiscoWorks MDCSupport Utility Generate?

After generating the **MDCSupportInformation.zip** file, it is very important to know what files and information this file collects pertaining to Common Services and Firewall MC. Following is a list of files that the **MDCSupportInformation.zip** file contains:

- **Configuration and log files for the Apache web server**—These files are located at **CSCOpx\MDC\Apache\conf** and **CSCOpx\MDC\Apache\logs**, respectively.
- **Configuration and log files for the Tomcat servlet engine**—These are located at **CSCOpx\MDC\Tomcat\conf** and **CSCOpx\MDC\Tomcat\logs**, respectively. The important logs here are the **stdout.log** and **stderr.log** for the Tomcat process.
- A full copy of the KRS database.
- A full copy of the Sybase database.
- **All the operations and audit logs for applications using Common Services**—These are located at **CSCOpx\MDC\log** and **CSCOpx\MDC\log\audit**, respectively.
- **The Core Client Registry (CCR)**—This is located at **CSCOpx\MDC\etc\regdaemon.xml**.
- Some diagnostic information collected about your system.
- Installation logs for all the CiscoWorks-related install activities on your system.

Other Useful Log Files Not Collected by mdcsupport

Not every file that can be used to diagnose all the problems is included in the **MDCSupportInformation.zip** file. Some of the files that are not included in the **MDCSupportInformation.zip** file are described in the list that follows:

- Any log file of the form **hs_err_pid*.log** located in the **CSCOpx\MDC\Tomcat** directory. For example, **hs_err_pid1396.log**. These log files are normally the result of hard crashes to the tomcat process and are not common.
- The **CoreTib.log** file, located in the **CSCOpx\logs**. This log file provides information about the Core tibco process.
- The log files for the JRun servlet engine. This file is located at **CSCOpx\lib\jrun\finish log pathMMF**.

Analysis of Problem Areas

This section looks into some of the problems based on their functional areas and how to resolve them:

- Installation issues
- Initialization issues
- Browser issues
- Authentication issues
- Activity and job management issues
- Device import issues
- Configuration generation and deployment issues
- Database management issues

Installation Issues

Once Firewall MC is installed successfully, it is very important to verify that it is running correctly. This section discusses how to verify and troubleshoot the Firewall MC Installation problem.

Installation Verifications

After installing the Firewall MC, the first step is to verify the success of the installation. Following are two ways you can verify if the Firewall MC is installed successfully:

- Firing up Firewall MCLog in to the CiscoWorks Server desktop, and then selecting **VPN/Security Management Solution > Management Center**. Click on **Firewalls** in the Management Center folder. Answer **Yes** in the Security Alert window. The Firewall MC home page displays. Finally click on **About** to verify if the correct version of Firewall MC is running on your system.
- Checking Package OptionLog on the CiscoWorks Server desktop, then selecting **Server Configuration > Administration > Package Options**. Scroll through the list of package names to see the installed options. If the installation succeeded, you will see **Management Center for Firewalls** in the list of installed options. Select **Management Center for Firewalls** from the Package Name list, and then click **Next**. The Package Options page displays the build information for the installed version of Firewall MC.

Installation Troubleshooting

If Firewall MC Installation fails on the Windows platform, you need to analyze the log in the **C:** directory. This is where you can find the log in the format of **C:\Ciscoworks_setupxxx.log** (for example, **C:\Ciscoworks_setup001.log**) file. The file name with the highest number is the most recent log file. Following are some of the probable causes of Firewall MC Installation failure on Windows platform:

- **CiscoWorks Common Services Installation is corrupt**—If the Common Services Installation is corrupted, the installation of Firewall MC will fail with one of the following messages:

  ```
  Unable to retrieve package name (pixmc)
  Unable to register Firewall MC Resource with CiscoWorks Common Services Client
    Registrar.
  Unable to initialize Firewall MC Configuration Manager database.
  ```

  To resolve the problem, uninstall and reinstall CiscoWorks Common Services. Then install the Firewall MC. Additionally, if you have problem with CiscoWorks Common Services Installation corruption problem, you might receive one of the following messages:

  ```
  Unable to launch KRS database process.
  Unable to launch LM database process.
  ```

  To resolve the problem, uninstall and re-install CiscoWorks Common Services. During the installation of Firewall MC, be sure to choose to initialize the database option of Firewall MC.

- **The Firewall MC installation is corrupt**—Uninstall Firewall MC and reinstall it.
- **Microsoft Terminal Services Issues**—You will receive the following message when terminal services are running at the time of installation:

  ```
  Unable to connect to the database.
  ```

  There is a known problem when installing Common Services on a system that has Terminal Services enabled in Remote Administration mode. The workaround is to go to the Services Control Panel, and manually stop or disable Terminal Services before you install Common Services. After finishing your installation, you can then restart or re-enable the Terminal Services.

  However, there are existing problems with the Sybase SQL wherever a database is running as a service on a machine that has Terminal Services enabled using Application Server mode. These problems are outside the control of Cisco, and are documented at this URL:

  http://www.microsoft.com/windows2000/docs/W2kTSApCmpt.doc#_Toc475940238

  Under the Terminal Services Application Server Mode, there is an entry for Sybase SQL Anywhere on Page 16 which reads: "When SQL Anywhere is run as a service, compatibility problems with Terminal Services may result." To avoid such problems, you must run SQL Anywhere as a regular process. Sybase is currently working on a solution for this problem.

- **VMS Interoperability Issues with Microsoft IIS Web Server**—VMS does not work well with IIS Web Server. IIS Web Server and VMS compete for port 443 during system startup. If IIS binds the port, then VMS will not work. It is recommended that you disable IIS to prevent port conflicts and other well-known IIS security problems.

- **Firewall MC Interoperations with Other Applications**—Other software running on the system can affect Cisco Works performance and cause port conflicts. The VMS processes can be memory and I/O intensive, so it is recommended that you run VMS on a dedicated system. Table 19-1 lists the ports used by VMS that cannot be changed.

Table 19-1 *Ports Used By Different VMS Components*

Processes part of VMS	Port Numbers
SSL port for Common Services web server	443
Normal port for Common Services web server	1751
Normal port for CMF web server	1741
SSL port for CMF web server (only used if the desktop itself is in SSL mode)	1742
JRun servlet engine	42343
JRun administration	57860
Cisco Works 2000 Daemon Manager	42340
Tibco port for Common Services	10032
Tomcat communications port to Apache web server	8007
Tomcat communications port to Apache web server	8009

Be sure that you do not run any application that is in conflict with the ports listed in Table 19-1. It is strongly recommended to remove any unnecessary service/ application (IIS, HP Services, Compaq Services, and so on) that you do not need before installing Firewall MC.

Initialization Issues

After successful installation of Firewall MC, it takes approximately one minute for all the services to reach the state of having been started. Once all the services are started, there still may be processing going on by the individual applications, including Firewall MC, as they are being initialized as well. It should not be uncommon to see high CPU activity while services are starting up, and immediately after all services have reached the **Started** state. When you try to open up Firewall MC, you may receive the following message at that time:

```
The MC is not fully initialized yet. Please clicks refresh (F5) to try again in a
  few seconds.
```

If you are unable to open Firewall MC even after waiting for a long time after the installation, work through the following steps to correct the problem:

Step 1 View the Process Status.

If you are unable to open up Firewall MC, go to **Server Configuration > Administration > Process Management > Process Status** from the CiscoWorks Server navigation tree. Be sure **Apache, SqlCoreDB, Tomcat, daframework**, and **lm** processes are running.

Step 2 Restart the processes.

To start the processes that are not running, go to **Server Configuration > Administration > Process Management > Start Process** page to start the processes. From the Start Process page, select **System** to start all processes, or select the specific process to start. You must be an administrator to CiscoWorks to be able to stop or start the processes.

Step 3 Wait and view the Process Status again.

After starting the Processes from the previous step wait for five minutes, and then check the status of the processes as described in Step 1.

Step 4 Restart the processes using CLI.

If any process is not running even after you restarted the process from CiscoWorks Desktop, you can restart the process directly from the command line of your CiscoWorks Server. Open the DOS prompt on the CiscoWorks server, and execute the following two commands:

```
net stop crmdmgtd
net start crmdmgtd
```

Be sure that you do not start the **crmdmgtd** process after you stop it.

Step 5 Check the Process Status again

Wait for five minutes after starting the **crmdmgtd** process that is described in the previous step, and then follow Step 1 to check the status of the Processes again.

Browser Issues

You might experience browser-related problems while trying to access or use Firewall MC. Some of these issues are discussed in the list that follows:

- **Desktop buttons do not work**—If the desktop buttons do not work, check whether Java and JavaScript are enabled. If not, enable Java and JavaScript.
- **Browser cache settings**—For successful Firewall MC Operations, be sure the browser cache is not set to zero.

- **Resizing browser window**—Do not resize the browser window while the desktop main page is loading.
- **Disable popup blockers on browsers**—If you use a popup blocker utility on any client you use to access the Firewall MC server, popup windows used by Firewall MC are blocked. So, be sure to allow the popup for at least the Firewall MC Server.
- **Open only one browser session from a single client**—Firewall MC supports only one browser session from a specific client PC. With Internet Explorer, even though you can create multiple browser sessions, it is strongly discouraged, because unpredictable results will occur.
- **Internet Explorer hangs after trying to close a dialog box**—You may experience a browser hang session, if the sessions between the web client and the CiscoWorks Server are canceled after a user-defined period of inactivity. For example, if you restore the database, a dialog box displays stating that the restoration is complete. If you do not click **OK** before the session times out, the web client can hang and cannot be closed. To resolve this issue, press the **Ctrl + Alt + Delete** buttons at the same time. This will bring up Windows Security window. Click on the **Task Manager** tab and then **Processes**. Then select the **iexplore.exe** process from the Process list and click **End Process**.
- **Other applications hijack Internet Explorer Windows for Firewall MC**—Internet Explorer provides an option that allows existing Internet Explorer browser instances to be used when a shortcut is selected or when a URL is entered in the **Start > Run** dialog box or at command prompt. You can change the default settings to prevent this level of reuse. Go to **Tools > Internet Options > Advanced** tab. Under **Browsing**, uncheck the "**Reuse windows for launching shortcuts**" checkbox.
- **Logout Error Message Number 500**—This message means that your session timed out and your Firewall MC window was left open. You must close all browser windows and then log in again to avoid this message. This error does not occur on a system on which Firewall MC is directly installed directly.
- **Changed IP address but did not restart the services**—If you changed the IP address but you did not restart the services, you will receive the following message on the browser while you are trying to access Firewall MC:

  ```
  Error 404: Page not found Message
  ```

  Stop and restart the services to avoid this message.

Authentication Issues

Authentication may take place among Firewall, Firewall MC, and Auto Update Servers in one of the following setups:

- Firewall MC authenticated by the Firewall during configuration import and deployment
- Firewall MC authenticated by the auto update server during configuration deployment

- Firewalls authenticated by the auto update server during configuration or image pulling

The sections that follow detail the points in the preceding list.

Firewall MC Authenticated by the Firewall During Configuration Import and Deployment

Before import or deployment of configuration, Firewall MC needs to authenticate with the firewalls. This authentication is performed either with AAA or with the enable password. When AAA is used, you must ensure that you provide both username and password on Firewall MC, by selecting **Configuration > Device Settings > Firewall Device Administration > Firewall Device Contact Info** on the Firewall MC.

If you run into a problem with authenticating Firewall MC with the firewalls, work through the following steps to correct the problem:

Step 1 Check syslog on the firewall and see why the authentication is failing.

Step 2 If AAA is used, analyze the log of the AAA server to find the cause of the authentication failure.

Step 3 Change AAA authentication to enable password authentication to rule out the possibility of an AAA issue.

Step 4 If the authentication problem occurs after you deployed the configuration, be sure to use current and future login credential options:

- **Changing Enable Password**—If you authenticate Firewall MC with the enable password of the firewall, and after the configuration import, you need to change the enable password, be sure to define the current and future password by selecting **Configuration > Device Settings > Firewall Device Administration > Firewall Device Contact Info**. Otherwise, Firewall MC will no longer be able to authenticate with the firewall after the configuration deployment.
- **Changing to AAA Authentication**—If you want to change the authentication method for Firewall MC from enable password to AAA-based authentication, be sure that the HTTP console setting is enabled and one AAA server is configured. To check the console setting in Firewall MC, select **Configuration > Device Settings > Firewall Device Administration > AAA Admin Authentication**. Next, set the AAA **future username** and **future password** settings. To set the future username and password, select **Configuration > Device Settings > Firewall Device Administration > Firewall Device Contact Info**.

Firewall MC Authenticated by the Auto Update Server During Configuration Deployment

Before Firewall MC can deploy to an AUS, Firewall MC must authenticate itself to the AUS with a username and password. You can either use CiscoWorks local user database or Cisco Secure Access Control Server (CS ACS) to authenticate the Firewall MC with the Auto Update Server. If CiscoWorks Common Services local database is used, the Username must be assigned the roles of system administrator or network administrator. On the other hand, if you need to use CS ACS for authentication, be sure Firewall MC roles are synchronized with the CS ACS server, and system administrator privilege is assigned for the user on the CS ACS Server.

On the Firewall MC, you need to provide the Auto Update Server contact information by going to **Configuration > Device Settings > Auto Update Server > Device AUS Settings**. The username and password entered here should be able to login to the CiscoWorks, bring up Auto Update Server and be able to perform administrative functions to the Auto Update server. Firewall MC communicates with the AUS using HTTPS regardless of whether the AUS is installed on the same or a different server.

Firewalls Authenticated by the Auto Update Server During Configuration or Image Pulling

Before Firewalls can contact AUS and pull the configuration or the image files from AUS, AUS will authenticate the firewalls. Hence, you must bootstrap the Firewall, which sets up the firewall with the minimum configuration needed. Example 19-1 shows the minimum configuration required on a PIX firewall to contact AUS.

Example 19-1 *Minimum Configuration Required on the PIX Firewall for Contacting AUS*

```
PIX# configure terminal
PIX(config)# auto-update server https://username:password@<AUSServerAddress>:port/
  autoupdate/
AutoUpdateServlet
PIX(config)#
```

You can configure the AUS server settings on the Firewall MC by selecting **Configuration > Device Settings > Auto Update Server > Server and Contact Information**.

If the firewall has problems with pulling the configuration or the image from the AUS because of authentication issues, work through the following steps to correct the problem:

Step 1 Revise the Firewall configuration.

If AUS is failing firewall, this can be because of either a bad username or password defined on the firewall. Revise the firewall configuration and ensure that the username and password defined can successfully log in to CiscoWorks Common Services, and bring up the AUS GUI.

Step 2 Verify the Login Role Privileges.

If you are using CiscoWorks Common Services local user database for authentication, be sure that username has the administrative privilege. If CS ACS is used as the authentication module, you must revise the configuration on the CS ACS server to ensure that administrative privilege is configured for the user.

Activity and Job Management Issues

You must open an activity to start any task on the Firewall MC. Also you need to define a job to perform configuration deployment. While working with activity or job, you might encounter the following problems, which are discussed in the sections that follow:

- Unlocking an of an activity
- Stopping a job from being deployed

Unlocking of an Activity

If an activity is locked, and if you try to edit the activity, you will receive the following message:

```
Scope already locked by activity name
```

To release an activity from the lock, you must either submit and approve the activity or undo the activity, which discards it from further use.

You could run into the locking up of an activity due to one or more of the following reasons:

- If you left an activity in the **Edit_Open** state (possibly due to a browser crash), the next time you log in, the Activity Management table displays the activity in the same state as before; however, the activity bar shows no activity opened (none) when you view the activity bar from the Devices or Configuration tabs. You must close the activity, and then reopen it to update the activity bar state.
- Another user has opened your activity and still has it open. The activity must be closed by the person who opened it or by an administrator before you can open the activity.
- Another user has opened your activity and has made changes to the activity that involves other devices. If you lack the needed privileges to modify the newly added devices, you no longer have access to your activity.

If you are unable to open an activity with the suggestions provided earlier, you may need to remove the activity from Firewall MC using the either of the following: Firewall MC GUI or Firewall MC Server CLI.

Using Firewall MC GUI

A pruning thread is run on demand or at midnight after a specified number of days to remove any terminal (approved or discarded) activities. Work through the following steps to remove the terminal activities from the Firewall MC using Firewall MC GUI:

Step 1 Select **Admin > Maintenance**.

Step 2 Perform one of the following tasks:

- To purge all terminal activities, click **Purge Now**. All terminal activities are removed from the activities page.
- To set a time for the Firewall MC to purge all terminal activities, enter the number of days in the field entitled **Purge approved/ discarded activities older than**, and then click **Apply**.

NOTE If you set the number of days to 0, then that night, any activity that is terminal and has its approved changes deployed will be deleted. All terminal activities that meet the requirements are removed from the activities page.

Using Firewall MC Server CLI

You can use a utility called *purge-mc-tasks* from a command prompt of the Firewall MC server to remove the terminal activities. It is strongly recommended to use this CLI utility as a last resort if you cannot close the activity and want to remove it from Firewall MC. Work through the following steps to perform the purging activity:

Step 1 Stop service CiscoWorks Daemon Manager. Wait for all CiscoWorks services to stop.

Step 2 Start the CiscoWorks KRS Database service. If you get a dialog about the service not starting in a timely manner, dismiss it, and watch the status of this service. Wait for it to change from **Starting** to **Started**.

Step 3 Start the CiscoWorks Lock Manager service. Wait for the CPU to become idle.

Step 4 Open a command prompt and type **purge-mc-tasks** (this should be on the path for an installed system). You should see output stating that tasks were purged or that no tasks were found.

Step 5 Stop the CiscoWorks Lock Manager service.

Step 6 Stop the CiscoWorks KRS Database service.

Step 7 Start the CiscoWorks Daemon Manager. The system should be usable after all the services come up.

Stopping a Job from Being Deployed

If a job is being deployed, you can select the job in the Job Management table, and then click **Cancel**. If a job has completed deployment, you can select the job in the Job Management table, and then click **Rollback**. The rollback feature allows you to select the device(s) for which you want to roll back to the last previously deployed configuration file.

Device Import Issues

You can import the device (PIX or FWSM) configuration from either a CSV file or the live device. Work through the following steps if you cannot import a device configuration using either method:

Step 1 Version information is missing on the CSV file.

When you import the device configuration from a CSV file, you must ensure that you have the version information on the CSV file; otherwise, import will fail with the following message:

```
No version found in the text
```

The image version information should be at the beginning of the file with one of the following two syntaxes:

```
! A comment should be following an exclamation point
:! PIX Version 6.n(n)
```

Or

```
PIX Version 6.n (n)
```

Step 2 The required configuration is missing on the firewall.

To import the firewall configuration directly from the device, you must ensure that firewalls are configured to communicate using HTTPS, and that Firewall MC is one of the listed addresses that are allowed to make an https connection to the firewall.

If you have the proper configuration for Firewall MC to be able to connect, you will see the verification process illustrated in Example 19-2. Assume that the Firewall MC Server IP address is 10.1.1.100 and that it is sitting on the inside network.

Example 19-2 *Verifying and Correcting the Configuration Required on the PIX Firewall for Firewall MC To Be Able To Import The Configuration*

```
pixfirewall# show version
Cisco PIX Firewall Version 6.2(4)
! Only showing the relevant information
Compiled on Mon 28-Jun-04 15:05 by morlee
Licensed Features:
Failover:            Enabled
! Make sure DES or 3DES feature is enabled for the PIX
VPN-DES:             Enabled
VPN-3DES:            Disabled
Maximum Interfaces: 6
Cut-through Proxy:   Enabled
! Removed the irrelevant portion of the output.
Configuration last modified by enable_15 at 01:26:55.309 UTC Thu Jun 30 2005
pixfirewall# configure terminal
! Check to see if the http server is enabled and if so, is Firewall MC allowed?
pixfirewall(config)# show http
```

continues

Example 19-2 *Verifying and Correcting the Configuration Required on the PIX Firewall for Firewall MC To Be Able To Import The Configuration (Continued)*

```
http server disabled
! As the http server is disable, you need to enable this server with the
! following command
pixfirewall(config)# http server enable
! Then you need to allow the Firewall MC with the following command
pixfirewall(config)# http 10.1.1.100 255.255.255.255 inside
! Verify the http configuration again
pixfirewall(config)# show http
http server enabled
10.1.1.100 255.255.255.255 inside
! If you still unable to connect, you may have certificate problem.  Verify if
! the certificate is generated
pixfirewall(config)# show ca mypubkey rsa
% Key pair was generated at: 19:07:14 UTC Jun 16 2005
Key name: pixfirewall.rtp.cisco.com
 Usage: General Purpose Key
 Key Data:
  30819f30 0d06092a 864886f7 0d010101 05000381 8d003081 89028181 00eb238b
  6b2dde82 2c3b1b69 02844257 c175e53a e204510c b2e71689 392de546 ec5f0857
  ebbcf8a3 116e5280 72fc3b26 13474501 ff49ba95 b8f37867 5de93a3e 9265745a
  8897da68 e17db40b d453a525 36578df7 c91583d0 96f268d8 b3aa2246 2db82b8d
  4dca775d da82314d d7256134 7250358a f37ecff0 e3090401 5375c8d7 db020301 0001
% Key pair was generated at: 01:26:21 UTC Jun 30 2005
Key name: pixfirewall.rtp.cisco.com.server
 Usage: Encryption Key
 Key Data:
  307c300d 06092a86 4886f70d 01010105 00036b00 30680261 00ac5034 7d9092f9
  fd4eaebe 124bb4d7 45a1c127 04733bfe 279b166f e90acaf0 bdaf462a c7876633
  62618542 55cb224b 1644866c 40ebc906 80c1a0d2 cc2c1b74 c1b8e31e f974f7ee
  fc80c688 8ff7ab19 0250702a eacf1c37 cd4e1b4f 12a0b63b 1d020301 0001
pixfirewall(config)#
! If the mypubkey exists but, then may be the key is corrupt.  You may want to
! remove the key.
pixfirewall(config)# ca zeroize rsa
pixfirewall(config)# show ca mypubkey rsa
! Regenerate the key with the following command. This example uses 512 as the
! key size as this activation key on the PIX supports only DES, not 3DES. You
! should choose this number based on your need.
pixfirewall(config)# ca generate rsa key 512
.
pixfirewall(config)#  show ca mypubkey rsa
% Key pair was generated at: 01:42:24 UTC Jun 30 2005
Key name: pixfirewall.rtp.cisco.com
 Usage: General Purpose Key
 Key Data:
  305c300d 06092a86 4886f70d 01010105 00034b00 30480241 00c61618 84bfa964
  bf5bd5ae a2116910 54f87e56 d4e213e9 c72e9f23 ffac73ac a811445b bda18805
  25777c1f 7d52eb9c 425bbc20 5c6fa9da 0c7b7d76 93d16671 6f020301 0001
! Finally save the key, otherwise a reboot will wipe out the key
pixfirewall(config)# ca save all
pixfirewall(config)#
```

Step 3 There are communication problems using HTTPS.

As the Firewall MC uses the HTTPS protocol to connect to the firewall to import the configuration, you must ensure that the firewall is configured to allow Firewall MC to connect to the firewall to pull the configuration as explained in the previous step. If HTTPS is blocked by a network device between the Firewall MC and the firewall, or if PIX is configured to allow the https connection from the Firewall MC server, you will receive the following message on the Firewall MC:

```
Failed to contact host: x.x.x.x
```

If there is a connection problem to the firewall, you can verify this with the following URLs from the Firewall MC Server browser to the firewall:

```
https://<device-IP/exec/show%20ver
https://<device-IP/exec/show%20run
https://<device-IP/exec/show%20config
https://<device-IP/config
```

If any of these URLs work for you, then you do not have a connection problem using HTTPS to the firewall from the Firewall MC server.

Otherwise, go through the previous step to make sure that you have the proper configuration on the firewall, and also revise the device configurations between Firewall MC and the firewall to ensure that one of the devices is not blocking the traffic.

Step 4 There is an authentication failure.

In this situation, the firewall can authenticate either with the AAA username and password or the enable password only. If you have the following command on the firewall and authentication fails, then the problem might be with the way the AAA server is configured.

```
aaa authentication http console server_tag
```

To eliminate the possibility that AAA is causing the problem, you can remove the AAA authentication for HTTP with the following command:

```
no aaa authentication http console server_tag
```

Open the browser on the server, and enter the following URL:**https:// <device ip> /exec/show version**. and be sure that you can authenticate with the enable password.

If enable password authentication works but AAA does not, be sure that the user defined on the AAA server has privilege 15 if the following command is turned on:

```
aaa authorization command {LOCAL | TACACS_Server_TAG}
```

If after checking everything, you still have problems generating the following message, then analyze the syslog on the firewall and the AAA server log.

```
"Unable to talk to the server x.x.x.x. Please check the username and
  password".
```

Step 5 Import fails with Interface error.

If you have multiple interfaces up but do not have the IP address, the import will fail with the following message:

```
*** Severe: Interface outside is not a valid interface
```

The interfaces need IP addresses to become valid for Firewall MC.

Step 6 You may import PIX configuration with unsupported commands.

If you are running a version on PIX that is higher than what is supported by the Firewall MC, you will receive error messages when try to import the configuration from the Firewall. Follow either of the following methods to work around this problem:

— Remove the commands for which you are getting errors. Import the configuration, and then insert the commands in the **Ending Commands** under **Configuration > Device Settings > Config Additions > Ending Commands**. Then push the configuration to the firewall.

— Copy the entire Configuration from the PIX into a text file, and remove the commands you are having problems with from this text file. Insert the "removed" commands in the "Ending Commands" under **Configuration > Device Settings > Config Additions > Ending Commands**. Then push the configuration to the firewall.

Step 7 Import is extremely slow.

If network connectivity is very unreliable, an import or deploy may take a long time. If so, you should copy the configuration from the firewall as an interim solution and import the configuration from the CSV file. If you have the large configuration on the firewall, then a delay is to be expected.

Step 8 Check if SSL communication is broken.

If you still cannot import, get the output of the following debug command and contact Cisco Support for additional help. Be sure to collect the debug output when you attempt to connect to the Firewall MC.

```
debug ssl cipher
debug ssl device
debug crypto ca
```

Additionally, the syslog with the debug level turned on may be required.

Configuration Generation and Deployment Issues

If you cannot deploy the configuration from Firewall MC to the firewall, go through the troubleshooting steps under the "Device Import Issues" section of this chapter. Additionally, this section lists some of the issues that are specific to the deployment of Firewall configuration.

- Firewall MC is unable to push the configuration to the AUS
- Getting "Incomplete Auto Update Server contact info." Message when pushing the configuration to AUS
- Memory Issues with Firewall Services Module (FWSM) during deployment

The sections that follow present detailed discussions of these topics.

Firewall MC is Unable To Push the Configuration to the AUS

Firewall MC may be unable to push the configuration to the AUS for either or both of the following reasons:

- Username or Password is invalid—If the username and password defined under **Configuration > Device Settings > Auto Update Server > Server and Contact Information** of Firewall MC, then Firewall MC will not be able to push the configuration to the AUS. Revise the configuration on both Firewall MC and the CiscoWorks Common Services local user database to make sure that the username and password match on both sides.
- Default Port is changed on the AUS—By default the AUS listens on TCP/443 for Firewall MC. However, at the time of installation, if you change the default port, then make sure to use that port under **Configuration > Device Settings > Auto Update Server > Server and Contact Information** of Firewall MC.

Getting "Incomplete Auto Update Server contact info." Message when Pushing The Configuration to AUS

When you import a firewall that is configured for use with an Auto Update Server, the contact information for the Firewall MC to the Auto Update Server communication is overridden. Therefore, after import, you must provide the correct information on the **Configuration > Device Settings > Auto Update Server > Server and Contact Information** page before you try to deploy. The best way to work around this problem is to define the settings for this page at the group level, import AUS enabled devices into that group, and select the Inherit settings from the parent checkbox at the device level.

Memory Issues with Firewall Services Module (FWSM) during Deployment

By default Firewall Services Module (FWSM) keeps the old ACL and compiles at the same time with the new ACL, while the new ACL is added to the FWSM. This is to make sure that there is no traffic disruption at the time of ACL updates. However, this may result in Firewall MC not being able to successfully push ACLs to an FWSM device because of an out-of-memory failure. You can get around this problem by requesting that old ACLs be removed from the device before target ACLs are deployed by the Firewall MC by selecting **Configuration > MC Settings > Management**. Select the **Clear ACLs before deployment** (FWSM only) check box.

However, if the deployment fails, and the new ACL is not successfully deployed to the FWSM, traffic will be blocked. This may be less than desirable for specific network. Hence, make sure that you deselect the **Clear ACLs before deployment (FWSM only)** check box under **Configuration > MC Settings > Management**.

Database Management Issues

As the Firewall MC can coexist with other Management Centers on the same CiscoWorks Common Services server, the backup and restore operations are not exclusive to the Firewall MC itself. If you perform a backup or restore, the operation includes all CiscoWorks Common Services components running on the Server. This distinction is important to consider when restoring a component. All components on the CiscoWorks Server are restored using the last backed-up archive. Therefore, you should consider the strategies for scheduling Firewall MC Backups within the context of all components running on the CiscoWorks Server. It is important to realize that the backup and restore functions do not perform backup or restore on the users created on the CiscoWorks Common Services for login to the CiscoWorks desktop using browser.

The sections that follow discuss the following database activities in detail:

- Backing up and restoring database
- Scheduling checkpoint events for the database
- Compacting database for performance improvement
- Disaster recovery plan

Backing up and Restoring Databases

You should back up the database regularly so that you have a safe copy of the CiscoWorks Common Services database. You can back up the database on demand, at a specific time, or at scheduled intervals.

When you back up the database, the data for all client applications is backed up; you cannot specify a backup of a single client application. User account information is not backed up. You must use the CiscoWorks Server utilities to back up user account information.

NOTE You can back up the data only to the server. You cannot back up the database to a client system, even if that client system is being used to connect to CiscoWorks Common Services and to initiate the backup. However, after you back up the database, it is recommended that you store the backup to a different computer to prevent data loss if hardware fails.

Database Backup Procedure

To back up the database, work through the steps that follow:

Step 1 Select **VPN/Security Management Solution > Administration > Common Services > Backup Database** from the navigation tree. The Backup Database page displays.

Step 2 Specify the path to the directory in which you want to store the backup.

Step 3 To send an e-mail to a designated recipient each time the database is backed up, select the E-mail Notification check box and enter an e-mail address in the field.

Step 4 To back up the database immediately, select the **Immediate** check box.

Step 5 To back up the database at a specific date and time, deselect the **Immediate** check box, and define the **Start Date,** and **Start Time**.

Step 6 To schedule a backup at regular intervals, enter a value in the **Repeat After** field, and select **Days, Hours,** or **Minutes** from the list. To limit the number of times the database backup occurs, enter a value in the Limit Occurrences field under Frequency.

Step 7 To back up the database according to the settings you have made, click **Finish**.

Step 8 Finally click **OK** to close the message.

Database Restore Procedure

You can restore the database from an existing backup. The backup contains data from all installed CiscoWorks Common Services client applications. Because user account information is not backed up, you cannot use restore to recover deleted accounts. Additionally, license information is not restored; the license in effect when the restore is performed remains in effect after the restore.

CAUTION Restoring the database restores the data for all client applications; you cannot restore the data for a single client application. Therefore, restoring the database resets all client application data to the state it was in when you created the backup.

To restore a database, work through the steps that follow:

Step 1 Select **VPN/Security Management Solution > Administration > Common Services > Restore Database**. The Restore Database page displays.

Step 2 Specify the path to the directory where the backup is stored.

Step 3 To send an e-mail to a designated recipient each time the database is restored, select the **E-mail Notification** check box and enter an e-mail address in the field.

Step 4 Click **Finish** to save your settings. A message provides the status of the database restore. Note that if you restore using a backup file from an earlier version of Firewall MC and the database tables must be upgraded, the restore progress bar moves quickly to 25 percent and remains at 25 percent until the table upgrade is complete,Then, the progress bar moves quickly to 100 percent. The progress bar does not move during the table upgrade portion of the restore, which can take from several minutes to an hour, depending on the number of items that must be upgraded.

Step 5 Click **OK** to close the message.

Step 6 Select **Server Configuration > Administration > Process Management > Stop Process**. The Stop Process page displays. Select **System** in the stop column, and click **Finish** to start the process.

Step 7 Select **Server Configuration > Administration > Process Management > Start Process**. The Start Process page displays. Select System in the start column. Click Finish.

Now you should have backup database restored to the system.

Scheduling Checkpoint Events for the Database

Checkpoint event is used to trigger the Firewall MC to write all information stored in the memory cache to data files on the hard drive. A log file tracks the changes made to the system. These changes signify information, such as configuration settings and audit records, which differ from the settings stored in the data files. If the server on which the database resides shuts down too early, when power fails, for example, the database uses the log file to recreate the state of the system before it was shut down. Checkpoints reduce the amount of time required to recreate this "last known good" state, because they reduce the size and number of changes in the log file. The database synchronizes its in-memory working data with the data stored on the hard drive when one of the following events occurs:

- The specified amount of time elapses.
- The size of the log file that is tracking the changes made since the last checkpoint exceeds the maximum specified file size value.

A disadvantage of checkpoints is that they use much of the system resources. Therefore, the number of audit records that can be recorded while a checkpoint is being performed is reduced. The smaller the difference between the in-memory data and the data files, the faster the server running the database can "recover" and resume normal activity. (Normal activity includes recording audit records and accepting changes to existing network policies.)

You can define a checkpoint rule to specify how frequently the database should write the information stored in its memory cache to the database files on the server hard drive. You can base checkpoint events on the size of the log file, the time of day, a set interval, or some combination of the three. You can also disable checkpoint events by disabling each type of checkpoint rule; however, we discourage this option.

NOTE Database check pointing affects only the KRS database used by the Firewall MC.

TIP If importing or generating large configurations in a client application takes a long time, increase your Checkpoint File Size value. It is likely that one or more checkpoint events are occurring during your import or generation.

Work through the steps that follow for configuring the checkpoints:

Step 1 Select **VPN/Security Management Solution > Administration > Management Center > Database Checkpoint**. The Database Checkpoint Settings page displays.

Step 2 Enter the maximum size (in megabytes) that the log file can reach before requiring a checkpoint in the Checkpoint File Size field. To disable the size checkpoint, enter **0** (zero).

Step 3 From the Schedule At lists, select the hour and minutes when the checkpoint should occur. To disable the time-of-day checkpoint, select **00** (zero-zero) for both the hours and the minutes. The time is shown in 24-hour format.

Step 4 In the Interval field, enter the interval, in hours, to specify how often to repeat the checkpoint.

Step 5 Click **Finish**. A message provides the status of the configuration change.

Step 6 Click **OK** to close the message.

Compacting a Database for Performance Improvement

Compacting the database eliminates space that is allocated for data that no longer exists in the database. Hence it decreases the amount of space required to retain existing CiscoWorks Common Services configuration data and can increase system performance and minimize startup time. Only the KRS database used by the Firewall MC is affected by this procedure.

You should compact the database at regular intervals to reclaim unused storage space. You can compact the database on demand or schedule the database to compact at a set time or at regular intervals. You cannot compact the database while backing up or restoring it.

TIP Use the scheduling feature to schedule database compactions weekly or daily, depending on how often you update your configurations. You should schedule the compaction to occur when the system is not being used, such as late at night or early in the morning. Also make sure to schedule backup before scheduling database compactions.

Follow these steps to compact the database:

Step 1 Close all instances of Firewall MC. Note that the CW2000 KRS database service is shut down while the database is being compacted and restarted when compaction is complete. If there are any instances of the Firewall MC being active when you compact the database, the connection to the database for those sessions will be terminated. You will need to close Firewall MC, and then log out and back in to the CiscoWorks Server before you can use Firewall MC.

Step 2 From the CiscoWorks Server desktop, select **VPN/Security Management Solution > Administration > Management Center > Compact Database**. The Compact Database page displays.

Step 3 To send an e-mail to a designated recipient each time the database is compacted, select the **E-mail Notification** check box and enter an e-mail address in the field.

Step 4 To compact the database immediately, select the **Immediate** check box.

Step 5 To schedule a specific date and time for the compaction, deselect the **Immediate** checkbox. Define the **Start Date** and **Start Time** list, and then click each displayed value to confirm.

Step 6 To schedule compaction at regular intervals, enter a value in the **Repeat After** field, then select **Days**, **Hours**, or **Minutes** from the list. To limit the number of times the database is compacted, enter a value in the **Limit Occurrences** field.

Step 7 Click **Finish** to save your settings.

Step 8 Click **OK** to close the message.

Disaster Recovery Plan

To lessen the possibility of data loss and decrease the time required to recover from a catastrophic hardware failure on the system hosting Firewall MC, you can configure a rapid recovery server. A rapid recovery server is a secondary CiscoWorks Server running Firewall MC that subscribes to a database backup of the primary server. If the primary server fails, you can enable the secondary server as the new primary Firewall MC server.

Configuring the Recovery Server

Work through the steps that follow to configure the Recovery Server:

Step 1 From the primary CiscoWorks Server, map a network drive to a local drive letter (for example, z:).

Step 2 From the desktop of the primary CiscoWorks Server, select **VPN/ Security Management Solution > Administration > Common Services > Backup Database**.

Step 3 In the Backup Directory field, select the local drive letter that you mapped in Step 1.

Step 4 Specify the backup interval that meets your needs.

Step 5 From the secondary CiscoWorks Server, map a local drive letter to the same network share used in Step 1.

Step 6 From the desktop of the secondary CiscoWorks Server, select **VPN/ Security Management Solution > Administration > Common Services > Restore Database**.

Step 7 In the Backed-up Archive field, select the local drive letter that you mapped in Step 5.

Step 8 **Authentication and Authorization with CiscoWorks Server Local Database**—If you are using the authentication and authorization services provided by your CiscoWorks Server, you must manually synchronize the account and authorization definitions between the primary and secondary CiscoWorks Servers.

Step 9 **Authentication and Authorization with Cisco Secure ACS**—If you are using Cisco Secure ACS for authentication and authorization, this server acts as a shared authentication server for both Firewall MC servers. Therefore, you must verify that both the primary and secondary severs have the appropriate permissions in the PIX Device Group definition of the Cisco Secure ACS server.

Step 10 **AUS Server**—Because you can specify only a single AUS server as a target deployment location in Firewall MC, your AUS server also acts as a shared server for both Firewall MC servers. Therefore, you must configure your AUS Server to be independent of both Firewall MC servers.

Enabling the Recovery Server

If you experience a catastrophic hardware failure on the Primary Firewall MC server, go to the secondary server, assign the IP address and domain name to be same as primary Firewall MC server, and restore the last database backup performed by the primary CiscoWorks Server.

NOTE The total data loss depends on length of time since the last backup (the backup interval) plus the time required restoring the data. In this sense, data loss refers to audit data that can be collected by other VMS components.

Common Problems and Resolutions

This section lists some of common problems that you may experience and explains how to resolve them.

1 Does the Firewall MC server require a valid DNS entry?

Answer: No it's not required, but for performance you must have DNS entry.

2 What other Cisco software is required for running Firewall MC?

Answer: Firewall MC is a tool that installs on top of the VMS Bundle, which includes CiscoWorks Common Services.

3 What regional settings can I use for my operating system?

Answer: Currently, only English-US regional settings are supported.

4 Can I upgrade my Firewall MC from Version 1.x to the latest release?

Answer: Yes, you can directly upgrade from Firewall MC 1.x to the latest release by installing the new version. The upgrade will automatically address data schema changes that have occurred between the releases. During installation, you can choose to re-initialize your database, or to keep the existing data. If you choose to keep your data, the upgrade framework will automatically convert the data to be compatible with the new version.

Backing up data from older versions to new versions is also supported by the same database upgrade framework, so you can take a 1.0 backup and restore it on a 1.3 version of Firewall MC.

5 What happens to my AAA roles during an upgrade of Firewall MC?

Answer: If you do not unregister Firewall MC from CS ACS before you run the upgrade, your CS ACS role settings will be retained and you will be constrained to making changes directly through the CS ACS user interface. If you do unregister Firewall MC, and then upgrade, you will have to re-register with ACS, and CS ACS will use the new settings that are installed with the new version of Firewall MC as its default. The changed files are pixmdc_cmfrolemap.xml and acsroles.xml.

6 How do I determine device deployment status after canceling a deployment to an AUS?

Answer: If you cancel a job that deploys to AUS, the status might show that the deployment of some devices was canceled even though deployment was completed. To work around this problem, select **VPN/Security Management Solution > Administration > Logging > Audit Log** to determine which devices were deployed.

7 How can I see my global and default rules while I am defining rules on my devices?

Answer: To see all rules that apply to a device, select **Configuration > Access Rules**. Select the rule table from the TOC, and then navigate to the device for which you want to see the rules. Click **View All**. A popup window displays all rules defined at all scopes that pertain to the selected device.

8 The default setting ensures that global settings are inherited by all children. How do I change this?

Answer: Default configuration settings are set at the global level, but you can override them for a subgroup or device. A setting is designated as default for a subgroup or device(s) when you select Inherit settings in the user interface. When you select Inherit settings, the subgroup or device defers the definition of any setting to a higher-level, enclosing group. You can override a default setting by deselecting the Inherit settings check box and specifying other values completely for that scope.

9 How should I order the Access Rules for firewall using Firewall MC?

Answer: Access rules are processed in first-matched order. Therefore, the first rule that satisfies the conditions of a session, regardless of how generally they are expressed in the rule, is the rule that is applied. You should organize the most explicit and most narrowly defined rules first, and then define the more general rules.

Dynamic and static translation rules are processed in best-matched order. NAT 0 ACL rules are processed in first-matched order.

10 Can I move rules after they are inserted in a rule table?

Answer: You can cut, copy, and paste rules within a rule table by using the buttons at the bottom of each rule table or by right-clicking inside the rule table, which brings up a menu with the same button options listed.

Note Because rules are applied to an interface, make sure the interface specified in a rule exists on the device to which you are pasting the rule. If the interface is not found on the device, an error results when the device configuration is generated. You cannot paste a rule before or after a rule created from an outbound rule. Outbound rules are sorted in the order in which a firewall device applies them to traffic.

11 Why are certain rules in the rule table not mapping to rules in the generated command sets?

Answer: Not every rule in the GUI translates to a line in the CLI. If optimization is enabled, some rules might be compressed.

12 How can I see all rules that will be deployed to a device?

Answer: Select the device whose configurations you want to view, generate the command sets, select **Deploy Later**, and then use the **Devices Settings** report.

13 I changed a global rule and need to regenerate all my device configurations before they can be deployed. Can I select devices to deploy instead of deploying all of them at once?

Answer: How you select devices depends on your workflow settings:

- If workflow is not enabled, select the **Deploy Later** button. This option saves your changes. You can then go to the **Deployment** tab and select one or more devices to deploy the changes.
- If workflow is enabled, you can select the devices to deploy in the Select Devices page of the Job Management wizard.

Best Practices

This section lists some of the practices that can help in improving performance and providing necessary security for the Firewall MC server:

- Always upgrade to the latest version of Firewall MC and apply new patches available on the Cisco Web Site.
- A valid DNS entry for the Firewall MC server is required for optimum performance. Remote access for managing the Firewall MC might be slow when connecting to Firewall MC without the appropriate DNS entry. If you do not have the DNS server configured for the Firewall MC server, be sure both the management client and the Firewall MC server hosts files have the host name for Firewall MC server mapped to the IP address of the Firewall MC server.

- If possible, install Security Monitor on a server that is separate from the Firewall MC server.
- Be sure to install Common Services and Firewall MC on a dedicated machine. This is because Common Services and Firewall MC have their own web server and database server, which might cause resource confliction issues if another application is installed. Be sure to fulfill minimum requirements for running VMS server. As performance depends on the configuration of hardware, not VMS software, it is always recommended that you have a fast and powerful server.
- It is recommended that you secure the VMS server with Cisco's Security Agent (CSA). CSA is Cisco's host-based IDS/IPS software.
- If the Firewall MC is in a different network (VLAN) than the firewalls (PIX firewall or FWSM), then be sure the network devices between the Firewall MC server and the firewall allow SSH (TCP/22) and SSL (TCP/443) in both directions.
- Do not install Firewall MC on Primary or Backup Domain Controller, IIS Server, Terminal Server, IEV, or CSPM.
- Implement a Disaster Recovery Plan as explained in the **"Disaster Recovery Plan"** of this chapter.

CHAPTER 20

Troubleshooting Router MC

Router MC is a software component that runs on Common Services to provide the management capability for the VPN configuration on the router or the VPN Services Module. As of the writing of this book, the latest version of Router MC is 1.3.1. Hence, the configuration and troubleshooting details of this chapter are based on Router MC Version 1.3.1. This same information may be used for troubleshooting a newer version of Router MC.

Overview of Router MC

Router MC is a web-based Application for setup and maintenance of large-scale VPN connections. It is intended for use in scalable configurations of hub and spoke (site-to-site) topology—not as a single device manager. It centralizes configuration of Internet Key Exchange (IKE) and IPsec tunnel policies on multiple devices, and hierarchical grouping and reusable components for simplified deployment and management. Literally hundreds of VPN configurations can be deployed with the same policy with Router MC, which addresses the scalability requirements of today's network. The sections that follow explain the following items in detail:

- Router MC processes
- Communication architecture
- Features introduced on different versions of Router MC

Router MC Processes

Several processes perform different tasks on Router MC. If one of these processes is not running, that specific process function will not work. If there are problems in running the application, it is always a good practice to check that all these processes are running. The processes and their main functions are listed as follows:

- **Apache**—This is the web server process. Be sure that the web server is running properly.
- **ASANYs_SqlCoreDB**—This a SQL database. For the Router MC to function properly, be sure this is running properly.

- **Tomcat**—Be sure that the Java servlets that make up the Router MC user interface are running properly.
- **AppSrv**—This is the Application Server process. This process must be running for Router MC to function correctly.
- **IOSMDCMain**—This is the Router MC main process. This is the core process for Router MC that must be running.

If one of these processes is not running, the task it controls will not run. To check the status of the processes and start them, go to **Server Configuration > Administration > Process Management**. From there you can view the status of the processes, stop the processes, or start stopped processes.

Communication Architecture

Router MC communicates with VPN devices using Secure Shell (SSH) protocol for both importing and deploying configuration from VPN devices.

Features Introduced on Different Versions of Router MC

While working on Router MC, it is important to know which features are introduced on which versions of Router MC. This information can be found under "Supported Devices, OS Versions" and "Commands for Management Center for Firewalls x.x.x" link under each release document. For example, if you want to know the features introduced on Firewall MC Version 1.3.3, you could go to the following link:

http://www.cisco.com/univercd/cc/td/doc/product/rtrmgmt/cw2000/mgt_pix/fwmc133/index.htm

Then go to the "Supported Devices, OS Versions and Commands for Management Center for Firewalls 1.3.3" link which will take you directly to the following link:

http://www.cisco.com/univercd/cc/td/doc/product/rtrmgmt/cw2000/mgt_pix/fwmc133/dvice133.htm

You can find out information for the other versions from the following link:

http://www.cisco.com/univercd/cc/td/doc/product/rtrmgmt/cw2000/cw2000_b/vpnman/index.htm

Browse to the appropriate version of Firewall MC to obtain supportability information for a specific version of Firewall MC.

Diagnostic Commands and Tools

There is extensive debug capability for troubleshooting issues with the VPN Router MC. This section explains how to use this capability efficiently.

Setting the Logging Level

There are two levels of logging available for Router MC: **debug** and **info**. The default logging level is information. With this level, only information and error messages are written to the log file. While troubleshooting issues on VPN Router MC, you might want to set the logging to the **debug** level. However, note that working in debug mode uses more system resources, which slows down the system. Hence, you must use the **debug** level only when it is required. Once you are finished with troubleshooting or collecting data for analysis, reset the level back to **info**. Work through the following steps to perform this task:

Step 1 At the command line of Router MC Server, execute the following command to turn the debug on:

```
C:\Program Files\CSCOpx\MDC\iosmdc\bin> setLoggermode -debug
```

Step 2 Allow a few minutes for the new mode to take effect, or restart the services.

Step 3 Simulate your problem; let the system run collecting debug information for the problem you are trying to troubleshoot. Then collect the debug information with the procedure explained in the next section.

Step 4 Once you have finished collecting debug information, revert the logging level back to **info** by using the following command:

```
C:\Program Files\CSCOpx\MDC\iosmdc\bin> setLoggermode -info
```

Collecting the Debug Information (Diagnostics)

After setting up the logging level to **debug**, you can collect or view the debug information in two ways: by using a Graphic User Interface (GUI) or the Command line Interface (CLI).

Using a Graphic User Interface

You can view the debug log messages in the Common Services user interface, by selecting **VPN Security Management Solution > Admin > Logging > Operation**. This is useful for viewing the information in real time without having the console access to the Router MC server. However, if you want to analyze the log offline or want to send this information to the Cisco support center for additional analysis, you might want to follow the procedure described in the section that follows.

Using a Command Line Interface

Using the CLI is more efficient than using a GUI to collect debug information from the Router MC Server. Work through the following steps to practice using the CLI:

Step 1 On the Router MC server, open the DOS prompt and type **MDCSupport**. If you do not specify a location, the **MDCSupportInformation.zip** file is created in this default location: the **$BASE\CSCOpx\MDC\etc** directory, where **$BASE** is the drive and directory where you installed CiscoWorks Common Services (for example, **c:\Program Files**). To save the file to a different location, enter **MDCSupport drive:\path** at the DOS prompt.

Step 2 Press **Enter**. The **MDCSupport** utility creates a .zip file that contains system and configuration information.

Step 3 You can transfer this resultant file into a different machine or send this information to the Cisco support Team for additional analysis.

The **MDCSupportInformation.zip** file does not include the Router MC database. However, this may be required by the Cisco Support team to replicate your setup. To collect the Router MC database, follow the procedure in the next section.

Collecting the Router MC Database

Work through the following steps to collect the Router MC database of the Router MC server:

Step 1 Stop the Daemon Manager.

Step 2 Go to the directory in which Router MC is installed, navigate to **CSCOpx\MDC\iosmdc\db**, and copy the following files: **iosmdcDB.db** and **iosmdcDB.log**

Step 3 To collect the device configuration files, go to the directory in which Router MC is installed, navigate to **CSCOpx\MDC\iosmdc\IOSMDCFS\import\current**, and copy the device configuration files.

Step 4 Restart the Daemon Manager

Using the Log Files

The **MDCSupportInformation.zip** file is made up of a number of files. Hence to analyze the problem efficiently, you need to know which files are pertinent to the Router MC and therefore need to be analyzed Each message in the log files contains the timestamp, the module that has written the message, its type (information, debug or error), and its data. The following list outlines some of the most important logs that you need to analyze first, based on the types of problem you are experiencing:

- **Tomcat Logs**—The tomcat logs are located at **\CSCOpx\MDC\tomcat\logs**. The most important files are **stdout.log** and **stderr.log**. If due to login failure or timeout problems, the devices are not accessible when you are trying to update the current configuration, live deployment will fail. This may happen if the IOS does not support the CLI syntax that is generated by Router MC.

- **Jonas logs**—The Jonas logs provide information on issues related to the database actions. The log files are located at **\CSCOpx\MDC\logs**. The most important Jonas log files that need to be analyzed first are **JonasStderr.log** and **JonasStdout.log**.

Reports

The Router MC can generate the following reports, which can be used for troubleshooting Router MC:

- **Audit Report**—Query-based report showing who did what to which objects in which activity
- **Device Status**—Last deployment status of all devices
- **Activity Status**—Summary of **active** activities and what objects are locked by each

Analysis of Problem Areas

The Router MC troubleshooting issues can be categorized as follows:

- Installation and upgrade
- Initialization
- Browser
- Authentication
- Activity and job management
- Device import
- Configuration generation and deployment
- Database management

The sections that follow discuss each of these issues in detail.

Installation and Upgrade Issues

If Router MC Installation fails on the Windows platform, you need to analyze the log in the **C:** directory. This is where you can find the log in the format of **C:\Ciscoworks_setupxxx.log** (for example, the **C:\Ciscoworks_setup001.log**) file. The file name with the highest number is the most recent log file. Following are some of the probable causes of Router MC Installation/Upgrade failure on Windows platform:

- **Installation directory already exists**—If the installation directory is not removed completely during a previous uninstall operation, the new installation process will fail. You may receive an error message indicating that the **iosmdc** installation subdirectory already exists under the Common Services installation directory. If so, you cannot install the Router MC.

To resolve the issue, you need to delete the **iosmdc** installation directory, and then start the installation process again. If some of the files are locked and cannot be deleted, restart your system, and then delete those files.

- **Insufficient disk space to invoke Router MC**—If you do not have sufficient disk space on the system on which you are trying to install Router MC, you may receive a message such as this:

  ```
  Router MC Installation file cannot be unzipped due to insufficient disk space.
  ```

  To install the Router MC, you must click **Cancel**, free up sufficient disk space, and then try again.

- **Application server not removed after Router MC uninstall**—When Router MC is uninstalled from a server on which QoS Policy Manager (QPM) is installed, the **Application Server** service, which is a required process for Router MC, is not removed even after removing the QPM. The Application Server service must not be left installed on a server after Router MC is uninstalled. Otherwise, re-installation of Firewall MC will fail.

  To resolve this issue, after uninstalling both Router MC and QPM, remove the Application Server open up DOS prompt and go to **\CSCOpx\MDC\Shared\Services\EJB_Server.** Then run the following command to delete the Application Server from the list in Windows.

  ```
  Exe2Service.exe REMOVE AppSrv
  ```

  In addition, run the following command to remove the Application Server service from the Daemon Manager:

  ```
  pdreg -u AppSrv
  ```

Initialization Issues

You might encounter problems with bringing up Common Services due to one of the following reasons:

- **Required process not running**—If you cannot log in to the Router MC, you should first verify that all processes required are running by selecting **Server Configuration > Administration > Process Management > Process Status** from the CiscoWorks desktop. Refer to the "Router MC Processes" section to find information on the processes that are pertinent to Router MC. If any of the processes are not running, you can start the processes by selecting **Server Configuration > Administration > Process Management > Start Process**. If you cannot start the required services from the CiscoWorks desktop, stop and restart all services from the command line on the server with the following commands:

  ```
  net stop crmdmgtd
  net start crmdmgtd
  ```

You can perform the same task by selecting **Start > Settings > Control Panel > Administrative Tools > Services**. If the problems persist, try rebooting the server.

- **Changing Windows account password**—If you install Common Services and Router MC using a specific admin account and password in Windows, and then change that Windows account password, the installed processes fail to start due to the change in password.

  To resolve this issue, change the password for all processes so that they match the current password of the Windows account within which they were installed. Common Services processes include **tomcat, fms, lm**, and **daframework**.

- **Port conflict issues**—Common Services use port 1741. So, if there is another application running on the server using the same port, Common Services will not be able to start.

  Under this circumstance, you must change the port for other applications, and then restart the server system.

- **Changed database password**—If you change the Router MC Database password by selecting **VPN/Security Management Solution > Administration > Configuration > Database Credentials** in the CiscoWorks desktop, you must restart the Router MC server. If try to start Router MC without restarting the Router MC server, the connection to the database will be lost.

- **Internal error on login**—Immediately after the installation, if you try to log in to Router MC, you may receive an internal error message. This may be because services for Router MC require a few minutes to start.

  Close your Router MC Browser window, then log into Router MC again from the CiscoWorks desktop. If this does not solve the problem, log out of Router MC and CiscoWorks. On the server running Router MC, restart the CW2000 Daemon Manager from the **Windows Control Panel > Administrative Tools > Services** window. After a few minutes, log into CiscoWorks and Router MC again. If the problem persists, reboot the Router MC server.

Browser Issues

Following are some of the problems that you may experience while working with Router MC on your browser:

- **Unsupported version of Java Runtime Environment (JRE)**—If you are running an unsupported version of Java Runtime Environment (JRE), you may get Java Runtime error messages while working with Router MC. To check the version of Java you are running, go to **Start > Settings > Control Panel > Java Plug-in** from the Windows taskbar. Select the **Advanced** tab. Under **Java Runtime Environment**, click on the drop-down menu and be sure the supported version of JRE is installed. For Router MC Version 1.3.1, JRE Version 1.4.1_2 is supported as per the "Product Overview" link of Router MC Version 1.3.x.

http://www.cisco.com/univercd/cc/td/doc/product/rtrmgmt/cw2000/cw2000_b/vpnman/vms_2_2/rmc13/insguide/ig13ovr.htm#wp1023534

Go thorough the Release notes of the Router MC Version, and search by Java to see if there is any known issue on a specific JRE version. For example, if you are running Router MC Version 1.3.1, there is a known problem with the JRE version 1.4.2_06 as per the Release note for Router MC Version 1.3.1, as shown in the following link:

http://www.cisco.com/univercd/cc/td/doc/product/rtrmgmt/cw2000/cw2000_b/vpnman/vms_2_2/rmc13/rmc131rn.htm#wp1087903

- **Popup blocker**—You must turn off the popup blocker on your browser to allow Router MC to come up. If the popup blocker is on, the Router MC Window will not come up at all.
- **Security warning popup**—When using Java plug-in 1.4.x, a security warning popup appears when you first navigate to a page that uses the Object Selector. If you try to navigate to another page or perform an action while the security warning popup is loading, the browser may freeze. To resolve this issue, close the browser and log out of CiscoWorks. Then log into CiscoWorks and Router MC again. The next time you get the security warning popup, wait a few seconds for it to load, and then click **yes** or **always** to accept the certificate. Refer to the following link for more details: http://www.cisco.com/univercd/cc/td/doc/product/rtrmgmt/cw2000/cw2000_b/vpnman/vms_2_2/rmc13/useguide/u13_gst.htm#wp1383679
- **User interface disappears while working**—While working with Router MC, the user interface might suddenly disappear, and you might get a message that you can no longer access Router MC.

  When working in Workflow Disabled mode, only one Router MC Session per user can be open on the same server at any given time. If you are working with Router MC and another user with the same username and password logs in, your access to Router MC is blocked.

  To resolve the issue, close your browser and log into Router MC again and you will observe the following:

  — If you log in with the same username and password, you will reopen your previous session with all your changes, and the other users' sessions will be terminated.

  — If you log in with a different username and password, a new session of Router MC will open and you will not see the changes you made in your previous session unless you saved and deployed them.

When working in Workflow Disabled mode, it is recommended to have only one session per username and password. If necessary, create new users from the Cisco Works desktop. Go to **Server Configuration > Setup > Security > Add Users** and add a user with the appropriate permissions. Click the **Help** button in the **Adding Users** page for more information.

- **Certification problem with Netscape Browser**—If you encounter a certification problem when trying to log in using the Netscape browser, the downloaded certificate might be corrupted. You can correct the problem by removing the certificate from the browser certificate storage as follows:
  - For Netscape on Windows 2000

    Go to **Edit > Preferences > Privacy and Security > Certificates > Manage Certificates > Authorities**, and delete the certificate that matches the Router MC server. Then, restart Netscape.
  - For Netscape on Solaris

    Go to **Edit > Preferences > Privacy and Security > Certificates > Manage Certificates > Web Sites**, and delete the problematic certificate. Then, restart Netscape.

  Now if you bring up the browser and try to log in to CiscoWorks Common Services, you will be prompted to download a new certificate.

Authentication Issues

Authentication can play a role in Router MC in one or both of these ways, which are detailed in the sections that follow:

- Authentication issues with the Router MC
- Authentication issues with the managed device using SSH

Authentication Issues with the Router MC

Once you log in to Router MC, you might see that many buttons in the User Interface are grayed out. The probable cause is that you do not have the correct user privileges to perform the tasks associated with the grayed-out buttons, or for the group or device currently selected in the object selector. For example, assume you have privileges to manage devices but some functions in the Devices tab are disabled. This might be because a group or device for which you have restricted privileges is selected in the object selector.

To resolve this issue, verify your user permissions in the CiscoWorks desktop or in ACS (depending on what method is being used for user authentication).

Authentication Issues with the Managed Device Using SSH

Router MC communicates with the devices using SSH. The Troubleshooting steps might differ depending on how you have configured devices to authenticate SSH connection. If AAA is implemented for SSH, refer to Chapter 9, "Troubleshooting AAA on IOS Routers" for troubleshooting details.

Activity and Job Management Issues

The sections that follow outline some of the issues that you may experience with the Activities.

- **Dangling locks**—If you experience a problem with Activity being locked by user X, even though user X is not logged in, or has closed the application, then there might be a dangling connection in the server.

  Dangling connections occur because browsing is connectionless, and therefore you cannot be sure if a user simply closes a browser window. Users must either explicitly close activities or use the Logout (top-right of every screen) to close the session completely with the server. If a user closes all windows without closing activities or logging out, the administrator can use **Close** from the Activities page, or an implied Logout will occur after the session time-out time has passed.

- **Inability to access an activity after closing and re-opening the Router MC**—If you close Router MC using the browser's close button and you do not log out of Router MC, your activity remains open. When you log into Router MC again, you will be unable to access it.

  Wait until the activity times out or ask your administrator to close the activity for you. In general, always close your open activity before closing Router MC.

- **Inability to create a new activity**—An activity of the same name might already exist in the system. Be sure you give the new activity a unique name.
- **Some activities do not display in the list of activities**—In rare cases, previously existing activities are no longer visible in the user interface. You need to log out of Router MC and CiscoWorks. On the server running Router MC, restart the CW2000 Daemon Manager from the **Windows Control Panel > Administrative Tools > Services**. After a few minutes, log into CiscoWorks and Router MC again.
- **Changes made within an activity were retained after the activity was deleted**—When you delete an activity, all the configurations that were made within the activity should be deleted. However, changes that are made to a device group name, device model, or device IOS version are not activity sensitive. This means that if the activity under which the changes were made is deleted, the changes will still be committed to Router MC's database.

  To resolve the issue, create a new activity and reverse the changes.

- **Object is locked by another activity**—Another user might be configuring that device or device group in a different activity, in which case it would be locked to other users. A red lock icon next to the selected object indicates that the object is locked by another activity.

  Point your mouse at the red lock icon next to the selected object. A tool tip will indicate which activity is locking the object.

Device Import Issues

The sections that follow outline problems with importing a configuration from a file or a live router into Router MC:

- **Import of configuration file fails**—If you try to import device configuration from a file, and if the file size is greater than 583 kilobytes, the import will fail. Hence, if you have a larger configuration, import it from a live device.
- **Import of live device(s) fails**—Importing the configuration from a live device might fail due to one or more of the following problems:
  - Connectivity problem

    To find out if you have connectivity problems by pinging the router from Router MC. If this is successful, try to establish an SSH connection with the router using a third party SSH client (puTTY client, for example, which can be downloaded free from the Internet). If this is not successful, the problem could be with the authentication failure. Or you might have mis-configured or not configured SSH on the router.
  - SSH Configuration problem

    Be sure that you have SSH configured on the device. If SSH is not configured, configure it as per the following link:

    http://www.cisco.com/en/US/products/sw/iosswrel/ps1829/products_feature_guide09186a0080088197.html#wp13995
  - SSH version mismatch

    If SSH version 2 is enabled on the device and Router MC supports only SSH version 1, you will run into SSH version mismatch issues. To resolve these issues, check which SSH version is enabled on the device by typing **show ip ssh** at the command line. If Version 2 is enabled, change to Version 1 using the command: **ip ssh version 1**.
  - Login information is incorrect

    If the login credential defined in the Router MC is incorrect, you will have login problem with the device, which will in turn cause the import process to fail. Revise the login information and correct any problem that you may have with either username or password. If Authentication,

Authorization and Accounting (AAA) is configured on the router, run the debug for AAA on the router (refer to Chapter 9, "Troubleshooting AAA on IOS Routers") to correct any authentication problems.

- **Group lock problem**—When selecting the target group, if you get the message **group x is locked by another activity**, then you need to select a different group, or approve/reject the locking activity.
- **Device already exists**—If you are trying to import a device that has the same hostname or IP address as an existing device, import will fail. Note that you cannot import the same device via different interface.

> **Note** Do not import a spoke via its inside (private) interface. This will cause a connection loss to the spoke while configuring it. It is recommended to import a spoke via its external interface, where VPN tunnel terminates.

- **Some imported devices do not show up in the device hierarchy**—If devices you imported into Router MC are no longer visible in the user interface, you must log out of Router MC and CiscoWorks. On the server running Router MC, restart the CW2000 Daemon Manager from the **Windows Control Panel > Administrative Tools > Services**. After a few minutes, log into CiscoWorks and Router MC again. Note that if you restart CW2000 Daemon Manager, the other management console also will be restarted.

Configuration Generation and Deployment Issues

The lists that follow outline issues that you may encounter while generating or deploying of device configuration from Router MC:

- **Configuration generation failure**—The configuration may fail if the current configuration of the device is edited manually after import and either has no exclamation marks in it or does not end with the command **end**.
- **Live deployment may fail**—If due to login failure or timeout problems, the devices are not accessible when you are trying to update the current configuration, live deployment will fail. This may happen if the IOS does not support the CLI that is generated by Router MC. For example, if the Router MC pushes a configuration with 3DES encryption, but the device only supports DES, the configuration deployment will fail.
- **The VPN policy changes were not deployed to the device**—Router MC might be set up to manage pre-shared keys only. In this case, only pre-shared key configurations are generated and deployed even though other VPN policy configuration changes have been made.

Go to **Configuration > IKE > Pre-shared Key**. A note at the bottom of the Pre-shared Key page indicates whether the application is set up to manage pre-shared keys only. You can change this setting from here, if necessary.

- **Required device does not appear in the device tree**—When creating a Job, if the required device does not appear in the Device tree to select, it can be for either of the following reasons:
  - The activity within which the device was imported has not been approved; therefore, the device is not yet included in the database. In this case, cancel the job creation, approve the activity, and create the job again. The device should now be available for selection.
  - The device is already included in another job that has not yet been deployed. In this case, cancel the job creation, deploy or reject the other job to free its devices, and create the job again. The device should now be available for selection.
- **Deployment fails because router mc is unable to log into the device**—The reasons for this failure are the same as those described in the section entitled "Import of Live Device(s) Fails" under "Device Import Issues." Therefore, follow the same troubleshooting steps as those described under "Import of Live Device(s) Fails."
- **Deployment hangs**—When deploying IPsec without generic routing encapsulation (GRE), if the job deployment remains in progress for a long time (approximately 10 minutes) and then fails, the causes could be as follows:
  - Connection to the spoke is lost because the same interface is defined as both the VPN interface (where tunnel terminates) and the inside interface. Redefine either the VPN interface or the inside interface on the device by selecting **Configuration > Settings**.
  - The interface IP address used to identify the device for import is the same as the inside interface. Delete the device from the inventory and then import it again using the IP address of its external interface as the device name. Select the **Devices** tab to access the options for device management and import.
- **Job action does not end and it remains in transient status**—A job action that does not end and remains in transient status (for example, generating, deploying, and so on) prevents the job from being deployed. The job remains active and the devices in the job cannot be included in other jobs.

  This might be due to the failure of one of the services associated with Router MC.

  On the server running Router MC, restart the CW2000 Daemon Manager from the **Windows Control Panel > Administrative Tools > Services**. This causes the job action to fail, thereby freeing its devices to be included in other jobs. After restarting the Daemon Manager, log into CiscoWorks and Router MC again.

- **Some of the hub configurations are not shown in the View Configurations Page under the Configuration tab**—Peer-oriented policies (such as pre-shared key and tunnel policies) are defined on spokes. Router MC mirrors these policies on the hub and generates the required configurations for the relevant hubs. This is done during job creation, not during policy definition. Therefore, the proposed configurations for the hub cannot be seen in the View Configurations page under the Configuration tab.

  Define the required policies, approve the activity, and then create a job that includes the spokes associated with the hub for which you want to see configurations. The View Configurations page under the Deployment tab will show the configurations that Router MC has generated for the hub, which are based on the policies defined on its assigned spokes.

- **Aggressive mode commands are not deployed to the device, although they appear in the View Configurations page**—If there is an existing pre-shared key defined on the device, the Aggressive mode commands might not be written to the device. Router MC generates the commands and deploys them, but they are not reflected in the device's show-run.

  Reboot the device. Then, re-import the device into Router MC, and deploy to the device.

Database Management Issues

The sections that follow cover some problems that you might encounter with Backup/Restore operation:

- Backing up and restoring database
- Troubleshooting Router MC backup/restore operations

Backing up and Restoring Database

You should back up the database regularly so that you have a safe copy of the CiscoWorks Common Services database, which includes Router MC. The next two sections discuss both the backing up and restoration of the Router MC Database.

Database Backup Procedure

To back up the database, work through the steps that follow:

Step 1 Select **VPN/Security Management Solution > Administration > Common Services > Backup Database** from the navigation tree. The Backup Database page displays.

Step 2 Specify the path to the directory in which you want to store the backup.

Step 3 To send an e-mail to a designated recipient each time the database is backed up, select the E-mail Notification check box and enter an e-mail address in the field.

Step 4 To back up the database immediately, check **Immediate**.

Step 5 To back up the database at a specific date and time, deselect **Immediate**, and define the **Start Date**, and **Start Time** time.

Step 6 To schedule a backup at regular intervals, enter a value in the **Repeat After** field, and select **Days**, **Hours**, or **Minutes** from the list. To limit the number of times the database backup occurs, enter a value in the Limit Occurrences field under Frequency.

Step 7 To back up the database according to the settings you have made, click **Finish**.

Step 8 Click **OK** to close the message.

Database Restore Procedure

You can restore the database from an existing backup. The backup contains data from all installed CiscoWorks Common Services client applications. Because user account information is not backed up, you cannot use Restore to recover deleted accounts. Additionally, license information is not restored; the license in effect when the restore is performed remains in effect after the restore.

Troubleshooting Router MC Backup/Restore Operations

Following are some of the possible problems you may encounter with the Router MC Backup/Restore operations:

- **Router MC is not included in the restore operation**—This problem occurs if you perform a second restore and you have not rebooted the server after the first restore. After restoring data, reboot the Router MC server.
- **The restore operation failed but all recent changes were lost**—When you start a restore, the current database is cleared. Therefore, even if the restore fails, your most recent changes within the Router MC GUI will not be retained. Hence, back up your database before starting the restore. If the first fails, try to run a second restore, or try to restart the CW2000 Daemon Manager, and then run another restore operation.
- **An internal error displays when launching Router MC after a backup and restore operation**—After performing a backup and restore operation, if you get an internal error when launching Router MC, reboot the Router MC server to resolve the issue.

- **Router MC crashes after a database password change**—This may occur if you change the database password using Cisco Works Common Services, and you do not restart the server that is running Router MC.

  To resolve this issue, after making a database password change, reboot the Router MC server.

Case Study

This section goes through the configuration steps required to integrate Router MC with Cisco Secure ACS Server for authentication and authorization.

Understanding User Permissions

To log into Router MC, your username and password must be authenticated. After authentication, Router MC establishes what your role is within the application. This role defines the set of Router MC Tasks or operations that you are authorized to perform. If you are not authorized for certain Router MC tasks or for certain devices, the related Router MC Menu items, TOC items, and buttons will be hidden or disabled.

Either the CiscoWorks server or Cisco Secure Access Control Server (ACS) manages authentication and authorization for Router MC. By default, authentication and authorization is managed by CiscoWorks. You can change to ACS using CiscoWorks Common Services. See the documentation for CiscoWorks Common Services for details on how to specify ACS for authentication and authorization.

The sections that follow cover user permissions for Router MC.

CiscoWorks Server Roles and Router MC Permissions

CiscoWorks has five role types that correspond to likely functions within your organization:

- **Help desk**—User has read-only access for viewing devices, device groups, and the entire scope of a VPN.
- **Approver**—User can review policy changes, and either approve or reject them. User can also approve or reject deployment jobs.
- **Network operator**—User can make policy changes (but not device inventory changes) and create and deploy jobs. Note that a network operator's activities and jobs must be approved by an Approver.
- **System administrator**—User can perform CiscoWorks server tasks and can make changes to the device hierarchy (such as move or delete devices). The system administrator can also change administrative settings.

- **Network administrator**—User can perform all CiscoWorks server and Router MC Tasks. A network administrator can also add users to the system with CiscoWorks or ACS, set user passwords and assign user roles and privileges. Table 20-1 shows how Router MC Permissions are mapped to these roles in ACS.

ACS Roles and Router MC Permissions

Cisco Secure Access Control Server (ACS) supports application-specific roles. Each role is made up of a set of permissions that determine the role's level of access to Router MC Tasks. Each user group is assigned a role and each user in the group can perform Router MC Actions based on the permissions in the role.

Furthermore, these roles can be assigned to ACS device groups, which allow permissions to be differentiated on different sets of devices. ACS device groups are completely independent of Router MC Device groups.

Router MC provides default roles and permissions in ACS. Some permissions must be configured on the managed devices and others on the Router MC Management Station, as specified in the list that follows. The available Router MC permissions in ACS are as follows:

- **View Config**—Users can view settings and policies but cannot make changes.
- **View Admin**—Users can view Router MC Application settings. This permission must be configured on the Router MC Management Station.
- **View CLI**—Users can view the current and previous configurations on managed devices and can preview the CLI commands to be generated for or deployed to the devices by Router MC.
- **Modify Config**—Users can define and modify policies.
- **Modify Device-List**—Users can make changes to the Router MC Device inventory. This permission must be configured on the Router MC Management Station.
- **Modify Admin**—Users can modify Router MC Application settings. This permission must be configured on the Router MC Management Station.
- **Approve Activity**—Users can approve activities. This permission must be configured on the Router MC Management Station.
- **Approve Job**—Users can approve jobs. This permission must be configured on the Router MC Management Station.
- **Deploy**—Users can deploy VPN and firewall policy configurations to devices or files.

These permissions are mapped to roles in ACS. These roles are the same as the CiscoWorks roles.

Table 20-1 *Router MC Permissions and Associated Roles*

Router MC Permission in ACS	Permitted Router MC Tasks	Help Desk	Approver	Network Operator	System Admin	Network Admin
View Config	**Activity and Job Workflow:** • View activities. • View jobs. • Create a job to generate configurations. • View job status. **VPN and Firewall Settings and Policies:** • View settings and policies in the Configuration tab.	Yes	Yes	Yes	Yes	Yes
View Admin	• View administrative settings for the Router MC application, in the Admin tab.	Yes	Yes	Yes	Yes	Yes
View CLI	• View CLI commands for policy definitions, per activity, in the Configuration tab. • View the CLI commands generated for the devices in a deployment job, in the Deployment tab.	No	Yes	Yes	Yes	Yes
Modify Config	**Device Management:** • Specify device credentials. • Import devices (also need Modify Device-List permission). • Reimport devices. • Edit devices. • Move and delete devices (also need Modify Device-List permission).	No	No	Yes	No	Yes

Table 20-1 *Router MC Permissions and Associated Roles (Continued)*

Router MC Permission in ACS	Permitted Router MC Tasks	Help Desk	Approver	Network Operator	System Admin	Network Admin
Modify Config *(cont.)*	• Create device groups (also need Modify Device-List permission). • Delete device groups (also need Modify Device-List permission). **Activity and Job Workflow:** • Create and submit activity. • Delete activity. **VPN and Firewall Settings and Policies:** • Define/modify general, hub, and spoke settings. • Create/modify IKE and VPN tunnel policies. • Create/modify access rules. • Create/modify transform sets. • Create/modify translation rules. • Create/modify network groups. • Upload policies to target device.	No	No	Yes	No	Yes
Modify Device-List	**Device Management:** • Import devices (also need Modify Config permission). • Move and delete devices (also need Modify Config permission).	No	No	No	Yes	Yes

continues

Table 20-1 *Router MC Permissions and Associated Roles (Continued)*

Router MC Permission in ACS	Permitted Router MC Tasks	Help Desk	Approver	Network Operator	System Admin	Network Admin
Modify Device-List *(cont.)*	• Create device groups (also need Modify Config permission). • Delete device groups (also need Modify Config permission). • Add unmanaged spoke. **Activity Workflow:** • Create activity. • Submit activity. • Delete activity.	No	No	No	Yes	Yes
Modify Admin	**Administration:** • Modify administrative settings for the Router MC application. **Activity Workflow:** • Close an activity opened by another user.	No	No	No	Yes	Yes
Approve Activity	• Approve a submitted activity, thereby committing its policy configurations to the database. • Reject a submitted activity.	No	Yes	No	No	Yes
Approve Job	Approve a job so that it can be deployed.	No	Yes	No	No	Yes
Deploy	• Deploy job to devices or files. • Redeploy job. • Rollback job.	No	No	Yes	No	Yes

Setting up Router MC to Work with ACS

You need Cisco Access Control Server (ACS) 3.2 to use ACS device groups and permissions with Router MC. To work with ACS device groups and user permissions, you must define your username in ACS and in CiscoWorks, and follow the setup procedure as follows:

Step 1 Define the Router MC server in ACS.

Step 2 Define the Login Module in CiscoWorks as TACACS+.

Step 3 Synchronize CiscoWorks Common Services with the ACS server configuration.

Step 4 Define usernames, device groups, and user groups in ACS.

The sections that follow provide details about the preceding steps.

Step 1: Define the Router MC Server in ACS

Work through the steps that follow to define Router MC in ACS:

Step 1 In ACS, select **Network Configuration**.

Step 2 Add the Router MC server to a device group, or add it as an individual device, depending on the ACS setup.

Step 3 Enter the ACS shared key in the **Key** field.

Step 4 Click on Submit + Restart button.

Step 2: Define the Login Module in CiscoWorks as TACACS+

Work through the steps that follow to define the login module in CiscoWorks as TACACS+:

Step 1 In the CiscoWorks desktop, select **Server Configuration > Setup > Security > Select Login Module**.

Step 2 If it is not already selected, select **TACACS+**.

Step 3 In the Login Module Options window, enter the ACS server name, change the default port if necessary, and enter the ACS shared key that you defined in ACS for the Router MC server.

Step 4 Click **Finish**.

Step 3: Synchronize CiscoWorks Common Services with the ACS Server Configuration

Work through the steps that follow for the synchronization:

Step 1 In the CiscoWorks desktop, select **VPN/Security Management Solution > Administration > Configuration > AAA Server**.

Step 2 In the AAA Server Information window, click **Synchronize**.

Step 3 Add login details. Enter the ACS shared key that you defined in ACS for the Router MC server.

Step 4 Click **Register**.

Step 5 Select **iosmdc**, and then click **Add** to add the Router MC Permission roles in ACS.

Step 6 Click **OK**.

Step 7 Click **Finish**.

Step 4: Define Usernames, Device Groups, And User Groups in ACS

Work through the steps that follow to configure user and group information:

Step 1 In ACS, select **User Setup** to define usernames. You must define the same username and password for both CiscoWorks authentication and ACS authentication.

Step 2 Select **Group Setup** to define permissions for device groups.

NOTE To remove the CiscoWorks permission roles from ACS, click **Unregister** in the AAA Server Information window. To restore CiscoWorks permission roles in ACS after you have deleted them with the Unregister button, click **Register** in the AAA Server Information window.

Best Practices

This section looks into some of the important issues with Router MC. Following is a list of good practices:

- Always apply upgrades to the latest version of Router MC and apply the new patches available on the Cisco website.
- Be sure to install VMS on a dedicated machine, as VMS has its own web server and database server, which may cause resource confliction issues if another application is installed. Be sure to fulfill minimum requirements for running VMS server. As performance is dependent on the configuration of hardware not VMS software, it is always recommended to have a fast, powerful server.

- If the Router MC is in a different network (VLAN) than the VPN device, be sure the network devices between the management server and the sensor allow SSH for Router MC in both directions.
- Do not install VMS (Router MC) on Primary/Backup Domain Controller, IIS Server, and Terminal Server.
- Be sure to back up the database regularly to prevent the loss of configuration on Router MC.

CHAPTER 21

Troubleshooting Cisco Security Agent Management Console (CSA MC) and CSA Agent

Although the networks intrusion detection sensor (NIDS) provides network-based intrusion detection and prevention, Cisco Security Agent (CSAgent) provides threat protection for servers and desktops with a combination of multiple security features such as host intrusion prevention, distributed firewall, malicious mobile code protection, operating system integrity assurance, and audit log consolidation. Unlike traditional personal firewalls, which are based on policy, and host IDS, which is based on signatures, CSA Agent is not limited to protecting the end host from existing attacks based on a knowledgebase. Instead, with sophisticated algorithms built into the software, CSA Agent protects the end hosts from many sophisticated new attacks such as Code Red, SQL Slammer, etc., without prior knowledge about the attack. CSA Agent identifies and prevents malicious behavior before it can occur, and removes potential known and unknown ("Day Zero") security risks that threaten enterprise networks and applications. This chapter examines the details of the CSA Agent and CSA MC.

Overview of CSA MC and Agent

CSA Agent is centrally administered, with a distributed, autonomous policy enforcement reference monitor for desktop, laptop, and server computers running operating systems such as Windows NT, Windows 2000, Windows XP, and Solaris 8. CSA MC is the management segment of the CSA Agent that configures Agents and also retrieves events from the Agents to display for the users. CSA Agent adapts defenses based upon the correlation of events from different hosts. It is very effective against existing and previously unseen attacks. An important point to note is that CSA Agents stopped Nimda and Code Red viruses unseen with out-of-the-box policies. Figure 21-1 shows the major components of Cisco Security Agent.

Management Model for CSAgent

As shown in Figure 21-1, many components go into the architecture of the CSAgent. Figure 21-2 shows a more detailed view of the CSA components.

Figure 21-1 *CSAgents Architecture Components*

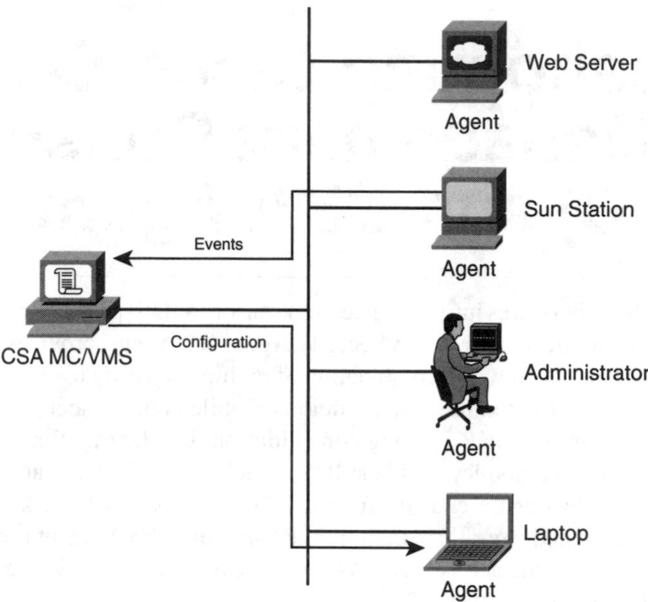

Figure 21-2 *CSA Components*

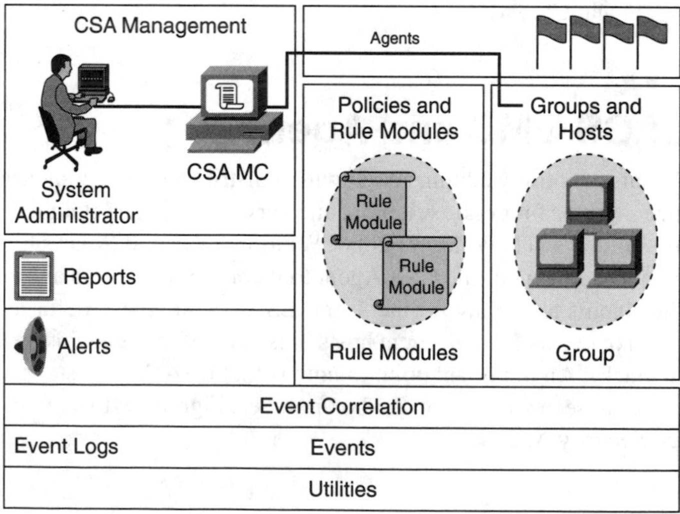

This section looks into the details of these different components:

- **Security administrators**—Security administrators are responsible for configuring the system via a browser connected to the Management Console. The jobs of the security administrators include reviewing security events, reports, and alerts, and modifying security policies. They can configure, deploy, and monitor roles.

- **Management Center**—Management Center is a server that runs the CSA MC (integrated with Common Services). As CSA MC is the data repository for the Agents, it is important to physically secure this server. Following are the some of the functions of the CSA MC server:
  - Holds the configuration and event databases (SQL server)
  - Distributes agent software to hosts
  - Deploys security policies to hosts
  - Receives events from agents and performs correlations
  - Sends alerts to administrators
- **Hosts**—Agents are deployed on hosts that have the following characteristics:
  - Are protected by Cisco Security Agents
  - Are members of one or more group
  - Obtain their security policies from the Management Center
  - Send security events to the Management Console
- **Groups**—Groups are used to organize logical collections of hosts. Examples of groups are IIS Servers, Executive Desktops, or SQL Servers.
- **Policies**—Policies are composed of logical collections of rules. They are attached to zero or more groups. Examples of policies are Common Security Module, or Microsoft Office Module.
- **Rules**—In Rules, security functions are specified and attached to policies. You may enable specific heuristics.

CSA MC Directory Structure

The default installation directory for CSA MC is **program files\CSCOpx\CSAMC**. This section discusses all the directories and files that make the CSA MC and Agent function correctly:

- **BIN**—This directory has a list of following files:
  - The Web Server (Apache) components
  - Physical location of the Agent Kits (deploy_kits)
  - Physical location of the agent upgrade executable (software_kits)
  - Physical location of import/export files
  - Physical location of the help guides
- **CFG**—This directory has the list of following files:
  - Configuration files for the CSA MC
  - SSL Certificates, license file (*.lic), kleidia, *.sql files, sysvars.cf

- **LOG**—This directory has a list of following files:
  - **csalog.txt**—Records Management Console transactions
  - **AgentInstallInfo.txt**—Record of the Management Console installation
- **DB**—This directory contains all the database-related files which are listed as follows:
  - **CSA MC.mdf**—CSA MC database
  - **CSA MC_log.ldf**—CSA MC database
  - **CSA MC_volatile_data.ndf**—Database for Stormtracker/tracker
- **Other directories**—Following is the list of other CSA MC directories:
  - **Cr**—Runtime version of Crystal Reports
  - **Doc**—User guide and install guide in PDF format And location of the **SNMPv2.MIB**
  - **Perl**—perl files
  - **Policies**—Profiler policies are stored here
  - **Samples**—Not used
  - **Tmp**—Not used

Communication Architecture

As mentioned before, network machines are assembled into specified groups and then security policies are attached to those groups in the CSA MC. All configuration is done through the Web-based user interface and then deployed to the agents. CSA MC Software is installed on a system, which maintains all policy and host groups. The administration user interface is accessed securely using Secure Sockets Layer (SSL) from any machine on the network that can connect to the server and run a Web browser. Use the Web-based interface to deploy your policies from CSA MC to the agents across your network.

Agents register with CSA MC. CSA MC checks its configuration database for a record of the system. When the system is found and authenticated, CSA MC deploys a configured policy for that particular system or grouping of systems. From then on, the Cisco Security Agent software continually monitors local system activity and polls to the CSA MC at configurable intervals for policy updates. It also sends triggered event alerts to the CSA MC's global event manager. The global event manager examines system event logs and, based on that examination, may trigger an alert notification to the administrator or cause the agent to take a particular action.

The Cisco Security Agent software installs locally on each system node and intercepts the operations of that system. A network application interceptor sits at the application level and intercepts all application operations. Other Cisco Security Agent mechanisms intercept network traffic, file actions, and system registry actions. At the same time, the rule/event correlation engine controls all agent mechanisms watching for any events that trigger an agent policy.

All communications between the Management Center for Cisco Security Agents server system and systems accessing the browser-based user interface are protected using SSL. Administrator authentication is also provided via the required entry of a username and password to authenticate and initiate each management session. Additionally, communications between the management server and the agents are passed over SSL.

How Cisco Security Agents Protect Against Attacks

Unlike anti-virus and network firewall software, Cisco Security Agent does not prevent you from accessing applications that you may require. Rather, it assumes that you are going to put the systems at risk by making use of a wide range of Internet resources. Based on this assumption, Cisco Security Agents install and work at the kernel level, controlling network actions, local file systems, and other system components, maintaining an inventory of actions that may be performed on the system itself. This way, malicious system actions are immediately detected and disabled, while other actions are allowed. Both actions take place transparently, without any interruption to the user. If an encrypted piece of malicious code finds its way onto a system via e-mail, for example, as it attempts to unexpectedly execute or alter Cisco Security Agent-protected system resources, it is immediately neutralized and a notification is sent to the network administrator.

The Cisco Security Agents protect systems using policies, which you as network administrators configure and deploy. These policies can allow or deny specific system actions. The Cisco Security Agents must check whether an action is allowed or denied before any system resources are accessed and acted upon. Specifically, rule policies allow administrators to control access to system resources based on the following parameters:

- What resource is being accessed?
- What operation is being invoked?
- Which application is invoking the action?

The resources in question here may be either system resources or network resources, such as mail servers. When any system actions that are controlled by specific rules are attempted and allowed or denied accordingly, a system event is logged and sent to the administrator in the form of a configurable notification type such as e-mail, pager or custom script.

Diagnostic Commands and Tools

Both CSA MC and CSAgent have extensive logging capability to troubleshoot issues on the CSA MC, on the CSAgent, or both. This section presents all the log files available on both the console and agent to troubleshoot any issue with the CSA.

CSA MC Log

As CSA MC is installed on top of Common Services, it's important to be sure that Common Services function properly for a seamless operation of CSA MC. In addition to what we have discussed in Chapter 17, "Troubleshooting CiscoWorks Common

Services," there are some additional log files that are necessary to troubleshoot issues with CSA MC.

Windows System Information

To get all the Windows system information in a single file, you can run the **winmsd** command on the server where you have installed CSA MC. This is particularly important if you want to analyze the problem offline or want to escalate the issue to the Cisco Support Team. To collect the information, work through the steps that follow:

Step 1 Go to **Start > Run**.

Step 2 Type **winmsd** in the text box.

Step 3 In the new window, select **System Information > and** click on **Action**. Select **Save As Text File** and name this file.

Server Selftest Information

Server selftest provides quick statistics on the health of the server. This test shows information on serious failures. To perform the **selftest**, go to **Server Configuration > Diagnostics > Self Test > Create** when you first log into CiscoWorks. The report appears in the same window. You can right-click it to either save it or view the report.

CSA MC Log Directory

The location of the log directory of CSA MC version 4.5 is **ProgramFiles\CSCOpx\CSAMC45\log**. This directory contains two very important files:

- **csalog.txt**—This file in CSA MC is used to record information about the health and state of the CSA MC. This is a very important file for analyzing troubleshooting issues with CSA MC itself, or connectivity issues with the CSA Agent.
- **CSAMC45-Install.log**—This is the installation log file. If there is an issue with the installation, this log file contains information about it.

CSA Agent Log

CSA Agent log provides details on issues pertaining only to CSAgent and its interactions with the CSA MC. Note that CSA MC has an agent installed to protect the CSA MC server. So, the log information discussion in this section can be found in CSA MC Server also.

CSA Agent Log Directory

This section examines the files that make up the log directory on the CSA Agent. There are three important log files in the log directory (program files\Cisco (or Cisco Systems)\CSAgent\log):

- **CSAgent-Install.log**—This file contains the CSAgent installation information. If you have an installation or upgrade failure, you need to analyze this log file.

- **Driver_install.log**—As the name implies, this file contains information about the driver that is installed with the CSA Agent. If there is an installation failure, you need to analyze this file.
- **csalog.txt**—This is the file where all events that are destined for the event log in the CSA MC are stored. Connectivity checks are logged along with other transactions between the CSAgent and the CSA MC. In addition, the health of the agent is recorded here (i.e., compile problems, etc). In a nutshell, it is the repository for events and troubleshooting information of the agent.

Turning on Debug Mode

To turn on debug mode for the agent to log more detailed messages in the CSAlog.txt, set **debug=1** and be sure that the value is not commented out with a **semi-colon** (;) in front of it in the **Program Files\Cisco (Systems)\CSAgent\cfg\sysvars.cf** file. This increases the level of detailed information about the agent's state and transactions. Stop the agent service with the **net stop csagent** command first, then make the changes and restart the service with the **net start csagent** command at the DOS command prompt. Once you collect the data for troubleshooting, turn the debug-level logging off by commenting the **debug=1** line out by placing a **semicolon** (;) in front of it.

Details Log—csainfo.log file

The **csainfo.bat** utility is used to collect a log you can use to troubleshoot general CSA issues, such as agent/MC communication issues, and system configuration issues. The file is in **Program Files\Cisco (Systems)\CSAgent\bin.** When executed, the **csainfo.bat** file generates a flat text file called **csainfo.log** (~2-3 MB). This file is created in the same directory as the **csainfo.bat** file. If you run into a blue screen problem, which is discussed next, you may need to provide a **csainfo.log** file in addition to the memory dump to Cisco Support Team. Following is some of the critical information that can be extracted from the **csainfo.log** file:

- Contents of **agent.state** file
- System OS information, including version and service packs
- Network cards present on the system
- Base system device configuration data
- Arp information
- System routes
- System interface information
- netstat command output
- nbstat command output
- Management center ping output

- BT management center ping output
- nslookup of management center output

Logs for Blue Screen

When your CSA Agent system crashes and the blue screen appears, there is not much troubleshooting you can do. However, with blue screen, the system produces a memory dump with a file name **memory.dmp**, which contains valuable information about what process caused the blue screen. This **memory.dmp** file is analyzed by the Cisco developers to find out the root cause of the problem. However, it's extremely important to know how to get the full memory dump file of the system. Work through the following steps to complete the task:

Step 1 Right click on **My Computer** > Select **Properties** > Click on **Advanced** tab > Click on **Startup and Recovery** button.

Step 2 On the Startup and Recovery window, change the drop-down under Write Debugging Information in the System Failure section to **Complete Memory Dump**.

Step 3 In the **Dump File: text box**, change the location and the name of the memory dump file as you desire. By default, it is located in %SystemRoot% and the file is called MEMORY.DMP. We recommend changing the name of the file to something more descriptive, for example yourcompanyname.dmp.

Step 4 Reboot to make this change take effect.

As mentioned before, memory dump is analyzed by the Cisco developer to find the causes of the dump. To extract information related to the CSAgent from the memory dump file, use the **extract.exe** utility, which is under **Program Files\Cisco (Systems)\CSAgent\bin.** Following is the command syntax for extracting the memory dump:

```
extract memory.dmp > filename.log
```

Here the **memory.dmp** is the name of the memory dump file and **filename.log** is the name of the file to which you want to extract memory dump information. Note that the **extract.exe** can be copied into any directory, and you can run it from there. It does not have to be run in the **Program Files\Cisco (Systems)\csagent\bin** directory.

Rtrformat Utility

This utility comes under the **Program Files\Cisco Systems\CSAgent\bin** directory. The syntax for running this utility is **rtrformat –s state**. Use this utility to get the exact state of your rules written to a state file (you can name the output file anything, but this example uses **state**). If there are issues with rules compilation or other rules-related issues, the Cisco Development team may ask for this information. The file is encrypted so that you cannot read it.

This same utility can be used to troubleshoot connectivity and transaction issues with CSA MC. Follow these steps to read the output of ***.rtr** files:

Step 1 Copy a specific ***.rtr** file from **Program Files\Cisco (Systems)\CSAgent\log** (for example, **request-27-22-17.rtr)** to the **Program Files\Cisco\CSAgent\bin** directory. You need to stop the **CSAgent** service with the command **net stop CSAgent** before you can copy the file over to the **\bin** directory. You also need to stop this **CSAgent** service to perform Step 2.

Step 2 Open CMD shell and type in the command: **rtrformat request-27-21-02.rtr > output.txt**. Here **request-27-22-17.rtr** is the ***.rtr** file you want to unscramble. You want the output to go to the **output.txt** file.

Step 3 Then start the **CSAgent** service with the command **net start CSAgent** at the DOS prompt.

Additional Logs Controlled by the **Sysvars.cf** file

This is the CSA MC and CSAgent configuration file. In Agent, this file is in **Program Files\Cisco (Systems)\CSAgent\cfg**, and in CSA MC it is in **Program Files\CSCOpx\CSAMC\cfg**. This file is not available in the CSA MC 4.5 version. Before you modify this file (**sysvars.cf**), be sure to back it up. You must stop **CSAgent** service with the command **net stop CSAgent** before you make any changes to the file. Otherwise, the change will not take effect. Following are some tasks you can perform after making some changes to this file:

- **Turning on Debug mode**—As mentioned before, to turn on debug mode for the agent to log more detailed messages in the **CSAlog.txt**, set **debug=1** and uncomment this value by deleting the semicolon (;).
- **Writing events to local file on CSA Agent**—Parameter **log_events_to_esl** dictates the writing of various events in readable format into **Program Files\Cisco (Systems)\CSAgent\Log\securitylog.txt** file. If the value is 0, then no events are written into this file. If it is 1, then all events destined to the MC are written to this file. Make sure to uncomment this parameter by removing the semicolon (;) in front of this value or creating another line without comment. Note, however, that for a standalone agent (for example, Agent runs on Call Manager) all security events are written to this file independently of this variable value. By default, the **securitylog.txt** does not exist and **log_events_to_esl=1** is commented with a semicolon (; **log_events_to_esl=1).** Once the **log_events_to_esl=1** is uncommented, the file will automatically be created in the **Program Files\Cisco (Systems)\CSAgent\log** directory.
- **Event limiting**—Under normal circumstance, you will probably not want to modify any values for Event Limiting parameters. This controls the number of events that you can log in the database before limiting occurs. **limit.info** controls the number of messages at which information level messages will no longer be logged. By default, the **limit.info** is commented, so it is turned off as follows:

```
;limit.info=500000
```

The other parameters are self-explanatory. Uncomment them as appropriate. These are the default values for MSDE. The limits for SQL Server are (by default) 20 times as big. Example 21-1 shows the limiting number by default.

Example 21-1 *The Default Limiting Number for the Event Logging to the Database*

```
;limit.notice=600000
;limit.warning=700000
;limit.error=800000
;limit.alert=900000
;limit.critical=1000000
```

- **Date and Time Formatting**—To format the date and time strings for the Management User Interface (UI), you can tweak the parameters shown in Example 21-2. By default, parameters are set to the U.S. version. Most likely, you will not have to change this setting, except for British English versions.

Example 21-2 *The Parameters in **Sysvars.cf** that Controls the Date and Time of the UI*

```
; US:   m/d/yy h:mm:ss tt
;date_format=M'/'d'/'yy
;time_format=h':'mm':'ss tt
; Unambiguous:   dd-mmm-yy HH:mm:ss
;date_format=d'-'MMM'-'yy
;time_format=HH':'mm':'ss
```

- **Monitor Disk Usage**—The services in CSA MC and Agent monitor disk usage on the partition containing the CSA MC or Agent installation. These services log a warning event when the amount of free disk space falls below the alert threshold. The alert threshold integer value is in megabytes. The default value for servers is 100 MB, and for agents it is 2 MB as shown in Example 21-3. Uncomment these tokens and change the values if desired.

Example 21-3 *Server and Agent Threshold Values for the CSA MC or CSA Agent*

```
;server_alert_threshold=100
;agent_alert_threshold=2
```

- **Limiting RTR File**—By default, the creation of RTR files is set to 10. The service in CSA MC or Agent checks the number of RTR files in the log directory once an hour with the following command:

  ```
  file_limit=10
  ```

Categorization of Problem Areas

The problem areas of CSA MC can be categorized as follows:

- Installation and upgrade issues
- Licensing issues

- CSA MC launching issues
- CSAgent communication, registration and polling issues with CSA MC
- Application issues with CSAgent
- Report Generation Issues
- Profiler issues
- Database maintenance issues

Installation and Upgrade Issues

CSA MC is installed as a component on top of Common Services. Hence, Common Services must be installed before you proceed with the CSA MC installation. Once the CSA MC is installed or upgraded, you can generate and download the CSAgents to install or upgrade on desktops or servers. This section explores both CSA MC/CSAgents installation and upgrade issues.

- New installation issues with CSA MC
- New installation issues with CSAgent
- Upgrade issues with CSA MC
- Upgrade issues with CSAgent

New Installation Issues with CSA MC

Starting with CSA MC Version 4.5, there are three installation configuration options:

- **Installing CSA MC and the database on the same machine**—Select the **Local Database** radio button during the CSA MC installation.
- **Installing CSA MC on one server and the database on a remote server**—Select the **Remote Database** radio button during the CSA MC installation.
- **Installing two CSA MCs on two separate machines and installing the database on its own remote server**—In this case, both CSA MCs use the same remote database. Select the **Remote Database** radio button during the CSA MC installation.

The following section elaborates on these options.

Local Database Installation

For a local database configuration, if you plan to deploy no more than 500 agents, you have the option of installing CSA MC and the included Microsoft SQL Server Desktop Engine (provided with the product) on the same system. In this case, the CSA MC installation also installs its own version of Microsoft SQL Server Desktop Engine on the system.

For a local database configuration, you also have the option of installing Microsoft SQL Server 2000 instead of using the Microsoft SQL Server Desktop Engine that is provided. Microsoft SQL Server Desktop Engine has a 2 GB limit. In this case, you can have CSA MC and Microsoft SQL Server 2000 on the same system if you are planning to deploy no more than 5000 agents.

NOTE If you are using SQL Server 2000, it must be licensed separately and it must be installed on the system before you begin the CSA MC installation. Also note that if your plan is to use SQL Server 2000, we recommend that you choose one of the other installation configuration options rather than the local database configuration.

Remote Database Installation with One CSA MC

Use this configuration option if you plan to deploy more than 5000 agents and are using a separately licensed, managed, and maintained SQL Server 2000 database. SQL Server 2000 must be installed and configured on the remote system before you begin the CSA MC installation.

If you are installing CSA MC and the database to multiple machines, be sure the clocks of each machine are in sync. If all clocks are not in sync, unexpected behavior may occur.

Remote Database Installation with two CSA MCs

This is the recommended configuration if you are deploying more than 5000 agents and are using a separately licensed, managed, and maintained SQL Server 2000 database. SQL Server 2000 must be installed and configured on the remote system before you begin the MC installations.

Using this configuration, you can deploy up to 100,000 agents. Having two CSA MCs lets you use one MC for host registration and polling, and another MC for editing configurations. This way, if your network is under attack and a flurry of events is causing one MC's CPU to spike, for example, your CSA MC configuration remains unaffected and you can still push configuration changes to your hosts.

When installing two CSA MCs, the first MC you install automatically becomes the polling and logging MC. The second MC acts as the configuration MC.

During the installation process, the CSA MCs know the order in which the MCs were installed. They direct polling, logging, and management tasks to the appropriate MC. The polling MC can also be used for administration if required.

Now that you are familiar with all the installation options, you are ready to learn the minimum prerequisites of CSA MC installation.

CSA MC Prerequisites

You must fulfill the minimum requirements before you proceed with the CSA MC installation. For the minimum requirements of different versions of CSA, refer to the following link: http://www.cisco.com/en/US/products/sw/secursw/ps5057/prod_release_notes_list.html

A summary version of the minimum requirements for CSA MC 4.5 is listed as follows:

- **Hardware Requirements**—Intel Pentium 1 Ghz or higher up to 2 processors, 1 GB of RAM, minimum 2 GB of virtual memory, and 9 GB free disk space at all times.
- **Software Requirements**—Windows 2000 Server or Advanced Server with Service Pack 3 and all the critical updates (Terminal Services turned OFF).
- **Networking Requirements**—Static IP address or fixed DHCP IP Address. Single NIC interface (Multi-homed systems are not supported for the CSA MC.)
- VMS version 2.3 with CiscoWorks Common Services must be installed before installing CSA MC 4.5.
- **Other Application**—No other applications such as web server, FTP server, and so on.
- **Web Browsers**—Internet Explorer 6.x or higher with cookies and JavaScript enabled, and Netscape 6.2 or higher.
- **Database**—No other instances of SQL databases installed on the CSA MC server. Multiple instances of a SQL Server database on the server on which CSA MC is being installed pose a security risk to CSA MC and to the server itself. Therefore, a server on which the CSA MC is installed (or about to be installed) that has databases other than CSA MC is not a supported CSA MC configuration.

  Check the registry to be sure there are no references to SQL Server. SQL Server 2000 full edition is available for installation (SQL Server Desktop engine supports up to 2 GB of data) if it is a large-scale deployment.
- **Login Account**—You must log in to the server on which you are installing the CSA MC as a local administrator.
- **File System**—You must be running New Technology File System (NTFS) file system.

Manually Remove CSA MC

If the CSA MC, for some reason, does not install properly, and you cannot uninstall it via Windows **Add/Remove Programs**, you will have to manually remove the CSA MC components and reinstall them.

NOTE These instructions are for failed installations of the CSA MC and are not meant to recover the CSA MC database, configurations, or other items within the CSA MC. The goal is to install the CSA MC after a failed initial attempt at installing CSA MC.

The following steps remove CSA MC manually. Note that some of these files, services, and registry keys may not exist, depending on how much of the installation completed:

Step 1 Uninstall CSAgent from the CSA MC server, and reboot the server.

Step 2 Open **Start > Settings > Control Panel > Administrative Tools > Services** applet and stop the following services (if applicable):

- Microsoft SQL Server (MS SQL Server)
- Cisco Security Agent Management Console
- CiscoWorks Daemon Manager
- Seagate Page Server
- Seagate Web Component Server

Step 3 Delete the **C: \Program Files\CSCOpx\CSAMC (45)** directory.

Step 4 Delete **C:\Program Files\InstallShield Installation Information\{F30535B5-5C0B-11D4-97C0-0050DA10E5AE}** file.

Step 5 Go to **Start > Run > regedit** and delete the following Registry keys:

- HKEY_LOCAL_MACHINE\SOFTWARE\Cisco\CSAMC(45)
- HKEY_LOCAL_MACHINE\SOFTWARE\Cisco\CSAgent
- HKEY_LOCAL_MACHINE\SOFTWARE\Seagate Software
- HKEY_LOCAL_MACHINE\SYSTEM\CurrentControlSet\Services\CSAMC(45)
- HKEY_LOCAL_MACHINE\SYSTEM\CurrentControlSet\Services\WebCompServer(45)
- HKEY_LOCAL_MACHINE\SYSTEM\CurrentControlSet\Services\pageserver(45)
- HKEY_LOCAL_MACHINE\SOFTWARE\Microsoft\Windows\CurrentVersion - uninstall the value {F30535B5-5C0B-11D4-97C0-0050DA10E5AE}

Step 6 Start the **MSSQLServer** service.

Step 7 Start the **CiscoWorks** Daemon Manager Service.

Step 8 Re-run the **setup.exe** for CSA MC.

CSA MC Installation Troubleshooting

To troubleshoot installation issues with CSA MC, you need to analyze the log file **CSAMC(45)-Install.log**, which is in the **C:\Program Files\CSCOpx\CSAMC(45)\log** directory. This section examines some common issues that you might experience during or after installation:

- Be sure to go through the earlier section entitled "CSA MC Prerequisites" to fulfill the requirements.
- If you try to install the MC when you are not logged on as local administrator (domain admin is not sufficient), CSA MC will not work.
- CSA MC Server's name should be resolvable by DNS. If not, the CSA Agent will not be able to register with CSA MC because the CSAgent needs to resolve the CSA MC via DNS or WINS (not IP).
- If you attempted to install CSA MC on a server with other databases running on it, the installation will abort because it detects other databases.
- The CSAgent (that comes with CSA MC) network shim may not be compatible with another application, especially Sniffer or personal firewall software.
- You must use Internet Explorer 6.x. Previous versions are not supported by VMS 2.3.
- If for some reason the CSA MC does not install properly, and you cannot uninstall it via Windows **Add/Remove Programs,** follow the procedure explained in the section entitled, "Manually Remove CSA MC."

New Installation Issues with CSAgent

Depending on the types of CSAgents that you are installing, the procurement process varies. The section that follows discusses how to get the CSAgent for different types of CSAgents and the minimum requirement for the CSAgents installation.

Procuring CSAgent Software

There are two types of CSAgent kits available:

- Headless CSAgent (for Call Manager)
- CSAgent managed my CSA MC

For the Headless CSAgent, you can refer to the following link:

http://www.cisco.com/cgi-bin/tablebuild.pl/cmva-3des

If you are using CSA MC to manage the CSAgent, you can generate the agent kit as follows:

Step 1 On CSA MC go to **Systems > Agent Kits.**

Step 2 Check to see if one of the available agents is what you want to use. If not, click the **Add** button to create a new one.

Step 3 Name the new CSAgent and the description.

Step 4 Under the Configuration section, select **groups with which this kit should be associated**.

Step 5 Choose additional options (for example **Force reboot after install**) under **Configuration** section.

Step 6 Then click **Make kit.**

Step 7 Click the **Generate rules** link.

Step 8 Finally click the **Generate** button.

Step 9 Once the CSAgent creation process is completed, go back to **Systems > Agent Kits** and be sure that you see your newly created agent kit.

Step 10 Click on the **CSAgent Kit** you have just created. In the next window, a link will be provided to download the CSAgent kit.

Step 11 You can copy the link and go to CSAgent machine, and point your browser to download the newly created Agent kit. This also can be transferred via CD once you download on the CSA MC server itself. To see all the available agents created, point the browser to: https://CSAMC45_Server_Name/csamc45/kits

Once you have downloaded the CSAgent, be sure to fulfill the minimum requirements for the CSAgent installation.

CSAgent Prerequisites

The minimum requirements differ for different versions of CSAgent. For the minimum requirements of a specific version of CSAgent, refer to the following link:

http://www.cisco.com/en/US/products/sw/secursw/ps5057/prod_release_notes_list.html

For CSAgent version 4.5, the following is a summary list of the minimum requirements:

- **Hardware Requirements**—
  - Pentium 200 minimum for Windows Operating Systems.
  - Sun Solaris 8 64-Bit Ultrasparc running at 400 MHZ or higher.
  - Linux Intel Pentium 500 MHz or higher.
  - Minimum of 128 MB of RAM (256 MB for Solaris 8).
  - 15 MB hard disk.
- **Software Requirements**—
  - Windows Server 2003 (Standard, Enterprise, Web, or Small Business Editions).
  - Windows XP (Professional or Home Edition) Service Pack 0, 1, or 2.
  - Windows 2000 (Professional, Server or Advanced Server) with Service Pack 0, 1, 2, 3, or 4.
  - Windows NT (Workstation, Server or Enterprise Server) with Service Pack 6a.

- Solaris 8, 64 bit 12/02 Edition or higher (This corresponds to kernel Generic_108528-18 or higher).
- Red Hat Enterprise Linux 3.0 WS, ES, or AS.

- **Web Browsers**—Internet Explorer 6.x or higher with cookies and JavaScript enabled, or Netscape 6.2 or higher.
- **Networking Requirements**—
  - CSA MC and CSAgents need to be able to communicate among each other on TCP/443, TCP/5401 and TCP/5402.
  - CSA MC Name must be resolvable via DNS (Domain Name Service) or WINS (Windows Internet Naming System).

Manual Removal of the CSAgent on Windows

You may want to remove the CSAgent manually from the machine because of the one of the following reasons:

- You are unable to uninstall the CSAgent with Add/Remove programs.
- CSAgent uninstall failed wholly or partially, leaving CSAgent files on the machine.
- The machine that has the CSAgent installed continuously shows blue screens and you cannot boot the machine.

Following are some of the steps that are necessary to remove the agent manually:

Step 1 Boot up CSAgent machine into Safe Mode (usually F8 or F2 during initial boot-up).This will disable all CSAgent drivers. VGA mode is not sufficient.

Step 2 If you have Windows 2000 or Windows XP, go to **Start > Programs > Administrative Tools > Computer Management**. Right-click on **Device manager > View > Show all hidden devices.**

Step 3 On Windows 2000 Professional or XP, highlight any entries that are under **CiscoCSA** and uninstall them (right-click on each device and select **Uninstall**). On the Windows 2000 server, you may need to go under **Non-Plug and Play Drivers** and remove all the drivers that start with **csa.**

Step 4 If asked whether you want to reboot, choose **No** until the other devices are uninstalled and the rest of this procedure is completed.

Step 5 Delete the following entries:

- **Program files\Cisco (Systems)** directory.
- **Program Files\InstallShield Installation Information\{DE49974667B9-11D4-97CE-0050DA10E5AE}**.
- **WINNT\system32\drivers\csacenter*.sys, csafile*.sys, csanet*.sys, csareg*.sys, csatdi*.sys.**
- **WINNT\system32\csafilter.dll** (Or WINDOWS\system32\).

— **WINNT\system32\csarule.dll** (Or WINDOWS\system32\).

— **WINNT\system32\csauser.dll**(Or WINDOWS\system32\).

— All references to Cisco CSAgent in the **Start > Programs > Cisco Security Agents** menu.

— All reference of CSAgent from **Start > Programs > Startup**.

Step 6 Select **Start > Run**, type **regedit**, and click **OK** to launch the Registry Editor. Then delete the following registry values:

— **HKEY_LOCAL_MACHINE > SYSTEM > ControlSet001 > Control > Session Manager > KnownDLLs > csauser.dll**

— **HKEY_LOCAL_MACHINE > SYSTEM > ControlSet002 > Control > Session Manager > KnownDLLs > csauser.dll**

— **HKEY_LOCAL_MACHINE > SYSTEM > CurrentControlSet > Services > csacenter**

— **HKEY_LOCAL_MACHINE > SYSTEM > CurrentControlSet > Services > csafile**

— **HKEY_LOCAL_MACHINE > SYSTEM > CurrentControlSet > Services > csanet**

— **HKEY_LOCAL_MACHINE > SYSTEM > CurrentControlSet > Services > csareg**

— **HKEY_LOCAL_MACHINE > SYSTEM > CurrentControlSet > Services > csatdi**

— **HKEY_LOCAL_MACHINE > SYSTEM > CurrentControlSet > Services > csagent**

— **HKEY_LOCAL_MACHINE > SYSTEM > CurrentControlSet > Services > csahook**

— **HKEY_LOCAL_MACHINE > SYSTEM > CurrentControlSet > Services >csafilter**

— **HKEY_Local_Machine > Software > Cisco > CSAgent**

— **HKEY_Local_Machine > Software > Microsoft > windows > currentversion > uninstall > {DE499746-67B9-11D4-97CE-0050DA10E5AE}**

Step 7 Finally, reboot the CSAgent machine.

For more details on this procedure, refer to the following link: http://www.cisco.com/en/US/customer/products/sw/secursw/ps5057/products_tech_note09186a00801e598b.shtml- #uninstall

CSAgent Installation Troubleshooting

If you encounter a problem with the CSAgent installation, always analyze the **C:\Program Files\Cisco Systems\CSAgent\log\CSAgent-Install.log** file (refer to "Diagnostic Commands and Tools" section of this chapter). Work through the steps that follow to troubleshoot any installation-related issues with CSAgent:

Step 1 Fulfill the minimum requirements outlined in the following link (Release notes): http://www.cisco.com/en/US/products/sw/secursw/ps5057/prod_release_notes_list.html

Step 2 Be sure the CSAgent machine does not have a VPN or firewall active when you uninstall/install the CSAgent. Having a VPN or firewall active will make it impossible to install at least the netshim.

Step 3 Be sure there is no network sniffer software installed.

Step 4 Be sure there is no load balancing software installed before installing the CSAgent. Some load balancing software (for example, Compaq load balancing) will work with the CSAgent only if the CSAgent is installed first, and the load balancing software installed second.

Step 5 Be sure that the user has LOCAL administrator privileges. Domain administrator privilege is not sufficient for installing the CSAgent.

Step 6 Get the log files found in **Program Files\Cisco (Systems)\CSAgent\log** and look for any errors.

Step 7 Get log files referencing CSAgent in the **TEMP** directory of the Agent machine (if applicable). When an install/uninstall fails, log files that are usually transferred from the **TEMP** directory to the **Program Files\CSAgent\log** directory are not transferred. Be careful to look at the correct temp directory. This is not usually the **WINNT\temp** directory. It is usually the **temp** directory under the user **PROFILE**.

Step 8 To find out which temp directory the user was using when the CSAgent was installed/uninstalled, do the following:

(a) Log into the machine as the same user as the one that installed the agent (remember, this user needs to have local admin rights to begin with).

(b) Open a CMD window and type: **set temp** (this will tell you the full path to the temp directory that is being used).

(c) Go to that directory and find any ***.log** files that reference CSA.

Step 9 Based on the error messages in the **temp** directory log pertaining to CSAgent, look for any bugs.

Upgrade Issues with CSA MC

In this section, while discussing the CSA MC upgrade, you will use CSA MC V4.5, because the upgrade procedure will be the same for future releases of CSA MC. If you install CSA MC 4.5 on top of CSA MC 4.0.x, the installation does not automatically upgrade or overwrite the V4.0.x installation.

NOTE Upgrading from versions of the product earlier than version 4.0.x to version 4.5 is not supported.

There are two options when upgrading from CSA MC 4.0.x to CSA MC 4.5.

- Install V4.5 on the same machine as V4.0.x. (If you select this option, note that you cannot apply any upgrades that may be released to the V4.0.x CSA MC.)
- Install V4.5 on a different machine with the knowledge that V4.0.x agents will eventually be migrated to the new V4.5 machine.

When you install CSA MC V4.5, a new *Security Agents V4.5* menu item appears in your CiscoWorks UI. If you install CSA MC V4.5 on the same machine as V4.0.x, your original Security Agents menu item remains in place and you continue to manage your existing V4.0.x configurations from there as well.

The CSA MC V4.5 installation also creates a new directory structure. (If you install CSA MC V4.5 on the same machine as V4.0.x, your original CSAMC directory structure remains in place, co-existing with the new V4.5 structure.) Note that subsequent releases of CSA MC will continue to include the new version number in the directory structure (Refer to Table 21-1 for Menu Item with the Directory Path).

Table 21-1 *Mapping Between the Menu and Directory Path*

	Menu Item	Directory Path
CSA MC V4.5	Security Agents V4.5	CSCOpx\CSAMC45
CSA MC V4.0	Security Agents	CSCOpx\CSAMC

CSA MC Upgrade Process on the Same System

If you're installing CSA MC V4.5 on the same server that is running CSA MC V4.0.x, an XML file containing V4.0.x configuration items and host information is automatically generated by the installation and ready for importing once the install is complete.

To upgrade and migrate V4.0.x agents to V4.5, schedule V4.5 software updates for V4.0.x agents. Schedule this upgrade from the CSA MC V4.0.x system. (Performing the V4.5 installation places a V4.5 software update on the V4.0.x machine.)

Once V4.0.x agents receive the scheduled software update, they will point to and register with the new CSA MC V4.5. The update contains the appropriate new certificates to allow this to occur.

When upgrading 4.0.x agents to software version 4.5, the upgrade program disables the system network interfaces to ensure that the upgrade process is secure. The agent service is also stopped to allow the update to occur. Once the update is complete, the agent service is restarted and the network interfaces are enabled.

This information applies only to 4.0.x to 4.5 software upgrades and not to the earlier versions.

CSA MC V4.5 ships with policies that contain new V4.5 functionality. This new functionality does not match all V4.0.x configurations. Beginning with V4.5, CSA MC Configuration item names are labeled with the release version number to distinguish them from older (or newer) configuration items or items created by administrators.

When you import your V4.0.x configuration, new V4.5 items are not overwritten. You likely will have items from both versions in your CSA MC V4.5. If the import process finds that two items have the exact same contents and the only difference is the V4.5 appended name field, the old V4.0.x item is not imported and the newer V4.5 item is used in its place.

When you import your V4.0.x configurations to the V4.5 system, old V4.0.x agent kits are also imported. When V4.0.x hosts perform software updates and register with the V4.5 system, they are placed in groups according to the group information that was part of their original installation kit.

If you want a host to be placed in a different group when it registers with V4.5, you have the ability to click on the original agent kit now listed along with the new V4.5 agent kits, and change the group association. You must generate rules after you change a group kit association.

NOTE Note that when hosts register with CSA MC V4.5, they appear in their assigned group(s), and they also appear in the mandatory V4.5 groups that match their OS type.

CSA MC Upgrade Process on a Separate System

If you are installing CSA MC V4.5 on a server that is different from the server running CSA MC version 4.0.x, after installing V4.5, you must copy and manually run an executable file on the V4.0.x machine to create the XML file needed for importing V4.0.x configuration and host information to V4.5.

If you are installing CSA MC V4.5 on a server that is different from the server running V4.0.x, after installing V4.5, you must copy and manually run an executable file on the V4.0.x machine to create the XML file needed for importing V4.0.x configuration and host information to V4.5.

Once you have installed CSA MC V4.5 and rebooted the system, navigate to the **CSCOpx\CSAMC45\migration** directory. Copy the file named **prepare_migration.exe** to your V4.0.x system. (You can copy it to anyplace on the system.)

On your CSA MC V4.0.x, disable agent security and run the **prepare_migration.exe** file that you copied from the V4.5 system. (You must disable security to run the executable file and create the import XML data.) This launches a command prompt that displays the progress of the migration.

When the prepare_migration.exe file is finished, on the V4.0.x system, navigate to the **CSCOpx\CSAMC\bin** directory and locate a newly created file named **migration_data_export.xml**.

From the V4.5 system, import the **migration_data_export.xml** file to the CSA MC V4.5 machine. Do this either by copying the XML file to the V4.5 system first and then importing it, or by browsing to it from the V4.5 system if you have network shares set up.

You must generate rules once the import is complete. If you do not generate rules at this point, you cannot upgrade and migrate agent hosts.

Naming Convention—After Upgrade

Configuration items shipped with CSA MC and provided by Cisco contain a version column with a version number. Administrator-created items have no version number.

When you import configuration items provided by Cisco, if you find that there is already an existing exact match for an item, the new configuration data is not copied over. Instead, the existing item is reused and the name reflects the new versioning.

If the import process finds that there is an existing item with the same name and different configuration components (variables, etc.), the newly imported item is changed by adding a new version number. The new item is always the item that is re-versioned. Existing items are not renamed or reversioned if there is a collision.

Also note that CSA MC automatically appends the name of the export file to any non-Cisco item collision it finds during administrator imports. The imported item is given a different name and both new and old items can coexist in the database.

CSAgent Update Issues

To update your CSAgent with CSA MC, work though the following steps:

Step 1 Navigate to **Maintenance > Software Updates > Scheduled Software Updates** on CSA MC.

Step 2 Click on **New** to display a window.

Step 3 Give the update a name, a target OS, and choose the appropriate software update and group to be applied.

Step 4 Choose the update time frame within which to run the update. This means that when a CSAgent polls in within this time frame and is entitled to an update, it will prompt the user to do so. Setting this time frame to **from 00:00 to 23:59** means that any time an agent polls in and is entitled, the update will be run on the CSAgent machine. There is no way to automatically update your hosts immediately.

If for some reason, CSAgent code is not getting updated, work through the following steps to resolve the issue:

Step 1 Find a host that you want to update and ensure that it can poll in to the CSA MC server. Double-click the **CSAgent** icon and then click **Poll**. On the CSA MC, find this host under **Systems > Hosts** and look at the field **Time since last poll**. Verify that the agent was able to communicate with the CSA MC.

Step 2 Ensure that the update you are trying to run on your agents is valid for the version of the agent code installed on your computers.

Step 3 Identify a host that you want to update and find this host under **Systems > Hosts**. Make a note of this agent version under **Product Information**.

Step 4 Then, go to **Maintenance > Software Updates > Available Software Updates** and click the **update** that you wish to run. Ensure that the agent version you recorded from your host is listed under **Target Systems**.

Step 5 The update will occur only if the agent polls in during the time specified in the update job. Check your agent poll interval by finding your agent under **Systems > Hosts**. Under **Group Membership and Policy Inheritance**, click the group that the host is a member of. Under the group configuration screen you will see the agent poll time. Try reducing this time to ensure that the agent polls within the time frame allowed for the update.

Licensing Issues

There are four possible licenses you may need to deal with for Cisco Security Agent Management Center (CSA MC). You must have common services license (see Chapter 17, "Troubleshooting CiscoWorks Common Services" under "Licensing Issues" for more details) installed before you proceed with any of the following licenses:

- CSA MC (required)
- Profiler (optional)
- Server Agents (specific number)
- Desktop Agents (specific number)

Each of these licenses can be in one ***.lic** file or separate ***.lic** files. The general recommendation is that you copy and paste each of these product license sections into their own separate files (using **Notepad**) and name them appropriately for better management. For example, a license file named 12345678.lic is not helpful. But if you change the name to server_20.lic, it tells you that this license is for 20 servers.

CAUTION Do not attempt to *manually* change or tamper with the license information in any way, or the license will become invalid.

To give a meaningful name to the license file, you need to be able to read and understand the content of the file (using Notepad). Example 21-4 shows the contents of the CSA MC file, which is required for CSA MC to function correctly. In the example, look for VENDOR_STRING = Count = x, where x is the number of valid seats for the license.

Example 21-4 *A Sample CSA MC License*

```
! The following line shows it's an MC license that expires on 10-apr-2006
INCREMENT managementcenter cisco 1 10-apr-2006 uncounted \
!Number of seat shows 1 in the following line
    VENDOR_STRING=Count=1 HOSTID=ANY ISSUER="Cisco Systems, Inc." \
    NOTICE="<LicFileID>XXXXXXXXXXXXXXXXX</LicFileID><LicLineID>1</LicLineID> \
    <PAK></PAK>" TS_OK SIGN=XXXXXXXXXXXX
```

Example 21-5 shows a license file for 10 Server Agents

Example 21-5 *A Sample CSA Agent License for 10 Servers*

```
! The following line shows that it's a server agent license
INCREMENT serveragent cisco 1 10-apr-2006 uncounted \
! The next line shows this license will allow 10 server agents registration to MC
    VENDOR_STRING=Count=10 HOSTID=ANY ISSUER="Cisco Systems, Inc." \
    NOTICE="<LicFileID>XXXXXXXXXXXXXXXXX</LicFileID><LicLineID>2</LicLineID> \
    <PAK></PAK>" TS_OK SIGN=XXXXXXXXXXXX
```

Example 21-6 shows a license file for 25 Desktop Agents.

Example 21-6 *A Sample CSAgent License for 25 Desktops*

```
! Following line indicates that it's a desktop license file
INCREMENT desktopagent cisco 1 10-apr-2006 uncounted \
! The next line shows 25 desktops are supported by this license
    VENDOR_STRING=Count=25 HOSTID=ANY ISSUER="Cisco Systems, Inc." \
    NOTICE="<LicFileID>XXXXXXXXXXXXXXXXX</LicFileID><LicLineID>3</LicLineID> \
    <PAK></PAK>" TS_OK SIGN=XXXXXXXXXXXX
```

Example 21-7 shows a license file for Profiler.

Example 21-7 *A Sample License for Profiler*

```
! The following line indicates that it's a profiler license
INCREMENT profiler cisco 1 10-apr-2006 uncounted \
! The next line indicates its for a single profiler
    VENDOR_STRING=Count=1 HOSTID=ANY ISSUER="Cisco Systems, Inc." \
    NOTICE="<LicFileID>XXXXXXXXXXXXXXXXX</LicFileID><LicLineID>4</LicLineID> \
    <PAK></PAK>" TS_OK SIGN=XXXXXXXXXXXX
```

With the knowledge gained from the preceding discussion, you can give meaningful names to the license files. All these files can be in the same file. In that case, be sure that the content of the CSA MC License information is on top of the other licenses. In the next section, we discuss how to procure the license.

How to Procure the License

To procure your CSA MC and Agent license key, you must use the Product Authorization Key (PAK) label affixed to the claim certificate for CSA MC, which is in the separate licensing envelope.

CSA MC does not run on the 90-day evaluation license that other Common Services applications use. You must register CSA MC and provide the PAK to obtain a valid CSA MC license.

To obtain a production license, register your software at one of the following Web sites. If you are a registered user of Cisco.com, use this Web site: http://www.cisco.com/cgi-bin/Software/FormManager/formgenerator.pl

If you are not a registered user of Cisco.com, use this Web site: https://tools.cisco.com/SWIFT/Licensing/RegistrationServlet

After registration, the software license will be sent to the e-mail address that you provided during the registration process. Retain this document with your VMS bundle product software records.

If you have any difficulties with Web registration, you can send an e-mail to licensing@cisco.com with your PAK number for advice.

How to Import the License

Once you receive the license, you can import the license in two ways to CSA MC:

- Using a GUI
- An alternate method

Using a GUI

Work through the procedure that follows to install the license using a GUI:

Step 1 Save the licenses to a safe location on a local or network drive.

Step 2 Make a copy of the license and then rename the copies to something more relevant as discussed previously.

Step 3 Log in to the **CSA MC**.

Step 4 Go to the menu item **Maintenance > License Information**.

Step 5 Click the **Browse** button, and locate the .lic file on your local or network drive where license files are saved.

Step 6 Click the **Upload** button on the lower-left corner of the screen.

Step 7 Repeat this for each license file (*.lic) that you have to install.

Step 8 Finally, click the **Generate Rules** link to generate the rules for the agents.

Alternate Method

If for some reason the GUI method discussed earlier does not work, or you want to copy the files to the appropriate directory manually, work through the procedure that follows to add the license to CSA MC:

Step 1 From a command shell execute the following commands to stop the CSA Agent and MC services:

```
Net stop csagent
net stop crmdmgtd
```

Step 2 Remove all **.lic files** from the **Program Files\CSCOpx\CSAMC(45)\cfg directory**.

Step 3 Copy the **license file(s)** into **Program Files\CSCOpx\CSAMC(45)\cfg directory**.

Step 4 Restart the CSA MC and agent services as follows:

Step 5 Net start crmdmgtd

Step 6 Net start csagent

Step 7 Log into CSA MC GUI and check to make sure the license is valid. If it is valid, you will be able to generate rules.

Step 8 Finally, click the **Generate Rules** link to generate the rules for the agents.

Determining the Number of Desktop/Server Licenses That Are in Use

For additional licensing information, you may want to investigate whether you are approaching the limit of purchased CSA Agent licenses. From the GUI, you can identify which agents are registered and find the number of agents based on group. But discovering how many server or desktop agents are registered is extremely difficult if you have hundreds of agents registering to your CSA MC. You can follow the procedures shown in Example 21-8 to obtain this information.

Example 21-8 *Determining How Many Servers and Agents Are Registered with CSA MC at Any Point in Time*

```
! Open up MS DOS command prompt and enter the following command
osql -E <enter>
! For CSA MC 4.5, use csamc45 instead of csamc
use csamc <enter>
go <enter>
! The following line will query the number of desktops are registered.
SELECT COUNT(*) FROM host WHERE  okena_system_type & 8 <> 0 <enter>
go
! The following line will provide the number of servers that are registered
SELECT COUNT(*) FROM host WHERE  okena_system_type & 16 <> 0 <enter>
go
```

Troubleshooting Licensing Issues

You may observe two behaviors on CSA MC when you have licensing issues:

- You see "license invalid" messages when attempting to upload the licenses.
- Or, you get "Internal Server Error" when logging into the CSA MC.

Work through the steps that follow to make sure you do not run into these licensing issues:

Step 1 If you cannot import the CSA Agent license, verify that the CSA MC license is installed and valid by going to the **Maintenance > License Information** screen and expanding the CSA MC license key by pressing the "+" next to the status. If you have a single file, be sure that the CSA MC License information is on the top of the file.

Step 2 For the CSA MC to load, it is necessary to have a CiscoWorks Common services license (refer to Chapter 17, "Troubleshooting CiscoWorks Common Services" under the "Licensing Issues" section).

Step 3 When you copy the license information from e-mail to the text file, be sure not to add characters accidentally (for example, the carriage returns on the license file).

Step 4 Be sure that the all files have the **.lic** extension.

Step 5 Do not add the same license twice. This can cause an internal server error.

Step 6 Try to upload the license files into a different CSA MC to verify their validity.

Step 7 Be sure that terminal services are disabled by going to the computer's services manager.

After going through the preceding steps, if you still have problems with license import or opening CSA MC, perform the steps that follow to work around the problem:

Step 1 Stop both CSAgent and CSA MC services with the following commands in the DOS prompt:

```
net stop csagent
net stop crmdmgtd
```

Step 2 Go to **Program Files\CSCOpx\CSAMC(45)\cfg** and delete all the license files that are showing up as invalid.

Step 3 Start both of the services with the following commands:

```
net stop crmdmgtd
net stop csagent
```

Step 4 Bring up **CSA MC** and upload the license key again.

Step 5 Finally, **Generate** the rules.

CSA MC Launching Issues

When you try to bring up CSA MC from CiscoWorks, you may encounter two problems:

- CSA MC does not launch.
- CSA MC launches slowly.

The sections that follow discuss the typical causes of these two types of problems and how to resolve them.

CSA MC Not Launching

In this section, we examine some possible causes of CSA MC launching issues:

- DNS issue
- CSA agent may block access
- No free disk space
- Web server is running on the CSA MC server
- Other management consoles are installed
- Licensing problem
- Browser and Java issues
- Certificate problem

Follow the discussions below for troubleshooting CSA MC launching issues.

DNS Issue

The requirement for correct DNS on both the CSA MC and CSAgent machines cannot be overemphasized. Without the proper name resolution of the CSA MC, agent will not be able to communicate with the CSA MC (this is discussed in detail in the "**CSAgent and Communication, Registration, and Polling Issues with CSA MC**" section). Also, there will be problems launching CSA MC unless you have the name resolution for the CSA MC server on both your machine from where you are accessing CSA MC, and the CSA MC server itself. If you do not have the name resolution configured by a DNS server for both CSA MC and your machine, then you can modify the **hosts** file, which is in the **C:\WINNT\system32\drivers\etc** directory.

CSA Agent May Block Access

Even though this is not very common, your CSAgent that is installed with CSA MC may block accessing the CSA MC from a remote machine. This can happen when the CSAgent that is installed on CSA MC is moved to a different group from **VMS CiscoWorks Systems** group, or rules are modified on the **VMS CiscoWorks Systems** group. This group on CSA MC Server should allow full access to the VMS server, yet also protect it. To verify if the CSAgent is blocking CSA MC access, you can stop CSAgent service with command **net stop csagent** in the DOS prompt of CSA MC Server. If the CSAgent stops the CSA MC access, then create an agent kit from the most up-to-date **VMS CiscoWorks Systems** group on the CSA MC, uninstall the existing CSAgent, and deploy this new kit on the VMS Server itself, then place it in test mode to watch for what is being blocked. Then you can tune your policies to be less restrictive on the VMS server, if needed. Once you have the policies tuned, you could take the agent out of test mode.

No Free Disk Space

If you have too many events on the database and run short of disk space, you may not be able to access the CSA MC. If everything is working, and suddenly you cannot access the CSA MC, the most likely cause is the free disk space issue. Work through the steps below to reclaim disk space:

Step 1 Check free disk space

Step 2 To free some up, try making the **pagefile** smaller (C:\pagefile.sys)

Step 3 Refer to the **Database Issues** section of this chapter to purge and compact the database.

Step 4 Then immediately do a backup.

Web Server is Running on CSA MC Server

If you have the web server running on the same server as CSA MC, you may be able to log in to all CiscoWorks, but when you try to bring up the CSA MC, it may not come up. Uninstall any web server or FTP server from the CSA MC server.

Other Management Consoles Are Installed

Any other Management Console (for example IDS MC, PIX MC, etc.,) must not be installed on the same server as CSA MC. Installing only Security Monitor along with CSA MC is supported. So, if you have other Management Consoles installed, be sure to remove them, and reboot the server.

Licensing Problems

If you have modified the license file after import or have the duplicate file for the same license (for example, CSA MC license), then your CSA MC may not come up. Refer to the "Troubleshooting Licensing Issues" section under "Licensing Issues" for additional details on how to get around this problem.

Browser and Java Issues

If you do not have the supported version of browser or Java, then you may get a certificate popup and then the browser says "done" in the bottom left hand corner and the page is blank. If so, be sure to fulfill the following requirements:

- You must be running one of the supported browsers. Refer to the Release Notes or the ReadMe file for the supported browser list. You can find out quickly if your browser is supported on the first page after you login to CiscoWorks.
- You must be running Java Runtime Environment (JRE) version at least 1.4.0.x. Warnings will pop up that the version is not recent enough.
- Be sure that you have only one instance of Java installed on your machine. If you have multiple versions of Java installed, uninstall both of them and install the latest version.
- You must turn off Proxy server on your browser. For example, in Internet Explorer, you can turn it off by going to **Internet Explorer > Internet Options > Connections > LAN Settings > uncheck "Use a proxy server for your LAN"**.

Certificate Problem

If everything else fails as described earlier, you may be running into an issue with certificate corruption. This is a costly procedure, because with the new certificate, your agents will not be able to register with CSA MC unless you copy the new CSA MC certificate over to all the agents. However, if your MC is unmanageable due to the certificate, as a last resort you may try the following procedure with the full consent of consequences:

Step 1 Stop both Agent and Console services as follows:

```
net stop csagent
net stop crmdmgtd
```

Step 2 Delete the files listed in Table 21-2.

Table 21-2 *Files That Need To Be Deleted*

Location	Files needed to be deleted
CSCOpx\CSAMC(45)\cfg	sslca.crt,sslhost.crt
CSCOpx\lib\web\conf	root.crt,server.key, server.crt
CSCOpx\mdc\apache\conf\ssl	chain.cer,root.cer, server.key,server.cert
CSCOpx\CSAMC(45)\cfg	Files with .lic extension

Step 3 Open a DOS window and type **cd CSCOpx\CSAMC(45)\bin** to change the directory.

Step 4 Type **perl.exe installcert.pl -forceinstall**

Step 5 Start both the CSA MC and agent services with the following commands:

```
net start crmdmgtd
net start csagent
```

CSA MC Is Launching, but Slowly

In the preceding section, we have explored how to resolve the issue with launching the CSA MC. This section will look at some of the probable causes of slow response when CSA MC launches up.

Database Size Is High

If your database size is high due to a huge number of events and configuration, the response time for launching CSA MC will be slow. Size is directly proportional to the CSA MC Launching time and query times for events. Refer to the **Database Issues** section for details on how to check the database size and how to purge, and then compact, the database to reclaim space.

Unsupported Installation

You must ensure that you fulfill all the minimum requirements for both hardware and software for installing the CSA MC. If you install the CSA MC on a server that doesn't fulfill the minimum requirements, you may be able to use the CSA MC, but the performance may degrade badly. In a lab environment for testing purposes this may not be a serious concern, but in production, this should be avoided by all means.

To find out if you are running any unsupported hardware or software configuration, you can analyze the **CSAMC(45)-Install.log** from CSA MC, which is in the **Program Files\CSCOpx\CSAMC(45)\log.** A snippet from **CSAMC(45)-install.log** shows below that CSA MC is running on an unsupported service pack:

```
Operating system is a server version.
Service Pack 4 of Windows 2000 is not installed on this machine. This product is
only supported on server versions of Windows 2000 with Service Pack 4 or higher. Do
you want to continue?
```

Look for Possible Bugs

After making sure that you are not running into any database or the incompatibility issues, look for a possible bug in the code. It is best is to look under the Release Notes of the newer version of CSA MC than that of the version you are running, and see if there is any known bug integrated on the newer version. If so, upgrade the code. One such example is that an SNMP problem may be reported on CSA MC Version 4.0(3.717), which will slow down the launching CSA MC. This issue is being integrated in the latest version of CSA MC 4.5. In the **Program Files\CSCOpx\CSAMC(45)\log\csalog**, you will see the following messages for the SNMP issue:

```
[2005-04-21 11:24:10.287] [PID=4501] [Csamcmanager]: Error sending trap to manager
at address [2005-04-21 11:24:10.287] [PID=4501] [Csamcmanager]: Error opening snmp
session
```

Look for these types of error messages for other processes and look for any possible bugs to find out if your version of CSA MC Code is running any software bug.

CSAgent Communication, Registration, and Polling Issues with CSA MC

CSAgents query the MC over SSL on port TCP/5401. If this fails, it will fall back to TCP/443. Profiler uses TCP/5402. If the CSAgent cannot communicate, register, or poll the CSA MC, walk through the following steps to resolve this issue:

Step 1 Read and learn and fulfill the requirements in the Release Notes from the following link: http://www.cisco.com/en/US/products/sw/secursw/ps5057/prod_release_notes_list.html

Step 2 First be sure network cables are plugged into the machines and into the proper network card. Also make sure the link lights are coming up fine.

Step 3 Use the **iccping** utility to perform the connectivity test between the CSAgent and the CSA MC. Work through the steps that follow to perform the **iccping** utility:

(a) Go into **Program Files\CSAgent\bin** directory from a CMD prompt from the machine that is having connectivity issues.

(b) Type **iccping.**

(c) This will give you syntax for running the utility and which ports it uses, as Example 21-9 shows.

Example 21-9 *iccping Options Available to Perform the Connectivity Test*

```
C:\Program Files\Cisco\CSAgent\bin>iccping
C:\Program Files\Cisco Systems\CSAgent\bin>iccping
Usage: iccping <component> [num_pings] [SSL] : to ping a component
       Where,
              <component> -> "leventmgr" | "webadmin"
! This will ping 4 times on TCP/80 to the CSA MC. You can define a different # than 4
Example: iccping webadmin 4    => will ping 4 times the remote component 'webadmin'.
```

Example 21-9 *iccping Options Available to Perform the Connectivity Test (Continued)*

```
! This will ping 4 times on TCP/5401. You can define a different # than 4
Example: iccping webadmin  4 SSL => will ping 4 times the remote component 'webadmin'
using SSL.
NOTE: set ICCPING_TIMEOUT=timeout   :in seconds; timeout for the ping transaction.
Default=15
NOTE: set ICCPING_INTERVAL=timeout  :in seconds; time interval between 2 consecutive
pings. Default=0
NOTE: set ICCPING_SIZE=size         :ping packet size in bytes
C:\Program Files\Cisco Systems\CSAgent\bin>
```

If the **iccping** fails, then you know that you have connectivity problem on **TCP/443** and **TCP/5401,** which are required for the connectivity between the CSA MC and CSAgent. If you are running Profiler on CSA MC, then you also need to open **TCP/5402**.

Step 4 Be sure the NAME of the CSA MC is resolvable via DNS or WINS. The Agent communicates with the MC via DNS or WINS names, not IP addresses (CSAgent machines can have different IP addresses if the environment is DHCP). If the client for some reason cannot or will not have a proper DNS or WINS setting, enter the IP address and FQDN of the MC manually into the CSAgent **C:\WINNT\system32\drivers\etc\hosts** file. This way the Agent will be able to resolve the CSA MC name.

Step 5 Check to ensure that the license file(s) are valid. If the license is not valid or is expired, newly installed CSAgents will not register with the CSA MC and pre-existing CSAgents will be placed into test mode. You might also run out of licenses. You might want to verify what types of licenses you are using, and how many desktop and server machines you have covered by your license by going to **Maintenance > License Information** (see **Licensing Issues** section of this chapter for more details). Check the **C:\Program Files\Cisco (Systems)\CSAgent\log\ csalog.txt** file from one of the agents that is failing for errors such as the following, which indicates a license problem.

```
[2005-05-02 10:21:25.131] [PID=672] [Csamanager]: Registration failed
without message Error ?code=2035'
```

Step 6 Be sure the CSAgent does not have the same IP address as another CSAgent machine. If it does, the CSA MC will not allow the same IP address to register for an hour.

Step 7 Be sure the CSAgents and CSA MC have the same time. If not, re-adjust the time, otherwise, you will experience certificate failure, which will result in the registration and Polling failure.

Step 8 If the CSA MC crashes or the CSA MC Database is renamed with a different DNS name, refer to the **Disaster Recovery Plan (DRP) for CSA MC** subsection under the **Database Issues** section of this chapter.

Application Issues with CSAgent

You might run into issues with launching different applications on the desktop or the server where you have installed CSAgent. Another problem, which is common, is to have issues with updating the anti-virus software update. In every incident, the CSAgent generates the events which can be viewed from the **Events > Event Log**. There are several ways to resolve these interoperability issues with CSAgent. The first part of this section introduces different procedures that we will use in the concluding sub-section of the section, which is "Troubleshooting Steps."

How to Create Exceptions

If you cannot perform certain tasks on the machine where CSAgent is installed, you might want to create exceptions so that the events are permitted. Work through the steps below to create an exception:

Step 1 Go to **Events > Event Log**.

Step 2 Find the Event that is being triggered by a specific CSAgent host.

Step 3 Click on **Wizard** of the event.

Step 4 You can either choose to **allow**, **stop logging**, or **behavior analysis** of the event.

Step 5 Follow the rest of the intuitive steps to complete the task.

Step 6 Once finished creating the exception, click the **Generate rules** link.

Step 7 Then go to the CSAgent and click the **Poll** button.

How to Disable Individual CSAgent Shims

To determine if a specific shim conflicts with other installed software, you might want to disable shims. Be sure to save your registry and back it up appropriately before making any changes. Work through the steps that follow to disable the individual CSAgent Shim:

Step 1 Open the Command prompt and type the following command to stop the CSAgent:

```
net stop csagent
```

Step 2 Run the command **regedit** from command prompt, which will bring up **Registry Editor.**

Step 3 Go to **HKEY_LOCAL_MACHINE > SYSTEM > CurrentControlSet > Services > csafilter,csahook, csanet, csareg, csatdi.** Table 21-3 shows the meaning of each value.

Step 4 Highlight the registry key for the shim you want to disable and look for DWORD **Enable**. If it doesn't exist, follow the next step to create one.

Table 21-3 *Values for Network Shim*

Registry Key Control Values	Description
csafile	File Interceptor—this is the fileshim.
csafilter	Http Interceptor—this is the http rate-limiting shim.
csahook	System Call Interceptor—for items within the Trojan Detection rule.
csanet	Network Traffic Interceptor—this is the lower level (level 3) network shim. Provides network hardening features such as syn flood and malformed IP packet protection—similar to a firewall.
csareg	Registry Interceptor—this is the registry shim.
csatdi	Network Application Interceptor— this is the upper level (level 5) network shim. Controls which applications can communicate with the network.

Step 5 Right-click and create new DWORD value, name it as **Enable,** and set its value to **0** as shown in Figure 21-2. If you need to re-enable it, just change this value from 0 to 1.

Step 6 Finally, reboot the CSAgent machine.

Step 7 Follow steps 1–6 for every shim, one by one, to find which one is causing the interoperability issue with other applications. Be sure that before disabling a new shim (see Figure 21-3), you re-enable the existing disabled one.

Figure 21-3 *Disabling Shims*

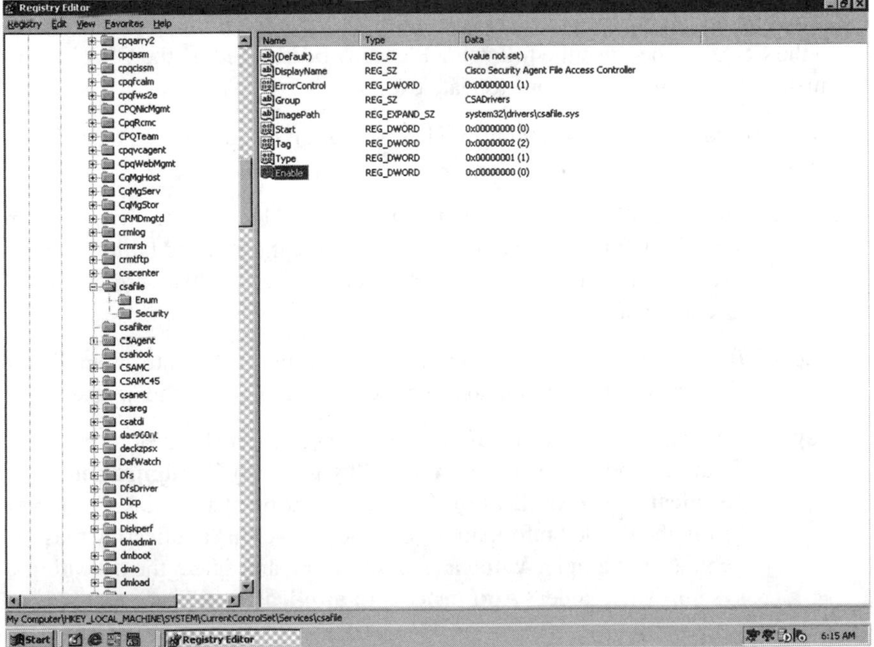

Disabling csauser.dll

Be sure to save your registry and back it up properly before making any changes. Work through the steps that follow to disable casuser.dll:

Step 1 Open a command shell (**Start** > **Run**) and type **cmd**.

Step 2 Type **net stop csagent** to stop the CSA agent.

Step 3 Type **regedit** to bring up **Registry Editor**.

Step 4 Go to **HKEY_LOCAL_MACHINE** > **Software** > **Microsoft** > **Windows NT** > **CurrentVersion**.

Step 5 Click on **Windows** to view the content of the keyword.

Step 6 Change the value of **AppInit_DLLs** from **csauser.dll** to **csauser.dll.org**.

Step 7 Reboot the machine.

Step 8 Once the test is completed, change the value of **AppInit_DLLs** in step 6 from "**csauser.dll.org**" to "**csauser.dll**".

Step 9 Reboot the machine.

Creating Buffer Overflow Exclusions

For any anti-virus software update, there are at least two executable files involved: one executable (.exe) file downloads the actual update file, which is the other executable (.exe) file. There may be more than two .exe files involved with the upgrade process. For example, automatic update for Trend Micro Client/Server Suite 6.5 (OfficeScan 6.5) may be blocked by the CSAgent because the following files may be blocked by the CSA MC: upgrade.exe, tmlisten.exe, spntsvc.exe, and stupdate.exe.

So, if your anti-virus software fails updating, work through the steps that follow to resolve the issue:

Step 1 On CSA MC, find the event that is triggered by the anti-virus software. Then look for the **Wizard** button. If you see the **Wizard** button, create an exception as outlined in the earlier section entitled "How to create Exceptions."

Step 2 If the Wizard button is absent from the event, then create an application class that has the executables defined as explained in the next step.

Step 3 For example, to create buffer overflow exceptions for acad.exe, you can create an application called Autocad by going to **Configuration** > **Applications** > **Application Classes [Windows]** and clicking on **New**. Fill in the needed information (in Bold). Give this application class a name (for example, **AutoCad**), description, and select the operating system. Then under "**Add process to application Class**", type

****\acad.exe**. Then click on **Save**. You have just created an application class called the **AutoCad** application, which needs to be applied either on a host or a group.

Step 4 Find a host that is having the problem (you can apply this in groups as well) and view its configuration by selecting it under **Systems > Hosts**.

Step 5 Scroll down in the host window to see all the rules that are applied to this host and find the rules that are of type **Trojan Detection Rule**. Click these rules to edit them.

Step 6 Under **Accessing system functions from code executing in data or stack space**, where it reads **Select any application classes to be excluded**, scroll down to find the **Autocad** application, and click on it to select it. If the .exe file has problems with updating the software, instead of just invoking it, define the application class created under the **Downloading and invoking executables** option, instead of defining the class under **executing in data or stack space**.

Step 7 Generate the rules and poll the new rules from the server on a CSAgent.

If the preceding procedure does not work, there might be another application executable that you would have to exclude from your Trojan detection file. Follow the directions that follow to learn how to use a file monitor rule to watch the exact executable that downloaded the file.

Assume that the Event Log shows executable "xyz.exe" is having problems with installation. The procedure explained here is based on the executable "xyz.exe" file. If your Event Log shows a different executable file name, the procedure remains the same. In the **Events > Event Log**, you see the following event:

```
The program 'C:\Program Files\CA\Common\ScanEngine\Incoming\xyz.exe' was recently
downloaded and attempted to execute. The user was queried whether to allow this
operation. The user chose 'Terminate (as default)'
```

You need to create an exclusion to exclude the application that is downloading the executable—not the actual executable itself (xyz.exe). The File Monitor rule that you will create here will capture the file that is executed for downloading the xyz.exe file.

Work through the steps that follow to create a file monitor rule and application class:

Step 1 Open any policy/module that is attached to the group to which the host is attached (or you can create a NEW policy/module and attach it to the group the host is a part of).

Step 2 Click on the **Add Rule** link (it is in blue) and select **File Monitor** for the rule type.

Step 3 Follow the steps in the explanation section on the values needed for the file monitor rule.

Step 4 Then once the process runs, the file monitor rule tells you which application wrote **xyz.exe.**

Step 5 Once you get the executable file name, go to **Configuration > Applications > Application Classes [Windows].** Click the **New** button and create a new application class with a descriptive name, and then add the EXE that downloaded **xyz.exe.** For example, the file monitor rule event triggered that bab.exe downloaded xyz.exe file. Hence, you may call the application **bab.** In the section **when created from one of the following executables:** type in **bab.exe.**

Step 6 Go back to the event in the **Events > Event Log,** and click on the rule ID (in blue) that generated the event. It will take you to the Trojan detection rule that gave rise to the event. Then in the section of the Trojan detection rule, **Downloading and invoking executable files,** select **Any application classes to be excluded** and select the application class you created (in this example, **bab**).

Step 7 Click on **Save** button and then click the **Generate rules** link.

Troubleshooting Steps

Using the procedures explained in the preceding sections, work trough the following steps to troubleshoot issues with CSAgent with any applications, or issues with updating applications:

Step 1 First be sure that CSA Agent is causing the application interoperability issue with the application. The quickest way to do that is to stop the CSAgent with the **net stop csagent** command. With that command, if the application functions well, then restart **CSAgent** with **net start csagent** command.

Step 2 Disable csauser.dll with the procedure outlined in the following section of this chapter: "How to disable csauser.dll."

Step 3 To find out which shim is causing the problem, follow the procedure outlined in section **How to Disable Individual CSAgent Shims** in the preceding section.

Step 4 In CSA MC, go to **Events > Events Log,** and check to see if the application in question generated any events. If an event is generated and there is a **Wizard** button, click it to create an exception. If there is no **Wizard** button, then you need to modify the rule manually.

Step 5 If there are problems updating anti-virus software, refer to the following section of this chapter: "How to create Buffer Overflow Exclusion."

Step 6 Look at the logs in the CSA MC for events. If there is an event, use the wizard to create an exception to allow the application to run.

Step 7 Check Windows Event Log on the affected system (CSAgent) if you do not see the events on the CSA MC.

Step 8 Decode and analyze the **.rtr** files in the log directory for rules/policy verification (refer to the "Diagnostic Commands and Tools" section of this chapter). If there are problems in the **.rtr** files output, poll the rules again on the CSAgent by clicking on the **Poll** button.

Report Generation Issues

In CSA MC you can generate reports in two ways:

- Using HTML
- Using Active X Control

If you are having problems with generating reports, work through the steps that follow:

Step 1 Supported Browser

Be sure you are running one of the supported browsers. Refer to the Release Notes of the respective CSA MC version at the following location: http://www.cisco.com/en/US/products/sw/secursw/ps5057/prod_release_notes_list.html

Step 2 Correct Browser Settings

If you are running Internet Explorer (IE), check the Internet Options on both Intranet and Internet settings, and be sure that all options are checked as either "enable" or "prompt" for both Active X and Scripting. Also clear the cache and close all open IE windows.

Step 3 Database size

Check to see if the database is approaching the Max limit (for MSDE the limit is 2 GB). If your database size is very high, then purge the events from the database and compact it with the procedure explained in the "Database Issues" section of this chapter.

Step 4 HTML Report is working but Active X Report is problematic

If you can run an HTML report, but you are having problems with generating an Active X report in CSA MC, open with **Notepad** the **httpd.conf** file (located at **Program Files\CSCOpx\MDC\Apache\conf**), and take a look at the line that contains **servername** (close to the end of the page) to determine whether it references **hostname.domain.com** or just the **hostname**. Then log in using whatever name the Apache server references, and run the report.

NOTE Do not change the name in the **httpd.conf** file because the name is automatically rewritten on startup. So, if you have just the server name written without the domain name, and your station is unable to resolve the name, then modify your hosts file to add the server name with the corresponding IP address of the CSA MC server.

Profiler Issues

The Profiler consists of following three separate components:

- The Management Console (CSA MC)
- The Analysis Workstation (Component of CSA MC from version 4.x)
- The Logging Agent (CSAgent)

All three components can be on the same machine, or two machines. For releases 4.0 and above, Profiler is installed on the same machine as the CSA MC. The Logging Workstation is any CSAgent that can communicate with the CSA MC and the Analysis Workstation.

Work through the following steps to troubleshoot issues with Profiler:

Step 1 Invalid license or no license

If you cannot see the Profiler menu on CSA MC, be sure that you have a valid Profiler license by browsing to **Maintenance > License Information**.

Step 2 Valid license, but still unable to see the Profile Menu

Sometimes, even if you have a valid Profile license, you may not see the Profiler menu. If so, follow the procedure in Example 21-10 to resolve this issue.

Example 21-10 *Procedure for Resolving the Profile Menu Not Showing Issues*

```
! Open up DOS prompt and then go to the following directory
C:\>cd  Program Files\CSCOpx\csaprofiler\bin
! To uninstall and install profiler execute the following two lines
C:\Program Files\CSCOpx\csaprofiler\bin>report_install u
C:\Program Files\CSCOpx\csaprofiler\bin>report_install i
! Then reboot the server
```

Step 3 Profiler job is not started

The CSAgent must poll after the Profiler job is scheduled. Otherwise, a Profiler job will not start. You need to go to the Agent manually and click the **Poll** button for on-demand polling.

Step 4 The job is completed without collecting data

If the Event Log says that the job is completed without collecting data, then the cause of the problem is that the application class selected is not correct (that is, it is misspelled), or the application has not been activated so that it can be analyzed. For example, if you choose notepad.exe as the application class and never launch it, then no data will be collected.

Step 5 Waiting for log data indefinitely.

If you have scheduled a job and the status of the job says waiting for log data indefinitely, then the port of the profiler may be blocked between the CSA MC and CSAgent. Open the TCP/5402 for the Profiler on the firewall between CSA MC and CSAgent (in both directions).

Database Maintenance Issues

Database maintenance is extremely important on the CSA MC. CSA MC database is the repository of configuration information for both the CSA MC and the agents, and it archives and stores events received from CSA Agents and MC itself. So, you must have a Disaster Recovery Plan (DCP) in place for the CSA MC database. Additionally, you must ensure that the database doesn't outgrow the capacity of the CSA MC server with numerous events. So, along with having the DCP in place, you must ensure that you purge the events and compact the database periodically so that enough space is reclaimed on the database to receive and write new events from the CSA Agent by the CSA MC. This section elaborates on how to perform the following database-related tasks for seamless operations of CSA MC and agents:

- Disaster Recovery Plan (DRP) for CSA MC
- Purging events from database
- Compacting the database

Disaster Recovery Plan (DRP) for CSA MC

The Disaster Recovery Plan for CSA MC (DRP) involves backing up the CSA MC Database and restoring it. The CSA MC has a built-in feature under the **Maintenance** menu called **Backup Configuration**. This feature allows you to perform the manual backup or automatic periodic backup of the database, certificates, and license, which saves the files and data necessary to perform a complete system restore quickly. To perform manual backup, go to **Maintenance > Backup Configuration >.** Select **"No database backup" &** specify **Backup directory.** Then click on **Backup now.** The restore can be done on the same machine or a different machine, *if the DNS name and IP address of the new server are the same as the original server's DNS name and IP address.* Because the restored configuration contains the original certificates, the Agents will find and communicate with the new Management

Console without any problems. The CSA MC will contain all the events, policies, groups, and host information as the original. There are three levels of backup:

- **Low Frequency Backup**—Full backup once a week, differential once a day, and transaction log every 24 hours
- **Medium Frequency Backup**—Full backup once a week, differential once a day, and transaction log every 8 hours
- **High Frequency Backup**—Full backup once a week, differential once a day, and transaction log every 4 hours

You may configure auto backup or manual backup. If the Auto backup is configured by selecting one of the backup types previously listed, you can perform manual backup by clicking on **Backup now** on the **Maintenance > Backup Configuration** page.

NOTE The backup *must* be to a local drive (a separate hard drive, for example) when originally saved to ensure that a network being down or another networking problem does not prevent the backup from completing successfully. Once the backup is completed, the files can then be moved to a secure site.

Back up the CSA MC Database

Work through the steps that follow to back up the CSA MC database:

Step 1 Open the GUI of the CSA MC (via a Web browser) and go to **Maintenance > Backup Configuration**. Click the **Backup** button and save the CSA MC Configuration locally. Copy these configuration files to a network drive for easier access. The main database file will be compressed and will be a combination of the database and the transaction logs (***.mdf** and ***.ldf** files, respectively). The backup database file will be approximately 50% smaller than the combined size of the ***.mdf** and ***.ldf** files. The certificate, pass phrase file and the license will be saved. If you are running CSA MC version 4.0.x, the backup files are **backup.vrs, full_backup_csamc.bak,kleidia, ssl-bundle.conf, sslca.crt, sslca.csr, sslca.key, sslca.sn, sslhost.crt, sslhost.csr, sslhost.key, sysvars.cf,** and ***.lic** files. If you are running CSA MC Version 4.5, the backup files are **backup.vrs, full_backup_ csaanalysis45.bak, and full_backup_csamc45.bak** files. In version CSA MC 4.5, back up the files as shown in Table 21-4.

Table 21-4 *Backing up Files to Keep the Certificates on the CSA MC*

Directory	Files
CSCOpx\CSAMC(45)\cfg	sslca.crt, sslhost.crt
CSCOpx\lib\web\conf	root.crt, server.key, server.crt
CSCOpx\MDC\Apache\conf\ssl	chain.cer, root.crt, server.key, server.cert

Step 2 To save the original agent kits that you created, back up the bin directory of **Program Files\CSOpx\CSAMC(45)\bin\webserver\htdocs** into the same location as the previously listed files. If this is not convenient, then you can re-create default agent kits, but you will lose any custom agent kits you might have created.

Restore the CSA MC Database on the Same Server

You can restore the CSA MC database on the same system or on a different system, with the same IP address or a different IP address. Work through the procedure that follows to restore the database on the same server with the same IP address and DNS name (this is useful if the existing VMS Server crashes and needs to be rebuilt). These directions assume you have *only* VMS Common Services and the CSA MC installed, and you want to completely reinstall *all* the components (VMS, SQL Server (or MSDE), and CSA MC). If you have other VMS components installed, you must uninstall *all* other components after uninstalling the CSA MC before uninstalling VMS.

Step 1 Be sure the server still has exactly the same machine name as before, and that the machine name is resolvable via DNS (this is required).

Step 2 Be sure the machine still has the same IP address. This is not absolutely required, but highly recommended.

Step 3 Uninstall the CSA MC by using **Start > Programs > CiscoWorks.** Uninstall **CiscoWorks** and keep the **Management Center for Cisco Security Agents** checked while unchecking the other components.

Step 4 When asked, you do not have to back up the files during the uninstallation of the CSA MC, because you have already backed up the files. In addition, the format used for backup during this stage is different than the backup files created via the CSA MC GUI.

Step 5 Reboot the server.

Step 6 Uninstall VMS via **Start > Programs > CiscoWorks**. Uninstall CiscoWorks. (These procedures assume you have no other VMS components on the system. If you have other VMS components, you must uninstall those before you uninstall VMS.)

Step 7 Reboot the server.

Step 8 Delete the **CSCOpx** directory.

Step 9 Uninstall **SQLServer** or the **MSDE.**

Step 10 Reboot the server.

Step 11 Delete **SQLServer** directories and references to **SQLServer** in the registry.

Step 12 Install the same version of VMS with Common Services onto the original server. Then reboot the server.

Step 13 Reinstall the CSA MC onto the original server. Reboot the server.

Step 14 Check to be sure you can log into VMS and the CSA MC.

Step 15 Move the backup configuration files that you moved to a network share down locally to the new machine (a folder of your choice).

Step 16 Uninstall the CSA MC Agent (this CSAgent will no longer be able to register with the correct CSA server). Reboot the server.

Step 17 Run the **Restore Configuration** utility located in **Program Files\CSCOpx\CSAMC(45)\bin** (and point to where the original configuration files are located that you just moved down from the network).

Step 18 Copy **\Program Files\CSCOpx\CSAMC(45)\bin\webserver\htdocs\deploy_kits** into the same directory on the new server (thus overwriting the agent kits with the original Agent kits). Reboot the server.

Step 19 Log into VMS/CSA MC to ensure that all the data is present and all agent kit links work as they did in the original CSA MC.

Step 20 Check to be sure that all the agents are polling into the reinstalled CSA MC.

NOTE Be sure to **manually copy** over the certificates for good measure. These certificates are crucial in maintaining communication between the Agent and the new CSA MC. Also run the following command via the command line interface to refresh all the default agent kits:

```
*:\Program Files\CSCOpx\CSAMC\bin\webmgr makekits_refresh
```

Be sure that the backup files are not transferred with a CD. To transfer the files, copy the files via a network share or thumb drive, or some other method besides a CD.

Restore the CSA MC Database on a Different Server with a Different Name and IP Address

To restore the database on a different server (for example, test machine) with a different name and IP address, use the following procedure:

Step 1 Be sure that the test machine has a different machine name and IP address.

Step 2 Install VMS and the CSA MC onto the new machine.

Step 3 Move the backup files from the network to a local drive.

Step 4 Run the **Restore Configuration** utility in **Program Files\CSCOpx\CSAMC(45)\bin** (and point to where the original configuration files are located that you just moved from the network).

Step 5 Create new certificates with the procedure in Example 21-11.

Example 21-11 *Creating a New Certificate*

```
! Stop the agent and MC services in DOS prompt
net stop csagent
net stop crmdmgtd
! Delete the following files
! In directory CSCOpx\CSAMC\cfg    delete files sslca.crt,sslhost.crt
! In directory CSCOpx\lib\web\conf delete files root.crt, server.key,
! server.crt
! In directory CSCOpx\MDC\Apache\conf\ssl delete files chain.cer, root.crt,
! server.key, server.cert
! From the DOS prompt change the directory to following
cd CSCOpx\CSAMC(45)\Bin
!Type the following command
..\..\bin\perl.exe installcert.pl -forceinstall

!The preceding command generates new certificate in CSAMC cfg directory and
!copies them in the appropriate files in the CMF and core apache. If you run it
!from the CMD as specified above, you will clearly see where it copies the files.
! Start the agents and MC services
net start crmdmgtd
net start csagent
```

Step 6 To refresh the kits, got to the **CSAMC(45)** bin directory and type **webmgr makekits_refresh** without the quotes.

Step 7 Log into VMS/CSA MC to ensure that all the data is present.

Step 8 Replace the **sslca.crt** file in the agent protecting the CSA MC (net stop the **csagent and** then replace the **sslca.crt** in **Program Files\Cisco (Systems)\CSAgent\cfg** with the one from the CSA MC's **Program Files\CSCOpx\CSAMC(45)\cfg**).

Step 9 Install an agent and be sure it works.

Purging Events from the Database

Purging allows you to remove events from the database. If there are a huge number of events occupying the database, you need to purge and then compact the database as discussed in the next section. Before considering purging, it is useful to know when to do it.

There are several methods to determine the size of the database, which will indicate when to purge the events. These methods are listed as follows:

- **Based on number of events**—Based on the number of events in the event log, you can determine if your database needs to be purged. If the total number of events is well over a million, you need to consider purging. Example 21-12 shows a sample of finding out the number of events in the event log file.

Example 21-12 *Finding the Number of Events in the Event Log File in CSA MC Version 4.5*

```
! Open a DOS prompt on the CSA MC server and type the following command.
! Make sure to type upper case E, this is case sensitive.
C:\>osql -E
! If you are running CSA MC 4.5, run the following command. If earlier version, then
! need to replace csamc45 with csamc.
1> use csamc45
! The following line will query the database to find out the number of events
2> select count (*) from formatted_event_log
3> go
 -----------
          61
(1 row affected)
1>
```

- **Based on database file size**—A quick way to find the size of the database is to check the **csamc(45).mdf** file located in **Program Files\CSCOpx\CSAMC(45)\db** and right-click on this file to see how large it is. If it is close to 2 GB, you need to delete events from the database.
- **Using a GUI**—You can determine the size of the file as listed in the previous item by going to **Maintenance > Database Maintenance**.

Once you know the size of the database and have decided to purge the events from the database, there are three options:

- Automatic purging
- On-demand purging
- Purging using CLI

Automatic Purging

With this option you can schedule the time for purging. Work through the steps below to accomplish this task:

Step 1 Create a new task that will purge the events. To do so, go to **Events** (**Monitor** on older version) **> Event Log Management.**

Step 2 Then click the **New** button.

Step 3 In the new window from Step 2, choose an event, set to delete, and set the deletion time.

Step 4 Finally, click the **Save** button to save this Event Managing Task.

This procedure will delete the events from the database as specified.

On-demand Purging

This type of purging allows you to remove the events when you want it. Work through the steps that follow to accomplish this task:

Step 1 Go to **Events (Monitor) > Event Sets**

Step 2 Choose an existing event or create a new one.

Step 3 After defining your event, click on **Purge events** at the bottom of the screen to purge them immediately.

Purging Using CLI

To purge the event correlation queue using the CLI, you can use the sql command in the example that follows. This sql command will delete some of the events in the event correlation queue. You can use the following syntax in the DOS prompt of your CSA MC server:

```
c:\>Program Files\Microsoft SQL Server\80\Tools\Binn\osql -d csamc(45) -E -Q "delete
from event_host delete from event_queue"
```

As previously mentioned, after purging, consider compacting the database as discussed in next section to reduce the physical size of the database files.

Compacting the Database

Regardless of whether you use the built-in MSDE or the full version of SQL Server 2000, you should compact the database after you have deleted large amounts of data from the CSA MC database (**csamc.mdf** and **csamc_log.ldf**), such as removing large numbers of events from the event log. This is because purging the events from the database does not really reduce the size of the database unless compacting is performed. This is very similar to an Outlook ***.pst** file after deleting e-mails. Compacting the database recovers disk space, increases efficiency, and reduces query time.

CAUTION Always back up the CSA MC database under the CSA MC GUI's **maintenance** section as discussed before purging events and compacting the database.

Compacting MSDE (CSA MC Built-in Database)

The MSDE, which ships with the CSA MC, does not have a Graphical User Interface (GUI), so database maintenance must be done through the command shell tool **osql –E**. Run these scripts as shown in Example 21-13 via the command shell when you are ready to shrink the database:

Example 21-13 *How to Shrink the Database of CSA MC When MSDE Is Used*

```
! Press <enter> after each line. E must be upper case as case sensitive
osql -E
! csamc45 in the case of CSA MC version 4.5. Earlier version used csamc.
use csamc45
backup log csamc45 with no_log
go
dbcc shrinkdatabase (csamc45)
go
update statistics host with fullscan
go
update statistics group_host with fullscan
go
update statistics event_log with fullscan
go
update statistics formatted_event_log with fullscan
go
update statistics rule_program_distribution with fullscan
go
```

Compacting Full Version Of SQL Server 2000

The full version of SQLServer 2000 has a GUI called **Enterprise Manager.** There are many tools that can ease the maintenance of the database.

Work through the steps that follow to shrink the database via Enterprise Manager:

Step 1 Expand a server group, and then expand a server.

Step 2 Expand databases, **right-click** on the **csamc** database to shrink it, point to **All Tasks,** and then click **Shrink Database.**

Step 3 Specify how much to shrink the database. For the maximum free space in files after shrinking, enter the amount of free space you want left in the database after shrinking. Use the **Database Size, Space free** value as a guideline.

Step 4 Select **Move pages to beginning of file** before shrinking to cause the freed file space to be retained in the database files, and pages containing data to be moved to the beginning of the database files.

Step 5 Click **Schedule** to create or change the frequency or time when the database is automatically shrunk.

Step 6 Click **Shrink files** to shrink an individual database's files.

NOTE You cannot shrink a database smaller than the size of the model database. Also, *do not* use the Enterprise Manager's **autoshrink** option, as this can cause database lockup.

Checking and Repairing the CSA MC MSDE Database

If your CSA MC is not functioning properly, for instance, if you cannot launch the CSA MC GUI or are unable to get the events, check to see if your CSA MC's MSDE database is working properly. There is a quick way to check that. Enter the following URL in the Web browser to perform the database check.

```
https://server_name/csamc/webadmin?page=db_checks
```

If the database check reports any error, you need to repair your MSDE database with the following procedure:

Step 1 Stop both Ciscoworks Daemon Manager and the sqlserver service.

Step 2 Launch DOS CLI and execute the following commands:

```
cd program files\microsoft sql server\mssql\binn
sqlservr.exe -c -m
```

Step 3 Launch a second DOS CLI and execute the following commands to launch the osql tool, and check if there is any report corruption issue on the database:

```
osql -E
alter database csamc set single_user
go
dbcc checkdb ('csamc')
go
```

Step 4 Review this report to see if it reports corruptions, and if it does, run the following:

```
DBCC CHECKDB ('csamc', repair_rebuild) with all_errormsgs
go
```

Wait until this completes.

Step 5 If you get an error saying it can't be fixed, you may have to allow data loss and run this:

```
DBCC CHECKDB ('csamc', repair_allow_data_loss) with all_errormsgs
```

This will allow a repair with some loss of data (most likely the event log data). Another option for repairing the database is **repair_fast.** Each time you run **DBCC CHECKDB**, it will suggest which repair command to run. It might be **repair_allow_data_loss** or **repair_fast** or both.

Step 6 Then run **repair_rebuild** as follows to rebuild your database indexes:

```
DBCC CHECKDB ('csamc', repair_rebuild) with all_errormsgs
```

Step 7 After Step 6 completes, run the following commands:

```
alter database csamc set multi_user
go
quit
```

Step 8 Then go to the first DOS CLI window and terminate the SQL Server session by pressing **ctrl + C** on your keyboard.

Step 9 Say **YES** to the prompt and reboot the machine.

Common Problems and Resolutions

This section examines some problems that often occur and how to resolve them.

1 Why can't I download the CSA Agent kit from CSA MC on Windows 2003?

Answer: You may have problems with downloading the CSA Agent kit on Windows 2003 directly from CSA MC due to the extra Internet Explorer (IE) security settings in Windows 2003. To take off the extra security go to:

Add/Remove Programs > Windows Components > Internet Explorer Enhanced Security Configuration

Removing this Windows component should remove some of the security on IE that could be blocking the download of the agent kit installer.

2 Where can I find CSA MC and Security Agent documentation?

Answer: For CSA MC and CSAgent documentation refer to the following:

http://www.cisco.com/en/US/products/sw/secursw/ps5057/tsd_products_support_series_home.html

3 Where can I download the latest versions and patches for CSA MC?

Answer: Go to the following location to get the latest version and patches of CSA (you must be a registered user):

http://www.cisco.com/pcgi-bin/tablebuild.pl/csa

4 Where can I find information on existing bugs for CSA MC?

Answer: You can go to the following link to find the details on existing bugs:

```
http://www.cisco.com/pcgi-bin/Support/Bugtool/selection.pl?cco_
product=Cisco&Security&Agent&mdf_label=Cisco&Security&Agent
```

5 CSA MC keeps saying I need to generate rules, even after I generate them. What should I do now?

Answer: This is a time issue. Set the clock to the correct time.

6 What ports do I need to open in my firewall to allow agents to communicate with CSA MC?

Answer: These agent components and relevant ports are needed for communication to the CSA MC:

— **Registration**—By default, the CSAgents communicate to the CSA MC on TCP port 5401. If that port is not available, the agents try TCP port 443 instead.

— **Browsing**—If you use a Web browser to communicate to the CSA MC, open TCP ports 1741, 1742, and 443.

— **Profiler**—The Profiler communicates with CSA MC on TCP port 5402.

7 I have disabled logging for a particular rule. However, I am still receiving logs for this rule. Is this normal?

Answer: In CSA MC Version 4.0.2 when the group is in test mode, these rule types are logged regardless of the configuration:

— Application control

— COM component access control

— File access control

— File version control

— Registry access control

For all other rule types, logging will be enabled or disabled as configured. In CSA MC Version 4.5 and later, the logging configuration is utilized for all rules types regardless of whether the group is in test or production mode.

8 How do I switch an agent from test mode to production?

Answer: To place a CSAgent in production mode, use the CSA MC to place the CSAgent's group into production mode:

Step 1 From CSA MC, go to **Systems > Groups**.

Step 2 Select the group that the agent is in.

Step 3 In the group properties, uncheck the **Test mode** check box.

Step 4 Click on **Generate rules**. The next time the agent polls the CSA MC and downloads the new setup, it is placed in production mode.

9 Where can I get information about each policy and a description for the rules?

Answer: In CSA MC, go to **Configuration > Policies** and select the policy you want to view. Then click the **Explain rules** link for a detailed description of each rule in the policy. This link is also available for a group in which multiple policies are applied, and for an individual host that may belong to multiple groups.

10 What are the run levels for the CSA Agent on UNIX?

Answer: These are the run levels for the CSA Agent on UNIX:

— /etc/rc0.d/K40csa

— /etc/rc1.d/K40csa

— /etc/rc2.d/S32csatdi

— /etc/rc2.d/S77csa

— /etc/rcS.d/K40csa

— /etc/rcS.d/S22csanet

For information about run levels, type the **main init** command to refer to the manual for init on UNIX.

11 Can I generate Reports Using Crystal Reports from CSA MC Database?

Answer: You can get events directly from the CSA MC DB if you choose, but Cisco changes the database schema often enough that any application written for a specific version of the CSA MC product will most likely not work when the next version comes out. It should not be a surprise that CSA MC DB will be modified whenever necessary to make the product better. However, there is a view in the product that you may use (or use a FULL version of SQL Server and look at CSA MC Schema). Refer to the following link for additional details: http://www.cisco.com/en/US/products/sw/secursw/ps5057/products_configuration_guide_chapter09186a0080424781.html#wp953202

12 How can I change the Profiler port from default?

Answer: If you have a firewall blocking the default port between the profiler and the CSAgent, use the following procedure to change the port from default:

Step 1 Open a DOS window and change the directory to **program files\Cisco\CSAgent\bin**.

Step 2 Type **report_install u** to uninstall the existing port number, which is 5402 by default.

Step 3 Type **report_install -p 8000 i** to install the new port number. In this example, 8000 is the new port number that you want Profiler to use.

To see which port is used by Profiler, look at **sfront.cf** in the **program files\Cisco\CSAgent\cfg** directory.

13 Is it possible to attach a saved database instead of export and import?

Answer: Yes, it is possible. Actually, if for some reason you forget to export the database and then uninstall the CSA MC, and during uninstall you save the database, you can attach the saved database files with the following procedure:

Step 1 Reinstall **CiscoWorks VMS**, and then reinstall CSA MC. This will install a generic database. You must first detach this generic database so you can use the saved database files.

Step 2 To detach the database, at the CMD prompt type the command on DOS prompt (**osql –E** is case sensitive) as shown in Example 21-14.

Example 21-14 *Detaching the Database Using SQL*

```
osql -E
osql>sp_detach_db csamc45   <enter>
osql>go  <enter>
osql>exit  <enter>
```

Step 3 Delete or rename the generic database files found in **Program Files\CSCOpx\CSAMC45\db\(csamc45.mdf** and **csamc45_log.ldf**)

Step 4 Copy or move the saved database files (**csamc45.mdf** and **csamc45_log.ldf**) into the **Program Files\CSCOpx\CSAMC45\db** directory.

Step 5 Open a CMD prompt and type the commands shown in Example 21-15 (anything after the at sign (@) is the exact path to your CSA MC system. This example uses the e:\ drive).

Example 21-15 *Attaching the Database*

```
osql -E <enter>
osql>sp_attach_db @dbname='csamc45' , @filename1='e:\program
files\CSCOpx\csamc\db\csamc45.mdf ', @filename2='e:\program
files\CSOpx\csamc\db\csamc45_log.ldf '   <enter>
osql>go  <enter>
osql>exit  <enter>
net start csamc.
```

Step 6 Restore the certificates used by this database.

Best Practices

This section examines some of the important issues involved in improving performance. Following is the list of some good practices:

Recommendation on Installation

Use a dedicated machine for CSAMC installation, and for better management and performance, use a separate machine for the Security Monitor. This also depends on the number of Agents deployed and other variables such as amount of logging turned on, etc. To support 5,000 agents, use approximately a quad processor, 2 GB of memory, and a RAID disk.

Test Mode

Test mode is used to find out what's normal for the machines in your network, and to see if you need to create any exceptions for certain applications to function correctly. However, be aware that there are performance issues with the agent installed and in testmode.

Testmode, as you know, logs all events regardless of whether logging is turned on or off. Once testmode is turned off, any rules that have logging disabled will no longer log the event. Testmode is meant for policy tuning and not for performance testing. Testmode logs more events than you will see if the agent is in protect mode.

The recommendation is this:

Step 1 Place agent into Testmode to tune the policies to meet your security objectives.

Step 2 Once the policies are tuned, take the agent out of Testmode and you will see a decrease in the performance impact of the agent. Furthermore, you can even turn off logging of some deny/query user rules if you do not want to see the event log messages that they generate.

Step 3 Turn off the network shim if the machine already has some kind of firewall capability or application already installed. Just by the nature of what it does, the netshim affects performance more than other CSA components.

Disaster Recovery for CSA

Disaster Recovery is discussed under the database management section of this chapter, so it is not discussed again here. This section focuses primarily on suggestions for Disaster Recovery procedures that were described in the Database Management Troubleshooting section earlier.

There is no need for a redundancy server at another site. However, if your current company policy calls for a redundancy server at another site, the backup procedure will work just as well as wherever that backup machine is located. This is true if the agents can resolve domain name via DNS server to that new MC.

A possible recovery scenario would be to run the Backup Configuration feature once a day (or just schedule the backup to be performed), and then run an automated script that will zip up the backup files and move them to a shared drive (or move them over without zipping them up). If the original server ever goes down, then you can use any machine that meets the hardware and software requirements to restore the MC quickly. Again, the new machine must be given the same DNS name and IP address as the original StormWatch Management Console.

In addition, the Agents that belong to that MC must be able to reach it via DNS/WINS to get their configurations changed, and to send events to the MC. Because the new MC has exactly the same configuration as the original MC, downtime and recovery of the MC is kept to a minimum. It would take approximately 10–15 minutes to reinstall the MC, and another 10–15 minutes (depending on the size of the DB) to restore the original configuration from our backup. Remember that the Agents are still protecting their hosts throughout any recovery process.

CHAPTER 22

Troubleshooting IEV and Security Monitors

The Security Monitor (also known as SecMon) is a component that is installed on top of CiscoWorks Common Services (see Chapter 17, "Troubleshooting CiscoWorks Common Services," for more details) to receive events, generate reports, and perform correlations. If you have more than three sensors, it is desirable to use a Security Monitor. However, with fewer than three sensors, you can use Intrusion Detection Event Viewer (IEV), which can be downloaded free. In addition to getting events from the IDS sensor (for example, sensor appliance, IOS IPS and so on), Security Monitor can also receive syslog messages from various devices such as Cisco Secure Private Internet Exchange (PIX) firewall, IOS Router, and so on. This additional capability motivates Security Administrators to deploy Security Monitor even with fewer than three sensors in the network. However, as Security Monitor is used primarily for receiving events and generating reports for IDS/IPS sensor, this chapter focuses primarily on how to configure and troubleshoot IDS/IPS-related issues with IEV and Security Monitor.

Overview of IEV and Security Monitor

Intrusion Detection Event Viewer (IEV) is a Windows program that you can download for free from Cisco.com and can install on your own desktop. You then need to configure it to connect to the sensor and pull alarms from the sensor. You can download the latest version of IEV from the following location:

http://www.cisco.com/cgi-bin/tablebuild.pl/ids-ev

As mentioned before, IEV is limited to pulling events from three sensors only, and doesn't have the syslog capability. So, if you have more than three sensors, or need syslog along with IDS sensor reporting capability, then you need to have the Security Monitor.

Security Monitor consists of a Web-based application with command line utilities for pruning and archiving the data in the database and Perl script files, which can be run through the **notifier** for notification purposes. Many of the components of the Web-based application run as services on Windows and are managed as daemons by the daemon manger.

The primary functions of Security Monitor include:

- Receiving and storing events and syslog messages
- Correlating events and providing a notification mechanism for filtered events

- Allowing dynamic (Event Viewer) and static views (Reports) of stored data
- Managing and archiving of received data

When installed on the same server, to IDS/IPS MC and the Security Monitor share many components, including database tables and Java objects.

The Event Viewer periodically polls events from the database. The polling rate is adjustable and affects the amount of delay that users will experience between when an event is received until it is displayed in the viewer. There are tradeoffs between how often the data is refreshed by the event viewer and the overall efficiency of the system.

The performance of the Security Monitor varies considerably with system resources. The default pruning rules are tuned to a system that meets the Bundle Hardware requirements. Systems with more resources may be able to adjust these rules to store more data before pruning.

You can filter event data three ways:

- **Event Rules (Correlation)**—These actively monitor filtered event data and send notifications when the rule triggers.
- **Reports (Static View)**—Reports are sometimes based on static analysis of filtered event data.
- **Event Viewer**—This is usually launched to display an active view of filtered event data.

Similar to Event Rules, Database Rules also send notifications. But they are based on the state of the database. The database state is periodically monitored and compared to the trigger condition of stored rules. When a rule triggers, it sends notifications. For example, a script notification runs default pruning when one of the default pruning rules triggers by default on Security Monitor.

There are three ways in which notifications can be triggered:

- The triggering of an event rule
- The triggering of a database rule
- When a scheduled report completes

The notification can be sent in the following ways:

- E-mail
- Console
- Script

Communication Architecture

Communication protocols between the Security Monitor and the reporting devices depend on the types of reporting devices. The Security Monitor is supported by the following list of protocols:

- **PostOffice (PO)**—This protocol is used for communication between IDS 3.x and the Security Monitor. This protocol uses the UDP port 45000. PostOffice requires the system to specify local parameters, and the PO parameters for each monitored PO device. The local data is initially set at install time.
- **Remote Data Exchange Protocol (RDEP)**—RDEP is used to connect to the sensor and pull alert data. It uses https (TCP/443-SSL) for communication.
- **Security Device Event Exchange (SDEE)**—SDEE protocol is the replacement starting from IPS version 5.0 on sensor and IPS on the IOS router. Security Monitor 2.0 supports **SDEE** protocol.
- **Syslog**—Syslog uses UDP/514. This is used by the reporting devices that cannot communicate by either of the two protocols mentioned previously.

How Does It Work?

As discussed previously, different monitoring devices use different types of protocols to forward events. For instance, IDS 3.x uses PostOffice for the communication, and pushes the events from the sensor to the Security Monitor, whereas in IDS 4.x, RDEP is used where Security Monitor makes the connection with the sensor and pulls the events over https (Secure Sockets Layer—SSL). In IPS version 5.0, Security Monitor uses SDEE as the communication protocol. Because IDS 4.x and IPS 5.x are the most frequently used monitoring devices for Security Monitor, this section explains the deeper details of how Security Monitor pulls the events from the sensor. For other devices (such as syslog from router), the mechanism is slightly different.

Figure 22-1 shows the system flow of Security Monitor with IDS 4.x sensor.

Figure 22-1 *System Flow of Security Monitor*

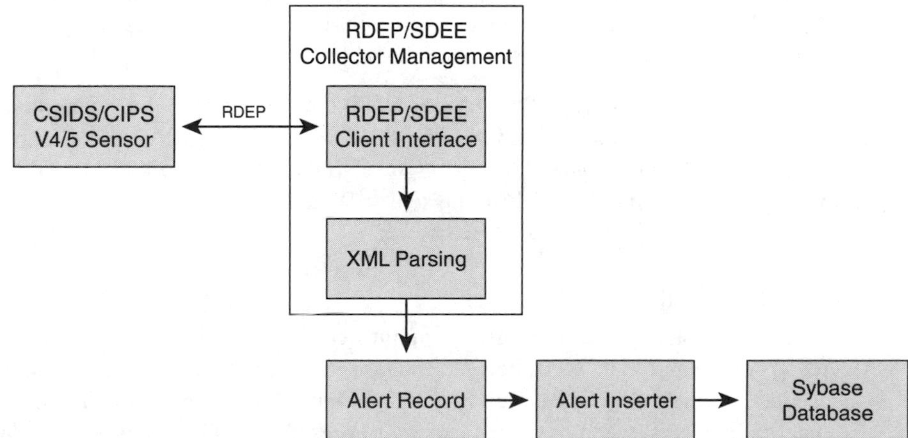

Following is a brief sequential discussion of every component required to pull the events from the sensor and insert them into the Security Monitor database.

RDEP/SDEE Collector Management

The RDEP/SDEE Collector Manager manages connection status, event retrieval subscriptions, and metrics. Items are added or deleted for monitoring by their placement in the **monitored_devices** table. A separate RDEP/SDEE Collector object is used for each CSIDS v4 or CSIPS v5 sensor listed in the **monitored_devices** table.

When a device is added to the table to be monitored, the collector opens an RDEP/SDEE connection to the sensor, starts a subscription and begins pulling alert data out from the sensor through the subscription. The alert data is parsed and inserted into the alerts table in the database. The RDEP/SDEE Collector manager keeps track of the timestamp and id of the last alert inserted. Knowing the id and timestamp allows the RDEP/SDEE collector to restart a subscription at a known location.

You can specify a minimum alarm level to be retrieved from the CSIDS v4 or CSIPS v5 sensor. The information for the minimum alarm level is specified in the GUI and passed to the receiver through the monitored_devices table.

The RDEP/SDEE collector continually pulls alerts from the sensor and sends them to the XML parser for insertion into the database. This continues as long as the device remains in the **monitored_devices** table and the device is connected. If the device is deleted from the monitored_devices table, the subscription is closed and the RDEP/SDEE collector disconnects from the sensor. If the connection goes down but the device is still in the **monitored_devices** table, the RDEP/SDEE collector attempts to open a new RDEP/SDEE connection to the sensor and re-attach it to the previously opened subscription. If the previous subscription is not valid, a new one is started using the timestamp of the last received event. If the reconnect attempt fails, the RDEP/SDEE collector logs the error in the **Audit Log** and sleeps for a second before attempting to connect again. This will continue until the device is removed from the table.

If there is a Network Address Translation (NAT) device between the sensor and the Security Monitor, then the NAT address for the CSIDS v4 or CSIPS v5 sensor is used for connection to the sensor. The NAT address is also the address stored in the alert record in the database **ALERT_TABLE** in the sensor IP address field.

Connection Status

The connection status with the sensor is monitored by the RDEP/SDEE Manager. A device is considered to be **Connected** if the last attempt to read through the connection succeeded. A device will be marked as **Not Connected** if the last read attempt failed. Connection status is stored in the database for access by the GUI. It will be updated dynamically by the **RDEP/SDEE** Collector. Table 22-1 explains the meaning of different connection statuses.

Table 22-1 *Connection Status*

Connection Status	Description
Connected	An insecure TCP or PostOffice connection has been established to the device.
ConnectedTLS	There is a secure Transaction Layer Security (TLS) connection
Created	This is a transitory state that occurs for a short period after the collector is created but before the first connection attempt is made.
Indeterminant	This can only occur when the IDS_Receiver process is not running; it means there is no connection information for the device.
Authentication Failed	The specified password or username is incorrect.
Paused	The receiver process has been paused and is not currently collecting events. This can happen if the receiver becomes overwhelmed with events.
Not Connected	For 4.x sensors, TCP connection did not complete. For 3.x sensors, any type of connection issue not related to authorization.

How Often Does Security Monitor Poll a Sensor?

The Security Monitor issues requests to RDEP/SDEE sensors at different rates at different times. When the collector first starts up, it builds the subscription and issues the initial get request (usually within a few seconds of placing the device in the monitored device table). The initial request asks for all events of the specified severity that are detected by the sensor from this point forward. The RDEP/SDEE sensor responds within 10 seconds with either an empty response (if no events have appeared) or with a document that includes up to 100 events (the maximum number of events retrieved with one get request). If the Security Monitor receives data in the initial request, it turns around and issues a new request immediately. If the initial request is empty, the Security Monitor delays one second before issuing the next request. When that response comes back, the Security Monitor issues a new request. If two empty requests are received in a row, the delay between requests is doubled. If the request contains data, a new request is issued immediately. The process continues in this manner with each successive empty response doubling the delay between requests, up to a maximum of five minutes—whenever a non-empty response is received, the next request is issued immediately and the process starts over.

One other thing complicates this process a bit. After the first request, the subscription timeout (the length of time the sensor waits for incoming data before returning the response) is set to 30 seconds. So the request turnaround time for an empty response is the delay between request and 30 seconds. This process ensures the following:

- The maximum delay between requests is five and half minutes.
- Requests that are taking this long only occur on sensors that have sent no event data for at least 15 minutes.
- Backlogs of events on any sensor are retrieved quickly with successive subscription reads. The Security Monitor receiver spends more time servicing sensors that are sending data than sensors that are not.

XML Parsing

The purpose of the XML parser is to parse a valid XML document that is received from the sensor to the Inserter to insert the information into the database. If the XML document is not valid, the parser will show an error. If the document is valid, it will be parsed. All required fields from the IDIOM Schema Specification must be present in the evAlert. If a required field is not present, there will be an error.

Alert Inserter

The purpose of the Alert Inserter is to write the alert to the database upon receiving the XML parsed data. This is done with an SQL statement and built into the Inserter; hence no user intervention is required.

IDS/IPS MC and Security Monitor Processes

There is a set of processes that manage the tasks that IDS/IPS MC and Security Monitor perform. If one of those processes is not running, the function they are responsible for will not work. If there are problems in running the application, it is always a good practice to check that all those processes are running. The processes and their main functions are the following:

- **IDS_Analyzer**—Processes event rules and requests user-specified notifications when appropriate.
- **IDS_Backup**—Is responsible for the IDS/IPS MC and SecMon backup and restore process.
- **IDS_DbAdminAnalyzer**—Periodically checks the Database rules created and starts the execution if the triggering conditions are met.
- **IDS_DeployDaemon**— Manages the configuration deployment.
- **IDS_EvsServer**—Is a daemon for the Event viewer.

- **IDS_Notifier**—Receives notification requests (script, e-mail, and/or console) from other subsystems and performs the requested notification.
- **IDS_Receiver**—Is a service that receives events and syslog and stores them in the database.
- **IDS_ReportScheduler**—Generates the schedules report.

If any of those processes is not running, the related task will not be performed. To check the status of the processes and start them, go to **Server Configuration > Administration > Process Management.** From there you can view the status of the processes, stop the processes, or start stopped processes. All the processes that start with **IDS_** are related to Security Monitor or IDS/IPS MC.

To identify the devices that are supported by different versions of Security Monitor, check this site: http://www.cisco.com/en/US/products/sw/cscowork/ps3991/products_device_support_tables_list.html

Following are some of the important points about supportability:

- IDS Sensor 3.0(1)S4 or better and IDSM 3.0(5)S23 or better requires Security Monitor 1.0 and above.
- IDS Sensor version 4.x requires Security Monitor 1.1 or above.
- Internet Operating System (IOS) IPS requires Security Monitor 2.0.
- IPS 5.0(1) requires Security Monitor 2.1

User Management for Security Monitor

You can create users for one of the following privileges for the Security Monitor:

- **Help desk**—Following are the privileges of the help desk:
  - Read only for the entire system.
  - View any report and alarm. Cannot delete reports or alarms, cannot generate reports.
- **Approver**—For the Security Monitor, this is the same as the help desk. Following are the privileges that the Approver has:
  - Read only for the entire system plus the privilege to approve configurations.
  - View any report and alarm. Cannot delete reports or alarms, cannot generate reports.
- **Network operator**—For the Security Monitor, this is the same as help desk plus the ability to generate reports.
  - Read only for the entire system plus the privilege to deploy configurations.
  - View any report and alarm, cannot delete reports or alarm, can generate reports.

- **Network administrator and system administrator**—For the Security Monitor, this is the same as the network operator plus the ability to delete alarms:
  - Edit anything in the system.
  - View any report and alarm.
  - Delete reports or alarms.
  - Generate reports.

Diagnostic Commands and Tools

Most of the problems with Security Monitor are with the Operations and Database Management issue. Log files in Security Monitor are used to log process state and error messages. The Security Monitor process log files are written at: **. . .\CSCOpx\log** and are generally named after the process that wrote them. Following is the list of files available to log information pertaining to different processes:

- **System log**—System log and login and logout information files are written at: **. . .\CSCOpx\MDC\log**
- **Apache server log files**—The Apache server logs errors under normal conditions, so you need to be careful while looking at these logs. In general, look for anomalies in error messages. The location of the log files is at: **. . .\CSCOpx\MDC\Apache\logs**
- **Tomcat log files**—The Tomcat directory has both log and logs (with an "s") subdirectories. The logs subdirectory is where the Security Monitor GUI sends its messages. It is probably the location of the most useful error information. The tomcat\log directory is usually empty. The location of the logs subdirectory is at: **. . .\CSCOpx\MDC\tomcat\logs**

If you are troubleshooting the problem with direct console access to the server in real-time, you can look into the files discussed above to isolate a problem with Security Monitor. However, if you need to engage Cisco support team for help, then you need to collect the **.zip** file generated by the **mdcsupport** utility as explained in the following link: http://www.cisco.com/en/US/products/sw/cscowork/ps3994/products_user_guide_chapter09186a00801f5963.html#wp1019256

Categorization of Problem Areas

The problem areas of the Security Monitor can be categorized as follows:

- Installation issues
- Unable to launch issues
- Licensing issues
- Device management issues
- Event viewer issues (real time)
- Report generation issues

- Notification Issues (e-mail notification)
- Database maintenance issues

Installation Issues

The Security Monitor can be installed through either of the two following scenarios:

- **Security Monitor only**—If you have multiple monitoring devices that need to send events to the Security Monitor, it is recommended to install the Security Monitor on a different server than the IDS/IPS MC. Installing only the Security Monitor on a different server gives you better management and performance of the Security Monitor. If the Security Monitor database is corrupted, you do not need to uninstall and re-install the IDS/IPS MC. This is required if both IDS/IPS MC and Security Monitor are installed on the same server, because both use the same Sybase database). Note that you only need to uninstall and reinstall the Security Monitor without using the old database, and then import the devices from IDS/IPS MC.
- **Both IDS/IPS MC and Security Monitor**—The advantage of installing the IDS/IPS MC and Security Monitor on the same system is the ease of management, as both of the components use the same database and share other files.

The installation procedures for different versions of the Security Monitor are listed in the following link and are not be discussed here.

http://www.cisco.com/en/US/products/sw/cscowork/ps3990/prod_installation_guides_list.html

You must install the Common Services first before proceeding with the Security Monitor installation. Core provides authentication and user management, and a host of other services. As mentioned before, when both Security Monitor and the IDS/IPS MC are installed on the same system, sensors configured to send their events to Security Monitor can be imported from the IDS/IPS MC. Otherwise, every sensor monitored by Security Monitor needs to be added manually. PostOffice devices must be in the device table to receive those events. Syslog devices do not need to be in the device table, but if they are, the device name will be displayed in the event viewer and reports.

Troubleshooting techniques related to the installation of Security Monitor are similar to those of IDS/IPS MC which is discussed in Chapter 18, "Troubleshooting IDM and IDS/IPS Management Console (IDS/IPS MC)" under the section entitled "Installation and upgrade issues." Therefore, the troubleshooting techniques are not discussed here.

Issues with Launching

To launch Security Monitor, first log in to Security Monitor server from your Web browser: **http://localhost:1741**.

Then, launch the Security Monitor by clicking **VPN/Security Management Solution > Monitoring Center > Security Monitor**.

When you launch, Security Monitor will land on the device table as shown in Figure 22-2.

Figure 22-2 *Security Monitor Shown After the Login*

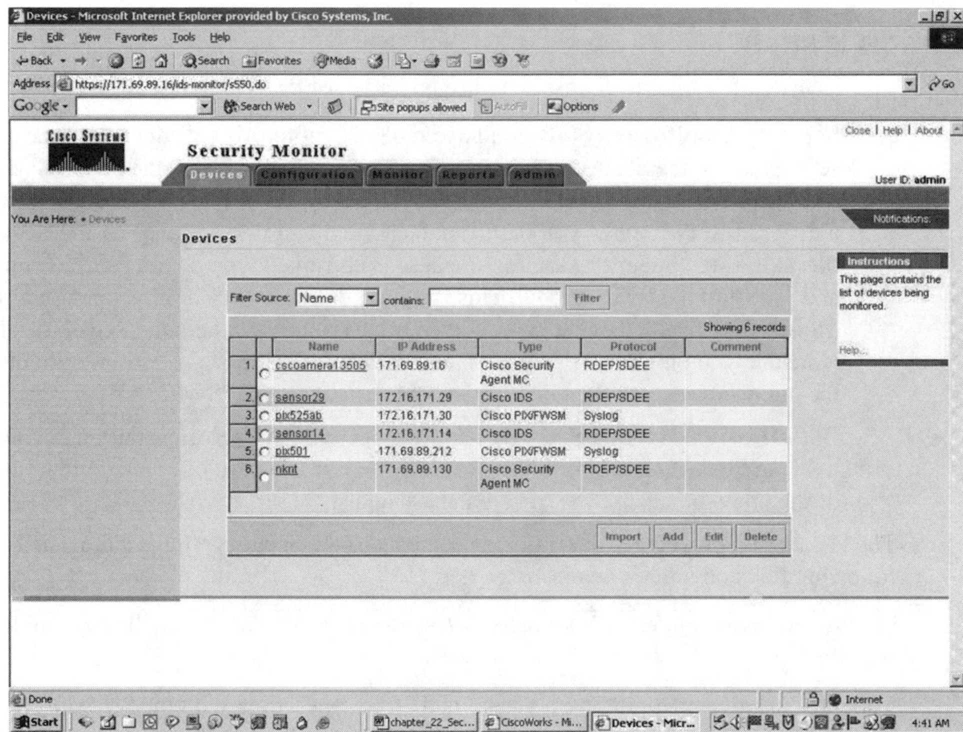

Following is the list of tabs available for different purposes in the Security Monitor GUI:

- **Devices**—Add, import, and edit devices.
- **Configuration**—Configure Event Rules. This tab is new to Security Monitor 2.0. The Event Rule configuration is performed under the **Admin** tab on the version earlier than 2.0.
- **Monitor**—Launch Event Viewer, and determine device status.
- **Reports**—Generate, schedule, and view reports.
- **Admin**—Configure database rules, system configuration, and event viewer preferences.

There might be several reasons for being unable to launch the Security Monitor or the CiscoWorks Common Services in general. The sections that follow explain some of these reasons.

DNS Issues

If you cannot launch CiscoWorks Common Services or the Security Monitor with the IP address, try the following:

- Enter the IP Address of the Security Monitor manually on the browser, without using its cache (clear the browser cache).
- Try connecting to the Security Monitor from a browser in a different machine and see if that helps.

  If both fail, add the Security Monitor server's hostname to the **hosts** file on your PC with the IP address, and browse to the Security Monitor via its hostname: http://hostname:1741

Issues with Enabling SSL

When SSL is enabled for CiscoWorks Common Services, its certificate must be selected for the Security Monitor. Otherwise you will get a Java error when launching the event viewer and the **untrusted server cert chain** error message will be displayed. A certificate is created when SSL is turned on in CiscoWorks Common Services. Since the Event Viewer uses the Java plug-in provided by the Cisco Works Common Services server, the Security Monitor server needs knowledge of this certificate before the Event viewer applet is launched.

Work through the following steps to enable SSL:

Step 1 Go to **Server Configuration > Administration > Security Management > Enable/Disable SSL.**

Step 2 In the new page, fill out the appropriate certificate information before clicking **Submit**. This certificate information may be presented to you when the Event Viewer Applet is launched.

Step 3 **Go to VPN and Security Management Solution > Administration > Configuration > Certificate**.

Step 4 In the next window, choose **Common Services Certificate** and click **Finish**.

Step 5 Restart the CiscoWorks Common Services Daemon Manager service.

NOTE If you are stopping and starting the daemon manager from the Process Management folder of the CiscoWorks Common Services GUI fails, you can perform this task from the service control applet or by using the **net stop crmdmgtd** and **net start crmdmgtd** commands in a command prompt window.

When you try to login for the first time, CiscoWorks Common Services shows a security alert for the CA root certificate. If this happens , view the certificate and install it before proceeding. If this warning does not appear, it probably means that you have already installed the certificate. You can proceed without installing the certificate by clicking **Yes**. There are no negative affects to this acceptance; however the warning message may be displayed again.

Getting **Internal Server Error** While Opening Security Monitor

If you receive an **Internal Server Error** message, first be sure that you have enough space on the drive where you have installed Security Monitor. For example, if VMS is installed at **E:\PROGRA~1\CSCOpx**, then you must have enough space on the **E:** drive.

MDCSupport Zip file does not show how much disk space is available for drive **E:**. However, **SysEventLog.evt** will contain messages that E:\ is at or near capacity. On the **IDS_Receiver.log**, you might see the following message:

```
Error writing Audit Log Msg: Security Msg INSERTER ERROR: SybaseESql::commit:
Disk full 'Fatal error: disk full E:\PROGRA~1\CSCOpx\MDC\Sybase\DB\IDS\idsmdc.log'
-- transaction rolled back
```

So, if you run into the disk space issue, to resolve the problem free up some disk space on drive E:\.

Security Monitor Takes a Long Time to Launch

The Security Monitor database is the file **install-dir\CSCOpx\MDC\Sybase\Db\IDS\idsmdc.db**. The **idsmdc.log** file in the same directory is used to keep track of database changes. It is important to maintain these files so that they do not become too large or consume all available disk space. Refer to the section entitled "Database Maintenance Issues" in this chapter for additional details on how to maintain the Database.

Page Cannot Be Found Error While Trying to Launch Security Monitor

You need to analyze the **SysEventlog.evt** file if you receive the "Page cannot be found" error message when trying to bring up the Security Monitor. You may receive multiple errors in the file (one caused by another).

An example of such a problem is that the CiscoWorks Common Services Tomcat **Servlet** Engine service failed to start due to the following error:

```
The service did not start due to a logon failure.
```

The probable cause of the problem is that Common Services is installed by user "X". Then, user "X" was either deleted from the computer, or more likely, his password was changed.

To resolve the issue, go into **Start > Settings > Control Panel > Administrative Tools > Services**. Then double-click on **CiscoWorks Common Services**, click on the **Log On** tab, click the **This Account** radio button, and browse to the user account. Then provide the password for that account. Next, stop and restart the services.

IDS/IPS MC Launches But Security Monitor Does Not

During the installation or upgrade, if the modification of the XML files that help to launch Security Monitor is corrupted, you might run into this problem: IDS/IPS MC may be working but there might be issues with the Security Monitor. The best way to determine the problem to analyze the installation log files. The file responsible for launching the Security Monitor is **ids-monitor.xml**. If the file is indeed corrupted, copy this file from another Security Monitor server that is working.

Security Monitor Behaves Strangely

If your Security Monitor behaves very strangely in terms of launching, reporting and so on, you need to look primarily at the Tomcat **stderr.log** file that contains stack traces from the Java code. You need to send these stack traces to Cisco Support, so that the development team can analyze the traces to find the root cause of the problem. The stack traces are found at **. . .\CSCOpx\MDC\tomcat\logs**

Licensing Issues

The license issue for Security Monitor is the same as for IDS/IPS MC. Hence, for details on licensing issues with Security Monitor, refer to the "Licensing Issues" section in Chapter 18.

Device Management Issues

Depending on the types of monitoring devices, you can populate the device tables of Security Monitor by importing the devices from IDS/IPS MC, or you can add them manually if you do not want to import them from IDS/IPS MC. It is important to understand that devices that are imported from the IDS/IPS MC cannot be edited by the Security Monitor. Also, if these devices are deleted from the IDS/IPS MC, they will not automatically be deleted from the Security Monitor. For a monitoring device that uses Syslog, you do not have to add the device in the device table. However, if you want to see the name of the device instead of the IP address on the Event Viewer or the reports, you need to add the device. In this section, we will look into the configuration and troubleshooting aspects of adding sensors to the Security Monitor.

Importing IDS Sensors from IDS/IPS MC

Work through the steps that follow to import an IDS Sensor from IDS/IPS MC to the Security Monitor:

Step 1 Click the **Import** button under the Device Table.

Step 2 Select the sensors you want to import from the MC.

Step 3 Click the **Import Sensors** button

Step 4 Now the Monitored Device table will show the imported sensors.

As mentioned before, monitored devices that are imported from the IDS/IPS MC are managed by the IDS/IPS MC. Their settings cannot be changed by the Security Monitor. There is a check box that is enabled by default in the IDS/IPS MC Add Device Page that will automatically add the device to the Security Monitor device table.

Adding Other Devices

Security Monitor can receive events from other hosts or devices such as PIX Firewall, IOS IPS, and Cisco Security Agents Management Console (CSA MC), and so on. The type of protocol used depends on the device type (IDS 3.x sensors use PostOffice, IDS 4.x uses RDEP, IPS 5.x uses SDEE, CSA MC uses RDEP, Router/PIX can use Syslog, and so on). The device table can contain different types of devices. Only sensor devices that are added to IDS/IPS MC can be imported; all other device types are added manually. Unlike IDS Sensor Import, sensors that are added manually may be deleted from the table.

Work through the steps that follow to add a device to the device table:

Step 1 Click the **Add** button under the Device table.

Step 2 Enter in the **IP Address** of your device.

Step 3 Select the device type.

Step 4 Click **Apply** when ready; you should see a new entry in the table.

Step 5 If the IOS device uses PostOffice, check the **Uses Postoffice Settings** check box and enter the appropriate PostOffice data; otherwise, if the IOS device logs syslog, Uses Postoffice should be left unchecked.

Step 6 The NAT address (if filled in) refers to the address of the device from the **Security Monitor Server's** perspective.

Follow these steps to configure the IOS device for logging:

Step 1 Use Telnet to access the IOS router.

Step 2 In configuration mode, enter the commands shown in Example 22-1.

Example 22-1 *Configuration for Forwarding Syslog to the Security Monitor*

```
c2600#
c2600#configure terminal
c2600(config)#logging on
c2600(config)#logging host 10.1.1.40
c2600(config)#exit
c2600#write memory
Building configuration...
[OK]
c2600#
```

Step 3 Save your configuration and exit the Telnet window.

IEV and Security Monitor Connect with Sensor

After importing or adding the sensor, go to **Monitor > Connections** to check the connection status. (Note that connection status is not displayed for devices that send events via Syslog.) Refer to Table 22-1 for connection status information and the reason for failure. If you see connection status other than "Connected" or "ConnectedTLS", then you know you have a problem with connectivity between the Security Monitor and the sensor. Use Table 22-1 as a reference to find the cause of the problem. For example, if your connection status shows "Indeterminate", as per Table 22-1, this means that the "IDS_Receiver process is not running". To resolve this issue, you might want to go to **Server Configuration > Administration > Process Management > Process Status** to check the status of the **IDS_Receiver** process on the VMS server. If the process has stopped, then restart it. If the process continues to stop automatically, then try the following:

- Check the **install-dir/CSCOpx/log/IDS_Receiver.log** file.
- Run an audit log report that shows the **IDS_Receiver** subsystem messages.

Depending on the log, you might analyze the issue further and resolve it. Work through the steps that follow as a general troubleshooting technique to isolate and fix the problem that occurs when connecting to a sensor using the IEV or Security Monitor:

Step 1 Ping to sensor's IP address fails.

If the ping to the sensor fails, check the network configuration. Run the **setup** command on the sensor to ensure that the sensor's IP address and gateway are set correctly. Also be sure that no router, switch or firewall is configured to interface with the sensor that may be blocking the traffic. If the network configuration is correct, verify that the sensor does not have an IP address conflict with another host on the network. Linux automatically prevents the command-and-control Ethernet port from activating if it detects an address conflict with another host. To check this, run the **show interfaces** command from the CLI. The output should say **command-control interface is up**. If the output says **command-control interface is down**, then there is a hardware issue, a cabling issue, or an IP address conflict.

Step 2 Ping succeeds but SSH fails to connect or the connection is refused.

In IDS 4.x, if ping succeeds but SSH fails, be sure the sensor's access list is configured to accept the user's address. This will have to be done from the CLI (run **setup**). If the access list is correct, be sure the sensor's SSH, Telnet, or web server ports are open in the firewall. Unlike IDS version 4.x, in IPS version 5.x and above if the sensor's ACL does not permit the host you are pinging from, the ping will fail. When you run setup, be sure that you include the IP address of the management station from where you are pinging the sensor. Also, be sure that the certificate Security Monitor you are using is valid (see Chapter 18 under the section entitled "Verifying If the IDS/IPS MC (Apache) Certificate Is Valid"). If the certificate is not valid, follow the procedure "Regenerating IDS/IPS MC (Apache) Certificate" as explained in Chapter 18.

Step 3 Sensor can be accessed via SSH but not via the Web browser.

If the sensor can be accessed through SSH, verify that you are accessing the correct port on the sensor (that is, http rather than https). This can be verified by logging into the CLI and displaying settings for the web server service. To verify the https connection, you can try to access Event Server directly through a Web browser through the following URL: **http(s)://<sensor's IP address>/cgi-bin/event-server**

Step 4 Access to the port and IP is right, but I am still being refused.

If you are correctly addressing the sensor, verify that the web server is still running by using the **show version** CLI command. If the web server is no longer running, look for a bug on Cisco.com for the specific version you are running. If an upgrade is available for the sensor, proceed with the upgrade. If the issue persists, run **show tech-support** and get the output file to Cisco Support. Restart the sensor.

Step 5 The web server process is running, but I am still unable to connect.

If the CLI indicates that the web server is still running, verify that the firewall has an open port for the sensor. Be sure that the firewall device between the port and the server allows SSL (TCP/443) and is open. If there is an NAT device, be sure to use the translated Sensor IP.

Step 6 I can connect and am getting a login prompt but fail on authentication.

Check to see if logins to the account have been disabled due to the failed login limit being reached. The sensor provides the configuration option to limit the number of consecutive failed login attempts. Once this limit is reached, the account becomes locked until it is administratively unlocked. This option is disabled by default. It can be enabled in the CLI. To determine if a failed login attempt limit is enabled, enter the authentication service configuration mode and **show settings**. If the **attemptLimit** is greater than zero, the failed login attempt limit is set to this value. Set the **attemptLimit** value to zero to disable this account locking feature. This feature is required to satisfy the government's Common Criteria for security devices. To check the failed login count, log into the service account, if possible. From the service account shell, run the command **pam_tally**. The output shows the number of failed login attempts for each account. To reset the count, run **pam_tally --reset**. This command resets the failed login counts.

Step 7 If directly accessing the event server or IDM succeeds, Security Monitor should be able to connect to the sensor. If it is unable to do so, delete the sensor and re-add.

Step 8 If removing and reading does not resolve the connectivity problem, then reboot the server, add/remove the sensor.

Step 9 If the problem persists, compact the database in the database issues section.

Step 10 If everything else fails, upgrade to the latest patch/version of Security Monitor to avoid any bug. As a last resort you may need to uninstall and reinstall the software.

Notification Issues

Notifications are performed by two daemons—**IDS_Analyzer** (for Event Rules) or **IDS_DbAdminAnalyzer** (for Database Rules) and **IDS_Notifier**. The Analyzer is the component that watches the incoming event, or database events, and triggers the notification. The Notifier is the component that builds and sends the notification. The notification can be sent to the console or by e-mail. If both of the Analyzer and Notifier daemons are running, then you need to determine if the Event Rules are indeed supposed to be triggered. Review the filter criteria of the event or database rules, and make necessary changes. To debug this issue further, collect the following information:

- Run "Subsystem Report" from the "Audit Log" report group and make the following choices: IDS_Analyzer (if problem is with event-related issues); IDS_DbAdminAnalyzer (if database related issues); and IDS_Notifier for the sub-system on the filter settings page of the report wizard. Also set the Time/Date filtering to cover the approximate time that you first noticed the problem.
- Look for messages in the corresponding log files of the daemons (for example, **IDS_Analyzer.log** and **IDS_Notifier.log** for events rules).

A more detailed case study on e-mail notification is analyzed in the "Case Studies" section of this chapter.

Event Viewer Issues

Event Viewer is used to view the events in almost real time. This window allows you to retrieve the events from the database based on the criteria you define.

Launching the Event Viewer

Follow these steps to launch the Event Viewer from the Security Monitor:

Step 1 Click the **Monitor** tab and select the **Event Viewer** option.

Step 2 Select the **Filter** options.

Step 3 Click the **Launch Event Viewer** button as shown in Figure 22-3.

Step 4 After loading the applet and the data, the Event Viewer is displayed. This page represents the filter used to screen data that is displayed in the Event Viewer.

Figure 22-3 *Launch Event Viewer Screen for Security Monitor*

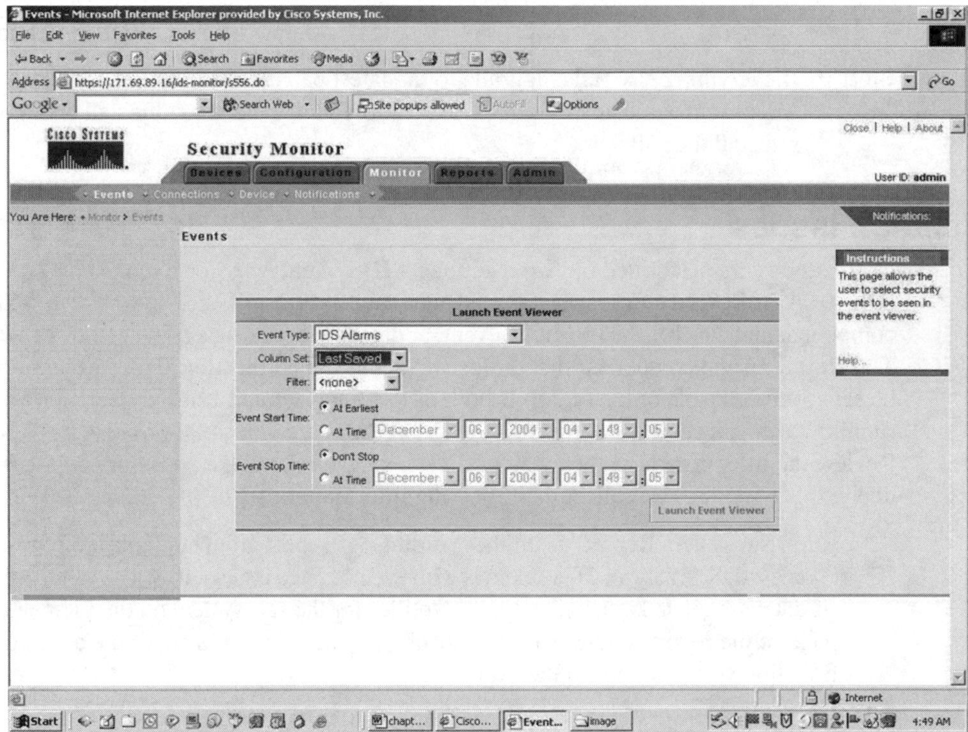

Event Viewer has the following two limitations:

- A user-configurable limitation on the maximum number of events to be shown in a grid (up to 32 million) with a default of 100,000. If there are more events than the limit, the oldest events are shown (this is done to allow the oldest data to be deleted from the grid).
- A hard-coded limitation exists on the number of rows to be displayed. This limitation depends on what data is being viewed (generally about 250000 rows).

Using the Event Viewer

Column headers and cell data depend on the type of data being displayed. You can drag columns and expand and collapse columns on the Event Viewer within the limitations of the user's Event Viewer preferences. When you drag a column or click a table of contents item, the system will do a round trip; this takes a variable amount of time (depending on the number of records in the database and the number of events being displayed). The column settings are reset by the launching of the Event Viewer in the version earlier than 2.0, but with version 2.0 and above, the settings are retained.

Generating Events for Test

For testing, events may be generated several ways. A simple form of event generation process is to generate the large Internet Control Message Protocol (ICMP) packet to a host that belongs to a VLAN where the sniffing port of the Sensor is connected. To generate a Large ICMP event, open a command prompt on the server and type: **C:\> ping 10.1.1.2 –t –l 5000**

Large ICMP events show up when the Event Viewer is refreshed.

NOTE You need to ensure that the Large ICMP event is configured with a severity high enough to be sent. You can verify this either by CLI on the sensor or on the IDS/IPS MC. The signature severity setting must be greater than the minimum level configured to be sent in the IDS/IPS MC.

What you see in the Event Viewer depends on several factors.

- The launch filter
- The level of expansion
- Timing
- The viewing preferences set for the user

You can expand columns and refresh events to update the view. One important point to note is that the event viewer Table of Contents is not used for navigation. New events are not necessarily displayed immediately.

Troubleshooting Steps

This section analyzes the issues that you might experience with the Security Monitor Event Viewer.

Cannot Load Security Event Viewer

If the Security Monitor Event viewer is not coming up, look at the **IDS_EvsServer.log** file. You will see a message such as: **ERROR: NrMainWidget::createDaemonMgrListener, daemon manager reported errors.** This is usually caused by a problem with the Java plug-in. Follow these steps:

Step 1 Verify that you are running a supported Web browser, and have the proper cookies, Javascript, or that Java is enabled, and verify that the client operating system is supported.

Step 2 Remove older versions of Java. If this does not work, remove all versions of Java, and CiscoWorks Common Services will prompt you to download the version that it is compatible with.

Step 3 Uninstall all "damaged" objects as reported in the: **Tools > Internet Options > General Tab > Settings > View Objects** panel.

Step 4 Delete all the cookies, temporary Internet files, history, and so on from Internet Explorer (**Tools > Internet Options > General Tab > Delete Files**).

Step 5 Shut down all open Web browsers.

Step 6 Delete the Java jar cache (**Start > Settings > Control Panel > Java Plug-In**, click on the **Cache** tab and press the **Clear** button).

Step 7 Be sure the proper Java plug-in is used. **Start > Settings > Control Panel > Java Plug-In**, click on the **Advanced** tab and be sure use Java plug-in default is selected.

Step 8 Add the Security Monitor server's hostname to the hosts file with the IP address, and browse to the Security Monitor server via its hostname http://hostname:1741.

No Events on Event Viewer from IDS/IPS Sensor Are Visible

If the Event Viewer on the Security Monitor does not show any events, then the problem can be either on the sensor or on the Security Monitor or even on both. Work through the steps that follow to troubleshoot the issue:

Step 1 Verify that Security Monitor shows the IDS/IPS Sensor connection status as **Connected** or **ConnectedTLS**.

Step 2 Be sure that the sensor is sending the events to the Security Monitor (see the "Events Issues" section in Chapter 14, "Troubleshooting IDS/IPS Sensor").

Step 3 Be sure to choose the proper filter when you bring up the Event Viewer. Otherwise, you may be blocking the alerts from being shown.

Step 4 By default, Medium is the lowest severity level for alerts sent from a sensor to Security Monitor. This means that only Medium and High severity alerts are shown in the Event Viewer. So, if the sensor is not generating and sending any Medium or High Severity events, then Security Monitor will not see anything. This could be because none of the signatures are configured to report High or Medium severity. Turn signatures 2000 and 2004 to High severity and see if they make it to Security Monitor. If you want to see lower severity events, in Security

Monitor, you can click the **Devices** tab. Then click the **radio box** next to the sensor name and click **Edit.** In this new window, there will be a drop-down box entitled **Minimum event level.** Set this to the appropriate value.

NOTE When the sensor is configured to generate events for lower severity and the Security Monitor is configured to pull lower severity events, the number of events sent to the VMS server increases dramatically. This could cause database issues if you do not perform regular database maintenance.

No Syslog Events from PIX Firewall Or IOS Router in Security Monitor Event Viewer Are Visible

Problems with being unable to see events on the Security Monitor Event Viewer are similar to those discussed in the previous section on the IDS sensor's events issues. If you cannot see any events on the Security Monitor Event Viewer from the PIX firewall or IOS router, the problem might be either on the Monitoring device or on the Security Monitor itself. Work through the steps that follow to troubleshoot this issue:

Step 1 Ensure that the PIX or IOS router is set up correctly to send syslog messages to Security Monitor (see Example 22-1 for syslog configuration on the IOS router).

Step 2 On Security Monitor go to **Admin > System Configuration > SYSLOG Settings** to check that the setting matches the UDP port number that the device uses. You do not need to check the **Forward Syslog Messages** box unless you want to forward the events to another syslog server.

Step 3 To ensure that the device name appears in the Event Viewer, add the device into Security Monitor from the **Devices** tab. When you start the Event Viewer, ensure that the **Event Type** is set to one of the syslog types. The PIX Security Summary should show you all syslog data received. To access the PIX Security Summary, in Security Monitor go to the tab Monitor, and select **Events** (the Event Viewer can be launched from there). Before launching the Event Viewer, select **PIX Security Summaries** in the drop-down menu for the Event Type field.

Step 4 Ensure that the **CWCS syslog** service on the VMS server has started correctly. If this service fails to start correctly, check the size of the ***install-dir*\Program Files\CSCOpx\log\syslog.log** file. If this file is quite large, clear the file or move it to an alternate location, and then restart the service.

Report Generation Issues

You can generate a static report based on different criteria and send out the report as e-mail in different formats. More details about generating and managing reports can be found at the following location:

http://www.cisco.com/univercd/cc/td/doc/product/rtrmgmt/cw2000/mon_sec/secmon20/ug/ch06.htm

If you find any issues with reporting, analyze the log file **<cw-install>\log\IDS_ReportScheduler.log.** This section examines the two primary problems that can occur with report generation:

- Report generation fails
- Report fails to complete

Report Generation Fails

If report generation fails, analyze the log **IDS_ReportScheduler.log** file. Work through the following steps to troubleshoot report generation failure issues:

Step 1 Be sure that the **IDS_ReportScheduler** process is running. Restart the process and re-run the report. If the process keeps dying and report generation keeps failing, apply the latest patch from the Cisco.com Web site.

Step 2 If the **IDS_ReportScheduler** is running but you are still having issues with report generation, the problem might be with the **TEMP** directory. Find the location of the temp directory by going to **Start > Run**, then type **cmd**, and press **Enter**. Type **Set** and press **Enter**. You will see a list of all the variables in use, and one of them will be the **TEMP** variable which points to the temp folder. Another quick way to find the path to the **TEMP** directory is to type **%TEMP%** in the command prompt. The report is temporarily created in the **TEMP** directory.

Step 3 Be sure the **TEMP** directory is not full. If it's full, then go to **Start > Run** > type **%TEMP%**. This will take you to the **TEMP** directory. Delete all the files in that directory and re-run the report.

Step 4 If the system fails to allow access to the temporary (TEMP) directory that is used during the report generation process, you will see the messages similar to those shown in Example 22-2.

Example 22-2 *Error Message in IDS_ReportScheduler.log*

```
Variable Query: "SELECT  COUNT(*) FROM tmpTableIdsTopSrcDestPairsAlarm"
getQueryVariableValue: var value "1729811"
Variable Query: "SELECT  COUNT(*) FROM tmpTableIdsTopSrcDestPairsAlarm WHERE
summary_count > '0'"
getQueryVariableValue: var value "0"
Variable Query: "SELECT  SUM(summary_count) FROM tmpTableIdsTopSrcDestPairsAlarm"
getQueryVariableValue: var value "0"
File error: The system cannot find the path specified
```

Example 22-2 *Error Message in IDS_ReportScheduler.log (Continued)*

```
File error: The system cannot find the path specified
getTimeSqlCondition: result is (event_time >= '1047136363531000000')
SqlResultTable.setResults: converting direct to XML
ResultSet err: null
java.lang.NullPointerException
```

Step 5 If you have restrictive permissions on the directory in which the **TEMP** files are created, the report generation will fail. So, be sure to provide the **Read/Write** permission to the **TEMP** directory for the user account that is used to run the CiscoWorks Common Services.

If the Security Monitor does not fail immediately but hangs instead, then follow the directions in the next section.

Report Fails to Complete

If you have a huge database full of events, report generation may take hours, as the Security Monitor may take hours to query and pull the events from the database. If so, the report generation process may seem to be hung. If you analyze the file **<cw-install>\log\IDS_ReportScheduler.log,** you may see messages similar to those shown in Example 22-3.

Example 22-3 *Error When Report Does not Completes*

```
!SqlResultTable.setResults: converting direct to XML
Cannot access a pooled DB connection java.lang.Exception: Cannot access a pooled DB
connection
query: DECLARE LOCAL TEMPORARY TABLE tmpTableIdsSrcDestPairsAlarm (severity tinyint
NULL, attacker_locality VARCHAR(17) NULL, victim_locality VARCHAR(17) NULL, sig_id
unsigned int NULL, sub_sig_id unsigned int NULL, event_time unsigned bigint NULL,
attacker_address unsigned int NULL, victim_address unsigned int NULL,
orig_app_ip_addr unsigned int NULL, summary_count unsigned int NULL) ON COMMIT
PRESERVE ROWS
query: INSERT INTO tmpTableIdsSrcDestPairsAlarm SELECT severity, attacker_locality,
victim_locality, sig_id, sub_sig_id, event_time, attacker_address, victim_address,
orig_app_ip_addr, summary_count FROM Correlated_Alerts WHERE ((1 & flags)  != 1)
SqlResultTable.setResults: converting direct to XML
SqlResultTable.setResults: done.
! There are the same log entries for another report being generated but then the entries
! stop.
SqlResultTable.setResults: converting direct to XML IDS_ReportScheduler rx
broadcast msg: jrm;IDS_Backup;3;0 IDS_ReportScheduler rx broadcast msg:
jrm;IDS_DbAdminAnalyzer;3;0 IDS_ReportScheduler rx broadcast msg:
jrm;IDS_DeployDaemon;3;0
! It looks like while it was converting some data into the finished XML format
!the process was stopped, possible by the daemon manager.
!From IDS_DbAdminAnalyzer.log file contents, this Security Monitor has almost
!2 million alarms. When the number of records approaches that level reports
!can take a long time to run to completion.
DbAdminAnalyzerApp.execute: done testing rules. Wed Mar 26 19:23:52 EST 2003
getDatabaseFileSize: result is 1907507200
getHddFreeSpace: result is 1,978,601,472
getTableRecordCount: ALERT_TABLE has 42427 records
getTableRecordCount: SECURITY_MSGS has 1830148 records
```

The solution to this problem is to re-adjust the default pruning value so that the alarms are deleted at a lower value (see the "Database Maintenance Issues" section, which is discussed next in this chapter).

Database Maintenance Issues

The Security Monitor receives data from different devices and stores the data in records in database tables for viewing and creating reports. The Security Monitor is designed to capture and store data flowing into its receiver process at high rates (on the order of 50 IDS/IPS events per second) for a sustained period or at even higher rates (up to 500 IDS/IPS events per second) for a short burst period of up to five minutes. Storing large amounts of data has its drawbacks, however, as both disk space requirements and query time increase with the amount of data stored.

Care must be taken to ensure that the Security Monitor's database environment is maintained. Devices sending information to the Security Monitor must be configured properly so that they do not send unwanted messages at the Security Monitor receiver and overload it with data. Be aware of these requirements and monitor the following:

- Amount of data (number of records) stored in the tables.
- Amount of space left on the database disk.
- Rate at which data is flowing into the Security Monitor's receiver.

The Security Monitor comes with several tools to help you keep the database size manageable. In particular, three default database rules are installed with the Security Monitor for maintaining the size of three database tables. These default rules are configured to:

- Run when the size of a specific table exceeds a set level (for example, 2,000,000 syslog alarms).
- Prune table data out of the database.
- Write the pruned records data out to archive files.

The sections that follow explain how to use the tools efficiently to maintain the database for the healthy operation of IDS/IPS MC and Security Monitor.

Proactive Measures Immediately After Installing the Security Monitor

It is extremely important to use the following proactive measures to avoid issues with the database:

- Redirect archive files away from the database disk
- Redirect backup files away from the database disk
- Create a new database rule

Redirect Archive Files Away from the Database Disk

When the database is pruned, by default it creates an archive of the pruned data in a flat file that is stored in **~\CSCOpx\MDC\secmon\AlertPruneData**. Monitor this directory very closely, because it can grow rapidly. Therefore, we recommend that you change the pruning directory to a network share, so that you do not have to worry about maintaining this directory. To change the directory, go to **Admin -> System Configuration -> Prune Archive Location** in Security Monitor version 2.0.

If you are running a version of Security Monitor that is earlier than 2.0, work through the steps that follow to redirect the archive files away from the database disk:

Step 1 Click the **Admin** tab and select **Database Rules** from the sub-area bar; the Database Rules table displays.

Step 2 Select the **Default Pruning** rule and click **Edit.**

Step 3 Click **Next** to go to the **Choose the Actions** page.

Step 4 The archive directory is specified in the **Arguments** list under **Execute a Script**. After installation, the argument contents look something like this: **-wc:\PROGRA~1\CSCOpx\MDC\Sybase\DB\IDS\AlertPruneData** This string specifies the root directory location where the archived files are stored. To redirect the archive files to another location (for example, d:\ArchiveData), change the argument string to this**:-wd:\ArchiveData**. Note that after installation, the root directory always points to the same disk where the database files are located. You must redirect the files away from this disk. You can specify a mounted network drive to redirect the archive files to a different computer.

Step 5 Click **Finish**.

Step 6 Repeat steps 1-5 for the other two rules (Default Syslog Pruning and Default Audit Log Pruning).

Redirect Backup Files Away from the Database Disk

A backup copy of the Sybase database is on the installation disk by default. Regularly scheduled backups can quickly consume a large amount of disk space, adversely affecting the performance of the installed management and monitoring centers. To prevent this problem, move the default location of the backups to a separate local disk or to a mounted network drive. Follow these steps for redirecting backup files away from the Database Disk:

Step 1 From the CiscoWorks Server Desktop, select **VPN/Security Management Solution > Administration > Common Services > Preferences** and the Administrative preferences page displays.

Step 2 Type a new path in the Backup Directory field. You should point the path to another local disk or to a mounted network drive.

Step 3 Click **Apply** and a confirmation dialog displays.

Step 4 Click **Yes** to confirm the change, and then click **OK** to return to the Administrative Preferences page.

Create a New Database Rule

In Security Monitor versions earlier than 2.0, when you delete data from the Event Viewer in Security Monitor, the records are marked for deletion. To remove these records from the database, create a new Database Rule that executes once daily to delete the records that are marked for deletion. Follow these steps to create a new database rule:

Step 1 Click the **Admin** tab and select the **Database Rules** sub-area bar item.

Step 2 Click the **Add** button.

Step 3 Name the rule, add a description, and check **Daily Beginning;** then enter the time that you want the rule to take effect and click **Next.**

Step 4 On the Choose the Actions page, check **Execute a Script**, select **PruneMarkedForDeletion.pl** from the drop-down list, and click **Finish**.

Reactive Measures During Run Time

At run time, you must periodically monitor the system for the following four items:

Flow Rates of Events and Syslog Messages

The **receiver** process on Security Monitor is responsible for receiving the events from various devices. You must not exceed the limit of the **receiver** capacity. Flow rates for the various devices are measured continually by the Security Monitor and are available for viewing in the **24 Hour Metrics** report. To run the **24 Hour Metrics** report, follow these steps:

Step 1 Click the **Reports** tab and select **Generate** from the sub-area bar.

Step 2 Select **IDS/IPS Alarms** from the **Report Group** drop-down box.

Step 3 Click to the **second page**, choose the **24 Hour Metrics** report radio button, and click **Select**.

Step 4 Click **Finish** to run the report immediately.

Step 5 After the notification displays, click **OK** and select **IDS/IPS Alarms** from the **Report Group** drop-down box. The report displays in the list (you may need to refresh the page a few times).

Step 6 To see the report, select it from the list and click **View**. The **24 Hour Metrics** report lists two measurements for each type of event:

- — The number that was received in the last 15-minute period
- — A running total

Each line indicates a five-minute period, and each row contains the timestamp for the time at which the measurement was logged. Pay particular attention to any measurement that is out of spec. (Security Monitor documentation specifies that it can handle a sustained rate of less than 50 IDS/IPS events per second—45,000 in 15 minutes. Syslog events are not specified in the documentation, but a good rule of thumb is that the system performance will start to suffer when syslog events approach 25 messages per second—or about 22500 messages in 15 minutes). If you find measurements out of spec, you should determine the cause and make necessary changes on the configuration of the monitoring devices, so that the events or the syslog messages are reduced.

Monitoring the Size of Log Files

Log files are used by the Security Monitor for error messages and state information, and for temporary data storage. Because log files reside on the same disk as the database, it is necessary to monitor their size and periodically move them off the system or delete them to ensure that the database has enough space to operate. There are two types of log files: CMF log files and IDS/IPS log files. There is no GUI method available for monitoring IDS/IPS log file sizes, so users need to monitor their sizes by other means. IDS/IPS log files are located in the ~CSCOpx/log directory and all begin with the characters "IDS_". Any IDS/IPS log file larger than 50,000 bytes should be deleted or moved away from the database disk.

You can monitor the size of CMF log files in the GUI by following these steps:

- Select the **Server Configuration** drawer from the CiscoWorks browser.
- Open the **Administration folder** and select **Log File Status.**

This page displays a list of the CMF log files and their sizes, and the **File System Utilization** for the database disk. The sizes of any of the log files that have grown larger than their recommended maximum size are listed in the table in red. These files may need to be deleted or moved to another computer. Both CMF and IDS/IPS log files are in the **~CSCOpx/log** directory. Follow these steps to move or delete files from this directory:

Step 1 Close all browser windows that are accessing CiscoWorks.

Step 2 Stop the **CiscoWorks Daemon Manager** service on the Security.

Monitor the server (either through the Windows Service panel or by using **net stop** from the command line). This will stop several associated processes and may take a few minutes.

Step 3 If you are deleting or moving **Syslog.log**, you must also stop the **CWCS syslog** service.

Step 4 Copy the files you want to move to another drive. (You may specify a mapped network drive to move them to another computer.)

Step 5 Delete the log files.

Step 6 If you stopped it, restart the **CWCS syslog** service. (You can use the services panel or "net start" from the command line.)

Step 7 Restart the **CiscoWorks Daemon Manager**. It might take a few minutes.

Monitoring Database File Size

You can monitor the size of the database by monitoring the disk utilization from the **Server Configuration > Administration > Log File Status** page. The **File System Utilization** column indicates the percentage of the database disk that is currently being used. The actual percentage of the disk that can be used without causing system degradation depends on the available resources. As a good rule of thumb, this number should not exceed 80 percent because the database will need extra space during operation to maintain its transaction log. The Security Monitor database is stored in two files in the **~CSCOpx\MDC\Sybase\Db\IDS** subdirectory: **idsmdc.db** and **idsmdc.log**. You can find out the size of the database by analyzing the **IDS_DbAdminAnalyzer.log** as shown in Example 22-4.

Example 22-4 *Determining Database Size*

```
*-- DatabaseRule -----------------------
ID:             2
Name:           Default Syslog Pruning
Desc:           Default pruning for syslog table.
Available:      0
Used:           0
IDS Count:      0
Syslog count:   2000000
Total count:    0
Exec Daily At:  2004-08-08 07:34:00.0
Is Exec Daily:  false
-----------------------------------------
isSyslogRecordCountTrigger: rule is asserted
insertNotification: inserted Notification record ID 199
DbAdminAnalyzerApp.execute: done testing rules. Wed Mar 26 19:23:52 EST 2005
! The following two lines show the database and disk space used
getDatabaseFileSize: result is 1907507200
getHddFreeSpace: result is 1,978,601,472
getTableRecordCount: ALERT_TABLE has 42427 records
getTableRecordCount: SECURITY_MSGS has 1830148 records
```

To maintain the database, use the pruning techniques that are discussed in the following section.

Pruning

Under normal operation, when events are flowing into the Security Monitor and the default database rules are in place, the system will prune excess data (the oldest data) automatically. The time at which this occurs depends upon the number of events that have been received and the sizes of the syslog, IDS/IPS events, and audit log tables. Whenever the pruning utility runs, it logs a message to the audit log table at the start of the process and again when it is completed. The user should check the audit log for these pruning messages to be sure that data is being pruned from the database as expected. In particular, if the pruning process is started but not completed, users should be aware of a problem. Starting from Security Monitor 2.0, the database pruning is handled automatically by a database pruning daemon. By default, it will prune the database when the volume reaches 2,000,000 events. This default value can be changed by logging into Security Monitor and going to **Admin > Data Management > Database > Pruning Configuration**.

To troubleshoot issues pertaining to pruning, follow these steps to run the Pruning subsystem report:

Step 1 Click the **Reports** tab and select **Generate** from the sub-area bar.

Step 2 Select **Audit Log** from the Report Group box.

Step 3 Choose the **Subsystem** report and click **Select**.

Step 4 Click **Select All** next to Event Severity, choose **IDS_Database Prune** from the Subsystem selection box, and click **Next**.

Step 5 Click **Finish** on the next page to run the report immediately.

Step 6 Select **Audit Log** from the **Report Group** and the report displays in the list (you may need to refresh the page a few times).

Step 7 Select the report and click **View**.

The pruning report lists a message, including a time stamp for each time the pruning utility started and was completed. If the user believes that the database should have been pruned but the process did not run, here are a few things to check:

- **Is the IDS_DbAdminAnalyzer process running?**—**IDS_DbAdminAnalyzer** process determines that the trigger condition has been met. If it is not running, the rule will not take effect. (You can stop and restart processes from the Server Configuration drawer, Process Management folder.)
- **Is the IDS_Notifier process running?**—The **IDS_Notifier** runs the specified script which attempts to run the pruning utility; if it is not running the script will not be executed. (You can stop and restart processes from the Server Configuration drawer, Process Management folder.)
- **Are any other instances of pruning running?**—Only one instance of the pruning utility can run at a time, so if someone used the utility from the command line to perform another task (for example, archiving data) the rule would attempt to take effect but the pruning would not run. Be sure that no other instances of the pruning utility are running.

Pruning trims records from tables in the DB. It does nothing, however, to the actual DB files, which are managed by the DB server. The Sybase DB, used by IDS/IPS MC/SecMon, does not give back space to the file system when table records are deleted; instead it keeps them as available space within the current DB file. Hence the DB file will not shrink in size even though data was purged from it. The sizes of the database files might be reduced by running the dbcompact utility, which will shrink the database by the amount of free space created when records were deleted. Database files themselves are never pruned.

The trick is to set up the DB record pruning trigger points as desired by the customer. When those trigger points are reached, the record counts in the DB will essentially remain at those counts, as pruning deletes older records to make room for new ones. The size of the DB should not grow by much past this point. Once at that point, you can reset the file management DB size limit value to that based on your actual steady-state size. If the DB grows to this new limit, then the dbcompact utility can be run again.

It is important to note that the pruning, by going to **IDS/IPS MC > admin > data mgmt > databases > pruning configuration,** affects the record counts of tables in the DB, not the size of the DB file. The other screen, **file management**, is used so that you can be alerted to files that are growing beyond a preset limit, which might require you to act.

DB Compact

If the database grows too large, you must run **dbcompact** to reduce the size of the dataset. The program is run by typing **IDSdbcompact**. You can find instructions for running the utility at: http://www.cisco.com/univercd/cc/td/doc/product/rtrmgmt/cw2000/mon_sec/secmon12/ug/ch07.htm#1824

Database Rules

Starting from Security Monitor version 2.0, database rules are now only used to set up e-mail notifications. With 2.0 and subsequent releases, the Security Monitor's pruning algorithm is no longer triggered by a database rule. Pruning (and archiving) now runs continuously once the pruning threshold has been reached. When archiving is enabled, event data is written to the archive files and pruned from the database at the same rate and at the same time that it is being received.

Case Study

Security Monitor has the flexibility to create your own custom script and integrate that with the Security Monitor. This section examines one of those scripts for e-mail notification. The discussion of this case study is based on the following Cisco document:

http://www.cisco.com/en/US/products/sw/secursw/ps2113/products_configuration_example09186a00801fc770.shtml#foursensor

Security Monitor has the ability to send e-mail notifications when an Event Rule is triggered. The built-in variables that can be used within the e-mail notification for each event do not include things such as the Signature ID, the source and destination of the alert, and so forth. This document provides instructions for configuring Security Monitor to include these variables (and many more) within the e-mail notification message. Follow the procedure outlined in the next section to configure e-mail notifications.

Configuration Steps

Configuration steps for e-mail notification with additional details on the e-mail involve writing Perl scripts to retrieve additional information and defining event rules for defining the triggering criteria. Follow this procedure to accomplish this task:

Step 1 Copy and paste the script into a Notepad file from the link that follow, name it **emailalert.pl** (if you want, you can give it a different name), and save it into the **$BASE\CSCOpx\MDC\etc\ids\scripts** directory on the VPN/Security Management Solution (VMS) server.

http://www.cisco.com/en/US/products/sw/secursw/ps2113/products_configuration_example09186a00801fc770.shtml#foursensor

This allows you to select it later in the process when you define an event rule. The script contains comments explaining each portion and any required input.

Step 2 Edit the emailalert.pl file with Notepad to modify the **$EmailRcpt** variable (near the top of the file) to be the e-mail address of the person who is to receive the alerts.

Step 3 Define an Event Rule within Security Monitor to call a new Perl script. To do this, from the main Security Monitor page, select **Configuration > Event Rules** and add a new rule.

Step 4 On the Specify the Event Filter screen, add the filters that you want to trigger the e-mail alert (in the sample that follows an e-mail will be sent for any high severity alert) as shown in Figure 22-4.

Figure 22-4 *Event Filter Screen*

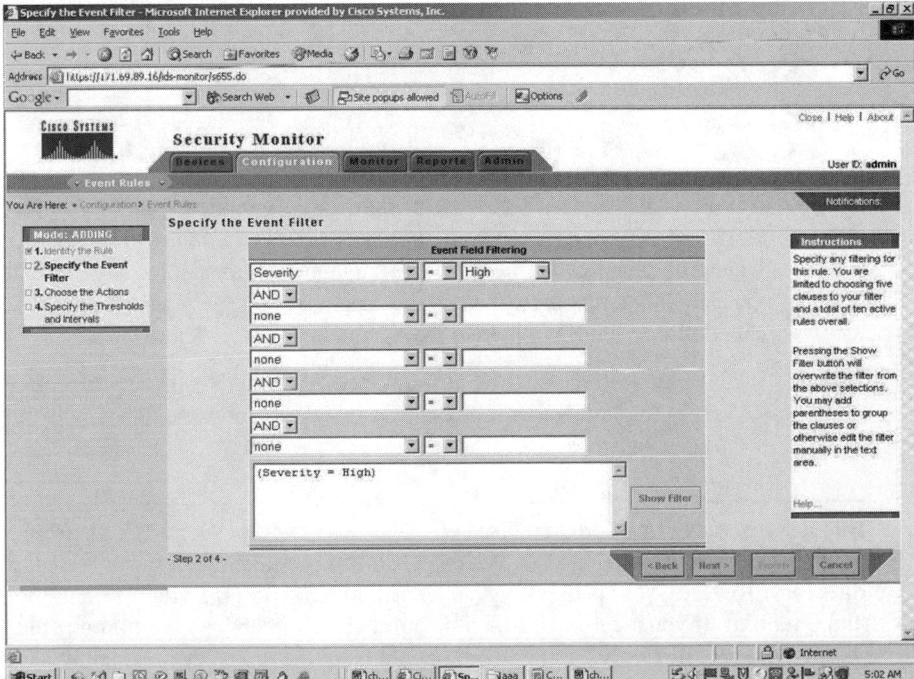

Step 5 On the Choose the Action screen, check the box to execute a script and select the script name from the drop-down box.

Step 6 In the Arguments section, enter "**${Query}**" as shown in Figure 22-5. Note that this must be entered exactly as it is here, including the double-quotes. It is also case sensitive.

Figure 22-5 *Event Filter on the Choose the Action Screen*

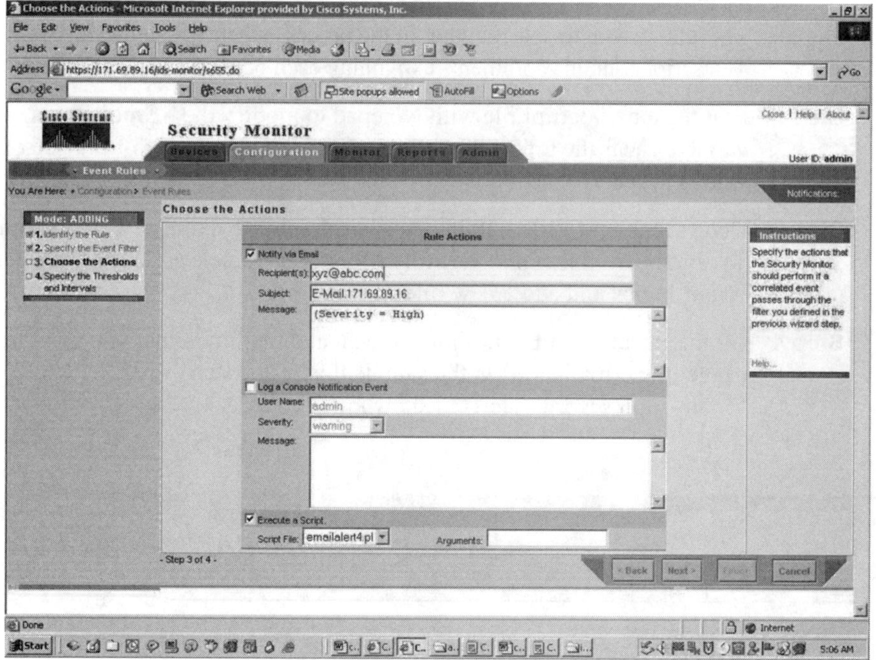

Step 7 At this point, when an alert, as defined in your event filters (in this example, a high severity alert) is received, the script called **emailalert.pl** is called with an argument of **${Query}** which contains additional information about the alert. The script parses out all the separate fields and uses a program called **blat** to send an e-mail to the e-mail recipient as defined in step 2.

Step 8 Install **blat** with the command: **blat -install <SMTP server address> <source email address>**. Once **blat** is installed, you are finished with the configuration steps.

NOTE Blat is a freeware e-mail program used on Windows systems to send e-mails from batch files or Perl scripts. It is included as part of the VMS installation in the $BASE\CSCOpx\bin directory. To verify your path settings, open a command prompt window on the VMS server and type **blat**. If you receive the **File not found** error, either copy the **blat.exe** file into the winnt\system32 directory, or find it and open it from the directory in which it is located.

Troubleshoot E-mail Notification

Follow these steps to troubleshoot the e-mail notification issue:

Step 1 Be sure your SMTP mail server is configured correctly. You can use the following commands in the command prompt of the Security Monitor server to verify that the SMTP server is working correctly:

```
telnet <mail server> 25
helo <your domain name>
mail from: notifier.<server name>@yourdomainname.com
rcpt to: <your email address>
data
(High Severity alert)
.
```

If your mail server is working correctly, you should receive this e-mail. It is important to note that you need to set your SMTP server to allow non-authenticated connections (i.e., no username/password has to be provided to submit e-mail).

Step 2 Next, check that blat is working properly by running the following from a command prompt: **blat <filename> -t <customer's email> -s "Test message"** where <filename> is the full path to any text file on the VMS system. If the user to whom the e-mail script is directed receives this file in the body of an e-mail, then you know that blat is working.

Step 3 If no e-mail is received after an alert is triggered, try running the Perl script from a command prompt window. This highlights any Perl or path type issues. To do this, open a command prompt and enter the commands shown in Example 22-5.

Example 22-5 *Commands Needed If No E-Mail Notification Is Received*

```
> cd Program Files/CSCOpx/MDC/etc/ids/scripts
> emailalert.pl ${Query}
```

Step 4 You might receive the following Sybase error:

```
C:\Program Files\CSCOpx\MDC\etc\ids\scripts>emailalert.pl ${Query}
ERROR: An Exception has occurred : SybaseESql::prepareSql: PREPARE
Syntax error
near 'Query'
```

This is because the **${Query}** parameter you are passing does not actually contain information, which is not the case when it is passed from the Security Monitor.

Step 5 Other than seeing this error, the script should run correctly and send an e-mail. Any alert parameters within the e-mail body will be blank. If you receive any Perl or path errors, they need to be fixed before an e-mail is sent.

Step 6 If blat is working correctly from command prompt, the next step is to verify whether the **IDS_Analyzer** daemon and **IDS_Notifier** daemons are running. If either one is not running, start these daemons.

Step 7 If you still have problems, generate an **Audit Log Report** for both **IDS_Analyzer** and **IDS_Notifier**. The **IDS_Analyzer** daemon will report when it submits a notification request, and the **IDS_Notifier** daemon will report success or failure messages when it receives the request. If any error messages display, correct the problem based on the message. Otherwise, go to the next step.

Step 8 If everything is working up to Step 6, then your event rule might not be getting triggered. This could be because of misconfiguration in the event rule. For example, if you have an event rule such as "SEVERITY = HIGH AND SEVERITY = MEDIUM", this rule will never trigger because a particular event will have only one severity and so it will not match any of the events. To get this working, either define one severity or change the "AND" to "OR." Then the rule will trigger on seeing both Medium and High Alarms.

Common Problems and Resolutions

This section looks into some commonly encountered problems that you might experience and how to resolve them.

1. I see a huge number of "ICMP Unreachable" syslog messages from PIX firewall in my Security Monitor. How can I resolve the problem?

   Answer: The problem can happen if the PIX is configured to send syslog messages to Security Monitor, but the syslog service on the VMS server that accepts these messages is down. The VMS server sends back an "ICMP Unreachable" message to the PIX. If IDS/IPS is enabled in the PIX firewall, the PIX receives the error message and sends another syslog message to Security Monitor to report the error. The two devices get stuck in an endless loop. So, to work around the problem, execute a **no logging message 400011** command so that the PIX does not report the ICMP error messages to Security Monitor. Then troubleshoot the Security Monitor server as follows:

   — Check for available disk space.

   — Ensure that the PIX sends the syslog messages to the same UDP port that Security Monitor uses to receive messages.

   — Be sure that the daemon responsible for syslog is running.

   — Be sure that the firewall or the Host IPS is on the Security Server, or that no Firewall in the network is blocking the UDP/514 traffic.

2. Can Sybase Database be installed and run on a separate computer for tasking like DB Backups?

Answer: Yes, you can install the Sybase database for IDS/SecMon on a different mounted drive. RAID disks are a better choice. Everything becomes I/O-bound in high volumes. You can schedule a prune and load the pruned data into another database (Sybase, Oracle, and so on). You can also perform a backup and load the IDS/IPS database into a Sybase installed on a different computer. This requires that you purchase an additional license for Sybase. The Security Monitor application uses the Sybase database shipped with VMS. There is no plugable replacement. To use the data on another database, you must replicate it to that database somehow. You can use the command line tools or any other means to do so.

3 How can I back up my alert database?

Answer: To back up the alert database, go to **VPN/Security Management Solutions > Administration > Common Services > Back up Database**. This option backs up the idsmdc.db and idsmdc.log files, which include your device and signature settings and all the received alerts.

4 How can I keep the customization of my columns in the Security Monitor?

Answer: Starting from Security Monitor 1.2, which is part of VMS 2.2, you can keep the customization of columns in the Security Monitor. When you have modified the columns, go to **Edit > Save Column Set. Then go to Monitor > Events** to ensure that the Event Viewer option for Column Set is set to **Last Saved**.

5 How do I view the Network Security Database (NSDB) from the Security Monitor?

Answer: From within the Event Viewer, click in any cell in the row to highlight the signature you are interested in. Then go to **View > Network Security Database**, or right-click on the cell and select **View NSDB**.

6 Is there a limit to the number of events I can receive through Security Monitor?

Answer: There is no configured limit to the number of events the Security Monitor can receive. The maximum suggested rate for received events, such as syslog and IDS/IPS, is 45 per second, with a burst rate of 500 per second for five minutes.

7 How do I get the Security Monitor to send me a daily report at a specified time?

Answer: Follow these steps to schedule a daily alarm report:

Step 1 Select the **Reports** tab.

Step 2 Select **Generate**.

Step 3 Choose the report that you want to run, such as IDS/IPS Summary Report.

Step 4 On the Schedule Report screen, select the **Schedule for Later** radio button and **Repeat Every Day** options for the report.

Step 5 Select the time that you want the report to be generated.

Step 6 Check the **Email Report To:** check box and enter the destination e-mail address for the report.

Step 7 Click **Finish**.

> **Note** If you want to schedule multiple reports, separate the reports by at least 30 minutes to avoid conflicts.

8 How can I increase the rather low number (50 events per second) sustained rate for Security Monitor?

Answer: The Security Monitor can sustain 500 events per second for several hours. Problems occur when you start doing something to the database at the same time, for example pruning. The default rule is designed to prevent the system from dying after a while. This pruning affects the rates. The author's tests show that the constant event rate forever is approximately 50 events a second. This is because Security Monitor is pruning. If you never prune, the rates are 500 events per second, however the data becomes so unmanageable that it is unusable. The problem is I/O bound. With RAID systems, it is expected that the rates may go up, but there are no guarantees.

9 Where are the results from the execution of the script sent/presented?

Answer: It depends entirely on the script and its arguments. Some scripts output results to a file, and the location of that file is controlled by the argument list of the script. For example, in version 1.x of Security Monitor, the default database rules that are shipped with the product reference the **pruneDefault.pl** script. This script controls where the output (the archived files) should be stored with the -w option in the arguments list. You can see that the rules are set up to output to this subdirectory: **...\CSCOpx\MDC\Sybase\DB\IDS\AlertPruneData**. You are encouraged to change this location by editing the rule and changing the argument text to point to another location (preferably on another computer). Of course, you can create your own scripts that can place results anywhere. In general, script results are not viewable in the Security Monitor.

10 When or how can I remove older reports from Security Monitor?

Answer: Reports are not automatically removed from the system, but you delete old reports. **Select Report > View** and select the reports from the table by checking the check box. Then click **Delete**. The selected reports will be deleted.

11 How can I develop my own scripts if I am not exposing the data structure?

Answer: You will not be able to develop your own scripts that interact directly with the security database. However you can create scripts to interact with Security Monitor database utility programs that Cisco has provided (**IdsAlarms.exe, IdsPruning.exe, IdsImportNrLog.exe**, and so on). These utility programs provide the capability of exporting table data to a file, importing data from a file in addition to pruning and archiving.

12 Can Security Monitor correlate alerts?

Answer: Yes, Security Monitor can correlate alerts based on different criteria.

13 How does Security Monitor treat PIX syslog messages?

Answer: PIX can generate two types of syslog messages: IDS/IPS and non-IDS security syslog messages. Security Monitor takes both types. The PIX IDS/IPS messages are stored with all other IDS messages. The non-IDS PIX messages are stored in a more generic security messages table. Viewing and reporting is available for both sets.

14 I have enabled SSL and when trying to access the event viewer I am getting different kinds of errors. What should I do?

Answer: The certificate that you are using is the wrong one. Synchronize the certificates as follows:

Step 1 Go to **VPN/Security Management Solution > Administration > Configuration > Certificate**, and change Certificate from **Common Services Certificate** to **CiscoWorks 2000 Certificate**.

Step 2 Exit Internet Explorer (IE).

Step 3 Then stop and restart the services.

15 Is it possible to forward an IDS event towards an external syslog server from the Security Monitor?

Answer: Yes, you can forward syslog events from Security Monitor to an external Syslog Server.

16 Where can I download the latest versions and patches for IDS/IPS MC/Security Monitor?

Answer: You can download the latest version and patches for IDS/IPS MC/Security Monitor software from the following location with cisco.com login id:

http://www.cisco.com/pcgi-bin/tablebuild.pl/mgmt-ctr-ids-app

17 From where can I download the latest signature and service pack updates for IDS/IPS MC/Security Monitor?

Answer: You can download them from the following location:

http://www.cisco.com/pcgi-bin/tablebuild.pl/mgmt-ctr-ids-ids4updates

IDS/IPS MC updates Security Monitor automatically if it resides on the same server.

18 How can I move the database after the installation?

Answer: This is not recommended by the author, as the process is complex and there is a chance of application corruption. However, if you really need to move the database from the location where it was installed in the beginning, you can do so by following these steps:

Step 1 Stop the Cisco Works Daemon Manager. (From **Start > Control Panel > Administrative Tools > Services**, click on the **CiscoWorks Daemon Manager** and then on **Dtop**.)

Step 2 Locate the file **SystemConfig.xml** in the three following directories:

— **<install-directory>\CSCOpx\MDC\etc\ids\xml**

— **<install-directory>\CSCOpx\MDC\tomcat\vms\idsconfig\WEBINF\classes\com\cisco\nm\mdc\ids\common**

— **<install-directory>\CSCOpx\MDC\tomcat\vms\idsmonitor\WEBINF\classes\com\cisco\nm\mdc\ids\common**

Step 3 In all the three files, change the line containing the **<DatabaseFile>** to point to the new location.

Step 4 Move the database files to these new locations: **idsmc.db** and **idsmc.log**, which are located in **<install-directory>\CSCOpx\MDC\Sybase\Db\IDS**.

Step 5 Start the CiscoWorks Daemon Manager again.

19 Is it possible to export IDS/IPS Event from VMS to a text file?

Answer: There is a way to export IDS/IPS events from a VMS server to XML and text files. This is possible through the CLI utility **IdsAlarms.exe**. The **IdsAlarms.exe** utility file is located in the **<install_path>/CSCOpx/MDC/bin/ids** folder. But it is not possible to export to .cab files.

The generic syntax for this utility is as follows:

```
IdsAlarms [-f"filename"] [-llevel] [-oformat] [-s"clause"] [-d] [-u] [-p] [-z]
```

In this, only the first three options are needed for exporting the events.

Example 22-6 shows how to use the **IdsAlarms** utility.

Example 22-6 *Usage of IdsAlarms Utility*

```
!To export all the events from the 3.x devices in NrLog text format,
     IdsAlarms -f"alarmsave.txt" -ll -on
!To export all the events from the database in IDIOM XML format,
     IdsAlarms -f"alarmsave.txt" -ll -oi
!To export only the Medium and High severity events from the database in IDIOM format,
      IdsAlarms -f"alarmsave.txt" -lm -oi
```

20 Why am I receiving multiple notifications while running prune jobs on the Security Monitor version earlier than 2.0?

Answer: The pruning can take several hours to run, depending on the size of the database and some other parameters. The notification for the execution of the script is sent when the script is started, and not when it actually ended. Therefore receiving the notification or seeing the notification message in the Audit Log file does not mean that the script is ended or that the script was successful. If the trigger for the script to run is a specific number of events in the database, since the prune job can be long, it can easily happen that the notification is sent multiple times for the same execution of the same script. This is because the IDS_DbAdminAnalyzer checks every half hour whether the conditions for a rule have been met. If the number of events in the database has not yet been reduced to a value that is under the trigger number, the script will be started again (even though it will fail when running since there is another script already running).

Best Practices

This section looks into some of the important methods for improving the performance and seamless operations of Security Monitor in particular and VMS in general. Following is the list of good practices:

- Always apply upgrades to the latest version of Security Monitor and apply the new patch available on the Cisco Web site.
- If you have more than one sensor to receive events, it is recommended that you install IDS/IPS MC and Security Monitor on a separate computer. If you have several sensors, depending on the amount of events you are getting, you might consider installing the Security Monitor on multiple servers for load-sharing purposes.
- Make sure to install VMS on a dedicated computer as it has its own web server and database server, which may cause resource conflict issues if other applications are installed. Be sure to fulfill minimum requirements for running VMS server. As performance depends on the configuration of hardware and not on the configuration of VMS software, it is always recommended to have a faster and more powerful server.
- It is recommended to secure the VMS server with Cisco's Security Agent (CSA). CSA is Cisco's host-based IPS software. If you have CSA MC installed with the Common Services, then the agent is installed for the server to protect VMS automatically. If you do not have the CSA MC installed, then be sure to install at least the headless CSA Agent to protect the VMS Server itself from any types of attack.
- If the VMS is in a different network (VLAN) than the sensor, then be sure the network devices between the management server and the sensor allows SSH (TCP/22), and SSL (TCP/443) for both IDS/IPS MC and Security Monitor) in both directions.
- Be sure to schedule for archiving and/or deleting the alarms to keep from filling the VMS database, as the more alarms stored in the database, the longer it takes your viewer to load the alarms for viewing.
- Do not install VMS on Primary/Backup Domain Controller, IIS Server, Terminal Server, IEV, and CSPM.

INDEX

Symbols & Numerics

***.rtr files, displaying output, 991**
.evt files, 887

50 percent rule, 148
802.1x
FAQs, 582–584
statistics, displaying, 555–557

A

AAA (Authentication, Authorization, and Accounting)
architectural components, 420
authentication, testing on VPN 3K, 593–594
authorization, troubleshooting on Cisco switches, 570–574
Auth-proxy, troubleshooting on Cisco routers, 457
communication protocols
RADIUS, 425–427
TACACS+, 421–424
configuring, best practices, 474
debug commands, 430–431
dial-up networking, troubleshooting on Cisco routers, 446–449, 452–457
FAQs, 472–474
on Cisco routers
accounting, configuring, 445
command authorization, troubleshooting, 443–445
exec authorization, troubleshooting, 440–443
troubleshooting, 432–440
VPDN case study, 458–462
on Cisco switches
802.1x, FAQs, 582–584
IBNS, 566–570
IBNSs, 541–545
switch management, 541, 558–566
on VPN 3K
FAQs, 611–612
session timeouts, avoiding, 593
troubleshooting, 587
show commands, 429
X-Auth, troubleshooting on Cisco routers, 457
access lists. *See* ACLs
Access-Accept messages (RADIUS), 427
Access-Challenge messages (RADIUS), 427
accessing
IDM sensor, 888
NM-CIDS console, 839
Access-Reject messages (RADIUS), 427
accounting
configuring
on Cisco routers, 445
on Cisco switches, 565
troubleshooting on Cisco switches, 566
ACL Partition Manager (FWSM), 168–169
ACLs. *See also* VACLs
Conduit to Access-list Converter, 53
downloadable, 652
PIX/IP ACLs, syntax, 606
troubleshooting, 654–655
effect on CBAC performance, 209
enabling/disabling on PIX Firewall, 35
established keyword, 180
implementing on PIX Firewalls, 34
IPS sensor blocking, 734–735
limitations of, 177
misconfigured, troubleshooting on CBAC, 202
on FWSM
ACL Partition Manager, 168–169
compilation process, 170–172
memory utilization, 164–166
outbound, applying on PIX Firewall, 35–36
performance impact on PIX Firewall, 101
Reflexive, 180
time-range keyword, 34–35
wide holes, 181
acquiring CSAgent software, 997–998
ACS. *See* CS ACS (Cisco Secure Access Control Server)
activating
syslog on Cisco routers, 193
URL filtering, 186
activation keys for PIX Firewall, 56

Active FTP connections, handling with CBAC, 180–181
active/active mode (PIX Firewall), 102
configuring, 105–106
active/standby mode (PIX Firewall), 102
activities
Router MC, dangling connections, 968
unlocking with Firewall MC, 941
AD (Active Directory). CS ACS integration, 627–629
adding
devices to device table, 1052
trusted hosts to sensors, 890–892
Administer Sessions window (VPN 3000 Concentrator series), 352
agent kits (CSA Agent), generating, 997–998
aggressive mode negotiation, 231–232
AH (Authentication Header), 226
alert database, backing up, 1073
Alert Inserter, 1044
alerts, configuring, 192–193
AnalysisEngine, 678
Analyzer daemon, 1055
analyzing MDCSupport file contents, 886–887
anti-spoofing, CBAC configuration best practices, 219
anti-virus software. creating buffer overflow exclusions, 1018–1020
Apache certificate
regenerating, 897
trusted host issues, resolving on IDS MC, 897–898
verifying on IDS MC, 896
APIs, IDAPI, 678
application issues, troubleshooting on CSAgent, 1016
application partition (NM-CIDS)
re-imaging, 854–857
recovering, 708–709
application-layer protocols, traffic inspection, 183
SMTP, 184
applications comprising IPS software
AnalysisEngine, 678
CLI, 678
MainApp, 677–678
application-specific roles (ACS), 975
application-to-port mappings, modifying, 188–189
architectural components of AAA, 420
archive files, redirecting away from Database Disk, 1063
arguments
for csutil.exe, 655–656
for show crypto ipsec command, 299
ARP spoofing, 80
ASA (Adaptive Security Algorithm), characteristics of, 29–30
assigning
IP address to IDS-Sensor interface, 839
privilege levels to VPN 3k users, 592
asymmetric cryptographic algorithms, 224
asymmetric routing
PIX Firewall support, 106
troubleshooting on CBAC, 205
attributes (VPN 3K), 589
audit reports (IDS MC), 885
audits, configuring, 193
AUS authentication
with Firewall MC, troubleshooting, 940
with firewalls, troubleshooting, 940–941
authentication, 592
AAA on VPN 3K, FAQs, 611–612
on Firewall MC firewalls, troubleshooting, 939
on Firewall MC with AUS, troubleshooting, 940
on Router MC, troubleshooting, 967
on VPN 3K, causes of failure, 607–608
PEAP configuration case study, 574–576, 580
testing, 593–594
authentication server (IEEE 802.x framework), 543
authenticator, 542
authorization
configuring on Cisco switches, 564–565
NARs, 648
configuring, 648, 651
troubleshooting, 651–652
troubleshooting on Cisco switches, 565, 570–574
Authorization cache, 212
auth-proxy, 177
authentication methods, 212
configuring, 213–215
on Cisco routers, troubleshooting, 457
operation, 212

supported Cisco router platforms, 213
troubleshooting, 216–217
avoiding AAA session timeouts on VPN 3K, 593

B

backing up data
alert database, 1073
CiscoWorks Common Services, 874–875
command syntax, 656
CS ACS, 665
CSA MC database, 1023–1024
IPS sensor configuration, 782–783
Router MC database, 972
backup files, redirecting away from Database Disk, 1063
backup/restore operations, troubleshooting on Router MC, 973
base group attributes (VPN 3K), 589
baselining, importance of, 6
best practices
for AAA configuration, 474
for CBAC
anti-spoofing configuration, 219
router security, 218–219
for CiscoWorks Common Services management, 881
for CS ACS Server, 670–671
for CSA MC installation, 1036
for IDS MC configuration, 929
for IDSM-2 blade implementation, 829
for implementing AAA on VPN 3K, 612
for IPS deployment, 781–785
for protecting PIX Firewall, 110–111
for Security Monitor operation, 1077
Bidirectional replication, 647
BIN directory (CSA MC), 985
blat, 1070
blocking issues on IPS sensors,
ACLs, 734–735
configuring, 737–740
for specific signatures, troubleshooting, 753
implementing, 736–737
MBS, 737, *741–743*
supported managed devices and versions, 735
verifying blocking processes, 923–924
blocking forwarding sensor, 737
blue screen, troubleshooting, 990
browsers. *See* web browsers
buffer overflow exclusions, creating, 1018–1020
Bugs Tracker, 54
bulk importing NASs, 667
Bypass mode (IPS sensor), 682

C

capture command, 47–49
capturing
debug command output, 199
IPS traffic
on MPLS IP IDS, 776–777
on RSPAN, 773–775
on SPAN, 763–770
on VACL, 775–776
on hub, 763
packets on FWSM, 123–124
sniffer traces, 199
"cascade" replication, 645
case studies
Hairpinning, configuring, 335–337
PEAP configuration, 574–576, 580
RADIUS configuration on Cisco IOS routers, 462–463
troubleshooting VPDN on Cisco IOS routers, 464–472
user permissions on Router MC, 974
ACS roles, 975, 978
CiscoWorks Server roles, 975
VPDN configuration on Cisco IOS routers, 458–462
Catalyst 2900/3500XL switches, configuring IPS traffic capture with SPAN, 765– 767
Catalyst 2900/3600XL switches, configuring SPAN, 765–767
Catalyst 2950 switches, configuring IPS traffic capture with SPAN, 767–770
Catalyst 2950/3550 and 3750 switches, configuring SPAN, 767–770
Catalyst 3550 switches, configuring IPS traffic capture with SPAN, 767–770
Catalyst 3750 switches, configuring IPS traffic capture with SPAN, 767–770
Catalyst 4000/6000 switches running CatOS, configuring SPAN, 770–771

Catalyst 4000/6000 switches running Native IOS, configuring SPAN, 771–772
Catalyst 6500, IDSM-2 blade
Command and Control port, configuring, 801–805
event generation, troubleshooting, 817–818
front panel indicator lights, 789
hardware issues on CatOS, troubleshooting, 797–800
hardware issues on Native IOS, troubleshooting, 793–797
hardware requirements, 788
installing, 789
Maintenance Partition, upgrading, 823–824
Promiscuous mode
configuring, 805–813
troubleshooting, 814–816
re-imaging, 818–823
removing from switch, 790
serial cable, connecting, 826
signature update, installing, 824–825
slot assignment, 788
sniffing ports, 791
supported ports, 790
TCP reset, 818
upgrading to version 5.x, 826
user passwords, recovering, 827–829
VACL Capture, 827
versus IDS Appliance, 787
categorizing CS ACS problem areas, 625
CatOS, Native IOS show commands, 792
CBAC (Context-Based Access Control), 177
Active FTP connections, handling, 180–181
anti-spoofing configuration, best practices, 219
asymmetric routing, troubleshooting, 205
Cisco IOS code base, upgrading, 209
connection states, 194–195
connectivity, troubleshooting, 201–203
CPU utilization, verifying, 205–206
FAQs, 217–218
half-open connections, manipulating threshold values, 208
HTTP inspection, verifying dropped packets, 208
interaction with IPsec, 193
interoperability with NAT, 188
IP fragmentation, mitigating, 191
Java blocking, configuring, 184
misconfigured ACLs, troubleshooting, 202
misconfigured IP inspection, troubleshooting, 203
misconfigured NAT, troubleshooting, 202
multi-channel protocols
inspecting, 187, 205
securing, 180
packet drops, troubleshooting, 210
packet flow across routers, 196
performance, troubleshooting, 205–210
protecting inside network, 179–180
router security configuration, best practices, 218–219
single channel protocol inspection, 182
application-layer protocols, 183
ICMP, 182
SMTP, 184
UDP, 182
switching path, troubleshooting performance issues, 209
TCP SYN flood attacks, mitigating, 189–191
troubleshooting, 199
UDP connection timeout, selecting, 207–208
UDP inspection, troubleshooting, 203–205
URL filtering
configuring, 185–187
troubleshooting, 211
CEP (Certificate Enrollment Protocol), PKI
configuring, 258–261
troubleshooting, 261–265
CFG directory (CSA MC), 985
challenge-response-based authentication, 546
changing database maximum event limit, 1066
check pointing CiscoWorks Common Services database, 951
checking status of Firewall MC processes, 931
CIDEE (Cisco Intrusion Detection Event Exchange), 679–680
CIFS access, configuring on VPN 3000 Concentrator series, 394
circular blocks, 737
Cisco AV-Pairs, 653

Cisco IOS routers
AAA
accounting, configuring, 445
Auth-proxy, troubleshooting, 457
command authorization, 443–445
dial-up networking, troubleshooting, 446–457
exec authorization, 440–443
router management, troubleshooting, 432–440
VPDN case study, 458–462
X-Auth, troubleshooting, 457
IPsec VPNs
PKI, troubleshooting, 258–265
Remote Access client VPN connections, troubleshooting, 265–270
NM-CIDS, managing, 848–849
RADIUS configuration, case study, 462–463
VPDN troubleshooting, case study, 464–472
VPNs, DMVPN, 270–280
Cisco IOS Software, upgrading code base on CBAC routers, 209
Cisco PIX firewalls. *See* PIX firewalls
Cisco Secure ACS mode (CiscoWorks Common Services), 862
Cisco Security Agent Management Center (CSA MC) license key, 865
Cisco switches
AAA
802.1x FAQs, 582–584
authorization, troubleshooting, 570–574
IBNS, 566–570
PEAP configuration, case study, 574–580
switch management, 541, 558–566
IBNSs, 541–542
IEEE 802.1x framework, 542–545
CiscoWorks Common Services database
backing up, 874–875
FAQs, 877–881
installing, 870–871
database management, 873
minimum requirements, 870
problems, troubleshooting, 871–873
user management issues, 873
license key, upgrading, 868
licenses, troubleshooting, 869
managing, best practices, 881
MDCSUPPORT, 863
files collected by, 864
MDCSupportInformation.zip file, file summary, 864
Privileges, 862
resolving DNS errors, 1048
restore procedures, 875–876, 950
Roles, 862
running on multi-homed machines, 879
user authentication, case study, 876–877
user management, 862
CiscoWorks Common Services Desktop, launching on browser, 861
CiscoWorks MDCSupportInformation.zip, file contents, 933
classifier, 84
clear crypto sa command, 238
CLI (command-line interface), 678
IPS sensors, licensing, 719–720
clientless SSL VPN mode (VPN 3000 Concentrator series)
configuring, 390
troubleshooting, 391–395
closing NM-CIDS sessions, 843
cluster redundancy on VPN 3000 Concentrator series, 412–414
collecting MDCSupport file on Windows platform, 886
combined sensor mode (IPS), 683
Command and Control port
on IDSM-2
5-minute output rate, checking, 803–805
configuring, 801–803
on NM-CIDS, 834
configuring, 844–845
command authorization, troubleshooting on Cisco routers, 443–445
commands
capture, 47–49
clear crypto sa, 238
debug, 300
debug aaa accounting, 430
debug aaa authentication, 430
debug aaa authorization, 430
debug application-protocol, 47
debug commands, FWSM-related, 122–123
debug fixup tcpludp, 47
debug icmp trace, 46–47
debug ip inspect, 197–198

debug pix process, 47
debug sanity, 24
debug tunnel, 257–258
diagnostic level complete, 795
for PIX flash file system, 33
intrusion-detection module, 808
ip port-map, 189
iplog, 691
nslookup, 19
packet, 692
ping, 17
recover application-partition, 709
service-module, connecting to NM-CIDS, 840
show authorization, 554
show aaa servers, 430
show aaa user, 430
show accounting, 554
show asp drop, 41–42
show blocks, 43
show commands
for IPsec Phase 1 tunnel negotiations, 233–235
for IPsec Phase 2 tunnel negotiations, 235–236
FWSM-related, 120–122
show configuration, 687
show connection, 40
show cpu usage, 42
show crypto ipsec, 299–300
show crypto map, 237
show dot1x all, 556
show dot1x statistics, 557
show events, 687
show interfaces, 689
show ip inspect, 194–195
show local-host, 40–41
show localusers, 552
show module, 791
show output filters, 44–45
show radius, 553
show radius statistics, 430
show running config, 15, 300
show running logging, 52
show security acl, 792
show service-policy, 41, 94
show span, 792
show statistics, 687–688
show tacacs, 430, 553
show tech-support, 45, 689
show test, 792
show traffic, 42
show trunk, 792
show users, 430
show version, 15, 200, 686–690, 791
show vlan brief, 558
show xlate, 39–40
tcpdump, 690
telnet, 18
time-range, 34–35
traceroute, 18
winmsd, 988
common services license key, 865
commonly asked questions. *See* FAQs
communication architecture
for CSA MC, 986
of Firewall MC, 932
of Router MC, 960
on IDS MC, 884–885
communication protocols, 678–681
RADIUS, 425–426
authentication operation, 426–427
authorization operation, 426–427
configuring, case study, 462–463
TACACS+, 421
AAA packet flows, 423
accounting operation, 424
authentication operation, 422–423
authorization operation, 424
versus RADIUS, 428–429
compacting
CiscoWorks Common Services database, 952–953
CS ACS database, 660
CSA MC database, 1029–1031
comparing RADIUS and TACACS+, 428–429
compilation process for ACLs on FWSM, 170–172
components of CSA, 983, 985
Conduit to Access-list Converter, 53
configuration files
for VPN 3000 Concentrator series, 354
sysvars.cf, 991

configuring
AAA
best practices, 474
on Cisco switches, enable password authentication, 563
accounting
on Cisco IOS routers, 445
on Cisco switches, 565
active/active failover on PIX Firewall, 105–106
alerts, 192–193
audits, 193
auth-proxy, 213–215
basic router security, best practices, 218–219
blocking, 737–743
CBAC anti-spoofing, best practices, 219
clientless SSL VPN mode on VPN 3000 Concentrator series, 390
Command and Control interface (NM-CIDS), 844–845
connectivity
on FWSM, 135–139
on PIX Firewall, 69–72
CS ACS
AAA Client definition for VPN 3K, 609
domain controller mode, 628
replication, 640, 644–647
email notification, 1068–1070
Firewall MC, Recovery Server, 953–954
FWSM
failover, 149–155
multiple SVI interfaces, 157, 161–162
GRE over IPsec, 256–257
Hairpinning, 335–337
IDM sensors, trusted hosts, 889–890
IDS MC, best practices, 929
IDSM-2
Command and Control port, 801–805
Promiscuous mode, 805–813
IPS sensor, Inline mode, 757–762
IPsec LAN-to-LAN VPN tunnels, 302, 305–308
crypto maps, creating, 305–306
transform sets, 304
tunnel groups, 305
IPsec over TCP, 339
Java blocking, 184
LAN-to-LAN tunnels on VPN 3000 Concentrator series, 356
LLQ on PIX Firewall, 93–94
local user authentication on VPN 3K, 597–599
login authentication, 559–560
MAPI Proxy on VPN 3000 Concentrator, 399–400
MBS, 741–743
MPLS IP IDS, IPS traffic capture, 776–777
NARs, 648, 651
NAT-T, 338–339
NDS database with CS ACS, 630
troubleshooting, 631–636
NM-CIDS, time stamping, 857–858
packet capturing on NM-CIDS, 846–848
PEAP
case study, 574–576, 580
Machine Authentication, 567–570
PIX Firewall
multiple context mode, 87–90
policing, 90–92
Remote Access VPN, 323–327
PKI, 258–261
RADIUS
dynamic filters, 604
on Cisco IOS routers, case study, 462–463
Remote Access VPN connections on VPN 3000 Concentrator series, 364–365
RSPAN, IPS traffic capture, 773–775
sensors
on IDS MC, 906
shunning, case study, 920–925
SPAN
IPS traffic capture, 763–770
on Catalyst 2900/3600XL, 765–767
on Catalyst 2950/3550 and 3750, 767–770
on Catalyst 4000/6000 running CatOS, 770–771
on Catalyst 4000/6000 running Native IOS, 771–772
Split Tunneling, 342–344
SSL VPN on VPN 3000 Concentrator, Thick Client mode, 402–403
syslog on PIX Firewall, 50–53
TACACS+ on VPN 3K, 590–592
traceback on PIX Firewall, 53

transparent firewalls, 193
on PIX Firewall, 79–82
URL filtering, 185–187
VACL, IPS traffic capture, 775–776
VPN 3000 Concentrator series
Cisco Secure ACS, 590–591
event classes, 348
group authentication with RADIUS, 599–600
Group feature, 608
Group Lock feature, 601
local group and user authentication, 595
RADIUS Server, 609
Windows NT/2000 Authentication, Unknown User Policy, 609–610
connecting
IPS sensor to network, 784
serial cable to IDSM-2, 826
to NM-CIDS console, 840–842
connection block, 734
connection states, CBAC, 194–195
connectivity
on CBAC, troubleshooting, 201–203
on FWSM
configuring, 135–139
troubleshooting, 134, 139–142
on IPS sensors, troubleshooting, 720–725
on PIX Firewall
configuring, 69–72
displaying details, 40
troubleshooting, 72–76
testing with ping command, 17
console access to NM-CIDS, troubleshooting, 843–844
console port (NM-CIDS), 835
Context-Based Access Control. *See* CBAC
CONTINUE packets (TACACS+), 422
control connection, 181
cooperation between SecOP and NetOP personnel, 7
core dumps
generating, 22
with Flash disk, 23
with FTP, 22
with rcp, 23
with TFTP, 22
testing configuration of, 24
corrupt IDS MC licenses, troubleshooting, 904
CP (control plane), FWSM architecture, 113–114
CPU utilization
on CBAC, verifying, 205–206
on FWSM, troubleshooting, 143
on PIX Firewall
displaying, 42
troubleshooting, 95–98
Cr directory (CSA MC), 986
creating
buffer overflow exclusions, 1018–1020
crypto maps for LAN-to-LAN tunnels, 305–306
database rules, 1064
DMVPN spoke-to-spoke tunnels, 275
dump text files, 657
dynamic crypto maps, 327
exceptions, 1016
securitylog.txt file, 991
transform sets, 304
CRSHDUMP.TXT file, 354
Crypto Errors (CS ACS), resolving, 661
crypto maps, creating for LAN-to-LAN tunnels, 305–306
crypto socket creation problems (NHRP), troubleshooting, 279
cryptographic algorithms, 224
cryptographic-based authentication (EAP), 546
CS ACS (Cisco Secure Access Control Server)
AAA Client definition for VPN 3K, configuring, 609
Active Directory integration, 627–629
application-specific roles, 975
as proxy server, 665
associated registries, 663
backing up, 665
best practices, 670–671
categorizing problem areas, 625
configuring, 590–591
FAQs, 661–670
database, compacting, 660
default NAS, adding, 663
domain controller mode, configuring, 628
domain stripping, 665
external user database integration, required components, 620
GUI, recovering lost passwords, 663
installing on Windows platform, 625–627
"Logged in Users" report, 668

NARs, 648
configuring, 648, 651
troubleshooting, 651–652
NASs, bulk importing, 667
Novell IDS integration, 630
troubleshooting, 631–636
packet flow, 619–620
password encryption, 668
RADIUS Server, communicating with VPN 3K, 597–599
replication
configuring, 640, 644
troubleshooting, 644–647
SDI integration, 636–638
troubleshooting, 638–639
services, CSAdmin, 615–616
setup procedures for Router MC, 979–980
Shared File Components, 653–654
uninstalling, 661
upgrading on Windows platform, 625–626
user/NAS import options, 658
exporting user and group information, 660
importing NAS to CS ACS database, 659
importing users to existing database, 658
user names, defining, 980
users, deleting, 659
CSA Agent, 983
application issues, troubleshooting, 1016
communication with CSA MC, troubleshooting, 1014–1015
csainfo.bat utility, 989
debug mode, turning on, 989–991
disk usage, monitoring, 992
installation
minimum requirements, 998–999
troubleshooting, 997, 1001
license, procuring, 1007
log files, 988–992
policies, 987
polling issues, troubleshooting, 1014–1015
registration, troubleshooting, 1014–1015
removing from Windows systems, 999–1000
rtrformat utility, 990
shims, disabling, 1016–1017
software, procuring, 997–998
stopping service, 991
update issues, troubleshooting, 1004–1005
CSA MC (Cisco Security Agent Management Console), 983
communication architecture, 986
database
compacting, 1029–1031
manual backups, performing, 1023–1024
purging events from, 1028–1029
repairing, 1031–1032
restoring, 1025–1027
database maintenance, 1023
default installation directory, 985
directory structure, 985–986
disaster recovery, 1036–1037
DRP, 1023
installation
best practices, 1036
minimum requirements, 995
troubleshooting, 993
launching
problems with, troubleshooting, 1010–1013
slow launches, troubleshooting, 1013–1014
license key, installing, 869
licenses, 1005–1006
importing, 1007–1008
procuring, 1007
troubleshooting, 1009–1010
local database installation, troubleshooting, 994
log directory, 988
log files, 987
management model, 983–985
manually removing components, 996–997
registration, 868
remote database installation, troubleshooting, 994
uninstalling, 995
upgrading, 1002
on same system, 1002–1003
on separate system, 1003–1004
CSAdmin, 615–616
csainfo.bat utility, 989
csalog.txt file, 989
csauser.dll, disabling, 1018
CSAuth, 616
CSDBSync, 616
CSLog, 616

CSMon, 616–617
CSRadius service, 618
CSSupport utility, files included in Package.cab file, 622–624
CSTacacs service, 618
csutil.exe, 655, 658
options, 655–656

D

daemons
Analyzer, 1055
Notifier, 1055
daily alarm reports, scheduling, 1073
dangling connections on Router MC, 968
data connection, 181
data not passing through IPsec LAN-to-LAN VPN tunnels, troubleshooting, 322–323
databases
backing up, command syntax, 656
CiscoWorks Common Services, 873
backing up, 874–875
check pointing, 951
compacting, 952–953
restoring, 875–876, 950
compacting, 660, 1068
CSA MC database
compacting, 1029–1031
purging events, 1028–1029
repairing, 1031–1032
restoring database, 1025–1027
disk utilization, monitoring, 1066
DRP, 1023
maximum event limit, changing, 1066
pruning issues, troubleshooting, 1067–1068
restoring, 657
Router MC
backing up, 972
restoring, 973
rules, creating, 1064
DB directory (CSA MC), 986
debug aaa accounting command, 430
debug aaa authentication command, 430
debug aaa authorization command, 430
debug application-protocol command, 47
debug commands, 195, 197, 300
FWSM-related, 122–123
guidelines for using, 16
output, capturing, 199
debug fixup tcp|udp command, 47
debug icmp trace command, 46–47
debug information
on Firewall MC, viewing, 932
on Router MC, 961–962
debug ip inspect command, 197–198
debug logging level (Router MC), 961
debug mode (CSA Agent), turning on, 989
debug pix process command, 47
debug sanity command, 24
debug tunnel command, 257–258
debugging
IDS MC, 887–888
turning off, 555
decryption, 223
default event limit (database), changing, 1066
default installation directory for CSA MC, 985
defining
tunnel groups for LAN-to-LAN tunnels, 305
usernames in ACS, 980
deleting
CS ACS users, 659
users in multiple group, 669
deployed jobs, stopping, 942
deploying
device configurations from Firewall MC, 947
device configurations from Router MC, 970–971
IDS MC configuration, 917–920
deployment architecture of IPS, 676–677
destination ports, 764
detecting IOS Firewall feature set, 200
device groups, defining in ACS, 980
devices
adding to device table, 1052
configuration files
deploying, 947
importing, 943–946, 969–970
flow rates, monitoring, 1064–1065
diagnostic commands, show ip inspect, 194–195
diagnostic level complete command, 795
dial-up networking on Cisco routers
accounting, 457
troubleshooting, 446–456

Digital Certificates
on VPN 3000 Concentrator series, 383–384
troubleshooting, 384–389
on VPN 3000 Concentrator series VPN client, 382–383
digital signatures, 225
directory structure of CSA MC, 985–986
disabling
CSAgent shims, 1016–1017
csauser.dll, 1018
disconnecting from NM-CIDS console, 842–843
disk space, reclaiming, 1011
disk usage, monitoring, 992
displaying
*.rtr file output, 991
802.1X statistics, 555–557
Firewall MC debug information, 932
Router MC debug information, 961–962
server selftest information, 988
Windows system information, 988
DMVPN (Dynamic Multipoint VPN), 270
configurable dynamic routing protocols, 280
crypto socket creation problems, troubleshooting, 279
dynamic spoke-to-spoke configuration, 273–276
mGRE interface, 271
NHRP, 271
mapping problems, troubleshooting, 278–279
DNS errors, resolving, 1048
Doc directory (CSA MC), 986
documenting network topology, importance of, 6
domain controller mode (CS ACS), configuring, 628
domain stripping on CS ACS, 665
DoS attacks
fragmentation, mitigating with CBAC, 191
TCP SYN flood, mitigating with CBAC, 189–191
downgrading PIX Firewall, 66
downloadable ACLs, 652
PIX/IP, syntax, 606
troubleshooting, 654–655
DPD (Dead Peer Discovery), 345
driver_install.log file, 989
DRP (disaster recovery plan), 1023
application partition, recovery procedures, 708–709
implementing, 707
dump text files, creating, 657
dynamic crypto maps, creating, 327
dynamic filters
active, viewing, 603
configuring on VPN 3K, 602
fields, 604
on RADIUS, configuring, 604
rules, syntax, 603
dynamic routing protocols for DMVPN networks, 280
dynamic spoke-to-spoke DMVPN configuration, 273–276
dynamically mapped users, replication, 670

E

EAP (Extensible Authentication Protocol), 545–546
EAPOL (EAP over LANs), 544
egress traffic, 764
email notification
configuring, 1068, 1070
troubleshooting, 1071–1072
E-mail Proxy (VPN 3000 Concentrator)
configuring, 401
troubleshooting, 401–402
enable password authentication
configuring, 563
troubleshooting, 562–564
enabling
Firewall MC, Recovery Server, 954
SSL, 1049
encryption, 223
of CS ACS passwords, 668
error messages, troubleshooting
Internal Server Error, 1050
Page Cannot Be Found Error, 1050
escalation procedures, documenting, 7
ESMTP (Extended Simple Mail Transfer Protocol), traffic inspection, 183–184
ESP (Encapsulating Security Header), 226
established keyword (ACLs), 180
establishing LAN-to-LAN tunnels, 240–246

Ethereal, 125, 199
web site, 20
Ethernet, interface IDS-Sensor, 834
event classes, configuring on VPN 3000 Concentrator series, 348
Event Limiting, 991
event log (VPN 3000 Concentrator series), viewing, 350–352
Event Viewer
launching, 1055
test events, generating, 1057
troubleshooting, 1057
events
Large ICMP events, generating, 1057
maximum event limit (database), changing, 1066
purging from CSA MC database, 1028–1029
writing to securitylog.txt file, 991
exception memory command, generating core dump, 23
exceptions, creating, 1016
exec authorization, troubleshooting on Cisco routers, 440–443
expired IDS MC licenses, troubleshooting, 905
exporting user and group information from CS ACS database, 660

F

fact gathering stage, production network troubleshooting, 10–11
Failed Attempts logs, 621
failover, 102
on FWSM
configuring, 149–155
forced reboot conditions, 147
initialization phase, 146
monitoring, 147–148
troubleshooting, 144–146, 155–157
on PIX Firewall
active/active failover, configuring, 102, 105–106
active/standby mode, 102
asymmetrical routing support, 106
failover groups, 104
hardware and licensing requirements, 104
failover groups, 104
failure of VPN 3K authentication, causes of, 607–608
FAQs
regarding 802.1x, 582–584
regarding AAA, 472–474
on VPN 3K, 611–612
regarding CBAC, 217–218
regarding CS ACS, 661–670
regarding CSA Agent/CSA MC, 1032–1035
regarding CiscoWorks Common Services, 877–881
regarding FWSM, 173–174
regarding IDS MC, 925–929
regarding IPS, 777–781
regarding PIX Firewall, 109–110
regarding VPN 3000 Concentrator series, 406–410
Fast Path packet flow through FWSM, 116–118
features of Router MC, 960
Field Notices, 54
fields
of dynamic filters, 603–604
of EAP frames, 546
file systems (PIX), commands, 33
files in MDCSupport, analyzing, 886–887
filters, configuring dynamic filters on VPN 3K, 602
Firewall MC
activities, unlocking, 941
authentication problems, resolving, 939–940
browser-related problems, resolving, 937
CiscoWorks Common Services database
check pointing, 951
compacting, 952–953
Common Services, installing, 935
communication architecture, 932
debug information, viewing, 932
device configurations
deploying, 947
importing, 943–946
initialization, 936, 964
installation issues, troubleshooting, 934
interoperability with other applications, 936
jobs, rolling back, 942
MDCSupport utility, generated files, 933
processes, 931
purge-mc-tasks utility, 942

Recovery Server
configuring, 953–954
enabling, 954
terminal activities, removing, 941–942
Firewall module administration on FWSM, troubleshooting, 128–133
firewalls
and IPsec, 284–285
deploying between IPsec peers, 340
on IPsec endpoints, 340
Flash disk, generating core dumps, 23
flow rates, monitoring, 1064–1065
fragmentation, mitigating with CBAC, 191
front panel indicator lights
IDSM-2, 789
NM-CIDS, 833
FTP, 21
generating core dumps, 22
packet flow through FWSM, 118
FWSM
access-lists
ACL Partition Manager, 168–169
compilation process, 170–172
memory utilization, 164–166
connectivity
configuring, 135–139
troubleshooting, 134, 139–142
CP, 113–114
CPU utilization, troubleshooting, 143
debug commands, 122–123
failover
configuring, 149–155
forced reboot conditions, 147
initialization phase, 146
monitoring, 147–148
troubleshooting, 144–146, 155–157
FAQs, 173–174
Firewall module administration issues, troubleshooting, 128–133
hardware issues, troubleshooting, 127–128
image upgrades, performing, 133–134
intermittent packet drops, troubleshooting, 144
licensing issues, troubleshooting, 126–127
Maintenance Partition, 130–132
multiple SVI interfaces, configuring, 157–162
NP, 114–116
packet capturing, 123–124
packet flows, 116
Fast Path packet flow, 116–118
FTP session packet flow, 118
Session Management Path packet flow, 118
password recovery, 132
show commands, 120–122
syslog, 125

G

generating
agent kits, 997–998
core dumps, 22
with exception memory command, 23
with Flash disk, 23
with FTP, 22
with rcp, 23
with TFTP, 22
Large ICMP events, 1057
test events on Event Viewer, 1057
GRE over IPsec
configuring, 256–257
troubleshooting, 257–258
group attributes (VPN 3K), 589
group authentication with RADIUS, configuring on VPN 3K, 599–600
group configuration on VPN 3K, 608
Group Lock feature (VPN 3K), 601, 607
groups, 985
GUI (Firewall MC)
lost passwords, recovering, 663
removing terminal activities from Firewall MC, 941–942

H

Hairpinning, 334
configuring, 335–337
half-open connections, manipulating threshold values on CBAC routers, 208
hardware
IPS support, 683–685
on FWSM, troubleshooting, 127–128
hardware requirements
for IDSM-2, 788

for NM-CIDS support, 832
for PIX Firewall failover, 104
Headless CSAgent software, procuring, 997
high availability of PIX firewall for VPN connections, 344–345
high CPU utilization, troubleshooting
on FWSM, 143
on PIX Firewall, 95–98
host block, 734
hosts, 985
HTTP inspection, Java filtering, 204
HTTPS, tasks performed on IDS MC, 885
hubs, capturing IPS traffic, 763

I

IBNSs (Identity-Based Network Services), 541–542, 555
802.1X statistics, displaying, 555–557
IEEE 802.1x framework, 542–545
standard operation, 544–545
machine authentication, 566–567
PEAP, configuring, 567–570
ICMP (Internet Control Message Protocol), traffic inspection, 182
IDAPI (Intrusion Detection Application Programming Interface), 678
IDENT protocol, troubleshooting on PIX Firewall, 102
identifying registered CSA MC agents, 1008
IDIOM, 681
IDM (IPS Device Manager)
IPS sensors, licensing, 719
sensors
accessing, 888, 901–902
trusted hosts, adding, 890–892
trusted hosts, configuring, 889–890
IDS MC
Apache certificate
regenerating, 897
trusted host issues, resolving, 897–898
verifying, 896
audit reports, 885
communication architecture, 884–885
configuration deployment, 917
troubleshooting, 918–920
configuring, best practices, 929
corrupt licenses, troubleshooting, 904
database pruning, 920
debugging, 887–888
device table, adding devices to, 1052
expired licenses, troubleshooting, 905
FAQs, 925–929
installing, 902–903
MDCSupport file
collecting on Windows platform, 886
file contents, analyzing, 886–887
processes, starting/stopping, 884
resolving connection problems with sensor, 893
secure communication with sensor, verifying, 893
sensors
configuring, 906
import process, troubleshooting, 907–908, 1051
shunning, case study, 920–925
updating signature level, 899–901
upgrading, 908–917
service pack version, verifying, 895–896
VMS Server, IP addressing, modifying, 898
IDS Sensor Software, naming conventions, 700
platform-dependent images, 700–701
platform-independent images, 701–702
IdsAlarms.exe utility, 1076
IDSdbcompact utility, 1068
IDSM-2 (Intrusion Detection Services Module 2) blade
Command and Control port
5-minute output rate, checking, 803–805
configuring, 801–803
event generation, troubleshooting, 817–818
front panel indicator lights, 789
hardware issues, troubleshooting
on CatOS, 797–800
on Native IOS, 793–797
hardware requirements, 788
implementing, best practices, 829
installing, 789
Maintenance Partition, upgrading, 823–824
Promiscuous mode, 805
configuring, 805–813
troubleshooting, 814–816
re-imaging, 818–823
removing from switch, 790

serial cable, connecting, 826
signature update, installing, 824–825
slot assignment, 788
sniffing ports, 791
supported ports, 790
TCP reset, 818
upgrading to version 5.x, 826
user passwords, recovering, 827–829
VACL Capture, 827
versus IDS Appliance, 787

IKE (Internet Key Exchange), 229
phase 1, 229–232
phase 2, 232–233

images
for NM-CIDS, 849
upgrading on FWSM, 133–134

implementing
AAA on VPN 3K, best practices, 612
access lists on PIX Firewalls, 34–35
outbound ACLs, 35–36
time-range keyword, 34–35
disaster recovery plan, 707–709
IDSM-2, best practices, 829

importing
CSA MC license, 1007–1008
device configurations
with Firewall MC, 943–946
with Router MC, 969–970
IDS sensors from IDS MC, 1051
troubleshooting, 907–908
NAS to CS ACS database, 659
users to existing CS ACS database, 658

inaccessible sensors, troubleshooting, 901–902

inbound connections, 69
configuring on PIX Firewall, 69–72

information logging level (Router MC), 961

ingress traffic, 764

initial IPS sensor setup problems, troubleshooting, 693–696

initialization problems, resolving
on Firewall MC, 936
on Router MC, 964

Inline Bypass sensor mode (IPS), 682

Inline mode (IPS sensor), 681–682
configuring, 757–762
troubleshooting, 762–763

inside network, protecting, 178–180

inspecting
multi-channel protocols, 187
single channel protocols, 182
application-layer protocols, 183
ICMP, 182
SMTP, 183
UDP, 182
URL filtering, 185–187

installation failures on Router MC, troubleshooting, 963

installing. *See also* removing; uninstalling
CiscoWorks Common Services, 870–871
database management, 873
minimum requirements, 870
problems, troubleshooting, 871–873
user management issues, 873
with Terminal Services in Remote Administration mode, 935
CS ACS on Windows platform, 625–627
CSA MC
best practices, 1036
license key, 869
minimum requirements, 995
problems, troubleshooting, 993–994
CSAgent
minimum requirements, 998–999
problems, troubleshooting, 997, 1001
Firewall MC, 934
IDS MC, 902–903
IPS Sensor Appliances, 703
with CD-ROM, 703–704
with TFTP server, 704–707
ISDM-2 blade, 789
NM-CIDS, 833
Security Monitor, 1047
signature update on IDSM-2, 824–825

integrating CS ACS
with Novell IDS, 630–636
with AD, 627–629
with SDI, 636–639

interfaces supported on IPS, 683– 685

intermittent packet drops on FWSM, troubleshooting, 144

Internal Server Error messages, troubleshooting, 1050

interoperability
of Firewall MC with other applications, 936
of NAT and CBAC, 188

inter-process communication, 678
intrusion-detection module command, 808
IOS Firewall feature set, 177
auth-proxy, 212
authentication methods, 212
configuring, 213–215
troubleshooting, 216–217
detecting with show version command, 200
supported Cisco router platforms, 213
IP addresses
assigning to IDS-Sensor interface, 839
DNS errors, resolving, 1048
on VMS Server, modifying, 898
IP fragmentation, mitigating with CBAC, 191
IP inspection on CBAC routers, troubleshooting, 202
ip port-map command, 189
iplog command, 691
IPS (Intrusion Prevention System)
AnalysisEngine, 678
best practices, 781–785
capturing traffic
with MPLS IP IDS, 776–777
with RSPAN, 773–775
with SPAN, 763–770
with VACL, 775–776
CLI, 678
combined sensor mode, 683
communication protocols, 678–681
deployment architecture, 676–677
FAQs, 777–781
Inline Bypass sensor mode, 682
Inline sensor mode, 681–682
MainApp, 677–678
monitoring device, troubleshooting event reception issues, 726–733
NM-CIDS, 831
ACL checks, case study, 852
application partition, re-imaging, 854–857
available images, 849
CEF forwarding path, case study, 850
Command and Control port, configuring, 844–845
connecting to, 840–842
console access, 839, 843–844
disconnecting from, 842–843
dropped packets, case study, 853
encryption, case study, 852
front-panel indicator lights, 833
GRE tunnels, case study, 853
hardware issues, troubleshooting, 836–838
hardware/software requirements, 832
installing, 833
IPS insertion points, case study, 851
managing from IOS router, 848–849
NAT, case study, 851
network setup, 831
packet capturing, configuring, 846–848
removing from router, 833
slot assignment, 833
supported ports, 834–835
time stamp configuration, 857–858
Promiscuous sensor mode, 682–683
sensors
blocking function, verifying, 744–745
blocking issues, troubleshooting, 733–743, 753
configuration, backing up, 782–783
connecting to network, 784
connectivity issues, resolving, 720–725, 746–752
initial setup issues, 693–696
Inline mode, 757–763
MBS, 754
NAC function, verifying, 745–746
software installation/upgrade issues, 699–717
TCP reset, 754–757
upgrading to IPS 5.0, 715–717
user management issues, 696–698
Sensor Appliances, installing, 703–707
show commands, 686–690
supported hardware and interfaces, 683–685
traffic, capturing, 763
IPS 5.0, licensing, 717–720
IPsec
aggressive mode negotiation, 231–232
AH, 226
backup servers, redundancy on VPN 3000 Concentrator series, 415
debug commands, 300
ESP, 226
firewall issues, troubleshooting, 284–285, 340

GRE over IPsec
configuring, 256–257
troubleshooting, 257–258
IKE, 229
phase 1, 229–232
phase 2, 232–233
interaction with CBAC, 193
IOS routers, VPN troubleshooting
debug commands, 238
PKI, 258–265
Remote Access client VPN connections, 265–270
LAN-to-LAN tunnels, 239
establishing, 240–246
phase 1 establishment failures, 247–251
phase 2 establishment failures, 252–254
traffic flow, troubleshooting, 254–255
LAN-to-LAN VPN tunnels between PIX firewalls
configuring, 302, 305–308
crypto maps, creating, 305–306
data not passing through, troubleshooting, 322–323
MTU issues, 340–342
Phase I failures, 309–319
Phase II failures, 319–321
transform sets, creating, 304
tunnel groups, creating, 305
main mode negotiation, 229–231
MTU issues, troubleshooting, 285–286
NAT-related problems, troubleshooting, 282–284
exemptions, 338
over NAT-T, configuring, 338–339
over TCP, configuring, 339
Phase 1 tunnel negotiations, show commands, 233–235
Phase 2 tunnel negotiations, show commands, 235–236
PKI
configuring, 258–261
troubleshooting, 261–265
Remote Access VPNs on PIX firewall
configuring, 323, 325–327
debug output for successful tunnel build-up, 328–331
split tunneling, 342–344
stateful failover, obtaining resiliency through, 287–288
stateless failover, obtaining resiliency through, 288–295
tunnel not passing through traffic, 333–334
unestablished tunnels, troubleshooting, 332–333
SAs, 228
split tunneling issues, troubleshooting, 286
transparent tunneling options, 340
transport mode, 226
tunnel mode, 227–228
tunnels,
tearing down, 238
verifying configuration of, 237

J-K

Java blocking, configuring on CBAC, 184
jobs (Firewall MC), rolling back, 942
Jonas logs, 963

keyed message digest, 225
Knoppix security CD, 21

L

LAC routers, troubleshooting, 464–467
LAN-to-LAN IPsec VPN tunnels, 239
configuring, 302, 305–308
crypto maps, creating, 305–306
data not passing through, troubleshooting, 322–323
establishing, 240–246
MTU issues, 340–342
on VPN 3000 Concentrator series, troubleshooting, 356–363
Phase 1 establishment failures, troubleshooting, 247–251, 309–319
Phase 2 establishment failures, troubleshooting, 252–254, 319–321
traffic flow, troubleshooting, 254–255
transform sets, creating, 304
tunnel groups, defining, 305
Large ICMP events, generating, 1057
launching
CiscoWorks Common Services on web browser, 861

CSA MC
problems, troubleshooting, 1010–1013
slow launches, troubleshooting, 1013–1014
Event Viewer, 1055
Security Monitor, 1050
LED indicator lights,
on Catalyst 6500 IDSM-2 blade, 789
on VPN 3000 Concentrator series, 354
on NM-CIDS, 833
libpcap format files, 691
license keys (CSA MC), installing, 869
licensing
for CiscoWorks Common Services, troubleshooting, 869
for CSA MC, 1005–1007
importing, 1007–1008
troubleshooting, 1009–1010
for FWSM, troubleshooting, 126–127
for IDS MC
corrupt licenses, troubleshooting, 904
expired licenses, troubleshooting, 905
for IPS software, 717–718
procuring license from Cisco.com, 718
sensors, 719–720
for PIX Firewall, 54–56
for VMS, 865–868
limitations
of ACLs, 177
of Virtual Firewall, 86
LLQ (Low-Latency Queuing), configuring on PIX Firewall, 93–94
LNS (L2TP Network Server) **routers, troubleshooting, 468–471**
load balancing on VPN 3000 Concentrator series, 413
loading Event Viewer, 1057
local database installation (CSA MC), troubleshooting, 994
local group authentication, configuring on VPN 3K, 596
Local mode (CiscoWorks Common Services), 862
local user authentication, configuring on VPN 3K, 597–599
locking VPN 3K users to specific groups, 601
log directory
CSA Agent files, 988
CSA MC, 986
log events, viewing on VPN 3K, 589
log files
CSA MC Log, 987
for CSA Agent, 988–992
securitylog.txt, writing events to, 991
size of, monitoring, 1065–1066
"Logged in Users" report, 668
logging
Event Limiting, 991
syslog configuration on PIX Firewall, 50–53
logical PIX firewalls
See Security Contexts
login authentication
configuring, 559–560
troubleshooting, 561–562
lost GUI passwords, recovering, 663
low memory issues, troubleshooting on PIX Firewall, 98–101

M

machine authentication
activating on Cisco switches, 566–567
PEAP, configuring, 567–570
Main mode negotiation (IPsec), 229–231
MainApp, 677–678
Maintenance Partition (FWSM), 130–132
major/minor software, upgrading, 710
to IPS 5.0, 716–717
managed devices, troubleshooting connectivity with sensor, 746–752
Management Center, 985
management model for CSA, 983–985
managing NM-CIDS from IOS router, 848–849
man-in-the-middle attacks, 80
manipulating half-open connection threshold values on CBAC routers, 208
manual operations
adding trusted hosts to IDM sensors, 892
performing backups on CSA MC database, 1023–1024
uninstalling CS ACS, 661

MAPI Proxy (VPN 3000 Concentrator)
configuring, 399–400
troubleshooting, 400–401
mapping
CS ACS group names to VPN 3K group names, 598
NHRP issues, resolving, 278–279
maximum event limit (database), changing, 1066
MBS (Master Blocking Sensor), 737
configuring, 741–743
troubleshooting, 754
MDCSUPPORT
MDCSupport, 863
collecting on Windows platform, 886
contents, analyzing, 886–887
files collected by, 864
MDCSupportInformation.zip file
contents of, 933
file summary, 864
installation log files, 864
memory utilization, troubleshooting on PIX Firewall, 98–101
memory.dmp file, 990
message digest, 225
messages, RADIUS, 427
mGRE interface, 271
minimum installation requirements
CiscoWorks Common Services , 870
CSA MC, 995
CSAgent, 998–999
misconfigured ACLs, troubleshooting on CBAC, 202
misconfigured IP inspection, troubleshooting on CBAC routers, 203
misconfigured URL filtering, troubleshooting, 205
mitigating
IP fragmentation with CBAC, 191
TCP SYN flood attacks with CBAC, 189, 191
mls ip ids command, 813
configuring on switch running Native IOS, 809
modifying
application-to-port mappings, 188–189
IP addressing on VMS Server, 898
monitoring
database, disk utilization, 1066
devices, flow rates, 1064–1065
disk usage, 992
log files, size of, 1065–1066
monitoring interface (NM-CIDS), 834
MPF (Modular Policy Framework), 37–38
MPLS IP IDS, configuring IPS traffic capture, 776–777
MSDE database
compacting, 1030
repairing, 1031–1032
MTU problems with IPsec, troubleshooting, 285–286, 340–342
multi-channel protocols
inspecting, 187, 205
securing with CBAC, 180
multi-homed machines, running CiscoWorks Common Services on, 879
multiple context mode (PIX Firewall), 84–90
multiple mode (FWSM), access list memory utilization, 164–166
multiple SVI interfaces, configuring on FWSM, 157–162

N

NAC (Network Access Controller) function, verifying, 745–746
naming conventions
after CSA MC upgrade, 1004
of IDS Sensor Software, 700
platform-dependent images, 700–701
platform-independent images, 701–702
NARs (Network Access Restrictions)
configuring, 648–651
troubleshooting, 651–652
NAS (Network Access Server), 421, 639
bulk importing, 667
NAT (Network Address Translation)
interoperability with CBAC, 188
troubleshooting on CBAC router, 202
with IPsec, 282–284
NAT exemptions, 338
nat-control, implementing on PIX Firewall, 36
Native IOS
IDSM-2, troubleshooting hardware issues, 793–797
show commands, 792
NAT-T (NAT Traversal), configuring, 338–339

NBMA (Non-Broadcast Multiple Access), 271
network analyzers, 20
network failures
proactive troubleshooting methods, 5–7
types of, 7
network resources, protecting on PIX Firewall, 111
NHRP (Next Hop Resolution Protocol), 271
NMBA addresses, 272
NM-CIDS (Cisco IDS Network Module), 831
application partition, re-imaging, 854–857
case studies
ACL checks, 852
CEF forwarding path, 850
dropped packets, 853
encryption, 852
GRE tunnels, 853
IP insertion points, 851
NAT, 851
Command and Control port, configuring, 844–845
console access, 839
console access, troubleshooting, 843–844
front-panel indicator lights, 833
hardware issues, troubleshooting, 836–838
hardware/software requirements, 832
images, 849
installing, 833
managing from Cisco IOS router, 848–849
network setup, 831
packet capture, configuring, 846–848
removing from router, 833
slot assignment, 833
supported ports, 834–835
time stamping configuration, 857–858
upgrading to version 5.0, 849
Notifier daemon, 1055
Novell IDS, troubleshooting CS ACS integration, 630–636
NPs (network processors)
FWSM architecture, 114–116
NP3, access-list utilization on FWSM, 164–166
NSDB (Network Security Database), 785
viewing from Security Monitor, 1073
nslookup command, 19
NT/RADIUS password authentication feature, testing, 610–611

O

obtaining
Common Services software production license, 867
IPsec resiliency
with stateful failover, 287–288
with stateless failover, 288–295
options for csutil.exe, 655–656
outbound connections, 69
configuring on PIX Firewall, 69–72
Output Interpreter, 54

P

Package.cab file, contents of, 622–624
packet capturing
configuring on NM-CIDS, 846–848
on FWSM, 123–124
packet command, 692
packet drops. troubleshooting
on CBAC routers, 210
on FWSM, 144
packet flows
through CS ACS, 619–620
through FWSM, 116
Fast Path packet flow, 116–118
FTP session packet flow, 118
Session Management packet flow, 118
packets, troubleshooting IPsec MTU issues, 285–286
Page Cannot Be Found Error messages (Security Monitor), 1050
PAM (Port Application Mapping), 188–189
Passed Authentication log, turning on, 621
Password Expiry, testing, 610–611
passwords
encryption (CS ACS), 668
recovering
from FWSM, 132
from IDSM-2, 827, 829
from PIX Firewall, 56–60
PEAP (Protected EAP)
configuring, case study, 574–580
machine authentiation, configuring, 567–570
performance issues on CBAC, troubleshooting, 205–210

Perl directory (CSA MC), 986
Phase 1 tunnel negotiations
IPsec LAN-to-LAN VPN failures, 309–319
show commands, 233–235
Phase 2 tunnel negotiation
IPsec LAN-to-LAN VPN failures, 319–321
show commands, 235–236
tearing down tunnels, 238
ping command, 17
pinging CBAC router incoming interface, 201
PIX firewalls
access lists
enabling/disabling, 35
implementing, 34
outbound, 35–36
time-range keyword, 34–35
activation keys, 56
ASA, characteristics of, 29–30
commands
capture, 47–49
debug application-protocol, 47
debug fixup tcp|udp, 47
debug icmp trace, 46–47
debug pix process, 47
show asp drop command, 41–42
show blocks, 43
show connection command, 40
show cpu usage command, 42
show local-host command, 40–41
show output filters, 44–45
show service-policy command, 41
show tech-support, 45
show traffic, 42
show xlate command, 39–40
connections
configuring, 69–72
troubleshooting, 72–76
CPU utilization, troubleshooting, 95–98
Downloadable PIX ACL, 653
failover
active/active failover, configuring, 105–106
active/standby failover, 102
asymmetrical routing support, 106
failover groups, 104
hardware and licensing requirements, 104
FAQs, 109–110
file system commands, 33
Hairpinning, 334–337
high availability on VPN connections, obtaining, 344–345
IDENT protocol, troubleshooting on PIX Firewall, 102
licensing issues, troubleshooting, 54–56
memory utilization, troubleshooting, 98–101
MPF, 37–38
multiple context mode, configuring, 87–90
nat-control, configuring, 36
packet processing, 30–32
password recovery issues, troubleshooting, 56–60
protecting network resources, best practices, 110–111
QoS issues, troubleshooting, 90, 92–94
Remote Access VPNs
configuring, 323, 325–327
debug output for successful tunnel build-up, 328–331
tunnel not passing through traffic, 333–334
unestablished tunnels, troubleshooting, 332–333
Security Contexts, 84
multiple context mode, 84–86
software upgrade/downgrade issues, troubleshooting, 60–68
syslog, 50–53
tools, 53
traceback, 53
Transparent Firewall, 38–39, 78
configuring, 79–82
troubleshooting, 82–83
Virtual Firewall, 84–86
PKI
configuring, 258–259, 261
troubleshooting, 261–265
platform-dependent images, naming conventions, 700–701
platform-independent images, naming conventions, 701–702
policies, 985–987
Policies directory (CSA MC), 986
policing, configuring on PIX Firewall, 90–92
polling issues with CSA MC, troubleshooting, 1014–1015

port forwarding, VPN 3000 Concentrator
configuring, 396–397
troubleshooting, 397–399
port-level authentication, 542
ports
ISDM-2 switch support, 790
mapping information, changing, 188–189
NM-CIDS, configuring Command and Control interface, 834–835, 844–845
Post-Block ACL, 735
Pre-Block ACL, 734
privilege levels, assigning to VPN 3K users, 592
proactive troubleshooting methods, 5–7
processes running
on Firewall MC, 931
on IDS MC, 884
on Router MC, 959
on SecMon, 884
procuring
CSA MC license, 1007
CSAgent license, 1007
CSAgent software, 997–998
IPS 5.0 license from Cisco.com, 718
production license for Common Services software, obtaining, 867
production network failures, 8, 12–13
defining the problem, 9–10
gathering the facts, 10–11
Profiler, 1022
Promiscuous mode (IDSM-2), 805
configuring, 805
on switch running CatOS, 810–813
on switch running Native IOS, 806–809
troubleshooting, 814–816
Promiscuous sensor mode (IPS), 682–683
protecting
inside network, 178–180
PIX Firewall, best practices, 110–111
protocol analyzers, 20
pruning
IDS MC database, 920
troubleshooting, 1067–1068
public key algorithms, 224
purge-mc-tasks utility, 942
purging CSA MC database, 1028–1029

Q–R

QoS, 90
LLQ, configuring on PIX Firewall, 93–94
policing, PIX Firewall configuration, 90–92
RADIUS, 425–426, 609
authentication operation, 426–427
authorization operation, 426–427
configuring on Cisco IOS routers, case study, 462–463
dynamic filters, configuring, 604
group authentication, configuring on VPN 3K, 599–600
user authentication, configuring on VPN 3K, 596–597
versus TACACS+, 428–429
rcp, generating core dumps, 23
RDEP (Remote Data Exchange Protocol), 1041
RDEP2, 679
real-time alerts, configuring, 192–193
reclaiming disk space, 1011
records, pruning from IDS MC database, 920
recover application-partition command, 709
recovering
application partition, 708–709
lost GUI passwords, 663
user passwords from IDSM-2, 827–829
recovering lost passwords
from FWSM, 132
from GUI, 663
from PIX Firewall, 56–60
recovery packages, 702
Recovery Server (Firewall MC)
configuring, 953–954
enabling, 954
redirecting archive/backup files away from Database Disk, 1063
redundancy
failover
active/active failover, configuring, 105–106
active/standby failover, 102
configuring on FWSM, 149–155
monitoring on FWSM, 147–148
troubleshooting on FWSM, 144, 146–147, 155–157

on VPN 3000 Concentrator series
clustering, 412–414
using IPsec Backup Servers, 415
using VVRP, 410–411
Reflexive ACLs, 180
regenerating Apache certificates, 897
registered CSA MC agents, identifying, 1008
registering CSA MC, 868
re-imaging
IDSM-2, 818–823
NM-CIDS application partition, 854–857
Remote Access VPN connections
on PIX firewall, troubleshooting, 323–327
debug output for successful tunnel build-up, 328–331
MTU issues, 340–342
tunnel not passing through traffic, 333–334
unestablished tunnels, 332–333
on VPN 3000 Concentrator series, troubleshooting, 364–371
client routing, 377–381
Internet inaccessibility, 381–382
local LAN inaccessibility, 382
tunnel establishment, 372–377
split tunneling, configuring, 342–344
remote database installation (CSA MC), troubleshooting, 994
removing
CSA MC components, 995–997
CSAgent from Windows systems, 999–1000
ISDM-2 blade from switch, 790
NM-CIDS from router, 833
terminal activities from Firewall MC, 941–942
repairing CSA MC database, 1031–1032
replication, 640
Bidirectional, 647
"cascade", 645
CS ACS
configuring, 640, 644
troubleshooting, 644–647
of dynamically mapped users, 670
REPLY packets (TACACS+), 422
reports
daily alarm reports, scheduling, 1073
generation failures, troubleshooting, 1060
pruning reports, 1067
Router MC, 963
resolving
connection problems between IDS MC and sensor, 893
CS ACS Crypto Errors, 661
DNS errors, 1048
restoring
CiscoWorks Common Services, 875–876, 950
CSA MC database, 1025–1027
data, 657
Router MC database, 973
Roles, 862
rollback feature (Firewall MC), 942
Router MC
ACS, setup procedures, 979–980
authentication problems, resolving, 967
backup/restore operations, troubleshooting, 973
browser issues, troubleshooting, 965, 967
checking status of, 960
communication architecture, 960
dangling connections, 968
database
backing up, 972
restoring, 973
debug information, collecting/viewing, 961–962
device configurations
deploying, 970–971
importing, 969–970
features, 960
installation failures, troubleshooting, 963
logging levels, setting, 961
processes, 959
reports, 963
user permissions, case study, 974–975, 978
RRI (Reverse Route Injection), 345
RSPAN (remote SPAN), configuring IPS traffic capture, 773–775
rules
CSA MC, 985
database/event, creating, 1064
for dynamic filters, syntax, 603
Rx SPAN, 764

S

Samples directory (CSA MC), 986
SAs, 228
saving crash information to Flash on PIX Firewall, 53
scheduling daily alarm reports, 1073
SDEE (Security Device Event Exchange), 679–680, 1041
SDI (Secure ID), CS ACS integration, 636– 639
SecMon
- database Pruning, 920
- processes, starting/stopping, 884

security administrators, 984
Security Contexts, 84
- multiple context mode, 84– 90

Security Monitor
- best practices, 1077
- database maintenance issues, troubleshooting, 1062
- DNS errors, resolving, 1048
- email notification
  - *configuring, 1068–1070*
  - *troubleshooting, 1071–1072*
- Event Viewer
  - *launching, 1055*
  - *troubleshooting, 1057*
- inability to launch, troubleshooting, 1050
- inability to receive events, troubleshooting, 726, 728–733
- installation guidelines, website, 1047
- Internal Server Error messages, troubleshooting, 1050
- licensing issues, troubleshooting, 1051
- NSDB, viewing, 1073
- Page Cannot Be Found Error messages, troubleshooting, 1050
- report generation failures, troubleshooting, 1060
- sensor connection status, troubleshooting, 1053–1055
- strange behavior, troubleshooting, 1051
- tabs, 1048
- user management, 1045

securitylog.txt file, writing events to, 991
selecting
- slot for ISDM-2 placement, 788
- traffic capture method on IDSM-2, 827
- UDP connection timeout for CBAC, 207–208

sensor modes
- combined modes, 683
- Inline Bypass mode, 682
- Inline mode, 681–682
- Promiscuous mode, 682–683

sensors
- active processes, verifying, 893–895
- blocking
  - *for specific signatures, troubleshooting, 753*
  - *process, verifying, 923–924*
- connectivity, 721–725
- IDM
  - *accessing, 888*
  - *trusted hosts, adding/configuring, 889–892*
- IDS, importing from IDS MC, 1051
- IDS MC
  - *configuring, 906*
  - *deploying, 917–920*
  - *import process, troubleshooting , 907–908*
  - *shunning, case study, 920–925*
  - *upgrade process, troubleshooting, 908–917*
- inaccessibility, troubleshooting, 901–902
- IPS, troubleshooting
  - *ACLs, 734–735*
  - *backing up configuration, 782–783*
  - *blocking, 734–745*
  - *connecting to network, 784*
  - *connectivity with managed device, 746–752*
  - *initial setup issues, 693–696*
  - *Inline mode, configuring, 757–762*
  - *Inline mode, troubleshooting, 762–763*
  - *MBS, 737, 741–744*
  - *software installation/upgrade issues, 699–717*
  - *supported managed devices and versions, 735*
  - *TCP reset, 754–757*
  - *user management issues, 696–698*

licensing, 719–720
with CLI, 719–720
with IDM, 719
resolving connection problems with IDS MC, 893
signature level, updating, 899–901
upgrading to IPS 5.0, 715–717
verifying secure communication with IDS MC, 893
serial cable, connecting to IDSM-2 blade, 826
server selftest information, displaying, 988
service packs, IDS MC
upgrading sensors, 908–910
verifying version of, 895–896
service-module command, connecting to NM-CIDS, 840
services, CSAdmin, 615–616
Session Management packet flow through FWSM, 118
Shared File Components (CS ACS), 653–654
Shared Profile (command authorization), configuring, 444
shims, disabling, 1016–1017
show aaa servers command, 430
show aaa user command, 430
show access-list command, 655
show accounting command, 554
show asp drop command, 41–42
show authorization command, 554
show blocks command, 43
show commands
for IPsec Phase 1 tunnel negotiations, 233–235
for IPsec Phase 2 tunnel negotiations, 235–236
for Native IOS, 792
FWSM-related, 120–122
show configuration command, 687
show connection command, 40
show cpu usage command, 42
show crypto ipsec command, 299–300
show crypto map command, 237
show dot1x all command, 556
show dot1x statistics command, 557
show events command, 687
show interfaces command, 689
show ip inspect command, 194–195
show local-host command, 40–41
show localusers command, 552
show module command, 791
show output filters command, 44–45
show radius command, 553
show radius statistics command, 430
show running config command, 15
show running logging command, 52
show running-config command, 300
show security acl command, 792
show service-policy command, 41, 94
show span command, 792
show statistics command, 687–688
show tacacs command, 430, 553
show tech-support, 45
show tech-support command, 689
show test command, 792
show traffic command, 42
show trunk command, 792
show users command, 430
show version command, 15, 686–687, 689–690, 791
verifying installed IOS Firewall feature set, 200
show vlan brief command, 558
show xlate command, 39–40
shunning on IDS MC sensor, case study, 920 –925
signature levels, updating on IDS MC sensors, 899–901
signature updates, installing on IDSM-2, 824–825
signatures, IDS MC
upgrading IDS MC sensors, 908–910
verifying version of, 895–896
single channel protocol
inspection
application-layer, 183
ICMP, 182
SMTP, 183
UDP, 182
securing on inside network, 179–180
single-mode (FWSM), access list memory utilization, 164–166
size of log files, monitoring, 1065–1066
slot assignment of NM-CIDS on router, 833
slow CSA MC launches, troubleshooting, 1013–1014
SMTP
email notification
configuring, 1068–1070
troubleshooting, 1071–1072
traffic inspection, 183–184

sniffer software, 49
Ethereal, 199
sniffer traces, capturing, 199
sniffing ports on IDSM-2, 791
software
installation/upgrade problems (IPS), troubleshooting, 699–717
requirements
for ISDM-2 blade, 788
for NM-CIDS support, 832
upgrade/downgrade issues, troubleshooting on PIX Firewall, 60–61, 63–66, 68
Software Advisor Tool, verifying correct IOS Firewall version, 200
source port, 764
SPAN (Switched Port Analyzer)
configuring
on Catalyst 2900/3600XL, 765–767
on Catalyst 2950/3550 and 3750, 767–770
on Catalyst 4000/6000 running CatOS, 770–771
on Catalyst 4000/6000 running Native IOS, 771–772
on switch running CatOS, 810
on switch running Native IOS, 806–807
IPS traffic capture, configuring, 763, 765
on Catalyst 2900/3500XL, 765, 767
on Catalyst 2950, 767–770
on Catalyst 3550, 767–770
on Catalyst 3750, 767–770
SPI (security parameter index), 228
split tunneling
configuring, 342–344
troubleshooting, 286
spoke–to-spoke tunnels, creating, 275
SQL Server 2000, compacting, 1031
SSH, tasks performed on IDS MC, 885
SSL
CSA MC communication architecture, 987
enabling, 1049
SSL VPN
clientless mode, 390
configuring, 390
troubleshooting, 391–395
thick client mode
configuring, 402–403
troubleshooting, 403–405
thin client mode, 395–396
E-mail Proxy, configuring, 401
E-mail Proxy, troubleshooting, 401–402
MAPI Proxy, configuring, 399–400
MAPI Proxy, troubleshooting, 400–401
port forwarding, 397–399
START packets (TACACS+), 422
starting IDS MC/SecMon processes, 884
stateful failover
for VPN connections, 345
obtaining IPsec resiliency, 287–288
stateless failover, obtaining IPsec resiliency, 288–295
static ACLs, established keyword, 180
status indicator lights
IDSM-2, 789
NM-CIDS, 833
status of Router MC processes, checking, 960
stopping
CSAgent service, 991
deployed jobs, 942
supplicant, 542
supported tokens on VPN 3K, 604
suspending NM-CIDS sessions, 842
switch management, 558
accounting
configuring, 565
troubleshooting, 566
authorization
configuring, 564–565
troubleshooting, 565
enable password authentication, troubleshooting, 562–564
login authentication, troubleshooting, 559–562
switching path on CBAC, troubleshooting performance issues, 209
symmetric cryptographic algorithms, 224
syntax
for database backups, 656
for downloadable PIX/IP ACLs, 606
for dynamic filter rules, 603
rtrformat utility, 990

syslogs, 21
activating on Cisco routers, 193
configuring on PIX Firewall, 50–53
on FWSM, 125
System Image, re-imaging IDSM-2, 818–823
system images, upgrading to IPS 5.0, 716
sysvars.cf file, 991

T

tabs, Security Monitor, 1048
TACACS+, 421
AAA packet flows, 422–423
accounting operation, 424
authentication operation, 422–423
authorization operation, 424
configuring on VPN 3K, 590–592
versus RADIUS, 428–429
TCP reset, 754–757
on IDSM-2, 818
TCP SYN flood attacks, mitigating with CBAC, 189–191
tcpdump command, 690
tearing down IPsec tunnels, 238
telnet, connecting to NM-CIDS, 841–842
telnet command, 18
terminating CSAgent service, 991
test events, generating on Event Viewer, 1057
testing
authentication, 593–594
core dump setup, 24
NT/RADIUS password expiration feature, 610–611
TFTP, 20
generating core dumps, 22
Thick Client SSL VPN mode (VPN 3000 Concentrator series)
configuring, 402–403
troubleshooting, 403–405
Thin Client SSL VPN mode (VPN 3000 Concentrator series), 395–396
"time exceeded" error messages, 18
time stamping on NM-CIDS, configuring, 857–858
time-range command, 34–35
Tmp directory (CSA MC), 986
tomcat logs, 962
traceback, configuring on PIX Firewall, 53
traceroute command, 18
traffic capture method on IDSM-2, configuring
with mls ip ids command, 813
on switch running Native IOS, 809
with SPAN
on switch running CatOS, 810
on switch running Native IOS, 806–807
with VACL
on switch running CatOS, 811
on switch running Native IOS, 807–809
traffic filtering, ACLs
limitations of, 177
wide holes, 181
traffic inspection
of multi-channel protocols, 187
of single channel protocols, 182
application-layer protocols, 183
ICMP, 182
SMTP, 183
UDP, 182
transform sets, 325
creating, 304
translation details, displaying for PIX Firewall, 39–40
transparent firewalls, 38–39, 193
configuring, 79–82, 193
troubleshooting on PIX Firewall, 78, 82–83
transparent tunneling options, 340
transport mode, 226
trusted hosts
adding to IDM sensors, 890–892
configuring on IDM sensors, 889–890
tunnel groups, VPN 3K, 326
attributes, 589
authentication, 588–589
defining for LAN-to-LAN tunnels, 305
tunnel mode, 227–228
turning off
debugging, 555
Passed Authentication log, 621
turning on CSA Agent debug mode, 989
Tx SPAN, 765

U

UDP
connection timeout, selecting, 207–208
traffic inspection, 182, 203–205
uninstalling. *See also* removing
CS ACS, 661
CSA MC, 995
Unknown User Policy, configuring, 609–610
unlocking Firewall MC activities, 941
updating
CSAgent, 1004–1005
signature level on IDS MC sensors, 899–901
upgrading
Cisco IOS code base on CBAC routers, 209
CiscoWorks Common Services license, 868
CS ACS on Windows platform, 625–626
CSA MC, 1002
CSA MCL
on same system, 1002–1003
on separate system, 1003–1004
IDS MC sensors, 908–910
failures, troubleshooting, 910–917
IDSM-2 to version 5.x, 826
IPS Sensor Appliances, 703
with CD-ROM, 703–704
with TFTP server, 704–707
Maintenance Partition on IDSM-2, 823–824
Major/Minor Software, 710
NM-CIDS, 849
PIX Firewall, 61–63
in failover setup, 68
ROM Monitor mode, 63–66
Router MC, troubleshooting failures, 963
to IPS 5.0, 715–717
URL filtering
activating, 186
configuring on CBAC, 185–187
on CBAC routers, troubleshooting, 211
troubleshooting, 205
user attributes (VPN 3K), 589
user authentication
on CiscoWorks Common Services, case study, 876–877
on VPN 3K, 588–589
with RADIUS, configuring, 596–597
user management
on CiscoWorks Common Services, 862, 873
on IPS, troubleshooting, 696–698
on Security Monitor, 1045
user passwords, recovering from IDSM-2, 827–829
user permissions on Router MC, case study, 974–975, 978
users, deleting
in multiple groups, 669
on CS ACS, 659
utilities
csutil.exe
arguments, 655–656
syntax, 655
IdsAlarms.exe, 1076
IDSdbcompact, 1068
MDCSUPPORT, 863–864
purge-mc-tasks, 942

V

VACLs (VLAN ACLs)
blocking, 736
configuring
on switch running CatOS, 811
on switch running Native IOS, 807–809
IPS traffic capture, configuring, 775–776
VACL Capture (IDSM-2), 827
verifying
active processes on sensors, 893–895
Apache certificate on IDS MC, 896
blocking process configuration on sensors, 744–745, 923–924
CBAC CPU utilization, 205–206
core dump configuration, 24
Firewall MC installation, 934
IPsec tunnel configuration, 237
NAC function, 745–746
network connectivity with ping command, 17
Router MC installation, 963
secure communication between IDS MC and sensor, 893
service pack version on IDS MC, 895–896
version of IDS MC, 895–896

viewing
event log on VPN 3000 Concentrator series, 350–352
Firewall MC debug information, 932
log events on VPN 3K, 589
NSDB from Security Monitor, 1073
processes on IDS MC/SecMon, 884
Router MC debug information, 961–962
Virtual Firewall, 84–86
Virtual Reassembly option (IOS Firewalls), 191
VMS (VPN/Security Management Solution)
CiscoWorks Common Services
backing up, 874–875
FAQs, 877–881
installing, 870–873
problems, troubleshooting, 871–873
user management issues, 873
managing, best practices, 881
restoring, 875–876
running on mult-homed machines, 879
user authentication, case study, 876–877
licensing issues, 865–866
obtaining Common Services production license, 867
upgrading Common Services license, 868
VMS Server, modifying IP addressing, 898
VPDNs (Virtual Private Dial-up Networks)
LAC router, troubleshooting, 464–467
LNS router, troubleshooting, 468–471
on Cisco IOS routers, case study, 458–462
troubleshooting on Cisco IOS routers, case study, 464–472
VPN 3000 Concentrator series
AAA
session timeouts, avoiding, 593
TACACS+, configuring, 590–592
Administer Sessions window, 352
authentication, 590
causes of failure, 607–608
FAQs, 406–410
Cisco Secure ACS server, configuring, 590–591
communicating with CS ACS RADIUS server, 597–599
concentrator management, 587
configuration files, 354
CRSHDUMP.TXT file, 354
Digital Cerficates, 383–384
on VPN client, 382–383
troubleshooting, 384–389
dynamic filters, configuring, 602
E-mail Proxy
configuring, 401
troubleshooting, 401–402
event classes, configuring, 348
event log, viewing, 350–352
failure, causes of, 607
group authentication with RADIUS, configuring, 599–600
group configuration, 608
group names, mapping to CS ACS group names, 598
LAN-to-LAN tunnel issues
configuring, 356
troubleshooting, 359–63
LED indicators, 354
local group and user authentication, configuring, 595–596
local user authentication, configuring, 597–599
log events, viewing, 589
MAPI Proxy
configuring, 399–400
troubleshooting, 400–401
port forwarding
configuring, 396–397
troubleshooting, 397–399
privilege levels, assigning to users, 592
RADIUS Server, configuring, 609
redundancy
using clustering, 412–414
using IPsec Backup Servers, 415
using VVRP, 410–411
Remote Access VPN connections
configuring, 364–365
troubleshooting, 365–382
SSL VPN
clientless mode, 390–395
Thick Client mode, 402–405
thin client mode, 395–396
supported tokens, 604
tunnel group authentication, 588–589
user authentication, 588–589
with RADIUS, configuring, 596–597

users, locking to specific group, 601
VPN client log, 354–355
X-Auth, troubleshooting, 594–596
VPNs
on Cisco IOS routers, DMVPN, 270–280
stateful failover, 345
transparent tunneling options, 340
VVRP (Virtual Router Redundancy Protocol), redundancy on VPN 3000 Concentrator series, 410–411

W

web browsers
CiscoWorks Common Services, launching, 861
on Firewall MC, troubleshooting, 937
on Router MC, troubleshooting, 965–967
websites
Ethereal, 20
Knoppix tool, 2
Security Monitor installation guidelines, 1047
well-known ports, changing port-to-application mappings, 188–189
wide holes, 181
Windows operating system
CS ACS
installing, 625–627
related registries, 663
CSAgent, removing, 999–1000
IDS MC
MDCSupport file, 886–887
MDCSupport file, collecting, 886
system information, displaying, 988
Windows NT/2000 Domain Authentication, configuring Unknown User Policy, 609–610
winmsd command, 988
worry state, IKE keepalives, 345

X-Y-Z

X-Auth, troubleshooting, 594–596
on Cisco routers, 457
XML parser, 1044

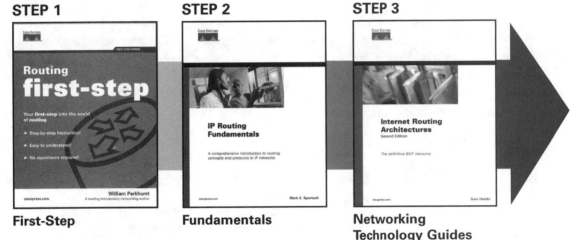